CASSELL'S
ENCYCLOPEDIA
OF

QUEER MYTH, SYMBOL AND SPIRIT

GAY, LESBIAN, BISEXUAL AND TRANSGENDER LORE

Randy P. Lunčunas Conner
David Hatfield Sparks
Mariya Sparks

Foreword by
Gloria E. Anzaldúa

CASSELL
London and New York

Cassell

Wellington House, 125 Strand, London WC2R 0BB
370 Lexington Avenue, New York, NY 10017-6550

Front cover illustration © 1993 Robert Lentz,
Natural Bridge, PO Box 91204, Albuquerque, NM 87199-1204

Back cover illustration © 1995 Paul B. Rucher,
209 E. 19th Street, No. 106, Minneapolis, MN 55403-3942

First published 1997. Reprinted with corrections in paperback 1998.

British Library Cataloguing-in-Publication Data

A catalogue record for this book is available from the British Library.

ISBN 0-304-33760-9 (Hardback)
ISBN 0-304-70423-7 (Paperback)

Printed and bound in Great Britain
by The Bath Press, Bath

Contents

Acknowledgements

This text could not have been written without the loving support of Yvette "Beto" Gómez and our families. We also wish to thank Gloria Anzaldúa, Aziz, Rebecca Baltzer, Doug Bonner and Gwynneth, Marty Boroson, Z Budapest, Ariban Chagoya, Priestess Mother Miriam Chamani, Gatsby Contreras, Steve Cook at Cassell, Matthew Daude, Tamara Diaghilev, Donald Engstrom, Arthur Evans, Laurie Fuchs, Christine Garrett, Babalorisha Omí Guillermo González, Judy Grahn, Kveldulf Gundarsson, Kandace Hawkinson, Harry Hay, Hai Hua, Keith Hennessy, Lisa Jones, Jonathan Katz, Joseph Kramer, Richard Labonté, Peter Limnios, James M. Martin, Mark Miller, Misha, Cherríe Moraga, Sheila Na Gig and Beth, Vicki Noble, our editor Rictor Norton, Sherry Peterson, Adrian Ravarour, Ana Rubinstein, Joan Sibley, Bill Stanton, Karyn Taylor, Mark Thompson, Shawn Tran, Kay Turner, Uma of Tools of Magick, Karen Vogel, Mitch Walker, Sheila Walker, Charles Whitenberg, the staffs of the libraries at the University of Texas at Austin, especially of the Harry Ransom Humanities Research Center, and the many others who shared information with us. Above all, we wish to acknowledge the Divine in its myriad manifestations, the spirits, the ancestors, and all other "powers that be" who have aided in the creation of this text.

Foreword

by Gloria E. Anzaldúa

For many years what kept my spiritual flame lit was the memory of the picture of *la Virgencita de Guadalupe*, a Mexican manifestation of the Virgin Mary, that Mamagrande Ramona kept on her dresser-top altar alongside *las velas*, the votive candles, and snapshots of family members, *muertos y vivos*, the dead and the living. That memory led me to *el hecho de altares* (the making of altars), *curanderismo* (healing), *nagualismo* (shamanism), and other indigenous Mexican traditions.

After being mugged and later suffering a near-death experience and a host of other traumas, I realized that I would go mad if I did not honor the spirit world. Meditational practice, altar-making, and other rituals helped me to cope with fear, depression, loneliness, poverty, and oppression. I learned that when I could not change external circumstances, I could at least alter my perspective regarding them. Altering my perception often led to the transformation of outer reality.

For me, spirituality is a source of sustenance, a way of knowing, a path of survival. Like love, spirituality is a relational activity leading to deep bonds between people, plants, animals, and the forces of nature. Spirituality not only transforms our perceptions of "ordinary" life and our relationships with others, but also invites encounters with other realities, other worlds.

When I began to suspect that I might be *una de las otras*, "one of the others," *una mita' y mita'*, "half and half," I went to one of those places I always go to for solace, for guidance, and to better understand myself and others – books. That part of myself which is of European heritage – primarily Spanish and Basque – finds resonance in the term "lesbian" and in the vision of Sappho's *thiasos* on the island of Lesbos. That part of myself which is of indigenous American heritage takes delight in *patlache*, Nahuatl for an Amazon- like, woman-loving woman. Yet I hunger for a spirituality that will embrace my *mestiza* ("mixed") as well as my Queer self.

I remember a night in the winter of 1980, when we were all living on Noe Street in San Francisco, shoving a note under Randy and David's door, asking, "Is there a Queer spirituality?" My question led us to many discussions over *lattes* at Cafe Flore.

As I read *The Encyclopedia of Queer Myth, Symbol, and Spirit*, I feel a sense of belonging to a vast community of *jotos*, "queers," who participate in the sacred and mythic dimensions of life. Again and again, I see parts of myself reflected in many of its narratives and symbols. Like one who was starving, once I tasted such articles as "Shamanism," "Tlazolteotl," and "Xochiquetzal," and other kernels of Aztlan (the mythical homeland of the ancient peoples of Mexico), I quickly lapped up the Queer stories of cultures beyond my own.

Years ago, when I first studied the Mayan glyph, or pictogram, that depicts a king covered in part by a jaguar pelt, and read that the glyph is called "the Way," the word and the image resonated throughout my being. "The Way" has multiple meanings. It refers simultaneously to the shaman, to an animal and/or spirit companion, to metamorphosis, to the art of "dreaming" worlds. For a "postcolonial" *mestiza* like myself, any single way is not "the" way. A spiritual *mestizaje* weaves together beliefs and practices from many cultures, perhaps including elements of Shamanism, Buddhism, Christianity, Santería, and other traditions. Spiritual *mestizaje* involves the crossing of borders, incessant metamorphosis. It is a spirituality that nurtures the ability to wear someone else's skin, its central myth being shapeshifting. In its disturbance of traditional boundaries of gender and desire and its narratives of metamorphosis – as amply presented here – as well as in its traversing of cultural and historical borders, Queer Spirit qualifies as a kind of spiritual *mestizaje*.

This encyclopaedia may disturb some Queer theorists and other academics in its focus on the mythic and spiritual aspects of erotic and gendered experience. It is time for us to move beyond confining parameters of what qualifies as knowledge. When we refuse to consider the value of knowledge that is rooted in the body, in the psyche, in paralogical experience, we fail to challenge colonialist, post-Renaissance, Euro-Western conceptions of reality. We need to move beyond the facile dichotomy of "essentialism" and "constructionism" to embrace other theoretical paradigms inclusive of embodied and in-spirited knowledge. In its comprehensiveness and inclusiveness, this encyclopaedia is a valuable reference work. But it is not simply a reference work. It challenges us to read history – the history of sexuality as well as the history of the sacred – differently, giving voice to knowledges that are deeply rooted in the realm of spirit.

At long last, here is an encyclopedia for *jotas y jotos* and all others who seek to recover, reinscribe, and re-vision myths and symbols of gender metamorphosis and same-sex desire.

(Gloria E. Anzaldúa is the co-editor of This Bridge Called My Back: Writings by Radical Women of Color *(1981) and the author of* Borderlands: La Frontera: The New Mestiza *(1987),* Prietita and the Ghost Woman *(1996), and numerous other works.)*

Introduction

"We are sacred because we are queer."
– Mark Leger/Trixie Glamourama

Have you ever heard the tale of Lu Yi Jing, whose male lover Wei Guo Xiu was abducted by a demon and who was aided by a spirit and a necromancer in making contact with his companion, now a ghost? Are you aware that the notion that a female soul might take up residence in a male body was popularized by Isaac ben Solomon Luria, the headmaster of a Qabbalistic center at Safed in Galilee, in the sixteenth century? Did you know that many persons living in Medieval and Renaissance France held that a person might change sex by passing under the rainbow? That in the world of the ancient Greeks, same-sex unions between women appear to have taken place within the structure of women's religious households, *thiasoi*, with the unions being referred to as "syzygies," meaning "to yoke together"?

In *Pure Lust* (1984), philosopher Mary Daly writes: "Symbols . . . participate in that to which they point. They open up levels of reality otherwise closed to us and they unlock dimensions and elements of our souls which correspond to these hidden dimensions and elements of reality."

A very powerful, yet often unacknowledged, aspect of the resilience of lesbian, gay male, bisexual, and transgendered (in this volume, also referred to as "androgynous," "third gender," "gender variant," and "two-spirit," to reflect a diversity of views) experience lies in the symbol-making process. Whether one believes that a divine presence or presences, or humans alone, fashion human experience, it is evident that for millennia, and in many cultures, humans have sought to symbolize a perceived association of eroticism, gender identity, and the realm of sacred or mythic experience. Within this association, and often in the face of oppressive forces, individuals and groups have continued to symbolize a perceived linking of same-sex-erotic, bisexual, or pansexual behavior, transgenderism, and spiritual experience. This association manifests itself in various ways, including in archetypal figures such as deities, spirits, and other divine beings and mythic figures; sacred narratives, including myths and legends; symbols and metaphors; spiritual functionaries such as shamans and priestesses, and spiritually-minded artists; and works of art.

Many lesbian women, gay men, bisexuals, and transgendered persons – all currently referred to as "queer" in a radical reclaiming of this term – living in the late twentieth century are becoming acutely aware of the suppression of knowledge pertaining to this domain. This suppression is rooted, incidentally, not only in religious fundamentalism, with its patriarchal, heterocentric biases, but also in many "New Age" texts, especially erotic manuals and texts pertaining to the men's movement, which tend to ignore or denigrate gender and sexual fluidity. Some Queer theorists, as well, have played a role in this suppression, in generally seeking to remove the spiritual dimension of experience from academic discussion (especially in terms of Goddess Reverence) and more particularly, in condemning works of feminist and gay spirituality as "essentialist" because they refer to a relatively stable feminine (as in the concept of a compassionate Goddess) or gay or queer identity which is multicultural and transhistorical.

A number of Queer theorists and lesbian-feminist scholars have further insisted that male homoeroticism and lesbianism share no common history. Yet ancient texts – despite what we might call today their homophobia, lesbophobia, and transgender-phobia – indicate the existence of such a shared history, one that is further shared with the history of bisexuality and that of transgenderism. For example, the Roman fabulist Phaedrus (fl. c. 20 BCE), whose work is reminiscent of Aesop's, speaks of gender and sexual variance in mythic terms. "Another asked," he writes, "why *tribades* (*tribadas*, lesbians) and *cinedes* (*molles mares*, effeminate, homoerotically inclined men) were created." Phaedrus replies that the hero-deity Prometheus – best known as the rebel who steals fire from heaven – is creating the first group of human beings from clay. He has just finished shaping genitalia that he plans to attach to the bodies he has made when the god Dionysus unexpectedly invites him to supper. At his host's home, Prometheus drinks too much wine. On returning home in a stupor, he completes his work, except that he joins "the female parts to the male bodies, and [affixes] male members to the women." It is due to Prometheus's mistake, Phaedrus explains, that "we find lust indulging in depraved pleasures." From the opening of the fable, we can readily see that by "depraved pleasures" he is referring to same-sex eroticism, and is clearly linking lesbianism, homoeroticism, and gender variance. This tale, furthermore, bears an uncanny resemblance to a Yoruba tale from West Africa which depicts the androgynous or transgendered deity Obatala creating persons with physical and mental differences as he-she grows increasingly drunk on palm wine. The second century CE Roman writer Lucian also links lesbianism and male homosexuality, albeit in a satiric condemnation of "the new age," writing: "Come, you man of the new age, you law-giver of unknown amours, if you open out new ways to the lubricity of men, you may grant to the women equal license. Let them cohabit together as the men do; let woman lie with woman . . . as man lies with man! Let the . . . lubricity of our tribades triumph without blushing." Also in the second century CE, the Christian polemicist Justin Martyr, in his "Discourse to the Greeks," writes: "And I say nothing of the masculine character of Minerva, nor of the feminine nature of Bacchus [in Greece, Dionysus] . . . Read to Jupiter [Zeus], ye Greeks, the law against . . . pederasty. Teach Minerva [Athena] and Diana [Artemis] the works of women, and Bacchus the works of men. What seemliness is there in a woman's girding herself with armor, or in a man's decorating himself with cymbals, and garlands, and female attire?" A third writer of the second century CE, Maximus of Tyre, also speaks of a shared history of lesbianism and male homosexuality; his depiction, however, is not clouded by hostility. He writes: "What then is the passion of the Lesbian songstress [i.e. Sappho] but the love-technique of Socrates? For both of them seem to me to have the same idea of love, the former the love of girls, the latter of youths. What then an Alcibiades, Charmides, and Phaedrus were to Socrates, a Gyrinna, Atthis, and Anactoria are to Sappho; what rivals such as Prodicus, Gorgias, Thrasymachus, and Protagoras were to Socrates, so are Gorgo and Andromeda to Sappho . . . The former [i.e. Socrates] is senseless before love of Phaedrus; love convulses the heart of the latter, as a storm on the mountains assails the oaks."

Those who prefer to avoid discussion of, or who consciously attempt to suppress discussion of, what we might refer to as "Queer-Spiritual" knowledge, might consider the role that destruction of the symbol-making process has played in colonialism. Oppressors have long understood that cultural domination requires the dismantling of a people's sacred narratives, the rites and symbols evoking those narratives, and the roles of persons whose responsibility it is to spiritually guide the people, whether by way of religion itself or by means of arts imbued with sacred impulse. In this way, the oppressor achieves his ultimate purpose – that of destroying the self-esteem, integrity, and independence of the individuals whose culture he wishes to dominate or decimate.

In dictionaries and encyclopedias of religion, mythology, and folklore, the result of this suppression is clear. Narratives or descriptions of gender fluidity and same-sex desire typically are reported in a hostile or apologetic manner; are mentioned briefly but relegated to the background, implying their insignificance; are camouflaged, as in a case where same-sex lovers become "friends" or where transgendered deities become "goddesses" or "male gods;" or disappear altogether. In many instances where multiple variants of a mythical sacred narrative exist, only the heterosexual or traditionally gendered account is given. More tragically, the suppression of this data has resulted in lesbians, gays, bisexuals, and transgendered persons reaching the conclusion that they (we) are without history – or herstory. As gay Beat poet Jack Spicer expressed it in 1953, "we homosexuals are the only minority group that completely lacks any vestige of a separate cultural heritage. We have no songs, no folklore." This suppression of knowledge is especially tragic where lesbian, bisexual, and transgendered women are concerned. As lesbian filmmaker Barbara Hammer observes, "When you look for . . . lesbian history, the gaps and silences are profound." Similarly, Gayle Rubin, in her introduction to lesbian writer

Renée Vivien's exquisite novella *A Woman Appeared to Me* (1904), writes, "Lesbians, suffering from the dual disqualification of being gay and female, have been repeatedly dispossessed of their history." In this respect, the authors of this volume would like to say that we hope that we may be forgiven for an imbalance of data relating to women and men. The relative absence of general works on lesbian history and spirituality (as distinguished from women's history and spirituality) has made our task extremely difficult. We have tried, however, whenever possible, to include data pertaining to women. Another difficulty presenting itself has centered on whether or not, or how, to include references to people of color, as we, the authors of this volume, are of European heritage, and it has been suggested to us that in presenting such data, we are in a sense appropriating it. After discussing this issue with many persons of color, we have decided to include this data. Ultimately, it is our feeling that to refrain from including this data would be to further the suppression of the history of people of color who have been same-sex oriented, bisexual, or transgendered and who have contributed to the world's spiritual traditions. In respect to inclusion or exclusion of data, we were, in the course of compiling this text, approached by several individuals who expressed concern as to our including material referring to sadomasochism and intergenerational love. While we respect their desire that we exclude this material from the text, we have decided to include the data because we feel that to exclude it would be to deny important issues and figures in our history. We recognize that in doing so, however, we risk challenging the well-established tradition of referring only to "positive role models" in works such as ours.

Given these conditions, we feel the reinscription into spiritual lore of narratives, figures, symbols, etc., pertaining to gender and sexual "variance" (or totality) to be a vital undertaking. As those among us who participate in religious services, storytelling, and other ritual events, as well as those of us who are drawn to myths and legends (often in the contemporary guises of horror and science-fiction), are aware, signs and narratives emerging from the symbol-making process can help us to "open up levels of reality otherwise closed to us," as Mary Daly has suggested. Moreover, drawing upon the experiences and writings of contemporary feminists and persons of color, we are made aware that such knowledge may also aid us in struggling against oppression and in honoring ourselves in a manner that embraces yet also reaches beyond the personal, toward the collective and transpersonal realms of experience.

It is, we feel, especially important to stress in this text that spiritual impulse has historically been manifested not only in strictly religious contexts but also within the realm of the arts. Artistic expression of the sacred appears, moreover, to have especially served persons and groups denied overt religious power as a means to speak of the spiritual dimension of experience. In the works of Caravaggio, Walt Whitman, Emily Dickinson, Tchaikovsky, Mikhail Kuzmin, Renée Vivien, Benjamin Britten, Christopher Isherwood, Kenneth Anger, Allen Ginsberg, Judy Grahn, Monique Wittig, Paula Gunn Allen, Audre Lorde, Derek Jarman, Gloria Anzaldúa, Rotimi Fani-Kayode, and many others, the weaving together of gender and sexual variance with spiritual impulse is evident.

In an effort to provide our readers with both the most current and the most accurate information pertaining to our subject, we have interviewed practitioners of many of the spiritual movements and traditions described herein. To aid our readers in exploring the *Encyclopaedia,* we have also employed small caps to refer to cross-referenced entries and have provided an index of spiritual/mythic traditions and attributes as well as a selected bibliography.

In recent years, Queer theorists and others have begun to recognize the potentiality of a history, and in particular, of a spiritual history, shared by lesbians, gays, bisexuals, and transgendered persons. This widening perspective was heralded by Hélène Cixous and Catherine Clément in *The Newly Born Woman* (1986), in which they wrote, "There have always been those uncertain, poetic persons who have not let themselves be reduced to dummies programmed by pitiless repression of the homosexual element. Men or women: beings who are complex, mobile, open. Accepting the other sex as a component makes them much richer, more various, stronger, and – to the extent that they are mobile – very fragile. It is only in this condition that we invent." This perspective has also been voiced by Andrea Juno and V. Vale in their introduction to *Angry Women* (1991), in which they write, "The gay and lesbian community are pioneers in . . . playing with the fixed biological gender identities of 'man' and 'woman' which our society has deemed sacred and untouchable . . . The very act of subverting something so primal and fixed in society as one's gender role can unleash a creativity that is truly needed by society – like a shamanistic act." In her queer-theoretical essay "Tracking the Vampire," postmodernist theorist Sue-Ellen Case, in describing what she terms a "queer compound," echoes this view, in linking same-sex desire, "gender inversion," and "ontological shift" (roughly, metaphysical shift in consciousness). Case observes that in the poems of the Spanish mystic San Juan de la Cruz (St John of the Cross), who writes of himself, in Christian manner, as a lover or beloved of Jesus Christ, the "queer compound" appears in this fashion: "The flame of this desire . . . sears into a world where being is reconfigured. John, the mystic lover, desires a being of a different order . . . In order to 'know' this being, the senses . . . must be reconfigured . . . [In] 'The Spiritual Canticle,' where his love finds full expression in the trope of marriage, John inverts his gender, writing his desire as if he were the bride with the other being [Christ] as the bridegroom. John, the bride, languishes for her lover, seeks him everywhere . . . The wound of love liberates the lover from the boundaries of being . . . Ontology shifts through gender inversion and is expressed as same-sex desire. This is queer, indeed." Such perspectives indicate that we may be entering into a period of rich discussion and creative expression in terms of the honoring and celebration of the interrelationship of eroticism, gender, and the spiritual in our lives.

Randy P. Lunĉunas Conner
David Hatfield Sparks
Mariya Sparks
San Francisco, 1996

A Note on Terminology

We feel it important to clarify the terms concerned with gender and sexuality which are employed in this text, as the language currently used to describe these arenas of activity remains in its infancy. We hope this explanation of terms will aid in familiarizing the reader with this rather complex discourse.

While we hold that gendered and sexual behaviors and identities probably result from a complex interaction of biology and societal shaping as well as, perhaps, spiritual embodiment of archetypal energies or forces, when we refer to "traditionally feminine" and "traditionally masculine" behaviors or identities herein, we are in this case referring to gender roles not as essential traits but rather as roles shaped by the cultures in which individuals have been reared.

The terms "transgendered," "gender variant," and "third gender" are used to refer to gendered behaviors, identities, or roles which do not conform to a particular culture's conceptions of "masculinity" or "femininity," which mix these conceptions in a fluid or relatively stable manner, which cross them in terms of traditional lines based on anatomical sex, or which constitute a fairly stable gender role rooted neither in traditional "masculinity" nor "femininity." "Transgendered" behavior or identity may be manifested in behaviors characterized as "tomboyish" or "sissyish," as well as in transvestism or "drag," and in transsexuality.

While "transgendered" may place emphasis on either a transformative process or on a stable identity, "gender variant" stresses process or fluidity, while "third gender" stresses stable identity. In no way is the term "gender variant" meant to imply that transgendered behaviour is a psychologically confused response to traditional gender roles or that transgendered behavior should be judged against a norm of traditional roles.

The transgendered community and writers concerned with that community differ in terms of how they describe anatomical males and females who manifest what are deemed transgendered characteristics. In this text, "transgendered female (or woman)" refers to an anatomical female (or woman) who exhibits transgendered characteristics, while "transgendered male" refers to an anatomical male who exhibits transgendered characteristics.

The more specialized term "two-spirit" refers to a transgendered or third gender role, in the past referred to as "berdache," occurring within Native American Indian, North Asian shamanic, and related cultures. The term

"Amazonian" is used in this text to refer to transgendered women who often serve as warriors in their respective cultures. The term "priest/ess" is used to stress the transgendered aspect of the role undertaken by certain transgendered spiritual functionaries.

We have avoided using the term "gay" in pre-twentieth-century contexts, opting to employ "homoerotically inclined" to refer to males engaging in affectionate and/or erotic relationships. We have employed "lesbian" and "bisexual" to refer to persons or groups of various cultures and epochs due to the fact that they are widely accepted in the discourse of sexuality and carry somewhat less cultural baggage than does the term "gay." In certain instances, especially concerning women of non-western heritage, the term "woman-loving" replaces "lesbian." We have used the terms "queer" and "queer-identified" to refer to persons or groups, especially of the late twentieth century, associated with lesbian, gay, bisexual, and/or transgendered behaviour or identity. We recognize, finally, that some transgendered persons describe their relationships in heterosexual terms. In this text, we have focused primarily on transgenderism where it is linked with sexual diversity.

Spiritual Traditions

African and African-Diasporic

In African cultures, same-sex EROTICISM and androgyny, or transgenderism, have often been linked to other traits, including military prowess. These traits have combined to form a domain or web of associations which manifests itself as a behavioral complex – a complex which has often taken the form of a gender variant, homoerotically inclined spiritual functionary. Africans have tended to focus, however, on spiritual role and not on sexual or gendered behavior or identity. Numerous spiritual traditions of Africa are shamanic in character. Elements of African religions, most if not all of which may be found in shamanic traditions, include ancestor worship, herbal medicine, animal sacrifice, complex systems of divination, initiation rites, and secret societies. In a number of African religions, as in shamanic traditions, an individual may be "possessed" or embodied by a deity or spirit of a gender or sex other than her/his own. The German ethnologist Hermann Baumann (b. 1902), tracking two key elements of Shamanism, belief in an androgynous, or transgendered, godhead and the process of gender transformation among practitioners, has documented the occurrence of one or both in many African spiritual traditions, including those of the Akan, Ambo-Kwanyama, Bobo, Chokwe, Dahomeans (of Benin), Dogon-Bambara, Etik, Handa, Humbe, Hunde, Iba, Jukun, Kimbundu, Konso, Kunama, Lamba, Lango, Luba, Lulua, Musho, Nuba, Ovimbundu, Rundi, Shona-Karonga, Venda, Vili-Kongo, and Yoruba. Contrary to the current Afrocentric view, both same-sex eroticism and gender variant behavior apparently were known to Africans long before Africa, except perhaps for Egypt and Libya, was subjected to non-African influences.

Among the Azande, living in what today is southwestern Sudan, northern Zaire, and the southeastern corner of the Central African Republic, a form of intergenerational homoeroticism was practiced from remote antiquity until the beginning of the twentieth century. Anthropologist Edward E. Evans-Pritchard has insisted that this and other forms of same-sex eroticism were indigenous and not the result of foreign influence. The typical intergenerational relationship was that between a ruler or warrior and a younger male. Azande women also practiced same-sex eroticism from the remote past until the present century, although this activity was apparently feared by most men. That same-sex eroticism was thought by men to double a woman's power indicates an earlier period in Azande history in which women held greater power. Lesbianism appears to have been especially common among women living in the courts of princes. The preferred form of sexual intercourse appears to have involved the use of a dildo fashioned from a root. Evidence suggests that Azande women engaging in same-sex eroticism also may have engaged in magical practices or served as spiritual functionaries. In folkloric belief, they were associated with witchcraft and were linked to the *adandara*, a supernatural wild cat with gleaming ebony skin and luminescent eyes. Indeed, lesbian lovemaking was referred to as *adandara*, and it was imagined that such lovemaking practices led to the birth of cat-people. The Nama(n), a tribe of Khoisan people, practiced from time immemorial a form of egalitarian homoeroticism. This relationship was formalized by means of a ceremony of communion at which a beverage, in earlier times water and in later times coffee, was shared by the lovers. Transgendered or gender variant homosexuality has been documented among the Nuba peoples of the Nilotic Sudan. The Nuba tribes have various names for gender variant males engaging in same-sex eroticism, including *domere* (Tira), *korre* (Nyima), *londo* (Korongo), *tomere* (Heiban, Otoro), and *tubele* (Mesakin). Among the Nuba, according to anthropologist S. F. Nadel, "homosexuals . . . wear women's clothing, do women's work, and adopt women's ways." Transgendered same-sex marriage is practiced by the Korongo and Mesakin; writes Nadel, "[Transgendered] 'wife' and 'husband' live together and keep a common household."

Transgendered, or gender variant, males and those engaging in homoeroticism have traditionally served as spiritual functionaries in a number of African cultures. Among the Lango, a Nilotic people of the Uganda, gender variant males engaging in same-sex eroticism were still being called *jo apele* or *jo aboich* in the early twentieth century. *Jo apele* saw themselves as the children of the gynandrous deity Jok. *Jo apele* dressed in women's garments, decorated their faces like Lango women, and wore their hair long. They took women's names and did the work of women, which may have included serving as spiritual intermediaries, delivering oracles while sitting beneath Atida-Jok's sacred banyan tree. They were formally wedded to men "without offending against Lango law." Among the Lugbara, spiritual functionaries are regarded as marginal persons and more specifically as gender variant; these qualities promote their serving as messengers between the human and spirit worlds. Transgendered, or gender variant, male mediums are named *okule* ("like women"), while female gender variant mediums are called AGULE ("like men"). Among the Kenyan Meru, the *mugawe,* a "powerful religious leader" who is "considered a complement to . . . male political leaders," wears women's clothing and often women's hairstyles as well. According to sociologist David F. Greenberg, the *mugawe* is "often homosexual, and sometimes marries a man." Gender variant male spiritual functionaries have also been documented among the Ila people of what is now southern Zambia. In the early twentieth century, such men were called *mwammi*, "prophets." They "dressed always as women, did women's work such as plaiting baskets, and lived and slept among, but not with, the women." Gender variant and/or homoerotically inclined male spiritual functionaries may also be found in the Kwanyama tribe, where they are called *"omasenge KIMBANDA,"* among the Zulu, where they number among the ISANGOMA, and in the BORI cult of the Maguzawa, the non-Muslim Hausa of Nigeria. Such spiritual functionaries, as well as transgendered and/or lesbian inclined female functionaries, also number among the practitioners of certain African-diasporic spiritual traditions such as Candomblé, Santería and Vodou.

To give the reader a more specific idea of how same-sex eroticism and transgenderism relate to an African-diasporic tradition, the remainder of this section will focus on the Yoruba-diasporic religion, which has its roots in Nigeria. It has been practiced for many centuries, although its exact date of origin is unknown. It has links to the religion of Dahomey (now Benin), and some scholars have further suggested associations with the ancient religions of Egypt and Phoenicia. The practice of the Yoruba and other African religions in the New World commenced in the early sixteenth century, with the arrival of the slaves. Many of the twelve million Africans who arrived in the Americas between the early sixteenth and the mid-nineteenth centuries were of Yoruba ancestry. In Brazil, the Yoruba came to be known as the Nagô; in Cuba, as the Lucumí. While they were forced to outwardly adopt Christianity, many continued to worship their gods, albeit in the guise of Catholic saints, and to hold their ancient celebrations, albeit on the feast days of the saints. The Yoruba religion is known by various names including [I]sin Orishá, roughly translated as "the way of the *Orishá*." The *orishá* are the divinities of the religion. The religion has many branches. The development of these branches, especially in the Americas, has depended upon which other indigenous religions it has come into contact with as well as upon the degree of influence exerted by Christianity – and, to a lesser extent, Islam – and other spiritual traditions and metaphysical systems, including ritual magic and spiritualism. In Brazil, the Yoruba religion is generally known as Candomblé. Brazilian branches include: Candomblé proper, Candomblé Caboclo, Macumba, Umbanda, Batuque, and Quimbanda. In Cuba, Puerto Rico, and the United States (especially in New York City, Miami, Oakland, San Francisco, and Los Angeles), the religion is known as Santería, Lucumí, Regla Ocha, or simply as "the religion." Where it has blended with Kongo religion, the tradition of Palo Monté has emerged; this tradition, in turn, is linked to the secret society of the Abakúa. The Yoruba religion has also played a role in the development of Vodou, the African-diasporic manifestation of Dahomean religion practiced in Haiti, New Orleans, and elsewhere. Likewise, Vodou(n) has influenced the Yoruba religion. In the Yoruba religion there exists a Supreme Being, Olodumaré, from whom all other *orishá* emanate. Practitioners hold that the *orishá*, as well as the/our ancestors, provide spiritual guidance and imbue those who believe with spiritual energy, called *ashé* (*aché, axé*). Practitioners often experience contact with the *orishá* by way of altered states of consciousness achieved through drumming, chanting, dancing, and other "techniques of ecstasy." Devotees learn of the future, and also what the *orishá* require of them, during these states and by way of divinatory consultations. Divinatory tools include palm nuts, cowrie shells, and pieces of coconut. Practitioners believe that offerings and sacrifices must be made to the *orishá* in order to honor and appease them and in order to obtain their blessings. The Yoruba religion has a hierarchical priesthood. Names referring to priests and priestesses include: *babalawo, babalaô, babalorishá, iyalorishá, pai de santo, mae de santo, santero, santera*. Each person – including non-practitioners . . . is believed to be the spiritual "son" or "daughter" of a "father" and "mother" *orishá*. One of these is generally claimed to predominate, to be the "owner of the head." Identity of one's spiritual parents is typically revealed or confirmed via divinatory consultations.

The Yoruba religion, primarily as practiced in the Americas, has carved out a niche for gender variant persons and persons engaging in same-sex eroticism. More than twenty-five terms, most of African origin, are employed to describe such persons. These include *adodi*, which may be applied to homosexual, bisexual, or transgendered males, and *alakuata*, which may be applied to lesbian, bisexual, or transgendered women. In *El Monte,* the classic work on Santería, Lydia Cabrera points out that many practitioners of the Lucumí branch of the religion are homosexually oriented. Seth and Ruth Leacock, in their study of Batuque, a Brazilian branch of the religion, report that almost one-third of all its male practitioners are either homosexual or alleged to be so: "there was often unanimity among our informants . . . that some male mediums lived with other men with whom they had sexual relations." Ruth Landes, René Ribeiro, Peter Fry, Hubert Fichte, and João Trevisan have documented the widespread presence of homosexual, lesbian, bisexual, and transgendered practitioners in Candomblé. Brazilian actor and gay activist João Ferreira relates that the *orishá* in general, and certain of them in particular, "defend their sons and daughters against . . . sexual prejudice." *Orishá* who are considered patrons of such persons include: OBATALA, OSHUN, YEMAYA, OLOKUN, YEWA, OYA, INLE, LOGUNEDE, OSHUMARE, and ORUNMILA. *Orishá* who demonstrate conflicting attitudes toward such persons include SHANGO and OGUN. An *orishá* who has recently become associated with HIV/AIDS and thus also with gay and bisexual men is BABALUAYE. A specifically Brazilian (and now also North American) *orishá* who is associated with gender variant, homosexual, and bisexual males is POMBA GIRA.

In the religion, male practitioners as a whole have tended to be divided – especially in Brazil, where relatively narrow definitions of gender identity and role are found – into camps of *homem*, or "real men," and what might be referred to as non-*homem*. Frequently, heterosexual and bisexual male practitioners have been lumped together as *homem*, while homosexual or gay male practitioners have been categorized as *adé*. It appears that while a heterosexual or bisexual male's *homem* status may be tempered by having a female *orishá* as a primary parent or by being temporarily possessed by a female *orishá*, causing that man to exhibit "feminine" behavior and/or to dress in feminine attire, his *homem* status is *not* thereby forfeited. There is disagreement as to whether or not homosexual males can be considered *homem*. Some practitioners and scholars have suggested that if a homosexual male generally conforms to a traditional male role and/or is the son of a male *orishá*, that male may be attributed an *homem* status. Most homosexual male practitioners, however, are categorized as *adé*, whether or not they exhibit traditionally masculine behavior. Thus, the category *adé* is similar to "homosexual" or "gay." *Adé* focuses primarily on sexual object choice; i.e., here is a male who desires what heterosexual women desire, regardless of whether he behaves in a "masculine" or an "effeminate" manner. *Adé*, however, also stresses that this male who desires other males also performs a spiritual function or fulfills a sacred role. Thus, *adé* suggests a homosexual spiritual functionary who may or may not behave in a gender variant manner. It would seem, however, that a majority of *adé* practitioners at least occasionally – if not frequently – perform behaviors regarded as transgendered. The term *bicha* ("bitch") is employed by Peter Fry in his article "Male Homosexuality and Spirit Possession in Brazil" to describe male practitioners who engage in same-sex eroticism, frequently assuming the "receptive" role, and who behave in a gender variant manner. While the term *bicha* is rejected by most of the practitioners with whom I have spoken, it may be useful in distinguishing a subgroup of *adé* practitioners who exhibit "effeminate" behavior and who are frequently, although not always, the children of female *orishá*. Among twenty-one practitioners of Candomblé studied by Maria Lina Leão Teixeira, eight of whom were women and thirteen of whom were men, Leão Teixeira discovered five of the men to be *adé* and one of the women to be *monokó* or lesbian. In this case, the males termed *adé* all appear to have been homosexual. Not all, however, could be properly termed *bichas*. Among the *adé* males, ages ranged from 27 to 42 years old; professions ranged from telephone operator to Navy officer. All but one identified as "mulatto." Of the five, two were priests, *pais de santo*. Three had female and two had male *orishá* as primary parents. Bene and Inacio were sons of Oxum [Oshún], while Lauro was a son of Iansã [Oyá]. Gustavo was a son of Oxossí [Ochossí], while Honorio was a son of Obaluayé [Babaluayé]. Tereza, the *monokó* or lesbian practitioner, a fifty-year-old Black female, was a daughter of Xangô [Shangó].

We have seen that all of these *orishá* are either directly or indirectly associated with same-sex eroticism and/or gender variance. The religion may appeal to gender variant, homosexual/lesbian, and bisexual persons because they discover within it deities who will defend them and whose sacred tales mirror their own. The religion may also appeal to them because it allows for, indeed often demands, the expression of behavior regarded as gender variant. Temples of the religion may also serve as sanctuaries for those who have been forced out of their homes by intolerant family members. Temples may also serve as meeting places for those seeking community among like-minded individuals. As mentioned above, Peter Fry has focused on the *bicha* practitioners of Candomblé. *Bichas*, while evoking fear and hostility in some practitioners, tend to be appreciated and respected because they are thought to be "more artistic" than other practitioners, "better equipped to organize and participate in ritual." They are – somewhat stereotypically – believed to be highly accomplished dancers, interior decorators, chefs, and costume designers, all of these professions playing key roles in the creation of a festive rite. What is more, Fry explains that supernatural power is often attributed to the *bichas* because, in deviating from prescribed gender and sexual roles, they are envisioned as inhabiting quasi-mystical "regions of the cosmos which are defined as outside society." This mystical difference between gender variant, homosexual practitioners and others is manifested in a ritual which, I am told, takes place in São Paulo. In this rite, "heterosexual men, who represent the sunrise, stand on one side; heterosexual women, who represent the moonrise, stand on the other; and gay people [of both sexes], representing the twilight, stand in the middle." This ritual gives expression to the belief that gender variant gay persons, in Fry's terminology, *bichas* and their female equivalents, may constitute an alternate gender role.

The *bichas* of Brazil seem remarkably similar to the drag queen practitioners of New York City described by Edouardo Mejía. Practitioner Mejía told writer Gloria Anzaldúa, "You visit any Hispanic drag queen's apartment and what do you see – a grand altar!" Some priests and practitioners insist that drag has nothing whatsoever to do with the religion – an opinion that is immediately challenged by the wearing of feminine attire by male sons of feminine *orishá* – and that drag queens are more representative of "Western decadence" than of the Yoruba religion. Others feel strongly that drag is intimately linked to spiritual practice. According to Mejía, "My friend dresses in drag, in red and white female garments, because Shangó wants him to dress this way." As for Mejía himself, he explained that he often wore a mixture of blue and white feminine and masculine garments, including "bracelets, a scarf, and a flower in [his] hair because Yemayá [wished] it." Mejía insisted that drag practitioners are considered especially skilled in the divinatory and magical arts. Said José, "In New York, a lot of transvestites read the *caracolés* [cowries]." He continued, "In the Bronx, a lot of them get the reputation of knowing how to work the *obra* [here, magic associated with Santería]."

Numerous gay, bisexual, and transgendered artists of various kinds have been practitioners of and/or deeply influenced by the Yoruba religion, including the Brazilian musicians Gilberto Gil, Caetano Veloso, Ney Matogrosso, and Maria Bethania, the African-American musician BLACKBERRI, and the Yoruba-British photographer Rotimi Fani-Kayode. A number of writers and practitioners have also spoken of the noticeable presence of transgendered, same-sex oriented, and bisexual priests and diviners in the Yoruba religion. In his monumental study of cowrie shell divination, William Bascom describes a diviner, Salako, who was born in Nigeria around 1880. As an infant, Salako was taken to a priest who "confirmed that he belonged to Orishalá [a manifestation of Obatalá]" and that Yemayá was also to play an important role in his life. Salako was initiated in 1895 and by 1926 had become chief diviner of the ruler Oyo. When Bascom met Salako in 1951, when the latter was about seventy, he described him in terms indicating gender variance, "slight and delicate of build . . . with his hair plaited like a woman's." In general, Salako was of "a somewhat effeminate appearance." Where

Nigerian priests are concerned, Margaret Thompson Drewal has recently described priests and initiates of Shangó in gender variant terms. They are often considered the "wives" of the god. This relationship of feminine male priest to masculine male deity is reflected in the priests' hairstyles. One of these hairstyles is the *shuku*, "which refers to the round basket in which the marketwomen carry their wares on their heads;" another is the "Yoruba bridal hairstyle known as *agogô*," resembling that worn by the male priest of Oyá. The relationship between priest and god is thought to be characterized in feminine-masculine terms because the Yoruba, like other peoples we have encountered, think of the state of possession as a receptive, hence traditionally feminine, state (i.e. to be possessed or "ridden" by the god is to be penetrated by the god). Drewal also mentions a priest of Oyá from the Ijebu remote area of Nigeria who wears "a women's-style wrapper tied under the arms and Oyá's cowrie vestment over his left shoulder." The transgendered appearances of Salako and the priests described by Drewal are reflected by the priests and other male practitioners of Candomblé Caboclo, a Brazilian branch of the religion. According to Ruth Landes, who published an article on the practitioners of Caboclo in 1940, the followers of this tradition hold that women possess greater and more immediate access than men to the realm of the *orishá* and other spiritual entities. They also believe, however, that certain men, whom they deem to be "like women," may possess this gift or power. For this reason, many of the original male initiates of Caboclo were homosexuals and bisexuals who exhibited behavior regarded as gender variant. Some were drag queens, some male prostitutes. As it happened, quite a number of these men were sons of Iansã (Oyá). In her study, Landes vividly describes a Caboclo priest, Father João, who wore "straightened hair . . . a symbol of male homosexuals" and "fancy blouses" and who was very open about his homosexuality, "writing love letters to the men of his heart." Of João and other homosexual and bisexual priests, Landes notes that they are believed to be especially gifted in the divinatory and magical arts, evoking their spiritual descendants, the *bichas* and drag practitioners of New York City. Their "fame as priests," writes Landes, is "overshadowed by their fame as sorcerers." Viewing the Caboclo priests as marginalized persons and perhaps also as religious radicals, Landes says of them, "Least of all do they reflect the masculinity of the patriarchal culture in whose heart they live." Serge Bramley, in his account of Macumba, another Brazilian branch of the religion, records priestess Maria-José as saying, "women make better mediums. But there are Fathers of the Gods . . . they are often homosexual." In Hubert Fichte's words, many Candomblé priests and priestesses "embrace . . . homosexuality." João Trevisan, in his interview with *babalorixá* M. Aparecida, asks, "Tell me something, Mario, do you know many gay priests [of Candomblé]?" to which Aparecida replies, "Most are gay." When Trevisan asks him why he thinks this is so, he responds, "I think it's the way things are." Ermeval, a member of Adé Dudu, a gay liberationist/African-Brazilian organization, writes, "In our religion, these persons are respected as *uma ponte dos Orixás*, a bridge to/of the *orishá*."

Ancient Near Eastern and Western Antiquity

While the spiritual traditions of Near Eastern and Western antiquity – including the religions of Egypt, Mesopotamia, Phoenicia, Canaan, Greece, Rome, Asia Minor, and Scythia, as well as the faiths of the Gnostics, the Celts and the Teutons (Germans, Scandinavians) – differed in many respects, they also shared much in common. Here, in an effort to be brief, we shall focus on their commonalities. One of their most noticeable shared characteristics was a belief that the Divine is multiple; in other words, either that more than a single divine being exists, or that the godhead may assume a nearly infinite number of forms. These traditions also maintained that reality is multidimensional, that is, that realms inhabited by beings such as ghosts exist, and, moreover, that they frequently impact upon life in the human realm. Within these traditions, many divine beings were associated with same-sex intimacy, bisexuality, or transgenderism, as the godhead was not required to represent male heterosexual or ascetic fatherhood only, at the expense of other traits. The Egyptian gods HAPY and SET, the Syrian goddess ATAGARTIS, the Greek deities ARTEMIS and DIONYSUS, the Gnostic deity NAAS, the Celtic CERNUNNOS and MACHA, the Teutonic ODIN and LOKI, and many others described in this text speak to the interrelationship of divinity and same-sex intimacy and/or transgenderism. It is important to note, however, that deities associated with such traits did not preside over gendered or sexual behavior or identity merely, but that they also functioned in other capacities, serving as creators, guardians, healers, peacemakers, psychopomps (guides of souls from this world to the next), and in still other capacities. These traditions also held in common that Nature was to be revered as a reflection of, or embodiment of, the Divine, that human beings were as well a reflection or embodiment of godhead, and that divine beings often led human-like lives. In part due to these beliefs, traits such as gender variance, or fluidity, and same-sex erotic orientation were often considered divine gifts, and less often, as divine punishments. Thus, ancient Mesopotamians considered transgenderism and homosexuality as MEs, or essential characteristics, distributed by a divinity. Further still, these traditions shared in common a strong belief in the continued existence of the soul, either by way of dwelling in a paradise or other afterlife or else by way of reincarnation or metempsychosis. Exemplary of this belief in our context is an Egyptian bas-relief from the Fifth Dynasty (c. 2600 BCE) which suggests that an intimate relationship between two male hairdresser-manicurists of Pharaoh Niuserre may have been represented in their tomb so that their relationship might continue in the afterlife. Beyond such beliefs, these traditions shared the concept of a multifaceted, often hierarchical, priesthood comprised of persons serving various functions and often possessing varying gendered and sexual, or erotic, identities. Even while some of these traditions might be described as patriarchal in character, they nevertheless admitted women, and often transgendered and same-sex inclined individuals as spiritual functionaries, a situation seldom occurring in so-called "living" patriarchal faiths. Such spiritual functionaries included the ASSINNU, KALUM, and KURGARRU priests and the SHUGIA priestesses of INANNA/ISHTAR, the KELABIM priests of the Phoenician goddess Astarte, the QEDESHIM priests of the Canaanite goddess ATHIRAT, the *arktoi* priestesses of Artemis/Diana, the GALLI priests of the Phrygian-Greco-Roman goddess CYBELE, the ENAREE priests of the Scythian goddess ARTIMPASA, the *ergi* priests and SEIDR magicians of the Teutonic deities FREYJA and FREYR, and many others described in this book. In terms of rites, all of these traditions emphasized the honoring of divine beings through prayers or invocations, offerings, and sacrifices, as well as the practice of the healing, divinatory, magical arts, the creation of sacred artworks including visual arts and crafts, MUSIC, dance, and drama, and participation in games and entertainments (such as CARNIVAL) linked to the realms of the spiritual and mythic. Some, like the *enarees* of Artimpasa, excelled at healing and divination, while the *assinnu* and other transgendered priests of Inanna/Ishtar were renowned as musicians and ritual actors. Within these spiritual traditions, ritual transgenderism was often undertaken, typically expressed in transvestism or mixed-gender attire and transgendered speech, gestures, and pursuits, as in the case of the priests of Inanna/Ishtar who spoke in the Emesal dialect, reserved for female and gender variant male worshippers of the goddess, and who at least occasionally dressed in a costume mixing traditionally masculine, feminine, and sacerdotal articles of clothing. Among the Celts, figures such as the FILIDH, the ancient Irish bard, and the GWIDINOT, societies of warrior women, suggest somewhat subtler links between spirituality, sexuality, and gender role. These traditions also held in common a profound reverence for both legendary and historical rulers, heroes and heroines, whose exploits were often grounded in, or otherwise bonded to, the realm of spirit. Such individuals include the Egyptian pharaohs AKHENATEN and HATSHEPSUT, the Mesopotamian ruler-hero GILGAMESH and his comrade Enkidu, the Amazons of Greco-Roman antiquity, the warrior HERACLES and his lovers IOLAUS and Queen OMPHALE, the Roman emperor HADRIAN and his beloved ANTINOUS, the Celtic heroes CÚ CHULAINN and Fer Diadh, the Teutonic women warriors ALFHILD and GROA, and many others mentioned in this text. Also within these traditions, ritual same-sex eroticism sometimes occurred, as in rites allegedly undertaken by the *qedeshim* of Athirat and the Gnostic NAASSENES and PHIBIONITES. What is more, rites commemorating same-sex union appear to have occurred among women dwelling at THIASOI, or religious households, in the ancient Mediterranean, as at the *thiasos* of SAPPHO on the island of Lesbos, as well as among male devotees of Greek and Roman deities. It is not surprising, given the impact that same-sex eroticism and love and transgenderism had upon the religions of antiquity in the areas of rites, spiritual functionaries, beliefs, and the envisioning of divine beings, that symbols would emerge which bore associations with, or correspondences to, these gendered and sexual behaviors or identities. Such symbols include animals like the HARE and the HYENA, articles of clothing including the SANDYX and KROKETOS, astrological signs like TAURUS, colors like SAFFRON, flowers including the HYACINTH and the POPPY, gemstones like AMETHYST, plants like the LETTUCE, sites including the islands of LESBOS and LEUKÉ, trees like the CYPRESS, and many others given in this text. In general, we find that the so-called pantheistic and/or polytheistic religions or spiritual traditions of Western and Near Eastern antiquity, due in great part to their embracing of multiple archetypal manifestations of divinity, engendered a cornucopia of deities, spiritual roles, rites, and symbols pertaining in some way to the interrelationship of the sacred or mythic and patterns of gender and sexual identity reaching beyond traditionally masculine or feminine heterocentric patterns.

Buddhism

Buddhism has been defined as the "tradition of thought and practice associated with Shakyamuni, the Buddha [the Enlightened One], who lived in India in the sixth/fifth century BCE, and is sometimes referred to by his clan name, Gautama [or by] his personal name . . . Siddhattha [or, Siddhartha]." Central to Buddhism is the doctrine of the Four Noble Truths: that life is full of suffering; that suffering is caused by desire; that in order to eliminate suffering, one must eliminate desire; and that one may eliminate desire by following the Middle Way. This Way is commonly referred to as the Noble Eightfold Path, the second doctrine central to Buddhism. This path consists of correct understanding, correct thoughts or motives, correct speech, correct action, correct means of livelihood, correct effort, correct concentration, and correct meditation. Also central to Buddhism is the idea that numerous BODHISATTVAS – typically, human beings who have become enlightened and who thereby have been delivered from the process of reincarnation – have declined, rather than accepted immortality, in order to return to earth to aid in the healing of the planet and the enlightenment of all sentient beings. *Bodhisattvas* associated with transgenderism and/or same-sex desire include AVALOKITESHVARA, KANNON, KUAN YIN, and TARA. Buddhism, while emphasizing correct ethical behavior, also imparts the notion that one must develop their own way of perceiving and experiencing the sacredness of life. Buddhism manifests itself in both religious and (purely) philosophical forms. Some Buddhist sects, like Zen, clearly emphasize the philosophical; while others, like those in which the *bodhisattva* Kuan Yin is revered, emphasize the spiritual, even, at times, the magical. Buddhism was brought from India to China before or during the first century CE; by the fifth century, it had become the major religion of China. It was introduced to the Japanese around 550. During the following centuries, many sects of Buddhism emerged in many other places.

The *Jataka* tales of early Indian Buddhism convey a rather positive attitude toward same-sex intimacy in their celebration of the Buddha's loving relationship with his disciple Ananda. J. I. Cabezón, in "Homosexuality and Buddhism" (1993), relates that in one of these tales, "the Buddha and Ananda are depicted as two deer who 'always went about together . . . ruminating and cuddling together, very happy, head to head, nozzle to nozzle, horn to horn.' In another, they are two handsome young sons of Brahmin parents who refuse to marry so that they may remain with each other." However, writings by Buddhaghosa (fl. c. 430) and other Buddhist scholars of the third through fifth centuries indicate that both same-sex intimacy and transgenderism were condemned in Indian Buddhism, with the greatest hostility being directed toward gender variant, third gender, or transgendered, homoerotically inclined males called *pandakas*. These persons were typically forbidden to become monks. If discovered already living in a monastery, they were expelled. Non-transgendered, homoerotically inclined monks, if and when discovered, also tended to be expelled, although punishment was usually less harsh. Indian Buddhist NUNS engaging in lesbianism were reprimanded and/or punished but do not appear to have been expelled. (This probably says more about patriarchal attitudes within Indian Buddhism than it does about respect for women-loving women within the tradition.) As Cabezón observes, "very little work has been done on Chinese Buddhist attitudes toward homosexuality or on its existence in monastic settings." This is also true where lesbianism, bisexuality, and transgenderism are concerned. Most of what we know derives from tales concerning lesbian and transgendered behavior among Chinese Buddhist NUNS. Sometime between the sixteenth and nineteenth centuries, a Buddhist nun founded the "Ten Sisters" society, which embraced resistance to heterosexual marriage, passionate friendship and lesbian intimacy and held ceremonies of same-sex UNION. This society became the prototype for other later societies including the GOLDEN ORCHID ASSOCIATION. In a drama of the seventeenth century written by Li Yu (1611-1680), *Lian Xiangban (Pitying the Fragrant Companion)*, two women, one a visitor married to a man and one a single novice, fall in love in a Buddhist convent, swearing their love to each other before an image of the Buddha. Ultimately, the novice becomes a second wife to the married woman's husband so that the two women may continue their relationship.

It appears that Chinese Buddhism may have shown greater tolerance toward persons engaging in same-sex and transgendered behavior than was shown in early Indian Buddhism. According to Noguchi Takenori and Paul Schalow in the *Kodansha Encyclopedia of Japan* (1983), "the practice of homosexuality in Japan is traditionally said to date from the early part of the Heian period (794-1185) when Buddhist monks introduced it upon their return from Tang (T'ang) China in 806." While they are quick to point out that "homosexuality surely existed in Japan before then," they emphasize that the "traditional account of its origins helps explain why homosexuality became a preferred form of expression among the Buddhist priesthood." By the end of the Heian period, they report, "homosexuality had become popular among the Kyoto aristocracy, perhaps because of the increased contact with the Buddhist clergy." The often open expression of affection and desire of Buddhist priests for those they loved appears to have grown stronger over the following four centuries. In the mid-sixteenth century, when Father Francis Xavier arrived in Japan with the hope of converting its people to Christianity, he was shocked upon encountering so many Buddhist monks involved in homoerotic relationships; indeed, he rapidly began referring to homoeroticism as the "Japanese vice." Needless to say, Father Xavier decided it was his duty to rid Japan of the "sin of sodomy." Xavier wrote, "We frequently tell the *bonzes* [i.e. Buddhist monks] that they should not commit such shameful sins; and everything that we tell them amuses them since they laugh about it and have no shame when they are reproached about so vile a sin." It appears, however, that Xavier and his fellow missionaries did not manage to convince a majority of Buddhists. It is reported that on one occasion, as he and a group of missionaries were walking through the streets of Yamaguchi, a gang of youths began yelling at them, "So you're the ones who forbid sodomy!" The youths then began throwing their shoes at them. On another occasion, Father Xavier and his companions paid a visit to the Sofuku-ji Zen-shu monastery in the city of Fukuoaka. The Buddhist monks there greeted them warmly at first, but when Xavier began to expound upon the evils of sodomy, several monks began laughing while still others, infuriated, demanded that Xavier leave the monastery at once. On a third occasion, Xavier and his entourage were invited to the court of the Duke of Yamaguchi, Ouchi Yoshitaka. The Duke, like the Buddhist monks, greeted the Catholics with hospitality, but when Xavier began reading in a very loud, hostile voice the story of Sodom and Gomorrah, Ouchi banished the priest and his companions from the court.

It should be noted that some Japanese Buddhists condemned same-sex relationships. The monk Genshin, for example, composed in the late tenth century an extremely homophobic treatise describing an inferno for same-sex lovers. It appears, however, that many Buddhists both accepted and participated in homoerotic relationships. While such relationships undoubtedly occurred in a great number of sects, the most prominent were Ji-shu, Hokke-shu, Shingon, Tendai, and Zen. Members of the Ji-shu sect revered several deities, chief among them Amida, known as the "Buddha of the Pure Land" or the "Buddha of the Western Paradise." They believed that Amida, the son of a king, had meditated for thousands of years in order to save humanity. He promised an afterlife in the Western Paradise to those who would follow him and practice *nembutsu*, in part by chanting his mantra, *Namu-amida-butsu*. Many of the members of this sect were warriors. Women were given great respect in Ji-shu. Father Xavier described the Ji-shu monks as "inclined to sins abhorrent to Nature." He explained that since same-sex relationships were "so very common" among the Ji-shu, they did "not regard it [i.e. same-sex eroticism] as strange or an abomination." He continued, "These *bonzes* have many boys in their monasteries, the sons of *hidalgos* [i.e. samurai], whom they teach how to read and write, and they commit corruptions with them." The Hokke-shu, or "Lotus" or "Black" Sect, was founded in 1253. Members of this sect revere Shaka, or Shakyamuni, the "first recognized Buddha." In the past, it is said that they also revered Dainichi Nyorai, the "Great Illuminator Buddha." Practitioners refer to the sect's founder, Nichiren, as "an incarnation of Bosatsu Jogyo, an early disciple of Buddha." Their sacred mantra is *Namu-myoho-rengekyo* ("Homage to the Lotus of the Good Law"). Georg Schurhammer explains that although the Hokke-shu or Nichiren monks officially disapproved of all forms of sexual intercourse, they nevertheless, at least into the mid-sixteenth century, openly engaged in homoerotic relationships. The relationship of the Shingon sect to homoeroticism is briefly discussed in the entry on its founder, KUKAI (774-835), while the relationship of the Tendai sect to homoeroticism is discussed in the entry on its founder, SAICHO (767-822).

Zen, that form of Buddhism with which, alongside Tibetan Buddhism, the West is most familiar, emerged in Japan in the ninth century. Zen stresses "meditation, the use of *koan* [paradoxes], tea-drinking, and sudden enlightenment." In the Zen monasteries, passionate friendships between priests and novices appear to have been so common that in 1303, the homophobic shogun Hojo Sadatoki attempted to eradicate homosexuality from the monasteries. Such relationships sometimes involved monks and *kasshiki* or *shami*, first and second stage novices. In *Five Mountains: The Rinzai Zen Monastic Institution in Medieval Japan* (1981), M. Colcutt emphasizes the dress of the *kasshiki*. With their hair "shoulder length and modishly" styled and with their faces "decorated with white powder," they were "dressed in finely wrought silken robes and vividly colored variegated underrobes." According to Colcutt, these "gorgeously arrayed youths became the center of admiration in lavish monastic ceremonies;" their beauty was even celebrated in the Noh theater, in the form of a "special mask known as the *kasshiki*." A body of homoerotic poetry had, moreover, begun to emerge from the Zen monasteries. The literature of the five Zen colleges (*Gozan Bungaku*) contained numerous love poems for young men who had been educated there. Unfortunately, the majority of these poems remain untranslated, due in part to the homophobic attitudes of otherwise competent translators and scholars who, like Zennosuke Tsuji, describe these poems as "repulsive," or who, like Marion Ury, hold the view that "around 1520 there was a further decline into homosexual love poems." Ury has, nevertheless, translated several poems which reveal the deep love felt by monks for novices and for other monks as well. In "Detaining a Visitor at Night," for example, the poet-monk Gakuin Ekatsu (1367-1425) writes, "With happy face I hasten to greet you at the shuttered window; / Since last we parted it's been colder at my heart than steel." In "Sent to a Friend," Ichu Tsujo (1349-1429) longs for an intimate friend who is far away. "So soon after parting," he laments, "you're a thousand miles away – / So far a distance, that no letter comes." And in "Yearning for My Friend on an Autumn Night," Sesson Yubai (fl. fourteenth century) echoes this theme: "I constantly long for a guest from the southeast . . . / I hum to myself, but you, dear friend, do not come, / And the bright moon shines vain in an empty sky." One of the first anthologies of homoerotic poetry appeared in Japan in 1676. This was Kitamura Kigin's *Iwatsutsuji* (*Cliff*, or *Rock, Azaleas*); many of the poems therein speak of the love of Buddhist monks for young men. In his preface to the anthology, Kigin notes: "for a man to take pleasure in the beauty of another man goes against nature. Nevertheless, as relations between the sexes were forbidden by the Buddha, priests of the law – being made of neither stone nor wood – had no recourse but to practice [same-sex love] as an outlet for their feelings." Kigin then proceeds to contradict his early statement concerning the unnaturalness of homosexuality, writing, "Just as the waters that plummet and flow below the pass at Tsukubané form the deep pools of the Mino River, so this form of love proved to be deeper than the love between men and women." Not only this, but same-sex love knows no class boundaries: "It afflicts the heart of the aristocrat and the warrior alike. Even the mountain dwellers who cut brushwood have learned of its pleasures."

One of the most beautiful tales linking homoeroticism to Buddhism (these are commonly referred to as *chigo monagatori*) is found in Saikaku Ihara's *The Great Mirror of Manly Love* (also translated as *Comrade Loves of the Samurai*), also composed in the late seventeenth century. In this tale, "Letter from a Buddhist Priest," one priest is writing to another, describing his affection for a young man of sixteen, also studying to become a priest. "My love became so violent," he writes, "that it seemed to me that my soul was breaking into a thousand pieces." He then shares with his friend a letter which he has sent to the young man. "I am a priest," he explains, "but alas! I have also the passions of a man, and I confess that I love you with all my being." His description of his own passion is reflected in his description of the young man's beauty, in which sensuality and spirituality are blended: "you are the most splendid flower of the Western province . . . the most precious jewel in the universe." He then describes the pain which he feels because he cannot be with the young man: "I cannot forget you even in my sleep; and when I awake I am excruciated. I have prayed to the god Fuyisaki to have pity on my unhappy love. I wish to drown myself in the river Kikutji, to put an end to my pain. I am ready to sacrifice my life for one evening's love with you." The letter to the young man ends, "I am cursed by a cruel Karma." But the tale does not end here. The priest relates that he has received a "kind answer" from the young man. "He is coming to spend a whole evening with me . . . His name is Aineme Okayima. When he comes to see me, we shall drink wine together and have a pleasant conversation by ourselves. I should like the night to last forever, and that the dawn should never come to put an end to our meeting." The influence of Buddhism upon BUSHIDO, or the "Way of the Samurai," was profound, as exemplified in the HAGAKURE, a work by Yamamoto Jocho (1649-1719). Little has been written concerning the relationship of lesbianism, bisexuality, or transgenderism to Tibetan Buddhism. Certain praise-hymns of Tibetan Buddhism, especially when uttered by a male devotee, assume a male-loving aspect. Exemplary of this is "The Ocean of Clouds of Praises of the Guru Manjughosha," composed by Je Tsong Khapa around 1394, which reads in part: "The complexion of your skin is pure and clear / Like dust of gold, fine, smooth and soft. / . . . Your organs are retracted like a superb horse, / Your fine and soft body hairs / Grow individually . . . / May the beautiful body of Manjughosa never leave my sight!"

Four major traditions of Buddhism emerged in Tibet: the Kagyu, the Sakya, the Nyingma, and the Gelug. It is the fourth tradition, the Gelug (or Gelugpa), which has been associated with homoeroticism. The Gelug, or "Yellow Hat," tradition was founded by Tsongkhapa Lozang in the early fifteenth century. Tsongkhapa was born in northwest China and later immigrated to Tibet. He was, according to W. Y. Evans-Wentz, "acquainted with Christianity through Roman priests who seem to have had a mission near the place of his birth" and was also deeply inspired by Bon, the indigenous, shamanistic religion of Tibet, claiming its deities for the Gelug tradition. According to Stephan Beyer, the "highest deity" of the Gelug tradition is the goddess or *bodhisattva* Tara. "Among the Gelugpas," Lama Anagarika Govinda has written, "intellectual knowledge . . . including history, logic, philosophy, poetry . . . medicine and astrology, was given particular prominence." The Gelug tradition, Christmas Humphreys explains, "soon became the most powerful in Tibet, and always [included] the Dalai and Panchan Lamas of the day." As Govinda reports, "their monasteries grew into cities in which up to ten thousand monks were residing." It has been only during the last half-century that the great power of the Gelug tradition has waned, largely due to the exile of the Fourteenth Dalai Lama, the Venerable Tenzin Gyamtsho. It is most probably in its adoption of the Vinaya rules of monastic discipline, inherited from Indian and Sri-Lankan, specifically Theravedan, Buddhism, that the Gelug tradition became linked to homoeroticism; ironically, in India, this was the same set of rules that forbade same-sex intimacy. According to the Vinaya rules, "no woman can stay overnight within the walls of the monastery." Indeed, the "sexual act [between men and women] was to be absolutely rejected." This rule against heterosexual relations appears to have encouraged same-sex relations. Numerous scholars, among them Heinrich Harrar, E. Schafer, and E. Kawaguchi, have reported that same-sex relationships were once very common in the Gelug monasteries: "the monasteries in Tibet . . . [have] a very strong reputation for male homosexuality . . . [especially] master-novice relations." Same-sex relationships appear to have been also particularly prevalent among the so-called "warrior" priests, the *lDab ldob*, who were skilled athletes and fighters and who protected and served the "scholar" priests. Kawaguchi relates that the warrior priests were often also ritual musicians who played "flutes, lyres, harps, flageolets . . . [and] drums" as well as preparers of "offerings for the deities." Same-sex relationships appear to have been especially prevalent at the Gelug monastery at Sera. These relationships were celebrated during the "festival of Lights" held in wintertime.

The impact of Buddhism upon American culture may be traced to the latter half of the nineteenth century, when writers like Henry David THOREAU (1817-1862) and Walt WHITMAN (1819-1892) – both lovers of men and perhaps also of women – began to explore in their writings and lives an integration of Eastern and Euro-western spiritual traditions, when organizations promoting such an integration (such as the Theosophical Society) were founded, and when Buddhist immigrants began establishing centers in the US. Anglo-American interest in Buddhism flowered from the 1950s to the 1980s, commencing with the Beat Movement and culminating with the Hippie movement of the late 1960s-early 1970s and the New Age movement emerging in the mid-1970s. Other than those reared in Buddhism (primarily Asian-Americans), the two branches of Buddhism to which Americans, Anglos as well as others, appear to be most drawn are Zen Buddhism and Tibetan Buddhism. The work of gay Beat poet Allen GINSBERG (b. 1926) is exemplary in revealing both of these influences, as does the writing of John Giorno (b. 1936), another gay poet allied with the Beats. Giorno's works include *American Book of the Dead* (1964), *Balling Buddha* (1970), and *Cancer in My Left Ball* (1973). In the early 1970s, Giorno's teacher was Dudjom Rinpoche of Darjeeling, India. At this time, Giorno also met and was profoundly affected by the Dalai Lama. When Winston Leyland asked him in a 1974 *Gay Sunshine* interview how his participation in Buddhism had affected his sexuality, if indeed it had, Giorno replied, "I've become like a rose. . . it has to do with openness, surrendering to the space around you . . . making love is meditation. It's surrendering . . . It seems to me gayness is just two people who are Buddhas . . . If you're making love properly there's no two guys . . . there is nothing there and it is blissful." Richard Ronan's *Buddha's Kisses and Other Poems* (1980) also reflects these influences and sentiments. In more recent years, Robert Aitken, a renowned Zen master and author based in Hawaii, has been particularly outspoken in his acceptance of queer-identified persons in Buddhist practice. For Aitken, "Buddha-nature" is neither homosexual nor heterosexual, "it is both." Contemporary African-American feminist scholar bell hooks, profoundly inspired by Buddhism, struggles similarly for the acceptance of queer-identified persons in society. In recent years, Buddhist gay-centered groups have been founded in northern California and elsewhere, one of the most well-known being the Hartford Street Zen Center in San Francisco, one of whose abbots was Issan DORSEY (1933-1990). Women-loving women like Sandi Boucher (b. 1936), author of *Turning the Wheel: American Women Creating the New Buddhism* (1988) have begun to emerge as teachers of the tradition.

Buddhists have also become active in the fight against HIV/AIDS, as exemplified by the emergence of such groups as the Buddhist AIDS Project of Los Angeles. Lesbian writer Jeanne DuPrau, in *The Earth House* (1992), explores the integration in of Buddhist principles and Zen practice in daily life in the experience of herself and her lover. This diary-like book focuses on their experience in helping to build a Zen retreat in the central California countryside. They also decide to build a house for themselves on the land. The choices they make, related to their Buddhist view and Zen practice, concerning these tasks and their impact upon both their lives and the environment are at the heart of the book. Unfortunately, DuPrau's lover dies before the house is finished. She is faced with finishing the house and continuing her Zen practice alone. DuPrau reminds us that while we have little control over the events in our lives, we can alter our reaction to them. "I can say, no, this isn't what I wanted . . . or I can say, Yes, I see. This is my life. It is being revealed to me, little by little. It could not be other than it is. The threads of [life] are connected everywhere, they extend into the far reaches of time and space, and they are winding together in a design that is far more rich and wondrous than the one I had in mind for myself." In Gavin Harrison's book, *In the Lap of the Buddha* (1994), the author, a teacher of Insight Meditation, employs scenes from the life of the Buddha as well as his gay identity and his HIV-positive status to illuminate his discussion of Buddhist principles. In the Buddha's first sermon, suffering, the second Noble Truth, lies in the inability to accept life as it presents itself. Here, Harrison explores his difficulty in accepting, and coming to terms with, his place in the universe as a gay man suffering oppression and as a person living with HIV/AIDS. Elsewhere in the book, he elaborates on his experience of the realization of death, commencing with his father's death and culminating with the acceptance of his own approaching death. Being present at the death of his father was, for Harrison, "one of the most sacred and special times of my life." He describes the experience of "letting go" not as a loss but rather as a gaining of potent spiritual force, invoking Chögyam Trungpa Rinpoche's metaphor of the "wind horse" as a "strong self-existing energy that is available to [one] after letting go . . . one can ride this hidden store of energy . . . like a horse."

In *Lesbian Sacred Sexuality* (1995), Diane MARIECHILD describes the interrelationship of Buddhism, lesbianism, and feminism in her own erotico-spiritual theory and practice. A practitioner of Buddhist meditation for over twenty years, she observes, "Being a lesbian was good preparation for my Buddhist practice [since it is often] concerned with change and transformation . . . Both Buddhism and feminism . . . emphasize individual responsibility and empowerment." Attitudes of Buddhists toward same-sex intimacy and transgenderism have varied according to culture and historical epoch. It was in Japanese traditions of Buddhism that male homoeroticism and spiritual experience became almost aligned. To a lesser extent, lesbianism and spiritual life appear to have intertwined in Chinese traditions of Buddhism. In general, it would seem that traditions hostile toward same-sex intimacy and transgenderism, as well as traditions in which same-sex-inclined and transgendered individuals played noticeable roles, have given way to a generlized acceptance of persons of differing gendered and erotoc identities.

Chinese Shamanism, Taoism, Confucianism, and Syncretism

The pre-Confucian and pre-Buddhist spiritual traditions of China were shamanic and pantheistic or polytheistic in character. Goddess Reverence was especially strong in southern and central China. Southern China was also the mythical birthplace of love between men, which is even today sometimes referred to as "South (or Southern) Wind." Where the natural elements are concerned, water deities dominated the Chinese pantheon, perhaps due to the importance of the rice-growing and fishing industries. Numerous divine beings were associated with same-sex intimacy, bisexuality, or transgenderism, including CHOU WANG, GUN, LAN CAIHE, SHAN GUI, and YU. While males do not appear to have been excluded from spiritual service, the chief functionaries were female shamans. Responsibilities of Chinese shamans, like those of other cultures, included communicating with deities and spirits, divining the future, diagnosing and healing illnesses, working magic (especially bringing rain), and guiding the souls of the dead to the next life. As in other shamanic traditions, ancestor reverence, sacrifice, and the attainment of altered states of consciousness via drumming, dancing, and other so-called "techniques of ecstasy" played key roles in early Chinese traditions. Among those males known to have practiced Shamanism are a number considered to have been gender variant or transgendered and/or homoerotically inclined, including the celebrated shaman-poet QU YUAN and numerous Chinese eunuchs who served in shamanic capacities (even in later times in Confucianist contexts). Shamanism may have been partly responsible for the emergence of Taoism (or Daoism) in the sixth century BCE. The Tao (or Dao) is the source of all that is, a divine energy pervading all life. In the Tao are contained all dualities, all oppositions. It is from the Tao that both YIN (traditionally feminine, receptive) and YANG (traditionally masculine, assertive) energies emerge; thus, the Tao reflects totality or wholeness, including gender wholeness. In China, as in many other places, this gender wholeness tends to be perceived as gender variance when it manifests itself in a mortal rather than a divine being. In Taoism, feminine, androgynous, and receptive energies are more highly valued than traditionally masculine energy. Taoists revere Nature as the earthly manifestation of the Tao and believe that individuals should seek to emulate its fluid patterns rather than accepting constricting patterns of thought and behavior. While Westerners are familiar with Taoism primarily as a philosophical movement, it is also a spiritual tradition, a polytheistic or pantheistic tradition in which the Tao may divide, or channel, itself into many divine beings. Belief in reincarnation is held in common by many Taoists and, as with the belief in the energies of yin and yang, reincarnation speaks to the *raison d'être* of both transgenderism and same-sex desire. As in Chinese Shamanism, healing, divination (especially employing the *I CHING*), and magic are practiced. One of the hexagrams of the *I Ching* has been documented by various scholars as pertaining to same-sex love. ALCHEMY also holds a special place in Taoism, one of its primary forms being erotic alchemy, which bears likeness to the TANTRIC tradition of India. Among China's most renowned practitioners of alchemy were two homoerotically inclined emperors, WENDI XIAO (reigned 179-157 BCE) and WUDI XIAO (reigned 140-87 BCE). Other renowned Taoists linked to same-sex love are the so-called "SEVEN SAGES OF THE BAMBOO GROVE" of the third century CE, especially Ruan Ji, Xi Kang, and Shan Tao, and WU TSAO (fl. c. 1830 CE), a Chinese poet-lyricist, Taoist priestess, and lover of women. Chinese Shamanism, Goddess Reverence, and

Taoism were all negatively affected by the philosophico-spiritual tradition of Confucianism, which stressed, among other things, respect for hierarchies and the repression of sensuality. Women were perhaps most negatively impacted by Confucianism, losing, with its ever-widening acceptance, not only spiritual but also political and economic power. In China, however, Confucianism was not entirely successful in overpowering the earlier traditions. Rather, over the centuries, a syncretic, eclectic spiritual tradition mixing elements of all of these traditions as well as of Buddhism has emerged; indeed, this syncretic tradition has become so widespread that it is often difficult when exploring Chinese beliefs and practices to determine where one tradition ends and another begins. This process of syncretization commenced at an early date. Wudi Xiao, mentioned above, sought to syncretize shamanistic practices with Taoism (especially Taoist alchemy) and Confucianism. Similarly, Wudi Xiao, also mentioned above, attempted to practice Confucianist rites honoring the spirits of the earth alongside Taoist alchemy, as did many Chinese eunuchs. This syncretic tradition supported intimate relationships between women, giving rise to spiritually-based groups including the CHAI T'ANG, GOLDEN ORCHID ASSOCIATION, and MOJING DANG. It also appears to have been somewhat supportive of both lesbian and homoerotic rites of UNION. It likewise engendered mythical figures such as STONE MAIDEN and STONE MAN as well as magical tales of homoerotic love, including "The Scholar and the Flower Spirit" and "Lu Yi Jing, Wei Guo Xin, and the Spirit." It also gave rise to legends concerning mythical lands, including BLACK TEETH COUNTRY, MEN'S COUNTRY, WOMEN'S COUNTRY, and WOMEN'S KINGDOM, as well as to legends concerning actual sites, such as CHAO TIAN GONG and the TWO FLOWER TEMPLE. Finally, the interwoven Chinese traditions engendered symbols bearing associations with, or correspondences to, gender and sexual variance or fluidity. Such symbols include animals like the DUCK and the EEL, articles of clothing like the cut SLEEVE of a garment, flowers like the CHRYSANTHEMUM, foods like TOFU, fruits such as the PEACH, musical instruments like the FLUTE, precious stones such as JADE, and objects like the MIRROR, with its simultaneous ornamental and divinatory functions.

Christianity

The Christian religion began as a movement within Judaism but distinguished itself from the former primarily (in the beginning) by stressing the teachings of JESUS (fl. first century CE) and his followers, and by identifying Jesus as the Son of God, the second figure of the Holy Trinity (God and the Holy Spirit being the first and third), and the savior of humankind. Spreading from Palestine to Rome and then to other parts of Europe and the world, Christianity was, after a period of persecution, proclaimed the official religion of the Roman Empire in 381. With this act, the marriage of Christianity and political power was secured, a bond which still endures. By the end of the eleventh century, a split had occurred in Christianity between Catholicism and Orthodoxy; in the sixteenth century, another split occurred between Catholicism and Protestantism. In the late twentieth century, yet another rift appears to be splitting both Protestants and Catholics (as well as members of other faiths) between moderates and Fundamentalists. Christian and other Biblical scholars differ greatly as to how same-sex intimacy and transgenderism were treated in early Christianity. Prior to the publication of Derrick Sherwin Bailey's *Homosexuality and the Western Christian Tradition* in 1955, a majority appear to have accepted common translations of the apostle Paul's words in Romans 2 (26-28) at face value: "For this reason God gave them up to dishonorable passions. Their women exchanged natural relations for unnatural, and the men likewise gave up natural relations with women and were consumed with passion for one another, men committing shameless acts with men and receiving in their own persons the due penalty for their error. And since they did not see fit to acknowledge God, God gave them up to a base mind and to improper conduct." (Oxford Annotated). With the publication of Bailey's book, however, Christian writers and religious leaders began to reexamine this passage as well as many others from the Bible to determine if anti-homoerotic (and occasionally also anti-transgender) sentiments were as intrinsic to Christianity as they had seemed. To date, the most important scholarly study of this type remains John Boswell's *Christianity, Social Tolerance, and Homosexuality* (1980). Another such study is gay priest Daniel A. Helminiak's *What the Bible Really Says*

About Homosexuality (1994). In general, these studies insist that the story of SODOM and GOMORRAH has much to do with inhospitality and very little to do with homosexuality. They also tend to question foreign (primarily Hebrew and Greek) terms which have been interpreted to mean "homosexual," suggesting that these terms have either nothing to do with homosexuality or that they refer not to homosexuality *per se* but rather to prostitution and/or to effeminate behavior. In most cases, the etymological arguments in these apologetic texts are weak, tending to demonstrate little awareness of eroticism and erotico-sacred roles in classical antiquity. The strongest arguments of such texts, on the other hand, concern the (potentially) homoerotic elements in Biblical narratives such as those of DAVID AND JONATHAN and RUTH AND NAOMI, as well as in Gnostic texts and in the tales of Christian saints and medieval Christian monks and nuns.

In terms of saints and spiritual functionaries, three exceptional works beyond Boswell's first book are his own *Same-Sex Unions in Premodern Europe* (1994) (aka *The Marriage of Likeness*); Janice Raymond's *A Passion for Friends: Toward a Philosophy of Female Affection* (1986); Judith C. Brown's *Immodest Acts: The Life of a Lesbian Nun in Renaissance Italy* (1986); and Paul Halsall's *Calendar of Lesbian, Gay Bisexual, and Transgender Saints* (1994). The majority of these works stress that in the ancient and Medieval worlds, "friendship" as a descriptive term for a relationship, as that between nuns or between monks, did not always preclude eroticism. As Raymond puts it, "The power of female friendship in convents derived from the fact that friendship is by nature a spiritual communion, but that women are not . . . pure spirits. With nuns . . . friendship is mediated through . . . the material world." The contemporary queer-centered Christian movement might be traced to early twentieth-century Germany when Elisàr von Kupffer (also known as Elisarion, 1872-1942), founded the KLARISTICHE MOVEMENT, which sought to weave together homoeroticism, Greek religion and mythology, and the Medieval European code of chivalry with Christianity. Von Kupffer wrote: "If we wanted to call Christian everything that has happened in the course of the past fifteen centuries, that would be ridiculous. Almost the entire history of Christianity is a protest against the personality of Christ . . . Truly Christ did not hold back his words, he reproves where he wishes to reprove. Relationships such as Lieblingminne [inspirited homoeroticism] entails, such he never judged with one public word." This notion, that Jesus remained silent of the subject of homosexuality – even if Paul did not – has been important in the development of queer-centered Christianity. Indeed, a number of years ago, a text titled *What Jesus Said About Homosexuality* contained only blank pages.

Following von Kupffer, one of the early exponent of the contemporary queer Christian movement was Father Michael Francis Augustine Itkin (1936-1989), who in 1957 became a priest in the Eucharistic Catholic Church, claimed by some to have been the first gay-centered religious body in the US. During the 1960s, Itkin developed a gay-centered theology, emphasizing links with pacifism and civil rights, and founded the Evangelical Catholic Community of the Love of Christ. This theological perspective and community inspired a pivotal work, *The Radical Jesus and Gay Liberation* (1972). A pivotal moment arrived in 1968 in terms of the relationship of Protestant lesbians and gay men to Christianity with the founding, by the Reverend Troy PERRY, of the Metropolitan Community Church, followed by his 1972 bestseller, *The Lord Is My Shepherd and He Knows I'm Gay*. In the years that followed, the Episcopalian group Integrity (founded by Louie Crew), the Catholic group Dignity, and many other gay-supportive Christian organizations were founded. Among these, the Unity Fellowship Church of New York and New Jersey focuses on outreach to lesbian and gay African-Americans. Two other books by renowned Christian leaders, former Catholic priest John J. McNeill's *The Church and the Homosexual* (1976), and Episcopalian priest Malcolm Boyd's *Take Off the Masks* (1978), also wielded a powerful influence upon open-minded Christians.

One of the most original contributions of this period was Catholic priest Richard Woods's *Another Kind of Love: Homosexuality and Spirituality* (1978). Woods moved beyond most other gay-focused Christian texts by defining "Gay Spirituality." Indeed, Woods appears to have been one of the first spiritual writers or thinkers to employ this term. For Woods, Gay Christian Spirituality consists of integrating gay sexuality and spirituality as well as working against injustice and oppression and employing creativity to enrich the gay community and the world at large. Among the most intriguing of Woods's components of Gay Spirituality is the expression of humor, joy, and resistance as exemplified by the archetypal image of the Clown. Building upon the clown or holy fool-like image of Jesus popularized by Harvey Cox in *The Feast of Fools* (1969), Stephen Schwartz in the musical *Godspell* (1972), and others in the late 1960s and early 1970s as well as upon the fools of Christ of Eastern Orthodoxy, and the Feast of Fools in the Medieval Catholic Church, and contemporary MARDI GRAS celebrations, Woods writes, "Despite persecution, suffering, even tragedy, gay men and women continue to endure, to hope, to rise again and to make festival . . . if gays are clown-figures, clowns are no less Christ-figures . . . Clowns liberate us from the tedium of the word's grind . . . They raise our levels of insight by displacing our dull and customary viewpoint, so that the incongruity and comedy of life are revealed to us . . . thus the clowns, the gay clowns . . . who bring all men and women . . . to the revelation, the re-evaluation of the meaning of sexuality and friendship, of hope and the persistent righting of wrongs, find something of their destiny in celebrating and thus overcoming . . . their outcastness."

At this time, gay and lesbian Christians began to receive support from some open-minded heterosexual and celibate religious leaders. In August 1978 the San Francisco-based African-American minister Reverend Cecil Williams said in *Jet* magazine that he had known for a long time that the majority of gay people were well-adjusted individuals and that religious institutions had condemned homosexuality as a sin in order to control people's lives. In this article, moreover, Williams linked homophobia to racism, sexism, and war. Similar support was noticeable in Letha Scanzoni's and Virginia Ramey Mollenkott's 1978 text *Is the Homosexual My Neighbor? Another Christian View*. In 1984 lesbian Episcopalian priest Carter Heyward published another pivotal work in the history of gay and lesbian-centered Christianity, *Our Passion for Justice: Images of Power, Sexuality, and Liberation*. In this work, Heyward identifies the "making" of love with the "making " of justice: "Our passion as lovers is what fuels both our rage at injustice . . . and our compassion . . . To really love is to topple unjust structures . . . To love you is to advocate your rights . . . To say 'I love you' means – let the revolution begin! God bless the Revolution!" The feminist Christian perspective of Heyward was reiterated and expanded upon by lesbian theologian Mary C. Hunt in *Fierce Tenderness: A Feminist Theology of Friendship* (1991). Hunt stresses friendship as opposed to eroticism in the bonds between lesbians and other women. She does, however, include eroticism as an aspect of "embodiment" in a very useful model of women's friendships also including the components of "love," "power," and "spirituality." As with Heyward, Hunt's emphasis is on the link between the love of women for each other and the displacement of injustice by justice and of oppression by liberation. Other important texts of the mid-1980s to mid-1990s include: Malcolm Boyd's *Gay Priest: An Inner Journey* (1984); *Lesbian Nuns: Breaking Silence*, edited by Rosemary Curb and Nancy Manahan (1985); Barbara Zanotti's anthology *A Faith of One's Own: Explorations by Catholic Lesbians* (1986); Presbyterian minister Chris Glaser's *Uncommon Calling: A Gay Man's Struggle to Serve the Church* (1988); Jeannine Gramick's and Pat Furey's *The Vatican and Homosexuality* (1988), Antonio A. Feliz's *Out of the Bishop's Closet* (1992), Thomas O' Neil's *Sex With God* (1994), and Michael S. Piazza's *Holy Homosexuals: The Truth About Being Gay or Lesbian and Christian* (1995).

The vision of lesbian and gay-centered Christian thought, writing, and practice has been profoundly affected by the emergence of Queer Spirit and the sociopolitical movements Act Up and Queer Nation. Four texts in particular reflect this innovative, indeed radical approach: the New Orleans-based journal *Second Stone*, edited and published by Jim Bailey since 1988; *Just as I Am: A Practical Guide to Being Out, Proud, and Christian*, by former Episcopalian priest Robert Williams (1992); *Jesus Acted Up: A Gay and Lesbian Manifesto*, by former Catholic priest Robert Goss (1992); and Reverend Nancy Wilson's *Our Tribe: Queer Folks, God, Jesus, and the Bible* (1995). All of these texts also reflect the inspiration of seminal non-Christian Gay-Spiritual and Queer-Spiritual texts, especially Judy Grahn's *Another Mother Tongue: Gay Words, Gay Worlds* (1984), which speaks of the connection of gay people to shamanic and priestly roles in pre-Christian and primal cultures. Further, they reflect the contemporary Queer inclusion of transgendered and bisexual persons alongside lesbians and gay men. They speak of Jesus himself as a loving, sensuous shamanic figure and suggest that he may have been lovers with LAZARUS (whom he is said to have raised from the dead), JOHN THE EVANGELIST, or both. By far the most radical (and speculative) of these texts is Wilson's *Our Tribe*. The senior pastor of the Metropolitan Community Church of Los Angeles, Wilson suggests that both eunuchs and angels may be Biblical ancestors of twentieth-century gay people, that LAZARUS may have been the "victim of gay bashing," and that the wise men of the Christmas story were "queer," "pagan," "gay fairy godmothers who dropped in on" Jesus.

Not surprisingly, many twentieth-century lesbians, gays, bisexuals, and transgendered persons who have been reared as Christians have distanced themselves from Christianity as a result of the intolerance they have experienced from other practitioners of the faith. In this century as well, many feminists, including lesbian-feminists, have found that Christianity, especially Protestantism (which tends to downplay the role of Mary, the mother of Jesus), has little to offer in women's terms of both divine or archetypal images and spiritual roles. Indeed, some feminists have seen in Christianity a peculiar paradox of homophobia and male (or phallic) adoration. In the mid-1970s, lesbian poet Elsa GIDLOW raised more than a few eyebrows when she observed, "Has it occurred to any psychological sleuths the extent to which male identification with a totally male God, Trinity, Christ-image . . . partakes of homosexuality? It would not be hard to see the Christian church as an exclusive male homosexual club." This notion has been taken up and profoundly illuminated by the Catholic-reared, lesbian-feminist theologian and philosopher Mary DALY in *Pure Lust: Elemental Feminist Philosophy* (1984) and other works. This has led many feminists and lesbian-feminists to become agnostics or atheists as well as to explore such spiritual movements and traditions as Goddess Reverence, Witchcraft, and Women's Spirituality. Nevertheless, many other women, as we have seen, have chosen to work for change within the Christian community.

Opposing Women's Spirituality and related paths as well as the Queer-Spiritual perspectives of Wilson and others and the more moderate positions of such leaders as Father McNeill are members of the burgeoning Fundamentalist Christian Movement, which has intimate ties to the most right-wing political groups now existing in the US and elsewhere. As Heather Rhoads observes in "Cruel Crusade: The Holy War Against Lesbians and Gays," "While accusing lesbians and gays of dismantling the foundations of Euro-western civilization, the religious Right itself has quietly and strategically mounted an all-out attack of hatred and bigotry against lesbians and gays. The culture war is on, and gays and lesbians are the enemy for the 1990s. The religious Right has made homosexuality the centerpiece of its [US] national agenda." The Religious Right, or Christian Fundamentalist movement, has witnessed a dramatic rise in the numbers of leaders, followers and groups in the past two decades. While the most well-known US leaders are probably the televangelist ministers Jerry Falwell and Pat Robertson (not to mention Anita Bryant in the 1970s), there are innumerable others, including Gary Bauer of the Family Research Council, Jay Grimstead of the Coalition for Revival (whose favorite remark concerning gays is "Homosexuality makes God vomit"), Beverly LaHaye of Concerned Women for America, John Land of the Southern Baptist Convention, and Ralph Reed of the Christian Coalition. Other US groups linking Christianity to right-wing politics which represent a serious threat to lesbian, gay, bisexual, and transgendered persons include Focus on the Family, Colorado for Family Values, and the Oregon Citizen's Alliance. One of the most disturbing texts published by the Christian Right in the early 1990s is *Death Penalty for Homosexuals Is Prescribed in the Bible*. This booklet, published by Scriptures in America, linked to a white supremacist church in Colorado, argues that Christians who do not do violence to gays are not fulfilling their responsibilities as Christians. The booklet comes with a promotional statement: "Use it as you will for the King." It is probably no coincidence that in the early 1990s, Colorado witnessed an 800 per cent rise in hate crimes.

Despite the massive effort of Fundamentalists to exclude lesbians, gays, bisexuals, and the transgendered from Christianity, they continue to struggle to find a place within the religion, they continue to be inspired by its symbols, narratives, and ethical guidelines, and they continue to express their relationship to their faith in artistic ways. One of the most poignant statements of this kind occurs in Catholic gay writer David Plante's "Images of the Body from My Religion," found in Brian Bouldrey's anthology *Wrestling with the Angel: Faith and Religion in the Lives of Gay Men* (1995); here Plante writes, "My religion gave to sex its greatest sense – and here once again I insist on the most acute sensuality of a sense that apprehends a whole larger than all its parts, in the same way this sense apprehends the beauty of a naked body as more than skin, hair, bone, blood, in the same way that the Catholic Church apprehends itself in all its parts as the living Mystical Body of Christ."

Goddess Reverence

This term is applied to ancient and primal (or tribal) worship of a female deity or deities as well as to a contemporary spiritual movement or tradition which is Goddess-centered. As archaeologist Marija Gimbutas (1921-1994) and others have amply demonstrated, Goddess Reverence may be traced to the Paleolithic era, as exemplified by a multitude of female figurines and by cave paintings such as that at ADDAURA. Goddess Reverence, as opposed to patriarchal spiritual traditions, does not seem to have excluded persons on the basis of transgendered orientation or same-sex inclination. Indeed, many of those serving the Goddess or goddesses of antiquity and primal cultures – as the Lesbian priestesses of APHRODITE belonging to the THIASOS of SAPPHO on the island of LESBOS, the gender variant male QEDESHIM of the Canaanite goddess ATHIRAT, the transgendered HIJRAS of the Hindu goddess BAHUCHARAMATA – have enacted lesbian, bisexual, homoerotic, and/or transgendered behaviors. In Europe and elsewhere following the emergence of patriarchal religions, Goddess Reverence survived in subtle forms, such as in celebrations of female saints and folk figures. As Witchcraft, Goddess Reverence was viciously attacked by Christian forces during the Catholic Inquisition and the Protestant Reformation, both in Europe and in the Americas, with many (alleged) practitioners, including transgendered and same-sex inclined persons, being tortured and executed. The contemporary movement or tradition of Goddess Reverence may be traced to two French salons – la Secte ANANDRYNE of the eighteenth century, and the salon of Reneé VIVIEN and Natalie Clifford BARNEY in the early twentieth century.

Goddess Reverence flowered, however, in the 1970s and 1980s, with the rise of the feminist movement. Among its many "mothers" are Z BUDAPEST and STARHAWK, who have (re-) linked Goddess Reverence to Witchcraft as well as to the emerging Women's Spirituality movement. The emphasis of many of those participating in contemporary Goddess Reverence is not so much upon the worship of an anthropomorphic deity as upon the seeking and celebrating of a "unity and wholeness" which, as Hallie Iglehart AUSTEN explains in *The Heart of the Goddess* (1990), "is the birthright and potential of every human being. All of us, all of existence, are the Divine. In order to complete this whole by bringing back that which has been denied, I name the Divine the Goddess." When Austen speaks of "that which has been denied," she refers to those values which patriarchal religions and cultures have tended to denigrate or suppress, such as "nurturance, cooperation, compassion, sensuality, peacemaking and egalitarianism." Goddess Reverence stresses embodiment, the honoring of the body and its processes, including maturation (as in menstruation), sexual union, aging, and death. "The Goddess," Austen writes, "is she who gives life and, when the form is no longer viable, transforms it through death. And then, through the exquisite pleasures of creativity and sexuality, she brings forth new life." Creativity expressed in visual art, music, literature, and other art forms plays as important a role as – indeed, perhaps more important than – theology in contemporary Goddess Reverence. Writers, musicians, and other artists who have celebrated the Goddess, goddesses, or female spirits in the mid- to late twentieth century have included many lesbian and bisexual women; among the writers are Paula Gunn ALLEN, Elsa GIDLOW, Judy GRAHN, Susan Griffin, Joy HARJO, Lynn Lonidier, Audre LORDE, Robin Morgan, and May Sarton. One of the most beautiful contemporary hymns to the Goddess, in which the deity is identified with the earth, is lesbian writer Susan Griffin's (b. 1943) "This Earth," which includes: "I have known her all my life, yet she reveals stories to me, and these stories are revelations and I am transformed . . . Now my body reaches out to her . . . and I know why she goes on . . . This earth is my sister . . . how we admire this strength in each other . . . we are stunned by this beauty, and I do not forget what she is to me, what I am to her."

Gay, bisexual, and transgendered males are also being drawn into the contemporary Goddess movement in increasing numbers; a common explanation given is that they wish to explore the "feminine" aspect of their nature. Others focus on alliance with women struggling against patriarchal, heterocentric religions. In "The Goddess in Every Man," inspired by the works of archetypal psychologist Jean Shinoda Bolen, Josef Venker expresses his desire to "reclaim the Goddess" within his own psyche, believing that cultivating his own femininity will help to restore him to a fuller humanity, of which the force of patriarchal ideology has previously deprived him. For Venker, this recovery of the feminine, of the Goddess within, is expressed through working in his garden: "The garden was perhaps the one place where the men in my family could be in touch with the nurturing and caring sides of themselves . . . a garden is a very personal expression . . . of [the] relationship with the Goddess within . . . Her name is Demeter." Others, like the SISTERS OF PERPETUAL INDULGENCE, an order of "genderfuck" drag nuns based in San Francisco, invoke the power of female deities in rituals meant to support and protect queer-identified persons and others. In their rites, as in those of the Radical Faeries, the Goddess is sometimes invoked in a "CAMP" or CARNIVALESQUE form. Some feminists see in such depictions of the Goddess an expression of misogyny. Gay, bisexual, and transgendered men, and more recently, lesbian, bisexual, and transgendered women, who honor the Goddess in CRONE form, however, see themselves as celebrating the powers of humor, wit, "gutsiness," and "bitchiness," which they link to queer expressions of rebellion in the face of a patriarchal tyranny.

Hinduism

In a recent article, "Homosexuality and Hinduism" (1993), Arvind Sharma, a professor of comparative religion at McGill University, states categorically: "Thus, although within classical Hinduism homosexuality was only a matter of marginal concern and disapproval, medieval and modern Hinduism tends to associate the practice with an outgroup [i.e. Euro-westerners] with whom its encounter has not always been pleasant or peaceful . . . if modern India is taken as a representative, Neo-Hinduism is now so hostile to it that 'no community admits of homosexual practices, though each accuses the others.'" Sharma is probably correct concerning the attitudes of many twentieth-century Hindus living in India. His certainty concerning earlier attitudes, while supported by other social constructionists like Nayan Shah, appears to be contradicted or at least modified by research undertaken by many other scholars, including Sadashiv Ambadas Dange, Alain DANIÉLOU (whose absence in his essay is conspicuous), Wendy Doniger, McKim Marriott, Subodh Mukherjee, Milton Singer, and Gita Thadani. What many persons of Hindu and non-Hindu heritage are unaware of – in part due to the idolization of Mohandas Gandhi (1869-1948), known as Mahatma, in the West – is that a massive campaign was launched in the period spanning the 1920s to the 1940s to erase all positive references to transgenderism and same-sex desire in Indian, especially Hindu, culture. Interestingly, Sharma says nothing of this in his article. Gandhi decided to send squads of his devotees to destroy the erotic representations, particularly those depicting homoeroticism and lesbianism, carved into Hindu temples dating from the eleventh century, as part of a program to encourage both Indians and non-Indians to believe that such behaviors were the result of foreign, namely Euro-western, influence. Fortunately the writer and philosopher Sir Rabindranath Tagore (1861-1941) was able to halt this violent action. Nevertheless, the campaign to erase the history of gender and sexual variance was continued by Prime Minister Jawaharlal Nehru (1889-1964), who held the office from 1947 to 1964. Like Gandhi, he had been educated in England, and like him, he wished to convey the message that it was the English who had imported the plague of queerness to India. He became extremely irritated with his friend Alain Daniélou when the latter, together with his lover, published photographs of the same-sex erotic and transgendered-themed sculptures. It was the socialist government of Nehru that inspired the first law in Indian history – article 377 – criminalizing same-sex intimacy. Research needs to be done exploring the possible relationship between this puritanical movement to erase history and the social constructionist view that same-sex and transgendered identities are recent inventions.

Thadani's research is especially illuminating in revealing that same-sex intimacy and transgenderism appear to be rooted in the pre-Hindu Indus Valley Civilization of India, the spiritual center of which was Mohenjo-Daro. Thadani explains that in this early civilization, in which prototypes of the Great Goddess(es) of Hinduism and SHIVA (as a phallic deity) were revered, "Importance was not attached to the 'male-female couple,' but on the notion of *yoni*, which signifies 'the womb, the infinite source,' the symbol of which was the triangle. The triangle consisted of two points of 'light' represented by female twins, symbols of fusion, and of a third point which was the earth. The notion of twins or *jami* also signifies, in various texts, 'homosexuality.' This triadic system goes back to a family structure in which importance is not attached to the notion of the 'social father' or the biological mother, but in which there is a notion of multiple mothers [as in a variant of the tale of the birth of the god GANESHA focusing on the goddess PARVATI and her handmaiden MALINI] . . . Sexuality was based on pleasure and fertility." While the religion of the Indus Valley was displaced by Hinduism, a basically patriarchal (and increasingly monotheistic) faith, many of its features survived (and were transformed), especially in the reverence of goddesses, Shiva, deities of sensuality like KAMA, KRISHNA, and VASANTA, and androgynous or transgendered deities like ARDHANARISHVARA, as well as in *puranas* (myths) of same-sex couplings and births resulting from these couplings (as in the myth of Parvati, Malini, and Ganesha or that of Shiva, AGNI, and KARTIKKEYEH), in spiritual paths like BHAKTI and TANTRA, in spiritual concepts like TRITITYA-PRAKRITI, in rituals like the AGNICAYANA, in spiritual functionaries including the HIJRAS, JOGAPPAS, SAKHIBHAVAS and VALLABHAS, and in the writings of BASAVA (fl. twelfth century CE), CAITANYA (b. 1485) and many others.

From the time of ALEXANDER THE GREAT (356-323 BCE), Euro-western culture, including its transgendered and same-sex oriented populations, has been influenced by Hinduism and its associated traditions. In the nineteenth and twentieth centuries, artists, including writers and musicians, as Henry David THOREAU (1817-1862), Walt WHITMAN (1819-1892), Edward CARPENTER (1844-1929), E. M. FORSTER (1879-1970), Gerald HEARD (1889-1971), Christopher ISHERWOOD (1904-1986), Charles Henri-Ford (b. 1910), the writers of the BEAT MOVEMENT, Andrew HARVEY (b. 1952), Kay GARDNER (b. 1941) and BOY GEORGE (b. 1961) have discovered inspiration in Hinduism and its associated traditions (Tantra, Vedanta, etc.). In recent years, gay, lesbian, bisexual, and transgendered persons of South Asian heritage and/or of Hindu background have begun to organize socially, politically, and spiritually. Such groups have also begun publishing journals including *Anamika* (US, commencing 1985), *Trikon* (US), *Khush Khayal* (Canada), *Shakti Khabar* (UK), and *Freedom* (India). It is important to note that while many regard spirituality as central to their lives, many also feel burdened by being perceived by Anglos and others as the bearers of a "spiritual culture." "I hate carrying that burden," relates Meera; "I think that it sets us apart. We are still perceived as exotic." Hindu-based groups involving both Indian- and non-Indian individuals, such as the SADHANA BROTHERS in San Francisco, have also been founded in recent years. Although not limited to Hinduism, the finest book to date on the interrelationship of queer-identified persons and the spiritual traditions of South Asia is Rakesh Ratti's anthology *A Lotus of Another Color: An Unfolding of the South Asian Gay and Lesbian Experience* (1993).

Islam

Both related to and diverging from Judaism and Christianity in important respects, Islam is rooted in a belief that the Biblical God's (called Allah in Islam) message was channeled most clearly by Muhammad (c. 570-622), the prophet of Islam, as expressed in the *Qur'an* (or *Koran*). Following *shari'a*, the "all-embracing law of Islam," is of utmost importance. While *shari'a* is supposed to be in accord with *tariqa*, the "way to salvation," they are often used to describe two very different ways of leading a spiritual life; for while *shari'a* stresses obeying the law, *tariqa* often places self-exploration and mystical experience above conformity to law. As Khalid Duran observes in "Homosexuality and Islam" (1993), "the primary source of Islam – its revealed scripture, *Al-Qur'an* – is very explicit in its condemnation of homosexuality, leaving scarcely any loophole for a theological accommodation of homosexuals in Islam." Islamic hostility toward same-sex eroticism is rooted in the tale of SODOM. While numerous Jewish and Christian theologians, especially in recent decades, have argued that the tale of Sodom concerns inhospitality rather than homosexuality, in Islam, the link between

Sodom and homosexuality is ironclad. Indeed, homoeroticism in general and anal intercourse in particular are referred to as *liwat*, while those (primarily men) engaging in these behaviors are referred to as *qaum Lut* or *Luti*, "the people of Lot." The Prophet Muhammad is believed to have said, "Doomed by God is [he] who does what Lot's people did . . . No man should look at the private parts of another man, and no woman should look at the private parts of another woman." Hostility toward both same-sex eroticism and transgenderism is also rooted in the pre-Islamic traditions of the Middle East, which included — one might say emphasized — Goddess Reverence, especially of the goddesses AL-LAT, AL-UZZA, and MANAT. These matrifocal traditions were led primarily by priestesses and by gender variant, often homoerotically inclined males called MUKHANNATHUN. These males bore kinship to the AL-JINK, who were in turn associated with the reverence of the JINN ("genii").

With the triumph of Islam, the earlier spiritual traditions were suppressed and their followers converted or slain. The spiritual — and general — authority of women diminished greatly, and those engaging in same-sex eroticism and transgendered behavior became outlaws. Aspects of the earlier traditions survived, however, in the subculture of MUJUN. They also survived in and were transformed by, a tradition growing out of Islam which focuses on *tariqa*, a path of self-awareness and mystical experience, the way of Sufism. The Sufis have for centuries suffered at the hands of other practitioners of Islam, due in part to their mystical focus and in part to their apparent acceptance of some forms of transgendered and homoerotic behavior. It is this tradition which has inspired some of the most beautiful — and some of the most humorous — male love poetry in world literature, including the work of Jalal Al-Din RUMI (1207-1273). In *Sexuality in Islam* (1985), Abdelwahab Bouhdiba explains that the Sufis were singled out by reactionary Islamic authorities not only because they were believed to engage in same-sex relationships, but also, and primarily, because they dared to look upon the male beloved as a reflection of God. This belief in embodiment, called *hulul*, was considered the "most heinous of Sufis heresies." Indeed, one Islamic text refers to the Sufis as a "community of sodomites." Various punishments were meted out by authorities to persons engaging in transgendered or homoerotic behavior, including stoning and burning (the authors have, unfortunately, been assured that these practices have not disappeared entirely). According to the twelfth century scholar Ibn 'Abbas, "the sodomite should be thrown upside down" — note the use of inversion in punishment — "from the highest building in the town and then stoned." Some Islamic faithful believed that in the afterlife, "punishment for sodomy will be even more terrible. On Resurrection Day, unless they repent, the guilty partners will find themselves stuck together." Clearly, there are contradictions within Islam concerning the afterlife, as this image hardly matches that of the faithful being served by handsome youths called WILDAN in the Garden of Paradise.

The oppression of same-sex inclined and transgendered persons has increased dramatically in the world of Islam since the late 1970s with the rise of Islamic fundamentalism. Ironically, US gay liberationists were actively encouraged to support the revolution led by Khomeini only to discover that hundreds, perhaps thousands, of their counterparts in Iran were being tortured and put to death by fundamentalist zealots. In 1991, Article 123 of Iran's Islamic penal code extended the death penalty for engaging in same-sex eroticism to women. Not surprisingly, hostility toward persons with AIDS/HIV is equally vicious. In autumn 1987, two Islamic physicians, Mustafa Sener and Ibrahim Geyik of Ankara, Turkey, described AIDS as a "divine warning to those who engage in corrupt lifestyles" and "immoral homosexual and extramarital sexual intercourse" and those who "do not live in accordance with Islamic ways." Sener and Geyik then condemned physicians providing condoms as a safeguard against AIDS, "instead of taking precise action against immoral and perverse sexual intercourse." Khalid Duran's concluding remarks seem especially pertinent in our context: "Religious gays [and here, we can probably also assume lesbians, bisexuals, and the transgendered] in the realm of Islam, then, would have to take recourse in antinomian Sufism . . . that puts *tariqa* in place of *shari'a*."

There are, however, indications that Islamic authorities and other practitioners are slowly beginning to reconsider the religion's — and the culture's — positions on same-sex eroticism and transgenderism. A 1994 editorial in *Islamic Canada Reflections* argues that while it "is true that Islam forbids homosexual practice . . . this does not mean that gay people should be 'subjected to violent crime' and other forms of persecution." This gradual shifting of positions is nurtured by the fact that increasing numbers of Muslims are "coming out of the closet," including individuals like Tinku Ishtiaq, a member of the International Gay and Lesbian Human Rights Commission, and groups like the Los Angeles-based Salaam. Writers like Shahid Dossani argue that Islam should be viewed as a vibrant faith which did not cease to evolve upon the death of the Prophet Mohammed, and that while insistence on heterosexual relationships may have once served an important social function, it may now be time to embrace stable same-sex relationships as well.

Judaism

"You shall not lie with a male as with a woman; it is an abomination . . . If a man lies with a male as with a woman, both of them have committed an abomination; they shall be put to death, their blood is upon them . . . A woman shall not wear anything that pertains to a man, nor shall a man put on a woman's garment; for whoever does these things is an abomination to the Lord your God" (*Oxford Annotated Bible*). These passages from the Biblical books of Leviticus (18: 22, 20: 13) and Deuteronomy (22: 5) have for millennia profoundly influenced the perspectives of Jews (as well as Christians and Muslims for lesser periods of time) concerning same-sex eroticism (especially pertaining to males) and transgenderism. Biblical scholars suggest that the harshness of these commandments may be rooted in the efforts of the ancient Israelites to distinguish themselves from the Canaanites, those who had inhabited the land previous to their arrival. In Canaanite religion, both gender and sexual variance were associated with Goddess Reverence; thus, in order to eradicate the religion of the Canaanites, it was deemed necessary to eradicate gendered and erotic practices linked to that faith. The most potent symbols of these practices were the hierodulic priestesses (*qedeshtu*) and priests (QEDESHIM), or "sacred" or "cult prostitutes," of the goddess ATHIRAT (or Asherah) and her male consort BAAL. Thus we find in Deuteronomy 23: 17, "There shall be no cult prostitution of the daughters of Israel, neither shall there be a cult prostitute of the sons of Israel." For approximately three hundred years, campaigns against the *qedeshtu* and *qedeshim* of Athirat were conducted by certain monarchs of Israel and Judah. The vehemence with which these campaigns were conducted may have arisen in response to more tolerant monarchs and others who, perhaps in an effort to syncretize Judaism and the Canaanite faith, housed *qedeshim* and *qedeshtu* in the Hebrew temples. By 600 BCE, due to these campaigns, the *qedeshim* and *qedeshtu* appear to have all but vanished.

Nevertheless, neither same-sex love nor transgenderism was to disappear entirely from the ancient Hebrew cosmos, nor were traces of the Canaanite reverence of the Goddess. Biblical scholars have observed all of these elements in the stories of NOAH and JOSEPH from the Book of Genesis. In this context, Biblical scholar Samuel Terrien has also argued that the *cherubim* (cherubs) of both Judaism and Christianity "may have been . . . related both to the . . . Magna Mater [i.e. the Great Goddess] and to the ritual of cultic male prostitution." These elements also seem woven into the Biblical tale of the destruction of SODOM and GOMORRAH. It would appear that despite the severe commandments of Leviticus and Deuteronomy, attitudes toward same-sex love and gender variance may have relaxed somewhat as struggles with the Canaanites lessened. At the very least, it appears as if passionate friendships between members of the same sex were tolerated and even celebrated. Evidence of this shift may be found in the tale of DAVID AND JONATHAN and in that of RUTH AND NAOMI. In later antiquity, however, as contact between Jews and others, especially Greeks and Romans, increased, particularly under Roman domination, hostility toward gender and sexual variance once again appears to have increased, exemplified by the writings of Philo Judaeus (fl. c. 50 CE), who specifically linked homosexuality to SODOM. Around this time, in the *Mishnah* (the first text of rabbinical Judaism, late second century CE) sexual intercourse between men became punishable by stoning. This rise in hostility continued throughout late antiquity and into the Middle Ages. Several beliefs gained strength, including that men engaging in same-sex eroticism would be visited by divine punishment in the form of early death, as well as that earthquakes and solar eclipses were punishments for the sin of male homosexual intercourse. Also at this time, the belief that homosexuality was associated with MAGIC and idolatry resurfaced. In the late twelfth century one of the first Jewish records specifically condemning lesbianism appears, in the writings of Moses Maimonides (1135-1204): "Women are forbidden to engage in lesbian practices with one another, these being the doing of the land of Egypt."

In spite of the rise in hostility, however, both esoteric and folk traditions of Judaism emerging in the Middle Ages, seem to have treated gender and sexual variance less viciously. For example, QABBALISTS explained androgyny as an attempt to restore the original androgyny of ADAM, while a folkloric tradition explained the allegedly transgendered hare as the result of a mishap on Noah's ark and as an animal blessed by the Lord. This greater tolerance was mirrored by the dramatic rise of male homoerotic poetry among the Jewish poets of Spain. While this poetry has often been described as "secular," this opinion rests upon an extremely narrow definition of the religious or sacred. Rather, the poetry attempts to bridge the secular and the sacred, drawing upon both erotico-mystical Islamic poetry (as the *ghazal*) and the Biblical Song of Solomon. If anything, it seems like an attempt to Biblically justify homoerotic love by alluding not only to the Song of Solomon but also other Biblical books including Psalms, Proverbs, and Jeremiah. This is suggested by images and phrases such as that of the beloved as a gazelle (Song of Solomon 2: 9 and Arabic/Moorish poets), the pubic area being "fenced with roses" (Song of Solomon 7: 3), and the phrase "I am sick with Love," (Song of Solomon 2: 5). The beloved, moreover, is compared to Biblical figures, including Joseph and David, both of whom were traditionally linked to same-sex love, with Joseph also being linked to gender variance. Beyond this, the beloved is almost always compared to the moon. Exemplary of such erotico-spiritual poetry is a poem by Yishaq ben Mar-Saul (eleventh century), in which he writes: "Gazelle desired in Spain / . . . / Lovely of form like the moon with beautiful stature: /. . . / Like Joseph in his form, like Adoniah [a son of David] his hair. / Lovely of eyes like David, he has slain me like Uriah. / He has enflamed my passions and consumed my heart with fire." In these poems, the younger beloved male is associated with a host of other symbols as well – he is a fawn, a "branch who has exalted my heart with its blossoms," and a "bough of myrtle which passion has planted." His cheeks are "apples of gold." His necklace "is the Pleiades," meaning that his neck is so beautiful that only stars might serve to ornament it. His chest and nipples are "like golden pomegranates fastened with silver." The beloved is most often a CUPBEARER. This image was most probably known to both Arabic and Jewish poets of Spain in reference to GANYMEDE, the beloved of the Greek god ZEUS; both were probably further aware of Ganymede's association with the astrological sign of AQUARIUS. Moreover, the cupbearer was the chief image of the beloved and at times the lover in Islamic mystical, especially Sufi, poetry. This was linked to the figure of the WILDAN or *ghilman*, the beautiful male youth who would serve the Islamic faithful in Paradise. The *wildan* was alternately compared to the beloved as the beautiful youth and to the lover (mystic-poet) as the servant of God. Beyond these associations, there may have been preserved the memory of a beautiful youth who served Baal, the male consort of the Canaanite goddess ATHIRAT. That the beloved was compared to God and that these were clearly erotico-spiritual poems as opposed to purely secular poems is perhaps most evident in the poem of Moses Ibn Ezra (1055- c. 1135/40), who is "considered the greatest of the Hebrew poets of Spain." In one of these, he compares the sight of his beloved to "the moon at the edge of a rainbow," an image alluding to the prophet Ezekiel's vision of God ("Like the appearance of the bow that is in the cloud on the day of rain," Ezekiel 1: 28). In another, apparently realizing the stigma attached to same-sex love and yet also realizing its divine aspect, Ibn Ezra writes: "Come, O gazelle, rise and feed me / With the honey of your lips, and satisfy me. / Why do they hold back my heart, why? / If because of sin and guilt, / I will be ravished by your beauty – God is there!" Among the Jewish poets who wrote poems of homoerotic love, the most renowned include Yishaq ben Mar-Saul and Moses Ibn Ezra (mentioned above), Yosef Ibn Saddiq (c. 1075-1149), Samuel Ibn Nagrillah (c. 993-1056), Solomon Ibn Gabirol (b. c.1021), Judah ha-Levi (1075-1141), Abraham Ibn Ezra (1082-1167), and Isaac Ibn Ezra (fl. twelfth century). It should be noted that poets writing homoerotic poems were typically also lovers or spouses of women and would be considered bisexual in today's terms. With the expulsion of the Jews – who, along with the Muslims, were accused by Spanish Catholics of importing homosexuality to Spain – in 1492, this enlightened era regarding homoerotic love appears to have ended. For the ensuing four-hundred-year period, little has yet been written concerning gender and sexual variance in Jewish life.

With the arrival of the late nineteenth and early twentieth centuries, the association of gender and sexual variance and Judaism began to surface once more, as numerous same-sex inclined and/or gender variant individuals of Jewish heritage rose to prominence in the world of art and social activism. These individuals, including the artist Simeon SOLOMON (1841-1905), the poet and early sexologist Marc André Raffalovich (1864-1934), the novelist Marcel Proust (1871-1922), the composer Reynaldo Hahn (1874-1947), the writer Gertrude Stein (1874-1946), and the dancer Ida RUBENSTEIN (c. 1885-1960), often struggled intensely to come to terms with what literary historian Ludger Brinker has aptly described as their "double otherness." Some, disillusioned by the lack of tolerance they discovered in Judaism, converted to Catholicism, (naively) imagining that Christianity would embrace them as they were, or else believing that their erotic inclinations would vanish upon conversion. Others sublimated their spiritual feelings or expressed them artistically. In contrast to such individuals, persons of Jewish heritage like Magnus Hirschfeld (1869-1935) and Emma Goldman (1869-1940) became activists in the early homosexual rights movements. The emergence of the contemporary movements for lesbian and gay rights, and more recently those of bisexuals and the transgendered, have already made, and continue to make, a powerful impact upon Judaism's relationship to gender and sexual variance. In 1972, partly inspired by the Christian gay-centered Metropolitan Community Church, Beth Chayim Chasdaim (BCC), or "the House of New Life," was established in the United States. Also that year, the Jewish Gay Group was founded in London. The next year, the Union of American Hebrew Congregations voted that BCC be accepted into that organization. Since that time, many groups and temples have been founded, including Am Tivka in Boston, Beth Ahavah in Philadelphia, Bet Havarim in Atlanta, Sha 'ar Zahav in San Francisco, and the World Congress of Gay and Lesbian Jewish Organizations. In the 1990s, smaller groups such as San Francisco's Dyke Shabbos, where lesbians and other women come together to celebrate Shabbat, are also prospering. Beyond the establishment of these groups and houses of worship, other Jewish organizations have followed the lead of the UAHC in adopting resolutions in support of same-sex inclined Jews, including the Central Conference of American Rabbis (Reformed) and the Reconstructionist Rabbinical Association. While the Knesset, the Israeli Parliament, is not bound by and thus does not necessarily reflect shifts in Jewish religious law (*halakh*), it is important to note that in 1988, the Knesset legalized sexual relationships between adult males – those between women, while generally considered immoral, had not been illegal – allowing gay men to enter the Israeli army.

Christie Balka, Evelyn Tornton Beck, Yoel H. Jahn, Andy Rose, Aliza Maggid, and Alan D. Zamochnick are among the many involved in this movement who have begun to write about their experiences in anthologies such as *Nice Jewish Girls: A Lesbian Anthology* (1982); *Twice Blessed: on Being Lesbian or Gay and Jewish* (1989); and *Lesbiot: Israeli Lesbians Talk About Sexuality, Feminism Judaism, and Their Lives* (1995). The rise of this spiritual movement is mirrored by a renascence in literature by persons of Jewish heritage including David Feinberg, Leslie Feinberg, Jyl Lynn Felman, Harvey Fierstein, Allen GINSBERG, William Hoffman, Melanie Kaye/Kantrowitz, Irena Klepfisz, Larry Kramer, Tony Kushner, David Leavitt, Elana Nachman/DYKEWOMON, Lesléa Newman, Adrienne RICH, Sarah Schulman, and Irene Zahava. As Ludger Brinker observes, "American Jewish gay and lesbian [and we might also add transgendered and bisexual] writers have tended to be secularists," relating to being Jewish in ethnic more than in spiritual terms. Nevertheless, for a number of celebrated writers, including Lev Raphael and Judith Katz, the spiritual dimension of Jewishness is an important concern. Raphael concerns himself with the relationship of gays to Judaism in both fiction, as in *Dancing on Tisha B'Av* (1990), and in nonfiction, as in *Journeys and Arrivals: On Being Gay and Jewish* (1996). In *Running Fiercely Toward a High Thin Sound* (1992) Katz depicts an inspirited cosmos where Jewish women and their female ancestors join together to heal humanity. One of the most powerful statements concerning queer Jewish identity occurs in Lev Raphael's "To Be a Jew" (1995) where he writes: "One of the most moving injunctions in the Torah is that 'the stranger in your midst shall be as the native' . . . This call is a central part of every Passover seder. Alienated for so long from other Jews, deeply divided about my own homosexuality, I have felt myself twice strange: Jewish in the gay community, gay in the Jewish community . . . but living with and loving a Jewish man . . . [has] made it possible for me to do what Evelyn Beck has called exceeding 'the limits of what was permitted to the marginal.'"

Mesoamerican and South American

The spiritual traditions of Mesoamerica and South America were, generally speaking, pantheistic or polytheistic traditions rooted in Shamanism, as exemplified by the traditions of the AZTECS, CHIMU, LACHE, LUPACAS, MANTA, MAYAS, MBAYA, MOCHE, TUPINAMBAS, and others. From the spiritual traditions of these and other peoples of Mesoamerica and South America, numerous deities and other supernatural beings linked to same-sex eroticism and/or transgenderism emerged, including CHIN, HEISÈI, IN P'EN, KUCUMATZ, NGENECHEN, TAWEAKAME, TEZCATLIPOCA, TLAZOLTEOTL, URUHÚ, XOCHIPILLI, XOCHIQUETZAL, and XOLOTL, as well as a mythical race of giants inhabiting sites in Mexico and in northwestern South America. Although many of the original names of their spiritual roles have not survived – ISHQUICUINK, MACHI, and possibly, PIACHE, being among the few that have – we know that many transgendered and/or homoerotically inclined or bisexual shamans and priests served in the villages and temples of these cultural areas. In twentieth-century Mexico, renowned shamans like María SABINA have continued in some respects to carry on the tradition of the androgynous shaman. Certain sites, including CULIACAN and PANUCO in Mexico, PUNÁ in Ecuador, and TRUJILLO in Peru came to be especially associated with the interrelationship of spirituality, transgenderism, and same-sex intimacy. The traditions of Mesoamerica and South America have further engendered symbols pertaining to same-sex desire and/or transgenderism, such as animals and insects including the BUTTERFLY, CRAB, DEER, GOAT, JAGUAR, and OWL, and foods including the AREPA, CAULIFLOWER, PAPAYA, RICE WITH PORK, and the TORTILLA. These traditions have also inspired many lesbian, gay, bisexual, and/or transgendered artists of the twentieth century, including the writers Gloria ANZALDÚA, Luis CERNUDA, Gil CUANDROS, and Cherríe MORAGA and the painters Frida KAHLO and Nahum ZENIL. They have also, in recent years, wielded a powerful influence upon the manner in which persons dying of AIDS-related illnesses have been remembered, especially in Mexico and in the southwestern and western US. In these regions, during the festival of the Dia de los Muertos (the Day of the Dead), the deceased are celebrated with music, dance, and altars combining personal favorite items of the deceased with candles, skeleton breads, sugar skulls, and marigolds.

Queer Spirit

In this volume, the reader will find both "Gay Spirituality" and "Queer Spirit" employed. In general, although Judy GRAHN's pivotal work *Another Mother Tongue* stands as a notable exception, Gay Spirituality has in the main referred to gay men's spirituality, referring only occasionally to lesbian concerns and rarely to those of bisexuals. To the contrary, Queer Spirit, emerging from the period of Queer political activism, speaks to the spirituality of gay men as well as lesbians, bisexuals, and transgendered persons. While the movements of Gay Spirituality and Queer Spirit are equally valid, we have chosen in this volume to focus on the latter due to its inclusiveness. We also feel that in certain respects such figures as "TWO-SPIRIT" shamans and transgendered priests, as well as bisexual or pansexual deities and living persons, cannot be adequately served under the rubric of Gay Spirituality. Nevertheless, in other respects, Gay Spirituality and Queer Spirit share much in common. Many lesbians, gay men, bisexuals, and transgendered individuals living at the end of the twentieth century have begun to (re-) claim the ancient association of same-sex EROTICISM, transgenderism, and sacred experience or role. This process often begins with "coming out," an experience that stresses not only self-acknowledgement but also public announcement. In recent years, the lesbian, gay, bisexual, and transgendered rights movements have facilitated the coming out process. Yet many queer-identified persons continue to experience coming out as a harrowing journey bringing them face to face with a "shadow" or "other" that they have kept locked inside but that they know must be retrieved if they are to survive. For many queer-identified persons, coming to terms with their erotic feelings for persons of the same sex and/or with transgendered identity constitutes the beginning, and not the end, of the coming out process. A second or later phase commences when they come out politically, as persons seeking human rights. For many queer-identified persons, personal and political coming out have been followed by a spiritual reckoning. This encounter with the sacred is sometimes expressed as a desire to secure a place for themselves within the spiritual traditions of the communities in which they have been reared. Others, however, search for spiritual traditions which may be more accepting of their sexuality or transgendered identity. Both of these choices constitute forms of what is today being referred to as Queer Spirit, insofar as they grapple with the role of queer-identified persons in the tradition.

Queer Spirit refers primarily, however, to an eclectic movement based in the beliefs that the divine source embraces homoeroticism, lesbianism, bisexuality, and transgenderism and that persons enacting these behaviors or holding these identities have served in many cultures as spiritual functionaries, which include the role of (ritual) artist or craftsperson as well as that of (spiritual) warrior. Queer Spirit emphasizes the weaving together of various beliefs and practices giving expression to these root concepts. Queer Spiritual practices include but are not limited to the reverence of divine beings or forces, healing, divination, and MAGIC, and the creation of art. In terms of a divine being or beings, Queer Spirit seeks to discover the potential queerness of divinities not commonly associated with gender or sexual variance (such as JESUS) – a task mastered by Shug AVERY in Alice Walker's novel *The Color Purple* – as well as to honor those which *are* commonly associated with these traits (such as ARTEMIS/DIANA). Bert Provost (1991) suggests that queer-identified persons might begin to envision divine beings which speak directly to sexual and gender variance. "I've grown tired of the divine heterosexual couple of contemporary Paganism," he writes. "While I continue to invoke a variety of spirits, both male and female, the emphasis is on linking them to my queerness. I might invoke the Goddess as the Sacred Bitch, Dyke Sister or Mother of Faggots. Her relationship to male spirits is anything but 'traditional.' The God I call on has a variety of names. He is the Rising Pillar of Flesh, the Open Hand, Boyfriend, Lover and Gate of Pleasure." In terms of the role of spiritual functionary, Arthur EVANS writes in *Witchcraft and the Gay Counterculture*, "We look forward to regaining our ancient historical roles as medicine people, healers, prophets, shamans, and sorcerers." Native American Indian writer Paula Gunn ALLEN speaks similarly of lesbian women who are beginning to embody the role of a "ceremonial dyke" who serves in a shamanic capacity.

Queer Spirit also seeks to sacralize same-sex and transgendered relationships, which have been denigrated by Church, State, and families. Eroticism becomes an encounter of Self and Self, experienced, in Harry HAY's terms, as "subject-subject consciousness." Queer Spirit may also include Tantric rites and other forms of ritualized eroticism. Because many queer-identified persons, perhaps especially gay men, have been led to think of themselves as "unnatural," Queer Spirit also emphasizes communion with Nature. It also acknowledges that because, in general, lesbians, gays, bisexuals, and transgendered persons have been barred from positions of spiritual authority, many have expressed their spirituality in works of art. A canon of Gay/Queer Spiritual literary texts has begun to emerge. It includes Arthur Evans's *Witchcraft and the Gay Counterculture* and *The God of Ecstasy*, Mitch WALKER's *Visionary Love*, Judy Grahn's *Another Mother Tongue*, Mark THOMPSON's *Gay Spirit and Gay Soul*, Will Roscoe's *Living the Spirit* (with Gay American Indians) and *Queer Spirits*, Diane MARIECHILD and Marcelina Martin's *Lesbian Sacred Sexuality*, and numerous other works. Others express their spirituality in music, painting, film, and other arts, as articles in this volume reveal.

Practitioners of Queer Spirit, living in the midst of the AIDS and breast cancer crises, are also (re-) claiming the ancient shamanic or priestly roles of healer and psychopomp ("guide of souls"), which have been attributed by many cultures to deities and fnctionaries also linked to transgenderism and/or same-sex desire. They have become involved in various healing practices believed to ease suffering, practices including established medical care as well as herbal medicine, massage, and visualization. In the words of Tom Cowan, a gay Wiccan, "the gods and goddesses [are] saying to us, 'Hey, wake up. This is your [time to reclaim the] ancient role of healer and death counselor, someone who understands what it means to move between the worlds.'" Queer Spiritualists have also begun to create rituals to honor their loved ones who have died.

Perhaps the most important contribution of Queer Spirit to the discourses of gender, sexuality, religion, spirituality, and myth, however, lies in the expression, often agonized, of its struggle to discover the origin(s) of gendered and erotic identities and its attempt to balance in consciousness two contradictory positions concerning identity. One is expressed poetically by Robin Morgan. "We are the myths," she insists. "We are the AMAZONS, the FURIES, the Witches. We have never not been here, this exact sliver of time, this precise place. There is something utterly familiar about us. We have been ourselves before." The second position is voiced by Paula Gunn Allen: "From a metaphysical point of view, everything will change into something else." In spiritual, mythic, archetypal, or transpersonal terms, this suggests that queer identity may be both stable and unstable. Harry Hay has described this form of consciousness as "both-and," as opposed to the dualistic "either-or" consciousness to which most of us are accustomed and which operates in many disciplines. Allen continues, reaching the heart of the paradox, the enigma: "That doesn't mean that there are no essences, it just means that all essences are subject to change." While social constructionists and biologists have been engaged in battle over whether the origin of queerness lies in nurture or nature, Queer Spiritualists offer – not surprisingly – a metaphysical response: Queerness may represent a form of embodiment, or what others might deem possession. The Greeks spoke of *en-theos*, from which our term "enthusiasm" derives. To "en-theos" is to "invite the god within." The Greek devotee did not merely worship the deity, but rather invited the deity in. In embodying Artemis or DIONYSUS, the male or female devotee gave expression to the mythos of that divine force, as does the devotee of DAMBALLAH, the RAINBOW SERPENT of Vodou, today. While this notion rests upon the very question of the existence of the spiritual realm and thus may not be tested scientifically, it may help to explain why so many queer-identified persons resonate so deeply with the shamans, priests, and priestesses of other times and places. "We are the myths . . . We have never not been here."

Radical Faeries

Stuart Timmons (1990) offers what is perhaps the most concise and tangible – if somewhat idealistic – description of the Radical Faeries. The Faerie Circle, as the group is commonly referred to, is a "mixture of political alternative, counterculture, and spirituality movement." It is a "networking of gentle men devoted to the principles of ecology, spiritual truth, and, in New Age terms, 'gay-centeredness.'" The Radical Faeries was founded in 1979 by Harry HAY, his companion John Burnside, and a small circle of friends. They chose the term "Faerie" in an attempt to transform or reclaim a term used to denigrate gay and transgendered men into a term by which to celebrate themselves (ourselves). The added "Radical" inferred an emphasis on radical politics, primarily of an anarchistic, communitarian nature, as well as a casting off of inauthentic identities (such as those assumed by "closet queens") and a psychic return to the root of one's being. On Labor Day Weekend in 1979, the first "Spiritual Conference for Radical Faeries" was held at the site of Sri Ram Ashram in Arizona, with over two hundred men attending. "A spontaneous theme of paganism emerged," relates Timmons; "Invocations were offered to spirits . . . [Hay] called on the crowd to 'throw off the ugly green frogskin of hetero-imitation to find the shining Faerie prince beneath.'" Many of the men saw themselves as free spirits communing with each other and with Nature; like Faeries, they were dancing, feasting, and creating spectacle in a natural setting. While a strong anarchistic tendency militates against the establishment of standardized rites, certain ritual practices, inspired by Wiccan and Native American traditions, have been generally accepted by many Faeries. These include: the creation of sacred space by way of "casting a circle"; the passing of a talisman from one speaker to another in the circle to encourage the direction of others' attention toward that person; ecstatic dance rituals, including the "Kali Fire," which often focuses on the banishing of that which is no longer needed or desired; and communal feasts (typically vegetarian). Beyond these events, one often finds at gatherings smaller circles devoted to sensuous massage, weaving and other crafts, and divination. Especially at larger gatherings, a tendency to create fantasy environments is pronounced.

The Faerie Circle has become an international movement. Its major voice is the journal *RFD*; its minor voice, *FDR* (the *Faerie Dish Rag*). In recent years, the Faerie Circle has experienced stresses from within which appear to be threatening its continued existence. Criticism has also come from without; e.g., many non-white gay men feel uncomfortable with the Circle's name, evoking as it does the Celtic or British pre-Christian tradition. At the same time, Faeries are encouraged by prospering communal households in Tennessee, North Carolina, and elsewhere, as well as a strengthening movement to establish a Faerie sanctuary on land purchased in Oregon. The Circle has inspired a variety of artists, including the musicians Charlie Murphy and Lunacy, Heartsinger, Ron Lambe, and Stephen Klein, the poet and filmmaker JAMES BROUGHTON, the filmmakers/video artists Bill Weber and Eric Slade (of the psychedelic-erotic short *Sex Life*, 1995), the essayists Arthur EVANS, Mark THOMPSON, Mitch WALKER, and Will ROSCOE, the visual artist Stevee Postman, the ritual-performance artists Keith HENNESSY, Jack Davis, Elk, and the connoisseur of chocolates, Jeoffrey J. Douglas, of Rococoa's Faerie Queene Chocolates in San Francisco. One of the most poetic texts expressing the resonance with the fairies of folklore that Radical Faeries have felt appears in Mitch Walker's *Visionary Love: A Spirit Book of Gay Mythology* (1980), an early "bible" of the Faeries and the Gay Spiritual movement; Walker writes: "Fairies see polarities dancing, changing everywhere, constantly . . . This wonderful paradoxical freedom from form . . . enables Fairies to fly . . . There is an essence, essence of an eternal, hidden, dark, shining, eerie secret: the simultaneous and continuous creation and annihilation of Form . . . all shapes, forms, are bendings and corners of this flowing-is . . . [Fairies] are not static things but riders of lightbeams, weightless dancers along the edge – indeed are the Dancing itself . . . they are flow, the wind."

Shamanism

During the Paleolithic period, men and women lived primarily by hunting, fishing, and gathering wild plants. Chief among their material concerns was survival, both individual and collective. They looked toward the female to perpetuate the tribe. They may or may not have recognized the role of the male in reproduction. Their spiritual beliefs and practices reflected their way of life. Above all, they worshipped female deities and spirits as the sources of life. To a lesser extent, they revered male deities and spirits as guardians and hunters. Males also appear to have been perceived as human reflections of "rising and dying vegetation . . . ephemeral and mortal." As such, they, like animals and plants, were seen as embodiments of the principle of sacrifice. Along with this, they represented the eternal return of animal and plant life in the springtime. The central themes of both Paleolithic and Neolithic religions appear to have been birth, death, rebirth, and metamorphosis. In terms of metamorphosis, it seems that two key themes, the belief in the power of theriomorphic transformation – that is, becoming an animal or hybrid human-animal – and the belief in the power of gender transformation – becoming a person of the opposite sex, an hermaphrodite, or a person of an alternate or 'third' gender role – may have emerged during these early epochs of humankind. With its reverence of the feminine and also of the male principle and of animals and plants – not to mention the elements of earth, air, fire, and water – we may say that the spiritual beliefs of the first peoples appear to have been matrifocal (or gynocentric) and pantheistic (or animistic) in character. These beliefs were often manifested in the practice of Shamanism.

While narrowly defined as the spiritual practices of the early peoples of Siberia, Shamanism may be more broadly defined as a cross- or multicultural spiritual pathway stressing the interrelatedness of all life, the reverence of Nature, and the recognition that we live in a multiverse wherein we dwell with spirits or divine beings who actively participate in our lives. Numerous shamanic traditions also tend to share a belief that transgenderism and same-sex eroticism, together with traditional gender roles and heterosexuality, are both natural and sacred. Indeed, they often look upon transgendered persons as especially capable of performing spiritual functions, as they are believed to hold the knowledge of gender transformation as well as other forms of metamorphosis. Shamanism tends to focus on the practices and character of the shaman and the beliefs he/she shares, often matrifocal or pantheistic, with his/her people. The shaman is a spiritual functionary who, in a state of trance – which has recently been termed a "shamanic state of consciousness" (an "SSC") and which is often triggered by the use of chant, drumming, ecstatic dance, and mind-altering substances or entheogens – travels mentally or spiritually to other worlds or realms of consciousness in order to retrieve a wandering soul (often believed to be a cause of illness), to escort the soul of the deceased to the afterlife, or to communicate with a deity or spirit. The shamanic trance is closely linked to the state of possession, the primary difference being that with possession (also referred to as "embodiment," "enthusiasm" [from *en-* + *-theos*, "taking the god within"], or CHANNELING) a spiritual functionary, rather than visiting a deity or spirit, is instead visited or ridden by that divine being. The shaman functions as a healer, psychopomp (guide of souls), intercessory, diviner, worker of magic, and teacher of the mysteries.

Persons traditionally become shamans because other family members have been shamans or because they are called upon to become such by deities or spirits while dreaming or experiencing an otherwise altered state of consciousness. Prior to becoming shamans, they often experience illness and death-like states. They frequently work with animal and spirit helpers, and they are believed to hold the power to transform themselves into animals (theriomorphic transformation) and other entities. At some point, certain shamans came to be looked upon as individuals belonging to an alternate gender, or genders. This gender category (or categories) represented a blending of traits assumed by the cultures concerned to be masculine, feminine, and godlike or supernatural. According to Joseph Campbell, such shamans represented a "sphere of spiritual power transcending the male-female polarity." Gender variant, or transgendered, shamans have found a place in many cultures. They have been called by many names – TWO-SPIRIT (general, Native American Indian), "soft" shaman (general, Alaskan, Siberian, North Asian), ALYHA (Mohave, male), BASIR (Ngaju Dayak, male), HWAME (Mohave, female), KWIRAXAME (Maricopa, female), MANANG BALI (Iban Dayak, male), MAHU (Hawaii, male), NADLE (Navaho, male) – and others. They have often revered or otherwise been associated with certain deities and spirits. Joseph Campbell maintained that these deities and spirits have generally pointed toward a "Primal Bisexual Divinity." Such deities and spirits include the Inuit (or Eskimo) Mother Goddess SEDNA, Sedna's companion QAILERTETANG, the Inuit WHITE WHALE WOMAN, the Koryak Big RAVEN, Raven's wife MITI, the Hidatsa triune goddess VILLAGE OLD WOMAN, ANOG ITE of the Lakota and Oglala Plains, WIYA NUMPA of the Lakota, the Ngaju Dayak androgynous deity MAHATALA-JATA, and the Iban Dayak deity MENJAYA RAJA MANANG.

Becoming a transformed shaman is often viewed as a process which includes several relatively distinct phases. Metamorphosis might commence as early as infancy. Among the Koniag Inuit, "When father or mother regard their son as feminine in his bearing, they will often dedicate him in earliest childhood to the vocation of *Achnutschik* [i.e. ANGAKKUQ, gender variant shaman]." Among the Koniag, Iban Dayak, and others, metamorphosis might also commence when a deity or spirit visited the young person in a dream or otherwise altered state. The young Mohave woman destined to become a *hwame* would begin dreaming of becoming such even before exiting the womb. The Maricopa female who "dreamed too much" as a child was believed destined to become a *kwiraxame*. Among Native American Hidatsa, young men destined to become gender variant MIATI shamans dreamed that the triune goddess instructed them to leave behind traditionally masculine attire, speech, behavior, and pursuits and to adopt those of women or individuals of alternate gender. Among the Plains Indians, especially among the Omaha and Lakota, young men destined to become gender variant shamans also dreamed of a feminine or gynandrous being. The Omaha youth would dream of the gynandrous deity of the MOON. Among the Oglala Sioux, gender variant shamans-to-be dreamed of the female divinity DOUBLE WOMAN, Anukite. There were, of course, those young persons who refused to accept the role. A young Native American male who was determined to escape the deity's call began to see loops of SWEETGRASS, emblematic of gender variant shamanhood, everywhere he looked. Should the young Iban Dayak refuse the deity's call, he would bring ruin not only upon himself but upon his entire family and, further, upon his entire community. Others who accepted and later rejected the calling, like the female *hwame* SAHAYKWISA (c. 1850- c. 1895), were often visited by great misfortune. The young person who accepted the call, whether he be Iban, Hidatsa, or of another people, would usually begin to dress in a combination of the attire usually attributed to the opposite anatomical sex as well as in attire signifying shamanic calling. The Maricopa female *kwiraxame* began to dress in men's clothes. The Yakut gender variant shaman of Siberia wore a "woman's jacket of foal-skins and a woman's white ermine cap." The Siberian soft male shaman often tattooed his face, TATTOOING being a sign of feminine beauty. With the onset of the next stage, the young person would leave behind "all pursuits and manners of his [or her] sex." The Maricopa female *kwiraxame* would begin to hunt and to fight in battle. Vladimir Bogoras wrote of the Chukchi soft male shaman: "He throws away the . . . lance, the lasso of the reindeer-herdsmen, and the harpoon of the seal-hunter, and takes to the needle and the skin-scraper . . . Even his pronunciation changes from the male to the female mode. At the same time his body alters . . . his psychical character changes. The transformed person . . . becomes . . . fond of small-talk and of nurturing small children." During this stage of transformation, an individual might even change the way in which he or she entered a dwelling. Among the Koryak, a young male shaman would now enter the opening reserved for females and soft men. He might also change the place where he slept. Also during this stage, or at the beginning of the next stage, training as a shaman would intensify. While some, like the Iban *manang bali*, were instructed primarily by deities in dreams, others, like the Ngaju *basir*, were taught by elder shamans or shamanesses.

During the next stage, same-sex eroticism and relationships were often emphasized. At this time, the Iban *manang* was said to move from being "unripe" to being "completely transformed," *bali*. This stage was marked by the Iban with an "elaborate and costly initiation" ceremony. Gender variant male shamans of Polynesia, and probably also those of Korea, Vietnam, and Japan, engaged in homoeroticism. Native American two-spirit shamans, including those of the Hidatsa and Oglala Sioux tribes, often married traditionally masculine males, while gender variant female shamans, like the *hwame* of the Mohave, typically married females. Of the Ngaju Dayak male shamans, Justus van der Kroef explains that the basir were expected to "act as women sexually." He stresses that failure to perform homosexually might place the *basir* in an "inferior position." Both the Ngaju *basir* and the Iban *manang bali* established marriage-like relationships with traditional males. Among the Chukchi, the young male shaman, according to Bogoras, "seeks to win the good graces of men, and succeeds easily with the aid of 'spirits.' Thus he has all the young men he could wish for striving to obtain his favor. From these he chooses his lover." The Chukchi are said to have celebrated marriages between gender variant shamans and their lovers "with the usual rites." Such relationships usually formed, in Bogoras's words, "a quite solid union, which often last[ed] till the death of one of the parties." Among the Chukchi, this earthly marriage was seen as a reflection of the divine marriage existing between the shaman and a deity or spirit. While scholars have tended to downplay the importance of transgendered homosexuality in shamanism, Krasheninikoff and Vladimir Jochelson believed that, at least among the Kamchadal (or Itelmensy), its role was crucial: "[It] may be inferred that the most important feature of the institution of the KOE'KCUC lay, not in their shamanistic power, but in their position with regard to the satisfaction of the unnatural inclinations of the Kamchadal. The *koe'kcuc* . . . were in the position of concubines." The relationship of shamans and their companions cannot, however, be reduced to a typical "husband-wife" relationship. Their spiritual function, combined with their special relationship to a deity or spirit, caused shamans, whatever their anatomical sex or gender role, to be regarded as the true heads of their households. If mortal companions failed to treat shamans with respect, the shamans' supernatural companions would punish them. That the male Chukchi shaman was head of his household is also evidenced by the fact that the mortal lover often took the shaman's name as an addition to his own name; for instance, Tilu'wgi-Ya'tirgin ("Ya'tirgin, husband of Tilu'wgi"). Relationships between shamans and their companions did not generally emphasize age differences. Bogoras, for example, mentions a sixty-year-old male Chukchi shaman named Kee'ulin who, upon the death of his companion of twenty years, now "was said . . . to have a new lover, – another old man who lived in the same house with him." The Kootenai female shaman KAUXUMA NUPIKA (c. 1790-1837) had a succession of female lovers prior to marrying a young woman. She and her female spouse acted as guides to Alexander Ross and other traders and explorers. While writers on Shamanism have tended to avoid explicit descriptions of same-sex eroticism, Bogoras infers that sex between the gender variant Siberian shaman and his male lover may have consisted largely of anal eroticism, with the shaman typically taking the receptive role. Certain myths, such as that of Big Raven castrating himself and that of an Inuit man exposing his genitals to the sun in order to cause them to shrivel, suggest that at one time, castration may have been practiced by transformed shamans. This hypothesis is strengthened by a statement made to Bogoras by Ya'tirgin, the male companion of the Chukchi soft shaman Tilu'wgi. Describing the shaman as "wholly masculine, and well developed," Ya'tirgin "confessed that . . . he hoped that in time, with the aid of the KE'LET [spirit], Tilu'wgi would be able to equal the real soft men of old, and to change the organs of his sex altogether." If castration had at one time been practiced by Siberian shamans, it is not difficult to see why anal eroticism may have become the primary erotic activity among shamans and their companions. Among Polynesian *mahu*, fellatio seems to have been practiced, with the *mahu* taking the role of fellator. Female two-spirit shamans were said to employ objects including animal horns and bones as dildoes while making love.

While gender variant shamans appear to have comprised a special class of shamans in numerous cultures, this categorization does not seem to have greatly limited their functions. Among the Chukchi, for example, soft shamans were said to "excel in all branches of shamanism." The same was said of female Mohave *hwame* shamans. Nevertheless, certain transgendered shamans were thought to be especially skilled in certain sacred tasks and arts. Some, like the Kootenai female shaman Kauxuma Nupika, were considered great mediators, peacemakers, and prophets. Ngaju *basir* were the "chief officials during new year's ceremonies." They were especially gifted as ritual chanters and singers. Koniag *angakkuq* not only practiced the arts of divination, magic, and healing, but also instructed young women in etiquette and dance. Navaho *nadle* and Lakota WINKTES were thought to be able to heal mental and physical illness and to aid in childbirth through the employment of magical songs. Mohave *hwame* two-spirit women were thought to be highly skilled at curing venereal disease. Among the Iban Dayak, the *manang bali* was believed to be able to heal the sick by way of prayers, the employment of crystals, and journeying to the realms of the gods and spirits in order to retrieve the wandering soul, which was at least partly responsible for the patient's illness. Similarly, gender variant shamans – like other shamans – often served as psychopomps, guiding the souls of the dying to the afterlife. Like other shamans, gender variant shamans were also thought to be capable of raising storms and of transforming into animals, plants, stones, and other entities. V. F. Trostchansky has suggested that among the Yakut of Siberia, the soft shaman may have mastered the art of destructive magic, a branch of magic thought to have originated among female shamans in response to hostile invaders. Soft shamans may have undertaken spells not only of a destructive but also of an amatory nature. Hidatsa *miati* shamans were thought to be especially gifted in hunting and agricultural magic.

Like other shamans, gender variant, transgendered, or two-spirit shamans are perceived as intermediaries or intercessories between the mortal and other realms. They typically visit other realms when in an altered state of consciousness such as possession or trance, often triggered by chant, dance, simulated or actual erotic activity, or the employment of hallucinogenic or intoxicating substances. Among the Inuit, the *angakkuq* would often begin his journey while naked, being bound, and having artificial wings tied to his back. In this manner he would embark on the treacherous journey to Adlivun, abode of Sedna. Among the Ngaju *basir*, communication and ultimately union with the deity occurs during a state of possession, when the deity (*sangiang*) enters the stomach – rather than the head, as is customary in African traditions – and begins to speak to and then through the shaman. During the time of possession, the *basir* is envisioned as a boat in which the deity sails. Gender variant shamans, like other shamans, frequently employ entheogenic substances in rituals. The Siberian soft male shaman often used the fly agaric mushroom (*amanita muscaria*) in this manner. Other participants in these rites, by way of drinking the shaman's urine, were able to share in his ecstasy. Tales of White Whale Woman suggest that female Inuit shamans may have also employed fly agaric in their rites. When a transgendered male shaman dies, he is sometimes buried "on the man's side of the cemetery," as were the Zuni LHAMANA. The Lakota shaman Lame Deer reported that in "the old days *winktes* . . . had a special hill where they were buried." It is conceivable that two-spirit female shamans were also buried in either of these ways, although little research has been published as yet in this area. Even when two-spirit males were buried alongside other males, their funeral dress, which they would wear into the next life, often reflected their alternate gender status; they would apparently remain persons of alternate gender in the afterlife. Lame Deer remembered asking a *winkte* "what he would be in the spirit land, a man or a woman." "Both," the winkte replied. The Ngaju Dayak not only believed that the gender variant *basir* would retain his identity after death but also that he would share a special "village of the dead in the Upperworld" with female *balian* shamanesses.

Shinto

In Japan, Shinto is the descendant of Shamanism. Like its predecessor and like religious Taoism, Shinto is deeply concerned with healing, divination, and magic. The chief deity, or *kami*, of the Shinto pantheon is the sun goddess AMATERASU OMI KAMI, who is, especially by way of two other deities, AME NO UZUME and ISHI KORE DOME NO KAMI, associated with transgenderism and possibly also with lesbian desire. Many *kami* are linked to forces of Nature and to geographical sites. Shinto ceremonies (*matsuri*) are "designed to appeal to the *kami* . . . for benevolent treatment and protection, and consist of . . . offerings, prayers, and purification." Tales of the *kami* are found in various texts, including the *Kojiki*, the *Nihon Shoki*, and the *Shoku Nihongi*. Shinto is concerned not only with the afterlife, which includes concepts of both reincarnation and an eternal paradise, but also with "life and the benefits of this world, which are seen as divine gifts." While attitudes toward transgenderism and same-sex desire are not altogether positive in Shinto, archaeological evidence suggests that at an early date, transgendered shamans or priest(esse)s may have served in Shinto rites as *miko*, that is, as spiritual functionaries capable of becoming embodied by *kami* – in this case, female or transgendered *kami* – during possession or trance states. C. Blacker, in *The Catalpa Bow: A Study of Shamanistic Practices in Japan* (1986) reports that evidence for this practice was discovered in the 1950s on Tanegashima Island, where the skeleton of a young male was found dressed in feminine sacred garments and jewelry, including an "extraordinary profusion of shell ornaments – necklaces, abundant bracelets, square brooches decorated with an endless knot pattern at the waist and loins."

The association of homoeroticism – often of a transgendered and intergenerational character – and Shinto is an ancient one. CHIGO, young men, were often "chosen to offer sacred wine, perform dances, and be archers" at Shinto ceremonies. These youths were chosen because they were believed to be "capable of divine possession" by the *kami*, thus serving as *miko*. *Chigo* were especially celebrated in July, when the *Chigo-kurai-morai* was held. At this time, one young man was honored by the emperor. Jean Herbert has emphasized the fact that this youth was "attended by male persons exclusively," a rather unusual situation in Shinto, in which many ceremonies involve women. Herbert's statement is echoed by Louis Frédéric, who describes *chigo* as "young males who acted in the place of women when the latter were not admitted in temples or shrines during certain ceremonies." Many of these *chigo* were studying to become Shinto priests. As novices, they often found themselves loved by their spiritual masters. In Japan, the term *chigo* eventually came to be employed in non-spiritual contexts as well, to refer to "effeminate boys loved by some lords," and as late as the Meiji period (1868-1912) to refer to a "male student who was the object of an older male student's affection." Figures associated with transgenderism and/or same-sex desire and Shinto, beyond those mentioned above, include: AMA NO HAFURI, KITSUNE, KUKAI, SHINU NO HAFURI, and SHIRABYOSHI. The MIRROR is also of relevance here.

Sufism

Sufis, or "wearers of wool," have been called by some "the mystics of Islam." Sufis numbered among the wandering seekers of the Middle Ages and later epochs. It should be noted that – as with the Greco-Roman priests of the Goddess – ridicule, banishment, and the fear of capital punishment also may have contributed to the itinerancy of the Sufis. Also called "dervishes," or "poor men," the Sufis seek ecstatic union with the Godhead. The *tariqah*, or "path to God," is a serpentine one, winding between ascetic and aesthetic extremes and embracing homoeroticism and, to a lesser degree, gender variance or transgenderism. Among Sufis, it is believed that the "path of love must lead directly towards God; but it may also pass through the intermediary of the SHAHED," the beloved disciple of the Sufi master. The *shahed* "reflects the splendour and perception of the divine." Contemplation of the beloved disciple is referred to as *nazar ill' al-murd*, "contemplation of the unbearded," or as *shahed bazi*, "witness play." The relationship of the master and the disciple also reflects the relationship between God and SATAN, also called Iblis or Shaitan. Sufi teachings relate that Satan was cast out of heaven because he, being solely dedicated to God, "refused to bow before Adam." The beloved is thus the reflection of God, while the lover is the reflection of Satan or Iblis, "the lover in agony over his separation from the Beloved." At the end of time, Satan or Iblis, revered in the form of a peacock, will be reunited with God, his beloved.

While the relationship between master and disciple sometimes extends only to embracing and kissing, anal and oral eroticism, at least in the past, were not uncommon. Same-sex eroticism also may have played a role in Sufi initiation rites. In *Sexuality in Islam* (1985), Abdelwahab Boudhiba writes: "In the sessions of mystical initiation, the accolade was frequently given by the adults to the young initiates behind and in front." One of the rites undertaken by the Sufis and their disciples is the *sama'*, or "spiritual concert," which brings the participants, by way of music and whirling dance, into a state of ecstatic drunkenness. P. L. Wilson relates in *Scandal: Essays in Islamic Heresy* (1988) that the Sufis Awhaddodin Kermani and Fakroddin Iraqi, "when overcome by ecstasy during the *sama'* . . . were inclined to rend the shirts of the unbearded and dance with them breast to breast." On occasion, "transvestite whirling dervishes [possibly the KOCEK] performed." These "spiritual concerts" in the past were often held in taverns or cemeteries, forming part of the subcultural or countercultural phenomenon of MUJUN, which includes musicians, dancers, "homosexuals of both sexes" (according to Boudhiba), and other marginalized persons and groups. According to Wilson, the relationship of the Sufi and the *shahed* may inspire a kind of madness, a deautomization of ordinary consciousness, an altered or chaotic state; he writes: "there is something mad about the metaphysical experience. There is a kind of cosmic playfulness about the deepest levels of reality which . . . approaches the most chaotic and primordial of essences . . . there really is something mad about . . . *shahed bazi* [contemplating the beloved] . . . To make a passionate rite of such a crazy Game [i.e. *shahed bazi*] is to set up a whirlwind, a vortex through which everything present . . . will be sucked into the Other World."

The Sufis have been targeted by Islamic fundamentalists because they are mystics whose tradition may be rooted in pre-Islamic Arabic religion and because they engage(d) in same-sex eroticism. Indeed, one Islamic text refers to Sufis as a "community of sodomites (*al-lutiyun*)." Sufis, it must be stressed, have not simply engaged in homoeroticism; they have dared to see in it a sacred dimension, have dared to see the beloved as a reflection or an embodiment of God. This belief in indwelling, embodiment, or incarnation, called *hulul*, is considered the "most heinous of Sufi heresies." Among the many Sufis believed to have participated in homoerotic relationships, the most renowned are probably JALAL AL-DIN RUMI (1207-1273) and SHAMS AL-DIN TABRIZI (d. c. 1246). Another, Attar (d. 1220), writes in a poem representative of the Sufi blending of homoerotic passion and spiritual fervour: "Love of the beauty of the One I adore is like an ocean of fire; / the candle lights up with luminous flames but the moth perishes in it." Homoerotic love has been a subject of numerous secular texts influenced by Sufism. One such text is the *Qâbûs-nama*, composed by the Emir Kai-kâ' ûs ibn Iskandar in the eleventh century. In this text, the Emir encourages his son to "fall in love . . . with a worthy object [who should] possess a sufficient degree of beauty . . . and be graceful, that loose tongues may be silenced." The Emir also suggests that this relationship should remain essentially private. Noting a difference between homoerotic and heterosexual passion, the Emir further encourages his son to be bisexual so that he might be able to enjoy the pleasures of summer (other males) and winter (women).

Witchcraft and Wicca

Although Witchcraft, or Wicca as it is often called in the late twentieth century, has been confused with Satanism, it is in fact a matrifocal, earth-centered religion or spiritual tradition with roots in Goddess Reverence and in the ancient belief systems of the Greeks, Celts, and numerous other cultures. Many Witches trace its origins to Shamanism, with the Witch being the spiritual descendant of the shaman. Due to the persecution of its adherents, it is difficult to speculate if Witchcraft was itself a clearly defined ancient religion, perhaps consolidating in Thessaly, or if it emerged in late antiquity or the Middle Ages as a blending of the vestiges of "pagan" religions devastated by Christians and others. Whatever the case, it is clear (from the

Daemonologie of King JAMES I, published in 1597, and other sources) that by the Renaissance, numerous paths of "Witchcraft" existed, including those which were gender-segregated and those in which all genders participated. These traditions shared in common the revering of Nature, ancient deities and spirits such as ARTEMIS/DIANA and HECATE, fairies including PUCK (or Robin Goodfellow) and Queen Mab, and the dead. Some paths, resembling Santería as practiced in the Americas, sought to syncretize the elder deities and spirits with manifestations of the Biblical God, JESUS, the Virgin Mary, Catholic saints, and ANGELS, perhaps sincerely viewing them as kindred or perhaps in an effort to avoid persecution. Most if not all of these traditions celebrated seasonal festivals such as Halloween (Celtic Samhain, corresponding to the Christian All Souls' Eve and the Mexican/Mexican-American Dia de los Muertos); and most if not all practiced the arts of healing, divination, and MAGIC. The various paths of "Witchcraft" were typically confused, or else purposefully identified, by Christians and others with Satanism as well as ritual magic (in both its positive, or "white," and destructive, or "black," forms), other pre-Christian and syncretic traditions, and even with Judaism and Islam. Forms of this confusion continue to be practiced in the late twentieth century by "mainstream" theologians as well as other academics, including numerous social-constructionist feminist and queer theoreticians.

In general, one may say that Witches, or Wiccans, of our time continue to celebrate Nature, the deities and spirits of ancient cultures, and ancestors. The primary deities revered are the Great Goddess, either as Artemis/Diana, Aphrodite, or one or more of her other manifestations, and the Horned God (or Horned One), as PAN, CERNUNNOS, or one of his other manifestations. The body and sexuality are honored rather than condemned, and, differing from patriarchal and androcentric traditions, women often play central roles in Wicca or "the Craft," as it is also called. Moreover, sacred experience is perceived as profoundly linked to everyday life and to the realm of politics, with Witches playing important parts in the environmentalist, feminist, and other such movements. Witchcraft's links to same-sex desire and transgenderism may be traced, if not to its controversial origins, at least to the late ninth century, with the publication of the *Canon Episcopi,* which describes women attending rites presided over by the classical goddess Artemis/Diana. Patricia Simons (1994) explains that in a "folkloric tradition pre-dating Christianity but continuing well into the fifteenth century, [Artemis/] Diana as goddess of the MOON would lead a group of people, chiefly women, in night-time processions or gatherings in the woods . . . At the close of the fourteenth century, several women in Milan were tried before the Inquisition for actually following Diana in a 'society' . . . A sermon by Nicholas of Cusa delivered at Bressanone in 1457 treated several women who had belonged to a 'society of Diana.' A trial in Mantua in 1489 mentioned a 'mistress of the game' [i.e. Diana] and in 1532 a Witch confessed to the Modenese Inquisition that she went 'to the games of Diana.'" By the Middle Ages, Artemis/Diana, as well as Hecate, had come to be called by various names, including Abundia, Benzozia, Herodias, Noctiluca, and the Queen of the Night; they had, moreover, become identified with goddesses of other cultures, including the Germanic Holda. The classical goddess Artemis/Diana is clearly linked to both lesbian desire and, by way of her Amazonian aspect, to transgenderism. Through her brother APOLLO and her servant CYPARISSUS, whom Apollo loved, she becomes linked as well to homoerotic desire. Similarly, Hecate's entourage included transgendered priests called SEMNOTATOI. The association of Diana and/or Hecate, Witches, lesbianism, and transgenderism survived into (at least) the eighteenth century, when William King wrote in *The Toast,* "Then by Hecate she swore, she was sated with men; / Sung a wanton Sapphic."

Contemporary Dianic Witches draw upon this rich heritage, infusing it with feminist and lesbian-feminist theory and practice. Dianic Witchcraft emerged in its current manifestation in the early 1970s, due in large part to the dreaming and effort of Zsuzsanna "Z" BUDAPEST. Dianic Witches include males in certain rites but tend to hold women-only gatherings, thus attracting many lesbians, including lesbian separatists. While some celebrations (such as Halloween, or Samhain) resonate with those held in other traditions of Witchcraft, many rites may be distinguished by a focus on life experiences pertaining specifically to women such as menstruation. Some of these women-centered rituals are rooted in the traditions of pre-classical and classical antiquity, including the Thesmophoria (October 11-13), sacred to the goddess DEMETER and her daughter PERSEPHONE. The "Great Rite" of UNION with the deity (or deities), typically expressed erotically, is common to most if not all traditions of Wicca, but among Dianics commonly takes the form of a woman-only, and thus lesbian-erotic-centered, ritual. Of this ritual Z Budapest writes, "Through our sexuality, the Goddess reveals Herself, energizes us ... The sexual mores of the Goddess are ... open and inclusive." The rite includes an invocation which is well known not only to Dianics but to other Witches as well: "Let my worship be in the heart that rejoices / For behold, all acts of love and pleasure are my rituals." The rite also includes the "five-point kiss," which is also known to, and practiced by, other Witches; indeed, the KNIGHTS TEMPLAR, alleged to have been homoerotically inclined, were said to have bestowed this kiss in rituals. The kiss begins with the forehead, then proceeds to the mouth, the breasts, the vagina (or penis), the buttocks, and the feet. Among Medieval Christians horrified by the practice, this kissing rite became known as the "dark" or "obscene" kiss, terminology later accepted by many Witches themselves. In a Dianic milieu, the "five-point kiss" clearly acquires woman-loving significance. The remainder of the rite is often given to safe-sex EROTICISM, drumming, dancing, and feasting. Many "New Age"-identified lesbians and others have been greatly disturbed by one of the magical practices undertaken by the Dianics, namely, the hexing of rapists. This curse includes, "In the most holy name of Hecate, the Goddess of life and death, She Who holds the key to ... the underworld, let this rapist be caught." Whatever objections to it others may hold, however, the authors of this text (not to mention members of the San Francisco police force) are aware that its pronouncement has led to the arrest and conviction, in the early 1980s, of at least one rapist. It should also be noted here that a number of feminist- and/or New Age-identified women practitioners of the Craft strongly disapprove of the words "Witch" and "Witchcraft." Objection to these terms is ostensibly due to their negative associations in the popular psyche. Conversations the authors have had with US practitioners taking such a position have revealed the position to be directly linked to a desire to forfeit certain beliefs and practices in order to be assimilated into the dominant culture, as well as a censorious tendency to condemn those practitioners who do not shirk from facing the "shadow" dimension of life.

In recent years, Dianic Witches have begun to be more inclusive of men in their rituals. Z writes in *The Holy Book of Women's Mysteries* (1989 ed.), "things are not as bleak as they used to be. There are natural allies of the Dianic Women ... [primarily] nonhomophobic men who respect the Goddess and Her privacy and gay men who search for Her." A pivotal event in terms of this shifting attitude toward men occurred in 1980 at the Pan Pagan Festival, held in the midwestern United States. As the Dianic Witches were convening in the rural setting, a number of heterosexual men, including some of the women's male lovers and husbands, began to taunt and threaten the women with physical violence. A group of queer male Radical Faeries aided the Dianics in fending off the men and in protecting the circle so that the women's rite might proceed. Since that time, Dianics have held rituals for men including those of honoring manhood in non- or anti-patriarchal ways. Some of these rites have been inspired by the COURETES of classical antiquity. Nevertheless, Dianic Wicca remains largely the province of women-identified women. In the groundbreaking *Witchcraft and the Gay Counterculture* (1978), Arthur EVANS foregrounds the roles played by homoerotically inclined and gender variant men from the ancient traditions of Shamanism through the religions of antiquity, the Craft traditions of the Middle Ages and the RENAISSANCE, and into the nineteenth and twentieth centuries. His painstaking research has helped greatly to diffuse the hostility of heterosexist Wiccan individuals and groups. Evans's study has since been extended and amplified in works including Judy GRAHN's *Another Mother Tongue* (1984) and Randy P. Conner's *Blossom of Bone* (1993). In *Witchcraft*, Evans posits a link between homoeroticism, Witchcraft, and FAGGOTS, bundles of sticks employed in cooking and in the burning of Witches, sodomites, and other "heretics." Despite vicious attacks on Evans's claim by Queer and other academics, it appears to contain more than a kernel of truth. Moreover, the term "faggot" is clearly linked to the realm of FAIRY.

From the Middle Ages and for centuries thereafter, many European men have occasionally taken the roles of fairies in traditional rituals; among certain groups, as among the CALUSARI, an interrelationship of the realm of fairy to male gender variance and homoeroticism has been reported. While the late-twentieth-century gay male Radical Faeries may, in some respects, mirror the Dianic Witches, as in embracing same-sex inclined persons, they differ in other important respects, especially in that Witchcraft, while an influence, is not foregrounded in Faerie gatherings. This is due in part to the Faeries' inclusion of men from many different spiritual paths and in part to the profoundly anti-organizational, anti-leadership stance of many individual Faeries. In some cases, the backgrounding of Wicca arises from misogyny. Nonetheless, many individual Faeries are practitioners of the Craft. Beyond the Faeries, many other gay and bisexual men are Wiccans. Some, unfortunately, remain, or have remained, closeted, including a very popular writer (on almost every other aspect of the Craft) who died of HIV/AIDS-related illness in the early 1990s. Others are, or have become, primarily solitary practitioners. Still others who are, or have been, openly gay or bisexual, including the writer Paul Beyerl and the writer and occult shop owner Herman Slater (recently deceased, of the Magickal Childe in New York) have chosen not to focus their work on the role of same-sex desire and/or transgenderism in Witchcraft. A number of gay and bisexual male Witches have, however, begun to write about their experiences as such, to construct a queer-positive and/or queer-centered Wiccan path, and to form groups of like-minded persons. These include: Michael THORN, a writer who formed the Kathexis Anthropos coven for gay men in the early 1980s; Sparky T. Rabbit and Greg Johnson, writer-musicians who co-founded the Sons of the Bitch Coven and the Faggot Witch Camp in the early 1990s; and Tom Cowan, who has published works on both the Craft and on lesbian/gay history. In Cowan's view, "one of the main skills gay people have is being able to move between the worlds, because we grow up in a world that we don't feel at home in. That gives us a particular aptitude for magic, because magic is based on the ability to shift consciousness at will." One of the most innovative writers and artists (primarily of installation art) of the 1990s to self-identify as a Queer Wiccan is Donald ENGSTROM. In his writings, he offers a new queer-centered mythology and an accompanying spirituality based upon spirits he has encountered in visionary work. These spirits, or "Mysterious Ones" – including the Queer God, Singing Bear, the Goddess Fee Fee, and the Green Gods – often manifest themselves as primordial, archetypal forces garbed in decidedly contemporary gear. In recent years, Engstrom has found himself increasingly assuming the role of psychopomp, or soul-guide – a role he refers to as the "death-priestess" – especially to persons dying of HIV/AIDS-related illness. He is also active in Reclaiming, a Wiccan-based group embracing queer people. Transgendered persons have also begun to discuss and write about their experiences in Witchcraft. In 1995, Valkyrie Cougar PenDragon, a transgendered Wiccan high priestess, described a difficult journey leading to self-acceptance of her transgendered identity and the integration of that identity into her Craft practice. Valkyrie was greatly aided, she explains, by performing a ritual constructed by the English Witches Janet and Stewart Farrar called the "Rite of the Thirteen Megaliths." According to PenDragon, it was the experience of the "twelfth megalith," also called "the Hermaphrodite," which brought a profound illumination of her embodiment of "both male and female characteristics." PenDragon feels that her ability to "assume either role" gives her a "unique perspective" which a "uni-sexual person cannot experience or appreciate." This perspective has led PenDragon to posit that "transsexuals exist on a higher plane of existence than do uni-sexed individuals." PenDragon, incidentally, appears to link transgenderism to the process of REINCARNATION.

A number of traditions of Witchcraft, however, continue to greet lesbians, gays, bisexuals, and transgendered persons with hostility. Negativity toward queer people appears to arise from five related sources: (1) dualism, especially in terms of biological determinism, wherein males are associated with traditionally masculine behavior and females with traditionally feminine behavior, and/or groups are divided into males/men and females/women (a practice found in numerous patriarchal traditions); (2) an exaggerated emphasis on sexual fertility, as opposed to mental and other forms of fertility; (3) the carrying of Biblical morality into the Craft, especially by those who have not been reared in Wicca; (4) the carrying of a reductionist version of Freudian psychology into the Craft, often including wholesale acceptance of the concept of the Oedipus complex; and (5) widespread ignorance concerning the roles that queer people have played in the world's spiritual traditions, including Witchcraft. Of (1) above, Paul B. Rucker (1995) argues that Wiccans who "subscribe to a purely binary concept of the world and its Powers," who declare "that no man can ever be May Queen, no woman the Green Man," are dependent upon a "heterosexist view of the universe." "Where," Rucker asks, "does that leave a person who agrees in heart and soul with everything Wicca has to offer except for the expectations laid upon him/her because of his/her biological sex?" In terms of (2), Sicilian-American Witch and gay activist Dr Leo Louis MARTELLO (1975) has said that "Witchcraft . . . was and is concerned with fertility, but it is not restricted to that alone . . . Those groups who insist on heterosexuality as a requirement for admittance into a coven cannot claim ancient precedence, since so many of the pagan religions had male prostitutes in their temples . . . To stress the fertility aspects is to discriminate against not only homosexuals but also all women who have had tubal ligations or hysterectomies . . . all men who have undergone vasectomies . . . [and indeed, all] those who use birth control." In spite of Martello's insight, however, many Witches continue to discriminate against queer persons in various ways. Certain inroads have nonetheless been made since the 1970s, due to queer- or queer-supportive writers, practitioners, shop owners and others like Budapest, Slater, Martello, Evans, Gwydion Pendderwen, Margot Adler (especially in *Drawing Down the Moon*, 1979, 1986), and STARHAWK. Starhawk's *The Spiral Dance* (1979) is considered a pivotal, indeed revolutionary, text by many Wiccans. In this book, as in her later works, Starhawk argues against exclusion and points to liberating lessons others can learn through encountering and embracing queer persons. "Sexual desire for a person of one's own gender," she writes, "challenges the idea that the only valid purpose of sex is reproduction . . . Lesbians, women loving women, are threatening because they are women refusing to serve as ground for the male self . . . The gay men's movement has aspects that are threatening to patriarchy and potentially liberating . . . Men who truly love men, who are willing to be each other's ground and support, are potential sources for far-reaching change." The woman-loving poet Emily DICKINSON (1830-1886) wrote: "Witchcraft was hung, in History, / But History and I / Find all the Witchcraft that we need / Around us, every Day."

Women's Spirituality

This is a spiritual – as well as psychological and political – movement emerging in the 1970s and continuing into the 1990s, rooted in feminism and in the alternative spiritual movements of the 1960s and 1970s. In *The Women's Spirituality Book* (1988), Diane STEIN describes Women's Spirituality as "a celebration of the lives, lifestyles and values of women, women's participation in the cycles of the earth and the universe, and women's working toward a better world." Women's Spirituality, while embracing numerous spiritual traditions, focuses on the role assumed by the Divine Feminine in these traditions, as the goddess in Witchcraft (or Wicca) and Goddess Reverence, KUAN YIN in Buddhism, or the Shekinah in Judaism. Special attention is also paid to the roles women play within these traditions. Beyond this, many involved in Women's Spirituality are practitioners of healing (typically with herbs and other items from nature, as well as meditation and body-work techniques), divination (astrology, the I CHING, TAROT, etc.), and magic – all associated in the popular psyche with wisewomen or witches. Many, beyond involvement in the women's movement, are also activists in the anti-war, animal rights, and environmental movements, looking upon the earth and all sentient beings as embodying the Divine – a perspective STARHAWK and others have named "immanence" as opposed to "transcendence" (the latter roughly implying that the Divine is "somewhere else"). As a spiritual path (or paths) linked to sociopolitical movements, Women's Spirituality has been referred to by Jane Caputi as "psychic activism." Women's Spirituality – like Queer Spirit – is often expressed in artistic ways, in visual arts, music, performance, and other forms. Emphasis is also placed upon honoring women regardless of economic class, ethnicity, physical or psychological difference, spiritual path, or sexuality.

Practitioners of Women's Spirituality, unlike many men's movement spiritual seekers, have generally embraced lesbians and, to a somewhat lesser extent, bisexual women and transgendered individuals, in part because many of the mothers of the movement have been women-loving women, and in part because heterosexual women involved in the movement seem less threatened by same-sex intimacy than heterosexual men in the men's movement. Because of this inclusiveness, lesbian and bisexual women who are involved in Women's Spirituality do not always feel it necessary to identify themselves as such. Thus, it is sometimes difficult to distinguish the contributions these women have made. Nevertheless, they represent a very powerful force in Women's Spirituality. A very partial listing includes: Paula Gunn ALLEN, Gloria ANZALDÚA,

Asungi, Hallie Iglehart AUSTEN, Z BUDAPEST, Mary DALY, Kay GARDNER, Sally GEARHART, Judy GRAHN, Susan Griffin, Audre LORDE, Diane MARIECHILD, Vicki NOBLE, Adrienne RICH, Monica SJOO, Starhawk, Diane STEIN, Kay TURNER, Karen VOGEL, Alice Walker, and Monique WITTIG. Anthologies on the movement containing works by lesbian and bisexual women include: *Womanspirit Rising* (1979), edited by Carol P. Christ and Judith Plaskow, *The Politics of Women's Spirituality* (1982), *Weaving the Visions* (1989), edited by Christ and Plaskow and *Uncoiling the Snake* (1993), edited by Vicki Noble.

A

Aakulujjuusi and Uumarnituq In Inuit (Eskimo) Shamanism, the first two humans, constituting a primordial male couple. Soon after emerging on the earth, on the island of Igloolik, they began to desire the company of other humans. They realized that they would have to mate if there were to be more humans. They did so, and miraculously, Uumarnituq became pregnant. It was only when he was ready to give birth that Uumarnituq realized that he did not possess a passageway large enough through which the child might pass into the world. Aalulujjuusi chanted some magic words, or *irinaliuti*, and this spell or charm caused Uumarnituq to transform into a woman. On doing so, he, now she, gave birth to a male infant, from whom the Inuit trace their descent. In those times, neither death nor war existed, and the human population began to increase at such a rate that the deities or spirits feared that the earth might be destroyed. In desperation, the elder Uumarnituq chanted the *irinaliuti*, "Now we shall have death! Now we shall have war!" Aakulujjuusi, still not wishing to permit death or war, cried out in opposition to his mate. But the CRONE Uumarnituq had already spoken, and the fate of humanity was sealed. Aakulujjuusi was able, however, to preserve the continuance of human souls by way of an afterlife existence inclusive of reincarnation.

A'anon'nin In the Western European and QABBALAH-inspired ritual magic system of twentieth-century occultist Kenneth Grant, a spirit described as the Lord of the Gates of Matter and represented by the All-Seeing Eye of the Egyptian god SET, itself symbolic of the anus.

Abaris Hyperborean priest loved by the Greek god APOLLO. As a love-gift, Apollo bestowed Abaris with a magical, winged arrow upon which Abaris was able to traverse the heavens. While Abaris ultimately exchanged the arrow for instruction in philosophy, he remained dear to Apollo. Abaris was widely invoked by ancient Greeks in rites of magic and divination.

Abban, Saint (fifth century CE) Irish Catholic abbot said to be an expert diviner, healer, and magician (or miracle worker). Abban was acquainted with an older couple who had tried unsuccessfully to have a child. After many years had passed, the wife gave birth to a daughter. While the husband was delighted to have a child, he also knew that this was to be their only child. He felt sad – we are not told what she felt – on realizing there would be no male heir. Abban, empathizing with him, blessed the infant and then magically transformed her into a male. St Abban is fêted on March 16.

Abbatá In Santería, a branch of the West African Yoruba diasporic religion practiced by Cubans and Cuban-Americans, a tale, or *pataki*, is told of the sea-goddess YEMAYA being seduced by one of her sons, SHANGO. Because the goddess was greatly humiliated by this action, she sent two of her other sons, INLE and Abbatá, who had witnessed the act, to live at the bottom of the sea. She cut out Inlé's tongue, so that he couldn't speak of the event; she also caused Abbatá to become deaf, so that he could not hear anyone asking him about what had transpired. Inlé and Abbatá were, however, able to communicate with each other empathically. In their loneliness and perhaps also in their suffering, they became passionately drawn to each other, and ultimately became lovers. This *pataki* is told in order to explain the origins of incest, muteness, deafness, and homoeroticism.

Abbot of Drimnagh Central figure in a fifteenth-century Irish tale of gender metamorphosis. The abbot of Drimnagh (near Dublin) does not seem to have actually been an abbot but rather a man in charge of preparing Church festivals. A handsome, young, married man, he had long, golden hair and wore a tunic with a mantle draped over his chest. He carried a sword resembling a cross. One afternoon, taking a break from preparing for an Easter feast, he took a long walk on his favorite mound nearby. Soon he felt very tired, and it was not long before he fell asleep. A great noise awakened him. He discovered that his sword had been replaced by a spindle and his tunic by a woman's dress. His long, golden hair was now bound by a net, and there was no trace of a beard on his chin. When he felt between his legs, he realized that he had been transformed into a woman. He began to think that this, his favorite mound, must be an abode of the fairies (indeed, from archaeological and botanical evidence, we know that in prehistoric times it was the site of a burial mound and probably also a sacred grove), especially when a strange old woman suddenly appeared and asked him, "So how did you, beautiful woman with golden hair, come to be on this deserted mound, and what will you do, now that the sun is setting?" The CRONE vanished, and the transformed abbot determined to walk toward Crumlin, which lay to the west of Drimnagh. Soon she (the abbot) encountered a handsome young man who fell instantly in love with the transformed abbot. He told her that he worked at the Crumlin church, and that he wished to marry her. She accepted his proposal. They lived together for seven years. During that time she gave birth to seven children. One day, they were invited to a great Easter feast at Drimnagh.

Although she became quite nervous when she thought of returning to Drimnagh, it had been a long time, and she was certain everyone there counted her among the dead, and surely no one, not even her wife, would recognize her, which made her a bit sad. But she agreed, and they gathered themselves and their children together. As they approached the Drimnagh mound, she began to grow very tired, and shortly thereafter fell asleep. A great noise awakened her. Once more, she was a man, with sword and male clothing and a male organ. The abbot's wife was chiding him, "Where have you been? I've been looking for you for over an hour!" When he told his wife the strange story, she might not have believed him had not the churchman, anxious to wake his wife up, cried out to her. There was the churchman, with his and the abbot 's seven children. Whatever were they to do? In the end, the court awarded four of the children to the husband and three to the wife, that is, the abbot of Drimnagh. The people of the region accepted the event as a trick of the fairies, and the two men remained great friends to the end of their days. British composer Thea Musgrave has written a chamber opera based on this folktale, *The Abbot of Drimock* (1955).

Abbott, Franklin (1950-   ) Queer psychotherapist, poet, and editor. Now living in Atlanta, Abbott was among the original Radical Faeries, helping to hold gatherings at Running Water, a communal sanctuary in North Carolina, and serving as poetry editor of *RFD*, a journal associated with the Faeries. In the early 1980s he was deeply inspired by his work with the Wiccan priestess STARHAWK. Shifting his focus to the pro-feminist branch of the Men's movement, he began sharing what he learned working with the Faeries and Starhawk with anti-sexist heterosexual and bisexual men. From his desire to explore commonalities between Gay Spirituality and Men's Spirituality, three books have emerged: *New Men, New Minds* (1987), *Men and Intimacy* (1990), and *Boyhood: Growing Up Male* (1993). In recent years, Abbott has played an important role in the Gay Spirit Visions conferences held in the southeastern US. He is currently at work on a psychospiritual guidebook for gay men.

Abderus In Greek mythology, a son of HERMES who became, as a young man, an armor-bearer and *eromenos* (beloved) of the hero HERACLES (Roman Hercules). Heracles was both horrified and heartbroken upon learning of the death of Abderus, who was fatally trampled and then torn apart by the wild HORSES of Diomedes. In honor of the young man, Heracles buried him ceremonially, placing a KALOS bowl (praising his beauty) in his tomb to commemorate their love. Beyond this, he established the Abdera games and founded the town of Abdera in memory of Abderus.

Abraham (fl. second millenia BCE)   Biblical patriarch of Judaism, Christianity, and Islam, sometimes portrayed as having a "bosom." While some perceive the "bosom of Abraham" as a positive symbol of androgyny or transgenderism, others, especially feminists, find it a disturbing signifier of the patriarchal assumption of both the role of the mother – and/or the Goddess – and of female anatomy.

Abrao According to the Akan of Ghana, the planet JUPITER is a transgendered or androgynous divinity named Abrao.

Abraxas (or **Abraxos, Abrasax**)   Gnostic deity associated with the power of the sun, often depicted as a man with the head of a rooster and two serpents for legs. Abraxas is invoked in a lesbian love spell of the early centuries of the Common Era belonging to the *Greek Magical Papyri* collection. In Hermann Hesse's *Demian* (1919), which focuses on the passionate friendship of two young men, Sinclair and Demian, and the goddess-like mother of the latter, the god Abraxas plays a key role.

Abu Nuwas (c. 757-c. 814)   Arabic-Persian Islamic poet whose writings celebrate the beauty of both women and young men. In part because wine was officially forbidden in Islam, leading to Christians operating taverns, one of Abu Nuwas's favorite themes is recounting drunken nights spent with handsome Christian youths. Speaking of a certain "wandering reveler," he writes: "A cross was loosed from the neck's place / It distinguished him from each friend / We turned the mill of pleasure thrice / And joined the waists hand in hand."

Acca In Roman legendary history and in Virgil's *Aeniad*, an intimate female companion of the Amazon CAMILLA. Acca's name may mean "She-who-is-a-maker;" she may have been nicknamed "Halfdreamer." When Camilla fell in battle, Acca, heartbroken, sought sanctuary in a forest. Legend has it that in her grief for her lost love, Acca wept so much that she metamorphosed into a fountain.

Achilles Semi-divine Greek hero-son of PELEUS and the goddess Thetis. As a youth Achilles was mentored and loved by the centaur CHIRON and by the god DIONYSUS. When his mother Thetis learned that he would die in the Trojan War, she sent Achilles to live at the court of King Lycomedes on the island of Scyros. There he was disguised as a maiden, given the name of PYRRHA, and housed in the women's quarters. Ultimately, however, Thetis was not able to prevent Achilles' entry into the Trojan War. During the war, Achilles fell in love with TROILUS, a Trojan prince. This was a tragic affair that ended in the young prince's death. Also during the war, Achilles also became comrade-lover to PATROCLUS. The love of Achilles for Patroclus was the subject of several Greek tragedies which are lost to us, as well as the theme of numerous works of art including *Achilles Receiving the Ambassadors of Agamemnon* by the painter Jean-Dominique Ingres (1780-1867). Both Achilles and Patroclus, incidentally, also became lovers with Antilochus, a fellow warrior. When Patroclus was slain, his spirit appeared to Achilles to beg him to hurriedly attend to his burial rites so that he might cease wandering the earth as a ghost, and to bid him farewell. Achilles buried Patroclus ceremonially, but when Achilles himself was later slain by being shot in the ankle (the single vulnerable spot on his body, hence "Achilles's heel"), the two appear to have been reburied in a single grave, with their bones being ritually mixed together. One account relates that they were buried on LEUKÉ (or Leucé), the White Isle, where they, along with their comrade-lover Antilochus and the divinized HELEN of Troy, were worshipped. Another account relates that Thetis, Achilles's mother, kept their mixed bones in a golden urn which she kept always nearby. The tragic playwright Aeschylus (525/4-456 BCE) wrote a tragedy celebrating the love of Achilles and Patroclus which was quite popular in antiquity but which has been lost or destroyed.

Acoetes (or **Acetes**)   In Greek mythology, a Tyrrhenian pirate who fell in love with the god DIONYSUS and ultimately became his priest. A band of pirates, having spotted a handsome young man, kidnapped him, not recognizing him to be Dionysus. They were about to gang-rape him when Acoetes, the pilot of their ship, stepped forward to defend the young man. Acoetes, too, desired him, but did not wish to take him against his will. He also had the uncanny feeling that someone so beautiful might well be a god in disguise. "I do not know," he thought, "what magic stirs in that beauty, but I do know this: it is divine." Just as Acoetes began to wrestle with the other pirates, gigantic grapevines wove themselves around the ship, producing enormous grapes. Just as suddenly, all the pirates except Acoetes were hurled overboard by invisible hands and transformed into dolphins. Dionysus then revealed himself to his defender, and the two set off for Naxos, as lovers delighting in a bounty of wine. Afterwards, Dionysus initiated Acoetes into his Mysteries.

Actaeon   In Greek mythology, a male hunter who was punished by being transformed into a stag after he spied upon the goddess ARTEMIS/DIANA bathing with her nymphs. As with the Hindu goddess PARVATI's bath, no male was to witness this female-only rite.

Adam   In Judaism, Christianity, and Islam, and in some traditions of Gnosticism, the father of humankind, with Eve being the mother. The NAASSENES, a Gnostic sect incorporating homoerotic intimacy, believed in a gynandrous or androgynous deity which they envisioned as a boundless ocean named BYTHOS or "The Deep" or as an UROBORUS, a serpent biting its tail, named NAAS or Ophis. They identified the feminine aspect of the godhead with CYBELE, ISIS, and DEMETER, while the masculine aspect was identified with an androgynous or gender variant male figure named Adam Aeon, or Adamas. "So God created man in his own image, in the image of God he created him; male and female he created them" (Genesis 1: 27). This verse, according to those learned in the QABBALAH (Kabbalah), a primarily Jewish mystical tradition, suggests that the God of the Bible is an androgynous or hermaphroditic being embracing both male and female aspects. Qabbalists further suggest that the first human fashioned by God was an androgynous being named Adam Kadmon. They have, moreover, indicated that the later account describing the creation of Eve from Adam's rib represents, along with the tale of the serpent and the apple, the Fall of humanity, when the androgynous being Adam, and perhaps also an equally androgynous (or gynandrous) mate, was, or were, divided into male and female creatures. This association of the Fall with the separation of male and female resonates with the account of the Fall given in PLATO's *Symposium*. The tradition of Adam Kadmon was especially preserved in the body of mystical, Qabbalistic texts known as the *Zohar*, and specifically in Abravanel Judah's *Dialogues of Love* (1536).

Addaura   One of the incised drawings of the Addaura cave near Palermo, Sicily represents one of the most provocative works of Upper Paleolithic art, executed around 10,000 BCE. Discovered in 1952 by Iole Bovio-Marconi, it depicts, in the words of archaeologist and linguist Marija Gimbutas (1921-1994), a group of "superbly drawn bird-masked male figures engaged in a ritual drama." Gimbutas suggests that these figures "were probably . . . participants in rituals . . . [dedicated to the] Goddess." From the bird masks, it appears that the men may have been honoring that aspect of the Great Goddess now referred to as the Bird Goddess. The bird-masked men are dancing in a circle. They are nude except for the masks, thick with plumage, that they wear. Their genitals are visible. At least two of the men have erections. In the center of the circle of dancers are two men, one lying above or beside the other, facing opposite directions. The figure above is facing eastward and looking slightly toward us, his legs bent at the knees. His penis is erect, or he wears an artificial phallus or penis sheath. He wears a bird mask, though his is without plumage. Parallel lines connect his neck to his buttocks or ankles. His arms cover the legs of the male below him. The man beneath, larger in size, wears a plumed mask. He faces downward. His arms appear to be outstretched before him. He, like the other man, has an erection. Parallel lines link the penis of the male above to the buttocks of the male beneath. While some art historians have described the Addaura ritual as a sacrificial rite and the two central figures as victims, with the parallel lines representing cords, the parallel lines might instead represent lines of energy – specifically, male erotic energy – and the ritual might be one of initiation, including same-sex eroticism, rather than one of sacrifice. That the lines might represent male energy rather than nooses is suggested by a seven-thousand-year-old figurine from the Dimini culture of northern Greece, described by Gimbutas in *The Language of the Goddess* (1989). Just above the genitals of this male figure, whom Gimbutas believes to be a "Year God symbolizing [the] revival of nature," is an arc with a series of parallel lines, perhaps representing male energy or even ejaculated semen. This possibility is strengthened by the fact that the man is holding his phallus. While later observers have tended to emphasize the sacrificial interpretation of the Addaura ritual, the discoverer of Addaura, Bovio-Marconi, referring to the pioneering work of Magnus Hirschfeld in what is today termed Queer, or Gay, Studies, first noted its potential initiatory, homoerotic connotation. The Addaura ritual may have combined homoeroticism and sacred experience, perhaps in the form of shamanic reverence of an avian goddess. Gender variance also may have been given expression at Addaura, as suggested by the bird costumes worn by the dancers. These costumes, by creating the image of a hybrid human-bird, suggest theriomorphic (or beastly) transformation, which is often linked in shamanic traditions to gender metamorphosis. If the men are indeed honoring the Bird Goddess, then they may also be celebrating a transgendered aspect of the divine and attempting to embody that aspect. The Bird Goddess's gender-mixing quality is indicated by a host of figurines showing her as having an avian torso, female human breasts, and a male human phallic neck. Gimbutas explains that these figurines appear to have been associated by early peoples with other depictions of androgyny.

Adhesiveness Term from phrenology, the occult art of shedding light on an individual's intellectual and emotional makeup by reading patterns, including bumps and lines, on the head. Adhesiveness originally referred to friendship, as opposed to amativeness, which referred to love. The American Transcendentalist poet Walt WHITMAN employed the term and its opposite, however, to distinguish between same-sex (adhesive) and heterosexual (amative) love. In doing so, he linked the phrenological concept to the distinction made in PLATO's *Symposium* between same-sex and heterosexual love, with the first being governed by APHRODITE Urania and the second by Aphrodite Pandemos. Further linking adhesiveness to democratic idealism, Whitman writes in *Democratic Vistas*: "It is to the development, identification, and general prevalence of that fervid comradeship, (the adhesive love . . .), that I look for the counterbalance and offset of our materialistic and vulgar American democracy, and for the spiritualization thereof. Many will say it is a dream . . . [but] I say democracy infers such loving comradeship, as its most inevitable twin or counterpart." As R. K. Martin (1979) observes, Whitman's adhesiveness may also be distinguished from the URANIAN movement of the nineteenth century, the devotees of which celebrated intergenerational love as linked to aristocratic ideals, as well as from the "intermediate sex," or third gender, concept put forth by Edward CARPENTER and others who sought to link same-sex desire not only to democratic (or socialist or anarchist) ideals but also to gender variance, or transgenderism.

Admetus King of Thessaly who became a lover of the Greek god APOLLO. When Apollo slew the Cyclops, ZEUS punished him by forcing him to serve a mortal for several years. It was while tending the cattle of Admetus that Apollo and the king fell in love. According to Plutarch, Admetus was also loved by HERACLES.

Adonai Deity, angel, or spirit of Gnostic magic originating in the Bible, where it is a name of God. Adonai is invoked in a lesbian love spell of the early centuries of the Common Era belonging to the *Greek Magical Papyri* collection.

Adonis Beautiful young man of Phoenician and Greco-Roman mythology, described by classicist and feminist theorist Eva Keuls as a "countercultural male sex symbol." Adonis was the son of Myrrha, who was transformed into a myrrh plant after having given birth to him. He was the consort of the goddess ASTARTE, who is sometimes equated with APHRODITE. Adonis himself is sometimes identified with Tammuz, the male consort of the Mesopotamian goddess INANNA/ISHTAR. Adonis was also loved by PERSEPHONE, after she had become Queen of the Underworld, and he was an *eromenos*, or beloved, of the god DIONYSUS. Most of what we know about Adonis concerns his death. One day, while hunting in the forest, Adonis was slain by a wild boar. Although he sought shelter from the animal in a lettuce bed, he was discovered and fatally wounded by being gored in the groin. None of the deities who loved him were able to save his life. Some said Adonis rose to the heavens following his death, while others suggested he lay eternally in a state of suspended animation, rather like a vampire between the hours of sunrise and sunset. What is more agreed upon is that from his mutilated genitals, beautiful scarlet anemones grew. The anemone became Adonis's sacred attribute. In the myth of Adonis, according to French classical scholar Marcel Detienne, myrrh (from Adonis's mother) and lettuce (his useless refuge) signify conflicting traits. While myrrh suggests sensuality, lettuce was associated in the

Greek psyche (as in the Egyptian) with eunuchs and also with death. Paradoxically, Adonis is also linked, along with Dionysus, to fennel, believed to produce an abundance of sperm. Taken together, says Detienne, these vegetal signs relay that "Adonis is not a husband." Rather, he is a "lover, and an effeminate one." Each summer in Athens and elsewhere, at the time of the rising of Sirius, the Dog Star, priestesses and gender-variant, homoerotically inclined male priests, the latter called *kelabim* as well as *gerim*, celebrated the festival of Adonia in memory of the youth. They did so by planting seeds in small pots. These "gardens of Adonis" were allowed to thrive for only a few days before they were uprooted. Detienne suggests that the gardens symbolized the youth's fragility, sexual precocity, and early death. Both the gardens that grow quickly and then die and the sensuous youth are manifestations of *aklosia*, or early and unnatural ripening. *Aklosia* was linked by the Greeks to nonreproductive ("unfruitful") sexual behavior, including homosexuality. The Lesbian poet SAPPHO writes, "Our tender Adonis is dying, O Kythereia, / What can we do? / Beat on your breasts, my girls, and tear your dresses." In the *Greek Magical Papyri* of later antiquity, Adonis appears as an ANGEL and as such is invoked in a lesbian love spell. In the court of homoerotically inclined King HENRI III his favorites, or minions, were frequently referred to as "Adonises." A poem by Ronsard (1524-1585) includes, "Minion, you are young and beautiful, / an Adonis." Henri's minion Quélus (also nicknamed SAINT LUKE) was specifically nicknamed "Adonis." William Shakespeare in his narrative poem *Venus and Adonis* (1593) depicts Adonis as androgynous or transgendered, having a voice like a mermaid (l. 429) and blushing like a maiden (l. 50). Adonis has survived into the twentieth century as a symbol of youthful male beauty. In the early 1900s in gay-centered cafes of New York City, it was observed that "Round the tables sat boys and youths, Adonises both by art and nature, ready for a drink or chat with the chance Samaritan."

Adrasteia Legendary adoptive mother of the Greek god ZEUS. Adrasteia was alternately depicted as a princess, a NYMPH, and a goddess of destiny. In Orphism she became a transgendered deity associated with PHANES.

Aegea Classical sea goddess of healing and protection worshipped by the Amazonian GORGONS of north Africa. Akin to the goddesses Hygeia and ATHENA, she gave her name to the Aegean Sea. Her symbol was the AEGIS, which is akin to the GORGONEION.

Aegis Symbol of Greco-Roman religion associated with the goddesses AEGEA, Hygia, ATHENA, and MEDUSA, as well as with the GORGONS and the AMAZONS. The aegis originated as a goatskin apron and later transformed into a goatskin shield. The employment of cowrie shells,

symbolic of the vagina, in the aegis suggests the African origin of both the apron/shield and the divine and legendary females it represents. As a shield, the aegis was painted with the terrifying face of Medusa. The aegis is symbolic of healing, protection, and the power of women (especially as healers and Amazons, or warriors).

Aelia Laelia Crispis Figure of the Western European tradition of ALCHEMY signifying androgyny. In 1567 Richard White of Basingstoke explained that Aelia Laelia Crispis is "the soul, which is male in women, female in men. Aelia is solar, Laelia lunar, Crispis earthly."

Aelred of Rievaulx, Abbot, Saint (c. 1110-1167) Homoerotically inclined Christian abbot and later saint. Of noble parentage, Aelred left the court of King David of Scotland to enter, in 1135, the Cistercian abbey of Rievaulx. Becoming abbot of Rievaulx a decade later, he remained so until his death in 1167, celebrating spiritual friendship in his writings, including this collect: "Pour into our hearts, O God, the Holy Spirit's gift of love, that we, clasping each the other's hand, may share the joy of friendship, human and divine, and with your servant Aelred, draw many to your community of love; through Jesus Christ the Righteous, who lives and reigns with you, in the unity of the Holy Spirit, one God, now and forever." St Aelred is fêted on January 12.

Aemilia According to Pontanus (1426-1503) and to the ritual magician Cornelius Agrippa (1486-1535), Aemilia was a woman who, living during the late Middle Ages or early Renaissance, magically transformed into a man after many years of heterosexual marriage and commenced a new life.

Agamemnon King of Mycenae and later of Argos, Agamemnon was the leader of the Greek forces in the Trojan War. He was the husband of Queen Clytemnestra and the father of IPHIGENIA. In Euripides' tragedy *Iphigenia*, Agamemnon is portrayed as a coward who becomes responsible for the unnecessary sacrifice of his daughter, despite the pleadings of her mother and the man-loving warrior ACHILLES. In other versions of the myth, Agamemnon is portrayed in a more positive light. Agamemnon was the lover of a young man named Argynnus. He spotted Argynnus bathing in the Cephisus River one day and fell instantly in love with him. Tragically, Argynnus drowned shortly thereafter, when he was swept up in the river's current before the king could save him. To commemorate their love, Agamemnon, as a devotee of the goddess APHRODITE, founded a temple to Aphrodite-Argynnus.

Agate Gem associated with the gender variant and bisexually or same-sex inclined classical deities

ARTEMIS/DIANA and HERMES/MERCURY and believed to possess or enhance magical powers, employed in such matters as drawing lovers and raising tempests.

Agathon (d. 401 BCE)   Homoerotically inclined and transgendered ancient Greek composer and writer of tragedies who flourished during the fifth century BCE. All his plays, such as *Telephus* and *Thyestes*, are lost, but fragments are quoted by Aristotle and Athenaeus. Agathon plays a central role in PLATO's *Symposium*. He appears to have been a devotee of the goddess CYBELE, the god DIONYSUS, and perhaps also the goddess DEMETER. Perhaps because he was a devotee of these deities, he frequently dressed in women's garments. In his erotic relationships, he preferred taking a receptive role; for this he was greatly ridiculed and maligned by the playwright Aristophanes. He is said to have introduced into Greek drama the "effeminate music" and "lascivious dances of Asia," rooted in the reverence of Dionysus, Cybele, and ATTIS. His "Phrygian-style" compositions were often written for the AULOS.

Agdistis   Lover of ATTIS, a beautiful youth of Roman mythology who was also loved by the goddess CYBELE. Zeus desired intercourse with Cybele. She was, however, able to resist him. He then masturbated, his semen falling onto a rock. From the rock sprang an androgynous being. Because of this creature's enormous physical strength, the gods decided to castrate the being; from that moment he-she was perceived as a male eunuch and was named Agdistis. Agdistis went to live in the forest and became a hunter. From the blood that had spilled when he was castrated, a pomegranate tree grew. Nana, daughter of the river-god Sangarios, ate a pomegranate from the tree and became pregnant. She gave birth to Attis. Sangarios, refusing to accept the miracle of virgin birth, forced Nana to surrender the infant to goatherds. One day, when the youthful Attis was hunting, he encountered the eunuch Agdistis, who immediately fell in love with him. The two became intimate companions, Agdistis presenting Attis "with the spoils of wild beasts." Attis, under the influence of wine, confessed to others that he and Agdistis had become lovers, and that Agdistis had honored him with many gifts. Attis satisfied Agdistis's "lust in the only way now possible," that is, either by allowing Agdistis to fellate him or by having Agdistis take the receptive role in anal intercourse. This topsy-turvy version of the Greek intergenerational model was underscored by the fact that both partners were intermittently portrayed as hunters and as gender variant. Attis the youth was loved by both Agdistis and Cybele, and was pledged to marry the daughter of King Midas. Opposing the event, Cybele and Agdistis brought chaos to the wedding. The young bride, Ia, chopped off one of her breasts, while Attis castrated himself beneath a pine tree. Attis, having castrated himself

and botched the job, offered his testicles, and perhaps also his penis, to Agdistis before succumbing to death.

Agido (fl. c. 600 BCE)   Priestess of a female spiritual household in ancient Sparta who revered the goddesses ARTEMIS/DIANA and AOTIS. Agido is remembered for the lesbian UNION which she allegedly celebrated with HAGESICHORA, another priestess of the household.

Agni   Hindu god of fire, creative energy, and wealth and the patron of human technological achievement, it is Agni who carries sacrifices to other deities. He is commonly depicted as a long-faced (sometimes two-faced), bearded man with flame-like skin, yellow eyes, and as many as seven tongues. He has four arms, which carry items including a banner made of smoke, an axe, a torch or flaming spear, a fan, a spoon, and a rosary. He is dressed in black. He sits on a ram or in a chariot drawn by red horses. While he is married to the goddess Svaha, he is primarily known for his relationships with the gods SHIVA and SOMA. When Agni swallows the semen of Shiva, he sets off a chain reaction that results in the birth of KARTIKKEYEH, a god of battle and male beauty. In the *Mahabharata*, the question is asked concerning Shiva, "Who is it whose semen was offered in sacrifice in the beginning of the world into the mouth of Fire, of Agni?" Linked to this passage is one from the *Saura Purana* which reads: "Agni said, 'Release your seed, the heavenly Soma, into my hands, and let the gods drink it immediately.' Then from his *linga* [i.e. his phallus] Shiva released his perfect seed which had the fragrant perfume of jasmine or the blue lotus. Agni took it into his hands and drank it, rejoicing, thinking, 'Elixir!' and then Shiva vanished." Elsewhere, Soma appears not as divinized semen, but as a god unto himself with his own semen, which Agni imbibes. While the heterocentricism of Hinduism is not so absolute as to forbid sexual exchange between two male – or two female – beings, Hindu sources stress that in this MITHUNA, or ritual sexual coupling, Agni's mouth in particular, and his erotic role in general, should be interpreted as feminine.

Agnicayana   Hindu ritual in honor of the god Agni in which a *mithuna*, an erotic-spiritual coupling, was comprised of a same-sex rather than a heterosexual pair, with one priest representing the so-called Cosmic Man and another the Man in the Left Eye.

Agnidhra   In the AGNICAYANA rite of Hinduism, the *agnidhra* priest took the active role in a male-male *mithuna* (ritual coupling), also embodying the Cosmic Man, the god MITRA, the human male, and the male sheep, in opposition to roles taken by the NESTR priest.

Agnodice (or **Agnodike, Agonodice, Hagnodike**; probably lived sometime between the sixth and third centuries BCE) Although a few scholars doubt her existence, the Athenian woman Agnodice appears to have been interested in the healing arts from an early age. As a woman, she was barred from practicing medicine in Greece. In order to study and later to practice medicine, she began dressing in male attire and behaving in a traditionally masculine manner. She studied under a doctor named Hierophilus. She commanded great respect as a gynecologist until the day her secret was discovered. Successfully battling against the law prohibiting women from studying medicine in Athens, Agnodice became an archetype of the woman doctor for other Greek women.

Agule Meaning "like men," *agule* refers, among the Lugbara of east Africa, to gender variant female spirit mediums.

Ah Pook In the visionary cosmos of queer-identified writer William S. BURROUGHS, a Mayan-inspired god who is a "patron of street boys, wanderers, and outcasts." Ah Pook has a "face of green marble" and "flaring eyes like jade slits." Burroughs continues in *The Western Lands* (1987), "His phallus is a smooth, translucent green, and he gives off a smell of fungus and toadstools, of jungles and untamed wild cats and orchids, of moss and stone."

Ahriman In the anti-homoerotic religion of Zoroastrianism, practiced primarily in Persia (now Iran), a demonic patron of males engaging in same-sex eroticism.

Ahsonnutli (or **Ashon Nutli'**) Gynandrous or transgendered creator deity in the Native American Navaho tradition whose name means "Turquoise Hermaphrodite."

Aido Hwedo (or **Aida-Wedo, Ayida Wèdo**) Gynandrous Rainbow-serpent *lwa* (deity or spirit) of the Vodou pantheon, described as the wife or female (or feminine) aspect of the *lwa* DAMBALLAH. Devotees pray to Aido Hwedo for prosperity and joy. She (-he) inhabits springs and rivers. Her (-his) sacred attributes include: the colors blue and white; the cotton tree, silk tree, calabash, palmetto, and tamarind; milk, eggs, and rice; Monday and Tuesday. She (-he) is syncretized with a Catholic manifestation of Mary, the mother of JESUS, known as Our Lady of the Immaculate Conception; as such, Aido-Hwedo is fêted on December 8. In "Call," a poem from *Our Dead Behind Us* (1986), African-American lesbian poet Audre LORDE writes: "Holy ghost woman / stolen out of your name / Rainbow Serpent / whose faces have been forgotten / Mother loosen my tongue or adorn me / with a lighter burden / Aido Hwedo is coming."

AIDS/HIV and Spirituality Don Lattin wrote in the 27 February 1989 edition of the *San Francisco Chronicle*, "in the darkening shadow of AIDS, a new spirituality is rising from San Francisco's gay community." He continued, "Its sacraments are long hugs and slow, sensuous massage. Its altars are votive candles burning wherever people with AIDS gather. Its great totem is a sprawling quilt imbued with sacred power. Its high priests are people living with AIDS and those accompanying them into death. It is a search for meaning in the face of a devastating plague . . . In San Francisco, the spiritual response to AIDS is a gay spiritual response." Indeed, a comment often heard during the late 1980s and early 1990s was that, despite bringing illness and death, AIDS/HIV seemed to be empowering and inspiriting the queer community and (especially in terms of gay men) to be transforming a generally narcissistic, self-centered community into a compassionate, nurturing one. Cheryl Daniels-Shoham, a coordinator of the AIDS project of the Center for Attitudinal Healing in San Francisco, observed, "What we're learning from people with AIDS is the beauty that exists in life and the inner healing that occurs when people let go of the fear of death." While more mainstream queer-centered religious groups like the Metropolitan Community Church, Dignity, Integrity, and Congregation Sh'ar Zahav developed AIDS/HIV-focused services, even the leaders of these organizations realized that, to some extent, what might be termed AIDS-centered Spirituality (clearly related to yet distinct from both Gay Spirituality and New Age spirituality) was emerging "home-grown" from an extremely eclectic community not bound to any single spiritual tradition. In the words of writer, PWA (person with AIDS), and Catholic priest Robert Arpin, who links living with AIDS to alchemy, "Pain and suffering and sickness is like fire. It can refine people into gold or reduce them to ash. In the AIDS epidemic, gay people have begun refining their lives into gold, finding meaning that [comes] not from the church or society but from themselves, from their own self-worth. It refines them into beautiful examples of the meaning of life . . . and love." Many persons other than gay people have participated in the creation of AIDS-centered Spirituality. One of the first spiritual responses to AIDS was voiced by the southern California-based metaphysician Louise Hay who, in 1983, released the cassette tape *AIDS: A Positive Approach*. In the years that followed, Hay released numerous other tapes and books and ministered to thousands of persons with AIDS (and others) at her Wednesday night "Hayrides" at West Hollywood Park. Hay was frequently attacked, however, by those who felt she was profiting from the illness, as well as by those (gay men in particular) who felt uncomfortable with what they perceived to be her "mother image." Following Hay's lead, many other leaders and groups have contributed to AIDS-centered Spirituality, including Dr Elizabeth Kübler-Ross, Dr Bernie Siegel, Dr Gerold Jampolsky, Irene Smith, Margo Adair, Kevin Ryerson,

Lynn Johnson, Steven Levine, RAM DASS, Marianne Williamson, The Radiant Light Ministries, the Course in Miracles, the Living/Dying Project, the Shanti Project, and the Center for Attitudinal Healing. To date, the best anthology on AIDS-centered Spirituality remains Jason Serinus's *Psychoimmunity and the Healing Process: A Holistic Approach to Immunity and AIDS* (1986). AIDS-centered Spirituality is an eclectic path drawing upon ancient, primal, and "mainstream" religions, and New Age concepts and techniques, as well as upon the CAMP aesthetic and on rites especially dear to gay and/or queer-identified persons, such as Halloween and MARDI GRAS. Judd Wozencroft, describing a typical AIDS-centered Spiritual service, said in the late 1980s, "It's not down and heavy. It's light and airy and gay. You start out dancing, then get into meditation, visualizations." As Wozencroft indicates, healing techniques or practices such as meditation, visualization, affirmations, laying on of hands, herbal medicine, and CHANNELING play an important role in AIDS-centered Spirituality. Also of prime importance in the movement are rites concerning the transition between life and death. One of the chief roles those involved in AIDS-centered Spirituality often find themselves assuming is that of the psychopomp or "soul-guide." In this capacity, one helps both the dying person and those near to them to accept, and in some cases to rejoice in (especially with those believing in an afterlife), the imminent arrival of death. This may include being with someone at the hour of death, sometimes described as "helping them to cross over," as well as presiding over, or taking an active role in the creation of, funeral rites and/or memorial services. The impact that AIDS-centered Spirituality has had upon the manner in which funerals are conducted has been enormous, particularly in the US. Although many funerals remain somber occasions, a great number have become joyful, festive celebrations of the deceased's life, honoring them with stories, songs, and balloons as well as objects and foods they enjoyed in life. In this way, funerals and memorials linked to AIDS-centered Spirituality much more closely resemble the jazz funerals of New Orleans and the Mexican/Mexican-American celebration of the Dia de los Muertos (the Day of the Dead) than they do traditional funerals of "mainstream" faiths. The concept and practice of "offering" in terms of memorials for the deceased in AIDS-Spiritual settings also bears a striking parallel to that of offerings made in Mexican and other Latin American folk-Catholic traditions and in African-diasporic traditions like Santería and Haitian- and New Orleans-based Vodou, in the sense that these offerings (*ofrendas* in Spanish) are often expressed aesthetically in the forms of ALTARS, ornamented fabrics, and other items bearing symbols and employing a variety of media. This is most apparent in the Names Project QUILT, a sacred patchwork created by a host of artisans and dedicated to those who have succumbed to AIDS-related illness. The central role of art in AIDS-centered Spirituality should come as little surprise, considering the high number of artists within the queer-identified and other "high risk" communities. Art, moreover, has traditionally served as a medium through which those who are not spiritual functionaries *per se* (often because they have been barred, as have many gays and lesbians, from positions of religious authority) may give expression to their spiritual sentiments. Artists affected by AIDS have begun to consider the spiritual dimension of life to be of much greater importance than many of them had previously thought. Writer and filmmaker Cyril Collard says, "I seem to have a spiritual tendency that I certainly didn't have before," while performance artist and choreographer Rick Darnell adds bluntly, "AIDS brought spirituality to our community . . . Death does that." Iranian-born playwright, director, and performer Reza Abdoh expands upon this theme: "AIDS has created a landscape in which the body and the spirit can be examined . . . destroyed, and re-formed. I think it's important for us as a people . . . to discover our own road to what you might . . . call redemption or salvation. It has nothing whatsoever to do with the Judeo-Christian idea of salvation or redemption. It has to do with a certain kind of peace that you find within yourself and [that] you transmit . . . through a generous act to your community." Kenny O'Brien, a designer who pioneered the use of jewelry on leather and who died of AIDS-related illness in 1991, said of spirituality: "The world is a psychedelic Sesame Street of the soul . . . The Indians say you can always take a step on the path of beauty. Look for the trail of beauty when you're in trouble and suffering. You can find it in a hummingbird or in a song or in a cloud." In recent years, the links between art and AIDS-centered Spirituality have been documented in such works as: *From Media to Metaphor: Art About AIDS* (1991), *Muses from Chaos and Ash: AIDS, Artists, and Art* (1993), *The Art of AIDS* (1994), and *Life Sentences: Writers, Artists, and AIDS* (1994). Works of art relating the sacred to AIDS are now so numerous that only a few may be mentioned here: Duane Michaels's photo series *The Dream of Flowers*, Edward Stierle's ballets *Lacrymosa* and *Empyrean Dreams*, Diamanda Galás's *Plague Mass*, Keith Haring's altarpiece *The Life of Christ* at San Francisco's Grace Cathedral, and Tony Kushner's drama *Angels in America*.

Aikane Hawaiian term for beloved one, an intimate relationship embracing passionate friendship and same-sex eroticism (often in a bisexual or pansexual context). *Aikane* appears to be related to *ai*, sexual intercourse, as well as to *'ai*, to eat. Revealing a spiritual component to this relationship, it is said: "He or she who eats of your soul is your true friend." Of *aikane* it is also said, "An *aikane* is a nest of fragrance."

A-Jami, Jami In the earliest spiritual tradition of India, the shamanic, matrifocal religion of the Indus Valley Civilization, the concept of *jami* appears to have arisen from the notion of a triadic or trinitarian relationship among the Goddess and a set, typically female, of twins. Indian scholar Gita Thadani has suggested that these twins and the term *jami* may have been associated with same-sex intimacy as well as with Goddess Reverence. In Vedic Hinduism, which displaced the Indus Valley religion (although aspects of it survive in TANTRA and elsewhere), persons participating in MITHUNAS, erotic-sacred couplings, must typically be considered *a-jami*, basically, 'unlike,' as opposed to *jami*, 'alike,' due to the patriarchal, heterocentric bias of the tradition. For this reason, if two males, ordinarily considered *jami*, participate in a *mithuna*, they must be distinguished from each other by having one represent the masculine, the other the feminine, one fire, the other water, and so on, in a manner resembling the YIN-YANG dialectic of Taoism.

Akhenaton (or **Ikhnaton**, c. 1379-c. 1362 [or 1354] BCE) Pharaoh of the Eighteenth Dynasty who ruled Egypt from 1372 until his death. Androgynous in appearance, Akhenaton was a religious zealot and monotheist who abandoned all of the deities of Egypt except for Aten, the god of the sun. While he is traditionally spoken of as the spouse of Queen Nefertiti (whose bust is perhaps the most renowned work of Egyptian art other than the SPHINX), he appears to have shared an intimate relationship with his son-in-law Smenkhare. In artworks they are shown in intimate situations, with Akhenaton stroking Smenkhare's chin or as being nude together, depictions not common in Egyptian art. After an apparent separation from Nefertiti, who rejected her husband's monotheism, Akhenaton made Smenkhare his co-regent and bestowed on him names of endearment usually reserved for a queen. Smenkhare also appears to have become for Akhenaton the mortal embodiment of Aten, the sun.

Aku Among the Akan of Ghana, the androgynous or transgendered deity of the planet MERCURY.

Alastair (c. 1887-1969) Alastair, whose name evokes a falling star, has been nicknamed "the illustrator of decadence." Born around 1887 and of mysterious origins, Alastair, as a youth, learned to speak French, German, and English fluently, to play piano, and to perform mime shows. As a young man, he studied philosophy at the University of Marburgh, where he met Boris Pasternak, the author of *Doctor Zhivago*, and Felix Noeggerath, the latter becoming his lover for several years. Alastair has been described as resembling both Pierrot and Nosferatu. Victor Arwas writes of Him: "Alastair frequently wore . . . makeup . . . [He was known for his] malicious high-pitched speaking voice, the glitter of his eyes, the studied gesture."

In the 1890s, Alastair began producing illustrations in a style influenced by Aubrey BEARDSLEY, his favorite subjects being Salome, Cleopatra, and androgynous or effeminate youths, including American dandies. His illustrations for Oscar WILDE's poem *The Sphinx* are considered among his finest works. In the early 1900s he performed erotic-mystical dances for the circle of the Italian Decadent novelist Gabriele d'Annunzio. Arwas writes of this period, "Alastair, who had by now accumulated a vast wardrobe of exotic costumes . . . needed little encouragement to dress and perform, creating curious ritualized scenes which appeared to conjure up the supernatural." In 1914 Alastair met André Germain, a writer who was fascinated with the poetry of the lesbian writer Renée VIVIEN. Alastair and Germain would share a long-lasting, tempestuous relationship. Nine years later, Alastair met the ritual magician and esoteric artist Austin Osman Spare, who was to wield a great influence upon his life and work. Also in the early 1920s, Alastair became friends with the homosexual or bisexual occultist Ludwig Derleth, a member of the circle of Stefan GEORGE, a homosexual German Decadent poet whose love for a youth named Maximin had inspired a cult upon the untimely death of the youth. Also during this period, Alastair became friends with the eccentrics Harry and Caresse Crosby, and a bit later with Pablo Cassals, whom he sometimes accompanied on the piano. Philippe Jullian (1975) describes the world of Alastair as one of "Black Masses in transvestite clubs." In the 1940s, Alastair began to withdraw more and more from the outside world; he did, however, continue to receive visitors in the evenings who would bring him bunches of "roses, lilies, chrysanthemums." He reemerged briefly in the 1960s, when his work again became fashionable. He died in 1969. His lover Germain wrote of him: "He travelled throughout Europe with a huge number of trunks containing the most magnificent clothes, but had no roof of his own. An air of splendour and decay hung around him . . . Moving with a kind of effort hieratic costumes resembling chasubles [i.e. mantles worn by priests], he executed, as though hypnotised, slow pantomimes which . . . transposed sacerdotal wails and recreated the splendours of an exiled court . . . He gave one the impression of emerging from a fairy-tale, but a rather 1890s fairy-tale, in which there was some Villiers de l'Isle-Adam as well as some Aubrey Beardsley, some perfected liturgies, and a degree of Witchcraft."

Albani, Cardinal Alessandro (1692-1779) Homoerotically inclined Italian Catholic cardinal, collector of art, and patron of artists. At his villa in Rome, Albani, his librarian Johann Joachim WINCKELMANN, the bisexual painter Anton Rafael Mengs (1728-1779), and others are believed to have formed a circle of passionate male friends or lovers and to have devoted themselves to the Greek gods PAN and PRIAPUS and the divinized lover of the Roman emperor HADRIAN, ANTINOUS.

Al-Basri, Abu Abdallah (fl. tenth century CE)   Bisexual Shi'i Islamic theologian and leader of a sect of Mu'tazili Muslims. His desire for young men led to his being nicknamed "Dung Beetle," as dung beetles were believed to be an all-male group, reproducing by placing their semen in, and then rolling in, dung (a belief traceable to ancient Egypt). His pupil Abu l-Qasim Isma'il b. 'Abbad (936-995) claimed that his own passion for other males had been inspired by al-Basri; "the doctrine," he wrote, "is that of Mu'tazilism (*i'tizal*) and intercourse with men (*rijal*) [the practice]." Al-Basri's most notorious student was Abu Ishaq al-Nasibi, nicknamed Maq'ada ("Backside") due to his enjoyment of the receptive role in anal intercourse.

Albina   In the visionary, lesbian-centered cosmos of Monique Wittig and Sande Zeig in *Lesbian Peoples* (1979), a Libyan Amazon of the DANAID tribe living during the Bronze Age. She was known as the "Fiery Chest."

Alchemy   Ancient science or art which seeks to spiritually transform the lives of individuals yearning for wisdom. Chinese alchemy accomplishes this by way of plant and gem elixirs, practices akin to Hindu TANTRA, and other means, while the Euro-western tradition, greatly indebted to Arabic alchemy, focuses on – primarily as a physical symbol of a spiritual process – the transformation of base metals into gold. Euro-western alchemy is especially rich in symbolism relating to the mixing or merging of genders or sexes. The so-called primary material of alchemy allegedly contains all colors and all metals within itself, corresponding to the fusion of body and spirit and the heavens and the earth, labeled by Marie Delcourt as "hermaphroditic." The so-called Philosopher's Stone of alchemy is often depicted as a crowned Hermaphrodite. Alchemy also embraces the Qabbalistic figure of ADAM Kadmon. Alchemy further portrays the classical deity HERMES/MERCURY as androgynous, often as a young man with feminine breasts. As an androgynous being, this deity is associated with numerous other alchemical symbols, including the mystic golden flower or alchemical ROSE, the BLUE SAPPHIRE, the PEACOCK, the PHOENIX (who rebirths or recreates itself from its own ashes), and the UROBORUS (i.e. the SERPENT devouring its own tail). In the metaphoric language of alchemy, Mercury is at once god, planet, and the alchemist's own gender-mixing nature.

Alcibiades (c. 450-404 BCE)   Athenian actor, politician and general ultimately assassinated by political enemies, Alcibiades is better remembered as a dandy and as the man-loving devotee, and probably lover of, the philosopher Socrates (469-399 BCE). Other male lovers of

Alcibiades included Anytus and Thrasyllus. Many spoke of the beauty of Alcibiades, especially of his long hair and elegant purple attire. It was widely believed in late antiquity that many of the herms, or phallic statues, erected in honor of DIONYSUS, HERMES, PRIAPUS, PAN, and other deities were modeled upon the phallus of Alcibiades. Alcibiades made a grave mistake when, at a private party, he and his companions allegedly parodied the Eleusinian Mysteries of Demeter and Persephone. He would have gone to trial for this offense had he not been called to head a military expedition to Sicily. Many believed that it was Alcibiades' ridicule of the goddesses and their mysteries that led to his demise. In the folklore of fashion, Alcibiades's memory survived for centuries in the form of an exquisite slipper named after him, the wearing of which came to signify male gender variance and receptive homoeroticism. By the late nineteenth century, Alcibiades, as the lover of Socrates, had been reclaimed by French bohemians as an archetypal figure signifying homoeroticism, so much that the term *alcibiadiser* (an active verb) was employed to refer to a male taking the receptive role in same-sex eroticism.

Alcuin of Tours, Saint (c. 735-804)   Homoerotically inclined Medieval English poet and educator who, in France, became an abbot and a friend of King Charlemagne (c. 742-814). Inspired by Greek mythology, religion, and philosophy as much as by Christianity, Alcuin and his pupils, whom he often referred to by pet names such as "DAPHNIS" and "Cuckoo," as well as certain French courtiers, appear to have formed a "circle of masculine friendship." Writers including John Boswell (1980), have noted the homoerotic quality present in Alcuin's correspondence and poetry. In "Lament for a Cuckoo," he writes, "O cuckoo that sang to us and art fled, / Where'er thou wanderest, on whatever shore / Thou lingerest now, all men bewail thee dead, / They say our cuckoo will return no more. / Ah, let him come again, he must not die . . . / Yet be thou happy, wheresoe'er thou wanderest / Sometimes remember us, Love, fare you well." And in a letter to a bishop friend, Alcuin writes, "I think of your love and friendship with such sweet memories . . . that I long for that lovely time when I may be able to clutch the neck of your sweetness with the fingers of my desires. Alas, if only it were granted to me . . . to be transported to you, how I would sink into your embraces, how much would I cover, with tightly pressed lips, not only your eyes, ears and mouth, but also your every finger and toe, not once but many a time." St Alcuin is fêted on May 19 or 20.

Aldinach   Egyptian demonic spirit "given to causing earthquakes, hailstorms, and tempests", Aldinach is depicted as a transvestite male or transgendered (male-to-female) being.

Alexander, Follower of Apollonius of Tyana (fl. c. 100 CE)   Devotee of the mystic APOLLONIUS OF TYANA. As a rather promiscuous young man who was considered very beautiful, he fell in love with a Tyanian *goes*, a magician or sorcerer, who was allied with the cult of Apollonius. This *goes* taught Alexander the arts of healing, divination, and magic. Alexander became especially skilled in discovering buried treasures. In later years, he founded a mystery cult devoted to the hybrid god ASCLEPIUS-Glykon.

Alexander the Great (356-323 BCE)   Warrior and king of Macedonia, Alexander as a youth was taught by the philosopher Aristotle (384-322 BCE). By the age of 24, Alexander had conquered the Persians and the Egyptians. In Egypt he founded the city of Alexandria, where Egyptian priests declared him to be a god. In 326 BCE, Alexander and his troops entered India; while unsuccessful in his attempt to conquer India, he is credited with having encouraged the cross-pollination of Greek and Hindu art and spirituality. He died at the age of 33. Man-loving, his most celebrated lovers were Hephaestion (d. 324 BCE), a Macedonian warrior, and the Persian eunuch Bagoas. When he and Hephaestion visited the site of ancient Troy, they placed wreaths on the tomb of ACHILLES and PATROCLUS, honoring them as kindred comrade-lovers. When Hephestion died, Alexander was so devastated that he demanded that the physician taking care of Hephaestion be put to death. The funeral rites prepared by Alexander for Hephaestion are believed to have been unsurpassed in grandeur in the ancient world. Never afraid to display affection, it was said that once, when attending the theatre at Ilium, Alexander was "so overcome with love for the eunuch Bagoas that, in full view of the entire theatre, he, bending over, caressed Bagoas fondly, and when the entire audience clapped and shouted in applause, he . . . again bent over and kissed him." Like Alcibiades, Alexander was a dandy. He delighted in rich fabrics, and clothed himself and his attendants in exquisite garments of purple. Even when at war, he slept on a golden couch, surrounded by flute-players. Alexander was a religious eclectic. He appears to have been initiated into the cult of the Egyptian god AMUN (Ammon). Amun, meaning the Hidden One, was a deity of creation, the air, the sun, fertility, healing, magic, reincarnation, and kingship, as well as a patron of travelers and the poor. On at least one occasion Alexander appeared dressed in the purple robes and ram's horn headdress of the god. He also appears to have been devoted to HERMES and ARTEMIS/DIANA, in whose costumes he would occasionally appear. He was a close friend of a *megabyzos*, a gender variant male priest of Diana, at Ephesus. He once wrote to the priest asking if a runaway slave finding sanctuary in the temple at Ephesus might be allowed to join him as a companion. Athenaeus (fl. ca. 230 CE), in the *Deipnosophistae*, describes Alexander's dressing as Diana: ". . . at another time [he

wore] the costume of Artemis . . . wearing the Persian garb and showing above the shoulders the bow and hunting-spear of the goddess." Following his death, Alexander was worshipped as a god, often being identified with APOLLO. The most popular work of twentieth-century fiction concerning Alexander's love of men is lesbian writer Mary Renault's (1905-1983) *The Persian Boy* (1972).

Alexander VI, Pope (1431-1503)   Pope who was allegedly bisexual. With the birth name Rodrigo Llançol, he was born near Valencia in Spain. Moving to Italy, he changed his name to Rodrigo Borgia. After studying to be a lawyer, he instead became a bishop, a cardinal, and finally a pope, thanks in large part to the homoerotically inclined popes PAUL II and SIXTUS IV. He and his mistress, Vannozza dei Cattani, had several children, including the infamous Lucrezia Borgia. His male lovers appear to have been handsome pages, and perhaps also a man named Jem, the brother of a Turkish sultan. A patron of numerous homoerotically and bisexually inclined artists including MICHELANGELO Buonarroti , Alexander delighted in theatrical performances and apparently also in orgies. Those who loved him were outnumbered by those who hated him; among his bitterest enemies was the Dominican priest Girolamo Savonarola (1452-1498), famous for his "BONFIRE OF THE VANITIES."

Alexandria   Legendary mecca of sensuality, especially homoerotic intimacy, since its founding by ALEXANDER THE GREAT, so much so that by the first centuries of the Common Era, young male prostitutes had become known throughout the Roman Empire – with little regard for their country of origin – as "Alexandrian" or "Egyptian" youths. Much of the literature referred to as Alexandrine is permeated with the theme of homoerotic love. Alexandria experienced a renaissance in the late nineteenth and early twentieth centuries, in part due to its poetic celebration by the man-loving C. P. CAVAFY, a native of the city, and in part due to the discovery of its charm by foreign writers including Mikhail KUZMIN, E. M. FORSTER, and Lawrence Durrell (1912-1990), whose writings occasionally explore the interrelationship of homosexuality and/or bisexuality and the mythic or mystical.

Alexis   In Roman mythology and in the *Second Eclogue* of Virgil (70-19 BCE), a shepherd loved by his fellow shepherd CORYDON. Alexis ultimately rejected Corydon in favor of a young woman.

Alfhild (fl. tenth century CE)   Daughter of King Seward of the Goths, Alhild was a woman warrior and pirate who dressed in traditional male attire, participated in Viking raids, and fought alongside her shieldmaiden and comrade-lover Groa.

Alger, Horatio (1832-1899)   Unitarian minister and writer of New England. His love for male youths was expressed not only in "rags-to-riches" popular novels but also in the financing of orphanages for runaways.

Alimontian Mysteries   Mystery cult revering the Greek god DIONYSUS, centered at Alimos (or Halimus) near Athens. The central ritual undertaken in these Mysteries commemorated the homoerotic relationship of the god Dionysus and the mortal PROSYMNUS. It appears that either simulated or real anal intercourse was engaged in during these Mysteries. Also at this time, Alimos was decorated with herms (phallic statues or pillars) in honor of Dionysus and Prosymnus. According to Arnobius, in the latter years of Dionysiac worship, many of these herms were modeled on the celebrated phallus of ALCIBIADES. The Alimos was also a dance of Attica.

Al-Jink (or **El-Gink[eyn]**)   Men, typically of Turkish, Greek, Armenian, or Jewish heritage, who wore female attire, including kohl eye makeup, braided and pomaded hair, perfume of attar-of-roses, and garments of muslin seemingly woven "of evening dew." They generally led an itinerant life and sojourned primarily in Egypt. They engaged in homoerotic relationships and found great pleasure in anal eroticism. They were associated with, believed to worship, and apparently named after the JINN (or *djinni, genii*), spirits whose behavior embraced gender metamorphosis and same-sex eroticism. Like the MUKHANNATHUN of pre-Islamic Arabia and the HIJRAS of India, the Al-Jink[en] assumed ritual roles as singers and dancers at weddings and other celebrations. In this capacity they appear in the tale of "Ma'aruf the Cobbler and His Wife" in the *Arabian Nights*. They were also associated with the Arabic concept of MUJUN, liminal space inhabited by marginalized persons.

'Alké 'na 'a cï   Navaho term meaning "One Who Follows The Other," a name given to an androgynous, transgendered, or TWO-SPIRIT being created by the god BEGOCHIDI. The being was later split into male and female halves, although its original, androgynous shadow appears to have survived in one of the Navaho lands of the dead.

Al-Lat   Arabian, pre-Islamic, gender variant goddess served primarily by women and by gender variant males known as MUKHANNATH(UN). A deity of love and a warrior, depicted as wearing a helmet decorated with spirals, Al-Lat was one of a trinity of goddesses, joined by AL-UZZA and MANAT. Al-Lat was also called Moawallidah, "She who bringeth forth." By the fifth century BCE, she was known to the Greeks; she became syncretized with other goddesses including ATHENA, ASTARTE, Baalat, CYBELE, INANNA/ISHTAR, and

VENUS. Her faithful would circle the Kaaba, the shrine of the sacred black stone, chanting, "By Al-Lat and Al-Uzza, and Manat, the third idol . . . Verily they are the most exalted females whose intercession is to be sought." Certain Sufis continued to worship her as Sayyidat al-Kabirah, or, the Great Lady.

Allen, Paula Gunn (1939-)   Laguna Pueblo/Sioux/Lebanese/Scottish lesbian writer. In her work, Allen weaves together the sacred narratives of Native American Indian divine female beings with contemporary feminist-spiritual, environmentalist, anti-racist, and, generally speaking, holistic thought. Her works include *The Sacred Hoop: Recovering the Feminine in American Indian Traditions* (1986) and *Grandmothers of the Light* (1991). A. Keating (1993) observes: "Unlike many feminist revisionist mythmakers who primarily identify goddess imagery and female power with childbirth, Allen associates women's creativity with the intellect . . . she equates myth with metamorphosis . . . by defining it as . . . 'a language construct that contains the power to transform something (or someone) from one state or condition to another' . . . She challenges Euro-western conceptions of mythic stories as falsehoods . . . and argues that they embody a mode of perception – 'the psychospiritual ordering of nonordinary knowledge' – shared by all human beings, 'past, present, and to come.'" In an interview in *Trivia: A Journal of Ideas*, Jane Caputi asks Allen if she thinks there might be a "female spirit or energy." Allen's reply indicates a belief in the spiritual association of this spirit or energy not only with women but also with queer-identified men and transgendered persons: "I think there are essential feminine spirits . . . I believe as a metaphysician that the physical reflects the spiritual, the temporary reflects the essential . . . How do you get a faggot? I think what happens is that their consciousness is moving towards the feminine . . . because we are in a process of transmutation and that's a liminal space. That is where magic is possible. You can't create it if you are absolutely male or absolutely female. Forget it. Nothing moves. And of course the fundamental concept is movement . . . the wind." Caputi follows with. "So are lesbians moving toward masculine energy?" to which Allen responds, "Well, dykes are." "So dykes are like indians," Allen writes in "Some Like Indians Endure," "like indians dykes / are supposed to die out / or forget." She continues, "they remember and they / stay / because the moon remembers."

Al-Marini (fl. thirteenth century CE)   Islamic poet whose writing is inspired by the sentiment of *carpe diem* ("seize the day"), which, at its source, is a profoundly spiritual concept linking a belief in the transitoriness of life on earth to a belief in the sacredness of all life, expressed in the celebration of simple pleasures. In a poem to a young man he has loved, Al-Marini writes: "What a splendid time did we spend together / At the Wall and at the Pulpit of Charm! / . . . / Many a night we spent there without sleeping, / In the carefree and fragrant days of youth."

Almond Sacred attribute of the Roman gods AGDISTIS and ATTIS and of the GALLI, the gender variant priests of Attis and the goddess CYBELE, almonds are associated with the testicles and semen, with potency on one hand and castration on the other. When Agdistis was born from ZEUS's seed falling upon a rock, it was determined that because of this creature's enormous physical strength, the gods would castrate the being, causing Agdistis to be transformed into a male eunuch. When he was castrated, Agdistis's testicles, falling to earth, metamorphosed into a tree bearing almonds. The god Attis was born when the daughter of the god of the Sangarius River ate the almonds from the tree. Resembling Agdistis, Attis, prior to death, castrated himself, also becoming a eunuch. The *galli* castrated themselves in memory of Agdistis and Attis. In the visionary, lesbian-centered cosmos of Monique Wittig and Sande Zeig in *Lesbian Peoples* (1979), almondines, rings bearing almond-shaped stones symbolic of the vulva, were once worn "by Lesbians as a sign of recognition."

Altar Public or private expression of spiritual practice in the form of a collection of symbolic items, including representations of deities, spirits, ancestors, seasons, elements (earth, air, fire, water, etc.), and other items, often of a more personal nature. Altars may be traced to the beginnings of humankind. Like others, those considered gender variant or transgendered and those engaging in same-sex eroticism have participated in constructing altars. An altar fashioned by the THIASOS (spiritual household) of SAPPHO on the island of Lesbos exemplifies such early altars. Upon the altar, located in a sacred grove of apple trees, were placed roses, anise, hyacinths, and wildflowers, as well as an incense burner containing frankincense, offered to APHRODITE and other deities. On or near the altar was a model of the plow, which was offered to ARTEMIS/DIANA and which appears to have symbolized not only fertility but also intimate UNIONS shared by women. While altars are transcultural and transhistorical, a remarkable surge in personal, or "home," and group altar construction has occurred since the late 1960s, a phenomenon which is now international. This renascence has clearly been fueled by the desire of many women, including lesbians, as well as bisexuals, gays, and the transgendered to express their spirituality in ways not sanctioned by the spiritual traditions in which they have been reared, or else to express their personal and gendered relationships to those traditions. This phenomenon, discussed by P. Gargaetas (1995), is especially observable in spiritual traditions or paths honoring nature and "the feminine," such as Goddess Reverence, Neopaganism,

Wicca, and Women's Spirituality. The altar renascence also owes much to the cross-pollination of Asian, Native American, African, European, and other traditions which has occurred widely since the late 1960s. Such altars often include elements akin to those placed on the Sapphic altar described above, with the noticeable addition of candles (borrowed from folk Catholicism and/or Santería) possessing divine images and appropriate color symbolism, as well as contemporary or reclaimed symbols of feminism, bisexuality, same-sex love, and/or transgenderism, such as the LABRYS representing lesbian desire and alliance. What is particularly noticeable, however, is the emphasis on eroticism, which may manifest itself in genital-shaped symbols including phallic- and vaginal-shaped candles. Also observable is the addition of the element of Camp, which includes (but is not limited to) the conferring of spiritual, magical, or otherwise transpersonal potency to icons of popular culture. This phenomenon is exemplified by lesbian altars displaying images of MADONNA and by Radical Faerie altars including images of Judy Garland in *The Wizard of Oz* as well as the KALI-like villains of animated Disney films. Since the emergence of HIV/AIDS in the 1980s, especially in US cities like San Francisco, Los Angeles, and San Antonio, this altar renascence has become intertwined with the Mexican/Mexican-American festival of the Dia de los Muertos (the Day of the Dead). On altars (*ofrendas*) constructed to honor the deceased, one often finds images of the divine, candles, marigolds, skeleton breads, skulls made of sugar, favorite foods of the deceased, photographs, and personal belongings. Kay TURNER and Dennis Medina, both living in Austin, Texas in the 1990s, are among those queer-identified persons well known for the construction of altars inspired by the Dia de los Muertos. When prominent and much-loved San Francisco gay socialist activist Tede Matthews died of AIDS-related illness in 1993, altars in this tradition were observed in various parts of the city, especially in the Mission District. Some see the Names Project QUILT for persons who have died of AIDS-related illnesses as a kind of altar honoring the dead in a fashion akin to that of the Dia de los Muertos altars.

Al-Uzza Together with the Arabian goddesses AL-LAT and MANAT, she formed a trinity, worshipped in pre-Islamic times primarily by women and by gender variant men known as MUKHANNATH(UN). Al-Uzza was often depicted as having black skin; she was thus associated with the Kaaba, the shrine of the black stone, and was sometimes thought to be of Black African origin. She was the desert goddess of the moon and the morning star and the patron of travelers and nomadic peoples. Her sacred attribute was the samura palm. Among Christians she later resurfaced as Our Lady of Mâdabâ.

Alyha Among the Mohave of the American Southwest, the third gender or TWO-SPIRIT male, who, in the past, often served in a shamanic capacity. Also a type of venereal disease (probably gonorrhea, as syphilis is *hikupk*), which the *alyha* male was believed to cure by way of shamanistic rites. Among the Mohave, music, in the form of chanting or singing, has been held responsible for the transformation of traditionally masculine males into third gender *alyha*, who often served in shamanic capacities. These songs, sung at initiation rites and other occasions, were called *alyha kwayum* or *alyha kupama*. *Alyha* songs were also sung in reference to HWAME, third gender females who served in similar capacities and/or who became warrior women. One such song describes the delight by an *alyha* on the making and wearing of a traditionally feminine skirt. Four male singers (traditionally masculine) braiding bark for the sacred skirt of the *alyha* sing: "*ihatnya vudi, ihatnya va'ama* (roll it this way, roll it that way), *istum, ucham* (I hold it, I place it), *hilyuvik havirk* (it is done, it is finished), *ka'avek, kidhayk* (listen)."

Al-Zahra In Arabian mythology, a magical mountain spring. When one drinks of, or bathes in, the water of Al-Zahra, one changes sex.

Ama No Hafuri In the Shinto religion of Japan, Ama No Hafuri was a servant of a primordial goddess and the lover of another of her male servants, SHINU NO HAFURI. While this myth is told from a homophobic point of view, the love of the two male beings for each other is not hidden. When Shinu No Hafuri died after a long illness, the grief-stricken Ama No Hafuri committed suicide beside the body of his companion. The two were buried in the same grave.

Amaesia Sentia (or **Maesia Sentinas**, fl. c. 77 BCE) An historical personage, she became legendary, during the course of a trial in which she pleaded her own cause before the Roman praetor c. 77 BCE, for being recognized legally as an androgyne, as possessing a man's spirit and a female body.

Amaterasu Omi Kami All-powerful sun goddess of the Japanese religion of Shinto. Once, when her brother Susa No O, jealous of her power, began wreaking havoc on the earth, Amaterasu retreated to a cave, either temporarily surrendering to him or in order to regain her strength so that she might subdue him. During her retreat, no light shone on the earth, and everything began to rapidly die. It was only when the goddess AME NO UZUME performed a shamanistic dance with elements of both humor and eroticism outside the cave's entrance, yet in Amaterasu's view, that the latter ventured outside. As she took a step outward, she noticed her own reflection in a magical mirror created and held up by the transgendered deity ISHI KORE DOME NO KAMI. So tantalized was Amaterasu by Ame No Uzume's bawdy dance and by her own brilliant reflection that she did not, or pretended not to, notice as several other deities shut the cave's door. On another occasion, Amaterasu Omi Kami, again struggling with Susa No O, did not retreat. She dressed herself in the combined garments of a warrior and a shaman, "putting up her hair like that of a warrior, wrapping herself in the magical *magatama* beads, and taking up a bow and quiver." Outfitted thus, she approached her brother suddenly, frightening him with a shamanistic, warlike dance (an interesting parallel to Ame No Uzume's bawdy dance). Her dance has been compared to a martial art performance. Some writers have also described the dance as "revealing a masculine side of the goddess . . . suggesting a hermaphroditic nature."

Amathaon (or **Amaethon**) Celtic deity of agriculture and magic, associated with the legendary GREEN Man. According to Robert Graves (1958), Amathaon may have made love to a priest of the god Bran – a less intriguing variant has him stealing a supernatural dog – in order to discover the secret, magical name of Bran. Both of these versions of the tale, however, may be colored by Graves's intense homophobia.

Amazon "Amazon," when employed in its most specific context, refers to a woman warrior of ancient Greek, otherwise Mediterranean, or North African ("Libyan") origin. Less specifically, it refers to women warriors of other cultures. Even more generally, it refers to women considered, or considering themselves, transgendered in the terms of the cultures in which they live. Amazons often share a domain of common traits; among the Greeks, the word *antianeira* signified this domain. *Antianeira* typically includes the rejection of heterosexual marriage (although numerous Amazons are portrayed as having love affairs with men), love of hunting, skill as a warrior, a sense of alliance with gender variant males (in Greco-Roman culture, exemplified by the alliance of Amazonian priestesses and the gender variant, often homoerotically inclined priests of the goddess CYBELE, the GALLI), and a desire to reside in the company of women, often in a territory occupied primarily or solely by women. While the ancient authors do not usually speak directly of lesbianism among Amazons, they frequently infer its practice in describing the Amazons as the beloved companions of female deities, as BRITOMARTIS is the companion of ARTEMIS and DIANA, or PALLAS is the companion of ATHENA. Among the most well-known of the Amazons of classical antiquity are: Myrina, a Queen of the Amazons, known as the conqueror of the Atlantians; Mytilene, the sister of Myrina, after whom the city of MYTILENE on the island of Lesbos was named; and SEMIRAMIS, an Amazon queen of Assyria and daughter of the goddess ATARGATIS.

The Amazons known to Greeks and Romans were believed to have originated in Libya. It appears that "Libya" served for centuries as a general term to refer to that part of northern Africa west of Egypt. If we rely on Diodorus Sicilus (fl. c. first century BCE), we place the original home of the Amazons in the vicinity of Lake Tritonis in Numidia, corresponding to the area now bordering central Tunisia and northeastern Algeria. The Amazons were thought by the ancients to have conquered numerous peoples and founded many cities. According to Diodorus Sicilus, Amazon armies were distinguished by their size as well as by their unusual weapons. The army of Myrina allegedly numbered 33,000. Amazon shields employed the skins of serpents. Their rites tended to be orgiastic, with the wild music of flutes, cymbals, and tambourines inspiring ecstatic dancing. These priestesses are said to have employed their shields and swords in a circular dance around a sacred oak or beech. When Amazons participated in relationships with males, these men were perceived as gender variant or transgendered. Diodorus relates: "The men . . . like our married women, spent their days about the house, carrying out the orders which were given them . . . they took no part in military campaigns or in [political] office . . . When their [i.e. the Amazons'] children were born the babies were turned over to the men, who brought them up." The philosopher Sextus Empiricus in the third century CE claimed that when Amazons gave birth to male children, they castrated them in honor of the goddess Cybele so that they would revere her and so that they would be unable to make war, which the Amazons considered their own prerogative. Diodorus relates that as Cybele considered the Amazons her daughters, the *galli* were her sons. When the Amazons departed the island of Samothrace for their native Libya, Cybele "settled in it . . . her own sons," the *galli*, so that her worship might continue there. According to the historian Herodotus (c. 484-c. 420 BCE), Amazons also occupied the area of ancient Russia at one time. He suggests that an armed struggle may have occurred between the Scythians on one side and the Amazons and other peoples of ancient Russia and neighboring lands on the other prior to the sixth century BCE. Female warriors who lived in the vicinity of the Sea of Azov engaged in battle with the Scythians. Conflict slowed temporarily when the two groups decided to intermarry. For a time, Herodotus reports, the "two camps were . . . united." He points out that while the "men could not learn the women's language . . . the women succeeded in picking up the men's." Ultimately, however, the female warriors decided to separate from the Scythian males. "We are riders," they said, "Our business is with the bow and the spear, and we know nothing of women's work . . . let us go off and live by ourselves." The historian and geographer Strabo (c. 63 BCE-c. 21 CE) tells a similar tale. A tribe of Amazons once lived in the Caucasus between the Kuban and Terek rivers. These women hunted, farmed, and

raised cattle and horses. They removed their right breasts to facilitate throwing the javelin, and they wore animal skins. In the spring, they journeyed to a sacred mountain, where they participated in ritual sexual intercourse with the men of a neighboring tribe, the Gargarenses. "The female children that are born," Strabo tells us, "are retained by the Amazons," while "the males are taken to the Gargarenses" – presumably an all-male community – "to be brought up." Like the men and women of Herodotus' tale, they decide that "there should be companionship only with respect to offspring, and that they should each live independent of the other." The strict separation of the sexes in these tales may be legendary rather than actual. Such tales suggest, however, that battles may have occurred between matrifocally oriented indigenous peoples, represented by the Amazons, and patriarchally oriented invaders. If such battles did in fact occur, they probably involved both the men and women of the indigenous groups struggling against the invaders. Such tales may also point toward earlier male-female arrangements, suggesting that sexual separation may have once been the norm, interrupted intermittently by periods emphasizing reproduction. As in certain primal cultures, such arrangements may have encouraged same-sex eroticism. While numerous writers have vociferously argued against the existence of Amazons or female warriors, archaeological evidence may ultimately settle this dispute. For example, "Excavations have uncovered the burials of wealthy [Sauromatian] women containing weapons, equestrian gear, and objects suggesting a priestly status." Archaeological evidence appears to confirm, moreover, that even among the Scythians, Amazons may have been esteemed. In a Scythian tumulus near the village of Balaban, for instance, "archaeologists have found a woman warrior, buried . . . with weapons. Beautiful earrings, shaped into animal headlets, lay at her head." Many goddesses of antiquity are associated with Amazons. Beyond those already mentioned, they include the Egyptian deities ANAT and SEKHMET, the Phoenician ASTARTE, and the Celtic MACHA. In terms of Celtic culture, also noteworthy are SCATHACH ("Shade"), who trained the foster-brothers and intimate companions CU CHULAINN and Fer Diadh in the martial arts, and that of the GWIDONOT, a particular group of warrior women who may have engaged in same-sex relationships. Among the Aztecs, the gender variant female who engaged in lesbian eroticism and who was roughly equivalent to the Amazons of the ancient Mediterranean and Russia, was referred to as the *patlache*. Goddesses associated with the *patlache* include TLAZOLTEOTL and XOCHIQUETZAL. In Native American cultures, one finds Amazons like the TWO-SPIRIT HWAME shamans of the Mohave and warrior women of other tribes like KAUXUMA NUPIKA as well as divine female beings like ANOG ITE, DOUBLE WOMAN, and WIYA NUMPA. In the shamanic cultures of Alaska and north

Asia, one find the warrior-shamans as well as the divine female beings SEDNA and QAILERTETANG. In African cultures, the *mi-no* (or *mimo*) Amazon warriors of the Dahomean (Benin) culture are representative, as are the Yoruba *orishá* OSHUN Yeyé Iponda, a manifestation of Oshun as a Yoruba woman warrior; YEMAYA Okutí, an aspect of Yemayá as an *obiní ologun*, an Amazon; and OYA, a woman warrior, bringer of tempests, and guardian of the dead. Roger Bastide has described Oyá as a "queen who vanquishes death," while Macumba priestess Maria-José depicts her as a warrior who dwells "in the sky, armed and helmeted . . . ready to combat injustice." In later European history, JEANNE D'ARC (Joan of Arc) and Doña Catalina de ERAUSO are representative of women considered Amazonian, transgendered, and possibly lesbian. In premodern France Catherine de' Medici was compared to Semiramis, while her man-loving son HENRI III loved to dress in Amazon garb at lavish banquets. In part due to the reign of ELIZABETH I (1533-1603), the figure of the Amazon experienced a vogue in Renaissance England, giving birth to memorable characters including BRITOMART in Edmund Spenser's *The Faerie Queene*, her own character inspired by Britomartis, the beloved of Artemis, and by Ariosto's BRADAMANTE in *Orlando Furioso*. In the early twentieth century, the association of Amazons and lesbianism was reclaimed by the lesbian (or, according to others, bisexual) writer Natalie Clifford BARNEY, an American living in Paris. Two of her book titles, *Pensées d'une Amazone* (1920) and *Nouvelles pensées de l'Amazone* (1939), reflected this linkage; moreover, she was nicknamed "the Amazon." In 1972, classical scholar D. J. Sobel, in *The Amazon of Greek Mythology*, lent his support to this association: "No scholar can ignore the current of homosexuality in Hellenic and classical times, or doubt the authenticity of Sappho's female coterie on the island of Lesbos . . . An all-lesbian force that fused relentless training, unfailing dedication, a superiority in archers, and a monopoly on cavalry would overcompensate for muscular shortcomings and the impairment of menstruation. The battlefield was their rightful setting, and they colored warfare female." With the emergence of lesbian-feminism in the late 1960s, and continuing into the 1990s, the association has reached a pinnacle. Politically oriented books like *Amazon Expedition: A Lesbian/Feminist Anthology* (1973) have multiplied alongside speculative fictions including Monique Wittig's *Les Guerrilères* (1969) and Joanna Russ's *The Female Man* (1975) which celebrate archetypal Amazons and envision Amazonian UTOPIAS. To date, the most accessible and comprehensive work available on Amazons is Jessica Amanda Salmonson's *The Encyclopedia of Amazons: Women Warriors from Antiquity to the Modern Era* (1991).

Amazonium General term used to designate cities founded by the Amazons, including Smyrna and Ephesus.

Amber Fossilized resin frequently employed in making amulets. In Greek mythology, amber was associated with the lovers CYCNUS and PHAETON, and in classical astrology with HERMES/MERCURY. Amber is also an attribute of the Yoruba-diasporic deities OSHUN and INLE, the goddess Oshun being a patron of sensuality, including same-sex intimacy, and Inle being a gender variant or androgynous male patron of homoerotic love.

Ambrosia Food, nectar, or ointment of the gods symbolic of the loving relationship between ZEUS and GANYMEDE.

Ame No Uzume Japanese Shinto goddess (*kami*) of shamanism, magic, humor, music, and dance; inventor of the bamboo flute and the koto; patron of spirit mediums and dancers; invoked by those desiring protection from evil and longevity. Once, when the goddess AMATERASU OMI KAMI had hidden herself in a cave, the gods asked Ame No Uzume to help them to cause her to come out of the cave so that the sun would shine upon the earth once more. Ame No Uzume agreed to help. Wearing garments made of plants and a shaman's headdress and brandishing a spear decorated with bells, she stood on a tub turned upside down and began to chant and to dance. She chanted to Amaterasu, "Majesty appear! Behold my bosom and thighs!" Then, employing bawdy movements, she revealed her breasts and vagina to Amaterasu who, enchanted, took a step outside the cave. R. S. Ellwood states that the "licentious dance, by which Ame No Uzume aroused . . . Amaterasu out of the cave, apparently included a . . . positive female genital magic." Ame No Uzume's dance is still performed in Shinto temples; according to Jean Herbert (1967), her dance is "considered as the prototype of all sacred dances which are offered to the *kami*." The myth of Ame No Uzume's dance for Amaterasu Omi Kami bears a striking resemblance to a bawdy performance undertaken by the Greek goddess BAUBO for the goddess Demeter.

Ameinas Like the nymph Echo, the youth Ameinas fell in love with the beautiful young male NARCISSUS; like Echo, he was rejected. Indeed, Narcissus went so far as to send Ameinas a sword with which he might kill himself. Ameinas did commit suicide, but not before he prayed to ARTEMIS/DIANA to ask that Narcissus also experience rejection one day. Artemis answered Ameinas's prayer by having Narcissus fall in love with his own, ever-elusive reflection.

Amen Among the Akan of Ghana, the androgynous or transgendered deity of the planet SATURN.

Amethyst Nymph of Greco-Roman myth, Amethyst was a devotee and beloved of ARTEMIS/DIANA, the goddess of the hunt, the moon, and women's Mysteries. Amethyst was on her way to the temple of Artemis when she met the god of wine, DIONYSUS, and his retinue. Dionysus, having been earlier offended by a neglectful worshipper, had decreed, in a moment of fury, that he would have his tigers kill the next person they encountered. When they saw the young woman approaching, the tigers leapt at her. Terrified, Amethyst cried out the name of Artemis. The goddess, at first imagining that Amethyst had planned to meet Dionysus for a rendezvous, lingered momentarily in her jealousy. The tigers attacked. Artemis, in despair, attempted to restore Amethyst to life, but because this gift was not among her powers, she was unable to do so. She could only transform the young woman into another natural object which might serve as a reminder of the nymph's brief life and of their love for each other. Because she had never been married, and was thus pure in Artemis's eyes, and because she had not, as the Goddess had at first imagined, sipped the wine of Dionysus, Artemis changed her body into a crystal formation. Dionysus, overwhelmed by guilt and realizing that the nymph had been loved by Artemis, asked forgiveness for his crime, and poured a libation of wine over the crystal. As if the compassionate spirit of the young woman were accepting his apology and his offering, the crystal absorbed the wine, becoming an exquisite purple gem. Artemis named the stone amethyst, which means "not drunk," in tribute to the nymph she had loved. The ancients paid homage to Amethyst when they wore jewelry of her stone and garments of amethyst hue. At EPHESUS, the color was especially associated with the cult of Artemis, and, as throughout Greece and later the Roman Empire, amethyst became associated with gender variant persons, particularly with effeminate men. Once worn as a protective talisman, today amethyst, the birthstone for February, symbolizes deep love, chastity, courage, penitence, meditation, and wealth. The color of amethyst is also akin to lavender, that hue most associated with the contemporary sociopolitical movement for lesbian and gay rights.

Amis and Amile (or **Amis and Amiloun**)   Medieval French pair of soldiers, resonating with the Christian saints SERGIUS AND BACCHUS. Both in appearance and demeanor, Amis (Friend) and Amile bore a striking resemblance to each other. Once when they were separated, they spent two years desperately seeking each other. When they finally found each other, they embraced and kissed, said a prayer of thanks to God, and swore eternal comradeship to each other on the sword of Amile. Amile, not wishing Amis to die, took the latter's place in a great battle. During the war, Amile contracted leprosy. One night, Amis dreamed that the blood of his children could cure Amile. His love for Amile was so great that Amis slew his own children. He fed their blood to Amile,

and the sick man was healed instantly. Because God knew of the love the two men shared, He sent the archangel RAPHAEL to restore Amis's children to life. Ultimately, Amis and Amile were killed while fighting side by side in battle. They were buried next to each other in a single grave, as those responsible for interring them discovered that their coffins, miraculously, could not be kept apart. Over the centuries they have become a symbol of friendship and love between men.

Amitabha   Buddha revered by the sect of the Pure Land Buddhism, which teaches that Paradise can be entered by anyone who utters Amitabha's name in sincere devotion. Amitabha's devotees include the homoerotically inclined HWARANG of premodern Korea, whose songs often contain references to him.

Ampelus (or **Ampelos**)   Young male SATYR loved by the Greek god DIONYSUS. In the *Dionysiaca* of Nonnos (fl. fifth century CE), Dionysus says to Ampelus, "If you have the short-living blood of the horned Satyrs, be king at my side . . . you have a . . . heavenly beauty." One afternoon, when Ampelus had climbed to the top of a very tall ladder in order to reach the sweetest grapes growing on the highest part of the vine, he slipped and fell to his death. Discovering Ampelus lying in a pool of blood on the ground, Dionysus was unable to revive him, but transformed his body into vines and his blood into wine. The young satyr is remembered in the words "ample" and "ampelography," the latter referring to the study of vines.

Amphiaraus   Celebrated warrior of ancient Greece, but even more renowned as a master of the art of divination. Amphiaraus was the husband of Eriphyle, an *eromenos* (beloved) of the gods ZEUS and APOLLO, and the *erastes* (lover) of his charioteer BATON. Just as Amphiaraus was about to be killed in a great battle, Zeus caused the earth to open up beneath him and to swallow him until his enemies departed. The site at which this event occurred was still familiar to Greeks during the first centuries of the Christian era. After this event, a kind of symbolic death/rebirth experience, Amphiaraus became an oracle, especially as an interpreter of dreams. He founded an incubation temple at Oropus where persons would come to sleep so that their dreams might be interpreted. After his death, Amphiaraus came to be worshipped as a divine being, and Olympic-style games were celebrated in his honor.

Amphion   Theban musician loved by the Greek god HERMES. "Overcome by love for him," Hermes presented Amphion with several love-gifts: an exquisite golden headband; a tunic whose color "does not remain the same but changes and takes on all the hues of the rainbow"; and the first lyre, a seven-stringed instrument which Hermes invented especially for Amphion. Philostratus (fl. c. 200 CE) describes Amphion as having beautiful curly hair and a soft golden beard. He also tells us that Amphion was a devotee of the Great Goddess in her manifestation as Gaia: "he is singing a hymn to Earth . . . creator and mother of all." Like the music of ORPHEUS, Amphion's music worked magic. By strumming his lyre, he caused stones to come together to form the wall around the city of Thebes; the seven gates of Thebes would serve to remind inhabitants of his seven-stringed lyre.

Amun (or **Amen, Amun-Re**)   Ancient Egyptian deity of creation, fertility, the sun, and rulership, possessing the power to procreate without the aid of another entity, suggesting primordial androgyny, the patriarchal assumption of the female role of giving birth, or a mixture of these. Masturbation, oral intercourse, and perhaps also latent homoeroticism play a role in the Heliopolitan story of Amun's creation of the male-female divine couple Shu and Tefnut: "I, even I, had union with my clenched hand, I joined myself in an embrace with my shadow, I poured seed into my mouth, I sent forth issue in the form of Shu, I sent forth moisture in the form of Tefnut." In his ability to create by way of masturbation Amun bears likeness to, and is sometimes identified with, the Egyptian god KHEPERA; Amun may also be compared with the PHOENIX. Amun was the special patron of numerous pharaohs; the Amazonian HATSHEPSUT was thought to have been the daughter of Amun and a mortal woman.

Amyclas   King of Sparta, he was a son of NIOBE, who had once known lesbian companionship, and AMPHION, who had been loved by HERMES. Amyclas was himself an *eromenos* (beloved) of APOLLO; and, according to some sources, he was the father of HYACINTHUS, who was also loved by Apollo.

Anactoria (fl. c. 600 BCE)   Companion-lover of the poet SAPPHO at her THIASOS, or religious household, on the island of LESBOS. Anactoria also appears to have been a lover of Sappho's pupil ATTHIS.

Anahita   In the view of Monique Wittig and Sande Zeig (1979), an AMAZON who lived during the Bronze Age in Anatolia, known as "the Devastating." Anahita's companion was Queen OMPHALE. Upon her death, Anahita was worshipped as a goddess (also known as Tanaquil).

Anandryne, La Secte (or **Anandrine**)   While the existence of an erotic-spiritual, lesbian-centered organization known as the Sect of the Anandrynes remains controversial, written evidence suggests that in or around 1770, a group of women led by Thérèse de Fleury founded this organization in Paris. They converted a house in the

Rue des Boucheries-Saint-Honoré into a temple, the reigning deity of which was the Roman VESTA (in Greek religion, Hestia), goddess of the hearth. While in Rome she was considered the goddess of family life, Vesta remained unmarried, and, in general, men were barred from her temple. Thus it is not surprising that Vesta would be chosen to preside over a spiritual family of women who swore to love one another and to refrain from heterosexual relations (hence the term *anandryne*, 'without men' – although not all kept their word). They also revered one of the Muses, Melpomene, who presides over Tragedy. Not only were a number of women who belonged to the Sect renowned actresses, but also Melpomene is represented as gender variant in Greco-Roman terms – besides the mask she wears or carries, she often holds a sword or club, suggesting an Amazonian figure. In *La Nouvelle Sapho, ou Histoire de la Secte Anandryne* (Paris, 1791), we learn that while the women who participated in the Sect were referred to by others as *tribades* (Greco-Roman term for women having sex with other women), they preferred to call themselves *anandrynes*, perhaps to stress an emphasis on gender identity rather than sexual activity – although it is clear from the evidence that theirs were, generally speaking, erotic relationships rather than so-called "romantic friendships." One of the most well-known of the Anandrynes, and allegedly at one time their leader or president, was the predominantly lesbian actress Françoise Marie Antoinette Joseph Saucerotte Raucourt. Called by her fans La Raucourt, she made her debut at the *Théâtre français* in 1772 in the role of Dido. Other roles included those of Cleopatra, Athalie, and Catherine de Médicis. Her portrayal of a male army captain in *Le Jaloux* was deemed a great success. During the French Revolution, she supported the royal family. In 1807, Napoleon gave her the task of organizing a French company for Italy. La Raucourt's primary intimate relationship was with Jeanne-Françoise-Marie Souck (or Sourques). On her death in 1815, it was reported that 15,000 people attended her funeral, even though the *curé* of the Eglise Saint Roch had almost succeeeded in preventing her having a Christian burial. Another renowned Anandryne was the actress Madeleine-Sophie Arnould (1740/4-1802/3). Known for her beautiful appearance and equally beautiful voice, she was compared by Madame de Pompadour to a "princess." She made her debut in 1757 at the Opéra. In 1774 she performed the title role in *Iphigenia at Aulis*. Apparently bisexual, she gave birth to several children fathered by the *comte* de Lauraguais; she remained, however, unmarried. Ironically, when La Raucourt and Arnould became embroiled in an argument concerning the admission of men into the Sect, it was Arnould who took the separatist stance, while La Raucourt suggested that gender variant, homoerotically inclined men like the poet Charles, the Marquis de Villette (1736-1793) should be allowed to join. In terms of other potential male candidates, it is suggested in *La Nouvelle Sapho* that the Chevalier d'Eon (1728-1810), who shifted from traditionally masculine to feminine attire and behavior throughout his life, might have also been an appropriate candidate. Other women alleged to belong to the Sect were the actresses Mademoiselle Claire-Joseph-Hippolyte Léris de la Tude Clairon (1723-1803) and Louise Contat (1760-1813). The Anandrynes traced their history to the Lacedaemonians of ancient Sparta, who, they said, established schools where women exercised and danced in the nude and engaged in intimate relationships. The Anandrynes linked these schools to the THIASOS of SAPPHO and her companions. At Rome, the Vestal Virgins, they claimed, carried on the tradition, from whence it spread to other parts of the world, ultimately as far as China. According to the Anandrynes, the tradition of lesbian-centered spirituality "has been perpetuated without interruption into the present." The ritual garb of the Anandrynes included head wreaths of myrtle and laurel; flame-colored gowns with blue belts for priestesses or "mothers"; and white gowns with pink belts for "novices" (or "pupils"). The sacred bird of the Sect was that of Venus/Aphrodite, the DOVE. In the elegant temple of the Anandrynes, one discovered exquisite art objects, including a life-size statue of Vesta and busts of Sappho, "the most ancient and well known of the tribades," and her companions. One also observed a central hearth-fire, a basket-shaped bed to be occupied by the president of the Sect and her beloved, and piles of Turkish cushions to be enjoyed by the others. As the rite of initiation commenced, the hearth-fire was lit and sprinkled with incense. The priestess sponsoring the initiate (presumably an intimate companion) addressed the president and the "companions": "Here is a postulant; she appears to me to have all the required qualities . . . I ask that she be admitted by us in the name of Sappho." The initiate was ceremonially undressed and her beauty praised in chant. She was then given a gold ring, signifying her union with the group and perhaps especially with the sponsoring priestess. A banquet followed, with Greek wine and sensuous songs based on Sappho's poems. The hearth-fire was rekindled – "O Vesta! Tutelary deity of this place, replenish us with your sacred fire!" – and an orgy of lovemaking commenced. The term *anandryne* was still being applied to lesbian women in late nineteenth-century France.

Anastasia the Patrician, Saint (or **A. Patricia**; fl. sixth century CE)   Byzantine noblewoman to whom the emperor Justinian (482/483-565) was attracted, thus inciting the jealousy of his wife. Anastasia withdrew to a convent to escape intrigue. After the death of the emperor's wife, he instigated a search for Anastasia, whereupon she assumed a male identity and spent the remainder of her/his life as a monk-hermit in Scythia. St Anastasia is fêted on March 10.

Anat (or **Anath**)   Amazonian warrior goddess of Egypt, her worship perhaps originating in Syria. She is typically portrayed as bearing a shield and sword or axe. While she is perceived as gynandrous or transgendered, little is known of her sexuality, except that she and her spouse, the pansexual god SET, occasionally engage in anal intercourse.

Anaxagoras (500-428 BCE)   Greek philosopher from CLAZOMENAE who moved to Athens when he was twenty years old, there becoming an intimate companion of Athenian general and statesman Pericles (d. 429 BCE). He also became a teacher of the tragedian Euripides (485-406 BCE). Anaxagoras rejected the deities of classical antiquity, but created his own spiritual-scientific system, believing that the creation and maintenance of the universe was directed by a supreme Mind, or Nous. For his beliefs, he was charged with impiety, and only his beloved Pericles (who also had a female lover, Aspasia) was able to save him from being put to death. Anaxagoras then retired to Lampsacus in the Troad where he founded a school promoting his spiritual-scientific philosophy.

Anderson, Margaret (1886-1973)   Known primarily as the editor of the *Little Review*, a Modernist experimental journal (whose editorship she shared with her lover Jane Heap), and as a force fighting censorship (especially as it pertained to James Joyce's *Ulysses*). Anderson and her lover Georgette LEBLANC were devotees of the mystics Georgei Ivanovich Gurdjieff (1872/7-1949) and Pyotr Demainovitch Ouspensky (1878-1947). Gurdjieff was the founder of a metaphysical tradition sometimes referred to as the Fourth Way School, with Ouspensky being the disciple who disseminated his ideas. Among their teachings was the belief that humans possess not one but four brains or minds and that one must engage in meditation and kindred practices if one is to fully empower and balance the four. Anderson wrote in spirited terms of Georgette Leblanc, "I felt at once – as if a prophecy were being made to me – 'There is something perfect in her soul.' For twenty-one years I never saw Georgette Leblanc do anything, never heard her say anything, that did not spring from this perfection. It is a quality, I think, that arises in the creative mind."

Andro   "Man," an Amazonian companion of the Amazon Queen PENTHESILEIA during the Trojan War.

Androphonos   "Slayer of Men." A black-skinned manifestation of the Greek goddess APHRODITE who ritually castrates her male lovers, linking her to the Greco-Roman cult of CYBELE and ATTIS. In this aspect, Aphrodite is sometimes considered transgendered. Her skin color suggests an African origin.

Anemone   This flower, especially in its red variety, is considered a sacred attribute of the beautiful youth ADONIS, who was loved by APHRODITE (Roman VENUS), ASTARTE, PERSEPHONE, and DIONYSUS. Upon being fatally castrated by a wild boar, the blood of Adonis was transformed into anemones, which preserve the memory of the beautiful young man.

Anethus   Young man of Roman mythology who loved another young man named PAPAVER ("Poppy"). When Anethus died, he was transformed into an ANISE plant. His memory was preserved in garlands given by homoerotically inclined lovers to each other in ancient Rome.

Angakkuq (or **Angakok, Angaqoq**)   Derived from *anga*, meaning "elder" or "ancient one," the name given to gender variant or third gender male shamans of the Inuit (Eskimo) of North America. Among the Inuit, becoming a transformed shaman is often viewed as a process which includes several relatively distinct phases. An early Russian explorer explained that among the Koniag Inuit, "When father or mother regard their son as feminine in his bearing, they will often dedicate him in earliest childhood to the vocation of Achnutschik [*angakkuq*, gender variant shaman]." Such children were "highly prized" by the Koniag Inuit. They were dressed and reared as girls by their mothers until they were fifteen, when they were given to an older man, a tribal leader or *anqakkuq* to focus on the process of becoming a shaman. Metamorphosis might also commence when a deity or spirit visited the young male in a dream or otherwise altered state. Among the Koniag, this sometimes occurred when a KE'LET spirit visited a young man in his dream and told him he was destined to become an *angakkuq*. The process would continue with the *angakkuq* being instructed in Shamanism by an elder *angakkuq* or shamaness. Koniag *angakkuq* not only practiced the arts of divination, magic, and healing, but also instructed young women in etiquette and dance. Their most important task, however, was journeying to the submarine abode of the goddess SEDNA to serve as an intercessory between her and the people. The *anqakkuq* would often begin his journey while naked, being bound, and having artificial wings tied to his back. Passing through the regions of the dead and places of terrible iciness and boiling water and cauldrons of ferocious seals, he would finally arrive at the dwelling of the Goddess. He would find her sitting inside, covered with dirt, her hair matted with the blood of slain and sacrificed animals. He would comb her hair and speak softly to her, and she would forgive his people for slaughtering too many seals, would tell him of things to come, and would grant his people's wishes. He would then return to his village to share the Goddess' words with the people. The *angakkuq* often shared long-term loving relationships with other males.

Angamunggi   Among Australians, a transgendered rainbow-serpent revered as a giver of life.

Angel   "Guardian angel I speak with eyes / that are rivers of words only you / can hear," gay Canadian poet Victor Borsa (b. 1931) writes in "I Speak with My Angel." Borsa's poem appears in Winston Leyland's *Angels of the Lyre: A Gay Poetry Anthology* (1975). In his introduction to the anthology, Leyland confesses, "I have been, like Jean COCTEAU, a life-long angelophile," noting, "Interestingly, there are a disproportionate number of contemporary Gay poems with angel themes or motifs." While the angel, typically an androgynous figure (there are of course exceptions), is frequently found in artworks (including literature, painting, music, and film) blending the male homoerotic and the spiritual, it does not appear to be a key icon in works linking lesbian desire and the sacred. This is somewhat surprising, in that the angel is profoundly rooted in Goddess Reverence, which a myriad women-loving women have referenced in their arts for millennia. IRIS, the Greek goddess of the RAINBOW, and ISIS, the Egyptian goddess of magic, fertility, and death-rebirth, are only two among many female deities depicted as winged, angelic figures. The very term "angel," as "*angelos*," may have first been used as a name for the Greek goddess HECATE. It was later used as a surname of the goddess ARTEMIS at Syracuse. Both of these goddesses were especially known for their rejection of heterosexual marriage, with the latter also being renowned as a lover of women. Other often-winged beings, such as the FURIES and the GORGONS, are associated with transgenderism. Despite these early associations, however, few references to angels occur in works of female-centered intimacy. In terms of male homoeroticism, the angel's iconographic resonance may be traced to EROS, the winged god of erotic passion in Greek myth and religion, and particularly to the Erotes, a multiplied Eros embracing himself, HIMERUS, and POTHOS. The Erotes are typically portrayed as nude, muscular, winged men with androgynous faces and beautiful hair; they often carry gifts associated with homoerotic courtship in ancient Greece, such as a HARE. In her masterpiece *Prolegomena to the Study of Greek Religion* (1908), classical scholar Jane HARRISON observes of Eros and the Erotes, "The Eros of the vase-painter is the love, not untouched by passion, of man for man, and these . . . Erotes help us to understand that to the Greek mind such loves were serious and beautiful." Other winged figures, as well as figures linked to wings and flight, associated with homoeroticism and occurring in classical myth, religion, and magic include ADONAI, GANYMEDE, HERMES, and ZEPHYRUS. In "The Omphalos Myth and Hebrew Religion" (1970), Biblical scholar Samuel Terrien suggests that the figure of the angel, especially as cherub, "may have been . . . related both to the . . . Magna Mater [i.e. the Great Mother] and to the ritual of cultic male prostitution." Terrien is referring specifically to the QEDESHIM, the HIERODULE-priests of the Canaanite goddess ATHIRAT. Terrien infers that despite the persecution of the followers of Athirat, particularly of her priestesses and the qedeshim, much of the lore and iconography of the Canaanite faith was appropriated by Judaism and later by Christianity and Islam. If observed from this perspective, the Biblical tale of the angels arriving at SODOM to purify that city seems especially fascinating. The angels' arrival at Sodom has inspired numerous works of art imbued with homoerotic-spiritual sensibility, including Gustave MOREAU's painting *The Angels of Sodom*; James Watson and Melville Webber's experimental gay film *Lot in Sodom* (1933); and Saint Ours's novella *Un Ange à Sodome* (1973), the powerfully moving tale of an angel who, on orders from a vengeful God, sets out to destroy Sodom, only to find its culture sophisticated, its inhabitants beautiful and wise, and his heart captured by a mortal male dwelling there. A lost, perhaps destroyed, surrealistic tragic drama by the homoerotically inclined Spanish poet Federico García LORCA, *La destrucción de Sodoma*, apparently intended to portray the angels as beautiful and as falling in love with the men of Sodom, according to his friend, the actor Luis Sáenz. According to A. Sahuquillo (1991), the play was also supposed to show the Sodomites being punished for sodomy and Lot escaping punishment for engaging in incest with his daughters. The archangels GABRIEL, MICHAEL, and RAPHAEL have not escaped the homoerotic gaze, as evidenced in the poetry of Lorca. In the European Middle Ages, the transgendered, possibly lesbian JEANNE D'ARC (Joan of Arc) was visited by angels, and in the early seventeenth century, her sister in spirit Benedetta CARLINI, abbess of the Theatine nuns of Pescia, Italy, was similarly visited. In terms of premodern female-centered literature, one of the most memorable references to angels occurs in Katherine Philips's (1631-1664) poem "Friendship's Mystery: To My Dearest Lucasia," in which the poet, insisting that "There's a Religion in our Love," describes herself and her beloved Lucasia "As Angels." In the early nineteenth century, both the transgenderism and the potentially bi- or pansexual character of the figure of the angel were celebrated in Balzac's 1835 novel *SERAPHITA*. Nineteenth-century fascination with the androgynous angel was, however, coupled with fear, especially among those surrendering to internalized homophobia, like the poet Lionel Johnson (1867-1902), the cousin of Lord Alfred Douglas (1870-1945). Johnson, who converted to Catholicism near the end of his life, betrayed his former friends who were homoerotically inclined, describing Oscar WILDE as the "destroyer" of Douglas's soul. In "Dark Angel," Johnson portrayed homoerotic desire as a "Malicious Angel" of "aching lust" bent on obliterating the world. In the early twentieth century, the homosexual writer and filmmaker

Jean COCTEAU in 1925 was visited, or rather embodied or possessed by, an angel. In the midst of a vision induced by opium, Cocteau became convinced that a brand name of an elevator in his friend Picasso's building revealed the name of the angel – Heurtebise. This angel demanded that Cocteau write, or rather channel, a poem, not surprisingly titled "L'Ange Heurtebise." The poem suggests an experience of roughly consensual SADOMASOCHISM, with the angel leaping on the poet "with incredible / Brutality"; it does not take a genius to decipher the symbolism of the angel's "heavy / male sceptre." In his brilliant biography of *Cocteau* (1970), Francis Steegmuller relates: "The angel is a figure that Cocteau had liked to use from the time he introduced it into his wartime preface to an airplane company's brochure . . . Gabriel was one of Cocteau's favorite angels: the Annunciation is the theme of several early poems . . . the poet constantly participates in the announcement of his own [artistic] pregnancy." Steegmuller observes that Cocteau thought of his beloved Raymond Radiguet (1904-1923), who died of typhoid at a very young age, as an angel. In March 1925, Cocteau said of him, "I knew he would die quickly . . . I respect his angelic exit." Two decades later, the contemporary musician Ned Rorem (b. 1923) set one of Parker Tyler's (1904-1974) most beautiful poems to music – "Dawn Angel" – which includes the lines "An angel sang from the highest place in my heart / with a voice thinner than light / yet an arm of dawn." In "L. A. Nocturne: The Angels," the homosexual Mexican poet Xavier Villaurrutia (1903-1950) depicted men – primarily young hustlers – seeking erotic encounters with other men as angels who have "come down to earth / on invisible ladders" to "sing the songs" of men's "ancient mysteries / of flesh, blood, and desire." In the early 1970s, a group mixing androgyny (expressed in "genderfuck" drag), pansexuality, radical politics, spirituality, and performance emerged in San Francisco, its members calling themselves the "Angels of Light." The Angels included Hibiscus, Coco Luna Vega, Pristine Condition, and many others. One of their most memorable operatic musical performances, which typically embraced elements of ritual such as the burning of incense, was the carnivalesque *Holy Cow*, inspired by the mythos of the Hindu deities KRISHNA and RADHA. During this same period, Winston Leyland described "Gay Poets" as "Androgynous Angels / Bastard Angels / Angels in Drag / Angels of Desolation / Angels of Liberation." In the 1980s, poems whose authors included the African-American gay writer Essex Hemphill (*Conditions*, "III," "XIV," 1986) and the Chicana woman-loving writer Gloria ANZALDUA ("My Black Angelos," in *Borderlands*, 1987) continued to reflect the queering of the angel. The angel plays a central role in Tony Kushner's epic drama *Angels in America: a Gay Fantasia on American Themes* (1992), and among the most important writers in the current explosion in metaphysical literature focusing on angels is gay US writer

Andrew RAMER, whose works include *Ask Your Angels: A Practical Guide to Working with Angels to Enrich Your Life* (with Alma Daniel, 1992) and *Angel Answers: A Joyful Guide to Creating Heaven on Earth* (1995).

Anger, Kenneth (1930-)   US avant-garde filmmaker and author of *Hollywood Babylon*. Anger's career began when he was cast as the changeling prince in Max Reinhardt's and William Dieterle's elaborate film production of *A Midsummer Night's Dream* in 1934, when he was only four years old. At the time, he was studying dance with Theodore Kosloff, who had worked with Sergei DIAGHILEV in the Ballet Russes. Anger, by the age of seven, had begun making his own experimental films. As a teenager, he rejected Christianity and began to study the works of the ritual magician Aleister CROWLEY. He began to think of himself as a disciple of Crowley and as a magician-in-training and came to see film as a potentially magical medium and the camera as a kind of magic wand. He patterned his films upon ritual structures, employed magical symbols in them, and wove spells into them. The type of ritual on which he focused was that of the invocation of the deity or Holy Guardian Angel into the person of the magus or priestess. He adopted the fairy trickster PUCK as a logo and chose a focus a great deal of his work on Lucifer, whom he viewed as a fusion of the rebellious SATAN and a bringer of illumination. Indeed, critic Robert A. Haller has suggested that in Anger's cinematic spirituality, Crowley, Puck, and Lucifer form a sort of trinity. From his earliest films, Anger has explored the interrelationship of transgenderism, pansexuality, and the realms of magic, myth, and dream. *Fireworks* (1947) centers on a young man's homoerotic dream of a sailor, while *Inauguration of the Pleasure Dome* (1954) is a fusion of pagan and masque, with celebrants/actors embodying/enacting ASTARTE (the bisexual writer Anaïs Nin), GANYMEDE, HECATE (Anger himself), ISIS, KALI, PAN, and SHIVA. *Inauguration* ends with Shiva transforming all the others into "spirits of pure energy." Anger's most blatantly homoerotic-ritualistic film is *Scorpio Rising* (1963), a surrealistic vision of queer leathermen engaging in a rite of SADOMASCOCHISM, celebrating male aggression, sexuality, and death to the beat of late 1950s rock 'n' roll songs. *Lucifer Rising* (1966, 1970-1980) is much more reflective of the hippie subculture of the late 1960s and early 1970s and a vision more akin to that of Wicca or Neopaganism. Haller descries *Lucifer Rising* – which includes pop singer Marianne Faithfull – as a "celebration, and an invocation, of the power of Magick to summon the forces of nature." The film focuses on the ritualistic encounter of the Egyptian deities Isis and OSIRIS. *Invocation of My Demon Brother* (1969) approaches a celebration of the Satanic, with High Priest of Satanism Anton Szandor LaVey enacting Satan and with music by Mick Jagger of the Rolling Stones. Of his fascination with magic, spirits, and the like, Anger relates, "One thing I've found is that my film is about demons . . . I have to work fairly fast because they tend to come and go . . . The devil is always other people's gods . . . Lucifer is the Rebel Angel . . . His message is that the Key of Joy is Disobedience."

Anise   The small, delicate flowers of this aromatic plant were employed in headwreaths worn by Lesbian women in the *thiasos*, or religious household, of SAPPHO in rites honoring the GRACES. The Graces, linked to the ocean, bestowed persons with the quality of grace and presided over banquets. Also associated with ANETHUS, a young man of Roman mythology who loved another young man named PAPAVER (Poppy), or who was loved by a male deity, and who was, upon dying, transformed into an anise plant. For this reason, anise appears to have been among the flowers, herbs, and other plants comprising a garland given by a male lover to his beloved in ancient Rome. In the poet Virgil's *Second Eclogue*, the shepherd Corydon offers such a garland to Alexis, a young man with whom he has fallen in love.

Anog Ite (also **Double-Faced Woman**)   "Double Faced Woman" of the Lakota and Oglala Plains people of North America, goddess of crafts and patron of female TWO-SPIRIT persons. A daughter of First Man and First Woman, she was married to the male deity of the wind and was lover to the male deity of the sun. Because her grandfather, the sky god, was upset with her for taking the sun as a lover, he transformed her into a double-faced woman, one face beautiful, the other not – at least not to men. One night, Anog Ite had a vision. She saw in it a garment decorated with the quills of a porcupine. She asked that a porcupine be brought to her. From its quills, which she dyed, she created a garment of great beauty and power. Anog Ite appeared in the dreams of young women who were destined to become two-spirits (persons who typically represent an alternate or third gender, perform tasks of the opposite sex, have intimate relations with the same sex, and perform spiritual work). In these dreams, she would teach them, among other things, how to quill. Quilling is used to decorate such things as shields, tipis, and buffalo robes. Sam D. Gill and Irene F. Sullivan explain that quilling is not merely a craft, but also a healing and a magical art: "When a person is ill, sees a bad vision, or has an intuition of trouble, a friend may vow to make and quill for him or her a shirt, moccasins, buffalo robe, and leggings. Making these items also brings purity, strength, health, and prosperity to the quiller." Gill and Sullivan also relate that quilling is "considered to be in conflict with the traditional roles of wife and mother, leading the dreamer to choose a Lesbian lifestyle (which would leave her free to develop her skills as a craftswoman)."

Anselm of Canterbury, Doctor, Bishop, Saint (c. 1033-1109)   Christian monk, bishop, archbishop, and theologian. Born in Italy, as a young man he entered the Benedictine monastery at Bec, in northwestern France, becoming abbot in 1078. Bec soon became renowned as a center of learning. Anselm was later appointed archbishop of Canterbury, England by the homoerotically inclined King WILLIAM II RUFUS (c. 1056-1100), whom Anselm despised. Of Anselm's own sexuality, Paul Halsall writes in the *Calendar of Lesbian, Gay, Bisexual, and Transgender Saints* (1994), "I make no claims about Anselm's sexual practices, but I am sure he was what we would now call gay." Anselm shared passionate friendships with a number of his male pupils and other men. To one he wrote, "Wherever you go my love follows you, and wherever I remain my desire embraces you . . . How then could I forget you? He who is imprisoned on my heart like a seal on wax – how could he be removed from my memory? Without saying a word I know that you love me, and without my saying a word, you know that I love you." St Anselm is fêted on April 21.

Ant   In Greek mythology, the goddess ATHENA fell in love with a young woman named MYRMEX, known especially for her industriousness. When, however, Myrmex claimed to have invented the plow, which in truth Athena had done, the goddess punished her by transforming her into an ant. This was an odd punishment, however, since ants were "honored as holy creatures" among Myrmex's people. In this form, Myrmex symbolizes "patience, endurance, and diligence."

Antenna   In the visionary, lesbian-centered cosmos of Monique Wittig and Sande Zeig in *Lesbian Peoples* (1979), an "invisible organ that one has at birth which allows for instantaneous perception of the possible alliances between Lesbians." In her 1960 poem "Of Forbidden Love, " lesbian poet Elsa GIDLOW speaks of antennae in this context: "Antennae: exploring: / Are you there? / Are you shadow / Or fleshed being / Of the long seeking? / Are you she?"

Antheus   Two Greek heroes were given this name. The first was the son of a king of Ionia who lived at Assesos and was loved by the god HERMES. The second was a Trojan warrior who was loved by Deiphobus and by the latter's brother PARIS, both Trojan princes. Paris allegedly killed Antheus accidentally during a discus match. When Antheus died, he was transformed into a flower. He is remembered in the English word "anthology," which literally means a "gathering of flowers." It seems likely that stories of older lovers killing younger lovers in this manner, as that of APOLLO and HYACINTHUS, may actually refer to a symbolic death-rebirth ritual representing a transition from late adolescence to adulthood, as a number of these tales also contain the image of the flower, linking the life cycle of the vegetable world to that of humans. B. Sergent (1986) writes: "Hence he [i.e. Antheus] belongs to the same family as Hyacinthus, CYPARISSUS, NARCISSUS, CARPUS, etc., all heroes for whom the plant kingdom signifies initiatory death and resurrection. Antheus was certainly the founder of initiatory homosexuality in Assesos."

Anticleia   Not only the mother of Odysseus but at another time an AMAZON, or woman warrior, and a companion of the goddess ARTEMIS/DIANA. Callimachus (fl. c. 250 BCE) relates that Artemis loved Anticleia deeply; he describes Anticleia and the other Amazon companions of the goddess as handsome women wearing "the gallant bow and arrow-holding quivers on their shoulders; their right shoulders bore the quiver strap, and always the right breast showed bare."

Antilochus (or **Antilochos**)   Son of King Nestor of Pylos, Antilochus was a renowned runner, charioteer, and warrior in the Trojan War. He is remembered for being a comrade-lover to ACHILLES and Patroclus in a triadic relationship. When Patroclus was slain in battle, it was Antilochus who brought Achilles the tragic news, and it was he who restrained Achilles from committing suicide on hearing of his lover's death. Not long after, Antilochus himself was slain in battle, leaving Achilles devastated. Antilochus, dying so young, soon became a symbol of children who die before their parents. Legend has it that his bones were mingled ritually with those of Achilles and Patroclus, and that the spirits of the three lovers lived out an otherworldly existence on the island of LEUKÉ, feasting and joining in mock combat.

Antinous (c. 110-130)   Beloved of the Roman emperor HADRIAN (76-138) who was divinized upon his death and whose worship continued until at least the end of the fourth century, when it was outlawed by Christina forces. Born in Bithynia on the northwest coast of Asia Minor, Antinous appears to have encountered Hadrian when he was about thirteen years old. At the time, the two entered into a loving relationship. Both the Emperor and his beloved appear to have been profoundly drawn to spiritual exploration. In 125, Hadrian had begun his initiation into the ELEUSINIAN MYSTERIES of DEMETER and PERSEPHONE, and in 128, Antinous accompanied him to begin his own initiation. In 129 and 130, the two continued their spiritual quest in Egypt, having extensive conversations with Egyptian priests and apparently participating in rites centering on ISIS and OSIRIS. In autumn 129, they probably witnessed the *Passion of Osiris*, a ritual-drama held on the bank of the Nile commemorating that god's death and rebirth or resurrection. In the summer of 130, Antinous and Hadrian were almost killed when they were attacked by a ferocious lion they had been pursuing. The lion had been ravaging the area to the west of Alexandria, and the two were determined to capture it. When it leapt on them, Hadrian managed to free himself in order to slay the animal and save Antinous's life. Sometime between that episode and the last half of October, Antinous and Hadrian may have been told by an Egyptian priest, possibly a diviner of the cult of THOTH, that Hadrian's death was imminent unless some great sacrifice was offered to the gods. This would not have surprised them, since Hadrian had been sick on and off for quite a while. It has been suggested that a priest then told Antinous in private that Hadrian's life would be spared only if he sacrificed himself willingly. He apparently followed this advice, as he drowned, apparently in an act of suicide, in the Nile on or near October 28, 130, at the time of the Passion of Osiris. The body of Antinous was mummified as if it were that of a pharaoh. Five months later, he was declared a god, offerings were made to him, games were established in his honor, and the city of Antinoopolis was dedicated to him – all this in Egypt. Within several years, the worship of Antinous had spread throughout the Roman Empire, with more than twenty-five temples dedicated to him, not to mention countless statues and coins bearing his image. Antinous, his followers believed, had sacrificed himself not only so that Hadrian might survive, but also, and more importantly, that Egypt and Rome might survive (the Empire was being attacked on various fronts at the time, and apparently there had been food shortages in Egypt due to the failure of the Nile to rise at its appointed time). More than this – and we can be sure that both Hadrian and the Greek, Roman, and Egyptian priests and priestesses he knew were acutely aware of their shaky position at the time – Antinous represented a "pagan" savior deity who might be held up to Christians insisting upon the destruction of paganism and the enforcement of Christianity. Antinous was, by way of his life experience, poised to become a syncretic deity: born in Bithynia, he had become the lover of a Roman emperor, with whom he had been initiated into the Eleusinian Mysteries, only to meet his sacrificial death in Egypt. Antinous came to be syncretized with the Egyptian Osiris as well as with the Greek deities DIONYSUS and HERMES, all gods associated with eroticism and with death and rebirth or resurrection. Antinous also came to be identified with GANYMEDE, the beloved of ZEUS. Shortly after his death, the reddish LOTUS growing beside the Nile was deemed sacred to Antinous, in memory of the blood he had spilled so that his lovers and others might live. The lotuses were woven into garlands and placed on his images and on the heads of those who won musical and athletic contests held in his honor. A constellation neighboring Aquila was also named after him; the constellation, also referred to as "Ganymede" and the "Cupbearer," speaks to his identity as the Beloved of God, as Aquila (the Eagle) represents the

form taken by Zeus when he carried Ganymede to Olympus. Little information has survived, or has yet been discovered, concerning the actual rites of Antinous. It seems fairly certain, however, that the delivery of oracles and cultic homoeroticism played key roles in his worship. Christians despised Antinous and were determined to destroy his cult. Clement of Alexandria (c. 150-220) was one of the cult's most vociferous opponents: "Another fresh divinity was created in Egypt . . . when the Roman King solemnly elevated to the rank of god his favorite whose beauty was unequaled. He consecrated Antinous in the same way that Zeus consecrated Ganymede . . . and to-day men observe the sacred nights of Antinous, which were really shameful . . . Why do you tell the story of his beauty? Beauty is a shameful thing when it has been blighted by outrage." Nevertheless, the worship of Antinous survived well into the fourth century, and his image has continued to inspire artists including painters, sculptors, and poets, into the present. In the eighteenth century, Cardinal Allesandro ALBANI, Johann Joachim WINCKELMANN, and others appear to have secretly revived his worship at Rome. In the nineteenth and early twentieth centuries, his tale was reclaimed by numerous poets including John Addington SYMONDS and Fernando Pessos (1888-1935). In "Antinous" (1891), the homoerotically inclined poet and essayist Charles Kains-Jackson (1857-1933) writes: "Glory throughout the world thy conquering name / Had celebrated, and through ages sung / The Asian youth whose cult's melodious flame / Lends bitter-sweetness to the poet's tongue."

Antiope   One of the queens of the AMAZONS. Antiope was abducted by THESEUS, whom she later married, making her the sole Amazon to wed a male. She was the mother of Hippolytus. Wittig and Zeig (1979) suggest that prior to her abduction and marriage, she may have been the lover of another Amazonian queen, HIPPOLYTA, although the latter is usually described as her sister.

Antony, Mark (Marcus Antonius, 82-30 BCE)   Roman ruler, bisexual in contemporary Euro-western terms, who loved not only Cleopatra (69-30 BCE), the renowned queen of Egypt, but also a number of men, including (according to the Jewish historian Josephus), ARISTOBULUS III (Jonathan; d. 35 BCE). Aristobulus was a high priest of Judaism and the brother-in-law of the Biblical Herod Antipater, the Great (c. 73-4 BCE). Antony was a worshipper of DIONYSUS and, moreover, believed himself to be an incarnation of the god. As the companion of Cleopatra, herself an embodiment of the goddess ISIS, Antony also came to see himself as an incarnation of OSIRIS; in Hellenistic Egypt, Dionysus was among the Greek gods identified or syncretized with Osiris. When Antony was betrayed by his fellow Romans, losing the Battle of Actium (31 BCE), he had a vision indicating that the god(s) had abandoned him; shortly thereafter, he and Cleopatra committed suicide. The man-loving Alexandrian/Greek poet C. P. CAVAFY in "The God Forsakes Antony," writes, "as a last enjoyment listen to the sounds, / the exquisite instruments of the mystical troupe, / and bid her farewell, the Alexandria you are losing."

Anubis (or **Anoubis**)   Jackal-headed god of the Underworld in Egyptian religion and later in Greco-Egyptian magic and in Gnosticism, invoked in an ancient lesbian love spell found in the *Greek Magical Papyri* as "Anoubis, the pious herald of the dead."

Anzaldúa, Gloria (1942-)   Chicana (Mexican-American) *patlache* (in Nahuatl, woman-loving, often transgendered female) writer, editor, illustrator, and instructor, born in south Texas and now living in northern California. While many of those who have analyzed and interpreted Anzaldúa's writings have ignored their spiritual dimension, choosing to focus only on their social and political aspects, it is nevertheless the case that religious, mystical, mythical, supernatural, and psychic elements pervade her work. Her family members were devout Catholics. When Anzaldúa's father died, she was instructed to mourn for three years; this meant dressing in somber hues and avoiding television and other forms of entertainment. One of her grandmothers was known as a healer. From her as well as from other family members and friends, Anzaldúa learned much about healing with plants as well as about supernatural figures dwelling in the valley of south Texas and the Southwest, foremost among them being La Llorona, a banshee-like figure who wails in the night for her lost children. She also learned to protect herself from *mal aires*, evil winds that cause illness, and *mal ojo*, curses dealt by envious eyes. Bridging Catholicism and *curanderismo* were such folk figures as the Virgin of Guadalupe, a source of inspiration for Anzaldúa and many other queer-identified persons. With her scholarly persona forming quite early, Anzaldúa soon began to interpret the religious and folk wisdom she was acquiring in the light of literary works, immersing herself in Gothic fictions, Christian mysticism, Aztec and Mayan mythologies. Later, during her college years, she found time to study the works of Jane Roberts (known for CHANNELING the entity Seth), Carlos Castaneda, the Theosophists (including Madame BLAVATSKY), and Aleister CROWLEY, at the same time enriching her knowledge of the Latin American aesthetic tradition of magical realism (including Borges, Cortazar, and Garcia Marquez) and of *nagualismo* (indigenous Mexican shamanism). From these and other sources, she began weaving her own eclectic spiritual path. This dimension of her life and work was greatly enhanced by her move from Texas to San Francisco in the late 1970s. There, she studied with Eastern spiritual masters and with women involved in Goddess Reverence, Witchcraft (or

Wicca), Women's Spirituality, and the psychic arts, including Angeles Arrien (a scholar of TAROT), Tamara DIAGHILEV, and STARHAWK. She also received potent, enlightening divinatory readings from Yoruba-Lucumí priestess Luisah Teish. In the later 1980s and early 1990s, Anzaldúa became somewhat withdrawn in terms of participation in spiritual groups. This shift resulted from several factors, among which were a much more intense focus on her writing, adapting to living with diabetes, and pressure exerted by political activists and social constructionist theorists to "tone down" the spiritual aspect of her work. Nevertheless, Anzaldúa continued her private spiritual practice, sharing her burgeoning wisdom in this arena with those nearest to her, who found it both disturbing and bemusing that those few critics daring to discuss the spiritual dimension of her work would speak only of her use of "metaphors" of ancient traditions, unaware of, or else disapproving of, the altars placed in every room of her house. During this period and continuing into the mid-1990s, Anzaldúa has nevertheless continued to imbue her work with spiritual elements. One of the ways in which she is currently giving voice to her spirituality is in children's books, her first two being *Friends from the Other Side: Amigos del otro lado* (1993), in which a *curandera* is a central character, and *Prietita and the Ghost Woman* (1996), which depicts a girl's encounter with La Llorona. Anzaldúa's other works – all of which speak of the spiritual dimension of life as well as the psychological and political – include: *This Bridge Called My Back: Writings by Radical Women of Color* (1981), co-edited with Cherrie MORAGA; *Borderlands: La Frontera: The New Mestiza* (1987), a postmodern meditation combining poetry and prose; and a second anthology, *Making Face, Making Soul / Haciendo Caras: Creative and Critical Perspectives by Feminists of Color* (1990). In *Borderlands*, she writes: "I've always been aware that there is a greater power than the conscious I. That power is my inner self, the entity that is the sum total of all my reincarnations, the godwoman in me I call *Antigua, mi Diosa*, the divine within, *Coatlicue-Cihuacoatl-TLAZOLTEOTL-Tonantzin-Coatlalopeuh-Guadalupe* – they are one." For Anzaldúa, the spiritual power of expressing queerness resides in its potential to liquify traditional boundaries of sexuality and gender – as well as other boundaries – thereby freeing the psyche or spirit of oppressive roles. Anzaldúa sees great power in the bonding of queer persons into a tribe or tribes to heal and transform the dominant culture. For Anzaldúa, the term "queer" embraces not only lesbians, gay men, bisexuals, and transgendered persons, but also others perceived as different, or who self-identify as being different from, "the norm." It should be noted here that she first used the term "queer" in this way in or around 1976, developing the definition in the early 1980s though she is seldom recognized as an early user of the term as it is currently employed. Also not recognized is that her use of the term embraced rather than rejected the realm of the spirit. In her theory as well as in her poetry and fiction, Anzaldúa defies the dualistic and reductionist paradigms of social constructionism and essentialism as relating to queer-identified persons, viewing both of these concepts as Euro-western, neither of them very useful in speaking of persons whose cultural systems include ceremonial roles for same-sex inclined and transgendered persons. The goddesses, gods, and spirits are "real," Anzaldúa insists, as queer energy is "real." They exist as energies that choose to embody us, or that we will to embody. Rooted in traditions like that of Native American TWO-SPIRIT shamans and transgendered priests and priestesses of Aztec deities, queer power and wisdom are to be discovered in "*loquería*," or "craziness," which is in truth a kind of holy madness available primarily to those who "live in the borderlands." She suggests that those most oppressed by the dominant culture are often those who possess the most potent form of this psychic "faculty," "*la facultad*," observing, "When we're up against the wall, when we have all sorts of oppressions coming at us, we are forced to develop this faculty." *La facultad* is "the capacity to see in surface phenomena the meaning of deeper realities . . . It is an instant 'sensing' . . . an acute awareness . . . that communicates in images and symbols." "*Cuando vives en la frontera*" ["When you live in the borderlands"], Anzaldúa chants, "you're a . . . / forerunner of a new race, / half and half – both woman and man, neither – / a new gender / . . . / To survive in the Borderlands / you must live *sin fronteras* [without borders] / be a crossroads."

Aotis Goddess of dawn invoked by women participating in what appear to have been lesbian union ceremonies in ancient Greece.

Ape Animal symbolic of wisdom and trickery in ancient Egypt, Greece, and Rome, allied with the gods THOTH and HERMES/MERCURY. For the ancient Aztecs, the ape, linked to TRICKSTERS and performing artists (especially singers, dancers, and jugglers), was placed on the astrological calendar as a day-sign of the West and was allied with the god XOCHIPILLI.

Aphrodite Goddess of love and later also of war, also known as the Lady of Byblos and the Queen of Heaven, and frequently identified with ASTARTE and VENUS. Believed by some to be of African origin, Aphrodite was worshipped at various times by the Egyptians, Canaanites, Phoenicians, Greeks, Romans, and even by heretical Hebrews. As a manifestation of the life-bestowing aspect of the Great Goddess, she is often depicted as a nude woman holding her breasts or raising her arms above her head. She sometimes wears a bird mask and is occasionally flanked by male goats. She may also appear as a gender variant goddess, as a woman warrior crowned with horns and driving a chariot, or as an hermaphrodite with female breasts and an erect phallus. In this aspect, she is known as Bearded Aphrodite, is identified with APHRODITOS and HERMAPHRODITUS, and is associated not only with the planet Venus but also with the MOON. Above all a goddess of love, Aphrodite was nicknamed Philommedes, "genital-loving." According to K. J. Dover, the Greek term *aphrodisia*, meaning the "things of Aphrodite," refers to sexual intercourse. She is the patron of both hierodulic priestesses and secular prostitutes. In SAPPHO's poetry, she becomes a patron of Lesbian women. In the THIASOS, or religious household, of Sappho on the island of Lesbos, priestesses and initiates honored Aphrodite – especially as the combined deity Aphrodite-HERA – and Sappho herself (after the poet's death) by singing and dancing. They circled an exquisite ivory statue of, and an altar dedicated to, the goddess. As Aphrodite Anosia, she also may have presided over rites of Lesbian sadomasochism at her festival in Thessaly. She was further called Androphonos, "Man-Slayer." In this aspect, she may have presided over rites of castration. This manifestation may be traced to her birth, brought about by the coming together of the maternal sea and the severed genitals of her father, Chronos (Cronus). Through her association with the castrated Chronos as well as her own gender variant aspects, Aphrodite becomes linked to gender variant males. She is also the mother of Hermaphroditus, the very emblem of gender variance or transgendered identity. Aphrodite's primary consort is the beautiful youth ADONIS – also loved by Persephone and Dionysus – whose life would end when he was castrated by a wild boar. Paris, another of Aphrodite's favorites, was, despite his role in the Trojan War, said to be "unwarlike and effeminate." He was blessed by the goddess with a retinue of eunuchs. Aphrodite is – especially as Aphrodite Urania – a patron of men-loving men. K. J. Dover notes that in the poetry of Theognis, the beloved is considered a "gift of Aphrodite." One of the goddess's loyal servants is EROS, a patron of homoerotic love. In nineteenth-century French bohemian circles, lesbian women were poetically compared to priestesses of Aphrodite, with the expression "*prêtresse de Venus* [Venus being the goddess's Roman incarnation]" becoming synonymous with "lesbian." In a survey of almost six hundred lesbians taken in 1989 and 1990, JoAnn Loulan (1990) found that among seven goddess archetypes from which the women could choose to identify both themselves and their lovers – Aphrodite, ARTEMIS/DIANA, ATHENA, DEMETER, Hera, Hestia, and PERSEPHONE – Aphrodite rated second, with Artemis being first. Loulan also discovered that in some contexts Aphrodite and Artemis may represent a lesbian "femme-butch" couple.

Aphroditus (or **Aphroditos**)   Hermaphroditic deity of Greco-Roman antiquity identified with the Bearded Aphrodite and with HERMAPHRODITUS. Aphroditus is depicted as bearded and as wearing feminine attire. From his/her garment, an erect phallus looms. At rites honoring Aphroditus, men dressed in feminine and women in masculine attire.

Apollinaris, Saint (fl. c. 450 CE)   While her actual existence is the subject of controversy, the story goes that Apollinaris was a young woman who assumed a male identity and, as a monk, became a disciple of Saint Macarius. Apollinaris is remembered on January 1 or 5.

Apollo   God of music, dance, poetry, fine arts, philosophy, science, physical education, and the healing power of the sun. Among his many male lovers were: ADMETUS, AMYCLAS, BRANCHUS, CYPARISSUS, DAPHNIS, HYACINTHUS, HYLAS, Iapis, ORPHEUS, Paros, Phorbas, Potneius, TROILUS, Tymnius, and ZACYNTHUS. As the lover of the ram-god CARNEIUS, Apollo was fused with the former and as such was revered by the COURETES. He is the brother and in certain aspects the male compliment of his Amazonian sister ARTEMIS/DIANA.

Apollonius of Tyana (c. 4 BCE–c. 96 CE)   Neo-Pythagorean philosopher of Cappadocia, wandering holy man, and worker of miracles. Most of what we know comes from the *Life* written by Flavius Philostratus in the third century CE, who implies that he was homoerotically inclined. Apollonius of Tyana, believed to have been born to a wealthy Greek family in Anatolia, was sent to school at Tarsus where he became a Pythagorean. He left for Babylonia, where he studied with magi, continuing on to India, probably studying with fakirs and Brahmans. He was in Rome during the reign of Nero and represented a "counterblast to Christianity." Condemned as a quack by the Church, he was charged with "magic and sedition" in 93 CE. Apollonius of Tyana, who as a youth may have served as a male HIERODULE-priest in a temple of ASKLEPIUS, founded a mystery school at Ephesus. Ironically, while apparently serving as a hierodule himself, he nevertheless condemned the GALLI, the male hierodules of the goddess CYBELE. After his death in 93 CE, he was said to have ascended to the heavens. His life inspired the twentieth-century Greek poet C. P. CAVAFY to write "If Dead Indeed."

Apostle   In Christianity, a term used to refer to a messenger of God or JESUS. In nineteenth-century French bohemian circles, homoerotically inclined men were nicknamed "Apostles of the anus." The poet Collé wrote: " Ah! in all of Christendom / It's important that society / send out missionaries / Saintly apostles of the anus / . . . / [who] Preach the Gospel of the ass."

Apothecary   Akin to a pharmacist, one who prepares medicines and who may also sell them. In nineteenth-century French bohemian circles, the term *apothecaire* was applied to homoerotically inclined males taking the active role in anal eroticism.

Apple   Sacred attribute of the goddess APHRODITE, a patron of gender fluidity and of many forms of love, including homoerotic and lesbian love. The theme of female companionship and indeed female separatism is found in the myth of the Hesperides, a band of women, possibly sisters, who lived on an island far to the west of Greece, perhaps in the vicinity of Africa, where they guarded the golden apples of immortality, given to the goddess Hera by Gaea, the Earth Mother. The Hesperides' sole male companion for many years was the dragon Ladon. A grove of apple trees, in which roses, anise, and wildflowers also grew, served as a religious site for the members of the *thiasos*, the spiritual household, of the poet and priestess SAPPHO. Here, rituals of union between women took place in which apples, as tokens of love, were exchanged. Sappho once compared a woman she loved to the "sweet apple turning red on . . . the top of the topmost branch." Lesbian and bisexual women poets of the nineteenth and twentieth centuries have reclaimed – as Judy GRAHN points out in *The Highest Apple* – the apple as a signifier of lesbian desire. H. D. (Hilda Doolittle), subtly comparing her desire for a woman to her desire for a celestial apple, writes in "Winter Love" that she wishes she ". . . could kneel / and savor the fragrance of the cleft fruit / . . . / I would be intoxicated with the scent of fruit, / O, holy apple, O, ripe ecstasy." And in her 1922 poem "The Artist," Elsa GIDLOW writes, "My Lady, loose me and rise. / We are brief as apple blossom."

Apple of Sodom   In Christian-inspired homoerotic literature, the so-called "apple of Sodom," or "Dead Sea fruit," is a symbol of the "sin of sodomy," as in the work of the poet John Addington SYMONDS. In Elsa GIDLOW's poem "Experience," the apple of Sodom becomes symbolic of the terrible emptiness and insatiableness the poet experiences after her female lover has left her in the morning, "Yea, I have loved and love is dead sea fruit."

Apricot   Because this delicate fruit is said to blend the flavors of the PLUM and the PEACH, the apricot has been deemed a symbol of androgyny. In ancient China, the apricot became a symbol of feminine beauty; in the European Middle Ages, a symbol for the vulva. At the TWO FLOWER TEMPLE in pre-modern China, named after two young men who loved each other deeply, the apricot served as a symbol of great affection. There, stems of apricot blossoms were offered as sacrifices and exchanged between lovers.

Aquarius In Euro-western ASTROLOGY, zodiac sign ruling from (approximately) January 20 until February 18, associated with hope, wonder, inspiration, open-mindedness, independence, imagination, spiritual nourishment, mysticism, humanitarian service, and liberation from oppression. Aquarius is typically depicted as a person carrying, serving from, or emptying water from, a vessel. Figures associated with Aquarius and with gender and/or sexual variance include: ANTINOUS, GANYMEDE, HAPY, and the WILDAN. In the late 1960s and early 1970s, the hippie movement embraced a collective vision of the Age of Aquarius, powerfully depicted in the musical *Hair*, when "peace will guide the planets and love will steer the stars." Many gay, lesbian, bisexual, and transgendered persons were profoundly inspired by this vision, and thus it played a prominent role in the creation of the liberation movements of that era. More specifically, it inspired a revival of belief in the androgyny and/or the "third sex," especially as manifested in "genderfuck drag." In her 1975 manifesto *Ask No Man Pardon*, Elsa GIDLOW wrote: "It is fashionable to speak of an 'Aquarian Age' . . . Many buds are bursting into flowers . . . in this turbulent time. Among them certainly [is] the Lesbian." In the late twentieth century, the figure of Aquarius, as reflected in the poem "Water-Bearer" by the bisexual poet Kenneth Pitchford (b. 1931), has become a symbol for males who are attempting to move beyond patriarchal attitudes and behaviors.

Aquila The EAGLE, a constellation recalling when the Greek god ZEUS, in the guise of an eagle, swooped down to earth and picked up GANYMEDE, a youth at play, to become his beloved and cup-bearer.

Arani Hindu goddess of fire, love and sexuality, families and tribes, nicknamed "Mistress of the Race." Her sacred attribute is the shami tree. She is invoked in a ritual in which she is represented by two pieces of wood, the *adhararani* and the *uttararani*, which are apparently both perceived as feminine, suggesting a lesbian *MITHUNA* (erotico-spiritual coupling), and which are rubbed together in order to make fire. This rite and others to Arani have linked the goddess to lesbian sexuality.

Aravan Son of the Hindu god-hero ARJUNA. On the eve of a great battle, that of Kurukshetra, between the Pandavas and their cousins the Kauravas, Sahadev determined that if the Pandavas (the side of Aravan and ARJUNA as well as the god KRISHNA) were to win, a perfect male must first be sacrificed at dawn. Aravan, not wishing his father or Krishna to be sacrificed, volunteered. He was beheaded at dawn, but not before Krishna had assumed the form of a woman and married him, so that he might die having first known love. Following Aravan's death, Krishna remained in female form, as a grieving widow, for

a period of time before assuming male form again. Each year, the HIJRAS, gender variant male or transgendered priest/esse/s of the goddess BAHUCHARAMATA and other deities, gather at the village of Koovagam (south of Madras) to take part in Thali, a rite commemorating the marriage of Aravan (sometimes known in the more specific manifestation of Kiithandavar) and Krishna and the death of the latter. *Hijras* take the role of Krishna as bride. At the mass wedding ceremony, a priest ties a *thali* (yellow thread covered with turmeric) around their necks to symbolize their marriage to Aravan. A great party follows, in which cultic eroticism and Camp-like antics play a central role. This phase of the rite is followed by the ritual death and burial of Aravan. At this time, Kavitha Shetty reports (in 1990), the *hijras* break the *thalis* and begin to "thump their chests in grief . . . in the best traditions of *opperi*, the Tamil art of mourning. Then they bathe . . . and change into the widow-white of mourning, marking the end of the festival."

Arcadia Rustic, fertile region of ancient Greece surrounded by mountains, inhabited by Arcadians (or Pelasgians), believed to have been an indigenous people. The primary deities revered by the Arcadians were ARTEMIS/DIANA and PAN – indeed, Arcadia was believed to be the birthplace of Pan. The reverence of these deities was linked to two of the chief professions of the people, hunting (Artemis) and shepherding (Pan). In "This Other Eden: Arcadia and the Homosexual Imagination" (1983) – one of the finest single works concerning Gay/Queer Spirituality – Byrne R. S. Fone writes, "Those who would dwell in Arcadia seek out that secret Eden because of its isolation from the troubled world and its safety from the arrogant demands of those who would deny freedom, curtail human action, and destroy innocence and love . . . Those who search for that hidden paradise are often lovers." Arcadia, in the Euro-western psyche, and more recently, cross-culturally, has been associated with a return to the joys of simple, rustic life, given voice especially in the pastoral poem. Fone suggests that while the dream of Arcadia speaks to persons of all genders and sexualities, it holds special importance for homoerotically inclined men. As forest, wood, grove, or wild garden, it is a place where such men may express their love for each other safely, may come to understand its naturalness, and may engage in rituals honoring same-sex love. "Only in this metaphoric land," he writes, "can certain rituals take place, rituals that celebrate this [homoerotic] mythology. These rites are transformational and involve the union of lovers . . . The symbolic events of the rituals include the offering of gifts, usually from nature, and the purification by water to prepare for an eternity of blissful habitation in the garden." This tradition of homoeroticism and the vision of Arcadia, Fone reveals, stretches from Virgil's (70-19 BCE) *Second Eclogue*, depicting the love of the shepherd CORYDON for ALEXIS, to Richard Barnfield's (1574-1627) Renaissance love poem *The Affectionate Shepherd*, portraying DAPHNIS's love for GANYMEDE, to the "paths untrodden, / In the growth by margins of pond-waters" where Walt WHITMAN (in *Leaves of Grass*, 1855) celebrates the "love of comrades," to the ideal valley of *Joseph and His Friend* (1869), Bayard Taylor's (1825-1878) novel of passionate friendship, to the "greenwood" of E. M. FORSTER's *Maurice* (1913), where Maurice and Alec Scudder discover love. Of rites taking place in Arcadian settings, Fone describes, among others, Whitman's distribution of symbolic tokens of love – lilac, pine, sage, and calamus – to his comrades. The dream of Arcadia has been shared by women-loving women. In the Euro-western tradition, Artemis is goddess of Arcadia. In the wild she lives and hunts with her Amazonian companions. In groves sacred to APHRODITE, SAPPHO and her companions celebrate the goddess of love. This tradition survived into the eighteenth century, when Anna Seward (1747-1809), paying homage to the "Ladies of Llangollen," the passionate friends or lovers Eleanor Butler and Miss Ponsonby, writes of their home, "Then rose the fairy palace of the Vale, / Then bloom'd around it the Arcadian bowers." In her poem beginning "Ourselves were wed one summer – dear," Emily DICKINSON depicts a ceremony of female union in a garden; in Christina Rossetti's "GOBLIN MARKET," Laura and Lizzie drift to sleep in an elfin wood. While "Moon and stars gazed in at them, / Wind sang to them lullaby," the young women lay "Cheek to cheek and breast to breast / Locked together in one nest." Mary Coleridge (1861-1907), in "Marriage," a poem reminiscent of Sappho depicting the loss of a female companion to heterosexual marriage, writes, "Thy merry sisters to-night forsaking; / Never shall we see thee, maiden, again. / Never shall we see thee, thine eyes glancing / Flashing with laughter and wild in glee, / Under the mistletoe kissing and dancing, / Wantonly free." For Amy Lowell (1874-1925), the site of love is the garden at evening, her beloved the "Madonna of the Evening Flowers," "Standing under a spire of pale blue larkspur / With a basket of ROSES." Baroness Gertrud Freifrau von Puttkamer, aka Marie-Madeleine (1881-1944), describing her lover as a "scarlet blossom," dreams in "The End is Now" of happier times, "the flight / Of stags along the mountain height; / The dripping grass; the trailing mist; / The wooded vale where last we kissed." Vita Sackville-West (1892-1962), renowned for her gardens, in *The Land: Spring* treks through "embroidered fields" and woods, knowing these Arcadian sites to be places of witchery and lesbian desire and fearing she will be seduced by a floral spirit taking the form of an "Egyptian girl," with an ancient snaring spell" or a "gypsy Judith, witch of a ragged tent." Elsa GIDLOW is that "witch," bringing, in "For the Goddess Too Well Known," a young woman to her "quietly dreaming garden." There,

she scatters "wild roses" over her, also covers her with "endless kisses," and leaves her at dawn in the "wakening garden."

Ardhanarishvara "The Lord Whose Half Is Woman" represents a transgendered being created by the union of the Hindu deities SHIVA (male) and SHAKTI (female). Ardhanarishvara, above all, speaks to the totality that lies beyond duality. In Chinese Taoism (or Daoism), this concept is symbolized by the coming together of YIN AND YANG in the Tao (or Dao). Like the Greek god HERMES, Ardhanarishvara is associated with communication; the intermediate being often serves to mediate between women and men, mortals and deities, and between other entities. For this reason, Ardhanarishvara is said to dwell in the *chakra* (sacred center of the human body) of the throat. In TANTRA, this *chakra* is also sometimes associated with oral intercourse, linking the deity not only to androgyny but also to homoeroticism. In the past, Ardhanarishvara was served by gender variant, cross- (or mixed-) dressing, priests. Alain DANIELOU writes, "The hermaphrodite, the homosexual, and the transvestite have a symbolic value and are considered privileged beings, images of the Ardhanarishvara. In this connection, they play a special part in magical and Tantric rites." To devotees, Ardhanarishvara, like GANESHA – Shiva's non-biological son and a companion of Ardhanarishvara – brings prosperity. In artistic depictions, Ardhanarishvara is typically shown with the left half of his body being female and the right half, male. The female (Shakti, or PARVATI, or Uma) half is usually garbed in red and often holds a lotus, while the male half (Shiva) wears a tiger skin or an ascetic's cloth around the waist. The skin of the female half is tan, while that of the male half is light blue. His/her gaze is pensive, serene; his/her pose sensuous, inviting. The cult of Ardhanarishvara appears to have reached a pinnacle during the tenth through the twelfth centuries and again in the eighteenth and early nineteenth centuries, when he-she became a popular subject in sculpture and painting.

Arepa In the Caribbean, and in Costa Rica, Colombia, and Venezuela, a fried griddle cake made of CORN meal corresponding to the Mexican tortilla. The *arepa* is symbolic of lesbianism, with lesbian women being referred to as *areperas*, "makers of *arepas*."

Ares and Menelippa In the visionary cosmos of Monique Wittig and Sande Zeig in *Lesbian Peoples* (1979), Amazon queens and lovers of the Thermodontine tribe who living during the Bronze Age and were honored for their outstanding physical prowess.

Arescontes (also **Arescon** and **Arescusa**, fl. c. 50 BCE) Young person living at Argos around 50 BCE who experienced transgender metamorphosis. According to Licinius Mucianus, who met this person, she/he had been reared as a girl, being given the name Arescusa. As a young woman, she was married to a man. A number of years later, however, Arescusa allegedly began to grow a beard and to display other masculine attributes. After separating from her husband and taking the name Arescon[tes], she, now he, married a woman of Argos.

Arete In Greco-Roman antiquity, the essence, or essential energy, of masculinity, comparable to the Chinese Taoist *yang*. *Arete* embraces virtue, heroism, and wisdom. It may be given by one male to another in a mentoring situation as well as in ritual homoeroticism. In esoteric, initiatory terms, the carrier of *arete* is generally the phallus, and more specifically the semen; the receptor is the anus of another male. Rites transferring *arete* appear to have been undertaken by COURETES and perhaps others in honor of the divine, often fused, male couple Apollo-Carneius on the island of Thera.

Argonauts In Greek myth, the crew of the Argo, the ship sailed by Jason on his quest for the Golden Fleece. Among the more prominent argonauts, several, including the sole female argonaut, are associated with gender variance and/or same-sex eroticism; these are: ATALANTA; CALAIS; HERACLES; ORPHEUS; PELEUS; POLLUX; and ZETES.

Argynnus (or **Argynnis, Argynnos**) Young man of Greek myth loved by King AGAMEMNON. After Argynnus drowned while bathing in the Cephisus River, Agamemnon founded a sanctuary to him and to the love-goddess Aphrodite in memory of their love. Argynnus also loved HYMENAEUS.

Ariadne Best known as the leader of the MAENADS of the Greek god DIONYSUS and as she who aided THESEUS in escaping from the Minoan labyrinth by giving him a magical spool of thread, Ariadne, whose name means "very holy," was in earlier times a goddess of fertility. On the island of Cyprus, an annual ritual took place during which a young male was chosen to experience couvade, simulated pregnancy. This mysterious rite, about which little is known, was dedicated to Ariadne, who, according to one legend, experienced pregnancy without giving birth to a child.

Aries In Euro-western ASTROLOGY, zodiac sign ruling from (approximately) March 20 until April 20, associated with ambition, courage, leadership, and a pioneering spirit, typically depicted as a RAM. Figures associated with Aries and with gender or sexual variance include: ALEXIS, AMAZONS, ATTIS, BRANCHUS, CARNEIUS, CORYDON, CYPARISSUS, DAPHNIS, FURIES, GLAUCON, GOPIS, GORGONS, HERMAPHRODITUS, KOTYS, KRISHNA, MA, MARSYAS, MIN, MINERVA, PALES, PAN, PELE, POMBA GIRA, RADHA, SEKHMET, SHANGO, and SHEPHERDS.

Aristobulus III, Jonathan (d. 35 BCE) Jewish high priest of the Hasmonean sect, brother-in-law of the Biblical Herod Antipater, the Great (73-4 BCE), and lover of Mark ANTONY (82-30 BCE). Perhaps because he disapproved of Aristobulus's and Antony's relationship and/or was jealous of his brother-in-law's popularity, Herod had Aristobulus drowned in a swimming pool at Jericho.

Aristodemus (or **Aristodemos**, fl. c. 650-600 BCE) Handsome young man at that time when EPIMENIDES was called upon to cure Athens of a plague, Aristodemus was the male lover (*erastes*) of a young man named CRATINUS (not the comedian of the same name). The two willingly sacrificed themselves upon learning that only human blood would cure the plague.

Aristogeiton (fl. 515 BCE) Athenian nobleman, lover of Harmodius. Together, they attempted the murder of the tyrant Hippias. While they did not succeed in this effort, they murdered his brother Hipparchus in 514 BCE. Though they suffered torture and were executed, the event eventually led to the banishing of Hippias and to the ritual honoring of Aristogeiton and Harmodius as martyrs for democracy.

Arjuna Son or incarnation of the Hindu god INDRA, Arjuna was the beloved companion of the god KRISHNA and the hero of the epic *Mahabharata*. Arjuna disguised himself as a eunuch in women's clothing and taught the young princess and her companions at the court of King Virata the arts of dancing, singing, and music. In the Javanese version of the *Mahabharata*, Arjuna is husband to the bisexual, Amazonian SRIKANDI.

Armpit In the transcendental poem "Song of Myself" from his masterpiece *Leaves of Grass* (1855), Walt WHITMAN expresses his belief that divine energy flows in all things and especially throughout the human body: "Divine am I inside and out, and I make holy whatever I touch or am touch'd from, / The scent of these arm-pits is aroma finer than prayer." In "Invocation to Sappho," Elsa GIDLOW writes: "in my own armpits I have breathed sweat of your passion." In the visionary lesbian-centered universe of Monique Wittig and Sande Zeig in *Lesbian Peoples* (1979), companion lovers magically transform their armpit aromas into exotic, musk-based perfumes.

Arsenothelys Primordial transgendered deity, possibly the same as ZEUS Arrhenothelus, worshipped by Simon Magus (first century CE), the Gnostic magician-priest condemned in the Christian Bible.

Artemis (Roman **Diana**)   Greek and Roman goddess of
maidenhood, the MOON, Nature, and the hunt, also
worshipped in Crete, England, France, Italy, Spain, and
elsewhere. The homoerotically inclined poet and librarian
Callimachus (c. 305-240 BCE), depicts the Goddess
primarily as an AMAZON and lover of women, her amours
including BRITOMARTIS, CYRENE, and ANTICLEIA.
"These were the first," he writes, who wore the gallant bow
and arrow – holding quivers on their shoulder." Among her
priestesses were the *melissae* ("BEES"), her high priestess
their queen. Diana also may have been served by
Amazonian or *antianeirian* priestesses. *Antianeira* refers to
a complex of traits including rejection of marriage, love of
HUNTING, skill as a warrior, hatred of traditionally
masculine men, a sense of comradeship with gender variant
males, and a desire to remain in the company of women.
These priestesses are said to have employed their shields
and swords in a circular dance around a sacred oak or beech
at EPHESUS. She was also served by the *arktor* ("BEAR"),
priestesses who might also be classed as Amazonian, and are
probably linked to the reverence of CALLISTO, a loving
companion of the Goddess. As Artemis Orthia, a lunar
manifestation, she was invoked by women participating in
same-sex unions in Greco-Roman antiquity, as well as by
young males – typically the *eromenoi*, or beloved, of older
males – undergoing ritual flogging in Sparta. As Artemis
Pergaea, she was celebrated in hymns by the lesbian circle
of Damophyle of Pamphilia. As Artemis Kordaka, she was
honored with the KORDAX, a dance-drama in which women
and men dressed in the garments of the opposite sex. In the
kordax, the women, wearing "*lombai*, enormous artificial
phalli," pretended to penetrate the male dancers. In
another rite, young Lakedaimonian males, in preparation
for combat, flagellated themselves and engaged in same-sex
eroticism at a festival honoring Diana. The Goddess was
also revered at the initiation rites of young men joining the
order of the COURETES, a band of warriors whose functions
may have included serving as guards at birthing rituals.
From rock inscriptions on the island of Thera, we know
that the rites of the *Kouretes* included homoeroticism. The
couples, usually initiator and initiate, dedicated their lives
to Diana and other deities. Among the Goddess's most
renowned worshippers was ALEXANDER THE GREAT, who
loved to dress as Artemis in parades honoring her. The
Christian Church played the greatest role in the destruction
of the religion of Diana and the deaths of her followers. The
apostle Paul said to early converts to Christianity, "The
temple of the great goddess Diana should be despised, and
her magnificence should be destroyed, *whom all Asia and
the world worshippeth*." Responding to Paul's invitation,
Christians destroyed the temple of Artemis at Ephesus in
the third century CE. It was rebuilt, but was again burned
by the Christians in 405 CE. At this time, the patriarch of
Constantinople proudly proclaimed that the Christians
succeeded in stripping "away the treasury of Artemis." As

John Holland Smith explains, the destruction of the temple
provided the funds and materials to build the Church of
Saints Mary and John at Ephesus and Hagia Sophia at
Constantinople. This did not prevent Christians from
worrying, however, that the stones used to build these
churches might still be "infected" with the "evil" energy of
the Goddess. A poet nearer our own time, perhaps
imagining how the few remaining faithful of Diana must
have felt as they looked upon the ruins of the temple at
Ephesus, wrote, "We now seek the Temple in vain: the city
is / prostrate, and the goddess gone." While the religion of
Artemis/Diana was in the main destroyed, a great amount
of evidence has surfaced or been reinterpreted in recent
years indicating that Witchcraft may have represented a
transformation of her worship. The Goddess and her
companions also survived in the arts, especially in painting.
A number of these works depict the interrelationship of
lesbian desire and the mythic or sacred. They include: the
Circle of Lorenzo di Niccolò's *Diana with Meleager and
Actaeon* (c. 1420), Paolo Schiarvo's (attributed) *The Story
of Diana and Actaeon* (c. 1440), Paolo Veronese's *Actaeon
Watching Diana and her Nymphs Bathing* (1560-1565),
Parmagiano's *Two Nymphs* (c. 1523), and Titian's *Diana
and Callisto* (1556-1559). In the twentieth century, with the
emergence of the Women's Spirituality movement as well
as the reclamation of Goddess Reverence and the revival
and transformation of Witchcraft, or Wicca, Artemis has
once more become a powerful embodiment of Amazonian
women who prefer the loving companionship of women to
that of men. The Goddess is especially honored in the
Dianic Witchcraft of Z BUDAPEST, Diane STEIN, and
others who focus on the interrelationship of lesbian-
feminism and spirituality. In a survey of almost six
hundred lesbians taken in 1989 and 1990, Jo Ann Loulan
found that among seven goddess archetypes from which
the women could choose to identify both themselves and
their lovers, Artemis rated highest (30-35%). Loulan
also discovered that Aphrodite and Artemis may in
certain contexts represent a lesbian "femme-butch"
couple.

Arthur, Gavin (**Chester Alan Arthur III**, 1901-1972)
American bisexual occultist, astrologer, philosopher, and
writer. He was the grandson and namesake of Chester Alan
Arthur, the twenty-first President of the United States.
Although from a wealthy and influential family, he became
a Merchant Marine, panned gold, and sold newspapers for
a living. During the 1920s and 1930s, he frequented the
artistic salons and communites of Europe and America. He
became famous in San Francisco for the people he had
encountered (including Magnus Hirschfeld, Havelock
Ellis, Edward CARPENTER, Alfred Kinsey, and Gertrude
Stein) as well as for his astrology charts and astrologically
based sexual theories. His book *The Circle of Sex* (1966,
introduced by Alan Watts) is both a memoir and a queer

sexological treatise. In this book, Arthur describes a "clock" of queer sexual types that moves far beyond simple definitions of homosexual, heterosexual, and bisexual. Each of us possesses differing combinations of YIN AND YANG. Like magnets, we attract or repel others in the circle of sex who balance our own combinations of these fluid essences. Arthur's clock employs the theory of correspondences, linking gender and sexuality to such things as times of the day and seasons. Profoundly inspired by Walt WHITMAN and Edward CARPENTER, Arthur suggests that only when heterosexuals are utterly liberated from procreation and from the constraints of marriage will bisexuals, lesbians, gay men, and the transgendered come to be liberated.

Artimpasa (or **Argimpasa**)   In ancient Russia and neighboring countries, priestesses and gender variant priests called ENAREES served the goddess Artimpasa. Although little information concerning this deity has survived, she appears to have been viewed as a Great Goddess. She was often accompanied by a lion and sometimes by a male consort. She appears to have been especially associated with plant life, and even more specifically with cannabis (or marijuana). The use of this magical plant, or entheogen, indicates, as does other fragmentary data, that her religion or cult included elements of Shamanism. Artimpasa was compared by Greeks and Romans to CYBELE, and also to APHRODITE Urania. As this aspect of Aphrodite, she was further linked to male gender variance and homoeroticism. It is conceivable that warrior women, or AMAZONS, also revered Artimpasa, as Amazons were frequently associated with Goddess Reverence, as numerous classical sources document such women living in the region, and as archaeological excavations of the remains of women warriors are beginning to lend credence to those documents. In a Scythian tumulus near the village of Balaban, for instance, "archaeologists have found a woman warrior, buried . . . with weapons. Beautiful ear-rings, shaped into animal headlets, lay at her head."

Asanga   In Hindu mythology, a male sage (*rishi*, or *rsi*) who metamorphosed into a woman.

Asclepius (or **Asklepios, Aesculapius**)   Greek divine or semi-divine being of healing whose name means "unceasingly gentle." The son of APOLLO (according to some accounts), Asclepius was as a youth mentored and loved by the wise centaur CHIRON, who taught him the art of healing. In later years, he married, and taught his daughter Hygieia the science of health, hence our term "hygiene." (Some sources maintain that Hygieia was originally a healing goddess independent of Asclepius who only later was depicted as his daughter.) Together, Asclepius and Hygieia are said to have established healing centers. One of the functions of these centers was to interpret the dreams of ill persons, in the belief that the interpretation of their dreams might guide the healers in diagnosing and curing their illnesses. As an adult, Asclepius is said to have loved HIPPOLYTUS, the son of the queen of the Amazons, Hippolyte. One account says that he actually raised Hippolytus from the dead on the request of the goddess ARTEMIS/DIANA. This capacity of Asclepius to revivify the dead so disturbed Zeus that he slew Asclepius by spearing him with a thunderbolt. On his death, Asclepius was transformed into the constellation *Serpens* (the Serpent). His sacred attributes are the caduceus (he shares this symbol of entwined serpents with Hygieia, Hermes, and Tiresias) and the plant serpentaria. It appears that homoerotically inclined sacred prostitutes, or HIERODULES, may have played a key role in the worship of Asclepius, union with them representing union with the godhead. Alexander, a man-loving follower of Apollonius of Tyana, allegedly founded a mystery school devoted to Asclepius during the first century CE.

Assassins   Islamic sect spreading throughout the Middle East during the eleventh and twelfth centuries . Its members were alleged to engage in ritual homoeroticism.

Assimilation   In the late twentieth century, great pressure is being applied to "queer" communities – from without and from within – to acknowledge the controlling paradigms of dominant cultures as desirable, on the sole condition that they/we be able to participate fully in institutions such as marriage and the armed forces. Many who identify as "queer" fear that such assimilation into dominant cultures may entail the sacrifice of such attributes as diversity, integrity, authenticity, and even marginality or liminality, in arenas ranging from fashion to language to spiritual life. In "Hapa Haole Wahine, " the bisexual feminist poet Lani Ka'ahumanu (b. 1943), of Hawaiian, Japanese, and Irish descent, expresses this concern in two brief lines: "Assimilation is a lie. / It is spiritual erasure."

Assiniboin Woman   According to an Assiniboin(e) legend of North America, a certain man's wife fell in love with his sister and eloped with her. The two women mated, and one gave birth to a child. Unfortunately, the tale ends tragically. The child was born without bones, and the husband, enraged, caught up with his wife and murdered her, the baby, and perhaps also her female spouse.

Assinnu   Gender variant male priests of the Mesopotamian goddess INANNA/ISHTAR. *Assinnu* were generally referred to as "*sal-zikrum*, women-men." As such, they were considered as being essentially different from other men, their collective identity a gift of the gods, a *me. Assinnu* appear to have dressed in a combination of feminine, masculine, and sacerdotal garments. They also appear to have let their hair grow long and to have worn colorful necklaces. A hymn to Inanna indicates that on occasion they may have worn a bifurcated costume, with masculine articles making up the left side of the costume and feminine articles the right. Certain texts indicate that at least some of the *assinnu* may have been eunuchs; at least one text indicates that they could not experience penile orgasm. Their gender variant status was expressed not only in dress but also in speech. During a certain period of their history, they spoke in the Sumerian dialect of *Emesal*. This dialect, opposed to *Eme-ku*, the dialect employed by traditionally masculine males, was spoken only by women and gender variant men and was believed to be an invention of the Goddess. Their gender variant status was further expressed in terms of a diet of delicate and exotic foods. This status was confirmed by the belief that the physical bodies of the priests differed from those of other men in that they carried magical power. For instance, simply touching the head of an *assinnu* would allow a warrior to conquer his enemy. *Assinnu* were, like Inanna/Ishtar's priestesses, considered the mortal representatives of the Goddess. The priests were also seen as human reflections of certain spirit-companions of the Goddess, in particular, the androgynous divine beings known as Asushunamir, or "He Whose Face Is Light," and the *kalaturru* (or *galatur*) and the *kurgarra*, created to rescue the Goddess from the underworld. During various periods of Mesopotamian/Sumerian history, the *assinnu* were persecuted. One such persecution occurred in the late second millenium BCE. In the *Erra-epic* we read: "In [the city of] Uruk . . . / . . . the *kurgarru* and *assinnu* . . . / Who regularly do [forbidden things] to delight the heart of Ishtar: / You set over them an insolent governor who will not treat them kindly, / (But) persecuted them and violated their rights. / (With the effect) that Ishtar became enraged." Despite periodic persecution, the *assinnu* nevertheless held respected positions in the worship of the Goddess, being employed as magicians, ritual artists, and HIERODULES (commonly, and somewhat incorrectly, referred to as "sacred prostitutes"). As magicians, they were said to excel in making talismans and amulets to protect the wearer from destructive magic and other dangers. As ritual artists, they functioned as singers, musicians, composers, dancers, and actors. Among their types of compositions was the *inhu*, a lament concerning the life of the Goddess. The term *inhu* refers to the sorrowful, melancholy song of the *ursanu* bird. "You seat the *assinnu*," an ancient text reads, "and he will sing his *inhus*." Of such laments, another text reads, "*in-hi-ia sunuhuti Istar ismema*, Ishtar (/Inanna) heard my sorrowful *inhu* songs." It is possible that a well-known gypsum statuette discovered at Mari and known as the "Singer Ur-Nanshe" represents an *assinnu*. As ritual actors, the *assinnu* took part in a ritual drama honoring both Inanna and the goddess Narudu, in which the priests dressed in the garments (*tillu*) of the goddesses. *Assinnu* also played a role in the ritual of the *hieros gamos*, or "sacred marriage," of Inanna/Ishtar and her consort Dumuzi, embodied by the high priestess and the king. This rite was celebrated each year in order to promote fertility. In a hymn dating from the third millenium BCE, composed during the reign of Iddin-Dagan (c. 2255 BCE), we read that in this ritual, the *assinnu* and other gender variant functionaries of both sexes wearing bifurcated costumes, the men carrying mirrors and combing their hair, joined in a procession, chanting, "Hail, Inanna!" Foremost among their functions, however, was that of engaging in eroticism with – in most cases – traditionally masculine worshippers in order to bring the latter into intimate contact with the Goddess. In this respect, the *assinnu* dedicated their bodies – including their anuses – to the Goddess. Like the priestesses of Inanna, they engaged in anal intercourse with male worshippers, usually taking the receptive role. In the *Summa Alu*, an omen collection, one finds: "If a man engage in coitus *per anum* with his (male) equal. If a man has intercourse with an *assinnu*."

Astarte Goddess of love and later also of war, also known as Ashtoreth, the Lady of Byblos, and the Queen of Heaven. She is frequently identified with APHRODITE and VENUS. She was worshipped by the Egyptians, Canaanites, Phoenicians, Greeks, Romans, and even heretical Hebrews. As a manifestation of the life-bestowing aspect of the Great Goddess, she is often depicted as a nude woman holding her breasts or raising her arms above her head. She sometimes wears a bird mask and is occasionally flanked by male goats. She may also appear as a gender variant goddess, however, both as a woman warrior crowned with horns and driving a chariot and as an hermaphrodite with female breasts and an erect phallus. A late Phoenician inscription makes mention of "King Astarte." The gender variant male priests of Astarte were generally known as the KELABIM, the "dogs" of the Goddess. It is conceivable, due to Astarte's transgendered aspect, that she was also served by gender variant or Amazonian women.

Astrology Since antiquity, astrologers have attempted to decipher signs of gender and sexual variance in the horoscopes of individuals and groups. As James R. Lewis suggests in *The Astrology Encyclopedia*, their findings have tended to "reflect the social conditions and the attitude toward homosexuals" and other persons and behaviors considered here which have been held by the cultures in which they have lived. One might also speculate that those considered or identifying as queer might have transformed a great deal across epochs and cultures and that these metamorphoses might be mirrored in their charts. Such transformations might well have to do with the degree of acceptance or respect experienced by such persons. They might also reflect shifting roles played or functions served by such persons in the societies in which they have lived. In a nutshell, even when it comes to astrological thinking, it is evident that both "nature" and "nurture" have played a role in shaping queerness. The ancient Mesopotamians (Sumerians, Babylonians) attributed male same-sex desire to the influence of the sign of SCORPIO, associated with sexuality, death, and rebirth. By the fourth century CE, as reflected in the works of astrologers including Claudius Ptolemaeus (of the second century) and Firmicus Maternus (of the fourth), predicting or interpreting an individual's chart as pertaining to sexuality and gender had become a fine art. At least half a dozen different "lesbian" (and/or possibly female-to-male transgender) configurations are offered. They include these combinations: (1) the SUN, MOON, and VENUS in "masculine" signs (i.e. AQUARIUS, ARIES, GEMINI, LEO, LIBRA, and SAGITTARIUS); (2) the addition of MARS in a masculine sign to the first configuration; (3) a morning birth time, a masculine rising sign, and a Mars-Venus conjunction in the first house (the self we present to the world); (4) the sun, MERCURY, and Venus in the seventh house (relationships); (5) Mars, Venus, and SATURN in the seventh house, especially with Mars in CAPRICORN or Aries; (6) Venus, Mercury, and Saturn in the ninth house (knowledge, especially philosophical or occult). Of these combinations, it is said, "Women who have this combination make love unchastely to other women;" "women will be born who take on a man's character and desire intercourse with women like men;" "[they] are what we call *tribades*; for they deal with females and perform the functions of males." It should be noted that most of these configurations refer to women enacting what today might be referred to as a "butch" role. What is most striking about these configurations, however, is that they differentiate between women who "do these things secretly, and not openly," and those who express themselves "without reserve." The latter are motivated, ancient sources report, by Mars, the planet controlling sexual passion and aggression. Of the latter, it is also said that they often refer to their female lovers "as their lawful wives." Of combinations pertaining to "androgynous" or "effeminate" men who are homoerotically inclined, the following are representative: (1) the sun, moon, Venus, and Mars, and possibly Saturn and/or Mercury in a feminine sign (i.e. CANCER, Capricorn, PISCES, Scorpio, TAURUS, or VIRGO); (2) Mars and Venus conjunct in the first house, an evening birth time, and a feminine rising sign; (3) Mars and Venus in Aries or Capricorn (see female combination 5 above); (4) Mercury and Venus conjunct in the nineteenth degree of Aries. In terms of such men, the ancient astrologers held that rising signs or "ascendants" played an important role; these include: 15 degrees Aries, 6 degrees Taurus, 26 degrees Gemini, 8 degrees Leo, 10 degrees

Libra, 2 degrees Scorpio, 25 degrees Sagittarius, 25 degrees Aquarius, and 4 degrees Pisces. These combinations are interpreted in such ways as: "These men are dealt with as pathics [receptive in homoerotic relations];" "[these men express] disgraceful sexual desires [as would a] . . . notorious male prostitute (*cinaedus publica damnatus infamia*);" "they will make eunuchs . . . [and] immodest male prostitutes (*turpes infames inpuros inpudices cinaedos*)." Some, especially those referring to males involved in the sacred arts, are much more specific. For instance, those whose charts include either male combination (2) or (3) above may be or become "perverts (*cinaedi*) who serve in temple choirs," possibly referring to such persons as the *galli* priests of the goddess Cybele. This sort of interpretation becomes even more specific in the case of those whose rising sign is 26 degrees Gemini. They will become *cinaedi* who will serve as priests, diviners, and/or prophets, being sought out by great rulers. If, however, this sign is thought to be "badly aspected," they may ultimately suffer betrayal and death at that ruler's hands. In the case of those with a rising sign of 6 degrees Taurus, the specificity is focused on physical and behavioral qualities, approaching what might be deemed today an archetypal drag queen. These males are "always involved in luxury and lust. They are always drenched in perfumes . . . in banquets . . . they attack their companions with a sarcastic wit . . . They twist their hair in ringlets [and wear wigs] . . . They soften their body with various cosmetics; pull out their body hair and wear clothes in the likeness of women." As with the women's configurations, Mars energy plays a role in whether or not these men conceal their behavior or openly express themselves. The Mars-Venus relationship in the charts of some homoerotically inclined, gender variant males is satirized in an anonymous poem appearing in the sixth century *Latin Anthology*. In "Of Martius, Cinaedus," the poet writes, "What good is it that your name is taken from the name of Mars / When it is Venus who itches in your notorious ass? / It would have been a better fate had you been named Cypridos [i.e., of Aphrodite, with a masculine ending]." It should be pointed out that these configurations differ somewhat from those applied to homoerotically or bisexually inclined males who were not perceived as gender variant or third gender. In the Near East and West of late antiquity, a more traditionally "masculine" form of same-sex love tended to be linked either to warriorhood (or comradeship), intergenerational love, or both. As with the males described previously, some of these men were linked to the sacred arts, as those having Mercury and Venus in the tenth house (career and recognition), with Mercury being in Aries, Gemini, Libra, Sagittarius, Scorpio, or Taurus. "[These men] will make musical composers . . . destined for the stage or public performances . . . some will be lovers of boys." Concerning the warrior/comrade, Ptolemaeus suggests that the astrologer examine the chart for a trine of Mars, the sun, and Jupiter. The man possessing this trine in his chart is described as a freedom-loving, benevolent, industrious, warrior who is "without passion for women" and who is "better satisfied with and more desirous of association with men." For such men, homoeroticism and gender variance or "effeminacy" are not linked; "nor do they become effeminate (*anandros*), and soft (*malakos*) thereby." Ptolemaeus further associates these warrior/comrades and the sun-Mars-Jupiter relationship with geographical sites including Sicily, Tuscany, western Spain, France, Germany, and the British Isles. Other configurations signifying "masculine" homoeroticism of a warrior/comrade and/or intergenerational kind include: (1) Mercury in the first or eighth house (heritage), with Mars squaring Mercury; (2) Mars in the sixth house (work, health), with Mercury squaring Mars; (3) the moon in the sixth house and Mercury in the fourth house (parents, home); (4) Venus in Aquarius in the fourth house, with the moon either squaring or in conjunction with Venus; and (5) Venus in the second house (possessions), with the sun and Saturn either squaring or in conjunction with Venus. It should be noted that it is said of those men possessing combinations (4) or (5) that they will "never marry" women (or "never enjoy conjugal life") and will "always prefer intercourse with boys" (or will "always be lovers of boys"). This potentially absolute homoeroticism runs counter to the image of Greek male eroticism promoted by social constructionists like Michel Foucault, David Halperin, and Eva Cantarella, who insist upon the bisexuality of such men. Nevertheless, some configurations speak clearly of bisexuality, especially among males: (1) possessing a rising sign of 5 degrees Virgo, a man will "hasten to the beds" of males or females; (2) having Venus and Mars and possibly also Saturn in the tenth or eleventh house (wishes, politics, spirituality), a man will tend to form relationships with either female or male prostitutes. A few examples are given of configurations clearly pertaining to transgendered persons, and these tend to focus (with the possible exceptions of those mentioned in reference to lesbianism above) on male-to-female persons and/or hermaphrodites. Such configurations include: (1) Venus and the moon in feminine signs, with Venus in the tenth house and the moon aspected with Mars; (2) the moon in Virgo, Capricorn, Taurus, or Leo; Mercury in the second or seventh house; Venus in the sixth house; (3) Saturn, Jupiter, Mars and the sun in feminine signs; the moon and Venus in masculine signs (Mercury is already considered androgynous, hermaphroditic, or transgendered). Chinese astrology, one of the most ancient non-western forms of the art, is almost silent where gender and sexual variance are concerned. Nevertheless, the signs of the TIGER and the SERPENT are sometimes associated with androgyny or transgenderism, while those of the HARE and the DRAGON

are occasionally linked to male homosexuality. The Middle Ages witnessed the rise and powerful influence of Arabic astrology and its cross-pollination with Euro-western astrology. In Da'Wah, certain signs associated with hermaphroditism as well with gender and sexual variance had equivalents for Gemini, Virgo, Capricorn, and Aquarius. In the Renaissance, men-loving men like the Florentine Neoplatonist Marsilio FICINO and the artist Michelangelo BUONARROTI were deeply inspired by astrology. The latter, possessing a Mercury-Venus conjunction, believed his love and desire for males to be directed by the stars. François Rabelais' (c. 1490-1553) sixteenth-century satire *Pantagrueline Prognostication* also indicates that the planet Venus was still believed to influence gender and sexual variance, ruling not only male "Ganymedes, Bardachoes [*berdaches*, and] . . . Ingles" – young males who took a receptive role in homoerotic relations, sometimes prostituting themselves to older men – but also "Fricatrices" – a sixteenth-century French term signifying lesbians. In the Americas, one of the richest and most complex systems of astrology belonged to the Aztecs. In terms of gender and sexual variance, Aztecs linked the *patlache* – the Amazonian, woman-loving woman – to the signs of the Rabbit or HARE (Tochtli) and the DEER (Mazatl). The sign of the Monkey or APE (Ozomatli), linked to tricksters and performing artists (especially singers, dancers, and jugglers), was allied with the god XOCHIPILLI, who was associated with sexual variance. Xochipilli was also associated, as was his sister XOCHIQUETZAL, with the sign of the FLOWER (Xochitl); persons born under this sign tended to be poets and artists. The sign of the Reed (Acatl) was ruled by the god TEZCATLIPOCA, sometimes considered a homoerotically inclined male being. The sign of the Knife (Tecpatl) was apparently associated at one time with ritual castration and eunuchs. In the late nineteenth and early twentieth centuries, astrologers in general adopted a queer-phobic perspective that attributed gender and sexual variance to certain "afflictions," or unfavorable aspects, in a horoscope. Both queer-phobic and queer-positive astrologers began to look upon the planet Uranus, discovered in 1781, as governing gender and sexual variance. This belief resulted from the weaving together of several items of mythic data, including (1) the tale of Uranus, who was castrated by Chronos, leading the former to be seen as a patron of eunuchs; (2) as the child born of the maternal sea and the severed testicles of Uranus, Aphrodite became known as Urania in her aspect of Queen of the Heavens, and in this aspect became further known, as in PLATO's *Symposium*, as a patron of same-sex love; (3) not long after its discovery, Uranus came to be perceived by astrologers as the patron planet of both personal and social rebellion or revolution. Indeed, persons expressing variant gender and sexual behavior, especially homoerotically inclined males, came to be known as

URNINGS, or URANIANS. Early twentieth-century astrologer Charles Carter (b. 1887) saw both Uranus and Neptune as governing variant erotic and gendered behavior; Neptune, discovered in 1846, is associated like Uranus with revolutionary activity and is also linked to eccentricity. Astrology experienced a great renaissance in the 1960s, a period when the gay San Francisco-based astrologer Gavin ARTHUR published the now cult-classic *The Circle of Sex* (1966), and when many gays, lesbians, bisexuals, and transgendered persons began to celebrate with others (prematurely) the "dawning of the Age of Aquarius," as the musical *Hair* proclaimed. As James R. Lewis explains, since the late 1960s, "astrological speculations that attributed same-sex preference [we might add other forms of queer behavior] to difficult aspects and unfavorable placements have been quietly put aside." Typical of contemporary attitudes is that voiced by Geraldine Hatch Hanon in *Sacred Space: A Feminist Vision of Astrology* (1990): "In my enthusiasm when I first came out over ten years ago, I hoped to find an astrological signature that indicated lesbianism. Today I feel quite the opposite and think the efforts to determine homosexuality in a chart rather homophobic, since most theories point to difficult planetary placements and aspects as if to imply that being gay cannot possibly be a chosen path to fulfillment and joy." Hanon does acknowledge, however, that Uranus seems to play a role in queer charts. That role, she maintains, is not to confer queerness, but to link it to political activism. In this, Hanon both echoes and amends the ancient notion that the bold expression of sexual and gender variance was linked to the energy of Mars. Other contemporary astrologers, in contrast to Hanon, do not frown upon deciphering signifiers of queerness, so long as this pursuit is not attached to anti-queer attitudes. Among these other astrologers is J. E. Kneeland. In researching his *Gay Signs* (1988), he found from an experiment involving over one hundred and fifty gay and bisexual men of various ages that certain astrological factors seemed to occur in relatively high percentages. For instance, his experiment revealed that gay and bisexual men are more likely to have Leo, Scorpio, or Sagittarius as sun signs or as rising signs than they are to have any other signs in these categories. He also learned that gay and bisexual men are more likely to have their sun signs in the tenth or twelfth (self-sacrifice, self-destruction, spiritual seeking) houses than in any other houses. While this information may prove to be very valuable to astrologers, it is rather unfortunate that Kneeland's experiment did not include lesbian or bisexual women or transgendered persons. It also might have been helpful if Kneeland had made some attempt to differentiate between men identifying as "masculine", "butch," "gender-bending," "drag queen," and so on, as well as between lovers of persons of relatively the same ages versus those loving persons of very different ages, etc., as this data might have been used to better

determine the presence of any resonances between the charts of antiquity and those of the present day. One intriguing observation made by Kneeland concerns the Venus-Mars connection (apparently) observed in charts of late antiquity. Kneeland found that "in 63% of the charts of homosexuals and bisexuals polled," Mars and Venus "do not aspect each other at all." While it is not clear from the text whether or not Kneeland is familiar with Ptolemaeus or with Firmicus Maternus, his data indicates that a deep connection once existing between love energy (Venus) and sex energy (Mars) has been severed, and it is his suggestion that this relationship needs to be integrated (or reintegrated) more fully in the lives of gay men. The participation of lesbians and (other) feminists in contemporary astrology, as evidenced in the work of Hanon, has brought insight especially in terms of associations of signs, planets, asteroids, and other heavenly bodies with ancient goddesses as inspirers of women and others living in the late twentieth century. While the vast majority of queer people may not choose to study astrology in depth, many purchase queer-positive guides to loving relationships like Michael Jay's *Gay Love Signs* (1980), John Savage's *The Gay Astrologer* (1982), and Aurora's *Lesbian Love Signs* (1991). Many more do not fail to "read their horoscopes" in newspapers or journals. A number of queer astrologers have in recent years become extremely popular, gaining audiences that stretch beyond the queer community/ies. The most renowned of these, reminiscent of Liberace, remains closeted in terms of his sexuality while dramatically expressing his gender-bending persona. In the San Francisco community of the 1980s and 1990s, it is beyond doubt Jack Fertig, once known as "Sister Boom Boom," who is most renowned. Fertig's column spices up astrological guidelines with CAMP; following his lead, this approach to journalistic astrology has become widespread in US queer journals and "zines." For instance, in his February 8, 1996 article in *San Francisco Bay Times*, "The Ache of Aquarius," Fertig, who has not given up on either Aquarius or Uranus as harbingers of Queer Spirit, writes: "What is really Aquarian and happening is that Uranus, the Queer Planet, has just gone into its own sign, Aquarius. The 'water carrier' was known in Greek culture (don't touch that one!) as Ganymede, the boy whom Zeus stole into the heavens. (Daddy Zeus, b.t.w., liberated the beautiful boy by taking the form of an Eagle. So it's said. Perhaps that was just the insignia on his bar vest)."

Asushunamir Androgynous male spirit-companion of the Mesopotamian goddess INANNA/ISHTAR. His name means "He Whose Face Is Light." He was created to rescue Inanna from the grip of her sister Ereshkigal, the Queen of the Underworld. For this action, Ereshkigal cursed Asushunamir: "The food of the gutter shall be your food! The drink of the sewer shall be your drink. In the shadows shall you abide." When Inanna learned of the curse placed upon him, she blessed Asushunamir with the gifts of prophecy, healing and magic.

Atalanta Originally an Arcadian, pre-Hellenic goddess, probably of death/rebirth, she later became a Greek athletic heroine renowned as a runner and a wrestler. Legend has it that she was abandoned by her father on a hill called Parthenia ("Virgin") and was discovered, nursed, and reared by bears. She was educated by a tribe of wandering Amazons. As a young adult, she became known as the Swift-Footed, the Unswaying, and the Impassable One, slaying centaurs and demanding the right to slay any man who did not beat her in a race. She was the first to wound the Caledonian boar in a great hunt for the legendary animal, and was the only woman taking part in the expedition of Jason and the Argonauts to capture the Golden Fleece. She was a lover of both men and women, her most renowned female lover being the goddess ARTEMIS/DIANA, who instructed her in the art of archery.

Atargatis (also called **Dea Syria**) Near Eastern – primarily Phoenician – goddess depicted as a young woman wearing an Egyptian dress or as a MERMAID wearing a fortress-shaped tiara. Atargatis is a lunar deity who presides over fertility and the hunt. Mother of the legendary Queen SEMIRAMIS, she has a male consort named HADAD (or Attah). Atargatis' seat of worship was at Hierapolis in Syria. Here she was served by a multitude of priests and priestesses, including the gender variant male GALLI. Many of Atargatis's male worshippers appear to have been slaves, freedmen, and peasant laborers. These men may have included sub-Saharan Black Africans. Some were married, but many others were gender variant males whose erotic partners were other males. The worshippers of Atargatis were among those participating in a great slave rebellion occurring in the Greco-Roman Empire between 135 and 131 BCE. While the revolt was crushed, this rebellion led by worshippers of the goddess nevertheless succeeded in encouraging numerous ancient writers to adopt anti-slavery positions. The faithful of Atargatis were the victims not only of Greeks and Romans but also of Hebrew zealots. Perhaps as many as 25,000, both men and women, died at Carnaim in 164 BCE at the hands of Judas Maccabeus. Her faithful were then persecuted by the Christians. Nevertheless, Atargatis was worshipped until at least the fourth century CE.

Ate Greek goddess of destruction, she appeared to the god DIONYSUS as a handsome youth in an attempt to destroy his love for the young satyr AMPELUS.

Athena Greek goddess of wisdom and war (as the former, identified with the Roman goddess Minerva) and patron of the city of Athens. According to most sources,

she is the daughter of ZEUS, springing from his forehead fully grown and ready for combat. Other accounts relate, however, that she is the daughter of POSEIDON and that her birthplace is LIBYA, suggesting an African and Amazonian (i.e. woman warrior) origin. Capable of transgender metamorphosis into a young man, Athena also holds the power of shapeshifting into a bird. Her intimate female companions include CHARICLO and MYRMEX. Chariclo is a nymph, the mother of the seer TIRESIAS, and at one time the companion of CHIRON. Unfortunately, Athena's relationships often end tragically or contain tragic elements. It is Athena, according to one legend (in other variants, it is HERA) who blinds Tiresias when he spies her and his mother Chariclo bathing. When she becomes angry at Myrmex, Athena transforms her into an ant. It is possible that these negative elements have been supplied by patriarchal mythographers, or that, like the myths of APOLLO and his lovers HYACINTHUS and CYPARISSUS, they may refer to the end of adolescence and to ancient rites of initiation into adulthood or into spiritual life. Athena was worshipped until at least 485 CE, when her temple at Athens was demolished and converted into a Christian church. In a survey of almost six hundred lesbians taken in 1989 and 1990, Jo Ann Loulan found that among seven goddess archetypes from which the women could choose to identify both themselves and their lovers, Athena rated third highest, with Aphrodite and Artemis ranking first and second.

Athirat (or **Asherah**) Primary goddess of the Canaanites, traditionally depicted as a nude woman with upraised arms or holding a lily in one hand and a serpent in the other, symbols of birth, death, and new life. Athirat is above all a goddess of the waters. She is also called Qudshu or Qadesh, the Holy One. As such, she is the goddess of erotic pleasure and is depicted as a HIERODULE (somewhat incorrectly described as a "sacred prostitute"). She is also known as the Mother of Kings. In this aspect, she is depicted as a horned female nursing male twins. While in Biblical times, Athirat was seen as the consort of a male deity, El, who became syncretized with the Hebrew Yahweh (or Jehovah), in earlier times she was depicted as a Great Goddess having a younger male consort named BAAL, who appears to have loved both women and men. Athirat was served by priestesses and also by gender variant male priests known as the QEDESHIM, or "holy ones." These men were also known as the KELABIM, or "dogs," the dog being the faithful companion of the goddess.

Atlantius Alternate name given to HERMAPHRODITUS, the androgynous child of HERMES and APHRODITE. This appellation emphasizes his, and also his parents', association with the god Atlas, a primordial giant who carries the sky on his shoulders. This god's link to the

beginnings of time have suggested to some mythologists a
link to primordial androgyny, which has led them to see a
cosmic pattern of original androgyny (Atlas) being split
into masculine (Hermes) and feminine (Aphrodite) and
then ultimately being reintegrated into an androgynous
whole (Hermaphroditus).

Atthis (fl. c. 600 BCE)   Beloved of the Greek poet-priestess
SAPPHO and member of the latter's THIASOS, or religious
household, on the island of LESBOS.

Attis   Youthful male consort of the Mediterranean
goddess CYBELE, revered by the gender variant, often
homoerotically inclined GALLI priests. Attis's name
suggests "goat" or "goatherd." He is commonly depicted
as a handsome goatherd or shepherd playing the pipes or
dancing. Maarten Vermaseren (1977) notes that "like the
Hellenistic dancing Erotes," Attis "sometimes wears
wings." He is also depicted as leaning on his staff in a
melancholy pose. Linked to the seasonal cycle, he
sometimes wears a wreath of pine cones and pomegranates
on his head and carries corn and fruit. He is, in the last
years of his worship, portrayed as a celestial deity, wearing
a "tiara set with stars" and associated with the moon, the
sun, and the Milky Way. The early Christian theologian
Arnobius writes, "When we name Attis . . . we mean and
speak of the sun." In the earliest times, Attis was compared
to ADONIS, PAN, and other vegetation deities. In later
times he, like Cybele and also like GANYMEDE, with whom
he came to be linked, was envisioned as a savior deity.
Holding within himself "the incorporeal cause of the forms
that are embodied in matter" and identified with aether,
the so-called "fifth substance," Attis had descended "even
unto our earth . . . from the stars" so that he might, through
self-sacrifice, teach mortals to prepare themselves for that
spiritual journey which would one day bring them to the
celestial throne of the Mother. Both male gender variance
and homoeroticism play a role in the myth of Cybele and
Attis. At the outset, ZEUS desires to have intercourse with
Cybele. She resists him, however. He masturbates, and his
semen falls onto a rock. From the rock springs an
androgynous being. Because of this creature's enormous
physical strength, the gods decide to castrate the being;
from that moment he is perceived as a eunuch named
AGDISTIS (sometimes mistakenly identified with Cybele).
Agdistis goes to live in the forest and becomes a hunter.
From the blood that spills when he is castrated, a
pomegranate tree grows. Nana, daughter of the river-god
Sangarios, eats a pomegranate from the tree and becomes
pregnant. She gives birth to Attis. Sangarios, refusing to
accept the miracle of virgin birth, forces Nana to surrender
the infant to goatherds. One day, when the youthful Attis is
hunting, he is encountered by the eunuch Agdistis, who
immediately falls in love with him. The two become
intimate companions, Agdistis presenting Attis "with the

spoils of wild beasts." Attis, under the influence of wine,
confesses to others that he and Agdistis have become
lovers, and that Agdistis has honored him with many gifts.
Attis satisfies Agdistis' "lust in the only way now possible,"
that is, either by allowing Agdistis to fellate him or by
having Agdistis take the receptive role in anal intercourse.
This topsy-turvy version of the Greek pederastic model is
underscored by the fact that both partners are
intermittently portrayed as hunters and transvestites.
Agdistis, however, is not alone in loving Attis; the young
man is also loved by Cybele. Together, they form a kind of
trinity. Attis, however, is pledged to marry the daughter of
King Midas. Opposing the event, Cybele and Agdistis
bring chaos to the wedding. The young bride, Ia, chops off
one of her breasts, while Attis castrates himself beneath a
pine tree. Attis, having castrated himself and botched the
job, utters these words before succumbing to death: "Take
these [i.e. my testicles or genitals], Agdistis, for which you
have stirred up so great and terribly perilous emotions."
From Attis's blood, violets spring, thus becoming his
sacred flowers. The Goddess weeps; from her tears an
almond tree emerges, signifying "the bitterness of death."
Cybele then bathes Attis's testicles or genitals, anoints
them with fragrant oils, wraps them in the youth's
garments, and buries them in the earth or conceals them in
a jar to be housed in a secret chamber. She then chops
down the pine tree, emblematic of self-sacrifice, and
transports it to the sacred cave in the vicinity of Pessinus.
While this tale might be read as one of jealousy and
intrigue, on a deeper level it speaks to a spiritual crisis
leading to enlightenment and reunion with the Goddess.
By the third century BCE, salvation had become an
important theme in religious thought, especially among
those participating in Goddess-centered and other
Mysteries. Perhaps influenced by Hinduism or Buddhism,
salvation had become linked – as is evident in Orphism – to
escape from the "wheel" of reincarnation or
metempsychosis which bound mortals to the earth. No
longer was the soul bound to return to the earth. The
Goddess now dwelt in the heavens, and it was the aim of
spiritually inclined mortals, often by way of rejecting
procreation (referred to as the "superabundance of
generative life"), to strive "upwards to the goddess of our
forefathers, to her who is the principle of all life." It was the
purpose and destiny of Attis to demonstrate that "in all
things the conversion to what is higher [i.e. spiritual
development] produces more power . . . than the
inclination to what is lower [i.e. reproduction]." Following
his act of self-sacrifice, Attis was "led upwards as though
from our earth" to resume again "his ancient sceptre." The
Roman Emperor Julian (332-363) writes, "immediately
after the castration, the trumpet sounds the recall for Attis
and for all of us who flew down from heaven and fell to
earth." Once more, and forever, Attis becomes the
"servant and charioteer of the Mother." Moreover, he is

made "the leader of all the tribes of divine beings" as well as the leader of the *galli*, "who are assigned to him by the Mother" and who are represented by her lions. Attis, now crowned with stars, is identified with the Milky Way. In one version of the myth of Cybele and Attis, Agdistis and Cybele plead with Zeus to restore Attis to life. Zeus refuses. He grants, however, "that the body should not decay, that his hairs should always grow, [and] that [one] of his fingers should live, and should be kept ever in motion." In this variant, Attis is neither reborn nor resurrected, but lives on eternally as, in Giulia Gasparro's terms, a *praesena numen* (numinous presence), in a kind of vampiric state, referred to as "survival in death." The finger has an erotic connotation in this context. Hugo Hepding points out that in Graeco-Roman iconography, the finger and the penis are often interchangeable symbols. Moreover, the finger in perpetual motion is a Greek sign signifying digital or penile stimulation of the anus, referred to as "siphnianizing," as the inhabitants of Siphnos were thought to be especially fond of anal eroticism. Arnobius links the moving finger of Attis with another legendary finger, namely, one of Zeus's on a statue created by Phidias. On this finger, the artist inscribed the name of Pantarces, a young man he loved. To inscribe the name on a finger suggested that the youth willingly yielded to anal eroticism. In the *Life of Apollonius* we find that the devotee of Attis, like that of ASCLEPIUS experienced sex with the high priest, the earthly incarnation of Attis: "The tie between god and man cannot be thought of in closer and stronger terms, and they are joined by a feeling not only of lifelong gratitude but of personal love, which in its expression passes over into sensual forms."

Attr (or **'Attar**)   Ugaritic and South Arabian androgynous or transgendered deity of VENUS as the star of morning. Attr is also a deity of war, water, and protection. His/her symbols include the spear and the antelope.

Atum   Creator deity and sun god of ancient Egypt, typically represented as a pharoah. Giving birth to himself from the primeval waters, Atum, by way of masturbation, created the primordial couple Shu, the god of sunlight and air, and Tefnut, the goddess of moisture. Occult tradition indicates that, much as in Gnostic myth, Atum (bearing a likeness to the Gnostic image of the God of the Biblical Old Testament) held power over Shu and Tefnut by sexually penetrating them. A coffin text states that Atum has no power over the man who has sexually penetrated him. This may indicate that the now deceased man once had intercourse with a priest or male devotee of Atum, but because of the esoteric nature of this text, it is hard to know. The passage does suggest that homoerotic (and perhaps also heterosexual) anal intercourse was related to one individual holding power over another.

Atymnius (or **Atymnios**)   Son of Cassiopeia, a Greek sea-goddess and at the same time a queen of Ethiopia, and Zeus. Atymnius as a youth was loved by the god APOLLO as well as by SARPEDON, a king of the Lycians. Atymnius was also desired by Sarpedon's brothers, MINOS and RHADAMANTHYS, but he rejected their advances. After Atymnius's death, his spirit was often seen riding beside his lover Apollo in the latter's solar chariot. Atymnius's name may mean "handsome youth whose praises must be sung."

Augustine of Hippo, Doctor, Bishop, Saint (354-430)   Educator, writer, theologian, and bishop of Hippo in North Africa, perhaps the most admired of the Church Fathers of Christianity. Virulently anti-pagan (especially against Goddess Reverence, and particularly against the reverence of CYBELE and ATTIS) following his conversion to Christianity, Augustine also became violently opposed to homoerotic and transgendered behavior (amply expressed in his *Confessions* and in *The City of God*) after having once loved another man very deeply. Describing his relationship with the young man in the *Confessions*, he writes: "My soul was sickly and full of sores . . . To love . . . and to be beloved, was sweet to me . . . I defiled . . . the spring of friendship with the filth of concupiscence, and I beclouded its brightness with the hell of lustfulness . . . I fell headlong then into the love wherein I longed to be ensnared." Having been this man's childhood friend, they met again when Augustine began teaching rhetoric. In the course of studying together, they fell in love. Augustine relates that also during the course of their relationship, he, still a pagan, encouraged his beloved, "sweet to me above all sweetness," to likewise devote himself to pre-Christian spiritual beliefs and practices. The Christian God, seeing what was happening, "tookest that man out of this life" when they had been together for only a year, causing the young man to die in the midst of a violent fever. As the young man lay dying and was temporarily unconscious, he was baptized as a Christian. During his final hours, he shrank from Augustine "as from an enemy." Of his despair, Augustine relates, "At this grief my heart was utterly darkened; and whatever I beheld was death . . . Mine eyes sought him everywhere . . . Wretched I was." Upon converting to Christianity, however, Augustine acknowledges the error of his ways. "Wretched is every soul bound by the friendship of perishable things," he now argues; "he is torn asunder when he loses them." Indeed, he rejoices that God has taken his beloved away from him. "Behold my heart, O my God, behold and see into me; for well I remember it, O my Hope, who cleansest me from the impurity of such affections, directing mine eyes towards Thee." Ironically, he is being claimed by some queer-identified Christians of the 1990s as a patron of same-sex lovers; he is fêted on August 28.

Augustus (Gaius Julius Caesar Octavianus, 63 BCE-14 CE)   Roman emperor known primarily for having lived during the lifetime of JESUS, he was depicted by those who knew him as a gender variant, homoerotically or bisexually inclined individual revering the goddess CYBELE.

Aulos   One of the principal wind instruments of ancient Greece, sacred to ATHENA, CALAMUS, CYBELE, DIONYSUS, KOTYS, MARSYAS, and OLYMPUS. The aulos, often described as a double flute, is perhaps better described as an oboe in which air is forced through a double reed to produce sound. The larger pipe acts as a drone tone while the other plays melody. The longer, sometimes curved, pipe is held in the left hand, while the shorter straight pipe is held in the right. The aulos is made of various materials, but most significantly of calamus reed. Among the five types of aulos, characterized by a range of pitches from lowest to highest, are the *parthenioi* (virginal) and the *paedikoi* (boy's pipes). Both of these are found at the high end and are considered more "feminine" than the others. The aulos is played alone, in pairs, or combined with stringed instruments and percussion. Some sources place the origin of the aulos in Phrygia, with one legend relating that Kotys, a Thracian or Phrygian goddess also worshipped in Greece, is the inventor of both the aulos and CYMBALS, the latter being especially linked to Goddess Reverence and to the cult of Dionysus. In the worship of Kotys the aulos, like cymbals and drums, were played by her gender variant male, or transgendered, priests, the BAPTAI. In another myth, Athena is attributed with the invention or discovery of the aulos. Seeing her reflection in the water, and displeased with the way her face is distorted while playing it – there is a suggestion in this myth that the image reminds her of oral intercourse – Athena throws the aulos away. It lands in Phrygia and is found and played by Marsyas, the legendary musician and lover of Olympus, who also plays the instrument. Still another legend concerning the aulos credits its invention to Cybele. In rites to this goddess, her gender variant priests, the GALLI, played the aulos.

Aurora   Goddess of dawn associated with Eos and Aotis, she is the "rosy-fingered" opener of the gates of heaven, the mother of the winds. Patron of ceremonies of UNION between women in ancient Greece, Aurora was among the deities worshipped by members of the THIASOS of SAPPHO on the island of LESBOS.

Ausonius, Decimus Magnus (c. 310-c. 395) Homoerotically or bisexually inclined French-Roman poet, teacher, and provincial governor. While Ausonius converted to Christianity, his poetry remains profoundly inspired by Greco-Roman paganism, as in a poem celebrating a young man's beauty, wherein he compares the youth to ADONIS and GANYMEDE. Ausonius shared a passionate relationship with PAULINUS OF NOLA (c. 353-431), a bishop who would later be canonized as a Christian saint. Though in later life, it appears, Paulinus distanced himself from Ausonius, he wrote to him during the halcyon days of their relationship, "Yea, when the prison of this flesh is broken, / And from the earth I shall have gone my way, / Wheresoe'er in the wide universe I stay me, / There shall I bear thee, as I do today." Ausonius is fêted on June 22, the official feast day of St Paulinus of Nola.

Austen, Hallie Iglehart (1947-   )   Priestess of Wicca and author of *Womanspirit: A Guide to Women's Wisdom* (1983) and *The Heart of the Goddess: Art, Myth and Meditations of the World's Sacred Feminine* (1990). A pioneer in the Women's Spirituality movement and in the contemporary manifestation of Goddess Reverence, Austen describes herself as a "pantheist and pansexual," viewing "spirituality and sexuality as inseparable." Living with her beloved companion, Gwendolyn Jones, "on the land" in northern California, Austen observes, "When we live close to nature, when we are not cut off from . . . life, we feel out true identity as part of the vast web of being. Then we experience the true nature of the erotic, the life force flowing through us and all of creation . . . Living erotically is being open to life in all its manifestations."

Autopator   "Self-Father," a name given by Valentinian Gnostics to the primordial deity, who embraces both male and female. Autopator is occasionally identified with ADAM Aeon.

Avalokiteshvara   In Mahayana Buddhism, a primarily male yet also transgendered BODDHISATTVA (here, an enlightened human being destined to become a Buddha) of compassion, whose name means "He who hears the sounds of the world." Avalokiteshvara serves as a savior to those who follow him and ultimately becomes a form of Amida Buddha. In Japan, Avalokiteshvara becomes the male *bodhisattva* KANNON; in China, the female *bodhisattva* KUAN YIN (Guanyin), the Goddess of Mercy. E. Zolla (1981) explains that the male Avalokiteshvara often transforms into the Kuan Yin when he becomes overwhelmed by compassion for children. "Soon, however, she will be ready to change back into her male form, becoming a fierce general in order to defend his devotees."

Avery, Shug   "Womanist" (i.e. caring deeply about women in multiple ways) character in Alice Walker's novel *The Color Purple* (1982). Literary critic SDiane Bogus (b. 1946) associates Shug with an archetypal figure she refers to as the "QUEEN B(EE)," who fuses a gift for music with spirituality, social conscience, and the love of women for each other. In Walker's novel, in which Shug and Celie, the central character, come to love each other deeply, it is

Shug who performs the role of erotic, political, and spiritual mentor, especially leading Celie to accept her love for women and to see God as a being embracing all ethnicities, genders, and sexualities.

Awo Transgendered divinity of the MOON of the Akan people of Ghana.

Awonawilona Androgynous, third gender, or TWO-SPIRIT creator of the Zuni people of New Mexico. Awonawilona creates the sky-father and the earth-mother by pulling skin off his/her body, rolling it into balls, and tossing the balls into the primeval waters.

Ayizan In Haitian- and New Orleans-based VODOU, the gynandrous female or transgendered (female-to-male) *lwa* (deity or spirit) of initiation. With the *lwa* Loco, she (-he) is primordial parent to the human race, their pairing akin to that of the Biblical ADAM and Eve (without, however, the patriarchal aspect). Together, Ayizan and Loco form a trinity with the *lwa* LEGBA. Ayizan is also sometimes said to be the wife of Legba. M. Deren (1983) writes, "Here, in Ayizan, are the last echoes of the androgynous divinity. In some regions she is referred to as 'he,' and in songs she is related to the ancient androgynous founders of the race: SILIBO-GWETO and NANAN-BOUCLOU, said to have preceded even MAWU-LISA." L. Hurbon (1995) observes that the *vèvè*, a symbolic drawing (or, in Robert Farris Thompson's terms, a "cosmogram") of Ayizan "basically consists of two conjoined Vs of primeval androgyny." As Hurbon points out, Ayizan is a *lwa* of great "authority and power." Especially presiding over the initiation process, Ayizan is a nurturer and guardian of humans, a great healer, a magician who protects her (-his) devotees from psychic harm, and a teacher of the arts of healing and magic. Her (-his) sacred attribute is the royal palm, its leaves depicted in her (-his) *vèvè*.

Aztec Religion Spiritual tradition of ancient Mexico, appropriating beliefs and practices of earlier and conquered peoples of the region, focusing on the reverence of the gods, above all the SUN, primarily by way of blood sacrifice. Aztec religion placed a great deal of emphasis not only upon the sun's movement but also on those of other celestial bodies, inspiring a complex calendar upon which the timing of rituals was based. While on the whole Aztec religion tended to be militaristic in character, the Aztecs were profoundly aware of the need to cultivate beauty and pleasure. At the time of the Spanish Conquest, Aztec religious authorities did not in the main sanction same-sex eroticism nor did they approve of gender variance. Punishment for same-sex eroticism was especially harsh; according to Fernando de Alva Ixlilxochitl: "To the one acting as a female, they removed his entrails from the bottom, he was tied down to a log, and the boys from the town covered him with ash, until he was buried; and then they put a lot of wood and burnt him. The one acting as a male was covered with ash, tied down to a log until he died." Individuals, both male and female, who dressed in garments traditionally worn by the opposite sex, were punished in a similar manner, as were women engaging in same-sex eroticism. At some as yet undetermined point in the development of Aztec culture, both transgenderism and same-sex eroticism generally came to be regarded as manifestations of illness. Indeed, one of the terms used to refer to a sick man, *cocoxqui*, also came to signify a gender variant, homoerotically inclined male. This "illness" due to homosexual and gender variant behavior was "discovered" by way of corn divination. One kernel falling upon another and causing the first to stand upright was all the evidence a diviner needed. By the time of the arrival of the Spanish conquistadors, a number of derogatory terms appear to have been in currency to designate such persons. A number of Nahuatl terms underscore the punishment awaiting them: *tlatla*, "he burns;" *tlatlani*, "he deserves the flames;" *chichinoloni*, "he deserves to be cast in the fire." In spite of the extreme hostility directed toward such men, however, Spanish chroniclers reported that not only was same-sex eroticism practiced among the Aztecs, but also that many men who dressed in women's garments and/or who engaged in same-sex eroticism were serving as HIERODULE-priests. Moreover, a number of Aztec deities, including TEZCATLIPOCA, TLAZOLTEOTL, XOCHIPILLI, and XOCHIQUETZAL were linked to transgenderism and/or same-sex passion. In general, these deities presided over realms of creativity, magic, and death/rebirth.

B

Baader, Franz von (1765-1841) German Romantic writer and Catholic mystical theologian. According to von Baader, the androgyne had existed in the beginning of time and would return, as Christ, at the end of time. Von Baader was inspired by Jacob Boehme (1575-1624), from whom he borrowed the notion that the Biblical Fall occurred not with the eating of the apple but with the dividing of an androgynous ADAM/Eve into male and female. During the period between the Fall and the Apocalypse, according to von Baader, marriage served to remind men and women of this original unity. At the end of history, however, men and women would be transformed into gynandrous angels, thus rendering marriage unnecessary.

Baal Male consort of the goddess ATHIRAT in Canaanite, or Ugaritic, religion and myth. Although Baal himself was later patriarchalized, becoming a god of war, he began as a god of agriculture. Between his first and final appearances, he was, as a patron of the cattle industry, depicted as a golden calf. He is linked to Dumuzi, the consort of the Mesopotamian goddess INANNA/ISHTAR, as well as to ADONIS. Ugaritic literature indicates that Baal also may have been a lover of men. Baal lived on the holy mountain Sapanu (also known as Mt Kasios or Jebel el-Aqra, forty kilometers north of Ras Shamra, or Ugarit). Here he was served by a "gracious lad" who sang to him in a sweet voice while playing cymbals or the lyre. This young man may have been the god Kinar, the ORPHEUS of Canaanite myth. The relationship of Baal and the youth, or Kinar, has been compared to that of ZEUS and GANYMEDE, suggesting a homoerotic aspect. Johannes DeMoor also maintains that a gender variant priest may have taken the role of the "sweet-voiced youth" in ritual dramas. The "sweet-voiced youth" or "gracious lad" has survived in the literature of both Judaism and Islam. In the Bible, DAVID assumes this role, while in Islamic literature, the figure survives as one of the WILDAN, "boys of perpetual youth," who serve divine liquor to the deceased in Paradise.

Babaluayé (also **Obaluayé, Omolu, Shapanna, Sopanna**) In the Yoruba-diasporic spiritual traditions of Santería and Candomblé, the *orishá* (deity) who may bring as well as heal life-threatening illnesses including smallpox, cancer, and HIV/AIDS. Thought to have emerged from the swamps, Babaluayé is a son of the goddess NANA BURUKU. Babaluayé is sometimes identified or syncretized with the Catholic saints Lazarus, Roch, and SEBASTIAN. He is depicted as a man whose skin is covered with lesions. He walks with a cane, and dogs lick his wounds. He wears a cape of purple velvet and burlap. Tradition has it that he was once very licentious. The *orishá* Olofí (related to OBATALA and sometimes identified with JESUS Christ) was offended by his excesses and punished him with venereal disease. The goddess OSHUN found him in great pain and healed him with her magical honey. She then went to Olofí and cried, "How dare you punish Babaluayé like this when you desire the very same thing!" In recent years, Babaluayé has become recognized by many practitioners as an *orishá* to be invoked in prayer if one or one's loved one has AIDS. Describing a Cuban sanitorium in which persons with AIDS were living fairly comfortably in the mid-1980s, Mark Kurlansky reports in *A Continent of Islands: Searching for the Caribbean Destiny* that by 1986, PWAs were allowed to make brief pilgrimages to the shrine of St Lazarus/Babaluayé, where they would pray to be healed. Eduardo Mejía, a practitioner of Santería in New York, related to the authors of the present text, "My mother has told me to pray to Saint Lazarus/Babaluayé [concerning AIDS]," and a priestess of the Yoruba-diasporic religion shared a ritual meant to ease the suffering associated with AIDS with the authors which includes: "Get an image of Saint Lazarus. Make a garment for him out of purple cloth and some old brown burlap. Wipe your body (or that of the person with HIV/AIDS) with the cloth and then drape it around the statue. The statue should be set on a plate, with different kinds of beans surrounding it. Then you should rub any lesions on you (his/her) body with unpeeled purple onions. No more than six onions. Then place the onions in a circle around the plate. Place a seven-day, deep purple candle near the statue and the plate. Remember not to use any water in your ritual, as Babaluayé does not like water. Every day at sunrise and sunset, meditate upon the statue and the candle and pray to Babaluayé, asking him to take your pain upon himself. Those onions should sit there until they absolutely rot. To end the ritual, take the cloak of the statue. Keep the statue, but go to a riverbank and bury the beans and onions. Should one of the onions begin to grow, that's a good sign."

Bahucharamata (or **Bouchera, Behechra**) Hindu goddess worshipped by many persons including the HIJRAS, gender variant male, third gender/sex, or transgender (depending upon one's perspective) priests and initiates. The popular image of Bahuchara is that of a goddess riding on a cock. S. Nanda (1990) observes that "all the *hijra* households in Bastipore have this very colorful print [of the Goddess] framed and hanging on the wall. Some Hindus," Nanda continues, "worship Bahucharamata in the form of a *yantra*, a conventional symbol for the vulva, and it is suggested that there is a relation between this representation of the Goddess and the emasculation ritual of the *hijras*." Bahucharamata is believed by some to be a sister of the goddess DEVI as well as the spirit of a martyred woman. A tale is told of a group of women travelers who were brutally attacked by a group of men. One of the women, Bahuchara, grabbed a sword from a man who was about to rape her and cut off her breasts, this leading to her death. As Bahuchara's self-mutilation led to her martyrdom and divinization, so her male followers, the *hijras*, practice self-mutilation.

Bajasa Gender variant, or third gender, male shamans of the Toradja Bare'e (Celebes) who dress in feminine attire, behave in a traditionally feminine manner, and relate intimately to men. *Bajasa* revere the goddess Ndo i Lino, the god Puë di Songe, and various other celestial deities. According to M. Eliade (1974), they act as "purifiers, healers, and psychopomps." Eliade relates that "their particular technique consists in ecstatic journeys to the sky and the underworld, which the *bajasa* can perform either in spirit or *in concreto*." In healing rituals, the *bajasa* often ascends the RAINBOW to the house of the deity Puë di Songe and returns with the patient's straying soul.

Baldwin, James (1924-1987) Writer who sought in his life and work to honor his love for men and his African/African-American heritage – embracing spiritual expression and political activism. Exemplary of his artistic interweaving of these dimensions of his life are episodes in the short story "Outing" (1951), a tale rooted in the Biblical story of DAVID AND JONATHAN, in which Johnny Grimes realizes, during a church picnic, that he has fallen in love with his friend David Jackson; and in the novel *Tell Me How Long the Train's Been Gone* (1968), in which a bisexual Black actor, Leo Proudhammer shares a loving relationship with a radical African-American activist named Christopher. Of this novel, Emmanuel S. Nelson writes: "Baldwin casts the homosexual in a redemptive role. Christopher's name itself . . . suggests his role as a racial savior. But Christopher is also comfortably and confidently gay;" the result is a potent interweaving of ethnicity, homoeroticism, and the spiritual.

La Baleine (or **Balaine**) Female, sometimes gynandrous, *lwa* (deity or spirit) of the ocean in African-diasporic Haitian- and New Orleans-based Vodou, depicted as a whale (*baleine*). She represents fertility (in terms both of reproduction and creativity), maternal compassion, receptivity, and the mystery of the depths. M. Marcelin (1950) relates that La Baleine joins with another Vodou goddess, LA SIRENE, to form a "single *lwa* : an androgynous deity." A chant evoking this female-female

being includes the line "La Sirène, oh, it's you! La Baleine, oh, it's you!" Many *houngans* (or *oungans*; priests of Vodou) envision La Baleine as the intimate companion of La Sirène. That is why it is said that the two "always walk together." It appears that La Baleine, in her relationship with La Sirène, assumes an Amazonian role. Further, it appears that both La Baleine and La Sirène share an intimate relationship with Agwe, the god of the sea; together, they form a kind of triad or trinity of marine deities. According to Mark Miller (b. 1965) and other practitioners of New Orleans-based Vodou, La Baleine often manifests herself as a lesbian being when she possesses a female devotee; she may also manifest herself as a homoerotically inclined male being, especially when possessing a male. La Baleine is sometimes associated with the Yoruba-diasporic transgendered submarine deity OLOKUN.

Ballanche, Pierre (1776-1847) French historian and utopian philosopher. In the *Vision d'Hébal* (1831) and other writings, he expressed the belief – in certain ways similar to that of Franz von Baader – that in the future, when women would no longer be oppressed by men, persons would become increasingly androgynous. Ballanche's conception of an androgynous utopia profoundly influenced the French social movement of Saint-Simonism, with the androgyne becoming one of its most potent symbols. Among those inspired by the vision of Ballanche as expressed in Saint-Simonism was the lesbian painter Rosa BONHEUR.

Banana and Plantain For African-American writer Audre LORDE, bananas and plantains are symbols of female genitalia and woman-loving desire. In *Zami: A New Spelling of My Name*, she writes, "There were green plantains, which we half-peeled and then planted, fruit-deep, in each other's bodies . . . There were ripe red finger bananas . . . with which I parted your lips gently."

Banda In Haitian- and New Orleans-based Vodou, an erotic dance of the GHEDES, the spirits of the dead, emphasizing grinding hip movements, performed by both same-sex and opposite-sex couples simulating lesbian, gay, and heterosexual intercourse.

Bankhead, Tallulah (1903-1968) Bisexual Hollywood icon of the queer community, among her greatest fans was the lesbian writer Radclyffe HALL. In the queer communities of the early 1970s, a series of jokes focusing on the flamboyant personality of Tallulah emerged. In one of these, Tallulah enters the Episcopal Church of Saint Mary the Virgin in New York. Terribly nearsighted, she cries out as the thurifer (the person carrying the censer) approaches, "Dahling, your drag is simply divine, but your purse is on fire!"

Bantut Gender variant, or third gender, male, often homoerotically inclined, spiritual functionaries among the Taosug people of the southern Philippines. Specialized roles for *bantut* in Taosug society include that of *fakil* (priest), *mangubat* (healer), *barbalan* (magician), and *mangangalang* or *manggagabbang* (ritual musician). One type of ritual music, *pagsindil* ("to express") is sung by *bantut* or women at weddings. *Bantut* singing style includes singing in the highest registers, traditionally linked to femininity. Transgendered ritual behavior among the *bantut* also includes gestures and body movements usually enacted by women.

Baphomet Deity worshipped since the Middle Ages, usually portrayed as a transgendered or hermaphroditic, hybrid human-goat figure, and occasionally as a handsome, burly man with curly, black hair and beard. Some scholars have suggested the name Baphomet may derive from "Mahomet," a corruption of Mohammed. Baphomet was believed to be worshipped by the ORDER OF THE KNIGHTS TEMPLAR as the source of fertility and wealth. In 1307 King Philip IV of France accused the Order of homosexuality and of worshipping Baphomet. Centuries later, Aleister CROWLEY (1875-1947) named himself "Baphomet" when he joined the Ordo Templis Orientlis, a secret sexual magic order.

Baptai Gender variant, transgendered male priest/esse/s of the Thracian/Greco-Roman goddess KOTYS. The "Baptists" were so called because they underwent a ritual cleansing, being smeared with a mixture of bran and clay and then bathed. After this baptism, they would celebrate communion – theirs included beer and rare or raw meat – and would chant in unison, "I have fled the evil, I have found a better way." From the seventh century BCE onward, male worshippers of Kotys were linked to homoeroticism and gender variance. They often dressed in feminine attire, which included wigs – probably blonde – and head garlands of poplar and fennel. The philosopher Synesius, equating the male *baptai* with homoerotically inclined, gender variant men, wrote, "One who partlcipates in the orgies of Kotys is identical with a *cinaedus*." In the Roman Empire, the term *baptai* came to mean "effeminate and licentious." Further, *baptai* became associated with another term, *impudicus*, which refers generally to lustfulness but "more particularly [to] sodomy." The *baptai* served primarily as workers of magic and ritual musicians, being especially celebrated as flute players and as drummers, their drums made of bronze cauldrons covered with hides. Leading a somewhat itinerant lifestyle, they often sojourned briefly in towns and cities, dancing wildly while waving serpents – sometimes real and sometimes made of gold – above their heads and shouting "*Evoe Saboi*, Hail Sabazius!" Their major rites, however, took place in the mountains by torchlight. Here, at the *kotyttia* or *sabazia*, they would again handle serpents, guiding them over their bodies, especially the genital region, and would dance furiously in a circle until they fell into an altered state. In this condition, as we have observed with other priests of goddesses, the *baptai* would become possessed by the Goddess and would utter her words.

Barbara, Saint (d. c. 200 CE) Amazonian Catholic saint depicted as bearing a sword and wearing a fortress-shaped crown. She actually may not have been a saint but instead a figure emerging from a popular yearning for the Goddess or goddesses of antiquity. Or she may have been a real person about whom legends arose after her death. Whatever the case, her iconography and mythology were blended over time with that of ARTEMIS/DIANA, ATHENA, CYBELE, and other classical goddesses. Popular belief maintains that Barbara was a beautiful pagan woman who rebelled against her father's wish that she marry not only by rejecting all potential suitors but also by converting to Christianity and by converting a bathhouse into a church. Enraged, her father dragged Barbara to a mountain top and slew her. As he was descending the mountain, he was struck by lightning and died. Thus it is that St Barbara is believed to control lightning and electrical storms. She is considered gender variant or transgendered by many practitioners of folk Catholicism and by practitioners of Santería, where she is syncretized with the "macho" male god of lightning, SHANGO. Barbara is the patron saint of drummers, architects, construction workers, firemen and -women, miners, and others. Protecting her faithful against fire and lightning and invigorating them with creativity, she is fêted on December 4.

Barbariccia (or **Barnariccia**) In Dante's *Inferno* (Canto 21), "Curly Beard" is a lord of demons associated with anal intercourse who makes his anus into a trumpet.

Barker, Clive (1952-) Gay English male writer and director of horror and fantasy fiction and films. His works include: *Hellraiser* (film, 1987), *Weaveworld* (novel, 1987), *Imajica* (novel, 1991), and *Lord of Illusions* (film, 1995). Many of his works depict the interrelationship of homoeroticism or pansexuality and the magical, mystical, or mythical. "In *Imajica*," Barker explains, "two of the heroes are gay. One dies of AIDS and is resurrected in the body of the lover." Barker has been profoundly inspired by contemporary mythology, especially by classics of children's literature including L. Frank Baum's THE WIZARD OF OZ (1900) and James Barrie's *Peter Pan* (1904): "The seeds of why I do what I do are in my childhood. I wouldn't let Narnia and Never-Never Land and Oz go . . . Why should I lose these wonderlands? They were the ways I best understood myself." Barker has little tolerance for Christianity as it is practiced today: "The Vatican sells lies . . . [The Reverend Jerry] Falwell does the same . . . these people are using the book [i.e. the Bible] for corrupt and divisive fascist intentions." When asked by interviewer Brandon Jüdell in 1995 what the "world might be like if Clive Barker had written the Bible," Barker replied, "There would be a lot more goddesses."

Barney, Natalie Clifford (1876-1972)   Bisexual or lesbian writer born in Dayton, Ohio who lived in Paris most of her life. In 1904, she traveled with one of her lovers, Renée VIVIEN, to the island of LESBOS, where, in memory of their poetic ancestor SAPPHO, they planned to establish a lesbian-centered artistic and spiritual community; unfortunately, it failed to materialize. In 1909, however, Barney, remaining faithful to their Sapphic dream, formed a Friday night salon, which became known as "Lesbos in Paris." Participants in the salon included Sylvia Beach, André GIDE, Wanda Landowska, Edna St Vincent Millay, Marcel Proust, Vita Sackville-West, Edith Sitwell, Gertrude Stein, Violet Trefusis, Oscar WILDE, and Marguerite YOURCENAR. Of Barney's works, *The One Who Is Legion* may be most appropriate in our context. Illustrated by Barney's lover Romaine Brooks, the tale is a macabre one centering on a hermaphroditic spirit inspired in part by Vivien. According to the bisexual actress-courtesan Liane de Pougy in *Idylle Saphique* (1901), Barney referred to lesbianism as "a religion of the body, whose kisses are prayers," and described lesbian love not as a "perversion" but as a "conversion."

Baron Limba   One of the family of Barons, who belong to the larger family of GHEDES, deities (*lwa*) or spirits of the dead in the pantheon of Haitian- and New Orleans-based Vodou. According to Michael Bertiaux (1988), Baron Limba is the intimate male companion of BARON LUNDY, also male. "These two barons," Bertiaux writes, "who are homosexual lovers, formed their own school for teaching nude wrestling." This practice is, for those devoted to Limba and Lundy, a way of accumulating magical force.

Baron Lundy   Like BARON LIMBA, one of the family of Barons within the greater family of GHEDES in the Vodou pantheon. According to Michael Bertiaux, Lundy is the lover of Limba. He is also alternately depicted, in Bertiaux's fusion of Gnostic-inspired ritual MAGIC and Vodou, as identical to, or as the high priest of, the spirit CHORONZON and as such is linked to the gateway of the QABBALAH known as DAATH.

Baron Oua Oua   Like BARON LIMBA and BARON LUNDY, one of the family of Barons, who belong to the greater family of GHEDES in the Vodou pantheon. Mark Miller (b. 1965) and other practitioners of New Orleans-based Vodou describe Oua Oua as the Baron "most closely linked to homosexuality." Often assuming a childlike appearance, Baron Oua Oua is especially associated, as are the other Barons, with ancestor reverence and MAGIC.

Baron Samedi (also **Baron Cimitière, Baron La Croix**) In Haitian- and New Orleans-based Vodou, a bisexual and occasionally transgendered dandy, leader of the Barons and the GHEDES, the spirits of the dead. He is married to Maman (or Madame) Brigitte (also known as Gran-N Brigit). They are especially known as the parents of GHEDE NIBO. According to African-American dancer, choreographer, and dance historian Katherine Dunham (1983), "Baron Samedi's dual sexuality is expressed in gesture and language as well as in clothing." Samedi wears a top hat or straw hat, sunglasses (often with one lens removed, suggesting one eye observing the world of the living and the other the world of the dead and spirits, reminiscent of the Greek prophet TIRESIAS), a black frock coat, and sometimes a skirt of raffia. His favorite colors are black and purple, the latter being the color most associated with Vodou in New Orleans. The Baron is well known for his "lascivious movements," which include both phallic thrusts and pelvic grinds, the latter (and perhaps also the former) indicating a desire to engage in anal intercourse. While Samedi is especially concerned with the realm of the dead, Laënnec Hurbon (1995) observes, "For most of the problems of daily life, he is the spirit most often appealed to." He is also invoked by those performing extraordinary feats of magic or sorcery. Samedi dwells in the cemetery. On his altar one finds a cross, a skull, candles, and a bottle of rum. He also accepts offerings of salted herring, black goats, and black hens. As his name suggests, his special day is Saturday. He is syncretized with the Catholic Saint Expedite (or Expeditus), who is fêted on April 19.

Basava (fl. twelfth century CE)   Hindu male poet, founder of a utopian community, treasurer to a king, and devotee of the god SHIVA. His community, *Shivanubhavamantapa*, encouraged the blending of manual labor with the search for enlightenment; promoted equality among men and women; and sought to abolish the caste system. Transgender and/or homoerotic elements associated with Shiva's worship resonate in Basava's poems. "Sometimes I am man," he writes, "sometimes I am woman. O lord . . . / I'll make war for you / but I'll be your devotee's bride."

Basir   Gender variant or third gender male shamans of the Ngaju Dayak of Borneo. The *basir* of the Ngaju Dayak of Borneo revered an androgynous deity named Mahatala-Jata. The *basir*, along with the female *balian* shamanesses, were seen as reflections of this androgynous deity; they were both referred to as *tambon haruei bungai*, "watersnakes which are at the same time hornbills." J. van der Kroef (1954) writes of the basir: "The transvestism of the *basir* and his homosexual practices are symbolic . . . of the total Ngaju godhead." Of the Ngaju, van der Kroef explains that the *basir* were expected to "act as women sexually." He stresses that failure to perform homosexually might place the *basir* in an "inferior position." H. Schärer (1963) indicates that the *basir*, like the female *balian*, functioned as HIERODULES. He also indicates that prior to or even during major ceremonies, *basir* might engage in public, cultic homoeroticism. Through the experience of sexual union with a *basir* or a *balian*, a traditional Ngaju male might be brought into the presence of the androgynous deity. Both the Ngaju *basir* and the Iban *manang bali* established marriage-like relationships with traditional males. Ngaju *basir*, along with the female *balian*, were the "chief officials during new year's ceremonies." They were especially gifted as ritual chanters and singers. Among the Ngaju *basir* and *balian*, communication and ultimately union with the deity occurs during a state of possession, when the deity (*sangiang*) enters the stomach – rather than the head, as is customary in African traditions – and begins to speak to and then through the shaman or shamaness. Among the Ngaju, as in some African traditions, the possessed individual, whether male or female, is perceived as feminine, while the deity, whether male or female, is perceived as masculine, during the time of possession; the *basir* or *balian* is a boat (*bandong*) in which the deity sails. In Ngaju, both *bandong* and *mangumpang*, another term referring to possession, are connotative of sexual intercourse. The Ngaju Dayak believed not only that the gender variant *basir* would retain his identity after death but also that he would share a special "village of the dead in the Upperworld" with the *balian* shamanesses.

Basket Crossculturally, the basket is primarily a feminine symbol. Among some, including ancient Greek and Maidu, a Native American Indian people, it is, by extension, a signifier of gender variant, transgendered, or TWO-SPIRIT male status. In ancient Greek theater, when a male carried a *kalathos*, a vase-shaped reed basket containing spinning work, it signified his gender variant status. In Maidu culture, one of the primary tasks of two-spirit males was making ceremonial baskets.

Bassareus Alternate name of the Greek god DIONYSUS referring specifically to his effeminate or transgendered appearance. The bassara is a woman's dress believed to be of Thracian or Lydian origin, associated with the goddess CYBELE and her cult. To the feminine bassara is added the masculine ending -eus to signify the transgenderism of Dionysus.

Bathala Transgendered or hermaphroditic deity worshipped by the BAYOGUIN and others of the pre-Christian Philippines. The name "Bathala" signifies "man and woman in one."

Baton In Greek mythology, "Blackberry" (or "Bramble") is the beloved charioteer of Amphiaraus. Just as AMPHIARAUS and Baton are about to be struck by an enemy, they are swallowed by the earth to prevent their deaths. Baton was revered as a deified warrior and had a sanctuary at Argos.

Battersea'd The homoerotically inclined, transgendered MOLLY subculture of seventeenth- and eighteenth-century England included a kind of health clinic that specialized in the herbal treatment of mollies and their male partners having venereal disease, which was rampant at this time. "Battersea'd," in molly slang, referred in part to a diseased penis, often found among sailors taking holiday at then notorious Battersea Park. B. Weinreb and C. Hibbert (1963) describe the park, prior to its dismantling and purposeful landscaping by the government, as a locus of "riff-raff" where brothels, theatres, taverns, and other sites were populated by "actors, dancers, conjurors and fortune tellers . . . and hawkers and vendors of all kinds of articles." A proverb among mollies, "you must go to Battersea, to be cut for the simples," referred to medicinal herbs growing at the Park. From these "simples" – including rhubarb, juniper, sassafras, saffron, cinnamon, nutmeg, and mace – mollies prepared ointments, also apparently called "battersea," which were smeared on the penis.

Baubo The ELEUSINIAN MYSTERIES were founded to commemorate the Greek goddess DEMETER's grief-stricken search for her daughter PERSEPHONE after the latter had been abducted by Hades, lord of the Underworld. During that period of grief, Demeter encountered two eccentric female figures, Baubo and Iambe. Baubo's name signifies "belly;" she is the goddess of belly laughter. She is sometimes associated with Heqt, the Egyptian frog goddess of birth, as well as with HECATE. Beyond her amphibian aspect, Baubo has been depicted as having a "headless and limbless body, with her genitals forming a bearded mouth, and her breasts staring like eyes." Iambe, portrayed as a mobilly impaired woman, is considered a twin or DOUBLE of Baubo. She is the goddess of obscene speech and iambic pentameter. Legend has it that Baubo and Iambe conspired to shake Demeter out of her depression, Iambe by telling her proto-limericks and Baubo by lifting her skirts. While most scholars have accepted the version of the myth which says that Demeter laughed when she looked upon the odd positioning of Baubo's body parts, a lesser known version of the myth recounts that Demeter smiled when Baubo lifted her skirts because she was delighted by the beautiful body of a young woman who had depilated herself. This lesbian variant of the myth was linked by Arnobius to a homoerotic myth concerning the god DIONYSUS and a mortal named PROSYMNUS who once fell in love with him. Baubo's name suggests transgenderism, according to Marie Delcourt (1961); while "*baubo*" refers to the belly, suggesting the womb, "*baubon*" refers to the phallus. In the *Companion to Literary Myths, Heroes, and Archetypes* (1992), Camille Dumoulié suggests that Baubo shares common traits with both Medusa and Dionysus, as indicated by German philosopher Friedrich Nietzsche in *The Birth of Tragedy* (1891) and *The Gay Science* (1892). Dumoulié further suggests that the tale of Baubo should be compared with the Shinto myth of AME NO UZUME's erotic, shamanistic dance to entice the sun goddess AMATERASU OMI KAMI from the cave in which she is hiding. The appearance of the fused Baubo-Iambe during the Eleusinian Mysteries occurred after the procession of worshippers left the temple of Zeus and crossed the bridge over the River Cephisus. This was the scene of the *Gephyrismos*. The role of Baubo appears to have been performed alternately by a female or male HIERODULE, the latter dressed in feminine attire.

Baudri of Bourgueil (1046-1130)   French Benedictine Catholic monk who became Archbishop of Dol near Mont St Michel in Brittany in 1107. According to T. Stehling (1984), Baudri appears to have been bisexually inclined. In "To Vitalis," he writes, "Vitalis will nowhere be separated from me, / Indeed till the savage day which takes his spirit away . . . / And even then . . . / Our two souls will become the breath of one spirit."

Bavent, Sister Madeleine (fl. mid-seventeenth century) French Catholic nun of the convent of Louviers, near Rouen, ultimately scapegoated and dying in prison, taking the heat (along with one of the priests of the convent) for the eccentric rites allegedly taking place at the convent. Led first by Father Pierre David, later by Father Mathurin Picart, and finally by Father Thomas Boullé, and carried out by Sister Madeleine and the other nuns, the rites supposedly included Goddess Reverence, particularly of a manifestation of ASTARTE, Witchcraft, and MAGIC. Father David was said to have encouraged the lesbian inclinations of Sister Madeleine and the other nuns. He did so by teaching that attending prayers in the nude honored the primordial innocence of ADAM and Eve and that the expression of the body in eroticism could not defile a pure soul. Following the deaths of David and Picart and the succession of Boullé, an Inquisitorial investigation resulted in the execution of Boullé and the imprisonment (for life) of Sister Madeleine.

Bayoguin   Gender variant or third gender male, or transgendered, shamans indigenous to the Philippines. While not all pre-Christian shamans were gender variant, "in most cases," as J. Fleras observes (1993) "a 'man whose nature inclined toward that of a woman,' called a *bayoguin*, was assigned the role of the *babaylan* [i.e. the shaman]." In the late seventeenth century, Father Domingo Pérez described the *bayoguin* as mixing masculine and feminine attire: "He wears a *tapis*, or apron, and ties up his hair like a woman . . . On the right side [he carries a] *yua* [a dagger] as other men [do]." According to the eighteenth-century Spanish Catholic priest Fray Juan Francisco de San Antonio, the *bayoguin*, whom he refers to as "*hombres maricones*," performed both traditionally feminine and shamanic tasks. One of the chief deities revered by the *bayoguin* was MALYARI, the "powerful" one; this deity may have been identified or associated with the androgynous deity BATHALA. The *bayoguin*, in a state of embodiment (possession, trance) would utter prophecies and communicate other messages of the deity. It was believed that the *bayoguin* was well-suited to this task, as, in his gender variance, he mirrored the transgendered, hermaphroditic, or androgynous character of the divine. The *bayoguin* performed various functions, including baptizing initiates (in the blood of a hog) into the worship of Malyari, or Bathala; making offerings and sacrifices; and acting as a psychopomp guiding the souls of the deceased to the afterlife. The *bayoguin* was deeply respected and, rewarded for his services, sometimes with gold, not infrequently became wealthy. *Bayoguin* were often joined in marriage to traditional males. Occasionally these unions were intergenerational in character; according to Fleras, "it was considered a great honor for a family to have its young son cohabit with [an] elderly *bayoguin*." With the arrival of the Spanish, many *bayoguin*, as victims of the Inquisition carried beyond the bounds of Europe, were burned at the stake. While the term *bayoguin*, which has survived in the Philippines as *bayot*, is now used to refer generally to a homoerotically inclined or transgendered male, *bayot/bayoguin* retain some ritual or ceremonial roles. Alongside women, they sometimes serve as healers. Also with women, they prepare and sell *tubâ*, an alcoholic drink made from the sap of the coconut tree, at weddings, funerals, and fiestas, as well as make the artificial paper flowers that decorate Catholic churches.

Bazzi, Giovanni Antonio (nickname **"I! Sodoma,"** 1477-1549)   Eccentric, homoerotically or bisexually inclined, possibly transgendered, Italian painter, nicknamed "the Sodomite" – a nickname in which he apparently took delight and pride. He was married with children, and had a favorite daughter with whom he seems to have occasionally shared male lovers. His entourage of male lovers was mirrored in a strange way by the menagerie of beloved animals he housed. He frequently transported both lovers and animals in a cart with him through the streets of Siena. In part due to holy cards printed for the Vatican, Bazzi's painting of *SAINT SEBASTIAN*, for centuries an icon of homoerotic desire, love, and suffering at the hands of oppressors, has become his best known work. Other works on sacred, mythical, and classical themes include *MARS and VENUS Trapped by Vulcan*, *Leda and the Swan*, *The Ecstasy* and *The Swooning* (of SAINT CATHERINE OF SIENA), and *The Flagellation of Christ*.

Bear Animal of special importance in Euro-western, Native American Indian, and North Asian spiritual traditions, particularly those of Shamanism and Goddess Reverence. During the Paleolithic period, it appears that males may have felt a need to consume semen and other "white" liquids due to a belief that while women stored in their bodies an immeasurable supply of blood, men's bodies carried only a small supply of vital energy. Thus, men needed to consume "white" liquids in order to replenish their strength. Because they imagined semen as having its source in the brain, and to be virtually identical to cerebrospinal fluid, and further believed that the semen and cerebrospinal fluid of the bear were roughly equivalent to those of human males, the Paleolithic consumption of semen may have been linked to practices including bear hunting, head hunting, cannibalism, and the preservation of human skulls. A carved bone discovered at La Madeleine in France seems to speak of this web of associations. It depicts an emanation flowing from a human phallus to the head of a bear. The emanation apparently signifies the divine liquor that is at once cerebrospinal fluid and semen. Among the Old Europeans, whose traditions have been illuminated by archaeologist Marija Gimbutas in *The Language of the Goddess* (1989) and elsewhere, the bear was revered as an embodiment of the Great, or Mother, Goddess. As such, the bear is seen as a creator, and, in part due to its hibernation, a bringer of death and regeneration. Having these associations, the bear is perceived as being both dangerous and nurturing, protecting animals as well as overseeing the hunt. In ancient Greek and Roman religion and mythology, several goddesses associated with transgenderism and same-sex intimacy, including ATHENA, ARTEMIS/DIANA and her beloved CALLISTO, are especially linked to the bear. Callisto's son Arcas ("Bear") is also represented as a bear. Both Callisto and her son are transformed into, or else as spirits inhabit, stars, Callisto becoming or dwelling in URSA MAJOR ("Great Bear"), Arcas becoming or inhabiting the constellation Boötes. Artemis' priestesses included not only the *melissae*, the "honey-bees," but also the *arktoi*, the "bears" – who love to eat honey – suggesting a coupling resonating with today's "butch"/"femme" pattern found in some lesbian relationships. In Teutonic or Germanic religion, the bear is sacred to the god ODIN; his warriors include the "bear-shirts," or "berserkers," who are believed by some to have engaged in cultic homoerotic SADOMASOCHISM. In Christian symbolism, the bear is linked to both the Virgin Mary, the mother of JESUS, and to SAINTS SERGIUS AND BACCHUS. Also in the Euro-western tradition, the nineteenth-century

French lesbian, transgendered painter Rosa BONHEUR, believing in reincarnation, felt that, where animals were concerned, she was most familiar with the spirit of the bear. Among Native American Indians, the TEWA have a saying concerning shapeshifting, especially as concerning the link between gender and animal metamorphosis: "If you are a man, and if you are a woman, then you can be a bear." After transforming into a TWO-SPIRIT person, the female Kootenai shaman and Amazon KAUXUMA NUPIKA, living in the eighteenth and nineteenth centuries took the spiritual name of Qanqon kamek klaula, "Sitting in the water grizzly bear." Contemporary Native American writers like Joy HARJO continue to honor the animal in their work. Artists and writers aligned with contemporary movements and traditions such as Women's Spirituality, Wicca (or Witchcraft), Gay Spirituality, and Queer Spirit, including Donald ENGSTROM (with his Singing Bear) and Rose FRANCES (with her *Mr Bear's Mantle* and other artworks), also celebrate the bear in their work. The bear has also become a cherished symbol for many gay men, and, to a lesser extent, lesbians, bisexuals, and transgendered persons, seeking to claim at once the nurturing, potentially dangerous, erotic, "natural," and "wild" aspects of their identities, as exemplified by the international Bear movement.

Beard Typically symbolic of mature manhood or masculinity, the beard may also signify the erotic power and danger associated with male, female, and assumedly, transgendered genitalia. In the traditions of ancient Greece and Islam, especially Sufism, the beard often signifies the lover, while beardlessness signifies the beloved, in an intergenerational and/or transgendered homoerotic relationship. In Greek mythology and religion, this dualism is exemplified by such couplings as that of PAN and OLYMPUS; in Sufism, by the master and his beloved disciple, or SHAHED. When a false beard was worn by an Egyptian female pharaoh such as Hatshepsut (d. c. 1479 BCE), it symbolized, at once, her political and spiritual authority, her devotion to the god AMUN, and a temporary or permanent third gender or transgender status conferred by the godhead. Similar symbolism may also be detected in the cult of the goddess APHRODITE, especially in that of her bearded or transgendered form of APHRODITUS. Kindred symbolism is echoed in images and accounts of miraculously or naturally bearded female Christian saints, including SAINT GALLA, SAINT PAULA OF AVILA, and SAINT WILGEFORTIS, where hirsuteness signifies merging with JESUS Christ.

Beardsley, Aubrey (1872-1898) Homoerotically or bisexually inclined British illustrator and writer associated with the Aesthetic, Art Nouveau, and Decadent movements of the fin-de-siècle. Beardsley is remembered especially for his illustrations of often sinister, transgendered and/or PAN-like mythical and sacred figures, such as *Man and Satyr* (1893) for Malory's *Morte d'Arthur* and *The Hermaphrodite* (1894) for Oscar WILDE's play *Salome*. These figures often inhabit landscapes reminiscent of ARCADIA.

Beat Movement In the Beat movement or "beatnik" scene of the 1950s (and continuing into the 1970s), bisexuality and/or homosexuality became interwoven with radical (left) politics and a spiritual vision linking elements of Buddhism, Hinduism, Judaism, Christianity, and Sufism, as well as elements of the nineteenth-century aesthetico-spiritual movements of Romanticism and Symbolism (especially as exemplified by William Blake, RIMBAUD, and Verlaine) and of the UTOPIAN vision of Walt WHITMAN. Gay or bisexual male Beat luminaries include William S. BURROUGHS, Neal Cassady (1926-1968), Allen GINSBERG, Jack Kerouac (1922-1969), and Peter Orlovsky (b. 1933).

Beauty and the Beast While ostensibly a fairy tale of heterosexual love, that of a beast – in truth, a handsome prince transformed by an evil spell – who falls in love with a beautiful young woman, the tale at its core speaks to all those who feel that their love will be rejected because they perceive themselves, or are perceived by others, as "beastly," i.e. different, and, on the other hand, to those who, fearing at first, learn to love that which they perceive as different. To date, the two most exquisite films created from the tale owe much to the creativity of gay male artists, the first being Jean COCTEAU's film *La Belle et la Bête* (1946), the second the animated Disney film *Beauty and the Beast* (1991). Rob Baker (1994) describes the Disney film as "probably the most touching example of AIDS as oblique reference." Baker, observing that the project was "largely conceived by lyricist Howard Ashman" just prior to his AIDS-related death, writes, "Drawing on the popular fairy tale about a handsome prince trapped in an ugly body, Ashman brings particular poignancy to the anger and despair of the character who is condemned to live out his life as a . . . 'Beast' unless he can find someone to love him before the last petal drops off a magical rose." "Beauty and the Beast" is also among those tales revised by Peter Cashorali for a contemporary gay male audience in his *Fairy Tales: Traditional Stories Retold for Gay Men* (1995).

Beaver In Greco-Roman antiquity, an animal symbolic of gender variant males, eunuchs, and specifically of the GALLI, the priests of the goddess CYBELE, primarily because male beavers were believed to practice self-castration when they felt they were in imminent danger. The semen of the beaver was highly praised as a medicine.

Bec Celtic woman warrior, sister or intimate companion of LITHBEN. They may have been members of a battalion of Amazonian, perhaps lesbian, warriors.

Beccarelli, Abbot (fl. c. 1700) Catholic priest, bisexual by today's standards, who became infamous for his eroticization of the Mass. He became especially known for the aphrodisiac pills which he allegedly created for and distributed to his devotees. On taking these, male followers believed they had been transformed into women, while women followers believed they had become men. Beccarelli was prosecuted for sacrilege and forced to row on a galley ship from 1708-1715.

Bee and Honey Symbolic of androgyny or asexuality as well as of eroticism, love, healing, eloquence, the soul, death, and immortality in Euro-western and in certain non-western traditions, such as that of the Yoruba of West Africa. A major sect of priestesses of the Greek goddess ARTEMIS/DIANA were the *melissae*, the "bee" or "honey priestesses." The Greek lyric poet Pindar (518-438 BCE) writes, "But I am like the wax of sacred bees / like wax as the heat bites in: / I melt whenever I look at the fresh limbs of boys." In a Medieval poetic letter written by "B," a Catholic Bavarian woman, perhaps a nun, to "C," a woman she loves, the former depicts the latter as "sweeter than honey and honeycomb." Richard Barnfield, in his 1594 poem *The Tears of an Affectionate Shepherd sick for Love*, has the shepherd DAPHNIS say to his beloved Ganimed (i.e. GANYMEDE): "O would to God . . . / My lips were honey, and thy mouth a Bee." He adds, "Then shouldst thou sucke my sweete and my faire flower / That now is ripe, and full of honey-berries," subtly evoking the act of oral intercourse. Similarly, Amy Lowell (1874-1925), in her poem "A Decade," writes: "When you came you were like red wine and honey, / And the taste of you burnt my mouth with its sweetness." Lesbian poet Elsa GIDLOW, in "Hymn to a Mystery," compares herself, the lover, to a bee and her beloved to honey, writing, "I, bee / To its honey, plunge / To being's core." In the Yoruba-diasporic religion, the *orishá* OSHUN heals the sick, including the *orishá* BABALUAYE (since the 1980s, associated with AIDS/HIV), with her magical honey.

Begochidi (or **Begochiddy, Be' gocidi, Be' gotcidi**) Navaho creator, TRICKSTER, healer, and artisan deity associated, as a TWO-SPIRIT being, with bisexuality or pansexuality and transgenderism. Begochidi is unusual in the Navaho pantheon in that he is described as having light skin, golden or red hair, and blue eyes. His hair color may have to do with his parentage, as he is considered the child of the Sun. Because of his coloring, however, he is also claimed by some Navahos to be the patron of Anglo-Americans and Mexican-Americans. Begochidi dwells in the heavens, and beyond his link to the sun, is also associated with the moon, one of his titles being "Moon Bearer." Begochidi is known – and revered – as a trickster, having roles as shapeshifter and clown or holy fool. G. A. Reichard (1983) observes that he can "move without being seen, and [change] into different forms at will – into rainbow, wind, sand, water." As a trickster, Begochidi delights in sarcasm. His being a trickster is linked to his inclination to cross or disrupt traditional borders of masculinity, femininity, and heterosexuality. Reichard relates that Begochidi is a transvestite; he is also thought to have sexual "intercourse with everything in the world." While his name suggests "One-who-grabs-breasts" – he likes to "make himself invisible, then sneak up on young girls to touch their breasts as he [shouts] 'be'go be'go' " – he also enjoys grabbing men's testicles. As a creator of plants (including cotton), animals, humans, and even worlds, he is called "One-who-made-everything." Begochidi is also the creator of the two-spirit being 'ALKE 'NA 'A CI. As a creator, he is further considered the god of sound and motion. Begochidi is not only a creator of animals but is also their guardian, especially BUTTERFLIES (he is said to be of the Butterfly Clan) and horses. He is a patron of hunters and riders of horses, teaching humans songs related to hunting. A healer, he is especially invoked to rid the body of sores on the skin. An artisan, Begochidi is, in Navaho belief, the world's first potter.

Bell In the Euro-western tradition, a symbol of the supernatural realm and of androgyny or transgenderism, with the bell itself being considered feminine and vaginal and its handle and/or tongue, masculine and phallic.

Bellona Warrior goddess of the Romans, syncretized with MA, whose devotees included Amazonian priestesses and gender variant male, or transgendered priest/esse/s as well as traditionally masculine priests. Associations of Bellona with AMAZONS and transgenderism survived into the Renaissance, as exemplified by *Macbeth* (1605), in which Shakespeare compares Lady Macbeth to Bellona and has her beg the spirits of darkness to "unsex" her (Act I, scene 5) so that she may commit murder without being troubled by traditionally feminine behavior.

Beowulf (c. eighth century CE) Old English *Epic* recounting the hero Beowulf's exploits, particularly the slaying of the monster Grendel and the latter's mother. Grendel and his mother may represent the older "pagan" religion that must be destroyed by Christian patriarchal warriors. The Danish King Hrothgar comes to love Beowulf. While this love is not (at least within the bounds of the surviving manuscript) expressed sexually, it reaches beyond the typical friendship between men found in Medieval European literature, affectionate though that was. "The peerless leader," we are told, "Kissed the good thane and clasped to his bosom . . . / so dear was the man."

The *Epic* continues, describing Hrothgar's "yearning love / For the dauntless hero, deep in his heart," which "burned through his blood." To insist upon the difference between this expression of love and homoeroticism, as social constructionist critics are wont to do, is to miss the point that much erotic passion between lovers – heterosexual, bisexual, homosexual, transgendered – was suppressed or sublimated in the world of Medieval Christianity, and that this suppression or sublimation in no way necessarily negates the presence of erotic passion.

Berenice Ancient legendary character, appearing as a queen of Egypt in Iamblichus' second century CE novel *Babyloniaca* (unfortunately lost or destroyed). Berenice, a passionate young woman, falls in love with another young woman, Mesopotamia. When the latter is captured by a man named Saka and given to his leader Garmos, Berenice's servant Zobaras rescues her. When Mesopotamia is returned to Berenice, the two women marry. A war between Garmos and Berenice ensues. The figure of Berenice was probably drawn from one or both of two renowned women of that name: Berenice (fl. c. 315 BCE), the half-sister and spouse of Pharaoh Ptolemy I, and Berenice of Cyrene (c. 273-c. 245 BCE), the wife of Pharaoh Ptolemy III Euregetes. Both of these women were AMAZONS who fought in numerous battles. The latter was a devotee of the Egyptian goddess ISIS.

Bernard of Clairvaux, Saint (c. 1090-1153) French Christian churchman who in 1115 founded a Cistercian monastery at Clairvaux where, as abbot, he remained for the remainder of his life. In some ways a merciless zealot, he was responsible for the condemnation of the brilliant philosopher-abbot Peter Abelard (1079-1142), known primarily as the secret spouse of Heloïse. On the other hand, his writings of love reveal a sublimated sensitivity and sensuality. As E. Begg relates (1985), "The heart of Bernard's spirituality is his devotion to JESUS Christ as lover of the soul, a devotion that . . . [has an] erotic quality . . . 'I do not want your blessing, it is you I want,' he cries to the one he referred to as 'the husband' or the 'the Word.' It is for this reason that the passionate, poetic imagery of the *Song of Solomon* is so much to his taste, as, identifying himself in soul with the black Shulamite, he abandons himself in soul to the spiritual caresses of the divine lover." The sublimated homoeroticism and transgenderism illuminated by Begg is echoed by sixteenth-century French folkloric tradition. Many French persons living at that time believed that "passing under the RAINBOW of St Bernard" could cause an individual to undergo gender metamorphosis. Canonized in 1174, St Bernard, patron of beekeepers and candle makers, is fêted on August 20.

Bernhard, Sandra (1955-) US comedienne, performance artist, and chanteuse of Jewish heritage. A master of cosmic humor, her sardonic tone is counterbalanced by a deep empathy for queer-identified persons – especially gay male friends who have died of AIDS-related illness – which reaches toward the spiritual. This aspect of Bernhard's work is exemplified by a recent performance piece, *Excuses for Bad Behavior* (1994), in which she appears almost possessed on stage as she communicates with the spirit of a beloved friend lost to AIDS.

Berry   Valerie Traub (1994) suggests that in Shakespeare's *Midsummer Night's Dream* (1595), berries may be symbolic of female-centered desire. Helena says to Hermia, "So we grew together, Two lovely berries molded on one stem; So, with two seeming bodies, but one heart (Act III, scene 2)."

Berthelot, le Sieur (fl. c. 1620 CE)   Little is known of this French writer's life, other than that he collaborated with the poet Théophile de Viau (1590-1626) on *Parnasse satyrique* and that he was condemned to be burned alive. In his poetry, however, he gives voice to the interrelationship of homoeroticism and the sacred, spicing the work with touches of sarcasm and pornographic imagery. "I am brave Ganymede," he pens, "Who wounds irremediably / A million souls. / King of sunken cities / My buttocks are crowned / With flowers of satyrion. / . . . / Bacchus crowned with ivy / And Venus inverted / These are the gods I wish to follow: / Under their laws shall I live / Honoring them in my verse."

Bhakti   In Hinduism, a type of yoga, or spiritual practice, described as the path of loving devotion. The practitioner of *bhakti* frequently looks upon the deity as a beloved or lover. The gender of the deity, at least in this context, remains relatively stable. In part due to the phenomenon of dualism and its support of (ostensibly or apparently) heterosexual relationships, the male devotee of a male deity comes to picture himself as feminine and as a bride, with the deity, e.g. KRISHNA, being masculine and the groom. As the beautiful RADHA is the chief female lover of Krishna, the practitioner of *bhakti* may come to identify specifically with Radha. This is the case in the VALLABHA sect of Hinduism. The ritual expression of this relationship is perhaps most noticeable during the festival of HOLI. It should be noted that in Hinduism, as in Sufism and to a certain degree in mystical Christianity (as expressed in the writings of SAN JUAN DE LA CRUZ [St John of the Cross]), it is the feminine bride (devotee) who takes the role of active lover, while the masculine bridegroom (deity) is the receptive beloved. Somewhat surprisingly, however, when a female deity becomes the beloved of the male *bhakti* devotee, while he may undergo gender metamorphosis, it is not to see himself as taking part in an apparently heterosexual relationship, but rather

to show his devotion to the Goddess (e.g. DURGA, KALI, RADHA, TRIPURASUNDARI) by identifying with her. This is especially noticeable in the case of the HIJRAS, devotees of the goddess BAHUCHARAMATA. A third reason for gender metamorphosis among male practitioners of *bhakti* consists in enacting the role of a transgendered deity with whom they identify, as with ARDHANARISHVARA or MOHINI. The latter is a transgendered manifestation of the god VISHNU, with whom *bhaktis* identify in order to demonstrate Vishnu's – and their own – love for Krishna. The relationships of *bhakti* practitioners to the Divine are often expressed in transgenderism (specifically in transvestism and in speech, gestures, and tasks traditionally assigned to Hindu women) and in homoeroticism – or what some would refer to not as homoeroticism but rather as "queer" behavior, in that the transgendered aspect of the erotic expression challenges certain conceptions of male-male eroticism. As M. Singer observes (1968), among *bhakti* devotees of Krishna who dress as women and "dream of making love to Krishna," the relationship is referred to as "the Sweet Mood" (*Madhura Bhava*). Singer relates that when he asked a *bhakti* practitioner "how the devotee's love for Krishna leads to mutual love among the devotees in the *bhajana* [spiritual household of *bhakti*], he replied spontaneously, describing three different incidents from the *Bhagvata Purana* in which the GOPIS [the handmaidens of Radha who also love Krishna] discover each others' love for Krishna, come to share that love with one another, and so develop a mutual love. He did not think it necessary to mention that something similar takes place with contemporary devotees [of *bhakti*] as they imitate the *gopis*." Unfortunately, the potential for female practitioners of *bhakti* to undergo similar gender metamorphosis has not been studied in depth to date.

Bhutamatr   Hindu "Mother of Spirits." At her festival, held in summer when crops are ripening, cultic eroticism and transvestism occur.

Biaggi, Cristina (1937-   )   Lesbian artist and writer, author of *Habitations of the Great Goddess* (1994). An activist in the feminist and the ecofeminist movements as well as a devotee of Goddess Reverence and Women's Spirituality, much of Biaggi's mixed-media art (primarily sculpture) bespeaks profound concern for women and children, animals, and the earth; such pieces include *Medusa* (1980), *GG* [i.e. *Great Goddess*] *Sculpture* (1983), *Birth* (1988), *Three-Dimensional Web* (1991), and *Women's Beijing Sphere* (1996). Together with Mimi Lobell, she has designed a temple to the Great Goddess (which is to be erected), based upon extensive research at Malta, the Orkney and Shetland Islands of Scotland, and other sacred sites. Of the temple and her work in general, Biaggi says, "Sculpture in the Western world has lost the mystical, magical presence that it had during the Neolithic period when a temple or sculpture was considered to be the body of the deity. In creating my sculpture, I wish to bring back some of this magic and mystery . . . [to evoke] rebirth and revitalized consciousness."

Bifrost In Teutonic religion or mythology, the RAINBOW bridge linking Asgard (heaven) and Midgard (earth), composed of precious stones of different colors. Seeing bisexuality as a bridge linking heterosexuality and homosexuality, a group of contemporary British bisexuals have taken the name Bifrost for their organization.

Big Nambas Among the Big Nambas of Vanuatu the older partner in a homoerotic relationship is called the *dubut. Dubut* probably means "shark" and refers to the hybrid human male-shark creator god Qat. Because the elder partner almost always assumes the role of spiritual guide and channel for the divine, the relationship is perceived as being both sacred and erotic in character and as being divinely sanctioned. J. Layard (1942) offers this observation: "Among the Big Nambas, [the act of] homosexuality [may well represent to the natives] a . . . transmission of male power [by physical means] . . . from the ancestors. . . and not merely from the active partner in the union. [It thereby] symbolizes a spiritual connection between the living and the dead in the male line of descent."

Bilitis Fictional character who gives her name to French writer Pierre Louÿs's (1870-1925) poetic prose masterpiece *Les Chansons de Bilitis* (*The Songs of Bilitis*, 1894). With the *Chansons*, Louÿs sought to create the illusion of a "found" text composed by a contemporary of SAPPHO – an ancient technique which remains popular in twentieth-century magical-realist literature like that of Jorge Luis Borges. Typical of the *Chansons* is "Chant pastoral," in which two female shepherds and lovers, Bilitis and Sélénis (the latter's name reminiscent of the Greek moon-goddess Selene, mother of DIONYSUS), watching over their flocks, "sing a pastoral song, invoking PAN, god of the summer breeze." In 1900, Claude Debussy set to music several of the poems in the *Chansons*. Del Martin and Phyllis Lyon honored the memory of Louÿs's sapphic poetess when in 1955 they named the early lesbian rights US organization the Daughters of Bilitis.

Bindhu Among some practitioners of TANTRA, an erotico-spiritual tradition linked to Hinduism, this mysterious somatic fluid is believed to bisexualize women and men.

Bird In many religious and mythological traditions, birds correspond to the upward flight of the soul, to transcendence. Birds are also frequently symbols of birth (often represented by the egg), beauty (the PEACOCK), love and peace (the DOVE), power (the EAGLE), death and rebirth (the SWAN and the PHOENIX). In numerous traditions, birds are feminine symbols and are related to Goddess Reverence. By extension, it appears, they have become linked to feminine-centered, or lesbian, intimacy as well as to transgenderism and homoeroticism (at least partly as an expression of the "feminine" element in men). In the worship of the Greek goddess APHRODITE, two male doves, represented as coupling and sacrificed to the goddess, appear to have depicted her gender variant male devotees; this tradition survived in Coptic Christianity. Other sacred and mythic figures associated with birds and with same-sex intimacy and/or transgenderism include APOLLO (swan), ATHENA (Roman Minerva, OWL), ATTIS (CAPON, ROOSTER), BAHUCHARAMATA (rooster), CORYTHUS (lark), CYCNUS (swan), EROS (dove), GANYMEDE (eagle), HYACINTHUS (swan), KARTIKKEYEH (peacock), RAVEN (RAVEN), SHANGO (rooster), TALKING GOD (eagle), THOTH (IBIS), TIRESIAS (various birds), YEMAYA (DUCK), and ZEUS (eagle). Akin to these are winged figures such as ANGELS and FAIRIES (or faeries). In terms of same-sex love between women, an anonymous Medieval female poet, a Catholic Bavarian woman, perhaps a nun, tells the woman she loves that in her loneliness she feels like both a "hungry little bird" yearning for its mother and a "turtledove" yearning for its mate. This symbolism is echoed in the work of Shakespeare, where the swan becomes a metaphor of female-centered desire, as well as in the poetry of Emily DICKINSON, who depicts apparently female lovers as ROBINS and SPARROWS, and in the work of Charles Baudelaire (1821-1867). In "Au milieu de la foule" ("In the Midst of the Crowd"), Baudelaire writes: "In the midst of the crowd, straying, lost, / Guarding the precious memory of another time, / The women search for the echo of their impassioned voices, / Sad as, when at evening, two lost doves / Call to each other in the wood." In terms of homoerotic love, the gay Spanish poets Federico García LORCA and Luis CERNUDA, aware of the expression *pluma de una misma ala* ("feather of the same wing", synonymous with "birds of a feather") often speak of gay men as *pájaros* ("birds"), as seen in Lorca's "Ode to Walt Whitman" and Cernuda's "The Eagle/Aguila," wherein the association of birds with gay men is specifically linked to the myth of Zeus assuming an eagle's form to carry his beloved Ganymede off to Olympus. In another poem, "The Young Sailor," Cernuda speaks of homoerotically inclined sailors as "the wings of love." A. Sahuquillo (1991) suggests that for these and other Spanish and Latin American poets, the association bird/homosexual is linked to their perception of gay men as constituting a tribe or even a race (*raza*). He also suggests that the association is linked to their belief, rooted in the *Symposium* of Plato, that homoeroticism may constitute a bridge to spiritual enlightenment or transcendence. Throughout Latin America, homoerotically inclined men are associated with birds: in Costa Rica, they are referred to as *aves* ("wings"); in Argentina, Bolivia, Costa Rica, the Dominican Republic, El Salvador, Guatemala, Mexico, Panama, Peru, and Puerto Rico, as *pájaros* and *pájaritos* ("birds" and "little birds"). Closely related to this is the Cuban designation of *pato* ("duck").

Bissu Also known as *banci*, *bencong*, *gemblak*, *wadon*, and *warok*, *bissu* are third gender male, or trans-gendered priest/esse/s of Hindu-inspired Indonesian religion.

Bitter, Bittersweet In her inspirited postmodern essay *Eros the Bittersweet* (1986), Anne Carson observes that "it was SAPPHO who first called eros 'bittersweet' [in Greek, *glukupikron*]." The Lesbian poet and priestess of APHRODITE, EROS, and other deities wrote of erotic desire, "It brings us pain and weaves myths." While Carson's definition of "bittersweet" is complex, it suggests a yearning for love that is "bitter," a finding of love that is "sweet," and a consequent sensing of the loss of one's boundaries and separateness or individuality as "bitter." In Spanish argot of the early twentieth century, gay and effeminate men are described as "*de la cáscara amarga*," as having a "bitter husk, shell, or peel." The poet Federico García LORCA, linking this slang usage to the ancient concept of "bittersweet," depicts unfulfilled homoerotic desire as "bitter"-"pure." This concept is found in numerous poems including the "Gacela de la raíz amarga" ("Gacela of the Bitter Root," 1932), dedicated to gay poet Luis CERNUDA, equally well versed in ancient Greek concepts. In her 1919 poem "For the Goddess Too Well Known" Elsa GIDLOW, a devotee of Sappho, writes, "Her flesh, bitter and salt to my tongue, / I taste with endless kisses and taste again," and a year later, in "Come and Lie with Me," "I have need of love that stings, / Come and lie with me and love me, / Bitterness."

Black A color rich in symbolism, alternately signifying absolute power (in Hinduism and in certain Native American Indian religions), evil (in the Biblical tradition), penitence (also in the Biblical tradition), and fertility (in the Old European tradition of Goddess Reverence and in certain African, African-diasporic, and Native American Indian religions). Among the Mohave of North America, black paint, when worn by HWAME, TWO-SPIRIT women, signified their transgendered status. During World War II, while lesbians, unlike gay men (who were forced to wear pink triangle badges), were not singled out as such by Nazi forces, many lesbians, as part of a larger grouping of women considered "undesirable," were branded with black triangle badges. This symbol was reclaimed and

transformed by lesbian-feminists in the 1980s. In Monique WITTIG's postmodern visionary novel *The Lesbian Body* (1975), black is one of the two colors – the other is lavender – most frequently signifying the beloved. In *Sister Outsider* (1984), Audre LORDE writes: "we must never close our eyes to the terror, to the chaos which is Black which is creative which is dark which is messy which is . . . erotic." A. Pratt (1994) writes: "Lorde entirely subverts the negative 'Terrible Mother' . . . affirming and assimilating a terror which consists in her natural, feminine power . . .".

Blackberri (1945-) African-American gay musician whose work is inspired by Christianity as well as by African-diasporic spiritual traditions. Reared in Baltimore, Maryland, Blackberri's first potent spiritual experiences occurred within the context of Pentecostalism. He later became involved with the alternative spiritual movement of the late 1960s and early 1970s, especially as a sojourner at Millthorpe, the communal residence of LSD pioneer Timothy Leary. Since the 1980s he has immersed himself in the Yoruba-diasporic spiritual tradition, developing a particularly powerful relationship with the *orishá* (deity) of thunder and the drums, SHANGO. Recently, having returned to his home in Oakland, California from a trip to Brazil, he was quite ill when he was visited by the spirits of three drag queens who, he believes, healed him with their powerful medicine. Beyond his album *Finally* (1981), Blackberri has provided music for, as well as performed in, numerous films of the African-American gay filmmaker Marlon T. RIGGS.

Black Teeth Country Chinese mythical country described in the eighteenth century novel *Ching hua yuan* (*Romance of the Flowers in the Mirror*), by Li Ju-chen. This is a country where "the women neglect their appearance to cultivate the mind and the merchant Lin finds no demand for his cosmetics."

Blavatsky, Madame Helena Petrovna (1831-1891) Russian mystic and medium versed in CHANNELING who, journeying to many parts of the world including India and Tibet in search of spiritual enlightenment, founded the Theosophical Society in 1875. Nevill Drury says of Blavatsky, "Her main contribution to mystical thought was the manner in which she sought to synthesize Eastern and Western philosophy and religion, thereby providing a framework for understanding universal occult teachings." What is less widely known concerning Madame Blavatsky is that at various times throughout her life she thought of herself as transgendered, linking this notion to her belief in reincarnation. Not only did she flee an unhappy marriage dressed as a male sailor, but in 1863, she joined the Italian patriot Garibaldi's guerrilla detachment, fighting in the battle of Mentana, in which she was severely wounded.

Moreover, she told those closest to her she was quite certain she would be reincarnated as a man.

Blue Color often symbolic of spirituality, tranquility, mystery, and melancholy. A. Sahuquillo (1991) observes that in Spanish writer García LORCA's poetry, blue alludes to homoerotic love experienced in natural surroundings, as celebrated by his hero Walt WHITMAN in *Leaves of Grass* (1855). This is exemplified by such phrases as "none loved the great leaves, none, the blue tongue of the beach." Lorca opposes blue to GREEN, the latter signifying homoerotic love expressed in urban environments such as New York, with Lorca believing that in the urban milieu, male-male love becomes tainted by prostitution and other related phenomena. Queer filmmaker Derek JARMAN chose the color as the subject of what was to be his final cinematic statement. In *Blue* (1993), a blue screen is accompanied by Tilda Swinton, Nigel Terry, and others reading from Jarman's journals. Jarman, in a meditative passage from *Chroma: A Book of Color* (1994), writes, "In the pandemonium of image / I present you with the universal Blue / Blue an open door to soul."

Blues African-American musical genre, the lyrics of which often concern spiritual malaise, disillusionment in love, and hope. Numerous performers of the Blues have been bisexually or same-sex oriented and/or transgendered, including Ma Rainey (1886-1939), Bessie Smith (1898-1937), and George Hannah (fl. 1930). Beyond these luminaries, African-American (and other) lesbian, gay, bisexual, and transgendered artists have been profoundly inspired by the Blues, including writers James BALDWIN and Alice Walker, musicians Jaqué DuPrée and J. Casselberry (fl. 1970s-1980s), dancer Bill T. JONES, filmmaker/writer Marlon T. RIGGS, and many others. The lyrics of Blues occasionally interface or merge same-sex intimacy and/or transgenderism and the spiritual or supernatural. This is due in no small part to the largely unrecognized role the West African trickster deity LEGBA (in Vodou), or Eleggua (in Yoruba-diasporic religions such as Santería), plays in the mythos of the Blues. In the Southern US, this deity – god of the crossroads associated with transgenderism and other forms of shapeshifting, now inhabiting a Christian milieu – came to be called "the Devil," with Blues becoming the "Devil's music." (It has been a tradition among bluesmen and blueswomen for many years to tell of meeting the Devil at the crossroads to exchange one's soul for mastery in music). Despite this potent association with non-Christian traditions, the Blues has played a central role in the development of African-American Christian music, including Gospel. One lyric speaking to the interpenetration of Blues, Christianity, and homoeroticism includes the lines: "Say, you may not know my people, I will tell you who they are (repeat) / Say, my daddy was a preacher, and my brother done the same old

thing (repeat)." "Peach Tree Blues" depicts a paradisal place resembling ARCADIA where gay men and perhaps other queer-identified, or "freakish," persons as well discover sanctuary. In this song, "Peach Tree" Payne (allegedly gay himself) sings of leaving his everyday life behind to live in Peach Tree Land. "My home ain't here," he sings, "it's down in Peach Tree Land. / My home ain't here, it's down in Peach Tree Land / Everyone at home calls me that Brownskin Peach Tree man."

Bly, Robert (1926-) US poet and storyteller and anti-war and men's movement activist. Since the 1980s Bly has influenced many gay and bisexual men who have participated in the men's movement and in the men's spiritual movement in particular, but his position in relationship to Queer Spirit is problematic. His non-poetic writings are fraught with a celebration of traditional masculinity supported by a reductionist revisioning of Freudian psychology, motivating him to condemn male gender variance or transgenderism and to blame primarily the mother for its presence. While he says very little concerning homosexuality itself, homophobia and effemiphobia ground his portrayal of the gender variant male. Exemplary of this, in "The Hawk, the Horse, and the Rider," an essay on male initiation, he depicts the gender variant male as a tragic, indeed pathetic, figure in that he is unable to – Bly would never consider that he might not wish to – conform to traditional Euro-western masculinity. In Bly's terms, this young man's tragedy, his infantile behavior, "point toward a failure in the very first stage of initiation."

Bodhisattva Individual who is destined to become a future Buddha. This individual has attained spiritual enlightenment and may enter the paradisal state of being referred to as *nirvana* but often chooses instead to return to earth to aid other humans, especially the downtrodden and those seeking wisdom. T. Watanabe and Jun'ichi Wata (1989) observe that angelic male youths appearing in visions to homoerotically inclined Japanese Buddhist monks of pre-modern Japan often revealed themselves to be *bodhisattvas*. *Bodhisattvas* linked to transgenderism include AVALOKITESHVARA, KANNON, KUAN YIN, and TARA.

Bogomil Dualistic Eastern European Christian sect acknowledging the power of both good and evil. The Bogomils were known in France as *bougres* ("buggers"). It is not certain how they came to be associated with same-sex eroticism, although numerous writers on the subject have suggested that same-sex cultic eroticism may have reflected their general antinomian perspective. The Bogomils, like the CATHARS, may have accepted same-sex eroticism to some extent on the grounds that it did not result in the birth of offspring, which would, like the eating of animal flesh, tie believers to the earth, which they desperately hoped to escape (implying a belief in reincarnation or metempsychosis). In this way, it is speculated that Bogomil/*bougre* became associated in France (and later in England, as "bugger") with persons engaging in same-sex eroticism, and more specifically, males engaging in anal intercourse.

Bohme, Jakob (or **Jacob Boehme**, 1575-1624)   German mystic known for his visionary work, *The Great Mystery* (1623). Boehme believed that the Biblical "Fall of Humanity" consisted not of the proverbial eating of the apple but rather of the separation of an androgynous ADAM into male and female.

Bona Dea   "Good Goddess" of Roman myth and religion. Bona Dea presides over healing (especially herbal medicine), prophecy, prosperity, and the life passages of women. Her rites apparently included the sacrifice of hens, a communal meal including wine, ecstatic dance, and possibly lesbian eroticism, perhaps involving the employment of dildoes. It is not, however, certain that we shall ever know exactly what transpired in the worship of Bona Dea, as only women were allowed to belong to her cult, and were forbidden (as in the Eleusinian Mysteries) to reveal her Mysteries in any depth. It is important to note also that most of classical literature that survives was written by and from the perspective of men. Indeed, women devotees knew her only as the "Good Goddess." Nevertheless, she was considered such a powerful goddess that she was offered sacrifices by Roman male officials which were given over to the devotees of Bona Dea by the Vestal Virgins of the goddess VESTA, who served as intercessories between the government and the cult of Bona Dea. The Goddess was said to be akin to HECATE and PERSEPHONE, suggesting that ceremonies also may have involved confrontations with the "shadow" aspects of life, as a kind of shamanic descent to the Underworld, echoing that experienced by INANNA/ISHTAR in her encounter with ERESHKIGAL.

Bonfire of the Vanities   Name given to the campaign undertaken by the Dominican Catholic priest Girolamo Savonarola (1452-1498). A religious fanatic, he despised the Neoplatonic reclamation of Greek paganism supported by philosophers like Marsilio FICINO, artists like MICHELANGELO Buonarroti, and popes like PAUL II, SIXTUS IV, and ALEXANDER VI. He was especially critical of those artists who indulged in the "abominable vice" of sodomy and whose paintings and sculptures of Biblical figures more closely resembled pagan deities than Judeo-Christian heroes or Christian saints. Following the exile of Piero de' Medici from Florence in 1494, Savonarola became spiritual ruler of that city. He and his "democratic" followers set fire to innumerable books and

priceless works of art as well as magnificent garments and even wigs. He supported the invasion of Italy by the French, believing that the country might thereby be purified of its decadence. Cecile Beurdeley (1978), describes a bizarre scene in which one of Savonarola's bonfires was accompanied by male youths in "white dresses wearing crowns of olive leaves [who] intoned the hymn specially composed for the occasion" by none other than the homoerotically inclined Neoplatonist Pico della Mirandola's intimate friend Girolamo Benevieni. Only after Savonarola had succeeded in destroying as many lives as he had works of art was he ordered to stop preaching and setting fires. Refusing to do so, he was executed as a false prophet.

Bonheur, Rosa (1822-1899)   French painter of animals. Bonheur was the daughter of Utopians of the SAINT-SIMONIST movement. Her father supported women's emancipation, believed in the positive potential of overcoming traditional gender roles, and encouraged his daughter's creativity. As a young woman, Bonheur dressed in male attire and enjoyed emulating traditional masculine behavior. Her primary loving relationships were with Nathalie Micas (for forty years) and Anna Klumpke. A mystical Christian, Bonheur envisioned herself as a third gender being reflecting the androgyny of JESUS CHRIST, whom she referred to as "beloved son, savior couple, Christ Androgyne." She pictured the wound in Christ's side as symbolic of the vagina. She linked these images of herself and Christ to that of an androgynous guardian angel. For Bonheur, the guardian angel was not a metaphor but a metaphysical reality, inspiring her as a muse and instilling in her a great sense of compassion for women and animals. Indeed, her dying words, spoken to her beloved Anna, were, "I . . . will . . . be . . your . . . guardian . . . angel." Her overwhelming compassion for animals, resonating with that of the poet Walt WHITMAN, was nurtured not only by her guardian angel but also by her love of myths of animal metamorphosis (which she linked to gender metamorphosis), her rearing of hundreds of animals (including two lions, Nero and Fathma), and her belief in reincarnation or metempsychosis. She felt she could recognize in certain animals human souls, and in certain humans, including herself, animal souls. Of herself Bonheur wrote – and again, *not* metaphorically, but metaphysically – "I am a mixture of dog and tortoise. However, on making a closer study of myself, it is the bear, I think, which predominates over the various animals that I am."

Boniface, Saint (680-755)   English-born Christian churchman who became bishop of Mainz, Germany and who established many abbeys, convents, and schools. Boniface condemned sodomy vehemently during his lifetime. From 1732 until the mid-nineteenth century, novena prayers were offered to him by Mexicans to rid the people of sodomites by whatever means necessary. Ironically, in more recent times, he, like SAINT SEBASTIAN (d. 287 CE), has become in Mexico a patron saint of men-loving men. He is fêted on June 5.

Bori Among the Maguzawa, the non-Muslim Hausa of Nigeria, gender variant, homoerotically inclined men comprise much of the male membership of the *bori* cult. This spiritual tradition involves a divine being or spirit called a *bori* or *iska*, nicknamed a "divine horseman," deciding to take possession or to "ride" a practitioner, a "horse" or "mare." Practitioners of *bori* tend to be regarded as marginal persons by Moslems. *Bori* faithful include the physically and mentally challenged, prostitutes, and gender variant and homoerotically inclined persons. Not finding a place in ordinary society, they are accepted and even exalted in *bori*. Gender variant, homoerotically inclined male practitioners wear a mixture of men's and women's clothes. While they wear somewhat masculine shirts and trousers, these garments are made from fabrics considered feminine. They speak in soft, high-pitched voices and mimic traditionally feminine gestures. Their functions include cooking for ceremonies and acting as intermediaries between female practitioners who are prostitutes and their male clients. While these men are sometimes parodied by traditionally masculine practitioners of *bori* and by Muslims, they are generally treated with respect in this primarily pre-Islamic spiritual tradition. They are revered as the children of the pansexual *bori* spirit Dan Galadima, the Prince. Galadima is a playboy who wears fancy clothes, reeks of perfume, and loves to gamble. Special songs are sung to him, and sacrifices of rams and cocks are made to him. When he "descends," gender variant practitioners dance for him "in an effeminate manner." As the children of Dan Galadima, gender variant, homoerotically inclined practitioners are called *'Yan Daudu* or *'yan hamsin*.

Boris, Saint (c. 985-1015) Scholar of Russian history and literature Simon Karlinsky has observed that "instances of homosexual love can be found in certain lives of saints that date from the Kievan period," that is, from the tenth through the thirteenth centuries, of Russian history. One such instance is discovered in "The Legend of Boris and Gleb." The "Legend" tells of the assassination of Prince Boris and his brother Prince Gleb, sons of Czar Vladimir of Kiev, by their brother Svyatopolk, who desired their property and who despised them because they were Christians. Boris had a favorite squire, George the Hungarian, to whom he gave a beautiful gold necklace because he loved George "beyond all reasoning." When Boris was about to be assassinated, George flung himself on Boris's body, crying out, "I will not be left behind, my precious lord! Ere the beauty of thy body begins to wilt, let it be granted that my life may end!" When Boris and his brother Gleb were assassinated, Svyatopolk treated their bodies disgracefully; a fourth brother, however, took them and buried them in the Cathedral of St Basil. The tomb soon became a site of pilgrimage and miraculous occurrences. Boris is the patron saint of Moscow. In the West, he is sometimes called Romanus, while Gleb is called David. Boris and Gleb are fêted on July 24.

Boudicca (or **Boadicea**, d. c. 61 CE) Celtic warrior-queen of the Iceni, the "People of the Horse," who led the struggle against Roman expansion into the British Isles during the first century CE. A tall, beautiful woman wearing a tartan plaid and a golden torque around her neck, Boudicca was a fierce fighter who, in her scythed chariot followed by an army of naked male soldiers, won many battles; she was especially known for setting fire to Londinium (present-day London). She was a devotee, and perhaps a priestess, of the battle-goddess Adraste (or Andraste), a deity whose sacred attributes appear to have been the RAVEN and the HARE, and to whom human sacrifices appear to have been offered. Ultimately, Boudicca and her army were not able to withstand the Roman onslaught. She seems to have been aware that her final battle would prove disastrous, as, after praying to Andraste and releasing a hare on the battlefield, she understood by the path it took that she would not win that day. It is believed that Boudicca committed suicide in order to avoid rape and slavery at the hands of the Romans. J. Grahn (1984) speculates that the expressions "bull dyke" and "BULLDAGGER" may be traceable to Boudicca. While Grahn's thoughts on the matter may strike more conservative scholars as somewhat fanciful, it is a certainty that in the twentieth century, the Celtic AMAZON has become an icon of strong, woman-loving women in the British Isles and in the US.

Boy George (stage name of **George Alan O'Dowd**, 1961-   ) Celebrated British gay pop singer and songwriter, often transgendered in appearance. From his earliest Culture Club lyrics including "Karma Chameleon" (c. 1983) to his more recent "Bow Down Mister" (c. 1991), dedicated to the Hindu deity KRISHNA (and possibly also to the Biblical God or JESUS, as suggested by the Gospel element of the song), Boy George has infused his music with spirituality. In his 1995 autobiography *Take It Like a Man*, Boy George says of spiritual life: "I'd been toying with spirituality since my first Buddhist meeting . . . I know I'm searching for something, inner peace or the answer to life's jigsaw . . . [God] might be Krishna, Allah, Jehovah, an energetic force . . . I don't see homosexuality as a curse or an affliction, though it is a cross of sorts. You're never going to convince everyone that you're happy defying God's so-called law." Of his participation with the International

Society for Krishna Consciousness in the late 1980s and early 1990s, inspired by his delight in their drumming and chanting and given voice in his "Bow Down Mister," George explains that while "none of the Krishnas ever made an issue of my sexuality . . . they clearly saw it as a fallen quality . . . Their official line was . . . sex purely for procreation or complete celibacy . . . [A] swami [friend] told me it was harder for homosexuals to enter the gates of heaven. I replied, 'Especially if you keep them shut.'"

Boyd, Malcolm (1923-) Social activist, Episcopalian priest, and one of the most successful Gay Christian writers. Studying with Reinhold Niebuhr at the Union Theological Seminary in the 1950s, Boyd became a powerful advocate of civil rights in the 1960s. His volume of unconventional prayers, *Are You Running with Me Jesus* (1965) quickly became a bestseller. He came out as a gay person publicly in the 1970s, publishing *Take Off the Masks* in 1978. In 1981 he was appointed chaplain to Integrity, the chief Episcopalian gay-centered organization. That same year his book *Look Back in Joy: A Celebration of Gay Lovers* was published. Since that time he has become even more visible a spokesperson for gay Christians with books including *Gay Priest: An Inner Journey* (1984), *Half Laughing/Half Crying* (1986), and *Edges, Boundaries, and Connections* (1992). It is Boyd's belief that through the theological concept of incarnation, or embodiment, the spirit of the Divine enters into the lives of all human beings, and that since God, in the person of Jesus Christ, has "fully embraced the human condition . . . there is simply no room for homophobia or racism."

Bradamante AMAZON character of Ariosto's *Orlando Furioso* (1531) who, having her hair shorn after being wounded in the head, is mistaken for her twin brother. A young Spanish princess, Flordespine, falls in love with Bradamante, presuming her to be a man. When Bradamante, who does not seem to be especially interested in Flordespine, tells her that she is a woman, the young princess does not flinch. Instead, she takes Bradamante to the palace and gives her elegant women's clothes to wear and invites her to stay with her. As the two lie in bed, Bradamante sleeps, while Flordespine "moans and weeps in piteous plight / Because her wild desire more fiercely glows." Ultimately, Bradamante's twin brother displaces her, with Flordespine assuming that some work of magic has caused Bradamante to transform into a man.

Brahma Creator deity of Hinduism, typically represented as male, although the term "*brahman*" is neuter, suggesting a eunuch or transgendered divinity according to the linguistics-associated rules of Hindu iconography. Brahma has the ability to divide "himself" into a male aspect, Manu Svayambhava, and a female aspect, Satarupa (also, Brahmani, or Brahmi).

Bran Celtic hero deity of healing, magic, and the Otherworld, having the power to resurrect the dead by way of a magic cauldron. According to Robert Graves (1981), Bran may have been worshipped by a "homosexual priesthood." His cult was virtually wiped out when AMATHAON was able to discover Bran's secret name by seducing one of the latter's priests. This version of the tale, however, may be (at least in part) a product of Graves's internalized homophobia.

Branchus (or **Branchos**) In Greek religion or mythology, a diviner whose father had founded the renowned oracles at Didyma. His mother suspected that her son might lead a spiritual life and that he might become linked to Apollo because, during her pregnancy, she had a mystical vision while observing through the branches the sun's descent, with the sun seeming to draw near to her. She named her son Branchus. One day when young Branchus was shepherding his flock in the mountains, Apollo noticed him and fell in love with him. The god bestowed Branchus with numerous love-gifts, including a crown of bay laurel and a branch of bay to serve as a wand. When Apollo kissed Branchus, he imparted to him the gifts of prophecy and healing. The Greeks claimed that Branchus founded at Didyma, near Miletus, a temple to Apollo and established there an oracular cult resembling that of Delphi. The oracle of Branchus was said to have been consulted by the Cumaeans and several pharaohs of Egypt. For many years following the death of Branchus, the bay laurel crown given by Apollo to Branchus was housed in the temple at Didyma. The temple was pillaged and burned by the Persians in 494 BCE but was later reconstructed; its remains were discovered by the archaeologists Haussoullier and Wiegand. Among Branchus's most renowned healing rites was one in which he cured the Milesians of a devastating plague by placing crowns of bay laurel on their heads while leading them in chanting hymns to Apollo.

Brant, Beth (1941-) Native American Indian woman-loving writer whose work often focuses on the interrelationship of eroticism and the sacred. A member of the Bay of Quite Mohawk of Tyendinaga Mohawk Territory in Ontario, Canada, Brant, also a mother and grandmother, is the editor of the ground-breaking collection *A Gathering of Spirit: a Collection by North American Indian Women* (1988). Brant writes in *Writing As Witness: Essay and Talk* (1994), "As a creative human being who is also Native and Two-Spirit, I will not make distinctions between sexuality and spirituality." Brant faults Euro-Americans for encouraging displacement of acceptance of queer-identified persons among Native peoples by anti-queer prejudice, which she explains many Natives have now assimilated and must attempt to eradicate. "The love that was natural in our world," she explains, "has become unnatural as we have become more consumed by the white world . . . Our sexuality has been colonized." By extension, Brant also argues that eroticism in general has been compartmentalized by Euro-American culture. "There is a broader cultural definition of sexuality that is at work here. Strong bonds to Earth and her inhabitants serve as a pivotal edge to our most sensual writing . . . Indeed, one could say that much of Native lesbian writing celebrates Earth as woman, as lover, as companion. Two-Spirit writers are merging the selves that colonialism splits apart." Like Maurice KENNY, Paula Gunn ALLEN and many other contemporary Natives, Brant perceives a strong bond between the two-spirit shamans of traditional Native America and twentieth-century queer-identified persons. Brant is enraged by what she sees as the appropriation of Native spiritual traditions by non-Natives. While it is certainly the case that many non-Natives have exchanged their Bibles for "dreamcatchers" and "medicine cards" made readily available by the New Age movement, her argument might be challenged to the degree that she disregards many pre-Christian European and other non-Native practices – ceremonial tattooing among the ancient peoples of the British Isles, sweat-lodges constructed by the ancient peoples of Russia, shamanic flight in the Teutonic religion of Northern Europe, to name only a few – the practice of which might well be misinterpreted by the uninitiated as "rip-offs" of Native American traditions. Brant does state that she does "not object to non-Natives praying with us (if invited)", and she encourages "lesbian and gay Natives," who are "becoming the Elders of our people, giving counsel and wisdom," to share their "particular kind of beauty," their "transformative love," with "those who would receive it."

Breechcloth Among the Mohave of the American Southwest, a breechcloth, when given to a young female, is symbolic of the recognition of her third gender status, her being HWAME.

Breeden, Jim (1953-) San Francisco-based painter, illustrator, and writer whose work is nurtured by Gay Spirituality, Queer Spirit, and AIDS-centered Spirituality. His works include *The Magician* (1993), depicting a beautiful, long-haired nude male surrounded by magical tools, based upon the TAROT (Major Arcana I), and *Choir of Skulls* (1996). This multi-plate colored etching, inspired in part by the image of a Cambodian wall of skulls, and involving the meticulous process of taking seventy-five photographs of human skulls, represents the still-singing voices of loved ones who have died of AIDS-related illness.

Britomart AMAZON character of Edmund Spenser's *The Faerie Queene* (c. 1590), who, in the view of M. Duffy (1980), "seems to have been very convincing" in her seduction of another woman, the hybrid fairy-human Amoret.

Britomartis Beloved companion of the Greco-Roman goddess ARTEMIS/DIANA. Originating in Crete, Britomartis is a guardian of animals and a patron of hunters, fishers, and sailors. Deified upon her death by Artemis, Britomartis came to be worshipped, primarily under the name of Dictynna, at Knossos and elsewhere. Callimachus (fl. c. 250 BCE) writes, "And beyond others thou [i.e. Artemis] lovest the nymph of Gortyna, Britomartis, slayer of stags, the goodly archer." In attempting to escape Minos, who loved her but whom she did not love, Britomartis leapt into the sea. Fortunately, she fell into the nets of some fishermen and was saved. Minos, thinking she had died, halted his pursuit. Following this event, Britomartis became known as Dictynna, "the Lady of the Nets." FISHING and HUNTING nets are her chief symbols, and PINE and mastich are sacred to her.

Britten, Benjamin (1913-1976) One of the most renowned British composers of modern music. His love for men and his spiritual vision, which included elements ranging from pacifism to Gothicism, were often blended in subtle ways in his works. This is especially noticeable in such works as: *Les Illuminations* (1939) based on the poetry of Arthur RIMBAUD; *Seven Sonnets of Michelangelo* (1940), written by MICHELANGELO Buonarroti to his beloved Tommaso de' Cavalieri, set to music for Britten's lover Peter Pears to sing; the opera *Billy Budd* (1951), based on the homoerotic novella by Hermann Melville; the opera *The Turn of the Screw* (1954), based on the novella of Henry James; *The War Requiem* (1973), based on the pacifistic, homoerotic poetry of Wilfred Owen; and the opera *Death in Venice* (1973), based on the homoerotic novella by Thomas Mann. *The Turn of the Screw* includes among its subjects same-sex intergenerational desire. Peter Quint, the former caretaker of the estate, returns from the grave to continue his influence over the youth Miles. Miss Jessel, the former governess, holds a similar influence over his sister Flora. Philip Brett, a Britten scholar, suggests that the composer has Quint sing alluring songs to which "Miles fully responds." *Death in Venice* likewise concerns the theme of intergenerational homoerotic love, specifically the erotic awakening of a celebrated novelist, Gustav von Aschenbach, for TADZIO, a young man reminiscent of GANYMEDE. While Aschenbach watches the boys strike poses on the beach, APOLLO sings, "He who loves beauty worships me." With Aschenbach's love for Tadzio complicated by a deadly plague, Death is a character in this opera whose visage slips from one person to another. The god DIONYSUS also plays a role in the opera, appearing in a dream sequence. Britten enhances

Tadzio's godlike, otherworldly character by pairing him with Balinese-influenced sounds "identifying him as a citizen of the seductive, magical world form which [Peter] Quint also come[s]." Following his climactic declaration of love for Tadzio, Aschenbach sings a litany inspired by Plato's *Phaedrus*, ending with Socrates's warning, "Beauty leads to wisdom, but also to passion and therefore the abyss."

Broughton, James (1913-   ) US gay writer and avant-garde filmmaker. In both his writings – chiefly poems – and his films, Broughton insists that eroticism and the sacred must be wedded to joy and humor, describing this fusion as a "gaiety of soul." Says Broughton in his whimsical manner, "Celebrate your existence. Gay soul dances on the grave of the deadly serious." Some of his more recent films, made in collaboration with his lover of many years, filmmaker Joel Singer, including *Devotions* (1983) and *Scattered Remains* (1988), as well as numerous poetic texts, including *The Androgyne Journal* (1977, 1991), *Hymns to Hermes* (1979), *Graffiti for the Johns of Heaven* (1982), and *Ecstasies* (1983), must be given a central place in the emerging canon of Gay Spirituality/Queer Spirit. In "Shaman Psalm" (1981), Broughton writes: "Be warriors of kiss / Prove in beatitude / a new breed of man / Prove that comradeship / is the crown of the gods."

Broumas, Olga (1949-   ) Greek-American poet whose *Beginning with O* (1976) introduced the US academic poetic community to the contemporary Women's Spirituality and Goddess Reverence movements as practiced by women-loving women. At the time, even the section title "Twelve Aspects of God," referring not to male but to female divinities, raised more than a few eyebrows as this young poet received the coveted Yale Younger Poets Prize. Among the goddesses and figures of myth and fairy tale honored by Broumas are the AMAZONS, Io, Thetis, Circe, the MAENADS, APHRODITE, DEMETER, ARTEMIS/DIANA, BEAUTY AND THE BEAST, Cinderella, RAPUNZEL, Sleeping Beauty, Rumplestiltskin, Little Red Riding Hood, and SNOW WHITE. While various influences permeate her work, including jazz, the inspiration of her spiritual ancestors SAPPHO and H. D. (Hilda Doolittle) is unmistakable. In a transformation of the myth of "Leda and her Swan," Broumas writes, " . . . Scarlet / liturgies shake our room, amaryllis blooms / in your upper thighs, water lily / on mine, fervent delta."

Bryallicha (or **Bryllicha, Brydalicha**) Ancient Greek dance incorporating ritual transvestism of male and female dancers, performed in honor of ARTEMIS/DIANA and APOLLO (sister/brother deities associated with same-sex intimacy). The male dancer's costume included stag antlers, padded buttocks, and feminine masks and attire,

while the female dancer's costume included a large, artificial phallus. Performance of the *bryallicha* was believed to promote fertility of the earth and to ward off demonic spirits. Eventually the term *bryallicha* (or *brydalicha*) came to refer to any man dressed in women's attire.

Bryant, Anita (1940-   ) Singer, orange juice spokesperson, Fundamentalist Christian zealot, founder of Save Our Children, anti-gay crusader, and author of *The Anita Bryant Story: The Survival of Our Nation's Families and the Threat of Militant Homosexuality* (1977). Her opposition to gay rights culminated in the 1977 repeal of an ordinance granting lesbians and gays protection in terms of employment and housing in Dade County Florida. It also fueled a massive anti-gay movement led by Fundamentalist Christians.

Budapest, Z (Zsusanna Emese Moukcsay Budapest, 1940-   ) Hungarian-born, lesbian-feminist high priestess of Wicca (or Witchcraft) especially of Dianic Wicca, one of the mothers of the contemporary movement of Women's Spirituality and the revival of Goddess Reverence. Reared in a family knowledgeable in pre-Christian traditions, Budapest, traveling from Hungary to California by way of New York, founded the Susan B. Anthony Coven in 1971 and opened The Feminist Wicca, a shop in Venice California. In 1975 she was arrested for reading TAROT cards for an undercover policewoman. The trial for Witchcraft that followed proved to be a powerful catalyst in mobilizing women involved in Wicca and Women's Spirituality. Now living in the Bay Area of Northern California, Budapest has served as director of the Women's Spirituality Forum and is currently playing a central role in the International Goddess Festival, held annually by the organization Goddess 2000. Since the 1970s she has performed lesbian ceremonies of UNION, invoking ISIS, VESTA, PELE, APHRODITE, DEMETER and other goddesses (or aspects of the Great Goddess). "Trystees," anointed with sacred oils and blessed water, exchange floral crowns and say to each other, "Thou art Goddess!", after which a great feast occurs. A prolific writer, Budapest's works include *The Holy Book of Women's Mysteries* (1980, 1989), *The Grandmother of Time* (1989), *Grandmother Moon* (1991), and *The Goddess in the Office* (1993).

Budur, Lady While Lady Budur, a character of the *Arabian Nights* (or *The Thousand Nights and a Night*), continued to love Jubayr bin Umayral-Shaybán, he separated from her because, on visiting her chambers one day, he found her being embraced and kissed by her handmaiden Lutf. "I was sitting here one day, " Lady Budur explains, "while my handmaiden combed my hair. When she had finished, she plaited my tresses. I suppose my beauty and loveliness charmed her, as she bent over and kissed my cheek. At that moment Jubayr came in unawares, and, enraged, he vowed eternal separation from me."

Bull   In ancient Egypt, symbolic of MIN, a god of fertility associated with homoeroticism; in Goddess Reverence, as in the worship of the Roman goddess CYBELE, a symbol of the male consort, as ATTIS, or beneficent male principle; in Greek religion, a sacred attribute of DIONYSUS; and in ASTROLOGY, symbolic of the sign of TAURUS. The origins of Spanish bullfighting and the US rodeo may be traced in part to the participation of young, Amazonian Cretan women in bull-jumping contests. These associations also may have played a role in the creation of the terms "BULLDAGGER" and "bull-dyke" to refer to "butch" women-loving women.

Bulldagger   African-American term for an assertive woman-loving Black woman, described in archetypal terms by S. Diane Bogus in "The Myth and Tradition of the Black Bulldagger" (1994). While in certain respects the Bulldagger is a "loner in both myth and reality," in others, she stands upon a rich cultural history, with forebears including: legendary or actual AMAZONS of northwest Africa linked by the ancients to Goddess Reverence, especially to the worship of African goddesses akin to ARTEMIS/DIANA, ATHENA, and CYBELE; Dahomean (Fon, Benin) Amazons, the *mimo* (or *mi-no*) of the fifteenth through nineteenth centuries, as well as OYA and other Amazonian deities of African and African-diasporic religions; CALIFIA, the legendary queen of a tribe of Black New World Amazons who gave her name to California; cross-dressing women of the nineteenth century like Cora Anderson; BLUES singers like Ma Rainey and Bessie Smith; and, most recently, the poet Audre LORDE, whose work abounds in imagery weaving together lesbianism, female gender variance, and the sacred. The Bulldagger is both akin to, and different from, the QUEEN B(EE).

Buonamici, Sister Caterina Irene (fl. c. 1780)   Nun of the Dominican convent of St Catherine at Prato in Tuscany, Italy. Sister Buonamici confessed to having participated in a woman-loving relationship with Sister Clodesinde Spighi as well as having made love to seven other nuns.

Burroughs, William S. (1914-1997)   US queer-identified writer, one of the leaders of the BEAT MOVEMENT. In his excellent biography *Literary Outlaw: The Life and Times of William S. Burroughs* (1988), Ted Morgan observes, "Although cast in the mold of the American original, as exemplified by Emerson and THOREAU, there was an added dimension to Burroughs, a dark side, which was his belief in a magical universe ... As Wordsworth ... trailed

clouds of glory, Burroughs trailed clouds of Witchcraft." Morgan adds, "To Burroughs, behind everyday reality there was a reality of the spirit, of psychic visitations, of curses, of possession and phantom beings. This was the single most important element of his life." Of his childhood, Burroughs relates, "My nannies brought me up on black MAGIC ... I would not have had such nurses had I not been receptive ground." As a boy, Burroughs was visited by spirits and placed curses on fellows who betrayed him. As a young man, he was profoundly inspired by Baudelaire's *Les Fleurs du Mal* (*The Flowers of Evil*, 1857), which he read while "burning incense." In college, he consumed texts on magic (including those of the Golden Dawn and Israel REGARDIE) and Tibetan Buddhism as well as ghost stories. Of his magical perspective, Burroughs relates, "In the magical universe there are no coincidences and there are no accidents. Nothing happens unless someone wills it to happen ... Of course if you put a curse on someone it may boomerang, but you take the chance ... It's nothing to be undertaken lightly, but in many cases it has to be done ... As for me, I've won some and lost some." Of the link between his writing and magic and spirituality, which he further links to film, he says, "All my writing comes from the psychic thing. You have *satoris* [moments of bliss and enlightenment in Buddhism], you have enlightenments. I couldn't write a word without them. You've got to put yourself into a state where the [film] projector is on." As early as 1961, Burroughs was weaving together elements of homoeroticism and pagan ritual, depicting in *The Soft Machine* the character Carl as the "Young Corn God ... the boy sacrifice [who] is chosen by ... universal erection ... [when] all pricks point to 'Yes.' Boy feels 'Yes' run through him and melt his bones to 'Yes' stripped naked in the Sacred Grove." The weaving together of these elements with transgenderism and, to a lesser extent, lesbianism – the view of Burroughs as a misogynist is exceedingly reductionist – is perhaps most successful in *The Western Lands* (1987), which continues the tale told in *Cities of the Red Night* (1981) and *The Place of Dead Roads* (1983). Two of Burroughs's most intriguing queer-magical characters appear here, AH POOK and FUKU, as well as SHRIEKING SCORPION, born of a lesbian UNION. *The Western Lands* is Burroughs's most powerful testament to date concerning his spiritual and/or magical views. Of monotheism, he writes of OGU, the "One God Universe": "The OGU is a pre-recorded universe ... It's a flat, thermodynamic universe ... the One God has time and weight. Heavy as the pyramids, immeasurably impacted ... His OGU is running down like an old clock." Centering upon the Egyptian religion on one hand and Christianity and Islam on the other, he depicts the destruction of ancient polytheistic (or henotheistic) spiritual traditions by patriarchal monotheists. "So the One God, backed by secular power, is forced on the masses in the name of Islam, Christianity, the State, for all secular leaders want to be the One. To be intelligent or observant under such a blanket of oppression is to be 'subversive.'" In one of his most potent attacks on Christianity, Burroughs writes: "I spit on the Christian God. When the White God arrived with the Spaniards, the Indians brought down fruit and corncakes and chocolate. The White Christian God proceeded to cut their hands off. He was not responsible for the Christian conquistadors? Yes, he was." Of the "Magical Universe," or "MU," which he contrasts with OGU, Burroughs explains that it is a "universe of many gods, often in conflict . . . The Many Gods may have no more time than the BUTTERFLY, fragile and sad as a boat of dead leaves." "Let the Shining Ones enter me," Burroughs chants, "I want to shine too." While Burroughs might well be called a "scribe" of the religions of antiquity, especially of Egyptian religion, he seems always to have set his gaze on the – or a – future. Of the elder gods and the Egyptian afterlife abode, the Western Lands, he writes, "What do they look like? The houses and gardens of a rich man . . . I say then it is time for new Gods . . . We can make our own Western Lands." When asked, "But how do we make it solid," Burroughs, through the voice of a character, replies, "We don't . . . When you do this, it ceases to be spirit."

Bushido Japanese spiritual path known as the "Way of the Warrior" or the "Way of the Samurai." Bushido is rooted primarily in Zen Buddhism but also contains elements of Shinto and Confucianism. Bushido is concerned most with dying an honorable death. Secondarily, it focuses on training in mental and emotional discipline, the martial arts, and aesthetics. The last of these embraces ritual arts such as *ikebana* floral arrangement and the tea ceremony. Bushido also centers on monogamous homoerotic love, *shudo*. The spiritual philosophy of Bushido, followed by the acclaimed writer Yukio MISHIMA and many others, is perhaps best expressed in Yamamoto Tsunetomo's (1649-1719) HAGEKURE.

Butter In Hindu symbology, butter is considered androgynous, comprised metaphysically of both milk (feminine) and semen (masculine).

Butterfly In Greek mythology and religion, the butterfly signifies eros, thanatos (death and immortality), and both the transitoriness of beauty and the beauty of transitoriness. The god EROS, frequently associated with same-sex desire (both homoeroticism and lesbianism, the latter observed in the poetry of SAPPHO, is sometimes depicted as having butterfly wings. In the Euro-western tradition, butterflies also signify frivolity, wantonness, and extravagant or gaudy taste in clothes, qualities (for better or worse) often associated with gender variant or transgendered, homoerotically inclined males. In this same tradition, red butterflies are said to be Witches in disguise. The folk figure SCRAT, an archetypal "hairy androgyne" revered in the Middle Ages by some Germanic and Anglo-Saxon groups, may also assume the form of a butterfly. In Aztec mythology and religion, the butterfly is associated with the goddesses XOCHIQUETZAL and TLAZOLTEOTL and with their devotees, including transgendered and same-sex inclined persons. In Native American Indian mythology and religion, BEGOCHIDI, a bisexual or pansexual, sometimes transgendered deity of the Navaho pantheon, is said to belong to the Butterfly Clan. The Spanish poet Federico García LORCA, drawing upon mythic associations as well as upon *mariposa* as a slang term for "gay male" or "queen," and upon a celebrated photograph of Walt WHITMAN, writes in his "Ode to Walt Whitman," "Not for one moment, beautiful aged Walt Whitman, / have I failed to see your beard full of butterflies." The butterfly, especially as red or lavender, came, in the early 1970s came to be employed as a symbol of gay liberation.

Bythos "The Deep"; among the NAASSENES, a Gnostic sect, the primordial, fluid, transgender essence. Synesius (fl. fourth century CE) transcribed a hymn which includes: "Male thou and female, / Voice thou and silence, / . . . the initiated mind . . . / Celebrates with dances / The Ineffable Bythos."

C

Cabeiri Divinities presiding over phallic and chthonic Mysteries, frequently depicted as having black skin and curly hair and as being small in stature, originating in Asia Minor and later accepted into the Greek pantheon, their cult center being on the island of Samothrace. They were especially associated with the deities CYBELE and DIONYSUS, the COURETES (divinized warrior-nurturers), and twins (particularly the Dioscuri). HERMS (phallic statues) were their sacred attributes. Male lovers swore allegiance to each other at shrines dedicated to them.

Caduceus Staff or wand depicting a pair of intertwined SERPENTS circling about a rod, familiar to us as a symbol of the medical profession. The caduceus is associated in Greek myth and religion with healing, magic, and metamorphosis, including gender transformation. It is a sacred attribute of numerous deities linked to transgenderism and/or same-sex desire, including ASCLEPIUS, HERMES, and TIRESIAS. It was when the prophet-magician Tiresias (before becoming blind) witnessed two serpents coupling and struck them with his staff, forming the image of the caduceus, that he was changed from male to female. Gay-Spiritual writer Mitch WALKER links the image of the caduceus to that of the DOUBLE or Magickal Twin, an archetypal figure embracing homoerotic passion.

Caenis Daughter of Atrax, she was transformed into a man by the Greek god POSEIDON and named Caenis, because she did not wish to serve the sea-god as a mistress or to marry one of the many suitors who desired her.

Caieteva According to the ritual magician Cornelius Agrippa (1486-1535), Caieteva was a woman who lived during Agrippa's time who magically transformed into a man after many years of heterosexual marriage.

Cainites Gnostic sect revering the Biblical Cain and practicing cultic homoeroticism and other forms of variant sexuality.

Caitanya (b. 1485 CE) Hindu mystic widely believed to be an incarnation of both the god KRISHNA and the goddess RADHA. Caitanya expressed his transgenderism by dressing in female attire. In artistic depictions, he is not shown as having Krishna's dark blue skin but rather Radha's fair skin. Caitanya and his devotees followed the path of BHAKTI, or "loving devotion."

Calais One of the Argonauts of Greek legend – indeed, his name signifies "argonaut" – who sailed with Jason on his quest for the Golden Fleece, Calais was a son of Boreas, god of the north wind, and the nymph Orithyia. He and his twin brother ZETES were bestowed with wings for recovering the seer Phineus from the Harpies. Calais became ORPHEUS's most treasured male lover, just as Eurydice had been the musician's most treasured female lover. When Calais died, he was reincarnated as a bird.

Calamus and Carpus In Greek religion and myth, Calamus, whose name means "reed," was in love with the beautiful youth Carpus. One day when they were both bathing in the Meander, Calamus challenged his lover to a swimming competition, during which Carpus drowned. Carpus, whose name signifies "fruit," was transformed into an unnamed fruit. Grief-stricken and inconsolable at causing his lover's death, Calamus's body withered until he was transformed into a reed. Calamus reed was used in ancient Greece for arrows, writing implements, and musical instruments. The latter included the Pan pipes and the aulos. The American Transcendentalist poet Walt WHITMAN chose calamus to signify homoerotic love, titling a section of his masterpiece *Leaves of Grass* (1855) after this aromatic plant. The American poet Jack Spicer (1925-1965), determining that Whitman's dream had failed, wrote of the mythical land of Calamus: "Calamus cannot exist in the presence of cruelty . . . Calamus is like Oz. One needs, after one has left it, to find some magic belt to cross its Deadly Desert, some cat to entice one into its mirror. There Walt is, crying like some great sea bird from the Emerald Palace, crying '*Calamus, Calamus.' One* needs . . . an Alice, a Dorothy, a Washington horse-car conductor, to lead one over that shimmering hell, that cruelty."

Califia Dark-skinned Queen of the AMAZONS, a fictional character in Spanish writer Ordoney de Montalvos's romance *Las Sergas de Esplandian* (1510) from whom the state of California derived its name.

Calling God (Xa'ctceogan) In the Navaho religion or mythology of Native America, a deity of the sunset, the west, farming, and the sense of sound. Calling God was created from yellow corn by the sister of Changing Woman (or of Turquoise Woman); hence his other name, Yellow Body. He also wears yellow feathers. He often helps mortals in need and is invoked in the Hail Chant and in other chants as well. Calling God is viewed as transgendered or two-spirited, described as "feminine" in relation to Talking God. Calling God lives in a sacred mountain in the west with one of the twin two-spirit deities named SHOOTING GOD.

Callisto Either a wood nymph or the daughter of Lykaon, Callisto was a beloved companion of the Greco-Roman goddess ARTEMIS/DIANA. One tale of Callisto relates how ZEUS, realizing Callisto's love for Artemis, transformed himself into, or disguised himself as, Artemis in order to arouse her passion. Unfortunately, it seems that before Artemis learned of Zeus's trick, she learned of Callisto's pregnancy and, letting her temper overtake her, slew Callisto. Unable to revive her beloved, Artemis transformed her spirit into the constellation of the Great BEAR. The child, named Arcas (the "Bear"), was ultimately transformed into a constellation as well. The tale of Callisto has led to speculation that the cult of Artemis may have included rites of lesbian and/or transgendered eroticism undertaken by the *arktoi*, her "bear" priestesses. The myth of Callisto is depicted in Thomas Heywood's English Renaissance play *The Golden Age*, wherein Diana and her "princesses," welcoming Callisto to their court, search for a "cabin fellow" to "sleep by her." In Renaissance painting, Diana (or Zeus posing as Diana) and Callisto were depicted by Titian in his painting *Diana and Callisto* and by Peter Paul Rubens in *Jupiter and Callisto*.

Calusari Group of male spiritual functionaries of Eastern Europe who have traditionally been linked to transgenderism and homoeroticism. According to Carlo Ginzburg and others, the *calusari* would dress in feminine garments, including white veils placed over their faces, and would speak or sing in falsetto. As evidence of belonging to a third or alternate gender (at least for the duration of a ritual), they would brandish swords while wearing feminine attire and behaving in an otherwise feminine manner. Joining together in groups of seven, nine, or eleven, they revered a goddess variously named Irodeasa (Herodias), Arada (Aradia), or Doamna Zinelor. The last name is associated with the goddess ARTEMIS/DIANA and refers to "the Mistress of the Faeries" (*zinê*). The *calusari* were, like transgendered male shamans and priests of goddesses, ecstatics who would enter into an altered state of consciousness as they danced faster and faster in a ring, "so fast that their feet seemed to fly." Their dances, which they would perform at the houses of the village during spring, were thought to bring health, fortune, rain, and abundant crops; they were also thought to exorcise evil spirits. The *calusari* were especially adept as healers. When someone became seriously ill and spirits were believed responsible, the *calusari* would be summoned. They would take the sick person to a crossroads, where he or she would lie down. Then they would begin to leap over the patient's body and dance in a circle around him or her. Eventually, one of the *calusari* would fall into an altered state, a

doborire, in which he would do such things as smash a pot and sacrifice a chicken. As the evil spirits left the body of the patient, the patient would rise up to his or her feet, while the "possessed" *calusar* would return to ordinary consciousness. In recent centuries, the role of the *calusari* – who have survived into the twentieth century – as gender variant spiritual functionaries appears to have diminished. Moreover, the emphasis on transvestism has been partly assumed by a comic figure called the "mute." Still, references to both transgenderism and homoeroticism (largely sublimated) abound in their rites. For instance, flirtation and simulated erotic activity sometimes occur between the mute and the other *calusari*. In another instance in which the androgynous mute's masculinity is emphasized, a possessed *calusar*, imagined as a woman dying in childbirth, must suck the mute's wooden phallus as part of his returning to ordinary consciousness. The *vataf*, the leader of the *calusari*, often warns them of punishments and loss of special powers they will suffer if they lose their virginity to women. These ritual situations serve to encourage temporary, if not permanent, homoerotic object choice.

Camilla Amazonian hunter, warrior and favourite of DIANA/ARTEMIS in Roman myth and religion. She was reared by her father alone in the wilderness, who dedicated her to Diana. Camilla ran faster than the wind and fought with one breast exposed. She was renowned as a military commander.

Camp Sensibility rooted in the interrelationship of gender fluidity, parody (or what some have termed cosmic humor), and the indivisible unity of "the gutter" and "the stars," often embracing elements of nostalgia, seductiveness, and shock and frequently expressed in drag, especially in "genderfuck," which mixes feminine, masculine, and occasionally magical attire. The term "Camp" derives from "kaemp," a Polari word signifying a male's display of transgendered behavior, Polari being a lingua franca employed by sailors, actors, carnival workers, prostitutes, vagabonds, homoerotically inclined men, and others from the fifteenth century onward throughout Western Europe. "Campy" behavior may be discovered in the narratives of various deities and other figures appearing in this text, such as in the dances of AME NO UZUME and BAUBO for the goddesses AMATERASU OMI KAMI and DEMETER, as well as in the plays of the SOTS of Medieval France, festivities involving the HIJRAS (transgendered male priest/esse/s of the Hindu goddess Bahucharamata), and the rites and performances undertaken by the Angels of Light, the Radical Faeries, and the SISTERS OF PERPETUAL INDULGENCE of the late twentieth century.

Campus Martius   The Field of MARS, a legendary "cruising" site for man-loving males in ancient Rome. Martial describes the search of a young man, Selius, in the Campus Martius for a male partner. Selius visits not only the shops of the Saepta and the baths of Fortunatus but also the Temple of ISIS in search of an erotic encounter.

Cancer   In Euro-western ASTROLOGY, zodiac sign ruling from (approximately) June 22 until July 22, associated with diplomacy, intuition, and sensitivity, typically depicted as a CRAB. Figures associated with Cancer and with gender and/or sexual variance include: AMAZONS, ARTEMIS, ATHENA, CYPARISSUS, KHEPERA, and MINERVA. In the *Tetrabiblos*, Ptolemaeus (second century CE), speaking of the astrological effect on women living in Cancer-ruled Asia Minor, writes: "Most of the women, through the influence of the moon's oriental and masculine aspect, are virile, commanding, and warlike, like the Amazons, who shun commerce with men, love arms, and from infancy make masculine all their female characteristics, by cutting off their right breasts for the sake of military needs and baring these parts in the line of battle, in order to display the absence of femininity in their natures."

Candi   Hindu and Javanese goddess of the moon, considered by some to be gynandrous or transgendered, her masculine aspect being named Candra (or Chandra). Ancient Hindu stone sculptures, such as one dedicated to Candi at Borobudur, linked the goddess to lesbianism.

Canidia   Legendary or actual Roman sorceress who worshipped the goddesses HECATE, ARTEMIS/DIANA, Tisiphone, and Nemesis and who belonged to a "college of witches" allegedly engaging in cultic lesbianism. She was also said to be the lover of her mentor, the witch Sagana.

Capon   Castrated cock, symbolic in Greece and Rome of eunuchs, transgenderism, and homosexuality. In the *Book of the Secrets*, attributed to Albertus Magnus (1205-1280), one finds: "A capon is a cock that is castrated and effeminate." It was believed that a stone (tumor?), referred to as the alectoria or "cock-stone," could be extricated from the liver of a capon after it had lived six years after castration, and that this stone held the magical power to quench thirst and assuage hunger. In the early twentieth century, in the West, the capon continued to signify transgendered homosexuality.

Capricorn   In Euro-western ASTROLOGY, zodiac sign ruling from (approximately) December 22 until January 19, associated with brooding, determination, honesty, industriousness, and lustiness, typically depicted as a hybrid goat-fish. Figures associated with Capricorn and with gender and/or sexual variance include: AMAZONS,

APHRODITE, ASTARTE, ATHENA, ATHIRAT, BAPHOMET, COURETES, DIONYSUS, GORGONS, HERMES, KUAN YIN, MEDUSA, PAN, SATAN, and SET.

Caravaggio, Michelangelo Merisi da (1571-1610) Homoerotically inclined Italian painter who frequently depicted the interrelationship of homoeroticism and the sacred, as in *Young Bacchus* and *Victorious Love*, the latter depicting EROS as a puckish, seductive youth. Derek JARMAN depicted the life of the artist in homoerotico-spiritual terms in his film *Caravaggio* (1986). Jarman has said of Caravaggio that he "breathed his life, himself, into old ideals. Bacchus [i.e. DIONYSUS] was an androgyne god and this was a reflection of the painter's sexuality . . . He [Caravaggio] brought the lofty ideals down to earth, and became one of the most homosexual of painters . . . From the moment he grew up and identified himself with the murderer in Saint Matthew – the murderer imaged as God – he unconsciously took on the Church as his true and deadly enemy – after all, its authority, its over-selective reading of its holy texts, had led to the outlawing of the centre of his life."

Caribou   Among the Inuit, when the image of a white female caribou appears on a male shaman's garment, it signifies his gender variant or third gender status.

Carlini, Sister Benedetta (1590-1661)   Abbess of the Theatine nuns of Pescia, Italy. Entering the convent at the age of nine, Benedetta began almost immediately thereafter experiencing visions, one of which focused on JESUS appearing to her and saving her from a horde of wild beasts, whom he explained were, in reality, demons she would be forced one day to confront. In another early vision, SAINT CATHERINE OF SIENA appeared to her. The visions receded somewhat until 1617, when they returned with greater intensity. At this time, she was given a companion, Bartolomea Crivelli, to watch over her during her lapses into altered states of consciousness. In 1618, Benedetta, during an erotically charged vision of JESUS and the Crucifixion, received the stigmata, bleeding nail wounds in her hands and feet. In 1619, she received even more powerful, erotic visions of Jesus, accompanied by St Catherine, with the former telling her that he wished to unite in mystical marriage with her. This resulted in an elaborate ceremony of UNION presided over by Father Ricordati. Around the time of this event, Jesus also bestowed Benedetta with a guardian angel, Splenditello, with whom she had numerous erotico-mystical encounters. Also at this time, Benedetta began to prophesy; in particular, she warned of a plague that would soon sweep through Pescia. Shortly after the *hieros gamos* celebration, suspicion surrounding Benedetta's visions and visionary powers arose. While a first Inquisitorial investigation revealed little, a second, greatly aided by nuns who had become jealous of Benedetta's growing fame, proved disastrous to Benedetta. Unfortunately, the most damaging testimony came from her beloved companion Bartolomea, who continued to believe in her visions and her powers, but who had also grown increasingly fearful of Benedetta. "At least three times a week, in the evening after disrobing and going to bed [Benedetta] would wait for her companion to disrobe, and . . . would call [to her]. When Bartolomea would come over, Benedetta would grab her by the arm and . . . embracing her . . . would put her under herself and [kiss] her as if she were a man, [and] she would speak words of love to her. And she would stir on top of her so much that both of them corrupted themselves." On these occasions, in which Benedetta appears to have enacted both lesbian and transgendered behavior, it seems that she would sometimes become embodied, or possessed, by Splenditello or Jesus, who would assure Bartolomea that she and Benedetta were not sinning but that she should nevertheless keep silent as to their lovemaking. Bartolomea explained that when this occurred, Benedetta's voice would deepen, and she would assume the appearance of Jesus or of a beautiful winged adolescent male (Splenditello). At the end of the second investigation, Benedetta, devastated, confessed that she was no longer certain of the origins of her visions or powers and conceded that they might be the work of the Devil. While she was not executed, she was given a sentence of life imprisonment. From 1626 until her death in 1661, she lived the miserable life of a prisoner, never seeing Bartolomea again. In her brilliant examination of Benedetta's trial, *Immodest Acts: The Life of a Lesbian Nun in Renaissance Italy* (1986), Judith C. Brown notes that word of Benedetta's death "spread quickly outside the convent walls . . . Forty years after the events that had brought her notoriety, the power of her personality could still move those around her." Demanding that she be given a proper burial by the Church, the people of Pescia, acknowledging her accurate prediction of the plague, wanted first "to see and touch her body." "In the end," Brown observes, "Benedetta triumphed. She had left her mark on the world and neither imprisonment nor death could silence her."

Carlos, Wendy (1939-) Born Walter Carlos, the most renowned transsexual musician of the twentieth century and one of the earliest composers for, and performers of, electronic instruments. Carlos studied with electronic music pioneer Otto Luening and also served as advisor to Robert Moog during the modification and perfection of the Moog synthesizer. While perhaps best known for her enormously successful 1968 recording *Switched-On Bach*, Carlos's later compositions embody a mythic and often utopian or dystopian ambiance. Her recording *Sonic Seasonings* (1971) evokes the cycle of seasonal changes, using the elements of nature (wind, rain, thunder, and

other natural, including animal, sounds), while her film score for *A Clockwork Orange* (1971) evokes a dystopian nightmare. Related works include *Time Step* (1970), the score for Disney's *TRON* (1982), the score for *The Shining* (1978-1980), the music of which evokes the ghostly and macabre world of Stephen King's novel, and *Digital Moonscape* (1984).

Carmina Burana Body of over two hundred, mostly irreverent Latin and German songs, including songs of eroticism, drinking, gambling, and parodies of religious songs and services collected in the thirteenth century at the Benedictine monastery of Benediktbeuern near Munich, Germany. Also included in this manuscript are six religious plays. The *Carmina Burana* collection includes several lyrics relating to transgenderism and homoeroticism. John Boswell describes one entitled *Iam mutatur animus*: "["I Am Changing My Mind"] relates an affectionate argument between two clerics who are lovers. One is sick and offers to become a monk if God will only grant him recovery. His horrified lover begs not to be abandoned. The ailing cleric is moved by his pleas but retains his resolve. A lengthy dispute follows, in which the lover tries every argument to dissuade his friend from entering a monastery, pointing out the rigors of monastic observances, [etc.] . . . Finally the lover . . . points out to the monk-to-be that they will be separated forever. At this his companion begins to have second thoughts: 'I am already changing my mind,' he declares, and he resolves never to become a monk." At least two lyrics from the *Carmina Burana* concern gender metamorphosis. Both *De vestium transformatione* and *Nullus ita parcus est* describe how, by way of the monks' refusal to throw away worn-out fabrics, garments once worn by nuns or simply considered feminine are transformed into masculine garments. For instance, a cape, perceived then as a feminine item of clothing, is transformed into a mantle, a masculine garment. The lyrics suggest that the old garments or pieces of fabric carry magical power that effect a kind of gender transformation in the monks. L. Barkan (1986) translates the first lyric as follows: "So in the style of Proteus clothing is tranformed; nor was the metamorphic law recently invented. As the princes of the church change their sex in outward appearance, so secretly they patch up torn garments. Nor are these given away, you can be sure, without first going through the experience of TIRESIAS. For indeed the cape is determined to be of the feminine gender, while the mantle is of the masculine. God makes a cape out of a mantle, and therefore it can be guilty of both sides of love." In the second lyric, the themes of the first are amplified: "So after the fashion of the Gorgon, he transformed the form; or rather the remarkable artificer changed their sex. He masculinized the feminine, he feminized the masculine, and going Tiresias one better, he trifurcated sex." Stressing the borrowing of lines from

Ovid's *Metamorphoses* and especially the appearance of the bisexual or pansexual Tiresias and ORPHEUS in the *Carmina Burana* lyrics, Barkan writes, "It is clear that unconventional sexuality is a vivid example within real experience for medieval learned men of both the passionate and transforming impulses behind myths and metamorphoses."

Carnation   During the final decade of the last century, a carnation dyed green, popularized by Oscar WILDE, signified homoeroticism and aestheticism. In memory of this, in 1972, Detroit, Michigan's first gay community was named The Green Carnation. In twentieth-century Guatemala and Chile, one of this flower's significations is love between men.

Carneius   Son of ZEUS and Europa worshipped as a ram-god of flocks and fertility. He was the beloved of APOLLO; their union was symbolized by the dual god Apollo-Carneius, the "Horned Apollo." Carneius was honored with homoerotic rites on the island of Thera. His festival, the Carnea, celebrated the arrival of the harvest and the first fruits of the vintage. The carnelian is sacred to him.

Carnival, Carnivalesque   A. Orloff writes of Carnival, "Nothing can resist this tidal wave of juggernauting chaos as it turns our ordered world on its head . . . this is a magical time outside of time in which one and all are changed, everything is reversed, inverted . . . Through orgiastic excess and folly, through the embrace of the opposite within us, through the baptism of frenzied chaos we are reborn." The association of homoeroticism and transgenderism with the carnivalesque is an ancient one. In late antiquity, Christian authorities commenced their attempt to control or abolish carnivals, which they correctly perceived as celebrations of the exiled gods. "The remains of heathen superstitions of all kinds are forbidden," the Quinisext (or Trullan) Synod found it necessary to declare almost seven hundred years after the triumph of Christianity: "the festivals of the Kalendar, the *Bota* (in honor of PAN), the *Brumalia* (in honor of Bacchus), the assemblies on the first of March, public dances of women, clothing of men like women, and inversely, putting on comic, satyric, or tragic masks, the invocation of Bacchus at the winepress, etc. . . . [All] these activities are forbidden." Despite such efforts to destroy Carnival, however, the phenomenon, including its expression of transgenderism through transvestism, persisted. Indeed, in many sectors during the Middle Ages, Carnival was quietly acknowledged as a necessary release of pagan expression in a Christianized world. In the words of Mikhail Bakhtin, "the carnival processions . . . were interpreted as the march of the [officially] rejected pagan gods." Among the figures featured in celebrations, those of the "beastly" (or vegetal) human hybrids and

transgendered figures (primarily transgendered males) predominated, including the Wild Man, the Green Man, Bessie, Judy, Mollie, and Our Old Lass. One festival which incorporated elements of gender and theriomorphic transformation and, by implication, cultic—however comic—homoeroticism was the *hieros gamos* of Maia, the goddess of spring (sometimes depicted as having pointed ears, like those of an ass, as well as being a grandmother and a relative of the fairies), and Orcus, god of the harvest and the underworld (apparently linked to HADES, CERNUNNOS, and FREYR). A penitential of the ninth century condemned those males who "wear feminine garb in their dances and carry on the monstrous fiction of being Maia and Orcus." Mock weddings like that between Orcus and Maia were common in Medieval and Renaissance European Carnivals (sometimes even surviving into the twentieth century). In the Eastern Balkans, a comic *hieros gamos* was celebrated between the Wild Man Kuker and his "pregnant," male transvestite "bride" Kukeritza or Baba. In France, similar ceremonies took place between Monsieur Henri and Dame Douce and between Caramantran and his "bride." In these rites, the "brides" were depicted as elderly prostitutes who, miraculously becoming pregnant, gave birth to "sons" at MARDI GRAS, while the "grooms," representing the old year, were symbolically slain. A similar rite was recorded by the Flemish painter Bruegel. Here, the bride, a male transvestite wearing a white mask, tempts a Wild Man with a ring. In London, the *hieros gamos* of the Lord and Lady was celebrated on May 1, or Beltane, an ancient Celtic festival, with the part of the Lady often being assumed by a transvestite male. On the Isle of Man on this day, a mock battle took place between the Queen of May and the Queen of Winter. While the May Queen might be represented by either a young woman or a young man, the Queen of Winter was usually portrayed by an older male. Other Carnival, or carnivalesque, rites emphasized the link between gender and theriomorphic transformation. According to Janet and Colin Bord, the "most frequent animal disguise recorded in Britain is the horse" (an archetypal shamanic animal). As recently as the nineteenth century, the central figures of the Samhain (Halloween) rite of the Hooden Horse included "Mollie," a male transvestite carrying a broom, and a man dressed as a horse. A similar ceremony was the Horn Dance, which took place at Abbots Bromley in England, originally at the winter solstice and more recently in September. In this dance, the central figures included six "stags" wearing reindeer antlers, a hobby horse, and Maid Marian, played by a man dressed in women's clothes. In some places, mock weddings took place between womanly and beastly figures. In the French Pyrenees, for instance, a man dressed in women's clothes was joined in marriage to a man costumed as a bear. Needless to say, the Church condemned such rites. "Whosoever, at the beginning of

January, ventures forth disguised as a young stag . . . or a calf," one document read, shall endure a "three-year penance, for such things are devilish." Another posed the question, "Have you done as the peasants do, who on the first day of the year, disguise themselves in masks representing deer or old women?" Nevertheless, these rites took place within the Church as without. During the Feast of Fools, monks dressed in women's clothes and bearded nuns sang hymns to asses in churches perfumed with the incense of burning shoes. In the mid-fifteenth century, despite the efforts of the Church, Ludovicus, the archbishop of Sens, was still complaining about individuals who during the Feast of Fools wore "masks with hideous features," in other words, those of beasts, and "dressed like women." They danced inside the church, running, leaping, and singing "indecent songs." Not only this, but the crowd included "naked men with even their private parts uncovered" who indulged in "infamous shows" too "shameful to remember." As Janet and Colin Bord suggest, the "she-male" is not a piece of "tomfoolery," but rather "an attempt to encompass . . . [the] Godhead . . . every polarity, including male and female . . . totality." Of Carnaval in Brazil, Richard G. Parker explains that it emphasizes the "erotic merging of the [individual] body with other bodies," those bodies together becoming the *povo*, the "people," and transforming into a "community" in which, for "a few brief moments, hierarch[ies] . . . collapse." Carnaval, Parker continues, "offers a utopian vision . . . of life in a tropical paradise . . . where the struggles, suffering, and sadness of normal human existence have been destroyed . . . In the *carnaval*, everything is permitted, as it would be in the best of all possible worlds." Parker, who maintains that "no symbolic form dominates the symbolism of the festival as completely as transvestism," makes it clear that queer-identified persons play a vital role in Carnaval. Like Brazilian Carnaval, in the US, the festivals of Mardi Gras (especially in New Orleans) and Halloween (especially in San Francisco) are greatly enriched by queer, and increasing by Gay- and Queer-Spiritual participants. In the early 1970s, a group of gay men based in Milwaukee, Wisconsin, naming themselves Les Petites Bonbons, sought to blend gay activism, spiritual experience, aesthetics, and the carnivalesque in their works and lives. "Les Petites Bonbons," they said of themselves, "are Gay Pansensualists. We acknowledge the gaily erotic nature of all things and we reject the forcible attempt of straight society . . . to define and thereby limit the human experience. We are poets and we are painters. We are a Feast of Fools. We are the surprise in your crackerjacks . . . Les Petites Bonbons is the name of a . . . traveling circus, a musical band of Gay guerillas." More recently, the carnivalesque, especially in its "high CAMP" form, has become an essential ingredient in ceremonies undertaken by the SISTERS OF PERPETUAL INDULGENCE, an

international Order of drag nuns, and in Radical Faerie rites. Of a festival honoring a carnivalesque goddess, reminiscent of MÈRE SOTTE, and her consort, the Radiant Poodle, the Faeries Gloria Mundi and Shastina have written: "Out of the deep and mysterious twilight of Faerie Dream World, clothed in the ecstasy of multitudinous paper carnations, rose a spectre of Radical Faerie essence. . . the Radiant Poodle . . . [The] chant 'WOOF WOOF ARF ARF' rose from the frenzied participants . . . The Faeries lined up behind the Goddess . . . [and] Radiant Poodle . . . carrying all manner of colorful banners . . . [and dancing to the] rhythms . . . of the drums." Carnivalesque activity has also increased dramatically in the lesbian aesthetic and spiritual communities of the West following the relaxing of lesbian-feminist stridency in the 1990s. This is especially evident in the performances of lesbian-centered musical groups such as Girls in the Nose, led by Kay TURNER. Exemplary is their performance of "Breast Exam," which, while seriously promoting women's health education, does so against a backdrop of Art Deco-like dancers with exposed breasts moving between fire-eaters and enormous papier-mâché breasts being carried across a stage.

Carpenter, Edward (1844-1929) Homoerotically inclined British writer, utopian communitarian socialist, early homosexual rights activist, and mystic (or, visionary). While expressing little if any of the heterophobia voiced by his late twentieth-century devotees, Carpenter believed that same-sex oriented persons, whom he also perceived as transgendered and whom he referred to as "URANIANS" (or "urnings"), "intermediates," and "homogenic" persons, constituted a special grouping of humans bearing certain "gifts" including those of artistry and psychic ability (shamans, priests and priestesses, ritual artists, etc.). Carpenter described this group as sharing the "Uranian temperament." It is crucial to note, however, that while both "essentialists" in the Gay Spiritual movement and social constructionists have reduced Carpenter's theory to one of genetics or biological determinism Carpenter did not himself rely on biology to explain the "Uranian temperament." Rather, as a mystic influenced by spiritual tradition including Hinduism (as described in *Adam's Peak to Elephanta*, 1902) and the Transcendentalism of American poet Walt WHITMAN, Carpenter, in the main, described the "Uranian temperament" as a psychospiritual complex, or what lesbian writer Judy GRAHN might refer to as a "metaform", which has come to be embodied by individuals living in many cultures and epochs, with its origin ultimately residing in the Divine, portrayed by Carpenter as a primordial "Ocean". Thus, while Carpenter might be faulted as being a Platonist or as a proto-Jungian (he loved the term "archetypal"), he should not be reduced to being a biological determinist. Indeed, in his works exploring the interrelationship of same-sex passion, transgenderism and spiritual role, Carpenter is careful to note that while certain cultures hold the "Uranian temperament" to be inborn, others believe that it is acquired or embodied later in life as the result of divine intervention. Still others voice a belief that appears to reside midway between the first and the second, wherein an individual may be born with a "Uranian temperament" but that this temperament must be activated, as from hibernation, by a divine force. This third notion, which Carpenter linked to the coming-to-the-fore of a heretofore sublimated identity (a "coming out," if you will), inspired much of his poetic work. In "The Secret of Time and Satan" (1888) which portrays Satan as the beautiful, rebellious angel of Romanticism, he writes: "You are that person; it lies close to you, so close – deep down within – / But in time it shall come forth and be revealed. / You must undo the wrappings, not case yourself in fresh ones . . . / When the body which thou now hast falls away, another body shall be already prepared beneath, / And beneath that again another. / And the pains which I endured in one body were powers which I wielded in the next; and I grew in strength, till at last I stood before him [Satan] complete, and with a body like his own and equal in might – exultant in pride and joy. / Then he ceased, and said, 'I love thee.'" This poem is important in our understanding of Carpenter's ideas not only because it speaks of the embodiment and revelation of the "Uranian temperament" but also because of its insistence on metamorphosis. Carpenter, it is clear, while attributing same-sex inclination, gender-transgressive and psychic and/or artistic ability to the temperament, did not wish to reduce the temperament to a static stereotype (archetypes, contrary to anti-Platonic and anti-Jungian critiques, are not assumed to be static). As he writes in the conclusion to *Intermediate Types Among Primitive Folk* (1919), "'Intermediate' hardly covers all the human types [associated with the "Uranian temperament"]. Between the normal [i.e. heterosexual, gender-traditional] man and the quite normal woman there are certainly a number of intermediate grades . . . the term 'intermediate' is not quite the fitting one; and I can only ask the reader to excuse its use in consideration of the difficulty of finding a term which really covers all the ground." He implies that if the term "intermediate" be useful in describing transgendered and homosexual/lesbian/bisexual behaviors, it must be employed in a generalized way to include not only androgynous expression but also gender-transgressive behavior that is considered ultra-masculine and ultra-feminine. This is not to suggest that Carpenter was not an "essentialist"; it is to suggest, however, that Carpenter's essentialism excludes neither "nature" nor "nurture" but is rooted in the realm of psyche or spirit, as well as that his essentialism is fluid rather than solid in aspect. Among Carpenter's works (other than *Intermediate Types*) which concern the interrelationship of same-sex passion,

transgenderism, and the sacred are: *Homogenic Love* (1894); "On the Connection between Homosexuality and Divination and the Importance of the Intermediate Sexed Generally in Early Civilizations" (1911); *Towards Democracy* (1912), a poetic cycle profoundly influenced by Walt Whitman; and *Iolaüs: An Anthology of Friendship* (1917), one of the first anthologies in the English language of literature concerning same-sex love, with many of the texts therein referring to the spiritual dimension of same-sex relationships.

Cathars Members of a Medieval heretical sect of Southern France who believed that JESUS was one of a number of "eons" sent to earth to enlighten humans, while the Biblical Lord of the Book of Genesis was the very source of evil, his plan being to create humans in order to be served by slaves who would remain ignorant. The Cathars were associated with the BOGOMILS, a dualistic sect known in France as *bougres*, hence "buggers," roughly, persons engaging in sodomy. The Cathars, like the Gnostics before them, believed that their spiritual task was to detach themselves from earthly existence. Hence they abstained from eating meat and from bearing children, which they saw as further tying them to the earth. In this light, they appear to have condoned homoerotic behavior among all practitioners except the chief male and female priests, who must not engage in any form of erotic behavior. The association of homoeroticism and Catharism is found in a poem or song composed by the minstrel Gautier le Leu in the mid-thirteenth century. In *The Widow*, an angry wife complains that her second husband pays less attention to her than to the local garbage dump. She's not surprised, however, because he doesn't really love women. He's like "those on Mount Wimer." The wife is referring to an event which took place on Mt Wimer (also known as Mt Aime) in Champagne in 1239. On this occasion, at Pentecost, Robert the Dominican, who had once been a Cathar himself, rounded up 183 Cathars living on the mountain and executed them. Other groups of Cathars met their deaths at the hands of Christian fanatics at Montségur and elsewhere. From *The Widow* and other texts, it appears that the association of homoeroticism and Catharism was commonplace. It has of course been argued that the Cathars, being heretics, were unfairly or conveniently linked to homoeroticism by an ill-informed Church. Although this early form of "fag-baiting" at times must have been employed to destroy the lives of individuals and groups, the doctrines of the Cathars would seem to promote same-sex EROTICISM as a "non-binding" form of erotic activity. On March 15, the stronghold of the Cathars, their fortress at Montségur was captured by Christian forces. On the following day, two hundred of the Cathars were burned alive, leaving their cult devastated.

Catherine of Genoa, Saint (also **Caterina**, 1477-1510) Of noble birth and married at sixteen, Catherine Fieschi, in later life, devoted herself to helping the poor and homeless. She is well known for her mystical treatises concerning purgatory and the relationship of the body to the soul. An official document of the time reports that in 1493, Catherine affectionately kissed a tertiary (a nun of the third order in rank in a convent). Art historian P. Simons (1994) observes that "although the incident is reported in terms of piety and healing, it points to the possibility of sanctioned, intimate contact between women." St Catherine of Genoa, canonized in 1737, is a patron of nurses. She is fêted on September 15.

Catherine of Siena, Saint (1347-1380) Italian Catholic nun and later saint who began to have visions at the age of six. Resisting all marriage proposals, she entered a Dominican convent, after which her visions of Mary, the Saints, and JESUS increased. She was known to be a peacemaker and healer, devoting herself to victims of the plague and leprosy. The authenticity of her spiritual visions and powers were often doubted, even by the future Saint Raymund of Capua (d. 1399), her spiritual advisor. These doubts were put to rest, however, when Raymund saw in a vision Catherine's face transforming into that of a bearded man. Catherine, Raymund believed, had achieved a mystical union with Christ, as a result of which she had become mystically transgendered. She spent the latter part of her life recording her mystical experience. The stigmata she had received in 1375 during a visit to Pisa reappeared at the time of her death. Patron of Italy as well as of nurses, philosophers, and spinsters, St Catherine is fêted on April 29 or 30.

Cauliflower In twentieth-century Mexico, a signifier of male homosexuality.

Cavafy, Constantine P. (1863-1933) Alexandrian-born Greek writer best known for his poems of homoerotic passion, often drawing upon ancient religion, myth, and history. Typical of this fusion is his "Before the Statue of Endymion," which depicts a wealthy devotee of ENDYMION, offering "sacrifices and libations." "Now ecstatic," related the worshipper, "I gaze / at Endymion's illustrious beauty." Another example is his poem "If Dead Indeed," inspired by APOLLONIUS of Tyana.

Cellini, Benvenuto (1500-1571) Bisexually inclined Florentine sculptor of the Italian Renaissance. While the elder Cellini, having been imprisoned for sodomy, did his best to repress his bisexual and pagan leanings, as a younger man, he honored both in bold fashion. Cellini's most celebrated homoerotic sculptures were executed between 1545 and 1548, their subjects figures from Greek mythology or religion: GANYMEDE, NARCISSUS, and

APOLLO and HYACINTHUS. Several of his intimate companions appear to have been of his own age, including Francesco di Filippo, son of the painter Filippino Lippi (c. 1457-1504). Of Francesco, Cellini wrote, "I formed a close and intimate friendship with a charming young man of my own age . . . We came to love each other so much that we were never apart . . . Francesco and I went together for about two years." When Cellini was in his twenties, he and "a female companion" were invited to a dinner party. At the beauty contest held during the party, his date won: Diego, a sixteen-year-old model in drag, to whom Cellini had given the name "Pomona," after the Roman goddess of apples. Another well known episode from the life of Cellini concerns his participation in 1534 in two consecutive rites of conjuring spirits in the ruins of the Coliseum at Rome. As was typical in rites of ancient, Medieval, and Renaissance ritual magic, Cellini was to bring as an apprentice, actually a kind of CHANNELER, a male youth who was still a virgin (at least in terms of heterosexuality). He also brought along his companions Vincenzio Romoli and Agnolino Gaddi. The magician performing the rites was a Sicilian Catholic priest. On the first night, little happened, but on the second, all were amazed by what occurred; of the event, Cellini writes: "Having entrusted the care of the perfumes and fire to my friend Vincenzio who was assisted by Gaddi, the magician handed me a pentacle, ordering me to turn it towards whatever direction he indicated. I instructed my apprentice [the youth] to sit beneath the pentacle. Now began . . . marvelous incantations during which the magician summoned by name a vast multitude of demons, leaders of several [infernal] legions . . . Almost at once the amphitheatre became filled with demons . . . there were four armed giants of tremendous size, each doing his best to force a way into our circle . . . Although I felt as scared as any of them I strove hard to conceal my fright . . . I shouted, 'Gaddi, at times like this a man should make himself useful instead of yielding to fear, so move yourself and help me with this incense!'"

Cerberus Monstrous DOG, usually depicted as having three or more heads, who guards the entrance to HADES, the Greek underworld. Cerberus is invoked as a deity in Coptic lesbian love and binding spells dating from the first centuries of the Common Era. In one such spell Cerberus is called a "jagged-toothed dog . . . turning three heads."

Cernuda, Luis (1902-1963) Spanish gay poet whose homosexuality and opposition to right-wing politics ultimately forced him to leave Spain and to settle in Mexico. A friend of Federico García LORCA and profoundly inspired by the Surrealists, Cernuda rejected Christianity, turning to Greco-Roman paganism and the religion of the AZTECS for spiritual sustenance as evidenced in "El águila" ("The Eagle"), "Quetzalcóatl," and many other poems, In "Dans ma pénische," he writes, "Young satyrs / That live in the forest, laughing lips before the pale Christian god, / . . . Dance faster when the lover cries, / While he launches his soft sad song."

Cernunnos Horned god of pre-Celtic and Celtic peoples. Cernunnos's worship almost certainly predates the arrival of the Celts. He is a god of the forest and its creatures, abundance, self-sacrifice, the underworld, and eroticism. Often seated in lotus position, either naked or clothed in a short tunic, he is bald or has long, curly hair and wears a torque (choker) around his neck and antlers on his head. His attributes include the cornucopia, a bag of coins, a RAM-headed SERPENT, the stag, the BULL, and the rat. His worship appears to have included shamanic elements. Certain artworks also indicate that his cult was linked to Goddess Reverence, such as a votive relief discovered at Nuits-Saints-Georges in France which portrays him seated beside a goddess holding a cornucopia. This goddess shares much in common with the Roman CYBELE; it is significant in this respect that one of Cernunnos's centers of worship was Autun, in France, also one of Cybele's cult centers. A third deity depicted on the relief just described, one seated between the goddess and Cernunnos, is an androgynous figure. Jean Markale suggests that this figure may represent at once a deity in his-her own right or perhaps Cernunnos's androgynous aspect. In another syncretic Celtic-Roman depiction, Cernunnos is shown flanked by APOLLO and HERMES. This votive stela emphasizes the androgynous aspects of both of these deities. Indeed, Apollo is portrayed almost as an hermaphrodite, with plump breasts and belly and a feminine hairstyle. Both deities are nude except for caps and shoulder wraps which do not cover their genitals, and both are standing in relaxed, sensuous poses. Another portrait of Cernunnos, discovered at Val Camonica in northern Italy and dating from 400 BCE, depicts Cernunnos standing "chastely in a full-length chiton" while "his worshipper, smaller in size and having his hands raised in the same . . . posture as the god," is naked and has an erection. This representation indicates, in the view of some writers, that cultic auto- or homoeroticism may have figured in the god's worship, and further, that the ithyphallic worshipper may have seen himself as the lover of the "chaste" and seated – hence receptive more than active – god. Cernunnos plays a central role in contemporary Wicca, or Witchcraft, as well as in the Radical Faerie circle, as the male consort of the Goddess.

Cervula Feast of Roman origin, celebrated in many parts of Europe during the month of January in late antiquity and the early Middle Ages. The Feast of Fools appears to have been modeled on the Cervula. During the festival, participants dressed as animals and as persons of the opposite sex, exchanged gifts, sang sacrilegious songs, and danced in the streets. Christian officials condemned the Cervula, especially outraged by the transvestitism occurring within it, which was linked to the reverence of the CRONE, or elder, aspect of the Goddess.

Cestos Name of a magical belt or girdle representing that of the Greek goddess APHRODITE. Just as the bride taking part in a heterosexual marriage ceremony wore the *cestos* on her wedding night, so the *cestos* was given by male lovers, or *erastes*, to their beloveds, or *eromenoi*. Aphrodite (or VENUS, her Roman manifestation) was, as Aphrodite Urania, envisioned as a patron of homoerotic love. While it is not clear whether or not lesbian lovers exchanged the *cestos*, it seems quite plausible that they did so, as Aphrodite was also a patron of lesbian love.

Chai T'ang Term for a philosophy as well as for dwellings for women in a Chinese Buddhist-Taoist syncretic milieu. Prospering in the mid-nineteenth century, the philosophy of Chai T'ang included communal living in "vegetarian halls," or "spinsters' houses". These had originally served as residential establishments for members of the Buddhist *sangha* as well as for members of sects allied with Taoism. Chai T'ang emphasized sexual equality and focused on the female BODHISATTVA KUAN YIN. Many women followed the pattern established by Kuan Yin in retreating from society in order to escape heterosexual marriage. Lesbian relationships between women known as "sworn sisters" appear to have been accepted and perhaps even encouraged in Chai T'ang households.

Chalcis In Greco-Roman antiquity, the men of Chalcis in Euboea (i.e. the Chalcidians) were especially known for their erotic preferences for men. According to the cultural historian Athenaeus (fl. c. 230 CE), they "zealously pursued . . . such liaisons." It was this pride and passion that perhaps led them to claim that it was in Chalcis, at a place called Harpagion ("the place of abduction") that ZEUS swept down from the heavens in the form of an eagle to carry off GANYMEDE to be his beloved and cupbearer.

Chalcon of Cyparissus Armor-bearer and beloved of ANTILOCHUS who was crucified by the Greeks after he attempted to defend Penthesilea, Queen of the AMAZONS, in her struggle with ACHILLES.

Channeling Contemporary term for spiritual mediumship. According to George Lawton in his 1932 essay "The Psychology of Spiritualist Mediums," a number of spirtual mediums of his day were known to have been homosexual men. He mentions two "effeminate male trumpet mediums" known to him who had "masculine spirit guides who [gave] messages in deep, booming voices unlike that of the mediums [themselves]." Spritual mediumship, now primarily referred to as channeling, experienced a renascence in the west in the 1970s and 1980s. The channeler or medium, often in trance, might (allegedly) channel a discarnate entity or else information from a celestial data-bank sometimes referred to as the Akashic Records. Subjects discussed in channeling dialogues include same-sex desire and love and transgenderism. While some channeled entities have displayed hostility toward lesbians, gays, bisexuals, and the transgendered, most have been queer-positive. Seth, the entity channeled by Jane Roberts (a graduate of Skidmore College whose best-selling books include *The Nature of Personal Reality* [1974] and *The Nature of the Psyche* [1979]), views same-sex eroticism as positive in terms of both slowing overpopulation and in demonstrating that sexuality with the goal of giving and receiving affection and pleasure should be as treasured as sex undertaken for reproduction. "Lesbianism or homosexuality is [a] quite natural sexual expression, biologically and psychologically," says Seth, "the species is blessed, if you will, with many avenues for sexual expression." For Seth, bisexuality represents a higher state of sexual consciousness than either heterosexuality or homosexuality. Of transgenderism, Seth speaks of the need or desire of many persons to metamorphose in terms of gendered or sexual identity, observing that physical illnesses often result from an individual's suppression of this need or desire. The spiritual philosophy of Michael, an entity who, by means of a Ouija board, first appeared in the 1970s to a group of Californians, has been recorded by Chelsea Quinn Yarbro in *Messages from Michael* (1979) and in subsequent "Michael" books. For Michael, sexuality can be experienced as a path toward enlightenment. The seeker of spiritual wisdom should realize that they may experience different forms of passion and love as they journey through this and other lives. "All of you will have homosexual lives." As Michael sees it, homosexuality, like other sexual patterns, results from a combination of psychological, cultural, biological, and spiritual factors. The choice to be predisposed to homosexuality is made prior to birth, while the choice to accept or reject homosexuality is usually made by – not for – the individual by the third year of life. Echoing Seth, Michael attributes hetero- and homosexuality to "infant," "baby," "young," and "mature" souls, while attributing bisexuality or ambisexuality to "old" souls who "have lost their strong sense of gender identity and have freed themselves up to love whoever comes along in whatever way seems most appropriate." Influenced by Christianity, Michael adds, "Remember that even Jesus said you should love one another." In 1985, Jason Serinus, gay male musician, healer, writer, and editor of *Psychoimmunity and the Healing Process: A Holistic Approach to Immunity and AIDS* (1986), conducted an interview with channeler Kevin Ryerson, who played himself in Shirley MacLaine's

television miniseries *Out on a Limb* (1986). In this interview, Ryerson channels John, "Son of Zebedee, [who] lived two thousand years ago as an Essene (Hebrew) follower of Christ, and [who] has been linked . . . to John the Beloved." According to John, who links same-sex intimacy and androgyny or transgenderism, "Homosexuality is but a sharing of intimacy . . . Homosexuality, whether it manifests in the relationship between man and man, or woman and woman . . . is manifested not so much on the level of the body's consciousness, but moreso upon the level of the soul through the body's consciousness . . . There are no divisions in God. There is neither male nor female." When Serinus asks John why there are "so many gay artists," John responds, "Because as androgynous beings, there's a breakdown of the ego that allows for higher thought to flow in." In terms of HIV/AIDS, John suggests that one of the factors contributing to the illness is the hostility of many in the dominant culture toward those now finding themselves in "high-risk" groups. When individuals are susceptible to such hostility, which has a psychic aspect, they become "dis-eased." John, like another of Ryerson's channeled entities, suggests that a combination of meditative and natural healing techniques may help those who are HIV-positive or who have HIV.

Chao Tian Gong Built around 920 CE, this Taoist temple in Nanjing, China gradually became known as a place of rendezvous for men-loving men, especially from the mid-seventeenth until the early twentieth century, with young Taoist monks engaging in homoeroticism, perhaps of a cultic nature, with other men.

Chariclo Nymph, beloved of the Greek goddess ATHENA and mother of TIRESIAS. One day when Athena and Chariclo were bathing, a man, searching for a drink of water, approached the pool. Athena, not realizing that this was Chariclo's son Tiresias, blinded him for seeing their nude female bodies. While Athena could not restore Tiresias' sight, she told Chariclo that since she loved her, she would bestow Tiresias with the gift of prophecy or "second sight."

Charites In Greek myth and religion, the three GRACES, who among their other duties and powers, fashion the bodies of beautiful males to be loved by other males. They are depicted as beautiful young women who accompany various deities including APHRODITE, APOLLO, ATHENA, DIONYSUS, and EROS. They are patrons of artists and of all who cultivate beauty.

Chariton and Melanippus (fl. c. 560 BCE?) Legendary or actual male comrade-lovers who have become symbolic of the struggle against tyranny. They were instrumental in the struggle against Phalaris, tyrant of Agrigentum, Sicily

(r. c. 570-554 BCE). When their plot failed they were tortured. The tyrant Phalaris, however, was so moved by their devotion to each other that he released them. An oracle of APOLLO reads: "Happy were Chariton and Melanippus, guides for mortals in divine loving."

Chartres French city associated in the Medieval period with homoeroticism. It was related in Medieval Latin poems that in Chartres, "Adonis prostitutes himself / According to the law of the whorehouse: there are acts of sodomy there."

Cherry Generally symbolic of desire, immortality, and the female genitalia, and in Shakespeare's *A Midsummer Night's Dream* (1594-1596) of female-centered desire, according to V. Traub (1994). In Shakespeare's play, Helena says to Hermia, "So we grew together Like to a double cherry" (Act III, scene 2).

Chibiabos In Henry Wadsworth Longfellow's (1807-1882) epic American poem *The Song of Hiawatha* (1855), Chibiabos is an Algonquin TWO-SPIRIT or transgendered male loved by the protagonist. In this poem "gentle" Chibiabos is described as the "most beloved of Hiawatha, the best of all musicians and the sweetest of all singers." Epitomizing the balance of opposites, Chibiabos is both brave and soft as well as "pliant as a wand of willow" and "stately as a deer with antlers."

Chigo Angelic male youth of Japanese Buddhism. In the opinion of Tsuneo Watanabe, *chigo* are "representations of a very ancient Japanese cult [in which] the god appears incarnate in the form of angelic boys . . . This contributed to the development of homosexual love, in the same way as the cult of the Virgin seems to have contributed to the evolution of the love of women in Medieval Europe." The Buddhist monk SAICHO, in the eighth century CE, had a vision of a *chigo*, which inspired him to compose the teachings of Tendai Buddhism.

Ch'i-Lin The Chinese unicorn, sometimes shown lying at the feet of the BODHISATTVA KUAN YIN, is often a symbol of androgyny.

Chimu Highly civilized people of Peru who absorbed the earlier Moche culture. The Chimu Empire lasted from c. 100 until 1460, when the Chimu were conquered by the Incas. The Chimu were master architects, building the magnificent city of Chan-Chan. They were also well known for their jet-black pottery, feathered weavings, and art objects made of gold, silver, and bronze. Women and gender variant persons seem to have been held in respect, and Goddess Reverence played a central role in spiritual life, with goddesses including Si, the MOON, and Ni, the sea. The great temple of the moon, called Si-an, was located in the Pacasmayo Valley. Here, colored cottons, fruits, animals, birds, and supposedly children, were sacrificed to the lunar goddess. From the observations of Spanish Catholic chroniclers, it appears that transgendered male shaman-priests served as HIERODULES and oracles of the goddess Si at the great temple of Si-an. A ceremonial vessel which appears to depict a shaman-priest and another male engaging in anal intercourse supports the literary evidence. From Spanish accounts we also learn that the Incas conducted a campaign against Chimu who were suspected of participating in same-sex intercourse.

Chin (also **Cu, Cavil, Maran**) This deity may be the Mayan "God K," depicted as a dwarf or child. From Chin's forehead emerges a smoking MIRROR and from this mirror an ax appears, associated with RAIN, lightning, and FIRE. One of Chin's legs sometimes becomes a serpent. Chin is a god of nurturance, maize, magic, divination and destinies of rulers. He is said to have introduced the Mayas to homoeroticism. Chin's association with same-sex EROTICISM led to the practice of Mayan nobles purchasing handsome youths of the lower classes to be the lovers of their sons. These relationships were, at least in legal terms, considered marriages. If a third party attempted to break up the relationship, or if one of the partners wished to dissolve the relationship, he might be forced to pay a fine.

Chios Island (now named Scio) between Lesbos and Samos near Clazomenae (on the Ionian coast, present-day western Turkey), famous for its WINE – Chianti. On this island APOLLO, CYBELE, DIONYSUS, and ZEUS were especially revered. The men of Chios were so associated in the Greco-Roman psyche with the receptive role in anal intercourse that both they and their island came to be symbolic of receptive homoeroticism. In Rome, the terms "*Chian*" and "*pedicatio*" became synonymous.

Chiron Centaur who loved and mentored ACHILLES, APOLLO, ASCLEPIUS and other male gods and heroes of Greek mythology. Chiron was considered the wisest of all the Centaurs, and the friendliest to humans. An immortal, he lived in a cave on Mount Pelion in Thessaly. Chiron instructed his beloved pupils in such things as hunting, the martial arts, and music. He was also renowned as a healer; Grimal notes that "when Achilles as a child had his ankle burned as a result of magical practices used on him by his mother, Chiron replaced the missing bone with one taken from the skeleton of a giant."

Chloris In the writings of Horace (65-8 BCE) a tale is told of Chloris, a Roman woman who abandoned her husband in order to "sport with damsels" in a lesbian-oriented "bacchanalia."

Choronzon Spirit also known as the Lord of Chaos, appearing in the ritual magic systems of certain twentieth-century occultists. According to E. E. Rehmus (1990) it is Choronzon's sexual union with another male spirit, Yog Sothoth, which produces the Biblical Beast 666.

Chou Wang (or **Tcheou Wang**) In Taoism, the god of male homoeroticism and specifically of anal intercourse. Accounts vary as to the identity of this deity. In one account, he is briefly mentioned as the spirit of the star Dian Xi (or T'ien-hsi). In another, he is described as the spirit of a bisexual emperor (usually depicted by homophobic scholars as evil) who lived during the twelfth or eleventh century BCE, who practiced magic, and who, together with his chief male lover, became the principal deity of an all-male cult devoted to the celebration of same-sex love. According to Edward T. C. Werner, there is a temple dedicated to him at Chi Hsien, Wei-hui Fu, Hunan Province in southeast central China.

Christsonday Androgynous male spirit of sixteenth-century Scottish Witchcraft, consort of the Queen of Elfland. In 1596 he appeared to the male Witch Andro Man, once as an angel and once as a stag, bidding Andro Man to kiss his buttocks as a sign of allegiance to him.

Chrysanthemum In Chinese symbolism, a flower which signifies (among other things) androgyny because it blossoms in autumn, an "intermediate" season.

Chryses His name meaning "golden," he was, as a youth, loved by the Greek god HERMES. He later became a priest of APOLLO and father to Chryseis.

Chrystos (1946-) Lesbian poet, artist, and activist of Menominee Native American Indian and European (Lithuanian/Alsace-Lorraine) heritage. Living with her lover on Bainbridge Island in the Pacific Northwest, Native culture and woman-centeredness inspire much of her work. In "Night Visits," she writes: ". . . I remember / dancing with you washed in light / Our spirits whirl / Step into / the still center / of a friendship drum."

Chubb, Ralph Nicholas (1892-1960) Artist, URANIAN poet, lithographer, and pacifist whose utopian vision fused the love of male youths, Anglo-Catholicism, Greek mythology, and the ideas of Edward CARPENTER. "I believe absolutely in masculine love," he wrote, "of which I claim to be an apostle and a forerunner." In "Note on Some Water-Colour Drawings" (1929) Chubb wrote "David and Jonathan, Harmodius and Aristogeiton, [Jesus] Christ and the youthful [Saint] John [the Evangelist], Plato, Socrates, Michelangelo and Shakespeare are company good enough for me." Chubb appears to have believed that on March 21, 1941 a "boy-

god Raphi" was born "who is the way, the truth, and the life" and who will lead us all into a New Age. In *A Vision of the Manchild* he describes this deity: "Enveloped in dazzling sunshine appears the naked form of a glorious Manchild. His golden locks, his smooth rounded and ivory limbs, his violet eyes and rosy lips, his countenance of serenest innocence and beauty – so perfect, so marvelous, so divine – this is very Love itself, Love manifest."

Church, the Reverend John (fl. early 1800s) Itinerant clergyman who ministered to the transgendered male MOLLY community of London. As a lover of William Webster, he founded a chapel in a whorehouse in the Soho district of London. Church later fell in love with the Reverend J. K. Garret, another "notorious sodomite." In 1808, Church was dismissed from Banbury parish church, north of Oxford when he was exposed as having had affairs with certain men of his parish. In 1810, he was invited to become chaplain of the "Chapel" or "Marrying Room" of an infamous molly-house called The Swan in Vere Street. Church presided over same-sex, transgendered "marrying" and "birthing" ceremonies and other rites, gaining such notoriety that leaflets were distributed naming him the "devil incarnate" for ministering to the mollies and their "filthy frolics in a temple of Sodom." A broadside ballad was circulated about Church and the mollies entitled "An Epistle From the Devil to his Friend and Follower John Church," in which the Devil, as "Old Nick," invites his brother John Church to a feast of "sulfur and brimstone." In Hell, Church will continue to preside over ceremonies undertaken by the souls of the deceased mollies, who will also be there.

Cithara Greek musical instrument resembling the LYRE, sacred to DIONYSUS, ORPHEUS, and APOLLO, all being divinities particularly linked to homoeroticism, with Dionysus also expressing transgenderism.

City of No Desire In "Eros the Bittersweet: An Essay" (1986), Anne Carson speculates on an existence and mythical place without desire. She invokes the visions of Socrates and SAPPHO who describes desire, in terms of Eros, as winged and in "metaphors of flying, for desire is a movement that carries yearning hearts from over here to over there." In this City of No Desire, a dystopian vision, Eros's wings must be "clipped" and fights of desire are "unimaginable."

City West of Urs Mythical city of women described by the Jewish Medieval traveler Ibrahim iba Jabub. In this metropolis, women are impregnated by their male servants and are served by male slaves. When a woman gives birth to a male child, he is killed. Described as AMAZONS, the women of the City West of Urs are experts in horseback riding and warfare.

Civet-cat Symbol of transgenderism, this feline animal hailing from Africa was once believed, according to ritual magician Cornelius Agrippa (1486-1535), to change sex periodically. The prized ointment-like substance from the region of its anus has been used as an ingredient in perfumes for centuries. Magicians of the European Middle Ages and Renaissance believed that various parts of the civet-cat could be employed to inspire erotic attraction and prophecy, protect against negative magic, and bring about justice.

Clark, J. Michael (1953-) Co-founder of the Gay Men's Issues in Religion Group of the American Academy of Religion, Clark has authored and edited numerous distinguished texts on Gay Spirituality, including *Beyond Our Ghettos: Gay Theology in Ecological Perspective* (1993) and *Embodying Diversity: Identity, (Bio)Diversity, and Sexuality* (1995, with Michael L. Stemmeler).

Clazomenae Coastal Ionian city (in present-day western Turkey) where ARTEMIS, APOLLO, and CYBELE were especially revered. The men of this city were so associated in the Greek psyche with the receptive role in anal intercourse that Clazomenae became a topographical symbol of receptive homoeroticism.

Clement of Alexandria (Clemens Alexandrinus, b. c. 150-d. c. 220 CE) Early Christian polemicist whose influence on the religion has been profound. His condemnation of Greco-Roman paganism emphasized its reverence of deities and heroes associated with homoeroticism. "One loved HYLAS, another HYACINTHUS, another PELOPS, another CHRYSIPPUS, another GANYMEDE," Clement wrote, "Let these be they whom your boys are trained to reverence, in order that they may grow to manhood with the gods ever before them as a manifest pattern of fornication!"

Cocteau, Jean (1889-1963) French gay filmmaker and writer who was profoundly inspired by religion, mythology, and fairy tales. Charley Shively observes, "Greece provided Cocteau a magical realm of transcendence. In his youthful poems . . . in his great dramas . . . and in his extraordinary films [including] *Orpheus* (1950) and *Testament of Orpheus* (1960), Cocteau reinterpreted the Greek myths in his own libidinal and liberating way." Incessantly seeking the magical realm of experience, Cocteau not only immersed himself in films like *Beauty and the Beast* (1945) but also turned to opium, believing that it might restore to him the magical power of shapeshifting he associated with childhood. Recovering from opium addiction, Cocteau looked toward Catholicism for spiritual nourishment but quickly became disillusioned with what he perceived as the narrow-mindedness and hypocrisy of Church officials. He appears,

however, to have become increasingly drawn to mystical Christianity. Cocteau, from 1918 until his death in 1963, was grand master of the ORDER OF THE PRIEURE NOTRE DAME DE SION, a French secret society.

Colette (1873-1954) Bisexual French writer best known for her novels featuring the character Claudine. A married woman, Colette was for a time the lover of "Missy," the Marquise de Belbouf. She was slso a member of the salon of Natalie BARNEY and Renée VIVIEN, Colette was keenly interested in clairvoyance and CHANNELING. Among mediums she visited, described in *L'Etoile Vesper* ("The Evening Star," 1946), was a woman named Elise, another woman who delivered oracles while in a sleep-like state, and a gender variant man named SAPHIRA. In her illuminating essay "Colette, Clairvoyance, and the Medium as Sibyl" (1984), Stephanie A. Demetrakopoulos observes that "Colette listened to her clairvoyants with careful attentiveness and learning, seldom questioning them, but just allowing them to talk . . . Like her spiritual daughters Naomi Goldenberg, STARHAWK and other modern feminist theologians, Colette lived out a pious, non-ego-centered attitude towards others and towards all of creation's manifestations." Maurice Goudeket wrote of her, "Before every manifestation of life, animal or vegetable, she felt a respect which resembled religious fervor. At the same time she was always aware of the unity of creation in the infinite diversity of its forms." It was this respect of, this fervor, that inspired Colette to embrace many forms of gendered and erotic expression.

Commodus, L. Autelius (161-192) Bisexual Roman emperor who enjoyed taking the receptive role in homoerotic relations and who envisioned himself as the reincarnation of Hercules Victor (Greek HERACLES). In this manifestation, Heracles is the mixed-dressing consort of the Amazonian Queen OMPHALE. Commodus, like the deity he embodied, wore a combination of masculine and feminine garments even while performing as a gladiator in the amphitheater at Lavinium. Condemned for his decadent lifestyle, Commodus was strangled by an athlete named Narcissus.

Comus Spirit of revelry invoked in Greco-Roman festivals. Comus carries a torch and wears a crown of yellow and purple roses. When he is embodied by revelers at a festival, they play castanets, flutes and cymbals and dance wildly. Philostratus (fl. c. 200 CE) links Comus to transgenderism and more specifically to transvestism, writing: "Peals of laughter rise [as] the revel permits women to masquerade as men, and men to put on women's garb and to ape the walk of women."

Constantine the Great (Flavius Valerius Constantinus, 272-337) By today's standards, an extremely homophobic, transgender-phobic, and anti-pagan Roman emperor. A convert to Christianity, Constantine did his best to destroy the cults of APHRODITE, CYBELE, HAPY, MITHRAS, and other deities of antiquity. He was particularly determined to raze the temple of Aphrodite which stood near the tomb of JESUS. Constantine is known to have ordered the slaying of many transgendered, homoerotically inclined priests of Hapy and ISIS in Egypt as well as of Aphrodite/ASTARTE at Aphaca (or Afqa) in present-day Lebanon. Eusebius states that Constantine, on discovering a "hidden snare of souls . . . at Aphaca . . . dedicated to Venus," gave orders to raze the temple and to slaughter its priests. "Here men undeserving of the name forgot the dignity of their sex," writes Eusebius, "and propitiated the demon [i.e. the Goddess] by their effeminate conduct." He continues, "The hand of military force was made instrumental in purging the impurities of the place."

Constitius, Lucius (fl. c. 50 CE)   The historian Pliny (23-79) encountered in Thysdritum, Africa a person who had experienced transgender metamorphosis. Reared as a maiden, Lucia had allegedly transformed into a male on the day of her, now his, marriage to a woman. He then took the masculine name of Lucius Constitius. While this tale may concern gender transformation only, it may also suggest, as do many others of classical antiquity, that societal difficulties (in terms of maintaining heterocentric institutions) generated by lesbian relationships may have been resolved by one of the women assuming a masculine identity.

Convent   In bohemian circles of nineteenth-century France, the abode of Catholic NUNS, comparable to the THIASOS of Sappho and long associated with lesbian affection, became a generic signifier for places where lesbian women gathered.

Corelli, Marie (pseudonym of **Mary Mackay**, 1855-1924)   Scottish writer and mystic who shared an intimate relationship with her housekeeper, Bertha Vyver. Her popular novel *A Romance of Two Worlds* (1886) blends elements of science-fiction and the occult, including astral travel.

Corn   In the Cherokee spiritual tradition of Native America, the deity most associated with corn is SELU, Mother (or Grandmother) Corn, who is a gynandrous or transgendered being. YELLOW corn is symbolic, in the Navaho spiritual tradition, of CALLING GOD, who lives in a sacred mountain with the TWO-SPIRIT twin deity SHOOTING GOD. White corn is symbolic of TALKING GOD, who dwells in another sacred mountain with the second of the two-spirit twin Shooting Gods. Calling God (also known as Yellow Body) and Talking God (also known

as White Body) were created from corn by Changing Woman (or Turquoise Woman) and her sister. Once, the Navaho say, when men and women were not getting along and decided to separate from each other, the two-spirit NADLE went with the men, whom he (-she) taught to plant corn. In the center Nadle began planting kernels, making a hole with a rainbow planting stick. Then Nadle planted kernels in the east, making a hole with a white shell stick. Nadle then planted kernels in the south with a turquoise stick. Nadle planted kernels in the west with an abalone stick. And Nadle planted kernels in the north with a jet stick. Nadle planted all these kernels, singing the sacred Corn Songs.

Corydon   In Roman mythology and in the poetry of Virgil, a shepherd of ARCADIA who loved his fellow shepherd ALEXIS. As tokens of his love, Corydon gives Alexis two male goats, fruits, flowers, and other offerings. Ultimately, however, Alexis rejects Corydon for a young maiden. Corydon reveres the god PAN, a Greco-Roman patron of shepherds. Corydon was also the lover of GLAUCON. In Virgil's *Second Eclogue*, Corydon sings: "In the woodland with me thou shalt mimic Pan in song: / – it was Pan who taught us to join reed to reed with wax: / – it is Pan who cares for the sheep and the shepherds of the sheep!" The French writer André GIDE invoked these figures of myth in his 1924 gay manifesto *Corydon*.

Corythus   Iberian man whose name means "crested lark," loved by the Greek hero HERACLES.

Cossitius, Lucius (fl. c. 150 CE)   Aulus Gellius (c. 130-180), a Roman lawyer and the author of *Attic Nights*, reported that while traveling in Africa, near Thysadrus, he encountered a man named Lucius Cossitius, who claimed that on his wedding day, he had been magically transformed from a woman into a man.

Cottabus   Greco-Roman entertainment also employed as a tool of divination. Cottabus involved drinking contests and emptying dregs of wine onto the ground. As a divinatory tool, the patterns formed by the dregs would tell the querent if he were loved, and by whom. Cottabus appears to have been played or employed by male lovers of men. It was patroned by the deities APHRODITE, APOLLO, and HELEN, the divinized hero HERACLES, the EROTES, the Dioscuri, and the satyrs.

Courage   Anti-gay organization associated with the Church of England which claims to be able to transform lesbians, gay men, and bisexuals into heterosexuals. In July 1995, a London gay activist group, OutRage!, protested the retirement address of the Anglican Bishop of St Albans, Rt Rev John Taylor, whose affiliation with Courage was well known. Protesters, blowing whistles, chanting, and storming the altar, shouted "Church of hatred, church of fear, stop crucifying queers." The Church of England has done little thus far in the way of condemning organizations such as Courage which have links to the Church.

Couros and Couretes The term "*couros*," or "*kouros*," refers simultaneously to a Greek deity, a class of spirits, and a group of historical male warriors. The deity is synonymous with ZEUS, except that he is viewed as the son of Rhea or CYBELE rather than as the patriarch of the gods. As a class of spirits, the *couretes* protect the infant Couros from his father, who wishes to kill him; by extension, they guard and nurture other infants and children as well as others needing protection. They were especially revered alongside the CABEIRI on the island of Samothrace. Both as spirits and as living warriors, the *couretes* were acclaimed as dancers who combined that art form with martial arts. As spirits and as historical personages, they were also said to serve as shield-makers, metallurgists, bee-keepers, healers (including as midwives), musicians, and makers of musical instruments, including cymbals and bullroarers. They were also said to practice magic in order to bring rain and ensure the fertility of crops and flocks. Some claimed that it was the *couretes*, either the spirits or the living warriors, who founded the Olympic Games. An Orphic Hymn to the Courete spirits reads: "Leaping Kouretes, stepping to the sound of arms, / howling mountaineers, whose feet pound the ground, / discordant is the lyre you strike as you pace, light of foot, / O renowned marshals and arm-carrying guards, / priests in the train of a mother struck with mountain frenzy. / Kindly visit those whose words praise you." In terms of the *couros* as a living male warrior, and the *couretes* as an historical association, it appears that the institution may have emerged in Crete and that it may have first been called the Society of the Clenoi, its primary purpose being to rear warriors. The term "Cleinoi," roughly, "ensigns," referred to the beloved in a homoerotic relationship with a mentor. The life of a *couros* began when the youth became an ephebe on reaching the age of thirteen or fourteen. At this time, he was ritually abducted by an older male who became his lover, mentor, and companion-in-arms. The *couros* endured an intense period of initiation rites, one of which appears to have been public sexual intercourse with his lover, at which time he, and the relationship as well, were dedicated to APOLLO CARNEIUS and to other deities and deified heroes associated with homoeroticism, including ARTEMIS, ATHENA, Boreas, Couros, CHIRON, the Dioscuri, HERACLES and HERMES. The *couretes* were sometimes described as being transgendered, suggesting that they may have alternated or blended their warlike personae with traits and attire (according to Halliday) considered feminine. According to Strabo (c. 63 BCE-c. 21 CE), "The Aitolians explained the name Kouretes as derived from the female garb they

wore." In recent years, the *couretes* have been acknowledged as a model for manhood by the lesbian-feminist Wiccan priestess Z BUDAPEST, who writes: "Kouretes were sons saved by the Goddess, becoming Her helpers to save the rest. They, as protectors and teachers of the young, constitute the Sacred Priesthood of the Mother Goddess . . . [They may serve as a] role model for matriarchal manhood."

Coyote Native American Indian TRICKSTER known among the Navaho, Lakota, Crow, Apache and other tribes. He is particularly known for his power of shape-shifting, including gender metamorphosis. In one story, Coyote transforms into a woman to seduce and marry Not Enough Horses, a handsome man he desires. When she gives birth to twin coyote-infants, however, Coyote's true identity is revealed.

Crab In Latin America and the Caribbean, gay men are associated with waterfowl (such as the DUCK) and shellfish such as crabs, possibly because of the general perception that they use "effeminate gestures which resemble those of crabs moving along the beach." The term *cangrejo*, "crab," is, in fact, currently employed by both Mexicans and Cubans to refer to gay men. The use of this term may date to ancient Mesoamerica. This is suggested by the proximate Nahuatl terms *tecuicitli*, "crab," and *tecuilonti*, "sodomite." In the Mexican Yucatán, male transgenderism and homoeroticism play a central role in the ritual humor of Carnaval. Gay men are linked in Carnaval to the sea, being referred to as both *b'usóob*, "divers," and *haib'aóob*, "crabs." In a CARNIVALESQUE rite, "crabs" are discovered by the character Juan Carnaval, who tells another character that he did not find these crabs "in the sea" but rather "in Hidalgo Park, a site in Mérida frequented by homosexuals." In the Zapotec town of Juchitán, where the people believe that transgendered and/or homoerotically inclined persons are created by the deity as such – "He is like God made him . . . it is a thing of the blood" – "lewd, stately, and powerful" women embrace each other, drink beer, and "laugh loud and hard," while a number of men "put on dresses, do the chores . . . carry water" and sell flowers in the marketplace. These transgendered men of Juchitán wear necklaces of crabshells.

Cratinus (fl. c. 650-600 BCE) In Greek history, the lover of ARISTODEMUS, who sacrificed himself, alongside with his lover and with the help of the prophet EPIMENIDES (b. c. 659 BCE), to aid in cursing a plague devastating Athens.

Crocale Hunter, nymph, and companion of the Greco-Roman goddess ARTEMIS/DIANA.

Crocus This beautiful flower, typically yellow (-orange) or purple, the autumnal variety of which yields SAFFRON, obtained its name, according to the Greeks, from a handsome, gentle young man loved by the god HERMES. Crocus was fatally wounded at play one afternoon when the discus of Hermes, who was momentarily blinded by the sun, hit the youth on the head. Although Hermes was unable to restore the young man to life, he transformed him into a golden flower, which he named after Crocus. The memory of the youth was preserved by the Greeks in dyes, medicines, spices, perfumes, and clothing employing the crocus or its saffron. The KROKETOS was a graceful, saffron-dyed garment worn only by women and gender variant males; it was the dress of women attending the all-female celebration of the Thesmophoria, honoring DEMETER and PERSEPHONE; and it was a favorite garment of the transgendered, bisexual DIONYSUS. Another type of saffron-dyed garment was the SANDYX, worn by the hero HERACLES when he was at the court of the Amazon Queen OMPHALE, who insisted that they exchange garments as well as gender roles. For many centuries, artists appear to have remembered the ancient association of saffron-yellow and male gender variance, as the image of Omphale and Heracles (or Hercules) dressed in her saffron *sandyx* was a familiar one in Renaissance and Baroque art. This myth, like that of APOLLO and HYACINTHUS, may be a metaphor for, or linked in some way to, initiation rites marking the transition from late adolescence to early adulthood. The lesbian poet Amy Lowell (1874-1925), in her poem "Summer Rain," employed the crocus as a symbol of lesbian desire: "But to me the darkness was red-gold / and crocus-coloured / With your brightness."

Crone Wise, elder aspect of the triune lunar Goddess (mother, maiden, and crone), compared to the waning moon. ERESHKIGAL, HECATE, KALI, and PERSEPHONE are among those goddesses associated with this aspect of divinity and with transgenderism and/or same-sex desire. Feminists including Barbara Walker have reclaimed the image of the crone as a source of power, with lesbian-feminist theologian Mary DALY invoking her as the "Great HAG of History . . . Survivor of the perpetual witchcraze of patriarchy [who] has Dis-covered depths of Courage, Strength, and Wisdom in her Self." The figure of the Crone has, especially during the past two centuries, become linked to the Femme Fatale, inclusive of such figures as the diva, the decadent woman (sometimes a lesbian), the VAMPIRE, and the figure increasingly termed the "Bitch-Goddess." This figure may appear as a seductive, sradonic, threatening woman such as certain personae portrayed by Joan Crawford, Bette Davis, Marlene Dietrich, Eartha Kitt, Gloria Swanson, and others. This figure has also found its way into such films as *Cat People* (particularly the original film), has appeared as Disney villainesses including the Wicked Queen of *Snow White* and Maleficent of *Sleeping Beauty*, and reaches a pinnacle in the portrayal of the vampire Miriam by Catherine Deneuve in the film *The Hunger*. Occasionally, a carnivalesque element, reminiscent of the goddesses BAUBO and MÈRE SOTTE, is added to the general figure of the Femme fatale, resulting in the creation of such Camp personae as the Spider Woman of Manuel Puig's novel – later a film and Broadway musical – *The Kiss of the Spider Woman*, and as Disney's Cruella De Vil of *101 Dalmatians*. Among queer-identified persons, gay and transgendered men have been especially drawn to the figure of the Femme Fatale in both her more sombre and more humorous aspects, with a myriad of drag queens seeking to emulate her. While many feminists, especially during the late 1970s and early 1980s, condemnded the figure of the Femme Fatale as a creation of misogyny, in more recent years younger feminists, particularly lesbians and bisexual women inspired by *The Hunger* and the NEO-GOTHIC MOVEMENT, have begun to look increasingly toward the figure of the Femme Fatale as an archetype of woman-centered sensuality.

Cross Multivalent symbol embracing the four directions, the crossroads, and the merging of masculine and feminine. Divine beings associated with the cross and with transgenderism and/or same-sex desire include ATTIS, HECATE, HERMES, ISIS, JESUS, and LEGBA. Focusing on the "divine androgyny" associated with the crucifix of Christianity, Elizabeth Nightlinger invokes St AELRED of Rievaulx: "Our savior hanging on the cross; that will bring before your mind his Passion for you to imitate, his outspread arms will invite you to embrace him, his naked breasts will feed you."

Crowley, Aleister (1875-1947) Occultist, writer, visionary. A bisexual, or more appropriately "pansexual" magician who worked with and/or alienated many in the vanguard of the British occult, Wicca, or Neopagan movement, including the Golden Dawn. Among the men and women with whom he engaged in magical ritual, which he called "workings" were Herbert Charles Jerome Pollitt, aka Diane de Rougy, and Victor Neuburg, whom he encountered in 1908. Crowley and Neuberg were inspired to explore a path of homoerotic occult ritual based on Crowley's studies of Edward CARPENTER, European ALCHEMY and mysticism, Hindu yoga, and other occult traditions. In Algeria in 1909, Crowley experienced a series of possession trances in which a series of messages from spirits and deities was CHANNELED that were to become the foundation of his mysticism. Employing rites of homoerotic sex MAGIC, often possessed by PAN, he and Neuburg gained access to altered or magical states of consciousness, which Crowley referred to as "aethyrs." Then in 1913, on the six-hundredth anniversary of the martyrdom of Jacques de Molay, founder of the ORDER OF

THE KNIGHTS TEMPLAR, Crowley and Neuberg undertook the so-called Paris Workings. These rites involved the invoking of JUPITER, MERCURY/HERMES, and Pan. Their purpose was to provide the magicians with material wealth and erotico-magical wisdom. These rites of homoerotic SADOMASOCHISM, which lasted for three-and-a-half weeks, involved bondage, whipping, and carving a cross on Neuberg's chest. One of the Latin chants used in this rite included, "Magician is joined with magician; Hermes, King of the Rod, appear, bringing the unspeakable word." During the Thirteenth Working, Crowley and Neuburg were swept to a previous incarnation in which Crowley had been a HIERODULE-priestess named Aia and Neuburg had been "her" male companion Mardocles. Crowley and Neuburg apparently believed that one was incarnated seven times as one gender, then seven times as the other, in alternating cycles. At the beginning or ending seven-lifetime cycles, homosexuality or lesbianism often occurred. Crowley learned much from the Paris Workings. He became convinced that all forms of EROTICISM should be accepted and that all could be employed in magical rites. He began to instruct male practitioners to worship the phallus and to practice ritual, including mutual, masturbation. Semen resulting from these rites was often offered to the Goddess, represented by the altar or a talisman. Crowley also came to believe that the power of heterosexuality lay in reproduction, whereas the power of homosexuality lay in the shamanic experiences of transformation and death/rebirth. Related to this, he viewed heterosexual relations as extending outward (as to children) and homosexual relations as creating a circuit or loop of magical energy or power. Crowley continued to experiment with homosexual magic, as he did with heterosexual magic, for the remainder of his life. An example of Crowley's pansexual approach is found depicted on a mural at the Abbey of Thelema at Cefalu in Sicily which Crowley founded. In the mural, a man is being anally penetrated by "the Great God Pan while his [own] semen . . . [sprinkles] over the body of the Scarlet Woman," one of Crowley's ideal archetypes for the female magician. His poem "Hymn to Pan," read at his funeral, expresses the essence of Crowley's experience of the sacred:" . . . Pan! Io Pan! / I am thy mate, I am thy man, / Goat of thy flock, I am gold, I am god. / Flesh to thy bone, flower to thy rod." Crowley was a voluminous writer in many genres including ritual plays, poetry, and magical and divinatory texts. Primarily written in an ecstatic, "purple prose" style, many explore the conjunction of homoeroticism, transgenderism, and the sacred.

Cú Chulainn and Fer Diadh Celtic legendary foster-brothers trained in the martial arts by the Amazon SCÁTHACH ("Shade"), only to later find themselves – due to the desire of Queen Medb of Connacht to obtain the Brown Bull of Cuailnge – forced to fight each other. Fer Diadh, not wishing to fight against Cú Chulainn, says of their relationship: "Fast friends, forest-companions / We made one bed and slept one sleep." They were, however, forced to battle one another. At the end of the first day, we are told, they found and kissed each other, traded food and herbal medicines, and placed their horses in the same stable. While they could not sleep together, "their charioteers slept by the same fire." These events repeated themselves on the second and third days. On the fourth day, however, Cú Chulainn slew Fer Diadh, perhaps mistakenly. Holding his dying companion in his arms, Cú Chulainn cried out, "Oh, Fer Diadh! your death will hang over me like a cloud forever." Hamish Henderson has pointed out the similarity between this episode and certain tales of Greek warrior-lovers; he writes, "[Cú] Cuchulain's lament over the body of his lover recalls ACHILLES's lament for his beloved."

Cuadros, Gil (fl. c. 1990) Chicano writer whose *City of God* (1994), a postmodern text mixing poetry and prose, powerfully evokes the interrelationship of same-sex love, HIV/AIDS, and the mythic or sacred. In "Conquering Immortality," the haunting, final poem of the book, Cuadros weaves together a contemporary experience of casual sex with ancient Egyptian religion, employing as a symbolic link the Egyptian Theatre in Hollywood. Cuadros focuses on the proximity of sex, death, and immortality. "This sacred space" of cult movies and passion, he writes, "can never die out. / I steal underneath the chained gate, / enter through shattered lobby doors." In the ruined theatre, the poet finds a magical "serpentine necklace" which he places around his neck; it is like a "green scarab the color of the Nile."

Culiacan Ancient city on the western coast of Mexico, now located in the state of Sinaloa. Homoerotically inclined, transgendered male priest/esse/s were reported here in the late sixteenth century by Pedro de Castaneda and others.

Cullen, Countee (1903-1946) African-American bisexual poet of the Harlem Renaissance. Many of Cullen's poems possess a religious focus and a homoerotic subtext. Exemplary of this is "The Black Christ," which concerns the lynching of an African-American man named Jim. Here, Cullen links Jim to PATROCLUS, JONATHAN, and other figures associated with love between men. Cullen was profoundly moved on reading Edward CARPENTER's early anthology of homoerotic literature, *Ioläus* (1917), referring to the perspective revealed therein as a "soul window."

Cupbearer Like the charioteer, a role often assumed by the beloved in a homoerotic relationship. The cupbearer is found in numerous spiritual and mythical traditions including those of the Canaanites (exemplified by the cupbearer of the god BAAL), the ancient Greeks (Ganymede), and the mystics of Islam (the *WILDAN*, or *ghilman*). The Arabic poet Al-Gobari writes, "The boy who pours the wine gives off an enchanting perfume. His saliva enters my mouth like steel from a Hindu saber."

Cybele Great Goddess probably first worshipped at Çatal Hüyük, one of the world's earliest cities, located near present-day Konya in Turkey. The inhabitants of Çatal Hüyük depicted Cybele as a powerful, heavy-set woman seated on a throne and flanked by leopards. The leopards, which became lions in later times, are thought to represent the Goddess' male sons, consorts, or priests. In her later Roman manifestation, Cybele is seated between lions, or sits in a chariot drawn by lions. She wears a fortress-shaped tiara and holds a tympanum or a pair of cymbals. While perceived as omniscient and omnipotent, Cybele came to be primarily associated with the concerns of women, protection against one's enemies, the healing of grave illnesses, guardianship of the dead, and the gift of prophecy. In the latter days of her worship, she was recognized as a savior who was accessible to prayer, granting boons and promising her worshippers a joyous afterlife. Cybele's male consort was ATTIS. She was also linked to the god DIONYSUS, to the androgynous male AGDISTIS – indeed, she was occasionally identified with him – and to the satyr MARSYAS. While the center of her worship was at Pessinus, near Sivrihisar in Turkey, Cybele came to be worshipped in many places including Macedonia, Thrace, Carthage, Spain, Gaul, Italy, Britain, and northern Africa. Her worship was carried to Greece during the eighth century BCE, where it became syncretized with the worship of Rhea, Gaia, and Meter. The majority of Greek male citizens did not, however, welcome her arrival; they only accepted her worship because a priestess of Apollo had warned that if they did not do so, then the wrath of the Goddess would surely follow. The male citizens of Rome, like the Greeks before them, felt compelled to accept the worship of Cybele in order to fend off ill fortune. In 204 BCE, when the Sibylline Books were consulted, the Romans were advised to import the worship of Cybele to Rome in order to ensure success in their struggle with the Carthagians. A temple to Cybele was dedicated in 191 BCE. After being destroyed by fire, it was rebuilt by Caesar Augustus, who acknowledged Cybele as the chief divinity of the Roman Empire. Walter Burkert writes, "It was from the new center in the *ager Vaticanus*" that "the cult of Magna Mater pervaded the whole Roman Empire." Cybele's retinue included many priestesses, including Amazonian, transgendered female priest/esse/s as well as traditionally masculine functionaries such as the *dendrophori* and *cannophori*, the "tree-" and "reed-bearers," and transgendered males known as GALLI. The early Christians were determined to

destroy the cult of Cybele. St Augustine's condemnation of the Goddess was especially vicious. Referring to her as a "demon" and a "monster," he concluded, "The Great Mother surpassed all the gods . . . not by reason of the greatness of her divine power but in the enormity of her wickedness." The faithful of Cybele did not, however, surrender without a struggle. When a Christian fanatic "made a demonstrative protest against a procession in honour of Cybele," her followers demanded he be punished, and he was put to death. From the first century onward, however, conflicts between "pagans" and Christians increased at an exponential rate. In the fourth century CE, Valentinian II officially banned the worship of Cybele, forbidding citizens to visit her temples or to make sacrifices to her. In sixteenth-century France, Queen Catherine de' Medici was compared to Cybele, as her homoerotically inclined, transgendered son, King HENRI III, was compared to Attis, and his minions to the *galli*.

Cycnus In Greek legend, a king of Liguria, and a male lover of PHAETHON. Cycnus's name means "SWAN." When ZEUS killed Phaeton with a thunderbolt, Cycnus mourned his death so keenly that he was transformed into a swan. APOLLO gave Cycnus a beautiful voice, a fact from which springs the belief that swans sing one last beautiful song just before they die. Hence the expression "swan song." The constellation called the Swan is also symbolic of either Cycnus the lover of Phaeton, or of another Cycnus, a son of Apollo and Thyria, who was the lover of Phylius. The latter Cycnus was considered a very handsome, but cruel, lover whose friends and lovers left him one by one until only Phylius remained. Cycnus then sent Phylius on a series of difficult and dangerous tasks which Phylius completed only with help of Heracles. When Phylius finished these, he abandoned Cycnus, who, ashamed and alone, drowned himself. Apollo took pity on him and transformed Cycnus into a swan.

Cymbals Percussion instruments, usually made of metal, dish-shaped, and held by a grip, found in ancient Mediterranean cultures since at least the third millennium BCE. Cymbals have been linked since antiquity to deities and spiritual functionaries associated with transgenderism and/or same-sex desire. Transgendered male worshippers of ISIS, KOTYS (who was thought to have the cymbals), DIONYSUS, and CYBELE, as well as transgendered or Amazonian devotees of ARTEMIS/DIANA, honored the deities with the clanging of cymbals. Cymbals were used in the theatrical performances of the Greek MAGODOS, a transgendered mime and singer believed to practice magic.

Cyparissus Shepherd loved by the Greek god APOLLO, and guardian of the sacred stag of ARTEMIS/DIANA. One afternoon, in the scorching heat of the sun, the stag, with its antlers of gold encrusted with jewels, lay down to rest.

Cyparissus, blinded by the sun (i.e. Apollo), accidentally shot the stag, believing it to be another animal. He then committed suicide. When Apollo saw what Cyparissus had done, Apollo changed him into a cypres tree, saying, "I shall mourn for you as you have mourned for the sacred stag of Artemis, and as the cypress, you shall be a companion to all those who grieve." The tale of Apollo and Cyparissus is the subject of an exquisite painting by Claude-Marie Dubufe (1790-1864).

Cypress Tree symbolic of the phallus, the union of male and female energies, grief, death, and resurrection or rebirth. The cypress is an attribute of various deities associated with same-sex intimacy and/or transgenderism, including APHRODITE, APOLLO, ARTEMIS, ATHENA, CYBELE, CYPARISSUS, PERSEPHONE, and SILVANUS.

Cyrene Known as "Leontrophonos" or "Lion-Slayer", an athlete, hunter, and beloved companion of both ARTEMIS and APOLLO. Despising traditional women's crafts such as weaving, Cyrene excelled in jogging and in swordsmanship. She is said to have founded the city of Cyrene in Libya. She is associated with both the Naiads and the Centaurs.

D

Daath Hebrew for "knowledge," Daath is known as the unseen – some say "false" – eleventh sephirah beyond the ten commonly acknowledged on the QABBALISTIC Tree of Life. ("Sephirah" is defined as a mystical "emanation," "sphere," or "light" bearing a concentration of archetypal energy, similar to the Hindu *chakra*.) As a gateway to other worlds or other mystical dimensions and enlightenment, Daath is part of the left-handed path of magic. It is a magickal pathway in the system of Aleister CROWLEY associated with the demonic spirit CHORONZON. In the occult tradition of QABBALAH, Daath is described as "an existing/non-existing" sephirah, which is associated with magical wisdom and with feminine mysteries. According to some writers on the Qabbalah, it is also associated with the so-called Tree of Death, or Tree of Night, found on the usually unseen, "dark" backside of the Tree of Life, its spheres harboring demonic energies. Many Qabbalists are dualists who divide everything into light-right-good-masculine/dark-left-evil-feminine. Thus Daath would be associated with feminine mysteries and magic as well as darkness, death, and demons. E. E. Rehmus views Daath as a gateway or threshold between the realms of life and death, as the "doorway through which death, non-existence and Hell come into life." Daath has been compared to the Egyptian goddess Sothis (a deity of fertility, the Underworld, and SIRIUS the Dog Star) and to the Biblical Whore of Babylon, who appears in the Christian New Testament Book of Revelation as "arrayed in purple and scarlet." (Revelations 17: 3-5). According to Lawrence Durdin-Robertson, one of Daath's manifestations is that of a lesbian, or "tribade," goddess. In this aspect, she parthenogenically creates a number of demonic and possibly also angelic spirits, including the concept/goddess or spirit Nephesch, who is considered the daughter of Daath. Nephesch is associated with fertility, sexuality, and the MOON. Nevill Drury notes, "It can be argued that modern Witchcraft is a form of Nephesch-worship." Some spiritual writers may see in the figure of Daath unsavory, patriarchally motivated associations of femininity and evil. On the other hand, Daath may be seen as a manifestation of the so-called "dark Mother" archetype, linked to SCORPIO-like goddesses of sex, death, and regeneration such as HECATE, KALI, and the vampiric Lilith.

Daksha Transgendered or gynandrous deity of Hinduism who split itself into male and female, their intercourse producing numerous goddesses. Daksha is associated with the god SHIVA.

Daly, Mary (1928-) Lesbian-feminist writer and instructor of theology and philosophy at Boston College. A brilliant wit and consummate stylist, Daly's satirical treatment of patriarchy in general and of patriarchal religion in specific is reminiscent of Swift's *Gulliver's Travels* (1726) and Carroll's *Alice's Adventures in Wonderland* (1865). Daly is concerned, however, not only with dismantling the nightmare of patriarchy but also with the creation of a female-centered cosmos where CRONES, FURIES, HAGS, Harpies, and SPINSTERS are once more revered. Acknowleding lesbian love as a source of spiritual inspiration and empowerment, Daly observes: "It was in the rich, ecstatic, powerful Aura (O-Zone) of that connectedness that my writing flowed and sparkled, deep into the Hag-Time of night and early morning." Daly's works include *The Church and the Second Sex* (1968), *Beyond God the Father* (1973), *Gyn/Ecology* (1978), *Pure Lust* (1984), *Websters' First New Intergalactic Wickedary of the English Language* (edited by Jane Caputi, 1987), and *Outercourse* (1992).

Damballah Rainbow-Serpent of the Vodou pantheon, the male spouse or masculine aspect of the *lwa* (deity or spirit) AIDO HWEDO. As the latter, Damballah is considered androgynous or transgendered. According to the late Priest Oswan Chamani of the Voodoo Spiritual Temple of New Orleans, Damballah may occasionally manifest himself (-herself) as a homoerotically or bisexually inclined male divinity. In Dahomey in West Africa, Damballah appears to have been served in the past by gender variant male HIERODULIC priests called KOSIO. Dwelling in springs and rivers, Damballah is a *lwa* of thunder, RAIN, and the RAINBOW. He (-she) is invoked especially as a bringer of peace and prosperity. His (-her) sacred attributes include the cotton tree, silk tree, palmetto, calabash, and tamarind. Offerings include rice, milk and eggs. Syncretized with the Catholic Saint Patrick and as such fêted on March 17, Damballah is also honored on Thursdays.

Damon and Pythias In Greek legend, male lovers believed to be Pythagorean philosophers. When Pythias attempted unsuccessfully to kill the Sicilian tyrant Dionysius, he was condemned to death. Damon begged to take his place. Dionysius was so impressed by the men's love for each other that he pardoned Pythias and let the lovers continue with their lives.

Danaids Gender variant nymphs of Greek mythology who, according to Athenaeus, differed from both traditional women and men. Suggesting a comparison to the AMAZONS, Athenaeus relates that the Danaids, who generally preferred the company of women to that of men, "bore not the form and look of men, and they had not the voice of women, but in boxed chariots they exercised throughout the sunny glades of the woodland" or gathered frankincense, dates, and cassia.

Daniel (fl. c. 600 BCE) Biblical hero and prophet. With a story akin to that of JOSEPH, Daniel, taken captive during the Judean exile in Babylon, was later bestowed with political authority by King Nebuchadnezzar (fl. c. 600 BCE) and given the name Belteshazzar, the king being awed by Daniel's power to interpret dreams. D. Helminiak (1994) observes that "Daniel's role in Nebuchadnezzar's court [may have] included a homosexual liaison with the palace master. The romantic connection would explain why Daniel's career at court advanced so favorably."

Daniélou, Alain (1907-1994) French musicologist, writer, translator, musician (especially of the vina), dancer, and sportsman known especially for his works on Hindu music, mythology, religion, and mysticism, which include *Hindu Polytheism* (1964), *The Ragas of Northern Indian Music* (1968), *Shiva and Dionysus* (1982), and *While the Gods Play* (1987). Inspired by a deeply religious mother, at age four he constructed a sanctuary in the woods with images of the Virgin Mary and small crosses. His attraction to the sacred eventually led him to explore other spiritual traditions, particularly Hinduism, and to view EROTICISM as a bridge to enlightenment. He described his first homosexual experience in beatific terms – he felt suddenly "infused with light." "In that moment of intense pleasure, a god of sensuousness, happiness, and light was revealed to me – that god of love whom mystics [of ancient Greek religion, Sufism, Christianity, and Tantra] write about, the god of Jalal al-Din RUMI and Saadi, of Saint John of the Cross [San Juan de la Cruz] and Saint Theresa of Avila [Santa Teresa de Avila], of Dionysian and Tantric rites." In the 1930s and 1940s, with his lover Raymond Burnier, Daniélou immersed himself in Hinduism, visiting, photographing, and writing about many otherwise neglected Hindu temples. In *Fools of God* (1988), one of his works which depicts the interrelationship of homoeroticism and the sacred, Daniélou describes the erotico-spiritual dimension of the lives of certain *sadhus* (Hindu ascetics). For these, he insists, "the repression of sex is out of the question. The path of complete abstinence is considered impossible in the age of strife in which we live . . . The man who wishes to conquer heaven and earth must cultivate both sexual and mental energies and at length learn to channel the one into the other." While some *sadhus* have female companions, others, for reasons including the desire to avoid fatherhood, have male companions. Daniélou confirms that "relations between persons of the same sex are . . . very widely practiced." Observing that "this connection between homosexuality and monastic and spiritual life, and the sacred view of this kind of relationship, are well known in all religions," he concludes, "Sex allows the pupil-teacher relationship to achieve a fullness in which the flowering of the body leads to an ennoblement of the soul."

Dante Alighieri (1265-1321) Italian poet and author of the *Divine Comedy*. After the death of his beloved Beatrice, he began a study of mysticism, philosophy, and Provençal poetry resulting in the long epic of his visionary journey through Hell, Purgatory, and Paradise. In this long poem, Dante places the troubadours Arnaut Daniel and Guido Guinizelli among the sodomites in Purgatory. In *Paradiso* (I, 67-71) Dante describes a transgendered or androgynous image of the Ideal Lady, often conflated with the Virgin Mary, suggesting a process whereby one may meditate upon the vision of this figure until that moment when one becomes embodied or possessed by her: "Gazing on her, such [as she] I became within."

Daphne Huntress and beloved companion of the Greco-Roman goddess ARTEMIS/DIANA. Her name means "laurel." When a young man named Leucippus fell in love with her, he decided to dress as a huntress in order to woo her, aware of her erotic inclination. Although Daphne was at first attracted to him, he was torn to pieces when his male anatomy was revealed.

Daphnis Shepherd of Greek myth and inventor of pastoral poetry. The son of HERMES and a nymph, Daphnis was taught by PAN, who loved him, to play the flute or syrinx. On Daphnis's death, Pan's grief was inconsolable. Deserting the mountains and forests, he cried, "He is dead, Daphnis, Daphnis who embraced my heart!"

Dates This fruit served as a love-gift among homoerotically inclined lovers in ancient Greece and Rome. Seedless or "stoneless" dates were associated with castrated males and were sometimes referred to as "eunuch dates." Dates were also a favorite food of the DANAIADS.

David and Jonathan In Biblical tradition, David was a warrior-king, prophet, and musician-healer, celebrated for killing the Philistine warrior Goliath. In the Book of Samuel, David is loved by Jonathan, the son of King Saul, who is jealous of their relationship. In their final meeting prior to Jonathan's death upon the battlefield, it is said that they "kissed and wept." Upon hearing of the death of Jonathan, David was devastated, explaining that his "love [for Jonathan] was wonderful, passing the love of women"

(2 Samuel 1: 26). In the European Middle Ages, Peter Abelard (1079-1142), philosopher, theologian, and ill-fated lover of his female pupil Heloïse, wrote in "David's Lament for Jonathan," " For you, my Jonathan, / I must weep more than for all the others, / Mixed in all my joys / There will always be a tear for you." Baroque composer George Friederic Handel (1685-1759) composed the oratorio *Saul*, wherein David sings, "What language can express my sorrow? Great was the pleasure that I experienced with you; And your love was more precious to me than the love of women." Marc-Antoine Charpentier (c. 1640-1704), inspired by his contemporary Jean-Baptiste Lully (1632-1687), composed the opera *David et Jonathan* (1688), written to be performed by young male singers at the Jesuit college of Louis-le-Grand. This love story has inspired many homoerotically-inclined and bisexual artists, including D. H. LAWRENCE and John Addington SYMONDS. In 1872, inspired by a painting by Edward Clifford and by his love for Norman Moor, Symonds wrote "The Meeting of David and Jonathan." The greater part of this poem, which portrays the lovers as warriors, makes much use of twin imagery, with David and Jonathan being depicted as "twin eagles" and "twin roes." The bulk of the poem is devoted to a description of a ceremony by which the souls of the lovers are welded together. Under "an ancient holm-oak huge and tough," Jonathan takes David into "his arms of strength" and kisses him. "In that kiss," Symonds tells us, "Soul unto soul was knit and bliss to bliss." Jonathan then undresses, giving his clothing, armor, sword, and bow to David as tokens of his love. He praises David's beauty and strength and explains that his love for David is greater than the love he holds for his wife. The two then fall to the ground "To swear a sacrament and solemn vow," with Jonathan assuring David that "neither time nor chance shall sever / The troth" they "have plighted." In recent years, queer-identified Jewish and Christian couples joining in ceremonies of same-sex UNION have reclaimed the tale of David and Jonathan, as they (we) have that of the Biblical RUTH AND NAOMI.

Day, F. Holland (1864-1933) Homoerotically inclined US photographer. A student of the occult and a devotee of early homosexual rights spokespersons Edward CARPENTER and John Addington SYMONDS as well as of Oscar WILDE and the Decadents, Day's photographs often weave together the homoerotic and the mythic or sacred, especially his studies of ORPHEUS, PAN, and JESUS (with himself posing as Christ).

Deer Often symbolic of the hunt, the season of autumn, sacrifice, and rebirth. The deer is sacred to numerous deities and mythic figures associated with same-sex passion and transgenderism including ARTEMIS/DIANA, CERNUNNOS, CYPARISSUS, OYA, and XOCHIQUETZAL.

TAŸGETE was transformed by Artemis, who loved her, into a doe so that the former would not be captured by Zeus. The Aztecs linked the deer to the goddess Xochiquetzal and to the *patlache*, the Amazonian, woman-loving woman.

Demeter Greek goddess of grain who presides over bountiful harvests. The ELEUSINIAN MYSTERIES were founded to commemorate Demeter's grief-stricken search for her daughter PERSEPHONE after the latter had been abducted by Hades, lord of the underworld. During that period of grief, Demeter encountered two eccentric female figures, BAUBO and Iambe. Legend has it that Baubo and Iambe conspired to shake Demeter out of her depression, Iambe by telling her proto-limericks and Baubo by lifting her skirts. While most scholars have accepted the version of the myth which says that Demeter laughed when she looked upon the odd positioning of Baubo's body parts, a lesser known version of the myth recounts that Demeter smiled when Baubo lifted her skirts because she was delighted by the beautiful body of a young woman who had depilated herself.

Devi Of the many goddesses of Hinduism, Devi is most often described as the Great Goddess of India. She represents a syncretic blending of the Goddess(es) of the pre-Hindu Indus Valley religion with those of Hinduism. Of DURGA, KALI, PARVATI, and other goddesses, it is said, "Distinctions are apparent rather than real; each is Devi and Devi is each of them and the sum of all that they represent." Devi's following includes third gender male, or transgender male-to-female, devotees. Wendy Doniger, in *Women, Androgynes and Other Mythical Beasts* (1980) suggests that a male may commit ritual castration both to identify more closely with Devi and to avoid incurring her wrath. A third motivation may be traced to myths concerning men metamorphosing into women on drinking water from, or bathing in, springs found in groves sacred to Devi.

Diaghilev, Sergei (1872-1929) In 1899 the homerotically inclined impresario Diaghilev founded the avant-garde journal *Mir Iskusstva* (*The World of Art*) and in 1906 left Russia for Paris, where he established the Ballets Russes. Diaghilev worked with many of the great artists of his time including Leon Bakst, Claude Debussy, Michel Fokine, Leonid Massine, Anna Pavlova, Maurice Ravel, Ida RUBINSTEIN, Igor Stravinsky, and Vaslav NIJINSKY. Diaghilev's tragic love affair with Nijinsky is well known. What many do not know is that Diaghilev was deeply immersed in pre-Christian ritual and sought to imbue ballets such as *L'Après-midi d'un faun* with magical power. Diaghilev's tomb is located at the necropolis of San Michele near Venice, where he died in 1929. His grave is a site of pilgrimage, where dancers, dance devotees, and others "leave red roses and worn ballet slippers" in memory of his patronage of the ballet.

Diaghilev, Tamara (1928-   )   Lesbian metaphysician of Russian heritage who heads Transformational Journeys in San Rafael, California. A close relative of Sergei DIAGHILEV of the Ballets Russes, she was, as a child, acquainted with the psychologist Carl Jung (1875-1961) and the writer Hermann Hesse (1877-1962), friends of her family. Holding degrees in anthropology, philosophy, and metaphysics, she has lived with tribal societies around the world and has been trained in Shamanism, Magic, Wicca, and the psychic arts by well-known teachers in Europe. She is learned in CHANNELING, Goddess Reverence and Women's Spirituality. Diaghilev has been instructing others in the psychic and intuitive arts since the 1960s. In the 1970s, she founded and directed an alternative school for children which was based on body-mind-spirit integration. In the 1990s, Diaghilev, who teaches internationally, blends ancient wisdom, earth magic, metaphysics, transpersonal psychology, and ritual into a process of transformation which activates self-healing at a core level. She introduces tools which build self-esteem, self-love and personal power. In recent years, she has created rites of passage to aid queer-identified and other persons in making their journey home in a state of peace and grace.

Diamond   Both a gem and a geometric symbol, the word comes from the Sanskrit *dyu*, which means "luminous being." The diamond can be symbolic of androgyny in linking two triangles, one considered "masculine," the other "feminine."

Dickinson, Emily (1830-1886)   Lesbian or bisexually inclined American Transcendentalist poet who shared passionate friendships with several women (including Susan Gilbert Dickinson and Kate Scott Anthon) and whose works include depictions of female intimacy in visionary settings. Exemplary of such poems is one commencing "Ourselves were wed in summer – dear," which describes a ceremony of same-sex UNION, with the participants being referred to as "Queen." This rite is attached to a visionary experience approximating death and rebirth, with the poet writing, "Your Vision – was in June" and "By Some one carrying a Light / I – too – received the Sign." Poet-lover and beloved are depicted as polar opposites, the former corresponding to winter, the north, and the west, the latter to summer, the south, and the east. According to literary theorist Paula Bennett (1990), Dickinson's poems are "imbricated with layer upon layer of female sexual imagery," much of it linked to lesbian desire, with symbols including flowers of various kind, nectar, berries, peas, nuts, pearls, rubies, bread crumbs, and dew. Her use of flowers as signifiers of lesbian passion is particularly obvious in her poem on picking a flower, in which she writes, "So bashful when I spied her . . . / And bore her struggling, blushing, / Her simple haunts beyond!" In the view of literary theorist Camille Paglia (1991), the poet's lesbian inclination is intimately linked to her transgendered persona – she refers to herself as an earl and other male nobles – which in turn appears to be linked to the power of shapeshifting – "I'm Czar – I'm 'Woman' Now." In Paglia's view, moreover, Dickinson's fascination with pain and death is also tied to "Voyeurism, vampirism, necrophilia, [and] . . . SADOMASOCHISM." For Dickinson, blood appears to be linked to both death and desire, and possibly as well to menstruation. In a portrait of autumn, Dickinson writes, "And Oh, the Shower of Stain – / When Winds – upset the Basin – / And spill the Scarlet Rain." While Paglia's portrait of Dickinson as a woman intrigued by pain and blood and death may seem a bit far-fetched to some, even the more moderate lesbian-feminist poet and essayist Adrienne Rich claims Dickinson as "the American poet whose work consisted in exploring states of psychic extremity." In "Vesuvius at Home: The Power of Emily Dickinson" (1975) Rich notes that the poet "often felt herself possessed by a daemonic force." In Rich's view, the daemon is the poet's "own active, creative power." Certainly this is one way to interpret the daemon; yet there remains in Dickinson's vision a Gothic, or Decadent, element that resonates with Poe and Baudelaire and that cannot be reduced to a metaphor for the creative urge. This is abundantly clear in one of Dickinson's poems concerning the soul, in which she writes, "Salute her – with long fingers – / Caress her freezing hair – / Sip, Goblin, from the very lips / The Lover – hovered – o'er – ." Rich is certainly correct, however, in pointing out that Dickinson was "heretical, heterodox, in her religious opinions, and stayed away from church and dogma." Looking upon the Bible as "an antique Volume – / Written by faded Men," she preferred ORPHEUS's "Sermon," which, unlike Christianity, "captivated – / It did not condemn," Nevertheless, Dickinson drew upon Christian symbolism and narrative in constructing her own mystical vision of life which embraced both lesbian desire and transgendered identity as well as Gothic or Decadent sensibility.

Dictynna   Her name meaning "She of the HUNTING Nets," Dictynna is a companion of the classical goddess ARTEMIS/DIANA and is herself a goddess of the MOON, hunting, and fishing. Jessica Amanda Salmonson suggests that Dictynna and BRITOMARTIS, who are often identified as being the same figure, may have once been perceived as "comrade-lovers in the Dorian manner of homosexual initiation ritual."

Dillard, Gavin Geoffrey (1958-   )   Poet, artist, actor, and songwriter, author of seven volumes of erotico-sacred verse, including *The Naked Poet* (1989) and *Yellow Snow* and Other Poems (1993). Dillard, who has been featured in erotic TANTRA "how-to" films, says of gay and bisexual "porn" stars he has known, "Al Parker was a tremendously spiritual man. I've known several Colt models who were spiritual – some in pagan ways." Dillard, who is a disciple of the lineage of Sri Ramana Maharshi and who has recently been given the Sanskrit moniker of Sankara, expresses his general spiritual perspective thus: "Love is radical. God is radical. Enlightenment is radical. All else is reactionary . . . Power comes from surrender to the divine."

Diocles In Greek legend, an Athenian hero who died while defnding PHILOLAUS, a young man he loved. Diocles and Philolaus were honored each spring at Megara with a festival, the Diocleia, in which a flower garland was given to the youth whose kisses were judged the most passionate.

Diomus Greek hero who, as a young man, was loved by HERACLES, who was a good friend of Diomus's father Colyttus. After Heracles's death, when Diomus was preparing to sacrifice an animal to the spirit of Heracles, a dog appeared and dragged the animal to a certain place and deposited it there. For this reason Diomus erected a shrine to "Dog-Headed" Heracles there.

Dionysia Renowned female Roman dancer and courtesan (fl. c. 100 BCE) named after the Greek god DIONYSUS. Her name eventually appears to have become an epithet for a transgendered, homoerotically or bisexually inclined male. When the great Roman orator Hortensius (114-50 BCE) was accused by a rival, Lucius Torquatus, of being a "Dionysia," he replied that he would rather be such than be like Torquatus, whom he looked upon as extremely dull and uninspired.

Dionysus (also **Bacchus, Evius, Liber**) Transgendered and bisexual Greek god of wine, ecstasy, sensuality, rebellion, and drama, frequently portrayed as wearing a feminine hairstyle and feminine attire. Dionysus was raised by HERMES and dressed as a girl so that ZEUS would not discover him. He was said to have been born as a serpent at the winter solstice. At the vernal equinox he reached puberty, when he assumed the form of a TREE, a LION, or a RAM. At the summer solstice, he was ritually sacrificed as a BULL, a GOAT, or a stag. Among his male lovers were ACHILLES, ACOETES, ADONIS, AMPELUS, HERMAPHRODITUS, HYMENAEUS, Laonis, and PROSYMNUS. PRIAPUS was also attracted to him. Seen as an effeminate, yet sexually potent male, Marie Delcourt points out that "ribald epithets" such as "the Testiculous" and "the Codded," were given to Dionysus. Actors in the Greek theatre wore a red leather phallus at the festival of Dionysus. Once, while searching for his mother, Dionysus

met Prosymnus, who promised to show him where his mother was if he would sleep with him. Dionysus swore his promise, but asked that he be allowed to sleep with Prosymnus upon his return. Unfortunately, Prosymnus died before Dionysus returned. Mourning Prosymnus and keeping his word, Dionysus carved a phallus of FIG wood, anchored it in the dirt on Prosymnus's grave, and sat down on it. Numerous scholars have suggested that this act of receptive anal eroticism is symbolic of the gaining of chthonic wisdom by descending to the Underworld. The condemnation of the Christian Fathers of Dionysus was extreme. Justin Martyr, comparing Dionysus to the gender variant female deities ARTEMIS/DIANA and MINERVA/ATHENA, condemns the "feminine nature of Bacchus." He is repulsed by the image of "a man's decorating himself with cymbals, and garlands, and female attire, and accompanied by a herd of bacchanalian women." One of the most celebrated works of art depicting the god is MICHAELANGELO's *Bacchus* (1496-1497), which the painter and art historian Vasari (1511-1574) described as "a marvelous blending of both sexes – combining the slenderness of a youth with the round fullness of a woman." Another Renaissance masterpiece is CARAVAGGIO's *Young Bacchus* (1595). In *The God of Ecstasy: Sex Roles and the Madness of Dionysus* (1988), classical scholar Arthur EVANS provides an illuminating discussion of the god in a Gay- or Queer-Spiritual context as well as a brilliant translation of Euripides's *The Bakkhai* (or, *Bacchae*), a tragedy concerning Dionysus, which was performed in San Francisco in 1984.

Diotima (fl. c. fifth century BCE) Priestess and Pythagorean philosopher, mentor of Socrates (469/465-399 BCE). While her existence remains somewhat controversial, scholars are increasingly accepting her identity as factual rather than as legendary. She was a native of Mantineia, located in the mountainous region of ARCADIA. In the *Symposium* of PLATO, Socrates describes her as a "wise woman in this [i.e. philosophy] and many other branches of knowledge. She was the same who deferred the plague of Athens [430-427 BCE] ten years by a sacrifice [note: an earlier plague had been banished by EPIMENIDES], and was my instructress in the art of love." It is Diotima who explains the *raison d' être* for same-sex love. While heterosexual relationships tend to produce children, same-sex relationships tend to produce (ideally speaking) wisdom, virtue, and art (specifically, poetry). "Who when he thinks of Homer and Hesiod and other great poets, would not rather have their children than any ordinary human ones?"

Dog In traditions of Goddess Reverence, an animal symbolic of the male consort or devoted companion. In ancient Syria, a signifier of anal intercourse. Among the Greeks, symbolic of companionship, the phallus, sacrifice, and underworld journeys. Dogs were given by male lovers to each other as courting gifts. A number of divine and mythic beings and spiritual functionaries are linked to dogs as well as to same-sex eroticism and/or gender variance; these include APOLLO, ARTEMIS, ASCLEPIUS, ATHENA, ASTARTE and her KELABIM priests, ATHIRAT and her QEDESHIM priests, DICTYNNA, HECATE, HERACLES, HERMES, INANNA/ISHTAR and her ASSINNU priests, PAN, and ZEUS.

Dolben, Digby Mackworth (1848-1867)   English homoerotically inclined poet who struggled with physical illness and who drowned while swimming at age nineteen. Dolben's most difficult battle lay in attempting to reconcile his devotion to Christianity with his love for men. In 1863 he burned most of his work and, converting to Catholicism and joining the Order of St Benedict, began to dress and behave as he imagined a Medieval monk would have behaved. Nevertheless, he continued to write poetry. Some of the poems cloak and/or fuse his love for men with his love for JESUS; in "Sis licet felix," he writes: "I marvelled not, although he drew / My whole soul to him, for I knew / That he was born to be my king, / And I was only born to sing / With faded lips and feeble lays / His love and beauty all my days." Other poems, addressed primarily to Gosselin, a young man who captured Dolben's heart, focus on an earthly homoerotic love, albeit one that archetypalizes or divinzes Love: "Ah Love, first Love, came gently through the wood, / Under a tree he found me all alone, / Gently, gently he kissed me on the cheek." Still other poems reveal Dolben's yearning for a world in which his spiritual and erotic feelings might have been more fully united and accepted and honored as such. In "Vocation," he envisions himself as HYACINTHUS yearning for APOLLO: "Dear bright-haired god in whom I half believe, / Come to me as thou cam'st to Semele, / Trailing across the hills thy saffron robe, / And catch me heavenwards, wrapped in golden mists."

Dolphin   Symbolic of eroticism, rebirth, and transcendence, the dolphin is sacred to the Greek deities DEMETER and EROS as well as to Pelops, the beloved of POSEIDON, and HYACINTHUS, the beloved of APOLLO and ZEPHYRUS.

Dominicus, Saint (c. 1000-1073)   Spanish Catholic abbot who eventually became one of the most beloved of that country's saints. Dominicus was perhaps best known as a lover of the arts, with artisans under his direction producing some of the most exquisite specimens of Spanish Christian art. Also renowned as a diviner, healer, and magician, one of his legendary acts involved transforming a woman into a man. St Dominicus is fêted on December 20.

Doris   In Greek legend, Amazonian spearwoman in the Attic War whose name means "Beautiful." She was named after Doris, a Greek goddess of the sea, beauty, and destiny.

Dorotheus, Saint and Saint Gorgonius (d. 303 CE)   Companion, possibly lover, of Gorgonius, both women possessing transgendered names. When Dorotheus and Gorgonius stood together firm in their faith as Christians, the Roman emperor Diocletian (284-305) ordered them hanged. Revered by many Christian women-loving women, Saints Dorotheus and Gorgonius are fêted on September 9.

Dorsey, Issan [aka **Thomas James Dorsey, Tommy Dee**, 1933-1990)   Gay abbot of the Hartford Street Zen Center (later named Issan-ji, "One Mountain Temple" in his honor) and located in San Francisco's gay Castro district. Dorsey also helped found the *Maitri* Hospice that cares primarily for gay PWAs (persons with AIDS), attending to their medical, emotional, and spiritual needs. He was installed as abbot in 1989 by Richard Barker-roshi, his mentor and the former head of the San Francisco Zen Center. Dorsey's ordination into the Zen Buddhist priesthood represents a rare example of an openly gay person's inclusion in the lineage originating in the US with Shunryu Suzuki-roshi, founder of the Zen Center and one of the primary bearers of Zen to the US. Born Thomas James Dorsey in Santa Barbara, California, he and his lover were discharged from the US Navy, in the 1950s. At that time, Dorsey began working in the gay and mixed clubs of North Beach's "Beat" scene. Adopting the drag name "Tommy Dee," he performed in clubs and musical reviews and, by the end of the 1950s, traveled with a musical drag group called "The Party of Four" from Alaska to New York City. By 1965, Tommy was involved with the growing alternative "hippie" culture centered in the Haight-Asbury district of San Francisco. In this milieu, Tommy explored alternative spiritual paths including Hinduism, Euro-western occultism, and Buddhism, holding LSD sessions inspired by *The Tibetan Book of the Dead*. Encouraged by gay poet Allen GINSBERG, Tommy read the Buddhist *Heart Sutra*. Shortly thereafter, he began attending the Sokoji Temple founded by Suzuki-roshi. By the late 1960s Dorsey had moved into the San Francisco Zen Center, and in 1970 was given his Buddhist name, Issan, in an initiation ceremony conducted by Suzuki-roshi. During these years of meditation, work, and study, Issan gained many friends and admirers who appreciated his approach to Zen. He had trouble, however, integrating his gay life and his spiritual life. His lovers were not openly acknowledged at the Center; most gay men and lesbians found the Center's halls icy. In 1980, after conferring with Baker-roshi, Robert Aitken-roshi, and other sympathetic Buddhists, Issan and a group of interested gay men initiated a series of Tuesday evening study, mediations, and talk sessions at 57 Hartford Street in San Francisco. The group was first called the Gay Buddhist Club and later, Maitri. In 1981 the group established a gay and lesbian-centered *zendo* (a Zen Buddhist monastery) with Issan as spiritual advisor. The Center has been officially recognized and blessed by several respected Buddhist teachers including Robert Aiken-roshi, Chogyam Trungpa-Rinpoche, and His Eminence Jamgon Kongrul, Rinpoche.

Double Archetypal figure associated with same-sex intimacy, traceable to numerous ancient and primal cultural and spiritual traditions. This archetypal figure was posited as distinguishable from the Anima (roughly, feminine spirit of the male psyche) and the Animus (masculine spirit of the female psyche) of Jungian psychology by Mitchell WALKER in 1976. More recently, women writers on psychology and spirituality, including Vicki NOBLE, have begun to explore the Double in relation to the female and lesbian psyche(s). In "The Double: An Archetypal Configuration" (1976), a pivotal article in terms of both Gay Spirituality and Jungian psychology, published in the prestigious journal *Spring*, Walker suggests that in terms of the male psyche, "the Anima contains the archetypal images of mother, daughter, sister, [and] lover," while the male double "contains those of father, son, brother, [and] lover." Taken together, the Anima and the Double "form a whole, androgynous in nature." This would suggest that such a whole is formed in the female psyche by way of the union of the Animus and the female Double. Represented mythologically, the male Double is revealed by such hero-pairs as DAVID AND JONATHAN, ACHILLES AND PATROCLUS, and GILGAMESH AND ENKIDU. Likewise, the female Double is revealed by such heroine-pairs as RUTH AND NAOMI, ARTEMIS/DIANA and BRITOMARTIS, and ALFHILD and GROA. Significantly, in the context of spirituality, Walker suggests that the Double, like the Anima/us, "can be part of a transcendent function," can, like the others, serve as a "soul guide." "As these myths suggest, " he continues, "the Double is a soul-mate of intense warmth and closeness . . . the Double is facilitative of rapport, [creating] . . . an atmosphere . . . of profound equality and deep familiarity." *In Visionary Love: A Spirit Book of Gay Mythology* (1990), Walker links the Double to a spiritual energy or process he refers to as "Magickal Twinning," clearly inspired, like the Double itself, by the Double beings of PLATO's *Symposium*. "The action of Magickal Twinning is a kind of duplication where the spirit-essence of one object is infused into another, making spirit-twins." Such a bond produces powerful "feelings of unity, strength, and [the] reinforcement of personal identity." Such a bond, Walker observes, is like that described in the *I Ching* (and shared by Xi Kang and Ruan Ji of the SEVEN SAGES OF THE

BAMBOO GROVE of third-century CE China), a bond that can "shatter even the strength of iron or bronze" and that partakes of the "fragrance of orchids." The Double is especially frequent in the literature of love between women, as in "To Mrs. M. A. at Parting," in which Katherine Fowler Philips writes, "Thus our twin-souls in one shall grow, / And teach the world new love." In "So Still the Dawn, " lesbian poet Elsa GIDLOW writes: "Gentle, gentle / The double kiss: / . . . / In mutual bliss / Each into each / Merging."

Double Woman Among the Native American Oglala Sioux, TWO-SPIRIT or third gender shamans-to-be dreamed of the female divinity Anukite, or Double Woman (akin to ANOG ITE). Double Woman had many faces: she could appear as twins, as a beautiful maiden, a woman warrior, an hermaphroditic buffalo calf, a vampiric deer. The young person who dreamed of her would become a two-spirit shaman and a member of the society of "they [who] dream of face-on-both-sides," *Anukite Ihanblapi*. Among the Lakota, Double Woman is called WIYA NUMPA. Devotion to Double Woman includes a ritual dance in which two female devotees of Wiya Numpa are joined in UNION by means of a coiled rope.

Dove In ancient Syria, a symbol of homosexual love and in particular of anal intercourse. Male doves alternately copulating were utilized in rituals of the Syrian Moon-goddess. Pairs of female doves are symbolic in the West of the Greco-Roman goddess ARTEMIS/DIANA, of female friendship, and of lesbian love. The Seven PLEIADES, companions of Artemis, being pursued by Orion, were first changed into doves in their flight from him across the meadows of Boetia, before being transformed into a constellation. In a Medieval poetic letter written by "B.," a Catholic Bavarian woman, perhaps a nun, to "C.," a woman she loves, the former depicts herself as a "turtledove after it has lost its husband," remaining forever "on its barren twig." In her 1922 poem "Love Song, " woman-loving poet Elsa GIDLOW begs her wild, swanlike lover to transform into a dove: "Fold your wings, brood like a dove, / Be a dove I can cherish / More calmly, my dear, my tempestuous Love."

Dragon In traditional Chinese myth, kings were imagined to be the offspring of human women and male dragons. As persons having dragon ancestry, kings were often drawn to other men as lovers. "Dragon" (*lung*) forms a part of one of the terms employed by Chinese to refer to men-loving men: *lung-yang jun*. In an Albanian folktale, a young woman who assumes a male identity and slays a dragon falls in love with a princess. When the princess discovers the dragonslayer's female anatomy, however, she tells her father, who tries to have the Amazon killed. In one of the attempts on her life, she is surrounded by serpents, who "curse" her by changing her sex. She, now he, returns to the castle, marries the princess, and the two live happily ever after. As reclaimed by the lesbian-feminist philosopher and theologian Mary DALY (b. 1928), the dragon is symbolic of the "Primordial Female Foe of patriarchy." A woman who challenges the patriarchal, heterocentric order "participates in the Powers of the Dragon . . . and breathes forth Words of Fire."

Drill Tool symbolic in Greco-Roman antiquity of the phallus and of anal intercourse, especially between men. As a phallic, pansexual deity occasionally engaging in anal eroticism, PAN is called the "Driller" (*trupanon*). Trupanon was also metaphoric and/or slang for "phallus."

Drum Percussion instrument of many varieties found in many cultures and frequently associated with deities and spiritual functionaries linked to same-sex intimacy and/or transgenderism, including transgendered TWO-SPIRIT practitioners of Shamanism; the Mesopotamian underworld goddess ERESHKIGAL; the Greco-Roman ARTEMIS/DIANA and her transgendered female or AMAZONIAN priest/esse/s; the Roman CYBELE and the GALLI, her transgendered male priests; the Shinto shaman AME NO UZUME; the Hindu god SHIVA; and the Hindu BAHUCHARAMATA and the HIJRAS, her transgendered male priest/esse/s.

Dryops Young man of Greek mythology whose name means "Oak Face" and who was loved by the divinized hero HERACLES.

Duck In Santería, the duck is a sacred attribute of YEMAYÁ, the goddess of the sea, who has transgendered aspects and who is a patron of homoerotically inclined men. It is possible, according to some practitioners of Santería, that a Cuban slang term for gay men, *pato* ("duck"), reflects – beyond its link to swaying movement of the body – this mythic complex. In some parts of China, the terms for "duck" and "penis" are synonymous. As late as the thirteenth century, some Chinese believed that ducks gave birth to offspring by way of male-male coupling, thus leading the duck to become a symbol for the man-loving male. A mysterious spiritual tradition known as the "Duck Egg Religion," still thought to be practiced in Taiwan, allegedly includes the reverence of KUAN YIN, a communal meal of duck eggs (all other animal foods are forbidden), and ceremonial homoeroticism.

Dumuzi (also **Tammuz**) Of Mesopotamian and Phoenician origins, the youthful male consort of the goddesses INANNA/ISHTAR and ASTARTE. In a hymn celebrating Dumuzi, akin to the Canaanite BAAL, he is depicted as androgynous or transgendered: "Lo, the youth

[Dumuzi], he is your father, / Lo, the youth, he is your mother."

Duncan, Robert (1919-1988) US gay poet and essayist whose work reflects a profound interest in the world's mythological and spiritual traditions. Duncan's diaries reflect participation in a kind of shamanic process concerning his coming to terms with his homosexuality, his transgenderism, and other challenging aspects of his life. Speaking of himself in schizophrenic terms, he wrote in 1941: "Robert . . . had made a cross with nails thru his body like wires and he is hung there. I hit him with a shovel cutting his head so that it hangs dangling from the neck. Like a rooster cut by a scythe." In *Young Robert Duncan: Portrait of the Poet as Homosexual in Society*, Eckbert Faas explains that Duncan was conscious of associating his confrontations with same-sex desire and gender variant behavior with Shamanism. Faas writes: "The surrealist self-portrait from Robert Duncan's diary of January 1941 recalls the dismemberment process undergone by the . . . shaman as described by . . . anthropologists. Robert, in fact, had recently read Edward Westermarck's study of homosexual and transvestite practices in shamanism, and as early as 1939 had proclaimed himself a shaman poet." Indeed, Duncan went so far as to compare his confrontation with same-sex desire and gender variance to a *bardo*, or mystical, after-death state, described in the *Tibetan Book of the Dead*, which his friend Anais Nin had suggested he read. In his diaries, Robert Duncan also speaks of gender metamorphosis, linking it to the experience of coming out: "I wore paint on my face and eye shadow . . . I would dress in the dyke end of it . . . but with my hair cut in bangs, and earrings . . . There is a madness that moves over me . . . A man will look at me with desire . . . and then I am caught, moving as in a dream, inevitably toward him . . . as . . . [a] woman."

Duquesnoy, Jerome (1602-1654) Homoerotically inclined Flemish sculptor, primarily of religious statuary. The tomb of Bishop Anton Trest in Ghent Cathedral (c. 1640) is considered his finest work. Duquesnoy was strangled and then burned at the stake after allegedly engaging in lovemaking with two acolyte-models.

Durga Hindu goddess depicted primarily as an AMAZON, a woman warrior. She is associated with numerous other goddesses including DEVI, KALI, and TRIPURASUNDARI. Durga is both beautiful and terrifying. Her body is golden; the crescent MOON is her crown. Her steed is a LION or tiger. She holds a spear and creates "female batallions from her sighs." As a goddess of wisdom, she is known as "Contemplation" and "All Knowledge." As the universal totality, she is called "One Whose Nature Is True Bliss" and "Essence of All." As with the other Hindu goddesses mentioned here, Durga's faithful include gender variant, or third gender, males who are sometimes referred to as SHAKTAS.

Dwarf, Hermaphrodite Among the Tsimshian people of the Northwest Coast of North America, the MOON, known as "the half-way house to Heaven," is inhabited by "Pestilence" and four hermaphroditic, transgendered, or TWO-SPIRIT dwarves. These dwarves demand offerings from the spirits of deceased persons. If the spirits do not comply, the dwarves attack them. If they do, the dwarves aid them in their journey from the Moon to Heaven. Like sirens, however, they attempt to lure the spirits of the deceased to remain with them on the Moon.

Dykewomon, Elana Nachman (1949-) Lesbian writer and editor of the influential lesbian cultural journal *Sinister Wisdom*, her work focuses on struggling against the oppression of, and encouraging empowerment among, lesbians and Jewish women. Born Elana Nachman into a Jewish family in New York City, her "Fourth Daughter's 400 Questions" is frequently studied in Jewish lesbian circles. Also inspired by Goddess Reverence, the cover of her classic text *They Will Know Me By My Teeth* depicts the GORGON as a powerful symbol of lesbian-feminism and separatism.

Dzonokwa Gynandrous, possibly TWO-SPIRIT female, giantess of the mythology or religion of the Kwakiutl people of the northwestern coast of the United States. Alternately depicted as an ugly, cruel being who steals children and as a guardian of children who bestows riches, Dzonokwa displays characteristics common to gynandrous figures of other northwestern peoples, including a mustache.

E

Eagle   In Greek myth, ZEUS abducted his beloved GANYMEDE in the form of an eagle. Due to this myth, the eagle is sometimes associated with the astrological sign of AQUARIUS, although it is more frequently associated with that of SCORPIO. Saint John the Evangelist, known as the "beloved disciple" of Jesus, is sometimes depicted with an eagle above him, echoing the myth of Zeus and Ganymede. In Navaho myth or religion, the eagle is associated with TALKING GOD, who wears white eagle feathers and who dwells with a TWO-SPIRIT deity named SHOOTING GOD.

Earthquake   The sea god POSEIDON, who loved Pelops, was held responsible for earthquakes in ancient Greek myth and religion. The Christian Roman Emperor JUSTINIAN (-us the Great, 482/483-565), the Emperor of Constantinople, held homoerotically or bisexually inclined males responsible for earthquakes; for this reason, he argued, they should be burned alive. In the fourth century, Rabbi Acha, a Palestininan sage, similarly claimed that earthquakes were a punishment for the sin of sodomy. In 1750, Benjamin Stillingfleet, in *Thoughts occasioned by the late Earthquakes*, reiterated this absurd belief. In the late 1970s and early 1980s, many queer-identified individuals living in northern California shared the apocalyptic belief that queer people would perform a necessary shamanic function at the time of the great earthquake – the "Big One" – that would (will) soon occur.

East   Direction associated with solar deities including a number linked to transgenderism and/or same-sex desire: APOLLO, AMATERASU OMI KAMI, HERMES, PHANES, SEKHMET and TALKING GOD.

E'chûk   Transgendered male Chukchi shaman encountered by the Russian ethnographer Vladimir Bogoras (1865-1936) at the Anui Fair. Bogoras described him as "about forty, tall and strong," demonstrating "indecent behavior and lewd talk". Bogoras reported that E'chûk boasted that he had given birth to two sons with the magical help of his KE' LET, or male guardian spirit.

Eel   In Chinese symbology, the yellow eel signifies a man-loving male. While from a European-based perspective, this might appear to be a slur, in traditional Chinese culture, both YELLOW and eel are positive symbols. The eel is symbolic of the penis and connotes protection and good fortune, while yellow signifies progress and success. In ancient Greek dance, the eel is symbolic of erotic, including homoerotic, movement.

Elagabalus (or **Algabal, El-Gabal, Heliogabal, Heliogabalus,** spiritual name of **Varius Avitus Bassianus**, 203/205-222)   Syrian born at Emesa who, through his grandmother Julia Maesa's scheming, was proclaimed Roman emperor in 219. Elagabalus also served as high priest of the solar deity SOL INVICTUS-ELAGABAL, an androgynous being represented by a large conical black stone. He later became a priest of the cults of the goddesses CYBELE, Dea Caelestis, and VESTA. A beautiful young man, he often dressed in feminine attire, employing elaborate makeup and wearing exquisite jewelry. In doing so, G. H. Halsberghe (1972) explains Elagabalus sought to "identify himself with the female principle . . . the Sol cult . . . wished to incorporate the female as well as the male principle in a single divine being." Although marrying women on several occasions to satisfy his grandmother and to win allies, he was homoerotically inclined; he took a man named Gordianus as his husband and another, Hierocles, as his wife. While some in the Empire appreciated him, including those women who took part in the women's senate he established and those sub-Saharan Africans who took part in his religious cult, many others despised him, especially for his luxury and effeminacy. Elagabalus and others close to him were beheaded in 222, ending his brief reign. In the late sixteenth century, the homoerotically inclined, gender variant French king HENRI III was often compared by the poets of his day to Elagabalus. An anonymous satirical poem reads, "This [Henri] is Heliogabal, Emperor of the Romans / He wishes to copy our most effeminate male whores (*nos damoiseaux mondains*)." The *fin de siècle* German poet Stefan GEORGE remembered him in the poetic cycle *Algabal* (1892), describing in "Days" the final legendary feast held by Elagabalus and his mother. Supposedly, this festivity was governed by pink, with foods, wine, attire, and decor all in the roseate hue. At the feast's culmination, when all the guests had become inebriated, Elagabalus let fall a curtain containing thousands of roses which fell upon the guests, suffocating them. "Bacchus be gone!" George cries, "Roses caress you . . . / Kiss and bless you."

Elephant   Sacred attribute of the Hindu god GANESHA, who is depicted as possessing an elephant's head. In Hinduism, the elephant signifies androgyny or transgenderism, with the trunk and the tusks being seen as phallic and the remainder of the body being perceived as feminine. Moreover, elephants are associated with both transgendered males, perceived as possessing flaccid genitalia, and transgendered females, perceived as possessing exceptionally large genitalia.

Eleusinian Mysteries Greek Mysteries founded to commemorate the goddess DEMETER's grief-stricken search for her daughter PERSEPHONE after the latter had been abducted by HADES, lord of the underworld. Legend has it that the goddesses BAUBO and Iambe conspired to shake Demeter out of her depression, Iambe by telling her proto-limericks and Baubo by lifting her skirts. Perhaps it was the tale of Demeter, Baubo, and Iambe which led to the participation of transgendered and homoerotically inclined male HIERODULES as well as female hierodules in the Eleusinian Mysteries as representatives of a fused Baubo-Iambe figure at Eleusis. The appearance of Baubo-Iambe occurred after the procession of worshippers left the temple of Zeus and crossed the bridge over the River Cephisus. This was the scene of the *Gephyrismos*, which means "to joke at the bridge." At this time, the gender variant priest, dressed in women's clothes, lifted his skirts. Certainly if he were a eunuch, the sight of his genitalia might provoke surprise or laughter. First mocking the worshippers, the priest playing Baubo-Iambe would then lead them in a chorus of obscene chants or songs composed in iambic pentameter. Following this, he led the others in chanting "Iakchos! Iakchos!," referring to an aspect of DIONYSUS appearing in the Mysteries. He then offered the participants a beverage akin to mead. Beyond the participation of transgendered hierodule-priests in the *Gephyrismos*, the Mysteries attracted a number of men whose homoerotic inclinations were well known. These included the Roman emperor HADRIAN and his lover ANTINOUS. In 125 CE Hadrian was initiated into the lower order of the Mysteries, becoming a *mystes*. Three years later, Antinous became a *mystes*, while Hadrian graduated to *epoptes*, "one who has seen." Antinous, whose life would soon end in suicide, an act of self-sacrifice performed in Egypt in order to save Hadrian's life, must have been deeply moved by experiencing Persephone's descent to the underworld and triumph over death. Following Antinous's death, Hadrian compared his young lover to Persephone (as well as to Dionysus and OSIRIS). He established a cult honoring him at Eleusis and elsewhere, and commissioned an altar frieze depicting Antinous "being presented by Demeter and Persephone to the enthroned Dionysus." For the remainder of his life, Hadrian remained a faithful devotee of Demeter and a generous patron of the Eleusinian Mysteries.

Elizabeth I, Queen of England (1533-1603) While we may never know for certain whether or not the gibe at Elizabeth and James I, namely, that "Elizabeth was King and James is Queen" fit the former as well as it did the latter, it is nevertheless the case that, above all other goddesses, Elizabeth was constantly compared to ARTEMIS/DIANA (in her Renaissance manifestation of Cynthia) and, by extension, to the Fairy Queen. It is conceivable that the Queen experienced passionate feelings for both women and men. Maureen Duffy (1980) points out that "Elizabeth was often identified with an AMAZON, usually HIPPOLYTA." Her perceived gender variant or transgendered nature seems to be depicted in Edmund Spenser's (1552-1599) *Faerie Queene* (vi, x, 41), wherein the goddess/queen is described as being "Both male and female. . . / She syre [i.e. father] and mother is her selfe alone, / Begets and eke [i.e. also] conceives, ne [i.e. nor] needeth other none."

Elxa TWO-SPIRIT or third gender person of the Native American Indian Yuma tribe. Among the related Maricopa such persons were called *ily axaí*. A young man's dream of a message spoken by an enspirited arrowweed plant often initiated the shamanic process. The *elxa* would allow the cross- or transgendered expression of his dress and behavior to emerge and have his/her first experiences in transgendered, often homoerotic relationships, and would eventually practice healing and divination.

Empedocles (c. 493-c. 433 BCE) Homoerotically inclined Greek philosopher, mystic, and magician, perhaps best known for his theory of the elements. Empedocles believed that everything in the universe is produced by the intermingling of various degrees of love and hate with earth, air, fire, and water. He was a vegetarian, believed in reincarnation, and healed people of grave illnesses. He was also a lover of males, his most intimate companion being a younger man named Pausanias. Empedocles dreamed of an age when men had worshipped the Goddess, had dwelt in peace rather than in a constant state of war, and had sacrificed honey, incense, and breads shaped liked animals rather than animals and humans. Empedocles wrote of a paradisal past: "Nor had they any War-god, or Battle-din, nor was Zeus their king, nor Cronus, nor Poseidon, but Cypris [i.e. Aphrodite] only was their queen. Her folk appeased her with pious offerings – painted animals and richly-scented salves, with sacrifices of pure myrrh and fragrant frankincense, while they poured upon the ground libations from the yellow honeycomb." According to legend, Empedocles ended his life by throwing himself into the crater of Mount Aetna in order to become one with the gods.

Enaree We do not know the name by which the Scythian priests of ARTIMPASA called themselves; the Greeks and Romans, many of whom strongly disapproved of them, called them the *enarees* or the *anandreies*, the "unmanly" or "effeminate ones." Numerous writers have suggested that the *enarees* may have been the spiritual descendants of Paleolithic shamans and may even have been directly influenced by Siberian shamans. Indeed, we might say that the figure of the *enaree* lies midway between the "transformed" or "soft" shaman and the gender variant priest of the Goddess, such as the KELABIM of ASTARTE, the MEGABYZOI of ARTEMIS, and the GALLI of CYBELE. Marie Delcourt writes: "It is in the bisexuality of the shamans that the explanation of the mysterious *Enarëes* must lie . . . Hippocrates . . . describes the *Enarëes* precisely enough for us to recognise in them shamans similar to those of Eastern Asia." Archaeological evidence supports this theory. From the Paleolithic period onward, peoples living in the vicinity of present-day Russia and the Ukraine practiced both Shamanism and Goddess Reverence, worshipping a "cave mother and mistress of the animals." Goddess worship is especially evidenced by a "profusion of female figurines from the Paleolithic and Neolithic eras." In terms of Shamanism the use of cannabis (as mentioned above) and other hallucinogens, employed to attain an altered, shamanic, or ecstatic state has been documented at various sites. The ancient Maeotae, a people living in the vicinity of the Sea of Azov, are believed to have worshipped a goddess and to have developed a matrifocal and possibly matrilineal culture resembling the Tripolye or Cucuteni culture of Old Europe. A group of proto-Adygeians dwelling in the northern Caucasus are also thought to have revered the Goddess, embodied in the moon, and to have practiced Shamanism. The Sauromatians, Sindians, and Sarmatians are also believed to have worshipped the Goddess. The *enarees* may have practiced ritual castration or may have simply abstained from heterosexual sex; they do not seem, however, to have practiced celibacy. Hippocratic writings and other texts indicate that they engaged in same-sex eroticism. We find that the *enarees* not only "live like women" but also "play the woman" in all things, suggesting their assumption of the receptive role in same-sex erotic encounters. The term *malakia* is employed by Aristotle to describe the *enarees*. This term refers not only to "softness," as some scholars (especially gay Christian apologists) would have us believe, but also to effeminacy or gender variance. It is further related to *malakos*, which signifies not only a gender variant male but also one who takes the receptive role in anal eroticism. Herodotus, moreover, uses the term "androgynous" to refer to the *enarees*. It is important to understand that in Greece, as is pointed out in PLATO's *Symposium*, this term carried not only the meaning of one in whom masculine and feminine traits are combined but also that of a male who engages in anal eroticism, a "catamite." The *enarees* wore a fusion of feminine and sacerdotal attire. They emulated the speech patterns and employed the linguistic register of the women of the region, and performed tasks traditionally assigned to women. The *enarees* appear to have been accepted by their fellows. While in later times, Greek and Roman writers became convinced that the *enarees* were products of either divine punishment or illness, becoming so after offending a

god or riding horses too much, the indigenous persons of the region appear to have "respect[ed] and worship[ped] these creatures." They held that the *enarees* were essentially different from other males, their condition being a divine dispensation. They further held that *enarees* were repeatedly born into certain families, suggesting either a belief in reincarnation or a proto-genetic theory. While ancient documents provide little information concerning the specific functions assumed by *enarees*, it seems safe to assume, with M. Rostovstev, that the "Enareans fulfilled the same function[s] . . . in the worship of the Great Goddess . . . as the eunuchs elsewhere." From a plaque which forms the frontal part of a queen's tiara, dating from the fourth or third century BCE, we learn that *enarees* officiated in a ceremony of holy communion. This plaque, discovered in a burial chamber at Karagodeuashkh, in the vicinity of the Kuban River, portrays a chief priestess of the Goddess, probably the queen herself, surrounded by spiritual functionaries and a traditionally masculine worshipper. Two priestesses stand behind the chief priestess or queen. To her left stands an *enaree*, "beardless . . . clad in a woman's garment." He holds a vessel containing the communion beverage in his right hand. It appears that he has filled a rhyton with the beverage and is handing it to the chief priestess, who will administer it to the traditional male devotee. According to Rostovstev, this beverage was believed to confer power upon the individual drinking it. The beverage may have been made of grain, or perhaps a concoction of herbs or hallucinogenic plants. From Herodotus, we learn that *enarees* acted as diviners by taking "a piece of the inner bark of the lime-tree [i.e. the linden]" and cutting it "into three pieces," "twisting and untwisting" the pieces around their fingers in order to arrive at information concerning the future or the truth of hidden matters. While Herodotus does not specifically describe the contents of oracles delivered by *enarees*, it is likely that they were called upon to determine, among other things, what might have led to the ill health of a ruler. This usually involved discovering the identity of a rebellious subject who had placed a curse upon a ruler. The *enarees* also may have taken part in shamanic, funerary rituals described by Herodotus and confirmed by archaeological evidence. According to Herodotus, upon the death of a ruler, his or her body was, rather like the Egyptian corpse, cleaned out and filled with "aromatic substances, crushed galingale, parsley-seed, and anise," after which it was covered with wax. After the corpse had been exhibited to the subjects and had been buried, the *enarees* took a ritual vapor bath, a "sweat." Herodotus, noting that "hemp grows in Scythia . . . wild as well as under cultivation," describes the bath as follows: "on a framework of three sticks, meeting at the top, they stretch pieces of woolen cloth . . . and inside this little tent they put a dish with red-hot stones in it. Then they take some hemp seed, creep into the tent, and throw the seed on the hot stones. At once it begins to smoke . . . The Scythians . . . howl with pleasure." Archaeological evidence confirms Herodotus's description. R. E. Schultes and A. Hofman (1979) report that "archaeologists have excavated frozen Siberian tombs . . . and have found tripods and pelts, braziers and charcoal with remains of *Cannabis* leaves and fruit . . . The use of *Cannabis* by the Scythians is evidenced by various objects excavated from a chief's burial in mound no. 2 at Pazyryk in the western Altai. The pot contained *Cannabis* fruits, and the copper censer . . . was used to burn the sacred plant." The rug found at Pazyryk, described above, which has been uncritically accepted as depicting the Goddess or a priestess may in fact portray an *enaree* holding a cannabis plant in the presence of an approaching horseman. Ceremonies involving the use of cannabis may have included both those of a communal and of a funerary or psychopompic nature. If these rites did indeed include the participation of *enarees,* then *enarees* may have been among the first spiritual functionaries to employ cannabis in order to trigger an altered state of consciousness. This would in turn suggest that the association of the gender variant spiritual functionary with mind-altering substances is an ancient one indeed. A controversial theory states that Scythian religion and the institution of the *enaree* priest may have, somewhat paradoxically, influenced one of its own ancestors, Paleosiberian Shamanism and that in doing so it may have thereby aided in the creation or shaping of the institution of the gender variant TWO-SPIRIT shaman of Native American Indian tribes. Mythologist Joseph Campbell, a proponent of this theory, writes, "It is not unlikely that some of the practices of the Scythian *anandreies* [i.e. *enarees*] crossed the Bering Strait." Not so controversial is a theory which suggests that beliefs and practices of the *enarees* survived in the Russian pagano-Christian cults of the KHLYSTS (Flagellants) and Skoptsy (Castrators, Eunuchs), which emerged in the seventeenth century as part of a radical spiritual rebellion associated with the rise of the so-called Old Believers.

Endymion Beautiful young man of Greek mythology or religion loved by Selene, goddess of the moon, and by HYPNOS, god of sleep and dreams.

Engstrom, Donald (1950-) Gay multimedia artist, writer, and practitioner of Wicca treasured in the Wiccan and Gay- and Queer-Spiritual communities of the US for the enchanting beings inhabiting his visionary universe. Among these are: the Queer God, aka the Purple One, He Who Transforms, and Black Stonie; the Goddess Fee Fee, aka Miss Thing, She Who Knows His Own Ways; and the Vicious Bitch. Of the former, Engstrom writes, "The Purple One can be seen in full leather walking through empty streets or silent country lanes in the wee hours of the morning. . . He has [also] been known to show Himself as a

tornado, a song of desire, and endlessly changing dark jewel . . . [One of his primary purposes is] to cultivate and to nurture Places of Power for His Queer People." To invite the Queer God into our lives, Engstrom explains, we must "light a black or deep purple candle. . . Light a pink candle when you are ready to be one of his lovers." The Goddess Fee Fee, Engstrom relates, is the "Divine Drag Queen of Heaven . . . [Her-His] primary job is creating and perfecting the illusions and glamour that make the Earth such an exciting and beautiful planet . . . [She-he] is the archetypal interior designer . . . She is a powerful street fighter with a divine attitude." If we wish to invite the Goddess Fee Fee into out lives, we should "light a candle of a current high fashion color" and burn her favorite incense, "blue roses."

Eon (or **Aeon**) Androgynous, eternally youthful deity of the Valentininan Gnostics.

Epaminondas (d. 362 BCE) Military commander of the SACRED BAND OF THEBES. He and his lover Caphisodorus were buried together.

Ephesian Letters The MEGABYZOI, the transgendered male priest/esse/s of the Greco-Roman goddess ARTEMIS/DIANA, were best known for their ability to divine the future by way of the Ephesian Letters. The poet Anaxilas refers to their "carrying in sewn leather bags / The Ephesian letters of gold omen." Roughly equivalent to Teutonic runes, the letters, made of wood and painted gold, were carried in pouches that hung from the waist. The letters were six in number and named *aschion,* *chataschion, lix* (or *aix*), *tatras, damsmeneus,* and *asia;* they may have referred to darkness, light, earth (or water), the seasons of the year, the sun, and truth.

Ephesus City in Turkey, site of the great temple of the Greco-Roman goddess ARTEMIS/DIANA, who was associated with both transgenderism and lesbianism, and whose devotees included both transgendered males and females. Her temple was considered one of the seven wonders of the ancient world. Christians destroyed the temple in the third century CE. It was rebuilt, but was again burned by the Christians in 405.

Epimenides (b. c. 659 BCE) Poet and spiritual functionary of ancient Crete whose actual and legendary traits and experiences are difficult to disentangle, as is common with many individuals regarded as spiritual teachers. Undergoing a kind of shamanic journey or vision quest as a youth, he slept in a cave for a very long period of time (according to legend, between forty and fifty-seven years). As a result of this experience, he gained magical, divinatory, and healing powers, as well as the ability to travel astrally. In or around 596 BCE, Epimenides was asked to help Athens rid itself of a plague; he was successful in his efforts. He may have been transgendered, perhaps dressing in a mixture of masculine, feminine, and sacerdotal attire. Halliday (1913) compares him to the transgendered male prophet TIRESIAS.

Erasmus, Desiderius (c. 1466-1536)   Dutch scholar, priest and theologian. He is best known for his satire *In Praise of Folly* (1511). Erasmus appears to have loved a fellow monk at Saint Gregory's Augustinian monastery at Steyn, near Gouda.

Erauso, Doña Catalina de (1592-1650)   Nicknamed "the NUN" (*La Monja*), a woman warrior who evoked the image of the ancient AMAZON. Reared in a convent in Spain, Erauso ran away at fifteen and made her way to Central and South America, dressed as a soldier and taking the name of Francisco Loyola. She fought in numerous battles and was condemned to death on several occasions. Both men and women were attracted to her; she became engaged to at least two women but vanished before the weddings occurred. After almost being condemned to death a final time, she begged the church's pardon, entering a convent in Peru once she had explained herself and revealed her anatomy. After two contemplative years, she returned to Spain. Journeying to Rome, she delighted Pope Urban VIII, who issued her a papal license to dress in masculine attire. The last years of her life are shrouded in mystery.

Ereshkigal   Mesopotamian Queen of the Underworld who imprisoned her sister INANNA there for a time. Ereshkigal was invoked in male homoerotic love and binding spells originating in Alexandria, Egypt in the third century CE as "Kore Ereschigal," linking her to PERSEPHONE, the Greek goddess of the Underworld. In *The Queen of Swords* (1987), Judy Grahn portrays Ereshkigal as "shamanic, and ruthless, a counterpart of KALI [or the Gemanic] Hell . . . With her shem drum, long fingernails, and tangled hair she is one with the truly ancient shaman figures such as BAUBO."

Erigena, Johannes Scotus (c. 810-c. 877)   Christian theologian who believed that the division of a primordial transgendered being into male and female lay at the heart of humanity's suffering. Moreover, he believed that in experiencing resurrection, JESUS had become, like that being, "neither man nor woman." Finally, Erigena envisioned that men and women would once again become androgynous at the time of Christ's return to earth.

Erikepaios   Androgynous or transgendered deity of Orphism, depicted as "woman and begetter and mighty god," Erikepaios is sometimes associated with the Greek god DIONYSUS.

Erinyes (also **Eumenides**)   Three demigoddesses, Megaera, Tisiphone, and Alecto, who were said to have been born from the blood that dripped on Gaia, or Mother Earth, when Uranus castrated himself. Older than the Olympian deities, they are also called the Daughters of Night and Darkness and said to be the sisters of the Moirae, or FATES. They are associated with the Amazonian FURIES, GORGONS, and VALKYRIES and depicted as possessing serpentine hair and as carrying daggers or whips made of scorpions. While the Erinyes's primary responsibility appears to have been punishing wrongdoers, in Greco-Egyptian magical texts originating in Alexandria, they were also invoked in ancient lesbian love and binding spells as "the Erinyes, savage with their stinging." Those invoking the Erinyes offered them sacrifices of black sheep, honey, narcissus, and white doves.

Eros   In Greek religion and myth, simultaneously the eldest and youngest of the gods, masculine and effeminate, warlike and loving. With APHRODITE, he presides over love; with ATHENA, over education. According to Michael Grant and John Hazel, "In the classical period [Eros] was often regarded as the protector of homosexual love between men and youths. His statue was placed in gymnasia, and he was taken by the Sacred Band at Thebes as their patron." In fact, Eros formed part of a homoerotic trinity, the second and third members of which were HERACLES and HERMES. Each of the three gods played a role in homoerotic relationships: Hermes bestowed lovers with the gift of eloquence; Heracles, with strength; and Eros, with beauty and loyalty. The Lacedaemonians prayed and sacrificed to Eros before going into battle because they believed that only the love of the men for each other could ultimately bring them military success. Athenians also believed Eros to be the god of liberty, as it was often the love of men for one another that caused them to bond together to struggle against tyranny; like the lovers Harmodius and ARISTOGITON, who fought against the tyrant Hipparchus and who became, for Athenians, champions of freedom and democracy. It is important to point out that the heterosexual image of Eros as Cupid was popularized by poets and painters but rarely worshipped, while the homoerotic Eros was worshipped on the battlefield by warrior-lovers and in the gymnasia by athletes. Eros was a chief deity of the Orphic pantheon. His sacred attributes are the DOLPHIN, FLUTE, LYRE, ROOSTER, ROSE, and torch. In the court of the homoerotically inclined French king HENRI III, his favorites, or minions, were sometimes compared to Eros, most often in his manifestation as "Amour." A poem by Ronsard (1524-1585) includes the lines, "Minion, you are young and beautiful, / an Adonis, an Amour in a painting." The San Francisco gay BEAT poet Jack Spicer (1925-1965) writes in "Five Words for Joe Dunn on His 22nd

Birthday": "The third word is eros / . . . / Whomever you touch will love you, / Will feel the cling of His touch upon you / Like sunlight scattered over an ancient mirror."

Erotes Manifestations of the Greek god EROS, usually three in number, which take on a life of their own. Their names are Eros, HIMERUS, and POTHOS. They are depicted as handsome, nude, winged men bearing objects which served as courting gifts in ancient Greece. Jane HARRISON was among the first classical historians in contemporary times to point out their connection to the "love, not untouched by passion, of man for man," in her *Prolegomena to the Study of Greek Religion* (1902, 1908). The Erotes are bearers of erotic energy in specific and of the élan vital, or life force, in general. The Erotes, like Eros, are included in the retinue of the goddess APHRODITE.

Eroticism and Lovemaking Same-sex and transgendered eroticism have been associated with the realm of the sacred since antiquity in many cultures. In this article, we must confine ourselves to giving a few brief examples. It should also be noted that most data available on the relationship of same-sex eroticism to the spiritual concerns homoerotic rather than lesbian intercourse. While we must be careful in not equating twentieth-century primal cultures with prehistoric cultures, an example taken from a culture of New Guinea may shed some light on the origins of the conjunction of male homoeroticism and the sacred. The belief that consuming semen may impart strength is held by the Sambian people of New Guinea, who also believe that the first human being was created by way of fellatio. Gilbert H. Herdt, in describing a Sambian initiation ceremony, writes in *Guardians of the Flutes*, "Now we come to the most important early ingestive rite of all: fellation . . . Homosexual practices are introduced through the most secret of all rites, the 'penis and flute' ceremony. For the first time novices are shown the flutes. Indeed, it is the bamboo flute that is used to illuminate the mechanics of fellatio . . . Along with the secrets of the flutes, they are told of the urgent requirement to consume semen. The Sambia believe that in order for males to grow strong, they must practice fellation frequently." While the Sambia believe that a parallel ingestion of menstrual blood by women is unnecessary, in that women are thought to carry an immeasurable quantity of blood, contemporary lesbian writers including Pam Kesey suggest that in some primal and ancient spiritual traditions, menstrual blood may indeed have been consumed, by women and perhaps also by men. Kesey speculates that the mythos of the VAMPIRE may in part be traceable to such rites. In ancient Egypt, the god of writing, THOTH, presided over the anus and anal intercourse. This may have been due in part to his being compared to the ibis, believed to clean its own anus with its

long beak, and perhaps also due in part to Thoth's role in a homoerotic episode involving the gods SET and Horus, mentioned elsewhere in this text. Other deities associated with anal intercourse were Set and his Amazonian spouse ANAT, as well as ATUM, who secured power over Shu, a male being he had created, by penetrating him anally. In Egypt, the deities most frequently associated with fellatio were Set and MIN. As J. G. Griffiths explains (1960), "Seth [i.e. Set], like Min, was obviously imagined as increasing his renowned sexual strength by partaking of it [semen]." Egyptians often used the symbolism of eating LETTUCES to describe fellatio, as the sap of lettuce was likened to semen; hence, the use of lettuces in rituals invoking Set and Min. KHEPERA, the scarab-god, was also linked to fellatio; according to some, he renewed himself by fellating himself. Benjamin Walker notes that "Semen was widely believed to be the materialization of a kind of fire, and was sometimes described as a vital fire-fluid . . . At the coronation of the pharaohs of ancient Egypt, a mystical fluid called *sa*, the invisible semen of the god Ra, magically infiltrated the veins of the pharaoh during the ceremony, filling him with a flame-like quality that gave him majesty, dignity and divine power." The beliefs and allied ritual practices held and carried out by the Egyptians echoes, in a sense, the belief and practice of the Sambians. They are also linked to certain beliefs and rites of the ancient Greeks and Gnostics. These suggest that anal intercourse either may grant the active partner power over the receptive partner, or else may empower the receptive partner. The Greeks believed that ARETÉ, an energy force carrying physical strength and wisdom, could be transferred to a receptive partner via anal intercourse, thus empowering the receptive partner. Among the Greeks, the deity most often associated with anal eroticism was DIONYSUS, one of whose attributes was a dildo of fig wood, another being a dildo of red leather. Among the Gnostics, the Naassenes believed that the wise serpent NAAS had imparted *gnosis*, or mystical wisdom, to the Biblical ADAM and Eve by penetrating both of them sexually, Adam anally. Had he not done so, they would have remained the robot-like servants of a tyrannical God. The Naassenes also attributed a magical significance to fellatio. They worshipped the SERPENT as the symbol of divine wisdom, and in particular, they worshipped it as the UROBORUS, viewing fellatio as "a strict enactment of the image of the snake biting its tail." The Naassenes thus believed that wisdom could be transmitted by way of both anal intercourse and fellatio. Most of what we know concerning links made by the Chinese between eroticism and the sacred derives from texts on Taoist alchemy. While "eating TOFU" referred to heterosexual lovemaking, "grinding tofu" referred to lesbian lovemaking. Women engaging in Taoist-alchemical-inspired lesbian lovemaking were believed to employ dildoes made of silk filled with dried tofu. In the seventeenth century CE, the people of Huichou referred to male same-sex coupling as "treading on tofu." Also in China, where the mirror is traditionally a feminine and a lunar symbol and an attribute of female royalty, employed by shamans and Taoist priests and priestesses in divinatory rites, lesbian lovemaking was referred to as "*mojingzi* ," as rubbing or grinding MIRRORS together. In some traditions of Hindu TANTRA, male-male anal intercourse is "believed to energize the artistic, poetic, and mystical faculties." In Hinduism, the anus and anal intercourse are especially associated with the elephant-headed deity GANESHA, in part because he controls the first *chakra*, or sacred center of energy of the subtle body, located at the base of the spine. According to Alain DANIÉLOU, cultic anal eroticism has been practiced by male devotees of Ganesha into the twentieth century. According to the *Kama Sutra*, "People of the third sex [*tritiya prakriti*] are of two kinds, according to whether their appearance is masculine or feminine . . . Buccal coition as practiced by both kinds is a part of their nature." Fellatio is called *auparishtaka*, "mouth congress." In Hinduism, the god of fellatio is AGNI, who swallows the semen of SHIVA. A second god, SOMA, is associated with fellatio; while Agni is called the "eater of seed," Soma is often thought of as the "seed" itself, hence, the man who is being fellated. It is believed that semen may have been part of the beverage "soma" consumed by priests during Vedic rituals. A third deity associated with fellatio is ARDHANARISHVARA, the androgynous child of Shiva and PARVATI, in part due to the god's transgenderism and in part due to the fact that he (-she) controls the throat *chakra*. Male practitioners of Tantra, including devotees of Shiva, participated in an elaborate form of ritual fellatio. This began with the worshippers bathing the penis of the other male, then massaging the penis, invoking the spirit of the deity into the penis, and praising the beauty and power of the penis. This act of worship climaxed with fellating the penis until orgasm and culminated with the "putting to bed" of the penis and the dismissal of the god. While some scholars suggest that homoeroticism was not widely practiced in ancient India, it is clear that oral intercourse was practiced enough to merit its own vocabulary of techniques. There were at least eight different techniques of fellatio. The most poetic of these expressions was *amrachushitaka*, "sucking the mango," which meant to place the other male's penis halfway into the mouth, then to press on the base while sucking the head. These techniques were especially practiced by the HIJRAS of the goddess BAHUCHARAMATA. In terms of lesbian lovemaking in the Tantric tradition, we learn from the *Kama Sutra* that women of the harem frequently engaged in lesbian lovemaking, often with some of the women dressed in male attire and using dildoes to penetrate the others. According to Daniélou, women who practiced lesbianism were referred to as *svairini*. They are said to have fashioned dildoes from such things as carrots,

turnips, bananas, sweet potatoes, and cucumbers. The practice of employing dildoes in lesbian lovemaking became, like fellatio among males, so commonplace that a vocabulary of lesbian erotic techniques emerged, including *chatakavilasa*, the "bird's amusement," alternately semi-penetrating and deeply penetrating the vagina, *manthana*, "churning" the dildo in a circling manner, *varahaghata*, and the "wild boar's thrust," striking the dildo from side to side. Female devotees of KRISHNA, emulating the GOPIS, his divine female cowherds, are believed to have engaged in lesbian eroticism, making use of dildoes representing Krishna's phallus. In terms of north Asian shamanic and Native American Indian cultures, the QA'CIKICHECA, the TWO-SPIRIT female shamans of the Aleuts of northeastern Siberia, often wore artificial phalli during lovemaking with female companions, while the HWAME, the two-spirit female shamans of the Mohave of North America, preferred rubbing genitals together, *hithpan kudhape*, and manipulation of the genitalia with the fingers. ALYHA, two-spirit males among the Mohave who served shamanic and other functions, engaged in various forms of lovemaking including anal intercourse. Their male companions were not supposed to touch their erect penises. Only during anal intercourse was this permitted. It was customary and acceptable for *alyha* to ejaculate while being penetrated. Anal intercourse was referred to as *hivey añienm*. With the rise of the gay and lesbian movements, texts exploring the interrelationship of same-sex eroticism and the spiritual in contemporary lovemaking have begun to be published. These include Mitch WALKER's *Men Loving Men: A Gay Sex Guide & Consciousness Book* (1977), PURUSHA's *The Divine Androgyne* (1981), Celeste West's *A Lesbian Love Advisor: The Sweet and Savory Arts of Lesbian Courtship* (1989), and Katon Shual's *Sexual Magick* (1989). The last of these, while not strictly focusing on same-sex eroticism, contains a wealth of esoteric information. Joseph KRAMER's work in the Body Electric School of Massage Therapy and more recently in EroSpirit Institute, both based in northern California, has also promoted the erotico-spiritual expression of same-sex desire. In recent years, "safer sex" practices have been emphasized. Also in recent years, self-identified "sex radicals" and others, including Raelyn GALLINA, Brian MURPHY, Jim and Drew WARD, and persons mentioned in our article on SADOMASOCHISM, have focused their erotico-spiritual practices on what is commonly referred to as "fantasy sex," with body modifications such as piercings and TATTOOS being among its expressions. Unquestionably, however, what is most noticeable in terms of the queer-identified community is the explosion of artistic expression centering upon lesbian and bisexual female erotic spirituality. The emergence of this expression owes much to the African-American lesbian poet and essayist Audre LORDE, who wrote in "Uses of the Erotic" (1984): "The very word erotic comes from the Greek eros, the personification of love in all its aspects – born of Chaos, and personifying creative power and harmony. When I speak of the erotic, then, I speak of it as an assertion of the lifeforce of women; of that creative energy empowered, the knowledge and use of which we are now reclaiming in our language, our history, our dancing, our loving, our work, our lives." While Lorde may not have approved of all that followed – including journals such as *On Our Backs*, which proudly displayed erotic, or what others would deem pornographic, photographs of lesbian nudes, as well as performances by such musical groups as Girls in the Nose, and Camille PAGLIA's defense of stripping – she must be acknowledged for heralding the dismantling of a monolithic puritanism firmly entrenched in the feminist and lesbian-feminist movements of the late 1970s. A decade and a year following Lorde's pivotal essay, Diane MARIECHILD wrote in *Lesbian Sacred Sexuality* (1995): "Erotic love between women can be a celebration and an initiation into the female creative spirit, the feminine mysteries . . . Lesbians hold the form of woman power at its most profound. Many lesbians seek to identify ourselves from an inner source of woman wisdom. With each act of loving we can embrace this deep inner space . . . Lesbian love is sacred when it is visionary, interconnected, and transformational." Exemplary of the poetic expression of lesbian sacred sexuality is Native American Indian poet CHRYSTOS's "Double Phoenix" (1988), in which she describes mutual cunnilingus as "sailing in a boat of brambles our lips ripe / Our purple tongues signal the full moon." In *Shakti Woman* (1991), the lesbian-identified bisexual writer and healer Vicki NOBLE, in describing her experience of embodying the energy of a goddess while in the act of lovemaking, writes: "When I 'am' the serpent woman, or Aphrodite, or Kali with a male partner, it is unforgettable and wondrous, and when I have 'become' Dionysus with a female partner, it has been awesome." Echoing this kind of transgendered desire is Myrna Elana's poem "Define Community: This is a test," in which she considers what might happen "If my lover / had a cloven hoof / and a cunt and a / penis."

Erzulie (or **Ezili**) *Lwa* (deity or spirit) of love and sensuality in the Vodou pantheon. She is the patron of all those who seek to achieve aesthetic beauty, including artists, musicians (primarily of stringed instruments), actors, models, fashion designers, interior decorators, and perfumers. In a number of manifestations, Erzulie is an extremely heterosexual coquette. Even in these aspects, however, she may choose to embody a heterosexual male devotee. He may temporarily behave in a manner evoking both transgenderism and homoeroticism as he approaches other men to whom Erzulie is erotically attracted. When Erzulie embodies a gay, bisexual, and/or transgendered male, her influence is often of a more permanent character.

According to H. Fichte (1975) Erzulie is the "patron of gay men." In other manifestations, as with Erzulie Taureau ("the Bull"), the *lwa* is perceived as gynandrous or Amazonian. In these aspects, she may express both anti-male sentiments and lesbian desire. These sentiments are often expressed by a female devotee possessed by Erzulie. Due to the miraculous fluidity of the phenomenon of possession, however, these anti-male and pro-lesbian sentiments may also be expressed by a male devotee embodied by Erzulie Taureau. When not admiring herself, dancing, or seducing others, Erzulie likes to swim in pools and lakes. Her sacred attributes include the MIRROR, the heart (depicted in her *vévé*, or sacred sign), perfumes, bay laurel, delicate and exotic foods, and the colors pink and pastel blue. Syncretized with the Virgin Mary of Christianity, in her manifestation of Our Lady of the Sorrows, Erzulie is fêted on September 15. Her special days are Tuesday and Thursday.

Eugenia of Alexandria, Saint (d. c. 257 CE) Noblewoman, known for her great intellect, who, intrigued by Christianity, decided to adopt a male identity and retire to an abbey, where she/he eventually became an abbot. Another noblewoman of Alexandria, on encountering Eugenia, fell in love with her/him. When the abbot spurned the noblewoman's advances, wishing to remain celibate and/or closeted, the woman accused Eugenia of taking advantage of her. Eugenia, not wishing to be thought of as an abuser of women, revealed her/himself to be anatomically female. Not long after, the noblewoman perished in a fire. Eugenia died a martyr, was canonized as a Catholic saint, and is fêted on December 25.

Eunuchs, Chinese In ancient China, eunuchs were considered transgendered, were often lovers of other males, and occasionally served as spiritual functionaries. While a eunuch is typically described as a male whose penis and testicles have been removed, Chinese texts indicate that many eunuchs were deprived only of their testicles. Still others retained both penis and testicles and merely pretended to be eunuchs. Young men usually became eunuchs for one of several reasons: because they had been taken captive; because they had committed a crime punishable by castration; because they had been born to poor parents who had sold them to wealthy individuals; or because they desired to become eunuchs. Poverty, however, appears to have produced the greatest number and, as Ulrich Jugel explains, this allowed many Chinese of low economic status to achieve both wealth and power. In 135 CE, eunuchs were first allowed to adopt children, this not only permitting them to parent but also increasing their power substantially. The Chinese eunuch parent may be one of the earliest examples in history of the gender variant and (often) homoerotically inclined father. Although later epochs witnessed anti-eunuch hostility, it is evident that a great number of eunuchs were still living in China at the end of the nineteenth century. Homoerotic relationships involving eunuchs often began in adolescence, when a eunuch was chosen to be the companion of a royal or noble youth. Eunuchs were chosen "according to criteria of beauty and willingness." Such relationships often lasted into and throughout adulthood, with the eunuchs enjoying "honors, wealth, favors, and political power." The preferred form of sexual intercourse in these relationships was anal intercourse, with the eunuchs taking the receptive role. Many non-eunuch males apparently preferred eunuch to either female or non-eunuch male lovers; some, like the ruler Yuan-ti, "preferred eunuchs exclusively." Eunuchs have traditionally been associated with sacred experience. Indeed, it was believed that the eunuch carried magical power with him wherever he went, in the form of an urn in which his genitalia were preserved. These urns were often exhibited in ritual manner on the occasion of the eunuch's attainment of greater political or spiritual power or wealth. When a eunuch died, the urn was buried alongside him. A number of myths link eunuchs with the supernatural. In one such myth, a man named Jen Ku is penetrated anally by a shaman wearing a feathered costume. As a result, Jen Ku becomes pregnant. When the time comes for him to give birth, the shaman reappears. He slices off Jen Ku's penis and proceeds to deliver the "child" – a serpent. In ancient Chinese sacred traditions, the serpent is a YIN symbol. In this particular context, it is linked to transgendered homoeroticism. Jen Ku, now a eunuch and a shaman himself, goes to live at the palace, where he becomes intimate companion to the emperor. During the Han Dynasty, Shamanism, which had experienced a decline with the emergence of Confucianism, enjoyed a vogue among those who felt Confucianism to be too constricting when practiced by itself. This led to the development of a syncretic spiritual tradition blending elements of Confucianism with Shamanism and Taoism. Women and transgendered males – in the form of eunuchs – once more became, for a time, the chief spiritual functionaries. As shamans, eunuchs took part in various significant rituals. Among these were sacrifices to the deities, ceremonies installing new rulers, hunting rites, funerals, and seasonal celebrations. At funerals, eunuchs acted as ritual musicians, playing flutes and drums to aid in transporting the soul from this life to the next. At the winter solstice, eunuch shamans, wearing black robes and red headdresses, exorcised demons and invoked the spirits of the twelve beneficent animals of Chinese ASTROLOGY. Eunuchs were also believed to be highly skilled in the magical, divinatory, and healing arts. They divined by observing the movements of the four winds and by interpreting the oracles of the I CHING and were said to be expert acupuncturists.

Euphorion The Greek god ZEUS fell in love with this winged son of ACHILLES and HELEN but slew him with a thunderbolt when Euphorion rejected him.

Euphrosyne, Saint (dates uncertain) Young Alexandrian woman of late antiquity or early Middle Ages, who, refusing a traditional feminine role, assumed a masculine identity, becoming a Christian monk. Canonized as a Catholic saint, Euphrosyne is fêted on either January 1 or February 2.

Eurotas River This river in Laconia in southern Greece, on the banks of which stood the ancient city of Sparta, was for the ancients symbolic of anal intercourse because it appears to flow between two thighs before reaching the sea.

Euryalus and Nisus Legendary comrade-lovers in Virgil's *Aeneid* (c. 30 BCE). Accompanying Aeneas to Italy, the lovers perished in an attack on the Rutulians. In a poem included in the sixth century CE *Latin Anthology*, it is written of Euryalus and Nisus, "The greatest part of life is the bond of friendship."

Evans, Arthur (1942-) US writer, gay activist, philosopher, classicist, and translator. An anti-war activist during the 1960s, Evans, while a doctoral candidate at Columbia University in New York, became in the early 1970s an activist in the Gay Liberation Front and the Gay Activists Alliance. He continued to struggle for gay rights in San Francisco, where he became known as the "Red Queen." In 1975 he formed the Faery Circle, one of the first Gay- or Queer-Spiritual groups. The following year, he gave a series of lectures titled "Faeries," focusing on the spiritual origins of the contemporary gay counterculture. These lectures, together with earlier journalistic articles, developed into *Witchcraft and the Gay Counterculture* (1978), now considered a cult classic. Shortly thereafter, he began translating Euripide's *Bakkhai*, a tragedy concerning the worship of DIONYSUS, which was performed in 1984. This translation, along with his commentary on the historical and spiritual significance of the play, was published in 1988 as *The God of Ecstasy: Sex Roles and the Madness of Dionysus*. Since that time, beyond devoting time to AIDS activism, Evans has been at work on a three-volume opus of gay-centered philosophy, the first volume titled *Critique of Patriarchal Reason*.

Evola, Giuilio (or **Julius Evola**, 1898-1974) Italian futurist who ultimately became a philosopher, much of his work focusing on the interrelationship of sexuality and the sacred. Despite the fact that Evola is known to have been a racist who profoundly influenced Italian fascism, his *Eros and the Mysteries of Love: The Metaphysics of Sex* remains a popular book among New Age readers. In *Eros*, Evola, who fails to acknowledge Eros as a patron of

homoeroticism, describes same-sex eroticism as a
"displaced eros." He insists that homosexuality "wholly
lack[s]" any "profound dimension" or "meaning higher"
than lust because it is devoid of the "necessary ontological
and metaphysical premises" effecting a link between sex
and the sacred. In Evola's view, only monogamous
heterosexual relationships can produce this link.

F

Faggot In *Witchcraft and the Gay Counterculture* (1978), Arthur EVANS posits a link between homoeroticism, Witchcraft, and faggots (bundles of sticks employed in cooking and in the burning of heretics). While Queer and other academics have challenged (often in an extremely vicious manner) Evans's claim, it contains, as Carlo Ginzburg might say, a "kernel of truth." One must, however, be willing to search beyond the English language to discover possible connections. By the sixteenth century, the French word *fagot* ("faggot") had come to enjoy multivalent significance. It had come to signify not only a bundle of sticks but also a symbol of the same, which, as Evans and others point out, heretics were required to wear. Moreover, to *fagoter* someone was to "fuck" them. Further, *fagot* was used interchangeably with *bourre* (related to *bourée, bourelé, bourrer*, and *bourreur*) which referred not only to a bundle of sticks but also to an individual who stuffs something or tortures or fucks someone. What is more, *bourre* referred to the "backe-part, of a man." There is also this proverb: "*Fagot cherche bourée*, Like will to like." Further still, the *bourée* was a lively round or spiral dance which, as evidenced by Medieval illuminations, clearly had pre-Christian roots in ecstatic dance, and was frequently condemned by Renaissance Christians. While this word chain proves nothing, it may indicate an association of the bundle of sticks, the heretic, one who sexually penetrates, the buttocks, attraction to likeness, and pre-Christian music and dance. In a Jewish legend of "Rabbi Akiba and the Wandering Dead Man," a dead man and his friend eternally gather "faggots to burn themselves as a punishment for engaging in sodomy." A connection, if only indirect or subliminal, can further be made between *fagot*, "faggot," and *fee*, "FAIRY." The term "faggot" is derived from *fagus*, the beech tree, ruled in antiquity by Fagus. By the Middle Ages, Fagus had diminished into a tree fairy, with the beech becoming known as that tree around which the fairies danced.

Fairy In the 1970s, various gay male individuals involved in the gay rights movement and in alternative spiritual movements, primarily Witchcraft (or Wicca), began (re-) claiming the term "fairy" – most often as "faerie" – as a positive term to describe radical gay identity inclusive of spirituality, as opposed to a term of abuse employed by homophobic persons. This (re-) claiming of "fairy," or "faerie," was promoted in the main by Arthur EVANS, who founded a fairy circle in San Francisco, and by Harry HAY, John Burnside, and others, who founded the Radical Faeries. While, as with "faggot," it is difficult to trace the development of this term's queer connotation(s), there does exist a tradition of males embodying the personae of fairies in European rites and festivals. In Germany, the fairy-goddess Holda, depicted as a beautiful woman wearing white who caused it to snow when she shook the feathers out of her mattress, was still being revered in the Middle Ages and the Renaissance. Linking backward to FREYJA and forward to Hans Christian Andersen's SNOW QUEEN, she would, at the winter solstice, fly over the earth in a wagon, stopping at the windows of her devotees to give them presents. At this time, alongside women, men dressed in feminine attire, carrying brooms, would, in Holda's name, travel from house to house, blessing families and distributing gifts. In Italy, a woman or transvestite male customarily took the role of La Befana, a kindly CRONE who, like Holda, blessed families and bestowed them with presents during the winter solstice. In England, male peasants dressed as fairies would enter a house and begin chanting "Take one and give back a hundred" and dancing wildly before stealing everything they wanted, promising to "return what they had stolen a hundredfold." Males dressed as fairies also performed at wedding ceremonies, as did the *Feien* in Prussian and Bavarian marriages. A more profound connection of fairies and transgenderism, as well as homoeroticism, is found among the CALUSARI of Eastern Europe.

The Falling Woman (1992) In this novel by Australian writer Susan Hawthorne, aboriginal myth plays an important role in the central character Stella's coming to terms with her lesbianism.

Fanatici Spiritual functionaries of the Roman goddess MÀ. Transgendered, including homoerotically inclined, male *fanatici* wore heavy black robes with necklaces and tiaras resembling flower garlands. They dyed their hair blonde and wore it in braids, or wore blonde wigs. In processions, they carried double axes and branches of leaves. Some appear to have been eunuchs. The rites of Mâ were wild and rather bloody. The *fanatici* would let their hair down and begin to dance faster and faster in a circle until they attained an altered state of consciousness. In this state, they would wound themselves with the axes, splattering the statue of the Goddess, which stood in the center of their circle, with blood. They would then begin to utter the words of the Goddess. There appears to be a connection between the opening of the flesh and releasing of blood and the ability to fully embody the deity; in numerous cultures, cutting and flagellation of the body are linked to possession and trance.

Faro Among the Bambara of West Africa, an androgynous or transgendered deity who gives birth to twins who in turn become parents to the human race. Faro, whose sacred color is white, also bestows mortals with language and the knowledge of fishing and farming.

Fates (also **Moirae**) Triune Goddess configuration of Greek and later British myth and pre-Christian religion, generally depicted as three sisters – Clotho (birth, the maiden, the new and waxing MOON), Atropos (maturity, the mother, the full moon), and Lachesis (death, the CRONE, the waning and dark moon) – weaving the destinies of mortals. The Fates came to be known in England as the Weird (Wyrd) Sisters. As in Shakespeare's *Macbeth*, they are frequently associated with Witchcraft. In *Gossips, Gorgons and Crones* (1993), Jane Caputi reclaims the Fates as images of the wisdom and power of women. Linking them specifically to transgenderism, she contends that the Fates "invite us to imagine a transmuted world . . . in which the sexes have multiplied beyond currently imaginable limits."

Féithlinn Amazonian fairy of Celtic belief who predicted the war between CU CHULAINN and MAEVE (Medb). Féithlinn lived west Ireland at *Cruachen*, or "the Gateway to Hell." She was known to appear dressed in a "golden crown with seven burnt-gold braids hanging down her shoulders." Dressed in this manner she revealed to Queen Maeve her imminent death.

Fellini, Federico (1920-1993) Italian filmmaker whose *Satyricon* (1970), based on the *Satyricon* (c. 64 CE) of Petronius Arbiter, explores the interrelationship of bi- or pansexuality, transgenderism, and Roman paganism, including a homoerotic or transgender wedding rite. Fellini, commenting on the film, said, "To be homosexual was just part of sex. All our information comes to us from the Catholic Church. The Latin texts were changed by the monks or censored, burned, condemned, or distorted . . . I try to forget the . . . Christian world, and try to love that pre-Christian world."

Ferro, Robert (1941-1988) Gay writer whose works, foremost among them the novels *The Family of Max Desir* (1983), *The Blue Star* (1985), and *Second Son* (1988), focus on gay male desire, family relationships, Italian-American identity, and death. His works include numerous episodes and elements partaking of the mythical, the spiritual, and the fantastic, including the founding of an underground Masonic Temple in New York, Vodou rites, and a "spaceship bound for the planet Splendora."

Fey Shamanism Group founded by gay Pagans John Dabell (b. 1966) and Bill Karpen (b. 1967) of the West Coast of the US. Dabell, an herbalist with a particular interest in entheogenic plants (especially of the nightshade family) and also the founder of the metaphysical healing center Earth and Spirit, and Karpen, a practitioner of Teutonic religion and of SEIDR magic, editor of the *Lavender Pagan Newsletter* (1990-1993), established Fey Shamanism to instruct gay men in working with ecstatic and altered states of consciousness, with particular emphasis placed upon trance journeying, dreamwork, spiritual healing, and developing relationships with totemic plants and animals.

Fichte, Hubert (1935-1986) Bisexual German writer born of a Protestant mother and a Jewish father. Fichte was inspired not only by Greek legendary figures such as the lovers ACHILLES and PATROCLUS, as evidenced in *Detlev's Imitations* (1971) but also – and it would seem much more profoundly so – by the African-diasporic religions of Candomblé and Vodou. His postmodern autobiographies/prose-poems *Xango* [SHANGO] (1976) and *Lazarus und die Waschmachine* (1985) and his essay "The Razor Blade and the Hermaphrodite" (1975) illuminate his reverence for these African-based faiths.

Ficino, Marsilio (1433-1499) Italian Renaissance philosopher and priest of the Catholic Church who, like other Neoplatonists, believed in: an archetypal universe of ideal forms reflected in various ways (often poorly) on the earth; the immortality of the soul, often embracing the concept of reincarnation; the desire of the physical or material, in spite of obstacles, to move toward the spiritual, the "true" and the "beautiful;" union with the Divine as enlightening and as possible through the merging of lover and beloved. This last notion (and there were many more) of experiencing Divinity through uniting with the beloved reflected not only the influence of the ancient Greeks but also of the Islamic mystics and Sufis upon Neoplatonism. These ideas were given expression primarily at the Florentine Academy. The Neoplatonists – like PLATO himself – did not accept the twentieth-century connotation of "Platonic love" as absolutely distinct from sensuous or erotic love. Rather, they recalled the distinction made in the *Symposium*: that while "earthly" love refers most often to heterosexual love that is directed toward the birthing and rearing of children, "heavenly" love refers most often to same-sex love that is directed toward the birthing and nurturing of ideas. While "heavenly" love should not focus on lust, it does not exclude eroticism. Rather, like alchemy, it seeks to transform the experience of eroticism from one that is lust-driven and genital-centered into one that is love-driven and celebrates the entire body as a manifestation of the Divine. Like many others of the pre-modern west, Ficino often employed the term "friendship" as both a code word and a term of emphasis for same-sex love. "Friendship," he wrote, "derives its power and name from love . . . it is nothing but mutual love strengthened by a stable . . . relationship . . . friendship always has the same quality as love." For Ficino, part of the process by which same-sex attraction became heightened into an experience of divine union was by way of a kind of circuit of loving energy. As the lover gazed into the beloved's eyes, energy traveled from the heart into the eyes and then traveled into the beloved's eyes and into his or her heart. This was mingled with the beloved's own energy, which traveled from the heart into his or her eyes and then into those of the lover, and so on. In this way, lover and beloved merge energies. Their further focus on the Divine creates from their passion a trinity or triad. Ficino further believed that once such a relationship had been established, it could be extended to embrace a community of loving companions. P. O. Kristeller (1964) explains that for Ficino, "mutual love . . . constitutes a real and concrete communion between several persons." This notion is indicated by a letter he wrote to Amerigo Corsini: "A principle of this kind, Amerigo, a long time ago united Giovanni Cavalcanti and Marsilio Ficino in divine love; happily the same principle now joins a third to us: Amerigo. And what shall I say about Bernardo Bembo, the Venetian? Not only has this principle united him with us, but so has divine providence." It was in this spirit that the Florentine Academy was founded. From fragmentary evidence, it seems that the members (most if not all were males) formed couples which at some point became triads with the addition of another member, and then perhaps quarters, extending to form a chain of loving companions. Ficino, beyond seeing himself as bonded to Cavalcanti, Corsini, and Bembo, appears to have also seen himself as forming a trinity with Filippo Valori and Filippo Carducci as well as one with Lotterio Neroni and Giovanni Nesi. Other members included Lorenzo de' Medici, Girolano Dona, Antonio Pelotti, Giovanni Altoviti, Francesco Bandini, Gionvanni Pico della Mirandola, Panezio Pandozzi, Carlo Marsuppini, Alamano Donati, and POLIZIANO. It is conceivable that MICHELANGELO Buonarroti also belonged. The Academy not only held classes but also great banquets such as that given on November 7 to honor their spiritual ancestor Plato on the (alleged) anniversary of his death.

Fidus (pseudonym of **Hugo Höppener**, 1868-1948) German painter and illustrator whose work brought together a celebration of nudism, especially of the nude male body, pantheism, and Buddhism. Hans Bethge (1876-1946), who translated the Chinese lyrics which Gustave Mahler used in *Das Lied von der Erde*, wrote of Fidus in the early homosexual journal *Der Eigene* in 1903: "he is a worshipper of nature. He sees the spiritual in all material things alike . . . the naked, juvenile body always

attracts him the most . . . they are true pictures of . . . nirvana . . . they awaken in us Buddhistic ideas . . . This is Fidus – a religious man without a religious confession."

Fife, Connie (1961-)   Native American Cree woman-loving writer whose spiritual vision profoundly influences her work. This is especially evident in poems such as "Stains," from *Beneath the Naked Sun* (1992) in which she weaves together the figures of divine female beings, female ancestors, and TWO-SPIRIT (gender variant, often same-sex inclined) beings and persons. Describing "a journey across twinned mountain," Fife writes: "twinned heart / reminders of all life found in this / plush forest of self / woman within man / man inside woman / twinned spirit."

Fig   The fig tree and its fruit bear homoerotic significance in ancient Greek religion, myth, and folklore. The fig tree is especially sacred to the god DIONYSUS. It was a phallus of fig wood that Dionysus used to penetrate himself anally. Perhaps due in part to this myth, many phallic HERMS were carved from fig wood. Of the varieties of figs, the *chian* fig, found on the island of Khios, whose male inhabitants were said to delight in anal intercourse, came to be a signifier of homoeroticism.

Filidh   Little is known of the Druid priesthood, even less of pre-Druidic spiritual functionaries. Still, it appears that the Celts may have embraced a spiritual functionary who came in Ireland to be called the *filidh*. The *filidh* was at once a poet, a storyteller, a composer, a singer, an historian, and a practitioner of the divinatory arts. In the earliest times, the *filidh* performed various shamanic-like rituals. One such rite included sacrificing a bull, eating its uncooked flesh, drinking its blood, and sleeping in its hide. Another involved sleeping on a grave. Both of these rites were thought to inspire prophetic dreams. The *filidh* also may have dressed in a cloak of bird feathers during certain rites. While it is not clear whether or not the *filidh* dressed in feminine attire, it does seem that, along with the priestess and the queen, he was considered a representative of the Goddess. In this association, he and the king or ruler might enter into a formal relationship, perhaps even a kind of *hieros gamos*, in which the king or ruler would become the representative of the male consort of the Goddess. Although it is not clear whether their relationship was openly erotic or expressed in sublimated form, it is evident that a kind of "romantic attachment" existed "between the ruler and the poet [i.e. the *filidh*], in which the poet play[ed] the role of the woman," or rather, the transgendered representative of the Goddess.

Filiger, Charles (1863-1928)   Homoerotically inclined French painter and Rosicrucian mystic. Filiger's works, frequently depicting saints and resembling Orthodox Christian icons or stained glass windows, celebrate the feminine, androgynous or transgendered, and homoerotic dimensions of the Divine. Exemplary of his work is *Saint Jean-Baptiste* (St John the Baptist), which depicts an adolescent John, crowned by a halo and nude except for a blue scarf swirling about his loins, preparing to baptize another adolescent male.

Fini, Leonor (1908-)   French painter born in Argentina whose works, which might be described as surrealistic or as magical-realistic, evoke a powerful, woman-identified spirituality embracing lesbian and bisexual desire and transgenderism. Typical of Fini's works are *La Leçon de botanique*, *Lointaine Parente*, *Le Carrefour d'Hécate*, and *Prima ballerina assoluta*. The first depicts a nude, goddess-like, muscular woman explaining to a female pupil the similarity of a woman's genitals to the inner parts of a flower. In *Lointaine Parente*, four women pay homage to their ancestor, a beautiful leonine sphinx. The third presents a group of partially clad mysterious women, perhaps priestesses of HECATE or Witches, who wander in the darkness, drawn to a central, lunar, pearl-like sphere. *Prima ballerina assoluta* portrays a bald goddess figure whose transparent aqua cloak embraces two nude handmaids who are placing earrings, reminiscent in form of the Venus of Willendorf, on her ears as she crowns herself with a golden tiara ornamented with flowers. Together, the three figures of *Prima ballerina* suggest a feminine trinity. Fini describes her work as "an incantatory autobiography."

Fire   In many cultures, fire is symbolic of erotic and spiritual energy; like water, it is also an agent of purification. In Greek mythology or religion, the god PAN is associated with fire. According to P. Borgeaud (1988), the energy released by Pan when having anal intercourse with a goatherd is compared to fire. In "Invocation to SAPPHO," Elsa GIDLOW describes the Lesbian poet as "fire-hearted" and as she "whose veins ran fire." Other deities associated with gender and/or sexual variance and the element of fire include AGNI, ERZULIE, FREYJA, HEPHAESTUS, LOKI, OGUN, PELE, POMBA GIRA, SEKHMET, SHAKTI, SHIVA, and VESTA.

First Man and Woman, Myth of   In Native American Navaho cosmology, the children born of First Man and First Woman, who were themselves created from CORN, were hermaphrodite twins.

Fish and Fishing   Numerous deities linked to same-sex desire and/or transgenderism are also associated with fish and fishing; these include ATARGATIS, BRITOMARTIS, DICTYNNA, POSEIDON, LA SIRÈNE, and YEMAYÁ. In Taoist eroticism, the expression "fish gobbling flies" refers to women rubbing their genitals together. In ancient China, we also find the tale of King An-hsi of Wei (275-245

BCE) and his beloved Lung-yang. Fishing with the King, Lung-yang, who had caught many fish, suddenly began to cry. When the king asked him why, he replied, "My fate is comparable to that of the fish I throw back into the sea. One day, when you tire of me, you will cast me into the sea like an unwanted fish." The king promised that he would never tire of Lung-yang; indeed, his love for him remained so strong that the beloved's name came to signify homoerotic love, as "*lung-yang jun.*"

Flora   In Roman mythology or religion, the goddess of springtime and flowers (identified with the Greek CHLORIS) and a patron of courtesans. It was believed that Flora possessed a magical flower that could make women pregnant without the aid of men. She allegedly gave one of these to Juno (Greek HERA), the wife of JUPITER (ZEUS), whereby Juno gave birth parthenogenetically to the god MARS (Ares). The month of April, when the Floralia was celebrated, was sacred to her; courtesans, or prostitutes, played a central role in this festival. In Medieval Europe the name "Flora" signified a courtesan and apparently also a "GANYMEDE" or "CATAMITE," that is, a young man who took the receptive role in same-sex relationships; there is also a suggestion of transgenderism in the form of cross-dressing or "drag." In 1097, a young Christian man named John who was much better known by the nickname of "Flora" was made Bishop of Orleans by his lover, the Archbishop of Tours. In the twelfth century, Serlo of Wilton (c. 1110-1181), a Cistercian monk, refers to the homerotically inclined companion as both a "Ganymede" and a "Flora." "Your Flora," he writes, "[is] drooping without you, thirsting without his flower."

Flower   Symbolic of many things including desire, love, immortality, and transitoriness. In Greek religion and myth, numerous divine beings, especially young males who die before reaching full maturity, as ADONIS (whose blood is transformed into the ANEMONE), ATTIS (whose blood becomes the VIOLET), CROCUS, HYACINTHUS, and NARCISSUS, are associated with flowers. Greek male lovers exchanged garlands of flowers, as did the women-loving women of SAPPHO'S THIASOS on the island of Lesbos, weaving garlands of ROSES, violets, and ANISE. Like the Greek divinities mentioned above and like the Hindu deities KALI and LAKSHMI, the Aztec deities of flowers XOCHIPILLI and XOCHIQUETZAL also have links to transgenderism and/or same-sex desire. In Nahuatl, the Aztec language, *xochiua*, "flower person," often refers to a transgendered, or *cihuayollo*, male. Among the ancient Chinese, the wearing and ingestion of flowers by males was linked to femininity, transgenderism, and spirituality, to the gathering of YIN energy into the male psyche and body. In the work of shaman-poet QU YUAN, floral terms such as the "Fragrant One" refer to his passionate devotion to a king. In traditional Chinese culture, a "golden ORCHID bond" (*jin lan qi*) often refers to an intimate same-sex relationship. In the ALCHEMICAL tradition, the androgyny of flowers is central, as exemplified by the image of the "sapphire blue flower of the hermaphrodite." In the nineteenth and early twentieth centuries, numerous flowers came to signify homoerotic love in the West, including PANSIES and CARNATIONS (especially those dyed green). Flowers abound in lesbian poetry of the nineteenth and twentieth centuries. The flower as a metaphor for lesbianism was nurtured by the proto-Decadent French poet Charles Baudelaire's (1821-1867) description of lesbian acquaintances as "*fleurs du mal*," "flowers of evil." Feminist theorists have generally labeled Baudelaire's metaphor as misogynistic; this, however, is a reductionist interpretation which fails to take into account his reverence of those whom and that which others of his time considered evil or perverse, as exemplified by his "Hymn to Satan." By the end of the nineteenth century, the expression "*fleur du mal*" had become synonymous with "*lesbienne*" in Parisian bohemian circles. Lesbian poets employing floral symbolism include Amy Lowell, who in "Frimaire," writes, "Dearest, we are like two flowers / Blooming last in a yellowing garden, / A purple aster flower and a red one," and CHRYSTOS, who writes in "Close Your Eyes," "Come into a deep dark flower / night woman inside / crescent moon petals." Spirit, a queer-identified male Radical Faerie, in "One Faerie's Garden," offers a list of flowers and herbs comprising a Faerie garden, including Love Lies Bleeding, Fairyland Columbines, Gay Butterflies, Fairy Changeling, Lavender Boy Four O' Clocks, and Lavender Wings.

Flute   The association of the flute with same-sex eroticism, transgenderism, and the sacred spans many cultures and epochs. Here used to refer to any cylindrical tube (aerophone) played horizontally or vertically, the flute has frequently served as a phallic symbol, with its player symbolically performing fellatio, or as an androgynous symbol, its phallic body blending with its tonal properties, sometimes described as feminine. Among the Sambia people of New Guinea, flute-playing was both symbolically and ritually linked to fellatio, from which act male energy was thought to be obtained. Greek divinities and figures of myth bearing such associations include EROS; PAN, who seduces his beloved DAPHNIS while instructing him in playing the flute; and MARSYAS, who teaches his beloved pupil Olympus to play the instrument. It is said that ATHENA also enjoyed playing the flute or pipes until she was repulsed by her image reflected in a pool, reminding her of fellatio. Because in Greece the flute appears to have been played primarily by women, particularly courtesans, male flautists were often linked to gender and sexual variance. In the seventh century BCE, the Greek poet Archilochus condemned an acquaintance by comparing him to a devotee of the goddess KOTYS,

suggesting that he played the flute (probably the aulos), wore women's clothes, and engaged in cultic homoeroticism. The Greek historian Duris (from Samos, fl. c. third century BCE), explains that the Greek poets described the flute as "Libyan" because Seirites, an African musician (apparently Black), had discovered the art of flute playing and was "the first to accompany the rites of the Mother of the Gods with the flute." These were the rites of the goddess CYBELE, suggesting that Seirites may have been among her GALLI, her transgendered male priest/esse/s, who became renowned as flautists. In Hinduism, the flute is the instrument of KRISHNA, who is frequently associated with transgenderism. In Taoist alchemical TANTRA, to "blow the jade flute" signified fellatio. LAN CAIHE, the transgendered male divinity of the Chinese Eight Immortrals of China, is often depicted carrying or playing a flute. In contemporary American culture, the slang expression "playing the skin flute" refers to fellatio.

Forster, E. M. (Edward Morgan Forster, 1879-1970) British homosexual author of such acclaimed novels as *Where Angels Fear to Tread* (1905), *A Room With a View* (1908), *Howard's End* (1910), *Maurice* (1913, published posthumously), and *A Passage to India* (1924). Many of Forster's works explore the interrelationship of (often sublimated) homoeroticism and the realm of spirit, including "The Story of a Panic," which depicts a youth's epiphanic encounter with a Pan-like, Italian young man; "The Curates Friend," wherein a young clergyman encounters a faun who awakens him to his homosexuality; and "The Life to Come," wherein a tribal chief is betrayed by the missionary to whom he is passionately devoted.

Fortune, Dion (pseudonym of **Violet Firth**, 1891-1946) English occultist and writer. During her lifetime, Fortune was a member of various occult organizations including the Theosophical Society and the Hermetic Order of the Golden Dawn. In 1922, she co-founded, with her husband, the Fraternity of the Inner Light. Several of her novels, including *The Sea Priestess*, experienced a vogue during the 1970s with the rise of Neopaganism, Witchcraft (or Wicca), Goddess Reverence, and Women's Spirituality. Somewhat ironically, Fortune was remarkably vicious toward those engaging in same-sex eroticism (many of her fans have been lesbians), especially toward gay men. In the 1930s, condemning Oscar WILDE (1854-1900) in particular, she described homosexuality as an "unnatural," "infectious," "very cruel form of vice" occurring solely between two types of persons, the victimizers who "proselytise" and their "victims." She further blamed gay men, and not Christianity, for the downfall of Greek paganism.

Found Goddesses (1988)   This witty, sardonic, totally late twentieth-century approach to Goddess Reverence by Morgan Grey and Julia Penelope, with illustrations by Alison Bechdel, introduces us to divine beings including: Aerea Corrida, She-Who-Flies-the-Friendly Skies; Digitalis, Our-Goddess-of-Computers and patron of Digital Manipulation; Eutopia/DYSTOPIA, "the two-faced goddess of all Lesbian visions"; Getuffe, Our-Goddess-of-Self-Defense; Moola-Moola, goddess of Financial Security; and Tofu-Miso-Soya, the "triple goddess of natural foods."

Foutin, Saint   A Christianized, sanctified incarnation of the Roman phallic god Priapus. St Foutin (whose name is related to "fuck") was worshipped in France, often in the form of phallic pillars, until at least the end of the sixteenth century, when he was allegedly revered by the gender variant, homoerotically inclined King HENRI III of France.

Frances, Rose Wognum (1951-   )   Lesbian-identified pansexual artist and educator. For Frances, the process of making art and spiritual practice are intimately related, often identical. Trained in academic art, Frances became disillusioned with this approach at an early age and turned to crafts, sensing in them a spiritual potency lacking in much twentieth-century art. She was determined to weave together in her art memories of childhood psychic experiences (such as seeing garden devas) and Nature reverence (as a young girl she would place offerings at the foot of "Old Mother Tree" near her bedroom window) with her adult knowledge of MAGIC, Witchcraft, and Goddess Reverence. Frances knew she was on the right path when, as she was working at her loom one day, an older woman approached her and said, "I stand by your loom every day because I want to carry the image of your work in my heart, because it feeds my spirit." Her desire to fashion a different kind of art was also fueled by a workshop in clay arts she took with gay artist Paulus Berensohn, who spoke of the interrelatedness of the sacred and art. In 1970, her desire was manifested in the form of a clay pot from which Frances is certain all her subsequent works have emerged. "The wise hands," she says, "teach us everything. The artistic process is a surrender to the spirit. Art is the manifestation of spiritual truth, rendering visible that which was previously invisible. It is at once a yielding, a revelation, and an offering." Among those who served as early muses to Frances were gay male friends, including drag queens; she delighted in their CAMP sensibility, while they were drawn to what they perceived as the magical quality of her work, referring to her affectionately as a "witch." After being married for a number of years, Frances left her male partner to "come out" as a lesbian, marking this desired but difficult journey with a work of art that displays characteristics common to much of her

subsequent work. Inside a black wooden box covered with writing (describing her shamanic-like experience of psychic descent, confrontation with the shadows, re-emergence, and metamorphosis) is an elegant black velvet evening glove pierced with spikes and revealing a blood-red vaginal-shaped interior. For Frances, the shadow box, which now frequently has doors which open and close, has assumed the character of an altar and as such has become a powerful container of spiritual or magical power. One of her most beautiful works is *The Crone* (1989), a golden altar-box with deep blue panels evoking a starry night. A crescent moon glows, and high above, an owl flies. From the depths of the heavens, the face of an elder woman smiles softly at the viewer. Beneath her, golden sewn hands clasp a feather. Frances's work has been shown throughout the US and in Canada and Europe, including at the Corcoran Gallery and the Smithsonian Institution in Washington DC, and at the Royal Palace in Monte Carlo, Monaco. She founded and was head of the Fibre Arts Program at Florida International University for nine years. In 1996, she is Program Director for the Women's Spirituality Program at the California Institute of Integral Studies in San Francisco.

French, Jared (1905-1988)   Bisexual American painter whom painter and critic Nancy Grimes has described as an "American symbolist" who sought to create a "mythic realm, one that, like Olympus, is separate from, yet linked to, the mundane order." She continues, "he fashioned an idiosyncratic visual language drawn from the Renaissance and ancient art and based on the figures and symbols of religious myth." Among his works depicting an interrelationship of bisexuality and/or same-sex eroticism and the mythic or sacred are: *Washing the White Blood from Daniel Boone* (1939), *Murder* (1942), *Music* (1943), *Learning* (1946), *Help* (1946), *Prose* (1948), *The Double* (c. 1950).

Freyja   As K. Gundarsson (1990) asserts, Freyja "was probably the most widely worshipped of the Norse goddesses." Although perceived as a Great Goddess, her primary concerns appear to have been agriculture, EROTICISM, and MAGIC. That her worship was linked to, or preserved elements of, Shamanism is inferred by her garment of falcon or hawk feathers, which she uses to "fare forth" into other worlds, and by the type of magic she practices and teaches to others, which incorporates the shamanic state of consciousness. That her worship was matrifocal in character is indicated by the fact that her type of magic, SEIDR, was practiced primarily by women and gender variant, or transgendered, men and was in later times branded "feminine magic." It was contrasted with *galdr*, or runic magic, the runes being a sacred and divinatory alphabet; *galdr* was "masculine magic." As a goddess of eroticism, Freyja is believed to have enjoyed pleasure with many divine and semi-divine beings, including her brother Freyr and the dwarfs who fashioned Brisingamen, her magic necklace or torque. A foremother of the fairy tale witch, Freyja rides upon a cat. In later centuries, Freyja, like other originally peaceful deities, becomes a goddess of battle, having the responsibility of overseeing the spirits of fallen warriors. The *jardarmen*, a (primarily) male ritual of initiation into warriorhood linked to the reverence of Freyja, appears to have included either sublimated, simulated, or actual homoeroticism. This was a rite of blood-brotherhood during which young men passed under three strips of turf, referred to as "earth-torques," referring to Freyja's Brisingamen torque mentioned above. The Brisingamen is at once a symbol of the Goddess' fertility (in the Germanic psyche, the necklace is a vaginal symbol) and of her death-wielding aspect (as a "choker"). It has been suggested that torques may have been used to strangle males being sacrificed to the Goddess. In her destructive aspect, Freyja is sometimes called Fordoeda. This name is also given to gender variant or Amazonian women who not only assume masculine roles but who are believed to be capable of rendering men *ergi* (roughly, "receptive homoerotically inclined, gender variant male"). The torque itself comes to signify the anus, anal intercourse, and *argr* behavior. By extension, to form the hands into a ring is to suggest that one holds the power to cause another to submit to, or to cause another to desire, anal intercourse. M. C. Ross (1973) reminds us of an incident when Odinn directs this gesture at the god Thor, boasting that he can render him *rassragr* – that is, penetrate him anally – whenever he likes. It is in the context of this rather complex set of associations that the *jardarmen* rite becomes linked to simulated or actual anal intercourse. Ross explains that in the rite, the three strips of turf under which the youths pass represent not only Freyja's necklace, her vagina, and the womb-tomb from which all life emerges and to which all life returns, but also the anus, anal intercourse, and yielding to a spiritual male elder. Ross concludes that since the *jardarmen* is "connected with ceremonies of *fóstbrœdralag* [foster-brotherhood], one might suspect that its significance in the . . . initiation ceremony . . . was anal rather than vaginal in that the boys might have participated in a rite of communal sodomy to mark their entry into adult male society." In remote areas of the north, Freyja was still being worshipped in the twelfth century CE. In recent decades, as a combined result of the emergence of the Germanic Revival, Women's Spirituality, and Neopagan movements, Freyja's worship has experienced a revival. As Gundarsson explains, "Freyja is particularly called upon today by women [including lesbian and bisexual women] who wish to regain the strength which Christian culture has denied them for so long." She is also called upon by queer-identified men who practice *seidr* magic.

Freyr Brother of Freyja in Teutonic mythology and religion, nicknamed "the Fruitful." Freyr is a god of earth, water, EROTICISM, love, MAGIC, self-sacrifice, and peace. That his worship, like Freyja's, employed shamanic elements is suggested by two vehicles attributed to him, a ship which is not confined to sailing on the water, and a golden boar which has the ability to fly through the air. A link to Shamanism is also indicated by Freyr's association with the horse and the stag, animals playing a key role in shamanic traditions. Freyr is also a patron of elves. He is especially honored at Yule, when boars and baked boars' heads and boar-shaped cakes were sacrificed to him. As a god of eroticism and love, Freyr is often depicted with an erect penis. Small images of this sort appear to have been carried or worn by his worshippers, while larger ithyphallic images were to be found at holy sites. As a seasonal or dying god, Freyr was thought to experience birth and death periodically. "We know that Freyr was said to have been laid in a mound," H. R. E. Davidson (1981) relates, "and to have rested there while offerings were made to him." When the old gods were being driven underground by Christian forces in the tenth century, Freyr was believed by some – who had apparently forgotten his demise at Ragnarok – to have died a final time; according to Davidson, his "death was kept secret from the Swedes for three years." Even so, among others Freyr was still being worshipped in the eleventh and later centuries. Today, as with Freyja, his worship is experiencing a revival, chiefly among men, including queer-identified men, who do not feel comfortable emulating a patriarchal, war-oriented deity. From Saxo Grammaticus, we learn that the god Freyr was served by transgendered male priest/esse/s who dressed in feminine attire, employed effeminate gestures, behaved generally in a "lascivious," "wanton" manner, and utilized bells, considered "unmanly," in their rites. Moreover, they appear to have participated in a symbolic *hieros gamos* which may have involved cultic homoeroticism, in order to "ensure the divine fruitfulness of the season." This rite appears to have been linked to the Fröblod, a sacrificial rite which took place at Freyr's temple at Uppsala, where the god was revered in his ithyphallic manifestation. At this rite, which was celebrated every nine years, on nine consecutive nights, nine "males of every living species – dogs, horses, men" were sacrificed to Freyr and then "hung from the trees near the shrine," grim ornaments which shocked Christian zealots. The priests of Freyr also may have experienced theriomorphic transformation during rites in which they donned boar masks. Unfortunately, little else is known of the *ergi* priests of the god. They have, however, been compared to other gender variant priests of Germanic antiquity, including the priests of the Alcis, twin warrior deities revered by the Naharvali during the third century. While it is as yet unclear, it seems plausible that the *ergi* priests of Freyr may have been associated with – and perhaps even identified with – the transgendered, SEIDR-magic-practicing priests of Freyja.

Frog Earrings Female deity or spirit of the Mandan people of Native North America. Mother of Buffalo Woman, Frog Earrings insures successful buffalo hunts and guides men in becoming TWO-SPIRITS (third gender males, often homoerotically inclined and often serving as shamans). Frog Earrings possesses a magical garment, a buffalo robe that protects the wearer against misfortune and aids in the transformational process undergone by males destined or chosen to become two-spirit persons. If she is not revered, she may inflict the disrespectful individual with mental or physical impairments. Frog Earrings is generally served by women and two-spirit persons.

Fuku "The God of Insolence . . . Chaos . . . pranksters and poltergeists," according to queer-identified writer William BURROUGHS in *The Western Lands* (1987). In this UTOPIA/DYSTOPIA populated by queers and other "edge" persons and bearing more than a little resemblance to the ancient Egyptian afterlife/underworld, Fuku, "dreaded by the pompous, the fraudulent, the hypocritical, [and] the boastful," is "wild, riderless." Fuku knows "no master but PAN, God of Panic. Wherever Pan rides screaming crowds to the shrilling pipes, you will find Fuku."

Furfur In the Western European Renaissance tradition of ritual magic, Furfur is a bisexual, possibly transgendered, spirit who, when he (/she) manifests himself (/herself) in human form, delights in lying between men and women as they make love. Furfur may also appear as a DEER or an ANGEL.

Furies Goddesses of Greco-Roman antiquity, the Furies were chiefly concerned with justice and retribution. They were especially severe in bringing torment to those who had mistreated the elderly, disrespected ancestors, or murdered their mothers (considered the most terrible of crimes). Referred to both as the "angry ones" and the "kindly ones," they were said to be the daughters of the earth-goddess Gaea, who had formed them from the blood of Chronos following his castration; in this, they are related to APHRODITE, who was born of the union of Chronos's blood with the maternal sea. Considered much older than Zeus and his Olympian company, they are synonymous with the ERINYES, akin to the Greek AMAZONS, Eumenides, FATES, GORGONS, HECATE, MEDUSA, Nyx (the goddess of Night), and PERSEPHONE, and also share kindred traits with the Teutonic/Norse VALKYRIES. Typically represented as HAGS, often with wings and serpentine hair, their sacred animal is the scorpion. Considered as a trinity, they are given the names Alecto, Megaera, and Tisiphone. They were honored at Athens and elsewhere with offerings and sacrifices of honey, narcissi, black sheep, and white doves. Radical bisexual women and lesbian-feminists, including Mary DALY and Jane Caputi, have found great sustenance in the archetype of the Fury, in being "furious," with numerous groups taking the name of this divine troupe, such as the Furies Collective of Washington, DC founded in the early 1970s.

Fusionisme Spiritual movement of mid-nineteenth century France led by Jean-Baptiste de Torreil which upheld androgyny as the highest state of existence. Fusionistes revered an androgynous or transgendered deity known as Map, meaning "Mother-Love-Father." Fusionistes believed that via reincarnation, by way of experiencing many lifetimes as male and as female beings, not only humans but also animals would ultimately arrive at an androgynous condition. According to Albert Boime, the "individual must perfect her/himself through various stages of existence until the androgyne is realized – the authentic image and likeness of God." Fusionistes linked androgyny to a UTOPIAN, terrestrial paradise which they envisioned as emerging in the not-too-distant future. They upheld the utopian socialist, or radical democratic, ideals of brotherhood, sisterhood, and solidarity. They rejected the Christian concept of damnation, instead believing that all individual souls would eventually perfect themselves. Fusionisme wielded a profound influence on the life and work of the gender variant, woman-loving painter Rosa BONHEUR.

G

Gabriel the Archangel, Saint In Judaism, Christianity, and Islam, a chief angelic messenger of the Lord. In the Christian tradition, Gabriel heralds the births of JESUS Christ and St John the Baptist. In the Islamic tradition, it is Gabriel who is sent to destroy SODOM; in Islam, this city is most definitely associated with homosexual practices. Ironically, in the visionary poetry of Spanish writer Federico García LORCA, particularly in his poem "San Gabriel (Córdoba)," the angel signifies homoerotic desire. Gabriel is fêted on September 29.

Galás, Diamanda (1955-) US singer, composer, and performance artist whose *Plague Mass* (1984), in memory of her brother Philip Dmitri Galás, who died of AIDS-related illness, secures her place in queer-spiritual history. First performed in 1990 at the Cathedral of St John the Divine in New York City, the Mass has been described by Rob Baker (1994) as a "work of undeniable power." During the course of the Mass, Galás screams, chants, sings, and drenches herself in a blood-like substance, railing against the government and the gods for allowing the slaughter of the innocent by AIDS/HIV, and serving as a kind of psychopomp, or guide to the spirits of the deceased. Strongly identifying with queer consciousness, Galás speaks of having always been drawn to the goddess ARTEMIS/DIANA as a hunter, warrior, and witch who does not bear children. In this vein, she also explains that the voice "has always been a political instrument as well as a vehicle for the transformation of occult knowledge or power. It's always been tied to witches and the shamanistic experience – the witch as transvestite/transsexual having the power of both male and female . . . simultaneously [a] political/shamanistic homosexual witch's voice." Viewing herself as a rebellious TRICKSTER, Galás chants, "I am LEGBA, I am the Holy Fool, I am the Scourge of God . . . I am all the things you are afraid of."

Galatians, Letter to the (c. 55 CE) Despite Saint Paul the Apostle's (d. c. 65 CE) apparently hostile attitudes toward those he perceived as transgendered and/or same-sex inclined, a verse from his *Letter to the Galatians* has, since the early days of Christianity, inspired those who seek to embrace such individuals as fellow Christians. It reads: "There is neither Jew nor Greek, there is neither slave nor free, there is neither male nor female; for you are all one in Christ Jesus" (Gal. 3: 28).

Galaturra Name given to both transgendered male spirit servants and priests of the Mesopotamian goddess INANNA/ISHTAR. As priests, the *galaturra* served primarily as sacred musicians, renowned as chanters of lamentations. They are often identified with the KALATURRU, the KURGARRU, and ASUSHUNAMIR.

Galla, Saint (d. c. 550 CE) Roman noblewoman who refused to marry again after her husband's death, choosing instead to devote herself to the study of Christianity as a hermit living in a small cottage on the Vatican Hill. Legend has it that upon assuming this masculine identity, Galla began to grow a beard. St Galla is fêted on October 3 or 5.

Gallina, Raelyn (1954-) Lesbian body modification artist and priestess of the *orishá* (deity or spirit) OYA in the Yoruba-diasporic religion who lives in northern California. Gallina is representative of many contemporary lesbians who have rejected the notion (espoused by some lesbian-feminists) that SADOMASOCHISM represents aping of patriarchal behavior. Because some practitioners of Yoruba-diasporic religions disapprove of practices associated with S/M, Gallina, generally speaking, keeps her religious and body modification practices separate. Nevertheless, she explains that Oya, the goddess of tempests and revolutions, inspires her artistic creations, including TATTOOS, skin cuttings, brandings, and piercings, and that these artistic processes often take on a ritual character, becoming ceremonies of initiation for clients, with Gallina enacting a shamanic role.

Gallos (pl. **Galli**) Name given to the transgendered male priest/esse/s of the goddesses ATARGATIS and CYBELE. The *galli* of Atargatis dressed as she and her gender variant male consort Hadad did, in Egyptian feminine attire. It is probable, although not certain, that they engaged in sex with males. Their duties included caring for the sacred fish kept in the pool on the temple grounds, and participating in the Feast of Fire in early spring. At this rite, clothes, jewelry, figurines, and other objects were cast upon a great bonfire in sacrifice to the Goddess. When *galli* died, they were not buried like other males, but rather carried on biers to a place beyond the city walls, suggesting their liminal status in society, where their bodies were covered with mounds of stones. The worshippers of Atargatis were among those participating in a great slave rebellion occurring in the Greco-Roman Empire between 135 and 131 BCE. While the revolt was crushed, it nevertheless succeeded in encouraging numerous ancient writers to adopt anti-slavery positions. The faithful of Atargatis were the victims not only of Greeks and Romans but also of Hebrew zealots. Perhaps as many as 25,000, both men and women, died at Carnaim in 164 BCE at the hands of Judas Maccabeus. This massacre, when combined with the slaughter of Eunus' comrades, must have devastated the congregation of Atargatis. We last hear of her gender variant *galli* in the fourth century CE. The *galli* of Cybele were variously known as *bakaloi, bakèles, bakides, kybèbes, metragyrtes*, and *metrizantes*. They were considered gender variant in terms of appearance and behavior, and they appear to have engaged in same-sex eroticism. While the term *gallos* is said to be derived from the Gallos River, a tributary of the River Sangarios in Phrygia, *gallos* became associated with the Latin term "*gallus*, ROOSTER," in the Roman Empire. This bird thus became a sacred attribute of Cybele and her male consort ATTIS and a symbol of the *galli*. At the same time, the erotic association of "rooster-cock-phallus," already in currency, served as an inside joke among the *galli* and was later used by Roman citizens to ridicule them. The high priests of Cybele were called *Archgalli, Battakes*, or *Attises*. Unlike many of the anonymous worshippers of goddesses, or of aspects of the Great Goddess, some of the *galli* are known to us by name: Publius Sulpicius Gallus, Genucius, Eutychès, Soterides, M. Modius Maximus, Baeticus of Andalusia, Moschos of Egypt, Caius Frontinus Dorphorus, Quintus Valerius Severus Platiensis of North Africa, Iddibal of Spain, T. Flavius Vibianus, and Dindymus. At least three of these *galli* were slaves who found freedom from their masters in the worship of Cybele. The name Dindymus, incidentally, is theophoric, fusing one of Cybele's appellations, Dindymene, with the masculine ending "-us." Such a name clearly suggests a transgendered male. Their gender variance also caused the *galli* to be labeled *gallae*, employing the feminine ending "-ae." The institution of the *galli* may date back to the religion of the Goddess of Catal Huyuk, believed by many to be an early manifestation of Cybele. It is almost certain that the *galli* were functioning as priests of Cybele in Phrygia by the third millenium BCE. As an institution, the *galli* remained most firmly established in Phrygia. According to one account, the *galli* actually ruled Pessinus until 164 BCE, when the city was ravaged by invaders. Outside Phrygia, however, the *galli*, until the latter days of the Roman Empire, led a mendicant, itinerant existence and were generally prevented from establishing stationary quarters by male citizens opposed to the worship of Cybele, to transgenderism, and more specifically, to ritual castration. It also seems that when a Greek or Roman male citizen chose to become a *gallus*, he came to be looked upon as a foreigner. Like other *galli*, he became the victim of various prejudices including homophobia (because his expression was not of the intergenerational, or pederastic, type), transgender-phobia, and xenophobia. While groups of *galli* may have journeyed to Greece or emerged from the

Greek population prior to the fifth century BCE, their presence in Greece remained largely undocumented until 415 BCE. As transgendered persons and particularly as eunuchs and transvestites, the *galli* were abhorred by the Greeks. Even after temples of Cybele were established in Greece, the *galli* were usually forbidden to enter them. Thus in Greece the *galli* became known as the *metragyrtes*, the wandering, begging priests of the Mother. If the Greeks were repulsed by the *galli*, they also feared them. The Athenian general Nicias, for instance, considered it an omen presaging defeat for the Greek fleet in the Sicilian expedition when, just prior to the embarkation of the fleet, "a young man," a *gallus* of Cybele, "ran up to Nicias . . . and emasculated himself." When Cybele's worship was officially introduced to the Romans in the third century BCE, *galli* had to be imported, as Roman citizens could not undergo ritual castration. In spite of this, a number of citizens formed fraternities to demonstrate their reverence for the Goddess. In 101 BCE, the law was amended so that certain citizens might become *galli* if they so desired, and between 41 and 54 CE, the emperor Claudius removed all restrictions preventing citizens from becoming *galli*. This period of tolerance ended with the accession of Domitian to the throne. Between 81 and 91, Domitian forbade citizens to become *galli*. By 239, however, this policy had been reversed. This second period of tolerance ended with the triumph of Christianity. While the poorest and least stationary of the *galli* may have been forced to wear whatever rags they possessed, fashion, as an expression of reverence for the Goddess, was of great concern to them. They generally appear to have dressed in a combination of feminine and sacerdotal attire, only infrequently donning men's garments, these last being chiefly of foreign design. They dressed in *stolae*, robes worn by Greek and Roman women, and *chiridotae*, tunics covering the arms and legs, almost exclusively worn by women and gender variant men. Such garments were usually made of silk or linen. They were typically of colors associated with transgenderism and with the receptive role in homoeroticism: "grass-green" or chartreuse, purple, and saffron. They may also have worn white *chiridotae* or *stolae* having designs of arrows, checks, and purple stripes. On their feet, they wore gold, red, or pink sandals or slippers, sarcastically referred to as "cymbals" due perhaps to the musical instruments they played. On their heads, they wore golden hairnets or wreaths of golden leaves. On more solemn occasions, the highest in rank among them would wear miters (or *mitras*), turbans or tiaras with ribbons falling to the shoulders. The miter was considered a "mark of effeminacy" by Greeks and Romans who did not revere the Goddess. Its association with transgenderism seems to have sprung from its being of Phrygian, and hence "barbarian," rather than of Greco-Roman origin. Among male gods, it was worn only by transgendered deities like DIONYSUS, ADONIS, and Attis. Given its association with transgenderism, "it is curious," writes G. W. Elderkin (1924), "that the western church should have made use of it as a name for a bishop's liturgical cap." The *galli* sometimes wore exquisite jewelry – necklaces, brooches, rings, earrings, and ankle bracelets. Pierced ears, incidentally, signified devoted service to the Goddess. Necklaces, quite often elaborate, displayed portraits of Cybele, Attis, and other deities. The *galli* also carried mirrors and scourges made of wool, leather, and sheep knucklebones as they processed. They also wore makeup. They began by rubbing their faces with pumice stones and smoothing their skin with salves of balsam and fenugreek. The face was then painted with a white ointment containing flecks of gold. The *galli* also wore rouge, plucked their eyebrows, and outlined their eyes with kohl. Some also appear to have worn TATTOOS. They let their HAIR grow long, frequently to their waists; indeed, they were nicknamed the "longhaired ones." They rarely let their hair down in public, however, except during ecstatic dance rituals. The rest of the time they wore elaborate hairstyles, having their hair curled, corkscrewed, or calamistred. Those who were partially or altogether bald wore wigs. The *galli* also employed rich oils, PERFUMES, and unguents to enhance their attractiveness and to serve as a sign of reverence for the Goddess. The *galli* also practiced depilation in order to more closely resemble the Goddess as well as to appear younger and to attract certain males. Certain gestures and speech characteristics were also attributed to the *galli*. One such gesture involved rolling the eyes and raising them toward the heavens, a gesture also attributed to HIERODULES and courtesans. Another consisted of holding the neck in a lilting or tilted manner. A third was ambulatory in kind; Saint AUGUSTINE (354-430) was especially perturbed by the "gliding," "languorous" stride of the *galli*. The *galli* were known especially for swaying the hips as they walked. Another gesture attributed to the *galli* consisted in reclining with the legs pulled up to the chest, with the buttocks on the floor and the legs raised, resting on a pile of cushions or on a small platform. Certain speech characteristics were also attributed to the *galli* as well as to other gender variant males. The *galli*, like female hierodules and courtesans, were said to converse with the palms of their hands turned upward, a gesture depicted on figurines portraying female deities. They were also said to speak in shrill tones, to lisp, to giggle and whisper, to use obscene language, to employ women's oaths, and to address each other in the feminine gender. Finally, the *galli* and other transgendered males were said to employ a verbal signal peculiar to them, the REGKEIS. Many *galli* appear to have viewed sedentary life and the owning of property as an obstacle to spiritual development. Many of them, moreover, were freedpersons, fugitive slaves, and persons from the poorest economic classes. They generally traveled in caravans. In a wagon or on the back of an ass,

they carried a small shrine containing a statue of Cybele. When they reached a town or a city, they would set the shrine on a rock or beneath a tree or on an improvised stage, and this would become the temporary temple of the Goddess. They would proceed to dance around the shrine, chanting, singing, and telling fortunes in exchange for alms – coins, cheese, and wine. If the *galli* could be said to have a true home, it would undoubtedly have been the mountain forests considered sacred to Cybele. The *galli* were carnivores, as opposed to many others leading spiritual lives who were vegetarians. They adhered to a diet consisting chiefly of wild game and birds. Considering such a diet "savage," they held that it was essential to follow because it reminded persons of that time when only Cybele, the Mother of the Beasts, ruled the earth, long before the arrival of Demeter and other deities associated with agriculture. The *galli*, for this reason, abstained from grain, as well as apples, pomegranates, dates, and pigs. They sometimes ate meat raw, tearing it apart with their teeth. On feast days, they prepared a sacrificial meal for Cybele (of which they also partook in communion) which included the Goddess' favorite dish, *moretum*. *Moretum* was prepared by blending garlic, celery, rue, coriander, vinegar and olive oil into feta cheese. Ovid explains in the *Fasti* that the *galli* prepared *moretum* so "that the ancient goddess may know [i.e., be reminded of] the ancient foods." During the period of initiation, the *galli*, like initiates of other Mysteries, were fed only milk; according to Sallust (86-34 BCE), this was because they were thought of as *hosper anagennomenon*, that is, "those who are being *born again*." Many *galli* underwent ritual castration. It is difficult to say whether only the testicles or both the penis and the testicles were removed, as different texts suggest either possibility. The ritual of castration took place on March 24, the Day of Blood. While this ritual undoubtedly originated in Phrygia, probably during the Neolithic period, it came to be performed at the Metroon in Athens, the Campus Matris Deum in Rome, in London near the Thames, and in many other places. Elder *galli* and initiates would begin to chant, sing, play their instruments, and dance in a circle. Soon they would attain a state of *mania* or *enthousiasmos*, in which they would begin to tear their clothes and to bite, cut, and flagellate themselves and each other. Their "womanish" blood, as Apuleius (b. c. 124 CE) called it, would splatter on the statue of the Goddess in the center of the circle. At the climax of this rite, ritual castration of certain initiates was performed. In the earliest times, the instrument employed in castration was a sharp, chipped stone of flint, an instrument which G. Zuntz (1971) indicates may be traced to Çatal Hüyük. In later times, knives, double axes, and potsherds were used. According to Pliny (23-79), "The priests of the Mother of the Gods called *galli*, castrate themselves . . . with a piece of Samian pottery, the only way of avoiding dangerous results." Finally, elaborate bronze instruments, clamps resembling those employed to geld horses, came into use. One such implement was discovered in the Thames near London Bridge, an elaborate clamp with ornamental busts of Cybele, Attis, and other figures. This instrument suggests that, at least in later times, only the testicles were removed. Found in London, it indicates the widespread diffusion of the institution of the *galli*. Following the ritual of castration, the organs were bathed in holy water and then wrapped in the old, masculine attire of the initiate, clothes he would not wear again. Occasionally the testicles were embalmed, allegedly even gilded. They were then buried in the earth or placed in an earthenware jar and stored in an underground chamber. "Here they became a cult object, and played a role in the mysteries." Throughout this ritual, devotees of Cybele and Attis showered the *galli* with coins and white roses. Slowly the chaotic atmosphere dissolved into joyous solemnity. Sometime thereafter, the initiates processed to the houses of priestesses or female devotees, where they were greeted with feminine garments, which they would wear henceforward. Several theories concerning the ritual of castration among the *galli* have been advanced. One suggests that the *galli* underwent castration in order to more closely resemble the Goddess and women. Another, espoused by Porphyry (c. 232-c. 305), suggests that it "is in memory of . . . Attis that the *galli* mutilate themselves" because they, like Attis (and perhaps also like Adonis, not to mention NARCISSUS and HYACINTHUS, other beloved youths of Greco-Roman myth), represent "the earth in spring . . . the flower [that] falls before the fruit." Others hold that the *galli* sacrificed their organs to the Goddess because it was thought that their seed would fructify the earth. Still others argue that castration symbolized leaving behind an ordinary for an extraordinary existence. W. Burkert (1982) insists that above all, ritual castration carries the message that these men are "totally different, both superior and inferior to average men, inferior in sexual status," in terms of their ability to reproduce, but "superior as to blood and death," in other words, superior in embodying the principle of sacrificial death and spiritual regeneration; "thus awe spreads from the holy beggars." It would seem that in the latter days of Cybele's worship, castration was no longer generally required of the *galli*, this rite being displaced by the *taurobolium*, a bull sacrifice, and by offerings of phallus-shaped breads. The Roman emperor Julian (332-363) tells us in his "Hymn to the Mother of the Gods" that he is grateful to the Goddess for not requiring his castration in order to be initiated into her Mysteries. In some places and among some groups, however, castration continued to be practiced. In the town of Autun, France, for instance, young men were still castrating themselves in honor of Cybele (as Berecynthia) in the fifth century. By Greco-Roman standards, the *galli* were alternately described as *semiviri*, "half men," and *anandreies*, "not men." They were not considered women,

however, nor do they appear to have thought of themselves as such. Obscene speech, which they employed, was not a marker of femininity; besides working-class traditional males, only prostitutes, devotees of BAUBO-Iambe, and perhaps lesbians or "tribades" might be expected to "talk dirty." Physical size also prohibited many *galli* from being perceived as women. The *castrati* voices of many the *galli* also differentiated them from women. There is also the suggestion that lisping (in Greek, a *batalos* is both a lisper and a *kinaidos* [Latin, *cinaedus*] or gender variant, homoerotically-inclined male) and the *regkeis* signal were specifically associated with the *galli* and other "not men." Nor did their ascetic character conform to standards of either femininity or masculinity. An itinerant, mendicant lifestyle including a rejection of procreation definitely represented an alternative to Greco-Roman concepts of masculinity and femininity. Sources offer contradictory explanations as to how a *gallus* came to be a *gallus*. A number of texts suggest that individuals became *galli* as a result of a psychological or spiritual crisis ultimately manifesting itself in physical transformation. Such a crisis might occur as the result of a sudden awareness of having behaved in a brutal manner and a desire to atone for that behavior. Others appear to have become *galli* after dreaming of the Goddess, from drinking or bathing in the rivers Gallos or Sangarios, after eating an herb growing along the banks of the Maeander River, or on seeing a reflection of the Goddess – perhaps merging with one's own image – in a piece of obsidian. Other sources suggest that certain individuals may have freely chosen to become *galli* after witnessing a ritual performance of theirs, while others may have done so in order to find sanctuary from slavery. There is also the possibility that individuals who were already eunuchs or otherwise transgendered may have found companionship among the *galli*. Still other sources indicate that *galli* were born, not made. These sources include texts on ASTROLOGY such as the *Matheseos* of Firmicus Maternus (fl. fourth century CE). In the view of astrologers, to become initiated into the worship of the Goddess and to undergo a process of gender transformation was to fulfill a destiny ordained before birth, a fate controlled by the Goddess and revealed by the stars. In the treatise of Firmicus Maternus, as John Boswell notes (1980), "Varieties of homosexual behavior are mentioned." Many of these references concern mundane as opposed to cultic behavior. Several, however, refer directly to the *galli*, emphasizing sacred function while also speaking of transgenderism and same-sex eroticism. We find, for example: "In general if the Moon, sun, and ascendant are in the face or back of CAPRICORN, ARIES, TAURUS, or LEO, they indicate all kinds of sexual impurities together with extreme effeminization of the body [*omniu libidinum inpuritates cum extreme corporis effeminatione decernunt*]. In all charts, if the Moon is found in the Tail of Leo, it will produce homosexuals who serve as tympany players to the mother of the gods [*cinaedos efficiet, matris deorum tympanis servientes*]." The writings of Firmicus Maternus and other astrologers clearly demonstrate that many individuals, especially those living in late antiquity, reckoned that to become a *gallus* was to live out a preordained destiny which, like the shaman's, could be ignored or rejected only if one were willing to accept divine retribution. These writings also indicate that linkages were made between *galli* and other transgendered persons and persons engaging in same-sex eroticism. The belief that *galli* were born as such clearly stood in opposition to the belief that one freely chose to become a *gallus* or that one became a *gallus* as a result of certain life experiences. As relates to psychological or spiritual transformation, it is possible to see in the visionary dream, the drinking or eating of substances, etc., fated occurrences which acted to trigger the awareness of one's destiny. Such experiences were said to cause an individual to experience *sophrene*, to "recover one's senses." Whether one sees the *gallus* as a product of destiny (genetics?) or social circumstance, it is evident that the ancients regarded him as "totally different" from other men – and women. This becomes remarkably clear in the case of Genucius, a freed slave who became a *gallus* in (or near) 101 BCE. When another freed slave, Naevius Anius, died, he left his possessions to Genucius. It is unclear but certainly conceivable that the two were intimate companions. Genucius was allowed to inherit the property, apparently in spite of the regulation against eunuchs inheriting such, by way of a decision handed down by the praetor Cn. Aufidius Orestes. This decision was appealed, however, by Sordinus Naevius, the previous owner of both parties. Despite the fact that he had freed both, he apparently felt that he still had a right to their belongings. Thus, in 77 BCE, the case was reopened. The consul Mamereus Aemilius Lepidus reversed the decision, insisting that Genucius had no right to inherit the property of Naevius Anius. In Rome, only men and women could inherit property, and Genucius, having "voluntarily mutilated himself" in order to become a "*gallus* of the Great Mother," had forfeited his (-her) claim to any inheritance because he (-she) could now be counted "neither male or female, *neque virorum neque mulierum*." While *galli*, as transgendered persons, were usually forbidden from owning property and from claiming inheritances and were essentially not protected by the law, they were *not* exempt from paying taxes. Due to their transgendered appearance and behavior, their rejection of reproduction, their mendicant existence, and other factors, the *galli* may well have come to be considered social or political radicals, perhaps even enemies of the State. Richard Gordon (1990) explains that Goddess-centered religions like that of Cybele, as well as other mystery religions, "should . . . be understood as implicitly opposed to elite culture" and "seen as forms of resistance to dominant elite goals."

Cristiano Grottanelli (1985) further points out that in the ancient world, forms of "archaic" sociopolitical rebellion included individual and mass flight (exodus), suicide, and tyrannicide. In Grottanelli's view, however, the *galli* engaged in other forms of rebellion as well, most important of which was their "refusal not only of production, but also of the sexual roles that guarantee reproduction," a refusal which has the potential of bringing about "the end of any social order based on marriage and reproduction," in other words, patriarchy. Grottanelli seems convinced that the Romans were acutely aware of the threat posed by the *galli*. From an early (although unspecified) date, the *galli* were associated with gender variant women, including AMAZONS. In a lengthy treatise on the Amazons, Diodorus Sicilus describes these women as worshippers of Cybele. A. W. Persson (1942) agrees with this view, and states that the Amazons were functionaries "of the same kind as the *galli* . . . consecrated to the Goddess." W. B. Tyrrell (1984) also makes this connection: "Amazons worship . . . the Phrygian Mother, Cybele . . . Their rites were orgiastic, attended by frenzied dancing and MUSIC; their votaries were women and eunuchs." *Galli* were also associated with *tribades* and *fricatrices*, women engaging in lesbian eroticism. Clement of Alexandria wailed that just as men of his day enjoyed playing the "passive role of women," so women enjoyed acting "like men, letting themselves be possessed in a way that is contrary to nature." Similarly, Tertullian states bitterly: "I do not call a cup poisoned which has received the last of a dying man; I give that name to one that has been infected by the breath of a *frictrix*, [or] of [the breath] a high priest of Cybele . . . and I ask if you will not refuse it [i.e., the cup] as you would such persons' actual kisses." Both *galli/cinaedi* and Amazons/*tribades* were associated with hierodulic priestesses and courtesans, or HETAERAE. As eunuchs, the *galli* were grouped legally with the courtesans or *hetaerae*. While neither group was supposed to inherit property, both were bound to pay poll tax. Prostitutes like *galli*, were considered gender variant. Perhaps their alleged participation in lesbian eroticism, coupled with the myth of an enlarged clitoris (attributed to both *tribades* and *hetaerae*) encouraged this perception. According to Clement of Alexandria, the *galli* and other gender variant males spent a great deal of time in the company of hierodules and *hetaerae*. "But these women delight in intercourse [and here he appears to refer to conversation] with the effeminate [also translated as 'androgynous males']," he writes; "among them may be found bands of infamous debauched males [*kinaides*]." Little is known concerning the erotic lives of the *galli*, and that which is known derives primarily from hostile sources. An epigram of Martial suggests that some *galli* may have occasionally, albeit rarely, engaged in cunnilingus with female companions; in one of his satirical poems, he reprimands the *gallus* Baeticus for engaging in oral sex with a woman.

Such relationships were outlawed in early Christian times. At the Synod of Elvira in Spain in 305 CE, it was declared that marriages between women and eunuchs were henceforth forbidden. While the *galli* were believed to occasionally engage in variant, or "filthy," forms of heterosexual lovemaking, they were much more frequently alleged to practice same-sex eroticism. As H. Graillot (1912) explains, the terms "*galli* and *cinaedi* ended up being synonyms." Several other terms first used to describe *galli* also came to be used interchangeably with *cinaedus*. These included: "*umbraticola*, one who carries a PARASOL or who stays in the shade;" "*cymbala pulsans*, pulsating cymbals," referring to the cymbals employed by the *galli* and connoting anal eroticism; and "*tympanotriba*, a drummer . . . an effeminate companion like one of Cybele's drumming priests." In twentieth-century terms, Burkert states that the *galli*, following initiation, "would present themselves as passive homosexuals." Apuleius (b. c. 123 CE) indicates that the *galli*'s erotic partners were traditionally masculine males who also may have been followers of the Goddess. He mentions, for instance, a "certain stout young man with a mighty body, well skilled in playing the flute," who leads a procession of *galli* and who (in this satire, unwillingly) plays an "active" role in same-sex erotic activities with them. Juvenal suggests that some *galli* or other gender variant priests may have even married other men. Cultic or ritual homoeroticism also appears to have played a role in the worship of Cybele and Attis. Firmicus Maternus writes: "In their very temples one may see scandalous performances . . . men letting themselves be handled as women, and flaunting with boastful ostentatiousness this ignominy of their impure and unchaste bodies." St Augustine also deplores the cultic homoeroticism "openly professed in . . . religious ceremonies" dedicated to Cybele. Although shrouded in mystery, it is conceivable that cultic homoeroticism as manifested in the worship of Cybele and Attis played a role in the Pannychis or Mesonyctium, an induction ceremony which usually occurred on the evening of March 24. On that night, the elder *galli* and the initiates processed to "a subterranean or hidden space in or near the temple" of Cybele. The ritual commenced with a series of laments sung over the effigy of Attis, which lay on a bier. A symbolic *katabasis*, or descent, followed; this represented Attis' death and "survival in death." At this time, the initiates may have repeated, "I have crept below to the bosom of the Mistress, I have entered the house of Hades." This shamanistic descent was followed by a rite of communion, in which a substance, perhaps *moretum*, was eaten from a tambourine, while a beverage, perhaps milk, was drunk from a cymbal. The ritual of induction climaxed with a *hieros gamos*, a sacred marriage ceremony, with the elder *galli* and initiates playing complementary roles. According to Philostratus (fl. c. 200 CE), the initiates assumed the role of yielding worshippers whose intimate interaction with the elders, playing the role of or embodying Attis, allowed the former to enter into an altered state of consciousness in which they, too, could come to embody Attis. Philostratus writes: "the initiate no longer beholds what the deity has experienced, but he himself experiences it and thereby becomes the deity . . . when the high priest himself is called *Attis*, he must be understood to be the embodiment of the deity already in his own lifetime. The tie between god and man cannot be thought of in closer or stronger terms, and they are joined by a feeling not only of lifelong gratitude but of personal love, which in its expression passes over into sensual terms." While writers agree as to the feeling of union with the deity during this ceremony, they do not always agree as to the roles assumed by participants. H. Willoughby (1929) writes: "As a new *Attis* the votary [i.e. initiate] assumed the role of a bridegroom to the goddess . . . From another standpoint [however,] the newly consecrated priest was thought of as a male counterpart of the goddess. Hence, he was called a *kubebos*." The *archgallus* was said to have concluded the induction ceremony with these words: "Be of good heart, you novices, because the god [i.e. Attis] is saved. / Deliverance from distress will come for us, as well." While the *galli* paid homage to Cybele and Attis throughout the year, the Goddess and her consort were especially honored in the spring, during the period between March 15 and April 10. This period was known as the Megalensia, *Megale* referring to the Great Mother. The first day of the festival celebrated the birth and infancy of Attis. On March 16, nine days of fasting began. Six days later, the passion of Attis was commemorated. An effigy of Attis tied to a pine trunk and decorated with bunches of violets and woolen bands, or perhaps purple ribbons, was carried in procession. This was the day of the "*arbor intrat*, the entry of the pine," and commemorated Attis' sacrifice and death. The effigy was mourned by Cybele's priestesses and the *galli* with "ululations . . . [and] the rhythmic beating of . . . tambourines." March 24 was known as the "*dies sanguines*, the day of blood." On this day, the *galli* participated in ritual dances involving flagellation and castration. In the evening of that day, the *galli* took part in the *hieros gamos* described above. On March 25, Attis's triumph over physical death was celebrated. In later times, this occasion took the form of the Hilaria, commemorating Attis's ascension to the heavens (in opposition to the view that he "survives in death"). Attis was carried by GANYMEDE to the heavens. The coupling of Ganymede and Attis links two important elements in the worship of Cybele: that of spiritual transformation, symbolized by ascension to the heavens; and that of cultic homoeroticism, as both Attis and Ganymede are loved by other divine male beings – the former by Agdistis and the latter by Zeus. On March 27, a statue of Cybele and other sacred objects were ritually bathed. Between April 4 and April 9, games and other entertainments were held. On April 10, Cybele's birthday was celebrated with banquets and sacrifices. On this day it was customary for Roman citizens to be especially generous with their gifts of food and money to the *galli*. The *galli*, like the priests of other deities, fulfilled an artistic function as ritual poets, musicians, dancers, and actors. It is ironic, and tragic, that while the priests of Cybele were especially well known as poets and composers of hymns, little work has survived which is undoubtedly that of *galli*. The *galli* are credited with inventing the *galliambic*, a poetic meter which has been described as a variant of ionic tetrameter, in visual terms, $\cup\cup--/\cup\cup--$ $//\cup\cup--/\cup\cup--$. This meter, also known as the *metroaic* or the Mother Goddess's meter, was appropriated by a number of ancient poets including Catullus and Callimachus. Many centuries later, Tennyson employed it in his poem *Boadicea*. Many, however, like Quintillian, were repulsed by the "wanton measures that suggest the accompaniment of castanets." Quintillian, criticizing the "effeminate modulations now in vogue," linked the *galliambic*, despite its ancient origin, with the "modern music" of his day, which he described as "emasculated by the lascivious melodies of our effeminate stage." It seems possible that the following poem may have been composed by a *gallus*: "Thou art powerful, of the Gods, Thou art the queen and also the goddess. Thee, Goddess and Thy power I now invoke, Thou canst easily grant me all that I ask, And in exchange I will give Thee, Goddess, sincere thanks." The *galli* were also known as singers and musicians. The *galli* employed ululation resembling that performed nowadays by women in the Middle East. It is not hard to imagine that the *galli*, who have been compared to the Sufis by Graillot and others, chanted, as they danced, the names of the Goddess and her consort in shrill tones, "faster and faster and ever more loudly," in an attempt to reach a "summit of ecstasy" in which they would participate in a "deep communal experience." Once the *gallus* had entered into the state of *enthousiasmos*, he would begin to utter the words of Cybele. J. Quasten (1983) writes, "Through the din of tambourines, cymbals and flutes the ecstatic worshipper of the goddess prophesied the future to those present." In the worship of the Goddess, music was frequently combined with dance. Like music, dance functioned to trigger an altered state. The *galli* were believed by many to be adept in divination, healing, and MAGIC. They employed a number of divinatory techniques, including: astrology, geomancy, ornithomancy (the observation of the songs and flight patterns of birds), astragalomancy (divination by hucklebones or knucklebones made to resemble dice), and oneiromancy (the interpretation of dreams). In sacred caves and dream temples, the *galli* would interpret the dreams of clients or would be asked to dream prophetic dreams themselves in order to determine a client's destiny. The *galli* were, however, most celebrated for their employment of divinatory techniques requiring attainment of an altered state. Iamblichus (c. 250-c. 330) writes: "many, through enthusiasm and divine inspiration, predict future events . . . Some also . . . energize enthusiastically on hearing cymbals or drums, or a certain modulated sound, such as those who are corybantically inspired [by Dionysus] . . . [or] those who are inspired by the Mother of the Gods." *Enthousiasmos* could also be triggered by descent into caverns called *plutonia*, a name suggesting descent into the underworld, governed by Proserpina (PERSEPHONE) and Pluto (Hades). These caverns allegedly emitted toxic vapors. Cattle approaching them were said to succumb to the vapors and die. Among humans, the *galli* and certain other priests and priestesses were the only ones thought to be able to withstand the experience. Surrounded by the vapors, they would become possessed by the Goddess. Emerging from the caverns, as if from a shamanic death/rebirth experience, they would begin to prophesy by speaking in verses, typically in *galliambic*, or in foreign or nonsensical tongues. When they prophesied, the *galli* were said to "*vaticinate*," a term later appropriated by Christians. The *galli* also served as healers. Many of the pilgrims who journeyed to dream clinics and to the vicinity of vaporous caverns were ill, physically challenged, or experiencing psychological crises. The *galli* were thought to be especially gifted in healing childhood illnesses, problems occurring during pregnancy, illness caused by the sirocco, and epilepsy. Such illnesses as epilepsy and schizophrenia were sometimes thought to be inflicted upon individuals because they had seriously offended the Goddess or, conversely, because their suffering and subsequent healing would lead them, like shamans, toward divine service. The *galli* also prescribed healing baths for clients, as well as prayers and sacrifices. One of the chief rites performed for Roman women by the *galli* was a rite of expiation. The *galli*, in the role of "sin-eaters," would have the women put on purple or magenta garments, directing them to transfer to, or infuse, the garments with their negative feelings. The *galli* would then take the garments and put them on themselves, using their ability to spiritually consume negativity and/or convert it into positive energy. The *galli* would complete the rite of expiation by purifying the women with eggs. As practitioners of magic, the *galli* composed spells, created philters, and fashioned amulets and talismans for persons seeking lovers, travelers making long journeys, and farmers desiring abundant crops. Graillot quotes from a spell which is believed to have been composed by a *gallus* and which may have been employed in later centuries by Christians. The spell, to be read by a farmer wishing to banish rats from his land, reads: "I exorcise the rats which I have spied in this place . . . I'm going to give you this field over here . . . but if I should come upon you again, I will, with the help of the Mother of the Gods, separate each of you into seven parts." The *galli* were thought to be highly skilled in fashioning talismans and amulets. Their specialty may have been designing amulets to be used in amatory magic. One such object was phallus-shaped, carved from a pomegranate root. Another, which may have been fashioned by *galli* and which must have been extremely rare, was prepared from the hairs encircling the anus of a HYENA, in order to protect them from violence while at the same time attracting lovers. The hyena was "popularly believed to be bisexual and to become male and female in alternate years." *Galli* were believed to hold the power to tame wild animals. Legend has it that Cybele granted this power to the *galli* in order to commemorate an event in the life of Attis. Once, when he was journeying from Pessinus to Sardis, Attis wandered into a cave, where he was confronted by a lion. He managed to tame the lion, however, by beating rhythmically on this tympanum. On the death of Attis, this power was transferred to the *galli*. The *galli* were also believed to be able to make rain, a power attributed to shamans and other gender variant functionaries such as the HIJRAS, devotees of the Hindu goddess BAHUCHARAMATA. It was also thought that, like certain shamans, the *galli* could exorcise evil spirits by circling rapidly around the possessed person while beating on their tympana or tambourines. This technique became known as *tympanism*; some believe it to be related to the tarantella of later centuries. The *galli* also appear to have engaged in, or directed others in performing, rituals of purification employing eggs resembling those undertaken by Latin American *curanderas*. When a *gallus* died, his (-her) hair was cut for a final time and sacrificed to the Goddess. Cult objects in his (-her) possession may have been sacrificed, given to others, or buried with him (-her). It is not clear whether his (-her) severed testicles or genitals were buried with him (-her). Although some *galli* may have been buried above the ground under piles of stones, others were buried in tombs, some even in elaborate sarcophagi bearing images of Cybele, Attis, lions, roosters, doors leading to Hades, and even the figures of *galli* themselves. When a *gallus* died, it was believed that Cybele, as Mother Earth, received him (-her) "into her bosom." F. Cumont (1956) writes, "The belief seems to have been that the deceased were absorbed in the Great Mother who had given them birth, and that they thus participated in her divinity." While Cybele's worship spanned several millenia, it was a cult or religion that was continually being attacked by hostile forces. St Augustine's condemnation of the Goddess and the *galli* was especially vicious. Referring to Cybele as a "demon" and a "monster," he concluded, "The Great Mother surpassed all the gods . . . not by reason of the greatness of her divine power but in the enormity of her wickedness." For Augustine, the priests of the Goddess were "mountebanks," "madmen," "castrated perverts," those "foully unmanned and corrupted." Many *galli* perished at the hands of zealous Christians. The patriarch of Constantinople praised John Chrysostom (347-407) for

leaving, in Phrygia, "without sons her whom they called the Mother of Gods." The Roman emperor Valentinian II (reigned 375-392) officially banned the worship of Cybele, forbidding citizens to visit her temples or to make sacrifices to her. Christian emperors – Theodosius (346-395), Justinian (527-565), and others – would stop at nothing to destroy the worship of the Goddess and to rid the earth of the *galli* and her other functionaries. Justinian was by far the most intolerant of worshippers of the Goddess, transgendered persons, and those engaging in same-sex eroticism. Such persons had their property confiscated, sacred texts burned, temples razed; they were tortured, forced to commit suicide, or burned alive.

Gambling Among the Mohave of Native North America, ALYHA, third gender males, were in the past thought to be especially lucky at gambling.

Gandarva Fairy-like musician-companions of the Hindu sky-god INDRA, associated with EROTICISM, healing, and ecstatic states. They are the subject of a song sung by the homoerotically inclined "flower boys" (HWARANG) of Korea.

Ganesha Plump, elephant-headed, androgynous Hindu deity of the threshold and of prosperity. While in some versions of his myth, Ganesha is the son of the goddess PARVATI and the god SHIVA, in others he is the child of Parvati only, and in still others, he is the child of the female-female union of Parvati and her handmaiden MALINI or of Parvati and GANGA, goddess of the Ganges. As P. B. Courtright observes (1985), Ganesha is "often said to be the most popular deity in the Hindu pantheon." Believed to have been created by Parvati to be her faithful servant as well as her son, Ganesha is often described as a son who "will not wander even a hair's breadth" from his mother's side. Ganesha is described as being androgynous. In general, his head is that of a female, or cow, elephant, while his torso is that of a human male. The elephant head also contains its own androgyny. The trunk and the tusks are seen as phallic, while the temples, "like a woman's breasts, give forth a . . . desirable fluid [i.e. ichor]." The elephant, moreover, is associated with both masculinity and femininity. Elephants are associated with rain, which is symbolic of "male seed", but also with "women with large sexual organs." Ganesha's trunk, while it is a masculine symbol, is flaccid and soft, as opposed to Shiva's erect phallus. This "perpetually flaccid trunk" indicates, according to Courtright, an association with eunuchs. It "poses no threat because it is too large, flaccid, and in the wrong place to be useful for [hetero-] sexual purposes." Even Ganesha's male torso is perceived as androgynous; his softness, plumpness, and especially his breasts are viewed as feminine; even his movements are described as being "graceful like a woman's." While Ganesha is occasionally said to be married, he is most frequently depicted as unmarried and as incapable of reproducing by ordinary means. The female beings around him "appear more like feminine emanations [that is, like *shaktis*] of his androgynous nature" than like wives; they are "like the figure of Ganesani or Vinayaki, a feminine form of Ganesha." As a figure associated with eunuchs, Ganesha is believed to inhabit the threshold between feminine and masculine space. His feet, however, are firmly planted in the feminine realm. As the goddess Diti decided to create a son without the participation of a male being in order to protect herself from "Indra's destructive power," so Ganesha came into being to protect Parvati's "inner chambers." Ganesha is also associated with homoeroticism. Courtright suggests that this association is symbolized by Ganesha's craving for sweets, which "evokes associations of oral eroticism." This association is also suggested, according to some scholars, by an event in Ganesha's life, when Shiva, having beheaded him, i.e. having taken away his sexual potency, gives him his own weapons, that is, gives Ganesha his own sexual strength. Courtright describes a Brahmanic ritual, the *upanayana*, which reveals an intimate relationship (union, initiation) between master and disciple in the worship of Ganesha. In this complex ritual, a young man is smeared with *gatra-haridra*. After spending a night in total silence and eating a ceremonial meal with his mother, he is conducted to a temple, where he is bathed and shaved. He is then given certain gifts including three sacred threads (representing VISHNU, Shiva, and BRAHMA) and is accepted as a disciple (*brahmacarin*) by his master (*acarya*). The acceptance of the disciple into the order is described in terms of birth; the master "gives birth to him [i.e. the disciple] androgynously into a spiritual lineage and a new life." It is not clear whether sexual intercourse takes place or not, but it is at the very least suggested symbolically. The relationship which develops between master and disciple "creates a new bond of affection." Their intimate relationship is in part symbolized by the giving of the *yogadanda* (courtship gift), the sacred staff, by the master to the disciple, echoing the giving by Shiva of his weapons to Ganesha. Ganesha is also linked to homoeroticism, however, by his association with the first *chakra*, the body's sacred power center located in the region of the anus. Alain DANIELOU writes in *Shiva and Dionysus: The Religion of Nature and Eros* (1984): "Ganesha is the guardian of the gate which leads to the coiled snake-goddess [Kundalini] . . . In the human body, the strait gate leading to the earth-center, or snake-goddess, is the anus. It is here that the center of Ganesha is found, the guardian of gates and mysteries, and servant of the Goddess." Daniélou indicates that cultic homoeroticism in the worship of Ganesha may have taken the form of anal intercourse. Because Ganesha controls the first chakra, he presides over a "ritual connected with anal penetration through the narrow gate opening on the

labyrinth," that is, Kundalini, here manifested physically by the rectum and intestines. Daniélou continues: "The male organ, in directly penetrating the area of coiled-up energy (Kundalini), may help its brutal awakening and thus provoke a state of enlightenment and sudden perception of realities of a transcendental order." Ganesha functions primarily as a guardian and as a bringer of both good and ill fortune. As a guardian, Ganesha is a "protean, liminal character" who "stand[s] on the threshold between the profane world . . . and the sacred territory," who "protect[s] the purity of the inner shrine," and who "provides access to the other gods and goddesses." As a bringer of both good and ill fortune, he holds the "power to bless and curse." Both his liminality and his power to curse and bless associate him with eunuchs; in India, eunuchs were thought to hold the power to bless and curse, and their chief responsibility was to guard the harem. Ganesha is also a bringer of rain – a power also attributed to eunuchs – and a god of music and of social justice. Ganesha is said to have been the first to play the *mrdanga*, the ancient and dominant drum used in the Karnatak music of South India to accompany the dance of Shiva. Ganesha is also a god of sacrifices. In Hindu tradition, the head is the container of semen – or SOMA, its sacred equivalent – and sacrifice of the head is viewed as the supreme sacrifice. In the *Kathasaritsagara*, for example, a male worshipper who has nothing to give the goddess Durga offers her his head. His sacred attributes include a hatchet to cut away illusions, a noose to restrain passions, thresholds, the color red and stones painted red, the number 21, and *modaka* cakes, sweet balls of rice or wheat. He is honored on the fourth day of the moon's waxing with gifts of *modakas* and other sweets. In Terence McNally's play *A Perfect Ganesh* (1993), two women in late middle age take a spiritual journey to India. The son of one of the women has been killed by gay-bashers shortly after his lover has died of AIDS; the other woman's son has also died. A third central character represents Ganesha, whose role in the drama is to impart wisdom.

Ganga Hindu Goddess of the Ganges River. According to some, Ganga and the Ganges came into being as SHIVA was making love to VISHNU, who had assumed the feminine form of MOHINI in order to seduce Shiva. Some of Shiva's semen spilled to earth, and from it emerged Ganga and the river. Ganga is associated with the goddess PARVATI, that goddess's servant MALINI, and the goddess LAKSHMI.

Ganneau, known as **Le Mapah** (fl. 1830s)   French sculptor and spiritual leader. The name "Le Mapah" was composed of the first syllables of *mater* ("mother") and *pater* ("father"). Le Mapah founded a spiritual movement in the late 1830s based on the principle of androgyny. According to Le Mapah, the union of the male and female principles was primal. He (-she) struggled against social barriers and laws which separated the sexes. He (-she) opposed the change of a woman's name to her husband's at marriage, proposing a new name be created using the first syllable of each name to create a collective name for the couple (e.g. Eve and Adam becomes Evadam). Le Mapah called his (-her) UTOPIAN movement Evadisme in honor of the primordial androgyne.

Ganymede   In Greek mythology and religion, the prince loved by ZEUS, who assumed the form of an EAGLE in order to carry Ganymede to his abode, where he would become his lover and CUPBEARER. By late antiquity in the West, the term "Ganymede," as well as its Latin equivalent, "catamite" (*catamitus*) had come to signify a male, usually young, who took the receptive role in homoerotic relationships. The Medieval Christian poet Hildebert of Lavardin (c. 1055-1133), in "The Wickedness of the Age," bemoans the presence of "countless Ganymedes." "Both boys and men . . . defile themselves / With this vice and no class escapes it." Meanwhile, Juno (Hera, the wife of Zeus) weeps, and Venus (Aphrodite) panics. Hildebert, asking the homoerotically inclined to "remember the lesson of Sodom," clearly links "the plague of sodomy" (*sodomitica pestis*) to the city of Sodom, the myth of Ganymede, and homoeroticism. Similarly, Bernard of Cluny (mid-twelfth century CE) condemns those who follow "Sodom's law" (*Lex Sodomae*); he is horrified by the presence of "countless Ganymedes." Juno, once more, is abandoned (i.e., sodomy here does not – as some social constructionists of the late twentieth century have suggested – apply equally to heterosexual and homosexual anal intercourse). Moreover, we find here that the ancient ascription of gender and sexual variance to the HYENA has been preserved, with Bernard wailing, "Men forget what is manly; o madness! o terror! they are like hyenas." On the other hand, the twelfth century poet Hilary the Englishman, in what is clearly a love poem, compared William of Anfonia, the "splendor of England," to Ganymede, writing, "Certainly if Jupiter now reigned . . . / He would . . . become a bird for you / So that you might be joined with him forever." In the thirteenth century, debates between Ganymede, representing homosexual love, and Helen or Hebe, representing heterosexual love, were composed by Christian writers attempting to convince homoerotically inclined males that the ultimate purpose of love was reproduction rather than affection or pleasure. In the Renaissance, Ganymede became extremely popular as a subject of painting and sculpture, as revealed in James M. Saslow's *Ganymede in the Renaissance* (1986). Among those artists portraying Ganymede were MICHELANGELO, Correggio, Giulio Romano, and Benevenuto CELLINI. The Elizabethan poet Richard Barnefield in his 1594 poem *The Tears of an affectionate Shepherd sick for Love*, names his shepherd's

beloved Ganimede, and in his *Tableau des Différends de la Religion*, Philippe de Marnix de Sainte-Aldegonde (1538-1598) compares the beloved of Pope JULIUS III (1487-1555) to Ganymede. In the court of the homoerotically inclined French king HENRI III, his minions were frequently referred to as "ganymedes." His beloved Quélus (also nicknamed Adonis and Saint Luke) was specifically nicknamed "Ganymede." In 1774, Johann Wolfgang von Goethe wrote in "Ganymede": "Up, up lies my course. / While downward the clouds / Are hovering, the clouds / Are bending to meet yearning love. / For me, / Within thine arms / Upwards! / Embraced and embracing!"

Gardner, Kay (1941-   ) US lesbian composer, flautist, conductor, and pioneer in the women's MUSIC and Women's Spirituality movements. Inspired by Goddess Reverence, Hinduism, TANTRA, Shamanism, African-diasporic, and other spiritual traditions, as well as by the poetics and vision of SAPPHO, Gardner's chief emphasis is upon the power of music to act as an agent of healing and transformation, as recorded in her book *Sounding the Inner Landscape: Music as Medicine* (1990). Connecting her lesbian identity to that of Sappho, Gardner has explored the power of poetic and musical forms – such as the Lesbian mode – originating on the island of Lesbos to empower her listeners. She speculates that the use of "cyclic forms with central point of climax" might be rooted in a feminine mode of expression. Gardner has also explored the interrelationship of music, the Hindu- and Tantra-based system of the *chakras* (spiritual centers of energy in the body/psyche, perceived as creating a RAINBOW of inner light), and healing. Her early works include: *Prayer to Aphrodite* (1974) for flute and string orchestra; *Three Mother Songs* (1977); *Sea Chantress* (1978) for voice and hammered dulcimer; *Moods and Rituals: Meditation for Solo Flute* (1980) which features pieces titled "Saraswati" (Hindu goddess of music, especially of stringed instruments) and "The Temple of Ishtar" (INANNA/ISHTAR). *The Rainbow Path* (1984) focuses on healing and empowerment by listening to music, chanting, and meditating upon the *chakras*. *Rainbow* represents one of the first efforts in contemporary music to produce an interactive event on a record (tape, CD). *Garden of Ecstasy* (1989), with Nurudafina Pili Abena, continues the work commencing in *Rainbow*. The most notable piece is "Viriditas," a composition in three movements, to nurture healing in persons with HIV/AIDS or other life-threatening illnesses. Centering on the heart *chakra* , "Viriditas" has been described as taking the listener "through the emotion of despair to a cosmic feeling of joy, and finally to a place of comfort and resolve." Gardner's most recent works include *Amazon* (1992) a meditation for alto flute which features the sounds of birds, tree-frogs, and other inhabitants of the Peruvian rainforest recorded by Gardner; *One Spirit* (1993, with

Abena) featuring flute, drums, and percussion, with sources including Shamanism, Goddess Reverence, and African-diasporic spiritual traditions; and *Ouroborus: Seasons of Life: Women's Passages* (1994) for female soloists, women's chorus, and orchestra, a celebration of the life passages inspired by the Celtic Wheel of the Year.

Gearhart, Sally (1931-) Lesbian US writer and political activist, much of whose work is spiritually focused. Reared as a Protestant, Gearhart taught for a number of years at a Lutheran college in Texas, where she began writing on religious subjects. After moving to San Francisco in 1968, her writing became increasingly grounded in lesbian-feminist politics and the emerging movement of Women's Spirituality. From this perspective Gearhart produced texts that have become "bibles" of Womanspirit, including *Loving Women/ Loving Men* (1974, authored and edited with William Johnson), *A Feminist Tarot* (1975, co-authored with Susan Rennie), "Womanpower: Energy Re-Sourcement" (1975, 1982), and *The Wanderground: Stories of the Hill Women* (1978). The last of these marks one of the finest contributions of a lesbian-feminist writer to the literature of UTOPIA or ARCADIA, depicting a tribe of women who are psychically bonded and who have evacuated the structures of heterocentric, patriarchal culture.

Gemeinschaft der Eigenen Organization of homoerotically (and perhaps also bisexually) inclined men led by Adolf Brand (1874-1945) and emerging in Germany in the 1920s. The GDE, or Community of the Self-Owners, gave official expression to followers of LIEBLINGMINNE, men seeking to combine intergenerational, and less often same-age, male love with the ideals of ancient Greek religion and culture as these men perceived them. They upheld restrained homoerotic love, condemned prostitution, and encouraged nudism. Brand writes: "The G. D. E. advocates above all the . . . rebirth of the love of friends . . . as it existed . . . in ancient Greece. The G. D. E. wishes to cultivate in word and picture, through art and sport, a cult of youthful beauty, such as was the custom in the golden age of antiquity."

Gemini In Euro-western ASTROLOGY, zodiac sign ruling from (approximately) May 21 until June 21, associated with intelligence, nonconformity, and sociability, typically depicted as twins. Figures associated with Gemini and with gender and/or sexual variance include: ANOG ITE, CALAIS, CHORONZON, DOUBLE WOMAN, the DOUBLE, MARTHA-MARY, SHOOTING GOD, and ZETES. Generally speaking, many of the lovers or intimate companions appearing in this encyclopaedia might be said to reflect the twin-like behavior or identity associated with Gemini.

Genet, Jean (1910-1986) Homoerotically inclined French writer, criminal, and political activist. In his introduction to Jean Genet's *Our Lady of the Flowers* (1942), which focuses on the life of a drag queen in prison, Jean-Paul Sartre stresses Genet's self-assumed role of the sacred artist, a role inextricably linked to Genet's homosexuality. Explaining that Genet perceived himself as a magician, Sartre writes, "He was forced from the very beginning into the solitude that the mystic and the metaphysician have such difficulty in attaining." Exemplary of Genet's blending of the homoerotic and the spiritual is his poem "Le Condamné à Mort" ("The Man Condemned to Death"), in which he writes: "O triumphant brat, / Terrible divinity, invisible and evil, / . . . Crush thy ravished body against mine." Exemplary also is a passage from *Our Lady of the Flowers*, in which the drag queen Divine searches in the night for the ingredients of a poisonous brew: "The Borgias, Astrologers, Pornographers . . . would receive him . . . Beneath the moon [he] became this world of poisoners, pederasts, thieves, warriors, and courtesans . . . possessing and possessed by an epoch . . . the murmur of a few magic words thickened with darkness . . . *Datura fatuosa, Datura stramonium*, Belladonna."

George, Stefan (1868-1933) German Symbolist poet, neopagan priest, and magician. After his lover, the beautiful youth Maximin, died in 1904, George and his friends established a cult to the young man as a god of homoerotic love. Celebrating male intimacy, George dreamed of a future in which same-sex love would be fully embraced. Typical of his mystical poems is the epic-lyric cycle *The Star of the Covenant*, in which he writes, "I am the One, I am the Two, / I am the womb, I am the sire, / I am the shadow and the true, / I am the faggot and the fire."

Geryon (also **Caulacau**) Among the NAASSENES, a Gnostic sect, a primordial androgynous, hermaphroditic, or transgendered deity alternately identified or associated with: the Roman goddess CYBELE; ATTIS, Cybele's gender variant male consort; the Biblical ADAM; and JESUS Christ.

Ghazali, Mehemmed (d. 1535) Born into Islam, Ghazali was a mystic, poet, pornographer, professor, and scholar, ironically nicknamed "Stupid Brother." A Sufi, he founded, in Istanbul and apparently also later at Mecca, an erotico-spiritual establishment blending Sufism and homoerotic (especially intergenerational) practices. In "The Repeller of Troubles and the Remover of Anxieties," he speaks of the healing potential of lovemaking, especially of anal intercourse. Ghazali's symbol for the anus as an organ of pleasure is the ROSE.

Ghede In Haitian- and New Orleans-based Vodou, occasionally depicted as a single *lwa*, deity or spirit, of the dead but more often as a family of such *lwas*. The Ghedes oversee the transition from life through death to the afterlife or rebirth; as such, they are said to dwell at the crossroads as well as in cemeteries. They are associated with ancestor worship and magic. A smaller, but very powerful, sub-family within the Ghede family is that of the Barons. The Ghedes and Barons often dress in black formal wear, including cane and top hat and they usually wear sunglasses, often with one of the lenses removed. They also frequently wear scarves and cummerbunds of purple and red. They are fêted on November 2, the Day of the Dead (also known as the Day of All Souls and the Dia de los Muertos); their celebration bears resemblance to Halloween (the Celtic Samhain). Ghedes and Barons especially linked to same-sex desire and/or transgenderism include BARON LIMBA, BARON LUNDY, BARON OUA OUA, BARON SAMEDI, GHEDE MASAKA, GHEDE NIBO, and GHEDE OUSSOU.

Ghede Masaka Androgynous male or transgendered *ghede*, or spirit of the dead, in Haitian- and New Orleans-based Vodou, a gravedigger who assists GHEDE NIBO. He (-she) is sometimes depicted as the companion of GHEDE OUSSOU; both are considered bisexual. Ghede Masaka wears a black shirt, white jacket, and white headscarf. He (-she) carries a sack containing an umbilical cord and poisonous leaves. A song to him (-her) includes the lines, "The moon is new. The evil spirits bar my path."

Ghede Nibo Son of BARON SAMEDI and Maman Brigitte and, following them, leader of the *ghedes*, the spirits of the dead, in Haitian- and New Orleans-based Vodou. Ghede Nibo is said to dwell "behind the cross" of the Baron. He dresses in black, often wearing old trousers, a riding coat, a crooked hat, and a black scarf around his neck. Occasionally, however, he appears in drag. He usually holds a staff in one hand and a bottle of peppered white rum in the other. He also usually smokes a cigar. He is described as being both extremely effeminate and phallic at once. His high, nasal voice indicates, at once, his gender variance and his membership in the community of the dead. M. Deren (1983) depicts Ghede Nibo as the "Lord of Eroticism" who "embarrasses men with his lascivious gestures," confounding "sex with sex, dressing women as men and men as women." H. Fichte (1975) portrays him as the "phallic god of the dead, who is homosexual." Songs and dances to Ghede Nibo suggest his homoerotic or pansexual and transgendered aspects. In the recent past, it was customary, each November, for Haitian farmers to sing a praise-song to him entitled "MASSISSI," a term signifying a homoerotically inclined male, typically one who enjoys the receptive role in same-sex lovemaking. This praise-song was accompanied by a dance in which the farmers employed phallic thrusts, grinding of hips, and other erotic gestures. Another popular praise-song to Ghede Nibo also alludes to his enjoyment of anal eroticism: "Ghede Nibo has a cinnamon anus! Just look at how Ghede walks!" While Ghede Nibo may choose to embody or possess a devotee of Vodou regardless of gender or sexual identity, he seems to take special delight in possessing female devotees. When this occurs, they exhibit transgendered qualities which some also interpret as lesbian, as they may, during possession, approach another woman in a sensuous manner. Ghede Nibo is portrayed as a witty, campy dandy and TRICKSTER. He can also, however, be deadly serious. He is a great healer, as represented by the *trempées* (bottles of medicinal leaves infused in white rum) on his altar, and in some respect, the archetypal houngan, or Vodou priest. He is also a special patron of children and of the souls of deceased children. And he is a powerful magician or sorcerer. On his altar one usually finds a small coffin. Offerings to him include calabash, fried plantains, pistachios, smoked herring, coconut, sweet sesame balls, cigars, black cocks, black goats, and white rum spiced with African bird pepper. His sacred attribute is the citron tree. Ghede Nibo bears more than a little resemblance to the Aztec deity TEZCATLIPOCA, also linked to homoeroticism, transgenderism, pranks, sorcery, and death. Nibo is frequently syncretized with the Catholic Saint Gerard Majella (1726-1755). This is due to the saint's being a patron of children as well as to his iconography, including a cross, a skull, red cloth, and an open book. As syncretized with St Majella, Ghede Nibo is fêted on October 16.

Ghede Oussou Androgynous male or transgendered *ghede*, spirit of the dead, in Vodou. He (-she) is sometimes seen as the intimate companion of GHEDE MASAKA. His (-her) primary female companion is Ghede L'Oraille. Ghede Oussou wears a black or mauve jacket, often marked on the back with a white cross, and a black or mauve headscarf. Like Masaka, he (-she) is a gravedigger. His (-her) name means "tipsy," and while he (-she) never becomes as inebriated as BARON SAMEDI, Ghede Oussou enjoys a bottle of white rum.

Giant A Mesoamerican myth concerning homoerotically inclined giants has been documented in sites as far apart as Cholula, Mexico and Manta, Ecuador. According to Mariano Veytia, the people of Cholula believed that the giants arrived during the year 3979 of their calendar, which some say corresponds to 107 CE. These giants were sometimes called the Quinames and were thought to be the ancestors of the Toltecs and the subduers of the Olmecs. Their race is also said to have emerged during the second cosmic age of Aztec myth. Their great strength allowed them to survive the hurricane which brought an end to the Second Sun. They were hunters and gatherers, having voracious appetites for food as well as sex. The men of Cholula (and elsewhere in other traditions) offered the giants their own daughters, but the Quinames were not interested, preferring male erotic companions. Because they allegedly coerced the men of Cholula into having sex with them, they were destroyed by a fiery conflagration or an earthquake – although this part of the myth may have been purposely Christianized in order for priests to connect this myth to that of SODOM in an effort to dissuade Mesoamerican males from engaging in same-sex eroticism or relationships.

Gide, André (1869-1951)   Bisexual or homosexual French writer. Born into a strict, Protestant family, his journey to North Africa in 1893 and meeting with Oscar WILDE in 1894 inspired Gide's coming to terms with his homosexuality. In the 1930s Gide embraced Communism, but became disenchanted with it on visiting the USSR. In 1947 he received the Nobel Prize for Literature. His works include *The Fruits of the Earth* (1897), *The Immoralist* (1902), *Corydon* (1924), and *I it Die* (1924). *Fruits of the Earth* has been described as a "hymn to the pleasures of life." Rooted in classical mythology and religion, in the *carpe diem* ("seize the day") sensibility of Near Eastern and Euro-western mysticism, in Walt WHITMAN's dream of male comradeship, and in the Decadent aestheticism of the late nineteenth century, this text should be considered a classic of spiritual literature in general and of homoerotic spirituality in particular. In it, Gide, speaking to a young man he calls Nathaniel, writes: "Life is more beautiful than men consent to make it. Wisdom lies not in reason but in love. Ah! I have hitherto lived over-prudently. One must be lawless to hear aright the new law. O deliverance! O liberty! As far as my desire is able to reach, so far will I go. O you whom I love, come with me; thus far I will carry you – so that you may go farther still."

Gidlow, Elsa (1898-1986)   Lesbian writer, philosopher, mystic, and foremother of the contemporary Women's Spirituality movement. Gidlow, born in Yorkshire, England, immigrated as a teenager to Canada and eventually settled in northern California. By 1916, while in Canada, Gidlow had begun to explore her love of women, had become comrades with a young gay man named Roswell George Mills, and, alongside him, had begun to immerse herself, quite consciously, in the works of lesbian, gay, and bisexual luminaries, including SAPPHO, WILDE, and Edward CARPENTER. Mills bestowed her with the nickname "Sappho." During this period, she began writing poems celebrating lesbian love and evoking the Goddess. In her 1919 poem "Love's Acolyte," she wrote, "But I who am youth among your lovers / Come like an acolyte to worship." In 1923, in "Is She Found?" she wrote, "Now, with love's old alchemy / We have made ourselves immortal." At this time she also became

interested in Theosophy, led by Madame H. P. BLAVATSKY, but was disillusioned by apparently homophobic and otherwise reactionary followers. During the period spanning the 1930s to the 1960s, she read deeply in Taoism and Buddhism and became especially devoted to the feminine *bodhisattva* KUAN YIN. Through her passionate friendship with Ella Young, she was also drawn to Celtic lore. In the 1960s and 1970s, Gidlow became friends with other artists steeped in Taoism and Zen Buddhism, including the mystical writer Alan Watts, the poet and essayist Gary Snyder, the Tai-chi master Al Chung-liang Huang, and the gay musician Lou HARRISON. With Watts, she co-founded the Society for Comparative Philosophy, which focused on applying Taoism and Buddhism to everyday life in the West. She also co-founded Druid Heights Artists' Retreat near Mt Tamalpais north of San Francisco, where she and those close to her celebrated the moon with rites and readings. During this period, she was nicknamed *yama bushi*, "Mountain Monk." Gidlow's participation in Goddess Reverence, as noted above, may be traced to her earliest poems. As early as 1918, at age twenty, she wrote in "To the Unknown Goddess," "Come to me at the top of the world, / Come soon. I have waited too long." In 1940, her devotion to the Goddess took the form of a Yuletide ritual. Alone, having lost almost everything, including a longtime lover, she lit a fire. "As I added twigs and dry boughs, then MADRONE logs, the firelit room became peopled by presences: spirits of women. Women I had known . . . all the women . . . who kindled and tended sacred and domestic fires." This ritual proved extremely beneficial to Gidlow; over the years, she shared it with others. In the 1970s and 1980s, Gidlow became increasingly involved in the lesbian-feminist and Women's Spirituality movements. During the last years of her life, she participated, as "Lady Clitoressa," in a group of women, including Celeste West, who convened to celebrate the Goddess. Weaving together her love of women and her devotion to the Goddess, she wrote in 1974 in "Love in Age": "Lover-beloved, Woman / Small and strong in my arms / I know in you / The Goddess / Mystery / fecund Emptyness / From which all fullness comes / And universes flower." Of this interrelationship, she also wrote in her 1975 manifesto *Ask No Man Pardon: The Philosophical Significance of Being Lesbian*, "the natural, undistorted Lesbian is by nature virgin [here she refers to the original meaning of the term, "a woman independent of men"], androgynous, priestess, dedicated to the Great Goddess. She is . . . daughter of the Amazons." In this document, Gidlow also expressed her accord with Essentialism: "She is from birth and perhaps prenatally an essentially different being with different needs and desires. She is constituted as she is because Nature has made her so . . . Nature needs the Lesbian as she is. She needs me as I am . . . The Lesbian is born, not made." Gidlow's autobiography *Elsa: I Come With My Songs*, published in 1986, the year of her death, culminates with a powerful meditation on the meaning of life, death, and the potential for rebirth: "I ask: if there is a reservoir of creative consciousness on which all emerging life . . . draws, and each returns . . . what shall I render back when breath is surrendered? . . . What, in the cauldron of my soul, has been invisibly alchemized for rendering back? I do not know. I am willing to abide by the mystery and to celebrate it."

Gilfaethwy and Gwydion Welsh legendary warrior and magician, respectively. Math, the lord of the Welsh province of Gwynedd and an ancestor of the Great Goddess of Wales and Ireland, was in love with the maiden Goewin. This young woman, however, was also desired by the warrior Gilfaethwy. The young warrior wished to take Math's place as lord of Gwynedd. To aid him in his efforts, Gilfaethwy employed his brother, the magician Gwydion. Because Math was also a very powerful magician, Gwydion and Gilfaethwy failed to achieve the latter's ends. Math decided to punish them by transforming them into animals of opposite anatomical sex and then having them mate. Together, they gave birth to a deer, a pig, and a wolf. Their "children" were then transformed by Math into human males, becoming the heroes Hyddwn, Hychtwn, and Bleiden. The shamanic elements of gender and theriomorphic, or animal, transformation are clearly present here. In veiled form, homoeroticism is also present; for even if on one level Gilfaethwy and Gwydion become female and male animals, on another they remain themselves. In the case of Gilfaethwy, he is made to take the receptive role in intercourse each time, probably because it was he who desired to take Goewin away from Math. In Bernard Sergent's view, based on the work of Georges Dumezil, this tale may refer to cultic homoeroticism occurring among Indo-European, here Celtic, warrior bands; the name Bleiden, "Wolf," is especially suggestive of this, as wolves were often linked in Euro-western lore to warriors. Reminiscent of the story of the Egyptian deities SET and Horus, while the sexual relationship of Gilfaethwy and Gwydion commences as a punishment, it culminates with the creation of great warriors, one known for his swiftness, the second for his strength, and the last for his cunning.

Gilgamesh and Enkidu The *Epic of Gilgamesh*, written down near 2100 BCE, concerns the life and adventures of the hero Gilgamesh, ruler of the city of Uruk. Gilgamesh actually may have lived some seven hundred years prior to the *Epic*'s composition. In the *Epic*, Gilgamesh has an insatiable appetite for intimacy, which is finally relieved when a deity creates not a female but rather another male, Enkidu, to become his intimate companion. Together, Gilgamesh and Enkidu journey into the wilderness, where

they conquer the giant Humbaba. During the course of their exploits, the goddess INANNA/ISHTAR attempts to seduce Gilgamesh. When he spurns her advances, she becomes infuriated. Her rage explodes, however, when Enkidu slays her sacred bull. She curses Enkidu, and he dies shortly thereafter. Gilgamesh then sets out on a journey in search of the secret of immortality. Near the beginning of the *Epic*, Gilgamesh dreams of a shooting star which he at first embraces "like a wife" and then presents to his mother. He then dreams of a supernatural ax which he likewise embraces. It is his mother Ninsun, the goddess of wisdom, who interprets his dreams. She explains that the shooting star and the ax both symbolize a man whom Gilgamesh will encounter shortly and whom he will love "as a woman." This lover will "never forsake" him. We then discover that it is another goddess, Aruru, who creates from clay the soon-to-be companion of Gilgamesh. In the Mesopotamian pantheon, Aruru is the creatrix and nurturer of all life. Enkidu, the creature she creates to be Gilgamesh's companion, is an archetypal "wild man" who dwells in the wilderness and lives on honey and wild foods. However, Enkidu is also described in androgynous, gender variant, or transgendered terms: "His whole body was covered thickly with hair, / his head covered with hair like a woman's." It is a hierodulic priestess of the Goddess who civilizes the wild Enkidu by first making love to him and then dressing him in her own garments; we are told that "she took off a part of her clothing and covered him." It is she who makes Enkidu aware that he will soon become Gilgamesh's companion, and it is she who leads him to the city to meet Gilgamesh. To return to Ninsun, she not only sanctions the relationship of Gilgamesh and Enkidu but also adopts Enkidu as her own son: "Enkidu, strong one, you are not the child of my womb – you. / Now I adopt you, / along with the cultic lovers of Gilgamesh." Finally, when Gilgamesh sets out on a journey to unravel the mystery of death and rebirth following the death of his beloved friend, he is aided by Siduri, the Celestial Barmaid, a manifestation of Inanna. It is she who directs him toward the abode of Utnapishtim, the Noah of Mesopotamian myth and the only human being to have escaped death, and she who cautions that this journey will involve a difficult shamanic descent. (In terms of this aspect of the Epic, knowledge of Gilgamesh's VAMPIRE heritage enhances the tale's richness.) Thus, while apparently due to his erotic orientation, Gilgamesh spurns the advances of one manifestation of Inanna/Ishtar, he remains, nevertheless, the loving son of a goddess who seeks counsel from goddesses, including another manifestation of Inanna. In other myths, moreover, Gilgamesh is the friend and helper of Inanna/Ishtar. As for Enkidu, while he makes the tragic mistake – under the influence of patriarchal-heroic passion – of slaying the Bull of Heaven, he remains the handiwork of a goddess, is civilized by a priestess of the Goddess, and is adopted by a goddess as the loving companion of her son.

Anne Kilmer has even suggested that Enkidu may have become a gender variant priest, an ASSINNU, of the Goddess. That Enkidu enters the city of Uruk wearing the garment of a priestess and that his adoption by Ninsun is linked to that of the hierodulic priestesses corroborates this interpretation. Kilmer observes that word-play is used in the *Epic* to inform the reader not only of Enkidu's possible role as an *assinnu* but also of the erotic nature of the relationship he shares with Gilgamesh. She suggests that the ax of Gilgamesh's dream is meant not only to convey the action of chopping – an action that has been linked to ritual castration – but also to indicate an association between this ax, called a *hassinu*, and a gender variant priest, an *assinnu*. She further suggests that the other object of which Gilgamesh dreams, the shooting star, or *kisru*, is employed to remind the Mesopotamian reader of the term *kezru*, which signifies a male wearing a feminine hairdo or a male hierodulic priest (or male prostitute). "The implication of the double pun is, of course," writes Kilmer, "that the often suspected . . . sexual relationship between Gilgamesh and Enkidu is, after all, the correct interpretation." If Enkidu is a wild man who "ranges over the hills with wild beasts and eats grass," he is also a mortal embodiment of the Goddess. His hair is specifically compared to that of the goddess Nisaba, patron of agriculture, divination, and the arts. The *Epic*, then, is not only the tale of a wild man for a ruler; it is the tale of a ruler's love for a gender variant priest of the Goddess. This love becomes tragic when patriarchal heroism rears its head. Within the psyche of Gilgamesh, matrifocal and patrifocal elements also do battle. When Enkidu dies, Gilgamesh himself metamorphoses into an *assinnu*-like figure. Referring to himself as Enkidu's mother and widow, he weeps "like a wailing woman" and paces back and forth like a "lioness whose whelps are lost." What is more, both Gilgamesh and Enkidu experience gender transformation in this scene, with the former becoming a widow and mother and the latter having his face covered "like a bride's." That both lovers are compared to women indicates a transgendered, homoerotic relationship of much greater complexity than scholars have imagined.

Ginsberg, Allen (1926-1997)   Gay poet of Russian Jewish heritage, luminary of the Beat Movement and the Hippie Movement, now one of the most honored poets of the US. Best known for his 1956 epic poem *Howl*, he has been deeply inspired by the writings of the English mystical poet William Blake (1757-1827) and by Tibetan Buddhism, as well as by periods of vagabondage and visionary experiences triggered by peyote. Actively involved in the anti-war movement during the US's conflict with Vietnam, he composed, in 1966, "Wichita Vortex Sutra," as an incantation meant to aid in ending the war. In a 1972 interview with gay activist and writer Allen Young, Ginsberg described a ceremony of UNION which

he had celebrated privately with poet Peter Orlovsky in 1954 in a cafeteria in downtown San Francisco. "We made a vow to each other . . . to do everything we wanted to, sexually or intellectually, and in a sense explore each other until we reached the mystical 'X' together, emerging two merged souls. We had the understanding that when our . . . erotic desire was ultimately satisfied by being satiated (rather than denied), there would be a lessening of desire, grasp . . . craving and attachment; and that ultimately we would both be delivered free in heaven together. And so the vow was that neither of us would go into heaven unless we could get the other one in – like a mutual Bodhisattva's vow . . . So we held hands, took a vow: I do, I do, you promise? yes, I do. At that instant we looked in each other's eyes and there was a kind of celestial fire that crept over us and blazed up and illuminated the entire cafeteria and made it an eternal place." In this interview, Ginsberg also spoke of his concern that the emerging gay liberation movement was not addressing certain issues, among them aging, death, sexual and/or relationship addiction: "An element in the gay lib struggle and metaphysics that I don't think has been taken up is that of disillusionment with the body. I'm not trying to be provocative in that – just the age-old realization of . . . [the] grinning skeleton, with the spiritual lesson behind it, of detachment from neurotic desire. I think there's a genuine eros between men that isn't dependent on neurotic attachment and obsession, that's free and light and holy and lambent . . . If there's too much of a neurotic grasping to gaiety, to gayness, even to gay lib, then it makes everything too tense, and the lightness of love is lost. So the gay lib movement will have to come to terms sooner or later with the limitations of sex." Typical of Ginsberg's (proto-) Queer-Spiritual poetry is his beautifully composed "Elegy for Neal Cassady" (1968), in which he chants: "Tender Spirit, thank you for touching me with tender hands / Sir spirit, give me your blessing again, Sir Spirit forgive my phantom body's demands, / Sir Spirit thanks for your kindness past."

Girodet de Roucy, Anne-Louis (1767-1824)   French male painter, illustrator and poet, whose works, including the painting *The Sleep of Endymion* (1791-1792) and sketches illustrating the myths of EURYALUS and NISUS and APOLLO and HYACINTHUS, as well as the poems of SAPPHO, often depict or imply the interrelationship of same-sex desire, gender variance, and the mythic or sacred. In *Le rapt de Ganymède* (1989), Dominique Fernandez relates that Girodet's *Endymion* became a "cult painting for the homosexuals" of his day, especially for those drawn to castrati singers.

Giton   Akin to GANYMEDE, the youth loved by the Greek god ZEUS, and, like HERMAPHRODITUS, a child of the deities HERMES and APHRODITE, Giton signifies a beautiful, androgynous young man who engages in homoeroticism. This is the role he plays in the *Satyricon* (c. 64 CE) of the Roman writer Titus Petronius Arbiter (c. 27-c. 66 CE), where he is a lover of the two central male characters, Ascyltos and Encolpio. In nineteenth-century France, the term *"giton"* referred to homoerotically inclined young men taking the receptive role in same-sex lovemaking.

Glaucon   Lover of the Greek legendary shepherd CORYDON (who had been rejected by ALEXIS). The poet Erucius (c. 50 BCE) wrote of their reverence of PAN, one of the chief deities of their native ARCADIA: "Glaucon and Corydon, mountain herdsmen and both Arcadian, pulled back the head of this horned bull-calf to sacrifice to the mountain-lover, Kyllenian Pan: then they fastened the yard-span of his horns with a long nail to the broad trunk of a plane-tree: a good offering to the god of grazing."

Gleim, Johann Wilhelm Ludwig (1719-1783) Eighteenth-century German poet who established a "temple of friendship," containing more than one hundred portraits of passionate male friends. The "temple" has been preserved by the Gleimhaus Museum, Halberstadt, Germany.

Glow-worm   The female of the insect *Lampyris noctiluca*, which emits a shining green light from the abdomen. In Medieval and Renaissance European ritual magic, it was believed that a drink containing the glow-worm might transform a man into a eunuch or castrato.

Glyphius   The attempted rapist of TIRESIAS in his transgendered-female manifestation, who was killed by Tiresias during the assult. POSEIDON loved Glyphius and avenged him by asking the FATES to transform Tiresias back into a man. They did as Poseidon requested and also took away temporarily Tiresias's gift of prophecy.

Goat   Of a she-goat as a sacrifice to the classical goddess APHRODITE, SAPPHO writes, "For you, Aphrodite, I will burn / the savory fat of a white she-goat. / All this will I leave behind for you." Also sacred to the Greek god PAN and DIONYSUS, the goat is symbolic of lust, creativity, humor, intoxication, sure-footedness, and bedevilment. In ASTROLOGY, the goat represents CAPRICORN. In Hindu religion the goat is sacred to Agni and KARTIKKEYEH. In Western European ritual magic, such as that practiced by Aleister CROWLEY, both the anus and the opening of the penis/phallus – together suggesting anal intercourse – have been referred to as the "eye of the goat." In twentieth-century Peru, the young male goat is symbolic of male homosexuality.

Goblin Market   Romantic poem by Christina Rossetti (1830-1894) considered a landmark of both lesbian-themed and Gothic literature. Rossetti appears to have been bisexual or lesbian and to have also pondered transgenderism, writing in "From the Antique", "I wish and I wish I were a man." As Lizzie and Laura, either sisters or friends referring to each other as such, are busy at work, they hear the voices of goblin men beckoning them to buy their magical fruits. Lizzie resists, but Laura succumbs. On returning home, Laura begins to hunger for more of the fruit and, refusing all other food, grows extremely ill. When she is approaching death, Lizzie, terribly worried about her, goes to the goblins to purchase more fruit. They do not want her money, however; they want her, and they are willing to force her to eat their fruit. While, for the most part, Lizzie manages to fend them off, the goblins smear her body with the juices of their fruits. When Lizzie returns home, she tells Laura to suck the juice off her body. This scene is depicted by Rossetti in a manner fusing the erotic and the magical, with Lizzie telling Laura, "Never mind my bruises, / Hug, kiss me, suck my juices / Squeezed from goblin fruits for you, / Goblin pulp and goblin dew. / Eat me, drink me, love me . . ."

Golden Bird, The   In this fairy tale collected by the brothers Grimm, a TRICKSTER fox helps a prince to obtain all he desires, including a princess; in turn, the prince aids in relieving the fox of a curse, with the latter returning to his original form, that of another prince. M. Duffy (1980) suggests that the "close relationship between the fox and the prince may be a homosexual one for which the rest of the story is an elaborate justification."

Golden Orchid Association   Rooted in the symbolism of the ORCHID, representing passionate friendships and embracing same-sex intimacy, this was a Chinese women's organization which emerged during or prior to the early twentieth century. Members of the Golden Orchid, or Jinglanhui (also *jin lan qi*), swore to help and protect each other. Many participated in ceremonies of UNION, which included a "wedding feast and an exchange of ritual gifts." Sexual practices of the women included "grinding TOFU." Some members married to one another adopted female children. To marry a man meant to be formally expelled from the Association.

Gomorrah   The Biblical city of Gomorrah does not appear to have become associated with lesbianism until the Middle Ages. The homoerotically inclined French writer Marcel Proust (1871-1922), in his novel *A La recherche du temps perdu* (*Remembrance of Things Past*, 1913-1927), was largely responsible for the popularization of the concept of Gomorrah as a lesbian utopia. In *Lesbian Peoples* (1976), Monique Wittig and Sande Zeig offer a magical, yet melancholy glimpse of Gomorrah: "That city . . . it is said, appears at times when the sun is particularly bright, with its golden roofs and its white marble terraces, in the bottom of the sea."

González, Babalorisha Omí Guillermo (1955-)
Cuban-American writer, artist, and priest of the Yoruba-diasporic religion. González, a spiritual son of the *orishá* YEMAYÀ, plays an important role in the religion by insisting upon the necessity of its spiritual authorities to move beyond personal homophobia and trans-phobia in order to embrace lesbian, gay, bisexual, and transgendered practitioners, as well as to acknowledge their contributions to the religion. González has also played an important role in the gay movement and in organizations helping persons living with AIDS as an openly gay priest of the Orisha tradition.

Goose In ancient Greece, a symbol of erotic love, sacred to APHRODITE; given by an *erastes* (lover) to an *eromenos* (beloved) as a courting-gift.

Gopi Female followers of KRISHNA, the Hindu god of music, dance, EROTICISM, playfulness, and beauty. The *gopis* are milkmaids or cowherds – or, in the world of Tom Robbins, "cowgirls" who worship the "blue" god – who are led by RADHA, his primary female companion. In certain tales told of Krishna and Radha's love, in which the *gopis* play a central role, female gender variance and lesbianism pervade the atmosphere. In one of these, from the *Brahma-vaivarta-purana*, we learn of a ritual dance carried out by the *gopis*. While a number of the *gopis* dress in male attire, others dress in female attire, playing "the parts of heroines courted by the males. Some assumed the form of Radha; and others, of Krishna. Some mixed freely with others. Some were embracing their companions."

Gorgoneion The face of a Gorgon as a symbol of protection against enemies or evil forces and of retributive justice. Linked to the AEGIS which by tradition belonged to ATHENA and primordial female power.

Gorgons Also called the Grim Ones, the Gorgons of Greek mythology are three sisters, Stheino ("Strength"), Euryale ("Wide Roaming"), and MEDUSA ("the Cunning One"). They have bronze claws and serpentine hair, golden wings, lizard-like skin, and the ability to turn men into stone at a glance. In contemporary lesbian feminism, Gorgons have been (re-) claimed as "symbols of women's rage." Emily Culpepper relates a story wherein she confronts and subdues an attacker who has entered her house by transforming her face into that of a "Gorgon, a Medusa." She continues, "the Gorgon has much vital, literally life-saving, information to teach women about anger, rage, [and] power . . . needed for survival." In Elana

DYKEWOMON's book of poetry *They Will Know Me by My Teeth*, the Gorgon becomes a potent signifier of lesbian-feminism and particularly of lesbian separatism. Freudian psychology has suggested that the Gorgons, especially Medusa, signify castration. Diana Russell concurs that the Gorgons can "signify women's capacity to emasculate men's nuclear phallacies." In a powerful anti-war poem Barbara Deming writes: "This is a song for Gorgons – / Whose dreaded glances in fact can bless. / The men who would be gods we turn / Not to stone but to mortal flesh and blood and bone. / If we could stare them into accepting this, / The world could live at peace." Mary Daly and Jane Caputi (1987) describe the Gorgon as "She whose face can stop a clock." Women become Gorgons, they say, because of the need to turn the "madmen into stone," to stop "the doomsday men with their doomsday clocks."

Gospel of Philip Gnostic Christian text suggesting that the division into male and female consititues the Biblical "Fall." JESUS Christ will return to reunite male and female into one androgynous being.

Gospel of Thomas Gnostic text of the second century CE in which JESUS suggests that it is necessary for women to transform from female into male to obtain salvation. Jesus relates that he must "attract" Mary Magdalene to him in order "to make her male so that she too might become a living spirit . . . For every female that becomes male will enter the kingdom of heaven." While some scholars view this passage as misogynistic, others suggest that it promotes transgenderism. .

Gouillé Dance performed, especially at CARNIVAL-time in Port-au-Prince, Haiti, by practitioners of Vodou and others. *Gouillé* refers to a grinding of the hips. The dance is frequently linked to cross- or mixed dressing, transgenderism, and same-sex eroticism. In *Dances of Haiti* (1983), African-American dancer, choreographer, and dance historian Katherine Dunham writes of the gouillé : "With nightfall, all possible remaining restrictions are automatically cast aside, and the play element becomes decidedly orgiastic . . . Homosexual activity is very common to these mass bands. It is not at all unusual to see two men in the embrace of the *gouillé*." Dunham notes that even a presumably heterosexual man "will, under the increasing momentum of the MARDI GRAS, seek out persons of his own sex for erotic dances."

Graces The Greek Charites, more commonly known by their Roman name, the Graces, were sea spirits who bestowed persons with the quality of grace, teaching etiquette and presiding over banquets. R. E. Bell (1991) notes that "none of the Charites [i.e. Graces] seems to have had a sexual liaison" with a man. Lesbian women in the THIASOS, or religious household, of SAPPHO participated in rites honoring these spirits. A contemporary queering of the spirits is offered by Della Grace in her photograph *Three Graces* (1992), which depicts three women with shaved heads who are wearing only black leather boots, standing in weeds, and embracing.

Grahn, Judy (1940-)   Lesbian writer, instructor, activist, and major force in Women's Spirituality and Gay Spirituality. In *The Queen of Wands* (1982), the first text in a poetic cycle inspired by the four Queens of the TAROT cards, Grahn weaves together the myths of many cultures with the experiences of living women to create an epic tale of a powerful woman/goddess, inspired by the Greek goddess/heroine HELEN, struggling both to survive and to transform the world in which she lives. The second text of this cycle, *The Queen of Swords* (1987), is based in large part on the Mesopotamian sacred narrative of the descent of the goddess INANNA/ISHTAR to the underworld and her encounter with the goddess ERESHKIGAL. In Grahn's verse play, Inanna, conflated with Helen, represents the maiden who must, with the crone (Ereshkigal) as soul-guide, come to confront and to honor her own shadow aspect. In Grahn's retelling, Ereshkigal becomes a dyke warrior-shaman, and the gateway to the underworld a lesbian tavern, the Crow Bar. Other figures appearing in the drama are the third gender or transgendered Kur and Gal here depicted as Radical Faeries. The two remaining texts in the cycle, *The Queen of Pentacles* and *The Queen of Cups*, have not yet appeared. Grahn's pivotal work on Gay Spirituality, *Another Mother Tongue: Gay Words, Gay Worlds* (1984), a postmodern collage, contains a wealth of information on the origins of numerous terms (such as "fairy") and symbols (such as green) blended with events from Grahn's own life experience. This work continues in *The Highest Apple: Sappho and the Lesbian Poetic Tradition* (1985), wherein Grahn meticulously traces the interrelationship of lesbian poetics and the mythic or sacred to antiquity, revealing how this tradition has survived, transformed, and been enriched by way of interaction with non-Euro-western woman-centered spiritual cultures. Women's spiritual bonding is also a focus of Grahn's speculative fiction *Mundane's World* (1988), which culminates in a celebration inclusive of honoring MENSTRUATION. This honoring of menstruation is the focus of Grahn's nonfiction text *Blood, Bread, and Roses: How Menstruation Created the World* (1993). In this richly documented text, Grahn reveals the multiple ways in which menstruation appears to have contributed to the development of human consciousness and cultures. Herein, she also introduces readers to the concept of the "metaform," defining the term as a metaphor that has moved from being a description of analogical similarity to an "embodied" concept. It is the difference between comparison and profound resonance or identity.

Grant, Kenneth (1924-)   English occult writer in the tradition of Aleister CROWLEY. While Grant is the author of numerous illuminating texts on MAGIC and mysticism, including *Nightside of Eden* (1977) and *Outside the Circles of Time* (1980), his prejudiced and homophobic evaluation of same-sex desire and transgenderism are curious; he considers these to be a "perversion of magical practice." This seems especially hypocritcal in light of both Crowley's bi- or pansexuality and Grant's acceptance of many other erotic activities generally considered perverse. While worlds apart in other respects, Grant shares this animosity toward same-sex desire and transgenderism with fellow occultists Dion FORTUNE, Gareth KNIGHT, and William Butler YEATS.

Graves, Robert (1895-1985)   British poet whose major work, *The White Goddess* has profoundly influenced neopaganism, Wicca, and the Women's Spirituality movements. The White Goddess is burdened, however, by Graves's internalized homophobia and transgender-phobia. As Diane Purkiss (1992) wisely and sarcastically points out, the Goddess, in Graves's view, "is important . . . chiefly because she prevents the dreaded onset of . . . homosexuality. Her function, rapidly equated with the function of woman-in-poetry, is to stand between men and other men, inspiring healthy heterosexual songs."

Green   At EPHESUS, the transgendered, often homoerotically inclined male priest/esse/s of the goddess ARTEMIS/DIANA – who was herself associated with gender variance as well as with lesbian desire – wore garments primarily of scarlet, violet, saffron, and yellow-green or chartreuse. In ancient Rome, as we discover in Martial's *Epigrams* and elsewhere, green, and especially yellow-green (in Latin, *galbinatus*), was likewise associated with male gender variance and the receptive role in homoeroticism. Indeed, gender variant, homoerotically inclined males came to be called *galbinati*. Martial describes an effeminate man, whom he nicknames Malchiones (after *malakos*, "soft, effeminate"), as "garbed in green" and as lying on a purple couch, fanned with red feathers by a like-minded man. Martial, assuming an anti-homoerotic pose, describes the morality of such men as "grass-green." In pre-modern France, green appeared as a color chosen for the tights of *mignons* (basically, gender variant, often bisexually- or homoerotically inclined male courtiers). According to Ida Nelson (1976), and exemplified by numerous tapestries and paintings, the colors of tights worn by *mignons* were often green, yellow, or red, or some combination of these. Indeed, *mignons* often wore bi-colored tights, as, for example, with one leg yellow and the other green. Nelson writes: "In the fifteenth century, this style, among young men . . . was emphasized and exaggerated . . . [They] would wear tights with one leg of one color and the second of another . . . This style was associated with a class of men whose homosexual behavior was known to all." The color combination employed in the costume of the *mignons* may be derived from three sources, namely, the costumes of historical troubadours, fools, and legendary fairies. From at least the twelfth century, troubadours (one might also say *jongleurs*) had traditionally worn costumes of yellow and green complimented by red cloaks. The costume of the fool was "traditionally of variegated yellow and green." Maurice Lever notes, "These are the colors of folly." In French, as in English, folklore, fairies typically dress in yellow, green, and red. French sophisticates remained aware of the ancient Greco-Roman association of *galbinus*, or yellow-green, with effeminacy and homoeroticism. Associations of green with figures on the margins or altogether outside society may have been partly responsible for green becoming equated with heresy; thus, explains Lever, "In the ceremonies of auto-da-fé, the heretic carried in procession a green cross." Green may have also served Andrew Marvell (1621-1678) and other British poets of the time as a signifier of homosexuality, in contrast to red and white, which in seventeenth century signified – generally speaking – women and heterosexual attraction. In "The Garden," Marvell writes, "No white nor red was ever seen / So amorous as this lovely green." The ancient association of green, male gender variance, and homoeroticism apparently survived into, or was reclaimed during, the nineteenth century, when a band of Parisian men adopted the green cravat as a badge of homoerotic inclination, and when the green carnation was adopted as a kindred symbol by Oscar WILDE and the English Decadents. In the early twentieth century, in his "Ode to Walt Whitman," the Spanish poet Federico García LORCA described men-loving men as those with a "green stare" (*mirada verde*). Since that time, green has continued to be associated with gay men; it has become linked as well to women-loving women. Both lesbian women and gay men have, for many years now, chosen to wear, or made certain not to wear, green (especially green socks) on Thursday, that day being designated "Fairy Day." In the 1939 film THE WIZARD OF OZ, starring Judy Garland – perhaps the best loved of all films among members of the queer-identified communities of the West – the Wicked Witch sports a chartreuse face, reflected in the glittering towers of the Emerald City.

Grey Enyo, latter associated with the goddess MA, was one of the Graeae, or "Grey maids." They were the protectors of the GORGONS. Also in the poetry of Elsa GIDLOW, grey is symbolic of ashes, the aftermath of fiery lesbian passion. In "The Artist," she writes, "Let us leave off loving, My Lady, / You have kissed me grey," and in "Constancy," she speaks of "Those first burned ash-grey – far too passionate."

Groa Amazonian companion of ALFHILD. Groa and Alfhid belonged to a group of Saxon, Goth, and Swedish women who fought against the Danes.

Gullveig Amazonian sorceress and warrior of Scandinavian, or Teutonic, religion or mythology whose name means "gold-madness" or "gold-might," referring to her flesh, which was made of gold. She was slain and subsequently returned to life on at least three occasions.

Gun In Chinese Shamanism (also referred to as traditional Chinese religion), a deity of agriculture who is credited with the invention of farming tools. Gun is also a god of FISHING and is frequently portrayed as a fish. He is alternately depicted as the father or intimate male companion of the god YU. Together, they are sometimes portrayed as intertwined male SERPENTS, possibly in the act of copulation. Ping-leung Chan (1972) writes: "This is reminiscent of the story in the *Kuo yu* that two male dragons copulated in Hsia court. My suggestion inevitably leads to the question of incest. In Genesis, Noah and his son Ham were incestuous. Therefore, it is not inconceivable that Kun and Yu were incestuous, too."

Gwidonot Society of pre-Christian Celtic Amazons possibly participating in lesbian relationships.

Gwrach y Rhibyn In the visionary cosmos of Jessica Amanda Salmonson and Jules Remedios Faye in *Wisewomen and Boggy-boos* (1992), this Welsh banshee mentioned by both Katherine Briggs and John Rhys, attains or reasserts a lesbian identity. Known as the "Washer of the Ford," Gwrach y Rhibyn is associated with the Celtic Mother Goddess Ana or Danu, as well as with the Medieval fairy-goddess Morgan Le Fay. She is alternately depicted as a beautiful maiden or a CRONE washing bloody garments in a stream. She is occasionally portrayed as a woman with bat wings dressed in black. Gwrach y Rhibyn strides invisibly alongside the woman she wants to warn of impending death. When they come to a crossroads or a river, she beats the ground or splashes the water, shrieking unhappily, "My wife! My Wife! My wife!"

Gymnopedia (or **Gymnopaedike**) At Athens this was a ritual dance performed by nude male youths who imitated the rhythmic movements of WRESTLING and boxing. Several styles of this serious and majestic ceremony are known, including the Bacchic, danced in honor of DIONYSUS, and the Oschophoria, in honor of ATHENA and THESEUS. At Sparta, the Gymnopedia was an annual festival held in honor of APOLLO, ARTEMIS/DIANA, and LETO. There, its primary participants were young nude females and males. Many of the young women among them, ancient sources indicate, shared intimate relationships with other women. The term *gymnopediste* survived into the late nineteenth century as a French bohemian expression for "lesbian." The French composer Erik Satie (1866-1925) reclaimed the ancient spirit of this festival in his piano pieces entitled *Gymnopèdies*.

Gypones Spartan cross-dressing male dancers who danced on wooden stilts using leaping movements.

H

H. D. (Hilda Doolittle, 1886-1961)   Bisexual poet and
novelist whose loves included Ezra Pound, Frances
Josepha Gregg, Richard Aldington, and Bryher (Annie
Winifred Ellerman). Profoundly influenced by SAPPHO,
H. D. was learned in ancient Greek religion and mythology
as well as in spiritualism (spirit mediumship, or
CHANNELING), numerology, the TAROT and the
QABBALAH. As a client of Sigmund Freud, she also
became versed in the interpretation of dreams. Her poem
"The Master" is among those which subtly refers to her
bisexuality, her gynandrous or transgendered identity, and
her spirituality (here, a syncretism of Christianity and
Goddess Reverence). "I had two loves," she says of her
bisexuality, "God who loves all mountains / alone knew
why." Of her gender variance, she writes, "she needs no
man, / herself / is that dart and pulse of the male." Of her
spirituality, she invokes APHRODITE, "that Lord become
woman," as "her limbs fling wide in dance / ecstatic."

Haakaulianani   In Hawaiian mythology or religion, a
male servant with whom both WAKEA, the sky father, and
PAPA, the earth mother, appear to have shared an intimate
(AIKANE) relationship. Haakauilanani's name contains the
element *kauila*, which is a kind of wood used in making
walking sticks and which is symbolic of the phallus.

Hadad (also **Attah**)   Male consort of the Near Eastern –
primarily Phoenician – goddess ATARGATIS. According
to Lucian (c. 120-c. 180 CE), Hadad castrated himself after
offending the Goddess by taking up with a mortal woman.
While divine or semi-divine himself, Hadad thereafter
became a GALLUS priest (a name also employed by the
priests of the goddess CYBELE), dressing in feminine attire,
leading an itinerant life, and singing praises of the Goddess
wherever he went. Indeed, Hadad is depicted as a messiah
who descended to earth in order to teach mortals how, by
following the path of the Goddess, they might achieve
salvation and everlasting life.

Hades (Roman **Pluto**)   Phallic god of wealth and the
Underworld in Greek mythology or religion, famous for
having abducted the maiden PERSEPHONE to become his
queen and co-ruler. He became associated with
ritual/cultic homoeroticism by way of the tale of
DIONYSUS and PROSYMNUS, in which Dionysus
promised the latter that he would have sex with him if
Prosymnus would give him directions to the kingdom of
Hades. Both Hades and Dionysus were honored in rituals
with trance-dances employing artificial phalli. Hades is

invoked in ancient lesbian love/binding spells given in the
Greek Magical Papyri as "Blessed lord of the immortals,
holding the scepters of Tartaros and of terrible, fearful
Styx and of life-robbing Lethe, the hair of Kerberos [or
Cerberus] trembles in fear of you, you crack the loud whips
of the ERINYES; the couch of Persephone delights you."

Hadrian, Publius Aelius (76-138)   Homoerotically
inclined Roman emperor, lover of ANTINOUS and initiate
in the ELEUSINIAN MYSTERIES of the Greek goddesses
DEMETER and PERSEPHONE. When Antinous died,
Hadrian established a mystery cult in his memory, likening
him to a savior deity.

Haecke, Father Louis van (1828-1912)   Belgian
Catholic priest alleged to have begun performing phallic,
possibly Satanic, masses in Belgium and in Paris in the
later nineteenth century. Known for his psychic powers,
van Haecke was a friend of the French occultist Stanislas
de Guaita (1861-1897). While van Haecke, wearing a
skullcap with horns, stood before an altar dressed with
phallic statues, reciting heretical prayers, a male servant
masturbated him, with van Haecke ultimately ejaculating
on the host, which was then shared by celebrants. Both
then removed their robes to display their erections. An
orgy followed. Somewhat ironically, van Haecke and de
Guaita became mortal enemies of Joseph-Antoine Boullan
(1824-1893), a defrocked Roman Catholic priest who also
performed phallic, perhaps Satanic, masses.

Hag(s)   Elder women, sometimes called CRONES, who,
especially in British folklore, are practitioners of
Witchcraft. The term also refers to the deceased female
ancestors of such women. According to Katharine Briggs
(1976), hags represent "the last shadows of a primitive
nature goddess [known as] the Cailleach Bheur, Black
Annis, or Gentle Annie." Lesbian-feminist theologian
Mary DALY (1987) has reclaimed "hag" as a term honoring,
rather than dishonoring, these ancient associations and the
power of independent, including lesbian, women. The hag
is "a Witch, FURY, [or] Harpy who haunts the
Hedges/Boundaries of patriarchy, frightening fools and
summoning Weird Wandering Women into the Wild."

Hagakure (c. 1716)   "A Life Hidden Behind the Leaves,
"a text of martial-spiritual philosophy explaining
BUSHIDO, or the "Way of the Samurai," by Japanese
samurai-author Yamamoto Tsunetomo (1649-1719).
Rooted primarily in Zen Buddhism, *Hagakure* stresses

dying a glorious death. One of its other primary subjects is *shudo*, the devotion of male warrior-lovers in long-term relationships. In this type of relationship, which often commences as a mentor-pupil relationship, the beloved is called the *shudo*, while the lover is called the *nenja*. Yamamoto relates: "[When] you have had relations with your *nenja* for five years or so and you have found him to be really loyal, you must then put your trust in him completely. Because he is the person for whom you sacrifice you life, you really must see into his heart." Ideally, the lovers should join one another in death by way of *seppuku*, roughly, ritual disembowelment. The acclaimed writer Yukio MISHIMA (1925-1970) was deeply inspired by *Hagakure*, writing, "[It is] the womb from which my writing is born."

Hagésichora (or **Hagesikhora**, c. 600 BCE) Chief priestess of a spiritual household, or THIASOS, of women in ancient Sparta which worshipped ARTEMIS Orthia and/or the dawn-goddess AOTIS. Hagésichora celebrated a ritual same-sex UNION with another priestess of the house, Agido, probably around 600 BCE.

Hair Generally symbolic of the life-force, hair in many cultures as an important signifier of gendered, erotic, and spiritual identity. In the ancient Near East as well as in ancient cultures of the Mediterranean, male deities and legendary figures thought to be transgendered, or to have transgendered manifestations, such as ADONIS, AMPHION, APOLLO, ASUSHUNAMIR, ATTIS, DIONYSUS, and TIRESIAS are often portrayed as having long, flowing hair, or hair dressed in a traditionally feminine style. In these regions as well, gender variant, often homoerotically inclined male priests, especially of female deities but also of androgynous male gods, frequently dressed in feminine attire, or in a combination of feminine, masculine, and sacerdotal attire, let their hair grow long, and dressed it elaborately, as did the ASSINNU of the goddess INANNA/ISHTAR, the MEGABYZOI of ARTEMIS, the FANATICI of MA, the BAPTAI of KOTYS, and the GALLI of CYBELE. The *megabyzoi* wore their hair in a feminine style with a plait of hair looped in front of each ear, while the *fanatici* dyed their hair blonde and wore it in braids, or wore blonde wigs. The *galli* let their hair grow long, frequently to their waists; indeed, they were nicknamed the "longhaired ones." They rarely let their hair down in public, however, except during ecstatic dance rituals. The rest of the time they wore elaborate hairstyles, having their hair curled, corkscrewed, or calamistred. Those who were partially or altogether bald wore wigs. The Roman rhetorician Quintillian (35-100) and the Christian bishop Clement of Alexandria (c. 150-c. 220) appear to have been especially irritated by this excessive attention to hair grooming, a fashion which seemed to be rapidly spreading to the male population at large.

Quintillian attacked the *galli* and other males for dressing "their locks by scorching them with the curling iron," while Clement complained of those who carried mirrors with them in order, so he thought, to comb their hair and clip stray hairs. "Oh, these preoccupations of immoral androgynes," Clement wailed, "and their coifing sessions!" The *galli*, moreover, like Mâ's *fanatici*, dyed their hair blonde, "from the religious belief that the Goddess would only accept offerings of blonde hair." The hair of the *galli* could be cut on only three occasions: when they wished to sacrifice a lock to the Goddess by hanging it from the branch of a sacred tree; when, due to grave illness or advanced age, they felt they could no longer actively serve the Goddess; and at the time of death. The *galli* also practiced depilation, using depilatories of "resin, pitch, white vine or ivy gum extracts, ass's fat, she-goat's gall, bat's blood, and powdered viper" or of a less Macbethian compound of arsenic and bryonia. The *galli* practiced depilation in order to more closely resemble women and the Goddess as well as to appear younger and to attract certain males. This custom, like that of wearing perfume, quickly spread to the general male populace. In *The Art of Love*, Ovid warned young men not to curl their hair or depilate their legs, telling them to "Leave such matters as those to the members of Cybele's chorus, / Howling their bacchanal strains under the dark of the moon." During the first centuries of the Common Era, salons for depilation may have outnumbered traditional barbershops. Dio Chrysostom especially condemns the depilation of the genital area as an action growing out of men's desire to become women, complaining that the men of his day see masculine males as "defective" and thus desire to become "whole beings and natural – epicenes!" Attacking depilation in particular and the "perversity of modern tastes" in general, Quintillian bemoans the fact that men's admiration of the artificial over the natural has led them to "glow with a complexion that is not their own." Arnobius insists that God has not created men to wear jewelry, curl their hair, wear makeup, or engage in gender variant or homoerotic behavior. Another writer poses this question, "Does anyone doubt that the man who wears perfume, who practices depilation, and who reclines in a full-length tunic on the inner side of a divan at a symposium is a *cinaedus*?" Aristophanes wrote that males, including the *galli*, who depilated themselves and who engaged in related practices should be burned alive "upon a heap of sixteen wooden phalluses." Also having long hair (or bald, its opposite) are deities and legendary figures also associated with homosexuality or bisexuality but usually not with transgenderism, including MARSYAS, PAN, and the SATYRS AND SILENOI. The latter two are hybrid goat-humans and horse-humans who are attendants of the effeminate DIONYSUS. These figures appear to have been represented by traditionally masculine men in ritual and in drama (especially in satyr plays), and portraits of them in the company of Dionysus and others suggest that they may have signified the masculine – or, in today's terms, "butch" – partners in same-sex relationships. Where female gender variance is concerned, goddesses, AMAZONS, and legendary figures are typically portrayed as having either short hair cut in a traditionally masculine manner, such as the haircut of PALAESTRA, goddess of wrestling, or wild, serpentine hair, like the hair of MEDUSA and the FURIES. RHODOGUNE (fl. second century BCE), an Amazonian warrior-queen of Parthia who fought against the Armenians, was famous for her disheveled hair, as she had gone into battle immediately following a bath. In terms of other ancient European cultures, most data collected to date concern males. The ENAREES of the goddess ARTIMPASA of Scythia wore their hair long. The Celtic deity CERNUNNOS, like the satyrs and silenoi above, is depicted as being bald or as having long, curly hair; in Germanic legendary history, Haddingr, a favorite of the gods ODIN and FREYR who practiced SEIDR magic, may have dressed his hair in a feminine style. SCRAT, a figure of Germanic and Anglo-Saxon myth, is described as a "hairy androgyne" (differing in this respect from the satyrs and silenoi), as is BAPHOMET, allegedly revered by the ORDER OF THE KNIGHTS TEMPLAR. In the Christian tradition, the cutting of men's hair signifies asceticism, while the cutting of women's hair signifies both asceticism and transgenderism, as in the case of SAINT MARGARITA, a beautiful noblewoman who, despising the institution of marriage, cut her hair, donned masculine attire, and sought refuge, as a young man named Pelagius, at a nearby monastery. Other female saints are also known for cutting their hair and wearing it in a masculine style, the most renowned being JEANNE D'ARC (Joan of Arc). In the legendary history of SAINTS SERGIUS AND BACCHUS, the identical "page-boy" haircut appearing on both members of this twinlike couple has over the centuries become an element of homoerotic iconography. The Church, employing the State to create sumptuary laws, has periodically condemned the wearing of certain hairstyles, especially those which have been linked to transgenderism, same-sex passion, and luxury or decadence. Exemplary of the Church's proscriptive attitude concerning hair is its campaign during the Middle Ages to outlaw hairstyles and garments associated with the Normans, especially long, curled hair and pointed goatees. In 1094, Christian authorities demanded that all males entering churches avoid these fashions. To refuse to obey would mean to sacrifice communion and proper Christian burial. The Church reiterated its edict in 1096 and again in 1102 and 1103 because so many, including members of the clergy, refused to submit. Turning to Hinduism, several deities associated with gender and/or sexual variance are depicted as having remarkable hair; these include the god VASANTA, who has beautiful curly, black hair, and the goddess YELLAMMA, who has matted hair. The JOGAPPA

and JOGAMMA, male and female devotees of Yellamma, wear a hairstyle meant to resemble this goddess' hair. Likewise, the transgendered HIJRAS of the goddess BAHUCHARAMATA wear a hairdo meant to resemble that of the goddess: "the hair of the head is put up like women's, well oiled, combed, and thrown back, tied into a knot, and shelved to the left side, sometimes plaited, ornamented . . . the whiskers, mustache and beard [are] closely shaven." In the Arabic world, especially in Egypt, the AL-JINK (or El-Gink[eyn]), males linked to pre-Islamic Goddess Reverence and the reverence of JINN, wore female attire, including kohl eye makeup, perfume of attar-of-roses, garments of muslin, and braided and pomaded hair. In Japan, the great Shinto goddess AMATERASU OMI KAMI, possessing subtle links to both lesbianism and transgenderism, is sometimes portrayed as a warrior-shaman who puts "up her hair like that of a warrior . . . taking up a bow and quiver." In the milieu of Japanese Buddhism, *kasshiki* were novices known for their magnificent costumes and "shoulder length and modishly" styled hair, to which older monks appear to have been greatly attracted. Among actors, especially of the seventeenth century, the so-called *mae-gami* locks of hair at the forehead, seen as a mark of beauty, signified homoerotic inclination and, occasionally, male prostitution. During the seventeenth century, a sumptuary law was made against the wearing of the *mae-gami* hairstyle, with theatres remaining closed until actors agreed to cut the *mae-gami* and to shave the front part of the forehead. Among African peoples, the gender variant male *jo apele*, who served as spiritual functionaries to the Lango, dressed in women's garments, decorated their faces like women, and wore their hair long. Among the Kenyan Meru, the *mugawe*, a "powerful religious leader" who is "considered a complement to . . . male political leaders," sometimes wears women's clothing and hairstyles. Among the Yoruba, the androgynous *orishá* (deity) OLOKUN is depicted as having beautiful, flowing hair. The Amazonian female *orishá* OYA is sometimes served by gender variant males who wear her bell-shaped or "beehive" hairdo; the male *orishá* SHANGO, who occasionally wears a feminine braided hairdo himself, is also served by men wearing feminine hairstyles. The *orishá* OGUN is the patron of hairstylists. In traditions of Shamanism, such as those found in North Asia and North America, female gender variance, as in the case of the goddess SEDNA, is often marked by wild or matted hair, while male gender variance, as among gender variant, third gender, or TWO-SPIRIT shamans, is commonly marked by the wearing of elegant feminine hairstyles, including the chignon braid and, as among Hidatsa two-spirit male shamans, special feathers worn in the hair. Noteworthy in this respect are the TUPILAK, figures carved by Inuits on the fronts of kayaks depicting androgynous or transgendered beings bearing feminine chignon hairstyles, mustaches, female breasts, and phalluses. In the Navaho tradition, the deity BEGOCHIDI is remarkable in that he is described as having light skin, golden or red hair, and blue eyes. His hair color may have to do with his parentage, as he is considered the child of the Sun. Also in the Navaho tradition, the two-spirit NADLE, the mythic ancestor of all other two-spirit males, invented the hairbrush. In the Aztec religion of Mesoamerica, transgendered, allegedly homoerotically inclined priest/esse/s of the goddess XOCHIQUETZAL wore the knotted braids of the goddess, while the hair of the priests of the god TEZCATLIPOCA, which the priests wore quite long, was thick and matted with blood. In Pacific cultures, gender variant male shamans also wore feminine hairstyles, with the pre-Christian Philippino BAYOGUIN tying "his hair up like a woman's," the Ngaju Dayak BASIR parting his hair in the middle, and the Iban Dayak MANANG BALI wearing a chignon braid. In the nineteenth century, Karl Heinrich Ulrichs (1825-1895) observed that in Constantinople (Istanbul), "even today the youths who have Mannlings [i.e. other males] as lovers carry a lock of their hair. A young person there who carries a lock of hair is considered without a doubt to be the lover of an Urning [i.e. a lover of men]." Although not as linked to religion or spirituality as in the past, the interrelationship of hair, transgenderism, same-sex intimacy, and the symbolic continues to express itself in the late twentieth century, especially as a way of expressing nonconformity to the dominant culture, alliance to a subcultural or countercultural group, or both.

Hairy Meg Female brownie (a type of British FAIRY) and TRICKSTER perceived as hairy and masculine or what we might term in the late twentieth century "butch". Associated with PUCK in Shakespeare's *Midsummer Night's Dream*, Hairy Meg is identified with, or resembles, Maug Moulach.

Hall, Radclyffe (1880-1943) British lesbian novelist best known for her novel *The Well of Loneliness* (1928). "John," as Hall preferred to be called, was fascinated by spiritualism, an interest nurtured by her relationship with Mabel "Ladye" Veronica Batten and carried into her relationship with Una Lady Troubridge. Commencing in 1916, Hall was a frequent client of Mrs Osborne, a renowned medium especially known for CHANNELING a young female spirit named Feda. Encouraged by Sir Oliver Lodge, Hall and Troubridge joined the respected Society for Psychical Research. In *Our Three Selves: The Life of Radclyffe Hall* (1985), Michael Baker writes of Hall's belief in psychic forces and reincarnation: "She and Ladye [Batten] had always believed in the existence of supra-normal forces . . . they [attributed] their own remarkable empathy to the fact that they had known each other in a former incarnation. They were receptive to instances of telepathy . . . They had always said that their love would

survive death." Baker adds that Hall "was much attracted by the ineffable, by a vision of life that emphasized the unity and timelessness of all creation."

Hamilton, Edith (1867-1963) Mythographer and historian born in Dresden, Germany and educated at Bryn Mawr College in the US. Her books include *The Greek Way* (1930), *Mythology* (1942), and *The Roman Way* (1932). She was also the translator of *The Trojan Women* (1937) and the *Collected Dialogues of Plato* (1961). *The New York Times* review of *Mythology* (1942) stated, "Its merit is largely derived from the author's interest in Greek and Roman myths, which she sees not merely as outworn fancies of dead antiquity, but as living fables not wholly deprived of meaning for our time." Her translation of Euripides' tragedy *The Trojan Women* was adapted by director/screenwriter Michael Cacoyannis in his powerful 1971 film starring Katharine Hepburn, Vanessa Redgrave, Genevieve Bujold, and Irene Papas. Hamilton was the lover of Doris Fielding Reid for sixty years.

Han Temple Mysterious homosexual organization and colony centered on an island near Thailand, established circa 1936 and apparently surviving into the early 1950s. The Han Temple appears to have been the brainchild of the equally elusive Homosexual World Organization, one of whose alleged sponsors was the French homosexual writer André GIDE. Affiliated with other secret societies including the Buddha-Shakti Sect of Siam, the High Rooms of Macao, the Moon Flower Rooms of China, and the Sons of Mauna Loa of Hawaii, the goals of the Han Temple appear to have been promoting gay political and spiritual consciousness. It seems that both Buddhism and Euro-western occult traditions, including astrology, wielded an influence on members of the Temple. The Temple also allegedly attempted to integrate Euro-western and indigenous Southeast Asian traditions of same-sex eroticism, members being of Thai, Chinese, Dutch, German, and other backgrounds. Scholarly research on the Han Temple and the other societies mentioned above remains to be done.

Hansel and Gretel This tale, as told to the brothers Grimm, concerns a young sister and brother who, while having a loving (although weak) father, are abused by their cruel stepmother. When the family is starving, the stepmother insists that she and their father take the children into the woods and leave them there to die. While in the forest, the children encounter a wicked witch who lives in a house made of sweets. She is ultimately cast into an oven meant for Hansel. In the opera by Humperdinck, first performed in 1893, the role of the witch is occasionally performed by a man. The tale is told as well in the contemporary musical *Into the Woods* (1988) by Stephen Sondheim and James Lapine. A transformation of the tale by poet Anne Sexton stresses the cruelty of the characters. At its culmination, Hansel and Gretel, "eating a chicken leg," their evil stepmother and the witch now dead, vaguely remember "the woe of the oven, / the smell of the cooking witch, / a little like mutton, / to be served only with burgundy / and fine white linen / like something religious." Occasionally, queer children and storytellers of the twentieth century transform the witch into a compassionate, wise crone, and her gingerbread house into a haven, a vision reflected in lesbian-feminist writer and activist Robin Morgan's poem "The Two Gretels" (c. 1976). Here, a good-natured Hansel stays at home "sending up flares" while Gretel and her twin or double sister/companion Gretel set out to explore the forest: "And eventually, they found the Gingerbread House, / and the Witch, who was really, they discovered, / the Great Good Mother Goddess, / and they all lived happily ever after."

Hapy (Roman **Nilus**) Androgynous god of the Nile in Egyptian religion and myth. Primarily male and depicted as bearded, Hapy nevertheless has female breasts. Hapy's head tops one of the four canopic jars, in which the internal organs of humans are housed when their bodies are mummified. Hapy's jar held the lungs of the mummified person. Hapy was sometimes depicted as a DOUBLE deity or as a pair of androgynous twins named Hap-Reset, Lord of the South Nile, and Hap-Meht, Lord of the North Nile. Egyptians believed that "without the waters of Hapy, every living thing would perish." In Roman times, Hapy became linked to the astrological sign of AQUARIUS. In this way, he also became linked to GANYMEDE, as a bearer of liquids. Hapy was served primarily by gender variant, possibly homoerotically inclined, priests. His (-her) cult was abolished formally by the Roman emperor and Christian zealot Constantine (306-337), in large part due to the emperor's hatred of transgendered male priest/esse/s. Papyrus and the lotus are sacred to Hapy; he (-she) is fêted on June 17. Practitioners of Islam have appropriated elements of Hapy's festival in their holiday Lêlet al-Nukta, the "Night of the Drop [of Celestial Water]."

Hare and Rabbit Kindred animals that are representative of the MOON, femininity, and erotic passion. In ancient Greek and Roman religion and myth, the animal is sacred to the goddesses ARTEMIS/DIANA (the Moon) – who has lesbian and Amazonian associations – and APHRODITE/VENUS (love and sexuality). The male hare was thought capable of bearing young and, perhaps for this reason, was associated with both transgenderism and same-sex eroticism. The poet Philostratus (fl. c. 200 CE) writes: "And let not the hare escape us, but let us . . . catch it alive as an offering most pleasing to Aphrodite . . . the hare . . . possesses the gift of Aphrodite [i.e. fertility] to an unusual degree . . . As for the male [hare], he not only [sires offspring], but also himself bears young, contrary to

nature." Men desiring other men, having "found in the hare a certain power to produce love," give hares as gifts, "attempting to secure the objects of their affection by a compelling magic art." The poet Ennodius (c. 473-521), in describing a man with a "masculine" face and "feminine" gestures who plays the active role in heterosexual relationships and both the active and receptive roles in same-sex relationships, chooses for the active role the symbol of a beast able to "trample the neck of a great lion," and for the receptive, the hare or rabbit. In Celtic legend, the hare was the companion of the Amazonian Queen BOUDICCA (fl. c. 60 CE). In Jewish and Christian folklore, the apocryphal *Epistle of Barnabas* claimed that Moses had condemned the eating of hares because he had felt this led to homosexuality. According to this view, the "hare grows a new anal opening each year, so that however many years he has lived, he has that many anuses." In the Middle Ages and the Renaissance, the hare retained its transgendered aspect. In "The Pregnant Monk," an anonymous Medieval tale (c. 1300) a monk, as the result of anal intercourse, becomes pregnant. The monk gives birth to a rabbit that appears at his side. In Renaissance ritual magic, hares were believed to change sex periodically, according to Cornelius Agrippa (1486-1535). P. Sébillot (1968) relates: "A storyteller of the sixteenth century reports . . . a legend . . . still popular at that time, which explains by way of episodes from the Biblical Flood the physical particularities of certain animals. In the course of a dispute on the question of knowing if there were in the Ark two beasts of every kind, one of the persons says, 'that there was only one hare, and that the female escaped from Noah and was lost in the water, and it's for this reason that the male carries himself like a female.' There has been collected in Anjou a variant of this little tale: 'Noah had cut a leg of the female rabbit to stop a leak, and she had died from this amputation, so that when the animals were leaving the Ark, there remained only the hare; in order to permit him to perpetuate the race, the All Mighty gave him the faculty of showing to the world the appearance of a young female rabbit, recognizable by the white star on the forehead'; certain hunters . . . affirmed that . . . hares (rabbits) changed sex each year." The hare also remained a signifier of same-sex love. John Boswell (1980) observes that the expression "a hare hunting hares" in a poem concerning the abduction of GANYMEDE by ZEUS refers to men passionately seeking others. Boswell speculates that "rabbit" or "hare" may have been employed as a slang term for homoerotically inclined men by homophobic persons as well as the homoerotically inclined themselves. In France, the connection between hares and those engaging in homoeroticism was strengthened as use of the term *bougre* ("bugger") became more widespread, as *bouc* (or *bougin*) was an alternate term for "hare" derived from the Old Norse *bukkr*. A French dictionary of the sixteenth century reports that Qabbalists believe that the souls of males engaging in same-sex eroticism are reincarnated as hares. In seventeenth-century England, many still remembered that rabbits with white stars or spots on their foreheads were sacred to Artemis/Diana and thus should be released by hunters. The term *"lapin"* ("hare", "rabbit") was used to signify a young male partner in same-sex eroticism in nineteenth-century French bohemian circles. In Chinese symbolism, the hare is also associated with male homosexuality. W. Eberhard (1986) notes that in China, "the belief that there are no male hares may be connected with the fact that the 'female' [i.e. receptive] partner in homosexual intercourse was known as the 'hare.' 'Hunting a hare' meant going to a brothel to look for a young man."

Harihara In Hinduism, male deity born of the union of the male deities SHIVA and VISHNU. His name means "Golden Ravisher." He is represented as a biune or double deity, akin to ARDHANARISHVARA, with Vishnu "occupying the female, left half" of his body and Shiva the "male," right half. Unlike Ardhanarishvara, however, he is depicted as a male-male being rather than as an androgyne *per se*. His left side is indigo, crowned, and holds a LOTUS and a mace; his right side is pale, wears Shiva's topknot, and bears the trident. As guardian of highways, he is represented as riding on horseback. Harihara is also thought to bring and to take away famine and PLAGUE, depending upon whether people make the appropriate sacrifices to him or not.

Haring, Keith (1958-1990) US gay painter and sculptor known primarily for his cartoon-like murals of dancing figures. Art historians and critics including Suzi Gablik, Robert Farris Thompson, Robert Pincus-Witten, and Maarten van de Guchte have observed in Haring's work the influence of the sacred arts of numerous cultures including those of the Inuit of East Greenland, the Nazca of Peru, and the Kongo of Africa and their descendants in the Americas. In "Requiem for the Degas of the B-Boys" (1990), Thompson notes that "from around 1981 onward Haring developed as his own spiritual copyright mark the Kongo sign of the solar round, a quartered circle signifying the cosmos," a sign upon which initiates stand to "seal a vow with God and the ancestors." When Thompson asked Haring about the use of the Kongo sign, or "cosmogram," Haring responded, "I had to draw a symbol to get the other world's [protection], a copyright mark that was more than legal, that was spiritually protective." Stressing the interrelationship of art and the sacred, Haring said in 1985, "art . . . should be something that liberates the soul." Haring died of AIDS-related illness at the age of thirty-one, having achieved international acclaim within a single decade.

Harjo, Joy (1951-) Native American Indian poet of the Creek nation. Harjo is also a screenwriter, literature professor, and player of tenor saxophone. Her works include *The Last Song* (1975), *What Moon Drove Me to This* (1980), *She Had Some Horses* (1983), *Secrets from the Center of the World* (1989, with Stephen Strom), and *In Mad Love and War* (1990). In her poems, Harjo's spirituality is rooted in Nature, in everyday life (reminiscent of the poetry of Adrienne RICH), and in those she cares deeply about, including women she has loved. The spirits she invokes have common names – Moon, White Bear, Wind, Coyote, Rabbit; these spirits are embodied in herself and those she loves. In "Remember," she writes, "Remember the sky that you were born under, / know each of the star's stories. / Remember the moon, know who she is. I met her / in a bar once in Iowa City." In "Grace," she recalls "Wind and her wild ways the year we had nothing to lose and lost it anyway in the cursed country of the fox," and in "The Book of Myths," she depicts an archetypally beautiful woman who might be named "Helen" or "Marilyn," but in Harjo's "subversive country," she is named "dark earth." Such women as this, Harjo relates, also call themselves "ripe, and pine tree."

Harpagmos Ritual abduction in ancient Greece of male youths by older lovers, often misinterpreted as "rape" (particularly by homophobic, otherwise puritanical, and simply ignorant writers). The rite was accepted by the families of the youths; their role in the drama was to pretend anxiety or disapproval. The lover, or *erastes*, would give the beloved, or *eromenos*, and his family gifts, after which he would carry him off to the wilderness to initiate him in the mysteries of manhood, including that of same-sex eroticism.

Harrison, Jane Ellen (1850-1928) One of the world's most brilliant classical scholars, who discovered evidence that a matrifocal civilization had preceded the establishment of patriarchal culture in the ancient Mediterranean. Inspiring such writers as Virginia Woolf, T. S. Eliot, and D. H. Lawrence, as well as a myriad of women of our day who are devoted to Women's Spirituality and Goddess Reverence, Harrison was the companion of writer Hope Mirrlees. One of Harrison's best known works is the *Prolegomena to the Study of Greek Religion* (1903).

Harrison, Lou (1917-) Openly gay American composer, many of whose works draw upon sacred and homoerotic themes. Harrison's music is informed by numerous non-western musics, including the gamelan music of Bali and Java. During the 1930s, he studied with Henry Cowell in San Francisco and Arnold Schoenberg in Los Angeles, California. During World War II, he joined John Cage in recitals of percussion music. Harrison has been inspired by spiritual traditions including the religions of Sumeria – he is especially drawn to the *Epic of GILGAMESH*-Greece, and Rome, and Renaissance mysticism. He is particularly drawn to angel imagery, especially as found in the work of the Medieval Persian philosopher Avicenna (980-1037). As a pacifist, Harrison is also inspired by Buddhism, employing Buddhist themes in works including *Avalokiteshvara* (1965), *Peace Piece One and Two* (1968, using passages from the poetry of Robert DUNCAN), and *La Koro Sutro* (1972). Many of his works draw upon the realms of myth, legend, and folklore, as well as ancient history, including incidental music for James Barrie's *Peter Pan* (1934) and Euripides's *Trojan Woman* (1938); the ballets *Orpheus* (1941), *Solstice* (1949), and *Io and Prometheus* (1951); the opera *Rapunzel* (1954); and the homoerotic puppet drama *Young Caesar* (1971, which concerns Caesar's affair with Nicomedes IV, King of Bithynia during the first century BCE). His 1955 work *Four Strict Songs for Eight Baritones and Orchestra* is exemplary in its focus on the realm of spirit. This is an avant-garde piece in which the musical elements include five note scales in equal temperament for mixed ensemble, percussion, including water bowls. The text is derived from a Navaho chant concerning the reverence of plants, animals, heavens, and minerals: "Here is Holiness – of the mountain's deer, and the scented fawn . . . / . . . Here is Nourishment of the tree, the fish, and the moon Ganymede encircling third, the largest planet . . . / . . . Here is splendor – Of the airplane, and the Cobra arching his head." Works which interweave same-sex desire and the spiritual or transpersonal include *May Rain* (1941) and *The Perilous Chapel*, both based on the work of lesbian poet Elsa GIDLOW; *Fragments from Calamus* (1946) based on the poetry of Walt WHITMAN; and *Scenes from Cavafy* (1979-1980), based on the work of homosexual poet C. P. CAVAFY. Same-sex love, Harrison believes, carries a spiritual force which can inspire both creativity and, like music, transformation. With his lover William Colvig, Harrison has created a number of musical instruments. Of Harrison's opus, one may safely say that the chief emphasis is on the "brotherhood and unity of all sentient beings."

Hartley, Marsden (1877-1943)   American poet and painter of homoerotic and mystical subjects. Hartley was profoundly inspired by the visions of the poets Walt WHITMAN and Setfan GEORGE. Hartley's visionary art was also inspired by the death of one of his lovers, Lieutenant Karl von Freyburg, who was killed during World War I in 1914, as well as by visions he experienced while living in Mexico and in Taos, New Mexico. His painting *Christ Held by Half-Naked Men* (1940-41) has been described as an "all-male pieta." Another painting, *Sustained Comedy; Portrait of an Object* (1939), depicts a tattooed man wearing lipstick who is being pierced in the eyes by arrows and in the forehead – which bears a triangle

– by a bolt of lightning, while butterflies circle his head. The butterflies may simultaneously represent the psyche, Whitman, and homoerotically inclined, gender variant men, playing on the Spanish slang term "*mariposa* " (effeminate gay man, or "queen"), while the arrows may allude to SAINT SEBASTIAN, a patron of homoerotically inclined men.

Harvey, Andrew (1952-   )   Gay writer and spiritual seeker of Anglo-Indian heritage, inspired primarily by Hinduism, Sufism, and Christianity. His works include *Hidden Journey: A Spiritual Awakening* (1991), *The Way of Passion: A Celebration of Rumi* (1994), and *The Return of the Mother* (1995). He is currently at work on a book concerning gay mystics.

Hatshepsut (d. c. 1479 BCE)   Egyptian transgendered female pharaoh of the eighteenth dynasty, portrayed as a man with a beard. The mortal representative of the god AMUN, her (-his) full name as pharaoh was Hatshepsut Khenemet-Amun – Hatshepsut "united with" Amun. V. L. Bullough and B. Bullough observe (1993): "Some have argued that Hatshepsut's cross dressing involved more than adopting the necessary symbolism to rule and expressed her desire to change her sex, since some surviving representations of her portray her with a penis."

Hay, Harry (1912-   )   Known to many as the "founder of the contemporary gay liberation movement," Hay, a native of Worthing, England now living in Los Angeles, is also one of the originators of the Gay Spirituality movement, and in particular, of the Radical Faeries. Hay's writings on the interrelationship of homosexuality or gayness and spirituality may be traced to the late 1960s and early 1970s when he began to speak of gay people organizing themselves into "far-ranging communities of Free Spirits". Since the mid-1970s, Hay and his lover John Burnside have been honing their vision of Gay Spiritual Consciousness. Of prime importance in this vision is the notion of gay people as constituting a "species-variant." As an effect of this separateness, this radical difference from others, gay people (and Hay refers primarily to gay men in his writings) view life experiences from a "gay window" which differs markedly from the view from the "window" of heterocentric patriarchal culture. Gay people, as an aspect of their separateness, also relate to each other in ways diverging widely from traditional heterosexual patterns. Specifically, Hay believes, gay men relate to each other as equal and kindred "subjects" rather than as "objects" (as is typical in heterosexist contexts). In recent years, Hay has begun to describe this radical separateness from others in terms of gays being "men of the third gender," drawing upon the Native American tradition of TWO-SPIRIT persons, which he has spent many years exploring. This separateness or third gender status links gay men or third gender men of many other epochs and cultures, men who have frequently made artistic and/or spiritual contributions to the societies in which they have lived. This different way of being, however, also carries with it responsibilities. In these, Hay includes not only nurturing other gay men but also struggling against racism, and guarding the earth from further devastation. While Hay is respected and loved by many in the gay and queer communities, he has not escaped controversy. His support of intergenerational relationships, his alleged negative attitudes toward heterosexuals and bisexuals ("Faeries must begin to throw off the filthy green frog-skin of Hetero-imitation"), and his alleged essentialism (gays constitute a "species-variant") have made many uncomfortable with his central role in Gay Spirituality and the Faerie movement. Hay, however, is constantly metamorphosing, as Stuart Timmons observes in his fascinating biography *The Trouble with Harry Hay: Founder of the Modern Gay Movement* (1990). Hay's writing is a remarkable brew of political manifesto, mystical treatise and Beat-inspired poetic prose. Typical of his writing is this passage from "A Separate People Whose Time Has Come" (1983): "We have been a separate people, drifting together . . . here and there as spirit-people . . . Shamans . . . priestesses and priests . . . healers and nurturers . . . [and] almost all of them were visionaries . . . Almost all of them were rebels."

Heard, Gerald (Henry Fitzgerald Heard, 1889-1971) Gay writer and mystic. Of Irish heritage, Heard was born in London. He attended Cambridge and intended to become a priest in the Church of England (as his paternal grandfather had been) until, near 1916, he realized that his conflicts with Christianity were insurmountable. After a lengthy illness, Heard spent several years in Ireland working with the Irish Agricultural Cooperative Movement. During this period, he became friends with a number of Irish writers and mystics associated with the Celtic Revival, including A. E. Russell, Lady Gregory, and even the homophobic William Butler YEATS. Returning to London, he became active in the London Society for Psychical Research; around this time he also became friends with Aldous and Julian Huxley. In 1937, he traveled with Aldous and his wife Maria to New York. On this trip, he encountered Swami Prabhavananda, ultimately becoming a disciple of the Swami and a follower of Vedanta, a philosophico-spiritual tradition rooted in, but departing considerably from, Hinduism. Settling in southern California, where he became friends with Christopher ISHERWOOD, fellow disciple of Prabhavananda, Heard established Trabuco College near Los Angeles. The goal of this college was to instruct students in comparative religion, with an emphasis on practice, including meditation and communal effort. Unfortunately, the experiment was ahead of its time and

failed, with Heard donating the facilities and property to the Vedanta Society of Southern California in 1949. During these years, he continued his friendship with the Huxleys, also becoming friends with other well-known artists, writers, scientists, and mystics, including Steve Allen, John Betjeman, Dave Brubeck, Kenneth Clark, E. M. Forster, John Gielgud, Edwin Hubble, Nancy Wilson Ross, and Igor Stravinsky. In the 1950s he began to consider in greater depth the relationship of his spirituality to his sexuality. Inspired by evolutionary theory as much as by Vedanta, he developed the sociobiological-spiritual concept of the "isophyl." Somewhat closeted, he published gay-related articles, such as "The Isophyl as a Biological Variant" (1958) – which appeared in the early gay liberation movement journal *ONE Institute Quaterly of Homophile Studies* – under the pseudonym of D. B. Vest. In these articles, and in lectures to gay men active in the Mattachine Society and other movement groups – including Harry HAY, John Burnside, and Jim KEPNER – Heard spoke of the isophyl as a same-sex-oriented individual who was biologically, psychologically, and spiritually distinct from the typical heterosexually inclined man or woman. Echoing in some respects the "third sex" or "third gender" concepts promoted by Edward CARPENTER, Magnus Hirschfeld, Karl Heinrich Ulrichs, and others, he described the isophyl as transgendered or as transcending gender. In this respect, he referred to the isophyl as the "intergrade," resembling Carpenter's "intermediate." He linked this transgendered or androgynous aspect of the isophyl to another archetypal figure, that of the child. In this respect, he referred to the isophyl as the "paidomorph;" we might refer to its female equivalent as "parthenomorph." While Heard focuses in his gay-related writings on men, it is clear from "The Isophyl as a Biological Variant" that he viewed lesbians as female isophyls. It must be said, however, that Heard, impressed by some aspects of the hippie movement of the 1960s, apparently believed that some heterosexuals might be included in the category of isophyl. When Jim Kepner attended lectures given by Heard in 1965, the latter was focusing on the "communal" or "tribal" spirit embodied by the isophyl, cautioning that same-sex-oriented, transgendered individuals must make a determined effort to "break free from the inherited tendency to imitate heterosexual marital patterns." Kepner (1971) writes: "He envisioned an isophylic elite rising above the outmoded ideas of sex. He saw a new kind of creativity in the erotic interplay of two or more persons who were . . . committed to exploring one another's potentialities." His vision at this time embraced the emergence of communal societies of isophyls which would be economically based upon cottage industries. Heard's work has been carried on to some extent by his longtime companion Jay Michael Barrie; his work has also been made accessible to a generation of younger gay men and others through the efforts of Jim

Kepner, Mitch WALKER (especially in his Voices and Visions workshops of the early 1980s), and Mark THOMPSON (1987). Heard's writings include *The Ascent of Humanity* (1929), *Man, the Master* (1941), *The Eternal Gospel* (1946), *The Human Venture* (1955), and *The Five Ages of Man* (1963).

Hecate Greek goddess of Witchcraft as well as a dispenser of justice, bestower of wealth, overseer of horses and dogs, and patron of sailors and fishers. She is especially associated with crossroads and trivia, places where three roads meet. As such, she is a goddess of liminality, of the threshold or edge, and a patron of liminal or marginal persons. SAPPHO (b. c. 630/610 BCE) describes Hecate as "shining of gold" and "a handmaid to APHRODITE." Hecate is invoked in male homoerotic love spells dating from the third century CE. One of these spells names her "Mistress ruler of all mankind, all-dreadful one, bursting out of the earth." Another appeals to the "true Hecate [to] come and accomplish for me this very act [of love and binding]!" Hecate was served by priestesses as well as by gender variant male priests called SEMNOTATOI.

Hé-é-é TWO-SPIRIT warrior woman of the Hopi people of North America who styled her hair in a split style, one side feminine (held up), the other masculine (falling down), to signify her gender variant or third gender status. Hé-é-é became legendary for defending her village against an attack when the men were far away.

Heiséi Deity of illness and death, viewed as necessary aspects of life, among the Kogi and Cagaba people of Colombia. As the representative of the dead, Heiséi is the complement of the Mother Goddess of Life. As a god of the dead, he is associated with the west, the tiger, the serpent, the arrow, and the crab. His color is blue, as it is the color of death, because the "dead live in the sky." Heiséi is also a god of sexuality, especially of homosexuality and other non-reproductive forms of sexuality. It is said that he visits men in homoerotic dreams. In rituals, Heiséi's dancers wear masks with long snouts and big teeth, with a serpent coiled about the face.

Helen Long before the birth of Helen of Troy, Helen – whose name means "fair one" or "bright one" – was worshipped at Argos, Sparta, and elsewhere in the ancient Mediterranean as a goddess of beauty, the moon, vegetation, and fertility. Offerings to her included figurines of her hung from the branches of fruit trees. According to Claude Calame (1977), Helen was invoked by women taking part in ceremonies of same-sex UNION. Eventually, the mythos of the goddess Helen became interwoven with the legend of Helen of Troy. As such, Helen was the sole female being revered on the island of LEUKE, known primarily as the afterlife abode of homoerotically inclined warrior-lovers including ACHILLES and PATROCLUS. Various contemporary lesbian and bisexual female poets have been drawn to the mythos of Helen, including H. D. and Judy GRAHN.

Helenus Prophet of Greek myth and religion, brother of the prophetess Cassandra, husband of Andromache, and beloved (*eromenos*) of the god APOLLO, who bestowed upon him the gift of prophecy by causing oracular serpents to lick his ears.

Hennessy, Keith (1959-) Queer-identified, San Francisco-based, internationally acclaimed performance artist, choreographer, and writer. Hennessy describes his work as "holy male performance ritual trickery." In the 1990s, he lives and works at a collective art space, 848 Divisadero, "an urban site for Art, Spirit, Sex and Justice." In 1991 he and fellow traveler Jack Davis founded Phallic/Image, a learning center focusing on the interrelationship of (safer) sex, creativity, and spirituality. In 1992 the "848" vision began to coalesce. "As the faggot liberationist, goddess-honoring, anarchist grand-children of . . . Emma Goldman . . . Walt Whitman [and others]," Hennessy relates, "we wanted nothing less than the abolition of sex shame, HIV ignorance, homophobia . . . Our work emerged from . . . feminism, earth-based spiritualities, gay lib . . . anti-racist [movements and] contemporary art movements." Hennessy's works of performance/dance/ritual include *Sacred Way*, *Saliva*, and *Sacred Boy*, all of which he is constantly re-visioning. In *Sacred Boy*, he chants, "Gods, I hope you're not expecting anything . . . I take a moment to acknowledge the lineage of voices of male ecstatic poets: Yo Rumi! Yo William Blake! Yo Walt Whitman! Yo James Broughton! . . . I am nijinsky, antonin artaud, anne sexton: crazy for experiencing the divine within."

Henri III (1551-1589) Homoerotically inclined, gender variant king of France, reigning 1574-1589. The son of Catherine de' Medici and Henri II, he often wore makeup and a mixture of men's and women's garments. In a celebrated etching, he wears earrings, has a thin beard and a feminine hairstyle, and wears a feminine cap decorated with a brooch and feathers. He also wore the infamous tights called *garguesques*, which were nicknamed *chausses à la bougrine*, "hose fit for buggery." *Garguesques* were extremely tight-fitting and were worn without codpieces beneath "excessively short tunics which . . . revealed the buttocks." The term *garguesque* is related to the French terms for "throat," "gargle," and "gargoyle," the last being not only a mythic figure but also a conduit, a channel for conveying fluids, thus signifying, in erotic terms, fellatio. *Garguesque* also may have been related to a word chain clustered around *gouge*, the cognates of which referred not only to Gentiles (*goy*, from Yiddish) but also to prostitutes and lesbian women. Henri occasionally appeared at parties dressed as an Amazon. The chief fool at court during this time was a gender variant, quite possibly lesbian, woman named MATHURINE. Henri's court overflowed with androgynous, homoerotically inclined minions who shared his taste in fashion and his interest in spiritual matters. Henri delighted in wearing a fusion of feminine and monastic attire. He was especially enchanted with the "fashionable Capuchin girdle of ivory skulls," which he wore around his waist. Henri founded the Order of the Holy Spirit, a monastic order comprised of himself and his minions. Besides spending long hours in devotions and taking pilgrimages, Henri and his companions engaged in essentially Catholic rites including flagellation. The historian l'Éstoile describes in his *Journal* a procession which took place on Holy Thursday, April 7, 1583: "at nine o'clock in the evening, the procession of the Penitents, in which the King appeared with all his *mignons*, journeyed for the remainder of the night through the streets and to the churches, in a great magnificence of illumination and excellent music . . . And there were among them . . . several who flogged themselves during the course of the procession, whose backs, one could see, were totally red from the blows they had inflicted on themselves." Many believed that Henri, like his mother, also practiced the divinatory and magical arts and worshipped, alongside Christ and the Virgin, the elder goddesses and gods. Catherine's interest in the occult was widely known. She was especially fascinated with astrology and scrying. Among her most prized possessions were a magic mirror in which the entire history of France might supposedly be observed, and a talisman depicting Jupiter (in his linkage to GANYMEDE), VENUS, and an androgynous ANUBIS. On both sides of the talisman were engraved the names of angelic and demonic beings. Of Henri's minions, Nogaret, the duke of Epernon, and Saint-Megrin, were believed to have practiced sorcery. Nogaret was thought to have instructed Henri in the magical arts, in particular the art of sex magic. A legendary account described Henri as waking up in Nogaret's arms only to realize that he had made love to, and at the same time sold his soul to, the Devil. Some suggested that paintings depicting Henri engaging in intercourse with the demonic Nogaret were housed in a secret gallery. If such paintings ever existed, they have been lost, destroyed, or remained a secret. Henri, Nogaret, and other minions of the Order were believed to engage in magical rites primarily in a tower room at his castle at Vincennes. The altar they employed displayed both Christian and pre-Christian elements, including an alleged relic of the cross on which Jesus was crucified and two crystal goblets held by silver Pans. The abundance of data, derived from various sources, suggests that there may be, at the very least, a kernel of truth in the tales of Henri, Catherine, and the minions. The minions were frequently compared to the GALLI of CYBELE, while Henri took the

role of ATTIS and Catherine, that of the Goddess herself. The alleged beliefs and practices of Henri and his companions were satirized by Thomas Artus in *L'Isle des Hermaphrodites*, published in 1605. In *L'Isle*, a traveler is carried to an exotic island ruled by a transgendered king/queen. The text opens with these lines: "The world is a fool, and man a comedy; one carries a *marotte* (a fool's, or rather SOT's, scepter), and the other is folly." Thus, from the outset, the island and ultimately Henri's court are associated not only with gender variance and homoeroticism but also with the world of fools or *sots* and the carnivalesque. When the narrator first steps onto the island, he sees a palace which more closely resembles a Greek temple, its columns topped with the heads of goddesses. Sensing a mystery, he follows a glittering path, which leads him to the royal bedchamber, where the king, at first a sleeping statue – perhaps a reference to the Greco-Roman sculpture of the *Sleeping Hermaphrodite* – is magically brought to life by his minions. The moment the statue comes to life, it begins speaking in an effeminate, sarcastic manner (*une parole toute effeminée, avec desdain*). The narrator leaves this scene only to witness a transsexual operation. Following this, he discovers a gallery filled with artworks depicting Pan, Ganymede, Dionysus, Hermaphroditus, and other gods, as well as homoerotically inclined, gender variant rulers of antiquity including Sardanapalus and Heliogabalus. The reigning female figure is Semiramis, a legendary Amazonian queen who serves here as another manifestation of Catherine de' Medici. He then discovers the sacred texts of the religion of the hermaphrodites; these include the works of Ovid, Catullus, and Anacreon. Rites include celebrations of Eros, Dionysus, and Aphrodite, as well as the Romano-Celtic rites of May. All religious observances which do not promote "voluptuousness" are forbidden. Articles of faith include the rejection of the concepts of damnation and of paradise as a realm other than the island itself. Some readers might interpret Artus's satire as little more than an attack on Henri's court and upon gender variant and homoerotically inclined males. This reading, however, ignores the important contribution which the text makes to our understanding of the development of Queer Spirit. The text inspired gay playwright Charles LUDLAM to write *Isle of the Hermaphrodites or the Murdered Minion* (published 1989).

Hephaestus Greek god of FIRE, iron, and metallurgy, he was the lover of numerous goddesses including APHRODITE, who left him for ADONIS. Hephaestus was also the lover (*erastes*) of PELEUS, who eventually became the King of Phthia in Thessaly, husband to Thetis, and father of ACHILLES, who loved PATROCLUS.

Hera In Greek religion and myth, ruler of the heavens, overseer of animals, and patron of women. In some accounts, she is gynandrous or transgendered, giving birth to HEPHAESTUS without the aid of a male. SAPPHO (b. c. 630/610 BCE) and her devotees revered the Goddess, singing, "Lady Hera, while I pray let your graceful form appear . . . be kind, as in former days, and now help me." Hera was served on the island of Samos not only by female priestesses but also by transgendered male priest/esse/s. According to Athenaeus, Hera's male priests dressed in feminine garments, "snowy tunics that swept the floor of wide earth." They also wore arm bracelets "wrought with cunning" and golden headpieces which "surmounted them, like cicadas." They grew their hair long, braided it, and decorated it with yellow or gold ribbons, hence the poetic fragment "marching to the Heraeum with braided hair." That sherds of Samian pottery were traditionally employed by the priests of another goddess, CYBELE, to perform ritual castration suggests that the priests of Hera may have also been eunuchs. While it is not clear whether or not the priests of Hera engaged in same-sex eroticism, it is highly probable that they did so. The island of Samos was a topos of luxury, known for its exotic foods and perfumes and its prostitutes of both sexes. The prostitutes, nicknamed the "flowers" of Samos, lived in a sort of French quarter designed by Polycrates, an effeminate man "passionately devoted to liaisons with males."

Heracles (Roman **Hercules**)   In Greek and Roman myth and religion, a divinized hero famous for carrying out the "twelve labors" forced upon him by Eurystheus. These labors included the slaying of several fabulous animals, the Nemean lion, the Hydra, the Erymanthian boar, and others. One of his labors, taking possession of the girdle of HIPPOLYTA, a Queen of the AMAZONS, resulted in his slaying Hippolyta. His relationship to Amazonian women was not, however, altogether negative. After murdering Iphitus, a celebrated archer, Heracles was forced, as punishment, to become a slave for three years. The Amazonian Queen OMPHALE of Lydia became his master. During this period, while he continued to perform heroic actions such as ridding the country of criminals, he and the Queen fell in love and eventually married. At home, they enjoyed a role-reversed relationship, with Omphale, the master, dressing in the lion-skin and brandishing the club, and Heracles spinning and wearing the elegant, transparent, saffron-colored feminine garment called the SANDYX. A hairy man, he soon became known as "Heracles of the Black Buttocks." When Heracles and Omphale were sleeping one night, the god PAN, creeping into their bedchamber, pounced on the beautiful Queen, leaping up when he realized it was Heracles he was embracing. It may have been in commemoration of this liaison that the priests of Heracles wore women's clothes, while the priestesses of Omphale wore masculine attire. On the island of Cos, the male priest/esse/s of Heracles referred to themselves as his "Brides." They were transgendered, homoerotically

inclined, and famous for wearing the *sandyx*. Many centuries later, the homoerotically inclined King HENRI III of France was compared to Heracles in this role of transgendered consort of Omphale. Heracles is associated not only with transgenderism but also with homoeroticism. Together with EROS and HERMES, he is a patron of same-sex liaisons commencing in gymnasia. His chief male lovers include ABDERUS, ADMETUS, Chonus, DRYOPS, Haemon, HYLAS, Iokastus, IOLAUS, NESTOR, PHILOCTETES, and POLYPHEMUS.

Herm   Stylized pillars of the ancient Mediterranean, often phallic in shape, or displaying an erect phallus, typically dedicated to the god HERMES. Herms were employed in erotic rites, not only to Hermes but also to DIONYSUS, PRIAPUS, and other deities. They were also used as boundary markers and as signposts. In a poem concerning a handsome young man named Philetadas, the writer Callimachus (fl. 250 BCE) suggests that the youth's beauty may have caused the erect phallus to appear on the herm that stands before the wrestling school (PALAESTRA). "Long-bearded Hermes," he asks, "why is your phallus pointing to your beard and not to your feet?"

Hermaphroditus   Son of the Greek deities HERMES and APHRODITE. The nymph Salmacis fell in love with the beautiful young man, but he spurned her. She prayed to the gods that they might be together forever. They answered her prayer, but not in the way she expected. When the young man next bathed in the pool she inhabited, she caught him in her arms. Suddenly, the two melted into one. Salmacis had won, but she had also lost. For Hermaphroditus, although now transformed into a being with both male and female characteristics, remained, Salmacis was no more. Hermaphroditus is usually represented as having a penis and female breasts. Following his metamorphosis, he was loved by the god DIONYSUS.

Hermes (Roman **Mercury**)   Greek god of the crossroads, communication, commerce, and flight, as well as being an intercessory, TRICKSTER, and guide of souls (or psychopomp) from this life to the next. His symbols include the palm tree, tortoise, cock, fish, honey, cakes, pigs, lamb, and goats. Hermes, together with EROS and HERACLES, formed a trinity of gods presiding over homoerotic love, their statues often housed together in gymnasia. Seldom associated with women, Hermes's male lovers include AMPHION, ANTHEUS, CHRYSES, CROCUS, Perseus, and Therses. He was invoked as "Hermes of the Underworld" in both homoerotic and lesbian love spells undertaken in Alexandria, Egypt during the third century CE, as evidenced in the *Greek Magical Papyri*. In this same Hellenistic system of magic, the "semen of Hermes" signified dill when named in ingredients for spells. George

Cecil Ives (1867-1950), founder of the homoerotico-spiritual ORDER OF CHAERONEA, wrote in his poem "Eocene": "I thought to be alone but Hermes stood / Against the bed and lifted up my eyes. / Gracious and strong in gallant hardihood, / Sprinkled with dew, he came to bid me rise."

Hermes Trismegistus "Thrice-great HERMES," a legendary or possibly historical figure serving as a spiritual guide and embodying attributes of the Egyptian god THOTH and the Greek Hermes. He plays a central role in a collection of mystical texts dating from late antiquity known as the *Hermetica*. In the *Perfect Discourse*, one finds Asclepius, a disciple, asking, "You say then that God possesses both sexes," to which Trismegistus replies, "Yes, Asclepius, and not only God, but all living beings."

Herrman, Bert (1946-)   Gay writer and publisher (of Alamo Square Press books in San Francisco). Of Jewish heritage, Herrman has written two books which explore the interrelationship of homoeroticism and spirituality: *Being, Being Happy, Being Gay*: *Pathways to a Rewarding Life for Lesbians and Gay Men* (1990); and *Trust: The Hand Book* (1991). In the first of these, Herrman blends the sharing of his own eclectic beliefs and practices with interviews of lesbians, gays, and bisexuals who belong to diverse spiritual traditions. The text concludes with a program of transpersonal growth that is laid out in well-defined steps and which includes meditation, creative visualization, and affirmations. *Trust* is devoted to gay male TANTRA.

Hesperus Greek deity of evening and the evening star, he was the lover of HYMENAEUS, who presided over ceremonies of UNION, which often took place in the evening. Hesperus was also considered a deity of MUSIC; as such he led "vespers," hymns sung at sunset or in the early evening. When he died, he was transformed into the evening star. SAPPHO (b. c. 630/610 BCE) writes to Hesperus in her lyric the "Evening Star," "Hesperos, you bring home all [that] the bright dawn disperses, bring home the sheep, bring home the goat, bring the child home to its mother." In his dramatic poem "Hesperus and Hymenaeus" (written near 1868), John Addington SYMONDS depicts a shepherd invoking Hesperus: "Trim thy lamp," he asks, "To guide me to the shepherd whom I love . . . how fair it is, / When friend meets friend sole in the silent night, / Thou knowest, Hesper." For leading him to his lover, the shepherd vows to make offerings to Hesperus: "Thy shrine shall never lack the gift of flowers / And golden honey and sweet myrrh and wine." The spirit of Hesperus tells the shepherd that if, on finding Myrtilus, he loves and remains faithful to him, they will one day, after death, dwell with Hesperus and Hymenaeus in "a

land behind the western cloud . . . of ceaseless spring and everlasting twilight."

Hetaira and Female Hierodule   Both "*hetaira*" and "*hierodule*" are much misunderstood terms often translated as "prostitute" and "sacred prostitute" respectively. In classical antiquity, they applied specifically to women who served as priestesses in cults typically devoted to Goddess Reverence, as in the worship of ASTARTE and INANNA/ISHTAR. More generally, however, the terms, especially "*hetaira*," applied to loving relations between and among women reflecting their love for the Goddess and often extending into EROTICISM. In this way, the terms have more in common with African-American writer Alice Walker's (b. 1944) concept of "womanism" than they do with the term "prostitute" or even "sacred prostitute." Exemplary of this signification, the Lesbian poet SAPPHO (b. c. 630/610 BCE) writes, "These joyous songs I will sing well today in honour of my companions [*hetairae*]."

Hexagram   As a six-sided figure, a symbol of androgyny or transgenderism, formed by the merging of "masculine" and "feminine" triangles.

He-Xiang-gu (or **Ho Hsien-Ku**)   In traditional Chinese religion and myth, usually linked to Taoism, the sole woman among the Eight Immortals, unless one counts LAN CAIHE. Those scholars who do so, however, tend to conceal that Immortal's transgendered status. He-Xiang-gu, usually represented as holding a LOTUS, is today considered a patron of housewives. This is somewhat ironic, however, given her story. One day, as a young woman, she was cooking rice in her stepmother's kitchen when suddenly she decided that she would never marry. Just as suddenly, she was lifted into the heavens to become an Immortal. In order to grasp the full import of this story, one needs to understand that in premodern China, resistance to traditional female roles and especially to marriage often went hand in hand with an acceptance of loving relationships between and among women.

Hierodule, Male   Like the HETAIRA, male hierodules, often gender variant or transgendered and engaging in same-sex eroticism, have served as spiritual functionaries in many of the world's spiritual traditions, especially those devoted to Goddess Reverence, as in the cults of ASTARTE (as KELABIM), ATHIRAT (as QEDESHIM), BAHUCHARAMATA (as HIJRAS), CYBELE (as GALLI), and INANNA/ISHTAR (as ASSINNU, KURGARRU, etc.). In these traditions, they are representatives of the primary deity. In others, such as in the cult of the Hindu deity KRISHNA, they represent the beloved or "bride" of the god, in this case, RADHA or the GOPIS. In still other contexts, male hierodules represent an androgynous, gynandrous, or transgendered deity, as do the devotees of the Hindu deity ARDHANARISHVARA. Of the last example mentioned, A. Daniélou (1984) "Male [sacred] prostitution, mainly in the form of transvestism . . . played a ritual role in connection with the Hermaphrodite [i.e. Ardhanarishvara] cult." Spanish Catholic chroniclers were shocked upon finding male hierodulic priests in the temples of Central and South America, as in the countryside near Lima, Peru and at Portoviejo and on the island of Puna in present-day Ecuador. Typically referring to the deities of the region as "the Devil," Pedro de Cieza de Léon (1520-1554) wrote, "The Devil made the Indians of these regions believe that it was pleasing to the gods for them to have Indians as temple assistants so that the chieftains could have carnal knowledge of them, committing sodomy." He quoted Father Domingo de Santo Tomás as saying, "In each important temple or house of worship they have a man or two, or more, depending on the idol, who go dressed in women's attire from the time they are children, and speak like them, and in manner, dress, and everything else imitate women. With these, almost like a rite and ceremony, on [feast] days and holidays they have carnal, foul intercourse, especially the chiefs and headmen. I know this because I have punished two, one of them of the Indians of the highlands . . . [the Devil had] made them believe that this vice was a kind of holiness and religion."

Hi'iaka In Hawaiian myth and religion, a goddess of the HULA and of magic. Hi'iaka was devastated when her sister PELE killed her intimate female companion (*aikane*) HOPOE after becoming jealous of Hi'iaka's relationship with LOHIAU, Pele's male lover.

Hiiakalalo and Hiiakaluna During a battle with the Hawaiian pig-god KAMAPUA'A, the volcano-goddess PELE sent her brothers Hiiakalalo and Hiiakaluna to attack him. Kamapua'a, however, won the round by sending the love-god LONOIKIAWEAWEALOHA to seduce her brothers. Hiiakalalo and his brother forgot their sister's orders as they made love to the handsome love-god.

Hijra Transgendered male priest/esse/s and devotees of the Hindu goddess BAHUCHARAMATA. *Hijras* believe that they are chosen to become so by the Goddess, their metamorphosis often commencing with a dream wherein Bahucharamata instructs young men to begin transforming their attire and behavior as well as their erotic and spiritual lives. Elder *hijras* have been known to ritually abduct young men they believe the Goddess has chosen. *Hijras* typically undergo ritual castration. They often dwell in communal households called *jemadh*, where they relate to fellow *hijras* as "sisters" and to their *hijra* guru, or master, as a "mother." Some *hijras*, however, live with male companions. The *hijras* earn their livelihood in

various ways, including begging for alms, prostitution (in the past, it appears they served as HIERODULE-priests) and singing and dancing at celebrations including births and weddings. The primary musical instruments employed by the *hijras* are the *dholak* (a small cylindrical folk drum) and small copper cymbals. They also employ special hand-clapping rhythms. They perform chants called *bhajan*, or *kriti*. Their dances tend to be sensuous. While they are often ridiculed, especially in twentieth-century India, *hijras* are nevertheless believed to carry magical power. For example, even those who ridicule them fear their curses, which are cast when they are not invited to sing and dance at special events or when they are refused alms. Moreover, they are believed by many to hold the power to bring riches and rain. While they are considered transgendered, they differ from traditional Hindu and Indian women in several key respects, foremost of which is their tendency to behave in a bawdy manner (such as lifting their skirts) and to use obscene speech. Recently, some *hijras* have become popular as singers in films. To date, the finest study on the *hijras* is Serena Nanda's *Neither Man Nor Woman: The Hijras of India* (1990).

Himerus In Greek religion and myth, one of the EROTES. Depicted as a beautiful, nude, winged man, Himerus, a bearer of erotic energy and the *élan vital*, or life force, carries a taenia, a headband of beautiful colors worn by athletes.

Hinemoa Maori AMAZON who, falling in love with the male hero TUTANEKAI, "deliberately masquerades as a man, as a [male] warrior, to lure him to her arms," as Ngahuia Te Awekotuku (1991) relates . This action infers Tutanekai's love for other men, which other tales confirm. It also suggests a kind of mirroring relationship between the Amazonian woman and the man-loving man.

Hintubuhet Gynandrous or transgendered supreme being of New Ireland, Melanesia. Hintubuhet's feminine aspect is identified with the moon and the butterfly Heba, while her-his masculine aspect is identified with the sun and the butterfly Talmago.

Hippo "HORSE," a queen of the AMAZONS, who, according to legend, founded the temple of ARTEMIS/DIANA at Ephesus. Callimachus (fl. c. 250 BCE) writes, "The Amazons . . . in Ephesus . . . established an image beneath an oak trunk, and Hippo performed a holy rite" for Artemis.

Hippolyta "Stamping Mare," AMAZON Queen of Greek legendary history who, according to some accounts, was slain by the hero HERACLES, when, as one of the "twelve labors" he was forced to perform by Eurystheus, he took possession of her girdle.

Hippolytus Handsome son of the Greek AMAZON HIPPOLYTA, a hunter devoted to the goddess ARTEMIS. When he spurned the advances of his stepmother, Phaedra, she accused him of raping her, for which reason he was slain or else committed suicide. He was revivified, however, by ASCLEPIUS, who loved him, after which he was carried away by Artemis to become her priest at her temple on the shore of Lake Nemi.

Hispo Name of a celebrated female courtesan of the Roman Empire. "Hispo" later became a more generalized term for a male enjoying the receptive role in anal intercourse. The term "Hispo" survived into the European Middle Ages, when Serlo of Wilton (c. 1110-1181) invoked it as a nickname for a male lover: "Naevolus without his mate can't play at night; / He says, 'Hispo, return; I have pledged myself to you.'"

Holi Hindu festival celebrating the love of the god KRISHNA, RADHA, and the GOPIS which includes elements of transgenderism and same-sex EROTICISM. McKim Marriot (1968), in describing an incident occurring during Holi, writes: "There was one great throng of villagers watching an uplifted male dancer with padded crotch writhe in solitary states of fevered passion and then onanism; then join in a remote *pas de deux* with a veiled female impersonator in a parody of pederasty, and finally in telepathic copulation – all this to a frenzied accompaniment of many drums."

Home, Daniel Dunglas (1833-1886) Spiritualist skilled in the arts of CHANNELING and levitating. Born in Scotland, Home was reared in the US, in Connecticut, and as an adult sojourned in England. While many were skeptical of his powers, the renowned psychical researcher Sir William Crookes determined Home to be an authentic psychic, and the Roman Catholic Church condemned him as a sorcerer. Among those who admired him, he was especially appreciated for his acceptance of gifts and refusal of fees. According to British-American writer and mystic Gerald HEARD, Home, although agreeing to an arranged heterosexual marriage, was homoerotically inclined as well as transgendered in terms of his behavior. Home's works include *My Life* (1863) and *Lights and Shadows of Spiritualism* (1877).

Hopoe In Hawaiian religion and myth, an intimate female companion (AIKANE) of the goddess HI'IAKA. Hopoe and Hi'iaka first met in the Puna district on the island of Hawaii. At this time, Hopoe danced the HULA for Hi'iaka, who had not seen it performed before. Hi'iaka was so delighted by the dance that she planted red and white blossoming *lehua* trees on the island for her new companion. Since that time, the flowering *lehua* has been Hopoe's sacred attribute. When the volcano-goddess

PELE, Hi'iaka's sister, became jealous of the friendship her sister had developed with Pele's male lover LOHIAU, Pele killed Hopoe by sending lava flowing over her. Hi'iaka was devastated upon the loss of her beloved Hopoe. Some say that when Pele realized how mistaken and how cruel she had been, she restored Hopoe to life. Others say that Hopoe transformed into a rock which appears to be dancing, still visible near Kea-au in Puna.

Horse Frequently symbolic of swiftness, skill in battle, mastery of the emotions, and sacrifice, the horse is an attribute of numerous deities and heroes associated with transgenderism and/or same-sex passion, including ACHILLES, the AMAZONS, ARTEMIS/DIANA, ASTARTE, ATHENA, BOUDICCA, INDRA, ODIN, PELOPS, PHAETON, POSEIDON, and the VALKYRIES. Ancient Greek poetry suggests that women-loving women were compared to horses. In a poem celebrating AGIDO and HAGESICHORA (both fl. c. 600 BCE), we find the former described as a "Kolaxaian filly" and the latter as a "splendid stallion." "Hippopornos," or "horse-whore," came into use as a slang term in the third century BCE to describe a gender variant male "reeking of perfume" and enjoying the receptive role in same-sex eroticism. In twentieth-century Mexico, the horse (*caballo*) is a signifier of male homosexuality.

Hortensius (114-50 BCE) Roman orator who may have identified himself – and clearly was identified by others – as gender variant or transgendered. When a colleague, Lucius Torquatus, called him "Dionysia," referring to a famous female courtesan-dancer of the time (whose name derived from the god DIONYSUS), Hortensius replied, "I'd rather be like Dionysia than you, Torquatus, whom the Muses, Aphrodite, and Dionysus have abandoned."

Hosmer, Harriet Goodhue (1830-1908) Woman-loving US artist, possibly a lover of the actress Charlotte Cushman (1816-1876, famous for her portrayal of Hamlet). Hosmer was profoundly inspired by classical myth and British folklore, the subjects of her sculpture including DAPHNE, HESPERUS, MEDUSA, and PUCK. In 1868 Hosmer, who had been reared as a boy, wrote, "I honour every woman who has strength enough to step outside the beaten path when she feels that her walk lies in another."

Hu Hsien In Chinese myth and folklore, the fox, as in Europe, is known for its cunning. It is also known for its longevity and for its power of shapeshifting, including gender metamorphosis, as well as for its extreme sensuality. For almost two millennia Hu Hsien has been linked to venereal diseases. Sometimes it happens that Hu Hsien falls in love with a human male. He may transform himself into a woman, or he may choose to remain male at this time. Because Hu Hsien brings wisdom and good fortune, men rarely refuse him. Whether Hu Hsien wishes to or not, it is his nature to drain his human lover of his vital essence, or *ch'i*, as their relationship grows stronger. If the human lover is to survive, Hu Hsien must ultimately leave the relationship and return to his animal-immortal state. Otherwise the lover will die. This results in many melancholy relationships between Hu Hsien and mortals.

Huckleberry Finn, The Adventures of (1884)   Classic of children's literature written by Mark Twain (pseudonym of Samuel Clemens, 1835-1910). In the novel, Huck Finn experiences a kind of shamanic initiation or vision quest which includes the weaving together of spiritual with homoerotic and transgender elements. Leslie Fiedler's controversial 1955 article "Come Back to the Raft Ag'in, Huck Honey!" and Harold Schechter's 1987 essay "Symbols of Initiation in *Adventures of H. F.*" illuminate this dimension of the novel. Huck's quest begins in the woman-centered cosmos of Aunt Polly, then moves on to a ceremony of blood-brotherhood with his male friends, followed by a violent confrontation with "Pap," who seems to have returned from the dead, followed in turn by Huck's staging of his own death. Huck then goes to live in the wild, where he encounters an African-American slave named Jim. The journey proceeds to include visions of death, trickster-like antics, and an episode involving Huck's dressing in a calico dress and sun-bonnet. Schechter describes Huck's friend Jim as a "genuine magus, a priest of the river god." Indeed, Jim seems to be a repository of the sort of knowledge one gains in such African-diasporic religions as Vodou. Jim is also depicted as androgynous; "it is he," Schechter observes, "who mothers Huck as they travel down the big river . . . it is he who . . . takes Huck to his own bosom to nourish him." Schechter's well-founded interpretation of the figure of Jim as a gender variant spiritual mentor-nurturer and Fiedler's equally well-founded interpretation of the love shared by Huck and Jim as homoerotic in character combine to illuminate a queer-spiritual reading of this classic work.

Hula   Traditional Hawaiian dance rooted in pre-Christian religion and myth, whose performers and teachers include women, homoerotically inclined males and transgendered males called MAHU. Among the famous Kane Hula (male hula performers) is Darrell Lupenui, said to be a *mahu* of great *mana* (spiritual power), and who created "for his *halau* (dance school) a strong aggressive male style of dancing including dressing in loincloths that left the buttocks exposed." Another is the transgendered Laulana Kasparovich, a celebrated teacher of hula, especially to children, who call him their "festive uncle;" still another is Auntie Moana. As a child he (-she) was active in the Catholic Church and called "Butchie" since he

(-she) reminded family members of a masculine girl. He (-she) studied hula with Auntie Harriet Ne, and at the "*uniki*" (hula graduation ceremony) danced in a costume designed to hide his male chest Auntie Moana is both respected as a performer and teacher and revered as a spiritual guide. In "The Ethnomusicologist as Midwife" (1993), Carol Robertson points out that the hula embraces the spiritual concept of *aloha*, which celebrates the "acceptance of diversity." For this reason, the contributions of the *mahu* and other homoerotically inclined men are considered by native Hawaiians as "sacred gifts."

Huligamma   Hindu goddess of Dravidian origin, worshipped by *basivis*, hierodulic priestesses, and by transgendered males akin to the HIJRAS. The center of her worship is on the left bank of the Tungabhadra River in South India. Devotees of Huligamma carry on their heads circular baskets containing small images of the Goddess as well as ornaments and toiletries.

Humboldt, Wilhelm Freiherr von (1767-1835) Perhaps in part because his celebrated brother Alexander, a naturalist and traveler, was homoerotically inclined, the German writer W. R. von Humboldt came to look upon androgyny as an ideal form of being, especially in his book *On the Manly and Womanly Form*. "Everything in the nature of divinity," he writes, "strives toward the purity and perfection of the archetypes of the species. Sexual character begins to disappear in the youthful figures of the gods . . . the sharp delineation of the male body loses itself in a milder grace . . . undeniably it happens sometimes . . . that a few isolated traits of a certain individual shine through and seem purely human, midway between masculine and feminine."

Hunting   Hunting variously signifies desire, nurturance, sacrifice, death, metamorphosis, and embodiment of animal spirits. M. Detienne (1979) and A. Daniélou (1984) suggest that hunting grounds symbolize territory which lies beyond the bounds of heterosexual marriage. This notion appears to be borne out by the myriad of sacred or mythic figures who are associated with hunting and with same-sex intimacy and/or transgenderism, including ACTAEON, ADONIS, AGDISTIS, the AMAZONS, ARTEMIS/DIANA, ATALANTA, ATARGATIS, ATTIS, BEGOCHIDI, BRITOMARTIS, CAMILLA, CHIRON, CROCALE, CYRENE, DAPHNE, DICTYNNA, DIONYSUS, the ERINYES, FROG EARRINGS, GIANTS, HIPPOLYTUS, INLE, KANYOTSANYOTSE, KARTIKKEYEH, KOTYS, LEUCIPPE, LOGUNEDE, MAENADS, NA THU PEN DO, ODIN, OSANYIN, OSHUMARE, PAVATAIRAYAN, PIKOE SENDO, QAILERTETANG, SEDNA, SILVANUS, SKADI, SYRINX, TALKING GOD, THESEUS, and WAKDJUNKAGA. Spiritual functionaries bearing these associations include the TWO-SPIRIT KWE'RHAME and MIATI of Native American Indian Shamanism. Animals which are hunted and which have connections to transgenderism and/or same-sex desire include the BEAR, the DEER, the HARE, and the PANTHER. ARCADIA is a mythical setting of Greco-Roman origin possessing these correspondences.

Hwame Name for the TWO-SPIRIT, third gender, or transgendered female among the Mohave of the American Southwest. Often serving as a shaman, the *hwame* was beloved to be especially skilled at curing venereal disease. Some *hwame* began to dream of becoming transgendered shamans while they were still in the womb. Among the Mohave, chanting or singing was also thought to nurture the transformation of women into *hwame*. The *hwame* usually took women as lovers or spouses.

Hwarang Known in premodern Korea as the "flower boys of Silla," the *hwarang* was a male institution comprised of military, spiritual, aesthetic, and homoerotic components. The term *hwarang* simultaneously connotes a shaman, a sage, a poet, a musician, a beautifully dressed male singer, a fairy, and a homoerotically inclined male. The *hwarang* arose during the sixth century CE. In terms of eroticism, the *hwarang* were usually said to engage in *lung-yang-chih-ch'ung*, a term of Chinese origin referring to homoeroticism. Spiritually speaking, the *hwarang* practiced a syncretized spiritual tradition embracing elements of Shamanism, Buddhism, Hinduism, and a belief in fairy-like spirits. Hwarang archetypal figures eventually emerged, e.g. the handsome and heroic devotee of Maitreya Buddha Kim Yusin, known as "Fragrant One," "Incense Man," or "Dragon Flower." While a majority of the songs of *hwarang* are praise-hymns, others promote healing and magical transformation. Two *hwarang* mythical companions, Ansang and Purye, the latter referred to as the "leader of a thousand men with jeweled shoes," are especially associated with two Korean musical instruments, the "harp" (probably a plucked zither, or the *yanggum*, a kind of dulcimer) and the "pipe" (either the "oboe-like" *piri*, or the *tanso*, a vertical notched flute). A typical *hwarang* song, "The Song of the Comet," composed during the seventh century, compares the *hwarang* to the GANDARVAS, the fairy-like celestial musicians of Hinduism: "See the fort by the Eastern Sea / Where the Gandarva used to play / . . . the moon, hearing, / The three Flower Boys are visiting the hills, / Quickly shows her beams."

Hyacinth Flower sacred to the Greek god HYACINTHUS, symbolic of beauty, springtime, tranquillity, ephemeral existence, heavenly aspiration, and rebirth.

Hyacinth (or **Jacinth**) Gem sacred to the Greek god HYACINTHUS, which protects travelers, induces sleep, and wards off negative energies.

Hyacinthus Philostratus (fl. c. 200 CE) writes, "Read the hyacinth, for there is writing on it which says it sprang from the earth in honor of a beautiful youth." Originally a god of the underworld, Hyacinthus was first portrayed as a dual male being, like the male-male being of PLATO's *Symposium*. Later, he became known as the beloved of the Greek god APOLLO, as a dancer, and as a Spartan youth riding a DOLPHIN. One afternoon, as he and Apollo were throwing the discus, ZEPHYRUS, the west wind, who also loved Hyacinthus, caused the discus to change its course and to strike Hyacinthus on the head. Zephyrus had decided that if he could not have Hyacinthus as a lover, then Apollo would not have him either. Hyacinthus was dying rapidly. His face had been smashed, and not even Apollo could bring him back to life. However, Apollo was determined that the youth's beauty should be immortalized, so he transformed Hyacinthus's body into a beautiful flower. The death of Hyacinthus came to symbolize the death of springtime, of adolescence, and of the "ego," while his rebirth came to signify the arrival of summer, of manhood, and the transcendent Self. His death and rebirth were celebrated at the Hyacinthia each year at the time of the rising of the dog-star SIRIUS. Eventually he also came to be seen as a patron of homoerotic love. In the sixth century CE *Latin Anthology* an anonymous poet says of Apollo and Hyacinthus, "Phoebus [i.e. Apollo] could not steal his lover back from fate, / But the dead boy's blood replenishes the flowering fields." Among the most memorable paintings of the myth are Anne-Louis Girodet de Roucy's (1767-1824) *Apollon et Hyacinthe* and Jean Broc's (1771-1850) *The Death of Hyacinthus*. Broc's painting represents one of the earliest post-antiquity depictions of the legendary lovers which does not attempt to conceal the homoerotic element. Dominique Fernandez (1989) writes, "*The Death of Hyacinthus* remains an example, unequaled in the world's paintings, of the celebration of homosexual union." In this effort, Broc may be differentiated from the composer Wolfgang Amadeus Mozart (1756-1791), who heterosexualized this tale in his musical intermezzo in one act, *Apollo et Hyacinthus*.

Hyena In Greco-Roman and possibly also Egyptian antiquity, the hyena was associated with transgenderism, homosexuality, and magic. The hyena was "fond of a great deal of sexual indulgence," "has certain magic arts by which it causes every animal at which it gazes three times to be rooted on the spot," and "geld[s] [its] male offspring." The GALLI, gender variant priests of the goddess CYBELE who were thought to be highly skilled in fashioning talismans and amulets, were said to prepare amulets from the hairs encircling the anus of a hyena. These hairs, explains Pliny (23-79; Pliny, a naturalist, was the lover of Titus, son of the Roman emperor Vespasian), were "reduced to ashes, mixed with oil, and used as an ointment" by effeminate men to protect themselves from violence while at the same time drawing lovers. A potion made of honey and the genitals of a hyena was believed to cause men to become sexually attracted to other men. Medieval bestiaries preserved the associations of classical antiquity, as did Medieval poets. Bernard of Cluny, in his twelfth-century "Contempt of the World," wails, "Unnaturally, outrageously, he becomes she . . . / Men forget what is manly; o madness! o terror! they are like hyenas." It was important for Medieval Christian writers to paradoxically stress both the beastliness and the unnaturalness of gender and sexual variance. The hyaenia stone, today called not a "hyena's eye" but rather a "cat's eye," was placed under the tongue by ancient Roman diviners and later by European Renaissance magicians in order to prophesy. It appears that this practice may have originated in Africa. In the alternately serious and satirical *Wisewomen and Boggy-boos* (1992), Jessica Amanda Salmonson and Jules Remedios Faye link the hyena to "lesbian sorceresses" of ancient Greece whose laughter was considered scandalous and who were thought to have lived as men in previous incarnations.

Hylas Beautiful young man of Greek mythology loved by HERACLES and perhaps also APOLLO. Hylas, a prince and the son of King Thiodamus, traveled on the ship Argo with Heracles and the other ARGONAUTS. During this period, Hylas was also admired and "caressed passionately" by the twins CALAIS and ZETES. Once, when Hylas went in search of water (perhaps possessing healing properties), he encountered a group of seductive nymphs who, pulling him under the water to their lair, drowned him. Heracles abandoned the Argonauts to search for Hylas but without success. Each year the people of CHIOS honored the love of Heracles and Hylas with a ritual drama enacting the search. Hylas was invoked by an anonymous sixth century CE poet in the *Latin Anthology*: "Hylas the waterboy is abducted: the nymphs' joys increase. / The wrath of Hercules swells."

Hymenaeus A god of MUSIC in Greek mythology or religion, envisioned as singing at ceremonies of union, hence the term "hymn." He is depicted as a beautiful, androgynous man with soft skin and luxuriant hair; he carries a basket or arrangement of roses, walnuts, pomegranates, and marjoram. His primary lover is HESPERUS. He is also said to have loved or been loved by APOLLO, ARGYNNUS, THAMYRIS, and DIONYSUS. When the last of these fell in love with him, ZEUS became jealous and caused one of Dionysus' arrows to strike Hymenaeus. Dionysus, however, restored Hymenaeus to life with magical wine and ivy.

Hypnos Greek god of sleep and dreams, depicted as wearing garments of black and white and as holding a crescent- or cornucopia-shaped horn from which dreams flow. Hypnos loved ENDYMION so much that he caused him to fall asleep with his eyes remaining open, so that he might "enjoy the delight of gazing upon them [i.e. his eyes] continually." Hypnos gave his name to hypnotism.

I

I Ching (or **Yi Jing, Yi King**) Chinese divinatory text dating from approximately the first millennium BCE, probably originating in Shamanism and later expanded and transformed by practitioners of Taoism and Confucianism. The *I Ching* guides the querent in a course of action based upon the hexagram (comprised of various combinations of YIN AND YANG energies) received in a consultation. One of the hexagrams is traditionally associated with same-sex relationships, including friendships and loving, erotic relationships. This is the thirteenth hexagram, T'ung Jên, or "Fellowship with Men," which reads: "But when two people are at one in their inmost hearts, / They shatter even the strength of iron or bronze. / And when two people understand each other in their inmost hearts, / Their words are sweet and strong, like the fragrance of orchids." Ruan Ji, Xi Kang, and Shan Tao, three male poet-philosophers of third-century CE China, members of the circle known as the SEVEN SAGES OF THE BAMBOO GROVE who were intimately involved with each other, were said to share the relationship described in this hexagram. In the *Kwan Yin Book of Changes* (1989) by lesbian-feminist writer Diane Stein, this hexagram is translated as "Sisterhood"; Stein writes, "In T'ung Jên, the women are not only the power of the community, but are also the empowerment and love in each other's lives." Twentieth-century US writer Jacqueline Lapidus is inspired by another hexagram, the fifty-eighth, Tui, known as "the Joyous" or "the Lake," to write in her poem "I Ching": "The query: / woman loving woman / what now? / The hexagram / Joyous / Youngest daughter doubled / a smiling lake . . ."

Ianthe In classical mythology, daughter of Telestes of Crete and beloved and later spouse of IPHIS. While she may have suspected Iphis, who had been reared as a male, of being female, she apparently did not make love to Iphis until the wedding night. Just prior to this event, the goddess ISIS had granted Iphis' mother's request to transform her daughter into a man.

Iao Sabaoth Gnostic manifestation of the God of Judaism and Christianity, employed in a sixth century CE Coptic MAGIC spell concerning homoerotic love.

Ibis Sacred bird of ancient Egypt associated with the god THOTH and with the anus, enemas, and anal intercourse, as the ibis was believed to clean its anus with its beak.

Ibn Dawud al-Zahiri (fl. c. ninth century CE) Spiritual master and writer of ninth-century Baghdad, he spoke of restrained homophilia (male-loving) as a path to enlightenment. Best known for his *Book of the Planet Venus* (also known as the *Book of the Flower*), he wrote to one young man, "To love you better, I want to remain unsatiated."

Idomeneas Commander of the Cretan contingent in the Trojan War, his comrade-lover was MERIONES. Mozart characteristically removed the homoerotic element from the tale of Idomeneas in his 1781 opera *Idomeneo, Rè di Creta*.

Ila / Sudyumna In Hindu mythology, Manu prayed to the god MITRA-VARUNA that his wife might bear a son. He did not, however, offer the appropriate sacrifice, and his wife consequently gave birth to a daughter, who was named Ila. (This aspect of the myth clearly reflects the patriarchal elements of Hinduism and the related social system of India.) Mitra-Varuna, despite Manu's error, ultimately changed Ila into a male. Although it is possible that numerous Ilas existed in the Hindu mythos, it seems that one day, Ila, now male, wandered into a sacred grove belonging to the spouse of the god SHIVA, the goddess PARVATI. Prior to this event, Parvati had made Shiva promise to transform any man wandering there into a woman, as she and her female companions (reminiscent of the Greek ARTEMIS and her retinue) had once been disturbed by male sages while taking a bath. In this way, Ila once more became a woman, reminding one of the Greek sage TIRESIAS, who underwent numerous sex changes during his/her lifetime, as well as of persons who changed sex, like NARADA, as a result of drinking or bathing in magical springs like the Arabic AL-ZAHAR or in water touched by the RAINBOW. Ila's brothers prayed to Parvati and Shiva that Ila might again become a male. Their prayer was answered, with Ila as a man taking the new name of Sudyumna. After a time, however, Sudyumna metamorphosed yet again, becoming a woman and marrying Budha (the planet Mercury as a god, not the Buddha of Buddhism), a son of SOMA. Sudyumna then gave birth to a son Pururavas. Following this event, certain sages prayed to VISHNU that Sudyumna might once more be changed into a male. Vishnu answered their prayer, and eventually Sudyumna, once Ila, became the father of several children. In a less mythological, more religious context, Ila is associated with Sarasvati, a Hindu goddess of writers and musicians.

Ilpindja A type of erotic, magical incantation employed by indigenous Australians, sometimes including heterosexual, bisexual, and homosexual/lesbian elements. In one *ilpindja*, two women (one older, the other younger, possibly suggesting initiation) are being carried by a magical bird toward a man who desires them. At one point in their journey, they find themselves in the upper branches of a tall tree. There they begin to "look hard at each other's genitals." The implication is that they are aroused by each other and that they commence mutual masturbation.

Imsety Androgynous son of Horus portrayed as a beardless man with the "yellow skin colour of a woman" (in Egyptian, as in Greek, art, darker and lighter colors frequently referred to gender rather than ethnic differences). His image (along with that of HAPY) is depicted on one of the canopic jars; Imsety's contains the liver. Imsety is associated with the direction of the south and with the goddess ISIS.

In P'en Transgendered deity of prosperity among the Chorti of Guatemala.

Inanna/Ishtar While empires rose and fell in the Fertile Crescent, the worship of the goddess Inanna/Ishtar remained a constant in the lives of Mesopotamians. Inanna/Ishtar controls the seasonal cycles as well as those of human life. She is a bestower of "bounteous crops," and a patron of artists and craftspersons. According to G. Leick (1994), "In the hymns and prayers it is Inanna/Ishtar who represents and controls the *me* (essential quality, inborn gift) and *garza* of sexuality . . . she is the patron of brides . . . and prostitutes, as well as of eunuchs and homosexuals. Her personality, which spans the roles of both genders, provides a unique frame of reference for all aspects of sexual behavior [and the] capacity for gender metamorphosis." Inanna is often depicted as a HIERODULE, "visiting 'taverns' and converting her own temples into such establishments." As a patron of prostitutes, she is sometimes depicted as an OWL, or hybrid human female/owl, "which, like the harlot, comes out at dusk." In this aspect, she is called Ninnina, "Mistress Owl." As a transgendered goddess, Inanna is portrayed as an armed and winged AMAZON. As a patron of gender variant women, Inanna was served by transgendered female, perhaps lesbian, priest/esse/s called *sinnisat zikrum*. As a patron of transgendered and homoerotically inclined males, she was served by the ASSINNU, KALATURRU, KALUM, KURGARRU, and others. An ancient text concerning Inanna and transgenderism, including transvestism, reads: "She [turns] a man into a woman, / She [turns] a woman into a man, / She adorn[s] a man as a woman, / She adorn[s] a woman as a man."

Indra Sky god of Hinduism. Both bisexual (or pansexual) and transgendered in today's terms, he loves his wife Indrani and the male lunar deity SOMA. His role as celestial deity and his love for Soma has elicited comparisons with the Greek ZEUS as the lover of GANYMEDE. Indra is associated with transgenderism in that Indra and Indrani are perceived both as a married couple and as the masculine and feminine aspects of a single androgynous deity. When Indra is seen as Indra/Indrani, he-she is described as being "marked with a thousand yonis" as well as "a man among men, and a woman among women." Indra/Indrani played a central role in early Vedic ritual. According to S. A. Dange (1979), Indra/Indrani was represented by two male priests joined in a symbolic, or possibly literal, intimate embrace or MITHUNA, with one of the priests taking the role of the masculine aspect and the other, that of the feminine. Dange compares this androgynous figure and accompanying mithuna to the embrace of SHIVA and SHAKTI and the androgynous "child" of their union, ARDHANARISHVARA.

Ingiet Initiation rites of certain Ingiet groups in Melanesia include ritualized homoerotic sexuality. Van Gennup describes one ritual in this way: "an elderly member of the group strips and covers himself with lime from head to foot. He holds the end of a plaited mat in his hand and gives the other end to one of the novices. They alternately pull and stuggle until the old man falls on the novice and the act is carried out."

Ini Goddess of Borneo revered chiefly by the Dayak. Her name simultaneously suggests "Grandmother" and "Medicine Woman." A celestial goddess of fortune, "she brings good luck to farmers and blesses them with abundance." She is perhaps the most important deity among those worshipped by the MANANG BALI, the transgendered male shamans of the Sea Dyak.

Inle (or **Erinlé**) The *orishá* Inlé, sometimes identified with Ochossí, the *orishá* of hunting, and also with Saint RAPHAEL, is a physician of the pantheon of the Yoruba-diasporic religion(s). Inlé is also a patron of hunters and fishers as well as – with ORUNMILA and YEMAYA – an *orishá* of divination. Once when Inlé was fishing, a beautiful siren or mermaid appeared to him. This figure was Yemayá (or Yemayá-OLOKUN). Inlé fell in love with the *orishá* at first sight, and the two became lovers. While together, Yemayá taught Inlé the art of divination. When he abandoned her, and she became worried that he might share her secrets with others, she cut out his tongue. Now when Inlé wishes to speak, he must do so through Yemayá. Inlé is sometimes envisaged as merging with Yemayá. In this androgynous/gynandrous aspect, he/she is known as Inlé Ayayá or as Yemayá Mayéweló (when the feminine nature predominates). In this manifestation, Inlé is considered to be the patron of lesbian women, "masculine homosexuals," and transgendered persons. L. Cabrera (1980) reports that many lesbian women in Regla Ocha (a Cuban term for Santería, a branch of the religion) "have Inlé for a patron." Cabrera also reports that in pre-revolutionary Cuba, there was a society of lesbian daughters of Inlé. Further, she reports that for many years, lesbian and gay children of Inlé would gather in Cuba on October 24 to pay homage to the *orishá*. Their festive procession included the lighting of a fish made of straw and filled with firecrackers.

Intestines In the past, among gender variant, third gender, or TWO-SPIRIT male shamans of northeastern Siberia, a symbol of the intimate relationship between an elder and a novice shaman, likely to have signified anal intercourse, according to J. Malaurie (1992). The elder shaman was thought to ritually extract the younger shaman's soul, or spirits, and intestines, both in order to protect these organs from dangerous shamans and spirits as well as to nourish (in an almost vampiric way) the elder shaman. Malaurie compares this pedagogical, intergenerational intimacy to that of the ancient Greeks.

Inyangba A feminine manifestation of the androgynous or transgendered Yoruba-diasporic deity OBATALA.

Iolaus An *eromenos*, or beloved, of the Greek divinized hero HERACLES. Iolaus is a divinized hero associated with the shamanic powers of healing and raising the dead. On his way to Libya, Heracles was killled by Typhon. He was revived by Iolaus, who knew that if anything would bring his lover back to kife, it would be the smell of roasted quail. He roasted the bird and placed it under Heracles' nose, and Heracles revived instantly. Plutarch tells us that male lovers pledged their lives to one another at the tomb and chapel of Iolaus at Thebes. Near the *héroon* of Iolaus stood a gymnasium or stadium where games in honor of him, the Iolaéia, took place. C. Calame (1977) describes the complex of tomb-chapel and gymnasium as a sacred site for "the religious consecration of homosexual relationships." One of the first anthologies of gay, or queer, literature as well as of Gay Spirituality or Queer Spirit, edited by Edward CARPENTER, was *Iolaüs* (1917), so named in memory of the beloved of Heracles.

Iphigenia In Greek legend, a princess, the daughter of Queen Clytemnestra and King AGAMEMNON. Agamemnon was told that if he wished to sail to Troy, he must sacrifice his daughter, as he had offended the goddess ARTEMIS by slaying a sacred deer of hers. While some say that the sacrifice went ahead as planned, others claim that Artemis, loving Iphigenia, rescued her at the last moment

and carried her to the land of the Taurians, where she became a priestess of the Goddess.

Iphis Young woman of Greek and Roman legend brought up as a male youth so that she would not be killed by her father, who had wanted a baby boy. On reaching adulthood, Iphis fell in love with a young woman named Ianthe. The two were engaged to be married. On the eve of the wedding, fearing that Iphis' anatomical identity would be discovered, her mother Telethusa prayed to the goddess ISIS to aid her daughter (-son) in some miraculous way. The Goddess responded by transforming Iphis into a male, and Iphis and Ianthe were married. While the tale has a double-edged ending involving the unfortunate dissolution of a transgendered, lesbian relationship, it is clear that the tale simultaneously acknowledges lesbian attraction and may in fact be a heterosexualized version of an earlier lesbian narrative.

Irinaliutiit "Magical words" employed by the ancient Inuit people to transform humans into animals, men into women, and women into men.

Iris In Chinese symbolism, a flower representing the "intermediate stage between man and woman."

Isangoma (pl. **Izangoma**; also **Sangoma**) Spiritual functionary of the traditional religion of the Zulu people of southern Africa. While in the late twentieth century it appears that neither transgenderism nor same-sex eroticism plays a central role in the tradition, it is nevertheless the case that some male *izangoma* are considered gender variant, or transgendered, and are homoerotically or bisexually inclined. The same may be true for some female *izangoma*, although the authors have not been able as yet to verify this. Among the Zulu, the gender variant male spiritual guide is also said to undergo a kind of shamanic transformation. This process is referred to as *ukuthwasa*, which suggests a "'coming out' or 'emergence,' as of the appearance of the new moon." The process begins when a certain spirit decides to take possession of, or become the spiritual guardian of, an individual. That individual will then proceed to become an *isangoma*, a diviner. The spirits that take possession of new *izangoma* are those that, unlike spirits of the newly deceased, have "reached the desired complete state of spiritual being," rather like BODDHISATTVAS. They tend to "return to this world through their daughters." Occasionally, however, an ancestral spirit of this type takes possession of a male. Contemporary Zulu anthropologist H. Ngubane (1977) writes, "Divination is a woman's thing, and if a man gets possessed he becomes a transvestite, as he is playing the role of a daughter rather than that of a son." As with female *izangoma*, the man experiencing transformation often falls ill. He begins to eat less and less and frequently experiences nausea. He may also experience nervousness, insomnia, and intense itching in the area of the shoulders. Eventually, he has a dream or series of dreams in which a spirit or spirits speak to him, telling him that he is destined to become a diviner. "We are your ancestors . . . We have long tried to make your people understand that we want you to be our house—to speak for us." The individual is then taken by one or more *izangoma* to be further healed and initiated. This process may last several months. During this time he is isolated from the community and associates only with *izangoma*. Here he will learn about healing, divination, magic, and other beliefs and practices. It is usually during this time that the male diviner-to-be undergoes gender transformation and may begin to engage in same-sex eroticism. At this time, he "adopt[s] female dress" and begins to "speak in high-pitched tones." The male *isangoma* finds his complement in the female *isangoma*, described as "active" and "masculine." Unlike other Zulu women, she is allowed to "carry a shield and a spear, those badges of manhood," and she enjoys "meat and beer." At the time of formal initiation, the initiate is adorned with "crossed strips of magical goatskin over the shoulders," his hair is plaited, he is given beads, and his face and body are painted. He may also carry a serpent. A celebration called the *ukuhunga* takes place at which goats and oxen are sacrificed. The initiate is now believed to have completed the process of *ukuthwasa* and will be allowed to become a full-fledged *isangoma*, called upon by his community to heal, divine, work magic, and perform sacrifices.

Iscariot, Judas (fl. first century CE)   In Christianity, a disciple of JESUS Christ who betrayed him to his captors by kissing him. Xavier Mayne (pseudonym of Edward Prime-Stevenson, 1869-1942) suggests in *The Intersexes* in 1908: "One may even ask whether the treason of Judas was the madness of a jealous homosexual." This view is echoed in the passionate relationship depicted between Judas and Jesus in the rock opera *Jesus Christ Superstar*.

Isherwood, Christopher (1904-1986)   Acclaimed gay male writer, born in England and settling in California, best known for his *Goodbye to Berlin* (1939) and *The Berlin Stories* (1945) that were developed into the musical and film *Cabaret*. Isherwood is also recognized for his translations of Hindu works and his writings on Hinduism including *Bhagavad-gita: The Song of God* (1944, trans. with Sw Prabhavananda), *What Vedanta Means to Me* (1951), *Approach to Vedanta* (1963), *Ramakrishna and His Disciples* (1965), and *Essentials of Vedanta* (1969). *A Meeting by the River* (1967) and *My Guru and His Disciple* (1980) speak to the interrelationship of homoeroticism and the sacred. In the former, Isherwood symbolically divides himself into erotic artist and ascetic seeker in the form of two brothers whose ultimate rapprochement represents

the writer's own integration of the homoerotic, the artistic, and the sacred. In the latter, Swami Prabhavananda, in attempting to persuade Isherwood to focus on the spiritual aspect of his love for the artist Don Bachardy, tells him, "You must try to see him as the young Lord KRISHNA."

Ishi Kore Dome No Kami   Transgendered or gynandrous deity of the Shinto religion of Japan who creates and holds the exquisite mirror that, along with the dance of AME NO UZUME, succeeds in bringing the sun goddess AMATERASU OMI KAMI out of hiding. Makers of mirrors and stonecutters worship Ishi Kore Dome No Kami.

Ishquicuink   Among the Kechki people of Guatemala, a term signifying a man who "sometimes acts like a man, sometimes like a woman." In the past, such men appear to have assisted *curanderas*, women folk healers. Today, the tradition of the *ishquicuink* is carried on by gay men who serve as ritual artists, as in stringing pine needles in decorative strands to be employed in festivals.

Isis   While the worship of the Great Goddess in Egypt appears to have commenced during the Paleolithic period, her manifestation as Isis dates from the period between 3600 and 3000 BCE. A goddess of nature, the arts, healing, and magic, she was called the Mother of the Pharaohs. Although her worship was eventually displaced by a state religion focusing on OSIRIS, Horus, and other male deities, a renascence of Isis reverence commenced in the seventh century BCE which reached its apex in the Hellenistic world of the fourth century BCE, coming to an end only with the triumph of Christianity over paganism. The revived religion of Isis gathered followers of both sexes, various ethnicities, and all economic classes; included among the faithful were gender variant, homoerotically inclined males. Isis appears to have been associated with gender variance from an early date. According to a papyrus in the Louvre (no. 3079), Isis says of herself in an early ritual drama concerning Osiris's death, "I turned myself into a man, although I was a woman in order to make your [i.e. Osiris's] name endure on earth." She was also associated with homoeroticism by way of her brother or son SET and his relationship with her son Horus. The transgendered male priest/esse/s of Isis appear to have comprised one of several groups of priests. They dressed in the linen garments of the Goddess. In *The Golden Ass*, the Latin writer Apuleius describes one such man as wearing "gilt sandals, [a] silken gown, and costly ornaments." While some of Isis's priests shaved their heads, ancient sources indicate that her gender variant priests may have grown their hair long or worn indigo wigs made of horsetail plumes. According to Ramsay Macmullen, "their long hair was thought to be a sign of inspiration, the longer the better." Some priests also grew their nails long; a horrified

Christian observer referred to these as "claws." Some shaved their faces daily and smeared them with milk-soaked bread to make them seem smoother. Some depilated their bodies, wore exotic perfumes, and walked "with a woman's mincing gait." At least some may have undergone ritual castration. Where same-sex eroticism is concerned, classical scholar Peter Green assures us that the Temple of Isis in the Campus Martius in Rome was "used as a rendez-vous by male homosexuals." We also know the names of several homoerotically inclined worshippers of Isis, one of the most well known being the Roman emperor Otho, a lover of Nero. One of the most important functions of the transgendered priests of Isis was to join her female priestesses in magically causing the Nile to rise so that the land might be made fertile. According to Aristainetos, a company of priests and priestesses would sail the Nile singing antiphonal hymns to encourage its rising. This ceremony appears to have been an ecstatic dance-drama which included the ritual raising of skirts by both the priestesses and the gender variant priests. While the priestesses' exhibition of their genitalia was believed to represent fertility, the priests' exhibition of their genitalia represented rather their forfeit of virility – via ritual castration, gender variant homoeroticism, or both – to the Goddess, and hence the earth, so that the crops might prosper. A similar dance-drama is depicted on a marble relief found in a tomb on the Appian Way at Ariccia, near Rome. Several, if not all, of the participants are of sub-Saharan African descent. Some are dancing ecstatically, shaking their buttocks, bending their knees, tossing their heads, and raising their arms toward the heavens. Others are clapping. Still others are playing cymbals and clappers. According to Frank Snowden, a number of those who carried the worship of Isis from Egypt to Rome were sub-Saharan Africans. Non-Black worshippers, however, may also have carried African elements of her worship to Rome, returning home from pilgrimages to her temple at Meroe. We know, for instance, of a Roman noblewoman who journeyed to Meroe to obtain holy water for the temple of Isis in Rome. While Snowden is to be commended for his observation that the rite depicted on the Ariccian relief is an African-based dance performed by Black Africans or Afro-Romans, he is incorrect in supposing all the dancers to be female. Indeed, some are clearly male, while others may be men dressed as women. According to Ramsay Macmullen, the male dancers are *cinaedi*, that is, gender variant and homoerotically inclined males, shown in the characteristic pose of shaking the buttocks (in Greek, *kinein*). Thus, in sum, the Ariccian relief depicts female and gender variant, homoerotically inclined African or Afro-Roman worshippers engaging in an ecstatic, African-based dance-drama in honor of the goddess Isis. Gender variant male priests continued to serve Isis until the fourth century CE, when the Christianized Roman emperor Constantine, as part of his campaign against paganism,

forbade them from participating in the rite of raising the Nile and in other ceremonies as well. When they refused, they were murdered. Not long after, the priestesses of Isis fell at his hands, and the temples of the Goddess were desecrated and destroyed.

Island Dialogues, The (1973)   This mysterious book by equally mysterious author Llee Heflin (fl.1970s) is an early cult classic of Gay Spirituality/Queer Spirit. The work is profoundly influenced by TANTRA, the Hindu system of *chakras*, QABBALAH and by the ritual MAGIC(K) of Aleister CROWLEY. Its form is that of a magical diary, written between 1971 and 1973. Its style is poetic prose, highly evocative and suggestive of CHANNELING. Its central message is that homoeroticism, when experienced in a magical, ritualistic context, can serve as a bridge to enlightenment. Another key message suggests that while homoerotic relations, like hetero-erotic ones, are governed by duality or binarity, this duality is expressed as "both-and" – resembling the image of twins and Mitch WALKER's concept of the DOUBLE – rather than "either-or." While a sort of YIN AND YANG dualism exists, it exists within both partners, creating a kind of four-way current. This "both-and" aspect of homoerotic relationships also infers that this type of relationship is one which thrives on paradox. Another way in which this "both-and" quality is expressed is in the ability, by way of meditative anal intercourse, to experience the full power of both the first and the final *chakras* or "lights" (*sephiroth*) of the Qabbalistic tree of Life at once. In this aspect, it is noteworthy that Heflin names the "feminine" or receptive aspect of the lover the "SHAKTI," as this term refers simultaneously to a Hindu goddess, the "feminine" aspect of the male psyche, and the serpentine current of energy (also referred to as Kundalini) which traverses the spinal column to link the various chakras in order to awaken and to fully empower the practitioner, especially of Tantra. Another key message is that in order to attain homoerotic enlightenment, one must: master the art of self-love, expressed in masturbation; confront, in a sort of vision quest or shamanic journey, one's "demons" and psychically experience one's death; make contact with a soul-guide, or psychopomp, who may appear as an angelic or alien being; experience a loving relationship with another man and/or a community of men undertaking this process. From such a relationship, a "Magickal Child" – similar to the spirit-children described by Diotima in the *Symposium* of Plato – is born. Eventually, such relationships will also give birth to erotico-spiritual, i.e. Tantric, communities of men-loving men. Such a relationship may also give birth to a magical force that can be manipulated to ameliorate life. Heflin asserts – in opposition to the brilliant but homophobic occultist Kenneth GRANT – that this process is what Aleister CROWLEY had in mind when he spoke of the "eleventh degree" of his system of ritual magic.

According to Heflin, the eighth degree focuses on self-love/masturbation; the ninth on heterosexual relations; the tenth on transgenderism, asceticism, and aestheticism; and the eleventh on homosexual relations. Heflin further links these degrees to cards of the Major Arcana of the TAROT, with the eighth represented by Empress and Death, the ninth by the High Priestess and the Hanged Man; and the eleventh by the Fool, the Aeon, and the Universe. Another key message will strike some today as mistaken, outdated, or irresponsible, yet one should bear in mind that *Island* was written many years prior to the emergence of AIDS. This is the belief that homoerotically inclined men are helped toward enlightenment by way of the ritual (and loving) ingestion of semen, which Heflin refers to as "Holy Star Food." "The come of our brothers," he chants, "links us with each other and their Stars." This belief is not a new one; Hindu deities and sages have long been aware of the potency of semen, as revealed in the *purana* (myth) of the fire-god AGNI swallowing the semen of SHIVA, an action that ultimately results in the birth of KARTIKKEYEH, god of war and beauty. Yet, perhaps aware that tales of Hindu divinities and sages suggest that a majority are incinerated by the fiery semen of Shiva, Heflin tempers this belief with the warning, "It [i.e. semen] is [both] the fruit of the Tree of Life and the key to Daath [here, Death] . . . it must be purified . . . in the living laboratory of the body . . . Its purity depends upon the purity of the man. Become aware of the quality of all the energy that comes into your body for it affects the quality of the Star Food you manifest. This means food, liquid, air, drugs, thoughts and ideas, sights, sounds, emotional vibrations, [and] the Star Food

of other men." Heflin also offers – again, in 1973 – an extraordinary prediction: "Our bodies will be persecuted severely as mutations and will be forced underground, as the mystery always is. Part of this mutation will have to do with our gaining the ability to physically absorb more and more of the rays above ultraviolet. The community of eleventh degree magickians will [then] establish itself." Heflin further speculates that, reminiscent of the ancient Gnostics, this community will ultimately evacuate earth to establish itself elsewhere. "Thus," he tells us, "does the body of migration mythology build itself."

Ithyphalloi Term given to phallic rites, dancers, and songs associated with the cult of DIONYSUS. Dancers were often cross-dressed. Some (presumably including women) wore or carried large artificial phalli. At the climax of a procession to the theater, the dancers chanted, "Give way, give way! Make room for the god; for the god wishes to pass through!"

Itijjuaq Inuit third gender being, "Big Anus," considered one of the world's first shamans (*angakkuq*). Itijjuaq is also the discoverer of the world's first amulet (*arnguaq*): the shell of the sea-urchin. Itijjuaq, employing his (-her) shell amulet, possesses the power to cure the most deadly illnesses.

Ivy Symbolic of comedy, wisdom, healing, and ecstasy, the ivy is sacred to the Greco-Roman deities DIONYSUS and CYBELE, with many of their priests and priestesses tattooing themseles with ivy-leaf patterns.

J

Jade In China, jade is symbolic of beauty, sexual intercourse, the coming together of traditionally feminine and masculine (YIN AND YANG) elements within the psyche, longevity, and immortality. As early as the third century CE, the "man of jade" referred to the "paragon of male physical beauty," as exemplified by the scholar Pei Kai (237-291). "Looking at Pei Kai," wrote an admiring observer, "is like walking on top of a jade mountain with the light reflected back at you." In Taoist ALCHEMY, the "jade stem" is the penis, while "jade fluid" refers to semen. The expression "to play with jade and blow the flute" refers to fellatio. The nickname of the Taoist alchemist Shan Tao, a bisexually inclined man who shared a homoerotic relationship with the sages Xi Kang and Ruan Ji (of the SEVEN SAGES OF THE BAMBOO GROVE) in the third century, was "Uncut Jade," signifying an impressive, uncircumcised penis. The "jade gate" is the vagina or vulva, with "jade sap" referring to vaginal secretions. "Handling jade" signifies cunnilingus. In Taoist alchemy, Mistress White Jade appears as a character who engages in woman-loving EROTICISM with Lady Precious Yin, their "jade gates" pressing together. In premodern China, lesbian lovers exchanged jade bracelets.

Jaguar In Aztec religion or mythology, associated with the god TEZCATLIPOCA, thus linked to Shamanism – especially to healing, divination, and shapeshifting – and to gender and sexual variance.

James I, King of England (and **VI of Scotland,** 1566-1625) Man-loving ruler whose place in queer-spiritual history is both noteworthy and problematic. James, responsible for the *King James Version of the Bible*, compared himself and his beloved George Villiers, the Duke of Buckingham, to JESUS and ST JOHN THE EVANGELIST, saying, "Christ had his John and I have my George." For the greater part of his life, James appears to have been viciously anti-pagan – as exemplified by his *Daemonologie* (1597) – especially against those who claimed to revere fairies, claiming that these individuals were more repellent than those who (allegedly) revered Satan, because the fairy worshippers did not seem as evil to the populace as the latter when in fact, according to James, they were. Those alleged to be practicing Witchcraft or kindred spiritual traditions did not, for the most part, care for James either. As one example among numerous others, John Fian and his coven were charged with raising a storm in an attempt to drown the King as he was returning from a journey to Denmark. Nevertheless, fragmentary evidence

suggests that the King's beloved George may himself have been reared to be a Witch or other sort of pagan, and that Katherine Manners, the female courtier George ultimately married, may have been as well. It seems that the anti-pagan James, lying on his deathbed, participated in a magical rite geared toward prolonging his life. The belief behind the rite was that if another person were sacrificed, the King might live. George and Katherine, leading the rite, could not procure a human and so dressed a piglet in infant's clothing and sacrificed it. Not surprisingly, the substitution proved unacceptable, and the King died shortly thereafter.

Jarman, Derek (1942-1994) Simon Field has written of the British filmmaker, "Jarman has . . . in utopian spirit, sought out angels, while celebrating visual pleasure and luxuriating in an excess of theatricality and painterly effect." Many of his films touch upon the interrelationship of same-sex passion and/or transgenderism and the mythic or sacred; chief among these are *Sebastiane* (SAINT SEBASTIAN, 1976), *The Tempest* (1979), *The Angelic Conversation* (1985), *CARAVAGGIO* (1986), *War Requiem* (1989), *The Garden* (1990), *Edward II* (1992), and *BLUE* (1993). Raymond Murray (1994) describes *The Garden*: "While director Jarman fitfully sleeps in his garden, his cryptic dreams . . . are played out in their fullest, queerest glory. The lyrical images of male love, tenderness, and art are interspersed with images of natural beauty; but all collide against a backlash of homophobia, persecution, and death. An allegory for AIDS, the film's main narrative thrust depicts two male lovers as they, in the manner of JESUS Christ, are taunted, arrested, tortured and are crucified for their beliefs. A stunningly filmed work of art, full of poetically realized images and fueled with an intense longing for understanding, peace and brotherhood."

Jeanne d'Arc, Saint (Joan of Arc, 1412-1431) French Catholic saint, woman warrior, and mystic. As a young girl living on a farm, Jeanne began to hear voices, allegedly those of Catholic saints, including St Michael, St Catherine, and St Margaret. Some have suggested that behind the masks of these saints, the young Jeanne may have been visited rather by pre-Christian Celtic deities or fairies believed to inhabit the region in which she was living, a focal point being certain trees, especially a wood known as Bois Chesnu, and a particular tree, a beech (*fagus*), known as "The Ladies' Tree" or "The Fairies' Tree." W. S. Scott in *The Trial of Joan of Arc* (1956), and Arthur Evans, in *Witchcraft and the Gay Counterculture*

(1978), relate that a prophecy attributed to Merlin, and linked to the Celtic faith and Bois Chesnu, claimed that a maiden would come forth from the wood, would perform miracles, and would unite the people. When Jeanne was about twelve, she ran away from home to Neufchateau, where she became the servant of an innkeeper known as La Rousse. This inn apparently also served as a brothel, and it is conceivable that Jeanne developed an affectionate bond with one or more of the young women housed there. She appears to have shared such a bond with a young woman named Catherine, with Jeanne and Catherine sleeping in the same bed so that Jeanne might also see the angelic "lady" who visited Catherine at night. Around this time, Jeanne's own visions seem to have increased dramatically. She also began to gain the reputation of being a powerful healer. She was told in a vision which included a host of saints, angels, and the Lord Himself that she was to relinquish feminine attire, behavior, and responsibilities and to assume a transgendered, Amazonian identity in order to serve France. The similarities between this vision and the ensuing gender metamorphosis experienced by TWO-SPIRIT shamans is uncanny. Jeanne was not exchanging a mystical role for a soldierly one; rather, like the HWAME and other two-spirit female shamans, she was transforming into a warrior-spiritual functionary. Jeanne is described as having "her hair cut around like a young coxcomb" and as wearing "shirt, breeches, doublet [and] buskins," and as bearing "sword, dagger, breast-plate, lance and other arms in the fashion of a man of war." Jeanne also began to prophesy. She was at first laughed at by the French military commander at Vauchuleurs, but he changed his mind after her prophesy of the French being defeated in the Battle of Herrings near Orléans in 1429 came true. At sixteen years old, at the commander's bidding, she approached the Dauphin, later Charles VII of France, asking him to grant her the right to join the French forces. While primarily in a leadership rather than a combat role, she was furnished with troops, raising the Siege of Orléans in the Hundred Years War in May 1429. Later that year, she defeated the English at Patay but was unsuccessful in her attempt to conquer the English at Paris. The following spring she was captured by the Burgundians, who sold her to the English, who desperately sought her death. She was ultimately brought to trial at the ecclesiastical court at Rouen, where she was tried for Witchcraft and heresy by French clerics who supported the English. While the court could not find enough evidence to condemn her as a witch, her belief that her transgendered identity and its expression in transvestism and soldiering were divinely inspired was enough to convict her of heresy, especially when combined with testimony suggesting possible lesbian intimacy. At the trial's climax, Jeanne, fearing the worst, recanted. She was sentenced to life imprisonment. Shortly thereafter, she retracted her statement, was found wearing male attire in

her prison cell, was turned over to the secular court as a relapsed heretic, and was burned at the stake on May 30, 1431. A court appointed by Pope Callistus II found her innocent in 1456. Almost five centuries later, in 1920, she was canonized. Today, she serves as an icon for women in the military and woman fighting for injustice. Known as the Maid (La Pucelle) of Orléans, St Jeanne d'Arc is fêted on May 30.

Jesuit In nineteenth-century French bohemian circles, the figure of the Jesuit priest became a signifier for male homosexuality.

Jesus (c. 5 BCE- c. 30 CE)   Founder of Christianity. Reared in Judaism, Jesus began to preach a radical variant of the religion in or near 27 CE which ultimately led to its splitting from the parent faith, the most divergent message being that he was himself the son of, and synonymous with, the Lord of Biblical tradition. For his beliefs, Jesus, who became known to his followers as (the) Christ, was crucified by the Romans holding power in the region. As Albert Boime (1981) observes, "The mystical tradition has always considered Christ an androgyne; the wound in Christ's side was the analogy for female genitalia, and the image of Christ producing his bride, the holy Mother Church, through the wound in his side in the same way as the first Adam produced Eve, is to be found in Orthodox Christian theology and liturgy." Some Gnostic Christians believed that Jesus had actually produced a woman from his side, with whom he then had intercourse, with the woman giving birth to mortal children. Others held that Jesus did have children, but that these resulted from a union with Mary Magdalene. Thus, while "mainstream" Christianity has held that Jesus was a celibate ascetic, minor traditions of the religion have suggested that he may have been transgendered and/or heterosexual. Still others have suggested that he may have been bisexually or homoerotically inclined. This notion is rooted in three events of the life of Jesus. The first concerns his healing and revivification of a man named LAZARUS, whom he is said to love. While it is clear that followers believe that Jesus loves all people, it is equally clear from this narrative (John 11: 1-44) that Lazarus held a special place in Jesus's heart. The second centers on the last Passover, or "Last Supper," that he celebrated with his primary disciples. In John 21: 23, we are told that "One of his disciples, whom Jesus loved, was lying close to the breast of Jesus." As with Lazarus, emphasis is placed upon the depth of Jesus's affection for this particular disciple, who has become known as "the beloved disciple." While many scholars and artists over the centuries have identified the beloved disciple with SAINT JOHN THE EVANGELIST, an increasing number are arguing that this disciple may have been Lazarus. The third event concerns Jesus's betrayal, when he is identified by his captors upon his disciple Judas

ISCARIOT's kissing him. This kiss has inspired both homoerotic and homophobic commentary and art for almost two millennia. A SECRET GOSPEL attributed to the apostle St Mark, a reference to which was discovered by Morton Smith in 1958, supports the notion of cultic homoeroticism occurring within the inner circle of Jesus. As John Boswell (1980) reveals, the tradition of Jesus' affection for the disciple John has been depicted in painting and sculpture since late antiquity, becoming especially popular in the European Middle Ages. Also in the Middle Ages, a legend, known as the TOLEDOTH YESHU, appears to have emerged which suggested that Jesus and Judas engaged in sexual intercourse. During the Renaissance, the Spanish mystic SAN JUAN DE LA CRUZ (Saint John of the Cross) described in a poem an erotico-spiritual encounter with Jesus, the English poet and playwright Christopher MARLOWE allegedly remarked, "John the Evangelist was bedfellow to Christ and leaned alwaies in his bosome," and King JAMES I, commenting upon his relationship with George Villiers, Earl of Buckingham, allegedly said, "Christ had his John, and I have my George." In the eighteenth century, the French philosopher Diderot (1713-1784) pondered, "What if, at the marriage of Cana, Christ . . . a bit of a nonconformist, had caressed the breast of one of the bridesmaids and the buttocks of St John?" Jesus's potential bisexuality or homosexuality continued to intrigue scholars, artists, and others of the nineteenth and early twentieth centuries. Jean Delville's (1867-1951) exquisite *Academy of Plato*, conflating the narratives of Plato and Jesus and their disciples, is clearly meant to infer the homosexuality of Jesus's inner circle. In 1908, in *The Intersexes*, Xavier Mayne (pseudonymn of Edward I. Prime-Stevenson, 1868-1942) named Jesus as a "URANIAN," that is, as one possessing homoerotic sensitivity. This notion was again reiterated in a biography of Walt WHITMAN by the US writer Edgar Lee Masters (1869-1950, renowned for his *Spoon River Anthology*), published in 1937. Jesus also made an appearance in Noel I. Garde's *Jonathan to Gide: The Homosexual in History* (1964). The love of Judas for Jesus was not lost to Andrew Lloyd Webber and Tim Rice in *Jesus Christ Superstar* (1972), especially in the London production of the rock opera. In the 1980s, US lesbian-feminist theologian Mary DALY (1984) attacked Jesus's transgendered aspect: "Androgynous, sweet Jesus, the misbegotten and transsexed parthenogenetic daughter who incorporated both masculine and feminine roles, being lord, savior, and sacrificial victim, was the logical surrogate for the female principle." Almost a decade later, Robert Williams (Episcopalian), Robert Goss (Episcopalian), and Nancy Wilson (Protestant), all ministers and all inspired by Queer activism, offered radical (re-) visions of Jesus and of Christianity as a whole. Williams, in *Just as I Am: A Practical Guide to Being Out, Proud, and Christian* (1992), argues that "Jesus was the

passionate lover of Lazarus, a young man who became his disciple." Goss, in *Jesus Acted Up: A Gay and Lesbian Manifesto* (1993), guided by the writings of Morton Smith, Tom Driver, Malcolm BOYD, and others, writes: "At the core of the Gospel traditions, Jesus is depicted as a shaman. He is portrayed as a spirit-filled charismatic, an exorcist, a magician, and a visionary . . . Queer Christians are called to be shamans like Jesus and embark upon a vision quest to integrate their vocation to be queer and serve God's reign." Wilson, who, in *Our Tribe: Queer Folks, God, Jesus, and the Bible* (1995), associates Jesus with queerness as well as with HIV/AIDS, writes: "The Jesus who said he wanted to be identified with 'the least of these' today has AIDS."

Jeto Legendary figure associated with the Hindu goddess BAHUCHARAMATA and honored by the HIJRAS. King Baria was unhappy because he had no son. He prayed to Bahucharamata, who granted him a son, whom he named Jeto. Baria, in turn, offered his son to the Goddess to be her servant. One night, the Goddess appeared to Jeto in a dream and told him to castrate himself and begin to dress in feminine attire. Jeto did so, and since that time, the hijras of Bahucharamata have followed his example.

Jinn Their name signifying "SERPENT-like," these spirits of pre-Islamic Arabic religion and myth have survived in Islamic folklore. They are depicted as "fairy-like" spirits born of wind or fire, neither angelic nor demonic, who possess shapeshifting powers, including that of gender metamorphosis. They also possess the gifts of comprehending and speaking all languages. While they may live for many centuries, they are usually not considered immortal. Their leader is sometimes said to be Iblis, the Arabic equivalent of SATAN, viewed in this context not so much as a force of evil but rather one of rebellion and magic. They appear to have once been associated with the cult of the goddess AL-LAT. Magicians or sorcerers posses the power to control *jinn* for certain period of time. The *jinn* are legendary especially as bringers of wealth. Among those said to be devoted to them are the AL-JINK and the MUKHANNATHUN, transgendered males of the Arabic cosmos. "*Jinn*" is also linked to "MUJUN," a concept of Arabic counterculture embracing same-sex passion, transgenderism, and mysticism.

Joan, Pope (papal name, **John VIII, Anglicus**; may have lived c. mid-ninth century CE)   While her existence remains controversial, many scholars have steadfastly maintained that Joan was an actual, historical personage and not merely a legendary figure. She was said to have been born in England (hence "Anglicus") and to have been dressed in male attire and placed by her parents in a monastery in Mainz, Germany so that she might be able to exercise her intellect to its fullest capacity. As she matured, she increasingly accepted the transgendered identity of John. As a monk and pilgrim, John developed a special friendship with another monk, Ulfilias, with whom s/he traveled to Greece, where the two passed their day studying theology, philosophy, and literature. John was thus devastated when Ulfilias died suddenly. Traveling to Rome, John quickly acquired the reputation of being a brilliant scholar and soon began to rise up the hierarchical ladder of the Church, ultimately being elected Pope John VII, Anglicus in or near 855 CE. Unfortunately, however, John's reign as Pope was brief. It seems that s/he fell deeply in love with a man who reminded him/her of Ulfilias, and, revealing his/her female anatomy to him, soon became pregnant. Certain sources suggest that high Church officials were made aware of John's condition and that a concerted effort was made to conceal his/her condition. Fortune was unkind to John, however, who was, according to the controversial tale, exposed and who either died in childbirth or shortly thereafter. What is perhaps the most intriguing element of this tale is that the Church appears to have been more willing to accept John's being a transgendered female-to-male than it was his/her "lapse" into sexual, and specifically heterosexual, relations, resulting in her pregnancy. If Joan/John's tale is true, however, the Church has proven to be ultimately intolerant, in denying her very existence.

Jogamma In Hinduism, transgendered women serving as priests in the worship of the goddess YELLAMMA.

Jogappa Transgendered male priest/esse/s of the Hindu Goddess YELLAMMA. The term *jogappa* is related to terms meaning "to wander" and "to swing" or "to rock," signifying both the itinerant asceticism and the sensuous dances of the *jogappa*. Males become *jogappa* if and when the goddess Yellamma decides to "catch" (possess, or embody) them. When they are "caught" the males are customarily taken by family members to be initiated at Sundatti, the center of Yellamma's worship. A diviner there confirms (or denies) the man's being "caught" by the Goddess. He is ritually bathed and bestowed with a red *sari*, red and white beads (alternating), an alms basket (*padalagi*), musical instruments (the *surati* and the *chaudiki*), and a copper water pot (*koda*), around the neck of which is a small image of Yellamma. He is given a female name. Now dressing in feminine attire, the *jogappa* lets his (-her) hair grow long and begins to practice depilation. The *jogappa* also receives TATTOOS customarily worn by women. He (-she) begins to perform tasks generally performed by women such as grinding grain. The *jogappa* also begins to carry out spiritual functions which are frequently blended with EROTICISM, such as performing erotic dances, with the copper pots balanced on their heads. While *jogappa* emulate women in some respects, they are considered as being very different from women,

especially in the way that they flaunt their sexuality. They also differ from the HIJRAS of BAHUCHARAMATA in that they do not undergo ritual castration. Moreover, whereas *hijras* often share intimate relationships with non-*hijra*, traditionally masculine men, *jogappa* appear to have sexual relationships primarily with other *jogappa*. Specific spiritual functions fulfilled by *jogappa* include: singing and dancing for Yellamma, especially at puberty rites, weddings, and celebrations of birth, where the presence of *jogappa* is thought to bless the event; collecting alms for Yellamma (again often by way of singing and dancing); making offerings to the Goddess (including betel nuts, turmeric, eggplants, sugarcane, and green onions); preparing ritual meals for the Goddess and her devotees; healing devotees; and leading and instructing devotees or pilgrims of Yellamma in her rites, often serving as village temple priests. *Jogappa* hold Tuesday and nights when the moon is full to be those times most sacred to Yellamma. On certain full moons, *jogappa* ritually destroy their necklaces, symbolizing the "widowhood" of the Goddess; on others, they are bestowed with new ones, symbolizing the "marriage" of Yellamma. The most important rite led by the *jogappa* is the Huttagi, a rite of purification for sick and otherwise afflicted pilgrims. Devotees are dressed in branches of the margosa tree and then ritually bathed in a spring believed to have cured Yellamma of leprosy. They then dress in clean clothes and perform a ritual dance around the temple of the Goddess, after which they partake of a feast prepared by the *jogappa*.

John the Evangelist, Saint, Apostle, called **the Beloved Disciple** (fl. first century CE) In Christianity, the "Beloved Disciple" also known as the "Divine." JESUS met the Galilean fisherman at Lake Genesareth, where he introduced John and his brother James into his mysteries. John is said to have had a fiery temperament; for this reason, he and his brother James were nicknamed the "sons of thunder." At the Last Supper, the final Passover celebrated by Jesus with his disciples, John, "whom Jesus loved, was lying close to the breast of Jesus" (John 13: 23, Oxford Annotated) when the disciples learned of Jesus's imminent betrayal. He was with Jesus during the latter's agony in the Garden of Gethsemane and the only male disciple believed to have been present at the Crucifixion. At this time, Jesus asked John to take care of his mother, Mary. In later years John traveled with Peter to Samaria. He almost certainly wrote the fourth Gospel and three Epistles. In the past, John was thought to have authored the book of Revelation, but both in content and style it differs so widely from his other works that many scholars no longer attribute the apocalyptic text to him. After settling in Ephesus, John was allegedly challenged as a Christian by a priest of ARTEMIS/DIANA to drink a cup of poison in order to see if his God would protect him; thus, one of his attributes is a chalice containing a serpent. It is possible, however, that this tale derives from an attempt to syncretize the cult of John with that of Artemis, or with one of the male gods she was associated with, such as her brother APOLLO, considered a healer and reptile-slayer, ASCLEPIUS, a god of healing whose attribute was the serpent, or HERMES, who was sometimes depicted as holding a chalice containing a serpent. John died at Ephesus. Of the passionate relationship between John and Jesus, John Boswell (1994) writes : "Certainly the most controversial same-sex couple in the Christian tradition comprised Jesus and John, the 'beloved disciple.' The relationship between them was often depicted in subsequent art and literature as intimate, if not erotic. John refers to himself six times as 'the disciple whom Christ loved,' causing one to wonder whether in John's view Jesus did not 'love' the other apostles. At the very least, he must have meant that Jesus had a special affection for him." The EAGLE as John's attribute suggests that this relationship may have been viewed by those of classical antiquity as comparable to the relationship of the Greek god ZEUS and his beloved GANYMEDE, whose other attribute is a chalice. The patron of writers, editors, publishers, booksellers, and theologians, St John is fêted on May 6 and December 27.

John XII, Pope (938-964) Born Octavian, the son of Alberic II of Spoleto, Italy, he became Pope in 955 due to his father's powerful connections. Octavian/John appears to have been drawn toward both men and paganism, with rites including homosexual orgies and the invocation of VENUS (Greek APHRODITE) and JUPITER (Greek ZEUS). Although Church authorities attempted to depose him, he remained Pope until his death in 964.

Johnson, Toby (1945-) Gay writer, therapist, and entrepreneur. A former Catholic monk, Johnson's interest in Gay Spirituality may be traced to the early 1980s, when he served as a counselor to young down-and-out gay men living in a tough area of San Francisco. His book *In Search of God in the Sexual Underworld* (1983) emerged from this experience. Johnson has also been profoundly inspired by his mentor, the mythologist Joseph Campbell, to whom he has dedicated *The Myth of the Great Secret* (1992, rev. ed.). He is also the author of three Gay-Spiritual-themed novels: *Plague: A Novel About Healing* (1987); *Secret Matter* (1990), a winner of the Lammy Award for science-fiction; and *Getting Life in Perspective* (1991). In recent years, Johnson, with the help of Kip Dollar, his companion of many years, has facilitated various Gay-Spiritual groups in Austin, Texas, including Shaman's Circle.

Johnson, Tom (1959-) Gay male writer and traditional Witch living in Oakland, California in the 1990s. An initiate of several traditions of Witchcraft including the Gardnerian tradition, the Faery tradition, and the Minoan Brotherhood, the last of these a gay male-centered path

based in the myth of the goddess Rhea (roughly equivalent to CYBELE) and her male consort, the "Divine Youth." Johnson is the author of numerous articles exploring the interrelationship of homoeroticism and Witchcraft, including "Gay and Gardnerian – Huh?" (1990) and "Scourging and Witchcraft" (1995).

Jones, Bill T. (1952-) African-American gay male dancer, choreographer, and writer. Together with Arnie Zane (1947-1988), Jones created a unique (homo-) erotico-sacred dance style, the two founding the now internationally acclaimed Bill T. Jones/Arnie Zane Dance Company in 1982. Works of special interest to devotees of Queer Spirit include: *The Devil's Gonna Get You*; *Last Supper at Uncle Tom's Cabin*; *ACHILLES loved Patroclus*; and *Last Night on Earth*. "I am Eros," Jones chants, "I am the possibility of Eros before you. I am your future lover. I am every orgasm you are ever going to have . . . I stand there in a short white skirt . . . confusing gender and time."

Joseph (fl. c. second millenium BCE) Biblical hero, whose tale is told in the Book of Genesis (30-50). The apple of his father's eye, Joseph was sold into slavery by brothers jealous of his beautiful coat and his prophetic dreams. After being unjustly imprisoned in Egypt, he rose to prominence there as a governor of Egypt and as a confidant of, and dream-interpreter for, the Pharaoh. A number of scholars, including Beatrice Brooks, W. F. Albright, Joseph L. Henderson, and Maud Oakes, have suggested that Joseph's coat may have linked him to the QEDESHIM, the gender variant hierodulic priests of the Canaanite goddess ATHIRAT. The garment has been linked specifically to Joseph's mother, Rachel, who is believed to have been a devotee or priestess of the Goddess; it may even have functioned as her wedding dress. "For Joseph to possess this [garment]," Henderson and Oakes write, would have "enraged his brothers as much as a group of college students today [they wrote this in 1963] would be enraged if one of their number appeared in women's clothes and expected to have his transvestism accepted." The gift of this garment to Joseph may have signified his father Jacob's desire to return to the worship of the Goddess. We are told in the *Midrash*, a collection of Biblical exegesis gathered between the fifth century BCE and the second century CE, that Potiphar purchased Joseph for the pharaoh of Egypt because of the young man's beauty. Potiphar is described in the *Midrash* as a eunuch priest of a pagan deity, probably the goddess ISIS. It is apparent that he and his wife, who also desired Joseph, did not have a monogamous marriage. While the *Midrash* tells us that Joseph, being a Biblical hero, did not yield to either Potiphar or his wife, various scholars have questioned this aspect of the story. Indeed, it seems that Joseph and Potiphar, or the persons on whom these characters were based, may have enjoyed a complex, transgendered relationship. Indeed, even when depicted as a prophet of the Lord, an interpreter of dreams, Joseph seems more like a qadesh priest, guided "by a secret knowledge of the feminine principle." Henderson and Oakes, following psychologist Erich Neumann, point out that both Joseph's experience in the pit at the hands of his brothers and his interpretation of the dream of seven lean cattle and seven fat cattle may be linked to the shamanic, underworld journey undertaken by the Goddess and her consort. Over the centuries, Joseph became, according to Norman Roth and others, "the ultimate symbol of the beautiful young man in Jewish, Muslim, and Christian" traditions. The Medieval Spanish Jewish poet Yishaq ben Mar-Saul (eleventh century), describing a young male beloved, writes, "Lovely of form like the moon . . . / Curls of purple / upon shining temple, / Like Joseph in his form." Thomas Mann (1875-1955) returned to this image of Joseph in his novel *Joseph and His Brothers* (1939), writing, "It was the mother-goddess who stood there before him [i.e. Jacob, Joseph's father] smiling, in the boy's [i.e. Joseph's] lovely guise."

Juan de la Cruz, San (Saint John of the Cross; Juan de Yepes y Alvarez, 1542-1591) Spanish Catholic priest, theologian, mystic, and writer, considered one of the world's finest poets. He was a close friend of SANTA TERESA DE AVILA (St Theresa of Avila, 1515-1582). Like Terésa, he was a leader of reform within the Carmelite Order. For his efforts, he was arrested and imprisoned at Toledo in 1577; there, he wrote his most beautiful works, including *Noche oscura del Alma* (*The Dark Night of the Soul*). While nothing is certain concerning Juan's sexuality, his work seems inspired by homoerotic desire. Perhaps this is one of the underlying reasons for his friendship with Terésa. In "Dark Night," Juan describes a secret rendezvous in a garden where JESUS awaits him. There, Jesus lays his head on Juan's "flowering breast." It seems that Juan is experiencing gender metamorphosis. Meanwhile, Juan runs his fingers through Jesus' hair. When Jesus serenely "wounds" his neck, Juan yields to him, in a state of bliss, which he depicts in mystical terms, as a sense of oneness with the "lilies of oblivion." San Juan is considered a patron of writers and fabric makers, especially of silk. One of his attributes is the eagle, which links him to SAINT JOHN THE EVANGELIST and the Greek divinized mortal GANYMEDE. He is fêted on December 14 and on June 24, his birthday as well as that of St John the Baptist.

Juana Inés de la Cruz, Sor (Juana de Asbaje y Ramírez de Santillana, c. 1648-1695) Catholic nun, intellectual, and writer living in Mexico, deeply concerned with improving the lives of women, indigenous Americans, and persons of African descent. As a young woman, she rejected not only the roles of "wife" and

"mother" but also that of "woman," writing, "I am not a woman . . . / I know only that my body / Is neither one gender nor the other." While it is uncertain as to whether or not Sor Juana ever acted upon her desires, it is clear that her affections were inclined toward women. Of the women she loved, two of the most well known were: Leonor Carreto, the Marquise de la Mancera, whose husband appears to have respected Sor Juana greatly and to have been comfortable with the bond she and his wife shared; and Luisa Manrique de Lara y Gonzaga, the Marquise de la Laguna and the Countess of Paredes, appearing as "Lysi" and "Filis" in Sor Juana's poems. In "Happy Easter, My Lady," dedicated to Luisa Manrique, reminiscent at once of Medieval troubadour lyrics and Renaissance sonnets, she writes, "Only your mirror can reflect you splendor , / For you are the proof of such heaven / Which only God can grant in its entirety." This poem, like others, speaks of Sor Juana's pain on not being able to be with often or completely the woman she loves. In "Happy Easter, " she continues, "Without you, even my own speech / Seems foreign to me," and in "My Divine Lysis," also dedicated to Luisa Manrique, "Finally, I plead guilty / Of adoring you; / If you wish to punish me / That punishment will be my reward." A feature film, *I, the Worst of All* (*Yo, La Peor de Todas*, 1990), directed by Maria Luisa Bemberg and starring Assumpta Serna and Dominique Sanda, powerfully depicts Sor Juana's love for women as well as the censorship of her literary work, and in general the admiration and subsequent repression of her genius, by the Catholic Church.

Julius II, Pope (1443-1513) Allegedly homoerotically inclined Pope. Born Giuliano Della Rovere, he was a friend of the artists MICHELANGELO and Raphael (1483-1520). A great patron of art and literature, he founded the Vatican Museum.

Julius III, Pope (1487-1555) Born Giovanni Maria Ciocchi del Monte, he became pope in 1550 and reigned until 1555. He encouraged the newly formed Society of Jesus (the Jesuits) and was a great patron of Renaissance humanist art. He appointed MICHELANGELO as the chief architect of St Peter and Giovanni Pierluigi da Palestrina (c. 1525-1594) its choir master. Not well regarded as a pontiff, his lovers were mainly youths about whom Julius often told lascivious tales. One special seventeen-year-old youth, named Innocente and nicknamed Prevostino, became a cardinal and was always at Julius's side. Satires were written and published about Julius and Innocente, calling the youth a "new GANYMEDE," while the Pope was compared to JUPITER (or ZEUS). Innocente was eventually adopted by Julius's brother, Baldovino del Monte. It is also said that Julius accepted the dedication of the infamous Latin poem *In Laudem sodomiae* ("In Praise of Sodomy") written by the archbishop of Benevento, Giovanni della Casa.

Jupiter In Euro-western ASTROLOGY, this planet governs accomplishments, fame, honor, legal matters, luck, political power, professions, and prosperity. In astrology, as well as in the Euro-western traditions of alchemy and ritual magic, the planets are considered to be ultimately androgynous or transgendered, their feminine and masculine aspects represented by the signs they govern. In the case of Jupiter, his masculine aspect is represented by Sagittarius, his feminine by Pisces. Figures associated with Jupiter and with gender and/or sexual variance include: AMUN, CYBELE, HERA, ISIS, KUAN YIN, MAWU-LISA, OBATALA, PHAENON, Thor, and ZEUS.

Justinian (-us) the Great (482/483-565) Roman emperor, Christian zealot, and lawgiver who conducted campaigns against pagans and against those participating in homoeroticism. Pagan teachers were forbidden to continue teaching, and persons who did not immediately submit to baptism lost all civil rights. Those men engaging in same-sex eroticism were to be tortured and then burned alive. While critics of Justinian "alleged that the trials [of such men] were a farce, that men were [being] condemned on the single testimony of one man or boy," the Emperor paid no attention. According to J. B. Bury, men found guilty of such acts were "shamefully mutilated, or exquisitely tortured, and paraded through the streets of the capital before their execution."

K

Kadesh Barnea   Biblical site shrouded in mystery, possibly modern-day En Qdes, lying south of Beersheba, which some scholars, including Warren Johansson, have perceived as rich in hidden and complex homoerotico-spiritual significance. Also called En Mishpat (Spring of Judgment, in Genesis 14:7), it may have been in pre-Biblical times the site of a temple to the Canaanite goddess ATHIRAT/Asherah, served by priestesses and male gender variant hierodulic priests (*qedeshim*). The historian Eduard Meyer (1885-1930) believed Kadesh Barnea to be especially linked to the bond between Moses and the Biblical Lord, a relationship which, based on the research of philologist Franz Dornseiff (1888-1960), may have paralleled that of ZEUS for GANYMEDE, or the Greek lover (*erastes*) for his beloved (*eromenos*). Also as concerns the site's link to Moses, Kadesh Barnea belongs to the tribe of Levi, whose members, over the centuries, "evolved from a warrior to a priestly caste." According to Epiphanius, the Levites inspired a Gnostic subsect of the PHIBIONITES that practised cultic homoeroticism. "Those among them who are called Levites . . . do not have intercourse with women, but with each other. And it is these who are actually distinguished and honoured among them."

Kahl, Regina (fl. c. 1935)   Woman-loving actress and high priestess of the Templi Ordo Orientis in Hollywood, California circa 1935. The OTO, an occult order devoted to ritual MAGIC, was founded in the late nineteenth century, its most (in)famous leader being Aleister CROWLEY. While priestess, Kahl hired Harry HAY to play the organ for ritual services.

Kahlo, Frida (1907-1954)   Bisexual painter of Jewish and Mexican heritage, the wife of artist Diego Rivera (1886-1957) and Mexico's most renowned woman painter. Numerous works of Kahlo's reflect the interrelationship of the sacred or mythic and transgenderism and/or lesbian desire, the most obvious of which is *The Earth Itself: Two Nudes in the Jungle* (1939).

Kahukura   Gynandrous or transgendered deity of the RAINBOW among the Maori, its feminine aspect referred to as Pou-te-aniwaniwa, its masculine as Kahukura-pango.

Kalathiskos   "BASKET dance" of the ancient Greeks, performed in honor of the god DIONYSUS. The *kalathiskos* dancer was typically a bearded male whose costume included artificial female breasts. Carrying a basket on his head, he danced on the balls of his feet, whirling frequently, to suggest tipsiness.

Kalaturru   Transgendered, homoerotically inclined male priest/esse/s of the Mesopotamian goddess INANNA/ISHTAR. They served as hierodulic priests, homoerotic union with them being deemed a sacred activity. Gender variant *kalaturru* were, like Inanna's priestesses, considered mortal representatives of the Goddess. They were also seen as human reflections of certain spirit-companions of Inanna, the androgynous beings *kalaturru* (or *galatur*) and KURGARRA, created to rescue Inanna from the clutches of death.

Kalbu   Babylonian term denoting "DOG" and connoting a male, often gender variant and homoerotically inclined, servant of the goddess INANNA/ISHTAR.

Kalebh (or **Caleb, Kelebh**)   Semitic term related to the Babylonian *kalbu*, denoting "DOG" and connoting a male, often gender variant and homoerotically inclined, servant of the Canaanite goddess ATHIRAT. "*Kalebh*" appears to have been roughly synonymous with the more common term *qedesh/ QEDESHIM*.

Kali   Wild, destructive, warrior goddess of the Hindus who may embody both female and male worshippers. A powerful fusion of beauty and terror, Kali has black, disheveled hair, her skin is midnight-blue, her tongue hangs from her bloodied, open mouth, she wears a tiger's skin and a garland of human heads, and she carries a sword. A patron of warriors, thieves, and Tantric adepts, she is mistress of the cremation grounds and a guardian of ghosts. D. R. Kinsley (1975) describes Kali as "the terrifying mother who destroys the ego." Kinsley writes, "Kali's dark, menacing appearance does not frighten but attracts one who has seen the world for what it really is: the ephemeral, phantasmagoric display of . . . the magic of the gods, a world fraught with pain and suffering, a world in which all things perish and pass away." The goddess Kali occasionally embodies or is otherwise represented by males, as when a male ritual participant wears an elaborate mask representing her face, a long black wig, and artificial breasts, or when another dresses as Bhagavati (or Vagesvani), a were-tiger manifestation of the Goddess. At an annual rite in Kerala, India, male worshippers of Kali cut themselves with swords in what may constitute an act of symbolic self-castration in honor of the Goddess.

Kallabis Ancient Greek dance, similar to the KORDAX, performed in honor of ARTEMIS by gender variant men. It is described as a "violent" and erotic dance in which "the hips are rotated." The term "*kallabis*" is also linked etymologically the word for "LIZARD," alluding to the lizard habit or ability to "to flick its tail."

Kalmakoff, Nicolas (1873-1955) Deemed the "Russian Beardsley," homoerotically or bisexually inclined Italo-Russian Symbolist painter. Spending most of his life in Italy, Russia, and France, Kalmakoff moved in various circles, including those of Rasputin and Sergei Diaghilev. According to one writer, he "frequented circles where mysticism and sexual orgy went hand in hand." Like Nikolai KLYUEV and Mikhail KUZMIN, he was inspired by the erotico-spiritual KHLYST and Skoptsy sects. Kalmakoff became extremely disillusioned when in 1908 a production of Oscar WILDE's *Salomé* for which he had designed the sets and costumes was canceled because "the decorative theme was the female pudenda." He spent his last years in Paris, where he allegedly "assisted at Black Masses," helping out with costumes and decorations.

Kalogheri Thracian dance still performed in the twentieth century in which two men wearing goatskins and headdresses with goat horns join in ritual combat, one carrying a bow, the other brandishing a wooden phallus. The latter chases, catches, and ritually weds a *koritsi*, a young male dressed in traditional feminine clothing. The "husband" is then slain by the other goatskinned male, after which he is mourned, symbolically buried, and made to rise again. The *kalogheri* mixes pagan and Christian elements and, pertaining to the latter, echoes or parodies the death and resurrection of JESUS.

Kalos Vase Love-gift given by ancient Greek male lovers (*erastes*) to their beloveds, or *eromenoi*. These often portrayed Greek deities, spirits, and heroes, including EROS, GANYMEDE, and HERACLES, as well as courting gifts such as the ROOSTER and the HARE, together with the name of the beloved one.

Kaluli According to the spiritual beliefs of the Kaluli people of Papua New Guinea, women mature of their own accord, symbolized by menstruation, while males, if they are to develop into strong, courageous men must, when young, ingest in rituals the semen of older males by way of oral intercourse. The older partners are typically selected by the younger males' fathers. The younger and older males frequently join in homoerotic relationships which tend to be disrupted by, or concluded with, the heterosexual marriage of the younger partner.

Kalum Gender variant, homoerotically inclined male priest(s) of the Mesopotamian goddess INANNA/ISHAR.

The *kalum* priests were especially known as composers of hymns, incantations, and *balag*-lamentations accompanied by the *balag*-instrument, which appears to have been either a harp or a drum. They chanted in the Emesal dialect of Sumerian, a dialect reserved for women and gender variant men. Like the other gender variant priests of Inanna/Ishtar, they served as HIERODULES, UNION with them being deemed a sacred activity.

Kalunga Supreme being of the Kwanyama, an African people of the Ambo group who live in southern Angola. This deity and a host of spirits associated with Kalunga were served in the past by female and gender variant male KIMBANDA. In the Americas, from the era of the slave trade, Kalunga became syncretized in African-Brazilian spiritual practice with Iemanja (YEMAYA), the Yoruba-diasporic goddess of the sea. So important was Kalunga's androgynous identity and that of the men who served him, the *omasenge kimbanda*, that in Brazil the term *calungagem*, directly derived from Kalunga, came to refer specifically to male gender variant behavior, to a swaying gait or a "languid inflection or gesture."

Kama Hindu god of eroticism, including homoerotic desire. In the *Shiva Purana, Rudra Samhita*, Kama is depicted as a paragon of Indian male beauty: "His complexion was golden, his chest strong and solid, his nose well-formed, his thighs, buttocks and calves were rounded and muscular. His black hair was curly, his eyebrows thick and expressive. His face was like the full moon. His hairy chest was as wide as a door . . . His hands, eyes, face, legs and fingers were red. His waist was slim, his teeth perfect. He gave off the odour of an elephant in rut. His eyes were like lotus petals, and he was perfumed like their stamens. His neck was a conch . . . His amorous glances seduced everyone. He winked at all around him. His breath was like a perfumed breeze. The feeling of love came from his whole person." Kama has at certain times two arms, at others, eight. He is draped in a blue robe. In his majestic stature he is compared to the heavenly elephant Airavata. His steed is sometimes a crocodile, sometimes a parrot. He carries a bow made from sugar cane; the bowstring is formed by a battalion of bees. In his pouch are five flower-arrows which inspire erotic passion, of blue lotus, jasmine, champak, s'irisa, and the flower of the mango. His traveling companions are the *apsaras* ("essences"), who are celestial dancers, and the GANDARVAS ("fragrances"), the musicians of the heavens. When not roaming the earth inspiring desire, Kama resides in his paradise of Kamaloka. Legend has it that upon seeing Kama, the sages ceased meditating in order to gaze upon him; one might say that they exchanged an ascetic for an erotic meditation. The god SHIVA, however, became infuriated when Kama disturbed his meditative practice, so much so that he slew Kama. When, however, Shiva grew calm again and realized that he had made a terrible mistake, knowing that neither he nor any other in the universe could survive without passion, he restored Kama to life. Kama not only inspires desire in others; the god himself occasionally desires another, often divine, being, such as the beautiful blue god KRISHNA. "Kama, seeing the jewellike toenails of Krishna, was intoxicated. He lost all notion of manhood and womanhood and said, 'Even if I have for countless lives to practice austerities I must in the end be born a shepherdess of Cow Land [i.e. one of the GOPIS, the legendary female companions of Krishna] to caress the toenails of Krishna.'"

Kamapua'a Hawaiian god of sexuality, agriculture, RAIN, divination, and battle, Kamapua'a is most commonly depicted as a hybrid human male-pig, although his most striking characteristic is his shapeshifting ability. As a deity of agriculture, he is the patron of sweet potato and taro farmers. Kaliuwa'a, O'ahu is the sacred center of his worship. Kamapua'a has both female and male lovers. His turbulent relationship with the volcano-goddess PELE is balanced by his love for Nihooleki, a legendary fisherman, and LIMALOA, a god of mirages and the sea. Kamapua'a is sometimes identified with LONO, a deity of weather, agriculture, eroticism, and war; like the former, Lono also loves both males and females. Kamapua'a is also attracted to one of Pele's brothers, and Pele is not above ridiculing Kamapua'a's enjoyment of anal eroticism. Indeed, his passion for this activity is so well known that his buttocks have been nicknamed Hamamailuna ("Gaping Above"). Once, when Pele and Kamapua'a were fighting, she sent two of her brothers to attack him, but Kamapua'a won the round when he determined to send one of his independent manifestations, the love-god LONOIKIAWEAWEALOHA, to seduce the brothers. So delighted were Pele's brothers with the love-god that they abandoned Pele's orders.

Kanekoa FISHING god of Hawaii, he is the AIKANE or loving companion of Makanikeoe, a god of love and the wind.

Kannaaluk Inuit TWO-SPIRIT female or transgender female-to-male divine being. This "Terrible One From Below" is, like SEDNA, opposed to participating in heterosexual marriage. Despite this, she-he is often regarded as the mother of the Inuit and of other indigenous Americans. She-he is believed to have created the sea animals from the blood of her own hands. She-he is a protector of animals, women, and lovers. Kannaaluk is revered by Inuit two-spirit shamans, who also honor NAARJUK, TAQQIQ, and other sacred beings.

Kannon Japanese BODHISATTVA of compassion identified with the Indian Avalokiteshvara and the Chinese KUAN YIN. Kannon manifests in female, male, and transgendered forms. In a fourteenth-century tale of same-sex love, a Japanese Buddhist monk who is a passionate worshipper of Kannon is rewarded for his faith by the *bodhisattva* with a young male lover who is himself a manifestation of Kannon. This tale exemplifies the Buddhist notion of *hoben*, or "expedient means." *Hoben* allows a *bodhisattva* to manifest as any form, including that of a homoerotic lover, that will nurture enlightenment. In the *Lotus Sutra* we are told, "To those who can be conveyed to deliverance by the body of a boy or girl he [Kannon] preaches *Dharma* [universal law or moral code] by displaying the body of boy or girl." Once, the tale goes, a monk asked Kannon if he might be granted a companion or disciple to assuage his loneliness. There on the desolate plain, bathed in moonlight, appeared a beautiful young man dressed in a lavender kimono and playing a flute. At first, the monk thought he must be dreaming, but he was soon convinced otherwise. The two spent three joyous years together. Then one day the young man fell ill and died. But as the heartbroken monk was praying over him, the spirit of the young man suddenly arose. The young man had been none other than Kannon himself, who, saying farewell to the now-joyous monk, returned to his abode in the heavens.

Kanyotsanyotse Man-woman shaman-deity of the Tewa people of southwestern North America. Long ago, the people lived beneath the surface of a great lake. For a long time, they lived without guidance. Then one day, Mother Summer and Mother Winter were born. Their births were followed by that of a mysterious being who was both male and female. When the people called upon this being, acknowledging him to be a man-woman, a *kwih-doh* (or *quetho*), the being denied being a man-woman three times. The fourth time, however, he-she told them, Yes, I am a man-woman. He-she then agreed to help lead them out of the lake into another world. He-she left the lake and traveled north, then west, then east, then south. The man-woman also asked the spirits and animals of various places he-she visited if they would be loving toward the people should they decide to journey and perhaps settle there. Finally the man-woman returned and led the people out of the lake. When the man-woman had completed this task, he-she taught the people how to hunt. They learned that the man-woman's name was Kanyotsanyotse.

Kapa'ihi Mysterious male figure of Hawaiian myth whose background is unknown, he appears suddenly beside the heroic deity LONO, who has set out on a long journey. When Lono asks him why he has appeared, Kapa'ihi replies, "I love you, so I followed you." The two become fellow travelers as well as AIKANE, loving companions.

Kapo Hawaiian goddess, a shapeshifter, sorceress, and poisoner as well as an herbal healer, associated with *kahuna*. Bamboo is her sacred attribute and she has a "flying vagina" (*kohe-lele*) which she sends out like a familiar to carry out magical work and which is itself revered by her devotees. Kapo belongs to the family of PELE and, like LAKA, is a master of the HULA. In her connection with hula, she is called "Red eel-woman." Laka is sometimes said to be the child of Kapo, although they are also depicted as a DOUBLE female being. Because Kapo can remove her vagina and because of her Amazonian behavior, she is associated with transgendered persons. Her priests and priestesses are especially renowned as prophets, due in part to Kapo's being patron of the dead, who often know what is to come. Kapo's traditional center of worship is on Maui.

Karezza Erotico-spiritual technique related to Hindu TANTRA whereby ejaculation is purposely prevented, in the belief that the energy of the orgasm will be redirected toward the head and nourish cosmic consciousness. This technique was practiced by the early homosexual rights activist and mystic Edward CARPENTER. Gavin ARTHUR, an astrologer who met Carpenter when he, Arthur, was around twenty and Carpenter around eighty, wrote of their lovemaking: "I just lay there in the moonlight that poured in at the window and gave myself up to the old man's marvelous petting . . . At last his hand was moving between my legs . . . And . . . when . . . I could not hold it any longer, his mouth closed just over the head of my penis and I could feel my young vitality flowing into his old age. He did not suck me at all. It was really *karezza*, which I know he recommended in his books. I had not learned the control necessary to *karezza* . . . The emphasis was on caressing and loving."

Kartikkeyeh (also **Guha, Kumara, Murugan, Skanda**) Hindu deity of war, occult wisdom, and male beauty. He is "the boy" (Kumara, Murugan), "the mysterious one" (Guha), and "the jet of semen" (Skanda). His complex birth process begins with a homoerotic act, when AGNI, the Hindu god of fire, swallows the semen of SHIVA, the god of meditation, eroticism, and asceticism. As an infant, he is nursed by the Pleiades. A god of male beauty, he remains forever young, with a delicate body, hair curly and black, and dark skin. He wears garments of yellow and fuchsia. "His ornaments are the moon and the snake." His home is on Krauncha, the Mountain of the Heron. His steed is a peacock or the celestial elephant Airavata. Like the Greek GANYMEDE, he carries a cock. A god of battle, he also carries a hunting-spear. He makes the gesture of shielding from harm. He is accompanied by a host of spirits and sorcerers. He is also a deity of esoteric wisdom. He "knows the meaning hidden in the teachings of the Vedas and other sacred texts. He knows the meaning of all ritual acts."

Kartikkeyeh never marries. "It is said that his only wife is the army." Perhaps because of this, his cult, A. Daniélou (1984) relates, "is strictly forbidden to women. He is the favorite deity of homosexuals."

Kathoey In the premodern spiritual system of Thailand, humans were thought to belong to three basic gendered groups: males (*phuuchai*), females (*phuuying*), and the transgendered or third gender (*kathoey*). R. C. Morris (1994) describes the *kathoey* as a "coherent identity attached to diverse and fluid practices." In today's Thailand, *kathoey* are often identified as either male-to-female transgendered persons or as gay males, with the term *thom*, apparently deriving from the English "tomboy," being applied to lesbian women. The origins of the *kathoey* may be traced to the *Pathamamulamuli*, an ancient text of Theraveda Buddhism. Herein, a primordial male-female couple creates females, males, and *kathoey*-like beings. Each type of mortal was bestowed with a kind of suffering; that given to the *kathoey* or third gender person was the burden of a "too-sensitive heart." According to Morris, the "potential [to become a *kathoey*] is preordained from birth. A young boy who is particularly graceful or delicate will be openly discussed by his parents and relatives as a future *kathoey*." As apparently linked to, or identified with, *krathoe-j*, *kathoey* may become KAW PHII practitioners of the Phii Puu Njaa spirit cult.

Katsotsi' Among the Zuni people of southwestern North America, the female TWO-SPIRIT person. The *katsotsi'* occasionally appears as a two-spirit kachina in masked dance rituals. Her male counterpart is the LHAMANA.

Kauxuma Nupika (also **Bowdash, Bundosh, Man-like Woman**, c. 1790-1837) Guide, woman warrior, and shaman, Kauxuma Nupika, whose name means "Gone to the spirits," was born to a Kootenai family living on the northwestern coast of North America around 1790. When still a child, she was given the nickname Ququnok Patke, "One standing [lodge] pole woman." At eighteen, she married an explorer named Boisverd, but he sent her back to her family after only a year or so. On returning home, she told her family that she had been magically transformed into a man, in other words, that she had become a TWO-SPIRIT person. She began to wear men's clothes, fight in battles, and to perform shamanic tasks. She also had a succession of female lovers prior to marrying a young woman. At this time she took a new name, Qanqon kamek klaula, "Sitting in the water grizzly bear." She and her female spouse acted as guides to Alexander Ross and other traders and explorers. She delivered numerous prophecies, including one forecasting a devastating epidemic. In 1837, while attempting to mediate peace between Blackfeet and Flathead warriors, she was slain by the former. It was said that she was so powerful that her wounds kept healing themselves miraculously, and that only after she had been shot, stabbed, and had her heart cut out did she perish. Tradition has it that she was especially mourned by her animal companions.

Kaw phii General term for ritual officiant or medium in the Phii Puu Njaa ancestor spirit cult of northern Thailand. Many practitioners are gender variant or third gender, possibly woman-loving, women called *tang khaw* (possibly related to *thom*, a twentieth-century term for "lesbian," which some writers suggest derives from the English "tomboy") and gender variant, often homoerotically inclined males who dress in feminine attire and are called *krathoe-j* (resembling, or identified with, KATHOEY). The spirits, who are worshipped in ritual trance dances, include Young Lord, a spoiled brat who wears dark glasses, and Grandmother Sae. Some spirits are referred to as *caw*; these include Buddhist spirits as well as Hindu gods like GANESHA. G. Wijeyewardene (1986) reports that "most female mediums are possessed by male deities [or spirits], often of princely or warrior rank." When female *kaw phii*, or *tang khaw*, are embodied by, or otherwise identify with male *caw*, they may, as Walter Irvine relates, "deny the fact of their own menstruation. Writers report that an elderly spirit medium from Chiang Mai demonstrated her 'masculine' . . . nature by saying that she had ceased to menstruate at the markedly early age of thirty." Other women mediums say that their headaches, like men's, are caused by looking upon women's underwear. Still others report that they can no longer function sexually with men. *Tang khaw* often claim that they do not eat phallic foods such as bananas because they, due to possession by a male *caw*, already carry an inner phallus. Irvine explains that the rejection of the male organ in heterosexual intercourse and the rejection of phallic symbols in diet are "connected with a spirit medium's identification with her *caw*'s masculinity, making her, when in the possessed state, a carrier of the phallus . . . another explanation in terms of the playing out by the medium of the homosexual component of her sexuality." Women mediums often compare themselves to Buddhist monks, claiming that their healing powers make them even more powerful than monk healers. Indeed, one female spirit medium living in the 1980s, embodied by the *caw* of a Buddhist monk named Mokhalan, was instructing more than a dozen *luug sid* (disciples), including three fully ordained Buddhist monks, in shamanistic tasks. The gender variant, homoerotically inclined, cross- or mixed-dressing male *krathoe-j*, when encountered by nineteenth-century European travelers, were thought to be hermaphrodites. In the twentieth century, Wijeyewardene reports, these male mediums often "adopt female gait and mannerisms, sometimes wear female clothes and adorn themselves with lipstick, rouge and eyeshadow. Men who will be appalled at the suggestion that they are homosexuals will flirt with them in public . . . and in local communities they fit into a recognizable public role . . . few of them [i.e. the male mediums] seem to have any marital relations with women."

Keawe-nui-a-'umi Ruling chief in Hawaiian myth, known especially for his skill as a warrior and for his love of storytelling. Keawe was the male AIKANE, or loving companion, of PAKAA. Pakaa served Keawe, as his father had before him, as a kind of shaman. When jealous courtiers succeeded in convincing Keawe that Pakaa was not trustworthy, Pakaa left the court, married, and raised a son. Keawe, regretting his mistaken belief in the courtiers, desperately sought Pakaa for many years. One day, when Pakaa's son, having learned his father's magical arts, caused a tempest to arise, the boat of Keawe and his men was cast upon the shore of the island where Pakaa lived. On seeing Pakaa, Keawe's men mutinied; they were defeated, however, by Pakaa and Keawe fighting together. Thus the chief and his *aikane* were reunited.

Kelab (pl. **Kelabim**) "DOGS," the gender variant priests of the goddesses APHRODITE and ASTARTE, the dog signifying the companion of the Goddess (the term *kelabim* being related to *kalbu* and *kalebh*). Some of them were also called *gerim*, a name that suggests either a mask wearer or a eunuch. The *kelabim* and *gerim* served Astarte at Kition on the island of Cyprus and in many other places. At Kition, where Astarte manifested as Aphroditos, her reverence was linked to moon worship as well as transgenderism and same-sex eroticism. Here, according to Philochorus, she was served by men "dressed as women, and women dressed as men, because the moon is thought to be both male and female." According to classical scholars O. Masson and M. Sznycer (1972), the *kelabim* at Kition functioned as HIERODULE-priests "employed for sodomitic purposes." *Kelabim* also served the Goddess at Afqa (in ancient times Aphaca, near the river Nahr Ibrahim, once the Adonis River, in present-day Lebanon). Here they also dressed in feminine attire and worked alongside the priestesses as hierodules. They maintained and protected the temple grounds and divined the future from the kidneys of sacrificed animals. They also participated in a springtime ritual in memory of ADONIS, the male consort of Astarte/Aphrodite. Each April, together with the priestesses, the *kelabim* formed a procession, walking from the temple at Afqa to the river. As they walked, they sang praises and laments recounting the life and early death of Adonis. At the river, which seemed red with the blood of Adonis, they gathered and cast into the water pieces of gold and silver, exquisite fabrics, and anemones. They then returned to the temple, where they gathered around a pool. By some feat of magic, a ball of fire would appear floating above the water. The ball of fire was associated in the minds of the *kelabim* and the female priestesses with both the planet Venus and Sirius, the Dog Star. This was a sign of Adonis's rebirth or resurrection and of his reunion with the Goddess. A massive attack on the *kelabim* and priestesses at Afqa was launched in the fourth century CE by the Christianized Roman emperor CONSTANTINE. Eusebius states that Constantine, on discovering a "hidden snare of souls . . . at Aphaca . . . dedicated to Venus [i.e. Astarte]," gave orders to raze the temple and to slaughter the *kelabim* and the priestesses. "Here men undeserving of the name forgot the dignity of their sex," writes Eusebius, "and propitiated the *demon* [italics ours] by their effeminate conduct." He continues, "The hand of military force was made instrumental in purging the impurities of the place."

Ke'let (or **Kele-uwä-quc**)   Guardian spirits of the Chukchi of Siberia whose "children" included male gender variant shamans. The *ke'let* played a major role in the process of gender metamorphosis and in the spiritual development of these shamans, and became in a very powerful sense a third partner in the relationships of gender variant male shamans and their male companions. If a shaman's companion failed to treat the *ke'let* with respect, he would surely be punished. If, however, the companion treated the shaman in a loving, respectful manner and revered the *ke'let* spirit, the latter would bestow him and his shaman-lover with joy and prosperity.

Kenny, Maurice (1929-   )   Mohawk writer whose work often reflects upon the interrelationship of same-sex desire, transgenderism, and Native American Indian spirituality, as in his pivotal essay "Tinselled Bucks: An Historical Study in Indian Homosexuality" (1975) and his poem "Winkte" (1979), in which he writes, "There was space for us in the village . . . / We were special to the Sioux, Cheyenne, Ponca / And the Crow valued our worth."

Kepner, Jim (1923-   )   Los Angeles-based, native Texan gay activist, historian, archivist, and writer. Kepner, a political activist for many years, while tending in recent years to avoid spiritually-oriented groups, has thought and written on the subject of what is now called Gay Spirituality for over two decades. He is currently integrating his writings into a book *Seeking the Spark: Exploring Various Paths to Gay Spirit*, in which he describes his experiences working with other seekers and records his private thoughts on the matter. "But what is Gay Spirit?" Kepner queries in his stream-of-consciousness style. "It is that 'ugly duckling' spirit which grows up alienated, and searches long and hard for its kind; it is an evanescent spirit which sees around corners, wriggles out of linear definitions to find new perceptions . . . It is that indomitable spirit by which we have persevered, laughed, danced, acted and created, through

centuries of persecution and shame . . . that campiness which . . . raises our voices and swings our hips . . . that delicate and wounded sissy-boy spirit, learning to survive and to be true to himself in a world he never made; that macho energy which loves to contend with the power of nature and with other males . . . It is that mystery of what we might become when we can each grow up without shame . . . when we can blossom according to our nature."

Keputren   Traditional to the Javanese court, an area set aside for the harem of the king in which women, according to B. J. D. Gayatri (1994), "could cultivate relationships with other women without fear of persecution." The *keputren* was justified by ancient Hindu myths, such as that of the goddess SRIKANDI, as the wife of the god-ruler ARJUNA, sharing an intimate relationship with Lavasati, another of his wives.

Keraki   As among the Kaluli, it is believed by the Keraki of Papua New Guinea that in order to grow strong, males must be nourished with the semen of elder men. Keraki practice differs, however, from that of the Kaluli: here it is by way of ritual anal intercourse, rather than via ritual oral intercourse, that the nourishment is obtained.

Ke'yev   Name given to TWO-SPIRIT males among the Koryak of North Asia. Ke'yev often took shamanic roles and chose men as lovers.

Khandoba   Androgynous or transgendered Hindu deity representing the union of sun and moon.

Khepera   "He who is coming into being," an Egyptian deity of creation and solar power represented by a scarab beetle and symbolizing self-creation and gender totality prior to division into male and female. Just as the dung-beetle seemed to recreate itself from the earth, so Khepera recreated himself. And just as the beetle spent its day rolling a ball of dung across the earth, so Khepera spent his rolling the SUN across the heavens. When he wished to create others, he masturbated, or else made love to his shadow.

Khlysts   Syncretic pagan-Christian spiritual tradition emerging in Russia in the seventeenth century which may have included gender variant, bisexual, and homosexual practices. The Khlysts, or "Flagellants" as they were otherwise called, formed, along with the Old Believers, Skoptsy (or Skopets) and others, a largely underground, radical spiritual movement persecuted by the Russian government as well as by the Russian Orthodox Church. The Khylsts did not believe that the spirit of JESUS Christ left the earth when he was crucified; instead "he was reincarnated in various individuals." They appear to have worshipped not only Jesus but also Mother Earth, whom they may have syncretized with the Virgin Mary. While some scholars suggest that the Khlysts were extremely puritanical, others suggest that they were more anti-patriarchal, anti-marriage, and anti- (traditionally organized) family than puritanical. They opted for more egalitarian relationships. Believing that every man and woman was potentially capable of embodying the Mother or Christ, they employed ecstatic dance (*radeniia*), flagellation, and "a kind of lucerna extincta [lights-out] rite, in which men and women . . . had intercourse . . . [including] homosexual intercourse," in order to attain an altered state of consciousness, in which they would deliver prophecies. The gay Russian poet and mystic Nikolai KLYUEV was at one time a member of, and remained deeply inspired by, the Khlysts.

Khoja In South India, a group of males, akin to the HIJRAS, who dress and behave in a manner regarded as feminine and who participate in sensuous ritual dances in public bazaars.

Khonsu Egyptian deity of the MOON, healing, and fertility, and a patron of SAILORS. Khonsu often takes the form of a young man who is naked or who wears a translucent linen garment and whose head is shaved except for a lock on one side, a traditional Egyptian youth's haircut. As ornaments he wears images of the full and crescent moons. The tale of Khonsu's birth embraces both heterosexual and homosexual variants. In one account, he is the son of the god AMUN and the goddess Mut. In another, he is the child of Horus, the falcon-headed god of the heavens, the sun, and kingship, and SET, Horus's brother or maternal uncle and a god of sexuality, sacrifice, and death/rebirth. Khonsu is produced by way of indirect homoerotic oral intercourse between Set and Horus, as a result of Set's ingestion – thanks to the goddess ISIS – of Horus's semen. Set's offspring first appears on his forehead as a golden disk, suggesting a "third" eye and spiritual rather than physical birth. When the god THOTH, who is standing nearby, sees the disk, he covets it, and takes it from Set's brow. As he does so, it magically transforms into Khonsu.

Khunsa Arabic term for "hermaphrodite," applied as well to eunuchs, transvestites, gender variant, third gender, or transgender male-to-female persons, akin to the MUKANNATHUN. In the past, despite periodic official condemnations and persecutions, they appear to have been generally accepted by many practitioners of Islam as long as they fulfilled religious responsibilities and demonstrated respect for the Islamic way of life. In the late nineteenth century, Thomas Hughes wrote of the *khunsa*, "In public prayer they must take their station between the men and the women, but in other respects observe the customs of women."

Khurafa Arabic legend of transgender metamorphosis. Khurafa had been a wealthy man, but now his wealth had vanished. Fleeing those he owed money, he was dying of thirst when he spotted a well and began to draw water from it. A voice cried out, "Stop! How dare you drink from my well." But Khurafa couldn't help himself. He drank, and drank, and drank. As he did so, the voice cried out again, "O Allah! Transform this man who is drinking from my well into a woman!" Suddenly, Khurafa became a woman. A woman who owed no one money, as no one knew who she was. Journeying to another country, Khurafa fell in love with a man. She gave birth to two children whom she loved dearly. Years later, while traveling, she became thirsty. Spotting a well, she began to drink its water. A familiar voice cried out, "How dare you drink from my well! O Allah, transform this woman who drinks from my well into a man!" Khurafa once more became a man. He could not return home to his husband, so he took the risk of returning to his former home. Thankfully, no one remembered him. He married a young woman who gave birth to two children, whom he loved dearly. While saddened by no longer being near his other children, Khurafa was grateful to Allah, for now he had four children whom he loved, "two sons of my loins and two of my womb."

Kiha (-nuilulumoko) Shapeshifting deity of Hawaiian myth whose manifestations include being a male tribal chieftain and a gecko goddess who, by hiding in treetops, warns others of the approach of enemies and whose challenges include fighting with the supernatural dog Kalahu-moko. Bisexual or pansexual in twentieth-century terms, Kiha (nuilulumoko) engages in heterosexual, homosexual, and presumably transgender relationships; indeed, as a male he not only has a male AIKANE or loving companion but also fathers a son, LILOA, who is, paradoxically, claimed by many Hawaiians to be the "inventor of homosexuality."

Kimbanda Spiritual functionary of the Kwanyama-Ambo people of southern Angola, Africa. *Kimbanda* serve a supreme being named Kalunga and a host of other spirits. In the twentieth century, a majority of *kimbanda* have been women. Apparently, however, some transgendered males have continued to serve alongside female *kimbanda*. In order to become a *kimbanda*, one has to be chosen by a spirit, following which one undergoes a kind of shamanic transformation. Frequently, divine choosing of a *kimbanda*-to-be first manifests as an illness that cannot be healed by way of herbs or sacrifices alone. The sick person becomes well again only when he or she recognizes and accepts the destiny of spiritual service. Transgendered male *kimbanda*, who engage in same-sex eroticism, are referred to as *omasenge*. "An [*oma-*]*senge*," ethnologist Carlos Estermann explains, is "essentially a man who has

been possessed since childhood by a spirit of female sex."
Omasenge kimbanda dress like women, do women's work,
and "contract marriage" with other men. *Omasenge* and
female *kimbanda* typically dress in a garment made of
genet, a kind of civet cat, decorated with cowrie shells.
Their spiritual tasks include performing sacrifices, healing
with herbs, divining by way of palmistry and other
methods, and working magic. *Omasenge* and female
kimbanda are apparently the only spiritual functionaries
among the Kwanyama-Ambo who are allowed to possess
or play the *omakola*, a musical instrument played at
initiation rites and other ceremonies to aid in summoning
divine beings. This stringed instrument is presented to the
kimbanda at the time of his or her initiation. This link of
music and the transgendered male worshipper is
noteworthy, since in certain African and African-diasporic
traditions, such men are forbidden to play sacralized
musical instruments, especially drums. When African
spiritual traditions, and with them, certain associations
with homoeroticism and transgenderism, were carried to
the Americas during the time of the slave trade, the
spiritual tradition of the *kimbanda* was syncretized with
other African-diasporic traditions, with the god Kalunga
becoming syncretized with the Yoruba-diasporic goddess
Iemanja/YEMAYA. The term *kimbanda* by the late
sixteenth century came to refer to a "passive sodomite,"
perhaps derived from omasenge *kimbanda*. Today
kimbanda – as Quimbanda – refers to an African-diasporic
tradition associated with destructive magic.

Kitsune Shapeshifting, primarily fox, TRICKSTER deity
of the SHINTO religion of Japan. A powerful magician, he
is greatly honored, especially by merchants, with offerings
of TOFU and sushi. Occasionally, without completely
transforming into a woman, Kitsune disguises himself as
such in order to engage in erotic relations with human
males.

Kiwai As among the Kaluli and the Keraki, the Kiwai of
Papua New Guinea have traditionally believed that in
order to grow strong, males must be nourished with the
semen of elder men. It is by way of ritual anal intercourse,
rather than via ritual oral intercourse (as practiced by the
Kaluli), that the nourishment is obtained.

Klah, Hosteen (also **tlah, Hosteen**, 1867-1937) Navaho
TWO-SPIRIT NADLE-shaman, chanter, sandpainter, and
weaver. Klah was the great-grandson of Narbona, a
celebrated Navaho chief. Klah's mother had made the
Long Walk three years before Klah's birth, when the
Navahos were forced to leave their homeland for Fort
Sumner. As a young man, Klah studied with his uncle, an
Apache shaman. He then studied for twenty-four years
with other shamans or medicine-people before holding his
first Nightway ceremony. In 1917, he held a Yeibichai

ceremony that firmly established him as a great shaman.
Klah shared some of his knowledge with anthropologists
and folklorists, including Mary Cabot Wheelwright and
Gladys Reichard. Klah trained only one other person,
however, without censoring esoteric wisdom; this was a
young man named Beeal Begay. Unfortunately Begay died
in 1931; thus much of Klah's knowledge was lost.

Klaristiche Movement Founded in Munich, Germany
in 1911 by Elisàr von Kupffer (also known as Elisarion,
1872-1942), a painter, writer, and philosopher, and his
companion Eduard von Mayer as a homoerotic-spiritual
movement. In the late nineteenth century, von Kupffer
immersed himself in the study of mystic Christianity as
well as in ancient Near Eastern and Greco-Roman
cultures. He also found inspiration in the early homosexual
rights movement, which was emerging at that time. His
works, including *The Dead Gods* and *Hymns of the Holy
Citadel*, reflected these interests, and fueled his and von
Meyer's dream of creating a UTOPIAN society embracing
neoclassical aesthetics and homoerotic intimacy, which
resulted in the founding of the Klaristiche Movement.
Around 1925, the couple began work on a neopagan temple
in Minusio, Switzerland in which to celebrate homoerotic
spirituality. For the inner sanctuary, von
Kupffer/Elisarion painted frescoes of comradely lovers
inhabiting ARCADIA.

Klyuev, Nikolai (also **Kliuev, Nikolai**, 1887-1937)
Russian poet, at one time a member of the Khlysts, and a
lover of men, including the bisexual poet Sergei Esenin
(1895-1925, who was also a lover of the dancer Isadora
Duncan [1878-1927]). Klyuev's spirituality was deeply
rooted in his Samoyed heritage and in Nature, in his
profound attachment, even as a poet courted by urban
bohemians, to rural, peasant life. "Seals frolic in the setting
sun," he wrote, "A tent is mirrored in the lake. / Here
browse my golden-antlered deer – / The thoughts I think,
the songs I make." Inspired and encouraged by his mother,
a professional singer of laments, he first joined the Khlysts
and later participated in the rites of the Skoptsy (or
Skopets). He was also drawn to the Old Believers; like
them he believed in Belovod'ye, an earthly paradise to
come. Blending elements of these traditions with a pre-
Christian reverence of nature – as crystallized in the image
of the Goddess, or Mother Russia – and with his passion
for men, Klyuev created his own spirituality. Images of the
Goddess abound in his work, as when he writes,
"Udilonya, mother of the rye, / Comb out your golden hair
from the straw / And plunge each ear into mead and
molasses." He once described himself as a "priest visiting
Baba-Yaga," who is, in Marija Gimbutas's (1921-1994)
words, "the ancient Goddess of Death and Regeneration in
Slavic mythology." His passion for young men like Esenin
and Nikolai Ilich Arkhipov was wedded to his reverence

for Mother Russia and nature. "My love," he wrote, ". . . is a thousand-faceted stone / In whose pools splashes Satan, the pike. / In a snake mask, on a gray boar / Carnality guards the dwelling of dream. / My lover is a harvest on a northern field." Klyuev envisioned a radical transformation of Russia, which he depicted in terms of a "fiery pheasant" flying over the land, which would bring about a classless society where peasant culture would triumph over industrialism, capitalism, and the general mechanization of life. Tragically, Klyuev was betrayed by the Russian Revolution. He was arrested in 1933 as an alleged counterrevolutionary and either died from a heart attack on the way to a labor camp or was executed in 1937. His essential themes – the reverence for the Goddess of Nature, or Mother Russia, blended with Christian sentiment; his passion for men; and his fear of modernization and specifically of westernization – are woven together in a 1914 letter to the poet A. V. Shiryaevets: "Every day I go into the grove – and sit there by a little chapel – and the age-old pine tree, but an inch to the sky, I think about you . . . I kiss your eyes and your dear heart . . . O, mother wilderness! paradise of the spirit . . . How hateful and black seems all the so-called Civilised world and what I would give, what Golgotha I would bear – so that America should not encroach upon the blue-feathered dawn . . . upon the fairy tale hut."

Knight In the Medieval European tradition, the knight is representative of ethically and spiritually oriented warriorhood, associated with such qualities as physical strength, courage, honor, and loyalty, and is frequently symbolic of a profound devotion to the deity. The knight is also singular in being a figure who garners respect even while leading an itinerant, relatively marginal (-ized) lifestyle. Deep affectional bonds which may have included same-sex eroticism developed among knights, in part as a result of their living together in the house of an overlord, sometimes for as long as twenty years. Unfortunately, it is difficult to distinguish between homoerotic affection and diplomatic expression (such as rulers embracing). This has led certain writers to insist that such expressions as male-male kissing do not signify homoerotic expression. This certainty, however, is complicated by the fact that many men of the period appear to have been acutely aware that open expression of homoerotic affection might well lead to accusations of sodomy or buggery. This latter notion is supported by the fact that while certain Medieval writers chose to depict embracing and kissing between men, others clearly chose to forgo such descriptions. As G. F. Jones observes (1966), while Gottfried von Strassburg in *Tristan* and Wolfram von Eschenbach in *Parzival* choose to portray some-sex kissing, the anonymous author of the *Nibelungenlied* "never lets men kiss men; and men usually seal their bargains with a handshake." Same-sex kissing occurring in a knightly or chivalrous context, which may or

may not signify desire or romantic love, may be found in numerous Medieval epics, including *Tristan* and *Parzival*, as well as in the *Rolandslied* (the *Song of Roland*), *Waltharius*, the *Ruodlied*, *König Rother*, *Erec*, and *Iwein*. N. Perella (1969) argues that kisses occurring between knights and other males do not merely represent diplomacy, but rather a profound bond that weds the physical to the spiritual which is reminiscent of that bond shared by warrior-lovers of classical antiquity. Observing that the "French *chansons de gestes* and their Middle High German imitations offer many examples of men kissing one another," Perella suggests that "behind such man-to-man kisses" lies the "magico-physical nature of the kiss as a bond uniting breaths, or souls." Such kisses not only knit souls together but, as Jones observes, "Both Gottfried [author of *Tristan*] and Wolfram [author of *Parzival*] stress the power of kisses to cure both physical injury and spiritual pain," as when one knight heals another by kissing him on the battlefield. Same-sex desire and transgenderism are occasionally linked in subtle ways in Medieval epics, as in *Lancelot*, wherein Sir Gawain prays to God to transform him into a beautiful woman so that he may be loved by a mysterious knight, and in *Huon of Bordeaux*, wherein the transgendered female knight Ide is given in marriage to Princess Olive, daughter of the Emperor of the Holy Roman Empire. In the latter, we are led to believe that the relationship might have survived as it was, between transgendered female and female, had not a page of the Emperor discovered what was going on. On learning of Ide's anatomical nature, the Emperor declared that Ide must be burned at the stake. Ide, not knowing what else to do, prayed to the Virgin Mary that she might be transformed into a man so that her life might be spared. The Virgin answered Ide's prayer, and the wedding went ahead as planned. While the tale culminates with the enforcement of heterosexuality and strict gender roles, it nevertheless acknowledges the possible linkages of same-sex desire, transgenderism, and knighthood, which partake of the spiritual. Kindred themes are echoed in Ariosto's *Orlando furioso* (1531), in the narrative of BRADAMANTE and that of BRITOMART in Edmund Spenser's *The Faerie Queene* (1590-1596). Perhaps the most well-known (allegedly) homoerotically inclined knight of English history is Richard I, the Lionhearted (1157-1199). Although not a knight *per se*, in many respects the transgendered possibly lesbian JEANNE D'ARC (Joan of Arc, 1412-1431), as a chivalrous warrior devoted to God, merits mention in this context. Among homoerotically inclined men of late nineteenth-century England, as among the Pre-Raphaelites and others, the figure of the knight and notions of chivalry experienced a renascence. In *The Artist*, in April 1874, Charles Kains-Jackson wrote in "The New Chivalry": "The flower of . . . perfect civilization will be found in the New Chivalry or the exaltation of the youthful masculine idea . . . The New

Chivalry. . . will not ask [Will an intimate relationship] lead to the procreation of children?' It will rest content with beauty . . . As in Sparta so once more, will the lover be the inbreather [and] the beloved the listener . . . Like will be drawn to like by each attempting to attain . . . to that which in the other is the Best." John Addington SYMONDS gave expression to this ideas in his poem "The Song of Love and Death," envisioning a UTOPIA or ARCADIA where "Chivalry / Long sought" is found and where "comrades thick as flowers," surpassing the chivalry of "Arthur or of Roland," shall "make the world one fellowship, and plant/ New Paradise for nations yet to be."

Knight, Gareth (pseudonym of **Basil Wilby**, fl. mid-twentieth century)   Described by N. Drury (1992) as a "leading contemporary authority on the magical applications of the Kabbalah (QABBALAH)," whose works include *A Practical Guide to Qabalistic Symbolism* (1965) and *A History of White Magic* (1978). Where same-sex desire and transgenderism are concerned, however, Knight takes an extremely reactionary position. In discussing the sphere of NETZACH (VENUS) on the Qabbalistic Tree of Life, he writes: "A high powered mutual stimulation on the mental and higher emotional levels can degenerate into homosexuality. In spite of the modern spate of apologetics for this form of lower emotional and physical relationship, it is a perversion and evil. It is perhaps as well to state this categorically, as it is a form of vice likely to be on the increase with lesser differentiation in physical sexual characteristics of the Aquarian type of human now coming into the world . . . Homosexuality, like the use of drugs, is one of the techniques of Black Magick." While worlds apart in other respects, Knight shares this animosity toward same-sex desire and transgenderism with fellow occultists Dion FORTUNE, Kenneth GRANT, and William Butler YEATS.

Kocek   Turkish term for gender variant, mixed-dressing male dancers, singers, and musicians, related to the pre-Islamic Arabic and early Islamic MUKHANNATHUN musicians who "dyed their hands and affected the habits of women." While the origin of the *kocek* performer remains unclear, dance historians Leona Wood and Anthony Shay have suggested that the *danse du ventre*, or belly dance, movements employed by such dancers as the *qawwal* of Egypt, the *batcha* of Iran, and the *koceks* of Turkey may have originated in the dance tradition of ancient Egypt (as early as the Eighteenth Dynasty, 1567-1320 BCE). They believe that this form of dance itself may have originated in the worship of the female deities. They point to a similar dance performed in the twentieth century in Malabar celebrating the "Goddess's invincibility when doing battle with her foes." They insist that belly dancing is "essentially female dancing, whether done by a male or female." When they danced, the *koceks* wore caps over

their long, braided hair, rings and bangles, and skirts of exquisite fabrics over their trousers. Their dances included employment of a symbolic language of gestures. When they sang, they often did so in falsetto. They accompanied themselves with finger cymbals and tambourines or wooden clappers. They were also accompanied by musicians including other *koceks*. Songs sung during their dances were often composed especially for them. The *koceks* were trained in a formal manner in the arts of mime, acting, singing, and dancing by the *kocek utasi* or master. When a *kocek* became too old to appear androgynous, he might become a master or a member of an instrumental group. *Koceks*, like *mukhannathun*, were associated with the world of MUJUN, in Arabic-Islamic culture a bohemian, marginal space, typically embodied by pleasure gardens, cafes, and taverns, where artists, mystics, prostitutes and others gathered to celebrate life. It was in the realm of *mujun* that, as the seventeenth-century Moldavian prince Dimitrie Cantemir observed and as exquisite illustrations demonstrate, Sufi mystics and *kocek* performers came together. Their association probably dates to the Ottoman Empire, with its support of the Sufis and its delight in spectacles. Both the *koceks* and the Sufis were well acquainted with same-sex intimacy, and both were accomplished dancers, the latter known popularly as the "whirling dervishes." While the Sufis emphasized the spiritual in their dancing, the *koceks* stressed the sensuous. Together, they must have given manifestation to the Sufi notion of SHAHED *bazi*, or *nazar ill' al-murd*, contemplation of the beautiful male being as an apparition of the godhead. This belief in indwelling or embodiment of the divine in the human, *hulul*, as in ecstatic dance, is considered by many Islamic traditionalists the most heinous of the Sufi heresies.

Koe'kcuc   Among the Siberian Kamchadal (or Itelmensy), TWO-SPIRIT, often homoerotically inclined male shamans. Koe'kcuc wore a mixture of feminine, masculine, and ceremonial attire. Their shamanic tasks included working magic and interpreting dreams. While scholars have tended to downplay the importance of transgendered homosexuality in Shamanism, Krasheninikoff and Vladimir Jochelson maintain that, at least among the Kamchadal, its role was crucial: "[It] may be inferred that the most important feature of the institution of the *koe'kcuc* lay, not in their shamanistic power, but in their position with regard to the satisfaction of the unnatural inclinations of the Kamchadal. The *koe'kcuc* . . . were in the position of concubines."

Kokk'okshi (or **Kokkookwe**)   Among the Zuni people of southwestern North America, Kokk'okshi are "Raw People," primordial beings who bring RAIN and who represent an "undifferentiated state of gender"; they constitute a prototype of Kolhamana, the TWO-SPIRIT kachina spirit. They are also related to the *koyemshi* clowns.

Kokopelli Mana Hopi female kachina spirit of erotic passion, mirroring the ithyphallic male Kokopelli. In masked rituals, she is impersonated by a man who dances sensuously, lifting "her" skirt and miming sexual intercourse with other male participants.

Kolhamana TWO-SPIRIT kachina of the Zuni people of southwestern North America, a warrior and mediator of polarities (masculine/feminine, solar/lunar, etc.). Kolhamana wears in masked dance rituals a male kilt over a woman's dress and his (-her) hair parted with half of it up in the women's style and half down in the men's style; he (-she) carries a bow and arrows or ears of corn and a rattle made of deer bones. Kolhamana is typically impersonated by male two-spirits (LHAMANA) and female two-spirits (KATSOTSI').

Kombabos The King of Syria once asked a young friend, Kombabos, to escort the Queen, Stratonic, to Hierapolis, where a temple to the goddess ATARGATIS was being built. Kombabos was afraid, as he was attracted to the Queen; he was certain that she was also drawn to him. Fearing the potential wrath of the King, he castrated himself. He placed his genitals in a pot with honey and balm. He then gave the pot to the King, telling him to guard it well until he and the Queen returned from Hierapolis. He did not, however, reveal to the King the contents of the vessel. While Kombabos and the Queen were sojourning at Hierapolis, rumors circulated that they had become lovers. When news reached the King, he became enraged, believing that he had been betrayed by his wife and his friend. He ordered the death of Kombabos. After their return, as Kombabos was being led away to be murdered, he begged the King if he might have the pot he had left with him. When Kombabos opened the vessel, the King wept with joy, apologizing to his wife and Kombabos for his lack of trust. He then told Kombabos that his love for him was now so great that he never wished to be without him, even when he and the Queen were in bed. From that time forward, Kombabos dressed in the garments of women. Legend has it that Kombabos's act of devotion led others to castrate themselves, to wear women's clothes, to perform tasks traditionally given to women, and to serve as priests of the goddess Atargatis at Hierapolis.

Komos Related to "comedy" and to the god Comus, the reigning deity of comedy, the *komos* was a Greek dance held in honor of the goddess ARTEMIS/DIANA. The *komos* included the wearing of artificial phalli by women dancers and padded buttocks by male dancers. The *komos* is akin to the KALATHISKOS, the KORDAX, the BRYALLICHA, and the *sikinnis*.

Koolau In Hawaiian myth, a god or spirit of the wind. Bisexual in today's terms, his female beloved was the beautiful Keaka, and his male AIKANE, or loving companion, the legendary male HULA dancer and chanter PAMANO.

Kordax The Greco-Roman goddess ARTEMIS/DIANA was honored with the *kordax*, a ritual dance, the name of which suggests a phallus. In the kordax, men dressed as women and women as men. Wearing "grotesque" masks, they "danced, sang, and bandied coarse jests," with the women wearing *lombai*, large, artificial phalli attached to their waists. In this capacity, the women dancers were referred to as the Lombai of the Goddess. The *kordax* was rooted in a "lewd rotation of the abdomen and buttocks." It employed figures or movements associated with other dances. From the *igde*, it borrowed the figure of the mortar, "characterized by rotation of the hips, with an occasional jerk of the body, suggestive of the stirring and pounding of a pestle." From the *maktrismos* it borrowed the figure of the "kneading trough," another movement based on rotation of the hips. Other movements or figures of the *kordax* included the *hygros*, a movement suggesting the slithering or wriggling of a serpent, the *proskinklizein*, a figure suggesting the flicking of a lizard's tail, and the *kallibis*, a figure expressing a delicate, mincing, voluptuous gait. The *kordax* is akin to the BRYALLICHA, the KALATHISKOS, the KOMOS, and the *sikinnis*.

Kosio *Kosio* were in the past, at least until the early twentieth century, HIERODULE-priestesses and priests of the Rainbow-serpent *lwa* (deity or spirit) DAMBALLAH (also called Da, Danhgbi) of the religion of Vodou of the Dahomean/Fon people of West Africa (present-day Benin). There appear to have been among the *kosio* transgendered males who engaged in cultic eroticism with men.

Koskalaka Among the Lakota people of North America, a term for women who exhibit transgendered behavior, who do not desire to marry men, and who may engage in same-sex relationships. Native American Indian writer Paula Gunn ALLEN suggests that "the proper translation [of *koskalaka*] is 'Lesbian' or, colloquially, 'dyke.'" These women are believed to be the spiritual daughters of the goddess or spirit WIYA NUMPA, Double Woman.

Kossa and Kwirana Among the Tewa people of North America, TWO-SPIRIT ceremonial clowns. Kossa and Kwirana are comparable to the KOYEMSHI.

Kothornos High boot worn by women and gender variant men in ancient Greece. The god DIONYSUS was thought to prefer the *kothornos* above all other footwear because of his effeminacy. Some Greeks even believed that the *kothornos*, when placed over a man's foot, might cause him to experience gender metamorphosis.

Kotys (or **Cotytto, Kotytto**)   Thracian or Phrygian goddess, and later Greek and Roman goddess of the hunt and the waning MOON. Kotys was worshipped in Greece by the seventh century BCE. In the Hellenistic Age, however, Kotys' worship experienced a great revival after lying dormant for several centuries. Her name probably derives from either *kued-* or *kuod-*, "energy" or "avenger." She is akin to the goddesses MA and ARTEMIS/DIANA. She is a patron of musicians and, along with the goddess CYBELE, is sometimes considered the inventor of cymbals and the AULOS. She is sometimes accompanied by a male consort, Sabazius. Devotees of Kotys and Sabazius included priestesses and gender variant, often homoerotically inclined male priests called BAPTAI ("baptists"). Pierre Le Loyer, Sieur de la Brosse, in his *Discours des spectres, ou visions et apparitions d'esprits* (1605), invoked Kotys as the "tutelary Goddess of *bardaches* [i.e. homoerotically inclined, often gender variant males] and prostitutes."

Koyemshi   Sacred "mudhead" clowns of the kachina spirit cult of the Zuni people of southwestern North America. The *koyemshi* represent a primordial androgynous, pansexual state. They are believed to be infertile but to have the power to inspire fertility in others. In rituals, they depict these characteristics by tying their foreskins and by giving seeds from deerskin pouches to others. They are liminal beings, dwelling between the realms of humans and spirits, the living and the dead. Their names tend to contradict their behaviors; e.g. Bat cannot see in, and is fearful of, the dark. Their mocking of traditions is itself a time-honored tradition.

Kramer, Joseph (1947-   )   Gay massage instructor, writer, theologian, sexual healer, and erotic visionary. Raised in the rural midwestern US, Kramer spent eleven years in a Roman Catholic religious order, the Jesuits. There, he learned to love men deeply and spiritually. He came to believe, however, that in order to fully experience the love of men, he could not continue to sublimate or repress the erotic dimension of this love. In 1979 he moved to Berkeley, where he attended the Graduate Theological Union as well as massage school. The weaving together of these pursuits culminated in the founding of the Body Electric School of Massage and Rebirthing in 1984. In the early years of the AIDS crisis, Kramer helped set up the first hospice massage team in the United States. As AIDS spread, Kramer, recognizing the need for a new, no-risk way of blending eroticism, play, and spiritual impulse, developed a technique or "Way" of Taoist Erotic Massage. Of this type of massage, Kramer explains: "According to Taoist sexual teaching, when the 'Jade Stalk' [i.e. the

penis] is massaged, a special energy called *ching chi* is unleashed in the body. We feel this erotic life-force energy as pleasure . . . as vibrancy." In 1993 Kramer left Body Electric to weave together a broader consortium of his skills by establishing the EroSpirit Research Institute. One of the most important ways in which erotico-spiritual information is being disseminated by EroSpirit is through videos, which include talks and demonstrations by luminaries of Gay Spirituality and Queer Spirit. Among these are: *Sex Magic, Male Sacred Prostitutes, and Sex Monasteries* (Kramer); *Sacred Boy* (Keith HENNESSY); *Both Lover and Priest* (Robert Goss); *Monogamy: The Container for Intimacy* (Andrew RAMER); and *Sluts and Goddesses* (lesbian ero-spirit, Annie SPRINKLE). The video *Fire on the Mountain: An Intimate Guide to Male Genital Massage*, narrated by Kramer, is an excellent introduction to Taoist Erotic Massage for men.

Krishna   Perpetually sixteen, Krishna is the blue-skinned god of Hinduism, a fusion of beauty, joy, playfulness, spontaneity, music, and dance. Large-eyed, full-lipped, and raven-haired, fragrant as a flower garland and crowned with a peacock feather, Krishna seduces the devotee, regardless of gender, into loving him, beckoning his devotees to forget their cares and join him in the *rasa lila*, the cosmic dance. Tales of Krishna abound in images of gender transformation and fluid sexuality. Once, long ago, Krishna gazed into a pool and, like the Greek NARCISSUS, fell in love with his reflection. Wishing to experience erotic union with the image in the water, he asked RADHA, his mistress, if he might exchange forms with her. Then, as Radha, he made love to the youth in the water who was none other than himself. On another occasion, following a quarrel, Krishna disguised himself as one of the GOPIS, the celestial milkmaids who have left their chores to dance with their companions and their lord, in order to be close to Radha. When they embraced, Radha was suddenly transformed into Krishna. On still another occasion, some of the *gopis* took the form of Radha and others that of Krishna as they danced, "embracing their companions." If one is to follow Krishna, one must come to see oneself as an embodiment of the feminine. As Ajit Mookerjee explains, in Hinduism it is generally believed that "all souls," and here he refers to worshippers, "are feminine" and active in relation to "the Supreme Reality," which is masculine and receptive. Krishnadas writes in *Krishna of Vrindabana*, "In truth every finite being is essentially an emanation or phase of Radha, to wit, a *manjari* [or *gopi*], or a milkmaid," and D. Kinsley (1975) relates, "The *gopis* beautifully . . . convey what man is like when he expresses his essential nature; indeed the essential nature of all men is that of a *gopi* . . . When a man expresses himself in devotion to Krishna, when he sports with Krishna in ecstatic bliss, all desires are fulfilled. Man becomes rapt in the intoxicating beauty of Krishna."

Among those who have identified with Radha and the *gopis* in their devotion to Krishna are the SAKHIBHAVAS, who dress as women and affect various behaviors regarded as feminine. Sakhibhavas come to know the state of pure bliss, *hladini-shakti*, by experiencing the union of Radha and Krishna, of the masculine and the feminine, within themselves, and as HIERODULIC priests, by "permit[ting] the sexual act on their persons" by traditionally masculine male worshippers. While many scholars and sages have ignored or suppressed materials relating to gender and sexual variance in the worship of Krishna, we know that, in the tradition of the Sahkibhavas, the fifteenth-century CE mystic CAITANYA, who was believed to be an incarnation of both Radha and Krishna, often dressed as Radha and described himself as the lover of Krishna. In the nineteenth century, the sage Ramakrishna, too, dressed as Radha and envisioned himself as the lover of God. And in the mid-twentieth century, Swami Pradhavananda suggested to gay writer Christopher ISHERWOOD that he sacralize an erotic relationship by viewing his lover as "the young lord Krishna."

Kroketos In Greco-Roman antiquity, a long-sleeved chiton worn by women, especially the devotees of the goddesses DEMETER and PERSEPHONE, and transgendered men, especially the male bacchants of DIONYSUS.

Kuan Yin (or **Guanyin, Goon Yam**) Chinese Buddhist BODHISATTVA of compassion depicted as both female and transgendered. "She who hears the cries of the world," who renounces her own divinity until she has aided humanity in becoming enlightened and in ending suffering, Kuan Yin is more popularly known as the Goddess of Mercy. In the late twentieth century, she is revered not only by Chinese but also by many Asian-Americans and others living in the United States and elsewhere. She is especially known as a guardian of women and children and as a patron of sailors and fishermen and - women. V. L. Bullough (1976) relates that "in one of the most interesting cases of sexual transformation, Kuan Yin change[d] from a male figure [AVALOKITESHVARA, of Indian origin, the male Buddha of the Pure Land or Western Paradise] to a female one . . . Because enlightenment is conceived as the union of male and female elements, Kuan-yin, the companion of the Buddha, may have come to be visualized [in the eighth century CE] in female form . . . At first, Buddhist theology preserved the maleness of Kuan-yin, but popular folk religion increasingly adopted the female. This was eventually accepted by scholars on the grounds that a *bodhisattva* could assume any form and shape to assist [hu-]mankind." Kuan Yin is believed to be able to transform into the primarily male Avalokiteshvara at will. Many Chinese women who in the nineteenth and earlier centuries

belonged to societies such as the GOLDEN ORCHID ASSOCIATION, which sought to integrate feminism, lesbianism, and spiritual practice, paid homage to Kuan Yin, as a goddess who not only watches over women but who also rejects heterosexual marriage in order to fully devote her life to the work of the spirit. The gay activist and social philosopher David Fernbach (1981) suggests that "the wonderful example of love shown by Kuan Yin requires, if it is to develop on any large scale in society, a process of de-masculinization, of reasserting the maternal culture, not as something ascribed solely to women, but as a quality that men must equally display."

Kucumatz Gynandrous or transgendered supreme being of the Quiché-Maya, the "heart of heaven" who created all life.

Kukai (posthumously known as **Kobo Daishi**, 774-835) Japanese spiritual teacher, writer/calligrapher, traveler, businessperson, sculptor, and founder of the Shingon sect of Buddhism. When Kukai was eighteen, he entered college with the goal of becoming a statesman. He soon became disillusioned with the Confucianist bias of the program, however, and withdrew. At this time he became fascinated with Buddhism and in 804 sailed for China, where he became the pupil of the Buddhist patriarch Hui Ge. Under Hui Ge, he began weaving together elements of Buddhism, Shinto, Confucianism, Taoism, and TANTRA, and in 806 he returned to Japan with a new sect, Shingon. Shingon is "essentially mystical and esoteric," a sect of "sacraments and elaborate ritual" which makes extensive use of "mantras, mudras . . . mandalas . . . [and] magical practices." Shingon embraces both Buddhist and Shinto deities. According to legend, not only the sect of Shingon but also homoerotic love was imported to Japan by Kukai on his return from studying in China. While it is clear from historical records that same-sex love (*doseiai*, or *nanshoku*) existed in Japan long before the birth of Kukai, this legend became so widespread that *doseiai* was from the ninth century onward associated with Buddhism. It became, indeed, the "preferred form of sexual expression among the Buddhist priesthood." While the exact reasons why Kukai became so intimately linked in the Japanese psyche to homoeroticism remain somewhat of a mystery, Tsuneo Watanabe and Jun'ichi Wata (1989) suggest that a text "highly regarded" by the Shingon master, the *Rishu-kyo Sutra*, may be partly responsible; in this text we read, "voluptuousness is pure, is a truth of the state of *boddhisattva* . . . physical pleasure is pure, is a truth of the state of *boddhisattva*," implying that sexuality may be a bridge to enlightenment and by extension, that devotees of Shingon may have practiced some form of Tantra. A text allegedly CHANNELED by the spirit of Kukai (as called by his spiritual name, Kobo Daishi), described by Paul Gordon Schalow in "Kukai and the Tradition of Male

Love in Japanese Buddhism" (1992), lends support to this notion. The *Kobo Daishi ikkan no sho*, roughly, *Kobo Daishi's Book*, recorded near 1598 by a Shingon monk, includes Tantric techniques for seducing potential male lovers as well as specific Tantric positions for anal intercourse, including "skylark rising" (buttocks lifted) and "turned up soles" (legs lifted). In the twentieth century, Shingon is considered to be the "third most powerful force in Japanese Buddhism." Devotees of Kukai, or Kobo Daishi, continue to make pilgrimages to his monastic center at Mount Koya; they believe that their master has not died but has "merely entered into eternal *samadhi*" and is "still alive there as a savior and teacher," comparable to or synonymous with a BODDHISATTVA.

Kulu'u Transgendered, often homoerotically inclined male priest/esse/s of the Mesopotamian goddess INANNA/ISHTAR. They served as HIERODULES, union with them being deemed a sacred activity.

Kumahumahuka'aka, Kumahumahukole, and **Kumahumaliukole** In Hawaiian myth, independent manifestations of the pig-man deity Kamapua'a whose names mean, respectively, "Ku the Great Homosexual, the Laugh," "Ku the Great Homosexual of the Buttocks," and "Ku the Homosexual Turning His Buttocks Towards One."

Kumarbi According to the Hurrians, an ancient Near Eastern people, Alalalu was king of the gods. He was defeated, however, by Anu, a lord of the sky. Anu in turn was defeated, although not entirely, by Kumarbi, a god of war. When Kumarbi had attacked Anu, he had bitten off his genitals and, swallowing Anu's semen, had become impregnated by the former ruler of the gods. Kumarbi subsequently gave birth to three gods: Teshub, the god of storms; Aranzah, the god of rivers; and the great god Tashmishu.

Kumukahi Hawaiian deity of healing, divination, and magic, luck and prosperity, male sexuality, and the power of the sun. A shapeshifter, Kumukahi often takes the form of a bird, particularly the Pacific golden plover. Both homoerotic and heterosexual versions of the tale of Kumukahi and his two loving companions are told. In one of the heterosexual versions, Kumukahi arrives from Tahiti (or Kahiki) with the volcanic goddess PELE, her entourage, and his two wives. In one of the gay variants, Kumukahi settles on the island of Hawaii with his male AIKANE LA, the sun god, and MAKANONI, a mysterious being perhaps linked to phallic mysteries. Together they form a homoerotic trinity. The three were represented by the sun – La – and by two phallic-shaped reddish stone pillars – Kumukahi and Makanoni – which stood on a cape – now Cape Kumukahi – on the eastern coast of the island

of Hawaii, with the Kumukahi-pillar standing to the northern of the Makanoni-pillar. N. B. Emerson (1986) relates that the "Hawaiians speak of them [i.e. the pillars] as *pohaku eho*, which . . . is the name given to a phallus." The midway point between the pillars and the place where the sun was believed to arise from the sea was referred to as the "ladder of the sun" or the "source of the sun." The Kumukahi-pillar represented sunrise and the Makanoni-pillar, sunset; they also signified the two solstices of the year. A chant concerning this triadic relationship was sung: "Awake, it is light, day is here, / The rays of the sun [La] prick the surface of the sea, / It pursues, just like Kumukahi, / Seeking to be friends [*aikane*, loving companions] with Makanoni." As a male trinity, the three were especially revered by fishermen, who offered sacrifices to them in exchange for good fortune. Sick persons also made pilgrimages to the site in the hope of being healed. The phallic shape of the pillars, coupled with the phallic expression *pohaku eho*, also suggests that male, possibly homoerotic, mysteries may have been performed at the site. In another homoerotic tale of Kumukahi, he was said to be the *aikane* or loving companion of PALA-MOA, a deity associated with shamans, fishermen, and birds. Together, Kumukahi and Pala-moa were revered, especially by practitioners of magic and sorcery, as powerful, shapeshifting shaman-deities. Potential priests of, or shamans allied with, Kumukahi were embodied or possessed by the god, after which they became capable of both causing and curing sickness as well as prophesying and performing great feats of magic.

Kurgarru Transgendered, often homoerotically inclined male priest/esse/s of the Mesopotamian goddess INANNA/ISHTAR. *Kurgarru* were seen as mortal embodiments of the Goddess as well as human reflections of certain spirit-companions of Inanna. In a myth concerning the Goddess's descent to the Underworld, the *kurgarru* (*kurgarra*) is one of two androgynous beings, "neither male nor female," along with the *kalaturru* (or *galatur*) that is created to rescue Inanna from the clutches of death. The transgendered status of *kurgarru* was confirmed in the belief that his physical body differed from that of other men, in that it carried magical power; simply looking upon a *kurgarru* could bring a change of fortune. As ritual musicians, the *kurgarru* played various instruments, including the lyre, the two-stringed lute (*zinnutu*, or *sinnatu*), the flute, and metal clappers. As ritual actors, the *kurgarru*, led by the *rabi kurgarri*, performed in dramas depicting epic struggles. The *kurgarru* also took part, with the *assinnu*, in a ritual honoring Inanna and Narudu, in which they dressed in the garments of these goddesses. Like the other transgendered priests of Inanna/Ishtar, they served as HIERODULES, union with them being deemed a sacred activity. In *The Queen of Swords* (1987), a poetic drama by lesbian writer

Judy GRAHN, the *kurgarru*, as Kur and Gal, are transformed into Radical Faeries.

Kuzmin, Mikhail Alekseevich (1872-1936)   Russian writer, musician, and mystic, perhaps best known for the Symbolist novel *Wings* (1906) and a series of poems titled *The Trout Breaks the Ice* (1928), both of which are infused with spirituality and same-sex desire. A student of the composer Rimsky-Korsakov, a friend of the early Soviet diplomat Georgy Vasilevich Chicherin, and a participant in the Russian art movement called "the World of Art" which included Sergei DIAGHILEV, Vaslav NIJINSKY, and others, Kuzmin's lovers included Vsevolod Knyazev, a poet whose life ended tragically in suicide, and the writer Yury Yurkun. An early supporter of the Russian Revolution, Kuzmin ultimately became a victim of Soviet oppression; dying of pneumonia in St Petersburg in 1936 saved him from being sent to a labor camp or from being killed. Yurkun was assassinated two years after Kuzmin's death alongside other artists who were thought to be counterrevolutionaries. Born into a family of Old Believers, Christian traditionalists who broke away from the Russian Orthodox Church in the mid-seventeenth century, Kuzmin spent several years, from 1898 until 1903, studying the music of the Old Believers and sojourning in several of their monastic communities in the Nizhny Novgorod and Kostroma regions. From them, Kuzmin inherited the dream of Belovod'ye, an earthly paradise to come. He was also greatly inspired by his study of ancient religions, especially of the Greeks and Egyptians, with Alexandria becoming for him the nearest manifestation in his lifetime to the terrestrial paradise. In his short story "Virginal Victor: A Byzantine Tale," a tale of spiritual passion and same-sex love, Victor lives in Byzantium in the early days of Christianity. His aunt, who has been his caretaker, determines to find Victor a wife so that she, Pulcheria, can fulfill her wish to become a nun. Victor, however, still a virgin at nineteen, finds no one of interest other than his personal slave, Andrew the Hungarian. As the two are leaving Church services one day, they are accosted by a group of persons which includes a holy fool, who mocks their relationship and refers to them as "demons," implying that theirs is a homoerotic bond. Soon afterward, Andrew becomes ill and dies. As Andrew is dying, he embraces Victor and kisses him on the lips. Some nights thereafter, as Victor prays to God to let him know if Andrew is at peace, his young companion appears before him, naked save for a loincloth. Andrew then recounts to Victor in detail the journey from this

world to the next. He describes a series of ordeals, including one that suggests otherworldly homoeroticism. Unfortunately, Andrew suggests that this "twentieth ordeal" may be associated with demonic rather than angelic activity. Nevertheless, before vanishing, Andrew kisses Victor once more on the lips. Kuzmin became increasingly disillusioned with organized Christianity's anti-erotic biases. Especially perturbed by Protestantism, he wrote, "I think that a true Protestant cannot be a true poet, rejecting as he does . . . sensuousness . . . Protestantism cannot give birth to genuine art – it is devoid of divine grace." He drew upon Christian mysticism and upon paganism to create his own syncretic spiritual vision, one which celebrated homoerotic love. Revering the gods and heroes of antiquity, he wrote in "Love": "Were I a second Antinous, / he who drowned in the sacred Nile – / I would drive all men mad with my beauty, / temples would be raised to me while I yet lived. . . ." Kuzmin's central concerns were art and love. In *Fish-Scales in the Net* (1916-1921), he returned to Christian metaphor to write of love: "Love joins. The source of love is God . . . The primal law – love . . . Truth and love – Divine Wisdom . . . Love for oneself is the primal instinct . . . the goal is love toward everything . . . Religion – the goal – is the union of our sensual with our intellectual nature, and love of self with love of God . . . Christ's passion is the exertion of the Divine love. Is it not sexual? The channel of love is the cross. The Phallus. Only in the life of the flesh is there the union of creation and oneness . . . The Annunciation (conception) was celebrated in ancient times on one and the same day as the Passion or the Resurrection. Does not this confirm my ideas about the erotic significance of the passion? . . . Love is the salt . . . Love is the source, the salt of all creation, it brings the Son of God down to earth." Kuzmin's most memorable lines in terms of homoerotic spirituality may be found, however, in *The Trout Breaks the Ice* : "We are two wings – a single soul, / Two souls we are – our maker one, / Two makers we – a single crown."

Kwe'rhame, Kwiraxame   If a young woman of the Yuma or Maricopa people of southwestern North America dreams "too much," she may transform into a man or a woman-man, a *kwe'rhame* (Yuma) or a *kwiraxame* (Maricopa). She will begin to wear men's clothes, hunt and fight in battle, and choose female companions. For the Yuma or Maricopa woman, dreaming provides a gateway not only to gender transformation but also to the acquisition of shamanic powers.

L

La Hawaiian sun god who shares a triadic, intimate (AIKANE) relationship with the male deities KUMUKAHI and MAKANONI.

Labarindja In Australian folklore, a wild woman or gynandrous figure who is depicted as having bluish skin and hair the color of smoke. The labarindja are alternately described as possessing "evil magic in their vaginas" and as having penises as well as female anatomical parts. They want nothing to do with men. If a man insists on having intercourse with a labarindja, he will probably die. In ritual, the labarindja is often enacted or embodied by a male dressed in feminine attire.

Labrys (also **Double Axe**) The double axe, or labrys, is an ancient ritual tool of Mediterranean Goddess Reverence and the weapon of choice of the AMAZONS of antiquity. In the late twentieth century it has been reclaimed by lesbians as a prominent symbol of lesbian-feminism. The labrys may be traced to Mediterranean antiquity, where it appears to have simultaneously represented the BULL, the MOON, and the BUTTERFLY, symbols associated with fertility, sacrifice, metamorphosis, and the spiritual life. The archaeologist Arthur Evans (1851-1941) interpreted the labrys in Minoan art as a symbol of androgyny. Together with the Amazons, numerous deities and heroes are associated with transgenderism and/or same-sex passion and the labrys, including ZEUS Labrandeus, also known as Zeus Stratios, a transgendered or androgynous manifestation of Zeus holding a double axe and possessing a beard and multiple breasts; the Mesopotamian heroes GILGAMESH AND ENKIDU; and the Yoruba god SHANGO. The Naassenes, a gnostic group, "adopted the double axe as a symbol for the eternal androgyne nature in man which they sought to restore." The related hatchet is an attribute of the Hindu god GANESHA which signifies his cutting away of illusions.

Lache The South American Lache attributed shamanic powers to transgendered or third gender males, whom they named *cusmos*. A mother who had already given birth to four male children was permitted to raise her fifth son as a *cusmos*; this process of rearing began when the child "had reached the age of twelve moon." On reaching adulthood, the *cusmos* often married a man of the tribe. Upon death the *cusmos* was given the same funeral given to a woman.

Lad's Love Also called "boy's love," a common name for southernwood (*artemisia abrotonum*), a variety of wormwood with pale yellow flowers once cultivated for perfume. Wormwood was also used in the making of absinthe, a favorite hallucinogenic drink of nineteenth-century bohemians including the homoerotically inclined French poet RIMBAUD. In the nineteenth century, Lad's Love was often employed by English poets as a signifier of homoerotic love. John Addington SYMONDS's "Clifton and a Lad's Love" (1862) evokes homoerotic desire, melancholy, and dreams, while John Gambril Nicholson in "A Chaplet of Southernwood" (1896) fuses visionary experience and homoeroticism with suggestions that dreams are an "anodyne" for his suffering brought on by loneliness.

Laius In Greek legend, a king of Thebes and the father of Oedipus. While at the court of PELOPS, who had once been loved by POSEIDON, Laius fell in love with Pelops' son CHRYSIPPUS. In one version of the myth, the young man was not in love with Laius. When Laius would not leave Chrysippus alone, the latter committed suicide. Pelops cursed Laius, who was eventually killed by his own son Oedipus.

Laka Hawaiian goddess of love and fertility, sometimes said to be the mother of KAPO, although they are at other times depicted as a dual female "being." As the goddess of love, Laka is calle *aloha* ("beloved one") and *alohi* ("shining one"). In her duel aspect, Laka is the patron of the hula and associated with healing and sorcery. As the patron of HULA Laka-Kapo is associated with the transgendered male MAHU.

Lakshmi Hindu goddess of love, beauty, and prosperity, associated with the goddesses GANGA and PARVATI (or Shakti). In the form of Lakshmi-Narayana, the goddess merges with the god VISHNU to become an androgynous, hermaphroditic, or transgendered deity. Lakshmi is evoked in Pierre Loti's novel *Le Mariage de Loti* (1880) and in Léo Delibes's opera *Lakmé* (1883). In the latter, an exquisite duet is sung by Lakmé and her handmaid Mallika. The duet greatly enriches a scene of lesbian lovemaking in the film *The Hunger* (1983). The scene commences with the beautiful VAMPIRE Miriam playing from the duet on the piano and explaining to the mortal Sarah that the opera concerns an Indian princess who falls in love with another woman. The goddess's memory has survived as well in the name and person of Lakshmi Bai, an AMAZON, or woman warrior, who fought against the British in the nineteenth century and who has become a national heroine of India.

Lalita A name of the Great, or Mother Goddess of Hinduism. According to the *Tantraraja Tantra*, "the entrancing person of the incarnate god KRISHNA ... was in fact a form assumed by the highest female Nitya [eternal one, i.e. Great Goddess] in the supreme mandala [here, pantheon] of TANTRIC female deities, who is called Lalita; the Great Goddess herself, embracing all women and entrancing the world." In other words, the male god Krishna, who often assumed the form of his female lover RADHA, may have himself been a manifestation of the Great Goddess Lalita.

Lambda Eleventh letter of the Greek alphabet, chosen as a symbol of liberation in the early 1970s by participants in the US gay rights movement.

Lan Caihe (or **Lan Zai He, Lan T'sai-ho**) Chinese deity, one of the Eight Taoist Immortals. Although "variously stated to have been a woman and a hermaphrodite," Lan Caihe is generally perceived as a male who "could not understand how to be a man (which is perhaps the reason why he has been supposed to be a woman)." Indeed, only one of the Eight Immortals of Taoism is female: the goddess Ho Hsien Ku. Lan Caihe is most appropiately described as a transgendered male wearing feminine attire. Lan Caihe is described as a pauper who once traversed the earth playing a FLUTE and singing of the transitoriness of life. Whenever he (-she) was given money, he (-she) would scatter it on the ground for the poor to retrieve. One day, he (-she) became intoxicated while singing and playing at an inn in Feng Yang Fu. The Immortals, then seven in number, noticed Lan Caihe and, admiring him (-her) for his (-her) wisdom and generosity, and amused by his (-her) tipsiness, lifted him (-her) into the heavens to join them as the Eighth Immortal. As he (-she) was ascending, one of Lan Caihe's shoes dropped. For this reason, he (-she) is sometimes depicted as wearing only one shoe. Over the centuries, Lan Caihe has come to be regarded as a patron of musicians (especially FLUTE players), vagabonds, the poor, and transgendered persons.

Lawrence, David Herbert (1885-1930) English bisexual writer, husband of Frieda Weekley, passionate friend of John Middleton Murry, and lover (for a brief period) of Cornish farmer William Henry Hocking (and perhaps of other men as well). D. H. Lawrence's works speak frequently (and ambiguously) of the relationship of bisexuality, same-sex intimacy, and/or transgenderism, to the realm of the mythic or sacred. This intermingling, while discovered in *The White Peacock* (1911), "The Prussian Officer" (1914), *The Rainbow* (1915), *Women in Love* (1920), *Aaron's Rod* (1922), and in many of Lawrence's poems, especially in "Snake" and "Rabbit Snared in the Night," is perhaps most apparent in *The Plumed Serpent* (1926). While this novel is considered by some scholars to be marred by anti-feminist, rightist, and racist elements, others see it as a paean to powerful women and non-white persons. The main characters Kate, Ramon, and Cipriano form the bisexual, erotico-sacred trinity of a new religion based in Mexico and centering on the Aztec deity Quetzalcoatl, the Feathered Serpent. Ramon, the pinnacle of the trinity, is compared to Quetzalcoatl, JESUS Christ, APHRODITE/VENUS, Lucifer, and Mephistopheles; he, like the Feathered Serpent, is "the lord of the two ways," of androgyny or transgenderism and of bisexuality or pansexuality. His sacred attributes are the serpent, symbolic in Lawrence's work of homosexuality, and the jasmine, symbolic of androgyny – or, more correctly, of gynandry, with emphasis being placed on the female component. In one of *The Plumed Serpent*'s most powerful scenes, elements of homoeroticism and sadomasochism mingle in a ritual in which Ramon binds Cipriano with fur. This ritual culminates with Cipriano entering into an altered state of consciousness, "as if his mind, his head were melting away in the darkness, like a pearl in black wine." The purpose of this rite, Lawrence relates, is to take Cipriano "to where there is no beyond."

Lazarus In the New Testament of the Christian Bible, the brother of Mary and Martha of Bethany who falls ill, dies, and is revivified by JESUS Christ (John 11: 1-44). In John 1: 3, one finds, "Lord, he whom you love is ill," implying that Jesus held Lazarus as especially dear. This notion is supported by the so-called SECRET GOSPEL OF MARK, quoted by Clement of Alexandria (b. c. 150-d. c. 220) in a letter discovered by classical historian Morton Smith and published in 1973. This text suggests that Lazarus may have been secretly initiated by Jesus in a mysterious rite possibly involving cultic homoeroticism. Perhaps it was knowledge of this now lost text that led certain Gnostics to look upon Lazarus as the *eromenos*, that is, the beloved, of Jesus. Robert Williams (1992) argues that it was Lazarus, and not SAINT JOHN (fl. first century) who was the so-called "Beloved Disciple" of Jesus. Moreover, he suggests that Lazarus whom Jesus raised from the dead may be identical to Lazarus the leper, who appears elsewhere in the New Testament.

Leadbeater, Charles Webster (1854-1934) Homoerotically inclined English writer, clergyman, and mystic. Leadbeater became a curate in the Church of England, especially attracted to the High Anglican tradition with its extravagant ritualism. In 1883 Leadbeater joined the Theosophical Society founded by Helena Petrovna BLAVATSKY, with whom he eventually traveled to India. With Blavatsky as his spiritual teacher, Leadbeater immersed himself in the study of clairvoyance, CHANNELING, and other psychic arts. He was instrumental in the establishment of the Theosophical

Society in Sri Lanka and, after Blavatsky's death, continued to work closely with her spiritual heir, Annie Besant. In 1909, Leadbeater was one of the people instrumental in recognizing the spiritual significance of the young Jiddu Krishnamurti (1895-1986) who would become an internationally recognized yogic philosopher and who would reject Leadbeater because of his mentor's homosexuality. In 1916 Leadbeater founded the Liberal Catholic Church in Sydney, Australia, an extremely eclectic body blending Christian , Eastern, and Euro-western occult beliefs and practices. Leadbeater authored many popular books on mysticism and occult traditions, including *Clairvoyance* (1899), *Thought-Forms* (1901, with Annie Besant), *Invisible Helpers* (1901) *The Astral Plane* (1905), *The Perfume of Egypt and Other Weird Stories* (1912), *The Life After Death* (1912), *The Science of the Sacraments* (1902), *The Hidden Side of Christian Festivals* (1920), *The Masters and the Path* (1925), and *The Chakras* (1927). His books have generally remained in print and have been very influential in the Neopagan and New Age movements. Gregory Tillet's biography, *The Elder Brother: A Biography of Charles Webster Leadbeater* (1982) discusses Leadbeater's homosexuality as well as the homophobia of those around him.

Leblanc, Georgette (1869-1941)   Singer, bisexual companion of Margaret ANDERSON, and devotee of Georgei Ivanovich Gurdjieff (1872/1877-1949) and Pyotr Demainovitch Ouspensky (1878-1947).

Lee, Travis   Female character in Ann Allen Shockley's novel *Say Jesus and Come to Me* (1982). After suffering physical abuse at the hands of Rudolph Valentino Jones, Lee, a singer, heals her wounds by becoming involved in a lesbian relationship with Myrtle Black of Myrtle's Universal Church for All People.

Legba   When the bluesman Blue Bob Crawford sang, "I stand at the crossroads, baby, / Now there's no turnin' back: / I'm here to make a deal / Let the Devil deal the pack!" he was most likely referring not to the Christian Devil, but rather to Legba, an African/African-American deity of the crossroads. The "Devil" was a code name for the god Legba (also known as Papa La Bas) during a time when religions rooted in Africa were being even more suppressed than at present in the Americas. Indeed, the nickname of the BLUES as "the Devil's music" might be said actually to mean "the music of Legba." Legba acts, like the Greek god HERMES, as an intercessory between the gods, living human beings, and the dead. He is master of the Great or Starry Road that leads to the city of Vilokan, where the *lwas* (deities or spirits) of Vodou dwell; he links past, present, and future. Legba is foremost the creative power of the sun, and as such is often honored with fires. This creative power, called *ashé* by the Yoruba, is thought

to be carried by Legba in a calabash. Some say that this calabash also contains the destinies of us all. In Vodou, this calabash has become a sack (*macoutte*) full of candies or foods that Legba likes. Legba also holds a cane or staff that carries multiple meanings: it is his elderly wisdom, his phallus, his warrior's club, his link to the world of the dead, his magic wand. Legba can guide us to paths which will lead us to success, to the fulfillment of our destiny. Legba can transform our fate positively if we honor him, or can mis-guide us into error if we do not. As a ruler of crossroads or intersections, Legba represents a place beyond duality, a realm of paradox, of "both-and" or "all-at-once" rather than "either-or." Young and old, he is sometimes portrayed as a child with an elder's face, or an elder with a child's face. He can be serious or silly, compassionate or cruel. This paradoxical nature is sometimes symbolized by his cap, red or white on one side and black on the other. As existing beyond duality, Legba is also thought to be androgynous or transgendered. Yoruba woman scholar Ogundipe says that Legba is "certainly not restricted to human distinctions of gender or sex; he is at once both male and female." This androgynous quality, L. G. Desmangles (1992) explains, is reflected both in his *vèvè* (Vodou sacred design) and in the design of the Vodou temple, the *ounfò*. While the "*potomitan* (central pole) . . . symbolizes his phallus . . . the open space around it . . . is his womb." It is because he (or perhaps he/she) exists beyond duality that Legba chooses the number 3 as his magic number. He is the "third" entity created by the merging of two: as the fusion of male and female on the physical plane, he becomes the child, as the fusion of male and female on the psychological plane, the androgynous or transgendered person. Offerings to Legba include candles, rum, cigar, coconuts, and peppermint candies. His special day is Monday.

Leo   In Euro-western ASTROLOGY, zodiac sign ruling from (approximately) July 23 until August 22, associated with adventurousness, authoritativeness, and vitality, typically depicted as a LION. Figures associated with Leo and with gender and/or sexual variance include: AMATERASU OMI KAMI, ARTEMIS, ATARGATIS, ATTIS, CYBELE, CYRENE, DIONYSUS, DURGA, HERACLES, INANNA/ISHTAR, SEKHMET, and the SPHINX.

Leonardo da Vinci (1452-1519)   Homoerotically inclined artist, scientist, and philosopher of the Italian Renaissance. Inspired by the androgyne of ALCHEMY, Leonardo frequently and subtly blended homoerotic desire, transgenderism, and the sacred in his works, such as in his painting *St John the Baptist*, a second version of which became a portrait of *Bacchus* (DIONYSUS). J. Saslow (1986) describes St John as a "truly androgynous being who so thoroughly integrates the polarities as to make them indistinguishable." Another work, a sketch titled

Allegory of Pleasure and Pain, depicts a double male being, undoubtedly inspired by the double, homoerotically inclined supernatural being of PLATO's *Symposium*.

Lesbos The association of the island of Lesbos and SAPPHO (b. c. 630/610 BCE) with lesbian love had become commonplace in Greco-Roman antiquity by the mid-sixth century BCE. Anacreon (c. 560-475 BCE) writes: "Now golden-haired Eros tosses at me his purple ball, and challenges me to sport with the maiden of the broidered sandal. But she – for she is from fair Lesbos – finds fault with my hair, for it is white, and is all agape for another – a woman!" By the late nineteenth century, the expression "a Parisian woman who seems to have been born on Lesbos" and the term "priestess of Lesbos" were being applied to lesbians. The woman-loving poet Renée VIVIEN, who, with Natalie Clifford BARNEY (1876-1972), hoped to create a lesbian-centered spiritual community on the island, wrote in "We Will Go to the Poets," "Remembering that there are vaster planets, / We will enter into the realm of the poets, / . . . We will enter, led by sister poets, / Into the land brought forth by their eternal lines . . ." This island paradise of women-loving women poets is lit only by the moon; the air is filled with music and perfume; and emerald palaces rise above "delicious gardens where the fountains rest."

Leto According to some traditions Leto was considered a goddess of the night and associated with Nyx. She was also the mother of APOLLO and ARTEMIS. Her name means "darkness." In her aspect as a goddess of fertility, one of her epitaphs was Leto Phytia, "the creator." She was given this name when she changed the daughter of Galateia into a man to avoid being killed by her father. The Lesbian poet SAPPHO (b. c. 630/610 BCE) writes, "Now Leto and Niobe were very dear companions." Athenaeus (fl. 230 CE) indicates that Leto and Niobe were lovers until they married men and became mothers.

Lettuce Sacred to MIN and SET of Egyptian religion, lettuce was associated with eunuchs and with men engaged in same-sex relations, its milky sap symbolic of semen. In twentieth-century Chile, *lechuga* (lettuce) is symbolic of male homosexuality. Puns are made with *leche* (milk), here metaphoric of semen, and *pechuga* (breast), here suggesting "to suck."

Leucippe / Leucippus Name of several AMAZONS of Greek legend. One was a daughter of the high priest Calchas. This young woman, dressing as a priest of APOLLO, was said to have awakened love in her own sister. A second Leucippe was born to a poor family. The father had said they could not afford to raise a girl should the wife give birth to a daughter. When she did so, she could not bear to abandon her and so raised her as a boy, Leucippus.

When the daughter reached adolescence, her mother prayed to LETO to change the girl into a boy, and the goddess granted her prayer. A third Leucippus was originally a man in love with Daphne. In order to seduce her, he dressed as an Amazon, inferring Daphne's lesbian-transgendered inclination. In female guise, Leucippus took the name Leucippe. Apollo, however, apparently did not approve of Leucippus's toying with Daphne and so either killed him or transformed him into a woman.

Leuké "White Island," located at the mouth of the Danube River, known as a paradise for warrior-lovers and sailors comparable to the Teutonic Valhalla. The lovers ACHILLES, PATROCLUS, and ANTILOCHUS were worshipped there. Helen of Troy, in this context a manifestation of an earlier goddess named Helen, was also honored there. The poet John Addington SYMONDS envisioned the island as a symbol of the emerging homosexual political and spiritual movements, particularized in the rebirth of Achilles on the island. "Thou shalt live," he writes in "Leuké," ". . . Men shall call to each other: / Behold a new star in the skies! / Our master, our Comrade, our Brother, / All hail for the light of thine eyes! / . . . / Come forth from thine island, and teach us / The truth of those excellent things. . ." The poet H. D., in "Helen in Egypt," envisioned Leuké as a UTOPIA of female artistry, linked in her visionary poetics to Atlantis and LESBOS.

Lewis, Mary Edmonia (1843-c. 1900) African-American/Ojibway (Chippewa) sculptor, thought to have been bisexually or lesbian inclined. Born in New York, she was an abolitionist who employed spiritual and mythic subjects in her artworks, with titles including *Forever Free* (1867), *Cleopatra* (lost), *Hiawatha's Wooing* (n. d.), and *Hagar* (1875).

Lewis, Matthew G. (1775-1818) Nicknamed "Monk" after his erotico-spiritual masterpiece *The Monk* (1795), which depicts Ambrosio's desire for another monk. While the latter turns out to be a woman in disguise, George E. Haggerty and other twentieth century critics insist that the novel remains "one of the great works in the gay and lesbian literary traditions." M. Praz (1963) relates that Lewis was homoerotically inclined. Haggerty notes that "chief among his attachments was his love for William Kelly," the son of a woman writer, Mrs Kelly, with whom Lewis corresponded.

Lhamana Term given to the TWO-SPIRIT male Zuni shaman. The lhamana We'wha (1849-1896) is the subject of Will Roscoe's acclaimed anthropological treatise *The Zuni Man-Woman* (1991).

Libra In Euro-western ASTROLOGY, zodiac sign ruling from (approximately) September 23 until October 23, associated with balance, harmony, justice, and partnerships, typically a scale. Figures associated with Libra and with gender and/or sexual variance include: ASTARTE, ATHIRAT, the FURIES, INANNA/ISHTAR, OYA, THOTH, and ZEUS.

Lieblingminne German neologism coined in the later nineteenth or early twentieth century by men-loving men who wished to distance themselves for the emerging movement for homosexual, lesbian, and transvestite rights led by Magnus Hirschfeld and rooted in the linkage of same-sex eroticism and gender variance. Elisàr von Kupffer (1872-1942) and other adherents of Lieblingminne, basically, "Chivalrous Love," promoted primarily intergenerational love and relationships between adult "masculine" males. They looked upon various writers, philosophers, and legendary and real-life military heroes as their spiritual ancestors. These included Theognis, Pindar, Socrates, ALEXANDER THE GREAT, Medieval KNIGHTS, Hafiz, Shakespeare, MICHELANGELO, Goethe, Schiller, and Friedrich the Great. They wished to found a kind of utopian society in which nudism, athletics, and male-male love would be prized above all else. They condemned theories depicting gays and lesbians as belonging to a "third sex." They also condemned theories supporting the idea that a primordial, matrifocal culture embracing Goddess Reverence had been devastated by hostile, patriarchal forces; not surprisingly, they condemned the rising German feminist movement and abhorred the idea, supported by Hirschfeld, of feminists, lesbians, and gays forming alliances. Led by Adolf Brand (1874-1945), devotees of Lieblingminne formed the GEMEINSCHAFT DER EIGENEN. Due to certain misogynistic and racist views, a number of adherents of Lieblingminne supported the burgeoning Nazi movement until realizing, far too late, its aim of annihilating Jews, the homoerotically inclined, and countless others.

Li-Liang-yü (fl. 1568)   Chinese laborer who, at age twenty-eight, as a married man, metamorphosed into a woman, becoming, after the annulment of his marriage, the wife of a man named Pai. Liang-yü's metamorphosis was credited to a mysterious "transformation of YIN AND YANG" energies occurring due to a strange interaction of "internal alchemy" with the powerful forces present during "the first month of the first year of the reign of a new emperor."

Liloa (if historical, may have died in 1575)   Historical or legendary chief of Hawaii. While KIHA (-NUILULUMOKO), the father of Liloa, had an intimate male companion, it is Liloa who is credited with formally introducing the Hawaiians to homoerotic lovemaking.

Lily Flower symbolic of desire, lovemaking, androgyny, self-sufficiency, receptivity, and ecstasy. In Chinese symbolism, it is among the flowers representing "the intermediate stage between man and woman." In Greek mythology or religion, the naiad Leiriope (Lily) is the mother of the androgynous youth NARCISSUS. To "feed among the lilies," as in the *Song of Solomon* (2: 1), is, in the Jewish tradition, to make love. In Christian tradition, lilies, as in the "lilies of the field" (Matthew 6: 28), are symbolic of trust in, and receptivity to, divine nurturing. SAN JUAN DE LA CRUZ (St John of the Cross, 1542-1591), in his poem "Dark Night," describes a secret journey to a grove of cedars where JESUS awaits him. There, Christ lays his head on the mystic's "flowering" breast; the latter undergoes gender metamorphosis as he plays with Christ's hair. When Jesus serenely "wounds" his neck, the mystic yields to him, now in a state of bliss, which he describes in terms of the "lilies of oblivion." In western art and in European occult traditions, especially in ALCHEMY, the lily is symbolic of gynandry, the stem being perceived as masculine and the flower as feminine. The symbolism of the lily is akin to that of the LOTUS. Lord Alfred Douglas (1870-1945) in his poem "Two Loves" describes the cheeks of the figure representing homoerotic love as "wan and white / Like pallid lilies"; similarly, for the poet Renée VIVIEN, the lily is symbolic of the lesbian lover. Vivien writes in "Like This Would I Speak": "I would learn that lilies are more lovely than ROSES . . . / And the maiden of my desire, like the lily, / Will seem to her [i.e. SAPPHO] more graceful and supple than ATTHIS." In the visionary cosmos of Jessica Amanda Salmonson and Jules Remedios Faye in *Wisewomen and Boggy-boos* (1992), Lily is a "genius or fairy of water-lilies" whose ancestors are "the naiads of Artemis," and also the kindly aspect of the vampiric goddess Lilith, the sister of Lotus, and has lived with her companion Iris, goddess of the RAINBOW, for seven thousand years.

Limaloa Hawaiian deity of the sea and mirages. Bisexual in today's terms, Limaloa was husband to a chief's daughter and an intimate male companion of KAMAPUA'A.

Linden Among the Scythians of ancient Russia, a symbol of feminine or third gender (male) identity. The ENAREES, gender variant priests of the Scythian goddess ARTIMPASA, twined or braided linden leaves and branches in divination. Although also called "lime," this tree of the genus *tilia* is not the citrus lime.

Lion Symbolic of strength and dominion, the lion is a sacred attribute of numerous deities, heroes, and heroines associated with gender and sexual variance, including ARTEMIS/DIANA, ATTIS, CYBELE, CYRENE, DIONYSUS, DURGA, HERACLES, and SEKHMET. The lion is also symbolic of the astrological sign of LEO. In twentieth-century Mexico, the lion is a signifier of male homosexuality.

Lithben Legendary Celtic woman warrior, sister or intimate companion of BEC.

Liwat "Anal intercourse." In Islamic tradition, sodomy derives its name from Lot (Lut) a figure of Judaism, Christianity, and Islam who is associated with the story of the destruction of SODOM. While a number of Jewish and Christian scholars have insisted that the Sodomites were damned not because of their homoeroticism but because of their inhospitality to the ANGELS sojourning there, the association of *liwat* with Lot indicates that in Islam, Sodom and the Sodomites are definitely linked to same-sex eroticism. The term for "active homosexual," *luti*, or *la'it,* is also derived from Lot (Lut).

Lizard In Greek myth and religion, the lizard is sacred to APOLLO. He is described as a "lizard-killer" in the erotic sense of bringing the "lizard," i.e. the penis, out of hiding and into a state of erection, and then "killing" it by bringing it to orgasm, ultimately resulting in the "perishing" of the "lizard," i.e. the decreasing in size of the penis. Also in Greece, to walk "like a lizard" was to saunter in an "effeminate" manner by swaying one's hips from side to side.

Logunedé Son of the Yoruba *orishá* (deity) INLE or Ochossí and OSHUN Yeyé Iponda. As the child of Inlé, patron of lesbian women and "masculine" gay men, and Oshún Yeyé Iponda, a woman warrior, Logunedé is linked to both transgenderism and same-sex eroticism. He is believed to spend half of each year as a "male hunter who lives in the forest" and the other half as a "beautiful, vain and honey-tongued nymph who lives in rivers and feeds on fish." Logunedé's androgynous character is represented in Candomblé in several ways. For instance, he holds the bow and arrow of Inlé-Ochossí and the fan or mirror of Oshún. His colors include indigo, here identified with Ochossí and masculinity, and yellow-gold, identified with Oshún and femininity. His androgynous nature is also manifested in one of his sacred animals, the seahorse, the male of which carries the developing offspring. The Brazilian musician Gilberto Gil, allegedly a son of Logunedé, has written a song celebrating the *orishá*'s androgynous character. In this lyric, Gil celebrates the deity as a potent blend of the *astúcia de cacador*, "the artfulness of the hunter," and the *"Paciência de pescador*, "the patience of the fisher." As a force depicting both traits simultaneously, Logunedé becomes a symbol for Gil of androgyny and bisexuality. Logunedé is depicted as the beautiful, tender *Mimo de Oxum* (Oshún), the fondling of his mother, who appears to have come into being primarily to be adored, desired, or embraced. As an openly bisexual musician who seeks to

blend the "masculine" and "feminine" elements of his own psyche, Gil has been acknowledged in Candomblé as a *filho* ["son"] *de* Logunedé. Logunedé is frequently identified or syncretized with SAINT MICHAEL the Archangel, SAINT SEBASTIAN, Saint Isidro, and Saint Expedite of Christianity.

Lohiau Prince of Kau'i in Hawaiian myth, his primary female lover being PELE, his primary male lover, PAOA. Upon the death of Lohiau – he seems to have been revivified or reincarnated later – Paoa sang the chant "The AIKANE is a beloved one" in his honor.

Loki Teutonic (Germanic, Scandinavian) TRICKSTER deity. While an Aesir – roughly, a member of the warlike "tribe" of ODIN, who arrived in the region already occupied by the Vanir, the "tribe" of the fertility deities FREYJA and FREYR – he often seems to express qualities associated with the Vanir and, indeed, in many situations acts as an emissary between the groups. In other situations, however, he seems to dwell outside both the Vanic and Aesic realms. Loki is above all a prankster, a sinister yet delightful brew of PUCK and Mephistopheles. He delights in mockery, gossip, scandal, and social chaos. Like the Greek HERMES, he is also a thief, stealing, among other things, Freyja's magic necklace. In his more sinister manifestation, he is the slayer of Balder (the Aesic APOLLO) and a catalyst of universal destruction. A protean being, Loki experiences both gender and theriomorphic (animal) transformation. Although scholars generally agree that he was not the subject of an independent cult, his reverence may have been linked to the cults of Odin, Thorr, or Freyja. Loki, for instance, often assumes Freyja's falcon or hawk-feathered cloak when he is "faring forth," which suggests at once an association with her cult, with Shamanism, and with both gender and theriomorphic transformation. Homoeroticism – specifically anal eroticism – and transgenderism play a key role in the tales of Loki and Odin. When Loki dons Freyja's feathered cloak, he becomes, as a mare, pregnant, giving birth to the eight-footed Sleipnir, which becomes Odin's mount. This tale, incidentally, links both Odin and Loki to the entheogenic mushroom fly agaric. Once, as Odin was being chased by hostile forces, he raced Sleipnir so hard that drops of blood began falling from the horse's mouth. Upon touching the ground, the drops became toadstools. Thus was the plant so essential to Shamanism a gift of the gods. In the *Lokasenna*, Loki and Odin engage in a "flyting" or verbal duel in which Odin attacks Loki for allowing himself to become feminized and impregnated. He accuses him of spending eight years as a female being, alternately a human female and a cow. "In that," says Odin, "I find the mark of one who is *argr*." According to Norse philologist Martin Larsen, *argr* is the "crudest term of abuse in old Norse. Applied to a man it indicated not only that he was effeminate but also that he submitted himself to being used sexually as a woman." In our terms, to be *argr* is to participate in both gender variant and homoerotic behaviors, taking the receptive role in anal intercourse. The noun *ergi* suggests that persons repeatedly and willingly engaging in such behavior may have been perceived as essentially different from other males. Loki counters Odin's remark by announcing that Odin practices *seidr* MAGIC – a practice associated with women – Odin having managed to convince Freyja to teach him this magical art. He has served as a *volva* or *seidkona*, practicing *seidr* on Sám's island in Denmark. F. Ström (1974) explains that *ergi* refers not only to a transgendered male who takes the receptive role in anal eroticism but also to a practitioner of *seidr*. In other words, the "true" *ergi* individual is one in whom homoerotic behavior, transgenderism, and spiritual function merge. Ström insists that it was the acceptance of the receptive role in anal intercourse, coupled with a yielding attitude toward the gods (as allowing oneself to be embodied by them), and not homosexuality *per se*, which caused a man to be looked upon – or to look upon himself – as *ergi*. In Ström's words, "the factor which . . . gave *ergi* its altogether special connotation . . . was the female nature of the *argr* man." *Ergi* may also refer to a cowardly male. This use of the term may have emerged from a Germanic perspective which equated non-violence (or pacifism, which characterized the early Vanir – no weapons in Freyr's temples, etc.) with cowardice. Edgar Polomé feels that the *Lokasenna* is "very. instructive because it tells us explicitly about his [i.e. Loki's] blood-brotherhood with Odin," because it states that "Loki was Odin's adopted son," and because it emphasizes Loki's "sexual inversion." The *Lokasenna* attributes *argr* behavior or *ergi* identity, which includes both gender variance and homoeroticism, to both Loki and Odin, further suggesting that their own relationship may have included an alternation of sex roles. The relationship of Loki and Odin is one partaking of both gender metamorphosis and theriomorphic transformation. In a wider context, the *Lokasenna* episode suggests how homoeroticism and transgenderism may have played a role in bridging the spiritual and, more generally, the cultural systems of the followers of the Vanir and those of the Aesir, with the former contributing the gender variant or transgendered model and the latter the intergenerational, military model of same-sex relations. The relationships of blood-brotherhood and adoptive father-son existing between Odin and Loki further indicate that same-sex relationships may have been cemented with formal rites. Sleipnir, the child of Loki who becomes the horse of Odin, may in some veiled way symbolize the magical power engendered by such relations. Indeed, the "gift" of the horse (often symbolic of the phallus) may even speak of a transference of masculinity from one male to another.

Lono   Hawaiian god of creation, weather (especially of storms), agriculture, war, and eroticism. Lono shares an AIKANE, or intimate same-sex, relationship with a mysterious figure named KAPA'IHI. Together, they search for the magical Koa tree. When Kapa'ihi leaves Lono, he is brokenhearted, becomes ill, and, according to some accounts, dies. Lono is sometimes identified with KAMAPUA'A.

Lonoikiaweawealoha   Hawaiian love-god sent by the pig-god KAMAPUA'A to seduce the volcano-goddess PELE's brothers HIIAKALUNA and HIIAKALALO so that they will forget her orders to attack Kamapua'a.

Lorca, Federico García (1898-1936)   Homoerotically inclined Spanish poet and playwright, self-described as an "impassioned and silent fellow" who liked "paper dolls" and who believed in spirits. He was deeply influenced by the myths and legends of the Spanish gypsies, as he was by the practitioners of the Yoruba religion he encountered in the Americas. His spirituality was also profoundly influenced by the writings of Walt WHITMAN (1819-1892) and Paul Verlaine (1844-1896) and by the Surrealist art of his intimate friend Salvador Dalí (1904-1989). Works exploring the interrelationship of same-sex desire and the realm of spirit include "Ode to Walt Whitman" and the *Sonnets of Dark Love*. The Lorca family is said to guard a manuscript of the poet written in 1918, "La religion del porvenir" ("The Religion to Come") which is thought to concern the emergence of a homoerotic spirituality.

Lord Abbot of Ninna-ji (fl. twelfth century CE)   Abbot of Ninna-ji, a Shingon Buddhist monastery in Japan, who fell in love with a beautiful young man named Senju, a talented flautist and singer. When the Lord Abbot became enchanted with a newly arrived novice, Mikawa, Senju appeared at a banquet and sang a song describing his suffering upon being treated so cruelly. The Lord Abbot, full of remorse, embraced Senju, while Mikawa departed for a distant monastery.

Lorde, Audre (1934-1992)   African-American woman-loving writer of Grenadian parentage, who spent most of her life teaching and writing in New York City, and who died in St Croix of breast cancer in 1992. Her primary companions following her marriage to Edwin A. Rollins were Frances Louise Clayton, whom she lived with for nineteen years and who helped her to raise her son Jonathan and her daughter Elizabeth, and Gloria I. Joseph, also a writer and scholar. Elaine Maria Upton relates that "before her death Lorde held an African naming ceremony and took the name Gambda Adira, which means Warrior: She who Makes her Meaning Known." Upton observes that "Lorde's writing is richly filled with the substance of her active life as lesbian, mother, friend, witness to our time, spiritual warrior, and woman of deep social conscience and commitment." Lorde (1978) asserts that the "erotic is a resource within each of us that lies in a deeply female and spiritual plane." As an aspect of patriarchal oppression, however, women have in general "been taught to suspect this resource" and to suppress it, the dominant forces recognizing that "eros" as a source of power "can provide energy for change." For Lorde, "eros" and eroticism embrace but are not merely equivalent to sexuality. "The very word 'erotic,'" she observes, "comes from the Greek word EROS, the personification of love in all its aspects – born of Chaos [it is] an assertion of the life-force [of] creative energy empowered." Lorde follows with an insistence that the erotic should not – indeed, cannot – be divorced from either the political or the spiritual. "Recognizing power of the erotic within our lives," she concludes, "can give us the energy to pursue genuine change within our world." Sacred and mythic imagery abound in Lorde's work. Especially noteworthy are her allusions to ancient Greek and African/African-diasporic mythology and religion. In "The Winds of Orisha," Lorde considers the Greek tale of TIRESIAS as well as tales of Yoruba *orishá* including Yemanja (or YEMAYA), OSHUN, SHANGO, OYA, and Eshu (or Elleggua; LEGBA). What many of Lorde's readers and hearers fail to realize is that for Lorde, these deities' names serve not only as poetic metaphors, but are at once metaphors and vessels of powerful, archetypal energies, akin to Judy GRAHN's term "metaforms." They are meant to function not merely aesthetically but also magically. The poet, in naming them, comes to embody them. As we read or hear the poem, we, too, become possessed by these healing, transformative forces. "Impatient legends speak through my flesh," Lorde intones, "changing this earth's formation / spreading / I will become myself / an incantation / dark raucous man-shaped characters . . ." Poems such as these serve simultaneously as praise-hymns (as in Yoruba, *oriki*) to the deities, as prayers thanking them and entreating their aid. In the event of embodiment, these functions merge as the deity works through the devotee to accomplish that which is needed or desired. This process is illuminated in "Call," in which the poet-narrator invokes the aid of AIDO-HWEDO (the Fon/Benin Rainbow serpent of Vodou), OYA, Seboulisa (Fon/Benin Mother Goddess), MAWU (primordial Fon/Benin androgynous deity of Vodou), and Afrekete (divine linguist, goddess and trickster equivalent to Fon/Benin Legba and Yoruba Elleggúa or Eshu), as well as mortal female ancestors of great courage. She writes: "I have written your names on my cheekbone / dreamed your eyes flesh my epiphany / most ancient goddesses hear me / enter / I have not forgotten your worship / . . . / my whole life has been an altar worth it ending." Lorde's lesbian passion and devotion to the spirits become powerfully linked in "The Winds of Orisha," in which she writes of

herself and Oshun, the goddess of love, beauty, and the arts, "the beautiful Oshun and I lie down together / in the heat of her body my voice comes stronger." Works of Lorde's which especially speak to the interrelationship of eroticism, gender, and the sacred, beyond *Uses of the Erotic*, include *The Black Unicorn* (1978), *Zami: A New Spelling of My Name* (1982), *Our Dead Behind Us* (1986), and *Undersong: Chosen Poems Old and New* (1992).

Lorrain, Jean (pseudonym of **Paul Duval**, 1856-1906) Homoerotically inclined French Symbolist-Decadent poet and novelist. Lorrain was drawn to both the figure of the androgynous male and the terrifying werewolf. Indeed, he occasionally disguised himself as a werewolf. He is said to have kept in full view in his living room a head made of wax painted so as to make it look like a decapitated human head. His erotic leaning was toward homoerotic SADOMASOCHISM. Lorrain was addicted to the consumption of ether as an intoxicant. He also became psychologically addicted to the drinking of fresh animal blood at abattoirs, cow's blood believed by many in the late nineteenth century to be a potential cure for tuberculosis. Lorrain's works include the poetic texts *Le Sang de dieux* (1992), *La Forêt bleue* (1883), *L'Ombre ardente* (1897) and the novel *Monsier de Phocas* (1899).

Lotus   The ancient Egyptians associated the lotus with HAPY, the androgynous deity of the Nile. In Greek mythology, Lotus (or Lotis) was a nymph loved by ARTEMIS/DIANA, who transformed her into a lotus so that she would not have to suffer being raped by PRIAPUS or PAN, who was pursuing her. In the cult of ANTINOUS, the beloved of the Roman emperor HADRIAN, the Egyptian lotus became a sacred attribute of the lover-become-god. At Alexandria, beautiful wreaths called "garlands of Antinous" were woven of red lotuses in memory of the young man who had sacrificed himself by drowning in the Nile. In ancient Chinese symbolism, the lotus signifies love; the red lotus, erotic love. While the flowers are perceived as feminine, the stem is seen as masculine; thus the lotus becomes a sign of androgyny or transgenderism. One of the five flower-arrows carried by KAMA, the Hindu god of eroticism, is the blue lotus. Kama's intimate companion, VASANTA, also a deity of desire, is compared to a "red lotus, [with] his eyes like open lotuses." In Hinduism, the lotus is also a sacred attribute of the god VISHNU and is further linked to eunuchs, in part because the linguistic gender of *padma* (lotus) is neuter. The Hindu goddess LAKSHMI also wears, carries, or sits upon a lotus. The lotus is symbolic of sensuality, fertility, the spiritual quest, revelation, rebirth, and immortality.

Lu Yi Jing (or **Leu Yi Chin, Lü Zijing**), **Wei Guo Xiu** (or **Wei Kuo Sui**) **and the Spirit**   A Chinese tale of love, death, and spirits. Lu Yi Jing's lover, Wei Guo Xiu, passed away suddenly and mysteriously. Lu grieved for him day and night. One evening, a spirit appeared beside Lu's bed. This was the spirit of a beautiful young man who had once been loved by a king, but who had been murdered while still young by a jealous courtier. The spirit told Lu that a demonic deity named Wutong (also Wulang) had fallen in love with Wei and had abducted him, carrying him off to live with him in the Underworld. Bisexual in contemporary terms, Wutong was well known for his desire for human males and females. The next morning, Lu found a Taoist necromancer, one who could contact the dead, to help him to retrieve his lover from the clutches of death. The necromancer, after performing intense rituals for three days, succeeded in calling up the spirit of Wei Guo Xiu. While the necromancer was not able to restore Wei to life, he was able to retrieve his spirit from the Underworld demon. Thus, while their relationship underwent a transformation, Lu and Wei were able to continue to be lovers as human and spirit. Together they made many journeys, accompanied in their travels by the spirit of the young man who had been loved by a king.

Ludlam, Charles (1943-1987)   Gay actor, playwright, and company director of the Theater of the Ridiculous in New York. Much of his work weaves together elements of homoeroticism, transgenderism, and the mythic with the CARNIVALESQUE, including his plays *Bluebeard* (1970), *Caprice* (1976), *The Mystery of Irma Vep* (1985), *Conquest of the Universe* (published 1989), and *Isle of the Hermaphrodites or the Murdered Minion* (published 1989).

Luke, Saint (fl. first century CE)   Christian evangelist, author of a Biblical Gospel, and saint. One of homoerotically inclined French king HENRI III's (1551-1589) most beloved minions, Quélus, was given the nickname "Luc" and specifically "St Luc," primarily by satiric poets of that era. Delighting in puns and anagrams, the poets reversed "Luc" into "*cul*" – "buttocks," "ass." In this way, St Luke became in late sixteenth-century France

an icon of male gender variance and same-sex intimacy. A typical satirical poem of the day reads: "Saint Mark is the patron of Venice / And Saint Matthew of usurers / Saint John accounts for millers . . . / Saint Luke is the minion of the King / And his feast [a pun on *fête* and *fesse*, "ass"], I do believe, / He loves the best, above all others." Patron of physicians, St Luke is fêted on October 18.

Lupacas   South American Indian people living on the shores of Lake Titicaca Basin, neighboring the Collas and Aymaras. According to Alonso Ramos Gavilan in 1621, the more powerful Inca, disapproving of the Lupaca institution of transgendered Shamanism "took away from them cattle and food, in order that their need and hunger should make them more subservient."

Lygismos   Form of the KORDAX dance honoring the Greco-Roman deities ARTEMIS/DIANA and DIONYSUS (Roman Bacchus) which survived well into the Christian era. In it, men wore feminine attire and performed voluptuous movements. Apparently the men's costumes included impersonations of the Maenads (or Bacchantes), the Nymphs, and the Horae.

Lyra   Constellation of the LYRE of ORPHEUS, the bisexual divinized Greek musician.

Lyre   Musical instrument found throughout the Mediterranean since c. 2600 BCE. The basic lyre is constructed with strings running from a round soundbox at the base to a crossbar or "yoke" supported by two arms and usually played with a plectrum. A type of lyre called the *chelys*, whose body was made of tortoise shell, was said to have been invented by the Greek god HERMES, who presented it to AMPHION, his beloved. Amphion, through the playing of the lyre, was said to have caused stones to form the wall surrounding the city of Thebes. The lyre is also an attribute of EROS, a patron of homoerotic love.

M

Mâ Mâ, or Enyo, is primarily envisioned as an Amazonian or transgendered death-wielding goddess. Her worship was centered at Comana in Cappadoccia. By the first century CE, more than six thousand, including HIERODULE-priests and priestesses, were serving in her temple at Comana. Her functionaries and worshippers were referred to as the FANATICI. The rites of Mâ were wild and rather bloody as her priests, in an altered state of consciousness, would splatter the statue of the Goddess with blood. At Rome, Mâ became fused with BELLONA. Comana, as the seat of Mâ's worship, came to be seen by more reactionary Greeks as a mecca of effeminacy and decadence, being nicknamed "Little Corinth."

Macareus In Greek mythology, the son of Aeolus and a beloved of APOLLO. Upon ending an incestuous relationship with his sister Candace and atoning for that relationship, Macareus became a priest and lover of Apollo.

Macha Amazonian or transgendered Celtic goddess of athletics and war. Beyond being gynandrous, Macha is envisioned as a hybrid human female-HORSE and thus is also associated with theriomorphic (i.e. animal) transformation. In legends, however, both her gynandrous and her animal nature are secrets, the discovery of which commands a great price. In the tale "The Sickness of the Men of Ulster," the male warriors of Ulster are forced to experience gender transformation by Macha. In this tale, Macha first appears as a beautiful fairy maiden who pays a visit to the house of a peasant named Crunniuc. She lies down on his bed, and the two become lovers. Soon he is no longer a peasant. He must never, however, reveal the identity of his lover. If he does so, all will be lost. One day, at a great assembly, Crunniuc becomes angry when the King brags about the swiftness of his horses. "My wife," he says unthinkingly, "can run faster than all your horses put together." "We'll see," says the King; "if you're lying, you'll find yourself headless." Macha, now pregnant, is dragged out of bed and forced to run with the horses. While she is a goddess, her involvement with a mortal results in her human feelings of great pain as she is forced to race against the horses. In a moment of great suffering, she gives birth to children on the track. Having experienced enough agony and humiliation among the mortals, Macha reveals her true identity, a fierce, horselike, gynandrous goddess. For their cruel treatment of her, Macha places a curse upon the men of Ulster. Periodically, and especially during moments of great crisis,

they will experience feminization and the pangs of childbirth. This will continue for nine generations. Jean Markale, whose work on the Celts is profoundly illuminating, suggests in *Mélusine, ou l'androgyne* (1983) that the men of Ulster must experience gender transformation because they have discovered the secret of the Goddess: "They had seen Macha in her androgynous reality; thus, they must also become androgynous."

Machi Traditional shamans of the Mapuche (also called Araucanian) people of Argentina. While usually women, *machi* shamans are sometimes transgendered males. These males must work to perfect their feminine aspect so that the gods will see them as "life givers" rather than "life takers." They undergo female initiation rites and symbolic monthly menstrual cycles. Among the *machi*'s primary responsibilities is learning the rituals and singing the songs that call the spirits, referred to as "pulling the ancestors."

Machlyes Ancient people of Libya who appeared to ancient Greco-Roman travelers as androgynous beings having masculine features on the left side and feminine features on the right side of their bodies. It is conceivable that gender-mixing clothing, such as that worn in Mesopotamian rites honoring the goddess INANNA/ISHTAR, may have aided in the formation of this perception. It has been suggested that they were devotees of the goddess NEITH. The Machlyes were depicted as performing tasks assigned to both male and female genders.

Madivinèz (also **Zami**) In Haitian culture, and especially within Vodou, a term meaning "my divine one" and signifying a woman-loving woman. *Mambos* (or *manbos*, high priestesses) of Vodou are often *madivinèz*. Both lesbian desire and transgenderism may be expressed within Vodou ceremonies, by those who are normally so inclined as well as by those who are heterosexual females adopting traditionally feminine roles. This occurs when an Amazonian (or gynandrous) *lwa* (deity or spirit) chooses to embody, or possess, a devotee. This is especially the case when GHEDE NIBO chooses to possess a female devotee.

Madonna (**Madonna Ciccone**, 1959-) Regardless of her own gendered and sexual identities, this Italian-American pop singer of the 1980s and 1990s has attained archetypal status in the psyches of many lesbians, gays, bisexuals, and transgendered persons. Kay TURNER, lesbian writer, musician, and folklorist, ponders this phenomenon in *I Dream of Madonna: Women's Dreams of the Goddess of Pop* (1993). Madonna is a shapeshifter; "she is APHRODITE, she is DIONYSUS," she is *the* Madonna. Turner sees Madonna as a narcissist, but of a different sort than we are accustomed to: "When Madonna gazes into NARCISSUS's pool, she sees not one but many images, and through her art she yields them to us for our own self-reflection." Turner has found that most women who dream of Madonna envision her not as an unattainable idol but as an empowering companion, a spiritual guide, a lover. It is conceivable that the dreams of bisexuals, gays, and transgendered persons concerning Madonna may mirror these. However near she seems, Madonna remains for most a divine being in the realm of dreams and, as Turner concludes, "The fact that her name happens to be Madonna is an even more intriguing emblem of the move from the dominance of the gods to a revived reign of the goddesses." Cultural theorist Camille Paglia's assessment in "Madonna II: Venus of the Radio Waves" (in *Sex, Art and American Culture*, 1992) resonates with Turner's. "Madonna, like Venus stepping from the radio waves, emerged from this giant river of music . . . I view disco . . . as a dark, grand Dionysian music . . . Like me, she [i.e. Madonna] sensed the buried pagan religiosity in disco . . . Responding to the spiritual tensions within Italian Catholicism, Madonna discovered the buried paganism within the Church . . . Madonna has both the dynamic Dionysian power of dance and the static Apollonian power of iconicism . . . Yes, Madonna has restored the Whore of Babylon, the pagan goddess banned by the last book of the Bible."

Madrone   Originally *madroño*, Spanish for "godmother," with a masculine ending; an evergreen tree of western North America, known especially for its reddish, satiny wood. Among northern Californians of the 1970s and 1980s, the madrone symbolized lesbian and, to a somewhat lesser extent, gay male and bisexual desire and love. This symbolic employment of the madrone may ultimately be traceable to the Native Americans once living in the region. Its current symbolism appears to date from the 1940s, when woman-loving poet Elsa GIDLOW kindled a fire with madrone which produced a vision of female ancestral spirits and women she had loved. In "Four Songs," gay male poet Robert DUNCAN depicts the madrone as a nurturing mother: "Madrone Tree, from your thirsty root / feed my soul as if it were your fruit."

Maenad   Nymphs and female companions of the Greek gods DIONYSUS and PAN. They are typically depicted as dancing wildly and as playing the AULOS and the tambourine. This altered state of "divine madness" was triggered in part by their ritual use of beer, wine, honey mead, bay laurel, and other mind-altering substances. They danced naked except for crowns of IVY or else dressed in the skins of wild animals. Perceived as transgendered women, they valued promiscuity and spent much time in hunting wild game and in making bloody sacrifices to the gods. While they revered the effeminate, bisexual Dionysus, they murdered men like Pentheus, a ruler of Thebes who dressed as a woman merely to gain entrance into their orgy. They also tore the singer ORPHEUS to pieces, not because he chose homosexual love after losing his wife Eurydice, but because he began taking away their male spouses and more so because he distanced himself from the worship of Dionysus. While the ancient sources remain virtually silent as to whether or not the Maenads engaged in lesbian lovemaking, the fact that theirs was a primarily female orgiastic band led by a bisexual god suggests that lesbian desire might well have found a place therein. The Maenads were invoked in ancient Greco-Egyptian lesbian love spells as the "maenads, frightful maidens."

Maeve   Queen of Connought in Celtic legend. Her tale apparently emerging from the worship of a warrior goddess, Maeve ultimately became Mab, the Fairy Queen of English Renaissance folklore, synonymous with Titania. As a martial figure, Maeve was responsible for the death of the hero CU CHULAINN. Certain tales suggest that she was pansexual by nature. J. A. Salmonson and J. R. Faye (1992) have speculated that Maeve was once a lover of the Amazon FEITHLINN.

Magic, Ancient Love and Sex   F. Graf (1991) describes several features of ancient spiritual practice which, while focusing on a prayer/spell composed by the poet SAPPHO (b. c. 630/610 BCE) described below, may be applied to the incantations of other cultures as well. Graf explains that "the magician felt no difference between . . . prayer [and] . . . incantation." That is to say, the religious and the magical are not severed in the ancient "pagan" traditions. Ancient prayers/spells are generally tripartite in character, containing an (1) invocation (a naming of the divine being and one or more of that being's epithets and/or attributes) and (2) a voicing of desire framing (3) a "narrative middle part." In terms of the invocation, Graf relates: "The meticulous listing of cult-places, myths, and epithets that follows assures that the divinity is addressed in all its relevant aspects, so that it will feel a real obligation to come." Many ancient love spells of the Near East and West do not place importance on whether the love desired is of a homosexual, heterosexual, or transgendered nature, but only on the gender or anatomical sex of the person performing the spell. For instance, a spell to be undertaken by a male desiring a lover whose gender and anatomical sex are unspecified reads, "Eternal spell for binding a lover: Rub together some gall of a wild boar, some rock salt, some Attic honey and smear the head of your penis." Other spells, however, focus on particular forms of desire and love. Another characteristic of many ancient love spells is their insistence that the desired party fall in love with the magician, even if this appears to be contrary to the desired one's will. In the late twentieth century, many practitioners of magic view this type of spell as unethical; some go so far as to categorize it as "black magic" (a term laden with dualistic, not to mention racist, signification). One needs to understand, however, that the practitioner sincerely believed, generally speaking, that it was primarily the will (we might say the intellect or else the self-repressive aspect of an individual's personality) of the desired one that need be conquered as the heart of the beloved was not necessarily opposed to the desire of the magician-lover. In some cases, of course, another lover or mate who stood in the way must also be conquered. To invoke a deity is not only to entreat their aid; it is to ask the deity to enter into one's self, one's own body, to become possessed or embodied by, or enthused (en-*theos*-ed, in-godded) with the archetypal force of the divine being. One of the earliest recorded spells of Greek origin is one composed by Sappho to call upon the goddess APHRODITE to come to her aid. Sappho's poetry is imbued not only with religious and/or mythical imagery or metaphor but rather exists as both a literary and a magico-religious text at once, as Fritz Graf has acknowledged. Sappho opens with an invocation of the Goddess: "Ornate-throned immortal Aphrodite, wile-weaving daughter of Zeus." She then voices her desire: "I entreat you: do not overpower my heart, mistress, with ache and anguish, but come here." This is followed by a dramatic account of the Goddess's helping her in the past. Sappho envisions Aphrodite pondering, "Whom am I to persuade this time to lead you back to her love? Who wrongs you, Sappho?" The Goddess approaches and commences to embody the poet-magician, "leaving your father's golden house, with chariot yoked: beautiful swift sparrows whirring fast-beating wings." Aphrodite then says to, or possibly through, Sappho, "If she runs away, soon she shall pursue; if she does not accept gifts, why, she shall give them instead; if she does not love, soon she shall love even against her will." The spell ends with a final, amplified invocation and voicing of desire: "Come to me now again and deliver me from oppressive anxieties; fulfill all that my heart longs to fulfill, and you yourself will be my fellow-fighter." Other ancient lesbian love spells, Greco-Egyptian in origin, have been brought to light in recent years. In *The Greek Magical Papyri in Translation* (1986, 1992), edited by Hans Dieter Betz, two are given. The first (PGM 32) is performed by a woman named Herais toward obtaining the love of another woman, Sarapias. The second lesbian love spell (PGM 32a), performed by Serapiakos upon Amoenios, emphasizes erotic passion, with the image of fire being employed – "inflame the heart and soul" and "burn the soul and

heart." It should be pointed out that others have determined this spell to be homoerotic rather than woman-loving in nature; whichever the case, it refers to same-sex love. Another ancient Greco-Egyptian lesbian love spell is given in R. W. Daniel and F. Maltomini's *Supplementum Magicum* (1990). Here, Sophia, daughter of Isara, seeks to inflame the heart of Gorgonia, daughter of Nilogenia. Once again, the Underworld deities are invoked, especially ANUBIS and the ERINYES (or FURIES). Sophia insists that the spirit of a deceased mortal which has since become a demon of fire be further transformed into a handmaid at a bathhouse. This handmaid-spirit, bathing Gorgonia in steamy water, will erotically stimulate her and then deliver her to Sophia, who will enjoy the fruits of the explosive passion. Male homoerotic spells are also being brought to light. One is given by J. D. Sager (1992) dating from the third century CE, from the city of Alexandria in Egypt. Ionikos seeks the love of another man, Annianos. He appeals to various Underworld deities including HECATE, HERMES, Pluto (Greek Hades), and Kore (i.e. PERSEPHONE, here identified with the Near Eastern goddess ERESHKIGAL). Here, love spell and binding spell become totally fused: "restrain for me – Ionikos . . . Annianos . . . melt away his body . . . so that he is unable to proceed against Ionikos." A gentler spell, also of Egyptian origin, although Coptic Christian as opposed to "pagan," is given by M. Meyer, R. Smith, and N. Kelsey (1994). This text is obviously important to us not only because it offers an example of homoerotic magic but also because it indicates an early acceptance of homoeroticism among (at least some) early Christians – not to mention an acceptance of magical practice. In the spell, Papapolo seeks the love of Phello. Invoking the aid of YAO (or Iao) SABAOTH, a manifestation of the Biblical God, Papapolo chants: "He must seek me from town to town, / from city to city, / from field to field, from region to region, / until he comes to me . . . / . . . Papapolo, son of Noe . . . / . . . until I satisfy him with the desire of my heart." At least one spell (PGM 12) given in *The Greek Magical Papyri* clearly speaks to bisexuality. In the incantation, which occurs within the context of a ritual invoking the aid of the god EROS, the magician chants, "Come to me, O master of forms, and arouse men and women for me," and "Cause all men and all women to love me." The ritual including this spell demonstrates the complexity of magical operations undertaken in antiquity. The magician first takes wax and mixes it with a variety of aromatic plants, creating from this substance a seven-inch tall figure of Eros carrying a bow and arrow. The magician then offers Eros seven fruits (including dates), seven little cakes, seven pine cones, and seven small lamps, as well as a bowl of honeyed wine. Next follows a sacrifice of animals – "one cock, a partridge, a wren, a pigeon, a turtledove," and two other small birds. This and other offerings and sacrifices culminate in a final series of invocations, including "I call upon you, you who are on the couch of beauty, who are in the mansion of desire: serve me . . . whether to men or women."

Magic and Ritual, Contemporary Magic is generally defined by its contemporary practitioners as "the art of changing consciousness at will." The practice of magic is commonly associated with a larger ritual encompassing the creation of sacred space, the invocation of divine beings and sometimes ancestors, dancing, and feasting. Magic is also commonly linked to a spiritual tradition, in the late twentieth century, especially to Witchcraft (or Wicca), Ritual Magic(k), and other "Neopagan" traditions. Magical transformation tends to be accomplished by way of casting spells or working charms, which involves the use of invocation or incantation coupled with the gathering together of symbols. Invocations or incantations are generally comprised of three elements: (1) praising the attributes of a divine being; (2) beseeching the aid of that being in granting one's wish; and (3) thanking the divinity. Symbols include colored candles, incenses and oils, flowers and foods, and artistic representations of divine beings (such as paintings or statues) believed to correspond to certain magical operations. Symbolic correspondences arising from what is termed the "theory of correspondences" also include geographical directions, seasons, particular times of the day, week, month, and year, as well as other elements. Thus, a practitioner desiring a lover might, if he/she wishes to achieve optimal success, invoke the goddess APHRODITE on a Friday at sunset or in the early evening in midsummer when the moon is approaching fullness, paying special homage to the direction of the south, gathering together on an altar draped with a rose-colored cloth elements including a pink rose, a pink candle, a stick of rose incense, a cup of rosé wine, and an image of Aphrodite. It is somewhat ironic that while a host of the most celebrated magicians, ranging from SAPPHO to Aleister CROWLEY, have been transgendered and/or lovers of persons of the same sex or bisexual, a number of nineteenth- and twentieth-century practitioners of, and writers on, magic have expressed ardent hostility toward such persons. Hostility on the part of such practitioners and writers as William Butler YEATS, Dion FORTUNE, Robert GRAVES, Gareth KNIGHT, and Kenneth GRANT has been documented by Katon Shual in *Sexual Magick* (1992, 1995) and by others. This hostility is related to that expressed by writers on sexual mysticism, as exemplified in the writings of Giulio Evola and especially in *Sexual Secrets* by Nik Douglas and Penny Slinger, as well as to that found in New Age writings pertaining to the Men's Movement, such as the works of Robert BLY. Shual remarks: "Homosexuality has a long and ancient association with the magickal tradition. Even so it is rare for magicians to express anything other than derision for homosexuals and homosexuality. The magical literature abounds in attitudes that can only be described as homophobic. Magicians may have radical . . . ideas in many things, but almost always adopt the reactionary views of the ruling orthodoxy in this matter." In spite of the hostility of some practitioners and writers, however, others have demonstrated tolerance and occasionally even acceptance of those expressing same-sex erotic and/or transgendered behavior. Exemplary of this more enlightened perspective is that expressed by David Conway in *Ritual Magic: An Occult Primer* (1978): "There is scope for all within the magic circle. You will often hear it suggested . . . that the most competent magician will be bisexual, since in this way he [/she] can combine within himself [/herself] both the male and female principles." A similar view is expressed by Paul B. Rucker, who writes in "People of the Rainbow" (1995): "Work with transgender is one of the most potent ways available for creating changes in the magickal mind . . . Unifying male/female/ etc. energies in one's magickal being provides one of the most direct and daring routes to expressing the true and whole inner self." Indeed, a number of the most pivotal texts treating contemporary magic have been authored by lesbians, gays, bisexuals, transgendered, and "queer"-accepting persons, including Margo Adler, Paul Beyerl, Z BUDAPEST, Tom Cowan, Scott Cunningham, the Reverend Dr Leo Louis MARTELLO, Rachel Pollack, Herman SLATER, and STARHAWK (as well as many others who unfortunately have remained closeted where gendered and sexual identities are concerned). We might add to this list a number of instructors of metaphysics who incorporate magic into their teachings, as do TAMARA DIAGHILEV and Donald ENGSTROM, as well as proprietors of metaphysical and magical shops and services such as Herman Slater of the Magickal Childe in New York, DREW WARD of San Francisco's Light and Shadow, Eric Pollard of Seattle's Tenzing Momo, and Papa Jim of San Antonio, Texas. However, it is generally the case that their focus is not upon the queer-identified community *per se* but upon all practitioners of magic (except perhaps in cases where the primary focus is on women). While this all-embracing perspective has been beneficial in terms of its respect for persons of differing sexual and gendered identities, it has also resulted in the virtual absence of a queer-centered magical tradition. Nevertheless, certain texts indicate that such a tradition might be emerging. These texts include Llee Heflin's *The Island Dialogues* (1973), which interprets Aleister Crowley's so-called "Eleventh Degree" of homoerotic magic, and Shual's queer-accepting *Sexual Magick*, as well as journals (unfortunately, often short-lived) such as the *Queer Pagans Newsletter* of New York and the *Lavender Pagan Newsletter* of San Francisco. Occasionally, mention will be made of an oil, incense, or powder employed by queer-identified practitioners, such as one finds in Slater's *The Magickal Formulary* (1981), wherein one learns that gay men sometimes employ a lavender-colored powder with a lavender base to attract a lover, as well as Satyr oil, the latter being a blend comprised of ambergris, cinnamon, musk, saturnian root, and other ingredients. Similarly, Tenzing Momo's Lavender Incense depicts on its packaging a winged, gay, bearded man wearing a T-shirt, boots, and a skirt, as well as text explaining that one of the primary purposes of the incense is to attract love, and that corresponding divinities and spirits include Hermes, Priapus, and Fairies. Certain texts treating magical practice in the context of rites focusing on gender and sexuality also allude to what might be termed queer-centered magic. These include Budapest's Dianic re-visioning of the so-called "Great Rite" in *The Holy Book of Women's Mysteries* (1980, 1989) – typically referring to a representational encounter of the Goddess and God of Wicca, or Witchcraft – as a woman-loving rite, wherein one finds the Priestess of the South chanting the invocation, "Conjure, conjure, O Goddess of Love! / Conjure and appear through us! / Fiery passions, woman-loving Goddess come!" Similarly, in a rite performed by the gay male members of the Scarlet Path, the Sumerian male moon god Nanna, the "Lord of Magic" and "protector of same-sex lovers everywhere," is invoked to cause a willing "god-vessel's" phallus to rise and ejaculate. "Fill his cock with magics," they chant, "so our spells [will] be done, our wishes granted." Occasionally, works of magic focusing on gender and sexuality are also linked to "coming out" as a lesbian, gay man, bisexual, or transgendered individual, as well as to political struggles for liberation. In Celeste West's *A Lesbian Love Advisor* (1989), in celebrating a woman's acknowledging of her lesbianism, practitioners call upon such figures as ARTEMIS/DIANA, AMAZONS, SAPPHO, JEANNE D'ARC, Emily DICKINSON, Rosa BONHEUR, and Gladys Bentley to empower the woman as she comes to terms with her love for other women. In terms of political struggles, Budapest remembers that in San Francisco in 1978, "we performed a spell against the Briggs Initiative [Briggs was a right-wing opponent of gay leader Harvey Milk], which would have made it illegal for gays to teach. The initiative bit the dust." Nevertheless, to date, groups and texts focusing on queer-centered magic remain surprisingly scarce and fragmentary. This differs somewhat from the field of divination, particularly astrology, which has attracted many lesbians, gays, bisexuals, and transgendered persons and has resulted in the publication of several texts on lesbian- and gay-centered ASTROLOGY. To a lesser extent, the TAROT has been enhanced by, and has enjoyed popularity among, queer-identified persons. This may be due in part to the widespread familiarity with daily horoscopes and Tarot readings as opposed to the general ignorance and fear of the magical arts. The emergence of, and published writings of, "grass-root" queer-centered magical groups such as the Scarlet Path suggest, however,

that a tradition of queer-centered magical practice may now be evolving.

Magnolia In Chinese symbolism, one of the flowers signifying "the intermediate stage between man and woman."

Magodus While the Great Mother as Meter, Rhea, or CYBELE never enjoyed the popularity in Greece that she would in Rome, a type of musician associated with her worship appears to have encountered both popularity and mockery among the Greeks. This was the *magodus*, described by the philosopher and musician Aristoxenus in the fourth century BCE as a performer who acted and sang both male and female roles. The *magodus* accompanied himself on the DRUM and cymbals, wore "all kinds of women's attire," behaved "in an effeminate manner, and [did] every sort of indecorous, indecent thing." *Magodus* is linked to the term "magic." According to Aristoxenus, as recounted by Athenaeus, *magodi* were "addicted . . . to the practice of magic, utter[ing] things like magical incantations, and often declar[ing] the power of various drugs."

Magpie Symbol of the triune deity or spirit of the Native American Hidatsa people called VILLAGE OLD WOMAN. In reverence of Village Old Woman, Hidatsa transgendered male shamans, the MIATI, wore magpie feathers in their hair.

Mahatala-Jata Transgendered or androgynous deity revered by the transgendered male BASIR shamans of the Ngaju Dayak of Borneo. The male aspect of this deity, Mahatala, is represented as a hornbill, lives on a mountain top high above the clouds, and is ruler of the Upperworld. The female aspect of the deity, Jata, is a water snake who dwells in the sea with her were-crocodile companions and rules the Underworld. The two aspects of the deity are joined by a jeweled bridge that is the RAINBOW. The *basir*, along with the *balian*, female HIERODULE- shamans, were seen as reflections of this androgynous deity; they were both referred to as *tambon haruei bungai*, "watersnakes which are at the same time hornbills." Justus van der Kroef writes of the *basir*: "The transvestism of the *basir* and his homosexual practices are symbolic . . . of the total Ngaju godhead."

Mahu Transgendered male spiritual functionaries of Hawaii associated primarily with healing and the HULA. They were said to engage in homoerotic relationships. The term *"mahu"* is sometimes used today to refer to a gay Hawaiian man.

Maitreya Manifestation of the Buddha, or BODHISATTVA, revered by the homoerotically inclined

HWARANG, or "flower boys," of premodern Korea, whose song repertoire included paeans to Maitreya. One such *hwarang* song, the "Tusita Hymn," composed in the eighth century CE by Wolmyong, includes this verse: "O flowers scattered here today, / As we sing the scattered petals song, / Heed the orders of this upright heart / And haste to serve Maitreya's throne."

Makanikeoe   In Hawaiian mythology or religion, a god of the wind and love who reconciles quarreling young couples. Makanikeoe sometimes takes the form of a plant or tree, a branch of which can be used as an amulet or love charm. Makanikeoe is the AIKANE, or *intimate male companion*, of KANEKOA.

Makanoni   Mysterious divine being of Hawaiian myth or religion, perhaps linked to phallic mysteries, sharing a triadic AIKANE (intimate companion) relationship with KUMUKAHI and LA.

La Malinche   Female figure in traditional Mexican and Native American (including Yaqui) ritual dance dramas, based on the Aztec woman (b. c. 1502) who acted as interpreter for Hernán Cortés (1485-1547). Malinche is alternately viewed as a traitor to, and a heroine of, her people. It is clear that for Malinche, little choice was given to her as to whether or not she would accept the role of translator for the Spanish conquistadores. When Malinche was forced to convert to Christianity, she was given the name Marina. In legend and ritual, Malinche came to be associated with various Mesoamerican and European divine beings and folk figures, including Cihuacoatl, Tonantzin, TLAZOLTEOTL, La Llorona, the Virgin Mary, and SAINT MARINA. In most dances in which Malinche figures, her part is performed by a boy or unmarried young man dressed in mixed feminine and masculine attire. In a couple of cases, this role appears to be linked to humor or mockery, or to an appropriation of a female ritual role. In the majority of cases, however, the mixed-dressed male appears to represent an androgynous or transgendered quality with which Malinche has come to be associated. This quality is manifested in Malinche's costume: the youth or man wears a white gown but carries a whip in one hand and a gourd containing a live snake in the other, attributes linked in Mesoamerican and European spiritual traditions to gynandrous or Amazonian deities and spirits. Late twentieth-century Chicana woman-loving writers and artists, including Gloria ANZALDUA and Esther Hernandez, have reclaimed La Malinche as a symbol of women who struggle to survive in the face of oppression.

Malini   In Hindu mythology or religion, one of the two "mothers" of the elephant-headed god GANESHA, according to one variant of the tale. Malini, an elephant-headed goddess and the maidservant of SHIVA's spouse PARVATI, initiates his birth process when she rubs Parvati's body with scented powders and unguents, including *gatra-haridra*, a mixture of turmeric and oil, sometimes described as red or yellow "dirt." When she has smeared these powders and unguents over Parvati's entire body, Malini scrapes them, now blended with Parvati's sweat, from her mistress' body. These substances, when combined with the sweat of the deity, her "dirt" (*lepa* or *mala*), are referred to as *tirtha*. The *tirtha* of the goddess holds great power and is "suggestive of seed, gestation, and power." Rather than casting the *tirtha* of Parvati away, Malini, out of love, ingests it. She then becomes pregnant and gives birth to Ganesha. According to P. B. Courtright (1985), Parvati "plays the male role" in this reproductive union while "Malini may be seen as Parvati's other self, her female aspect, because she [has] taken on the role of the male in giving the seed. These two mothers together make up a single androgynous parent." Her name meaning "bedecked with a garland of champa blossoms," Malini is sometimes associated with the goddess DURGA.

Malyari   Pre-Christian Philippine androgynous or transgendered deity whose name means "Powerful One." The image of the god was usually made of wood (the head) and straw (the body). Malyari was served especially by the transgendered male BAYOGUIN shamans.

Manang Bali   Transgendered male shaman of the Iban Dayak of Borneo. The *manang bali* was "set apart from normal people . . . he does not fully belong to the world in which Iban men and women live." As a marginalized individual, the *manang bali* was both ridiculed for his alleged weakness – "To be like a *manang* . . . implies that a man grows insufficient rice" for his family – and admired for his skill as a shaman. A young man who was destined to become a *manang bali* might be "summoned in a dream" by the god Menjaya Raja Manang or by the goddess Ini. In this dream, the young man would experience "himself in a new way, commonly in the dress of the opposite sex." He would see himself as wearing a chignon braid (*besanggol*) and a woman's skirt (*bekain*) and as performing feminine and shamanic tasks. He would also begin to participate in same-sex eroticism and in homoerotic relationships. At this time, the Iban *manang* was said to move from being "unripe," *mata*, to being "completely transformed," *bali*. This stage was marked by the Iban with an "elaborate and costly initiation" ceremony. Among the Iban Dayak, the *manang bali* was believed to be able to heal the sick by way of prayers (*pelian*), the employment of crystals (the *bata ilau* or "stones of light"), and journeying to the realms of the gods and spirits in order to retrieve the wandering soul, which was at least partly responsible for the patient's illness.

Manat   Arabian goddess of time and destiny, identified in later antiquity with APHRODITE (or VENUS),

INANNA/ISHTAR, and Nemesis. Along with the Arabian goddesses AL-LAT and AL-UZZA, with whom she formed a trinity, Manat was served by hierodulic priestesses and gender variant male, or MUKHANNATH(UN), priests.

Manta Civilization of ancient Ecuador including the island of Puna. The Manta spoke a language and possessed a culture similar to those of the MOCHE (or Mochica) and the CHIMU (or Chimor). They worshipped goddesses of the MOON and the sea, one or both symbolized by a giant emerald, the location of which remains a mystery. The Manta believed that homoeroticism had been introduced to their culture by a race of GIANTS. Apparently this was their reason for placing gender variant male, or third gender, mixed-dressing priests in temples at Puna and Puerto Viejo (or Portoviejo). These priests served primarily as oracles and as HIERODULES, or sacred prostitutes. Incisions made on their lips and noses marked such persons. The Manta culture was virtually destroyed by the Incas. Nevertheless, some gender variant priests, among others, continued to serve in the temples. The last of their kind were believed to have been slain by the Spanish conquistador Juan de Olmos, when he allegedly conducted a campaign against homoerotically or bisexually inclined and gender variant males in the region in the mid-1500s.

Mardi Gras Such celebrations as CARNIVAL and Mardi Gras serve to remind us of the ancient association of gender variance, same-sex desire, the sacred, and the carnivalesque. In Medieval and Renaissance Europe (sometimes even surviving into the twentieth century), mock weddings involving transvestism frequently occurred during Mardi Gras. In France, such a ceremony celebrated the marriages of "Monsieur Henri" and "Dame Douce" and "Caramantran" and his "bride." In these rites, the brides, enacted by cross-dressing males, were depicted as elderly prostitutes who, miraculously becoming pregnant, gave birth to sons at Mardi Gras, while the grooms, representing the old year, were symbolically slain. Cross-dressing, together with queer erotic expression, continues to play a role in Mardi Gras and in kindred celebrations. In New Orleans' Mardi Gras, the first openly gay krewe was founded in 1958 – the Krewe of Yuga (or KY). In 1961 the Krewe of Petronius was founded; others followed, including: Krewe of Amon Ra, Krewe of GANYMEDE, Krewe of Armenius, Krewe of APOLLO, Krewe of Olympus, Krewe of DIONYSUS, and the lesbian Krewe of ISHTAR. Of queer participation in New Orleans's Mardi Gras, R. Paul (1984) explains that queer krewes have grown into extravagant spectacles reminiscent of those held at the court of the homoerotically inclined, transgendered French king HENRI III (1551-1589), frequently incorporating pre-Christian and otherwise pagan themes. "Like the early court entertainments in

France and Italy," Paul observes, "the krewes and associated balls "rely heavily on mythological themes, especially . . . Mediterranean ones . . . because of the intuitive resonance with the homoeroticism of the Greeks and with the mystery cults of Egypt and the Fertile Crescent."

Marées, Hans von (1837-1887) German homoerotically inclined painter of Symbolist environments whose works, such as *Three Men in a Landscape* (1875), *Paris and Mercury* (1880-1881), *The Riding School* (1881-1882), *Chiron and Achilles* (1883), *The Abduction of Ganymede* (1887), depict the interrelationship of homoeroticism (especially of a traditionally masculine and occasionally intergenerational type) and the mythic or sacred.

Margarita, Saint (dates uncertain; late antiquity or early Middle Ages) Beautiful noblewoman who, despising the institution of marriage, fled from her parents' home on the eve of her wedding, after cutting her hair and donning masculine attire. Seeking refuge, as a young man named Pelagius, at a nearby monastery, she/he later became the prior of a convent. When one of the nuns there accused her/him of impregnating her, Margarita/Pelagius left the convent to become a hermit, spending her/his remaining years in a cave. Before dying, Pelagius told an abbot friend the tale of her/his earlier incarnation as Margarita. The abbot proclaimed the innocence of Margarita/Pelagius upon her/his death. Canonized as a Catholic saint, Margarita/Pelagius is commonly fêted on July 4.

Margherita de Parma (1522-1586) Bisexual writer and ruler of the Netherlands. Married first to Alessandro de'Medici and later to Ottavio Farnese, her greatest love appears to have been another woman, Laudomia Forteguerra Petrucci (who was also married). Petrucci was not only a celebrated Italian poet but a powerful Amazonian soldier leading a band of female soldiers in defense of Siena against a Florentine attack. Margherita apparently conceived of her relationship with Laudomia in Neoplatonic terms outlined by Marsilio FICINO, as did her supporters. In *Discourse on the Beauty of Women* (1548), Agnolo Firenzuola specifically referred to the *Symposium* of PLATO in speaking of their relationship, explaining that it was natural for certain women to fall in love with other women. Ironically, her detractors compared Margherita to "Sappho the lesbian," who may well have agreed with Platonic – which are not deprived of an erotic component, as most of us have been led to believe – conceptions of love.

Mariechild, Diane (1942-) Spiritual counselor, leader in the Women's Spirituality movement, and writing instructor who lives in northern California with her life partner. A student of Ruth Denison since 1976, Mariechild teaches Vipassana Meditation. She has also studied

Theravadan and Tibetan Buddhism as well as certain Native American spiritual traditions. Her works include *Crystal Visions* (1985), *The Inner Dance* (1987), *Mother Wit* (1988), *Lesbian Sacred Sexuality* (1995), and *Open Mind: Women's Daily Inspiration for Becoming Mindful* (1996).

Marina, Saint (dates uncertain; late antiquity or early Middle Ages)   When Marina's father Eugenius decided to become a monk, Marina, apparently by choice, assumed a male identity in order to follow him, changing her name to Marius. After a certain woman accused her/him of impregnating her, Marina was cast out of the monastery. She/he raised the child, keeping her/his earlier life as Marina a secret. Only upon the death of Marius was her/his female anatomy discovered. She/he was then officially forgiven and eventually canonized as a Catholic saint. St Marina, whose name derives from a title of the Greek goddess APHRODITE signifying "of the sea," is sometimes associated with the planet VENUS. She is fêted on February 12, June 18, or July 4 or 17.

Marlowe, Christopher (1564-1593)   Bisexual or homoerotically inclined English Renaissance poet and playwright profoundly inspired by classical mythology and Euro-western ritual MAGIC. Swinburne is quoted as saying of Marlowe, "From Heaven he got his mind, from Hell his vice." What an iconoclast, a veritable Doctor Faustus, Marlowe must have seemed. Beyond his own wide reading of hermetic texts, his dabbling in the magical arts, and his association with Sir Walter Raleigh's mysterious salon, the School of Night, Marlowe espoused views even today considered controversial. "Moses was but a Juggler," and "all protestantes are Hypocritical asses," Marlowe was heard to say. "[JESUS] Christ was a bastard and his mother dishonest . . . [SAINT] JOHN THE EVANGELIST was bedfellow to Christ and leaned alwaies in his bosome, that he used him as the sinners of Sodom." And this Wildeian epigram: "All they that love not Tobacco & Boies were fooles." In Marlowe's works, the elements of same-sex passion, transgenderism, and the mythic or sacred are woven into an exquisite tapestry. In *Hero and Leander*, a story of heterosexual love, Neptune (POSEIDON) desires the androgynous hero Leander. "Some swore he was a maid in man's attire, / For in his looks were all that men desire." Jove (ZEUS) fondles an equally androgynous, though far more mischievous GANYMEDE in *Dido, Queen of Carthage*; and in *Edward II*, brilliantly revivified by the filmmaker Derek JARMAN, Gaveston, the beloved of the King, dreams of the court he and Edward will not live to share: "Like sylvan nymphs my pages shall be clad, / My men like satyrs grazing on the lawns / Shall with their goat feet dance in antic hay; / Sometime a lovely boy in Dian's shape, / With hair that gilds the water as it glides, / Crownets of pearl about his

naked arms, / And in his sportful hands an olive-tree / To hide those parts which men delight to see." Marlowe's death remains a mystery. Some said he and another drunken man fought over a youth, and that Marlowe lost. Others claimed that Marlowe knew too much of a government grown corrupt. Still others suggested that Marlowe had been slain by one who disapproved of his erotic interests and irreligion.

Maron   Priest and beloved of DIONYSUS in Greek mythology or religion, depicted as a WINE maker. Maronian wine became extremely popular in Greco-Roman antiquity.

Mars   In Euro-western ASTROLOGY, this planet governs anger, combat, courage, defense, endurance, energy, sexual passion, and strength. In astrology, as well as in the Euro-western traditions of alchemy and ritual magic, the planets are considered to be ultimately androgynous or transgendered, their feminine and masculine aspects represented by the signs they govern. In the case of Mars, his masculine aspect is represented by ARES, his feminine by SCORPIO. Figures associated with Mars and with gender and/or sexual variance include: ACHILLES, AIDO WEDO, AMAZONS, ANAT, ARTEMIS, ATHENA, FURIES, GORGONS, HERACLES, HORUS, KARTIKKEYEH, MA, PATROCLUS, and SHANGO.

Marsyas   In Roman myth and religion, a satyr associated with the worship of the goddess CYBELE and her male consort ATTIS and hence also with the GALLI, the transgendered male priests of these deities. Music teacher and lover of the youth OLYMPUS, Marsyas was a *gallus* of Cybele who "roamed the country[side] with the disconsolate goddess to soothe her grief for the death of Attis." According to the Celaeneans of Phrygia, Marsyas was the legendary composer of "the Mother's Air, a tune played on the flute in honour of the Great Mother Goddess." Marsyas was crucified on a pine tree and then flayed by APOLLO after having lost in a musical competition to the latter. It is quite possible that this competition reflected a larger struggle between the worshippers of the Goddess and those of the Olympian pantheon. As a worshipper of Cybele, Marsyas, although vanquished, was revered by the Calaeneans and others as semi-divine musician. It was believed that his flayed skin, which hung in a cave at Calaenae, would dance when Phrygian melodies were played, while remaining motionless when hymns to Apollo were played. Marsyas is a subject of the painting *Apollo and Marsyas* by the Italian Renaissance painter Pietro Perugino (c. 1445/50-1523). He is also honored in Oscar Wilde's *De Profundis*.

Martello, the Reverend Dr Leo Louis (1931-)
Celebrated Sicilian-American gay male practitioner of

Witchcraft. Reared in Massachusetts, Martello is the descendant of Sicilian witches (*streghe*). He "came out" both as a Witch and as a gay person in 1969 (the year he published *Weird Ways of Witchcraft*) and immediately thereafter became an activist in both the Wiccan rights and gay liberation movements, playing a central role in the first "Witch-In" in recorded history, held in Central Park in New York on October 31, 1970. A prolific writer, his work most relevant to this encyclopaedia is *Witchcraft: The Old Religion* (1973). Martello describes Witchcraft as "an underground spring which has occasionally broken through the surface in rivulets and then continued on its way underground, sometimes manifesting as a pond. Now all these rivulets and ponds are merging into a raging river which cannot be dammed up by the Judaeo-Christian tradition." Concerning the place of gay people in Wicca, he writes: "Those [Witchcraft] groups who insist on heterosexuality as a requirement for admittance into a coven cannot claim ancient precedence, since so many of the pagan religions had male prostitutes in their temples. And the eunuch priests, most notably of CYBELE, would be disqualified." Martello, now in his sixties, lives in a Manhattan flat overflowing with old books, ritual paraphernalia, and stuffed animals. It is his carnivalesque attitude toward life that is perhaps most striking about the elder Martello. While he says that he has generally "given up on people," his sardonic, campy humor keeps him afloat. When he was recently asked if he believed in reincarnation, he replied, "No, I once did, but that was in a former life." In the neopagan journal *Fireheart*, he remarks: "There is a greater Magick . . . That is . . . the magick of humor, of laughter . . . The sacredness of silliness. Wouldn't Miss Piggy make a marvelous High Priestess? Or imagine Mae West greeting a visiting [Wiccan] high priest in that undulating way of hers, asking, 'Is that an athame [i.e. a ritual knife] in your pocket, or are you just glad to see me?'"

Martha-Mary   In the *Amphitheatre of Dead Sciences*, the mystic Joséphin Péladan (1859-1918) describes a DOUBLE female being, based on that figure in the *Symposium* of PLATO, as a Catholic fusion of Saint Martha and Saint Mary Magdalene (or the Blessed Virgin Mary, the mother of Jesus).

Massalia   The city of Marseilles, France, as known to the ancient Greeks. The male inhabitants of Massalia/Marseilles were said to be effeminate and homoerotically or bisexually inclined and to enjoy the receptive role in same-sex intercourse. The slur "May you sail to Massalia!" might be translated as "Get screwed!"

Massissi (also **Macici, Desikole, Madoda, Makòmè, Nan Metye**)   In Haitian culture, and especially within Vodou, a term for a homoerotically inclined and often gender variant or transgendered male. *Houngans* (or *oungans*, priests of Vodou) are often *massissi*. Although the origin of the term is not clear, it may derive from the French *ma soeur*, meaning "my sister." One of the alternate terms, *madoda*, may derive from the Yoruba term *adodi*, referring to a homoerotically inclined male, found in the Yoruba-diasporic religions of Santería and Lucimi. The term *massissi* is used to refer to the homoerotic aspect of one of the spirits of the dead, GHEDE NIBO; it is also the title of a song and accompanying dance dedicated to him.

Mastamho   Divine ancestor of the Mohave of the American Southwest. Mastamho created the sun, moon and stars, and instructed the Mohave in agriculture and in the arts. Mastamho also presided over initiation ceremonies undertaken by ALYHA, third gender males often serving in shamanic capacities.

Mastic (or **Mastich**)   An evergreen shrub or the gum it yields, the latter used in incenses and as a chewing gum, sacred to the lesbian goddess BRITOMARTIS.

Mathurine (d. 1625)   Chief fool at the court of both the homoerotically inclined, transgendered HENRI III (1551-1589) and Henri IV (1553-1610) of France, possibly a transgendered and/or lesbian woman, in some ways comparable to the male fool RAHERE. Mathurine wore mixed masculine and feminine attire; she was typically depicted as carrying a woman's handkerchief in one hand and a sword in another. Frequently seen in the streets of Paris around 1600, Mathurine was usually mounted on a large white gelding (horse) and followed by a crowd of ass-eared SOTS behaving lewdly and crying out in a braying manner, "Aga, aga, Mathurine!" People would gather to ask her questions to which she would respond with a mixture of prophecy and gossip. The transgendered and lesbian associations surrounding her survived into the seventeenth century, when, in a pamphlet titled *La Métempsychose de la reine Christine* (1657), Queen Christina of Sweden was said to be the reincarnation of both Mathurine and the legendary transgendered Queen SEMIRAMIS.

Mawu-Lisa   Celestial *lwa* (deity or spirit) of the Vodou pantheon, alternately depicted as linked to female (Mawu) and male (Lisa) twins and as a single gynandrous or transgendered divinity, described by L. Hurbon (1995) as an "androgynous double god." Mawu-Lisa, according to African-American lesbian writer Audre LORDE, is "west-east, night-day, moon-sun." Some say that Mawu-Lisa created the first human beings from clay. As a divine artisan, Mawu-Lisa is a patron of artists and craftspersons.

Maximus the Confessor, Saint (c. 580-662)   According to the Catholic monk, theologian, and mystic Maximus,

JESUS Christ is androgynous. Moreover, males and females will become androgynous at the time of the Resurrection.

Mayas Ancient civilization of Mexico and Guatemala. In the early phases of development, the Mayas were extremely hostile toward the practice of homoeroticism. In fact, they murdered many Itza men on this account. By the time of the Spanish Conquest, however, the Mayas appear to have become much more tolerant, for in the early fifteenth century, parents had begun acquiring young men to be the lovers of their own male offspring, explaining that the god CHIN had introduced and sanctified this practice. Juan de Torquemada wrote in 1615: "From that also began the law that if anyone approached the boy (the younger of the two men), they were ordered to pay for it, punishing them with the same penalties as those breaking the condition of a marriage." In 1569, Tomas Lopez Medel reported homoerotically inclined, transgendered priest/esse/s in the Mayan temples of the Yucatan and Guatemala; during the same period, Bernal Diaz reported seeing statues of men engaging in anal intercourse in the Mayan temples at Cape Catoche, Yucatan.

Mbaya Tribal people of the Gran Chaco, in the vicinity of Paraguay. TWO-SPIRIT persons were very common among the Mbaya. They dressed and spoke like women, simulated menstruation, performed traditionally feminine tasks, and served as HIERODULES, or "sacred prostitutes."

Me In Mesopotamian religion, where same-sex desire and transgenderism are concerned, it appears that both traits or behaviors may have been considered as *me*s, qualities distributed by the gods. Homoerotically inclined (and apparently also bisexual and lesbian) and transgendered persons were considered as being essentially different from others, their identities being a gift of the gods.

Medusa In Greek mythology and religion, one of the GORGONS. Although later Greeks explained that Medusa's once beautiful locks of HAIR had been turned into serpents by the goddess ATHENA after the latter had discovered her making love to POSEIDON, Medusa's origins may actually lie in Africa, where under another name, she may have been a serpentine, lunar, Amazonian goddess of metamorphosis or regeneration. Medusa holds the power to turn men into stone. Her blood is used by the god ASCLEPIUS to heal the sick, by sorcerers to create poisons. She is slain by Perseus, who decapitates her, yet she survives as a protective and oracular symbol, returning to guard and guide her faithful. Greek bakers painted her image on ovens to keep the curious from ruining the bread. Late nineteenth-century French Symbolist writers and artists, many of whom were transgendered and/or same-

sex inclined, reclaimed the image of Medusa as the mask of the creative individual who reflects truth to the world, no matter how disturbing. For this, the poet is cursed by the world, becoming the *poète maudit*, at the same time being conferred with semi-divine status by the gods. Lesbian-feminists of the late twentieth century have claimed the image of Medusa as a symbol of female power, including the power to protect oneself from violence. The US lesbian writer May Sarton (1912-1995) discovered that Medusa could act as an inspiring force. In the poem "The Muse as Medusa," she relates that even though she has beheld Medusa's glance, she has not been turned to stone: "I turn your face around! It is my face. / That frozen rage is what I must explore – / Oh secret, self-enclosed, and ravaged place! / This is the gift I thank Medusa for."

Megabyzos (pl. **Megabyzoi**) While the gender variant priests of the Greco-Roman goddess ARTEMIS/DIANA may have been divided into various groups, perhaps including the *essenes* (referring to male bees), those about whom we know most are the *megabyzoi*. While gender variant males probably served Diana for several millenia, the particular institution of the *megabyzos* – a Persian term – dates from the seventh century BCE. As with other gender variant priests, the appearance of the *megabyzos* was of great importance. While Quintillian, a Roman rhetorician of the first century CE, insisted that painters and sculptors would refrain from depicting a *megabyzos* on both aesthetic and moral grounds, a number of ancient artists, including Zeuxis, Apelles, and Nicias painted portraits of *megabyzoi* to hang in the Goddess' temples and sepulchers. Unfortunately, these portraits have apparently been lost. Most of the representations of *megabyzoi* which remain are in the forms of statuettes, columns, and literary descriptions. Contrary to Quintillian's view, the *megabyzoi*, who arrived at EPHESUS from all parts of the known world, were celebrated for both their beauty and their wisdom. The *megabyzoi* were clean-shaven and powdered their faces or painted them with an ointment containing flecks of gold. They wore their hair in a feminine style, "with a plait looped in front of each ear." Their attire mixed feminine, masculine, and sacerdotal articles. In early times, they may have worn panther skins in emulation of the Goddess, as evidenced by columns at Ephesus. In later times, they wore long-sleeved garments, *chitons* or *calasires*, decorated with meanders, flowers, and animals sacred to the Goddess. These garments were of different colors, including saffron and sea-green. The garments most frequently worn by the *megabyzoi* were PURPLE, the dye made from the murex shell. This dye was associated with royalty and effeminacy. The most exquisite purple garments were the *actaea*, sewn with purple and gold threads and ornamented with golden sheaves of millet. The *megabyzoi* also wore turbans or tiaras, often of gold, necklaces resembling rosaries, and delicate slippers. The *megabyzoi* were often eunuchs. In the latter days of the worship of Artemis/Diana, however, it appears that ritual castration was replaced by sacrifices of phallus-shaped breads. Texts dating from the fourth century BCE suggest that the rite of castration was partly undertaken to sever family ties, and that upon becoming a eunuch, the initiate was adopted by an elder member of the *megabyzos* community. The *megabyzoi* performed various functions, including the composition and performance of hymns, the casting of horoscopes, the overseeing of temple finances, and the organization of public festivals. The great festival of Artemis/Diana took place each year on May 25, the birthday of the Goddess. Gold, silver, and other images of the Goddess were carried by the *megabyzoi* and priestesses to all parts of the city for public viewing. At least one of the statues was dressed in an ornate purple and gold *actaea*. *Megabyzoi* and priestesses dressed as Artemis/Diana also rode through the city in stag-drawn chariots. ALEXANDER THE GREAT was among those who participated in this rite. The *megabyzoi* were best known, however, for their ability to divine the future by way of the EPHESIAN LETTERS. Roughly equivalent to Teutonic runes, the letters, made of wood and painted gold, were carried in pouches that hung from the waist. They were employed not only as a divinatory tool but were also believed to function as amulets or talismans, protecting the wearer from harm.

Melanippe Queen of the AMAZONS and sister of HIPPOLYTE. Her name means "Black Mare." At first defeating HERACLES, she eventually became one his shipboard prisoners who, J. A. Salmonson (1991) speculates, may have escaped with other Amazons to found settlements in Scythia.

Meliouchos In Hellenistic, or Greco-Egyptian, magic, a mythological figure associated with a number of deities, including ADONIS, Serapis, ZEUS, Helios, HECATE, ERESHKIGAL, and Mithras. Meliouchos's name may derive from the Greek word for honey, *meli*. Apparently a handsome or beautiful male figure, Meliouchos was invoked in male homoerotic love spells in Alexandria, Egypt during the third century CE.

Melusine Medieval French legendary figure whose identity may be partly based in fact. Hybrid human and SERPENT, the beautiful noblewoman Melusine, keeping the latter aspect of her anatomy concealed, married Raymond, nephew of the count of Poitier. She told Raymond, however, that she must always be left alone on Saturday nights. One Saturday evening, however, her husband surprised her as she was taking a bath and saw her serpent's tail, which it seems appeared only on that day of the week. Melusine, both infuriated and humiliated, fled from Raymond. She did, however, leave two children

behind, and is even today regarded as an ancestor of three noble French families. In *Mélusine ou l'androgyne* (1983), Jean Markale suggests that the serpent's tail may be a signifier of transgenderism or transsexuality, leaving one to conclude that the children may have been adopted. The portrayal of Melusine as a DOUBLE female being with a serpent's tail in alchemical texts has led some scholars to consider the possibility that she may have been considered as both transgendered and lesbian inclined, her double femaleness traceable to the lesbian figure of PLATO's *Symposium*. Melusine is the subject of Felix Mendelsshon's *The Legend of the Fair Melusina* (1833) and appears as the subject of a poem by a fictional character, the bisexual or lesbian poet Miss Christabel LaMotte in A. S. Byatt's novel *Possession: A Romance* (1990).

Menestratus Young hero of Greek legend who offered himself to a dragon ravaging the Boetian city of Thespiae so that his lover Cleostratus, who had been chosen by lot to be the annual sacrificial victim of the dragon, might be spared.

Menjaya Raja Manang Spirit or deity revered by the Iban Dayak of Borneo, including by the transgendered male *manang bali*. It is said that Menjaya was a male being until he decided to become the world's first healer when his brother's wife became ill. Upon curing the wife of Sengalang Burong, Menjaya transformed into a female or androgynous being.

Men's Country Chinese legendary society depicted in *The Classic of Mountains and Seas*. On a journey to obtain the drug of immortality from the Queen Mother of the West, Wang Meng discovers the Country of Men, where he remains for the rest of his life. In Men's Country, where only men live, Wang Meng gives birth to two sons who emerge from his belly.

Menstruation Not surprisingly, considering the taboos surrounding both menstruation and same-sex intimacy (as bisexuality and lesbianism), little has yet been written linking these two phenomena, especially their association with the realm of the sacred. While works such as Penelope Shuttle and Peter Redgrove's *The Wise Wound: The Myths, Realities, and Meanings of Menstruation* (1990 ed.), inspired by Women's Spirituality and Neopaganism, impart fascinating information concerning menstruation and the mythic or sacred, they tend not explore the linkage of these with same-sex intimacy. To date, US lesbian writer Judy GRAHN's *Blood, Bread, and Roses: How Menstruation Created the World* (1993) is apparently the first to do so. Commencing with the statement "Images of blood are all around us," Grahn observes that menstrual blood is the only source of blood that is not related to trauma. "Menstrual blood, like water, just flows. Its fountain existed long before knives or flint; menstruation is the original source of blood." Grahn links menstrual blood to lesbian desire and love primarily through images of fluidity (of both blood and passionate expression), flowers, Goddess Reverence, and ritualistic blood-sisterhood. She points out that "an approving Spanish name for lesbians is *las flores*, 'the flowers,'" and she quotes a Caribbean proverb which goes, "When a woman loves another woman, it is the blood of the Mother speaking." Of her own experience, Grahn writes, "I remember lesbian lovers with whom I have shared moments of spontaneous and exultant love and trust as we painted stripes on our bare torsos with our own fresh menstrual blood. We were 'blood sisters,' initiating each other into women's power." The authors of the present text have found that in certain cultures, Amazonian or gender variant lesbian or bisexual women have concealed their own menstruation while respecting cultural taboos concerning that of their female companions. This appears to have been the case among the Mohave people of North America, where the TWO-SPIRIT HWAME "submitted to the taboos of the husband of a menstruating . . . wife." To the contrary, Mohave two-spirit males, ALYHA, simulated menstruation by scratching themselves with sticks between the legs until blood flowed. Recently, as exemplified by Pam Keesey's anthologies *Daughters of Darkness* (1993) and *Dark Angels* (1995), menstruation, lesbianism, and the mythic or sacred have been further linked to the archetype of the VAMPIRE.

Mercurius Figure of ALCHEMY linked to the Greek god HERMES and variously depicted in female, male, and transgendered form. In *De alchimia*, a sixteenth-century text, Mercurius is shown as a female deity or queen holding a dragon. Similarly, in *Turba philosophorum*, also from the sixteenth century, Mercurius is a nude woman with long hair holding the moon in her left hand and the sun (as fire) in her right. In *Philosophia reformatat* (1622), another alchemical text, Mercurius is shown as a double male figure (the sun and moon his two heads), linking him to the homoerotically inclined, once-double male figure of PLATO's *Symposium*. In *Mutus liber* (1702), another text on alchemy, Mercurius is shown as an androgynous figure bearing likeness to ARTEMIS or Luna (the left side of his/her body) and to APOLLO or the sun (the right side). Mercurius's left foot stands on the moon, with the right foot touching the sun. He (-she) is contained within the alchemical vessel or "philosopher's egg," which is held afloat by two winged *erotes*. In *Rosarium philosophorum* (1593), an alchemical text, Mercurius is depicted as a winged, double female being, wearing a single crown, linking Mercurius to the lesbian, once-double female figure of Plato's *Symposium*. A TRICKSTER by nature, alternately helping and hindering the seeker, Mercurius is sometimes associated with MELUSINE, Mephistopheles, and PUCK. He (-she) has also been compared to other

alchemical symbols of androgyny or transgenderism, including the SAPPHIRE, the UROBORUS, the PEACOCK, and the PHOENIX.

Mercury In Euro-western ASTROLOGY, this planet governs androgyny, communication, creativity, diplomacy, journeying "between the worlds," magic, memory, prank-playing, shapeshifting, and transgenderism. In astrology, as well as in the Euro-western traditions of ALCHEMY and ritual magic, the planets are considered to be ultimately androgynous or transgendered, their feminine and masculine aspects represented by the signs they govern. In the case of Mercury, his masculine aspect is represented by GEMINI, his feminine by VIRGO. Figures associated with Mercury and with gender and/or sexual variance include: ANUBIS, ATHENA, Coatlicue, DEMETER, DEVI, Elleggua, HERMAPHRODITUS, HERMES, KALI, Mephistopheles, ODIN, OYA, PUCK, and THOTH. In the European Renaissance ritual magic application of the theory of correspondences, the planet Mercury is linked, according to Cornelius Agrippa (1486-1535), with "all animals that are of both sexes, and those which can change their sex, as the hare, the civet cat, and such like."

Mère Sotte Goddess-like figure celebrated by the SOTS, Medieval French fools who appear to have included transgendered and homoerotically inclined males. Those who speak of retentions and survivals believe that this figure, known variously as Mère (Mother) Sotte, Mère Folle, and Folle Bobance, may have at one time been linked to the Greco-Roman goddess CYBELE, as both were revered at Autun, a veritable citadel of Romano-Gallic paganism. The goddess BAUBO also may have played a role in the creation of the Mother of the *sots*. Mère Sotte was typically portrayed as an elderly woman wearing a multicolored skirt and a cap with asses' ears. While P. Berger (1985), views her as a "figure of ridicule only," I. Nelson (1976), perhaps more sensitive to CAMP, sees Mère Sotte as a creative force, a figure bringing joy, and, above all, celebrating the "joy of receptive homosexuality." "As soon as I'd cease being perverse," Mère Sotte tells us, "I'd die." Each February, from the Middle Ages until at least the mid-seventeenth century, the *sots* would parade through the streets of Autun pulling a cart in which Mère Sotte, represented by the local leader of the *sots*, would be seated. This figure may be the seated transvestite, nunlike figure being pulled by two similarly dressed figures in Bruegel's *Fight Between Carnival and Lent*. The male consort of Mère Sotte was the SEIGNEUR DE JOYE.

Meredites As late as the end of the nineteenth century, a ceremony focusing on gender metamorphosis among women was still being performed by the Meredites, a people living in Dalmatia in Eastern Europe. The ceremony commences when a young woman goes to the priest and announces, "From now on I want to be considered a man and live as one." The priest brings this to the attention of the congregation. Shortly thereafter, the young woman is given a man's name. She then dresses in male attire and begins to arm her (-him) self. From this time forward she will be treated as a man by all who encounter her. This means that she, now he, is free to love and to marry a woman.

Meriones Second in command of the Cretan contingent in the Trojan War, his comrade-lover was IDOMENEAS.

Merlin Wizard of British legend whose existence remains controversial. The mentor and advisor of King Arthur, Merlin was believed to excel at shapeshifting, including metamorphosing from male into female. Fortunio Affaytati (fl. c. 1550), an Italian scientist who taught mathematics in London and who published *Physical and Astronomical Considerations* in 1549, claimed that Merlin had been born around 446, without the aid of a male. He and others, apparently including midwives, suggested that the birth might have resulted from lesbian lovemaking.

Mermaid Beautiful hybrid woman-fish who customarily sits on a rock in the sea, combing her long, flowing hair and singing in the company of other mermaids. Hans Christian Andersen (1805-1875) wrote the tale that remains the most beloved concerning the mermaid. It is a bittersweet story of a young mermaid who yearns for a human prince so deeply that she is willing to sacrifice her identity to be with him. Numerous critics have suggested the fairy tale may reflect in part Andersen's struggle to accept his homosexuality or bisexuality, and that for him both mermaids and prince are representative of homoerotic fantasies. One of the most delightful paintings of a mermaid is *Mare-Maid*, an American primitivist watercolor painted in 1820 by the romantic friends or lovers Mary Ann Wilson and Miss Brundage, who have been immortalized in Isabel Miller's (pseudonymn of Alma Routsong) 1967 novel *Patience and Sarah* (also called *A Place for Us*). Emily Culpepper, in her article "Mermaids: A Symbol for Female-Identified Psychic Self-Reflection," sees in the mermaid as symbol of women loving together in harmony and tranquillity. "Because the mermaid's realm is not invaded by men," she writes, "it can represent a place where there is female freedom and self-sufficiency. Living in water . . . physically conveys the idea of a different world, different from the patriarchal land in which we find ourselves struggling for female liberation."

Merrill, James (1926-1995) Gay male American poet who, with his lover David Jackson serving as a second medium, employed a Ouija board to summon angels and spirits of deceased writers, these experiments resulting in a poetic trilogy, *The Changing Light at Sandover* (1982).

Mestra (also **Hypermestra**) Legendary shapeshifter of Greco-Roman mythology. As a young woman, she loved the god POSEIDON, who bestowed her with the power of shapeshifting. She used this power to obtain food for her n'er-do-well father Erysicthon. She would periodically serve a male master to obtain material goods and would then transform herself into a man in order to disentangle herself from the situation.

Metamorphoses, The Celebrated work by the Roman poet Ovid (P. Ovidius Naso, 43 BCE-18 CE) which contains many references to mythic or spiritual figures embracing gender and/or sexual variance, including IPHIS and TIRESIAS, and which may be read as an erotico-sacred text. Thomas Stehling notes that "in the twelfth century, imitations of Ovid became the vogue . . . In Medieval poems of male love and friendship, we repeatedly find figures from the *Metamorphoses*." Among these, CYPARISSUS, APOLLO, HYACINTHUS, ZEPHYRUS, ORPHEUS, and GANYMEDE are the most prominent.

Metamorphosphere Term coined by twentieth-century lesbian-feminist philosopher and theologian Mary DALY. In *Pure Lust: Elemental Feminist Philosophy* (1984), Daly explains that patriarchal culture deprives women of vision in its insistence on "reality," which is, of course, identical to patriarchal culture. New metaphors, like symbols, can aid women in burning through barriers and spinning new, liberating worlds, new "metamorphospheres."

Metis In Orphism, a Greek Mystery cult allegedly founded by the musician-mystic ORPHEUS. Metis is a transgendered deity associated with PHANES. Originally a nymph seduced by Zeus, when Metis was pregnant and about to give birth to ATHENA, Zeus swallowed Metis and the unborn child, not knowing that the child would be a girl, thinking it might be a male who would one day displace him. Thus, Athena was not only the child of Zeus but also of Metis.

Miao Shan In Chinese Buddhist folklore, a manifestation of the BODHISATTVA KUAN YIN. Miao Shan, rejecting marriage, entered a Buddhist convent. This, however, proved an unfortunate experience, as the monks visiting the NUNS would not leave them alone. Miao Shan, in the depths of disillusionment, was miraculously carried to the heavens on a RAINBOW. In premodern China, a profound connection existed between resistance to marriage, determination to lead a spiritual life, and love between women, as demonstrated by such groups as the GOLDEN ORCHID ASSOCIATION.

Miati "Woman-inclined," TWO-SPIRIT male shamans of the Hidatsa people of North America. Among the Hidatsa, young men destined to become miati dreamed that the female divinity VILLAGE OLD WOMAN instructed them to leave behind traditionally masculine attire, speech, behavior, and pursuits and to adopt those of women or individuals of alternate gender. Following such dreams, the young men came to be viewed as "mystic possessors of unique ritual instructions secured directly" from the divinity and were therefore "treated as a special class of religious leaders." *Miati* wore magpie feathers in their hair and white dresses made of sheepskin, white being the symbolic color of ash and oak, sacred trees in which the magpies lived. They also carried staffs made of ash and decorated with white sage, sacred to the goddess. Beyond this, they painted red ovals on their cheeks and foreheads, wore braids of sweetgrass looped around their left shoulders, and carried red blankets. They were thought to be especially gifted in hunting and agricultural magic. *Miati* often became possessed by Village Old Woman during the course of dance rituals; when this occurred, they would chant, "You can't kill me, for I am holy. I am holy, I can do anything."

Michael the Archangel, Saint Usually depicted with a sword and/or standing over a dragon he has conquered, he is one of the archangels of Christianity. Michael is often thought of as spiritual warrior who leads the hosts of heaven and protects the soul at the hour of death. In the work of Spanish poet Federico García LORCA, Michael becomes an icon of homoerotic love. In "San Miguel (Granada)," Lorca depicts the archangel as a beautiful young man "fragrante de agua colonia" ("fragrant with cologne"). In the Yoruba-diasporic religion of Candomblé, Michael is associated with LOGUNEDE, an androgynous deity. Saint Michael the Archangel is fêted on September 29.

Michelangelo Buonarroti (1475-1564) Bisexually or homoerotically inclined Florentine painter, sculptor, architect and poet of the Italian Renaissance. Inspired by Greek religion and mythology and by Neoplatonism as taught by Marsilio FICINO, Michelangelo often evoked the interrelationship of homoeroticism and the sacred (and occasionally also transgenderism) in his works, including such sketches as *Ganymede*, *The Fall of Phaethon*, and *The Dream* and sculptures including *Bacchus* (i.e. DIONYSUS) and *David*. His sonnets to his beloved Tommaso de' Cavalieri (b. 1509) likewise evoke this interrelationship. Love for the beautiful, strong, compassionate, and creative de' Cavalieri was for Michelangelo the earthly manifestation of his love for the Divine. Drawing upon images of GANYMEDE, ZEUS, EROS, as well as upon the Greek notion of lover and beloved as inspirer and inspired, he writes, "Wingless upon your pinions forth I fly; /

Heavenward your spirit stirreth me to strain." Unfortunately, Michelangelo's Neoplatonic spirituality, which nurtured his love for men, was counterbalanced and eventually overcome by a zealous Christian leaning, with Michelangelo coming to passionately admire the fanatical Savonarola (1452-1498) who, in his so-called BONFIRES OF THE VANITIES, destroyed many of the greatest artistic and literary works of the Renaissance and of previous eras on account of their alleged "pagan, decadent, and demonic influences." Michelangelo also quit loving de' Cavalieri, turning to Vittoria Colonna, a "pious noblewoman," according to J. Saslow (1986), "with whom he shared his growing religious fervor."

Midas One of several men named Midas was a transgendered male king of Phrygia who, after acquiring ass's ears, fell in love with a satyr and had him taken captive and brought to his court. Some say this satyr was Silenus himself. Midas was given ass's ears after telling the Greek god APOLLO that he was a more talented musician than the latter. Midas was able to hide his ears from everyone but his hairdresser. Unfortunately for Midas, the hairdresser whispered the secret to a hole in the earth, and Philostratus (fl. c. 200 CE) relates, the "bushes that grew there when shaken by the wind told the story to the world." Even with his ears, Midas remained an attractive man. Philostratus continues, "How dainty Midas is and how he takes his ease! He is careful of his headdress and his curling locks, and he carries a thyrsus and wears a robe woven with gold."

Midwife's Tale, The (1995) Film directed by Megan Siler which tells the tale of a noblewoman, Lady Eleanor, who cannot bear children until she is aided by Gwenyth, a young midwife. When the latter's mentor is put to death as a Witch and Gwenyth is herself accused of Witchcraft, the young midwife flees. Lady Eleanor, unable to tolerate her husband's abusiveness, and realizing that she has fallen in love with Gwenyth, drugs her husband and his men and, dressing in men's clothes, escapes, ultimately being reunited with the young midwife she loves.

Mihdacke Name of the TWO-SPIRIT male shaman of the Mandan people of North America. The Mihdacke are associated with the mythic figure Wolf-Black.

Mihri Hatun (d. 1506) First major female poet of the Ottoman Empire, a lengendary beauty who was learned in both Arabic and Persian and who is thought to have been loved by both women and men. She writes to a beloved of risking traditional religious beliefs in order to express desire: "At one glance / I loved you / With a thousand hearts / They can hold against me / No sin except my love for you / Come to me / Don't go away. / Let the zealots think / Loving is sinful / Never mind / Let me burn in the hellfire / Of that sin."

Miletus In Greek mythology, a young man loved by SARPEDON, founder of Miletus in Asia Minor.

Min Among the myriad of deities of the Egyptian pantheon those most closely linked to homoeroticism are Min and SET. Like Set, Min is associated with ISIS, as the "BULL of the Mother." Min is the god of storms, flocks, agriculture, travelers, and sexuality. He is often portrayed as a Black African holding a flail and as having an enormous, erect phallus. His chief attributes are the bull and the LETTUCE plant. The bull is associated with the moon, with the worship of the feminine principle, and with semen. The lettuce, because of its milky sap, is likewise associated with semen. This association caused the ancient Egyptians to consider lettuce the favorite food of eunuchs, effeminate men, and possibly, the homoerotically inclined. Min was often invoked by a worshipper who sought either to overpower a rival or to establish peace with him. The worshipper would journey to Min's temple at Edfu, where he would make a sacrifice of lettuces to the god. He would ask Min to eat the lettuces, to transform their milky sap into semen, and to cause, by magical means, his rival to swallow the sap and thereby become pregnant. In this way, the rival would eventually give birth to the worshipper's son, who would magically spring forth from his forehead. This magical child would symbolize either conquest or truce, depending upon the desire of the worshipper. In later times, Min was syncretized with the Greek god PAN. His sanctuary at Chemmis [or Akhmin] in the Delta then became known as Panopolis. Invoked by travelers and traders, he was also syncretized with HERMES. In the 1990s, certain practitioners of S/M (SADOMASOCHISM) revere Min, in part due to his depiction as a phallic god holding a flail.

Minerva Roman goddess of wisdom, arts (especially music), crafts, and commerce, sometimes identified with the Greek goddess ATHENA. The Christian writer Justin Martyr (c. 100-c. 165), who rejected the pagan faith of his parents, especially despised Minerva. He linked her to ARTEMIS/DIANA, as another gender variant female deity, and also to DIONYSUS/Bacchus, as a gender variant male deity, writing in the *Discourse to the Greeks*: "And I say nothing of the masculine character of Minerva, nor of the feminine nature of Bacchus . . . Teach Minerva and Diana the works of women . . . What seemliness is there in a woman's girding herself with armor?"

Minos Of the numerous Greek figures who are named Minos – the name signifying "the moon's creature" – one is a judge of the dead and the brother of Rhadamanthys and Sarpedon. According to the Cretans, it was Minos and not

Zeus who abducted GANYMEDE. Minos was also, according to Zenis of Chios, a lover of Theseus.

Minquga TWO-SPIRIT (transgendered, or third gender) individuals of the Omaha people of North America who begin to discover their destiny when they are visited by the MOON, usually during puberty. The deity or spirit of the Moon holds out bow and arrows and a woman's pack strap to the young person. If a male takes the pack strap, or a young woman takes the bow and arrows, that individual is destined to become a two-spirit shaman or medicine-person. They begin to wear the attire of, and behave in ways associated with, the opposite anatomical sex. They may even marry persons of the same anatomical sex. S. D. Gill and I. F. Sullivan (1992) write, "The *minquga* are publicly accepted by the tribes, and many are considered to be powerful medicine people."

Mirror In China, where the mirror is traditionally a feminine and a lunar symbol and an attribute of female royalty, employed by shamans and Taoist priests and priestesses in divinatory rites, lesbian lovemaking is referred to as "*mojingzi*," as rubbing or grinding mirrors together. In Japan, the mirror remains a feminine symbol and an attribute of female royalty but now becomes a solar symbol. The mirror, or *kagami*, found in many Shinto temples, also symbolizes meditation or reflection, purity of soul, and the linking of the heavens and the earth. As a solar symbol, the mirror is linked to the great Sun-goddess AMATERASU OMI KAMI, who is associated with both gender variance and woman-loving eroticism. In the myth of Amaterasu, the mirror which, coupled with the dance of the goddess AME NO UZUME, draws Amaterasu (the light) from the cave in which she has been hiding (the darkness) is the creation of a transgendered deity, ISHI KORE DOME NO KAMI. For this reason, Japanese makers of mirrors have traditionally paid homage to Ishi Kore Dome No Kami. Poets, philosophers, psychologists, and others have linked the mirror to the Greek deity NARCISSUS, who fell in love with his reflection while gazing into a pool. While some have condemned Narcissus as a selfish youth interested only in himself, hence our term "narcissism," others, including André GIDE (1869-1951), Paul Valéry (1871-1945), and Herbert Marcuse (1898-1979) have interpreted the myth of Narcissus and the mirroring pool as an honoring of the process of self-discovery or exploring one's inner depths – paralleling the lesbian poet Adrienne RICH's (b. 1929) voyage in "Diving into the Wreck" – of self-purification or self-baptism, of a man's experiencing of and uniting with his "feminine" self (symbolized by the water). Valéry writes, "Admire in Narcissus the eternal return toward the mirror of the water which offers his image to his love, and to his beauty all his knowledge." Indeed, some say that the myth of Narcissus and the mirror celebrates homoerotic love, one's uniting with a twin-like companion. The philosopher Marcuse writes, "He does not know that the image he admires is his own." Perhaps Narcissus imagines he has discovered his reflection in another beautiful young man, one dwelling in the water, with whom he might be lovers.

Minstrel Wandering musicians, used primarily to refer to those of the European Middle Ages and Renaissance, including French *jongleurs* and troubadours and Irish *filidh*. While many admired the minstrels, many others treated them as outcasts. The Church generally refused to administer communion to them. The Church's hostility toward them conspired with their itinerant lifestyle to place them in a subculture comprised of dancers, jugglers, prostitutes, card players, thieves, homeless persons, persons with physical and mental impairments, practitioners of magic, and the transgendered and homoerotically inclined. Minstrels typically dressed in garments of red, yellow, and green, resembling those worn by fools. During CARNIVALS, they would disguise themselves as women or beasts; some even went about naked. They were frequently condemned as effeminate, foolish, or both. Their behavior seems to have been perceived as belonging to a third or alternate gender category. While their graceful body movements and alleged delight in gossip were categorized as feminine, their love of belly laughter, yelling, obscene gestures, and equally obscene language were perceived as crudely masculine. In terms of erotic behavior, minstrels were generally depicted as ribalds, as erotic rebels having multiple partners. They were often grouped with female prostitutes, and they appear to have been associated with both male prostitution and homoeroticism. As the spiritual descendants of ORPHEUS, they were often thought to have forsaken the love of women for that of men. These associations are reflected by word chains. For instance, the term *jongleur* is related to *jogleor*, which in turn is linked to *burdoun* (*bourdon, bordon, burdon*, etc.). *B[o]urd-* refers to a young woman or to a jest, while *bourdon* refers to a scepter or staff, with all its phallic import. A *burdon* is a ninny or a mule, a sterile animal, while *burdoun* refers to a strong bass voice or a ground melody. *Jongleur*, via *jogleor*, was also linked to *galiard* and its cognates, referring to a "gaily dressed" male, a description which may have indicated transgenderism and/or homoeroticism. *Jogleor* was further linked to *pauton(n)ier* and *poltron*, words describing a "saucy," "base," and "knavish" male. *Pauton(n)ier* and *poltron* were in turn linked to *femmelette*, an effeminate male. While some writers described minstrels as mercenaries and male prostitutes, others reported that it was their *savoir gai* ("gay wisdom") that attracted noblemen to them, and that many intimate relationships were thus formed between nobles and minstrels. Of individual minstrels, three are believed to have engaged in same-sex relationships: Arnaud Daniel (fl. twelfth

century), Blondel (twelfth century), and the (possibly transgendered) woman troubadour Bieiris de Romans (thirteenth century). Several lyrics suggest that Daniel may have been a lover of men – beyond the fact that in *The Inferno*, Dante placed him among the homoerotically inclined. An exemplary lyric reads, "I am Arnaut who gathers the wind / and hunts the HARE with an ox / and swims against the tide." In Medieval iconography, as John Boswell (1980) points out, the image of the hare and the pursuit of hunting were both associated with homoeroticism. "Swimming against the tide," by indicating a reversal of the natural, may also speak to transgenderism and homoeroticism. Blondel, a chevalier of Artois, was, according to some historians, the handsome, golden-haired lover of Richard I, the Lionhearted (1157-1199). Legend has it that when Richard was imprisoned in Austria, Blondel stood beneath the fortress tower, playing on the lute and singing to his beloved. The song was one they had composed together in happier times. Of Bieiris de Romans, unfortunately, little is known, other than that a surviving chanson appears to be passionately addressed to another woman. Minstrels were believed to practice sorcery, and were often referred to as the "Devil's Disciples." Through the use of ecstatic music and dance, it was believed that they led many women and men away from the Church. Perhaps they were using music to facilitate an altered state of consciousness. Thomas de Cantimpre told a story of one *jongleur* who "caused young men and women to dance in circles whenever he played. One evening, when he began playing . . . the Devil himself appeared, dancing before him."

Misa Transgendered or gynandrous deity originating in Phrygia, later adopted by practitioners of the ELEUSINIAN and Orphic Mysteries of Greece, the former focusing on the goddesses DEMETER and PERSEPHONE, the latter said to have been founded by ORPHEUS. Misa was associated in classical antiquity with many deities, including CYBELE and DIONYSUS. In the Eleusinian rites, Misa was depicted as a daughter of the goddess BAUBO.

Mishima Yukio (1925-1970) Japanese writer, athlete, warrior, and mystic. From early childhood – as he relates in his roughly autobiographical novel *Confessions of a Mask* (1949) – until his death in 1970, Mishima linked homoerotic desire to athletics, war, SADOMASOCHISM, an archetypal struggle between transgenderism and ultra-masculinism, martyrdom, and transcendence. Primarily influenced by Catholicism and the Buddhist-based tradition of BUSHIDO, the "way of the Samurai," as expressed in the *HAGAKURE*, Mishima recalls in *Confessions* that he experienced his first ejaculation upon observing a reproduction of Guido Reni's (1575-1642) painting of SAINT SEBASTIAN. "The arrows have eaten into the tense, fragrant, youthful flesh" he writes, "and are about to consume his body from within with flames of supreme agony and ecstasy." A short time before his ritual suicide and murder, when he and his beloved Masakatsu Morita committed *seppuku* and were beheaded by a comrade as a form of political protest against the increasing westernization of Japan, Mishima posed as St Sebastian, his handsome, nearly naked, muscular body pierced with arrows. For Mishima, the ultimate aesthetic experience, as well as the ultimate spiritual experience, was to be found in the encounter of male beauty and death. As he wrote of Sebastian, "was not such beauty as his a thing destined for death? . . . His was not a fate to be pitied . . . [It was] a fate that might even be called radiant."

Mithuna (or **Maithuna**) In Hinduism and in TANTRA, a coupling, involving either symbolic or actual sexual union, with the purpose of inducing spiritual embodiment and/or enlightenment. While *mithuna* are usually comprised of one "masculine" and one "feminine" individual, these need not be anatomical males or females. Many *mithuna* are comprised of two males, with one taking the "masculine" and the other the "feminine" role. These roles are typically associated with Hindu deities. Hence two males may join in a *mithuna* representing the male deities MITRA and VARUNA, with Mitra and his representative being considered masculine and Varuna and his representative being considered feminine. A similar *mithuna* occurs between the male representatives of AGNI, the fire and the feminine, and of SOMA, semen and the masculine. The male taking the masculine role is often the AGNIDHRA or *hotr* priest, while the one taking the feminine role is the NESTR or *adhvaryn* priest.

Miti The wife of Big RAVEN, she is a Koryak deity associated with transgendered shamans. In one tale, Miti transforms herself into a man by creating a phallus from a stone hammer.

Mitra-Varuna The male Hindu gods Mitra and Varuna conjoined. The name "Mitra" means "companion" and is akin to MITHUNA, referring to a couple, often carrying sexual meaning. Together, Mitra and Varuna are described as "handsome, young, shining, sunlike and terrible." They uphold the law, encourage discipline and bravery, heal the sick, and help persons to attract lovers. In the Varunapraghasa ritual, Mitra-Varuna represents an androgynous figure as well as an implicit or symbolic homoerotic active-receptive union, or possibly a male/male-to-female transgender union. In this union, or *mithuna*, Mitra takes the "active" role, while Varuna takes the "receptive" role. They are represented by the AGNIDHRA and NESTR priests, respectively.

Moche People of ancient Peru, c. 500 BCE-1000 CE. The Moche were master architects, constructing great

pyramidal temples in honor of the Moon Goddess and other deities. They were likewise masters of the arts of weaving, pottery, and metallurgy. Their concern with the afterlife paralleled that of the Egyptians; funerals were costly and graves cluttered with sacred staffs and stirrup-spout vessels. These vessels, which normally contained *chica* (a beverage resembling beer), were ceremonial in nature, portraying religious scenes, from shamanic healing to sex magic. Many of the vessels were representations of the penis, the user necessarily imitating the act of fellatio if he wished to drink from the vessel. Others represented couples of the same and different genders engaging in cultic eroticism. One such vessel depicts a person in a bird mask and costume pouring a liquid from a jar between the legs of what appears to be a male-male couple engaged in ritualized sexual intercourse. This couple lies under a temple-like structure and canopy. Beside them is an iguana and another masked, costumed figure receiving the liquid or praying. The man on the bottom or underneath wears attire that is said to symbolize the shaman, including a helmet of catskin and a belted garment of snake skin. The male on top wears a great headdress with giant feathers decorating a similar helmet. These vessels are important to us not only because they suggest a Moche way of weaving together the elements of homoeroticism and the sacred but also, because they were deposited in graves, indicate that the Moche may have believed that the homoerotically inclined, including shamans, would continue this existence in the next life.

Mohini In the beginning of time, that is, at the time of the Churning of the Ocean, according to Hinduism, the gods and demons were arguing over which of them would have the first sip from a great chalice of nectar that had suddenly appeared on the surface of the primordial ocean. In the midst of their argument, one of the demons managed to steal the chalice. Then, suddenly, a beautiful woman with long, flowing, raven hair and wearing a shimmering, translucent blouse, a scarlet skirt, and a veritable treasure-chest of jewelry, appeared out of nowhere and charmed the demon into giving her the chalice. He did so, and she promptly granted the gods a taste of the nectar of immortality, *amrta*. Then, just as suddenly, both the beautiful woman and the chalice of nectar vanished. The beautiful woman was none other than the god VISHNU, assuming the transgendered form of Mohini. Accounts vary as to whether Vishnu undergoes complete gender metamorphosis when becoming Mohini or instead dresses in feminine attire, while remaining a male. In contemporary terms, Vishnu-Mohini is alternately perceived as a transsexual and as a drag queen. The name Mohini, however, signifying "delusion," "illusion," or "disguise," suggests the latter. Some say that when the god SHIVA learned of Mohini's true identity, he asked Vishnu what wish he would have granted in return for his having protected the magical nectar from being consumed by the demons, to which Vishnu replied, "I fell in love with you while playing that part; now I want you to embrace me." Others say that Shiva had fallen deeply in love with Mohini when she first appeared, and that he pleaded with Vishnu to take on the persona once more. Accounts vary as to whether Vishnu assumed the form of Mohini or remained in male form as the two deities united in a passionate embrace. The other gods, it is said, pondered "in their hearts how the two gods, Hari [another name of Vishnu] and Ishvara [i.e. Shiva] could have entered into one." They then beheld a miraculous sight: the phallus of Shiva, lying on Vishnu's heart. From the union of Vishnu-Mohini and Shiva, the child HARIHARA was born. In the worship of the god KRISHNA and also in that of the goddess BAHUCHARAMATA, served by the transgendered HIJRAS, strikingly similar tales are told, except that in these it is Krishna who takes the role of Shiva, while Harihara is called by the alternate name of ARAVAN.

Mojing Dang The "Rubbing Mirror Party" was founded in Guangdong Province (Canton) in or near the seventeenth century CE, where it had first been called the "Ten Sisters." Founded by a Buddhist NUN, the women who comprised its membership resisted heterosexual marriage and participated in rites of same-sex UNION. By the nineteenth century, the organization had been renamed the Mojing Dang. It was still in existence in Shanghai in 1925.

Molly Traditions of "womanish" men can be traced in England to pre-Christian rites such as those of the Celtic feast of Samhain, roughly synonymous with Halloween, and the rite of the Hooden Horse, which includes a male transvestite carrying a broom. When the molly subculture of transgendered, homoerotically inclined males flowered in eighteenth-century England, accusations of paganism – and of Catholicism ("Papistry") – were hurled at the mollies. The rise of the molly subculture was often attributed, in texts like *Satan's Harvest Home* and *Plain Reasons for the Growth of Sodomy*, to institutions such as taverns and theaters. Masques and operas, as decadent spectacles reviving pagan symbols and ceremonies in public, were especially condemned as encouraging molly behavior. Most disturbing to the reactionaries of the day, however, was the emergence of the molly house. The molly houses, such as the famous Mother Clap's and Bevell's molly club, were more than dance bars and whorehouses; indeed, like today's community centers, they also provided a place for mollies to discuss politics, participate in religious ceremonies, musical activities, and sexual entertainments. This kind of socialization also encouraged the use of *polari*, a linguistic code employed primarily by marginal persons linked to the realms of the theater, naval

ports, and homoeroticism. Molly houses further served as ritual spaces in which the mollies, and those who visited them, performed rites forbidden to them by the Church. Rituals included ceremonies of same-sex unions and mock birthing rituals. Weddings took place in the "marrying room" or "the chapel," a room especially set aside for this purpose. Ordained clergymen (such as John CHURCH) sometimes performed the services. These same-sex marriage ceremonies were a mixture of CAMP and seriousness, at once mocking the institution of marriage and solemnizing the relationship of the two men. The ceremony ended with the couple's having intercourse in a room decorated for the occasion. One rite, which took place around 1728, involved two mollies, a blacksmith nicknamed "Moll Irons" and a molly who was a butcher. They were attended by two bridesmaids, "Princess Seraphina," another butcher, and "Miss Kitten." The mock birthing rite seems to have been one of the most important rituals performed during an elaborate CARNIVALESQUE celebration called "Festival Nights." The molly "mother-to-be" sat in a birthing chair and was attended by a midwife and helper, who often had names like "Mrs May," "Madam Blackwell," and "Aunt England." The rite culminated with the birth of the "infant, a doll or sometimes a great hunk of cheese [and] who was christened by a mock bishop wearing a mitre." Following the eighteenth century, the mollies took the second name of "Margery", and by the advent of the early twentieth century, the terms "molly-dyke" and "margery" were being employed by lesbian women to describe those who played femme (rather than butch) roles in role-defined relationships.

Moon In Euro-western ASTROLOGY, this celestial body governs birth, dreams, feminine mysteries, inspiration, magic, meditation, motherhood, travel, and visions. According to *The Book of the Secrets*, attributed to Albertus Magnus (1205-1280), persons ruled by the Moon, that is, born under the sun sign of CANCER, will tend to behave in a "feminine" manner regardless of genital anatomy. Figures associated with the Moon and with gender and/or sexual variance include: ARTEMIS, DIONYSUS, Elleggua, ERZULIE, GANESHA, GANYMEDE, HECATE, ISIS, KHONSU, MAWU-LISA, Nana Buruku, NEITH, and SOMA. In one of the earliest works of science-fiction/fantasy, *True History*, the Greek writer Lucian (c. 120-c. 180) told of a journey to the moon, which was inhabited entirely by man-loving men who gave birth to children through the calves in their legs. In China, where the Moon is considered "yin" (roughly speaking, feminine), the phrase "admiring the full moon," according to W. Eberhard (1986), "refers to a homosexual's bottom." The Islamic poet Ibrahim Ibn Saul wrote of himself and a male beloved: "Like a jealous guardian, the moon on the horizon / watched over our playfulness . . . / and we kissed the breast of the moon." Envisioning the moon as an androgynous being, the Spanish poet Federico García LORCA linked it to the classical divinities Artemis, Dionysus, and Ganymede. In her 1933 poem "Would She Vanish, Kissed?" Elsa GIDLOW compares her female lover to the moon: "She glimmers with light / Like a moon. / . . . She is the moon's ghost."

Moonstone   Stone precious to the Greco-Roman goddess ARTEMIS/DIANA.

Moraga, Cherrie (1952-)   Chicana woman-loving poet, playwright, acting instructor, and director whose works frequently intermingle same-sex desire and spirituality, especially folk Catholicism, as exemplified by the figure of the Virgen de Guadalupe. Moraga's poetic prose work "La Ofrenda" ("The Offering") concerns the narrator's love for a woman named Tiny/Tina, who ultimately dies of breast cancer. Moraga, in depicting their lovemaking, evokes images of both Mesoamerican Shamanism and the Catholic rite of Holy Communion. "So, I put my hands inside her. I did. I put them all the way inside her and like a fuckin' shaman I am working magic on her . . . Tiny, Tina who stood in front of me in the first holy communion line smells like fucking copal." The story ends with the narrator performing an *ofrenda* to Tina/Tiny: "I burn copal. / Her name rising up with the smoke, / dissolving into the ash morning sky."

Moreau, Gustave (1826-1898)   Homoerotically or bisexually inclined French Symbolist painter profoundly inspired by the mystic Edouard Schuré (1841-1929), who believed that in each epoch of humankind, *illuminati* (divinely inspired persons) appear to guide us into the next era. Schuré, also holding Moreau in the highest regard, named him one of the "Great Initiates" of all time. Many of Moreau's works subtly depict the interrelationship of androgyny or transgenderism, same-sex desire, and the spiritual or mythic; these include *Les Chimères* (*The Chimeras*), *Les Licornes* (*The Unicorns*), and *Sappho*. Of Moreau's work, M. Praz (1963) writes, "Moreau's figures are ambiguous . . . lovers look as though they were related, brothers as though they were lovers, men have the faces of virgins, virgins the faces of youths . . . [The] most exalted figure [of Moreau's art is] the Androgyne."

Moret, Alfonso (1954-)   Gay artist, educator, and practitioner of the Yoruba-diasporic religion of Santería of African, French, Spanish, and Cherokee heritage. Reared in the vicinity of Los Angeles and receiving an MA in Visual Arts from the University of California at San Diego, it was when he was living in Santa Fe, New Mexico, that he began to focus on his spirituality. Commencing with the TAROT cards, he was eventually drawn to Santería, by way of an installation art piece, an altar to his ancestors and to

loved ones who had died of AIDS-related illness. This ALTAR/art installation, titled *A House of Spirits*, was constructed as a house with church windows, inside which was a collage of Catholic, African-diasporic, and Native American ritual paraphernalia as well as white (artificial) doves from which streamers of bright colors representing the major deities, or *orishá*, of the Yoruba-diasporic pantheon hung. "The making of this altar," Moret relates, "was what drew me further into the religion of Santería and encouraged me to further explore my cultural values as an Afro-Latino gay man." When interviewer Jaime Cortez of *A La Brava: A Zine of Queer Raza Spirit* asked Moret what particular role he might play in the religion, Moret replied: "I feel I am responsible for working with ancestors. I've contacted an ex-lover who died of AIDS. I never used to believe that he had really died because his family wouldn't let me see the body, and one day, he come back to me to say good-bye, in the form of golden light. He took me in his arms and said I shouldn't be sad. The other day I was preparing my Bóveda (water altar), and my dead grandfather suddenly appeared . . . I ask my ancestors to be with me and support me and guide me, and they manifest themselves and teach me."

Morgaine of the Fairies   In British folklore, an Amazonian sorceress, typically depicted as evil in terms of her relationship to King Arthur. Of Fairy blood, Morgaine's roots may be traced to ancient Celtic goddesses of the sea and of death and regeneration, especially to the Morriggu, a trinity of battle goddesses. Morgan's sacred attribute or familiar is the crow. In Marion Zimmer Bradley's brilliant retelling of the Arthurian legends, *The Mists of Avalon* (1982), she is a fairy and priestess of the Goddess who shares an intimate relationship with Raven, also a priestess. Bradley writes, "Raven's fingers covered her [Morgaine's] lips, in the old gesture of silence; she came to Morgaine's side, bent over and kissed her. Without a word, she threw off her long cloak and lay down at Morgaine's side, taking her in her arms . . . again she was in the shadows of the fairy country, held close in the arms of the lady."

Morgan, Ffiona (1941-)   Describing herself as a "wild Welsh witchwomon who loves the Goddess and the earth with a passion," Ffiona Morgan, a lesbian Canadian of Welsh heritage now living in the US, is a Dianic Wiccan high priestess. Linked to her devotion to ARTEMIS/DIANA and her practice of Goddess Reverence, Women's Spirituality, and Wicca (or Witchcraft), Morgan is learned in ASTROLOGY and TAROT, as well as in divination, healing, and MAGIC employing crystals (she is the creator of "Magical Crystals"). Her works include the *Daughters of the Moon Tarot* (1984, 1991), *Mysteries of the Goddess* (1995), and the *Goddess Spirituality Book* (1995).

Morris, Mark (1956-) Gay US-born dancer, choreographer, and company director, a number of whose works focus on the life of myth and the spirit. Inspired by Christianity (he was raised as a Presbyterian) as well as by what writer/dancer Joan Acocella refers to as "West Coast pantheism" and by the spiritual crisis brought about by the AIDS epidemic, Morris's spiritually-themed works include *Gloria* (1981), *The Vacant Chair* (1984), *O Rangasayee* (1984), *Lovey* (1985), *Stabat Mater* (1986), *Strict Songs* (1987), *Dido and Aeneas* (1989), *Beautiful Day* (1992), and *Jesu, Meine Freude* (1993). Of these, Strict Songs, a dance that has "angels flying at the end," employs the music of gay composer Lou HARRISON. Acocella writes, in her biography *Mark Morris* (1993), that this dance is accompanied by a musical score that includes performance of water bowls (crossculturally important sacred instruments). The text is "based on Hopi chants and its dancers dressed in the colors of earth, water, and sky, Strict Songs is a 'dance doxology' of the kind that Ted Shawn used to do, except that the religion is not Christianity but West Coast pantheism."

Moth In ancient Greco-Roman symbolism, the moth is named "phallaina," derived from "phallus," with the addition of a feminine ending, suggesting a gynandrous creature. Like the BUTTERFLY, the moth serves as a symbol of the psyche or soul.

Mother of the First Cause Transgendered, or hermaphrodite, hermit of Chinese Taoist legend. Living only upon sunbeams and moonbeams, she (-he) is the mother of the creator deity P'an Hu, who creates the world out of YIN AND YANG.

Mothon Dance performed in honor of the Greek deities including ARTEMIS and DIONYSUS by sailors and the Helots, who were the slave-companions and often lovers of Spartan youths. It is also related to the KORDAX and sikinnis dances. The mothon was a sensuous dance emphasizing rotation of the hips combined with a sharp thrust of the genital area. It was accompanied by bawdy songs, quite possibly of a homoerotic nature.

Mountain Person (also **a vial y xa'**) Among the Maricopa people of Arizona (related to yet in conflict with the Yuma), a TWO-SPIRIT (third gender or transgendered, often homoerotically inclined) holy being dwelling in Sierra Estrella Mountain. For this reason, the mountain was usually referred to as *a vial y xa'*, although it was also called, still referring to Mountain Person, "Two Heads" or "Man Lying on His Back." In later times, the figure of Mountain Person appears to have become conflated with that of the Aztec emperor Montezuma (c.1480-1520), perhaps because it was popularly believed that Montezuma was homoerotically inclined. For this reason,

Mountain Person's abode also became known as "Montezuma's Head" and "Montezuma Sleeping." The Maricopa relate that Mountain Person gambles with a two-spirit being of the Yuma people who also dwells in a mountain. They also maintain that a young man who is, or is destined to become, a two-spirit person, may learn of his destiny by dreaming of Mountain Person or of the mountain.

Mujun "*Mujun*," A. Boudhiba (1985) relates, "is the art of referring to the most indecent things, speaking about them in . . . a lighthearted way." While in the world of Islam, *mujun*, in principle, "ought not to go beyond words," beyond the realm of "fantasy," it in fact bridges the realms of the physical and the spiritual, in part by way of eroticism. A multivalent term, *mujun* is associated with madcap behavior, luxury, bohemianism, transgenderism, and same-sex eroticism. *Mujun* is a hedonistic celebration of the pantheistic realization that the Divine permeates all life. It is philologically related to JINN, a fairy-like spirit, which is itself related to AL-JINK, referring to gender variant, or transgendered, homoerotically inclined males. Culturally speaking, *mujun* refers to the bohemian subculture of the Arabic world, that which Hakim Bey (fl. late twentieth century) might name a "TAZ – a Temporary Autonomous Zone." Boudhiba describes it thus: "Arab civilization integrated *mujun* as much as faith. The cities had in their suburbs or in the surrounding countryside highly frequented pleasure gardens, with open-air cabarets and cafes." In the contexts of both *mujun* and Sufism, the cabaret, cafe, or tavern is at once an actual site and a temple, the symbol of a mystery. The universe is itself "intoxicated," existing in a permanent state of "unfolding, unveiling." In the tavern of *mujun*, one comes to understand that wine and Sufi contemplation of the beloved (SHAHED *bazi*) are at once triggers to activate an altered state of consciousness and symbols of this mystery. "Do you want a guided tour / of the Mecca of Love?" the thirteenth-century poet Fakroddin Ibrahim al-Iraqi asks; "Come, sit in the tavern." "The whole universe is His [i.e. God's] winehouse," writes Shabestari; "the heart of every atom is His winecup." "These taverns," Boudhiba continues, "were places where many kinds of pleasure were served up without shame . . . Singers, dancers . . . pleasure-seeking young fellows, homosexuals of both sexes, taught the art of pleasure, without . . . hindrance . . . *mujun* was an *ars vitae*, a permanent carpe diem." In the milieu of *mujun*, "homosexuality, so violently condemned by Islam, could be . . . widely practiced among both men and women." Among the chief expressions of homoeroticism occurring in the taverns of *mujun* were those linked to the *sama'*, the "spiritual concerts" of Sufism, which were frequently held there.

Mukasa   Supreme deity of the Baganda of the vicinity of Victoria Nyanza Lake in Uganda, comparable to the Rainbow serpent DAMBALLAH of the pantheon of Vodou. A god of abundance, his priests include women who, by way of embodiment by Mukasa are spoken of in terms of a "marriage," undergo gender metamorphosis, expressed in the adoption of masculine attire and behavior.

Mukhannath (pl. **Mukhannathun**)   Transgendered male, homoerotically inclined musicians and dancers of Arabic, pre-Islamic culture. They have been described as an "effeminate class who dyed their hands and affected the habits of women." The *mukhannathun* appear to have served the Arabian goddess AL-LAT, in her aspect of Moawallidah, "She Who Brings Forth." The most renowned *mukhannath* was the musician TUWAIS. As ritual musicians, the mukhannathun sang and danced employing tambourines, aulos-like reed aerophones and finger cymbals. Their ritual performance helped trigger an altered state of consciousness, in which they delivered prophecies.

Mule   In Medieval and Renaissance European ritual magic, an animal symbolic of male gender variance, linked specifically to eunuchs and castrati.

Muret, Marc-Antoine (1526-1585)   Homoerotically inclined Humanist philosopher imprisoned in 1553 for sodomy. While his friends obtained his release, after which he fled for Italy, his lover Luc Menge Fremiot was burned at the stake.

Murphy, Brian (1970-   )   Performer and master of the art of body piercing who self-identifies as an "infected faggot." Murphy, who lives in San Francisco in the mid-1990s, is in a sense representative of many "post-Stonewall" queer-identified persons. While intensely spiritual, he finds little sustenance in the New Age movement, which he perceives as a futile attempt to ignore the shadow dimension of life. He discovers inspiration rather in the "death spirits" of Tibetan Buddhism. His spiritual practice takes the forms of body art and performance art linked to SADOMASOCHISM. As a member of a queer performance troupe, Retarded Whore Productions, which performs at "Club JESUS," he and his fellow performers create tableaus including mock crucifixions and mock human sacrifices, in part to shock their audiences into taking responsibility for their lives – and their deaths. While this may seem hypocritical or paradoxical to some, Murphy explains that this form of theatrical expression has aided him in ceasing to use drugs. Like many other queer persons, he keeps an altar for loved ones who have died of AIDS-related illness. Believing that we must accept not only death but also the pain, suffering, and horror often accompanying it, rather than focusing

solely on "going toward the light," Murphy states in a nonchalant yet deadly serious manner, "It's OK to choose or even will [one's] death."

Musaeus   Among the Greeks, either a master and lover (*erastes*) or pupil and beloved (*eromenos*) of ORPHEUS. Musaeus was thought to be able to heal the sick with his MUSIC.

Mushroom   Stir-fried mushrooms were symbolic in seventeenth-century northern China of longevity and immortality as well as male same-sex coupling.

Music, Ancient Near Eastern and Mediterranean
The interrelationship of music, the sacred, same-sex intimacy, and transgenderism may be traced to antiquity. Many deities give expression to this interrelationship, including ARTEMIS/DIANA, CYBELE, DIONYSUS, HECATE, HERMES (who invented the seven-stringed lyre to give to his beloved AMPHION), INANNA/ISHTAR, ISIS, KOTYS, and ORPHEUS (whose music was known for its healing and magical powers), as do figures including the AMAZONS and the COURETES, the musician-priests and priestesses of the above-mentioned deities, historical musicians (particularly SAPPHO), musical instruments, musical modes, and even astrological discourses. The transgendered male priest/esse/s of Isis employed hand-clapping, CYMBALS, clappers and the sistrum as they sang magical incantations to encourage the rising of the Nile and as they participated in dance-dramas performed on the river. The transgendered male priest/esse/s of Isis were also skilled in the art of ritual wailing. The ASSINNU, KURGARRU, and other transgendered male priest/esse/s of Inanna/Ishtar were renowned as composers of hymns, lamentations, and incantations, which they chanted in the Emesal dialect of Sumerian, a dialect reserved for women and gender variant men. They were especially known for their laments, called *balag*, which were accompanied by the *balag*-instrument (according to some, a harp; to others, a drum), the *zinnitu* (a two-stringed lute), and metal clappers. Some of these laments were more specifically referred to as *inhu*, connoting the melancholy song of the *ursanu* bird. Priestesses of Artemis/Diana employed swords and shields as percussive instruments to accompany their sacred circle dances performed around sacred trees at Ephesus. Women devoted to Artemis also played *crembala*, bronze castanets. Timotheus, the musican of Miletos (c. 450-c.360 BCE), is said to have composed the hymns of consecration for the temple of Diana at Ephesus. His music was in the Ionian mode and as such was associated with softness and effeminacy. The hymns to Diana he is said to have composed were called *upingi* and were sung by antiphonal choirs who were accompanied by stringed instruments, tuned triangles and *auloi*. Amazons, who are associated with the worship of

Artemis, are depicted as playing the *salpinx*. This was a trumpet made of brass and/or of horn and played with a mouthpiece, reserved for military and religious ceremonies. An Attic black-figure vase depicts an Amazon playing the salpinx while riding a horse. The BAPTAI, male transgendered priests of Kotys, played flutes and bronze cauldrons covered with hides, while the kindred SEMNOTATOI priests of Hecate led "choruses of children in singing hymns to Hecate." Devotees of Dionysus, including transgendered and same-sex inclined individuals, played the cithara and joined together in performing the dithyramb, a musical and theatrical rite, in the god's honor. The GALLI of Cybele were noted for their unusual vocal style, which blended falsetto and a nasal technique of vocal production combined with ululation to produce the *rigelos ulagmos*, or "shuddering yelp." Their music was described as blending an extreme use of cacaphony (musical "noise") of vocal and instrumental sounds with songs and chants to honor and invoke the Goddess, for the purpose of entering into ecstatic states and to facilitate prophesying, healing, and working magic. The *galli* favored the timbrel, or tympanum, a large circluar drum which symbolized Cybele as the center of the earth. They also employed bronze cymbals and *krotala*. The concave-shaped cymbal was, like the tympanum, an important symbol in Cybele's worship, signifying the cup from which the bounty of the Goddess is drunk. "I have eaten from the tympanum," the *galli* would chant, "I have drunk from the cymbal." As composers they wrote hymns to the Goddess in their special "galliambic" meter. The Couretes, associated with the cult of Cybele, differed from the galli in being warrior-like, but resembled them in engaging in homoeroticism and in celebrating the Goddess with cacophonous music and ecstatic dance. Due in part to the somewhat wider gulf existing today between poetry and music than that which existed in classical antiquity, and in part to the loss of Greek musical compositions, many of us tend to think of SAPPHO (b. c. 630/610 BCE) as a poet rather than as a singer of lyrical compositions. Yet in her own time, Sappho was renowned as a composer of lyrics, a musician, a singer, and a music instructor. At her THIASOS at MYTILENE on the island of Lesbos, she led young women in musically praising Aphrodite and other deities. She was especially renowned for her love lyrics which honored the bond between the physical and the spiritual. As one of her fragments contains the term *olisbos*, "leather phallus," it would not appear that she shied away from erotic expression in her work. Her compositions are thought to have been performed by antiphonal choirs. She is said to have played the barbiton, a large lyre with a deep tone used in the worship of Dionysus and Cybele. The barbiton was also considered the proper instrument to employ with the Sapphic dialect and Sapphic stanza. Sappho also mentions the chelys, a lyre made of tortoise shell. Sappho mentions other stringed instruments

including the flute and the Lydian petkis, described as either "harplike" or as similar to the sambyke, a triangle-shaped stringed instrument played with a plectrum. Where musical modes are concerned, the Ionian, Lydian, and the Phrygian were associated with Goddess Reverence, Dionysian ecstasy, transgenderism, and sexual variance. Bearing such associations, they were condemned by many, especially by philosophers and theologians who considered them to be capable of disrupting the moral order. In astrological texts written during the first five centuries of the Common Era, gender variance, same-sex inclination, and musicianship were often linked. For example, those males possessing Mars and Venus in either Aries or Capricorn were destined to become "perverts (*cinaedi*) who serve in temple choirs," while males having Mercury and Venus in the tenth house might well become "musical composers . . . destined for the stage or public performances" who will also "be lovers of boys, involved in licentious vices."

Music, Contemporary Popular (including Folk, Jazz, New Age, World Beat)   The contemporary gay liberation movement – like the contemporary women's movement – arose in the era of the "flower children," a fact downplayed by many activists in the 1990s. This was an era of folk music, radical protest, erotic experimentation, and spiritual exploration. Among the first albums to emerge from the gay movement following the Stonewall revolt were folk-rock albums bearing these themes. They included Michael Cohen's *What Did You Expect?* (1973), an album of love and rebellion including a haunting rendition of Leonard Cohen's magical poem "Bitterfeast," which depicts a lover transforming a beloved into various animals, and Steven Grossman's *Caravan Tonight* (1974) which, in the title song, employs a Biblical metaphor to conjure an image of the lover's arms as an oasis. "And if the freedom of heart embraces / Is nothing but a vision in the sand," sings Grossman, "I'll be your oasis / I'll be your promised / Your promised land." Among the first contemporary lesbian musicians to focus on spirituality in her work was Chris Williamson. Songs on her album *The Changer and the Changed* (1975) included lyrics such as "Born of the earth, a child of God / . . . I will fold you in my arms like a white winged dove / Shine in your soul, your spirit is crying" ("Sister") and "When you open your life to the living, all things come spilling in on you. / And you're flowing like a river, the Changer and the Changed" ("Waterfall"). In "Song of the Soul," she sings, "Open mine eyes, illumine me / Spirit divine" and in "Wild Things" "It's the spirit of the wild things / That you love so much to see. / But wild, wild things can turn on you / And you got to set them free." As the 1970s progressed, folk music and the culture it had nurtured and been nurtured by were, in the main, discarded by the gay male communities of the US and elsewhere, largely exchanged for disco and its concomitant culture. Lesbian-feminists, however, did not seem as enchanted as their male counterparts were with either the new music or disco culture, instead choosing to preserve, refine, and amplify the music and culture of folk/folk-rock, which seemed to better suit lesbian-feminist political and spiritual concepts. This divergence in musical taste played a key role in terms of the development of what we might now call "Queer-Spiritual" music. Basically, it resulted in the production of many spiritually-oriented albums by lesbian musicians and very few such albums by gay men, other than Christian-based choruses and those few gay male artists associated with the anti-sexist men's movement (of the "pre-Robert BLY" era). Chief among these latter were Charlie Murphy and BLACKBERRI. When spiritual messages – perhaps "transpersonal" or "empowering" might serve as more appropriate terms here – were communicated in disco songs, they tended to be voiced by pro-queer, heterosexual female divas rather than by queer people themselves, or else by closeted queer men. This is not to criticize the women performers who have supported us, but rather a culture and a specific industry that has forced queer people who wish to succeed to remain in the closet. The authors of this encyclopaedia, like so many others, revere Judy Garland, Grace Jones, Patti LaBelle, Liza Minelli, Diana Ross, Barbra Streisand, Tina Turner, and others who have embraced us when others have denigrated us. One notable exception to this rule was the African-American performer Sylvester. While some might suggest that he was closeted concerning his sexuality, he rarely if ever attempted to conceal his gayness, or his transgendered identity, in live performances, especially those occurring in San Francisco. Famous for his "You Make Me Feel Mighty Real," revivified by performance artist/chanteuse Sandra BERNHARD, Sylvester's career began in the Palm Lane Church of God and Christ in South Los Angeles. It progressed through involvement with the Cockettes (a group of San Francisco genderfuck drag queen performance artists, some of whom were skilled in the divinatory and magical arts), and culminated in the discos of San Francisco's gay community. The emphasis on spirituality in lesbian-centered music and its lack of emphasis in queer male-centered music has continued into the 1990s. Perhaps, as celebrated, now openly gay musicians like BOY GEORGE and Elton John begin to incorporate spiritual themes in their music, as the latter does in his exquisite rendition of Bernie Taupin's "Blessed" on the 1995 release Made in England, and as music videos begin to incorporate images of spirit by artists like Pierre and Gilles, this tendency may shift. Where lesbian and bisexual female music is concerned, the shift may be seen more in terms of music genres than in content, with performers like Melissa Etheridge, k.d. lang, the Indigo Girls, and Girls in the Nose (and many other semi-closeted individuals and groups) venturing into rock and "alternative" music; with these more mainstream women performers, however, there seems to be a de-emphasis on the spiritual dimension of life somewhat mirroring the earlier tendency among queer male musicians. We may roughly classify contemporary popular queer-themed music and music by queer performers into eight general categories of spiritual source of inspiration. Many artists cross and blend these categories in their work, and it should also be noted that most of these categories may be subsumed under the umbrella categories of "New Age" and "World Beat." They are: (1) Goddess Reverence, Wicca, and related pre-Christian-based and Neopagan traditions, including the Radical Faeries; (2) African and African-diasporic traditions (like Santería and Vodou) and Shamanism; (3) Judaism, including QABBALAH; (4) Christianity; (5) reaction to the Religious Right; (6) Hinduism and related traditions (as TANTRA and the chakras); (7) general spiritual or transformative themes, often focusing on empowerment and liberation; and (8) AIDS-centered healing and empowering themes. Musical works inspired by the first category include: most if not all of the albums of Kay GARDNER; Libana's (some of whose members are woman-loving) A Women's Choir (1979), A Circle Is Cast (1986), and Fire Within (1990); Charlie Murphy's (with Jami Sieber) Catch the Fire (1981) which includes "Gay Spirit," "Double Love," "Under Capricorn," and "Burning Times" (re-released in 1993 on Rumors of the Big Wave, Burning Times); Jana Runnalls's Ancestral Drum (1985), which includes chant, flute, drums, and dulcimer and features invocations to ARTEMIS/DIANA, Kore (PERSEPHONE), KALI, and TIAMAT, and Who Gave Birth to the Universe (1988) with Rosemary Schonfeld, together as the British lesbian duo Ova; Heartsinger Sings Ron Lambe's Songs of Love and Nature, with Stephen Klein, Piano (1988); the queer male British group Coil's Love's Secret Domain (1991), inspired by the ritual magick of Aleister CROWLEY; Lunacy's (Sparky T. Rabbit and Greg Johnson) Hand of Desire (1992); Terry Garthwaite's AffiRhythms (1992), vocal and percussion, including "Sacred Within" and "Mother Earth"; Karen Beth's To Each of Us (n. d.), which includes "Full Moonlight Dance"; Jami Sieber's Lush Mechanique (1995), electric cello; Susan Herrick's Soul Chant (1994); and Jennifer Berezan's In the Eye of the Storm (1988), which features Charlie Murphy's "Burning Times," and She Carries Me (1995), which has been described as a "highly original weaving of gorgeous layers of vocals and instrumentation a powerfully evocative and meditative piece of healing music to the Goddess in her many forms," featuring as a special guest the acclaimed actress Olympia Dukakis reciting the "Charge of the Goddess." Also noteworthy here is lesbian-identified Kathryn Warner's contribution to the group Desert Wind, whose albums, employing electronic keyboards, flute, and voice, dating primarily from the 1990s, include Gaia, Earth Goddess,

Kali Ma: Dances of Transformation, and *Return to the Goddess: Chants and Song*, which includes Z BUDAPEST's "From the Goddess." While not lesbian-identified, another duo should be mentioned in this context due both to their drawing upon lesbian spiritual sources and their great popularity among lesbians as well as among queer men allied with the Radical Faeries: Ruth Barrett and Cyntia Smith, whose works have been described as "woman-oriented ballads, with themes of goddesses, magic, ritual, witchery. Melodies are traditional, with vocal harmonies, dulcimers" and other traditional instruments. *Aeolus* (1981) includes songs like "The Mermaid" and "Every Woman Born", the latter written to celebrate the birthday of Z Budapest and to commemorate a Take Back the Night March in Los Angeles, while *Music of the Rolling World* (1982) focuses on seasonal celebrations as well as the assumption of transgendered identity. *A Dulcimer Harvest* (1991) includes "Faerie's Love Song," while *The Heart is the Only Nation* (1993) features "Apples of Avalon" and "The May Queen Is Waiting." In 1987, Barrett also performed with F. Artemis Flowers in *Invocation to Free Women* with sources including STARHAWK, Z Budapest, and Shekinah Mountainwater as well as African-diasporic spiritual traditions. Musical works inspired by African, African-diasporic, and shamanic traditions include: Blackberri's *Finally* (1981); Casselberry-DuPrée's *City Down* (1986), which features an "Opening Elegba (LEGBA)/OBATALA" and *Hot Corn in the Fire* (1994), which includes the lesbian-gay liberation anthem "The Last Pioneers" by Steven Grossman; Barbara Borden's *All Hearts Breathing: Drumming from the Source to the Core* (1990); Melanie DeMore's Share *My Song* (1992), which includes "Lady of Peace" and "I Hear the Mother Calling"; Ubaka Hill's *ShapeShifters* (1995), drum and chant, including "Motherbeat" and "If the Drum is a Woman"; Carolyn Brandy's *Skin Talk* (1995); and Linda Tillery's (with the Cultural Heritage Choir) *Good Time, A Good Time* (1995), which features a chant to the Yoruba-diasporic maternal sea goddess YEMAYA. While Sweet Honey in the Rock is not a lesbian or bisexual-centered group, its women-centered spiritual music is extremely popular in the lesbian and other queer communities of the US and has inspired many queer-identified artists, including writers, visual artists, and performers as well as musicians. An often-quoted lyric from Bernice Johnson Reagon's "Every Woman" reads, "Every woman who has ever loved a woman / You oughta stand up and call her name / Mama – sister – daughter – lover." Sweet Honey's chant "Breaths" based on an African poem has taken on new meaning for many of those who have lost loved ones to AIDS-related illness and it has been performed in this context on numerous occasions. Musical works inspired by Judaism and the Qabbalah include Kathryn Warner's contribution to Desert Wind's *Shekina, Hebrew Goddess* (1993), and The Klezmatics's

Jews with Horns (1996), Jewish klezmer music with lesbian fiddler Alicia Svigalis and gay male lead vocalist and accordionist Lorin Sklamberg. Christian-inspired musical works include: the Dallas, Texas-based Turtle Creek Chorale's *Testament* (1992), *Requiem* (1994), and *United We Sing* (1994), the last of these inspired by African-American sacred musics and performed with the male chorus of the First Baptist Church of Hamilton Park and the Women of New Arts Six; and the Boston Gay Men's Chorus's *Visions: Words for the Future* (1994), featuring an arrangement of African-American musician Bobby McFerrin's version of "The Lord Is My Shepherd" (which employs the feminine pronoun for the deity). Musical works responding to the Religious Right include *Lesbian Concentrate* (1977), a response to Anita Bryant's homophobic crusade, with various artists including Linda Tillery, Meg Christian, Teresa Trull, Chris Williamson, Judy Grahn, the Berkeley Women's Music Collective, Gwen Avery, Sue Fink, BeBe K'Roche, Mary Watkins, and Pat Parker; Queer Conscience's *Back to the Other World?* (n. d.), Ron Romanovsky and Paul Phillips's song "Homophobes in Robes" on *Let's Flaunt It!* (1994), and Jallen Rix's "We Have Learned to Hate Each Other" on *The Sacred and the Queer* (1995). Among musical works drawing upon Hinduism and related traditions are Boy George's *The Martyr Mantras* (1990), especially the song "Bow Down Mister," a paean to KRISHNA, and Kay Gardner's *A Rainbow Path* (1984), which interweaves music with meditation upon the *chakras*. In the category of general spiritual or transpersonal themes are Frankie Goes to Hollywood's *Welcome to the Pleasuredome* (1984), The Flirtations's *The Flirtations* (1990), an acapella quintet, this album including a rendition of Sweet Honey in the Rock's "Breaths"; and Grant King's *Let Love Out* (1994) featuring the anthem "Common Ground." Of the growing list of AIDS-centered spiritual- or transpersonal-themed songs and albums, one of the most memorable is Michael Callen's *Legacy* (1995), which includes the anthem "Healing Power of Love" and a haunting rendition of Bernice Johnson Reagon's "They Are Falling All Around Me" performed with Chris Williamson, Holly Near, and John Bucchino. Beyond musicians inspired by these categories are those who, while not emphasizing the sacred in their work in an obvious way, are nevertheless contributing to the Queer Spirit conversation. Exemplary of this type of musical performer is the African-American, openly gay, (often) transgendered Ru Paul, who speaks of his drag in terms of reflecting an awareness of the ancient association of transgenderism, homoeroticism, and the sacred: "Drag is the ultimate in power dressing. When you're in drag . . . you become the God of your imagination, and that's powerful medicine, baby. I'm definitely a ruling diva when I'm in my Goddess Drag . . . My masculinity really comes out when I use my Goddess Drag. With my drag, I encompass both male and female. I

become a microcosm of the whole universe, the yin and
yang, and people pick up on that and are enthralled by the
power." While the canon of Gay Spirit/Queer Spirit,
strongly linked to the canon of Women's Spirituality,
music is gradually increasing in size as well as in artistry, it
is extremely difficult to find the above-mentioned works in
a single venue; in this respect, Ladyslipper Records, based
in North Carolina, performs an invaluable role in
providing this music to its listeners.

Mut Gynandrous or transgendered Egyptian goddess
known as the "Mother of him who begat her", depicted
occasionally as a person having female breasts and a
phallus.

Mwari Among the Shona people of Zimbabwe, the
androgynous supreme being and creator who sometimes
splits into female and male manifestations.

Myrmex Young woman loved by the goddess ATHENA
but later changed by her into an ant after Myrmex claimed

to have invented the plow, which Athena had actually
invented. ZEUS, however, felt pity for Myrmex and so
returned her to human form.

Myrtle In Greek religion or mythology, a sacred
attribute of the god HESPERUS. In 1894, the British poet
and criminologist George Cecil Ives (1867-1950) founded
the ORDER OF CHAERONEA, a secret (proto-) Gay-
Spiritual organization. He chose as one of its chief symbols
a wreath of myrtle, emblematic of glory and strength.

Mytilene (or **Mitylene**) City of the island of LESBOS
symbolic of lesbian desire and love, named after a Libyan
AMAZON general by her sister, Queen Myrene (or
Myrina). The Lesbian poet SAPPHO was reared in
Mytilene. In her "Invocation to Sappho," poet Elsa
GIDLOW beckons "Psappha of Mitylene on / sea-lapped
Lesbos."

N

Na Thu Pen Do Among the Miao of China, the gynandrous or transgendered spirit who rules over all other spirits. Na Thu Pen Do, also guardian of animals, is especially revered by hunters. Considered a great healer, Na Thu Pen Do is believed to be able to end epidemics.

Naarjuk Inuit childlike or youthful divine being conceived as a giant infant of questionable gender, described as "not-man, not-woman" or as "a tiny bit of man and a tiny bit of woman." Naarjuk breathes the breath of life into living creatures and also controls winds and storms. He-she is especially revered by Inuit TWO-SPIRIT shamans, who also honor KANNAALUK, TAQQIQ, and other sacred beings.

Naas, Naassenes, Ophites The Naassene sect or branch of Gnosticism has been described as "an altogether Hellenized Phrygian mystery-community that worships the Mother of the Gods and ATTIS, but at the same time appeals to the Jewish prophets and writers;" moreover, the Naassenes are said to have taken part in the rites of the Roman goddess CYBELE and her consort Attis as well as in their own mysteries. The Naassenes believed in a gynandrous or androgynous deity which they envisioned as a boundless ocean named BYTHOS or The Deep or as an OROBORUS, a SERPENT biting its tail, named Naas or Ophis (hence their appellation as Ophites). They identified the feminine aspect of the godhead with Cybele, ISIS, and DEMETER, while the masculine aspect was identified with the androgynous figure ADAM Aeon. They also spoke of a son-consort of the deity whom they identified with Attis, JESUS Christ, ADONIS, OSIRIS, ENDYMION, and Brimo. It was this being whose destiny it was to stop himself or be stopped from reproducing so that he might pass "from the material condition . . . to the eternal essence" without participating in the cycle of reincarnation. The Naassenes also believed in the Biblical Lord. Naming him Ialdabaoth, they saw him as a cruel tyrant who created Adam and Eve to be his slaves. Naas, taking the role of the serpent in the Garden, granted both Adam and Eve *gnosis*, mystical wisdom, by sexually penetrating them. In their communion rite, Naassenes honored Naas by having a live serpent slither over the consecrated bread and by then passing the serpent to each other as they, in a circle, joined in the "kiss of peace." The Naassenes insisted that if an individual wished to become enlightened and to return to the godhead at the end of his or her life (rather than be reincarnated), he or she must undergo a process by which he or she might become "neither male nor female, but a new creature . . . who reunites the two sexes." In defense of this belief, the Naassenes quoted the words of St Paul: "Therefore, if any one is in Christ, he is a new creation; the old has passed away, behold, the new has come . . . there is neither male nor female; for you are all one in Christ Jesus." For the Naassenes, however, becoming "neither male nor female" did not require ritual castration. Linking castration with circumcision, they again quoted Paul: "For neither circumcision counts for anything, nor uncircumcision, but a new creation," inferring that just as Jesus's sacrifice had rendered circumcision unnecessary, so Attis's sacrifice had rendered castration unnecessary. Still, while the Naassenes did not ritually castrate themselves, male adherents were required to "abstain, as if they were emasculated, from intercourse with a woman." Similarly, female adherents were also to abstain from coitus with males. Again, the Naassenes believed that abstaining from phallic-vaginal intercourse might free one from becoming attached to the "wheel" of generation and mundane existence. In the case of male adherents, such abstention would allow Naas-Cybele-Adam Aeon to recall "the male power of the soul to itself." According to the Naassenes, "the intercourse of woman with man is demonstrated to be exceedingly wicked." With typical idiosyncrasy, they understood Jesus' words "Do not give dogs what is holy . . . do not throw your pearls before swine" to mean that one should abstain from phallic-vaginal intercourse. On the other hand, the Naassenes appear to have approved of masturbation to celebrate the phallus. From the Egyptians, they borrowed the image of the phallic Osiris, while from the Greeks, they appropriated the phallic image of Hermes as depicted on herms. The Naassenes linked these phallic figures with the reborn Attis and Christ, whose phalli had not been employed for procreative purposes but were considered instruments of erotico-spiritual transformations. Like other Gnostics, the Naassenes held that certain Biblical passages were meant to be interpreted in one way by non-mystics and in another, often a reversed or inverted way, by mystics like themselves. Thus, when St Paul spoke in condemnatory terms of women exchanging "natural relations for unnatural" and men giving up "natural relations with women" for "passion for one another . . . committing shameless acts with men," the Naassenes heard something like this: "While same-sex eroticism is to be considered inappropriate behavior when undertaken by non-mystics, for mystics such behavior represents a path to spiritual enlightenment." As Hippolytus relates, "in these words which Paul has spoken they say the entire secret of theirs, and a hidden mystery of blessed pleasure, are comprised." What is more, a certain group of mystical images suggests that Naassene rituals may have included the use of semen, in the form of the "ineffable *alale* ointment" rubbed on the forehead and used as an ingredient in the sacred beverage. Semen was referred to by the Naassenes as the "beauteous seeds of Benjamin," "the water in those fair nuptials which Jesus changing made into wine," and as "the great and ineffable mystery of the Samothracians." The Naassenes allegedly borrowed an image from the Samothracians to express the mystery of fellatio (and perhaps other forms of homoerotic activity), that of two "naked men . . . their pudenda turned upwards as [is the case with] the statue [or herm] of Mercury on Mount Cyllene." In their peculiar, syncretic way, they associated this image of two sexually aroused males, presumably side by side and perhaps facing each other, with the words of Jesus. Hippolytus explains: "the aforesaid images are figures of the primal man, and of that spiritual one that is born again, in every respect of the same substance with that man. This is what is spoken by the Savior: 'If ye do not drink my blood, and eat my flesh, ye will not enter into the kingdom of heaven.'" Of the possible function of cultic homoeroticism among the Naassenes, Lacarriere writes: "for the Gnostics, this act [of anal intercourse, as performed by Naas in the Garden] evidently had the force of example and no doubt certain of them did *also* practice sodomy in the name of the serpent, as a ritual repetition of his first act, a way of opening up the 'passages' of knowledge and thereby unsealing the blind eyes of the flesh . . . no doubt fellatio (a strict enactment of the image of the snake biting its tail) [was also practiced] . . . The term *inversions*, so oddly used by sexologists to designate these . . . erotic practices, would certainly have delighted the Gnostics." Whether or not male Naassenes dressed in women's garments is unclear. It is more likely that they attended rituals wearing simple tunics or nothing at all. According to Hippolytus, they believed that "those who come thither ought to cast off their garments, emasculated through the virginal spirit." Like the *galli* of Cybele, the Naassenes were renowned musicians. Indeed, they described the cosmos in musical terms. As Amygdalus, Naas-Cybele-Adam Aeon was the source of music and hence of all creation. As Syrictas the Piper, Attis was the "harmonious spirit" given birth by the God/dess. A Naassene hymn praising Attis reads: "Whether [Thou art of] the race of Saturn or happy Jupiter, or mighty Rhea [i.e. Cybele], Hail Attis, gloomy mutilation of Rhea. Assyrians style thee thrice-longed-for Adonis, and the whole of Egypt [calls thee] Osiris, celestial horn of the Moon; Greeks denominate [thee] wisdom; Samothracians, venerable Adam; Haemonians,

Corybas; and the Phrygians [name thee] at one time Papa, at another time Corpse, or God, or Fruitless, or Aipolos, or green Ear of Corn that has been reaped, or whom the very fertile Amygdalus produced – a man, a musician."

Nadle (or **Nádleehé, Nadleh**)   Among the Navaho of North America, a TWO-SPIRIT, or third gender, male who often serves in a shamanic and/or artistic capacity. "Nadle" also refers to the legendary ancestor(s) of these persons. The ancestor of the *nadle*, sometimes called Nadleh, taught the people how to plant corn as well as watermelon and squash. He-She also taught them how to make flour, bake bread, and observe agricultural rites. Nadleh is sometimes identified with Kaydestizhi, "Wound in the RAINBOW"; as such she is said to have been created by BEGOCHIDI and is depicted as wearing a rainbow robe. The first *nadle* "invented pottery, the gourd dipper, the metate, the hairbrush, the stirring sticks, and the water jar." Because there is a tradition that a primordial hermaphrodite has to die so that males and females could be born, *nadle* are sometimes associated with death. Nadles, like WINKTES, were thought to be able to heal mental and physical illness and to aid in childbirth through the employment of magical songs.

Namsadang   Korean ritual folk theater form possessing homoerotic, transgendered, and spiritual associations. Until the early twentieth century, these all-male theater troupes could be commonly found traveling the countryside performing traditional ritual entertainments including *sokak*, shamanic music. On arriving at a new village, the *Namsadang* troupe plays loud and boisterous farmer's music to get the attention of the people and permission from the village authorities to perform. This important form of ritualized political and popular theater "appears to have been [the artistic creation of] a homosexual community." *Namsadang*, while rooted in ancient court traditions, has been de-classed and all but outlawed, especially because homosexuality is considered extremely immoral in Confucian society. The troupes perform for food and lodging. The troupes have included forty to fifty males, comprised of a hierarchy of master performers, regular performers, and novices. Each troupe has been further divided into the *sutdongmo* ("butch") and *yodongmo* ("queen"). The head of a *Namsadang* troupe, called the *Kkoktusoe*, has been elected by the *Ddunsoe*, supervisors and expert performers representing different units. Next in rank have been the *Kayol*, junior performers, and finally the novices, called *Ppiri*, who have taken care of the chores. Until the novice has become a *Kayol*, he has performed the transvestite roles and, if so inclined, a sexually receptive role in homoerotic relations. Novices have also been known to engage in prostitution with village men. In the *Namsadang* performance, some sections are particularly rich in folkloric, or religious significance, including the *totbegi* and the *kkoktukaksi norum dolmi* , or puppet show. The *totbegi* emphasizes dance, pantomime, humorous stories, songs and conversations among the stock characters which include parodic religious and transvestite figures including Sannim (or Yangban), an old woman; Ch'wibari, the prodigal; and Mockjung (or Omjung), a Buddhist monk. Although *Namsadang* is no longer a flourishing form, its dances and music are sometimes still performed. As late as 1979 the actor/performer, Yang Do-il, reminisced about leaving home at the age of six to follow a *Namsadang* troupe.

Nanan-bouclou Gynandrous of transgendered *lwa* (deity or spirit) of the Vodou pantheon. M. Deren (1983) describes Nana-bouclou as "both male and female" and as an ancient androgynous Dahomean deity, who even preceded MAWU-LISA. She is the "Great Mother" who includes both female and male in her being. R. Thompson (1983) depicts her/him as a "superlative warrior, utterly fearless." Nanan-bouclou is today considered primarily a *lwa* of herbal medicine. She is linked not only to Mawu-Lisa but also to SILBO-GWETO and to the Yoruba *orishá* Nana Buruku.

Napunsaka "Nonmale," a term used in Hinduism to refer to transgendered or third gender males. Alain Daniélou writes in *While the Gods Play* (1987), "Once a certain level of androgyneity develops in living beings [they are] called . . . nonmale (napunsaka)." "Napunsaka is akin to the terms PRAKRIT-PURUSHA and TRITIYA PRAKRITI.

Narada (dates unknown, may be legendary)   While his existence is controversial, Narada is considered to be one of the seven great Hindu mythical seers, a master of TANTRA, and the composer of several hymns of the Rig Veda as well as several works on music theory. Credited with the invention of the *vina*, he is the *guru* of the celestial musicians and patron of itinerant musicians. Narada once took a bath in a magical pool which caused him to transform into a woman. As such, he married King Taladhuaja and became mother to several sons. One day, the god VISHNU changed him back into a man. Narada had ecome a much wiser person by coming to experience the feelings of both men and women.

Narcissus Young male of Greek mythology renowned for having fallen in love with his own reflection, hence our term "narcissism." Tradition has it that Narcissus not only fell in love with himself but also rejected the love of both men, namely Ameinas and women, namely Echo. Some writers, both ancient and contemporary, argue that he did not realize the object of his affection to be his own reflection, but rather assumed it to be the face of another

young man, a twin or double, reminiscent of the double, homoerotically inclined figure of PLATO's *Symposium*. As social philosopher Herbert Marcuse (1955) observes, "he does not love only himself . . . He does not know that the image he admires is his own." While numerous homoerotically inclined artists have been inspired by Narcissus, including the painter Pierre Yves Tremois, whose nude *Narcissus* (1955) contemplates his twin or reflection in a pool of planets and spermatozoa, and the Spanish poet Federico García LORCA who has written, "I would remain at your verge. / Flower of love. / Narcissus," it is Marcuse who perhaps most profoundly comprehends the young god's archetypal or symbolic meaning. Linking Narcissus to ORPHEUS and DIONYSUS in a paean to "phantasy," which Marcuse views as the opposite of productivity (and specifically capitalism), he writes: "If Prometheus is the culture-hero of toil, productivity, and progress through repression, then . . . [Narcissus, Orpheus, and Dionysus] stand for a very different reality. They have not become the culture-heroes of the Western World: theirs is the image of joy and fulfillment; the voice which does not command but sings . . . the liberation from time which unites man with god, man with nature . . . the opposition . . . between subject and object, is overcome . . . the things of nature become free to be what they are." Narcissus, together with Orpheus, participates in that which Marcuse has termed "the Great Refusal." This act refers to the "refusal to accept separation from the libidinous object (or subject). The refusal aims at liberation, at the reunion of what has become separated." This "Great Refusal," Marcuse clearly states, includes a "protest against the repressive order of procreative sexuality."

Narcissus Flower symbolic of youth, beauty, desire, impermanence, and the cycle of birth, death, and regeneration, known for its intoxicating perfume, associated with the Greek deities NARCISSUS and PERSEPHONE.

Neboutosoualeth Mysterious figure of Greco-Egyptian MAGIC, most probably a goddess of the underworld associated with HECATE and ERESHKIGAL. Neboutosoualeth was invoked in male homoerotic love spells, in Alexandria, Egypt, during the third century CE.

Neith Gynandrous or transgendered creator goddess of Egyptian religion bearing the epithet "father of fathers and mother of mothers." She (-he) was sometimes identified with the god Khnum. Neith was said to have been worshipped in Libya by AMAZONS.

Nemesis Greek goddess of fate and retributive justice, or vengeance, associated with the FURIES. She is depicted as monstrous, further associating her with MEDUSA and the GORGONS. As her name indicates, Nemesis is also the guardian of trees and sacred groves; in this aspect, she is exceedingly beautiful. A shapeshifter, Nemesis may manifest as a female, gynandrous (or transgendered), or male being. Associations of Nemesis with the goddesses ARTEMIS and DICTYNNA may suggest that she bears a lesbian aspect.

Nemien Celtic warrior goddess, according to some the beloved of Badb, another warrior goddess. She forms a trinity with Badb and Macha, a third warrior goddess. She also has a male lover or spouse, the war god Neit (or Nuada). Nemien is said to have invented the caltrop, a Medieval weapon.

Neo-Gothic Movement Inspired by Romanticism and especially by Gothic novels, the Neo-Gothic Movement emerged in the early 1980s. While in many urban centers it reached a pinnacle in the late 1980s, it continues to flourish in certain quarters. Its primary aesthetic, like that of its predecessors, concerns the interface of beauty, the grotesque, eroticism, melancholy, nihilism, death, and the supernatural. Its adherents chiefly wear black, occasionally wear white facial makeup and dye their hair raven black, pierce and tattoo their bodies, read vampire fiction (especially the novels of Anne Rice), listen to the music of Bauhaus, Siouxsie and the Banshees, and other kindred groups, and delight in films like *The Hunger* and *Gothic*. Neo-Gothicism has proven especially appealing to bisexuals or pansexuals and to transgendered or gender-bending individuals. As Linda Howard observes in "The Black and the Velvet: Experiencing the Dark Passion and Mystery of Gothic Androgyny" (1996), Neo-Gothicism represents "an outlaw mentality that encourages the exploration and deconstruction of societally set boundaries . . . From a bisexual standpoint, the gothic/freak subculture is practically unique. Here, bi-eroticism and gender fluidity are the norm, both openly accepted and openly practiced." As exemplary of a Neo-Gothic response to a particular situation, Howard describes how a young man named Magpie dealt with a breakup with a male lover. "Lighting candles all over his room, turning off the lights," Magpie stayed "in his room all weekend listening to dark, depressing music: a proper gothic wake." It is not surprising, however, that many find Neo-Gothicism disturbing, particularly those wishing to deny the certainty of, or else not wishing to romanticize, loss, suffering, and death. Howard suggests, however, that ultimately, the Neo-Gothic aesthetic encourages us not only to celebrate death but also to celebrate being alive: "In its celebration of the senses, it urges us to be sensual, to feel and experience all that we can."

Neptune In Euro-western ASTROLOGY, this planet governs chaos, freedom, idealism, imagination, music, and psychic ability. R. Zoller (1989) suggests that Neptune also governs lesbian desire. Figures associated with Neptune and with gender and/or sexual variance include: AEGEA, LA BALEINE, GRACES, HERA, KANNAALUK, LIMALOA, MERMAIDS, OLOKUN, POSEIDON, SEDNA, LA SIRENE, and YEMAYA.

Nereids Tribe of sea-nymphs, originally fifty in number, said to be the daughters of DORIS and Nereus. The Nereids, dwelling together at the bottom of the sea, appear to have preferred each other's company to that of either mermen or human men, except for an occasional affair. The Nereids were known for their oracular and shapeshifting powers. They were worshipped in ancient Greece, particularly in port cities, and especially by fishermen and SAILORS. Beyond their subtle connection to women-loving women, they were also associated by the ancient Greeks with male couples, including ACHILLES and PATROCLUS. It was said that the Nereids wept when these comrade-lovers met their deaths.

Nestor Warrior in the Trojan War loved by HERACLES. Nestor was the father of ANTILOCHUS. Eloquence and strategic planning are among those qualities for which Nestor is remembered.

Nestr In the Agnicayana rite of Hinduism, the Nestr priest took the receptive or "feminine" role in a ritual MITHUNA, also embodying the man in the left eye, the god Varuna (as his feminine aspect, or SHAKTI, Varuni), the human female (or a person of third sex/gender), and the ewe, as opposed to the AGNIDHRA priest.

Netzach In the Qabbalistic "Tree of Life," the sphere of VENUS (APHRODITE), which ritual magician Aleister CROWLEY associated with female gender variance.

Neuburg, Victor (1883-1940) Poet, critic, and magician. Neuburg was also known as Frater Omnia Vincam in Aleister CROWLEY's magical Order, Argenteum Astrum. Neuburg was both sexual and magical partner to Crowley and remained his lover until 1914. In 1909, Crowley initiated Neuburg into magic during an intense sadomasochistic homoerotic ritual. Neuburg envisioned Crowley as an androgyne, naming him "sweet wizard," "the most obscene god" (i.e. PAN), and "queen." In his poem "The Romance of Olivia Vane," Neuburg wrote: "O thou who hast sucked my soul, lord of my nights and days, / My body, pure and whole, is merged within the ways, / That lead to thee, my queen." In December 1909, in Algeria, the two men engaged in another rite of homoerotic sex MAGIC. During this rite Crowley was anally penetrated by Neuburg, who allegedly became possessed by Pan. Four years later in 1913, Crowley and Neuburg undertook the so-called "Paris Workings," during which they summoned Jupiter (Zeus), Mercury (Hermes), and Pan in order to be provided with material abundance and magical wisdom, especially of an S/M and erotic nature during which Neuburg was whipped, cut, and bound with chains. As a result of the Paris Workings, Neuburg deserted Crowley, apparently unable to handle the erotico-magical power that dominated their relationship. Neuburg married, and Crowley cursed him. Years after the relationship with Crowley had ended, a friend of Neuburg's, seeing him sitting on a pedestal in the garden, remarked, "Great Gods, does Vicky [i.e. Victor] look like Pan, or a goblin, or what?" The poet Ethel Archer said of Neuburg, "He was absolutely fay! . . . He was a leprechaun! No, not a leprechaun . . . Puck! . . . It was quite unearthly . . . He wasn't human!"

Ne-uchica Among the Aleuts of northeastern Siberia, a term meaning "appareled like a woman," referring to gender variant, third gender, or transgendered male [-to female] shamans. The *ne-uchica*'s intimate relationships were often with traditionally masculine men.

Ngenechen Gynandrous or transgendered deity revered by MACHI, the gender variant male, third sex/gender, or transgendered (male-to-female) spiritual functionaries of the Mapuche (or Araucanians), an indigenous South American people. It is Ngenechen who demands that *machis* undergo gender metamorphosis in order to become shamans.

Niantiel In the ritual MAGIC system of the twentieth-century occult writer Kenneth GRANT, a demonic spirit of the QABBALISTIC Tree of Death. Niantiel is associated with the scarab, the scorpion, the Death card of the TAROT, and anal-erotic sex magic.

Nihooleki Mighty fisherman of Hawaiian mythology and religion. Inventor of the pearl fishhook and the double canoe, Nihooleki might be considered bisexual in today's terms; he was married to a woman and was also an AIKANE, or intimate companion, of the pig-god KAMAPUA'A.

Nijinsky, Vaslav (1890-1950) Bisexual Russian ballet dancer, lover of the impresario Sergei DIAGHILEV, director of the Ballets Russes, and husband of Romola de Pulszsky. During his brief career, cut short by schizophrenia, Nijinsky performed numerous roles evoking the interrelationship of pansexuality, transgenderism, and the sacred. In 1911 he played the spirit of a rose in *Le Spectre de la Rose*. Nijinsky performed this role as an androgynous persona fusing flower, human, and insect. Dressed in a leotard sewn with pink, red, and purple petals, his "face was like that of a celestial insect, his eyebrows suggesting some beautiful beetle which one

might expect to find closest to the heart of a rose, and his mouth was like rose-petals." R. Buckle (1971) relates that as "ever, when costumed and made up, he became possessed. As he danced the endless dance . . . weaving evanescent garlands in the air, his lips were parted in ecstasy, and he seemed to emit a perfumed gaze." In similar fashion, Nijinsky incarnated the spirits of NARCISSUS (in *Narcisse*, 1911), a JINN in *La Péri* (1911), KRISHNA (in *Le Dieu bleu*, 1912), and PAN (in *L'Après-midi d'un faune*, 1912). He is perhaps best remembered for his performance in the last of these. Wearing a spotted leotard that Léon Bakst had purposely designed to make him look *"plus nu que nu "* ("more naked than naked"), Nijinsky appears to have become totally possessed during the final moments of the ballet and, in this state, to have masturbated (at least in simulation) on the scarf of the Nymph, a ritualistic event that caused a scandal in the world of ballet. W. Russo (1978) writes of Nijinsky, "[he] seemed to possess something of the divine . . . From playing a series of roles that included demi-gods, androgynous slaves, and mythological beings, Vaslav was given the sobriquet of 'The God of Dance.'" Russo further points out that Nijinsky inspired Jean COCTEAU – who fell in love with him but who did nothing about it, so as not to upset Diaghilev – "to conceive the theory of a poet-angel [i.e. Cocteau] who would serve as a guardian of the divine [i.e. Nijinsky]." In a subtle love poem to Nijinsky, Cocteau depicts him as a "Hermes, eager to perform his mysterious errands" who "carries off all hearts on his invisible wings." Due to his descent into madness, Nijinsky never completed his ballet based on the lesbian-themed *Chansons de Bilitis* of Pierre Loüys and Claude Debussy. The life of Nijinsky, especially concerning his relationship with Diaghilev and containing a superb recreation of the final scene of *L'Après-midi d'un faune*, is the subject of the 1980 film *Nijinsky*, directed by Herbert Ross and starring George De La Peña in the title role and Alan Bates as Diaghilev.

Niobe The Lesbian poet SAPPHO (b. c. 630/610 BCE) writes, "Now LETO and Niobe were very dear companions." Athenaeus (fl. 230 CE) indicates that Leto and Niobe were lovers until they married men and became mothers. Niobe often bragged that she had given birth to more children than Leto. Resentful of Niobe's remarks, the deities APOLLO and ARTEMIS avenged their mother, Leto, by killing all but two of Niobe's children, Amyclas and Chloris. Chloris, ashamed of her mother's excessive pride, had prayed to Artemis to spare her, which she did; Chloris then honored Artemis by building a temple to her. In a version of the story recounted by Hyginus (fl. first century BCE) in his *Fabulae*, Niobe was punished after criticizing Leto for rearing what we might term transgendered children: "[Niobe] spoke rather contemptuously against Apollo and Diana [i.e. Artemis] because Diana was girt in man's attire, and Apollo [wore] long hair and a woman's gown."

Noah (dates uncertain, possibly second millenium BCE) Biblical hero who, directed by the Lord, built an ark to protect representative animals and humans from being drowned in a great flood, the Lord's way of punishing the sinful. Following the flood, Noah became a wine-maker, winemaking having been the chief industry of the "pagan" Canaanites. One day, the Book of Genesis (9: 20-25) relates, he "drank of the wine, and became drunk, and lay uncovered in his tent." Jewish folkloric tradition suggests that Noah was anally penetrated by his son Ham. Noah, in being associated with wine and homoeroticism, evokes the QEDESHIM, the gender variant hierodulic priests of the Canaanite goddess ATHIRAT. In later Bible-based folklore of the European Middle Ages, Noah's links to gender and sexual variance were both preserved and transformed in his association with the HARE, thought to be a transgendered animal.

Noble, Vicki (1947-   )   Lesbian-identified bisexual writer, artist, performance artist, educator, healer, and ritualist. Learned in the TAROT, Noble is the co-creator of the *Motherpeace Round Deck* (1981). Her interests in Goddess Reverence, healing, Shamanism, and Women's Spirituality are woven together in her book *Shakti Woman: Feeling Our Fire, Healing Our World: The New Female Shamanism* (1991) and her anthology *Uncoiling the Snake: Ancient Patterns in Contemporary Women's Lives* (1993). Noble currently holds shamanic healing circles and teaches classes in Female Shamanism at the California Institute of Integral Studies in San Francisco. Of her work, Noble says, "We are giving form and expression to the return of the Goddess through a global recovery movement that is the modern-day equivalent of a shamanic healing crisis." Noble is also at work on *The Double Goddess*, a book which will include an exploration of lesbian-centered Goddess iconography.

Nous   In Gnosticism, the primordial "Intelligence," a "male and female power," which first created human beings as androgynous, but later divides them into male and female.

Numboolyu   His age-mate lover fellated him, became pregnant, and gave birth to a female via a slit Numboolyu had carved in his belly. The Sambians (a pseudonym for a tribal people of New Guinea), who believe that this act of fellatio was responsible for the creation of the first human being, also hold that, while women are by nature healthy and strong, men, in order to become strong, must ingest semen frequently.

Nun   Generic name (in English) for an ascetic female spiritual functionary, most often associated with Christianity, especially Catholicism, and with Buddhism. J. Raymond (1986) suggests that women dwelling in CONVENTS have often, over the centuries, developed intimate (usually referred to as "special" or "particular") friendships which have occasionally included erotic expression. While some Catholic authorities have encouraged non-erotic bonds of this nature, many others, including SAINT AUGUSTINE of Hippo (354-430) and SANTA TERESA DE AVILA (1515-1582) have, perceiving the lesbian potential in such bonds, discouraged them. In 423, Augustine warned, "The love which you bear one another ought not to be carnal, but spiritual: for those things which are practiced by immodest women, even with other females . . . ought not to be done . . . by chaste virgins dedicated by a holy vow to be handmaidens of Christ." Judith C. Brown notes in *Immodest Acts: The Life of a Lesbian Nun in Renaissance Italy* (1986) that to "remove temptation, the councils of Paris (1212) and Rouen (1214) prohibited nuns from sleeping together and required a lamp to burn all night in dormitories." Still, three hundred years later, Terésa, who appears to have been intimately acquainted with lesbian desire, continued to rail against bonds established by nuns: "These intimate friendships are seldom calculated to make for the love of God; I am more inclined to believe that the devil initiates them." While, due to a chauvinistic dismissal of women and their activities, some authorities condemned but did not physically persecute women believed to be engaging in lesbian lovemaking, others, like Gregorio Lopez of mid-sixteenth century Spain believed that women "sinning in this way" should be "punished by burning according to the law of their Catholic Majesties . . . since the said law is not restricted to men." Even his more lenient compatriot, Antonio Gomez, felt that while certain forms of lesbian activity should be punished less severely, those women employing dildoes should be burned at the stake. While nuns are no longer executed for expressing female-centered affection, they are still likely to be severely reprimanded, told to leave the convent, and/or excommunicated. In *A Passion for Friends*, Raymond describes a walk in the woods one day during a period when she was a novice in a convent. She and a fellow novice, holding hands briefly during their walk, were spotted by a peer, who reported them to the novice mistress. They were reprimanded severely and encouraged to confess "illicit affection" for each other. Ultimately, both left the convent, extremely disillusioned. Experiences such as Raymond's and her friend's have caused many nuns and other Catholic women to leave the Church, as documented in *Lesbian Nuns: Breaking Silence* (1985), edited by Rosemary Curb and Nancy Manahan. Such experiences have, on the other hand, nurtured women in discovering spiritual paths such as Women's Spirituality and Goddess Reverence, which are a great deal more inclusive of what Raymond, following philosopher Mary DALY, terms "gyn/affection." They have also nurtured those who intend to struggle within the Church until it is forced to revise its stance on loving friendships between women. Catholic nuns and saints associated with the love of women and/or transgenderism include: Sister Benedetta CARLINI (1590-1661), Doña Catalina de ERAUSO (1592-1650), Sister Madeleine BAVENT (fl. mid-seventeenth century), SOR JUANA INES DE LA CRUZ (c. 1648-1695), Sister Caterina Irene BUONAMICI (fl. c. 1780), Sister Clodesinde SPIGHI (fl. c. 1780), SAINT MARGARITA (late antiquity or early Middle Ages) and SAINT CATHERINE OF GENOA (1477-1510). In the Middle Ages, nuns were parodied by Catholic males, just as monks were parodied by Catholic females, in celebrations including the Feast of Fools and the Feast of the Ass. This has inspired a number of late twentieth-century gay men and, more recently, women of various sexual orientations, to adopt identities as transgendered, "drag queen" nuns. These individuals and groups, while seen as expressing misogyny by some, blend social and political activism with a CAMP sensibility. In San Francisco, the SISTERS OF PERPETUAL INDULGENCE were among the first to dispense information relating to AIDS/HIV, and have more recently devoted much effort to combating the Religious Right. Where Buddhist nuns are concerned, little information is yet available, especially in English translation. R. H. van Gulik (1961) relates, "The monastery . . . offered refuge to . . . women with sapphic inclinations . . . Buddhist nuns . . . had free access to women's quarters, [and] were the favorite counselors of the ladies . . . Buddhist nuns officiated at intimate household ceremonies . . . and were also employed . . . as teachers." An unusual tale of thirteenth-century China describes a Buddhist nun who went to live with a wealthy family in order to instruct their daughters in embroidery. "One day, one of the daughters was found to be pregnant." She explained to her parents that the nun had impregnated her. The nun, when confronted by the parents and later the authorities, allegedly explained, "I have two sexes. When I encounter yang (here, the masculine or the male), I become yin (here, the feminine or female). When I encounter yin, I become male." Her (-his?) explanation, while it may seem strange to us, is not unrelated to concepts of Taoist alchemy concerning YIN AND YANG energies. The authorities were less than pleased with the nun's explanation, and she (-he?) was beheaded. While we shall never know whether the nun was in fact a man in disguise or a woman, perhaps lesbian inclined, unjustly blamed for causing another's pregnancy, the tale is clear in terms of revealing an association of nuns, transgenderism, and lesbianism in the context of Buddhism. In southern China, sometime between the sixteenth and nineteenth centuries , a Buddhist nun founded an all-female society known as the "Ten Sisters"; its members participated in ceremonies of

same-sex UNION. This society became the prototype of nineteenth- and twentieth-century Chinese societies such as the GOLDEN ORCHID ASSOCIATION.

Nureyev, Rudolf (1938-1993)   Closeted gay Russian ballet dancer who defected to the US in 1961 and who, after achieving international acclaim, died in 1993 of AIDS-related illness. Often compared to NIJINSKY, a number of Nureyev's roles subtly reflected the interrelationship of homoeroticism and/or transgenderism and the mythic, including the ROSE in *Le spectre de la rose* (a role initiated by Nijinsky), the faun in *The Afternoon of a Faun* (also first performed by Nijinsky), and the evil fairy Carabosse (*en travesti*) of *Sleeping Beauty* by Peter Illyich TCHAIKOVSKY. The French ballerina Violette Verdy has said of Nureyev: "Rudi [was] a dancer of such multiple beauties that you can almost say he has no sex. Or you could say that, as a dancer, he has both sexes . . . the matter is beyond one of simply having feminine qualities. It's almost as if he creates another type of sex altogether . . . Something like a faun or a bird . . . He has all sexual qualities."

Nursery Rhymes   Our research has turned up little in the way of queer nursery rhymes. Several, however, invite queer readings. The first of these concerns two young men, Robin and Richard who may have been brothers, or lovers, with "brother" used as a term of affection. Popular in 1765, "Robin and Richard," reads: "Robin and Richard / Were two pretty men, / They lay in bed / Till the clock struck ten." The second concerns Anne, Queen of England (1665-1714). Known as a skilled huntress and horsewoman, Queen Anne appears to have cultivated the image of the AMAZON and to have surrounded herself with female companions who likewise dressed and behaved as Amazons and "sapphists," women-loving women. "Lady Queen Anne she sits in the sun, / As fair as a lily, as white as a swan; / Come taste my lily, come smell my rose, / Which of my maidens do you choose?" The third centers on Bessie Bell and Mary Gray, two women who actually lived and who set up house together in the mid-seventeenth century. "Bessie Bell and Mary Gray, they were "two bonny lasses," the rhyme goes, "They built their house upon the lea, and covered it with rushes." Their tale appears to be rooted in the story of two Scottish women, Mary Gray, the daughter of the Laird of Lednock, and Bessie Bell, daughter of the Laird of Kinvaid. I. and P. Opie (1983) write, "They were both very handsome and an intimate friendship subsisted between them." When a plague broke out at Perth around 1645, they moved to a quiet place called Burn-braes, where they lived happily for a time. By today's standards, the two women might be described as bisexual as they appear to have participated in a ménage à trois with a young man who occasionally visited them. Unfortunately this young man may have unknowingly infected them. When the two women ultimately succumbed to the plague, they could not, as plague victims, be buried in a churchyard. Thus, they were buried side by side in the Dranoch-haugh, near the bank of the river Almond. Their burial place may still be visited in the twentieth century. Their nursery rhyme was transformed around 1720 into a song by Allan Ramsay and W. Thomson.

Nyame Gynandrous or transgendered supreme being of the Akan of Ghana. Nyame's feminine aspect is identified with the MOON, her/his masculine aspect with the SUN. It is Nyame who decides the fate of each human prior to birth. Five is her/his sacred number.

Nymph Beautiful female nature spirits of Greek religion and mythology who typically live together in all-female bands, occasionally having affairs with male spirits of mortal men. Nymphs of the water include Oceanides, NEREIDES, and Naiades; of mountains and grottoes Oreades; and of plants and trees, Dryades and Hamadryades. A number of the goddess ARTEMIS/DIANA's most beloved companions, including Chariclo, are nymphs. Places sacred to them include Cyrtone, Athens, Olympia, Megara, and Sicyon. Sacrifices to the nymphs include goats, lambs, milk, and olive oil. While in the mid-twentieth century the nymph surfaced in the derogatory term "nymphomaniac," a century earlier, in the bohemian subculture, or *demi-monde*, of Paris, "nymphe" referred to a bisexual or lesbian woman, recalling the female spirit tribes of antiquity.

Nzambi Androgynous or transgendered supreme being of the Bakongo people of the Kongo (or Congo) region of Central Africa. Nzambi created all life, and it is Nzambi who cares for those who honor him/her and who punishes those who do not. According to R. F. Thompson (1983), Nzambi's "illuminating spirit and healing powers are carefully controlled by the king (*mfumu*), the ritual expert or authority (*nganga*), and the sorcerer (*ndoki*)." In the Americas, it is the latter two who, in the Kongo religion, guard Nzambi's powers.

O

Obatala (also, in certain aspects, **Oxalá, Olofí**)   In the
Yoruba-diasporic pantheon, the *orishá* Obatalá is the
demiurge, lawgiver, and peacemaker. Obatalá is
commonly depicted as an androgynous being having long
white hair and dressed in white garments. Obatalá is
generally identified with that aspect of the Virgin Mary
known as Our Lady of Mercy. According to one *pataki* or
myth, Obatalá is believed to be androgynous. In order to
bring about human reproduction, he-she divides him-
/herself into a male-female pair, Oddúdua and Yemmú. As
the original androgyne, he-she is called Oddúaremu or
(I)Yekú-(I)Yekú, and is variously syncretized with St
Anne, La Purisima Concepcion (Mary of the Immaculate
Conception), and la Santisima Trinidad (the Holy
Trinity). It is this aspect or "road" (*camino*) of Obatalá,
Oddúaremu, that has been linked by Cabrera, Trevisan,
and others to both transgenderism and homoeroticism. As
Oddúaremu, the *orishá* is believed to be an *adodi*, a
homosexual male. As such, he is said to have fallen in love
with another *adodi*, with whom he dwells in the shade of a
cotton plant.

Odin   Teutonic (Germanic, Scandinavian) deity
associated with Shamanism, battle, and sacrifice. An Aesir
deity, as opposed to a Vanir deity (e.g. the fertility deities
FREYJA, FREYR) in the Teutonic pantheon. Odin, whose
name signifies "fury," "wildness," and "inspiration," is
primarily a god of "battle, death, and spiritual wisdom."
As a battle god, he is the leader of a band comprised of the
souls of fallen warriors. The approach of this band,
nicknamed "the Wild Hunt," often signals death. Odin is
also the master of Valhalla, the paradise of warriors. As a
diviner whose cult appears, like those of Freyja and Freyr,
to have been inspired by Shamanism, Odin is master of the
runes and a necromancer who divines the future by way of
communicating with a skull. That his worship is linked to
Shamanism is indicated by the manner in which he
acquires the knowledge of the runes – by hanging himself
on a sacred ash tree, by his possession of the eight-legged
horse Sleipnir (the horse being an archetypal shamanic
vehicle), and by his avian companions, the ravens Huginn
and Muninn, who function as all-seeing eyes. Like many
shamanic figures, Odin is often depicted as one-eyed,
another sacrifice to gnosis. In this respect, he resembles the
blind Greek prophet TIRESIAS. As a magician, Odin is
owner of a ring and a spear possessing supernatural
powers. Odin is said to have assumed female clothing on
various occasions. Moreover, one of his aspects or
nicknames is Jalkr, which means "gelding." K.

Gundarsson (1990) suggests that this appellation may refer
to "Odinn's initiation into the art of SEIDR MAGIC . . . [To]
assume the feminine powers of vision and understanding
or to give himself up totally to the feminine principle, a
man had to be capable of giving up his masculine identity,
even to the point of dressing and living as a woman for a
time – a practice common to many forms of shamanism,
and something which Odin is implied to have done in his
practice of *seidr* magic." Through a complex set of
associations, primarily through his relationship to the
trickster LOKI and through warriors devoted to him, Odin
becomes linked not only to *seidr* and gender variant
homoeroticism (*argr, ergi*) but also to outlaws or outlaw-
warriors (*vargr*, which is linked semantically to *seidr*), the
ritual use of psychotropic substances, wolves, werewolves,
and binding rituals suggesting SADOMASOCHISM. M. R.
Gerstein (1974) explains rather cryptically: "The binder
god of the Old Norse pantheon is, of course, Odin . . .
patron of outcasts and leader of the *berserkir* ["bear-
shirts," and *ulfhednar*, "wolf-shirts"], frenzied,
shape-changing warriors . . . Odin differs ideologically
from other binder gods in his essential amorality . . . Odin
is the embodiment of every form of frenzy . . . from the
insane bloodlust that characterized the werewolf warriors
who dedicated themselves to him, to erotic and poetic
madness." The relationship between *argr* (roughly,
"receptive homosexuality") and *vargr* ("outlaw-[wolf-]
warrior") is expressed in a "'wolf charm" which reads:
"Call me *varg* [*r*] / and I'll be *arg* [*r*] / Call me golden, / I'll
be beholden." In "You, Father Odin," lesbian poet Renée
VIVIEN (1877-1909) writes, "Come, my Gods of the North,
with your warlike faces, / You, our Father Odin and Freya,
of the golden hair."

Ogun   In the Yoruba-diasporic pantheon, the *orishá*
Ogún, identified with Saint George, Saint Anthony, and
Saint John the Baptist, has been described by priestess
Maria-José as a "brave young god . . . full of fire . . . pure of
body and spirit." Like ARES or MARS, Ogún is a god of
war; like HEPHAESTUS or Vulcan, he is a god of
metallurgy. He is a patron of steelworkers, ironworkers,
farmers, hairstylists, and taxi drivers. It is Ogún who
teaches us to combat injustice. In 1986, Eduardo Mejía, a
practitioner of Santería, related, "Ogún doesn't like gays
very much. Still, some of his *hijos* [sons] are *bugarones*
["buggers;" here, men who are married to women but who
also have male lovers]." In one of his Brazilian
manifestations, however, as Ogum Xoroquê – an aspect in
which Ogun merges with Exú – this male-male being is a

patron of, surprisingly, lesbian women. João Trevisan asserts that when Ogum Xoroquê "falls on the head" of [i.e. decides to parent] or possesses a female practitioner, she will be "revealed as gay."

Olive Sacred to PALAESTRA, Greco-Roman goddess of WRESTLING, "since its oil is useful in wrestling" and mortals "find great pleasure in it."

Oliveros, Pauline (1932-) US avant-garde lesbian composer . One of the first women composers to receive acclaim in the academic music world (she has won numerous international awards and taught at many colleges), Oliveros's work is chiefly experimental and in electronic media. Her "sonic meditations" tend to employ natural and droning sounds. Her works frequently bear spiritual or metaphysical themes and contexts. These works often utilize audience participation, chiefly in the forms of improvisational chant and movement transforming what might be a strictly musical into a ritual event. Works relevant to this encyclopaedia include *Bigmother is Watching You* (1966), *Participle Dangling in Honor of Gertrude Stein* (1966), *To Valerie Solanas and Marilyn Monroe in Recognition of their Desperation* (1970), *Crow Two* (1974), *Mother's Day* (1981), *Rattlesnake Mountain* (1982), *Oh Sister, Whose Name is Goddess* (1984), *Songs for the Ancestors* (1984), and *Nzinga, the Queen King* (1993).

Olokun Sometimes identified as an aspect of the *orishá* YEMAYÁ, Olokun is, in the Yoruba-diasporic pantheon, the androgynous ruler of the depths of the sea. He-she is not only transgendered but also a hybrid human-fish (or sea serpent) linked to both gender and theriomorphic transformation. He-she is sometimes depicted as having aquamarine skin and long, flowing, indigo hair. He-she lives in a magnificent palace with his-her intimate companions, mermaids and mermen. Legend has it that Olokun once fell in love with Orisha-Oko, a phallic god of the earth and agriculture. At first Olokun was afraid to tell Orisha-Oko of his-her love. But Oko also loved Olokun. Olokun then became concerned that if their love for each other were made public, they might suffer ridicule. He-she finally confided in Obatalá, who said to Olokun, "Stop worrying. After all, both you and Orisha-Oko are greatly respected by the gods and humankind. What is more, you are the perfect couple, since Oko is the earth and you are the sea."

Olympus Male youth loved by the satyr MARSYAS, who taught him to play the pipes or flute. In Philostratus's (fl. c. 220 CE) *Imagines*, we find a portrait of Olympus: "Your breast . . . is filled not merely with breath for the flute but also with thoughts of music and meditation on the tunes you will play." Breath, as breath shared between lovers, is a

spiritual concept signifying union, cross-pollination, and metamorphosis in Greek and later in Neoplatonic homoerotic discourse.

Omeo In Hawaiian mythology or religion, an intimate female companion, AIKANE, of HI'IAKA. She made a sacrifice to PELE of a hog and accompanied Hi'iaka on her journey to bring LOHIAU to Pele. Also linked to PAUO-PALAE, another companion of Hi'iaka.

Omphale AMAZON Queen of Lydia who enjoyed a transgendered relationship with the divinized Greek hero HERACLES. Her attribute is the LABRYS, or double axe. She may originally have been a chthonic or earth goddess, as her name signifies "navel."

Onion In seventeenth-century China, in Longyou, scallions or "green onions" (*cong*), nicknamed "women's fingers" and associated with cleverness and love MAGIC, also signified homoerotic coupling.

Onkoy Ancient Peruvian hybrid deity, transgendered and trans-species, male and female, feline and reptile.

Opera A form of theater that, by way of fusing text, music and dramatic action, reclaims the aura of ancient ritual theatre. In part due to its bond to the iconography and ritual of ancient Greece, opera since its inception has spoken, albeit in an often sublimated manner, to the relationship of gender and sexual variance to the sacred or mythic. This relationship is most frequently expressed in the idealization of androgyny as depicted by transgendered figures, their roles often being performed by castrati (in the past) and counter-tenors, by mezzo-sopranos, and by singers *en travesti*. As Wayne Koestenbaum elucidates in his operatic confessional *The Queen's Throat* (1993), opera is experienced by many queer-identified persons as a form of spiritual experience in which they willingly become embodied by the personae of opera, their identification with these promoting healing and metamorphosis. Opera was inspired, of course, not only by Greek ritual theatre but also by pre-Christian festivals which continued into the Middle Ages and the Renaissance, and by Christian ritual performances as well. By the fifteenth century, elaborate spectacles including parades and pantomimes, with musical *intermezzi* (musical pieces performed between sections of a spoken performance), often depicting "queer"-related divine and mythical beings, were held by, and in honor of, the nobility. The *intermezzi*, along with pastoral plays inclusive of madrigals, greatly contributed to the formation of opera. Such pastoral plays with music included Poliziano's *Orfeo* (1480), which employed homoerotic lyrics. Many pivotal operas from the late fifteenth century onward centered on the myth of ORPHEUS, the most famous from the early period being

Orfeo (1607) by Claudio Monteverdi (1567-1643), in which the part of Eurydice was sung by a castrato. In terms of Amazonian figures and lesbian references, in Pietro Francesco Cavalli's (1602-1676) *La Calistro* (1651), Jove, the Roman Zeus, transforms himself into ARTEMIS/DIANA in order to attract her beloved Callisto. The influence of the Vatican, in terms of the employment of castrati singers, profoundly influenced the development of opera in general and its transgendered and homoerotic components in particular. Between the sixteenth and nineteenth centuries, castrati became extremely popular in both church music and in opera. They had been employed as singers for centuries in the Eastern Orthodox Church, reflecting the transgendered, often eunuch, male priest/ess-singers of the goddesses of antiquity. St Paul's ban on women speaking or singing in church has often been cited as influencing the flourishing of castrati. When Pope Clement VIII (1592-1605) officially sanctioned the use of castrati in choirs, their numbers greatly increased. In 1762, Casanova (1725-1798) noted in his memoirs that he was so entranced by the beauty, power and grace of castrati in Roman opera that it might "force every man to become a pederast." The castrato who especially charmed Casanova was the *mignon* of Cardinal Borghese. In France, the homoerotically inclined Jean-Baptiste Lully (1632-1687) wrote many opera-ballets which drew upon Greco-Roman mythic themes with "queer" connotations. These include the pastorale *Pomone* (1671), *Atys* (1676), *Isis* (1677), *Psyché* (1678), and *Phaëton* (1683). Although the same-sex subtexts of these operas are submerged in heterosexual contexts, they are nurtured by transgendered interpretation and performance. Other early French operas noteworthy here are *Castor et Pollux* (1737) and *David et Jonathan* (1668) by Jean Philippe Rameau (1683-1764), and another *David et Jonathan* (1693) by Marc-Antoine Charpentier (1634-1704). The most celebrated opera diva of the late seventeenth century was the bisexual Mademoiselle d'Aubigny de Maupin (1670/1673-1707), who performed the roles of numerous goddesses including Pallas, Minerva, Cybele, and Artemis/Diana in works by Lully, Campra, and others; who often dressed as a man and won duels; and who was almost burned at the stake after rescuing her female lover from a convent. Baroque English operas bearing homoerotic, transgendered, and mythic elements include *Venus and Adonis* (c. 1682) by John Blow (1649-1708), a three-act masque/tragedy, and *The Fairy Queen* (1692) and *Dido and Aeneas* (1689) by Henry Purcell (1659-1695). These have continued to provide in modern times an opportunity for transgendered performances by counter-tenors and female mezzo-sopranos *en travesti*. The homoerotically inclined George Frideric Handel (1685-1759) wrote several operas evoking our subject. His opera *Alcina* (1716) tells of Celtic women warriors and sorceresses who, in performance, "display transgendered

pleasures" involving conscious "allusions to sexual ambiguities." While his personal homoerotic relationships remain obscure, it is widely believed that Handel loved for a time the famous bisexual castrato Farinelli (Carlo Broschi, 1709-1782), whose voice was claimed to exert magical and erotic powers. From the 1790s there was a decline in the popularity of the castrati and by 1844, few were heard beyond the walls of the Vatican. Alessandro Moreschi (1858-1954), said to be the last of the Papal castrati, was recorded before his death. With the demise of the castrati, the yearning for transgendered performance was fulfilled by women singers, especially mezzo-sopranos *en travesti* ("in pants") performing in the roles of gods, rulers, and warriors. Feminist scholars C. E. Blackmer and P. J. Smith (1995) suggest that such roles infer "same-sex desire between men and between women through the medium of classical mythology and cross-gendered casting." These become thinly veiled ritualistic performances in which the spiritual elevation of "same-sex desire can parade before an . . . adoring public." Exemplary of such performances is Pietro Cavalli's (1602-1676) *Eliogabalo* (1668) in which the male roles of Eliogabolo (ELAGABALUS), Alessandro, and Cesare were written for castrati or women, while the female role of Zenia was written for a male tenor. Transgendered performances referencing the sacred or mythic are also found in *Andromeda* (1637) by Manelli, who wrote the role of Venus to be sung by a male, reminiscent of Venus APHRODITOS, or the "Bearded Venus;" in *Hansel and Gretel* (1893) by Engelbert Humperdinck (1854-1921), with the role of Hänsel performed by a woman; in Jules Massenet's (1842-1912) *Le Jongleur de Notre-Dame* (1902), with the role of Jean, a holy fool, performed by a woman; in Christoph Gluck's (1714-1787) *Le Nozze d'Eroite e d'Ebe* (1747), the role of Heracles taken by a woman; and in Metastasio's *Achilles in Sciro* (1737), with Achilles played by a woman, wherein the hero is disguised as a woman (Pyrrha) to enter a harem "in order to escape the call to arms for the Trojan War." Other operas with *travesti* roles include Giacomo Castoreo's *Pericle Effeminato* (1653) and Charles Gounod's (1818-1893) *Faust* (1859); Gounod also wrote an opera on *Sapho* (1851). As the nineteenth century progressed, allusions to same-sex desire and transgenderism became somewhat more subdued, unless they were presented in a context of generalized decadence. Many of the most well-known operas also emphasized what French feminist theorist Catherine Clément has described as the "undoing of woman." Such references were not to disappear entirely, although there has been a tendency, since the late nineteenth century, among composers of operas, especially those who are homoerotically or bisexually inclined, to avoid directly referencing these subjects, with notable exceptions including Benjamin BRITTEN and Lou HARRISON. The narrative of the transgendered Saint JEANNE D'ARC (Joan of Arc) is treated in operas including *Giovanna d'Arco* (1845) by Giuseppe Verdi (1813-1901) and *The Maid of Orleans* (1881) by Peter Illyich TCHAIKOVSKY (1840-1893). In Verdi's *Un Ballo in Maschera* (1859), romantic and political intrigue, poisonous herbs, and murder are foregrounded, while the bisexuality of the Swedish King Gustavus III (1746-1792) is masked. A majority of the operas of Richard Wagner (1813-1883) focus on mythic and magical themes linked to Teutonic religion; many of these reference androgyny and same-sex passion. Many biographers and commentators have pointed out the importance of androgyny and (generally repressed) homosexuality in Wagner's personal life and works. In a letter to Peter Cornelius, Wagner begged him to come to live with him because he "belongs to him as a wife [and] will share fortune and failure." Wagner also made passionate declarations to King Ludwig II of Bavaria, which deeply troubled Cosima Wagner. Jean-Jacques Nattiez, in *Wagner Androgyne: A Study in Interpretation* (1993), suggests that a key to the homoerotic elements in Wagner's work and life can be found in his obsession with androgyny, with "the act of suspending the divided unity of male and female," as expressed in mystical twinships, incest, androgyny of siblings, and passionate friendships between men. His operas bearing these elements include *Der Ring des Nibelungen*, especially *Siegfried* (1871) and *Götterdämmerung* (1874), *Tristan and Isolde* (1859), *Lonhengrin* (1848) and *Parsifal* (1882). Wagner appears to have believed and hoped that his operas would, in their bold references to pagan religion and their more subtle references to transgenderism and same-sex desire, promote the coming into being of a "new man, a new woman, and a new religion of the future." A duet from *Lakmé* (1883) by Lèo Delibès (1836-1891), inspired by the Hindu goddess LAKSHMI, evokes (positive) lesbian desire within a larger (negative) heterosexual context comparable to that depicted in *Madame Butterfly* (1904) by Giacomo Puccini (1858-1924). Gender lines blur and intertwine as well in the operas of Richard Strauss (1864-1949), as in *Salomé* (1905), wherein Herod's wife and daughter hold power over both the King and John the Baptist, and in *Der Rosenkavalier* (1911), wherein Octavian, whose nickname is Hyacinth (alluding to HYACINTHUS, the beloved of Apollo), is performed by a transgendered mezzo-soprano. She (-he) presents a numinous silver rose to Sophie, who instantly falls in love with Octavian. Two operas by the possibly bisexual Eric Satie (1866-1925), *Socrate* (1920) and *La Piège de Méduse* (1913), bear subtle homoerotic and transgendered references. The opera *Turandot* (produced 1926) by Puccini tells a tale of a princess refusing both men and marriage, who poses impossible riddles that must be solved before she will submit her body and spirit. Due to her devoted female companions and to her depiction in art, Turandot has been associated with lesbianism as well as decadence. In requiring sacrifices of males, Turandot is

related to many goddesses of antiquity, including APHRODITE and CYBELE, as well as to such figures as the BODHISATTVA KUAN YIN and Buddhist and Christian nuns who enter cloistered life partly to escape domination by men. The operas of Dame Ethel SMYTH (1858-1944), remembered for her passionate attachment to Virginia Woolf, explore the sacred and mythic, although the lesbian and transgendered aspects are sublimated. Virgil Thompson (1896-1989), employing a text by Gertrude Stein, composed the opera *Four Saints in Three Acts* (1934) for African-American singers, to celebrate both "saintly" and "artistic life." The opera *Les Mamelles de Tiresias* (1944), written by the homorotically inclined French composer Francis Poulenc (1899-1963) and based on a text of the Surrealist poet Guillaume Apollinaire, focuses on the transgendered Greek shaman Tiresias. In the opera, a husband gives birth to forty thousand babies, while his wife grows a beard. Poulenc's opera *Dialogues de Carmélites* (1957) has inspired a lesbian interpretation. While avoiding direct references to same-sex passion or transgenderism, the homoerotically inclined Gian Carlo Menotti (b. 1911) explored the mythic and sacred in *The Medium* (1946) and *Amahl and the Night Visitors* (1951), while his companion Samuel Barber (1910-1981), in *Anthony and Cleopatra* (1966), with a libretto by Franco ZEFFIRELLI, allowed Marc Antony and his shield-bearer a tender farewell scene. The operas of Benjamin Britten (1913-1976), including *Billy Budd* (1951), *The Turn of the Screw* (1954), and *Death in Venice* (1973), are far less reticent in their exploration of these themes, as is Lou Harrison's *Young Caesar* (1971). In recent years, operas have been written on the theme of lesbian VAMPIRES, including *Carmilla* (1970) by Ben Johnston, based on Sheridan La Fanu's tale, and *La Contessa dei Vampiri* (1987) by David Clenny, who also sang the *travesti* title role. While not focusing on homoeroticism or transgenderism, John Corigliano (b. 1938), an openly gay American composer known for his *Symphony # 1* in tribute to persons with AIDS, delves into the realm of the supernatural in *The Ghosts of Versailles* (1991), an opera which centers on the ghost of Marie Antoinette and other spirits of Revolutionary France. Corigliano believes in the power of music and art to transform and, so to speak, "raise the dead." William M. Hoffman, the librettist of *Ghosts*, also acknowledges the spiritual dimension of opera; it is "dedicated to things of the spirit, [providing a] glamour [that] elevates the spirit" and that brings us "into contact with the spirit." This opera, Corigliano and Hoffman explain, is, above all, about "the love that transcends death."

Orchid   In China, symbolic of beauty, grace, elegance, and love. The orchid is a spring flower. While the flowers of summer and winter – including the peony and the plum – tend to represent traditional gender roles and heterosexuality in Chinese symbolism, the flowers of spring and autumn – including the orchid, iris, lily, magnolia, and chrysanthemum – represent the "intermediate stage between man and woman. "A "golden orchid bond," or jin lan qi, signifies an intimate relationship, not excluding eroticism, between two persons of the same sex. In the *I CHING*, this bond is described as one that is as "fragrant as orchids." It may be for this reason that the name GOLDEN ORCHID ASSOCIATION was given to a Chinese organization promoting resistance against heterosexual marriage and encouraging bonds between women.

Order of Chaeronea Deriving its name from the final battle fought by the SACRED BAND OF THEBES in 338 BCE, this clandestine British homosexual spiritual organization was founded in the 1890s by George Cecil Ives (1867-1950), a criminologist, poet, essayist, and early homosexual rights activist (co-founder of the British Sexological Society). A friend of Oscar WILDE and Edward CARPENTER, Ives used texts by them as well as by Walt WHITMAN in the construction of initiation ceremonies and other rites. Ives also employed passages of his own work in these rites, some of which appear in *A Book of Chains* (1897), *Eros' Throne* (1900), and *The Graeco-Roman View of Youth* (1926). The primary goal of the Order was to form a global chain of lovers, building upon the Platonic ideal of the "army of lovers" first realized by the Theban Band. The "bibles" of what amounted to a homosexual-centered (or proto-Gay/Queer-Spiritual) faith included Ives's own books of ritual as well as the *Greek Anthology* and Whitman's *Leaves of Grass* (1855). The god of the Order was EROS, that "gay, capricious" "angel of night" with "vast wings" of Ives's poem "With Whom, then, should I Sleep?" (1896). The messiah or prophet of the faith was Whitman, the disciples or saints, Wilde and Carpenter, the missionaries, Ives and the other members of the Order. Another prominent member of the Order was the writer Laurence Housman (1865-1959), the brother of poet A. E. Housman (1859-1936). It has been suggested that while the Order was comprised primarily of men, the lesbian writer Radclyffe HALL and her lover Una Lady Troubridge (1887-1963) also may have been members. While Ives appears to have preferred intergenerational love, he and members of the Order honored same-age relationships (which they linked to the warrior-comrades of antiquity as well as to Medieval knight pairs) and transgendered relationships. At the time of initiation, the novice was entreated to "love someone, for as the prophet Whitman says, that is the beginning of knowledge." The initiate was then instructed to follow a set of guidelines based primarily in self-esteem and respect of others, after which he joined others in reciting quotations from Whitman, Wilde, and others. He then formally agreed to struggle against the oppression of others

like himself. This was apparently followed by a love-feast, including a tongue-in-cheek recitation of Wilde's dictum, "Love is a sacrament that should be taken kneeling." The seal of the Order is comprised of: a double wreath of CALAMUS (sacred to Whitman) and MYRTLE (sacred to the Greeks); a chain signifying the "great chain of lovers;" the number 338 referring to the Sacred Band; the letters D (for "discipline"), L (for "learning"), and Z (for "zeal"); and the mystical word AMRRHAO. While, beyond the seal, some of the correspondence of members and a copy of the text used at the initiation ceremony also still exist, the Order remains a mystery in many respects.

Orestes and Pylades Brothers-in-law and comrade-lovers of Greek legend. Pylades assisted Orestes in his vengeance on his mother Clytemnestra, whose death had been ordered by the god APOLLO in return for her having murdered his father, AGAMEMNON. Although Orestes was hounded and temporarily driven mad by the ERINYES (or FURIES) for murdering his mother, he was ultimately purified of the crime. Together, Orestes, Pylades, and IPHIGENIA built a temple to the goddess ARTEMIS at Attica. The sixth century CE *Latin Anthology* includes an anonymous poem which says of Orestes and Pylades, "Love kindles quarrels so it can burn the lovers more seductively."

Orlando Central character of fantasy novel so titled by Virginia Woolf (1882-1941), rooted in the writer's love for Vita Sackville-West (1892-1962). Orlando, who comes to experience both gender transformation and a kind of immortality, commences as a handsome, somewhat powerful male in the Renaissance. Then, one day, he metamorphoses into a woman. Remaining a woman through the remainder of the tale, Orlando continues for awhile to dress in masculine attire, and, as a woman who has been a man, experiences sensations and desires which, while clearly gender variant or transgendered, are otherwise difficult to label as heterosexual, bisexual, or lesbian – as the answer seems to be "all of the above." In terms of the meeting of transgenderism and lesbianism, Orlando finds that "though she herself was a woman, it was still a woman she loved; and if the consciousness of being of the same sex had any effect at all, it was to quicken and deepen those feelings which she had as a man." In writing *Orlando* (1928), Woolf both reclaimed the ancient archetype of the androgynous/gynandrous or transgendered goddess and gave birth to a modern mythic figure blending, among other traits, lesbianism, bisexuality, transgenderism, and feminism. In 1993, *Orlando* further metamorphosed into a witty, exquisitely made film by Sally Potter, starring Tilda Swinton and Billy Zane and co-starring gay luminaries Quentin Crisp as Queen Elizabeth and Jimmy Somerville as an angelic spirit.

Orleans French city associated in the Medieval period with homoeroticism, especially intergenerational desire. Graffiti of the twelfth or thirteenth century declares, "The men of Orleans are the best, if you like / The customs of men who sleep with boys."

Orpheus Greek legendary hero and musician. In today's terms, Orpheus would probably be described as bisexual. He is most often remembered as the lover of Eurydice. When the latter died at an early age, Orpheus pleaded with Hades to release her from the Underworld so that they might remain lovers and so that she would be able to experience motherhood and other joys. Hades agreed, but only if Orpheus, clasping Eurydice's hand at the entrance to Hades, did not look back until they had reached their home. Orpheus, however, could not resist gazing upon his beloved. When he did so, Eurydice vanished forever. Perhaps because he had already known the love of such a kind and beautiful woman, Orpheus directed his love toward young men. Of those he loved, CALAIS, the son of Boreas, was his favorite. The MAENADS, however, became infuriated with Orpheus due to his rejection of the love of other women, and for this reason, tore him apart. According to myth, it was the lesbian poet SAPPHO, Orpheus's beloved friend, who buried his head and his lyre beneath a tree on the island of LESBOS after the Maenads had dismembered him. Before his death, Orpheus was said to have founded the Orphic Mysteries, the hymns of which we still possess. Central to Orphism is a belief in the healing and magical powers of MUSIC. Many artists have been inspired by the tale of Orpheus, including the Mannerist painter Agnolo Bronzino – who painted a portrait of Cosimo I de' Medici as a nude Orpheus, a stringed instrument and bow dangling between his legs – the Symbolist painter Gustave MOREAU, the choreographer George Balanchine, the poet W. H. Auden, the playwright and poet Tenneesee Williams, and the filmmaker and writer Jean COCTEAU.

Orunmila (also **Ifá**) The *orishá* Orúnmila, identified with Saint Francis of Assisi, is the Yoruba god of divination. It is he who controls the Table of Ifá, which reveals "the ultimate destiny of each individual." Orúnmila is, in one of his manifestations, an *adodi*, a transgendered male who engages in same-sex eroticism.

Osanyin (or **Osain, Ossãe**) In the Yoruba-diasporic pantheon, the *orishá* of herbal healing, sometimes envisioned as an androgynous being with female breasts and male genitalia.

Oschophoria Ancient Greek festival taking place in late November or early December, established, according to legend, by THESEUS, a hero and ruler of Athens, in honor of DIONYSUS. The name of the festival comes from the grape vines bearing clusters of grapes that were carried by two young males who were deemed the most beautiful in the region. These youths were dressed in feminine attire. Originally they were said to have been intimate companions of Theseus who "combined a bold and undaunted courage with a womanish and delicate appearance." The costumes were meant to honor Dionysus, who is sometimes portrayed as wearing feminine attire.

Oshumare (or **Oxumaré**) The *orishá* Oshumaré is the rainbow-serpent of the Yoruba-diasporic pantheon, associated with the Vodou(n) deity DAMBALLAH Awedo and identified with Saint Bartholomew. As a serpent, Oshumaré is the ruler of cycles – rain and drought, winter and summer, poverty and wealth. Oshumaré is the god of movement, of action. Occasionally depicted as a servant of SHANGÓ, Oshumaré's "office consists of taking water from the earth to his [i.e. Shangó's] palace in the clouds." As the RAINBOW, Oshumaré is a bridge linking the various worlds. As Saint Bartholomew, Oshumaré is associated with Exu, a sometimes sinister manifestation of Eleggúa, the *orishá* of the crossroads who acts as intercessory between the *orishá* and humankind. In this connection, he is especially invoked by practitioners of Quimbanda, a branch of the religion blending Yoruba and Kongo beliefs and practices and emphasizing sorcery or magic. As the rainbow, Oshumaré is an androgynous *orishá*, his/her nature represented by the oppositional colors "violet (internal, feminine) and vermilion (external, masculine)." As an androgynous deity, Oshumaré, like Logunedé, spends – according to some scholars and practitioners – one half of each year as a hunter and the other as a mermaid or nymph, evoking the above-mentioned *orishá* Inlé, Osanyin, and Logunedé. Oshumaré is a son of the goddess Nana Burukú, who is thought to be, along with Onilé, one of the eldest female deities of the Yoruba pantheon. He is the brother (or half-brother) of the *orishá* Babaluayé. He is also said to be the *ade* or "crown" of Yemayá. In Umbanda, Oshumaré is an aspect of Oshún; as Oxum Marê, s/he is nicknamed Oxum-of-the-Tides. Esther Pressel notes that in Umbanda, the "bisexual nature of Oxum Marê is emphasized." As an androgynous deity, Oshumaré is perceived by many worshippers as a patron of gay, lesbian, bisexual, and transgendered persons. Brazilian priest M. Aparecida explains that when "this saint talks in a man's head, he becomes gay." Thus, in Aparecida's view, to banish a queer-identified person from a Candomblé household, which sometimes happen, is to "kick out the rainbow."

Oshun (or **Ochún, Oxum**) In the Yoruba-diasporic pantheon, the *orishá* of rivers and lakes, sensuality, and the fine arts. Christianized as Our Lady of Caridad del Cobré, Oshún's counterpart in Vodou is Erzulie, patron of prostitutes and gay and transgendered males. Oshún is also associated with transgendered and lesbian women in her manifestations as Oshún Yeyé Iponda, Oshún Yeyé Karé, and Oshún Panchagayé (or Panchagárra). Eduardo Mejía, a gay practitioner of Santería living in New York, related in 1986: "I have heard it said that Oshún is a woman in love with women, a *cachaporra*. [*Cachaporra* is Portuguese for "bludgeon" or "cudgel" and is employed in Latin American slang for "lesbian" or "dyke."] There is a story that she and Yemayá love each other." A lesbian daughter of Oshún living in Oakland related that same year: "She has made me aware of all of the realms of sensuality. She finds sensuality in everything. Pansensuality is Oshún's dream." In "The Winds of Orisha, " the African-American lesbian poet Audre LORDE writes, "the beautiful Oshun and I lie down together / in the heat of her body truth my voice comes stronger."

Osiris Egyptian god of the dead, fertility, and MAGIC, spouse of the goddess ISIS. As a god of fertility, Osiris is depicted as having an erect phallus. Osiris was invoked as the "star of the land of Egypt" in a Greco-Egyptian lesbian love spell dating from late antiquity.

Otrera In Greek legendary history, the mother of the AMAZONS, in particular, of HIPPOLYTA, ANTIOPE, and MELANIPPE. According to J. A. Salmonson (1991), Otrera "built a temple and bird sanctuary upon a flat island in the Black Sea when the Amazons first settled the coast. It was here the Amazons retreated to worship and sacrifice horses before their major battles."

Owl Symbolic of wisdom as well as of divination and of death and regeneration. Sacred and mythical beings and spiritual functionaries associated with the owl and with transgenderism and/or same-sex intimacy include ATHENA, CALLING GOD, the FURIES, HECATE, MINERVA, PERSEPHONE and practitioners of Witchcraft.

Owu (also **Obukele, Obukere**) Deity of Nigerian traditional religion usually depicted as a shark and represented by a shark- or fish-shaped helmet. In the past, his worship apparently included cultic homoeroticism, especially by numbers of the Obukele (or Obukere) Society.

Oyá (also **Iansa, Yansa**) In the Yoruba-diasporic pantheon, the *orishá* Oyá, identified with Our Lady of the Candelaria, is a woman warrior, a bringer of tempests, and a guardian of the dead. Roger Bastide has described Oyá as a "queen who vanquishes death," while Macumba priestess Mari-José depicts her as a warrior who dwells "in the sky, armed and helmeted . . . ready to combat injustice." G. Edwards and J. Mason (1985) describe her as "the fury of the tempest . . . the sweeping winds of change . . . revolution . . . the destruction of the old society making way for the new." Ruth Landes, Hubert Fichte, and others have spoken of Oyá as a patron of gender variant and homoerotically-inclined males. Landes reported in 1940 that a number of male practitioners of Candomblé Caboclo whom she had encountered in Brazil were homosexual and bisexual "votaries of Yansan [i.e. Oyá]." Fichte writes, "In Colombia, homosexuals [in the religion] address their prayers to the Afro-American goddess Yansá." Oyá's association with male gender variance – if not with homosexuality – may be traced to Yorubaland. One exquisitely crafted Yoruba statue depicts Oyá riding on horseback, her skin painted white and her hair dyed indigo. She holds a fan plaque in her right hand and a sacrificial cock, also indigo, in her left. Among several figures flanking her is a small male figure who clutches her back and sits on the horse's rump. His hair, according to William Fagg, "is styled in the fashion of a woman," that is to say, his hair has been shaped into the "bell jar" or "beehive" hairdo of the goddess and, like hers, has been dyed indigo. This suggests that the figure may represent a gender variant male initiate or priest of Oyá.

Oyamakui Japanese transgendered mountain deity presiding over childbearing as well as industry.

P

Padmasambhava (also known as **Guru Rinpoche**, 755-797) Alongside his companion, Vajrayogini, who is known as the female "lineage holder" of Tibetan Buddhism, Padmasambhava, due to his own powerful shamanic and magical abilities, was able to triumph over the Bon-po shamans of pre-Buddhist Tibet. A shapeshifter, he possessed the ability to metamorphose from human into animal and from male into female. M. Jamal (1995) explains that Padmasambhava's "supreme mission was to liberate all sentient beings," and that "every metamorphosis was a means to that end," as such metamorphoses ultimately represented the "illusory nature of . . . identities."

Paimon In the western European tradition of ritual magic, Paimon, whose name means "tinkling sound," is distinguished from other male spirits in being described as possessing an "effeminate countenance." Wearing a crown and riding on a dromedary, he is preceded by a host of other male spirits resembling the GALLI of the goddess CYBELE; these spirits herald him with trumpets and cymbals. Associated with the direction of the northwest, Paimon is invoked by those wishing to know the future or wishing to instruct animals how to become familiars who will assist them in works of magic.

Pakaa In Hawaiian mythology, a shaman possessing great magical powers who served his male AIKANE, or intimate companion, Chief KEAWE-NUI-A-'UMI.

Paksu Mudang In Korea, where Shamanism was greatly influenced by Tungusic tribes journeying from Siberia between 1000 and 600 BCE, a majority of shamans have been women. There have, however, been male shamans. One class of these has been comprised of traditionally masculine males who are visually impaired. The other class of male shamans, the *paksu mudang*, have been described as transgendered, gender variant, or third gender males who wear feminine attire. They have been linked to the HWARANG, the so-called "flower-boys," who formed a military elite in Buddhist Korea.

Palaestra Greco-Roman goddess of WRESTLING. Philostratus (fl. c. 200 CE) tells us that when the Olympic Games were first established, there was no prize for wrestling, nor was there "even any love of wrestling." This would wait until Palaestra, a daughter of HERMES, reached maidenhood in Arcadia. Palaestra discovered the art, which was praised by the gods, who believed that if

anything could make mortals put an end to war, it would be their delight in this sport. "War will be laid aside . . . during the truce, and the stadium will seem . . . more delightful than armed camps." Palaestra was a handsome young woman. "The figure of Palaestra, if it be compared with a boy, will be that of a girl; but if it be taken for a girl, it will seem to be a boy. For her hair is too short even to be twisted into a knot; the eye might be that of either sex . . . the breasts themselves, as in a boy of tender years . . . She cares for nothing feminine; hence she does not even wish to have white arms . . . she begs Helius [the Sun] for color . . . the branch of olive on her bare bosom is . . . becoming to her." The olive tree was sacred to Palaestra, "since its oil is useful in wrestling" and mortals "find great pleasure in it." As the patron of wrestling schools, the *palaistra*, the goddess became as well a patron of love between men and perhaps also of lesbian love. Indeed, the *palaistra* became so linked to homoerotic love in the minds of Greeks, Romans, and others in western and Near Eastern antiquity that they were often set ablaze by tyrants fearing that male lovers would emerge from them who would, beyond wrestling, attempt to eradicate tyranny.

Pala-Moa In Hawaiian mythology, AIKANE, or intimate companion, of another male, KUMU-KAHI, with whom he practiced magic. Pala-Moa took possession of persons in order to aid them in becoming shamans who would be capable of healing, divining, working magic, and shapeshifting. The lord of birds, he also may have been especially associated with fish, as fishers sacrificed to him in exchange for bountiful catches.

Pales In Roman mythology or religion, a deity overseeing sheep and cattle and the patron of shepherds and cowherds. Pales was thought to be either transgendered, hermaphroditic, or a female possessing shapeshifting powers. Pales is fêted on April 21.

Pallas Daughter of the Greek river-god Triton and beloved companion of the goddess ATHENA. Triton, wishing Athena to be his daughter's companion, reared her. This did not please her own jealous father, ZEUS. One day when the two young women were engaged in spear-fighting, one of their favorite pursuits, Zeus, looking down, imagined that he saw Pallas's spear wounding Athena. Jealousy having blinded him from seeing clearly, he struck down Pallas. It was, unfortunately, not in Athena's power to revive her beloved Pallas. Thus she carved a statue of her from wood, and placed it on an altar in a shrine dedicated to her. Moreover, she honored her by joining their names; this fused female couple became known as Pallas Athena.

Pamano Legendary hero of Hawaii known for his mastery of the HULA and ritual chanting, restored to life, after being killed by men jealous of him, by his sisters. Bisexual in today's terms, Pamano's primary female companion was Keaka, while his primary male companion was KOOLAU, who also loved Keaka.

Pan In Greek religion and myth, goat-footed god of creativity, music, poetry, sensuality and sexuality, panic, and nightmares who haunts forests, caverns, mountains, brooks and streams. His favorite hour is noon, that time of day when he seduces young men while teaching them to play the SYRINX, or pan-pipe. Pansexual, his female lovers include Echo and Selene, his male lovers CYPARISSUS, DAPHNIS, OLYMPUS, and several of his music students. In an early pottery illustration, Pan is shown leaping from an ithyphallic HERM and throwing himself on a young goatherd, who is running away. The god's hands are outstretched, his member erect. In Renaissance symbology, Pan became linked to both GANYMEDE and JESUS Christ, a rather odd conflation subtly playing upon the idea of lover (devotee) and beloved (god). In the nineteenth century, the French Symbolist poet Paul Verlaine, the lover of RIMBAUD, continued to link Pan to Christ, and in the early twentieth century, the Spanish poet Federico García LORCA linked Verlaine himself to Pan and Christ, as well as to DIONYSUS. This linkage is revealed in "Responso a Verlaine" and elsewhere.

Pansy Also called "Heart's ease," "Call me to you," and "Love in idleness," this velvety, multicolored flower is symbolic of love, passion, remembrance, and reflection. As Judy Grahn (1984) suggests, its pansexual symbolism may be traceable to Shakespeare's *Midsummer Night's Dream*. In this magical comedy, a potion made of pansy "juice," distributed by the TRICKSTER fairy PUCK, holds the pansexual power, when dropped in someone's eyes, to cause that person to fall in love with the first creature they see on waking from sleep, whether male or female, human or another species. By the late nineteenth century, the pansy had become, primarily in England and the US, a signifier of homoerotic love. In an 1892 poem, "Heartsease and Orchid," Percy Osborne writes, "Heartsease it was from his dear hand I took, / A dainty flower that loves the garden air." While in the early to mid-twentieth century "pansy" became a derogatory term for an effeminate gay man, it was reclaimed by radical-spiritual gay men in the early 1970s as a positive symbol of gay love, becoming the primary symbol for *RFD*, a US gay men's rural journal. In the 1990s, the symbolism of the flower survives in the name of the queer rock group Pansy Division.

Panther Simultaneously symbolic of beauty, terror, and exoticism, the panther is sacred to numerous Greek and Roman deities associated with transgenderism and/or same-sex passion, including APHRODITE, CYBELE, DIONYSUS, and ORPHEUS. In the nineteenth and early twentieth century, the panther became a signifier of both homoerotic love and homophobic cruelty appearing as such in the works of Oscar WILDE, Federico García LORCA, and others.

Panuco Capital city of the Huastecs of Mexico described by the so-called "Anonymous Conquistador" in 1519 as a place where men "adored the penis and kept phallic images in their temples alongside images in relief of all manners of sodomitic pleasure which can be executed."

Paoa His name meaning "fruitless," in Hawaiian traditional religion Paoa was the primary male AIKANE (intimate companion) of LOHIAU. Paoa loved Lohiau deeply, calling him "the beauty of Kaua'i" and saying of him, *He aikane he mae aloha e* ("An *aikane* is a beloved one"). Bisexual in contemporary terms, Paoa also may have shared relationships with the goddesses HI'IAKA and PELE. After his death, apparently a suicide, Pele took his name for her digging stick or divining rod.

Papa Female creator and earth mother of Hawaiian traditional religion, Papa shares with her spouse WAKEA an apparently bisexual servant and AIKANE (intimate companion) named HAAKAUILANANI.

Papaver Young man of Roman mythology who loved another young man named ANETHUS ("ANISE"). When he died, Papaver was transformed into a POPPY. His memory was preserved in garlands given by male lovers to each other in ancient Rome.

Papaya In twentieth-century Chile, a fruit symbolic of male homosexuality. The papaya is also symbolic of the vulva and possibly of lesbianism.

Papyrus Sacred attribute of HAPY, the androgynous or transgender deity of the Nile.

Paradjanov, Sergei (1924-1993) Georgian filmmaker of Armenian heritage, imprisoned for homosexuality and other alleged "crimes" by the Soviet government. Despite suffering great persecution, Paradjanov created a number of exquisitely crafted films including *Shadows of Forgotten Ancestors* (1964), *The Color of Pomegranates* (1969), *The Legend of Suram Fortress* (1985), and *Ashik Kerib* (1988). Leonid Alekseychuk has described Paradjanov as a "bewitched and reverent pantheist, for whom everything in existence is full of spirits and universal harmony [who] worshipped icons and carnival masks . . . folk embroidery

[and] smooth skin on a handsome youth." While in prison, he painted and designed women's hats and founded a drag theater, but more importantly, he served as a healer and psychopomp. Paradjanov wrote of this experience: "They sent me to . . . zones where they expected me to perish . . . It's only because I have a clever and cunning character that I managed to survive . . . I painted a picture of Jesus on the cloth they put over a cadaver . . . I became the priest of the zones. I began to close the eyes of corpses and to tie up the jaws. I began healing people, listening to their fates."

Parasol In classical antiquity, a general symbol of effeminacy, and more specifically a symbol of the GALLI, the gender variant male priests of the Roman goddess CYBELE. *Galli* were sometimes referred to as *umbraticola*, "Those who carry parasols and stay in the shade."

Parenting and Mentoring In many cultures, divine beings and spiritual functionaries linked to bisexuality or same-sex eroticism and/or transgenderism are especially associated with parenting and mentoring. These include, from Hinduism, the deities SHIVA and AGNI, who, from their union, brought forth KARTIKKEYEH; Shiva and VISHNU, from whose union HARIHARA was born; and PARVATI and MALINI, from whose union GANESHA was born. In Greek religion, the centaur CHIRON is especially associated with rearing and mentoring children, while the *kourotrophoi* were both semi-divine beings and actual persons who served as parents, mentors, nurses, and companions to young persons, deriving their authority from goddesses including Ge Meter, Eileithyia, and Rhea or CYBELE and gods associated with homoeroticism, including APOLLO, HERMES, and POSEIDON. Among the Mohave people of North America, "TWO-SPIRIT" male ALYHA shamans emulated pregnancy by first stuffing rags under their garments, then constipating themselves, and then ritually defecating, "giving birth" to "stillborn children" who were buried, after which followed a grieving process. Also among the Mohave, whenever a "two-spirit" female HWAME shaman claimed "paternity" for the pregnancy of a woman, she took care of the child, loving it and raising it as its parent. Among the Yuki and Pomo tribes, "two-spirit" persons were sometimes allowed to adopt children. In Inuit (or Eskimo) culture, in the past, transgendered male ANGAKKUQ were responsible for rearing and educating certain young women. "The tribe confide[s] to him the girls most suitable in bodily grace and disposition; he has to complete their education – he will perfect them in dancing and other accomplishments . . . If they display intelligence, they will become seers and medicine-women . . . The summer *kachims* (assemblies), which are closed to the women of the community, will open wide before these."

Paris Trojan prince, brother of Deiphobus, abductor of HELEN, male lover of ANTHEUS and male beloved of HERMES (Roman MERCURY), and devotee of APHRODITE. The poet Luxurious (early sixth century CE) invoked Paris as a symbol of effeminacy and receptive homoeroticism, comparing an "effeminate" lawyer to "a Paris to be used as a woman."

Paris (City of) French city associated in the Medieval period with same-sex eroticism. Graffiti of the twelfth or thirteenth century declares, "Now CHARTRES and Paris make themselves filthy continually / With SODOM's vice," and "Paris is happy to be married to a soft and delicate master." The latter puns upon PARIS, the Trojan prince. Catholic authorities seemed especially concerned that NUNS dwelling in Parisian CONVENTS might be tempted to engage in lesbian lovemaking; in 1212 the Council of Paris "prohibited nuns from sleeping together and required a lamp to burn all night in dormitories."

Parjanya Androgynous or transgendered rain god of Hinduism who, though sterile, gives birth. Also described as a bull and cow, the "rain" Parjanya produces is at once rain, milk, semen, and offspring.

Parmenides (b. c. 515 BCE) Founder of the Eleatic school of Greek philosophy and intimate male companion of ZENO OF ELEA. Parmenides taught that "unchanging being is the material substance of which the universe is composed" and that growth and destruction are "illusions of the senses."

Parsifal (or **Perceval**) In British legend, an Arthurian knight and Grail seeker. Parsifal is said to have been raised in the forest by his mother to protect him from the ways of the world. On meeting the knights of King Arthur, however, Parsifal followed them and was eventually knighted in a ceremony employing the Grail, the sacred cup used by JESUS at the Last Supper. According to J. Huneker (1904), Parsifal signified for composer Richard Wagner a man-loving, possibly transgendered, hero mirroring King Ludwig of Bavaria, with whom Wagner shared an intimate friendship. A homoerotic interpretation of the Parsifal legend has also been advanced by Oskar Panizza, Hanns Fuchs, and Richard D. Mohr.

Partridge In Egyptian and later in Coptic Christian symbolism, a pair of male partridges signified homoeroticism.

Parvati "Lady of the Mountain," Parvati is a manifestation of the Hindu Great, or Mother, Goddess; as such, she is sometimes identified with SHAKTI, the goddess and principle of feminine energy. She is the spouse of SHIVA, the mother of GANESHA, and beloved of her handmaid MALINI. When Parvati (or Shakti) and Shiva merge, they become the androgynous or transgendered ARDHANARISHVARA.

Pashupata Branch of the Hindu cult of the god SHIVA as the "lord (*pati*) of cattle" who "helps his creatures (*pashu*) to free themselves from the bondage (*pasha*) of this world." Allegedly founded by Shiva and first led by Lakulisha (fl. c. 200 CE). The sect flourished from the seventh through the twelfth centuries. The Pashupatas chiefly revered Shiva as a liberator, a deathbringer, and as an erotic force. As the last of these, Shiva was represented by the *lakula*, or *danda*, a club signifying his erect phallus. Much like the GALLI priests of the Roman goddess CYBELE, the Pashupatas employed meditation, the chanting of mantras, ritual noises including yells and bull-like roars, and ecstatic dance to aid in triggering an altered state of consciousness in which they envisioned themselves as achieving erotico-spiritual union with Shiva. B. Walker (1968), infers that the Pashupatas, in honoring the phallus, may have practiced ritual mutual masturbation and homoeroticism.

Patlache Ancient Mexican Nahuatl term for Amazon-like, woman-loving woman. *Patlaches* were described as women who sought other women as intimate companions, *mocihuapotiani*, and who "liked to rub their vulvas on the bodies of other women," *tepixuia*. *Patlaches* were protected by the goddesses TLAZOLTEOTL and XOCHIQUETZAL, and as such were said to "follow the path of the rabbit and the deer."

Patroclus Comrade-lover of ACHILLES in Greek legend. After Patroclus was killed in the Trojan War by Hector, Achilles avenged his death by slaying Hector. Moreover, twelve Trojan nobles were sacrificed on Patroclus's funeral pyre. On the death of Achilles, his ashes and bone fragments were mingled together with those of Patroclus in a golden urn. Both Patroclus and Achilles were divinized and worshipped on the White Island (Leucé, or LEUKÉ). In the *Iliad*, a tale is told of the ghost of Patroclus appearing to Achilles shortly after his death, pleading with his lover to give him a speedy burial: "Sleeping Achilles, bury me quickly [Patroclus pleads] – let me pass the Gates of Hades. Oh give me your hand – I beg you with my tears! . . . A last request – grant it, please. Never bury my bones apart from yours, Achilles, let them lie together." Achilles replied, "I will obey your demands. Oh come closer! Throw our arms around each other, just for a moment – take our fill of the tears that numb the heart!" In the same breath "he stretched out his loving arms but could not seize him, no, the ghost slipped underground like a wisp of smoke."

Paul II, Pope (1417-1471) Born Pietro Barbo in Venice. Known for his beauty, vanity, and extravagance in clothes,

he originally intended to take the name Formosus I, "the well-shaped." His vestments and robes were lined with gold and sparkled with diamonds. He was known for his effeminate behavior and especially for crying in public, for which he was nicknamed Maria Pientissima, Our Lady of Pity. It was rumored that he died during the "act of sodomy" of a heart attack. His main accomplishments were urban beautification and the introduction of printing to Rome.

Paula of Avila, Saint (late antiquity or early Middle Ages) Transgendered female saint also known as St Paula the Bearded. Once when, as a young woman, she was being pursued by a man, Paula knelt before a crucifix and begged Jesus to shield her from unwanted advances. Christ did so by giving her a BEARD, and perhaps also by transforming her anatomy from female to male. Paula was compared to Aphroditos, a bearded, transgendered form of the Greek goddess APHRODITE. She is fêted on February 3.

Paulinus of Nola, Bishop, Saint (c. 353-431) Convert to Christianity who was passionately drawn to his teacher AUSONIUS, writing passionate poems to him. In later life, however, Paulinus, retiring to a chapel in Spain, distanced himself from Ausonius, apparently feeling guilty due to the homoerotic aspect of their relationship. St Paulinus is fêted on June 22.

Pauopalae Fern goddess and divine nurse with whom the Hawaiian goddess Hi'iaka shares an AIKANE, or intimate same-sex, relationship.

Pavatairayan D. Shulman (1980) recounts the legend of the South Indian hero Pavatairayan, the "King of the Long Skirt." Pavatairayan was out hunting one day when he shot an arrow into an ant hill by mistake. To retrieve it, he chopped a hole in the earth and accidentally wounded the Goddess who was dwelling there. When he asked the Goddess how he might atone for his error, she told him to bring her something to eat. As he had no food with him he offered her his own entrails. So honored was she by his sacrifice that she granted him eternal life, if he would but abandon his male attire and be her attendant. According to Shulman, "The transvestite Pavatairayan stands to this day outside the shrines of Ankalamman."

Pea In the poetry of Emily DICKINSON (1830-1886), the pea in the pod appears to be symbolic of the clitoris, and, by extension, of female, especially lesbian, sexuality.

Peach In Chinese mythology and symbolism, the peach, signifying immortality, may also refer to homoerotic love. Once, King Ling of Wei (534-493 BCE) fell in love with a handsome young man named Mi Tzu-hsia. As they were walking one day in the King's garden, Mi picked a ripe, sweet peach. Rather than eating the whole peach, however, Mi saved half of it for the King. Ling was deeply moved by Mi's generosity and told his courtiers of the event and of his great love for Mi Tzu-hsia. After this, the love of man for man became known as "*yu-tao*," or "sharing the peach." In a BLUES song by "Peach Tree" Payne, he describes a queer-centered ARCADIA called "Peach Tree Land." In the 1990s, in the US South, peaches continue to signify, among other things, transgendered homosexuality. In "Looking West to China" (1933), woman-loving poet Elsa GIDLOW writes: "Had I a garden / I would open its gate to you only / At the time of peach blossom."

Peacock   Steed of the Hindu deity KARTIKKEYEH, who is associated with homoeroticism. The peacock represents the ability to transform ugliness and death (in this context, signified by the SERPENT) into beauty and immortality (the peacock). In the Euro-western tradition of ALCHEMY, the peacock is symbolic of androgyny or transgenderism. The Arabian gender variant MUKHANNATH musician TUWAIS was referred to as "the little peacock."

Peirithous   In Greek legend, son of NESTOR and lover of TELEMACHUS, whom he accompanied to Sparta. Legendary ruler of the Lapiths, he also shared an intimate friendship with THESEUS, the ruler of Athens. They were revered as semi-divine heroes at Athens.

Péladan, Joséphin (1859-1918)   French occultist and novelist associated with the aesthetic movements of Symbolism(e) and Decadence. A student of the QABBALAH and other esoteric systems, Péladan was obsessed with androgyny, his long beard offset by mixed-gender attire. Alternately – or simultaneously – drawn to and repulsed by both gender and sexual variance, he wrote in a "Hymn to the Androgyne": "Intangible Eros, Uranian, in the eyes of coarse men of moralistic epochs, you are only an infamous sin. They call you 'Sodom' . . . It is the need of hypocritical centuries to attack Beauty . . . Protect your monstrous mask from profanity! Praise to you!"

Pelagia, and **Saint Pelagia** (no date; probably late antiquity)   One of the names of APHRODITE in her association with the planet VENUS; a beautiful dancer and courtesan of Antioch who has ultimately become a transgendered saint. Upon her conversion to Christianity, Pelagia began to identify as Pelagius. By the end of his life Pelagius had found refuge in a monk's cell on the Mount of Olives in Jerusalem and had become known throughout the Holy Land as the "wise Brother Pelagius monk and eunuch." Upon Pelagius's death, when the body was discovered to be anatomically female, the mourners chanted, "Glory be to thee, Lord Jesus, for thou hast many hidden treasures on earth, female as well as male." Canonized as a Catholic saint,

Pelagia/Pelagius, also known as Pelagia the Penitent and as St Margaret, is fêted on October 8.

Pele   Goddess of volcanoes in traditional Hawaiian religion and myth, still revered by many in the 1990s, primarily as Madame Pele. Pele is a jealous goddess. When she became convinced that her sister HI'IAKA had commenced an erotic relationship with her male lover, LOHIAU, she punished Hi'iaka by killing the latter's AIKANE (intimate companion) HOPOE by flowing over her with burning lava. Nevertheless, many lesbian and bisexual women are drawn to the fiery, Amazonian Pele. In *Lesbian Sacred Sexuality* (1995) Diane MARIECHILD writes: "I found a marvelous picture of Pele, her hair waves of fire extending out from her head. She stood, a fiery being in the ocean . . . I placed it on our altar and Barbara and I sat together and repeated our vows . . . I asked that we call upon Pele, thank her for cradling us to her breast."

Peleus   King of Phthia in Thessaly and father of ACHILLES, he was one of the ARGONAUTS, and a beloved of the Greek god HEPHAESTUS.

Pelops   Greek god of the sea, dolphins, and erotic passion, grandson of the Greek god ZEUS, son of Tantalus, beloved of POSEIDON, and husband of Hippodameia. When Tantalus was given the task of serving up a meal to the gods of Olympus at a banquet, he cooked his own son. The gods were horrified on seeing this and refused to eat, all except DEMETER, who, consumed in grief over losing PERSEPHONE, was not paying attention, and so ate a piece of PELOPS's shoulder. When the gods revivified Pelops, Demeter bestowed upon him an ivory shoulder. Tantalus, who had tantalized the gods, was punished. Pelops, whom Poseidon had fallen in love with, was carried off to live in the sea god's palace. Later on, Pelops married Hippodameia and also became lovers with his charioteer Sphaerus, who was revered on the island of Sphaeria or Hiera.

Penthesileia   A Queen of the AMAZONS who, after many triumphs, was defeated and slain in battle by the Greek hero ACHILLES. The hero wept over her body, despairing of his act.

Peony   In the work of woman-loving poet Amy Lowell (1874-1925), one of whose primary lovers was Ada Dwyer Russell, nicknamed "Peter", this flower was symbolic of lesbian desire. In "Reflection, she writes: "When I looked into your eyes / I saw a garden / With peonies."

Perpetua, Saint and Saint Felicitas (d. 203 CE) Perpetua, a noblewoman of Carthage, and Felicitas, a slave woman, were converts to Christianity who were arrested for their religious beliefs. When they were arrested, Perpetua had a young daughter, Vivia, and

Felicitas was pregnant. In a dream while in prison, Perpetua saw herself "borne into the amphitheater, stripped of her clothes, and changed into a man." Not long after, she and Felicitas, who had given birth to a daughter in prison, were taken to the amphitheater, where they were to be attacked by wild beasts. As the beasts did not harm them, however, they were stabbed to death. Sts Perpetua and Felicitas were described by early Christian fathers as "neither male nor female" due to the "manliness" of their souls. In part due to the scholarship of John Boswell, especially in his *Same-Sex Unions in Premodern Europe* (1994), contemporary lesbians and other Christians are beginning to honor Sts Perpetua and Felicitas as a sanctified female couple. Sts Perpetua and Felicitas are fêted on March 7.

Perry, Troy Deroy (1940-   ) Founder of the Universal Fellowship of Metropolitan Community Churches. At fifteen he was licensed to preach in Florida by a local Baptist church. Drawn to Pentecostalism, however, at sixteen he became an evangelist minister for the Church of God in Tennessee. Coming out as a gay man in the early 1960s, he settled in Los Angeles, where he founded the Metropolitian Community Church in 1968. In 1972 he published *The Lord Is My Shepherd and He Know I'm Gay* and in 1990 *Don't Be Afraid Anymore*. In recent years, Perry has become interested in the spiritual aspects of "leather," or S/M, concluding in a tongue-in-cheek manner in "A Meditation on Religion and Leatherspace," "Why else would the Christian scriptures tell us that John the Baptist, the person who proclaimed the coming of the One we believe is the Christ, the Promised One, wore leather?"

Persephone Primarily known in Greek myth and religion as the daughter of the goddess DEMETER who is abducted by the god HADES to the Underworld, commemorated in the ELEUSINIAN MYSTERIES. The poet SAPPHO refers to death as "Persephone's dark bedroom." Persephone was also invoked in same-sex-oriented love and binding spells in the *Greek Magical Papyri* of third-century CE Alexandria.

Phaenon Beautiful young man loved by the Greek god ZEUS. Phaenon was created from clay by Prometheus when the latter was fashioning humankind. Prometheus, familiar with Zeus's attraction to young men, decided not to introduce Phaenon to him. EROS, however, happened to see the youth as he was flying overhead and told Zeus of the handsome Phaenon. Zeus then demanded that Prometheus introduce them. They fell in love the instant they met. Some versions of the myth say that at the time of Phaenon's death, Zeus immortalized him by transforming him into the planet JUPITER. Others report, however, that HERMES stole Phaenon away by suggesting that they live together in

the heavens as immortal, and that it was Hermes, not Zeus, who transformed Phaenon into the planet Jupiter.

Phaeton In Greek mythology, the son of Helios and Clymene. When Phaeton learned that his father was the god of the sun, he journeyed west to find him. When at last they met, he begged his father to let him drive the solar chariot for a day. Helios reluctantly agreed, and Phaeton, unable to handle the chariot, set the world aflame. Zeus punished him by killing him with a thunderbolt. He fell into the Eridanus River. His lover CYCNUS, son of Sthenelus of Liguria, unable to find his body, lost in grief, was changed into a swan. Phaeton's grieving sisters, the Heliades, were changed into alder trees, while their tears transformed into amber. In some traditions, Phaeton came to represent the destructive power of the sun, while Cycnus came to represent the healing power of water. Attributed to Phaeton are EARTHQUAKES, volcanoes, FIRES, droughts, famines, burns, and sunburns. According to the Mithraists, a cult comprised primarily of Roman soldiers, Phaeton's ride symbolizes the final destruction of the world as we know it, and the birth of a New Age. For many centuries, the chariot will drive smoothly. Then one day, the horse of fire will breathe upon the horses of earth, air, and water, and will set the chariot and then the world on fire. Unbelievers will be burned alive or turned to stone, while the faithful will relinquish their physical bodies for spiritual ones. In some traditions, Phaeton is transformed into the constellation Auriga, the Charioteer. Homoerotically and bisexually inclined artists have been particularly drawn to the tale of Phaeton, with Jean Baptiste Lully (1632-1687) composing an opera and Camille Saint-Saëns (1835-1921) composing a tone poem, both titled *Phaeton*. More recently, Brazilian writer Aguinaldo Silva, in his *Primeira carta aos andróginos* (*First Letters to the Androgynes*, 1975) depicts the extraterrestrial journey of Davi/Salomao to Phaeton, an ARCADIA/UTOPIA where communitarian socialism and pansexuality are the order of the day. D. Foster (1991) writes of this novel: "Phaeton, whether as an alternative physical reality or as an emotional escapist fantasy, offers . . . the vision of a realm where the monsters of hatred, exploitation, and oppression can be conquered in order to (re)attain a Marcusian Eden of integral human sexuality."

Phanes In Orphism, a Mystery cult of classical antiquity allegedly founded by the musician-mystic ORPHEUS, Phanes is an hermaphroditic or transgendered deity of light and creation, possessing two faces, four eyes, golden wings, and the voice of a bull or lion. Despite this strange appearance, Phanes is described as a being "of wondrous beauty." According to the Orphics, Phanes created a universe of great beauty and joy which came to an end when the Greek god ZEUS displaced him. Phanes is akin to both PRIAPUS and HERMAPHRODITUS.

Phibionites Branch of Gnostics who revered the
Goddess as CYBELE Barbelo and whose rites embraced
sexual and gender variance. As Barbelo, Cybele was
associated with other Gnostic goddesses including Sophia,
Prunikos (the Lewd One), and Norea. It was the desire of
the Goddess, said the Phibionites, to gather to herself and
to replace in her womb the "light" that had been scattered
upon the earth when she gave birth to human beings, as
well as to gather the "light" which had divided itself from
her when Attis or Christ had descended to earth. This
"ingathering" was to be accomplished in part by her
worshippers, both men and women, who engaged in an
agape rite or "love feast" involving the "extraction,
collection, and solemn, sacramental consecration of bodily
fluids," namely, semen and menstrual blood, in an effort to
recover the lost "light." Only in this way might men and
women avoid "the further propagation of the human race,
and . . . the continued entrapment of divine substance" in
matter, linked in Gnosticism to evil. By way of the *agape*
rite, Goehring explains, the lost "light" was "gathered and
offered to the divine." This belief in the necessity of
gathering bodily fluids and sacrificing them was called
syllexis. Where male worshippers are concerned, it appears
that they often employed ritual masturbation, both of self
and other males, and fellatio, in order to gather semen. It is
possible that interrupted forms of anal and phallic-vaginal
intercourse were also undertaken. Of ritual masturbation,
the male devotees would recite passages from the New
Testament: "These hands were sufficient, not only for me
but for those with me" and "Working with your own
hands, so that you may have something to share with those
who have nothing." A male worshipper would take his own
semen or that of another, would offer it in prayer to the
godhead, and would consume it, invoking ATTIS-Christ:
"This is the body of Christ; and this is the Pascha, because
of which our bodies suffer and are made to acknowledge
the passion of Christ." Of the centrality of homoeroticism
among the Phibionites, Epiphanius writes: "since they are
not satiated with their promiscuous intercourse with
women, [they] are inflamed towards one another, men with
men, as it is written . . . for these, who are utterly
abandoned, congratulate each other, as if they had received
the choicest distinction." Within the Phibionite sect or
branch, moreover, there was the Levite subsect, whose
members appear to have been "exclusively homosexual"
and "regarded as the élite of the [Phibionite] sect."
According to Epiphanius, "Those among them who are
called Levites . . . do not have intercourse with women, but
with each other. And it is these who are actually
distinguished and honoured among them." As a sacred text
defending their autoerotic and homoerotic practices, the
Levites quoted from the apocryphal *Gospel of Philip,*
which speaks of "knowing oneself," which they interpreted
as masturbation, of "collecting all that has been scattered
of oneself into oneself again," which they interpreted as

saving or eating one's own semen, and of "sowing no
children" for the evil God of the Old Testament, which
they interpreted as sanctioning auto- and homoeroticism.

Philoctetes In Greek legend, an accomplished archer, an
ARGONAUT, and a lover of HERACLES. When Heracles
died, Philoctetes, whose name signifies "love of
possessions," kept his bow and arrows. Later, after being
bitten by a serpent and forced to remain on the island of
Lemnos, where he lived for ten years, Philoctetes was
visited by Odysseus and Neoptolemus, who, believing that
the Trojan War could be won only by using the arrows of
Heracles, demanded them from Philoctetes. This being
the only treasure Philoctetes possessed of his lover, he
refused to part with them. Only when the spirit of
Heracles, or, according to other accounts, the revivified
body of the hero, appeared to Philoctetes and beseeched
him to part with them did he surrender them to Odysseus
and Neoptolemus.

Philolaus In classical antiquity, a legendary Theban or
Corinthian hero whose name suggests an association of
love (*philo-*) and the army (*-laus*). Philolaus was the lover of
another warrior named DIOCLES. Lovers pledged
themselves to each other at their tomb at Thebes, and it
was in honor of their relationship that the Diocleia games
were founded.

Phoenix In Egyptian, Greek, Roman, Chinese, and
alchemical symbolism, a signifier of creativity,
transformation, rebirth, and androgyny or
transgenderism. In ALCHEMY, the phoenix is sometimes
depicted as having scarlet, blue, mauve, and gold feathers.
Due to its beauty turning to ash and again to beauty, the
phoenix has been compared to incense. In "Hymn to a
Mystery," poet Elsa GIDLOW compares lesbian
lovemaking to the self-creating, self-destroying, self-
recreating phoenix, writing: "Phoenix flesh that / Living,
dies / And dies / To live again / In ecstasy." In 1989 the US
lesbian comedienne Robin Tyler proposed the adoption of
the phoenix as a new symbol for the gay and lesbian
movement because of the power of queer-identified
persons to survive and replenish themselves (ourselves) in
the midst of great adversity.

Photography The study of the relationship of
photography to transgenderism, same-sex intimacy, and
the mythic or sacred is in its infancy. Among the first
photographers to explore the interrelationship of male
homoeroticism and the spiritual were Baron Wilhelm von
Gloeden (1856-1931), renowned for his portraits of nude
male youths of Taormina, Sicily posing in stylized Greco-
Roman poses among ancient ruins, and F. Holland DAY,
remembered for his subtle, homoeroticized depictions of
ORPHEUS, PAN, JESUS, and other mythic and religious

figures. A third photographer weaving together the mythic and the homoerotic was George Platt Lynes (1907-1951), whose work was inspired by friends and acquaintances including André GIDE, Pavel TCHELITCHEW, Jean COCTEAU, Marsden HARTLEY, and Jared FRENCH. More recently, Steven Arnold, Efren Ramirez, and Rotimi Fani-Kayodi have explored the interfacing of the homoerotic, the transgendered, and the spiritual. Of these, Fani-Kayodi (1955-1989), a British photographer of Yoruba heritage, said of his work, "If I ever manage to get an exhibition in, say Lagos [Nigeria], I would certainly be charged with being a purveyor of corrupt and decadent Western values." He was certain that, whatever their opinion might be of his work, practitioners of the Yoruba religion would resonate to his "smallpox gods," referring to the *orishá* BABALUAYE, his "transsexual priests," and his "images of Black men in a state of sexual frenzy." Other gay male photographers who have explored this interrelationship as well as it linkage to HIV/AIDS are Duane Michaels, whose *Dream of Flowers* (1986) evokes death as an "expanding veil of flowers that envelops the head of his model," and Robert Mapplethorpe, whose *Self-Portrait* (1988) depicts his head floating in darkness, his right hand bearing a jester's scepter mounted with a skull. By far the most popular of the photographers currently exploring our present subject are Pierre and Gilles. Shortly after meeting in 1976, they began collaborating on exquisite, Campy portraits of mythical and religious subjects including *Bacchus* (DIONYSUS), *Neptune* (POSEIDON), *SHIVA* (with BOY GEORGE as a model), *Le Diable* (SATAN), and *SAINT SEBASTIAN*. Since the 1980s, lesbian photographers have also begun to turn their attention to the mythic and sacred. Among the most well-known of these are Tee Corinne, who has published her photos in *Yantras of Womanlove* (1982), Della Grace, and Marcelina Martin, whose work appears in *Lesbian Sacred Sexuality* (1995, with text by Diane MARIECHILD).

Piache General Spanish term for male shaman of Colombia, Venezuela, and Brazil who, as leader of the men's house, led initiation rites including cultic homoeroticism. The *piache* served as "priest, physician, magician, and counselor." According to some accounts, the *piache* was considered gender variant or transgendered; according to others, he was not.

Pikoe Sendo Among the Tewa, an indigenous American people, a legendary leader of the hunt, sometimes perceived as a third gender or TWO-SPIRIT male.

Pikoi Hawaiian hero or demigod, hybrid rat-human male, somewhat ironically called the "rat shooter." Child of Crow and Bat, Pikoi was AIKANE (intimate companion) to the male beings Pueo ("Owl") and Waiakea.

Pilpili Mesopotamian spiritual functionary; synonymous with ASSINNU and SAG-UR-SAG, a gender variant, possibly homoerotically inclined, male priest of INANNA/ISHTAR.

Pine Symbolic of immortality, the pine tree is sacred to the Greco-Roman deities ATTIS and BRITOMARTIS.

Pisces In Euro-western ASTROLOGY, zodiac sign ruling from (approximately) February 19 until March 20, associated with artistic ability, empathy, and healing ability, typically depicted as a pair of FISH. Figures associated with Pisces and with gender and/or sexual variance include: APHRODITE, ATARGATIS, LA BALEINE, JESUS, KUAN YIN, MERMAIDS, ORPHEUS, PELOPS, POSEIDON, LA SIRENE, and YEMAYA.

Plague Since the sixth century CE and perhaps earlier, homoerotically and/or bisexually inclined and gender variant males have been accused by some Christians of causing – and of constituting – plagues, as well as earthquakes. Justinian (-us the Great, 482/483-565), Christian zealot and Emperor of Constantinople, was among the many who insisted that such men be executed in order to avert plagues. Six hundred years later, in the mid-twelfth century, Bernard of Cluny, in his poem "Contempt of the World," echoed Justinian in voicing this view: ". . . even churches are awash with this filthy plague . . . / . . . hermaphrodites are now very much in fashion! / Husbands recite empty marriage vows, / Unnatural sins persist . . . / This leprosy clings." On Christmas Day, 1497, Jimeoto da Lucca of the Order of the Observants of St Francis in Venice preached: "My lord, you close the churches for fear of the plague . . . This could be avoided if you would eliminate the causes that lead to the plague, which are the horrible sins that are committed [here], the blaspheming of God and . . . the societies of sodomy . . . Overcome this and you will overcome the plague." In 1519 another violent example of homophobia occurred when the Spanish city of Valencia was suffering from the plague. On June 14, the day of St Mary Magdalene, Father Luis Castelloli condemned sodomites for bringing God's wrath in the form of the plague. The people of Valencia became so anxious on hearing the sermon, that they hunted down five alleged sodomites and saw that they were burned alive. This tradition has experienced a revival with the emergence of HIV or AIDS in the late twentieth century, with Fundamentalist Christians claiming that the illness – unlike cancer, sickle cell anemia, and other devastating illnesses – has been sent by God to punish homosexuals, and further, that homosexuals are solely responsible for others acquiring the illness. One of the Catholic saints to whom the faithful have prayed to avert plagues is SAINT SEBASTIAN, associated since at least the Renaissance with homoeroticism. Another saint believed to hold the power to avert plagues is SAINT LAZARUS. St Lazarus, associated especially with leprosy, is identified in the African-diasporic religion of Santería with the *orishá*, or deity, BABALUAYE. This saint/*orishá* has been invoked since the mid-1980s by those wishing to heal and/or be healed of HIV/AIDS.

Plato (c. 427-347 BCE)   Greek philosopher and writer, pupil of Socrates (469-399 BCE), and founder of the Academy at Athens, the first permanent institution devoted to philosophy and the prototype of Euro-western universities. Two of his *Dialogues*, the *Symposium* and the *Phaedrus*, have since antiquity inspired those seeking to realize the interrelationship of same-sex passion, to a lesser degree transgenderism (as in the embodiment of a divinity of the opposite sex), and the sacred. While these dialogues are often discussed in the context of classical philosophy, they are immersed in religious and mythic belief and in ritual, including divinatory and magical, practice. "When Socrates had settled himself," we are told, "we poured libations and sang a hymn to the god and performed all the customary ritual actions." The *Symposium*, composed near 385 BCE, documents a celebration occurring in 416 BCE, attended by Plato, Socrates, the woman philosopher-mystic Diotima, Aristophanes, Alcibiades, and others. Without exaggerating, this dialogue might be described as a manual for those embarking on the homoerotic-spiritual path. It considers male-male relationships from their commencement to their end, suggesting practices such as participation in athletic and musical events, to be undertaken by lovers, as well as spiritual exercises. What is most striking, perhaps, about the *Symposium* is, however, its acknowledgement of the goddess Aphrodite-Urania as the patron of same-sex love, its myth explaining the origin of erotic identities related by Aristophanes, and its suggestion that same-sex relationships produce spiritual offspring. Originally, we are told, the gods created giant double beings to aid them in maintaining the cosmos. These were male-male, female-female, and male-female beings, the first created from the sun, the second from the earth, and the third from the moon. They became so powerful, however, that they threatened the authority of the gods. Thus, it was decided that they should be divided into solitary beings. That is why those males split from males search for their other halves, while "women who are halves of a female whole direct their affections towards women . . . Lesbians belong to this category." And that is why those males and females who are halves of a male-female whole search for one another. At first glance, one is struck that androgyny seems to be associated here not with homosexuality or lesbianism but with heterosexuality. Elsewhere in Plato, however, as in the *Phaedrus*, it is explained that same-sex directed couples often embody transgenderism in being the spiritual children of deities of the opposite sex. Of the birth of spiritual, or creative,

offspring by same-sex couples, it is the wisewoman Diotima who explains: "Those whose creative instinct is physical have recourse to women, and show their love in this way, believing that by begetting children they can secure for themselves an immortal and blessed memory hereafter for ever; but there are some whose creative desire is of the soul, and who long to beget spiritually, not physically, the progeny which it is the nature of the soul to create and bring to birth. If you ask what that progeny is, it is wisdom and virtue in general; of this all poets and such craftsmen as have found out some new thing may be said to be begetters; but far the greatest and fairest branch of wisdom is that which is concerned with the ordering of states and families, whose name is moderation and justice." The *Phaedrus* was composed near 370 BCE and said to have been delivered by Socrates near 410 BCE. While Socrates here focuses on male-male relationships, his ideas are clearly applicable to other relationships as well. In the *Phaedrus*, Socrates speaks of "divine madness," by which he refers to the embodiment of divine force in relationship to love: "When a man sees beauty in this world and has a remembrance of true beauty, he begins to grow wings . . . He gazes upward as though he were a bird and cares nothing for what is here below, so that he is accused of being mad . . . this, of all forms of divine possession, is the best . . . the man who partakes of this madness and loves beauty is called a lover." This "madness" involves a remembering, by way of a vision, of a deep love which one has experienced in one's after-death/pre-birth experience; and it is the sight of another man to whom one is attracted that triggers this memory. The love which one remembers has consisted of an erotico-spiritual union with a deity, "some of us with Zeus, others with another god." This union is described as "that mystery which it is right to call the most blessed of all." It is described as a celestial initiation rite. Socrates suggests that love, triggered by beauty (chiefly gauged by internal beauty, as in Native American spiritual traditions), is the chief soul-making experience to be learned during our sojourn on earth. "As for beauty," he explains, "we can still recapture it, gleaming most clearly as it does, through the clearest of our senses." Socrates warns us, however, that a man "whose [celestial] initiation is long past" or who has lived a corrupt (he is *not* referring to homosexuality) life on earth "feels no reverence" for beauty. Instead, "like a great beast he proceeds to lust and procreation." When, however, a man whose initiation has been relatively recent or who has lived an ethical life "sees a god-like countenance . . . a faithful imitation of true beauty . . . a shudder runs through him. Beholding it, he reverences it as he would a god; and if he were not afraid of being accounted stark mad, he would offer sacrifice to the beloved as to a holy image of divinity." Socrates describes the encounter of lover and beloved in passionate terms, indeed, as a "flood of passion," employing images blending flight and phallic tumescence:

"as nourishment streams upon it the stump of the wing begins to swell and grow from the root upward . . . During this process the soul is completely in a state of ferment and palpitation . . . the soul is irrigated and warmed and rejoices at the abatement of pain." Socrates explains that for each lover or beloved, there exists a deity whom he reveres above all others, and whom he seeks to emulate. When an individual falls in love with another, it is often because the other reminds him of his patron deity. "So each selects his love," he explains, "according to character . . . So the followers of Zeus desire that the soul of their beloved should resemble that god; they look for one who loves wisdom and has a commanding nature . . . Again, those who followed Hera look for a kingly nature . . . And similarly the followers of Apollo and the other gods" seek a beloved "whose nature corresponds to their god." It is, moreover, the responsibility of the lover to bring the beloved to be as "much as possible like . . . the god they honor." The homoerotic-spiritual path, Socrates explains in mystical terms, is linked to the cycle of rebirth. "For it is the law that those who have once begun the journey to heaven shall never pass down into the dark path beneath the earth. Their life henceforward shall be a journey of radiant happiness together, and when they grow their wings, these shall be alike, because of their love." Indeed, Socrates cautions those who are considering *not* taking up this path that if they do not, they may "float for nine thousand years around the earth and beneath it – a fool!"

Pleiades In Greek myth and religion, priestesses loved by ARTEMIS who, in attempting to escape the unwanted embraces of the hunter Orion, were transformed into a constellation. In the poetry of SAPPHO (b. c. 630/610 BCE) and in the female-centered THIASOI of the ancient Mediterranean, the Pleiades came to be associated with love between women. One of Sappho's most beautiful and melancholy fragments reads, "The moon has set, and the Pleiades. It is Midnight. Time passes. I sleep alone."

Plum In Chinese symbolism, plum blossoms represent androgyny, because they blossom in spring, an "intermediate" season.

Pluto In Euro-western ASTROLOGY, this planet governs disasters, revolutions, spiritual movements, the underworld, wealth, and the expression of one's sexuality. Figures associated with Pluto and with gender and/or sexual variance include: BARON LUNDY, BARON SAMEDI, CERNUNNOS, the GHEDES, HECATE, POMBA GIRA, and SET. J. E. Kneeland (1988) notes that the "house placement of Pluto in gay [male] charts has shown a marked preference for the ninth, the house of . . . philosophy, higher education, publishing, and long distance travel." In terms of possessing Pluto in the ninth house, F. Sakoian and L. S. Acker (1973) observe : "People

with this position have little tolerance for hypocrisy and social injustice. Sometimes they become revolutionaries, if they feel that existing institutions are unworthy of their respect."

Poliziano (pseudonym of **Angelo Ambrogini**, 1454-1494) Poet, instructor, and Neoplatonic philosopher of the Florentine Academy. Taught (and perhaps loved) as a young man by Marsilio FICINO, he became a celebrated teacher, with five hundred students attending his lectures at any given time. Unlike some of the Neoplatonists, he openly displayed his affection and desire for other men, among them Panezion Pandozzi. His passion for classical antiquity and for other men are interwoven in his works, especially in his pastoral poetic drama *The Fable of Orpheus* (1480), in which he writes: "Of the other love, ZEUS . . . / He who . . . / Sported in the heavens with handsome GANYMEDE. / APOLLO, on earth, sported with HYACINTHUS, / To this sacred love HERACLES also yielded, / By handsome Hyacinth was vanquished . . ." *The Fable of Orpheus* culminates with ORPHEUS urging "all married men to seek divorce" and to give themselves to male love. The *Fable* inspired Monteverdi's *Orfeo* (1607).

Pollux Ptolemeus Chemnos related in his *New History* that the Greek god HERMES loved Pollux, one of the Dioscuri, the other being his brother Castor. The Dioscuri were the sons of ZEUS. They were ARGONAUTS and patrons of sailors, as POSEIDON had bestowed upon them the guardianship of winds and waves. Hermes gave Pollux a love gift of a Thessalian horse.

Polyeuctus, Saint (d. 259 CE) **and Nearchus** (fl. c. 250 CE) Pagan Roman soldiers of Greek heritage stationed at the Armenian city of Melitene. The two were depicted as "brothers, not by birth, but in affection." After Nearchus converted to Christianity, he convinced Polyeuctus to do so. They were both tortured and executed as martyrs. However, Nearchus's sainthood is controversial. St Polyeuctus (and possibly also Nearchus) is fêted on January 9 or on February 13.

Polyphemus Son of POSEIDON, a giant blinded by Odysseus. Some say that he and HERACLES were once lovers. When inebriated, Polyphemus becomes overwhelmed by desire for the satyr Silenus.

Pomba Gira Brazilian deity (*orixa*, or *orishá*) of Candomblé, Macumba, and to a lesser extent in New Orleans-based Vodou, where she is identified with ERZULIE la Flambeau or Erzulie Taureau. The spouse or female aspect of Exu (comparable to Elleggua and LEGBA), Pomba Gira is primarily associated with sexuality. She dresses in red, wears heavy makeup, strong perfume, and costume jewelry. She haunts crossroads and nightclubs. At the crossroads, she is offered sacrifices of dresses, watches, rings, champagne, beer, cigarettes, goat, chicken, apples, and red roses. Her worship has spread to the US, where she is revered by Cuban-Americans, Brazilian-Americans, and others. One often sees her image in shops where ritual implements, necklaces, candles, herbs, statues, and other items are sold, in Los Angeles, San Francisco, and New Orleans. Around her statue, devotees often place offerings of cigarettes, tiny bottles of wine and perfume, gum, candy, lottery tickets, and coins. Pomba Gira can be very shocking and cruel, telling "men the truth in the very crudest terms and in a very loud voice," thus revealing in public their "vices and flaws." In queer-identified subcultures, this action has been a function of drag queens, referred to in the 1970s as "reading someone's beads." Pomba Gira can, however, be very helpful to those who call on her, especially when devotees wish to attract a lover, patch up a relationship, or "wreck a marriage." When Candomblé priest M. Aparecida "like[d] a man's face," he would offer Pomba Gira a bottle of beer, a red rose, a pack of cigarettes, and "a pork chop, cooked in very hot palm oil and Rio flour and lettuce." According to Aparecida, Pomba Gira is a patron of queer men because she is "unisex."

Pomona   Roman goddess of APPLES and other fruits. Vertumnus, a Roman god of change, fell in love with Pomona, but she was not interested. When, however, he dressed in feminine attire, wearing a brightly-colored turban, and approached Pomona once more, she, seeing him as a beautiful older woman, was charmed by him.

Popovici, Vasil (1815-1905)   Monk of the Tzibucani Monastery in Romania from about 1880 until "his" death, "he" was revered as a compassionate, contemplative mystic. Many considered "him" a saint. Only on washing the body after "his" death did they discover Popovici to be anatomically female.

Poppy   Flower often symbolic of fertility and dreams, an attribute of the Greek goddesses DEMETER and PERSEPHONE, as well as of PAPAVER, a young man of Roman mythology who loved a young man named ANETHUS ("Anise") and who was transformed into a poppy upon his death. For many queer-identified persons the poppy is especially remembered as a flower employed by the Wicked Witch of the West to drug Dorothy and her friends just as they are on the brink of entering the Emerald City in the 1939 film of *The Wizard of Oz*.

Poseidon (Roman **Neptune**)   God of the sea, of SAILORS and FISHERS, and of the depths of the earth. Poseidon brings tempests and earthquakes. He is called "He who gives drink from the wooded mountain." Poseidon is the lover of numerous individuals, including: PELOPS, whom he carries to Olympus in a golden chariot; the transgendered CAENIS; and Leander, a young mortal who, preferring the love of women, leaves him to marry Hero. As Poseidon Phutalmios, the "fostering one," the god appears to have presided over rites of initiation including transvestism and cultic homoeroticism. In his poem *Hero and Leander*, the homoerotically inclined Renaissance poet-playwright Christopher MARLOWE writes: "Leander made reply, 'You are deceived, I am no woman, I,' / Thereat smil'd Neptune, and then told a tale, / How' that a shepherd, sitting in a vale, / Play'd with a boy so lovely fair and kind / As for his love both earth and heaven pin'd . . .

Pothos   One of the EROTES, together with EROS and HIMERUS. While Eros carries a HARE and Himerus a headband, Pothos carries a vine, suggesting a connection to wine and to the Greek god DIONYSUS. Like the other Erotes, Pothos belongs to the retinue of the goddess APHRODITE and is a carrier of erotic energy and of *élan vital*, the life force. Like the others, Pothos is specifically associated with homoerotic love.

Potiphar   We are told in the *Midrash*, a collection of Biblical exegesis gathered between the fifth century BCE and the second century CE, that Potiphar purchased Joseph for the pharaoh of Egypt because of the young man's beauty. Potiphar is described in the *Midrash* as a eunuch priest of a pagan deity, probably of the goddess ISIS. It is apparent that he and his wife, who also desires Joseph, do not have a monogamous marriage. While the *Midrash* tells us that Joseph did not yield to either Potiphar or his wife, various scholars have questioned this aspect of the story. Indeed, it seems that Joseph and Potiphar, or the persons upon whom these characters were based, may have enjoyed a complex transgenderal relationship. Indeed, even when depicted as a prophet of Yahweh, an interpreter of dreams, Joseph seems more like a QADESH priest, guided "by a secret knowledge of the feminine principle." The Biblical/Midrashic tale of Potiphar and Joseph was remembered in nineteenth-century French bohemian circles, where to *putiphariser*, or "potipharize," a young man was to reach inside his trousers and grab his genitals.

Prajapati   Hindu deity, alternately phallic and ultramasculine or androgynous, "endowed with a womb and breasts" and capable of producing "milk and butter."

Prakriti-Purusha   The "Third Nature" in Hinduism, referring to third gender or transgendered, often bisexually or homoerotically inclined, persons who mirror the UNION of the god SHIVA with the goddess PARVATI (or SHAKTI), resulting in the creation of an androgynous or gynandrous being, sometimes identified as ARDHANARISHVARA. Persons such as the HIJRA devotees of the goddess BAHUCHARAMATA are described as manifesting *prakriti-purusha*.

Prayer Stick   Ritual tool of Navaho religion comprised of a "male" and "female" prayer stick made of wood "with eyes and mouth of inlaid jewels, bound together with yarn or twine decorated with feathers and jewels." The two bound together signify the ALKE 'NA 'A CI, meaning "one-who-follows-the-other," originally a hermaphroditic being created by BEGOCHIDI until it was cut into a male and female by Black God.

Priapus   Ithyphallic deity of Greek religion, presiding over erotic rites, fertility of crops, and boundaries. While some claim that Priapus is the son of DIONYSUS and APHRODITE, others say that he is a lover of Dionysus. Priapus punishes thieves that he catches by commanding them to engage in fellatio and in anal intercourse with him.

Prieuré Notre-Dame de Sion, The Order of the   Mysterious French spiritual organization, allegedly existing since the eleventh century. One of its primary aims is the restoration of the Merovingian bloodline as heirs to the throne of France. In French esoteric lore this royal family is descended from a child born to Mary Magdalene and JESUS Christ. One of its central beliefs is that the Black Virgin, whether worshipped as DIANA, CYBELE, or ISIS, now called "Our Lady of Light," is the "true goddess of France." The Grand Master of this society is called the "Nautonnier," or "the invincible helmsman of the baroque of Isis." The homoerotically inclined writer and filmmaker Jean COCTEAU was grand master from 1918 until his death in 1963.

Procris   Princess of Athens, once married to Cephalus, who deserted him to join ARTEMIS and her companions.

Prospero   In Shakespeare's *The Tempest* (1611), a magician who loves his fairy servant. When Ariel asks, "Do you love me master? No?", Prospero replies, "Dearly, My delicate Ariel" (act IV, sc. 1).

Prosymnus   The Greek god DIONYSUS, wishing to know the way to Hades, asked directions of the mortal Prosymnus, but the latter would give him directions only if the former would engage in anal intercourse with him. Dionysus agreed, if Prosymnus would but wait until his return. Prosymnus agreed, but died before Dionysus returned. In order to fulfill his promise, Dionysus carved a HERM from a fig branch and, using it as a dildo, sat on Prosymnus' grave in order to "satisfy [his] shade [i.e. his spirit]."

Prthivi   Earth goddess of Hinduism, comparable to the Greek Gaia. In the *Shatapatha Brahmana* Prthivi is

referred to as the "womb" of the male god of fire, AGNI, suggesting a gynandrous or transgendered deity.

Ptah   One of the primordial gods worshipped in Egypt. He (-she) was god of craftsman, the arts, and called "Creator-by-Word-of-Mouth." Regarded as both male and female, he (-she) is often depicted with female breasts.

Puck   TRICKSTER FAIRY of Shakespeare's *A Midsummer Night's Dream* (1594-1596), beloved servant of Oberon, the Fairy King. Whether or not Shakespeare intended it, Puck has, over the centuries, become linked to transgenderism and same-sex desire. This may be due in part to the fact that his part is often played by an androgynous young man or, increasingly, by an equally androgynous young woman, and in part to the magical love ointment he employs, with its potential to cause an individual, when it is rubbed in the eyes, to fall in love with whomever he/she first beholds on waking. The very close bond shared by Puck and Oberon may have also inspired these associations. In *Another Mother Tongue* (1984), Judy Grahn describes Puck as an archetype of both the "faggot" and the "ceremonial dyke," that is, of gay men and lesbians who are spiritually or magically oriented. Of her personal relationship to the archetype, Grahn remembers: "When I was fifteen I was lucky enough to see *A Midsummer Night's Dream* . . . I identified completely with the character of Puck and within weeks of seeing him was able to understand that I was a Lesbian. I knew that in some way Puck is what I am. He is also what I look for . . . in my lovers and in Gay men." In Angela Carter's "Overture and Incidental Music for *A Midsummer Night's Dream*" (1985), Puck is a pansexual spirit who falls madly in love with (the) Herm, an hermaphroditic spirit. Indeed, Puck desires Herm so greatly that, as Salmacis once merged with Hermaphroditus, so Puck merges with Herm as the tale reaches its climax.

Pukkumina (or **Pocomania**)   African-American religion in which homosexual and bisexual men are said to act as leaders. This religion emerged in Jamaica during the middle of the nineteenth century. According to Edward Seaga, approximately two thousand Jamaicans were members of Pukkumina congregations in 1982. About four hundred and fifty of these persons lived in Kingston and the surrounding area. According to Seaga, "Pukkumina followers work primarily with 'ground' spirits and 'Fallen Angels,' who in their value system are not considered evil." A religion in which magic plays an important role, "the Pukkumina cult is primarily concerned with the rapidity with which the various supernatural forces work and their availability, not with their characteristics of good and evil." Pukkumina priests are called "Shepherds;" directly beneath the priests are the "Mothers" of the "Bands" and the "Shepherd Boys." "Shepherds" commonly practice cultic homoeroticism and gender variant behavior. A "Shepherd" named Ronnie is reported to have worn "bracelets, earrings, and a braided wig at ceremonies" and to have used "patterned feminine gestures in his dance." Further, it is reported that "most urban Pukkumina leaders are either homosexuals or satyrs" and that "men frequently form strong emotional attachments to their Shepherds." It appears that in the late 1940s, a split occurred between those Pukkumina groups in which the membership was predominantly gay and those in which it was heterosexual. In recent years, heterosexual Pukkumina members as well as homophobic scholars have attempted to deny the importance of gays in the religion. It has been reported, however, that in one Pukkumina band, "the members . . . were all homosexual, both male and female."

Puná An indigenous people of present-day Ecuador (in documents of the past, referred to as Peru) conquered by the Inca ruler Huaina Cápac. These people and their ruler Tumpalla lived in luxury, worshipped feline deities, and participated in same-sex relations. The Punás were linked culturally to the Mantas and the Huancavilcas.

Punchinello Italian transgendered, hunchbacked CARNIVAL figure. Punchinello's ancestors include the Greco-Roman deities ATTIS (whose cap he-she wears), CYBELE, and PRIAPUS. Unfortunately, Punchinello's English descendant, Punch, has not only lost his-her transgendered aspect but has become a chauvinist who beats his wife Judy.

Purple Color symbolic of royalty, magic, and spiritual enlightenment, frequently associated with androgyny and same-sex passion, its various hues including lavender, lilac, magenta, mauve, and VIOLET. In Greco-Roman antiquity, purple was worn by the priestesses and transgendered male priest/esse/s of ARTEMIS and CYBELE. Especially as mauve, it was considered, when worn by men, a color signifying transgendered homosexuality

(*amethystinasque mulierum vocat vestes*, Martial I. 96.7). In seventeenth-century Japan, purple, employed as a headband worn by Kabuki actors, likewise came to signify homoerotic love. In the late nineteenth century, with its final decade referred to by the British as the "mauve decade," the color celebrated both homoeroticism and a Decadent lifestyle. In the early twentieth century, purple, especially as violet, served in the West as a signifier of lesbian desire. As lavender, the color was claimed by the contemporary gay liberation movement. In Monique Wittig's *The Lesbian Body* (1973), the color, alongside black, stands as an "epithet for the beloved." While purple is not directly associated with same-sex love in bisexual African-American writer Alice Walker's acclaimed novel *The Color Purple* (1982), the association may be inferred, as the color refers to a God transcending race and gender and accepting of all people.

Purusha In Hinduism, according to the *Brihadaranyaka Upanishad*, a primordial androgynous or transgendered being. Purusha divides him-herself into male and female in order to create humanity. In 1981, Christopher Larkin, once a monk, later a filmmaker, published an erotico-spiritual manual, *The Divine Androgyne*, under the spiritual name of Purusha.

Pu'uhele Hawaiian hill deity and sister of PELE whose name means "Traveling Hill." She is the AIKANE (intimate companion) of the female being Puuomaiai. Pu'uhele, born prematurely, was thrown across the channel to Maui. After traveling she remained at Wananalua. When she died she was transformed into a seaside hill called Ka'uiki.

Pyrrha Transgendered or "drag" name of the Greek hero ACHILLES when he was hidden in the court of Lycomedes by his mother Thetis. Portraits of Achilles as Pyrrha showed him wearing a blue woman's garment and holding an olive branch and a spray of vine.

Q

Qa 'cikicheca Among the Aleuts of northeastern
Siberia, a term meaning "appareled like a man," referring
to a TWO-SPIRIT female shaman. *Qa 'cikicheca* often
shared intimate relationships with traditionally feminine
women.

Qabbalah (or **Cabala, Kaballah, Qabbala**) From the
Hebrew *qbl*, "to receive," the Qabbalah is a body of
mystical knowledge of essentially Jewish origin which
emerged in southern France in the eleventh or twelfth
century and was greatly strengthened in the thirteenth
through sixteenth centuries in Spain, North Africa, and
the Holy Land. The best-known Qabbalistic text is the
Zohar, which was circulated in the thirteenth century.
While the Qabbalistic tradition was initiated by Jews, over
time it became practiced by many non-Jews as well,
especially by ritual or ceremonial magicians, who brought
other influences, including Egyptian, Greek, Christian,
and other elements into the tradition. The
correspondences drawn here derive primarily from
ceremonial magician Israel Regardie's interpretation of the
Qabbalah in *A Garden of Pomegranates* (1932, 1978); in
strictly Jewish interpretations of the Qabbalah, non-
Biblical correspondences would be regarded as
inappropriate. For Qabbalists, the universe (Ain Soph
Aur), as "the sum total of all things and living creatures, is
conceived as having its primeval origin in Infinite Space."
The Ain Soph Aur has been compared to the Tao of
Chinese Taoism, a transgendered symbol containing both
YIN (roughly, feminine) and yang (roughly, masculine)
energies, as well as to the UROBORUS, the serpent biting its
tail, a symbol of infinity linked by certain practitioners of
Gnosticism, including Naassenes, to masturbation and
homoeroticism. Within the universe stands the Tree of
Life. Qabbalists maintain that the creation of the universe
took place through series of emanations from the godhead,
ten archetypal energies called *sephiroth* (spheres) that
comprise this cosmic Tree, sometimes also depicted as a
cosmic humanoid being, ADAM Kadmon. The sephiroth
are: Kether ("crown"); Binah ("understanding");
Chokmah ("wisdom"); Geburah ("power"); Chesed
("mercy"); Tiphareth ("grandeur" or "beauty"); Hod
("splendor"); Netzach ("eternity"); Yesod ("foundation");
and Malkuth ("kingdom"). This belief is linked to the
Biblical tale of Ezekiel's vision of a celestial chariot. As
with the Ain Soph Aur, the ten spheres (and sometimes an
"invisible" or "false" eleventh, DAATH) and the pathways
connecting them correspond to certain deities, concepts,
and attributes associated with gender and sexual variance

or totality. The first sphere, Kether, signifying the creation
of life from thought and/or spirit, has been compared by
Nevill Drury to the "heavenly androgyne," representing a
"state of mystical transcendence." Chokmah, the second
sphere, while frequently identified with father-gods, also
corresponds to THOTH, PALLAS-ATHENA, and other
deities linked to gender and sexual variance. The third
sphere, Binah, corresponds to various goddesses appearing
in this text, including KALI and KUAN YIN, as well as the
god/planet SATURN. The fourth sphere, Chesed, is
depicted as a "feminine" male ruler, while the fifth sphere,
Geburah, conjures the image of an AMAZON. Regardie
writes, "Despite the fact that Geburah is a feminine
potency . . . practically all its attributions are male and
vigorous . . . The magical weapons of Geburah are the
Sword, Spear, [and] Scourge." Tiphareth, the sixth
sphere, said to be the child of Chesed and Geburah (i.e.
traditionally "feminine" male plus "masculine" female), is
described as either an androgynous male or a
transgendered being who rules over beauty and harmony.
Tiphareth corresponds to a number of deities and symbols
described in this text, including ADONIS, APOLLO,
KRISHNA, the LION, and the PHOENIX. Regardie also links
DIONYSUS to Tiphareth "because of his youth and
gracious form, combining effeminate softness and
beauty." Netzach, the seventh sphere, ruling love,
creativity, inner strength, and victory (as in athletics),
corresponds primarily to goddesses of love such as
APHRODITE and of athletic prowess like PALAESTRA.
Some ceremonial magicians claim that Netzach rules
lesbian desire. Hod, the eighth sphere, who rules the
intellect and acts as a psychopomp or guide of souls who
transports the soul of the deceased from this world to the
next, corresponds to ANUBIS and HERMES. Paralleling
Netzach, some ceremonial magicians claim Hod to be the
sphere of homoerotic male desire. Yesod, the ninth sphere,
is associated with the MOON, dreams, feminine mysteries,
Witchcraft, and sexual passion. Corresponding deities
linked to gender and/or sexual variance include ARTEMIS
and GANESHA. The color of Yesod is also noteworthy:
PURPLE. The tenth sphere, Malkuth, is associated
primarily with the earth and Nature, with relevant
corresponding deities including DEMETER, LAKSHMI,
PERSEPHONE, and the SPHINX. The spheres on the Tree of
Life are categorized in various ways, including the
"worlds" of archetypes, creation, formation, and action.
While associations with gender and sexual variance may be
discovered throughout the Tree of Life, they seem most
concentrated in the world of formation, Ruach. While this

"world" is often described in fairly negative terms (perhaps due to a bias toward transcendence rather than immanence on the part of some Qabbalists), it nevertheless harbors valuable attributes, including desire, imagination, reason, and will. If one examines a diagram of the world of formation, one sees that the beautiful androgynous or transgendered Tiphareth dwells at its center, with Geburah, Hod, Chesed, and Netzach encircling it and linked to it by various pathways. One also notices that the Amazonian Geburah is, by way of Tiphareth, linked to the beautiful, athletic Netzach, just as the "feminine" male Chesed is linked to the androgynous male Hod. Further, the gender variant females appear to share relationships with the gender variant males, all these relations seeming to merge in the transgendered Tiphareth. Of special interest in terms of a potential homoerotic relationship between Chesed and Hod are the pathways linking them to each other by way of Tiphareth. Yod, the twentieth path, is associated with semen and with the deities ADONIS and NARCISSUS, while Ain, the twenty-sixth path, corresponds to Dionysus, PAN, and PRIAPUS. Many Qabbalists have also accepted the doctrine of transmigration, whereby the soul, upon death, passes into another body. The notion that a female soul might take up residence in a male body was discussed in the mid-twelfth century by Jacob ben Sheshet Gerondi and was popularized by Isaac ben Solomon Luria, the headmaster of a Qabbalistic center at Safed in Galilee, in the sixteenth century. Luria's disciple Hayyim Vital published his master's ideas in *The Gate of Transmigrations* (c. 1573-1576). According to this view, Tamar, who appears in Genesis 38, was believed to have possessed a man's soul. Tamar was a young woman who disguised herself as a HIERODULIC priestess, or sacred prostitute, so that she might bear her father-in-law's children, after his sons had died before impregnating her. Judah the patriarch, her father-in-law, on the other hand, was believed to have possessed a woman's soul. It was further believed that the Biblical heroine RUTH inherited the masculine soul of Tamar. Some Qabbalists, it seems, extended the doctrine of transmigration to include transference of a human soul into the body of an animal. In sixteenth-century France, it was reported that Qabbalists believed that the souls of *bougres* (buggers), men engaging in anal eroticism, entered, upon their death, into the bodies of hares. In Greco-Roman antiquity and into the Renaissance, the HARE was widely associated in Europe and elsewhere with homosexuality and transgenderism.

Qadesh (pl. **Qedeshim**)   Gender variant or transgendered priest/esse/s of the Canaanite or Ugaritic goddess ATHIRAT, known as the "holy ones," as well as the KELABIM or "DOGS," the faithful companions of the Goddess and her consort. In most respects, the *qedeshim* resembled the priests of the Mesopotamian goddess INANNA/ISHTAR. They served in Canaanite temples stretching from Ugarit to Jerusalem from 1400 BCE onward, if not much earlier. They typically dressed in long-sleeved, multicolored caftans. These garments were meant to evoke the Goddess and the vision of the earth in springtime, described in the *Epic of Gilgamesh* as a "couch of many colours." The *qedeshim*, or *kelabim*, also may have veiled their faces. Their functions included maintaining the temple grounds and sacred groves as well as making ritual objects, especially pots and weavings. They also appear to have been credited with the power to bring rain. They participated in sacred dances employing self-wounding and flagellation in which altered states were attained. They may have played a role in the *hieros gamos* of Athirat and the god Baal or El, embodied, as in Mesopotamia, by the priestess and the king. During this rite, a gender variant priest or *qadesh*, taking the role of the "gracious lad" or "sweet-voiced youth," chanted as he performed a ritual involving the mixing of milk, butter, mint, and coriander in a cauldron and lighting seven cakes of incense over this brew. His chant or song celebrated Athirat and her sister Anat as the nurturers of kings. He, or perhaps another *qadesh*, also sang of the Goddess's seductive powers and of the strength of Canaanite warriors. The *qedeshim* were primarily known, however, as HIERODULES. While some scholars, including Raphael Patai, do not believe that the *qedeshim* engaged in cultic homoeroticism, others, including Michael Grant, Samuel Terrien, and W. L. Moran have asserted that the *qedeshim* did indeed participate in same-sex eroticism, primarily with traditionally masculine worshippers of the Goddess. If, as the term *gerim* suggests, they were eunuchs, it seems plausible that they may have engaged in anal intercourse, taking the receptive role. Like their female counterparts the *qedeshtu*, they may have employed dildoes in erotic situations. Union with a *qadesh* priest was believed to bring the worshipper into intimate contact with the deity. It also served to activate total embodiment of the deity in the body of the priest or priestess. Terrien and Moran have further suggested that the *qedeshim* may have employed sexual intercourse as a means of triggering an altered or shamanic state of consciousness. Of this TANTRA-like endeavor among the *qedeshim*, Terrien writes, "the function of the male prostitutes . . . was related to an ecstatic . . . divination technique," while Moran asserts that the *qadesh* priest "may well have obtained his oracular function through sophisticated techniques of sexual trance." Most of what we know of the *qedeshim*, unfortunately, concerns the campaigns conducted against them by Israelite zealots. These campaigns, commencing in the tenth century BCE, lasted more than four hundred years.

Qailertetang   Amazonian Inuit (or Eskimo) divinity who dwells with her female companion SEDNA at the bottom of the sea in the company of seals, whales, and other sea creatures. Qailertetang is depicted as a "large woman of very heavy limbs." In rituals, she is served by a TWO-SPIRIT male shaman "dressed in a woman's costume and wearing a mask made of seal-skin." Qailertetang is a weather goddess or spirit, a guardian of animals, and a patron of HUNTERS and FISHERS.

Qu Yuan Historico-legendary poet and shaman of ancient China. Qu Yuan is considered China's first major poet, author of the epic *Li Sao (Encountering Sorrow)*, the *Tian Wen (Heavenly Questions)*, and various other works. He was born around 340 BCE in the kingdom of Chu, on what was said to be the most auspicious day of the first month of the lunar calendar. From the time of his birth, astrologers realized that he was destined to become a poet and a shaman. He was bestowed with two sacred names, True Exemplar and Divine Balance, the latter a nickname of a mountain goddess. The people of Chu were of Mongolian heritage and had long been practitioners of Shamanism and Goddess Reverence. By the time of Qu Yuan's birth, however, Shamanism and Goddess reverence were being displaced even in the kingdom of Chu by Confucianism. Nevertheless, when Qu Yuan was still a youth, he began to study with an elder shamaness. As a shaman, he would learn how to divine the future by reading bones, and to exorcise demons with "bundles of reeds and branches of peach;" how to heal the sick by way of attaining a shamanic state of consciousness, induced by drumming and dancing, in which he would retrieve the client's wandering soul. He would learn to make objects fly through the air, to make spirits appear, and to bring rain. Qu Yuan's gender variant status is suggested partly by his attire, which appears to have blended feminine, masculine, and sacerdotal articles. Referring in a poem to his primary garment as a skirt, he infers that its design was floral. In ancient China, floral garments were worn primarily by women and shamans, flowers generally evoking femininity and spirituality. The garment may have included designs of selinea, angelica, water chestnuts, ORCHIDS, and LOTUS blossoms, the latter two signifying the "intermediate stage between man and woman." The Chinese shaman, like shamans of other cultures, often dressed in the garments of a divinity he served. If devoted primarily to a goddess, he might dress in feminine garments. He might also dress in feminine attire if, in revering a male deity, he considered himself that deity's bride. The wearing of feminine garments sometimes appears to have suggested homoerotic inclination; Qu Yuan is referred to by women jealous of his beauty as a "wanton." Qu Yuan's diet, like that of Taoist sages, or *hsien*, probably included herbs and flowers as well as mushrooms and gem elixirs. Such substances were considered essential because they provided a rich supply of *ch'i* or vital energy, because they satiated the body so that one did not crave mundane foods, and because their

ingestion allegedly prolonged life. Ingesting such substances lightened the physical body, allowing shamans and sages, freed from gravity, to fly. The drinking of gem elixirs was thought not only to prolong life but also to prevent decomposition of the flesh, thus conferring not only spiritual but also physical immortality. While Qu Yuan undoubtedly served both male and female deities, it is evident that in his life Goddess Reverence predominated. In ancient China, the worship of goddesses remained strongest in his homeland, southern China, the northern Chinese adopting more patriarchal traditions at a much earlier date. Among the goddesses mentioned in works by, attributed to, or about Qu Yuan are Fu Fei, Nu Wa, Xi Ho, Nu Qi, the Lady of Tu Shan Mountain, Xian E, Xi Wang Mu, and the goddess(es) of the Xiang River. Qu Yuan offered sacrifices to the goddesses he revered. Sacrifices to aquatic goddesses were often dropped into the water. The shaman would sail out in a boat, often one painted with floral designs or decorated with fresh or dried flowers and embellished with figures of phoenixes and dragons. He would sail to the middle of a body of water, or to an island or shoreline shrine, where he would shower the water with offerings. Preparing to meet the Goddess was an important rite undertaken by shamans. They would first bathe in purified water scented with iris and orchid, after which they would dress in the garments of the deity they intended to visit or summon. They would then, holding a bouquet of herbs and flowers, begin to dance until they fell into a shamanic state of consciousness. In this state they would journey to the submarine, subterranean, or celestial abode of the deity. Perhaps reflecting the rapid patriarchalization of the world in which Qu Yuan lived, the shaman's ability to communicate with the Goddess had become impaired. The Goddess had come to be seen as somewhat distant, evasive, unapproachable. Because the Goddess frequently chose not to appear, the relationship between the shaman and the Goddess came to be marked by an element of disappointment or sorrow – a relationship which Professor David Hawkes describes as "larmoyant" or "lachrymose," that is, "tearful." The "larmoyant" relationship with the Goddess experienced by Qu Yuan and other Chinese shamans is mirrored by his relationship with the King of Huai. It seems that as a young man, the shaman-poet came to live at the palace, where he became intimate with the King. Same-sex unions were common in ancient China, and shamans rarely joined in traditional marriages, as they were already considered married to deities. In a rather apologetic tone, Ping-leung Chan writes: "If Ch'u Yuan happened to be a homosexual, it is by no means a disgrace . . . [His] originality and creativity may also be the result of homosexuality." Among the ancient Chinese, the wearing and ingestion of flowers was linked to femininity, androgyny or gender variance, and spirituality, to the gathering of yin energy into the male psyche and body.

According to Chan, a "predilection for flowers" also served
in China as a sign of homosexuality. In the *Li Sao*, the
shaman-poet describes not only his journey in quest of the
Goddess, but also his love for the King, in floral terms. He
refers to the King as the "Fragrant One" and the "Fairest
One." The term used for "fragrant" is *quan*, which literally
refers to an iris. The term used for "fairest one" is *ling xiu*,
which suggests not only a shaman but also a beautiful
person. In Hawkes' view, Qu Yuan's use of *ling xiu*
indicates that he may see the King as an embodiment of a
goddess, perhaps Fu Fei, crowned with "feathers, flowers,
and jewels." While stressing that the use of such terms is a
poetic convention in Chinese literature, Hawkes
nevertheless suggests that these terms may imply a
homoerotic relationship: "Is the poet imagining himself as
a handsome, flower-decked youth and his king as a
beautiful maiden whom he seeks to woo? . . . One
possibility . . . is that the relationship here imagined is a
homosexual one: flower-decked male in pursuit of a
beautiful male lover." In traditional Chinese culture,
"golden orchid bond" (*jin lan qi*) is a nickname for a
passionate same-sex relationship. What is especially
interesting is that both the shaman-poet and the King are
described in feminine terms, implying a sophisticated
form of a transgendered homoerotic relationship. If Qu
Yuan did indeed look upon the King as a mortal
embodiment of the Goddess, then it becomes clear why he
chose to interweave the tale of his search for the Goddess
with that of his love for the King. He apparently viewed
both the Goddess and the King as forms of the Divine
Beloved. The shaman-poet realized, however, that unlike
the Goddess, the King of Huai was not immortal, that he,
like the flower, was destined to bloom and fade. The
shaman-poet employs other similes and metaphors to
describe his relationships with the Goddess and the King.
For instance, he compares himself to a horse and the
Goddess and King to riders, a comparison found in
shamanic and possession-trance traditions. In Chinese
symbology, the horse is a symbol of androgyny. While the
horse itself is perceived as feminine or yin, its eyes are
symbols of the "orifice of the penis." He also associates
these relationships with his shamanic chariot, of phoenix
design and pulled by dragons. Again, this hybrid symbol
suggests androgyny, with the dragons representing yang
and the phoenixes yin. Other symbols of androgyny
employed by the shaman-poet in describing his
relationships with the Goddess and the King are bridges,
gates, and RAINBOWS, all serving to connect yin to yang.
In Chinese alchemy, bridges may represent the area
between the genitalia and the anus, while gates may
represent either the vagina or the anus. According to Ping-
leung Chan, the rainbow is an "ambisexual" symbol
associated with the serpent (as in certain African and Afro-
diasporic traditions) and represents the "copulation of the
two ethers [i.e. yin and yang]," often but not always

embodied by females and males respectively. Beyond his
utilization of floral and other imagery, the shaman-poet
employs a term which indicates the attraction Qu Yuan felt
for the King as well as the latter's gender variance. This is
the term *mei-ren*, "beautiful person," usually employed to
refer to females. In early times, however, it was also used to
refer to "sexually ambiguous" individuals. Qu Yuan's
relationship with the King appears to have begun on a
joyous note and to have been a source of nourishment and
inspiration to both partners. "There was a time," the
shaman-poet recalls, "when he spoke with me in
frankness." This period of joy was, however, brief. From
the outset, the King's love of flattery and his apparent
inability to distinguish trustworthy from untrustworthy
persons negatively affected his relationship with Qu Yuan.
Although Qu Yuan warned the King that both the males
and females of the court were jealous of their relationship
and would stop at nothing to destroy their love for each
other, the King ultimately placed his trust in those who
claimed Qu Yuan was only seeking wealth and political
power. "The Fragrant One refused to examine my true
feelings," the poet tells us. "He lent ear instead to slander,
and raged against me." After declining to appear at a
farewell rendezvous, the King banished the shaman-poet,
who wandered in exile, emotionally devastated, until his
death. Meanwhile, the King's trust in the untrustworthy
led to his downfall and imprisonment. Some say that he
died in captivity. On the fifth day of the fifth lunar month,
probably during the final decade of the fourth century BCE,
Qu Yuan drowned himself in the Miluo River, a small river
in the vicinity of Lake Dong Ting, sacred to the Xiang
goddesses and near the city of Changsha. It is believed that
Qu Yuan committed suicide for two reasons: first, because
of the King's betrayal; and second, because this was a day
on which shamans traditionally sacrificed themselves so
that the gods might be pleased and humanity prosper. It is
further conceivable that his suicide was linked to the anti-
shamanic, anti-matrifocal forces that were then impinging
upon the cultures of southern and central China. In the late
twentieth century, the Chinese, Chinese-Americans, and
others continue to honor the shaman-poet Qu Yuan
annually on the fifth day of the fifth month of the lunar
calendar with such things as dragon boat races and
offerings of *zongzi* dumplings, which are often cast into
bodies of water.

Queen Female ruler, in some instances viewed as
transgendered, as in the cases of Pharaoh HATSHEPSUT (d.
c. 1479 BCE) and Queen Christina of Sweden (1626-1689).
Images of queens frequently occur in literature, especially
poetry, celebrating Amazonian women and lesbian love.
The American Transcendentalist poet Emily DICKINSON
was especially fond of the image, penning such lines as
"And I choose, just a crown," "Neither would be a Queen /
Without the Other," "And yet, one Summer, we were

Queens – / But you – were crowned in June." This tradition continues, exemplified by contemporary US lesbian writer Judy GRAHN's *The Queen of Wands* (1982) and *The Queen of Swords* (1987). In terms of slang usage, however, the term "queen" refers to a gay male, usually one who behaves in a manner considered effeminate or transgendered. As employed negatively, "queen" is linked to "queane," a premodern European term for "prostitute;" as employed positively, however, the term attributes a grandeur akin to that experienced by a female ruler to a gay man, often a "drag queen" who has mastered transgendered expression in terms of behavior and attire.

Queen B (or **Queen Bee**)   A kind of archetypal figure posited by SDiane Bogus (b. 1946) which weaves together African/African-American heritage, the love of women for one another, artistry, political practice, and spiritual vision. Her love of women finds resonance in Alice Walker's (b. 1944) concept of womanism. The Queen B often expresses her erotic and spiritual aspects in musical terms, frequently in the forms of Blues, Gospel, and Soul. She appears in Alice Walker's *The Color Purple* (1982) as Shug Avery, and as Travis Lee in Ann Allen Shockley's *Say Jesus and Come to Me* (1982). The Queen B is both akin to, and different from, the BULLDAGGER. Although Bogus does not directly pair the two, one might suggest that they form a kind of "butch"-"femme" woman-loving couple, with the "bulldagger" typically taking the "butch" role.

Quicksilver   Element of MERCURY, whose symbolic meaning in ALCHEMY is androgynous – referring to both the sun (masculine) and the moon (feminine).

Quilt, Names Project AIDS Memorial   Traveling exhibit of ornamented cloth panels commemorating persons who have died of AIDS-related illness. The Quilt was conceived by San Francisco gay activist Cleve Jones. The idea was inspired by a candlelight march in November 1985 in memory of Harvey Milk (a leader of the gay community who was slain by fellow city supervisor and right-wing ex-cop Dan White in 1978), when marchers attached pieces of paper listing the names of those lost to AIDS on a statue near City Hall. It began to materialize in the following year, when Jones and a friend began painting the names of those they had loved and lost on a large piece of cloth. In 1987, forty panels comprised the Quilt. As of February 15, 1996, the number of panels had risen to 32,646. In commemorating the deceased, the Quilt itself clearly qualifies as sacred art. But the Quilt, unlike most paintings hanging in museums, is also the locus of ritual. Wherever it rests or is housed, mourning, honoring, healing, and celebration occur. Describing the Quilt as "volumes of hieroglyphs" and comparing it to the Vietnam Veterans Memorial in Washington, DC, P. S. Hawkins (1993) writes, "To forget a name is in effect to allow death to have the last word . . . they [the Quilt and V. V. Memorial] are the destination of pilgrimage, the occasion for candlelight vigils and song," and S. G. Rosen (1993) adds, "The Quilt exists to honor the survivors along with the dead." For Elinor Fuchs and many others, part of the magic of the Quilt lies in its patching together the somber and the lighthearted; "imagine a cemetery," she writes, "of marble headstones etched with teddy bears . . . and Mickey Mouse . . . Imagine finding . . . 'Comfort, oh comfort my People' [stitched] in Hebrew and English right next to a splash of sequins . . . The Quilt is cemetery as All Fool's Day, a carnival of the sacred, the homely, the joyous and the downright tacky, resisting, even *in extremis*, the solemnity of mourning." Some of the most illuminating observations on the Quilt are found in Rob Baker's *The Art of AIDS: From Stigma to Conscience* (1994).

R

Radegunde Legendary AMAZON queen of Edmund Spenser's *The Faerie Queene* (1590, 1596) who subdues the male knight Artegall, dresses him in feminine attire, and orders him to perform traditionally feminine tasks such as spinning flax. He is rescued by BRITOMART, another Amazon, the daughter of King Ryene of Britain. In Joanna Russ's (b. 1937) short story, "Souls" (appearing in *Extra[Ordinary] People*, 1984), an abbess who is described as having great gifts, particularly the gifts of healing and knowledge of all languages. The wisewoman of her community, she is ultimately displaced by a male Christian priest. Upon her mysterious disappearance, it is suggested that she belongs to the Sidhe, the Faery-Folk. According to G. Griffin (1993), the character pivots on "the notion of a continuity between present-day lesbianism and myths of fairy-folk."

Radha With a name meaning "beloved one" or "attainment," Radha is best known as the female lover of the Hindu god KRISHNA. The daughter of Nanda, "Delight," she is associated with LAKSHMI, the goddess of love, EROTICISM, and beauty. Radha is commonly depicted as a beautiful, bejeweled young woman decked in flower garlands. She is the leader of the GOPIS, the female followers of Krishna. As Krishna's companion, Radha represents, according to D. Kinsley (1986), "one who willfully steps outside the realm of *dharma* [roughly, responsibility] to pursue her love." Possessing the power of shapeshifting, Radha and Krishna occasionally exchange forms so that each may experience what it is like to be loved by the other. In one tale, suggesting not only gender variance but also lesbianism, Krishna dresses as a woman, presumably a *gopi*, "in order to be close to Radha." Radha responds by embracing "her" passionately. Among those who revere Radha are the SAKHIBHAVAS, males who undergo gender or sexual metamorphosis in the process of worshipping her.

Rahere (fl. c. 1100 CE) Renowned court fool of King Henry I of England (r. 1100-1135). Rahere, alleged to have been homoerotically inclined, established St Bartholomew's Fair in London in 1102 following a vision of the saint.

Rain Crossculturally symbolic of nurturance, purification, and rebirth. Deities associated with transgenderism and/or same-sex desire, like the Hindu god GANESHA, as well as transgendered or third gender male spiritual functionaries, including the QEDESHIM of the Canaanite goddess ATHIRAT, the GALLI of the Roman goddess CYBELE, and the HIJRAS of the Hindu goddess BAHUCHARAMATA, are frequently depicted as bringers of rain. In the work of Native American writer Paula Gunn ALLEN, rain is a symbol of openness to, and acceptance of, lesbian desire. In her book *The Highest Apple: Sappho and the Lesbian Poetic Tradition* (1985), Judy GRAHN notes that "perhaps it is only natural from . . . a member of a tribe calling itself Laguna, 'Lake,' that Allen would associate intimacy with rain." Allen writes in "He Na Tye Woman (Female Rain Woman)," " Water (woman) that is the essence of you / . . . / Rain. The rain that makes us new. / That rain is you. / How did I wait so long to drink."

Rainbow In ancient Greece, the rainbow was associated not only with the goddess IRIS but also with the god HERMES, due to his protean nature, and with AMPHION, a young musician whom Hermes loved. To Amphion, Hermes gave a lyre and a beautiful garment: "its color does not remain the same," wrote Philostratus (fl. ca. 200 CE), "but changes and takes on all the hues of the rainbow." Many persons in Medieval and Renaissance France held that "a person might change sex while passing under the rainbow." In the nineteenth century, this belief was reported as being shared by Russians, Rumanians, Serbs, and other Eastern Europeans: "Any male creature that passes under the rainbow turns into a female, and a female into a male." Some Rumanians further imagined that "the rainbow stands with each end in a river, and anyone creeping into its end on hands and knees and drinking the water it touches will instantly change sex." In the Yoruba religion of West Africa and in its African-diasporic manifestations including Santería and Candomblé, the deity of the rainbow is OSHUMARÉ (also Oxumaré). As the rainbow, Oshumaré is a bridge linking the world of mortals to the world of the gods. He-she is androgynous, this nature represented by violet (here, feminine) and red (masculine). In Brazil, Oshumaré is perceived as a patron of gender variant, transgendered, gay, lesbian, and bisexual persons. In the view of Candomblé priest M. Aparecida, to banish a gay person from a Candomblé household is to "kick out the rainbow." Oshumaré's equivalent in the religion of Vodou is the rainbow-serpent, whose masculine aspect is called DAMBALLAH and whose feminine is called AIDO-HWEDO. Audre LORDE, an African-American Lesbian poet, chose the Rainbow-Serpent, as Aido Hwedo, to symbolize not only the power of women who have struggled against oppression but also the radical transformation of patriarchal society. "Aido

Hwedo is coming," she writes, "Rainbow Serpent who must not go / unspoken / . . . / I am a Black woman stripped down / and praying / my whole life has been an altar / worth its ending / and I say Aido Wedo is coming." Since the film *The Wizard of Oz* in 1938, based on L. Frank Baum's novel of 1900, queer people in general, and gay men in particular, have increasingly linked the rainbow to the magical world of Oz, located "over the rainbow" and offering freedom from oppression and delight in companionship and in being oneself. Indeed, this significance attached to the utopia beyond the rainbow has become so powerful that attending a screening of the film at San Francisco's Castro Theatre might be said to constitute a contemporary pilgrimage. The past several decades have witnessed the emergence of the "Rainbow Gathering," a "hippie"-like celebration of Nature, as well as the "Rainbow Coalition," a sociopolitical movement honoring diversity, spearheaded by the Reverend Jesse Jackson, both of which embrace gay, lesbian, and other "queer" people. Beginning in 1978, however, the rainbow acquired special meaning for those involved in the gay liberation movement. At that time, Gilbert Baker, living in San Francisco, California, created a rainbow flag with bands of colors symbolizing gay pride and the theme of unity in diversity. In the 1990s, the rainbow flag has become an international symbol in the struggle for 'queer' liberation.

Raja's Daughter Long ago, in India, each raja was required to send a princess to the seraglio of the ruler of Delhi. Once a raja lied about having a daughter so as to not have to send her to the ruler. When this was discovered, the ruler of Delhi sent emissaries to demand that the raja surrender his daughter. The daughter, however, had run away, taking refuge in a temple of DEVI and praying that she might be rescued from this fate. The goddess answered her prayer by transforming her into a man. The legend tells that she emerged from the temple changed into a boy. Her – now his – father, in gratitude to the goddess, constructed a mile-long avenue of temples to commemorate the event.

Raja-suya In India, among Hindus, this was a rite of royal consecration undergone by the ruler-to-be which included transgender metamorphosis in the psyche of the individual. In this state, the ruler supposedly experienced greater power than that known by men or women.

Rajneesh Movement Founded by Mohan Chandra (Bhagwan) Rajneesh (1931-1990) in an ashram in Poona, India 1974, this international spiritual movement once included many queer-identified disciples, or *sanyassins*. Bhagwan Rajneesh's spiritual philosophy was an eclectic one which, inspired by TANTRA, emphasized the merging of eroticism and spiritual impulse. In the late 1970s and early 1980s, he encouraged polygamous (presumably

"safe") "free love." During this period, as recorded in the *Darshan Diaries*, he told a gay male disciple that homosexuality could serve as a valid path to superconsciouness. In the early 1980s, a gay male household of *sanyassins* was established in the Castro district of San Francisco. Members of this household dressed in the typical gay male "clone" garb of the era, except for dyeing their jeans and T-shirts saffron, then vermilion, then fuchsia, and finally purple. These *sanyassins* played a key role in the development of gay male massage workshops employing techniques of Tantra. By the mid-1980s, however, with the emergence of AIDS, Rajneesh was condemning homosexuality as "perverted, against nature, and devoid of any creative or spiritual dimension," describing AIDS as "the ultimate development of homosexuality." He and those in positions of authority demanded that the Castro district household disband immediately. Shortly thereafter, Rajneesh fell into disgrace in the eyes of many of his followers. He was forced to close a commune he had established in Oregon, left the US, and died – according to sources close to Rajneesh, of AIDS-related illness – in 1990.

Rakusin, Sudie (b. c. 1950) Lesbian American artist best known for her illustrations of goddesses (or aspects of the Great Goddess) and AMAZONS, which are reminiscent of Art Nouveau and which blend ancient and twentieth-century iconography. In *The Once and Future Goddess* (1989) by Elinor Gadon, Rakusin says of her artistic process and her spirituality, "all this energy – spiritual, psychic, emotional, creative, sexual – comes from the same source . . . We are of the goddess – strong, brave and angry . . . as I create I discover myself."

Ram Often associated with male energy and lustfulness, the ram corresponds to the zodiac sign of ARIES. Deities associated with the ram and with transgenderism and/or same-sex passion include the Egyptian god MIN, CARNEIUS (a companion of the Greek god APOLLO), and the Yoruba god SHANGO.

Ram Dass (Richard Alpert, 1931-) Homoerotically inclined US spiritual teacher and writer. In the 1960s, Ram Dass attained notoriety due to his experiments with LSD arising from a desire to explore the workings of human consciousness. Leaving a teaching post, he journeyed to India in 1967, where he met a spiritual teacher, Neem Karoli Baba. Four years later, Ram Dass published *Be Here Now*, a best-selling spiritual guidebook. Since that time, he has published numerous other books which, like the first, have become "bibles" of the New Age movement, including *Grist for the Mill* (with Steven Levine, 1977), *The Only Dance There Is* (1979), and *Journey of Awakening: A Meditator's Guidebook* (revised edition, 1990). Believing that the ego and desire call forth suffering, Ram Dass generally shuns the concept of queer identity and downplays not only his attraction to other men but also a same-sex relationship in which he has been involved for many years. Nevertheless, he honors the great "tenderness, softness and compassion" he has observed among gay men and acknowledges that loving men can serve as a bridge to enlightenment. Since the 1980s, Ram Dass has worked with PWAs (persons living with AIDS). He, like many others in the New Age movement, holds that HIV/AIDS, although a devastating experience, can serve to teach us a great deal about "death, loss, and grief."

Rama   In Hinduism, an incarnation, or avatar, of the god VISHNU. Rama is depicted as a brave warrior and a compassionate ruler in the *Ramayana*, an epic probably composed near the third century BCE. He is also associated with the MOON. A. Daniélou (1964) relates that once, when Rama was in the forest protecting a group of sages from some demons, the sages were suddenly struck by his magnificent beauty. "Who is there with a physical body," they exclaimed, "that would not feel attracted at the sight of his form." Thus even the most ascetic of men were erotically drawn to Rama. They begged the god to allow them to embrace him passionately. He would not allow this, but he promised that when he – and now he was speaking of himself as an avatar of Vishnu – returned to earth, he would return as Vishnu's avatar KRISHNA. He would make certain that the sages returned as well, except that they would be reborn as the GOPIS, the female entourage of Krishna. In those future forms, the souls of the sages would at last be allowed to passionately embrace the deity.

Ramer, Andrew (1951-   )   US gay writer and mystic. Of Jewish heritage, Ramer is the author of two best-selling books on the phenomenon of ANGELS, *Ask Your Angels: A Practical Guide to Working with Angels to Enrich Your Life* (with Alma Daniel, 1992) and *Angel Answers: A Joyful Guide to Creating Heaven on Earth* (1995). He is also the author of *Two Flutes Playing: Spiritual Love/Sacred Sex: Priests of Father Earth and Mother Sky* (1990, 1996). The focus of *Flutes* is gay male spirituality. Ramer, versed in the art of CHANNELING, employs this metaphysical technique in presenting information relating to gay identity, homoerotic TANTRA, and other erotico-spiritual subjects. Among the insights imparted by Ramer (and channeled entities) in *Flutes* is that "gayness . . . is a matter of vibration. Gay men are 'tuned' differently than other men. This difference is what allows men who are drawn to men to recognize each other." This vibration, which Ramer describes elsewhere as "GREEN," is comprised of various elements, which he outlines in an interview with Mark THOMPSON (1994). These elements include: a role referred to as "consciousness scout"; artistic pursuits; the role (or roles) of healer and psychopomp (guide of souls);

and the role of the "hunter," which expresses the sexual drive of gay men. Of the first, Ramer says, "Any tribe has scouts that run ahead to see what's beyond the next mountain"; i.e. gay men often serve as pioneers, risk-takers, style-setters, and visionaries, leading a culture from one epoch to another. Ramer explains that "gay people . . . exist in a state of internal fluidity compared to the average human being that will make them, make us, vital in this time of planetary challenge." Recently, Ramer has begun to link his exploration of Gay Spirituality or Queer Spirit to his exploration of the angel phenomenon. "Since angels have no gender or the same gender," he speculates, "the relationships they share might be considered homosexual." He adds, "And just as there are gay guides and gay angels, there are gay heavens." Ramer's forthcoming book, *Revelations for a New Millennium* (1997), will speak to the "wisdom that the soul stores in the bones."

Raphael the Archangel, Saint   One of the seven archangels of Biblical tradition, his name means "God heals" in Hebrew. Raphael's association with passion between men may be traced to the Medieval French tale of AMIS AND AMILE. The homoerotically inclined Spanish poet Federico García LORCA depicts Raphael as a beautiful man of Moorish appearance "dressed in dark spangles" and reminiscent of the Greek deities DIONYSUS and GANYMEDE. Lorca describes a ritual honoring him as one embracing sublimated homoeroticism, its participants, including "slender-waisted Merlins" and youths ("disciples of Tobias," a mortal companion of Raphael), undressing "among the rushes." In the Yoruba-diasporic religion of Santería, Saint Raphael is identified with the homoerotically or bisexually inclined deity INLE. Saint Raphael is fêted on September 29.

Rapunzel   Fairy tale recorded by the Brothers Grimm which concerns a witch who steals a female infant because the father has dared to enter her herb garden to steal some rampion for his wife. The witch rears the maiden, keeping her locked in a tower. Rapunzel's long hair, however, allows a prince to visit her and ultimately to steal her away. In twentieth-century American poet Anne Sexton's transformation of the fairy tale, Mother Gothel, the witch, and the maiden Rapunzel come to love each other, in spite of their prison guard/prisoner relationship. Sexton writes, "A woman / who loves a woman / is forever young." Ultimately, however, the maiden abandons the older woman for a prince, with the poem ending on a Sapphic, melancholy note: "As for Mother Gothel, / her heart shrank to the size of a pin, / never to say: Hold me, my young dear, / hold me, / and only as she dreamt of the yellow hair / did moonlight sift into her mouth." Twentieth-century Greek-American poet Olga Broumas's revision of the tale honors Sexton's poem but moves beyond its parameters in more fully celebrating lesbian love. "Climb / through my hair, climb in / to me, love," Broumas writes, "I'll break the hush / of our cloistered garden, our harvest continuous / as a moan."

Ravarour, Adrian (1943-   )   Los Angeles-based gay male choreographer and writer who holds that dance, body movement, and eroticism may be employed as techniques of ecstasy and as pathways to spiritual enlightenment. He is the inventor of Energy Flow Dance and the author of *Energy Flow Choreography* (1986) and *Energy Flow Dance* (1992). Since 1970, he has published poetry chapbooks centering on Gay Spiritual themes, including *Free: Poems of Flow* (1970), *Wings of Flow* (1971), *Angels of Night* (1975), *Déjà Vous* (1995), *Male Love Poems* (1995), and *Homo Erectus* (1996). In "Dance Hall Ghosts," he writes, "There is a river / of silence / which songs / bring alive / Certain music / recalls / your presence / dancing alive."

Raven   Koryak deity or spirit associated with third gender or TWO-SPIRIT male shamans. In one tale, Raven and his son Eme'mqut are shamans who turn into ravens after putting on cloaks of raven feathers. Tales such as this one are linked to others focusing on sex and/or gender metamorphosis. In one of these, Raven transforms himself into a woman by castrating himself. From his penis, he fashions a needle-case; his testicles become bells. Among the ancient Greeks, the raven was a symbol of the lover (*erastes*). Likewise, in ancient Rome, the raven signified the active male partner in oral intercourse. In the late twentieth century, the raven has become a signifier of lesbianism, as female ravens are known to couple. Raven is the name of a lesbian swordswoman in Samuel R. Delany's *Tales of Neveryon* (1979). In Marion Zimmer Bradley's *The Mists of Avalon* (1982), Raven is a priestess of the Goddess who joins in a blood-sisterhood ritual with MORGAINE OF THE FAIRIES. Their union is described as weaving together the relationship of worshipper to Goddess, mother to daughter, sister to sister, and lover to beloved. Pat Califia's *Doc and Fluff* (1990) also includes a priestess named Raven.

Rebis   Androgynous figure or double same-sex (or same-gender) being of ALCHEMY representing the union of opposites including male and female, sun and moon, heaven and earth.

Red   In many cultural and spiritual traditions, a color symbolic of blood, vitality, aggression, erotic passion, and sacrifice. Red is the favorite color of the Amazonian Egyptian goddess SEKHMET. In Hinduism, red is sacred to numerous deities associated with transgenderism and/or same-sex desire, including AGNI, BAHUCHARAMATA, GANESHA, LAKSHMI, TRIPURASUNDARI, and VASANTA. In Hinduism, red is also associated with the HIJRAS, the gender variant male, or transgendered, priest/esse/s of Bahucharamata. In ancient Greek religion, red was especially sacred to ARTEMIS of EPHESUS and when worn by male devotees signified both allegiance to the Goddess and gender variance, or transgenderism. In the later Euro-western tradition, the interplay of red and white in a single being functioned, as in Richard Barnfield's poem *The Affectionate Shepherd* (1594), as an alchemical symbol of the androgynous merging of masculine (red, Mars) and feminine (white, the Moon). Among the Mohave of the American Southwest, the TWO-SPIRIT male ALYHA painted their bellies with red stripes, symbolic of their gender variant status. Hidatsa gender variant male shamans painted red ovals on their cheeks and carried red blankets. Among homoerotically inclined men living in the late nineteenth and early twentieth centuries, wearing a red scarf or tie around the neck signified homoerotic desire. This tradition was observed in places as far apart as Venice, Italy and Austin, Texas. By 1915, especially among the "fairies" of New York City, red had become synonymous with "sexual inversion." Early sexologist Havelock Ellis was told that red served, whether in the form of attire or interior decoration, "as a badge of all their tribe."

Regardie, Francis Israel (1907-1985)   Bisexual or gay (closeted) English-born ritual magician and writer. At one time the personal secretary of Aleister CROWLEY, Regardie was a member of the Hermetic Order of the Golden Dawn (which also included the homophobic William Butler YEATS and Dion FORTUNE). Regardie's works include: an anthology of *The Golden Dawn* (1937-1940, 1978); *The Eye in the Triangle*, a biography of Crowley (1970); and *Ceremonial Magic* (1982). According to N. Drury (1992), Regardie was "widely considered to have been the foremost authority on modern Western magic."

Regkeis   Verbal signal employed by the GALLI, the gender variant priests of the Greco-Roman goddess CYBELE and her male consort ATTIS. Eventually, it appears, other gender variant, often homoerotically inclined males also began to employ the *regkeis*. Unfortunately, we are familiar with the *regkeis* only from hostile sources; still, from these sources, we can guess at what this signal may have sounded like. Dio Chrysostom, in a speech to the men of Tarsus, names this signal the *regkeis*, commonly translated as "snort." From Clement of Alexandria, who also suggests that the *regkeis* signal was nasal in character, we learn that the men employing this signal "make a sound in their nose like a frog." The *regkeis* signal may have actually sounded more like heavy breathing or hissing. Dio Chrysostom describes the *regkeis* as "belonging to neither man nor woman." In another place, he asks, "But who are they who make that sort of sound? Are they not creatures of mixed sex? Are they not men who have had their testicles lopped off?" He answers himself, "It [i.e. the *regkeis* signal] is reserved for themselves, a sort of password of their own." The *regkeis*, while apparently inciting laughter in hostile males, was clearly employed with the intention of announcing to the listener one's erotic desires; Clement refers to it as a signal of "lewdness and fornication to provoke lust," continuing to say that it sounds as if its users have "concentrated their bad behavior in their nostrils." Dio Chrysostom insists that, even more than appearance, the *regkeis* may reveal a man to be a *cinaedus*, a gender variant male engaging in same-sex eroticism. He relates the story of an elderly man who is brought before a certain sage in order that the latter might determine what sort of man he is. Even though the elderly man is a "person of rugged frame and knitted brows . . . with calluses on his hands, [and] wrapped in a sort of coarse, gray mantle," the sage recognizes him to be a *cinaedus*, and perhaps also an elderly gallus, because he utters the *regkeis* during their brief encounter.

Reincarnation Among numerous spiritual groups, reincarnation is linked to transgenderism and/or same-sex orientation. In a majority of these, as among the Dhanwar of India and the Urabunna and Waramunga tribes of Central Australia, a soul that is reincarnated as a person of opposite sex or gender may come to express transgendered behavior and/or fall in love with an individual of the same anatomical sex. Taoists often explain lesbian relationships as resulting from reincarnation: "A woman may be predestined to marry a certain man over and over again in different incarnations; even if her predestined husband should in one incarnation be born a female, she is nonetheless attracted to her predestined partner." Similarly, some Chinese hold that women who have been abused by their husbands will be reincarnated as men, in order to take revenge on their husbands, who will be reborn as women. In the Euro-western tradition, some of those following PLATO appear to have believed that those drawn toward members of the same sex might trace their inclination to previous homoerotic or lesbian incarnations and ultimately to a divine double being. Moreover, it is suggested in the *Phaedrus* of Plato that those who are the spiritual children of a particular deity will be drawn toward other children of that deity. In the nineteenth and twentieth centuries, many lesbian, homoerotically inclined, bisexual, and transgendered individuals, including Walt WHITMAN, Madame Helena Petrovna BLAVATSKY, Edward CARPENTER, Arthur RIMBAUD, Aleister CROWLEY, Renée VIVIEN, Radclyffe HALL, Christopher ISHERWOOD, and Gloria ANZALDUA have expressed a belief in reincarnation. Renée Vivien, in *A Woman Appeared to Me*, has her character San Giovanni voice a feeling of her own, "If it is true . . . that the soul is reborn in several human bodies, I was certainly born once on Lesbos," and in "I was a Page in Love," she writes: "It

seems as though we come one to the other / From some deep unknown past that was ours, / . . . / On my lips a charming memory lingers. / Who can know? I was perhaps your love . . . / My remembrances are more tenacious than a hope / A page who sang beneath your balcony at night."

Relaxation of the Poor Mystical initiation rite of the Sufis in which it seems that male initiates and masters engaged in both anal and oral intercourse, with initiates taking the "receptive" role.

Remember the Tarantella (1987) In this novel by Australian writer Finola Moorhead, ASTROLOGY, MAGIC, and ceremonial dance aid in the weaving together of the lives of a group of lesbians. Patrick Holland observes, "Since dance is one situation that can combine individual expression with community celebration, Moorhead recuperates the tarantella – once associated with reaction to a deadly . . . bite – as a joyous female rite, an answer to Dionysian revel."

Renaissance With the emergence of the European Renaissance, the divine beings of classical antiquity discovered a refuge in the world of art. In describing the painting *Pan* by the artist Luca Signorelli (c. 1441-1523), Michael Levey describes the god and his companions as the "banished creatures of mythology who had always existed and who . . . now crept back in the welcoming Renaissance air." Renaissance artists, James Saslow explains, recognized "androgyny as the type of male beauty appropriate in a homoerotic context." Shakespeare (1564-1616) sang of the "master mistress of [his] passion," and paintings depicting GANYMEDE and a paganized SAINT SEBASTIAN proliferated. The myth of Ganymede was reinterpreted in the Renaissance to symbolize "divine Charity," the "divine fury" of a saint's experience of ecstasy, and the ascent of the soul upon death. If Ganymede and St Sebastian were the predominant symbols of homoerotic love and male gender variance in the Renaissance, the Greco-Roman goddess ARTEMIS/DIANA, her beloved CALLISTO, and the poet SAPPHO were the predominant symbols of lesbian love – as well as transgenderism where Artemis and Callisto are concerned. While most of the paintings referring to lesbian intimacy (with which we are familiar) were painted by male artists, they nevertheless suggest how such desire was perceived and how it may have been expressed. These paintings include *Diana with Meleager and Actaeon* (c. 1420, attributed to the Circle of Lorenzo di Niccolò), *The Story of Diana and Actaeon* (c. 1440, attributed to Paolo Schiarvo), *Diana and Actaeon* (c. 1540-1545, anonymous Italian work), *Actaeon watching Diana and her Nymphs Bathing* (1560-1565, by Paolo Veronese), *Two Nymphs* (c. 1523, by Parmagiano), and *Diana and Callisto* (1556-1559, by Titian). Other artists and writers of the Renaissance who gave expression to androgyny, or transgenderism, and/or to same-sex passion include Marsilio FICINO, Christopher MARLOWE, LEONARDO DA VINCI, MICHAELANGELO Buonarroti , Giovanni Antonio BAZZI ("Il Sodoma"), and Benvenuto CELLINI. For most of these artists and writers, the legendary landscape of ARCADIA signified a safe haven for the expression of same-sex passion. MUSIC of the period likewise is imbued with references to transgenderism and same-sex love. Texts of occult arts practiced in the Renaissance, such as those on ASTROLOGY, also reference these subjects. Beyond the realms of art and esotericism, incidences of same-sex passion and transgendered behavior may be discovered in the lives of Christian NUNS like Sister Benedetta CARLINI and even in those of saints, including that of SAINT CATHERINE OF GENOA. While in some respects the Renaissance might be described as a period of relative tolerance where same-sex passion and transgenderism are concerned, in other respects it represents one of the most hostile epochs in our history. The burning of sodomites, commencing in late antiquity, continued with the Inquisition. During the Renaissance, the real or imagined bond of sodomy and, to a lesser extent, lesbianism and Witchcraft resulted in the torture and execution of many individuals. This destruction of lives was coupled with the destruction of many great works of art, as exemplified by the popular BONFIRES OF THE VANITIES led by the Catholic zealot Girolamo Savonarola. Among the most illuminating works treating our subject in this period are Judith C. Brown's *Immodest Acts: The Life of a Lesbian Nun in Renaissance Italy* (1986), James Saslow's *Ganymede in the Renaissance: Homosexuality in Art and Society* (1986), and Patricia Simons's "Lesbian (In)Visibility in Italian Renaissance Culture: Diana and Other Cases of *donna con donna* " (1994).

Renart Medieval French fox, TRICKSTER, and rake. Although he does not appear to have been worshipped, Renart seems to have played a central role in the Medieval Feast of Fools. While rape, murder, and robbery were all credited to him, he somehow remained an amiable character and was admired as an outlaw. Patricia Terry explains that tales of Renart functioned to attack, "with gusto and subterranean idealism, the government . . . [and the] Church." A great sinner, Renart delights in confession. As Gerald Herman notes, "Renart . . . recites his past sins in the same manner that a warrior might display old battle scars." Not surprisingly, one of these "sins" is homoerotic activity. In the *Roman de Fauvel*, a propagandistic Christian text of the early fourteenth century, Renart appears not as a fox but as Fauvel, a "fawn-coloured stallion" who, in being linked to the KNIGHTS TEMPLAR, is credited with introducing humankind to homosexuality.

Renvoisy, Richard de (1520-1586)   French composer, lutenist and *"maître des enfans de choeur"* at the Sainte-Chapelle in Dijon who, convicted of sodomy, was burnt at the stake. Before his cruel trial and murder, Renvoisy enjoyed great respect. Most of his work was burned when his belongings were confiscated. His *Psalmi Davidici* for four voices is one of those works lost to us. A part of his 1559 chanson text based on a French translation of the erotico-spiritual *Odes of Anacreon* has survived. One of the most beautiful pieces therein tells of a lover smitten by Eros longing for his beloved.

Rhadamanthys   "He who divines with a wand," a brave, wise, and compassionate Cretan lawgiver. Rhadamanthys was the brother of MINOS and SARPEDON. The husband of Alcmene and the father of Gortys and Erythrus, he was also a lover of other males, including ATYMNIUS (who ultimately rejected him) and TALOS. Upon his death, Rhadamanthys became one of the judges of the dead in Hades.

Rhinoceros, Lavender   Symbol of gay pride in the early 1970s, especially on the East coast of the US, originating in Boston. Symbolically, the rhinoceros fuses gentility (its usual placidity, represented by its often large, round frame) and force (its rage when threatened, represented by its horn). The rhinoceros was depicted as lavender in order to secure its link to the gay movement.

Rhodogune (fl. second century BCE)   Amazonian warrior-queen of Parthia who fought against the Armenians. Her victory was celebrated in poems and works of art. Her trademark was her disheveled HAIR, as she had gone into battle immediately following a bath. Ancient sources indicate that she may have preferred the company of women to that of men.

Rhodopis   In Greek legend, a beautiful young woman from Ephesus who was loved by the goddess ARTEMIS/DIANA. The goddess APHRODITE succeeded in convincing Rhodopis to engage in heterosexual lovemaking by having her encounter a young man named Euthynicus. Upon learning this, Artemis, refusing to lose Rhodopis to a man, transformed the maiden into a spring.

Rice with pork (arroz con chancho)   In twentieth-century Latin American culture, this dish occasionally serves as a symbol of male homosexuality.

Rich, Adrienne (1929-   )   Lesbian-feminist US poet and essayist of Jewish heritage whose works have been inspired by, and in turn inspire, spiritual traditions including Judaism, Goddess Reverence, and Women's Spirituality. In poems such as *Sources* (1981-1982), "Eastern War Time" (1989-1990), and "Tattered

Kaddish" (1989), Rich draws upon her Jewish heritage. In
the last of these, she alludes to the QABBALAH, particularly
to the sphere of Malkuth, which is sometimes depicted as
an apple field. This field, in Jewish esotericism, is
associated with the fertile process of discovering hidden
meanings in the Torah. Rich also draws upon the Kaddish,
a Jewish prayer of praise, thanksgiving, a plea for peace,
and especially, an honoring of the dead, the ancestors.
Further, the poet draws upon ASTROLOGY, employing the
sign of TAURUS. "Taurean reaper of the wild apple field,"
she writes, "speak your tattered Kaddish for all suicides."
In other poems, Rich alludes to figures and rites of classical
antiquity, especially to the ELEUSINIAN MYSTERIES of
DEMETER and her daughter PERSEPHONE. In
"Cartographies of Silence" (1975), she envisions herself as
"the Eleusinian hierophant / holding up a simple ear of
grain," and in the sixth of her "Twenty-one Love Poems"
(1974-1976), she speaks of "figures of ecstatic women
striding / to the sibyl's den or the Eleusinian cave." In still
other poems, Rich invokes images from other spiritual
traditions and esoteric systems, as in "Nights and Days"
(1976), where she depicts two women walking along the
beach as "Norns, perhaps, or sisters of the spray," and in
the "Twenty-one Love Poems," where, as C. P. Christ
(1980) explains, Rich alludes to the twenty-one Major
Arcana (plus one, the Fool, her "floating poem") of the
TAROT. Rich has also written on her relationship to
Judaism and Women's Spirituality in her essay "Split at
the Root" (1982) and her book *Of Woman Born:
Motherhood as Experience and Institution* (1976). The heart
of Rich's own spiritual vision may be discovered in poetic
statements in "Natural Resources" (1977) and "The
Desert as Garden of Paradise" (1987-1988). In the former,
she writes, "I have to cast my lot with those / who age after
age, perversely, with no extraordinary power, /
reconstitute the world," and in the latter, "I don't pray
often / Never to male or female / sometimes to music or the
flask of sunset." This is, above all, a spirituality that is
embodied, frequently in persons and events the world
deems commonplace. Like the women divers, miners, and
mountaineers of her works, Rich discovers treasures in
places unreachable to most. Like the woman of the apple
field, she "grows sprouts of secrets," bestowing fresh
meaning to the sacred.

Riggs, Marlon T. (1957-1994)   African-American gay
filmmaker and writer whose works explore the
interrelationship of Black identity, gay identity, and
spiritual life (especially in terms of African-American
Christianity and traditional African-diasporic religions).
His films include *Ethnic Notions* (1987), *Tongues Untied*
(1989), and *Black Is, Black Ain't* (1995), the last film
released following his death due to AIDS-related illness.
In "Tongues Untied," Riggs, disillusioned with San
Francisco's gay Castro district, finds that the beat of his

own heart guides him beyond feelings of alienation and
toward salvation: "older, stronger rhythms resonate within
me, / sustain my spirit, silence the clock. / Rhythms of
blood, culture, / history, and race." Shortly before his
death, Riggs dreamed that the African-American
abolitionist and early women's rights activist Harriet
Tubman (c. 1815-1913) appeared to him as a spiritual
guide or psychopomp, guiding him to the other bank of the
river of life. Despite great suffering, Riggs accepted death,
transforming it into a potent, intensely creative experience.
"My work," said Riggs as he lay dying, "is the living spirit
of me."

Rimbaud, Arthur (1854-1891)   Homoerotically or
bisexually inclined, bohemian French Symbolist poet
profoundly inspired by classical mythology and the occult.
It was a work of "rough MAGIC" undertaken by the
sorcerer Bretagne which delivered the young poet and
vagabond Arthur Rimbaud into the arms of the Symbolist
poet Paul Verlaine (1844-1896). Rimbaud, born on
October 20, 1854, ran away from home at sixteen following
a violent argument with his mother. At Paris, he was
introduced to Verlaine, ten years his senior. The two
became lovers. Their relationship was a passionate one,
filled with quarrels, love letters, obscene poems, and even a
shooting. By twenty, Rimbaud had left Verlaine and
poetry forever. He died at thirty-seven, the name of Djami,
an Abyssinian youth, on his lips. If Rimbaud believed in
anything, it was that poet and sorcerer are one. As a youth,
he spent many hours in the library reading treatises on
ritual magic, Witchcraft, and the QABBALAH, including
Jules Michelet's *La sorcière* and Eliphas Levi's *Les Clefs
des Grands Mystères*. He was also enchanted with
Baudelaire's poems, perceiving them as verses inspired by
SATAN. As a devotee of Bretagne, he witnessed the
practice of the magical arts, and was apparently instructed
in telepathy and astral projection. Rimbaud was also no
stranger to opium. His earliest poems already reflect his
identification with the magician or priest of antiquity. His
Credo in Unam, a hymn to Greco-Roman paganism, opens
with a hymn to the SUN. Perceiving the earth as "VENUS,
goddess," he beseeches her, "Bring back those ancient days
when all was young; / Days of lascivious satyrs, animal
fauns." Rimbaud sees the "modern" individual as a
soulless robot and believes that the spirit of paganism has
the power to restore our humanity, our passion.
Rimbaud's reverence focuses on the Goddess in her
various guises and on her male consort, who resembles, at
once, PAN, a VAMPIRE, and an androgynous youth. In
"Antique," he depicts a "Graceful son of Pan" as having
gleaming fangs, a lyre-shaped breast, and "loins / That
cradle a double sex." He believes that men will be healed
only when they have returned to the Goddess and have
reincorporated into their psyches her male/transgendered
consort(s), when they have thrown off the chains of

Christianity. "Bring back the days of almighty CYBELE," he chants, "I believe! I believe in Thee, Divine Mother, / Aphrodite of the sea! Oh, the way is hard; / That other God has bound us to his cross! / Flesh, Marble, Flower, Venus – in thee I believe!" In "Tale" Rimbaud tells of a Prince who destroys everything around him, including his wives, in order to be able to "see the Truth," to know "satisfaction" in a way he has never known it before, to confront "essential desire." In "Genie," the Prince and the Genie merge into a single being: "The Prince was the Genie. / The Genie was the Prince." This being is then annihilated, becoming one with the cosmos. Nick Osmond, in *Illuminations: Coloured Plates* (1976), writes: "The meeting with the Genie represents the sexual revolution which Rimbaud hoped to enact through his relationship with Paul Verlaine, unbearable in its intensity, unspeakable . . . in the sense that it constitutes an almost religious mystery." In his illuminating essay "Visions of Violence: Rimbaud and Verlaine" (1979), Paul Schmidt describes the relationship of the two poets as one in which the roles of abandoned children were acted out, in which a "disordering of the senses" was cultivated. This disordering, which triggered an almost constant altered state of consciousness, was accomplished in part via drugs and same-sex eroticism, echoing the practices of gender variant shamans and priests. Schmidt stresses the disordering potential of homosexuality: "Homosexuality is a permanent extension of . . . liminality . . . It is an alienation from the order of society, and it provides, as all alienations do, a view of that order from outside, from the other side. But being permanent, it is more – it is a refusal of that order . . . it [i.e. homosexuality] is [thus] able to constitute itself as an exemplary and natural state of exaltation. Schmidt suggests that a type of sex magic partaking of SADOMASOCHISM may have been undertaken by Rimbaud and Verlaine as a means of achieving an altered state of consciousness. In their relationship, it would seem that Verlaine often played the role of "bride" or "slave," recalling the HIERODULE of antiquity, while Rimbaud acted as "the Infernal Bridegroom." Rimbaud suggests, however, that these roles occasionally may have been reversed. In "Farewell," he speaks of "the thousands of loves who nailed me to the cross," an image used by Rimbaud's circle to indicate "passive homosexuality," while in "Night in Hell," he cries, "Satan, you clown, you want to dissolve me with your charms. / Well, I want it. I want it! Stab me with a pitchfork, sprinkle me with fire!"

Ring   In the twentieth century, wearing a ring on the little finger, usually on the left hand, has become a sign for same-sex erotic orientation. While its origin may be Euro-western, the tradition has become an international one. The ring is typically symbolic of love and commitment to a relationship, nobility, wholeness, infinity, and magic (especially blessings, curses,

protection, and healing), while the left hand typically corresponds to the feminine, the exotic or eccentric, and the so-called "left hand path" of occult knowledge. Recently, queer-identified persons have begun to wear neck chains from which hang numerous rings which together signify the RAINBOW; these symbolize the joyful, empowering, and community-building aspects of the gay rights and/or queer rights movement(s).

Robin   In the work of lesbian or bisexually inclined American poet Emily DICKINSON, symbolic of one who travels far from her lover but who ultimately returns. In "I have a Bird in spring," Dickinson relates that when "the Rose appears / Robin is gone." Yet the poet/narrator does not despair, "Knowing That Bird of mine" will return, having "Learned beyond the sea / Melody new for me."

Rochel, Hannah (1805-1892)   Transgendered, possibly lesbian or bisexual Chasidic Jewish leader, known as the "Maid of Ludomir." Near the time of her wedding – an arranged marriage – Rochel fell into an altered state of consciousness, during which she claimed to have experienced gender metamorphosis. Halting the wedding ceremony, she began to dress in traditional male attire and to study in the synagogue. After a time, she began instructing others in the faith. The Zaddik of Chernobyl was, however, greatly disturbed by Rochel's assumption of male dress, behavior and religious role. After the Zaddik finally convinced Rochel to marry, her "femininity" seemed to return. With its return came the loss of her religious authority.

Rocky Horror Picture Show   Musical film (1975) directed by Jim Sharman and starring Tim Curry and Susan Sarandon, now a cult classic. Drawing upon Romantic and Gothic imagery, especially the figures of Frankenstein and the VAMPIRE, as well as the imagery of mid-twentieth-century science fiction, *The Rocky Horror Picture Show* raises the tragicomic, ultra-CAMP Dr Frankenfurter (Curry) – the "sweet transvestite transsexual from Transylvania" – to archetypal status. In the 1990s, Frankenfurter's sleazy vampire/femme fatale drag continues to inspire not only fans attending late-night showings of the film but also countless Radical Faeries dancing in moonlit groves.

Rolfe, Frederic William, Baron Corvo (1860-1913)   Homoerotically inclined Decadent Catholic writer whose 1904 novel *Hadrian VII* tells the tale of George Rose, an expelled seminarian who becomes Pope, sells the treasures of the Vatican, and reestablishes the Roman Empire, only to be assassinated by a socialist.

Rome   Center of the worship of the goddess CYBELE and her male consort ATTIS, served by the gender variant, homoerotically inclined GALLI, this ancient city was associated in the minds of nineteenth-century French bohemians with homoeroticism. One who had "attended school at Paris" referred to a heterosexual male, while one who had "attended school at Rome" signified a homosexual male.

Rooster Bird alternately symbolic of the sun, fire, vitality, nobility, masculinity, sacrifice, and rebirth. Deities and spiritual functionaries associated with the rooster and with transgenderism and/or same-sex intimacy include ATTIS, BAHUCHARAMATA and her HIJRA priests, CYBELE and her GALLI priests, DIONYSUS, EROS, GANYMEDE, and SHANGO. In ancient Greece, the rooster was a symbol of homoerotic love, given as courting gifts by lovers (*erastes*) to their beloveds (*eromenoi*).

Rope Baby Among the Lakota of North America, the "rope baby", a coiled rope linking two women in a UNION blessed by the goddess WIYA NUMPA, or Double Woman, symbolizes the creativity generated by that union.

Roscoe, Will (1955-) Gay anthropologist, historian, and writer who has been active in the Gay Spirituality movement and who has authored and edited numerous texts pertaining to the interrelationship of homoeroticism, transgenderism, and the sacred, including *Living the Spirit* (with Gay American Indians of San Francisco, 1988), *The Zuni Man-Woman* (1991), and *Queer Spirits* (1995).

Rose Primarily a symbol of love, passion, suffering (its thorns), ephemerality, and spiritual perfection, the rose is associated in Greek mythology or religion with numerous deities linked to same-sex intimacy and/or transgenderism, including ADONIS, APHRODITE, DIONYSUS, and EROS. Like the ROOSTER, the rose was given by the Greek lover to his beloved as a courting gift. The rose thus came to represent the beloved, or *eromenos*. Philostratus (fl. c. 200 CE) writes, "So must you beautiful boys arm yourselves with roses, and let that be the equipment that your lovers will present to you. Now the hyacinth suits a fair-haired boy well, the narcissus a dark-haired one, but the rose suits all, since once it was itself a boy." As emblems of Aphrodite, roses, together with violets and other flowers and herbs, were woven into garlands worn by the women of SAPPHO's THIASOS on the island of LESBOS. In Medieval European ALCHEMY, the rose became symbolic of androgyny or transgenderism; as such it was associated with the god/planet/spirit HERMES/MERCURY/MERCURIUS. In a Medieval poetic letter written by "A.," a Catholic Bavarian woman, perhaps a nun, to "G.," a woman she loves, the former depicts the latter as "her unique rose" to whom she "sends the bonds of precious love." The *Roman de la rose* was begun by Guillaume de Lorris in 1223 and completed by Jean de Meung two

decades later. The part of the text written earlier is more concerned with, as well as more positive toward, homoeroticism, bi-eroticism, and transgenderism than the part written by de Meung. In de Lorris's original version, a youth has a dream in which, after much wandering, he finds a "garden of love surrounded by high walls." He is befriended by Lady Idleness, who opens the door of the garden for him, and by Amor who leads him to the fountain of NARCISSUS. In the fountain lie two crystals which make it possible to see a reflection of the entire garden, especially its roses. The youth becomes entranced by a particular rosebud. While the open rose is symbolic of the feminine, the rosebud is symbolic of the masculine, as the French word for "bud," *bouton*, is masculine, suggesting that the youth is attracted to same-sex love rather than opposite-sex love. This homoerotic symbolism is lost in the version of de Meung. In Middle Eastern and later in Euro-western symbolism, the rosebud becomes a signifier of the anus and anal intercourse. In a sixteenth-century allegorical work, the Islamic writer Mehemmed Ghazali (d. 1535) compares the open or relaxed anus to the "laughter of a thousand roses" and the closed or tight anus to a "silent rosebud." In nineteenth-century French bohemian circles, the *rosette*, the "petite rose," signified the anus as an erotic organ, with men-loving men being deemed the *Chevaliers de la Rosette* ("the knights of the petite rose"). In the work of the Spanish poet and playwright Federico García LORCA, the rose, especially when linked to blood, as in "Poema doble del lago Eden," frequently signifies the homoerotically inclined male and love between men. In "La oracion de las rosas," Lorca compares the homoerotically inclined French Symbolist poet Paul VERLAINE to a "bloody rose" ("*rosa sangrienta*"). The rose evokes the short, intense life of a beautiful being that does not bear fruit. For the twentieth-century homosexual writers Jean GENET, especially in *The Miracle of the Rose*, and Yukio MISHIMA, especially in the sensuous photograph album *Barakei* (*Tortured by Roses*), the rose also stood for the beauty, suffering, ephemerality, and transcendence they associated with same-sex love. In twentieth-century lesbian symbolism, the rose signifies the vagina and love between women. This symbolism is discovered in the work of Gertrude Stein (1874-1946), Judy GRAHN, and many other woman-loving writers. The poetry of Elsa GIDLOW is particularly rich in rose imagery. The yellow rose, the state flower of Texas, was chosen in the early 1970s as the emblem and name of an Austin, Texas-based group, the Yellow Rose Tribe, of gay men and their friends, founded by Dennis Paddie, Calvin Doucet, and other local artists. The Tribe would meet to commemorate the birthdays of gay luminaries – Whitman, Cocteau, Spicer, and others – as well as to celebrate the solstices and equinoxes.

Rose of Lima, Saint (d. 1586)   Born in Lima, Peru, Isabel de Santa Maria de Flores born at Lima, refused to marry, rejecting the advances of men captivated by her beauty. Dedicating herself to religious life, she constructed a shack in her parents' garden which eventually became a spiritual center of the city. Here, her praying and singing of hymns not only drew pilgrims but also "beetles, spiders, snails and all creeping things" who yearned to be in her presence. A mystic, prophet, and miracle-worker, Rose was believed to have saved Lima from what might have been a devastating earthquake. So beloved of the Virgin Mary was Rose that the Virgin would reach out, from her fresco on the wall of the Church of Saint Dominic in Lima, to embrace her. On the day of her death, it is said, Rose dressed as a bride. The Virgin descended and, kissing her on the forehead, carried her to the heavens. The *fin-de-siècle* British artist Aubrey BEARDSLEY perceived in the legend of St Rose of Lima and the Blessed Virgin Mary a lesbian mystical dimension. In his drawing "The Ascension of Saint Rose of Lima," Beardsley depicts the "adorable intimacy that [exists] between her and Our Lady," portraying a gynandrous or transgendered Virgin embracing Rose. St Rose was canonized by Pope Clement X in 1671 as the first saint of the New World and in particular of South America. Patron of gardeners and florists, she is fêted on August 23.

Rôti le balal (or **Rosty boully**)   Originally referring to French Medieval Witches riding to sabbats on broomsticks and especially to their heating the brooms over the sabbat fire in order to keep warm on the return journey, *rôti le balal* , or *rosty boully*, eventually came to refer to a folk dance related to those performed by the Witches. By the sixteenth century, to "roast the broom" became, in the CARNIVALESQUE performances known as SOTTIES, symbolic of homoerotic lovemaking. In the nineteenth century, it came to refer more generally to anyone possessing numerous lovers.

Rubinstein, Ida (birth name **Lydiya Lvovna Rubinshtein**, 1885-1960)   Russian-born, Jewish bisexual or lesbian dancer, actress, and dance company director. Married to Vladimir Horwitz in 1907, she appears to have become increasingly drawn to women, falling in love briefly with Natalie Clifford BARNEY's lover Romaine Brooks (1874-1970), the latter painting Rubinstein as *The Weeping Venus* (1915). Rubinstein performed in Sergei DIAGHILEV's Ballets Russes during the early 1900s; there, she worked with many homosexual and bisexual luminaries of her day, including Vaslav NIJINSKY and Jean COCTEAU. Rubinstein frequently performed roles which gave voice to the interrelationship of transgenderism and/or same-sex desire and the mythic or sacred; such roles included: the title role in Oscar WILDE's *Salomé* (1908, 1918); SAINT SEBASTIAN in *Le Martyre de*

Saint-Sébastien (1911), by Gabriele d'Annunzio, with music by Claude Debussy; ARTEMIS in *Artémis troublée* (1920); ORPHEUS in *Orphée* (1927); the Biblical DAVID in *David* (1928), choreographed by Leonine Massine (a lover of Diaghilev); and Joan of Arc in *Jeanne d'Arc au bûcher* (1938).

Rumi, Jalal al-Din (also **Jalalu' ddin Rumi, Jellal-ed-din Rumi,** 1207-1273)   Sufi mystic, poet, and dancer. Born in Balkh, Afghanistan on September 30, 1207, Rumi's family moved to Konya when he was a small child. By the time he was six years old, he was having visions, engaging in philosophical discourse, and fasting. At Konya he was exposed to the Sufis, and in 1230 began a nine-year initiation into the Sufi brotherhood, soon thereafter becoming a spiritual master, nicknamed "Mevlana" ("Our Master") by his disciples. In 1244 he met and fell madly in love with SHAMS AL-DIN TABRIZI (or Shamsi Tabriz, d. 1247), a "rare beauty wrapped in coarse black." As the SHAHED of Rumi, Shams became for him the embodiment of the Divine Beloved. Shams convinced Rumi to discard his theological texts and begin to experience life to the fullest. They left Konya, living in the desert together in "close communion and discussion of mystical philosophy." The disciples of Rumi, becoming extremely jealous, persecuted Shams, who fled their desert hermitage. During their separation, Rumi wrote *ghazals* describing their love for each other and their mutual love of God. "Be drunk with love," he wrote, "All is love. / Without performance of love there is no access / to the Loved One." After Shams came out of hiding, he was murdered in May 1247 by the jealous followers of Rumi. For forty days after Shams's death, Rumi, putting on mourning robes, a white shirt open at the chest, a honey-colored wool fez, and rough sandals, began to dance a whirling dance of lamentation and love around the poles in the garden in which Shams had been killed. From this dance emerged the *sama*, the trance dance ritual that is central to Sufism.

Rusla   "Red," a Danish AMAZON who terrorized the Irish coast alongside her beloved shield-maiden STIKLA. According to J. A. Salmonson (1991), such women-warriors "have been mythologized as VALKYRIES."

Ruth and Naomi   Numerous Biblical scholars have seen in this tale of Ruth's refusal to desert her mother-in-law Naomi the suggestion of passionate same-sex attachment. "Entreat me not to leave you," Ruth pleads with Naomi, "or to return from following you; for where you go I will go, and where you lodge I will lodge; your people shall be my people, and your God my God; where you die I will die, and there I will be buried' (Ruth 1: 16-17, Oxford Annotated). As Raymond-Jean Frontain observes, the narrative has inspired lesbian literature, as exemplified by

Helen Anderson's *Pity for Women* (1937), in which Ann and Judith ceremonially recite the passage to sanctify their love for each other, and by Isabel Miller's *Patience and Sarah* (1969), in which one of the lovers, Patience, paints a scene depicting the tale. In recent years, the passage has been used by women participating in rites of lesbian UNION.

S

Sabina, María (b. 1894)   Mazatec female Shaman of Mexico. During a shamanic or altered state of consciousness, triggered in part by the entheogenic use of mushrooms, María Sabina experiences shapeshifting, including transgender shapeshifting. She chants: "Male saint I am. / Woman of pure spirit / . . . / Man who stays and stands, and / Woman root below water am I. / . . . / Whirling woman / In the whirlwind I am. / Male saint I am. / It's a holy man, says [the mushroom]. / It's a holy woman, says [the mushroom]."

Sacred Band of Thebes (also **Theban Band, Army of Lovers**)   Force of the ancient Greek army created in 378 BCE by the Theban general Gorgidas. The notion of such a force can be traced to PLATO's *Symposium* (c. 385 BCE), in which Phaedrus envisions an "army of lovers." "And if there were only some way of contriving that a state or an army should be made up of lovers and their lovers," he argues, "they would be the very best governors of their own city . . . and when fighting at each other's side, although a mere handful, they would overcome the world. For what lover would not choose rather to be seen by all mankind than by his beloved, either when abandoning his post or throwing away his arms? He would be ready to die a thousand deaths rather than endure this. Or who would desert his beloved or fail him in the hour of danger? The veriest coward would become an inspired hero, equal to the bravest, at such a time; Love [i.e. EROS] would inspire him." The Greeks offered hymns and sacrifices to Eros, the god of love, especially of homoerotic desire, prior to entering into battle. Just as the statue of Eros was housed in gymnasia, PALAESTRA, and academies, so it was where warriors were being trained, as these were institutions fostering bonds of male intimacy. Members of the Theban Band also paid homage to the divinized hero HERACLES (Roman Hercules) and to his beloved IOLAUS. The Band's leaders include Gorgidas, Pelopidas, and Epaminondas. Comprised of 150 pairs of male lovers, the Band became for four decades the pride of the Greek army, obtaining victory in numerous conflicts including that between Thebes and Sparta, one of the most decisive battles in Greek history. The Band met its end, however, in its struggle with the powerful army of Philip of Macedon in 338 BCE. By the end of the Battle of Chaeronea, all 150 pairs of lovers lay dead on the battlefield. Plutarch (c. 46-c. 126 CE) relates that Philip of Macedon, on surveying the field and learning that "this was the band of lovers and beloved[s], burst into tears," cursing any who disrespected the dead warrior-lovers. The memory of the Sacred Band was honored by the members of a late nineteenth-century British homosexual organization, the ORDER OF CHAERONEA.

Sa'd and Isa   Sa'd, an Islamic poet and bookseller living at Edessa, fell in love with Isa, a young man attending poetry readings at Sa'd's book shop. The Syrian poet Sanaubari (d. 945), also attending, described Isa as "the handsomest of God's creation; of the finest build and endowed with the richest gifts of mind and conversation." Sa'd began writing love poems to Isa, "with the result that his passion for him became widely known." Isa, a Christian, increasingly drawn to spiritual life, entered a monastery. He invited Sa'd to join him. So the Islamic bookseller closed his shop, moved into the monastery, and continued writing love poems to the young man. When the other monks realized what was happening, they insisted that Sa'd leave the monastery at once and never return. Devastated, Sa'd set fire to his book shop and house, tore his clothes, and began to "live in the desert close to the cloister, naked, mad, tearful, composing verses." He attempted to send messages and poems to Isa by way of birds. One day, he was found dead near the monastery's walls. "The monks have killed him!" the people cried out. They demanded that the Christians be punished. The local ruler, Emir Abbas ibn Kaigalag, did not set fire to the monastery as the people had wished, but did demand that the Christians pay an enormous fine for their inhumane (and extremely un-Christian) treatment of Sa'd. Isa left the monastery. On returning to Edessa, boys began throwing stones at him, shouting, "You're the murderer of Sa'd the bookseller!" Isa left Edessa and spent the remainder of his life in another monastery.

Sadhana Brothers   Gay male-centered Hindu group founded in San Francisco in 1993. Its members come together to affirm their sexuality and to honor the Hindu deities with *pujas* (rites including invocations, offerings, etc.).

Sadomasochism   Derived from two writers focusing on sexuality, the Marquis de Sade (1740-1814) and Leopold Sacher-Masoch (1836-1895), the term "sadomasochism," or S/M, as it is more commonly called at present ("leather" is also used as a general term), refers to a form of eroticism which may be practiced by persons of any gender or sexual identity and which centers on the exploration of such dualistic or polar relationships as those between pleasure and pain, dominance and submission, and fantasy and "reality." S/M, like intergenerational intimacy, is one of the most controversial subjects debated by queer-identified persons in the late twentieth century. Many feminists, including lesbian-feminists, object to S/M as duplicating patriarchal structures and as encouraging violence against women, while many persons of Jewish heritage object to the use of Nazi symbolism by some practitioners of S/M. Supporters of S/M, on the other hand, describe it as a "means of radically contesting the sexual assumptions of the majority culture." While the term "sadomasochism" is young, S/M-like practices may be traced to ancient and primal cultures, where rites include(d) such practices as whipping or flagellating, bondage, and piercing, cutting, or otherwise wounding the flesh, as well as ornamenting the body with TATTOOS, facial marks, and so on. Homoerotic S/M-like practices appear to have occurred among bands of "wolfish" warriors in ancient Greece devoted to lycanthropic manifestations of APOLLO and ZEUS. The Greek goddess APHRODITE, in her aspect of Anosia, may have presided over lesbian S/M-like rites. ARTEMIS, whose cult practices included both flagellation and ritual hanging from trees, may have also presided over such rites. The transgendered GALLI priest/esse/s of the Roman goddess CYBELE practiced ritual flagellation, castration, and tattooing (with ivy-leaf patterns). In northern Europe, "wolfish" and "bear-like" warriors devoted to ODIN and other Teutonic deities appear to have practiced S/M-like rites, including bondage and suspension from trees. Castration ceremonies undertaken by the transgendered HIJRAS of the Hindu goddess BAHUCHARAMATA might also be interpreted as containing an element of sadomasochism. It is possible that transgendered and/or same-sex inclined persons were also among those Native American Indians taking part in such rituals as the Sun Dance, in which intense pain and ecstasy intermingle. With the arrival of the eighteenth century and the Enlightenment, however, associations of S/M, ritual, transgenderism, bisexuality, and/or same-sex eroticism become more obvious and more plentiful. Homoerotic or bisexual as well as transgendered S/M-like rituals, including group masturbation and mock crucifixions, were undertaken at this time by members of erotico-Satanic clubs such as the Hell-Fire Club, Medmenham Abbey, the Tuesday Club, the Dublin Blasters, and the Somerset Club. Also during the eighteenth (and continuing into the twentieth) century, Russian KHYLSTS (Flagellants) and Skoptsy (Castrators) participated in S/M-like rites including cultic bisexuality or homosexuality. Many "queer" writers of the nineteenth and twentieth centuries have employed S/M ritual associations in their works though they may not have actually enacted them in their lives. These writers include Charles Baudelaire (1821-1867), Emily DICKINSON (1830-1886), Algernon Charles Swinburne (1837-1909), Renée VIVIEN (1877-1909), Baroness Gertrud Freifrau

von Puttkamer, aka Marie-Madeleine (1881-1944), and Elsa GIDLOW (1898-1986). Of Renée Vivien, S. Gubar (1985) observes, in "both her poetry and her novel . . . Vivien appropriates [a] sadistic [image of] Sappho . . . prevalent in the late nineteenth century . . . The unholy excess and implacable cruelty of lesbian desire in Vivien's fiction and poetry, the tormented hair, unappeased breasts, insatiable thighs, and ardent hands of the lovers described by Vivien – uncover the demonic power that drew Baudelaire and Swinburne to the lesbian femme fatale." In her poem "Crucifixa," von Puttkamer writes: "I saw you tortured on a stake, / high on a dark cross I saw you tied. / The marks of my sinful kisses glowed / on your white flesh like purple wounds. / . . . / I want to kneel before the altars / My own wanton daring destroyed. . . / Madonna with a whore's eyes / I myself crucified you!" Lesbian poet Elsa GIDLOW pleaded in "Come and Lie With Me" (1920): "Kiss me, as you lean above me, / With your cold, sadistic kisses; / . . . / Hurt me even, even wound me, / I have need of love that stings." A current argument against S/M (voiced in numerous texts including Joan DeJean's *Fictions of Sappho: 1546-1937* [1989] and Lilian Faderman's anthology *Chloe Plus Olivia* [1994]) insists that women alone could not conceive of such practices, and that such desire depends upon being poisoned by decadent, male writers. Whatever the case, lesbians and bisexual women have played, and continue to play, a dominant role in the production of ritualistic S/M works of art. Other writers inspired by S/M include Jean GENET (1910-1986), William BURROUGHS (b. 1914, and Yukio MISHIMA (1925-1970). Mishima clearly enacted his desires, especially in his obsession with the arrow-pierced SAINT SEBASTIAN, which led him to pose as the saint in photographs, and more importantly, in his bloody ritual suicide undertaken with his intimate male companion. More contemporary writers inspired by S/M include Samuel R. Delany (b. 1942), John Preston (1945-1993), and Clive BARKER (b. 1952). Anne Rice (b. 1941), the celebrated author of vampire and S/M novels, while heterosexual, merits honorable mention here. In recent years, Pat CALIFIA (b. 1954) and Artemis Oakgrove (fl. late twentieth century) have emerged as prominent writers in this tradition; both refer to Goddess Reverence and Neopaganism in their works, Califia in "The Calyx of Isis" (c. 1988) and *Doc and Fluff* (1990), the latter including a high priestess named Raven, and Oakgrove in the *Throne* trilogy (c. 1984). The ritual practice of S/M appears to have gained strength in proto-"queer" communities of the period spanning the post-War 1940s to the early 1960s, attached to the subcultures of sailors and motorcyclist "hoods," romanticized in such films as Kenneth Anger's *Fireworks* (1947) and *Scorpio Rising* (1963). Since that time, the S/M community (both queer and non-queer) has flourished internationally. Jungian writer Robert H. Hopcke suggests in "S/M and the Psychology of Gay Male

Initiation: An Archetypal Perspective" (1991) that the attraction to S/M may be due to its serving to initiate men in several ways. S/M, Hopcke explains, brings them into contact with an eroticized, ritual-making community of other men who are willing to explore the "shadow" aspect of male eros. In 1995, Gauntlet, Inc., the premiere US corporation where piercing and other body arts related to S/M are concerned, celebrated its twentieth anniversary. Gauntlet's founder, JIM WARD, a self-identified neopagan who has participated in rites inspired by the Sun Dance, is well acquainted with both S/M and magical practices, as is his companion, DREW WARD. In the late 1970s, the lesbian-feminist S/M group Samois (the name taken from *The Story of O* [1954] by Pauline Reage) was founded. In *Coming to Power* (1981, 1987), an anthology edited by members of Samois, a number of texts refer to S/M in a spiritual context. "Juicy Lucy," for instance, describes herself as a "femme . . . [lesbian-] separatist psychic witch astrologer" who finds in S/M the exorcism of unwanted memories and fears as well as a passionate, blissful, altered state of consciousness. In the recent past, at the strongly lesbian-identified Women's Music Festival in Michigan, a number of women have begun participating in a controversial nocturnal S/M rite including mock crucifixions referred to as the "Stations of the Cross," evoking the "Crucifixa" of the Baroness von Puttkamer. In 1989, a group of men associated with the Radical Faeries and inspired by S/M writer-activists like Geoff Mains (author of *Urban Aboriginals: A Celebration of Leathersexuality* [1984]) formed Black Leather Wings, wishing to explore rituals, such as ones rooted in the Sun Dance and those undertaken by fakirs, seldom occurring at Faerie gatherings. In "I Am the Leatherfaerie Shaman" (c. 1991), Stuart Norman gives voice to the spiritual perspective of this group. "[In] the use of ritual, rites of passage, initiatory practices," Norman explains, "the ordeals of shamanic training and those of S/M are similar . . . S/M has been referred to as an Apollonian way of reaching the Dionysian state – in other words, a controlled, skillful, and thought-out process for reaching the intuitive/ecstatic state . . . S/M is magical practice." In "Black Leather Wings," included in his masterful anthology *Leatherfolk: Radical Sex, People, Politics, and Practice* (1991), Mark Thompson observes that queer practitioners of S/M "pay homage to weighty lords, the dark male gods [and we would add goddesses and transgendered deities and spirits] of the underworld, of catharsis and . . . apotheosis." Such deities and spirits might include BARON LUNDY, BARON SAMEDI, COATLICUE, DIONYSUS, DURGA, GHEDE MASAKA, GHEDE NIBO, GHEDE OUSSOU, HADES, HECATE, KALI, LUCIFER, MADAME BRIGITTE, MEPHISTOPHELES, MIN, OYA, POMBA GIRA, SATAN, SEKHMET, SET, SHIVA, and TLAZOLTEOTL.

Saffron Flowering plant native to Asia Minor symbolic of the healing power of the sun, nobility, passion, magic, self-sacrifice, and spiritual enlightenment. In numerous cultures of antiquity, saffron was used as an ingredient in MAGIC. As a spice, it was used in special cakes, often designed to cause one person to fall in love with another. As a perfume, it was strewn in halls, courts, theaters, baths, and beds. As a dye, it was used to color garments. As a drug, it was said to produce a pleasant mania with sudden changes from hilarity to melancholia. In Greco-Roman antiquity, saffron was attributed to the goddesses DEMETER and PERSEPHONE and was a color normally worn by women. But "womanish saffron" was also attributed to CROCUS, a youth with whom the god HERMES fell in love, and was further associated with male gender variance and homoeroticism. It was the color of the transparent SANDYX worn by the gender variant, or transgendered, priest/esse/s of HERACLES on the island of Cos. The KROKETOS, a long-sleeved chiton dyed with saffron, was worn by DIONYSUS and his gender variant male bacchants. In the pre-Islamic Arabian world, its spiritual functionaries including women and gender variant MUKHANNATHUN devoted to Goddess Reverence, saffron was considered a powerful aphrodisiac and was employed in lesbian lovemaking.

Sagana (fl. first century CE)   Actual or legendary priestess of the Greco-Roman goddess HECATE at Rome. Sagana allegedly participated in a "cult of lesbian sorceresses" whose tasks included the ritual castration of young males, probably those destined to become SEMNOTATOI, the gender variant eunuch priests of Hecate. Sagana's companion was Candidia.

Sagittarius In Euro-western ASTROLOGY zodiac sign ruling from (approximately) November 22 until December 21, associated with frankness, generosity, hunting, philosophy, and swiftness, typically depicted as a centaur or satyr carrying a bow and arrow. Figures associated with Sagittarius and with gender and/or sexual variance include: ADONIS, AGDISTIS, AMAZONS, ARTEMIS, ATALANTA, ATHENA, BRITOMARTIS, CAMILLA, CHIRON, CROCALE, CYRENE, DAPHNE, DICTYNNA, FROG EARRINGS, KANYOTSANYOTSE, KARTIKKEYEH, KOTYS, MAENADS, PALLAS, SEDNA, and TALKING GOD.

Sag-ur-sag Like the ASSINNU, KURGARRU, and others, a class of gender variant male spiritual functionaries of the Mesopotamian goddess INANNA/ISHTAR. The *sag-ur-sag* were especially known for their bifurcated masculine/feminine ritual attire decorated with brightly colored ribbons. Like other servants of the Goddess, they were especially skilled in composing hymns and playing harps.

Sahaykwisa (c. 1850-c. 1895) Native American Indian Mohave TWO-SPIRIT woman, or HWAME, whose name means "Childless Woman Shadow/Soul." A powerful shaman, Sahaykwisa was especially skilled in the areas of healing and magic. She was renowned as a healer of venereal disease, and was said to fashion spells to protect her female companions from men. When in later life she began having affairs with men, her shamanic powers dwindled. Ironically, she was murdered by two men who had accused her of being a "witch."

Saicho (767-822) Japanese Buddhist monk and founder of Tendai Buddhism. Saicho founded the sect after its teachings were revealed to him by a BODHISATTVA, a vehicle of Buddha-energy, who manifested in the form of a beautiful angelic youth, or CHIGO, on Mount Hiei in 785. The spirit appearing to Saicho is known by various names, including Master Juzen, the *deva* of Nissho, the god of Dosei, and the god of Yugyo. The appearance of the beautiful being, and Saicho's love for him, apparently led the Buddhist master to encourage the love of beautiful young men as embodiments of the Divine. Saicho felt such an affection for his pupil Shinpan.

Sailor In numerous spiritual traditions, female divine beings associated with transgenderism and/or same-sex intimacy are patrons of sailors; these include BRITOMARTIS, KUAN YIN, the NEREIDS, OSHUN, and YEMAYA. Male divine beings also serve as patrons to sailors, including KHONSU and POSEIDON. In pre-modern France, several maritime roles, including that of the *fadrin*, were, as R. P. Conner (1996) indicates, associated with male homoerotic and possibly also with male gender variance. One of these was the *fadrin*, a "young sailor, a novice." The term *fadrin* is related to *fatrouiller*, to "play the fop" and to "copulate." It is also linked to *fadas*, *fadhas*, *fadet*, and *farfadet*, Portuguese-derived terms for fairies, more particularly, for those types of fairies referred to as *follets* and *lutins*. Thus, in the folklore of pre-modern France, we discover an association, albeit somewhat complex and indirect, of homoeroticism, transgenderism (possibly), sailors, and fairies. A. Sahuquillo (1991) observes that the sailor appears as an archetype of homoerotic passion in numerous twentieth-century works of fiction, including Ernest Hemingway's "The Sea Change", Jean COCTEAU's *Le Livre blanc*, and Jean GENET's *Querelle de Brest*, as well as in the poetry of Federico García LORCA, Hart Crane, and Luis CERNUDA. The sailor also appears as an archetype of gay eros in the works of numerous visual artists, including Paul Cadmus (b. 1904) and Jared FRENCH.

St Louis Women's Club Early twentieth-century US club for transgendered, lesbian, and bisexual women. The St Louis Women's Club's constitution stated: "Each woman who enters the group is duty bound to wear men's clothing, to smoke, to drink . . . Women's handicrafts are forbidden . . . riding, fencing, and gymnastics [are celebrated] . . . Each member who enters marriage leaves the club." This club took on a religious aura by choosing an elder member of the group as "chaplain" to head a prayer service based on "Christian or Islamic beliefs."

Saint-Simonism French utopian movement of the eighteenth and nineteenth centuries, based on the ideas of Claude Henri de Rouvroy, comte de Saint-Simon (1760-1825), influential in the development of socialism. The Saint-Simonists revered God as an androgynous or hermaphroditic Mother-Father. In the Saint-Simonist UTOPIA, the androgyne came to represent social harmony, which included the emancipation of women and a non-gender-defined approach to the rearing of children.

Sakhibhava Sect of devotees of the Hindu deities RADHA and KRISHNA. With a name meaning "unmanning men," the Sakhibhavas are variously described as gender variant or third gender/sex males, or transgendered (male-to-female) persons. R. G. Bhandarkar relates that the Sakhibhavas "assume the garb of women with all their ordinary manners and affect to be subject even to their monthly sickness [i.e. menstruation] . . . Their goal is the realization of the position of the female companions and attendants of Radha [i.e. the GOPIS]." The Sakhibhavas, as part of their identification with Radha and the *gopis*, permit "the sexual act on their person," i.e. they take a receptive role in erotic relations with men, "as an act of devotion." Ajit Mookerjee explains that in Hinduism, it is generally believed that "all souls are feminine [in relation] to the supreme Reality," presumably even if that Reality is itself sometimes considered feminine. For some, Krishna is the supreme Reality, and Radha the divine image of the disciple as the active, feminine lover of the receptive, masculine Beloved. Krishnadas writes, "In truth every finite being is essentially an emanation or phase of Radha . . . or a milkmaid [i.e. *gopi*]." W. D. O'Flaherty (1980) suggests that the Sakhibhava ideal is expressed in a myth wherein Krishna, following a quarrel with Radha, dresses in feminine attire, presumably as a *gopi*, in order to regain her affection. Radha responds by embracing "her" passionately. Then, Radha transforms into Krishna. O'Flaherty explains: "The worshipper who imagines himself as female, and dresses like one, in order to be with Krishna, is expressing the explicitly heterosexual (and perhaps implicitly homosexual) erotic relationship with the god [i.e. Krishna]; but that god himself [Krishna] is also imagined as participating in an explicitly homosexual [i.e. lesbian] embrace (he [Krishna], as female, embracing the female Radha)." M. Singer (1968) relates that the identification of the devotees and priests with Radha and the *gopis* as lovers of Krishna is often referred to as

Madhura Bhava, the "Sweet Mood." Singer notes that when he inquired about the love experience among the devotees, a devotee he calls "K" told him of a number of "incidents from the *Bhagavata Purana* in which the *gopis* discover each others' love for Krishna, come to share that love with one another, and so develop a mutual love. He did not think it necessary to mention that something similar takes place with contemporary devotees as they imitate the *gopis*." The Sakhibhavas come to know the state of pure bliss, *hladini-shakti*, by experiencing the union of Radha and Krishna the male and female principles, within themselves and serve as HIERODULES ("sacred prostitutes") by experiencing union with male devotees.

Salmacis Nymph who fell in love with the youth HERMAPHRODITUS, the child, then the son, of the Greek deities HERMES and APHRODITE. When he spurned her, Salmacis begged the gods to cause their bodies to merge into one. The gods granted her request. Her identity, however, was submerged in that of the now androgynous being, Hermaphroditus. Her memory lingered, however, in legends of men who, bathing in her pool, were transformed into androgynes or women.

Sandyx Garment associated with male gender variance, worn by the transgendered (anatomically male) priest/esse/s of HERACLES, especially on the island of Cos. While often SAFFRON in color it was sometimes transparent or opaque, flesh-colored, bright red, or floral-patterned.

Sanghyang Tjintiya "Divine Slippery One," he-she is the primordial, fluid being of Balinese religion or mythology who predates the division or "fall" into the male and female anatomical sexes. Sanghyang Tjintiya, who floats above the Middle World or stands on a lotus, is depicted as an androgynous young male dancer with elaborate eye makeup whose body is painted white and who wears only gold trefoil leaves, including a crown of these. Victoria Ginn, in her exquisite photographic study *The Spirited Earth* (1990), compares Sanghyang Tjintiya to the Hindu deity SHIVA as Nataraj, the Dancer.

Santa Maria del Carmine Monastery in Naples which became a site of pilgrimage for male lovers following its becoming the final resting place of Conradin (1252-1268), the last Hohenstaufen ruler, and his lover Frederick of Baden.

Saphira (fl. c. 1920) Male medium of aristocratic Russian (-Jewish?) heritage visited by French bisexual writer Colette (1873-1954), depicted by her as a gender variant, witty and campy individual (drag queen?) wearing makeup, numerous large finger rings, and (metaphorically at least), "a mass of tinsel." Colette also comments on "his

very beautiful eyes [of] velvet blue." Colette does not give his real name, but notes that he derived his magical name from the QABBALAH, from *sephir*, a sphere on the Tree of Life. Once, Colette took Rhodis, a young lesbian friend, with her. Saphira infuriated Rhodis by telling her that she was going to run off with a man very shortly. The following day, Rhodis's female lover began shooting at her and the new boyfriend with whom she was running down the street.

Sapphire In ALCHEMY, a symbol of androgyny or transgenderism associated with the shapeshifting Greek deity HERMES (Roman MERCURY) and his alchemical manifestation MERCURIUS. In Santería, this gem or jewel is associated with the aquatic *orishás*, or deities, YEMAYA and OLOKUN, who harbor gynandrous aspects. The sapphire is also linked, by way of the theory of correspondences, to the planets SATURN and VENUS. It is believed to promote tranquillity.

Sappho (or **Psappha**, b. c. 630/610 BCE) Greek lyric poet, musician, and priestess of APHRODITE and other goddesses of classical antiquity. Sappho's name and her home, the island of LESBOS, have survived as "sapphic" and "lesbian" to refer to women-loving women. While some writers have argued that Sappho was bisexual or even heterosexual, her primary male lover being a man named Phaon, other writers, particularly ancient writers such as Maximus Tyrius (fl. c. 185 CE) and Athenaeus (fl. c. 230 CE), insist upon her lesbianism, her primary female lovers being Atthis and Anactoria. Maximus Tyrius, linking lesbian love to homoerotic love, writes, "What then is the passion of the Lesbian songstress but the love-technique of Socrates? For both of them seem to have the same idea of love, the former the love of girls, the latter of youths. What then an Alcibiades, Charmides and Phaedrus were to Socrates, a Gyrinna, Atthis, and Anactoria are to Sappho." Athenaeus explains that there were two celebrated women named Sappho who lived during the latter part of the sixth century BCE, one a courtesan of Eresus who loved Phaon, the other the Lesbian poet. Sappho was associated by the ancients not only with lesbianism but also with gender variance; she was, for example, described by the Roman poet Horace (65-8 BCE) as "masculine." Numerous scholars have suggested that the term "lesbian" to refer to female same-sex desire and to allude to Sappho does not appear to have been employed until the late eighteenth or even the nineteenth century. They are quite mistaken. In the latter part of the sixteenth century, for instance, Pierre de Bourdeille, Seigneur de Brantôme (1535?-1614) referred to women-loving women as "*ces Lesbiennes*" ("these Lesbians") and wrote, "They say that Sappho of Lesbos was a very powerful mistress in this profession, indeed, they say that she invented it, and that since [that time] lesbian women [*les dames lesbiennes*] have imitated

SARAPIS 294

her in this, and have continued to do so up to this day; thus
Lucian said that such women are the women of Lesbos,
that do not wish to put up with men, but approach other
women." Pierre Bayle (1647-1706), in his *Dictionnaire
historique et critique* (published 1720), similarly wrote of
Sappho's love for women, noting, "some are of the opinion
that this was the reason why she was surnamed 'Masculine'
[*Hommasse*]." Of Sappho's work, only one complete poem
and some two hundred fragments survive of at least nine
books of poetry she was said to have written. Sometime
during the second century CE and again in the fourth
century, much of her work was burned by Christians. It
was not until the nineteenth century that a number of
fragments were discovered on the papyrus wrapping of a
mummy. Surprisingly few twentieth-century writers,
other than Claude Calame in *Les choeurs de jeunes filles en
Grèce archaïque* (1977), Judy Grahn in *The Highest Apple:
Sappho and the Lesbian Poetic Tradition* (1985) and Fritz
Graf in "Prayer in Magic and Religious Ritual" (1991),
have acknowledged the spiritual or magical function of
Sappho's writings or her role as a lesbian inclined spiritual
leader. Yet a number of her surviving works may be read as
invocations or incantations, such as an invocation to
Aphrodite culminating in "Come to me now again and
deliver me from oppressive anxieties; fulfill all that my
heart longs to fulfill, and you yourself will be my fellow-
fighter." Since the eighteenth century, when
women-loving members of the French sect of the
ANANDRYNES paid homage to Sappho, it appears that
lesbians and bisexual women have been consciously
revering Sappho as an erotic, artistic, and spiritual
ancestor. In nineteenth-century Parisian bohemian circles,
a lesbian (*lesbienne*, also *gougnotte, fricarelle*) was "a
follower of Sappho" or "a devotee of the cult of Sappho,"
suggesting a continuation of such reverence, and in the
early twentieth century, the lesbian writer Renée VIVIEN,
desiring to return to the Goddess-centered religion of
Lesbos, wrote in "Sappho Lives Again," "Some of us have
preserved the rites / Of burning Lesbos." In "Like This
Would I Speak," she chants, "Sappho will shower us . . . /
With the odes whose melodies charmed Mytilene / . . . And
we will prepare the flowers and the flames." Amy Lowell
(1874-1925), lover of Ada Russell, wishes she "could have
talked to Sappho / Surprised her reticences by flinging"
her own "Into the wind." Radclyffe HALL (1880-1943),
lover of Una Lady Troubridge and others, writes, "Oh!
Sappho, sister, by that agony / Of soul and body hast thou
gained a place / Within each age that shines majestic'ly." In
Sophia Parnok: The Life and Work of Russia's Sappho
(1994), Diana Lewis Burgin writes of Parnok's
relationship to Sappho, "Parnok [1885-1926] seemed to be
inspiring herself through belief in the eternal coming of
Sappho to her co-religionists in posterity. Like other
European lesbian poets of her generation, she sensed that
being a lesbian privileged her relationship with the Tenth

Muse. It put Sappho in the special relation to her that
Aphrodite occupied in Sappho's life." The mystical
Parnok appears to have believed that in an earlier
incarnation she numbered among the members of
Sappho's THIASOS on Lesbos: "Clearly in this life I have
not forgotten unforgettable raptures from unforgettable
songs that of old, my companion lovers sang in Sappho's
school." As S. Gubar (1985) observes, the bisexual poet H.
D. (Hilda Doolittle, 1886-1961), identifying Sappho with
Lesbos, envisions her as the "island of artistic perfection
where the lovers of ancient beauty . . . may yet find foothold
and . . . dream of yet unexplored continents and realms of
future artistic achievements." Lesbian writer Elsa
GIDLOW (1898-1986) invokes Sappho as "Sister-Mother /
free- / souled, fire-hearted;" "now now," Gidlow chants,
"let me declare / devotion." This is not to say that all
lesbians and bisexual women feel deep kinship with
Sappho. Muriel Rukeyser, Susan Griffin, and Robin
Morgan are among those twentieth-century writers who
have distanced themselves from Sappho. SDiane Bogus
(1994) rejects Sappho as an archetypal image of, and
"lesbian" as a term for, female same-sex desire on the
grounds that the figure and the term are ethnocentric or
racist, rooted in European culture, and irrelevant to the
sensuous experience of non-white women. Nevertheless,
many women of varying ethnicities and walks of life,
especially those participating in Goddess Reverence,
Witchcraft (or Wicca), and/or Women's Spirituality,
continue to invoke Sappho in the 1990s in rituals paying
homage to deities and spiritual ancestors. In a rite
performed several years ago, meant to nurture and
empower a young woman "coming out" as a lesbian to her
mother, a circle of women chanted, "We call on the spirit of
the Moon Goddess, Diana . . . We call Sappho, Madame de
Staël, Emily Dickinson, Willa Cather . . . Gladys Bentley,
Josephine Baker and Janis."

Sarapis Syncretic Hellenistic deity blending attributes of
the Egyptian gods Osiris and Apis with the Greek gods
ASCLEPIUS, DIONYSUS, HADES, Helios, and ZEUS. A
deity concerned with sexuality fertility, death, and healing,
Sarapis is invoked in a Greco-Egyptian lesbian love spell of
late antiquity as "immortal Sarapis, whom the universe
fears."

Sardanapalus (also **Ashurbanipal**, 668-626 BCE)   King
of Assyria, perhaps the most representative transgendered,
apparently bisexual, ruler of Near Eastern ancient history.
Athenaeus (fl. 230 CE) describes him as having a closely
shaven beard, his face painted with white makeup, his
eyebrows darkened, and eyelids colored. Dripping in
jewelry, Sardanapalus would often sit, knees uplifted,
combing purple wool in the company of female friends.
Ultimately either murdered by a general named Arbaces or
else committing suicide during a war Assyria was losing,

Sardanapalus was said to have composed his own epitaph, inscribing therein his philosophy of hedonism: "I have been a king . . . I have eaten, drunk, and done homage to the joys of love, knowing that the lifetime of men is short and subject to much change and misfortune, and that others will reap the benefit of the possessions that I leave behind me. For this reason I let no day pass without living in this manner."

Sarpedon King of Lycia, son of the Greek deities ZEUS and Europa, and brother of MINOS and RHADAMANTHYS. Sarpedon was the lover of several young men, including ATYMNIUS, Maris, MILETUS, and Scylaceus.

Satan In the Biblical tradition, the personification of evil, with other names including Beelzebub, Lucifer, and Mephistopheles (although, strictly speaking, these are names of his servants). Among Satanists and numerous writers including John Milton (1608-1674), Percy Bysshe Shelley (1792-1822), and the man-loving Paul VERLAINE (1844-1896) as well as visual artists like the bisexual Jean Delville (1867-1951), Satan becomes a Prometheus-like rebel against authority who often delights in sensuality and other pleasures. In Delville's magnificent painting *Trésor de Satan*, the demonic spirit, merging with the Greek god Dionysus, is a graceful yet muscular, orange-golden-skinned nude male with long locks of vermilion fire. He is followed by a train of male, female, and androgynous bacchants lost in sensuous dreams. The name of Satan may be traced to the Egyptian god SET, the rebel of Egyptian religion, and to a Hebrew term meaning "the enemy." While, in an effort to disentangle Witchcraft from Satanism, numerous twentieth-century writers on Witchcraft have suggested (either from ignorance or dishonesty) that Satanism did not, or does not, exist, it is abundantly evident from historical sources that it did, and does. Satanism, like Witchcraft, may have been maligned by Christians and others and it may be difficult to disentangle veritable elements of a Satanic cult (or cults) from the fantasies of Christian zealots. It does appear that during the European Middle Ages and Renaissance, alongside Witchcraft, ceremonial magic, and other forms of (neo-) paganism and syncretism, a tradition (or traditions) of Satanism emerged or flowered. It seems that worshippers participated in various rites including an abnegation of Christianity, a ritual honoring the acquisition of worldly possessions or powers, and rites of pansexual eroticism. Two of the most infamous rites in which practitioners were alleged to have engaged were the so-called "five-point," "dark," or "obscene" kiss, which included kissing the buttocks or anus and the phallus of the person embodying Satan, and sexual intercourse (not limited to heterosexual) with that person. Numerous writers have related that the phallus of Satan's priest was more often than not a dildo, black in color and cold to the touch, suggesting that the role of Satan might have been taken by persons of various gendered and/or sexual identities. That Satan was (and is) frequently perceived as transgendered is evident from Medieval accounts, such as one from France dating from the Merovingian era (c. 500-751), which describes how Euparchus, a bishop of Auvergne, discovered that his church was filled with "demons" and that, sitting on the episcopal throne, was Satan, or a representative of Satan, in male transvestite or transgendered form. It was said of Saint-Mégrin, one of HENRI III's (1551-1589) minions, that "he gave his soul to God, his body to the ground, and his arse to the Devil." The worship of Satan, or Lucifer or Mephistopheles (other manifestations or kindred spirits) apparently continued into the eighteenth century, when it experience a countercultural vogue with the establishing of erotico-Satanic clubs. The most infamous of these clubs were undoubtedly the Hell-Fire Club and Medmenham Abbey where "Do what thou wilt" was the motto of the "monks." In some of these, like the Tuesday Club, the Dublin Blasters, and the Somerset House Club, men would meet to hold "Corybantic orgies" and to reenact "the rites of Priapus," often engaging in "group masturbation." The leader of these rites was typically a "merry Gentleman" who took the role of Satan. This man, a spiritual functionary of sorts, would sometimes wear a bearskin, suggesting animal transformation. On other occasions, the priest of Satan would appear naked. Transvestites, drag queens, and/or transgendered persons with names like Lady Gomorrah would drink a brew of whiskey, butter, and brimstone, would kiss a cat on its backside, and perform mock crucifixions. In the nineteenth century, with the emergence of the artistic movements Romanticism, Symbolism, and Decadence, the image of Satan as transgendered and/or pansexual rebel experienced yet another renascence. In Johann Wolfgang von Goethe's (1749-1832) *Faust* (1808), Mephistopheles is depicted as homoerotically inclined. At the moment when Faust's soul is saved, Mephistopheles's gaze is directed toward the voluptuous buttocks of nude male angels. Later in the century, Mephistophela appears as a lesbian in Catulle Mendès's (1841-1909) novel of 1890 bearing her name as its title. The Decadent woman-loving writer Renée VIVIEN wove together in her works a complex association of Satan, Sappho, lesbian desire, rebellion, and aestheticism. In "The Profane Genesis" (1902), she depicts Biblical religion as a dualistic faith whose supreme deities are Jehovah and Satan, linking the former to heterosexuality, conformity, Homer, and the east, and the latter to same-sex eroticism, non-conformity, Sappho, and the west. For Vivien, Satan is the more admirable of the two gods. While Jehovah forces men and women to couple in "the violence of the embrace," Satan "leaned toward the west, over the sleep of Sappho, the Lesbian" who, on waking, "sang the fugitive forms of love." In or around

1907, the homoerotically inclined, occult writer Montague SUMMERS seems to have begun participating in or holding Satanic Black Masses which apparently included the sacrifice of a black cock; others suggest that he was holding Catholic-like masses save for ritual homoeroticism. The homoerotically inclined Spanish poet Federico García LORCA associated Satan, as fallen angel Lucifer, with Aphrodite/Venus, goats, the sea, the heavens, transgenderism, and same-sex desire. In *Lolly Willowes* (1926), lesbian writer Sylvia Townsend WARNER echoes Vivien's associations described above. According to J. Garrity (1995), Satan is depicted as "a feminized figure, a homosexual signifier." Garrity suggests that Lolly's attraction to Satan is related to her "repressed lesbian identification," noting that "When Lolly first encounters him at the Sabbath he is disguised as a woman . . . a man in drag." Warner, maintains Garrity, "codes Satan's campy performance as gay."

Saturn In Euro-western ASTROLOGY, this planet governs death and dying, devastating illnesses, difficult lessons, limitations, regeneration, reincarnation, and retribution; it is also associated, somewhat paradoxically, with a paradisal "Golden Age" which humanity witnessed in the beginning of time and which will one day return. In astrology, as well as in the Euro-western traditions of alchemy and ritual magic, the planets are considered to be ultimately androgynous or transgendered, their feminine and masculine aspects represented by the signs they govern. In the case of Saturn, his masculine aspect is represented by CAPRICORN, his feminine by AQUARIUS. Figures associated with Saturn and with gender and/or sexual variance include: ANAT, ATHIRAT, CHRONOS, CYBELE, DEMETER, HECATE, ISIS, KALI, PAN, SATAN, SET, and Tonantzin. In ancient Rome, and later throughout much of Europe, the winter festival of Saturnalia, evoking the "Golden Age" of Saturn, included in its celebration of reversals and inversions ritual transvestism and orgiastic eroticism. A. Sahuquillo (1991) suggests that in the mid-nineteenth century, the association of Saturn with homoeroticism (and possibly also with Satanism) became prevalent among bohemians in France. This association was imported to Spain during the late nineteenth or early twentieth century, ultimately finding its way to the Americas. In Sahuquillo's view, the writers Paul VERLAINE (1844-1896), Marcel Proust (1871-1922), Federico García LORCA (1898-1936), and José Lezama Lima (1910-1976) were among those linking Saturn to homoeroticism in their works. Indeed, the Cuban writer Lezama Lima, in his epic novel *Paradiso* (1966), identified the anus with one of Saturn's rings.

Satyrs and Silenoi Hybrid goat-humans and horse-humans, respectively, they are attendants and devotees, mostly male, of the Greek god DIONYSUS (Roman Bacchus). Inhabiting forests and mountains, they are typically depicted as hairy, having long hair (often in tight curls) or balding and as having beards, pointed ears, large lips and noses, muscular torsos (a few have "pot bellies"), ample thighs, large genitalia, and animal tails and hooves. Always lusty, they are alternately portrayed as jovial and as terrifying. They are also represented as grape harvesters, wine makers, dancers, and musicians, especially as players of the aulos and the lyre; these may have been roles performed by satyr-like males in the cult of Dionysus. In terms of sexuality, satyrs and silenoi, as depicted on Greek vases, might be best termed "pansexual." They are often shown in scenes of ritual group eroticism in the vineyard of Dionysus, engaging in anal, oral, and other forms of eroticism, with other male satyrs and silenoi as well as with female or transgendered sphinxes. One vase depicts a satyr masturbating with his right hand while using his left hand to penetrate himself anally with a dildo. Certain vases suggest that the satyr (or silenus), or his ritual representative, and Dionysus, or his representative, may represent a sort of "butch/femme" relationship. These works, exemplified by one depicting an ithyphallic, handsome satyr dancing the *sikinnis* for an effeminate Dionysus, further suggest that, in contrast to popular twentieth-century theories, satyrs may not always have been perceived as "ugly" or CARNIVALESQUE but rather as attractive men who simply did not conform to the image of the young, virtually hairless male. In the scene of the satyr dancing erotically for Dionysus, it is quite clear that both are enjoying themselves, and there is no hint of mockery. This is not to say that satyrs were humorless. Indeed, they were the central characters in satyr plays, from which the English term "satire" is derived. Philostratus (fl. 200 CE) describes a painting of Olympus, Marsyas and a group of satyrs, in which Olympus is sleeping after a music lesson from Marsyas. "A band of satyrs gaze lovingly upon the youth, ruddy grinning creatures, one desiring to touch his breast, another to embrace his neck, another eager to pluck a kiss; they scatter flowers over him and worship him as if he were a divine image; and the cleverest of them draws out the tongue of the second pipe which is still warm and eats it, thinking he is thus kissing Olympus, and he says he tasted the boy's breath."

Scáthach "Shade," a Celtic AMAZON, renowned as a poet, prophet, warrior and teacher of warriors. Among those she trained at her military academy on the Isle of Skye were the foster-brothers and comrade-lovers CU CHULAINN and Fer Diadh.

Schemen German CARNIVAL spirits who, depicted as androgynous and as linked to Witchcraft, are represented by maskers who take part in a great spiral dance.

Schlegel, Friedrich von (1772-1829) German Romantic philosopher who, prior to becoming a conservative Catholic, envisioned, especially in his essay "Über die Diotima," androgyny as a goal of spiritual enlightenment.

The Scholar and the Flower Spirit In a tale of the Chinese Ming Dynasty (1368-1644), a scholar sojourning in a Taoist temple falls in love with a handsome youth who proves invisible to all but him. The scholar discovers that the youth is a flower spirit. This is somewhat unusual, as in Taoist tradition, most flower spirits are female. The male flower spirit is searching for a human male to love because, we are told, he was a female in a previous incarnation, and also he wishes to become human again by taking some of the scholar's energy into himself.

Schubert, Franz Peter (1797-1828) Austrian Romantic composer, known especially for his song cycles, symphonies, and chamber works. While his sexual orientation remains a subject of controversy, numerous contemporary musicologists have suggested that Schubert may have been homoerotically inclined. He is believed to have belonged to a salon comprised primarily of homosexual and bisexual Viennese artists and to have cultivated passionate relationships with other men. In an autobiographical text, "My Dream," written in 1822, Schubert subtly reveals, according to M. Solomon (1992), his homoerotic orientation as well as his mystical devotion to a Goddess-like spirit. In this dream, Schubert rejects his father's invitation to a brothel, instead wandering until he arrives at the funeral of a virgin, around whose shrine beautiful youths and older men circle.

Scorpio In Euro-western ASTROLOGY, zodiac sign ruling from (approximately) October 23 until November 21, associated with death and dying, mystery, sexuality, transformation, and wit, typically represented as a scorpion, but also as an eagle and/or a serpent. Mesopotamians linked Scorpio specifically to homoerotic desire. In charts of gay and bisexual men born in the years spanning 1915 to 1970, Scorpio appears as one of the three most frequent sun signs. Figures associated with Scorpio and with gender and/or sexual variance include: BARON LUNDY, BARON SAMEDI, DICTYNNA, DURGA, the GHEDES, HECATE, KALI, Lucifer, Mephistopheles, SATAN, SET, and SHIVA.

Scrat Androgynous male forest spirit revered in the seventh century by some Germanic and Anglo-Saxon groups. The term "scrat" is related to the Germanic practitioner of SEIDR magic while also carrying the meanings of "monster," "hermaphrodite," "eunuch," and "prostitute." Apparently Scrat was an archetypal "hairy androgyne." A shapeshifter, he might also appear as an infant, a giant, a bear, a horse, a butterfly, or a red-capped dwarf resembling Rumplestiltskin. His nickname "Katzaus" (also "Katzenveit") may suggest a linkage to the cult of the goddess FREYJA and may also indicate an association with *katzenmusik*, a "deliberately distorted and noisy" musical performance elsewhere known as *charivari* or "rough music." Scrat was honored with gifts of food, often placed in houses or at forest shrines. His cult may have survived into the sixteenth century. Places sacred to him include Scrathawe, Strathawe, Scrachawe, and other sites in England and elsewhere. Eventually he became identified with the Devil, taking the nickname of Old Scrat or Mr Scratch.

Seabrook, William Buehler (1886-1945) US writer on the occult. During his lifetime, he studied with Sufis, Spiritualists, Witches, and practitioners of Vodou. His best known works are *Magic Island* (1929) and *Witchcraft: Its Power in the World Today* (1940). According to Francis King and Stephen Skinner in *Techniques of High Magic* (1976), Seabrook and Aleister CROWLEY (1875-1947) participated in magical rites together from 1917 to 1919 and also may have shared an erotic relationship at this time, which may have included Seabrook's wife Katherine Pauline Edmondson.

Sebastian, Saint (d. 287 CE) In Christianity, the patron saint of archers, athletes, and soldiers, and the protector against plague, associated since the Renaissance, if not previously, with homoerotic love. Sebastian was apparently a very beautiful young man who, according to legend, captured the heart of the Roman emperor Diocletian. When Sebastian, the commander of a company of archers, protected two Christians, Marcellinus and Mark, against being tormented by soldiers, Diocletian, despising the new religion, became infuriated with Sebastian, and demanded that his own archers slay him. Although he was left for dead, he survived, only to be beaten to death shortly thereafter. Commencing in the Renaissance and continuing into the present, Sebastian has signified the fusion of sensuilty and spirituality, and beauty and suffering, in a homoerotic context, in paintings by artists including Mantegna (1431-1506), Botticelli (1444-1510), Perugino (c. 1445-1523), Giorgione (1476-1510), Giovanni BAZZI ("Il Sodoma", 1477-1549), Titian (c. 1485-1576), Tintoretto (1518-1594), Guido Reni (1575-1642), Gustave MOREAU (1826-1898), and Odilon Redon (1840-1916). Sebastian has also been remembered by writers including Tennessee Williams (1911-1983), in his play *Suddenly Last Summer*, and Yukio MISHIMA (1925-1970), in *Confessions of a Mask* and in a celebrated photograph. The composer Claude Debussy (1862-1918) paid tribute to him, in *Le Martyre de St Sébastien* (1911), a performance piece starring the Jewish lesbian dancer Ida RUBINSTEIN in the title role, as did the early photographer

F. Holland DAY (1864-1933) and filmmaker Derek JARMAN (1942-1994), in his film *Sebastiane* (1976). In the 1990s St Sebastian is widely recognized as a patron of same-sex lovers and as a healing force in the struggle against AIDS. He is fêted on January 20.

Secret Gospel of Mark   Text of early mystical Christianity referred to in a letter of Clement of Alexandria (b. c. 150-d. c. 220 CE). Clement's letter, discovered in 1958 by classical historian Morton Smith, includes a description of a mysterious rite of initiation undertaken by JESUS and his disciples which suggests that cultic homoeroticism may have occurred therein. In *The Secret Gospel* (1973), Smith writes, "It was a water baptism administered by Jesus to chosen disciples, singly and by night. The costume, for the disciple, was a linen cloth worn over the naked body. This cloth was probably removed for the baptism proper, the immersion in water, which was now reduced to a preparatory purification. After that, by unknown ceremonies," which may have included "the recitation of repetitive hypnotic prayers and hymns," yogic breathing, and massage, "the disciple was united with Jesus . . . Freedom from the law [i.e. Hebrew and Roman] may have resulted in completion of the spiritual union by physical union. This certainly occurred in many forms of Gnostic Christianity." Smith and others have suggested that LAZARUS, whom Jesus raised from the dead, may have undergone this rite.

Sedna   Gynandrous, Inuit (or Eskimo) Mother Goddess, served by TWO-SPIRIT shamans. Sedna is the mother of wild animals – especially of seals, walruses, and whales – who gives "her children to the hunter" or fisher if he or she conforms to the hunting or fishing ritual but who withdraws the game if the hunter or fisher fails to observe her rites. Sedna is not only the patroness of animals, hunters, and fishers, however; she is also a goddess of destiny, death, and the afterlife. As ruler of the afterlife, she reigns over three heavens of the Inuit, including Omiktu, where the souls of deceased humans and whales live in harmony. Once a young woman who refused to marry, Sedna lives with her Amazonian female companion QAILERTETANG at the bottom of the sea in the company of seals, whales, and other sea creatures. Sedna's rejection of marriage and her wild appearance – her matted hair is thick with the blood of her "children" whom hunters and fishers have killed – have contributed to her identity as a gynandrous goddess.

Segarelli, Gherardo (or **G. Cicarelli, Sagarelli, Segalleli**, d. 1300 CE)   Italian spiritual seeker who, desiring to emulate the early Christians, sold his house and lived in poverty, wearing sandals and a gray robe, letting his hair and beard grow long, and begging for alms. By 1282 he had gathered so many followers that a sect was founded and named the Apostolici. As Segarelli and his devotees believed the end of the world was near, they frowned on reproductive sexual intercourse but apparently did not forbid other forms of eroticism, including same-sex eroticism. The Catholic Church condemned the Apostolici. After suffering imprisonment and torture, Segarelli was burned at the stake as a heretic (and apparently also as a sodomite) at Parma on July 18, 1300. His successor Dulcin, was shortly thereafter hunted down and burned in 1306.

Seidr   Tradition of Teutonic MAGIC related to Shamanism, associated primarily with the goddess FREYJA and to a lesser extent with her brother FREYR and the trickster LOKI. The warrior deity ODIN is linked to transgenderism in part because of his knowledge of *seidr*, in which Freyja instructed him. Women have been and remain the primary practitioners of *seidr*, but it has been, and is being, practiced also by gender variant and/or homoerotically/bisexually inclined men. In the past, the terms "*argr*" and "*ergi*" were applied to these spiritual functionaries. It is fairly certain that the *ergi* priest-magicians wore a mixture of feminine and sacerdotal attire. Like the priestesses and female *seidkonur,* they may have dressed in either feathered cloaks or blue, hooded cloaks, and worn necklaces of glass beads, bearskin belts, calfskin shoes, and catskin gloves. *Seidr* practitioners also carried magical staffs inset with jewels. *Ergi* priests of Freyja who practiced *seidr* apparently performed tasks traditionally assigned to women. These may have included planting, weaving, and childrearing. It is not clear whether or not the *ergi* priests-*seidrmen* were eunuchs, although Odin's nickname or aspect Jalkr, or "gelding," as well as other data indicate that ritual castration was not unknown. This may have accounted for the "strange" quality of their voices, though it is possible that like other gender variant male functionaries, they employed falsetto, especially during rituals. Homosexual behavior does not appear to have been restricted to *ergi* individuals, but it does seem that *ergi* priests-*seidrmen* were clearly differentiated from men who occasionally had sex with other men and who took the active role when they did. Truly bisexual men seem also to have been viewed as essentially different, sharing close ties with *ergi* individuals. These men, usually "passive" in terms of their male partners, were often imagined to undergo gender metamorphosis every ninth night, when, like werewolves or VAMPIRES seeking victims, they would go out hunting other men. *Ergi* priests-*seidrmen* were associated also with animal transformation, much like the gods Loki and Odin. This is suggested by the term *seidberender*, with *berendi* referring to a female animal. While F. Ström (1974) stresses the derogatory nature of this term, beyond its derisive use, *seidberender* might refer to becoming both the Goddess and the falcon by donning the feathered cloak of Freyja, or to alternately embodying the Goddess and another of her sacred animals by wearing the mask of the boar, these costumes employed in "faring forth" shamanically into other worlds. One of the services which may have been performed by the *ergi* priests-*seidrmen* involved journeying about the countryside, stopping for festivals and on other occasions when people felt the need to communicate with the Goddess and other divine beings. The *seidrman* (or -woman) would be offered a sacrificial meal, sometimes comprised of the hearts of various animals. He would then mount a high platform called the *seidjaller*, where he would begin to chant, as others below accompanied him. The *vardlokkur* songs they sang (from which the English "warlock" may come) were used to summon spirits, protect participants from harm, and facilitate a shamanic or an altered state of consciousness. The *seidrman* would then journey, often in the form of a falcon or cat, to the world of the gods. Upon his return, he would share the words of the divinity or spirit with the other participants. He would answer questions concerning the destinies of persons in the year to come, the probable abundance or failure of crops, and other matters. Other types of divination, perhaps even including runic divination were also practiced by *seidrmen*. Two of the runes, Berkano and Ingwaz, seem especially linked to the worship of Freyja, the other Vanir, and practitioners of *seidr*. Berkano speaks of the Goddess as the giver and taker of life and of the need for her "powers of fertility . . . [to be] renewed by the sacrifice of her consort each year," either by death, castration, or some other means. Ingwaz echoes this theme of sacrifice but focuses on the male consort, functionary, or devotee rather than on the Goddess. The central meaning of Ingwaz is a familiar one: in order to "assume the feminine powers of vision and understanding," a man must be willing to give up "his masculine identity, even to the point of dressing and living as a woman for a time." K. Gundarsson (1990) who specifically links this rune to the gender transformations of Odin and Loki, and to their child-producing relationship, describes Ingwaz as hieratically expressing either semen or a "castrated male." Working magic, however, appears to have been the chief function of the *ergi* functionaries. While their rituals have generally been lost, we know that they held the power to bestow wealth and fame and to take these away. They could bring plenty during a time of famine, or cause the land to be blighted. They could cause persons to fall ill, just as they could heal them with herbs and charms. They could bring lovers together, and sever relationships. In later times, they aided warriors by magically dulling enemies' swords, halting enemy arrows in flight, raising storms at sea, and unbinding the chains of imprisoned comrades. Indeed, they were believed capable of bringing an end to war. They were also thought to be able to transform persons into animals and to transfer speech, knowledge, and power from one person to another and from human beings to animals. It appears that *ergi*

priests-*seidrmen* may have engaged in rites of sexual magic by which the body of a male, via anal intercourse or other means, became feminized, transformed into a vessel or channel of the divine. This state of being *ergjask* (or *sordinn, strodinn, sannsordin, rassragr*), of being "fucked," becomes the erotico-sacred expression of surrender or yielding of the masculine to the feminine, the mortal to the divine. *Seidr* practitioners were even thought to be able, after having passed away, to pay visits to the living. A curious passage in the *Laxdaela Saga* suggests that practitioners of *seidr* may have sometimes been associated with the *draugr*, or "undead." In this passage, the bones of a *seidkona* are unearthed. Described as "blue and ill-looking," they conjure images of the corpses of the undead, depicted as showing signs of "swelling or changing color." This brings us to a controversial subject regarding the deaths of *ergi* priests-*seidrmen*. According to Tacitus, *ergi* males were drowned in mudholes and marshes. While he suggests that it was due to their being *ergi*, it is not clear that he was certain of this. A number of writers have suggested that these men may be among those whose corpses have been discovered in peatbogs. Folke Ström has argued, however, that the male corpses discovered in peatbogs appear to have been hanged first before being lowered into the bogs, which he believes represents a more honorable punishment than that allotted to *ergi* males. He insists that the "last resting-place[s] of the 'unmanly'" were not peatbogs but rather "morasses, quagmires, and swamps," which have "not attracted archaeologists." Nevertheless, a theory voiced by P. V. Glob (1971) suggests that while in later, increasingly patriarchal (or Aesic) epochs, such men probably did suffer the fate described by Ström, in earlier times, *ergi* priests-*seidrmen* may well have ended up in the bogs. According to Glob, "the circumstances of the bog people's deposition . . . have many of the characteristics of . . . sacrificial deposits." As evidence in support of Glob's theory, one may point to the nooses encircling the necks of a number of male corpses, which Glob sees as "replicas of the twisted neck-rings which are the mark of honour of the goddess, and a sign of consecration to her." Perhaps Glob is correct as concerns earlier epochs, while Ström is correct as concerns later times. The chief problem with Ström's theory is that, *within* the worship of Freyja, Freyr, Nerthus-Njord, Yngvi, and the Great Goddess as opposed to *without*, *ergi* priests-*seidrmen* appear to have been respected and not looked upon as degenerates or criminals. Further, we are fairly certain that human sacrifice was practiced in the worship of the Germanic Goddess(es) and, as male representatives of the Goddess and her consort, *ergi* functionaries may have been considered especially appropriate sacrifices. If *ergi* males were *not* placed in bogs, the peatbog may have been the final resting place of traditionally masculine devotees of the Goddess who were sacrificed during the Fröblod. It should be noted that whether Ström or Glob is correct, or whether the truth lies somewhere in the middle, *ergi* males were being drowned, burned, and otherwise tortured and slain at the time of Christianity's triumph. As late as the mid-twentieth century, the Nazi leader Himmler, in an attempt to demonstrate his admiration for the ancient practice of drowning *ergi* men, suggested that homosexuals should be disposed of in this manner. "That was no punishment," said he, "merely the extinction of an abnormal life." We know of several legendary men who were said to have been *seidrmen*. Haddingr, son of Gram of Denmark, was raised by a priestess of Freyja named Hardgrep(a). As a young man, Haddingr was said to have been a favorite of Odin. Later he established an annual sacrifice to Freyr. He is said to have ended his life in suicide, "in Odinic fashion," after his companion Hundingr drowned. Jaan Puhvel points out that the life of Haddingr reveals an intermingling of both "Odinic and Vanic features." The name Haddingr is associated with the Haddingjar, twin warrior deities who are in turn linked to the Alcis who were served by gender variant priests. The name Haddingr is also related to the word *hadr*, "denoting a feminine hairdo." Two other men who practiced *seidr* were Ragnvaldr Rettilbeini and Eyvindr Kelda. Rettilbeini lived during the ninth century and was a son of King Harald Fairhair. When his father, who despised *seidrmen*, sent a threatening letter to Vitgeir, another *seidrman*, the latter responded: "It is little strange / If we do wizardry, / Who are the sons of carls / And of low-born mothers, / When Ragnvald Rettlebone, / Harald's noble son, / Can be a wizard / In Hadeland [Hadalandia]." Not long after, King Harald sent another of his sons, Erik Bloodaxe, to Hadalandia, where Ragnvaldr lived. There Erik carried out the royal father's orders, burning his brother and eighty other *seidrmen* alive. Eyvindr Kelda, related to Rettilbeini and King Harald, practiced *seidr* during the tenth century. For this, he was brought before King Olaf Tryggvason, a Christian zealot, in 998. Tryggvason, who found pleasure in threatening to sacrifice pagans to their own gods, prepared a feast for Kelda and other *seidrmen* whom he was holding captive, causing them to think he had a change of heart. When he was certain that all the men were drunk, Tryggvason ordered the doors locked and the house set on fire. Kelda and a few other *seidrmen* managed to escape. They were eventually caught, however, and in chains were taken in a boat to a rock in the water, where they were left to drown. For this reason, the rock at Karmoy, near Haugesund, is called Skrattasker or Skrattaskerry, the "place where the *seidrmen* perished." The term "Skrattasker" is derived from the old Norse *skratta*, which appears in old Icelandic, Old High German, Old English, Middle English, and other tongues in such variants as *scarte*, *schrat*, *scraette*, *scritta*, *strac*, and *strat*, and signifies – at once – a monster, a sorcerer, an hermaphrodite, a eunuch, and a promiscuous person. *Skratta* and *seid-skratti* were also employed

interchangeably to refer to a practitioner of *seidr*. *Skratta* was also synonymous with *seid-læti*, the term describing the strange noises made by *seidrmen* during rituals.

Seigneur de Joye (also **Seigneur de Gayècté**)   Among the Medieval French fools called the *SOTS*, the male consort of MÈRE SOTTE. Dubbed the "Lord of Joy" or the "Lord of Gaiety," he is traditionally depicted as a handsome *galant*. As his name suggests, a link may indeed exist between *gai* or *gay* in Medieval and Renaissance French and the concepts of homoeroticism and transgenderism, although this link, rather than being a direct one, may refer to a complex web of associations embracing not only homoeroticism and gender variance but also foolishness, or "sottishness," and sacred or mythic experience (however carnivalized). In French and English dictionaries of the Middle Ages through the seventeenth century, the synonyms *gai/gay* and *joyeux* were linked to joyous and sensuous behavior – "loose, immoral, wanton, lewd, lascivious." Terms such as "wanton" and "lascivious" more often than not signify gender variant, homoerotic behavior when applied to males. John Palsgrave, in *Lésclarissement de langue française*, suggests that *joyeux* may also connote a "blythfull glad *co[u]e*," in other words, a "joyful ass or anus." Both *joyeux* and *gai/gay* also frequently referred to the behavior of horses and fools.

Seises   Spanish dance-drama linked to the *morisca* (or "morris"), traceable to the Middle Ages, in which six or ten youths, one or more of whom is dressed in women's attire, participate.

Sekhmet   Amazonian Egyptian goddess of war and divine vengeance, depicted as a hybrid female human-lioness crowned with the sun. She is believed to cause, and hold the power to cure, PLAGUES. Her color is scarlet, signifying the "blood-soaked garments of her enemies." Red beer is one of her favorite offerings.

Selu   In the Native American Indian Cherokee spiritual tradition, Mother, or Grandmother, CORN, a gynandrous or transgendered being. In *Selu: Seeking the Corn-Mother's Wisdom* (1993), Marilou Awiakta writes, "The Corn-Mother was born as an androgynous plant, one that incorporates the balance of genders not only in sexual parts of silken ear and tassel, but also in the forces of nature that female and male represent – continuance in the midst of change."

Semiramis (Sammuramat, ninth century BCE ?)   While her existence remains controversial, Semiramis appears to have been a queen of Assyria whose life experiences became interwoven with legends, as is often the case with great spiritual and political leaders. Semiramis was depicted as the daughter of the goddess ATARGATIS; this may have referred to a spiritual bond with the deity similar to that shared by Egyptian pharaohs with their gods. An Amazonian warrior, Semiramis was said to have conquered India and other countries, to have founded Babylon, and to have been responsible for the construction of the magnificent Hanging Gardens of the City (one of the Seven Wonders of the ancient World). As an AMAZON, Semiramis was associated with female gender variance. She is believed to have said of herself, "Nature made me a woman yet I have raised myself to rival the greatest men." Like the goddess Atargatis, who was served by transgendered male priest/esse/s named GALLI, she was also linked to male gender variance. Her servants were said to be eunuchs (perhaps some of whom were *galli*), and in ancient legendary history, her male parallel is the allegedly effeminate ruler SARDANAPALUS (668-626 BCE). This association is taken up (albeit in a negative manner) in the opera *Semiramide* (1823) by Rossini, based on the play by Voltaire, wherein her male lover Arsace (sung by a mezzo-soprano, a female singing *en travesti* with associations with the voice and roles of the male castrati) is ultimately revealed to be her own son. While Semiramis is thought to have been married, her husband seems incidental in her history, and it is not clear exactly where her sexual desires lay. Over time, however, her transgendered persona gave rise to an association with lesbianism. A satiric pamphlet focusing on the transgenderism and bisexuality/lesbianism of Queen Christina of Sweden (1626-1689), *La Métempsychose de la reine Christine* (1657), claimed that the Queen's past lives included being Semiramis as well as MATHURINE, the transgendered, possibly lesbian, court fool of King HENRI III (1551-1589). By the late nineteenth century, this link was secured, especially in urban France, where Semiramis became a signifier of love between women, even being chosen as a nickname by lesbians and as a name for lesbian bars. Around 1910, the bisexual French writer Colette began frequenting a bar run by a woman named Sémiramis. Of the bar and its operator she wrote, "I go to the bar kept by Sémiramis, appropriately named – Sémiramis, warrior queen, helmeted in bronze, armed with the meat cleaver . . . while dining at Sémiramis's bar I enjoy watching the girls dancing together, they waltz so well."

Semnotatoi Transgendred male priests of the Greek goddess HECATE. Undergoing ritual castration, it was said of the *semnotatoi*, "The revered ones of the Goddess are eunuchs." They were also known as the *demosioi*, a name suggesting "belonging to a tribe." It is probable, although not certain, that the *semnotatoi* engaged in homoerotic relationships. Their functions included casting horoscopes, performing spells, and maintaining the temples and sacred groves. Their chief function appears to have been directing choruses of flower-garlanded children in singing hymns to Hecate.

Senju (fl. twelfth century CE) Japanese novice of the Shingon tradition of Buddhism. Senju was the beloved of the LORD ABBOT OF NINNA-JI during the reign of the Emperor Toba (1103-1156). Once, however, when the Abbot became fascinated by a new male novice and deserted Senju, the spurned beloved arrived at a monastery banquet dressed in a dazzling violet robe, singing: "What shall I do? I am abandoned / Even by the innumerable ancient Buddhas. / Among the innumerable paradises I find / None where I may be reborn. / Buddha Amida, my last resort, / Though I am such a sinner, / May I be saved by your hand!" When Senju ceased singing, the Abbot embraced him and the two proceeded to the Abbot's bedchamber.

Sens French city associated in the Medieval period with homoeroticism. There, "ADONIS prostitutes himself / According to the law of the whorehouse: there are acts of sodomy there."

Séraphita Beautiful, androgynous, angelic spirit of Balzac's novel *Séraphita* (1835). The lovers Wilfrid and Minna are both passionately drawn to Séraphita/Séraphitus, Wilfrid perceiving the being as a female, Minna perceiving him/her as a male. Balzac suggests that where heterosexually inclined persons are concerned, a yearning for androgyny may be satisfied in a marriage based upon mutual respect. He hints, however, that transgenderism and same-sex passion may also lead to spiritual enlightenment, as these also seem to reside within the persona of the angelic Séraphita.

Sergius and Bacchus, Saints (d. 303 CE) High officers of the Roman army in Syria and Christian martyrs. For refusing to enter the Temple of Zeus with fellow officers to make offerings there, they were stripped of their military garb, dressed in women's clothes and heavy chains, and led through the streets of Arabissus. In prison, while singing and praying, they were visited by angels who comforted them. Calling each other "brother", they claimed that in their "union" they became as one, as well as at one with JESUS. Before Sergius was beheaded, Bacchus, who had been killed first, appeared to him as an angel wearing military garb. Sergius and Bacchus were not martyred because of their passion for one another, as many of their comrades were homoerotically or bisexually inclined, but rather because of their rejection of the elder gods of the Romans. Since the sixth century, continuing into the twentieth century, Sergius and Bacchus have been invoked in some Eastern European Christian congregations by those participating in ceremonies of same-sex UNION. Depicted as twins with identical page-boy haircuts and dressed in military apparel, riding on the same horse or side-by-side, Sergius and Bacchus are fêted on October 7.

Serpent Animal frequently symbolic of EROTICISM, the feminine, the masculine, fertility, metamorphosis (including of gender or sex), death, regeneration or rebirth, and infinity. The serpent is frequently linked to, or identified with, the RAINBOW. In the Biblical tradition, the serpent becomes linked to evil, specifically to SATAN. Figures associated with serpents and with transgenderism and/or same-sex eroticism include ABRAXAS, ADAM AEON, AIDO HWEDO, ANGAMUNGGI, ASCLEPIUS, ATHIRAT, DAMBALLAH, DIONYSUS, FURIES, GUN, JINN, JOHN THE EVANGELIST, KOTYS, MEDUSA, MELUSINE, MERCURIUS, NAAS, SHAKTI, SHIRABYOSHI, SHIVA, TIRESIAS, TROPHONIUS, UNGUD, and UROBORUS. Spiritual functionaries include BAPTAI, KOSIO, and SHIH-NIANG. Spiritual traditions include ALCHEMY, Goddess Reverence, and the NAASSENES.

Set Brother or son of the Egyptian goddess ISIS and maternal uncle or brother of Horus. Set is a god of sexuality, sacrifice, and the mystery of death. He is frequently depicted as a gender variant, bisexual – or more appropriately, pansexual – male. Two of his attributes, the LETTUCE plant and the flint knife, are associated with eunuchs and ritual castration. The lettuce plant, however, is also an aphrodisiac, suggesting Set's paradoxical erotic-ascetic character. Set's gender and erotic variance are also revealed in his relationship to his wife, the Amazonian ANAT, whose favorite sexual activity is anal intercourse. His gender variance and homoerotic desires are manifested in his relationship with Horus. While Osirian religion tends to demonize Set on a superficial level, portraying him as the enemy of Horus – an Apollonian god of harmony, order, and light – it implies that, on a more mystical plane, Set and Horus merge to form an indivisible union, rather like the Tao. This mystery, known as the "Secret of the Two Partners," is envisioned, as H. Te. Velde tells us, as "a union consisting of a homosexual embrace." In Egyptian myth, as in Hindu myth, reproduction is not an activity limited to a heterosexual couple, at least not in the realm of the gods. Thus, the Egyptian gods are not especially surprised when Set gives birth to Horus's child. While it is the case that in the Osirian, or patriarchalized, version of the myth, Set is ridiculed as a *hmty* – a word meaning "vagina" and here connoting a transgendered, homoerotically-inclined male – it is also true that even in this version, Set's offspring is coveted by the gods. The "child" first appears as a golden disk on Set's forehead, suggesting his "third eye" and hence a mystical rather than a physical birth. In one version, the god THOTH, the Egyptian judge, takes the child from Set. Upon his doing so, the disk transforms into the youthful lunar deity KHONSU. In another version, the child produced is Thoth himself. Thus, Thoth is sometimes referred to as the "son of the two lords." Due to the manner of his conception, as

well as his association with the self-douching ibis, Thoth is also referred to as the "Shepherd of the Anus." The pharaoh was also sometimes considered the product of this homoerotic union, containing within him- or herself (as in the case of HATSHEPSUT) "the dual power in which the two gods are at peace."

Seuse, Heinrich (1295-1366) Medieval Christian mystic whose "erotic yearning for union with God," according to Simon Richter, professor of German literature at the University of Maryland (in 1995) "can only be described as homoerotic."

Seven Sages of the Bamboo Grove (Zhulin Qi Xian) In the third century CE, homoeroticism, male gender variance, and sacred experience became intertwined in a Taoist circle known as the Zhulin Qi Xian, the "Seven Sages of the Bamboo Grove." The founding members of the circle were Ruan Ji, Xi Kang, Shan Tao, Ruan Xian, Liu Ling, Xiang Xiu, and Wang Rong. At their meetings, they wandered about in a bamboo grove (the perfect topos), drinking, dancing, playing music, and discussing aspects of Taoist philosophy and ALCHEMY. At least two of the circle's founders, Ruan Ji and Xi Kang, are "generally regarded as homosexuals." Xi Kang (or Hsi K'ang), born in 223, spent his youth "sitting under a willow tree . . . practicing the art of breathing with a view to securing immortality" and "experimenting in the transmutation of metals." In later years, he became an accomplished lutenist, poet, and essayist, the author of a number of Taoist treatises including *Poetical Essay on the Lute* and *Dissertation on the Nourishment of the Vital Principle*. Although Xi Kang married into the "imperial family, and received an official appointment," neither marriage nor political power seemed to interest him. Indeed, it was lack of interest in these matters which cost him his life. The emperor who admired Xi Kang, announced under great pressure that Xi Kang was a traitor and that he should be put to death. Although "three thousand disciples offered to take the place of their beloved master," the execution was carried out, Xi Kang meeting his fate with "fortitude, calmly . . . playing upon his lute." Bret Hinsch points out that Xi Kang was described in Taoist (or Neo-Taoist) terms as having the "grace of a dragon and the beauty of a phoenix." What Hinsch does not say, however, is that this expression, in describing Xi Kang as exhibiting both dragon-yang and phoenix-yin qualities, is depicting him in androgynous terms. Although in his youth, Xi Kang was deeply attached to a man named Lu Ngan, Ruan Ji was to become his most intimate companion. Born in 210, Ruan Ji (or Yüan Chi) was a wild, rebellious young man who spent much of his time wandering in the hills and shutting himself up in his room reading. Extremely close to his mother, it is said that he wept tears of blood when she died. As a musician, he was known especially for his whistling and for a treatise on the wind instrument called the *cheng*. Although he married, the great love of his life was Xi Kang. Ruan Ji spent the final years of his life wandering about naked, drinking excessively, and performing erotic dances. All these were elements of his own path, which had been inspired by Taoism and the Seven Sages circle and which came to be called "free wandering." By the time of his death, he had gathered many disciples who became known as the "unimpeded ones." Ruan Ji celebrated same-sex love in his poetry. Not only were Xi Kang and Ruan Ji lovers, but they also may have shared a brief erotic interlude with a third member of the circle, Shan Tao, a Taoist alchemist. Like Xi Kang and Ruan Ji, he was married and held political office, but also like them, he enjoyed being with male companions. One day, after talking with a friend whose husband had been having an affair with another man, Shan Tao's wife asked her husband if he might also be so inclined. His reply to her was generally affirmative. She then asked her husband, desiring to understand this type of relationship better, if he might invite Xi Kang and Ruan Ji to spend the night at their house and then allow her to secretly observe them making love. She did so, and was quite impressed. Incidentally, Shan Tao was nicknamed "Uncut Jade," which in Taoist erotic alchemy signifies an uncircumcised penis. It is conceivable that all three men, and probably Shan Tao's wife as well, were familiar with and perhaps even practiced Taoist erotic alchemy. The relationship of the three men was described as one with "the power to break metal and the fragrance of ORCHIDS," an image discovered in the I CHING.

Sexual Secrets: The Alchemy of Ecstasy (1979)   In this best-selling New Age sex manual (still popular in the 1990s), Nik Douglas and Penny Slinger manage, in three or four pages, to link male homosexuality to hormonal imbalance, patriarchal aggression, promiscuity, rape, suicidal tendencies, homicidal tendencies, the loss of magical energy, the decline of empires, and global apocalypse. Of course, homosexuality will go away if we as a species will simply learn to breathe properly and refrain from violent fantasies while engaging in heterosexual, reproductive intercourse. Lesbianism, while perverse, is not so monstrous as homosexuality, Douglas and Slinger explain, so long as it serves only as an hors-d'oeuvre or aperitif to the main and "real" meal.

Shahêd   In Sufism, the disciple who incarnates the Divine Beloved. The desire inspired by the *shahêd* is said to "exalt the soul." Ibn 'Arabi', an Andalusian philosopher, defined "God" as "one who manifests himself to the eyes of any lover in the loved one." Numerous Sufi poets, including 'Attâr (d. 1220), Sa'di (1193-1280), and Maghribi (d.1406), sing praises to the *shahêd* as the embodiment of Divine Love. Omar Khayyam (d. 1132),

who, if not a Sufi himself, was profoundly inspired by them, addresses some if not all of his verses to a male *shahêd*. (His work has been bowdlerized in order to make him appear exclusively heterosexual.) Omar Khayyam also celebrates other homoerotic relationships, including that of the love of the Sultan Mahmud of Ghazna (d.1030) for a young man. Another Sufi poet, Hâfiz (d. 1389), the lover of Shâh Shujâ the Magnificent of Shiraz, refers to his lover as the "king of beauty." Hâfiz's book of *ghazals*, many of which have homoerotic themes, has come to be used as a tool of bibliomancy, as the Bible is used in certain American folk traditions; that is, it is employed as a divinatory text, its messages revealed by randomly opening the book and meditating on the *ghazal* which appears. The most celebrated relationship of a Sufi master and his *shahêd* is that of JALAL AL-DIN RUMI (1207-1273) and SHAMS AL-DIN TABRIZI (d. 1247).

Shakta   Devotees of the Hindu goddesses DEVI, DURGA, PARVATI, SHAKTI, and TRIPURASUNDARI as well as those working with that feminine energy known as *shakti* or *kundalini* in Tantric rituals. Among Shaktas, women and transgendered (male to female) persons predominate.

Shakti   Hindu Great Goddess, sometimes identified with PARVATI as the spouse or "feminine" nature (or aspect) of SHIVA. "Shakti" is frequently employed, somewhat as "YIN" is employed by Taoists, to refer to "feminine" energy in general, wherever it is discovered. For instance, Parvati's bath symbolizes "the locus of power associated with her sexuality, her *shakti*." Similarly, while the god GANESHA is occasionally said to be married, he is most frequently depicted as unmarried, as incapable of reproducing by ordinary means, and as surrounded by feminine beings who are in truth "feminine emanations" – *shaktis* – "of his [own] androgynous nature."

Shamba   Son of the Hindu god KRISHNA. An unsavory character, he dons women's clothes in order to seduce, mock, and abuse women. For this and other acts, he is cursed by the gods. Over time, the more negative aspects of his character have been submerged, and Shamba has become a patron of eunuchs, transgendered persons, and homoerotically inclined men.

Shams al-Din Tabrizi (or **Shamsi Tabriz**, d. 1247) Sufi master, beloved SHAHED of JALAL AL-DIN RUMI (1207-1273). Shams, as beautiful as he was wise, was reared by women, who instructed him in the feminine "art of embroidering gold." His life ended when disciples of Rumi, jealous of the latter's love for Shams, assassinated him.

Shan Gui   The "Mountain Spirit," a Taoist deity sometimes regarded as a transgendered, homoerotically inclined or pansexual male. While some scholars and spiritual practitioners consider Shan Gui to be a goddess, others, including Arthur Waley and Ping-leung Chan, have described the deity as male. As such, Shan Gui bears likeness to the Hindu deity KAMA, the lord of erotic love. Shan Gui is described as wearing a garment made of vines with a belt of mistletoe, and as reeking of galingale perfume. He drives a chariot decorated with magnolias and pulled by red leopards. In an ancient poem, Shan Gui asks a worshipper if he (or possibly she) is attracted to him. The worshipper explains that while he (or she) had originally come to Shan Gui's grove to console him- (or her-) self after being treated cruelly by a lover, he (or she) now realizes that the true object of his (or her) affection is indeed Shan Gui. This experience, the poem suggests, culminates in erotic union between the worshipper and the deity, Shan Gui perhaps being represented by a spiritual functionary. Ritual sexual intercourse often occurred in the bamboo grove over which Shan Gui presided. While the ambiguity of Chinese pronouns does not allow us to confirm absolutely the gender of the worshipper, Peng-leung Chan is among those who believes that "the love in this poem is homosexual." Ritual homosexual intercourse, nicknamed "upside down clouds," appears to have been associated with certain topoi including mountains and bamboo groves.

Shango (or **Changó, Xangô, Hevioso**)   Of all the *orishás* of the Yoruba-diasporic pantheon, Shangó is most often associated with "machismo." As González-Wippler explains, Shangó is an "incorrigible woman-chaser . . . He is invoked for works of domination, passion." Some practitioners of Santería and other Yoruba-based spiritual traditions maintain that Shangó is extremely hostile toward transgendered, gay, and bisexual males, whom he occasionally punishes with death. In spite of his macho image, however, Shangó has been linked to homosexuality, lesbianism, bisexuality, and transgenderism. He is said to have an "effeminate road," in which he dresses and behaves as a sensuous woman. This includes putting on rouge and braiding his hair in a traditionally feminine style. In this manifestation, he may appear on horseback seated in a woman's position. He sometimes appears as a woman warrior or Amazon. As such, he may also manifest himself as a lesbian woman. Shangó has been syncretized with the female Saint BARBARA, who is herself considered gender variant. Reminiscent of Atargatis and Cybele, she is depicted as crowned with a tower and as holding a sword. What is more, in Nigeria, Shangó, like OYÁ, has a transgendered male servant. His name is Iwèfà; he is a eunuch and, according to Nigerian playwright Duro Ladipo, Shangó's "best praise-singer." Benjamin G. Ray tells us that some of Shangó's male devotees emulate the gender variant aspect of the god by dressing in women's clothes and braiding their hair in feminine style. Shangó's

most important tool is his double axe. This axe often takes the form of a staff crowned by a "woman with a double-edged axe . . . balanced upon her head." Called the *edun ara*, it holds the power to "create or destroy." In agreement with Hubert Fichte, João Ferreira reports that in Brazil, the double axe of Shangó has become "a symbol of the struggle for liberation among Black homosexuals." It is noteworthy that in ancient Crete, the double axe was a sacred attribute of the Minoan goddess, its form evoking that of the butterfly; and that in twentieth-century America and elsewhere, the double axe became a symbol of the lesbian-feminist liberation movement. In "The Winds of Orisha" the African-American lesbian poet Audre LORDE (1934-1992) writes, "Shango will be my brother roaring out of the sea / earth shakes our darkness swelling into each other."

Shepherd   Frequently symbolic of a compassionate person – especially a spiritual teacher – who cares for his/her "flock." The shepherd may also stand for the rustic ideal of ARCADIA, as well as for the psychopomp, the guide of souls. Divine beings associated with shepherding and with same-sex intimacy and/or transgenderism include ADONIS, ALEXIS, BRANCHUS, CORYDON, CYPARISSUS, DAPHNIS, DIONYSUS, GLAUCON, HERMAPHRODITUS, HERMES, HESPERUS, JESUS, MARSYAS, ORPHEUS, PALES, PAN, SILVANUS, and THOTH. One of the most celebrated literary works bearing these associations is the English Renaissance poet Richard Barnfield's *The Tears of an Affectionate Shepherd Sick for Love* (1594).

Shih-Niang   In ancient China, shamans were generally known as *wu*. Gender variant shamans, however, were specifically referred to as *shih-niang*, a term meaning "master girl," which indicates gender transformation. Shih-niang dressed in a fusion of feminine, masculine, and priestly clothes. They were described as "not dreaming and not awake," the latter phrase suggesting that they operated in an altered or shamanic state of consciousness. They were employed in various cults, including that of the canine warrior deity Pan Hu and the serpent king Ta Wang Shen.

Shikhandin   Individual experiencing sexual or gender metamorphosis in Hindu mythology. According to a story told in the *Mahabharata* (5. 189-193) King Drupada wanted a son. He prayed to SHIVA for one. Shiva said, "You shall have a child who shall be male and female," or depending on the translation, "you shall have a male child who is a woman." The queen gave birth to a daughter. Trusting Shiva, they decided to raise it as a son. When the "son" grew up, he was to be married to a young woman. When the woman discovered Shikhandin's female anatomy, she was upset, and told her father who decided to go to war with King Drupada because of this "treachery." Shikhandin became suicidal and went to the forest to kill herself. There she met Sthuna, a Yaksha (demi-god), who told her that rather than have her kill herself, he would exchange sexes with her for a while, as long as she would agree to give his penis back one day. When Shikhandin told her father what had happened, he was delighted; he called on the bride's father and told him. He had some female courtiers check; they reported that Shikhandin was now indeed a male. The two were married. Shikhandin, however, worried constantly that the Yaksha would one day demand the return of his penis. One day, however, Shikhandin learned that Kubera, the lord of the Yakshas, was annoyed with Sthuna for having changed his sex – which is odd, considering that Yakshas were known to change sex frequently – and that he had decided to require Sthuna to remain female. Shikhandin was overjoyed.

Shinu No Hafuri In the Shinto religion of Japan, along with AMA NO HAFURI, his lover, he was credited with introducing homosexuality (here, *azunai*) to the Japanese. Shinu no Hafuri and Ama no Hafuri were servants of a primordial goddess. When Shinu no Hafuri fell ill and died, Ama no Hafuri was so devastated that he committed suicide. The lovers were buried together in the same grave.

Shirabyoshi Female, sometimes transgendered, deities or spirits (*kami*) of the Japanese religion of Shinto depicted as half-human, half-serpent. Also the name of female, sometimes transgendered, shamans or priest/esse/s (*miko*) thought to be linked in some way to the *shirabyoshi* spirits, originating in Shinto and later playing a lesser role in Japanese Buddhism. Frequently dressing in male attire, *shirabyoshi* most frequently served as performers in ritual dance-dramas.

Shiva Phallic deity of the Hindu pantheon, the lord of yoga, the guardian of animals, the conqueror of fear and suffering, whose worship probably dates to the second millenium BCE. It is Shiva, as Nataraj, who dances the world into and out of existence. His attributes include the trident, the crescent moon, the serpent, the tiger, the drum, and the datura flower. The husband of the goddess PARVATI, Shiva also shares intimate relationships with the gods AGNI and VISHNU. His union with Agni ultimately results in the birth of the god KARTIKKEYEH, while his union with Vishnu results in the birth of the god HARIHARA. Shiva is also parent to ARDHANARISHVARA, born mysteriously when Shiva and Parvati merge into a single transgendered being. He is also parent to GANESHA, who is born, according to some traditions, of a union between Parvati and her handmaiden MALINI. Shiva is occasionally invoked by males engaging in cultic masturbation and homoeroticism.

Shooting God In the Navaho religion or mythology of Native America, twin deities, both possessing the name of Shooting God. Both are TWO-SPIRITS, third gender males. One dwells with TALKING GOD in the east, and the other with CALLING GOD in the west. The Shooting Gods twins are depicted in rituals, such as the Night Chant, by men wearing female costume.

Shrieking Scorpion In the visionary cosmos of queer-identified writer William BURROUGHS in *The Western Lands* (1987), the daughter of the lesbian union of the Egyptian cat goddess Bast and the scorpion goddess Selket. "With her lashing tail loaded with deadly venom," Burroughs relates, "her rending cat claws and insect mandibles, she is evoked only by the most terrible curses." It should be noted that Burroughs is not averse to curses when all other means to an end have failed.

Shugia (or **Sugia**) Mesopotamian Amazonian, possibly lesbian, priestesses, also called SINNISAT ZIKRUM, who served INANNA/ISHTAR. They are depicted as carrying swords and double axes (LABRYS) in rites.

Silibo-Gweto (or **Shi-Li-Bo**) In Vodou, a gynandrous or transgendered *lwa* (deity or spirit) said to be one of the primordial parents of the human race. Sometimes associated with the *lwas* AYIZAN and NANAN-BOUCLOU, Silibo-Gweto is described as a being loved by the Sun, implying a relationship to the *lwa* LEGBA. Also linked to streams and ponds, Silibo-Gweto presides over the psychic art of clairvoyance. She (-he) is a special protector of young women.

Silvanus Roman deity of fields and forests, patron of farmers, shepherds, and hunters. Silvanus, like APOLLO, loved CYPARISSUS and was devastated when the young man died. For this reason, Silvanus is sometimes depicted wearing a cypress wreath or carrying a cypress staff.

Singh, Ranjit (1780-1839) Sikh ruler known as the "Lion of the Punjab." As a Sikh, Ranjit Singh believed that while God is ultimately unknowable, the enlightened believer may come to experience a kind of intimacy with him. As a Sikh, he also believed stongly in the use of war to bring justice to the enemeies of the Sikhs. He was widely known as a lover of male youths, especialy dancers; his favorite lover was Gulab Singh. While Sikhs in the past were well known for their acceptance of intergenerational homoeroticism, they have generally become, in the twentieth century, extremely hostile toward sexual and gender variance, especially in the western movement of Sikh Dharma founded in 1971 by Yogi Bhajan.

Sinnishanu "Woman-like one," a type of gender variant male priest of the Mesopotamian goddess INANNA/ISHTAR who served as a HIERODULE, with whom other male devotees might have UNION.

SIPINIIT

Sipiniit Among the Inuit (or Eskimo), individuals reputed to have miraculously changed sex between conception and birth. Some Inuit envision a life inside the womb inclusive of a prenatal abode in which the not-yet-born is presented with symbols signifying masculinity and femininity and is encouraged to choose between them. Occasionally, a spirit about to be reborn will seemingly split into more than one spirit previously incarnated, an event which may result in a kind of tug-of-war as to whether the unborn will pass from the womb as male or female. This tug-of-war can sometimes result in a person of third gender, or TWO-SPIRIT status being born. This person is described as a *sipiniit* which translates roughly as "transgendered person."

Siproites Cretan male changed into a woman for having spied upon the Greco-Roman goddess ARTEMIS/DIANA and her companions bathing.

La Sirène *Lwa* (deity or spirit) of the sea in the pantheon of Haitian- and New Orleans-based Vodou. La Sirène, the siren, is depicted as a beautiful mermaid with long, flowing hair. Like ERZULIE, she is a *lwa* of love and beauty, except that, as M. Deren (1983) observes, "blue is her color and her voice contains a hiss, as though the sea were in it." La Sirène might be considered bisexual or pansexual in today's terms. Her male lover or spouse is Agwe, *lwa* of the sea, her female companion, LA BALEINE. Together they form a trinity of marine divinities. La Sirène's attributes and offerings include mirrors, combs, perfumes, powders, and orgeat syrup. Tuesday and Thursday are her special days. Bearing relationships to the Yoruba-diasporic *orishá* YEMAYA, the West African/African-diasporic goddess Mami Wata, and the folk figure Mexican La Sirena, she is syncretized with the Catholic Saint Philomena (fêted on August 11) and the aspect of the Virgin Mary known as Our Lady of the Assumption (fêted on August 15).

Sirius The "Dog Star." In Egyptian mythology and religion, Sirius is linked to ISIS, SET, HAPY, and ANUBIS. In Mesopotamian epic, it is the star of which GILGAMESH dreams, which serves as a symbol for his beloved ENKIDU, whom he will shortly encounter. In ancient Greece, its rising heralds the celebration of the Carneia, which commemorates the love of the Greek deities APOLLO and CARNEIUS, and, according to some, the Hyacinthia, commemorating Apollo's love for HYACINTHUS. In classical antiquity, generally speaking, Sirius seems to be linked to both the heat of passion between men and the death of youths loved by the gods, perhaps ritually marking transition to adulthood. Its rising is associated as well with celebrations of love between women. The lyric poet Alcman (fl. late seventh century BCE), writes of AGIDO and HAGESICHORA, "They are the white star Sirius rising / In the honey and spice of a summer night."

Sirius is also considered to be in the vicinity of the true home of the Gnostic NAASSENES, whose rites included cultic homoeroticism.

Sisters of Perpetual Indulgence Spiritual, political, CARNIVALESQUE Order of (primarily) gay men identifying as NUNS, centered in San Francisco, founded circa 1979, and now an international phenomenon. There are now houses in Seattle, England (two in London), France, Germany, Australia, New Zealand, and elsewhere. The Sisters are deeply inspired by the ancient "tradition of religious parody," as Kevin Starr observes in "Indulging the Sisters" (1981), drawing especially upon the Medieval European Feast of Fools, which was itself inspired by the Roman Saturnalia. The Sisters are also inspired by Goddess Reverence and Women's Spirituality as well as by the Radical Faeries, as exemplified by a chant composed by Sister Boom Boom (aka Jack Fertig) in support of the "Take Back the Night" march of women against violence: "Black Goddess KALI, mother of all, / creator of all, destroyer of all . . . / AMAZON warrior goddess of wisdom, / ATHENA, endow us with might . . ." As Starr observes, "individuals among the Sisters who are of Catholic background [many are not] exorcise themselves of rage and guilt over what they consider the Church's hostility to their homosexuality." At the same time that they hold up a mirror to what they see as the hypocrisy of the Church, they honor the compassion and insight of certain Catholic saints and mystics. Since the early 1980s, the Sisters have been activists in the battle against AIDS; their *Play Fair* was the first of safe-sex pamphlets. In recent years, they have begun to campaign against the Religious Right. In the 1990s, the Sisters have also begun to embrace female drag nuns. Ian Lucas (1994) writes of the Sisters that they "might be seen as queer – undefined and outside of definition – in the most literal sense, taking on the role of the cross-dressing shaman."

Sithon In classical mythology, a king of Thrace, son of the nymph Ossa and Ares (or POSEIDON), said to be able to transform gender at will. In doing so, he was said to have "turned backside nature's law."

Sixtus IV, Pope (1414-1484) Born Francesco della Rovere, he entered the Franciscan order and studied philosophy and theology at the Universities of Padua and Bologna. He was made a cardinal by Pope Paul II in 1467 and elected pope in 1471. Known as a patron of the arts – commissioning paintings from Botticelli and others – he founded the Sistine Chapel and the first orphan's hospital. He became controversial not only for granting asylum to Spanish Jews but also for falling in love with his beautiful nephew, Raphael Riario, whom he made Papal Chamberlain and Bishop of Ostia. It was during his reign that a certain cardinal presented an official "petition to practice sodomy during the warm season, a suggestion to which, it was said, Sixtus IV gave serious consideration."

Sjöö, Monica (1938-)   Swedish bisexual artist, writer and leader of the Women's Spirituality movement. She has been inspired by "woman experiences of natural childbirth . . . bisexuality, menstrual creative and psychic powers . . . visions and dreams of the Goddess and . . . journeys to Her sacred sites." Since 1967, her works have expressed her devotion to Goddess Reverence and "earth magic." She is co-author with Barbara Mor of *The Great Cosmic Mother* (1987).

Skadi   Teutonic goddess of death and rebirth, and the shadow into which all the gods are drawn at Doomsday, or *Götterdammerung*. Daughter of the giant Thjazi, Skadi is an Amazonian hunter and warrior who shuns all men save ODIN. She is believed to demand the sacrifices of men's genitals, which she collects. In this respect, Skadi is associated with the castration of the god LOKI. While some say that she castrated Loki, others claim he emasculated himself in order to make her laugh.

Slater, Herman (1935-1992)   Gay high priest of Wicca (or Witchcraft), writer, and proprietor of The Magickal Childe occult shop in New York. One of his most popular works is *The Magickal Formulary* (1981).

Sleeve, Cut (or **Torn Sleeve**)   Among Chinese, homoeroticism is often referred to in the twentieth century as "*dong xian*," or "cut" or "torn sleeve." This nickname is derived from a tale concerning the Han emperor Ai (reigned 6 BCE-1 CE) and his lover, nicknamed Dong Xian. Legend has it that one morning, the Emperor wished to get out of bed without disturbing his still sleeping beloved. In order to do so, he tore or cut the sleeve of the garment he was wearing. In naming the love of one man for another *dong xian*, it would seem that the Chinese paid homage to these lovers. It is evident from literary texts that men-loving men of later epochs looked upon Emperor Ai and Dong Xian as non-biological ancestors. It is conceivable that when certain men, especially poets, expressed their love for one another, they viewed themselves as ritualistically remembering these lovers of long ago.

Smyrna, Female-Male of (fl. c. 50 CE)   Woman of Smyrna who transformed into a man, encountered by Licinius Muscianus (fl. c. 50 CE).

Smyth, Dame Ethel Mary (1858-1944)   Acclaimed British lesbian composer, perhaps most remembered today for her friendship with Virginia Woolf and for composing "The March of the Women" (1911), an early women's rights anthem. Many of Smyth's works were inspired by the sacred and the mythic, including *Mass in D*, the fairy tale opera *Fantasio*, the cantata *The Song of Love* (based on the Biblical *Song of Solomon*), and the opera *Fête Galante*. One aria from *Fantasio* is based on the Irish folksong "Come O'er the Sea," which in Smyth's life served to woo Lady Ponsonby, by inviting her "over the sea" to a place where they would be "free" and "no longer slaves." Sharp-witted Smyth told a story in her book *Female Piping in Eden* (1933) which reflected in a mythic manner her experience in the male-dominated world of music. "One afternoon while Adam was asleep," she relates, "Eve, anticipating the Great God Pan, bored some holes in a hollow reed and began to do what is called pick out a tune. Thereupon Adam spoke: 'Stop that horrible noise,' he roared, adding after a pause, 'besides which, if anyone's going to make it, it's not you but me!'"

Snow Queen, The   On the surface, this fairy tale, attributed to Hans Christian Andersen, is a tale of a young girl's search for a boy who has been abducted by the cruel Snow Queen. The figure of the Snow Queen, however, represents an archetype to which many homoerotically inclined men (perhaps including Andersen himself) have been drawn – simultaneously maternal, powerful, icy, and threatening. Lesbian women are also drawn to "The Snow Queen," perhaps because, as M. Duffy (1980) has suggested, the tale includes a sublimated lesbian relationship between Gerda and the "butch" robber girl who "sleeps with one arm around Gerda's neck, clasping a dagger with the other hand."

Snow White   In this well-known fairy tale attributed to the Brothers Grimm, a young princess who, escaping from her stepmother, a wicked queen who is also a witch, encounters seven dwarves with whom she stays until she is rescued by a handsome prince. In the retelling of the tale by Anne Sexton (1928-1974), the wicked queen's cruelty is surpassed by that of Snow White, who invites the former to her wedding only to clamp burning "red-hot iron shoes" on her feet when she arrives. Excepting her cruel streak, Snow behaves as a mindless doll, "rolling her china-blue doll eyes open and shut." In Olga Broumas's (b. 1949) complex revision of the story, an unnamed Snow White leaves an unnamed prince to return to the unnamed queen, who manifest herself as goddess, grandmother, mother, and lover. "I'm coming back / back to you," Broumas chants, "woman, flesh / of your woman's flesh, your fairest, most / faithful mirror." In his queer revision of the tale, "Snow White Revisited," Brazilian writer Darcy Penteado (b. 1926) tells the story of Antonio Matoso Nunes de Alvarenga, aka Snow White. Antonio is loved as a child, but as he grows up and becomes a drag queen, he begins to experience oppression as well as a certain degree of notoriety. As "she" ages, Snow grows determined to remain forever in the wooded park she has come to claim as her own. She waits to die until the major agrees to her wish, then buys an apple, injects it with insecticide, and dies. A miracle ensues: Snow in death, appears more youthful than ever, and her tomb becomes the "greatest tourist attraction" in Brazil. Thousands of pilgrims pay homage to her and ask her to answer their prayers. The tale ends, "Brazil . . . will be blessed with the joy . . . of having a saint of its own: Saint Snow White or the Saintly Faggot . . . May God and Holy Mother Church see fit to grant us that favor."

Sodom Biblical narrative occurring in the Book of Genesis (18 and 19) wherein Lot, a man devoted to the Lord, is visited by angels who destroy Sodom, the corrupt city in which he lives. Legend has it that the pillar of salt into which Lot's wife was transformed when she gazed at the burning city still exists. Afterwards, Lot engages in incest with his daughters. A number of Jewish and Christian apologists have argued that the tale of Sodom concerns *not* homosexuality but rather inhospitality, with the men of Sodom expressing rudeness toward Abraham and the angels. While they may be correct in their assumption as to the original meaning of the tale, it is evident that by the time of Philo Judaeus (fl. 40 CE), the tale of Sodom had become linked to homoeroticism. Islamic tradition clearly associates Sodom with homosexuality, with, ironically, Lot giving his name to sodomy, "*liwat*." In the Holy Quran (7: 81) the sin of "*sudum*" is described as "Lust with men in preference to women." Many others share the view that the tale focuses on divine vengeance visited upon practitioners of homoeroticism, gender variant behavior and Goddess Reverence, although many of these do not share the hostility of Islamic and other theologians. Classicist Michael Grant observes: "Sodom and Gomorrah [were] . . . representatives of Canaanite religion. The shrines of Canaan harboured male prostitutes [i.e. the QEDESHIM of the goddess ATHIRAT], [thus] the cities of the plain became emblems of the homosexuality that Yahweh so strongly condemned." Some archaeologists believe they have located the site of the city of Sodom in the vicinity of the Dead Sea, its contemporary name being Bab edh-Dhra. Beginning as a sacred site and necropolis, Sodom, or Bab edh-Dhra, later became a prosperous agricultural community producing grapes, pistachios, and chick peas. It appears to have been destroyed by fire, perhaps linked to an earthquake, near 2300 BCE. While remains have not yet revealed evidence of the institution of the *qedeshim*, they have verified the worship of the Goddess at the site, burial chambers yielding "clay figurines of the mother goddess." One such figure is gynandrous, indicating a recognition of transgenderism and possibly linked to the *qadesh*. For centuries, the story of Sodom has fueled the fires of persecution against the same-sex inclined and the transgendered. In the eighteenth and early nineteenth centuries, a British folkloric belief perceived the molly

culture as the reemergence of the city of Sodom, as exemplified by the pamphlet *The Phoenix of Sodom*, which was widely circulated in the early 1800s. In the 1990s, Fundamentalist Christians continue to employ the tale in order to secure continued prejudice against gays, lesbians, bisexuals, and transgendered individuals. Nevertheless, many homoerotically inclined artists have also been inspired by the tale of Sodom, including: the Symbolist painter Gustave MOREAU (1826-1898); the writer Marcel Proust (1871-1922), who, in *Cities of the Plain*, from his epic *Remembrance of Things Past* (1913-1927), warned against the "lamentable error of proposing (just as people have encouraged a Zionist movement) to create a Sodomist movement"; the French writer Saint Ours, who, in *Un Ange à Sodome* (1973), tells the tale of an angel who, falling in love with a beautiful, sophisticated man of Sodom, turns away from a vengeful God's orders; the filmmakers James Watson and Melville Webber, directors of the 1933 Camp film *Lot in Sodom*; and the poet Robert Duncan (1919-1988), who writes, "This place rumord to have been Sodom is blessed / in the Lord's eyes."

Soft Man In a tale widely circulated among the Chukchi of North Asia, a "soft man," i.e. a transgendered male practioner of Shamanism, clad in a woman's dress, takes part, with other members of the family, in corralling the reindeer herd. The wife of his brother taunts him, saying, "this one with the women's breeches does not seem to give much help." The "soft man" takes offense, and leaves the family camp. He goes away to the borderland of the Koryak, who assault him in his traveling tent. He, however, snatches his fire-board implement, and with its small bow of antler, shoots the wooden drill at his adversaries. Immediately it turns into a fiery shaft and destroys all of them one by one. He then takes their herd, and, coming back to his home, shows his newly acquired wealth to his relatives, saying "See now what that of woman's breeches was able to procure for you."

Sol Invictus-Elagabal The invincible Sun, an androgynous or transgendered deity whose cult gained great popularity in the late second and early third centuries CE. Sol was represented in the form of a large black conical stone, a meteorite. Women and persons of African descent played significant roles in the cult, as did homoerotically or bisexually inclined, gender variant males. Persons were encouraged to explore the feminine and masculine elements within themselves. For this reason, male devotees often dressed in feminine attire. Some practiced ritual castration. The most well known practitioner of the cult was one of its high priests, the Roman emperor ELAGABALUS.

Solomon, Simeon (1840-1905) Jewish, mystical, pre-Raphaelite artist and writer. Solomon wrote this brief autobiography: "As an infant he . . . developed a tendency toward designing. He had a horrid temper . . . He illustrated the Bible before he was sixteen. He was hated by all of his family before he was eighteen. He was eighteen at the time he was sent to Paris. His behaviour there was so disgraceful that his family – the Nathans, Solomons, Moses, Cohens, etc., et hoc genus homo – would have nothing to do with him. He returned to London to pursue his disgraceful course of Art . . . His 'Vision of Love Revealed in Sleep' is too well known. After the publication of this his family repudiated him forever." Born in London on October 9, 1840, Solomon was the youngest son of Meyer Solomon. Simeon's brother Abraham and his sister Rebecca were both artists. As a young man, Solomon became friends with Burne-Jones, Dante Gabriel Rossetti, Walter Pater, Swinburne, and others of the Pre-Raphaelite circle. Parties given by this circle allowed Solomon to express himself in wild drag; on one occasion, Solomon and Swinburne allegedly "chased each other naked down the staircase" at Rossetti's, much to the latter's dismay. Swinburne is to be credited with introducing Solomon to SADOMASOCHISM and to Walt WHITMAN's *Leaves of Grass* (1855). Solomon and Swinburne became enemies after Solomon, in a state of dire poverty, sold intimate letters that Swinburne had written to him. In 1868, Solomon and Oscar Browning, an Eton schoolmaster, became lovers; this was to be the happiest period of Solomon's life. In 1871, having achieved some notoriety as a painter and illustrator, Solomon published his erotico-spiritual prose-poem, *A Vision of Love Revealed in Sleep*, which was praised by John Addington Symonds but condemned by many others. Two years later, on February 11, 1872, Solomon was caught in a public urinal having sex with a man named George Roberts. The two were arrested and convicted. After a time in prison, Solomon may or may not have entered an asylum. Following his arrest, his friends deserted him. One story has it that Solomon took a room in the house of a dealer who would lock him in his room for long periods of time, passing food and drink under the door in exchange for a sketch or painting. Another relates that Solomon became a pavement artist and sold matches and shoe laces. Beyond these stories, it is certain that he spent the last years of his life as an inmate of the St Giles Workhouse in London, where he died of heart failure on August 14, 1905. While the rampant homophobia of his day clearly had much to do with Solomon's demise, it is evident that anti-Semitism and alcoholism, from which his sister also suffered, played a role in his destruction. Throughout his life, Solomon attempted to blend elements of Judaism, Catholicism, Graeco-Roman paganism, and western mysticism in his works. For Solomon, it was the archetypal figure of the androgyne in whom these elements merged. The androgyne became not only a symbol of spiritual totality but also one of gender and sexual identity. Figures of the androgynous male, representative of transgenderism and homoerotic love, abound in Solomon's work, being portrayed in *Amoris Sacramentum* (1868), *Dawn* (1870), *Love Dreaming By the Sea* (1871), *An Angel* (1887), *Love at the Waters of Oblivion* (1891), and many other works. The Goddess with her son or consort is also a favorite theme of Solomon's, depicted in *Night and Her Child Sleep* (1875) and elsewhere. Works especially revealing the intermingling of transgenderism, same-sex eroticism, and sacred experience include: *David Playing to King Saul* (1859), in which David, having long, flowing hair and wearing only jewelry, recalls the image of the QADESH of ATHIRAT as he entertains Saul; *The Bride, The Bridegroom and Sad Love* (1865), which depicts a nude heterosexual couple and a winged androgynous youth, showing the right hand of the "heterosexual" male grasping the genitals of "Sad," i.e. Homoerotic, Love, while the woman, in ecstasy, remains ignorant of this action; *Spartan Boys About to Be Scourged at the Altar of Diana* (1865), in which mothers lead their adolescent sons to the altar, where a bearded priest holding a figurine of the Goddess greets them, behind him a statue of the Goddess against which two effeminate priests or devotees lean; *Heliogabalus, High Priest of the Sun* (1866), showing the gender variant, homoerotically-inclined ruler leaning languidly against an altar. In *A Vision of Love Revealed in Sleep*, which might be described as a vision quest in search of love, Solomon writes: "A weakness fell upon me, but my Soul supported me; we looked forward, and saw one approaching clothed with a soft light; he moved towards us, gently lifted by the spirit from the ground . . . Ever and again his feet, wherefrom sprang glowing wings, touched the earth and caused it to bring forth flowers; his head was bound with a fillet of violet . . . he carried a mystic veil of saffron . . . and his shining body was half girt with fawn-skin . . . I went forward until I set myself in front of him who bore the saffron veil; the waves of Love that move about him laved my face, they refreshed me." In 1989, London-based writer, actor and theatre director Neil Bartlett (b. 1958) honored the memory of Solomon in creating and performing in a poetic drama based on Solomon's *Vision of Love*.

Soma In Hinduism, a god of the MOON, a priest, and a divine beverage. As a god, Soma is sometimes depicted as forming a male same-sex couple with AGNI, the god of FIRE. In this relationship, Soma represents the offering, envisioned as semen, while Agni represents that which, or he who, consumes the offering.

Sophia, Saint (n. d.) While her existence is controversial, and her origins may well lie in pre-Christian Goddess Reverence, Saint Sophia is depicted in some traditions of Christianity as the feminine or transgendered aspect of JESUS or of God the Father. A mystical tradition of

Christianity holds that Sophia entered into the body of Mary in order to cause her to become pregnant with Jesus. Generally regarded as a source of wisdom and compassion, St Sophia is fêted on August 1.

The Sorcerer and the Young Cook of Baghdad A tale found in the *Arabian Nights*, in which a sorcerer convinces a vizier to plunge into a magic cauldron. The vizier finds himself in a great sea. Swimming to shore, he discovers that he has become a woman. He, now she, eventually marries and gives birth to seven children. One day, she grows weary of life, and jumps into the sea. She suddenly finds herself in the cauldron once more. She has returned to being a man. The sorcerer tells him that he has been in the cauldron only for a few seconds.

Sots and Sotties Of the various types of fools wandering the earth or living at court during the Middle Ages and the Renaissance, the *sot*, most frequently associated with France and the Netherlands, was among those associated with gender variance, same-sex intimacy, and a CARNIVALESQUE spirituality. In Mikhail Bakhtin's view, the *sots*, while they performed in dramas called *sotties*, were not actors as such, but "remained fools and clowns always . . . They stood on the borderline between life and art." A. Struebel describes them as the children of pre-Christian worshippers, "banished from the sanctuaries." The history of the *sots* is a complex one, as clerics and others who joined them in performing *sotties* and who further joined fraternities organized by the *sots* also claimed or pretended to be true *sots*. The *sots per se* were often vagabonds who performed plays and other feats in exchange for food and lodging. Eventually some of them became more established, even renting a building in the Rue Darnetal in Paris which they named La Maison des Sotz Attendans. Cutting a figure which might remind us of Harlequin or Pierrot, the *sot* often dressed in a costume of green, yellow, and red, sometimes wearing artificial asses' ears attached to his cap, as well as articles of feminine attire such as aprons and head scarves, suggesting both theriomorphic (animal) and gender transformation. He sometimes appears also to have dressed in more somber tones, as a peasant woman or a nun. He might paint his face white, or cover it with flour, conveying a mime-like presence and perhaps, as one scholar has suggested, indicating his desire to be "whitened" with another man's semen. He frequently carried a *marotte*, a scepter topped by a bladder or a doll head depicting a *sot*. His costume appears to have inspired a fashion craze among bisexually and homoerotically inclined, gender variant courtiers. Ida Nelson explains in *La Sottie Sans Souci: Essai d'interprétation homosexuelle* (1976) that the "gallants of the court, in order to attract male minions, would wear tights with one leg of one color and the second of another." If the courtier's tights

opposed green and yellow, he might wear a red cap. The *sottie* was a type of burlesque performance meant to celebrate sex, food, games, and other pastimes, and to ridicule Church and State. Bawdy and outrageous, the *sotties*, says Ida Nelson, "were founded on gay (*gai*), homosexual desire." Indeed, the use of the word *gai* to refer to persons engaging in same-sex eroticism may have originated in the *sottie*, through its relationship to the word *joyeux*. The *sotties*, through their characters, reveal a complex Medieval French categorization of homoerotic activities and relationships. The *sot* himself signifies the receptive partner, while the *galant* represents the active partner. The *fol*, or "fool," signifies a bisexual male. While all three characters display gender variant traits, the *sot* is considered the most effeminate, while the *galant* is considered the most masculine. Even the structure of the *sottie*, developing from the rondeau, an Old French poetic form in which the opening lines also serve as a refrain, seems to underscore its relationship to homoeroticism. As Nelson explains, the circle functioned in Medieval France as a multivalent sign. Included among its significations were spiritual, divinatory, and magical ones linking the circle to the cycle of birth, death, and regeneration and to the related Wheel of Fortune. Among its other significations were erotic ones. One of these linked the circle to the "roundness of the anus, that part of the body which is indispensable to anal intercourse." Another of its erotic connotations linked the circle to the loop or cycle believed to be generated by the practice of simultaneous fellatio by both parties in a homoerotic relationship. The *sots* appear to have been not only homoerotically inclined, gender variant males but also pagans. They honored, albeit in their own carnivalesque style, a Goddess-like figure and her male consort. Those who speak of retentions and survivals believe that this figure, known variously as MÈRE (Mother) SOTTE, Mère Folle, and Folle Bobance, at one time may have been linked to CYBELE, as both were, like the Celtic CERNUNNOS, revered at Autun, a veritable citadel of paganism. If she has Greco-Roman roots, however, we would venture to guess that BAUBO and Iambe may be other figures which played a role in the creation of the Mother of the *sots*. Mère Sotte was typically portrayed as an elderly woman wearing a multicolored skirt and a cap with asses' ears. While P. Berger (1985) views her as a "figure of ridicule only," Nelson, perhaps more sensitive to CAMP, sees Mère Sotte as a creative force, a figure bringing joy, and, above all, celebrating the "joy of receptive homosexuality." "As soon as I'd cease being perverse," Mère Sotte tells us, "I'd die." Each February, from the Middle Ages until at least the mid-seventeenth century, the *sots* would parade through the streets of Autun pulling a cart in which Mère Sotte, represented by the local leader of the *sots*, would be seated. This figure may be the seated transvestite, nunlike figure being pulled by two similarly dressed figures in

Bruegel's *Fight Between Carnival and Lent*. The male consort of Mère Sotte was the SEIGNEUR DE JOYE (the Lord of Joy), also known as the Seigneur de Gayècté (the Lord of Gaiety); he is traditionally depicted as a *galant*. We know that in the fourteenth, and perhaps as early as the thirteenth, century, homoeroticism was linked in the popular psyche to the world of fools, including the *sots*. In an unfortunately homophobic and effemiphobic, dystopian novel of this period, *Berinús*, we read of a "sodomite" king, Agriano, who rules the inhabitants of the isle of Gamel. Here, homoeroticism and gender variant behavior are mandatory. The author of *Berinús* refers to the practice of same-sex eroticism as "foolish," not only because it is performed in defiance of God but also, and more importantly, because it "goes against reason." Thus, while we may not be able to posit a direct connection between *gai/gay* and "homosexual," an indirect connection may be posited – one which links *gai/gay* behavior not only to homoeroticism and gender variance but also to carnivalesque realm of the *sots* and their transformation of pre-Christian rites.

Soul Windows   Term used by African-American poet Countee CULLEN (1903-1946) to describe his reaction to reading Edward CARPENTER's *Iolaus*. "It opened up for me soul windows which had been closed; it threw a novel and evident light on what I had begun to believe, because of what the world believes, ignoble and unnatural. I loved myself in it."

Sparrow   In the poetry of Emily DICKINSON (1830-1886), alongside other small birds, symbolic of the lover who humbles herself before the beloved.

Sphinx   Hybrid being of Egyptian and Greek religion and mythology. Already part lion and part bird, the Sphinx is not only trans-species but also transgendered, appearing alternately as male, female, and androgynous. The Sphinx represents the riddles or mysteries of life, the trials presented to those seeking answers, and the key to the mysteries.

Spighi, Sister Clodesinde (fl. c. 1780)   Nun of the Dominican convent of St Catherine at Prato in Tuscany, Italy. She confessed to having participated in a woman-loving relationship with Sister Caterina Irene BUONAMICI, explaining that it was her belief that paradise might be experienced while one was still living by way of making love to a human incarnation of the Divine.

Spinster   This solitary, often elder, female figure of fairy and folk tales and nursery rhymes becomes, in the visionary cosmos of lesbian-feminist theologian and philosopher Mary DALY (b. 1928), an archetypal figure who, defining "her Self . . . neither in relation to children

nor to men," "participates in the whirling movement of creation" by spinning – in every sense of the term.

Sprinkle, Annie (aka **Anya,** birth name, **Ellen Steinberg**, b. c. 1955)   Lesbian – although "pansexual" might be a more appropriate term – ritual performance artist, (former) porn star, AIDS activist, and erotic healer. Sprinkle describes her transition from pornography to performance art as a "liberation from 'junk sex' toward an eclectic exploration of the outer reaches of sexuality, combining Eastern philosophy, yoga, meditative breathing, spirituality and healing." Viewing sexuality as a "path to enlightenment," she celebrates sex "as the nourishing, life-giving force. We embrace our genitals as part of, not separate from, our spirits . . . We empower ourselves by this attitude of sex-positivism. And with this love of our sexual selves we have fun, heal the world and endure." In the early 1990s, Sprinkle assumed another persona, that of Anya. "Anya is neither Ellen nor Annie . . . Anya's . . . a goddess . . . older and wiser." In 1995, Sprinkle, "presently in her 'lesbian separatist phase' and loving it," leads workshops in woman-centered TANTRA.

Srikandi   Javanese goddess bearing likeness to the Hindu goddesses CANDI (or Chandi), DURGA and KALI. Candi links Srikandi to the moon and to gynandry or transgenderism; while Durga and Kali link her to warrior women, or AMAZONS. In the Javanese version of the *Mahabharata*, Srikandi takes the role of the Amazonian wife of the hero-deity ARJUNA and the intimate companion of Lavasati, another of Arjuna's wives.

Stapleton, Douglas (aka **Gurlene Hussey**, 1963-   ) Queer-identified performance artist, poet, and dramatist living in Chicago in the 1990s. Inspired by such diverse traditions and movements as Christianity, Goddess Reverence, the Radical Faeries, Sufism, and Vodou, Stapleton juxtaposes humor and sadness, exemplified by the archetypal figures of the TRICKSTER and the CRONE, to "create a mood of extremes" and to nurture in both himself and his audience a "heightened state of passion." Stapleton's "performance alter-ego" is Gurlene Hussey, whom he describes as "that channeled demi-urge and progenitor of my creative self. She, as art priestess/critic of social and gender constructions, cajoles, threatens, beseeches and prophesies her way into understanding her relationship with the Beloved . . . [who is] both human and divine." Deities with whom Gurlene resonates, Stapleton notes, include the Togo mermaid-goddess Mami Wata and the Vodou *lwa* ERZULIE, the latter "an embodiment of sensual pleasures, love, and devotion as well as the wellspring of deep sorrows. Many times, she cries the inconsolable tears of the world – the deepest, unspoken pains of loss." In *Our Whirling Endures* (1996), a performance piece written by Stapleton and Beth Tanner,

Gurlene chants, "two passions / the erotic and the mystical / speak one language / one tongue."

Starhawk (birth name **Miriam Simos**, 1951-) Bisexual feminist Witch, writer, and political activist of Jewish heritage. Her book *The Spiral Dance* (1979) has been pivotal in shaping Witchcraft, or Wicca, as it is practiced in the final decades of this century, in its weaving together of the personal, the political, and the spiritual, and more particularly in its linking of Goddess Reverence to both Shamanism and feminist theory, and its insistence upon the acceptance of sexual and gendered diversity within the Craft. A gifted essayist as well as writer of fiction, Starhawk's more recent works include *Dreaming the Dark* (1982), *Truth or Dare* (1987), and *The Fifth Sacred Thing* (1993). Founder of Reclaiming, a Wiccan group based in San Francisco, Starhawk teaches internationally. She appears in Donna Read's highly acclaimed documentary on Witchcraft and the Inquisition, *The Burning Times* (1990).

Stein, Diane (1948-) Writer, healer, activist in the anti-war, lesbian feminist, and gay movements in the US, and Wiccan priestess of the Goddess. Her works include *The Kwan Yin Book of Changes* (1985), *The Women's Spirituality Book* (1986), *Stroking the Python: Women's Psychic Experience* (1988), *The Goddess Book of Days* (1989), and *Casting the Circle: A Women's Book of Ritual* (1990).

Stikla In Teutonic lore, woman warrior and intimate female companion of RUSLA.

Stoicism Philosophical tradition founded by ZENO OF CITIUM (335-263 BCE) emphasizing rationality, duty, virtue, and harmony, holding that "divine reason [is] a Natural Law leading to a universal brotherhood of men." Many Stoics appear to have been homoerotically inclined and, while preferring shaven faces, were (in contrast to many Greeks) more given to relationships with adult males than with youths.

Stone Maiden (Shih Fu) Chinese term used during or prior to the eighteenth century to refer to a basically biological female with certain hermaphroditic characteristics or to a female-to-male transgendered person. Such a person was described as "not male not female" but "one of those stone maidens." A celebrated Ming Dynasty play, *Peony Pavilion*, suggests that "stone maidens," of which the character Sister Stone of Purple Light Convent is a bawdy representative, often became shamans or nuns. From certain stories of the period, it appears that many believed Buddha or the gods to be responsible for the creation of "stone maidens."

Stone Man (Shih Nan) Chinese term used during or prior to the eighteenth century to refer to a basically biological male with hermaphroditic characteristics or to a male-to-female transgendered person. Such persons were often identified with eunuchs and transvestites (*yaojen*). From certain stories of the period, it appears that many believed that, as was the case with "stone maidens," the Buddha or the gods were responsible for the creation of "stone men."

Strirajya Meaning "female realm," *strirajya* are female kingdoms of Hindu legend. *Strirajya* were said to be located in northern India as well as in Afghanistan, Orissa, Nepal, and Tibet, and on distant islands. Many atrocities committed during wars had resulted in women taking over men's responsibilities, including governance. In the *Mahabharata*, we learn of *strirajya* where lesbian eroticism, including cunnilingus, mutual masturbation, and copulation with dildoes, was widely practiced. In the *Ramayana*, we learn that in the palaces of Lanka, women likewise often joined in passionate embraces. Women of the *strirajya* kingdoms were believed to be especially adept at sorcery.

Strophios In ancient Greece a broad band, usually made of leather, worn around women's breasts for support. When worn by men, the *strophios* signified transgenderism.

Subrahmanya Name of a chant as well as an ancient Dravidian folk divinity in India who became identified with the Hindu god KARTIKKEYEH. A weather deity, Subrahmanya is considered transgendered. His-her chants are noted for their magical powers to summon the winds, thunder, and rain (the last of which is itself considered transgendered). His-her priests, also called *subrahmanya*, are likewise described as being of "three genders – man, woman, and neuter."

Summers, Montague (1880-1948) Associated with the URANIAN POETS, his relationship to Queer Spirit is problematic. In or around 1907, Summers seems to have begun participating in or holding Satanic Black Masses which apparently included the sacrifice of a black cock; others suggest that he was holding Catholic-like masses save for ritual homoeroticism. In a poem written in 1907, "To a Dead Acolyte," he conjures a vision of these ceremonies, this one centering on the death of a young man: "Thy lips are still and pale / Pale from Death's icy kiss," he writes, "No mass more sweet than this is, / A liturgy of kisses." Studying at the Anglican theological college at Lichfield in England, he took deacon's orders in 1908. After being appointed to a curacy in Bath followed by one in Bitton, his position was terminated when he was accused of practicing intergenerational male eroticism. In reaction to this and other events, Summers embraced Catholicism; he claimed to be a priest, referring to himself as a Reverend. Nevertheless, he seems to have performed a Satanic Black Mass at his home chapel regularly through at least 1918. That year, he met Anatole James (pseudonym of Geoffrey Evans Pickering) with whom he became intimately involved. He quickly became disillusioned with James, however, due to the latter's disinterest (James was an agnostic) in his spiritual pursuits, especially in his boredom with the Black Mass. At this time, Summers also knew the ritual magician Aleister CROWLEY and participated with Edward CARPENTER and many other homoerotically and bisexually inclined and transgendered persons in the British Society for the Study of Sex Psychology (BSSSP). In 1923 he had a serious falling out with James which appears to have been linked to a growing self-hatred both in terms of his homosexuality and his spiritual eccentricities; around this time he also severed ties with members of the BSSSP. In the mid- to late 1920s, he began writing fairly well researched yet extremely subjective, virulent tracts on Witchcraft and Satanism, making no distinction between them. Among these books are *The History of Witchcraft and Demonology* (1926), *The Geography of Witchcraft* (1927), and *Witchcraft and Black Magic* (1946). When others were fighting to remove laws against the practice of Witchcraft, or Wicca, he was insisting upon the death penalty for the practice. For the remainder of his life, it seems, he struggled within himself to bury his attraction to other males and to non-Christian spiritual paths. Nevertheless, he seems never to have given up wearing makeup and a treasure-chest of jewelry.

Sun   In Euro-western ASTROLOGY, this celesial body governs gradual change, creativity, growth, health, hope, prosperity, success, and vitality. According to *The Book of the Secrets*, attributed to Albertus Magnus (1205-1280), persons ruled by the Sun, that is, born under the sun sign of LEO, will tend to behave in a "masculine" manner regardless of genital anatomy. Figures associated with the sun and with gender and/or sexual variance include: ADONIS, AMATERASU OMI KAMI, APOLLO, CALLING GOD, KRISHNA, LEGBA, MAWU-LISA, OSHUMARE, SEKHMET, TALKING GOD, and VISHNU. In twentieth-century Mexico, "sun and shadow" (*sol y sombra*) is symbolic of homoeroticism.

Svin-fells-âs (or **Snoefells-âs**)   In Teutonic folklore, a male, fairy-like spirit of the mountains. Svin-fells-âs lives with another male being whom he transforms into a female every ninth night. It is suggested that the two spirits share an intimate relationship.

Swan   Bird frequently symbolic of purity, grace, melancholy, music, death (hence the expression "swan song") and rebirth, spiritual enlightenment, and androgyny or transgenderism, with its neck being perceived as phallic and its body as feminine. In Greek religion and myth, the swan is an attribute of APOLLO, CYCNUS, and HYACINTHUS. Certain North Asian myths allied with Shamanism depict swans as female beings who occasionally become lovers of males only to yearn to return to the all-female societies in which they have been reared. In Shakespeare's *As You Like It*, the swan becomes a metaphor for female-centered desire, with Celia saying to Rosalind, "We still have slept together, / . . . And whereso'er we went, like Juno's swans, / Still we went coupled and inseparable." In her 1922 poem "Love Song," lesbian Elsa GIDLOW writes, "You are a wild swan I have caught and housed in my heart."

Sweetgrass   Hidatsa TWO-SPIRIT male MIATI wore braids of sweetgrass looped around their left shoulders. One young Native American male who was determined to escape a deity's call to transgendered shamanhood began to see loops of sweetgrass everywhere he looked.

Sx'nts   Among the Bella Coola Indians of British Columbia, Sx'nts is a TWO-SPIRIT guardian of female spirits as well as of the two-spirit persons of the tribe.

Symonds, John Addington (1840-1893)   Homoerotically inclined British writer and classicist. In a letter to Edmund Gosse dated February 28, 1890, Symonds wrote: "You will not doubt, I am sure, that what you call 'the central Gospel' of that essay on the Greeks, has been the light and leading of my own life." Symonds' journey toward the recognition of his own homosexuality, as well as of the interrelationship of homoeroticism and the realm of spirit, commenced around 1848, when he began having dreams in which naked sailors would appear to him and he would have sex with them. Around this time, he was also experimenting in same-sex eroticism with an older cousin, especially fellatio. Around 1855, these dreams faded, but were replaced by dreams of a "beautiful ideal youth, who clasped him round." Later, this vision was displaced by dreams of "the large erect organs of naked young grooms or peasants." In 1858, when Symonds was eighteen, he read both the *Symposium* of PLATO and Walt WHITMAN's *Leaves of Grass*. These, more than any other texts, would become Symonds's bibles. This was also the year he fell in love with a young man named Willie Dyer. In 1864, Symonds, writing a poem to the spirit of a deceased young man who knew his father but whom he had never met, imagines that they might have been lovers. The poem is important because it heralds three of the central themes of Symonds's developing homoerotic spirituality: (1) the deep soul connection felt between men-loving men, expressed as "We should have gauged each other's soul;" (2) the possibility that men-loving men constitute a different species, expressed as "And learned the secrets of our blood;" and (3) that love between men could initiate utopian society, expressed as "Till Truth and Peace [are] multiplied." Symonds was, however, to experience great oppression during his life, including an operation on his genitals which was believed to cure homosexuality and marriage to a woman whom he did not love and who destroyed much of his homoerotic work. In "How Shall I Speak?" written in 1867, Symonds speaks of the isolation he feels: "the great Zeus hath hid / This love within a labyrinth each soul / must tread unfriended and without a clue." Later in life, however, he came to be increasingly more at peace with his homosexuality, returning to his early image of homoerotic desire as flowing from the spirit. In 1878, at Davos Platz, Switzerland, Symonds became lovers with a nineteen-year-old Swiss athlete named Christian Buol, whom he described as having "the vast chest of a young Hercules" as well as a "young Achilles." Three years later, he met and fell in love with the bisexual Venetian gondolier Angelo Fusato, who had blue eyes and raven hair and who became an "ANGEL" in many of Symonds' poems, especially in the cycle *Stella Maris*. In poem 16 he wrote: "I saw thee slumbering in the gates of dreams, / And seemed to see beneath the calm moonbeams / Thy pure white bosom all uncovered, / Thou loveliest angel flown from paradise!" In a letter to Havelock Ellis dated May 6, 1890, Symonds expresses his belief, inspired by his love for men as well as his reverence for the homoerotic expressions of Greek and Renaissance culture and for Whitman's "Calamus" poems, that a spirituality "lurking in manly love" may represent "the stuff of a new spiritual energy, the liberation of which would prove of benefit to society." In a letter to Edward CARPENTER March 20, 1892, Symonds referred to this homoerotic spirituality as "the new religion," and in another letter to Carpenter dated December 29, 1892, he wrote: "You raise a very interesting question with regard to physiological grounds for this passion. I have no doubt myself that the absorption of semen implies a real modification of the physique of the person who absorbs it, and that, in these homosexual relations, this constitutes an important basis for subsequent conditions – both spiritual and corporeal. It is a pity that we cannot write freely on the topic. But when we meet, I will communicate to you facts which will prove beyond all doubt to my mind that the most beneficent results, as regards health and nervous energy, accrue from the sexual relation between men: also, that when they are carried on with true affection, through a period of years, both comrades become united in a way which would be otherwise quite inexplicable." In one of his final poems, "Leander," published in *The Spirit Lamp* in February 1893, Symonds depicts the spirit of homoerotic love as the "Live image of URANIAN love." APOLLO is the central deity of Symonds's homoerotic pantheon, described in "Love and Death" as "A mightier spirit than my own," bestowing him with the courage to both accept and reveal

his feelings of love for other men. Apollo is the god of the sun, health, athletics, heroism, male beauty, and homoeroticism. If Apollo is the central deity of the "new Religion," it is Whitman who becomes its messiah. Whitman is described as "Bard sublime / To whom the keys of mysteries are given, / Throned in thine orb, filfilling Space and Time." He is further compared to a "new-born star" and specifically to the Star of Bethlehem, suggesting a relationship to JESUS Christ. This "new religion" will be founded on homoerotic love: "New laws of love to link and intertwine / Majestic peoples: Love to weld and weave / Comrade to comrade, man to bearded man." The disciples of this "new religion" will come from various walks of life. They will include poets, athletes, and soldiers. They will reside "On every upland and in every town." They will share homoerotic love. Together, they will form an army of lovers that will be even "nobler than that ancient vaunt / Of Arthur or of Roland" or the "Sacred Host" of "Theban Lovers." As such, they will fulfill the ideals of "Chivalry" and "Freemasonry." "Through love, they / Shall make the world one fellowship, and plant / New Paradise for nations yet to be." If Apollo is god, and Whitman messiah, then Symonds is a priest of the "new religion." "At this shrine," he writes, "I bid the nations to their feast / Of sacramental bread and hallowed wine, / Outpoured and broken in far distant days / For lips of Lovers holy and divine." The rituals of the new faith will include the reverence of Apollo as well as the honoring "bygone bards and athletes" and other lovers of men with "nard and frankincense and myrrh."

Syrinx "Reed." A huntress loved by the Greco-Roman goddess ARTEMIS/DIANA who, not impressed by PAN or his enormous phallus, ran from his embrace, begging the Naiads to save her. They did so by transforming her into water reeds. Pan, feeling guilty, made his pipes from the reeds, naming the instrument the syrinx in memory of the young woman.

Szymanowski, Karol (1882-1937) Polish composer and director of the Warsaw Conservatory from 1927-1931. Visits to Sicily, Algeria, Tunisia, and Cuba appear to have encouraged him to come to terms with his sexuality. *Ephebos*, a novel written in 1918, which unfortunately perished in the bombing of Poland in World War II, celebrated male beauty and homoeroticism. His opera *King Roger* integrates homoeroticism and the mythic or sacred. Written near the same time as his novel, it reveals musical influences of Wagner, Chopin, Scriabin, and Bartok; literary influences of Euripides, Walter Pater, and the composer's cousin Jaroslaw Iwaskiewicz; and spiritual influences of Christianity, Islam, and ancient Greek religion. The opera (which was not performed in the United States until 1988) depicts the legendary conversion of King Roger II to the cult of Dionysus; the king is

convinced to do so by a young shepherd devotee with
whom he falls in love. D. Fernandez (1989) describes *King
Roger* as a "magnificent work of sonorous mysteries, at
once oratorio, mass and drama, this opera . . . exalted
homosexuality." Others have, to the contrary, condemned
the opera as being extremely homophobic.

T

Ta-chueh and Chih-yan The central figures of a Chinese tale of the late sixteenth or early seventeenth century, probably based on living persons. Ta-chueh was a bisexual Taoist monk, Chih-yan his younger lover. According to the tale, they lived at a monastery called Tai Ping in Sichuan province. "Their erotic passion was said to be beyond description."

Tadzio One of the most haunting figures of twentieth-century literature and film, the beloved male youth of Thomas Mann's 1913 novella and Luchino Visconti's 1971 film *Death in Venice* (starring Dirk Bogarde, Silvana Mangano, and Bjorn Andresen). Gustav von Aschenbach, a writer in the novella and a composer (resembling Gustav Mahler) in the film, journeys to Venice to find himself in the midst of a powerful visionary experience weaving together Greek paganism, homoeroticism, death, immortality, and art, crystallized in his difficult attempt to relate to the ADONIS-like Polish youth Tadzio as a PLAGUE engulfs the city. "Often, when the sun was sinking," Mann writes, and von Aschenbach was observing Tadzio from a distance, "it was HYACINTH[US] that he seemed to be watching, Hyacinth who was to die . . . he, too, growing pale, caught the drooping body – and the flower, sprung from this sweet blood, bore the inscription of his unending grief."

Tages Magical child who sprang miraculously from the earth in Etruria. While he remained only long enough to utter a prophecy to those who witnessed his emergence before vanishing, his great beauty caused him to become, like EROS in Greece, an Etruscan patron of homoerotic love.

Takahashi Mutsuo (1937-) Homoerotically inclined Japanese writer. Takahashi began writing as a youth, his childhood marred by the "death of his father, separation from his mother, poverty, and . . . Japan's defeat in World War II." His first book, *Mino, atashi no oushi* (*Mino, My Bull*, 1959), a collection of poems, was published when he was twenty-two. This book has been followed by numerous others, including a novel, *Zen no henreki* (*Zen's Pilgrimage*, 1974), in which a "young provincial journeys through Tokyo's erotic underground, seen as a transmutation of the various realms of the Buddhist cosmos," and two other collections of poems, *Poems of a Penisist* (1975) and *A Bunch of Keys* (1984). In the *Kodansha Encyclopedia of Japan* (1983), Takahashi's work is described as focusing on an "intense dual preoccupation with eroticism and religion . . . His eroticism is homosexual . . . [and] in the area of religion, Takahashi's interests extend from Roman Catholicism . . . to Eastern Orthodoxy and Mahayana Buddhism" – not to mention Euro-western mythology, Goddess Reverence, and Shinto. Burton Watson stresses that it is the "rapt integration of the physical with the spiritual that is the whole point" of Takahashi's work. Takahashi's own term for this integration is "sacred pornography." In *Poems of a Penisist*, Takahashi distinguishes between homosexuality as practiced by the Greeks and as practiced by Japanese "penisists." The "penisist," he claims, confines his activities to masturbation and oral sex; he views anal intercourse as an imitation of heterosexual coitus. The "penisist" holds that the action of the penis filling the mouth is the "essence" of homosexuality. Furthermore, the "essence of homosexuality is not on the side of the phallus, but on the side of the oral cavity." The penis, according to Takahashi, represents the "absolute other, which is perfect," while the mouth represents "emptiness . . . the imperfection of human existence." Moreover, the "homosexual" is concerned primarily with sex, while the "penisist" is concerned primarily with eroticism; Takahashi explains that "eroticism" embraces sexuality as well as creativity and spirituality. In "penisism," the "male homosexual and the penis go toward . . . prayer and the supernatural." In his poetry Takahashi vividly demonstrates the "rapt integration" of the physical and the spiritual. In "Ode," for example, he describes the glans penis as an "infant in the straw of a stable" (alluding to JESUS) and the "dome of a great temple that the tongue / of the rain goddess wets on a bright / summer evening." The trunk of the penis is transformed into a "decorative sword inlaid with agate and jade." Testicles become "mandarin oranges guarded by Hsi Wang-Mu's / ladies in waiting / Litchi nuts with a taste of tears," as well as an "amulet bag." Semen is envisioned as "Sacred water that wells up on Okeonos' purifying island / . . . carried in the beak of a sapient dove / To Olympus, to the lips of the gods." A shadowy rendezvous for gay men is transformed into a celestial paradise. "At this very moment, in heaven's lavatory," the poet inquires of his reader, "among young ANGELS, / Are you dreamily jerking off?" "To climb and descend are one," Takahashi observes, "As in the Eleusinian mysteries." Jesus Christ becomes for Takahashi a patron of gay men or "penisists." "Be the father for homosexuals," he pleads of Jesus in "Christ for Thieves" – "One infinitely gentle . . . And give me a tiny, tiny happiness / A manly lover."

Talan Dish of fried pastry served as an offering to the Hindu goddess BAHUCHARAMATA and to her transgendered devotees, the HIJRAS.

Taledhek In Javanese culture, court servants who were said to be homoerotically inclined and transgendered and whose songs accompanying the *gamelan* were believed to carry magical power.

Taliesin (may have lived during the sixth century CE) Legendary Welsh bard and wizard "of the shining brow," compared to MERLIN. Renowned as a poet and riddler, Taliesin was especially skilled at raising storms and at shapeshifting, including metamorphosing from male to female.

Talking God (Xactceoltohi) In the Navaho religion or mythology of Native America, a deity of the dawn, the east, and hunting. He is a guardian of animals and serves mortals as a mentor being invoked in the Nightway and in other chants. Talking God was made from white CORN by Changing Woman (or Turquoise Woman); hence his other name, White Body. He is frequently paired in a relationship of polarity with CALLING GOD. Talking God lives in a sacred mountain in the east with one of the twin TWO-SPIRIT deities named SHOOTING GOD.

Talos A lover of RHADAMANTHYS, Talos was either (according to various accounts), a masculine robot fashioned by Daedalus or the Greek god HEPHAESTUS, created to protect Crete, or a young hero named after this robot.

Tan, the Lord of An-Ling (or **Lord An-Ling**, fl. c. 350 BCE) Male lover of King Chu Xiang Wang (ruled 369-340 BCE), who became an archetypal image of the beautiful male beloved in Chinese poetry.

Tano Among the Akan people of Ghana, an androgynous or transgendered deity of both the earth, and thus fertility, and the heavens.

Tantra Spiritual path, most probably of pre-Hindu, Indus Valley origin, absorbed into Hinduism and referred to as a type of yoga. Tantra generally emphasizes the interrelationship of the sensuous and the sacred. The Divine Feminine is revered in the form of the goddess or feminine principle SHAKTI, who manifests herself in serpentine form as Kundalini. Through certain Tantric practices, which may include meditational techniques and the eating of certain foods, such as fish and wine, as well as cultic eroticism, Tantrists experience within their own and at times their partners' bodies the merging of Goddess (Shakti, Kundalini) and God (SHIVA) to attain the state of divine androgyny (ARDHANARISHVARA). Although

certain Tantrists, influenced by patriarchal customs, have abused women in order to achieve an altered state of consciousness, Tantra is not inextricably bound to patriarchal or heterocentric beliefs or practices; indeed, when divorced from such mores, it stresses a transgender process. V. L. Bullough (1976) observes, "There is obvious homosexual connotation in some Tantric theory. It seems clear that each partner in the sex act must reorient and refashion his personality, recognizing the elements of the opposite sex in himself or herself." Alain Daniélou and others have suggested that homoerotic Tantric rites have been undertaken by devotees of the Hindu god GANESHA. Although little research has been done on Tantra where lesbianism is concerned, a form of lesbian Tantra is indicated by works of sacred art including stone sculptures, such as those portraying cultic lesbianism at the Hindu temple at Khajuraho and at Borobudur in Java, the latter dedicated to the goddess CANDI, as well as paintings, such as the "Lesbian Scene" in the Hindu-inspired Islamic *Koka Shastra*, a seventeenth-century treatise on physical love. In *Lesbian Sacred Sexuality* (1995), Diane MARIECHILD describes Tantra as a "radical understanding of the inherent unity of the universe . . . Our sexual communion becomes Tantric when it serves as initiation to the 'body' of the universe."

Taqqiq TWO-SPIRIT male or transgender male-to-female Inuit deity or spirit. Nicknamed "Brother Moon," Taqqiq is said to be a "great dispenser of shamanic 'light'" and is invoked especially during periods of great crisis. Taqqiq is a protector of orphans and of abused women; he (-she) also provides wild game and inspires fertility. Typically invoked when the moon is full, Taqqiq is revered by Inuit two-spirit shamans, who also honor KANNAALUK, NAARJUK, and other sacred beings.

Tara Star-goddess or BODHISATTVA revered in Hinduism, Tibetan Buddhism, and TANTRA. As a compassionate divine being, she is compared to the Chinese *bodhisattva* KUAN YIN. As a goddess of death and regeneration, she is associated with KALI. Tara is above all a divine instructor in mystical practices, including erotico-sacred practices, leading to enlightenment. Men meditating upon Tara are said to undergo a transgender process as the Goddess or *bodhisattva* enters their bodies in the form of a ray of light, often green in hue. Diane MARIECHILD (1995) describes a vision in which she discovers herself once more in a cave in Katmandu, in which Tara appears to her seated on a throne. In this vision, Mariechild merges with the consort of Tara. "The Goddess," she writes, "began making love to me . . . I felt great bliss as the Goddess melted into me . . . the pleasure of our union spread from my *yoni* [the vagina inspirited] throughout my entire body." Mariechild relates that this vision has found its way into her lovemaking in this reality:

"My lover becomes a Goddess or the Buddha Tara, and I am her devotee."

Tarot Pack of seventy-eight cards (typically) used in divination. The Tarot is divided into: the Major Arcana, representing archetypal forces and major life experiences; the Court Cards, representing aspects of the Self and others one may encounter; and the Minor Arcana, representing lessons and opportunities. The Minor Arcana are usually divided into four suits: pentacles, associated with earth and material reality; cups, associated with water, the emotions, and intuition; swords, associated with air, the intellect, and decision-making; and wands, associated with passion, in terms of erotic desire as well as artistic, political, and spiritual passion. The precise origins of the Tarot are unclear. The Tarot contains a vast amount of data gleaned from many cultures and historical epochs and, in the manner of a syncretic religion, adapts to the symbols and values of cultures and periods interacting with it. Thus, in the twentieth century, the Tarot, both in terms of new decks and interpretations of older ones, has begun to reflect the rise in queer consciousness as well as feminism, multiculturalism, and alternative spiritual paths. Already in the early to mid-twentieth century, Tarot scholars and practitioners including Oswald Wirth and the bisexual magician Aleister CROWLEY were suggesting that certain cards might be associated with gender and/or sexual variance. Wirth, for example, in *Le Tarot des imagiers* (1927), indicated that the Death (XIII), Temperance (or Art, XIV) and Devil (or Pan, XV) cards of the Major Arcana form a triadic relationship, with the Death card being neither male nor female, the Temperance card being gynandrous or Amazonian, and the Devil card being bisexual or pansexual. According to Crowley in *The Book of Thoth* (1944, 1981), several cards reflect gender and/or sexual variance, including the Fool (0), the Magician (I), the High Priestess (II), The Hierophant (V), the Lovers (VI), and Temperance/Art (XIV). The Fool, signifying innocence, wonder, risk-taking, and the beginning of a great journey, corresponds, says Crowley, to Zeus Arrhenothelus, who represents the fusion of "masculine and feminine . . . the true Hermaphroditic nature of the symbol," as well as Dionysus Zagreus (or Bacchus Diphues), "double-natured . . . more bisexual than hermaphroditic . . . a young and virile, but effeminate man." The Magician, representing communication, magic, and the role of psychopomp or soul-guide, corresponds, suggests Crowley, not only to the Hermaphrodite but also to an aspect of the god HERMES (or Mercury) invoked in homoerotic sex MAGIC. The High Priestess, signifying feminine wisdom and independence, corresponds to the Amazonian, lesbian goddess ARTEMIS/DIANA. The Hierophant, signifying esoteric knowledge, for Crowley corresponds not only to the high priest of the ELEUSINIAN MYSTERIES but also to "the

woman girt with a sword . . . Venus as she now is in this new aeon; no longer the mere vehicle of her male counterpart, but armed and militant." As the Lovers card is usually the most heterocentric of all the cards of the Tarot deck, it is somewhat surprising that Crowley attributes to it both gender variant and homoerotic significance, giving it the alternate names of The Twins and The Brothers, subtly referring to the homoerotic myth of Horus and SET, and asserting that its mystery concerns "some form of Hermaphroditism." Crowley links the Temperance/Art card, signifying the creative process, synthesis, and metamorphosis, to Artemis/Diana, this time as a huntress and, like Wirth, claims the card for the gynandrous figure. Crowley describes the alchemist portrayed in the card as a black king merging with a white queen. While the card, like that of the Lovers, clearly speaks to interracial desire and harmony, it is also quite evident that Lady Frieda Harris – the artist of *The Book of Thoth* – has not painted the alchemist as a typical androgyne but rather as a DOUBLE female being. The two heads, beyond color, match in terms of both facial appearance and hairstyle. The figure is multi-breasted, recalling Artemis of Ephesus, and wears a single feminine emerald gown covered with BEES, symbolizing the *melissae*, the bee-priestesses of Artemis. More recently, the political and spiritual liberation movements of the later twentieth century have demonstrated a profound impact on the Tarot; this has been especially true in terms of its interaction with feminism and lesbian-feminism. The illuminating work of writer Rachel Pollack, an activist in the transgender movement, has also proven a major influence. Gay and bisexual men have not made as much of an impact as have others in this area, but gay activist Carl Wittman wrote an article on the subject for the gay men's journal *RFD* as early as 1974. Wittman wonders, "What would a gay Tarot be like? . . . What light does this system shed on my growth as a faggot?" Wittman links the spiritual journey depicted in the Tarot to the process of coming out as a gay man. In 1976, Sally Gearhart, a lesbian-feminist activist and writer of the San Francisco Bay Area, and Susan Rennie published a pivotal work, *A Feminist Tarot: A Guide to Intrapersonal Communication*, which offered a woman-identified interpretation of the popular Smith-Waite deck. This work, as well as a Tarot renascence occurring in the Bay Area from the mid-1970s through the mid-1980s, inspired numerous woman-identified decks and interpretations inclusive of lesbian desire, love, and community and very much linked to the rising movements of Goddess Reverence and Witchcraft (or Wicca). These decks include: the *Motherpeace Round Tarot*, created by Vicki NOBLE and Karen VOGEL; *Shekinah's Tarot*, by Shekinah Mountainwater; the *Amazon Tarot*, by Billie Potts, Susun Weed, and River Lightwomon; *Daughters of the Moon Tarot*, by Ffiona MORGAN; *Thea's Tarot*, by Ruth West; and *The Book of*

Aradia, by Jean Van Syke. As Diane STEIN (1988) explains, the major differences between these and traditional Tarot decks "is in their emphasis on personal power and transformation, on female and goddess images of all races and cultures, and on women's spirituality." Especially noticeable in these decks is the celebration of woman-identified/lesbian desire, love, and community, as in the Lovers card of the *Amazon Tarot*, which portrays three women embracing. Also noticeable are such cards as the Emperor (IV) and the Hierophant (V), which may not speak to the political and spiritual power of these figures but to the abuse of that power in a patriarchal system. Rachel Pollack, activist in the transgender movement, has written some of the most influential interpretive texts on the Tarot published in the twentieth century, including *Seventy-Eight Degrees of Wisdom* (1980, 1983), *Salvador Dali's Tarot* (1985), *The New Tarot* (1989), and *The Haindl Tarot* (1990). For Pollack, one of the cards richest in transgender symbolism is the final card of the Major Arcana, the World, or Universe (XXI). In *Seventy-Eight Degrees of Wisdom*, comparing the image portrayed on the card to ARDHANARISHVARA, the androgynous form of the Hindu deity SHIVA as he merges with the goddess PARVATI, Pollack writes, "The World dancer is hermaphroditic, the dual sexual organs concealed by the banner, as if to say that the unity they represent lies beyond our knowing . . . The dancer expresses and unites all the different sides of being."

Tattoo J. E. Cirlot (1962) describes tattooing as an "expression of cosmic activity," writing, "a mystic purpose lies at the root of the mark or sign of identification: he who brands himself seeks to display his allegiance to that which is signified by the mark." Affiliatory tattooing may designate such things as one's devotion to a deity, one's tribe, one's gender, one's desires, one's fears, one's lover. The tattoo may also, or simultaneously, serve as a marker of an initiation undergone or sacrifice made and as a magical talisman serving to protect or attract. More directly relating the tattoo to queerness, G. Woods (1987) speculates: "The frequency with which tattoos are mentioned in the literature of male homoeroticism has to do with a number of discernible connections between male homosexual activity and the practice of tattooing. Both have been outlawed by the [Christian] Church . . . Both occur, in various forms, in initiation ceremonies. Both are considered to be predominant in groups of men forced to live closely together. Both are concerned with the beauty of flesh." Woods then quotes H. Ebenstein, who in *Pierced Hearts and True Love* (1953) stresses the ritualistic weaving together of erotic pleasure and pain in the tattooing process. Judy Grahn (1984) observes that "Most lesbians who get tattooed do it as a form of self-assertion, of pride, and as the expression of a daring personal aesthetic . . . [of] 'dykeliness'." To date, little has surfaced in terms

of the historical relationship of sexual and gender variance to the ritual art of tattooing. We do know that in some North Asian shamanic cultures, gender variant or transgendered individuals wore the tattoos of the opposite anatomical sex. As G. H. von Langsdorf noted in 1812, "Aleutians raise some boys totally as females; they pluck out the budding beard and tattoo them around the mouth as women." B. Sergent (1986) suggests that "tattooing may have been practiced in [Greece] in early periods in connection with [homoerotic] initiation." We also know that the GALLI, the transgendered priest/esse/s of the Greco-Roman goddess CYBELE, and perhaps also the *bacchants* of DIONYSUS, whose membership included those engaging in transgendered and same-sex erotic behavior tattooed themselves with ivy leaf patterns. Japanese samurai-lovers following BUSHIDO also practiced tattooing. Tsuneo Watanabe and Jun'ichi Wata (1989) relate that during the Genroku period of Japanese history (1688-1703), male lovers ritualized their relationships by "tattooing or cutting each other's arms or thighs so as to mix their blood." Homoerotically and bisexually inclined pirates are also thought to have tattooed themselves. In more recent times, French prostitutes of the nineteenth century tattooed the names of their lesbian lovers on their bellies, according to L. Adler (1990). Sailors of the nineteenth and twentieth centuries, homosexual and bisexual as well as heterosexual, seem to have been especially receptive to tattoos. Judy Grahn remembers that in 1961, "The first lesbian I met with a picture inked into her skin was a handsome blond woman who . . . had been in the Navy . . . The design was of a seahorse." In the 1960s, Robert Giraud, in "The Skin Artists," noted that "The young man proclaims his dedication to Greek love by means of a rose placed on his heart." In the gay male and later the lesbian and bisexual communities, tattoos became associated with world of "leather" or SADOMASOCHISM.

Taurus In Euro-western ASTROLOGY, zodiac sign ruling from (approximately) April 20 until May 20, associated with earthiness, enjoyment of luxury, musical ability, pragmatism, strength, and wit, typically depicted as a BULL. Figures associated with Taurus and with gender and/or sexual variance include: APHRODITE, CYBELE, DIONYSUS, MIN, POSEIDON, and SHIVA. According to Manilius (b. c. 50 BCE), those males whose sun sign is Taurus are ruled by Aphrodite (Roman VENUS) and Dionysus (Roman, Bacchus). They are more likely than men born under other signs to cultivate elegance and luxury and, *in extremis*, effeminacy and receptive homoeroticism. They are described as persons whose "insouciance runs free at feasts and banquets and who strive to provoke sweet mirth and biting wit. They will always take pains over personal adornment and an elegant appearance: they will set their locks in waves of curls or confine their tresses with bands, building them into a thick topknot." They enjoy wearing wigs, and they practice depilation, "craving for sleekness of arm. They adopt feminine dress [and] footwear . . . and an affected effeminate (*mollia*) gait . . . in their hearts dwells a senseless passion for display."

Taweakame Among the Huichols of Mexico, a transgender, shapeshifting spirit associated with sexual passion and with the altered state of consciousness triggered by peyote. In a traditional chant, Taweakame sings, "I'm the air tree you betcha / I can change / into a man or woman."

Taygete Beloved companion of the Greco-Roman goddess ARTEMIS/DIANA. After Artemis saved Taygete from the unwanted embraces of ZEUS by transforming her into a doe, Taygete dedicated to Artemis, according to various accounts, either a pair of horns made of gold, inscribed with the name of the Goddess, or a living doe with golden horns.

Tayu Gay male spiritual group founded in the late 1970s in San Francisco, led by Daniel Inesse. Described by Inesse and Ezekiel Wright in *God Is Gay: An Evolutionary Spiritual Work* (1982) as an "Hellenic spiritual order," members look toward the deities of Greece for spiritual – especially ethical – guidance, revering GANYMEDE as the "personification of the new Aeon."

Tchaikovsky, Peter Ilyich (1840-1893) Homoerotically inclined Russian Romantic composer, profoundly inspired by the sacred and mythic, and especially by fairy and folk tales. Suffering in a heterosexual marriage which was partly responsible for his wife's mental collapse, Tchaikovsky was happiest when in the company of male companions, including his servant Aloysha and his brother Modest. Russian scholar Simon Karlinsky relates that the so-called "secret program" of the Symphony No. 6 in B minor (Op. 74) is same-sex passion. The story of the "secret program," mentioned by both Peter and Modest Tchaikovsky, was shared with Karlinsky by the artist Pavel Tchelitchew, who had been told the tale by Sergei Diaghilev, founder of the Ballets Russes and a close friend of Modest. The French term "*pathétique*", "arousing pity," obscures the Russian "*pateticheskii*," signifying "passionate" or "enthusiastic," as well as the intended allusion to the Greek "pathic," signifying the receptive role in anal intercourse. If the Symphony gives expression to the physical aspect of homoerotic passion, however, it also speaks to the spiritual component of the act or relationship. In drawing upon a Russian Orthodox funeral canticle, it speaks of the holiness of love, as well as upon the repose following lovemaking, and the death of love or of lovers. Thus, the theme of the symphony is not the "pathetic" or suicidal but rather an erotico-spiritual

meditation upon love, repose, and death. Beyond the *Pathétique*, many of his works speak in subtle ways, often through the figures of women, of his love for men and his devotion to the magical and the spiritual, including *Romeo and Juliet* (1869), *Undine* (1870), *Nakula the Smith* (1876), *Swan Lake* (1877), *The Maid of Orleans* (1881), *The Sorceress* (1887), *Sleeping Beauty* (1889), and *The Nutcracker* (1892).

Tchelitchew, Pavel (1898-1957) Russian-born, homoerotically inclined painter, perhaps best known for *Hide and Seek*. His works are filled with goddesses and androgynous figures; in his final paintings, they become luminescent, as if painted with neon or lasers. We know from his biographer and friend Parker Tyler and from his lover, the poet Charles Henri-Ford, that Tchelitchew was deeply interested in the occult. From the time he was a child, Tchelitchew experienced visions of a goddess whom he named "the White Lady." In later years, he came to look upon both Gertrude Stein and Edith Sitwell as avatars of the Goddess. Believing in reincarnation, he spent a great deal of time trying to determine whom he might have been in former lives. Many of his arguments with Henri-Ford concerned their astrological differences; Ford, he felt, possessed too much Aquarian energy. He became possessed with the notion that water, in some form, would bring about his death. Tchelitchew, a child of earth, sought to become less earthy and more a creature of the air. Tchelitchew, also a student of TAROT, saw himself as the card of Strength (which often depicts a woman taming a lion) and Ford as the Wheel of Fortune. Tyler says of him and his work: "I could not forget that Tchelitchew's imagination was dominated by Astrology . . . by the Tarot pack . . . All Tchelitchew's close friends knew that he imagined himself in the occult tradition of the magus, the ancient wise man . . . Hermetic tradition . . . Egypt . . . Orphism, Neo-Platonism . . . Gnosticism and Alchemy . . . Tchelitchew became a painter who portrayed Hermetic eclecticism in a conscious series of real and ideal prisms."

Te Rongo Polynesian hermaphroditic deity, portrayed with a large phallus and female breasts, with three sons springing from her-his body.

Telines Transgendered male priest of the Greek earth goddess Gaia, he was, according to legend, born on the island of Talos near Rhodes, migrating in later life to Gela in southern Sicily. Telines has been compared to the transgendered seer TIRESIAS.

Templar, Order of the Knights Founded in 1188 by Hugh de Payens, the Order of the Knights Templar began as an anti-Arabic, Christian military organization. While numerous scholars deny the alleged ritualistic and erotic practices attributed to the Templars, others are certain that the Order developed a syncretic cult focusing on an androgynous deity, Baphomet, and that the Templars engaged in cultic homoeroticism, in rites including the *osculum obscoenum*, the kiss on the anus or phallus. For these and other alleged beliefs and practices, as well as for the enormous wealth they had managed to collect quite rapidly, many were tortured and burned at the stake.

Temple of Peace According to classicist Peter Green, the shrine of GANYMEDE in the Temple of Peace at the Roman Forum was, during the second century CE and perhaps earlier as well, "used as a [place of] rendezvous by male homosexuals."

Terésa de Avila, Santa, (Saint Theresa of Avila; Terésa de Cepeda Dávila y Ahumada,1515-1582) Entering the Carmelite convent at Avila at eighteen years old, over the following years Terésa opened at least fifteen convents, giving her the nickname of the "Roving Nun." Her writings, especially her autobiography and *The Way of Perfection*, drawing upon her many mystical experiences, are considered classics of sacred literature as well as of Spanish and world literature. Just prior to entering the convent, Terésa appears to have become passionately involved with a female cousin. This relationship seems to have ended rather abruptly. As a nun, Terésa appears to have not only sublimated any yearnings she might have felt for other women, but went further in suggesting that "special" or "particular" friendships between nuns were the work of the Devil. It is nevertheless the case that in Spain "the name of Terésa has been associated with SAPPHO," as bisexual writer Vita Sackville-West (1892-1962) points out in *The Eagle and the Dove*. In this context, Terésa has often been described as a female parallel to her friend SAN JUAN DE LA CRUZ (Saint John of the Cross, 1542-1591). Canonized in 1622, St Terésa of Avila is fêted on October 15. In her epic lyric, "Holy Relics," Chicana woman-loving writer Gloria ANZALDUA (b. 1942/5) describes the death, burial, and repeated disinterment and reburial of Santa Terésa. She envisions the spirit of the saint riding on horseback to collect her bones from those who have severed her body in order to obtain relics. "We are the holy relics," Anzaldúa writes, "the scattered bones of a saint, / the best loved bones of Spain. / We seek each other."

Terragon The gender variant, homoerotically inclined King HENRI III of France (1551-1589) was said to have engaged in a passionate relationship with this transgendered spirit.

Tewa Among the Tewa people of southwestern North America, young people participate in several initiation ceremonies in which they ritually pass from one stage of life to another and in which they are granted knowledge concerning spiritual beliefs and practices. In one of these rites, in which both the young females and the young males participate, they are lined up against one wall of the *kiva*, the subterranean sacred center. During a part of the rite, each one is asked "Are you a man?" and then "Are you a woman?" by the spiritual leader. Both females and males reply "yes" to both questions. This aspect of the ceremony introduces the young people to the notion that they are composed of both masculine and feminine elements, just as they partake of both summer and winter, north and south, pain and joy, and various other polarities. This rite is echoed by another in which some of these young persons will participate, where one receives shamanic powers if she or he is to become a spiritual worker. In this rite, the same questions are asked of the novitiate. She or he responds to both in the affirmative. The elder shaman or cult leader then says to him or her, "If you are a man, and if you are a woman, then you can be a bear." This rite reminds the man or woman that he or she represents a mixture of traditional femininity and masculinity, and also strengthens the primal belief that human beings and animals are intimately linked in the web of existence. And it speaks to the protean quality of the magical power which the shaman wields in order to transform her- or himself into a being of another gender or even species.

Tezcatlipoca Aztec deity whose name refers to the "smoking" obsidian MIRROR he carries, a mirror in which the future may be seen. Able to transform himself into a woman, a jaguar, a coyote, and a monkey, Tezcatlipoca has been compared to the Native American TRICKSTER COYOTE and to shapeshifting shamans. He is the left-handed god of the crossroads and the night sky, a shadowy sorcerer who holds the power to "steal the sun and plunge all things into night." Like the shaman, he is a skilled healer of life-threatening illnesses. In one of his aspects, he is a transgendered male, a *cihuayollo*, wearing women's clothes, engaging in same-sex eroticism. As such, he is referred to as a "male whore." The priests of Tezcatlipoca painted themselves black from head to foot with a mixture containing tobacco, morning glory seeds, and sacred mushrooms; one might say, echoing Peter Furst, that they "psychedelized" their own bodies. They pierced themselves repeatedly with maguey thorns; their hair, which they allowed to grow past their buttocks, was thick and matted with blood. Many, apparently, were the sons of chiefs who served in the temples as HIERODULE-priests, having sexual intercourse with other priests and devotees in order to commune with Tezcatlipoca.

Thamyris Legendary Thracian musician, at once an accomplished composer, lyricist, lyre-player, and singer, credited with inventing the Doric musical mode. After challenging the Muses to a contest of musical skill and losing that contest, Thamyris was blinded, his voice destroyed, and his lyre broken. Prior to his unfortunate downfall, Thamyris was considered by many Greeks to be the "inventor" of love between males; among those he loved were HYACINTHUS (also loved by APOLLO and others), HYMENAEUS (also loved by HESPERUS), and NARCISSUS (who may not have returned his love). When he died, his soul immediately entered the body of a newborn nightingale.

Theseus Legendary ruler of Athens who, as a young man, formed an intimate friendship with PEIRITHOUS, ruler of the Lapiths. Together, they hunted the Caledonian boar, attempted (unsuccessfully) to rescue PERSEPHONE from the Underworld, and shared numerous other adventures. They were revered as semi-divine heroes at Athens. Theseus was also said to have loved MINOS and to have established the festival of OSCHOPHORIA.

Thiasos Greek term for spiritual household which often also served as a center of learning. At the *thiasos* of SAPPHO (b. c. 630/610 BCE) at LESBOS, young women were instructed in music, dance, drama, and other arts and sciences, as well as in the worship of HERA, APHRODITE, ARTEMIS, and other deities. The *thiasos* sometimes also provided a setting in which intimate relationships might be formed, such as the lesbian relationships formed in Sappho's *thiasos*.

Thokk Giantess of Teutonic mythology. When the hero Balder was slain by the god LOKI, the gods commanded that all beings in the universe weep for the fallen hero so that he might rise from the dead. All except Thokk complied. It was ultimately discovered that Thokk was none other than Loki in transgendered form.

Thompson, Mark (1952-) Gay male journalist and essayist, an editor at *The Advocate* (Los Angeles) for many years, and editor of several anthologies pertaining to Gay Spirituality including *Gay Spirit* (1987), *Leatherfolk* (1991), and *Gay Soul* (1994). Thompson is among the few writers involved in this field who has focused on the subject of the soul. While he acknowledges that the soul itself may transcend gender and sexuality, he nevertheless maintains that gayness is a force that is born in the depths of the soul. Thompson also believes that in order to know the soul, we must be engaged with it by means of "ecstatic sexuality, breath and body work, psychotherapy and dream work." He further observes that what needs attention most among gay people is the awareness of, confrontation with, and healing and transforming of, the soul-wounding they (we) have experienced while living in a hostile milieu. Thompson is currently at work on *Gay Body*, which will discuss, among other things, the archetypal figure of the Shadow from the perspective of depth psychology.

Thoreau, Henry David (1817-1862) US naturalist, social philosopher, and writer best known for his retreat to the Maine woods, described in *Walden* and elsewhere, and for radical political beliefs expressed in *Civil Disobedience*. Much of his writing, however, concerns his belief in the power of friendship, which he sees as blending the physical and the spiritual. Although we possess no definitive proof that Thoreau was homoerotically inclined, numerous scholars have suggested that he may have loved Tom Fowler, a guide, and Aleck Therien, a Canadian woodchopper. It is clear that he cared for men deeply and that he was physically attracted to males. We also know that he admired androgyny or gender variance. Further, we know that Thoreau had a deep respect for the religions of antiquity, which he associated with his reverence for nature. Passages from his journals reveal his thoughts concerning gender variance, same-sex relationships, and the sacred. In January, 1840, he spoke of a dream he had of founding a community of passionate male friends or lovers, writing, "Constantly, as through a remote skylight, I have seen glimpses of a serene friendship-land – and know the better why brooks murmur and violets grow." In this community, he imagined living "henceforth with some gentle soul such a life [as] may be conceived, double for variety, single for harmony, – two, only that we might admire at our oneness, – one, because indivisible, such community to be a pledge of holy living." Thoreau believed that the affinity he felt for those he considered comrades was a human expression of the "friendliness of nature," embodied by the "goddess Ceres who presides over every sowing and harvest." On other occasions, this loving goddess took on the appearance of Diana. In this manifestation, both the goddess's and his own gender variance were celebrated. He wrote: "My dear, my dewy sister, let thy rain descend on me . . . . I am as much thy sister as thy brother. Thou art as much my brother as my sister . . . O my sister! O Diana, thy tracks are on the eastern hills . . . I, the hunter, saw them in the morning dew." Of his passionate attraction to men, he wrote, "All men and women woo me. There is a fragrance in their breath . . . I love men with the same distinction that I love woman – as if my friend were of some third sex." For Thoreau, the love of other men was both a private and a sacred matter. "Friendship," he wrote, "is by necessity a profound secret which can never be revealed . . . There is no need that a man should confess his love of nature – and no more his love of man . . . That person is transfigured is God in the human form – henceforth – The lover asks no return but that his beloved will religiously accept and wear and not disgrace this apotheosis."

Thorn, Michael (1956-) Writer and activist initiated into the Gardnerian tradition of Witchcraft, or Wicca, in 1974, and into the Faery Tradition of Wicca (as imparted by Victor Anderson) in 1978, Thorn founded Witches and

Pagans for Gay Rights in 1983 and Kathexis Anthropos, a queer-sensitive coven, in 1984.

Thoth Egyptian god of writing and justice, associated with the moon. One of his sacred attributes was the ibis, thought to clean its anus with its beak. For this reason, as well as his role in a homoerotic episode occurring between the gods Horus and SET, he was sometimes referred to as the "Shepherd of the Anus" and linked to anal intercourse.

Thug (or **Thuggee**) Secret society of certain male devotees of the Hindu goddess KALI who, until the early twentieth century, tortured and/or slew unwelcome strangers. Thugs often hunted in pairs; some of these pairs appear to have been comprised of male lovers.

Tiamat Gynandrous, Amazonian, primordial goddess of Sumeria who created, either by parthenogenesis or with the male deity Apsu, the remainder of Sumeria's first deities and spirits. Depicted as a DRAGON or sea monster, Tiamat was ultimately raped and cut into pieces by the warrior Marduk. Many scholars of religion and mythology observe in the tale of her demise a narrative of the transition from a pre-patriarchal to a patriarchal spiritual system. "She fertilized her own body, / and bore her own seed," lesbian poet, musician, and artist Fran Winant (b. 1943) writes in "She Was Called Tiamat," "giving birth . . . / to women like herself, / powerful, enduring."

Tiger In Chinese symbology and astrology, the tiger, especially the white tiger, is considered androgynous, partaking of YIN AND YANG.

Tiki Polynesian deified hero associated with eroticism and the arts, Tiki was a musician who played the *koauau*, a short, three-holed, end-blown FLUTE of wood or bone. Bisexual by contemporary western standards, Tiki spent many evenings making music with his intimate male companion (*hoa takatapui*) TUTANEKAI.

Tiresias Ancient Greek shaman whose name means "interpreter of signs," associated with transgenderism and with bi- or pansexuality. One day, while walking on Mount Cyllene, Tiresias witnessed two serpents coupling. On striking one of them, perhaps out of fear or as a magical gesture, he was transformed into a woman. He, now she, then lived as a woman for seven years until, after the same event repeated itself, he once more became a man. Other storytellers claimed that Tiresias had actually been female at birth and had changed sexes six times afterwards, his-her experiences including motherhood and warriorhood. According to these storytellers, he-she ended life as a wise-woman or CRONE. Also among some of these latter storytellers, it was believed that between Tiresias's phases as traditional male and traditional female, he-she

experienced being a "man-woman," or *kinaidos*, and a "woman-man," or Amazon. Still others told a tale of Tiresias being asked to settle an argument between the deities Zeus and Hera as to whether males or females experience greater pleasure when making love. After Tiresias had enjoyed a ménage à trois with them and reported that it was clearly the woman who experienced greater pleasure, Hera, suddenly becoming enraged, blinded him. Zeus responded by giving Tiresias the gift of prophecy, or "second sight." In this way, Tiresias's transgenderism, pansexuality, and visual impairment (common to many shamans) became interwoven in his legendary history. According to Fabius Planciades Fulgentius, Tiresias represented to many Greeks an allegory of the seasons. Spring, considered a masculine season, is that time when Tiresias, as a male, comes upon the two serpents coupling. As he strikes at them, he metamorphoses "into the feminine gender, that is, into the heat of summer," a season envisioned "in the form of a woman because at that season all things blossom forth with their leaves." When the season of blossoming draws to a close, Tiresias returns to being male in autumn; at this time, he is asked to judge the debate between Zeus and Hera. When Hera becomes enraged by Tiresias's judgment and blinds him, he transforms once more into a woman. For this reason, winter, a feminine season controlled by Hera, "grows black with dark clouds in the air." When Zeus rewards Tiresias with second sight, however, winter changes into spring, and Tiresias becomes male yet again, the cycle beginning anew. As a gender variant, homoerotically inclined male, Tiresias was sometimes depicted as the beloved of HERMES, the god of messages and himself a shaman. Classical scholar L. Brisson (1976), in describing a portrait of Tiresias on a fifth-century BCE Etruscan mirror, writes: "Tiresias here appears as a young being. His traits, his hair and his garments recall those of a woman . . . His garment looks at once like a masculine mantle and a feminine chiton." Tiresias's fluidity, like that of other shamans, extended beyond fluidity of gender role and erotic expression. Like other shamans, he was capable of transforming into animals. He experienced being, among other things, a badger, a mole, a hare, a lizard, a mongoose, a monkey, and a hyena. A number of the animals into which he transformed were thought to be either transgendered or hermaphroditic, especially the hyena and the hare. Once, during one of his incarnations as a woman or man-woman, depending upon the storyteller, Tiresias was sexually penetrated by the spiderman Arachnos. The latter may himself have been a man-woman, a male-gender variant form of the spiderwoman Arachne. At the moment of orgasm, Tiresias changed into a mouse, while Arachnos became a weasel. In our view, suggested by Brisson, this tale may mask a sex-magical encounter, as the animals into which the two transform place them into contact with the goddess Hecate and especially with her knowledge of necromancy. The animal, however, that looms above all others as a manifestation or attribute of Tiresias is the serpent, a multicultural and multihistorical symbol of the archetypal feminine and of fluidity. Serpents, associated with water, change skins, identities, lives. Not only were they guardians in Greece of sacred, oracular springs; they were also, like butterflies, vehicles of human souls. "It is in the form of a serpent," Brisson tells us, "that the soul leaves the earth, and in this form that it returns." As a shaman and prophet, Tiresias was believed to have mastered a great number of divinatory techniques, including two that depend upon the interpretation of chaotic patterns: pyromancy, divination by way of tracking the movements of flames; and libanomancy, divination by tracking the spiralings of incense. When it was decided that Tiresias should depart from the earth, he did not die but rather was carried to the otherworld, to Hades. Here, with Eros (as Eros-Amor), he serves Persephone and Hades as a mediator between the realms of the living and the dead.

Tlazolteotl "Shit goddess" of the Huastecs and Aztecs, deity of illicit sexuality and destructive magic. Tlazolteotl is often depicted as partially nude, as crowned with a horned or conical headdress, as clutching a serpent, and as riding on a broomstick or a bundle of magico-medical herbs. Above all, Tlazolteotl is associated with gender and sexual variance and with the Huastecs. Of the Aztec transgendered, woman-loving woman, the *patlache*, it was said, "She follows the broad road, the path of the rabbit, of the deer." To Aztecs, this meant that the goddesses XOCHIQUETZAL, represented by the deer, and Tlazolteotl, represented by the rabbit, were the protectors of *patlaches*. It is by way of her role as mother of the Huastecs that Tlazolteotl becomes linked to homoeroticism. According to the Anonymous Conquistador the Huastecs depicted scenes of phallic worship as well as of heterosexual and homosexual coitus in their temples, seeing eroticism as a bridge to the divine. The Conquistador also mentions the Huastec use of pulque enemas, which they employed in erotico-visionary rites. Even Tlazolteotl's Aztec devotees living in Tenochtlitlan, site of present-day Mexico City, were referred to as Huastecs, especially when they attended ceremonies wearing only masks, headdresses, and artificial phalli. The association of Tlazolteotl with homoeroticism is underscored not only by her association with Huastec erotic practices but also by her appellation Tzinteotl, "Goddess of the Anus."

Toad Among inhabitants of Zixi, China during the seventeenth century (and perhaps earlier), toads, generally linked to the moon, mushrooms, longevity, and erotic unions, became specifically symbolic of male same-sex coupling. In *Moriz von Craun*, a novel of thirteenth-century Germany, the character Nero, described as the

"antithesis of the ideal knight" because, in part, he was both sexually "active and passive," becomes pregnant with a toad.

Tofu (also **Bean-curd**) Food symbolic of lovemaking in Chinese spiritual and folkloric traditions. While "eating tofu" refers to heterosexual lovemaking, "grinding tofu" refers to lesbian lovemaking. Women engaging in Taoist-alchemical-inspired lesbian lovemaking were believed to employ dildoes made of silk filled with dried tofu. In the seventeenth century, the people of Huichou referred to male same-sex coupling as "treading on tofu."

Toledoth Yeshu (or **Toledoth Jeshu**) Legend, perhaps of German-Jewish origin and linked in some way to the *Talmud* (a major text of rabbinical Judaism) probably emerging around the ninth century CE (perhaps earlier) depicting celestial combat between JESUS and Judas Iscariot. Satirical and burlesque in nature, *Toledoth Yeshu* depicts Judas temporarily winning the struggle by breaking a spell cast upon him. He does so by having sexual intercourse with Jesus. Some Talmudic scholars have claimed that the legend concerns another man named Yeshua who lived a century before Jesus of Nazareth; this argument fails to explain, however, the presence of Judas Iscariot in the legend. The legend was revived in the later Middle Ages by Christian theologians seeking to promote anti-Semitism.

Tompa, Uncle Tibetan Buddhist TRICKSTER who sometimes employs his power of shapeshifting to transform into a woman. He does so at certain times to gain access to women, at others, to "have intercourse with men, and give birth."

Tornaq Name often given to the guardian spirit or spirit-husband of the TWO-SPIRIT male, or transgender male-to-female, ANGAKKUQ, or shaman, of the Inuit. *Tornaq* is comparable to *kele-uwä-quc*, used by the Chukchi of northeastern Siberia.

Tortilla In Mexico, a flat, thin cornmeal or flour cake symbolic of the vagina and of lesbianism. Lesbian women are sometimes called *tortilleras*, "tortilla makers." This symbolism is closely related to the Caribbean and South American *arepa/arepera*.

Tortoise and Turtle Among the Azande of Africa, the tortoise is sometimes symbolic of the phallus and/or homoeroticism. In Euro-western symbolism, the celebrated LYRE fashioned by HERMES for his beloved AMPHION is formed from the shell of a tortoise. In the West, the turtle often signifies androgyny or transgenderism, with its round shell being perceived as womb-like and its head as phallic. Among the Native

American Fox people of the Midwest, legend has it that two young women who were close friends fell into lovemaking in the woods one afternoon when they were unknowingly spied upon by two young men. The youths claimed that one of the maiden's clitorises resembled a turtle's penis. The other young woman became pregnant, giving birth to a child that bore likeness to a soft-shell turtle.

Tree In Greco-Roman mythology and religion, trees are often associated with young men who experience untimely deaths, such as the pine with ATTIS and the cypress with CYPARISSUS. Other Greco-Roman deities having trees as sacred attributes include: AGDISTIS, the almond and pomegranate; APHRODITE, the apple; DIONYSUS, the fig; HERMES, the palm; and PALAESTRA, the olive. In Hindu symbology, the shami tree is sacred to ARANI, and the margosa to YELLAMMA. In Hawaiian symbology, the lehua is sacred to HOPOE. The gender variant male ENAREES of ancient Scythia practiced divination with pieces of LINDEN bark. The expression "like trees which are joined by shared branches" was used to refer to female lovers belonging to lesbian-centered organizations emerging in China prior to the nineteenth century. In the Blues, the PEACH tree is sometimes associated with homoeroticism. West Coast US lesbian and, to a lesser extent gay male, poets and lovers of the mid- to late twentieth century have revered the MADRONE.

Triangle In numerous cultural and spiritual traditions, including Old European and Hindu, the downward-pointing triangle is a feminine symbol, signifying the vagina or womb. As an outgrowth of this symbolism, the upward-pointing triangle is employed as a masculine symbol signifying the phallus. Two attached triangles, one downward-pointing, the other upward-pointing, as in the Star of David, may represent not only faith in Judaism but also androgyny. During World War II, homosexual men were forced by the Nazis to wear a downward-pointing pink triangle badge. While lesbians did not wear the pink triangle, many of them, as part of a larger grouping of women considered "undesirable," also including prostitutes, were forced to wear black triangle badges. Gay liberationists of the 1970s adopted the pink triangle as a symbol of their movement to make others aware of their oppression as gay people and to transform a negative symbol into one of empowerment. In the 1980s, lesbian-feminist activists similarly adopted the black triangle, while persons involved in ACT UP employed an upturned pink triangle to represent the struggle against the AIDS/HIV epidemic.

Trickster S. D. Gill and I. F. Sullivan (1992) describe the trickster as a "complex character type known for his trickery, buffoonery, and crude behavior but also as a creator culture hero, and teacher." Tricksters are also frequently shapeshifters, and it is primarily in this aspect that those like BEGOCHIDI, COYOTE, CROKESOS, GHEDE NIBO, HAIRY MEG, Hu Hsien, KITSUNE, LEGBA, LOKI, MERCURIUS, PUCK, RENART, Uncle TOMPA, and WAKDJUNKAGA become associated with transgenderism and/or same-sex eroticism.

Tripurasundari Hindu goddess whose name means "Fair One of the Triple City." Tripurasundari is akin to the goddesses DEVI, DURGA, and LALITA. She is especially revered by practitioners of TANTRA and by gender variant males, or transgendered male-to-female persons, known as SHAKTAS. Depicted as a beautiful woman dressed in scarlet and bedecked with a garland of hibiscus flowers, she reclines in her palace playing a golden vina and singing. In another aspect, she is an AMAZON, a woman warrior. Offerings to her include hibiscus flowers, red meat, and wine. She is symbolized by the Shri (or Sri) Yantra, an abstract representation of the vagina, or yoni. Of the gender variant or transgendered Shaktas of the Goddess, R. G. Bhandarkar explains that it is the "ambition of every pious follower . . . to become identical with Tripurasundari, and one of his religious exercises is to habituate himself to think that he is a woman."

Tristan, Flora (1803-1844) Celebrated political and spiritual feminist of nineteenth-century France who described the godhead as a Divine Androgyne having male, female, and "embryonic" aspects. This androgynous deity appeared on her seal and stationery in the form of a TRIANGLE, its sides constructed of the words "*mère*" ("mother"), "*père*" ("father"), and "*embryon*" (embryo), with "*Dieu*" ("God") appearing inside.

Trititya Prakriti The "third nature," a term used in Hinduism to refer to third gender or transgendered persons. Alain Daniélou writes in *While the Gods Play* (1987), "Once a certain level of androgyneity develops in living beings, it is called the Third Nature (*Tritiya Prakriti*)."

Troilus Prince of Troy, according to varying accounts either a son or beloved of the Greek god APOLLO. It was prophesied that Troy would not fall to the Greeks if Troilus reached the age of twenty. During the Trojan War, Troilus, almost twenty, was slain by ACHILLES, who was familiar with the prophecy. Achilles, however, had fallen in love with the young man at first sight, and took no joy in slaying him. Another version of the story claims that Achilles offered to spare Troilus's life if the young man would make love to him; the passion of their lovemaking was so violent, however, that Troilus died in Achilles' arms.

Trophonius Gender variant male architect, oracle, and ultimately god loved by the Greek god APOLLO. Trophonius and his twin, Agamedes, helped to design and build the temple of Apollo at Delphi. On completion of the temple, an oracle was delivered to them: "Live merrily and indulge yourselves in every pleasure for six days; on the seventh, your hearts' desire shall be granted." On the seventh day, the young men were discovered dead in their beds. A second oracle read, "Those whom the gods love die young." Upon the death of Trophonius, Apollo honored him with immortality and with an oracular shrine at Lebadeia (present-day Livadia) in Boetia. Here, the spirit of Trophonius, akin to that of TIRESIAS, was embodied by an oracle and by a magical SERPENT, speaking through these. Those desiring prophecies would dress in the manner of sacrificial victims and would climb down a hole, where an underground river would carry them to the oracle. They would offer a honey-cake to the oracle and/or oracular serpent and then be told of their destinies. The oracular shrine of Trophonius was in use for over six hundred years, and its ruins may still be observed.

Trujillo City in Peru where hierodulic, gender variant male priests continued to serve in the temples long after the CHIMU had been conquered by the Incas and the matrifocal faith of the former supplanted by the patriarchal faith of the latter. According to Blas Valera (1590), these priests castrated themselves in the manner of the GALLI of the goddess CYBELE. Beyond serving as HIERODULES, or "sacred prostitutes," to male worshippers, their special responsibility was caring for, and receiving the confessions of, the priestesses of the temple.

Tsilth-'tsa-assún In Navaho religion or mythology, "Mountain Person," a TWO-SPIRIT being who, according to Hosteen KLAH, "looks like a woman but is a man" and/or "is both man and woman."

Tsze-too (or **Tsze-chung,** dates uncertain, first millenium BCE) "The most beautiful gay man of his time," Fang Fu Ruan relates in *Sex in China: Studies in Sexology in Chinese Culture* (1991). Due to his great beauty and perhaps also a TRICKSTER-like persona, Tsze-too had already achieved archetypal status by the time of the writing of the *She King* (*Shi Jing*, or *Shih Ching*, the *Book of Poetry*, or *Odes*), between 1000 and 600 BCE. In "On the Mountain Is the Mulberry Tree," the poet writes, "In the marsh is the lotus flower. / I do not see Tsze-too, / But I see and like this mad fellow."

Tuisto According to some sources, the first human of Germanic mythology. Tuisto, whose name means "dual (being)," was perceived as androgynous or transgendered. Tuisto may be related to the Hindu deity TVASTR.

Tupilak Among the Inuit, figures carved on the fronts of kayaks. Prior to the arrival of Christians, many *tupilak* depicted androgynous or transgendered beings bearing feminine chignon hairstyles, mustaches, female breasts, and phalluses. A great number of these *tupilak* were destroyed by shamans who feared their discovery by Christians.

Tupi, Tupinamba A people of the Amazon region of Brazil. A French tale of the sixteenth century, recounted by S. Mullaney (1988), concerns a bizarre encounter of Tupis or Tupinambas with the French court in 1550. The tale reveals an extremely cavalier attitude on the part of royalty, nobles, and courtiers towards imperialism, colonialism, and ethnocentrism. It also reveals, however, the manner in which persons of the Renaissance attempted to establish associations or correspondences between those of various cultures perceived as engaging in homoerotic, transgendered, and ritual behaviors or roles. On the occasion of Henri II's royal entry into Rouen, a meadow was dressed to resemble a Brazilian rainforest village. Not only had parrots and other animals been imported from Brazil to create the scene, but also around fifty "Tabbagerres" (*tyvires*) and "Toupinaboux" (Tupinambas or Tupis). Two hundred and fifty French sailors and other Frenchmen costumed as Brazilian men and women joined them. They performed supposedly authentic ritual dances as well as scenes of Brazilian life. In their books *La cosmographie universelle d'André Thevet cosmographe du roy* and the *History of a Voyage to the Land of Brazil, Otherwise Called America*, André Thevet (1502-1590) and Jean de Léry (1534-1611), respectively, reported that men whom we might now refer to as gender variant and as homoerotically or bisexually inclined had been encountered among the Tupis of Brazil. The indigenous people referred to these men as *tyvire* (also spelled in French and other European languages as *tebiró*, *tevir(a)*, and *tivîro*), hence, "Tabbageres." When Thevet described the androgynous, homoerotically or bisexually inclined Tupis to a fascinated Catherine de Médicis, he explained to her that the term *tyvire* might be translated into French as *bardache*. In using this term, Thevet was implying not only that these men were homoerotically or bisexually inclined but also that they may have performed shamanic or priestly roles. From the onset of its reemergence in sixteenth-century French, *bardache* was linked to the realm of myth and the sacred. Pierre Le Loyer, Sieur de la Brosse, in his *Discours des spectres, ou visions et apparitions d'esprits* (1605), invoked the Greco-Roman goddess KOTYS as the "tutelary Goddess of *bardaches* and prostitutes [*Deesse tutelaire des bardaches et des putains*]." Indeed, Le Loyer appears to have accepted a mythic or sacred origin of the term: "AGDISTIS, who was the lover of ATTIS of whom Arnobius speaks, derives from *Hasdesch*, which signifies 'bardache,' 'effeminate' [*effeminé*], as were those of the band and troop of CYBELE [i.e. the GALLI]." Thevet would have been aware that Catherine, her son HENRI III, and their courtiers were frequently compared to Cybele, Attis, and the *galli*, as well as that Henri and his mignons were often referred to as *bardaches*. Thevet further explained of their homoerotic relations that erotic roles (as described above) were divided into "the *bardache* and the *bougeron* ." In this way, the terms *tyvire*, *bardache*, *b(o)ugre*, and even *Tupi/Tupinamba* soon became linked in the French psyche. Sir Richard Burton, writing of this event in his *Terminal Essay to "The Thousand and One Nights,"* observes: "*Bougres* and *bougrerie* date . . . from the thirteenth century . . . [The] term[s] gained strength in the sixteenth when the members of the *Bugres*, or the indigenous Brazilians, were studied by [the French]." The *tyvire* of the Tupis thus represent one of the first indigenous groups linked in a cross-cultural manner by Renaissance persons to Europeans also associated with homoeroticism, transgenderism, and the sacred. The term *bougeron*, mentioned above, indicates the possible presence among the Tupis of a non-transgendered manifestation of homoerotic identity or behavior. This appears to be confirmed by the Portuguese chronicler Gabriel Soares de Souza, who reported in the sixteenth century that male "brothels" existed among the Tupis where warriors would go to strengthen themselves by engaging in oral or anal intercourse with other men.

Turlupins Referring to themselves as the Fraternity of the Poor, the Turlupins ("Fools") were a fourteenth-century French Christian sect labeled as heretical by the Catholic Church. They especially honored women as embodying the Divine, one of their chief leaders being Jeanne Daubenton. They were pantheists and mendicants who taught that when humans arrived at "a certain degree of perfection," they were "freed from the yoke of divine law." They are said to have expressed their beliefs in nocturnal rites in which, naked or "sky-clad," they engaged in cultic eroticism, including same-sex eroticism. Daubenton was burned, along with her books, in Paris in 1372. Many others were tried, tortured, and executed on the authority of the "Inquisitor of the Sodomites," deputized by Pope Gregory XI (1330-1378) in 1373 and the years that followed.

Turner, Kay (1948-   ) Austin, Texas-based lesbian writer, musician, artist, folklorist, educator, editor, and activist. Turner, who holds a doctorate in Folklore from the University of Texas, has been actively involved in the contemporary movements or traditions of Goddess Reverence and Women's Spirituality since the early 1970s. From 1976 until 1983, she edited *Lady-Unique-Inclination-of-the-Night*, a beautiful, handmade journal devoted to these movements. Also commencing in the 1970s and continuing into the 1990s, Turner has constructed ALTARS and installation artworks inspired by these movements and in particular her reverence for Our Lady of Guadalupe. Her altars are frequently miniature and housed in such items as match boxes and aspirin tins. In the 1980s, Turner, somewhat disappointed by the "women's music" scene as it existed, formed, with Gretchen Phillips, the hard-rock, all-female band Girls in the Nose. Seeking to weave together the ecstatic experience of women's ritual with that of the rock concert, Girls presented "edgy" musical performances such as "Breast Exam." Here, the pounding melody with its political lyrics was sometimes accompanied by bare-breasted female dancers evoking a KALI-, HECATE-, or DIONYSUS-like deity, some of them carrying enormous breasts across the stage while other women (and occasionally queer men) peered through the cut-out face of a giant many-breasted ARTEMIS. In 1993, Turner published *I Dream of* MADONNA: *Women's Dreams of the Goddess of Pop*, an anthology revealing the powerful archetypal, catalytic role this icon of popular culture plays in the dreams of twentieth-century women, with many of the dreams expressing lesbian or queer desire. In her most recent book, *Dear Sappho: A Legacy of Lesbian Love Letters* (1996), Turner examines the evolution of lesbianism through letters that privately evoke the spiritual sgnificance of lesbian love. Her study of women's altars, including altars by lesbian and bisexual women, will be published in 1997.

Tutanekai Polynesian deified male hero. Bisexual by today's standards, he loved both the goddess HINEMOA – who, some say, charmed him by dressing as a male warrior – and the male hero TIKI. Tutanekai, like his *hoa takatapui* (intimate companion) Tiki, was a musician; he played a wooden flute.

Tutu, Desmond (**Archbishop**, 1931-   ) South African Anglican priest and Archbishop of Capetown. He remains a seminal figure in the struggle against racism and injustice. Tutu is outspoken in his support of the political and religious rights of queer-identified persons. In 1996 he became the highest ranking Anglican to support the ordination of non-celibate gay priests – a position that in 1995 had brought retired American bishop Walter C. Righter to trial for heresy (the charges being dismissed following a hearing by the Episcopal Church Court). Tutu supports his position with theology, asserting that if Christians reject and despise gay and lesbian people they "negate" not only their humanity but also "their own baptism." Indeed, he refers to the "rejection of [the] homosexual [as] the ultimate blasphemy," insisting that gay and lesbian people are "the children of god," a fact "which must not be doubted."

Tuwais (c. 632–c. 700) Gender variant, homoerotically inclined MUKHANNATH, Arabic musician. Nicknamed "Little Peacock," Tuwais, according to H. G. Farmer (1967), is regarded as the "first male professional musician in the days of Islam." According to Ahmad al-Tifashi (1184-1253) in *The Delight of Hearts*, Tuwais "was the first person in al-Medina to sing in classical Arabic according to the rules of the new music," referring to the use of "strict rhythmic and melodic principles," especially of the *hazaj* rhythm. He composed, sang, and played the duff, a kind of tambourine. He also served as a music instructor to other *mukhannathun*, his most renowned (or infamous, depending on one's point of view) pupil being al-Dalal Nafidh, also gender variant and homoerotically inclined, depicted as beautiful and charming. While his art was greatly respected by many people, he was, as Farmer relates, "like the majority of the first male musicians in al-Medina at this period . . . socially an outcast." This was due to (1) his being an "idol worshipper," in other words, a devotee of the goddesses AL-LAT, AL-UZZA, and MANAT, as well as, perhaps, other pre-Islamic, Arabic deities; (2) his being a musician, associated – correctly so – by the first Muslims with Goddess Reverence and paganism; (3) his transgendered behavior which included transvestism or mixed-dressing; and (4) his expression of homoerotic desire. Indeed, an expression arose, "more effeminate than Tuwais," and al-Tifashi noted that he was "also said to have been the first to practice sexual inversion" at al-Medina. Thus, despite his mastery, he was forced, during an anti-*mukhannathun* campaign conducted (c. 670) by Marwan ibn al-Hakam, the governor of al-Medina, to seek refuge at Suwaida, or al-Martad, where he remained, "full of bitterness," until his death. One of Tuwais's most celebrated lyrics reads, "Love has so emaciated me / that through it I am almost melting away."

Tvastr Androgynous or transgendered deity of Hinduism, who both impregnates and is impregnated, alternately depicted as a BULL and a cow. Tvastr's milk is considered a divine beverage resembling *soma*, associated with the deity SOMA. Tvastr may be akin to the Germanic deity TUISTO.

Two Flower Temple Also known as Apricot Blossoms Temple and, much later, the Temple of Virtuous Female Ancestors, located near Guilin (or Kuei-lin) in southern China. In the late seventeenth or early eighteenth century, in springtime, a handsome scholar named Choy (or Chai) was enjoying a theatrical performance when he felt someone touch his buttocks. He became infuriated and turned around to reprimand the person. When he did so,

he saw a very handsome young man. Rather than reprimanding him, Choy touched the young man's crotch. The young man told Choy that while he was wealthy, he was very unhappy because he had no companion to study with or with whom to enjoy life's pleasures. It was love at first sight. At a nearby inn they celebrated their meeting with a great banquet, swearing to remain companions forever. From that time forward, they were rarely apart. Their many friends loved them dearly. One day, however, when they were traveling together, they were ambushed by a rogue named Wong. When they refused to submit sexually to him, he murdered them. When they failed to return home, their parents became very worried and notified the authorities. Wong was arrested and executed. The lovers' parents, friends, fellow scholars, and townspeople decided to dedicate a temple to Choy and his lover to honor the memory of their loving relationship. It was not long before pilgrims were journeying to the Two Flower, or Apricot Blossoms, Temple to ask the spirits of the lovers to bring them companions or to bless their relationships. As offerings, the pilgrims brought stems of apricot blossoms representing Choy and his lover. One day, however, the temple was destroyed by a large, bearded man who believed that same-sex love was evil. That night, the man dreamed that the spirits of the lovers appeared to him, wrestling with him and insisting that it was he, and not they, who represented evil. The man, feeling ashamed of his action and realizing the truth of the vision, rebuilt the temple. The Two Flower Temple once more attracted pilgrims wishing to celebrate same-sex love, and perhaps heterosexual love as well. During the nineteenth century, however, homophobic sentiment caused it to be rededicated as the Temple of Virtuous Female Ancestors, its earlier history purposely buried. The temple was destroyed by the Japanese army in 1894.

Two-spirit General term employed in the 1990s by Native American Indians and others to describe a ceremonial identity, found in many tribal cultures, which frequently incorporates transgenderism, same-sex intimacy, the undertaking of tasks normally assigned to an individual of the opposite anatomical sex, and the pursuit of shamanic arts including healing, magic, divination, and the guiding and retrieval of souls. Such individuals are commonly believed to be chosen by a divine force to realize a two-spirit destiny. In the past, the French term *berdache*, or the Spanish *bardaje*, was commonly used to refer generally to persons possessing this ceremonial identity. Two-spirit persons include the HWAME of the Mohave people, the MIATI of the Hidatsa, the NADLE of the Navaho, and many others found in this encyclopaedia.

U

Ulanah (fl. late twentieth century) Lesbian healing artist, poet, and performer of African-Caribbean descent born in Jamaica and making her home in England. Inspired by Buddhism, Women's Spirituality, Goddess Reverence, the Yoruba-diasporic religion (e.g. Santería), and other spiritual traditions, Ulanah explains that for her, poetry and ALTAR-building are forms of MAGIC and healing. In "Healing Through My Own Eyes," in *Talking Black: Lesbians of African and Asian Descent Speak Out* (1995), Ulanah says of the power of words, "I breathe them and speak them out aloud to my reflection in the mirror. I shout words to the trees, whisper them beneath my bed sheets and visualize them in emblazoned neon lights." Of her altar, she speaks of the centrality of flowers. "The flowers and their powerful healing are always pleasing to me . . . The flowers honour . . . my Godself . . . and give thanks for life."

Ultramontanist Catholic who believes in the absolute authority of the Pope. In nineteenth-century Parisian bohemian circles, the term signified a homoerotically inclined man who was "faithful to his cult" and who would never allow himself to participate in heterosexual lovemaking.

Ungud Androgynous or transgendered rainbow-serpent deity – similar to DAMBALLAH in the African-based pantheon of Vodou – among aboriginal, or indigenous, people of northwestern Australia. According to Manfred Lurker, "Medicine-men believe that their erect penis is identical with Ungud." To reflect the androgyny of the rainbow-serpent, some native Australians undergo ceremonies of subincision of the penis.

Unification Church Also known as the Holy Spirit Association for the Unification of World Christianity (HSAUWC), founded in Seoul, Korea in 1954 by the Reverend Sun Myung Moon. While practitioners suggest that God may be androgynous, the Unification Church is virulently anti-feminist and anti-queer. The extremely right-wing Reverend Moon condemns homosexuality as "the most unnatural kind of love . . . Homosexuality is . . . against God's law." The most favored form of relationship among Church members is patriarchal, monogamous, heterosexual arranged marriage.

Union Karin Loftus Carrington writes in "Women Loving Women: Speaking the Truth in Love," "A lesbian woman is drawn to a union and merger with another woman, to a kind of *participation mystique*, which involves a deep identity with the loved one. This union, which is a numinous experience, beyond the personal, also deeply embodies the personal." This sentiment has also been expressed by homoerotically and bisexually inclined men. The French writer Michel Eyquem, seigneur de Montaigne (1533-1592) wrote of his love for Etienne de la Boétie (1530-1563), "If any one should importune me to give a reason why I loved him, I feel it could no otherwise be expressed than by making answer, 'Because it was he; because it was I.' There is, beyond what I am able to say, I know not what inexplicable and inevitable power that brought on this union. We sought one another long before we met . . . [as if it were] some secret appointment of heaven . . . In the friendship I speak of, [souls] mingle and melt into one piece, with so universal a mixture that there is left no more sign of the seam by which they were first conjoined." Similarly, the American Transcendentalist Henry David THOREAU wrote of a beloved, "My friend, thou art . . . flesh of my flesh, bone of my bone . . . grain from the same field compose[s] our bodies . . . our elements but reassert their ancient kindredship . . . Our kindred, of one blood with us. With the favor and not the displeasure of the gods, we have partaken the same bread." And Walt WHITMAN in "Whoever You Are Holding Me Now in Hand," tells his lover, "Here to put your lips upon mine I permit you, / With the comrade's long-dwelling kiss or the new husband's kiss, / For I am the new husband and I am the comrade." While tales of loving companions may be found throughout this encyclopaedia, the in-depth exploration of lesbian, gay, bisexual, and transgendered rites of union and their history is only now emerging as a focus of study as the twentieth century draws to a close. To date, the finest explorations of same-sex unions, with some references to transgenderism, are Becky Butler's *Ceremonies of the Heart: Celebrating Lesbian Unions* (1990) and Suzanne Sherman's *Lesbian and Gay Marriage: Private Commitments, Public Ceremonies* (1992). Both of these texts examine the sacred dimension of loving unions. Butler's text in particular initiates the historical examination of such unions. Unions among males in ancient Greece were more likely to be commemorated publicly if they were formed between an older and a younger male rather than between two adult males of roughly the same age. The struggle between democratic and patriarchal attitudes resulted in a wider acceptance of same-sex love than in other patriarchal cultures while simultaneously encouraging role-differentiated, including age-differentiated, relationships. It is important to note, however, that many same-age, role-differentiated relationships, such as mentor-pupil, lover-beloved, etc., have been, and continue to be, misinterpreted as pederastic. As numerous writers have pointed out, the fact that many male couples fought side-by-side in battle challenges the notion that these were consistently man-boy relationships. In *A Problem in Greek Ethics* (1901), John Addington Symonds names ACHILLES and PATROCLUS, ORESTES AND PYLADES, DAMON AND PYTHIAS, CRATINUS and ARISTODEMUS and HARMODIUS and ARISTOGEITON, and the paired lovers of the SACRED BAND OF THEBES as exemplary of warrior-lovers whose relationships were not pederastic in nature. When an adult male fell in love with an adolescent male, he would let the younger man's parents know of his desire to form a relationship with him. If they agreed to this union, all would shortly thereafter participate in a ritual abduction ceremony, perhaps mirroring the abduction of GANYMEDE by ZEUS. The lover would take his beloved to his home, where they would live together for two months. During this period, the lover would instruct the beloved in the martial as well as in other arts. At the end of this period, the beloved would be returned to his family bearing gifts, "a suit of armour, an ox, a drinking cup, and other things of value." This ritual and initiatory period did not, however, bring the relationship to an end. Rather, it announced and secured a commitment of the lovers to each other. While little has yet surfaced concerning roughly same-age male union ceremonies in the ancient Mediterranean, warrior-lovers are known to have ritualized their commitment to each other at the tombs of numerous heroes. In "First Love Poem," Theocritus (fl. c. 270 BCE) stresses the long-term potential of homoerotic relationships: "Choose rather to be friends with the same body so long as you shall live; for if you do so, you will have both the honour of the world." The Roman poet Juvenal (c. 60–c. 130 CE) refers to an actual marriage ceremony which took place in Rome during the first century between a gladiator named Gracchus and an unnamed horn player. While a majority of scholars describe Gracchus as a *sallus*, or priest of Mars, it is clear that, although "once/ [he] Was a priest of Mars," he has now become a priest of the Goddess CYBELE, MA, or BELLONA, as is evident from his apparel, which includes a "mitre with dangling ribbons," and a male bride. Juvenal reports: "the blessing / [was] Pronounced and the blushing bride hung round / 'her' husband's neck / At a lavish wedding-breakfast." According to C. Calame (1977), same-sex unions between women were not uncommon in the ancient Mediterranean. They appear to have taken place primarily within the structure of women's religious households, or THIASOI. While in many cases the women participating in these unions would later marry men, some of these unions may have been of a more permanent character. The union was referred to by various names, primarily as a *parthenion*, a "maiden rite," and as a

syzygos, a "syzygy," meaning "to yoke together." These unions clearly possessed an erotic component; the passion of SAPPHO (b. c. 630/610 BCE) for Atthis was described as "erotic madness." The lovers were referred to as the "praiser" and the "praised," employed by the poet Callimachus (fl. 260 BCE) to refer to the love of the goddess ARTEMIS for ATALANTA. The beloved was also referred to as the "renowned one". Calame attempts to reconstruct these ceremonies of same-sex union. Of central concern is the union of two priestesses, Agido and Hagesichora, probably of a Spartan *thiasos*, around 600 BCE. Same-sex ceremonies between women typically took place at the time of the rising of the PLEIADES (a galactic cluster in the constellation Taurus representing seven virgin companions of Artemis), or else at the time of the rising of SIRIUS, the Dog Star. Formal rites of separation may have been conducted at the time of the setting of the Pleiades. The ceremony of union most likely commenced at dawn and ended at sunset. Deities who appear to have been invoked at the weddings would have included: two aspects of the goddess Artemis, Artemis Orthia and Artemis Pergaea; AURORA and AOTIS, goddesses of the dawn synonymous with Eos; Aphrodite; Hera; the divinized Helen of Troy; the Graces; EROS; and APOLLO. The lovers and perhaps the other participants as well wore primarily RED (here, sacred to Aphrodite) and PURPLE (here, sacred to Eros) garments; golden bracelets of SERPENTS; necklace-garlands of ROSES and VIOLETS; and head-wreaths of ANISE or perhaps miters. Such rites probably occurred at a central ALTAR in a sacred grove of APPLE trees; and on the altar, among other ritual paraphernalia, may have been placed roses, anise, HYACINTHS, and wildflowers, as well as an incense burner containing frankincense. The most important object placed on or near the altar was a model of a plow, which was offered to Artemis. The plow may have been symbolic of the lovers' syzygy and possibly also of the erotic dimension of their bond, as in Greece "plowing the earth" connoted sexual intercourse. Ritual foods probably included honey, apples, and cakes in the form of breasts. Numerous hymns were sung. One compared the lover and beloved, here Hagesichora and Agido, to horses. Another hymn may have compared them to the Pleiades; perhaps yet another compared them to Sirius: "They are the white star Sirius rising / In the honey and spice of a summer night." The late gay Christian historian John Boswell, attacked as an "essentialist" for his views concerning gay identity in the pivotal study *Christianity, Social Tolerance, and Homosexuality* (1980) by the same social constructionists who used without gratitude the information he had so painstakingly gathered, aroused the ire of academics once more upon the publication of *Same-Sex Unions in Premodern Europe* (1994), when he suggested that marriage rites for same-sex couples had been performed, in a relatively clandestine manner, by certain Christian bodies from late antiquity forward. In 1581, while sojourning in Rome, Montaigne learned of same-sex male wedding ceremonies that had been performed at the Church of St John several years previously. Certain Catholic church officials, determining that the only way to legitimate these relationships was to follow the marriage ceremony for heterosexual couples, performed numerous ceremonies of this nature. In the 1570s, it seems that four (or possibly five) Portuguese male couples were married by a priest at the Church of St John. The existence of this rite and its performance by a priest did not confirm its universal approval by the Church. Indeed, it would appear that the ceremonies were conducted by a maverick priest and were so strongly disapproved of by the Vatican that the male couples were rounded up and burned at the stake sometime prior to Montaigne's arrival. This piece of evidence strongly suggests that this was not simply a ceremony concerning "platonic" friendship but rather one recognized as the equivalent of a heterosexual wedding service, embracing sexual as well as spiritual commitment. Moreover, the fact that Montaigne's informant referred to the men as belonging to "this beautiful sect" suggests that men who participated in same-sex unions were considered as belonging to a particular group. A number of late nineteenth- and twentieth-century scholars have suggested that the priest of St John's may have actually been privy to and employing a ceremony continued primarily in the Greek and Russian Orthodox Churches. This Orthodox ceremony is the one described by Boswell in *Same-Sex Unions* and previously by Karl Heinrich Ulrichs (1825-1895). Writes Ulrichs, "The beginnings of a sanctioning ceremony were evident . . . in ancient Rome, and are evident again today in Christian Epirus (in Greece)." In 1857, Ulrichs relates, two German-born URNINGS (i.e. men-loving men) living in Moscow married themselves to each other by sharing in Holy Communion, having "discovered their own form of sanction for the Uranian bond of love," and in 1865-1868, other male couples were being married in Epirus in Greece, in remote areas of Turkey, and in Albania, by priests and according to traditional ceremonies. An anonymous writer, in a letter to Ulrichs, clearly links this ceremony to homoerotic passion and not solely to friendship, citing the *Symposium* of PLATO as the ultimate source of the rite. "On the Balkan Peninsula," he writes, "the antique cult of ["manly"] beauty was thoroughly penetrated by the Christianity of the Middle Ages. So, the Asian warmth and ardor became fanciful, sensual mysticism. The word given and accepted: this led to the altar. Custom demands a ceremony. The way in which it is carried out is a meaningful symbol for the seriousness with which both parties perceive the union. It loyally carries on its name inherited of old." The writer goes on to say, "The blood, once mixed and joined, according to divine ritual, forms a union that is absolutely inseparable," implying that the ceremony of same-sex marriage includes a rite of blood-brotherhood; this aspect

of the ceremony is also inferred by his mention of "its name inherited of old," which may refer to the Serbo-Croatian "*pobratimstvo* " ("blood-brotherhood"), usually combined with "*prichestno* " ("Holy Communion"), or a kindred term. In the eighteenth century, the Abbé Alberto Fortis wrote of the ceremony in *Travels into Dalmatia* (1778), "They have made it a kind of religious point and tie the sacred bond at the foot of the altar. The Sclavonian ritual contains a particular benediction for the solemn union of two male or two female friends." Women also took part in this ceremony. Fortis continues, "I was present at the union of two young women who were made *posestre* in the Church of Perussich." In the early twentieth century, Mary Edith Durham, in *Some Tribal Origins, Laws, and Customs of the Balkans* (1928), described the ceremony in some depth: "The two parties went together to church. The pope [i.e. priest] read a prayer. The two then took a large goblet full of wine, and both, setting their lips to it, sipped at once. They then broke bread and each ate a piece. They sipped and ate together thus three times and then kissed the cross, the Gospels, the icon, and lastly each other." Durham also points out that the performance of *pobratimstvo prichestno* was becoming less and less commonplace as the twentieth century progressed. Her remarks concerning this are extremely important in that they cause us to consider if a relationship might exist between the social constructionist insistence that queer-identified persons are without history and the purposeful burial of that history by puritanical authorities. Durham's friend Pope Gjuro of Njegushi, describing the ceremony as a "marriage of two men and against all nature," railed that "the Church should have never permitted" its performance because it "had been used as the cloak for vice [i.e. same-sex intimacy]." In *Same-Sex Unions*, Boswell confirms what earlier writers have said in terms of these unions being blessed by SAINTS SERGIUS AND BACCHUS (d. 303) and occasionally by other same-sex saintly couples, as Saints Bartholomew and Philip (fl. first century), SAINTS PERPETUA AND FELICITAS (d. 203), and SAINT POLYEUCTUS AND NEARCHUS (fl. c. 250), as well as by the Virgin Mary, the mother of JESUS. Boswell points out that while the ceremony may have survived the longest in the Balkans, it was known throughout Europe, experiencing a kind of vogue in twelfth-century Western Europe. Among the many examples of the ceremony given by Boswell, one tenth-century Greek version reads in part: "O Lord our God . . . thou who didst consider thy saints and martyrs Sergius and Bacchus worthy to be united, bless thy servants, N. and N., joined by nature . . . [Grant them] to love each other . . . all the days of their lives, with the help of the Holy Mother of God and ever virgin Mary." Among the Azande of Africa, a form of intergenerational homoeroticism was practiced from remote antiquity until the beginning of the twentieth century. Anthropologist Edward E. Evans-Pritchard has insisted that this and other forms of same-sex eroticism were indigenous and not the result of foreign influence. The typical intergenerational relationship was that between a ruler or warrior and a younger male. Younger males who were the intimate companions of rulers were sometimes referred to as the "king's old barkcloth" and as the *amoyembu,* "those who could be summoned." The most common form of sexual intercourse practiced between warriors and youths was interfemoral, a practice also popular among the Greeks. Relationships were formalized by way of marriage ceremonies. The ritual of betrothal included the older partner giving spears to the younger's parents, building a hut for his mother-in-law, his *negbiore,* and giving the younger partner "pretty ornaments," this last gift suggesting that the relationship may have included a transgender (gender variant) element. The older partner now addressed the younger's father as *gbiore* (father-in-law), while the partners addressed each other as *badiare* ("my love[r]"). The relationship stressed the training of the younger partner as a warrior. When two Azande women, often married to men, wish to enter into a formal relationship with each other, they participate in a *bagburu* ceremony. This ceremony centers on a ritual object, a cob of red maize called *kaima,* symbolizing blood, which is divided between the women. The women recite a spell, presumably a spell of binding and love, over the cob. Then, one of the women holds the bottom of the cob, the other the top, and it is broken between them. Each then plants the seeds in her garden. On conclusion of this rite, the women refer to each other "not by their proper names" but as *bagburu.* One of the women is considered more masculine, the other more feminine. "The one who is the wife cooks porridge and a fowl and brings them to the one who is the husband." Their relationship is erotic in character; in lovemaking they employ dildoes made of sweet potatoes, manioc, and BANANAS. Among other African groups, the Nuer of the Upper Nile practiced woman-woman marriage into the twentieth century, although its erotic component appears to have diminished over time. Nuer "woman-husbands," like Native American TWO-SPIRITS, often served as "magicians or diviners." The Nama(n), a tribe of Khoisan people, practiced into the early years of this century a form of egalitarian male homoeroticism. This relationship was formalized by means of a ceremony of communion at which a beverage, in earlier times water and in later times coffee, was shared by the lovers. This relationship was referred to as a *sore//gamsa,* a "water bond." The relationship was thought to be rooted in "deep friendship" and aimed at "mutual assistance." The preferred form of sexual intercourse appears to have been *oa/huru* (mutual masturbation). Transgender same-sex male marriage was practiced by the Korongo and Mesakin into the early twentieth century; writes Nadel, "[Transgendered] 'wife' and husband live together and keep a common household." In the Hindu-inspired *Kama*

Sutra of Vatyayana (fourth century CE), one finds, "There are also citizens [of the same sex], sometimes greatly attached to each other and with complete faith in one another, who get married [*parigraha*] to each other." While some scholars do not agree with this translation of the passage by the scholar Alain DANIELOU, commentaries linked to the passage seem to support it. "Citizens with this kind of inclination, who renounce women and can do without them willingly because they love each other, get married together, bound by a deep and trusting friendship." One commentary infers that such formal ceremonies of union also occur between women. Same-sex unions, including transgendered and intergenerational ones, have a long history in pre-twentieth-century China. An ancient Chinese ceremony celebrating same-sex union may have included these words: "For death, or life, or toil, / To thee myself I join / I take thy hand in mine, / With thee I would grow old." Numerous Chinese texts of the seventeenth century indicate the existence of male-male marriage in southern China. In Shen Defu's description of this institution in Min, a region corresponding to present-day Fujian, one finds: "Whether rich or poor beautiful or ugly, each unites with his kind . . . Some among them are so devoted to each other that even past the age of thirty they still share a bedchamber as husband and wife." These marriages, like other Chinese relationships of the period, followed Confucian principles, including lovers' accepting filial duties to each other's families. Same-sex unions between women in China were common during the nineteenth and early twentieth centuries and may reflect an ancient practice. The ritual structure of these unions is attributed to a Buddhist NUN who, several hundred years ago, founded, in Guangdong Province, a group called the Ten Sisters, which appears to have survived into the 1920s as the Mojing Dang, the "Rubbing Mirror Party," in Shanghai and the Jinglanhui, the GOLDEN ORCHID ASSOCIATION in Hong Kong. Companions could only marry other members. The ceremony included the taking of various vows, including one that if one or both of the women were pressured into a heterosexual marriage, she, or they, would commit suicide or find a way to eliminate the male partner(s). The wedding feast was an all-night celebration which included an exchange of ritual gifts – peanut candies, honey, and other items – and which culminated in lovemaking, referred to as "rubbing MIRRORS" or "grinding bean curd." After the marriage ceremony, the couple lived together. Some couples adopted children; these children were naturally allowed to inherit the property of their lesbian mothers. In North Asian shamanic and Native American Indian traditions, same-sex eroticism often led to relationships and marriage-like relationships. The Chukchi are said to have celebrated marriages between gender variant shamans and their lovers "with the usual rites." Such relationships usually formed, in Bogoras's words, "a quite solid union, which often last[ed] till the death of one of the parties." Among the Chukchi, this earthly marriage was seen as a reflection of the divine marriage existing between the shaman and a deity or spirit. Their spiritual function, combined with their special relationship to a deity or KE'LET spirit, caused shamans to be regarded as the true heads of their households. If mortal companions failed to treat shamans with respect, the shamans' supernatural companions would punish them. That the Chukchi shaman was head of his household is evidenced by the fact that the mortal companion often took the shaman's name "as an addition to his own name"; for instance, Tilu'wgi-Ya'tirgin ("Ya'tirgin, husband of Tilu'wgi"). Relationships between shamans and their companions did not generally emphasize age differences. Bogoras, for example, mentions a sixty-year-old male Chukchi shaman named Kee'ulin who, upon the death of his companion of twenty years, now "was said . . . to have a new lover, – another old man who lived in the same house with him." Among the Mohave – as among many other Native American Indian peoples – two-spirit, or third gender, shamans, the ALYHA (male) and the HWAME (female) often married individuals of the same anatomical sex. Among the Lakota, according to Native American woman-loving writer Paula Gunn ALLEN, same-sex unions traditionally occurred among women revering the goddess or spirit Wiya Numpa, Double Woman. The rite centered on a ritual object, a rope which was "twined between them and coiled to form a 'rope baby.'" In the nineteenth century, rites of same-sex union, often based on the Christian service mentioned above, began to be performed more frequently. In a letter to Havelock Ellis dated January 17, 1893, John Addington Symonds described a same-sex union involving his friend Amelia B. Edwards, an "eminent" writer of the day, author of *Egypt and Its Monuments* (1891) and other works. Edwards, "who made no secret to [Symonds] of her Lesbian tendencies," found herself deeply in love with the wife of an English "clergyman and inspector of schools," whom Symonds also knew "quite well." "The three made a menage together; and Miss Edwards told me that one day the husband married her to his wife at the altar of his church – having full knowledge of the state of affairs." In the late twentieth century, especially in the West, lesbian and gay weddings and other rites of union, such as "trystings," are becoming increasingly common in Jewish, Christian, Goddess-revering, and other spiritual communities. In many cases, these are unofficial "holy unions" which do not guarantee the partners the benefits enjoyed by married heterosexuals. One such union occurred on the evening of July 23, 1978, when poet and filmmaker James BROUGHTON and Joel Singer, also a filmmaker, were wedded on a ferryboat in Sausalito, California. "These holy mysteries elucidate," chanted the Priest, "the great

enigmas of mankind. We are all incarnations of the Androgyne. We are all mirrors of the Godbody." The Bridegrooms repeated after the Priest: "You are my Parent You are my Child . . . You are my Fate You are my Soulmate . . . You are my Bridegroom You are my Bride." Another exemplary ceremony of union took place on March 20, 1988, in New York City, when physician Rosanne Leipzig and laboratory clinician Judy Marble celebrated a "Brit Ahavah," roughly, a "covenant of love," ceremony at Congregation Beth Simchat Torah, with heterosexual feminist Rabbi Helene Ferris presiding over the ceremony. At the height of the ceremony, the women recited to each other, "*Zot dodati, zot ra-ayati*" ("This is my beloved, this is my friend"). Several months later, on July 17, 1988, psychotherapist Sheila Horowitz and realtor Shelley Pearlman celebrated a similar Jewish ceremony of commitment in California. The ceremony included a poetic reading from the Siddur of Shir Chadash, the New Reform Congregation: "May the door of this home be wide enough to receive all who hunger for love, all who are lonely for friendship." Wiccan high priestess Z BUDAPEST has been performing ceremonies of lesbian union for over twenty-five years. She insists, following Wiccan tradition, that couples must be engaged for a year and a day before committing themselves to each other in a formal ceremony. Typical elements in "trysting" ceremonies presided over by Budapest are reminiscent of those discovered in early Sapphic unions – engraved chalices, wreaths of YELLOW and white roses, purple garments, and fruits including DATES and oranges. The ceremony should be performed as near to the full moon as possible. Goddesses, or aspects of the Goddess, invoked may include ISIS (corresponding to the east), VESTA (the south), APHRODITE (west), and DEMETER (north). The ceremony includes trystees being anointed with oil, jumping over a myrtle broom, and joining other participants in a great feast. On March 25, 1996, San Francisco Mayor Willie Brown and City Supervisor Carole Midgen led the celebration of 166 lesbian and gay weddings in a crowd of over a thousand loved ones at the Herbst Theatre, with "I now pronounce you Domestic Partners" echoing over the loudspeakers. According to reporter Ann Rostow in the local journal *Bay Times*, the "men and women publicly affirming their vows – some of twenty years or more – each represented thousands of gay and lesbian couples who have merged their lives without the benefit of social approval or legal credit." While today some queer-identified persons look upon marriage as a patriarchal, heterocentric institution, others insist that, like heterosexuals, they (we) should honor our relationships with formal rites and, moreover, should be granted the same rights and privileges awarded to married heterosexuals. Even those skeptical of the institution have become aware that situations experienced by same-sex partners, such as being prohibited from visiting ill or dying lovers or spouses in hospital rooms and having no control over funeral rites, can be devastating. Whatever one's position on the issue, it is clear that the struggle to secure same-sex marriage is intensifying, and it is equally clear that religious and political conservatives intend to do everything in their power to prevent same-sex unions from becoming legal.

Upanaya In Hinduism, a ritual solidifying the relationship between a guru and a disciple which may include either sublimated or expressed cultic homoeroticism.

Uranian, Urning *Uranian, urning,* and numerous kindred terms signifying transgendered and same-sex oriented persons are attributed to the German lawyer and essayist Karl Heinrich Ulrichs (1825-1895). Ulrichs derived these terms – which preceded "homosexual" – from the *Symposium* of PLATO, wherein the goddess Aphrodite Urania is proclaimed the patron of same-sex love. In part because the terms were rooted in classical literature and in Greek religion and myth, they appealed to writers and other artists of the day. Exemplary is John Addington SYMONDS's poem "Midnight at Baiae," in which he writes, "Uranian Love, a god / Carved out of marble for some labyrinth / Of Academic grove where sages trod." For Ulrichs, homoerotic and lesbian orientation as well as transgenderism were essential traits. The *Urning* (or Uranian, homosexual), *Urninde* (lesbian), and *Uranodionings* (bisexuals) were creatures of Nature, just as heterosexuals (*Dionings/Dionindes*) were Nature's children. In the early 1860s, Ulrichs argued that *Urnings* and *Urnindes* "make up a third sex," a "special class of people . . . coordinate with that of men and that of women." He further divided *Urnings* and *Urnindes* into those of the "*mannling*," what we might today term "butch," and the "*weibling*," roughly, "femme," varieties, acknowledging a range between these poles. In his writings, Ulrichs paid equal attention to the biological, anthropological, psychological, sociological, political, and spiritual dimensions of Uranian existence. Not only employing terms rooted in religion, myth, philosophy, and classical history, Ulrichs constantly referred to transgendered and same-sex oriented persons and narratives linked to these realms. He was especially intrigued by the tale of ANTINOUS, the beloved of the Roman emperor HADRIAN. He was also concerned with the spiritual lives of persons living in his own time, was moved by accounts of priests performing clandestine same-sex UNIONS, and sought to ritualize relationships by way of legalizing same-sex and transgendered marriages. Unfortunately, Ulrichs lived in a world in which, beyond such pioneers as Edward CARPENTER and John Addington Symonds, his ideas were generally met with hostility. He wrote in 1894, the year before his death, of the hopefulness he had once felt, the disillusionment that followed, and the small ray of hope

returning to him at the end, quoting lines from a poem he had written in 1862: "Hope, yet hope a little while . . . / Uranians, uranians, your spring is coming without fail!"

Uranian Poets Associated with yet differing from the general nineteenth-century concept of "Urning" or "Uranian," this was the term given to a group of poets spanning the late nineteenth and early twentieth centuries who celebrated intergenerational male love in their works by weaving together elements of everyday life with figures of Greek mythology or religion and classical history. They were especially drawn to the tale of ZEUS and GANYMEDE and that of ACHILLES and PATROCLUS. Unlike Edward CARPENTER and others employing the term "Uranian" or "Urning," they did not typically link male love either to gender variance or to same-age love; and, primarily aristocratic in terms of values if not wealth, they rarely shared the utopian socialist visions of Carpenter and his comrades. The Uranian poets included: John Leslie Barford (1886-1937), author of *Ladslove Lyrics* (1918); Ralph Nicholas CHUBB, author of *Manhood* (1924); George Cecil IVES, author of *Book of Chains* (1897); and Marc-André Raffalovich (1864-1934), author of *Cyril and Lionel* (1894). Also associated with this group were those drawn to the occult, the writers Stanislaus Eric, Count Stenbock (1860-1895) and Montague SUMMERS. In his poem "The Urning," Ralph Chubb depicts the deity revered by the Uranian poets as a "wanderer" in all epochs and cultures, "from farthest ages of the Earth the same, / Strange, tender figure, full of grace and pity, / Yet outcast and misunderstood of men."

Uranus In Euro-western ASTROLOGY, this planet governs earthquakes and tempests, free-spiritedness, marginal(-ized) persons, and rebellion. Numerous astrologers have further claimed that Uranus governs same-sex eroticism. J. E. Kneeland reports in *Gay Signs: An Astrological Approach to Homosexuality* (1988) that a Uranus-MOON connection, or aspect, is extremely common (93%) in the charts of gay and bisexual men, whereas in the charts of heterosexual men, Kneeland finds no such connection, except in the case of heterosexual performing artists. Of the Uranus-moon connection, Kneeland writes, "This tends to imply that 'homosexuality' is . . . a mental and emotional relationship that finds outlet or expression through sex . . . Uranus frees the emotional [moon] nature from conventional responses." The specific types of aspect Kneeland finds are the moon trine Uranus and the moon sextile Uranus, aspects which describe "ambitious, imaginative, psychic, romantic," and generally energetic individuals. For Geraldine Hatch Hanon, in *Sacred Space: A Feminist Vision of Astrology* (1990), Uranus does not so much reveal same-sex desire as it shows "how eccentric and outrageous we are willing to be regardless of sexual orientation. As for lesbians and gays, I have found that the more prominent Uranus is in our chart, the less closeted and more visible we are with our gayness. Ultimately, the purpose of Uranus is . . . to enable us to push society beyond its established . . . values. Lesbians and gays [and the authors of this text would add bisexuals and the transgendered] have certainly been doing this during the past two post-Stonewall decades, intensifying with the advent of AIDS." Figures associated with Uranus and with gender and/or sexual variance include: AIDO WEDO, APHRODITE (URANIA), DAMBALLAH, OYA, and SHANGO.

Uroborus Serpent biting its tail, an image, like those of the PHOENIX, the mystical ROSE, and the scarab, of infinity. Also associated with androgyny or transgenderism and homoeroticism, especially with oral and anal intercourse, the uroborus was identified with the godhead by Gnostics including the NAASSENES.

Ursa Major Northern constellation linked to the Big Dipper. In classical antiquity, "Big BEAR" signified CALLISTO, loved by the goddess ARTEMIS.

Uruhú Male ancestor spirit of homoeroticism among the Cagaba and Kogi peoples of Colombia.

Utah Game Euro-American term for a woman's gambling game popular among the Mohave of the American Southwest. In this game, red and black dice, representing women and men, are thrown. When a red die falls on top of a black one, transgenderism is indicated. Earlier in the twentieth century, a young male's fascination with the Utah game was perceived as an indicator of TWO-SPIRIT, ALYHA identity. A popular *alyha kwayum* (two-spirit song) focuses on a young two-spirit male creating the dice from wood, painting them, and then playing the game: "He-she advances stealthily toward the willow, he-she stands there and cuts the branches and gathers them up . . . He-she divides them up, he-she tosses them up and tells the girls about it . . . He-she cannot do otherwise."

Utopias and Dystopias Queer-centered ideal societies are uncommon in literature prior to the late twentieth century. Indeed, homoerotically inclined men including the Greek philosopher PLATO (c. 429-347 BCE), in the *Republic*, and the English Renaissance philosopher Francis Bacon (1561-1626), in *New Atlantis* (1610, 1627), depict utopias in which homoerotic love is nowhere to be found. Dystopian literature, both in terms of queer characters and queer-identified writers, is, to the contrary, voluminous. Indeed, some of the most vicious portrayals of queer-identified persons, especially gay men, occur in speculative fiction. Two of the first contemporary fictions of this sort are Charles Beaumont's short story "The Crooked Man,"

published in *Playboy* in 1955, and Anthony Burgess's (of *Clockwork Orange* fame) novel of 1962, *The Wanting Seed*. In these works, overpopulation has forced the government to mandate homosexuality and to outlaw heterosexuality. Same-sex-oriented persons are depicted as foolish, lustful, intolerant, and cruel. In *Where Late the Sweet Birds Sang* (1976), Kate Wilhelm, following in the footsteps of Beaumont and Burgess, depicts a society overtaken by evil, telepathic, queer-identified clones who are eventually destroyed by heterosexuals. In the late 1970s and 1980s, however, dystopian fictions written by queer-identified and pro-queer writers began to emerge. These include: *Project Lambda* (1979), by Paul O'm Welles, which portrays a US controlled by political and religious fascists, wherein gays are sent to internment camps; Alabama Birdstone's *Queer Free* (1981), in which, similarly, gays suffer when the US is taken over by Christian Fundamentalists; and Tim Barrus's *Genocide: The Anthology* (1989), influenced by the AIDS epidemic, wherein persons with AIDS, primarily gay men, are incarcerated in internment camps in a misguided attempt to control the disease. The most well-known dystopian work of this period concerning the treatment of queer-identified persons, as well as women, African-Americans and others is, however, Canadian writer Margaret Atwood's *The Handmaid's Tale* (1986). In this terrifying novel, Atwood depicts a dystopia resulting from a right-wing takeover of the US government. In this police state, called the Republic of Gilead, an extreme form of fundamentalist Christianity is employed to utterly control and destroy the lives of the majority of its citizens. "Gender traitors" including gay men, lesbians, and feminists are dealt with most harshly. While Offred is heterosexual, her closest friend, Moira, is a lesbian. Because she is attractive, Moira's fate is not that of the majority of lesbians; she ultimately becomes a prostitute to avoid death in one of the "Colonies" where lesbians and other feminists work at toxic waste sites. Utopian literature concerning same-sex intimacy and transgenderism does, however, exist, and is slowly emerging as a literary genre. One of the first such works is James Sadeur's (fl. seventeenth century) *A New Voyage into Terra Australis* (printed 1692), in which the narrator discovers a utopian or paradisal "Australia" populated by hermaphrodites. One of the few pre-twentieth-century utopias depicting same-sex love, and the acceptance of such, is Scottish philosopher and historian David Hume's (1711-1776) Fourli, described in "A Dialogue" (1751). In Fourli, bisexuality, at least among the male population, is common, often taking an intergenerational form paralleling that of the ancient Greeks. We encounter the Fourlian man Alcheic, who has been, as a younger person, loved and mentored by the sage Elcouf; now, as an elder himself, Alcheic loves Gulki, a male university student. "It seems Alcheic had been very handsome in his youth, had been courted by many lovers, but had bestowed his favors chiefly on the sage Elcouf, to whom he was supposed to owe, in a great measure, the astonishing progress which he had made in philosophy and virtue." Alcheic is so esteemed that he is compared to "the great god Vitzli . . . the supreme deity among the Fourlians," perhaps an allusion to the Aztec deity Huitzilopochtli. American poet Walt WHITMAN, envisioning a socialistic-democratic future in which same-sex intimacy will be highly valued, writes in "I Dream'd in a Dream," "I dream'd in a dream I saw a city invincible to the attacks of the whole of the rest of the earth, / I dream'd that was the new city of Friends, / Nothing was greater there than the quality of robust love, it led the rest, / It was seen every hour in the actions of the men of that city, / And in all their looks and words." Whitman returns to this queer utopian theme in other poems including "For You O Democracy," in which he imagines founding "inseparable cities with their arms about each other's necks, / By the love of comrades, / By the manly love of comrades," and "I Hear It Was Charged Against Me," in which he resounds, "I will establish in the Mannahatta and in every city of these States . . . / . . . The institution of the dear love of comrades." Early homosexual rights activists like John Addington SYMONDS and Edward CARPENTER shared Whitman's vision (with the exception that Symonds was much more conservative politically than either Whitman or Carpenter). The dream of a queer-centered, or even queer-positive, Utopia virtually vanished, however, until the emergence of the contemporary feminist and gay liberation movements in the 1960s and 1970s. In 1962, in a brief description of the year 2060, "The Homosexual Aid Society in the Middle of the 21st Century," Roger Barth sketches a portrait of a society in which lesbians and gay men have established their own cultural institutions including academies and museums. It is primarily from the lesbian-feminist community – especially the lesbian-separatist community – that visions of Utopia have arisen. Many of these actually weave together the concepts of Utopia and ARCADIA, the wild, paradisal landscape of ancient myth. In *The Female Man* (1975), Joanna Russ paints a portrait of the utopian lesbian society of Whileaway, while Marge Piercy, in her 1976 novel *Woman on the Edge of Time*, portrays an environmentally-concerned, anti-racist, feminist-centered future society accepting of bisexuality and lesbianism. The "Bible" of lesbian-feminist utopian literature remains to this day, however, Sally Miller Gearheart's (b. 1931) 1978 visionary romance *The Wanderground: Stories of the Hill Women*. The women of *The Wanderground*, having vacated patriarchy, live together in harmony with themselves and with Nature, communicating telepathically. The only positive male figures existing in their universe are the Gentles, inspired in part by the Radical Faeries. Gearhart was followed by Katherine V. Forrest who, in *Daughters of the Coral Dawn* (1984), introduces us to utopians including

DEMETER, Diana, and VENUS who establish an extraterrestrial utopia with topoi named after celebrated lesbians, for example Radclyffe Falls, Vivien Lake, and Stein Lake (alluding to Radclyffe HALL, Renée VIVIEN, and Gertrude Stein). In a similar vein, Merrill Mushroom, in *Daughters of Khaton* (1987), depicts a group of space explorers who land on a paradisal all-female planet, and Donna Allegra, in "A Toast of Babatine" (1988), portrays a young Amazonian woman who lives in an egalitarian, tribal society. Jan Stewart's *Return to Isis* (1993), *Isis Rising* (1994), and *Warriors of Isis* (1995) echo Forrest's Coral Dawn in naming characters and settings after female figures associated with Goddess Reverence and love between women. One of the most memorable utopian texts composed by a gay male writer is Larry Mitchell's *The Faggots and Their Friends Between Revolutions* (1977). This postmodern collage of poetic prose depicts, however, not so much a utopia *per se* as a utopian manner in which to live in the midst of oppression. It is a revolutionary manual meant to aid radical queers – faggots, fairies, queens, dykes, and their friends – in surviving the twilight of patriarchy. "As the energy of the [chauvinistic heterosexual] men decreases, the faggots and their friends come aboveground. They know they do not have much time before the men will notice. So, as quickly as they can, they begin to arrange themselves into an intricate new world . . . The great gardens of the fairies begin to expand . . . The fairies have left the men's reality in order to destroy it by making a new one." Michael Swift, in "For the Homoerotic Order" (1987), offers up a utopia created from gay rage resulting from the continued repression of homosexuality, in which "all laws banning homosexuality will be revoked," "writers and artists will make love between men fashionable and *de rigeur*," "churches who condemn [gays] will be closed," "vast, private [gay] armies" will conquer surviving oppressors, and a government ruled by a homosexual elite will "demonstrate that homosexuality and intelligence and imagination are inextricably linked." While Hakim Bey's concept of Utopia is both temporary and not as queer-centered as the majority of those mentioned above, his concept of T. A. Z., the "Temporary Autonomous Zone," does include queer-identified persons, and his book *T. A. Z.* (1991) is a thrilling read. Inspired by Shamanism, Sufism, Gnosticism, anarchism, the BEAT MOVEMENT, postmodernism, punk rock, and chaos theory, Bey envisions the creation of "t. a. z."s, zones where "Wild Children," "Rootless Cosmopolitans," "Psychic Travelers," queers, and other "poetic terrorists" may find haven – temporarily. In the early 1970s, groups of women – or "wimmin" (or "womyn") as many of them chose to spell the term – began attempting to manifest the dream of Utopia/Arcadia by establishing urban collectives and rural communities. In the US, the birthplace of this movement was probably Oregon, where dozens of such women-only, primarily lesbian-separatist, sanctuaries sprang up, including Cabbage Lane, Womanshare, Fishpond, Owl, Fly Away Home, Rainbow's End, We'Moon Healing Ground, and Womanspirit, the last of these linked to a popular Women's Spirituality journal founded by Ruth and Jean Mountaingrove. In the years that followed, many other communities emerged, including Amazon Acres in Arizona, Arco Iris in Arkansas, Pagoda in Florida, A Full Circle in Georgia, ARF in New Mexico, Beechtree in New York, Raven's Hollow in Wisconsin, and Spinstervale in British Columbia. While the women's land movement has subsided, many communities nevertheless continue to exist in the 1990s. Sandia Bear writes in "Lesbians on Land: A Tribe of Womyn" (1995), "The experience of living on the land day to day allowed them to participate in a natural cycle quite different from city life. One governed by the sun. The Moon. The seasons . . . Women learned how to find their own rhythm . . . To open like a vessel,

receptive to transformation . . . [the women learned that] there was an intrinsic relationship between being a lesbian, living on land, and connecting to one's spirituality." The Radical Faeries are among those queer male seekers who have, like their women (or womyn) counterparts, taken steps to realize the dream of Utopia/Arcadia. Since the mid-1970s, Faerie communal households, farms, and sanctuaries have existed in various parts of the United States, in Oregon, North Carolina, Minnesota, Tennessee, in Ontario, Canada, and elsewhere. In Tennessee, the members of Short Mountain Sanctuary – not only Faeries but also other queer men as well as women and children – have kept bees, raised goats, hosted Faerie gatherings, and published the journal *RFD* for a number of years. In 1987, the Faeries, along with the organization Nomenus, purchased land in Oregon on which gatherings have been held for many years and on which they plan to establish a sanctuary.

V

Valkyries AMAZONS and divinized heroines of Teutonic religion and myth. Unmatched in terms of skill in battle, the Valkyries defer only to the god ODIN. They convene in Valhalla, the paradise of warriors, to determine the fates of heroes and heroines. They also serve as psychopomps who lead the souls of warriors to the afterlife. Related to the Valkyries are the *polyanitzi*, Slavic Amazons, and *veela*, Serbian Amazons, the latter of whom are also linked to the reverence of the Greco-Roman goddess ARTEMIS/DIANA. Due to Richard Wagner's operatic cycle *The Ring of the Nibelung* (1848-1874), Brunhilde, Queen of the matrifocal country of Iceland and a general of a women's army, is the most renowned of the Valkyries.

Vallabha Hindu sect whose male devotees experience gender metamorphosis in worshipping KRISHNA and RADHA.

Vampire Humanoid or human-bat (occasionally wolf or other animal or alien) hybrid figure who survives for centuries, if not for millennia or eternity, by drinking the blood of humans or animals. "Vampire" is applied as well to humans who are drained of blood and who, by sharing the blood of the former, become like the former following a process of death and "rebirth." "Vampire" is also used to refer to persons who, while not assumed to be or to have become immortal, find nourishment, healing, passionate fulfillment, and/or union with the Divine in consuming blood, often in a ritual context. While the term "vampire" is Euro-western, the phenomenon is discovered in the sacred and mythic traditions of many cultures. In her illuminating introduction to *Dark Angels: Lesbian Vampire Stories* (1995), Pam Keesey reminds us that blood, as the "very essence of life," "has always had an important symbolic power. In ancient times, blood offerings implored protection, purification, and salvation. Blood was, and is, a covenant. In some cultures, to be 'blood brothers/blood sisters' was as important as having the same kin . . . The belief that the dead crave blood in order to live [again] is deeply imbedded in the belief in the magical properties of blood." As hunters, the men and women of early history experienced a constant and intimate awareness of death. Some of them came to view themselves as eaters of life, their strength or vitality restored by the essences of wild animals and plants. They appear to have envisioned certain bodily fluids, including menstrual blood, semen, bone marrow, saliva, sweat, cerebrospinal fluid, and the synovial fluid of the knee, to have carried the essence of life, the *élan vital*. For this

reason and others, they consumed these substances. It is conceivable that from the consumption of these life-essences, the legendary and historical phenomenon of vampirism may have arisen. Keesey maintains that in terms of specific spiritual practice, "The roots of the vampire can be found in early images of the Goddess" and in Goddess Reverence. "The Goddess and the vampire share two very important symbols: blood and the moon. Vampires, like the Goddess, are associated with life, death, and rebirth." In Euro-western culture, the third aspect of the tripartite Goddess, that of the CRONE (the first two are Maiden and Mother) is most often identified with blood, death, and regeneration. "The vampire," in Keesey's view, is intimately linked to the Crone, "the dark moon Goddess who receives the dead into her womb and prepares them for rebirth." Many of the world's cultures are familiar with such goddesses or aspects of the Goddess; they include the Mesopotamian Lilitu (later to become Lilith in Jewish folklore), the Hindu KALI, the Aztec Coatlicue. In numerous patriarchal (or post-matrifocal) religions such as Christianity, the revering of the transformative power of, and the ritual consumption of, blood – most often in the metaphoric form of wine – survives. As Keesey notes, "In taking Holy Communion, the recipient is accepting 'the flesh of my flesh, the blood of my blood' in holy sacrament with Jesus Christ." The phenomenon of vampirism is common to many cultures and epochs, as it is common to individuals of varying gendered and sexual identities. While vampirism is, in most cultures, linked primarily to heterosexuality and traditional concepts of masculinity and femininity, its associations with same-sex desire (as linked to homosexuality, bisexuality, pansexuality) and transgenderism are noteworthy. In the legendary history of Mesopotamia, the hero GILGAMESH, ruler of the city of Uruk and the intimate male companion of ENKIDU, was believed to be of mixed human-vampire (*lilitu*) descent. In the *Epic of Gilgamesh*, Enkidu is cursed with a "wasting disease" by the goddess INANNA/ISHTAR after he slays her sacred bull. With the loss of Enkidu, Gilgamesh, who has loved him, is also cursed. But the cursing of Gilgamesh does not end with this event. He is forbidden from possessing a plant which carries the power to bestow immortality. The loss of both Enkidu and the plant signify the severance of Gilgamesh's connections to his immortal lineage. Greek and Roman mythological and spiritual traditions associate vampirism primarily with heterosexuality, but it appears that the belief in the potential pansexuality of vampires may have been nurtured in classical antiquity, particularly embodied by the figure of the shapeshifter Lamia, or her multiple form as the Lamiai. She (or they) was (or were), as Camille Paglia (1991) notes, "a bisexual . . . succubus [or succubi]" who drank the blood of others. While not vampiric (or blood-consuming) *per se*, the importance of blood in Greek and Roman myths, such as those concerning anemones springing from the blood of ADONIS, hyacinths from the blood of HYACINTHUS, and VIOLETS from the blood of ATTIS, as well as the ritual spilling of blood in the worship of Attis and CYBELE may be indirectly linked to the phenomenon of vampiric death/regeneration. In one of the myths of Attis, Cybele and AGDISTIS plead with ZEUS to restore the deceased Attis (who expires following ritual self-castration) to life. Zeus refuses. He grants, however, "that the body should not decay, that his hairs should always grow, [and] that [one] of his fingers should live, and should be kept ever in motion." (This was the finger which in Greco-Roman symbolism signified anal intercourse.) In this myth, as Giulia S. Gasparro explains in *Soteriology and Mystic Aspects in the Cult of Cybele and Attis* (1985), Attis is neither reborn nor resurrected but lives on eternally in a kind of vampiric state Gasparro calls "survival in death." Closer to our own time, the two figures of the European past which are most often identified as linking same-sex desire (and, to a lesser extent, transgenderism) to vampirism are Gilles de Rais (1404-1440) and Erzabét Báthory (1560-1614). These two have been as important as Vlad IV (Prince of Wallachia, son of Dracul and called "the Impaler," fl. c. 1450) in the creation of the literary vampire of the nineteenth and twentieth centuries. Once a Christian soldier fighting alongside his friend Joan of Arc against the English, Gilles de Rais, following Joan's execution, appears to have become embittered and, wasting huge sums of money, to have turned to MAGIC and ALCHEMY in an attempt to once more attain wealth and power. In this attempt, he was ill advised by a Catholic priest and ritual magician, François Prelati, who insisted that the blood of young persons must be spilled if de Rais were to obtain his desires. We must avoid accepting at face value confessions taken by Inquisitors. According to these, however, as well as subsequent legends, de Rais sacrificed numerous youths in rituals over a period of ten years. In doing so, he allegedly grew to love some of the male youths. This, however, did not stop him from killing them, unless, we are told, they could sing beautifully. In de Rais's tale, it is not clear whether or not he was believed to have vampirized his victims; nevertheless, the linkage of blood sacrifice and homoerotic intergenerational desire resulted in de Rais's becoming associated with vampirism. On the day before he was executed, a large demonstration unsuccessfully demanded his release. A fountain was built in his memory over the place of his execution, and it was believed that water from this fountain could bring fertility and prosperity. The Countess Báthory, allegedly believing that only blood could keep her young, and given to lesbianism or bisexuality and to SADOMASOCHISM, engaged in eroticism with female servants and later with noblewomen before slaying them and either drinking or bathing in their blood. Ultimately, the Countess was sealed within a wall of her own estate. We should take note of an image in a celebrated poem of Saint John of the Cross (SAN JUAN DE LA CRUZ, 1542-1591), brought to our attention by queer theorist Sue-Ellen Case in "Tracking the Vampire" (1991). In "Dark Night" ("Noche oscura"), in the course of an erotico-mystical vision including elements of homoeroticism and transgenderism, with John envisioning himself as the Bride of JESUS, the latter "wounds" John's neck, upon which the yielding mystic/bride falls into an altered state of consciousness. In Case's terms, "The [vampiric] wound of love liberates" the loved one "from the boundaries of being . . . Ontology shifts through gender inversion and is expressed as same-sex desire. This is queer, indeed." The most renowned poetic work of English Romanticism which includes a vampire, or vampire-like, character is Samuel Taylor Coleridge's "Christabel" (1816). Rich in Celtic/Druidic, Gothic, and occult elements, the poem concerns a maiden, Christabel, who, pining for her male lover, a knight, escapes at midnight to pray beneath a sacred oak for her beloved's safe return. In the wood, a mysterious woman, Geraldine, appears. She tells Christabel of being the victim of male abuse. Christabel, concerned for Geraldine's well-being, takes her back to the castle to care for her. As they prepare for bed, Christabel notices that one of the breasts (and surrounding area) of the beautiful Geraldine's body appears to belong to a much older woman. Geraldine initiates lovemaking and, as Christabel falls into a trance, chants a spell. When Christabel awakens the next morning, she notices that Geraldine's wrinkled breast appears youthful; indeed, Geraldine appears more beautiful than ever. Three years after Coleridge penned "Christabel," the apparently homoerotically inclined Dr John Polidori (1795-1821) wrote *The Vampyre: A Tale* as a result of an exercise in writing proposed by the bisexual poet George Gordon, Lord Byron during a strange evening spent with Percy Bysshe Shelley and Mary Wollstonecraft Shelley (who wrote *Frankenstein* in response to Byron's exercise) at the Villa Diodati near Geneva, Switzerland. The central character of *The Vampyre* is Lord Ruthven, a nobleman and vampire whose suave, aloof, pansexual persona continues to inspire literary portrayals of vampires in the late twentieth century. Vampirism, like other supernatural phenomena, inspired a number of Romantic, Symbolist and Decadent writers, including French poet Charles Baudelaire (1821-1867), who linked vampirism to lesbianism, and Oscar WILDE (1854-1900), whose central character Dorian in *The Picture of Dorian Gray* (1890, 1891) has been described by numerous literary critics (including Camille Paglia) and vampire afficianados (like

Leonard Wolf) as vampiric. Even poets like the American Transcendentalist, lesbian or bisexually inclined Emily DICKINSON (1830-1886) seem to have discovered – as Paglia (1991) observes – the thrill of blood. In a portrait celebrating autumn, Dickinson writes, "And Oh, the Shower of Stain – / When Winds – upset the Basin – / And spill the Scarlet Rain." Perhaps the most renowned vampire fiction of the late nineteenth century other than Bram Stoker's *Dracula* (1897, wherein passion between women occurs briefly) is J. Sheridan Le Fanu's *Carmilla* (1871). This is the tale of Carmilla (Millarca Karnstein), a noblewoman who returns after being dead one hundred and fifty years as a beautiful, seductive vampire. She and a young woman named Laura become lovers; Laura enjoys the passionate embraces, but her vital energy is nevertheless depleted. Carmilla is, however, depicted somewhat sympathetically, pleading with Laura, "Think me not cruel because I obey the irresistible law of my strength and weakness; if your dear heart is wounded, my wild heart bleeds with yours." The beautiful, seductive, vampiric female lover of women – as well as men – returns in Cora Linn Daniels's 1891 novel *Sardia: A Story of Love*. In this novel, Lulu is a young, dazzling woman loved by a man named Guy as well as by Countess Sybil Visonti, a vampiric figure if not a full-fledged vampire. "You cannot get rid of me," the Countess whispers to Lulu, "Nothing shall drive me away." Reminiscent of Carmilla and the Countess, lesbian writer Renée VIVIEN (1877-1909), weaving together the influences of SAPPHO and Baudelaire and depicting herself as a vampire (as observed by Susan Gubar [1985]), tells her lover, "I believe I take from you a bit of your fleeting life when I embrace you." In 1884, early homosexual rights activist Karl Heinrich Ulrichs (1825-1895) published a vampiric homoerotic tale titled "Manor." Har, a fifteen-year-old youth living in the Faeroe Islands, is rescued from drowning during a tempest by a nineteen-year-old named Manor who lives on a neighboring island. The two young men fall in love. Several months later, Manor drowns in a storm while on a whaling expedition; his body is washed ashore. Har throws "himself sobbing over the beloved body and [tastes] again for a moment the bliss of an embrace." Manor is buried, but afterward visits Har as he lies in bed, kissing him with icy lips. The following night he visits Har again, this time wounding his chest and sucking blood as the two make love. When the villagers discover what has transpired, they destroy Manor with a stake. Har, devastated, still very much in love with Manor, dies of loneliness. Har's mother honors his last request, that he be buried alongside Manor. In several works of fiction of the early 1900s, vampirism and homoeroticism are associated with creativity, as in George Sylvester Viereck's *The House of the Vampire* (1907), in which a young writer, Ernest Fielding, falls in love with Reginald Clarke, a vampiric figure who drains Fielding's creativity rather than his blood, and in Thomas

Mann's 1913 novella *Death in Venice*, in which the writer Gustav von Aschenbach envisions his beloved TADZIO and other young men taking part in a ritual to a phallic god. "His senses reeled," Mann writes, "in the steam of panting bodies . . . They laughed, they howled, they thrust their pointed staves into each other's flesh and licked the blood as it ran down." Lesbian-themed vampire novels experienced a renascence in the 1930s and 1940s, with the appearance of Francis Brett Young's *White Ladies* (1935) and Dorothy Baker's *Trio* (1943). As Andrea Weiss observes in *Vampires and Violets: Lesbians in Film* (1992), lesbian, bisexual, or pansexual vampires also began to appear in films from the 1930s onward, commencing with *Dracula's Daughter* in 1936. Many of these portrayals, while alluring, were not, however, sympathetic; this began to change in the late 1960s and early 1970s, paralleling the emergence of the civil rights, countercultural or "hippie," women's rights, and gay rights movements, with their emphases on honoring those the dominant culture had relegated to the margins. Commencing in 1972 with the publication of Leonard Wolf's anecdotal history *A Dream of Dracula: In Search of the Living Dead* (1972), which includes encounters with sympathetic, self-identified gay male vampires, and especially in 1975 with the release of the camp rock opera THE ROCKY HORROR PICTURE SHOW and the following year with the publication of Anne Rice's enormously successful novel *Interview with the Vampire*, wherein we meet a host of strangely familiar, pansexual vampires, the phenomenon of vampirism flowered, a flowering which has continued into the 1990s. While Rice has continued to publish texts belonging to her "Vampire Chronicles" into the 1990s, other writers have joined her in evoking the interrelationship of sexual and gender variance and vampirism. Among the qualities one observes in these texts are their potent interfacing of the ancient and postmodern, the beautiful and the grotesque, eros and thanatos. Works of this nature include: *Hotel Transylvania* (1978) by Chelsea Quinn Yarbro; *The Hunger* (1981) by Whitley Strieber; *Vampire Lesbians of Sodom* (1986) by Charles Busch; *The Blood Countess, Erzabét Báthory of Hungary: A Gothic Horror Poem* (1987) by Robert Peters; *Lost Souls* (1992) by Poppy Z. Brite; and *Minimax* (1992) by Anna Livia. The last of these is especially noteworthy, as it presents, in a comic manner, the lesbian writers Renée VIVIEN and Natalie Clifford BARNEY as vampires. Two superior anthologies of lesbian-themed vampire stories have also been published in recent years, *Daughters of Darkness* (1993) and *Dark Angels* (1995), both edited by Pam Keesey. Since the 1970s, vampire films linking the phenomenon to same-sex desire and/or transgenderism have also blossomed. The most popular of these include: *Daughters of Darkness* (1970), based on the legend of Erzabét Báthory, directed by Harry Kumel and starring lesbian cult idol Delphine Seyrig; *The Hunger* (1983), based on the novel by Whitley Strieber, directed by Tony

Scott and starring Catherine Deneuve, Susan Sarandon, and David Bowie; and *Interview with the Vampire* (1994), based on the novel by Anne Rice, directed by Neil Jordan and starring Tom Cruise, Christian Slater, and Antonio Banderas. Two writers whose works demonstrate the imaginative innovation and stylistic richness characteristic of contemporary queer-themed vampire literature are Gary Bowen and Jewelle Gomez. Bowen, of Apache and Welsh descent, born in Texas and now living on the East coast of the US, has published numerous works related to our subject, including a novel, *Diary of a Vampire* (1995) and *Winter of the Soul* (1995), a short story collection. Most impressive in Bowen's work is his poetic sensibility – enhanced by his familiarity with the works of Sappho and other of the world's greatest poets – as seen in this brief passage from "Dream-Eater": "There are many breeds of vampires . . . I eat dreams . . . I perch high above the city, roosting among the gargoyles of the cathedral . . . I crouch with my brothers along the gutter, their mouths gaping to spew forth the acid rain collected from the roof of this holy place . . . The men below me are shadows to my vision . . . If I am lucky I will meet a real demon tonight, a daemon with a name and history . . . And if it ends in my death, so be it. I have lived a long time and I am lonely." In *The Gilda Stories* (1991), Gomez achieves a literary victory in her sympathetic portrayal of lesbian, African-American, and Native American Indian vampires. Like Bowen, Gomez is a born poet. What is perhaps most noticeable, however, in *Gilda* is Gomez's sensitivity to persons – and vampires – of differing cultural backgrounds and her depiction of the profound love that allows them to discover a terrain beyond these differences. In *Gilda*, describing a young African-American woman's transformation in the arms of a white lesbian, transgendered vampire, she writes: "the Girl felt herself drawn into the flowing energy . . . She couldn't look away from Gilda's gaze . . . Yet she felt free . . . She curled her long body in Gilda's lap like a child safe in her mother's arms. She felt a sharpness at her neck and heard the soothing song. Gilda kissed her on the forehead and neck where the pain had been." Also representative of contemporary queer-themed vampire literature is Carol Leonard's short story "Medea," found in *Dark Angels*. In this tale, told in a matter-of-fact style, Hannah, on a bicycling adventure, encounters a vampire, Medea, who, in her conversations with the young woman, returns us to the possible origins of the vampire mythos. "Lunar blood," Medea tells Hannah, "was the basic ingredient in the Great Rite. Menstruating priestesses of the Goddess would collect their holy blood for the sacrament – the blood of the goddess Charis, goddess of sexual love. Did you know that the word *eucharist*, meaning communion, comes from the name Charis?" Numerous writers, chief among them lesbian and bisexual women, have explored in recent years the possible reasons for the attraction of queer-identified persons and women to the phenomenon of vampirism, as well as to the related phenomenon of Neogothicism. While specifically concerning lesbians and bisexual and other women, their positions suggest a range also assumed by other queer-identified persons. Lillian Faderman suggests that in terms of lesbianism, the attraction to vampirism lies not in women themselves but in men's fear of lesbianism; she views the adoption of the vampiric image by lesbian and female writers (other than Jewelle Gomez) as unfortunate and exemplary of assimilation to men's consciousness. At the opposite extreme, Camille Paglia sees the association of women and vampires as rooted in a Nietzschean Nature, describing a "fetus [as] a benign tumor, a vampire who steals in order to live" and explaining "Woman's latent vampirism" not as a "social aberration but a development of her maternal function." Less extreme positions on this subject are taken by Bonnie Zimmerman, Sue-Ellen Case, and Pam Keesey. In *The Safe Sea of Women: Lesbian Fiction 1969-1989*, Zimmerman argues, "In self-defense, if for no other reason, we claim alienation as superiority and specialness, and glorify the status of the outlaw . . . a creature of tooth and claw, of passion and purpose: unassimilable, awesome, dangerous, outrageous, different: distinguished." Case, in "Tracking the Vampire," echoes, "The queer is the taboo-breaker, the monstrous, the uncanny. Like the Phantom of the Opera, the queer dwells underground, below the operatic overtones of the dominant; frightening to look at, desiring, as it plays its own organ, producing its own music." For Keesey, fascination with the vampire lies in a desire to confront and overcome phobias associated with sexuality. "In embracing the vampire," she ventures, "we are embracing our shadow selves, our brightest hopes as well as our darkest desires. The vampire in each of us reminds us that we are human after all."

Vasanta Companion of KAMA, the Hindu god of love. Like Kama, Vasanta has the ability to stir desire in persons regardless of their gender. He is described as very beautiful, dark and handsome with black curly hair, his face shining like the moon and his muscular yet graceful body glowing like the rising sun or like a red lotus.

Vathek (1786) Gothic, hedonistic novel by homoerotically inclined William Beckford (1760-1844) which tells the tale of Vathek, the ninth Caliph of Abassides, who, as George E. Haggerty explains, "indulges his appetites in a fantasy of sensual power." In the person of Gulchenrouz, Beckford celebrates male intergenerational love.

Venus In Euro-western ASTROLOGY, this planet governs artistic talent, beauty, children, friendship, harmony, and love. In astrology, as well as in the Euro-western traditions of ALCHEMY and ritual MAGIC, the planets are considered to be ultimately androgynous or transgendered, their feminine and masculine aspects represented by the signs they govern. In the case of Venus, her masculine aspect is represented by Libra, her feminine by Taurus. Figures associated with Venus and with gender and/or sexual variance include: AL-LAT, APHRODITE, ASTARTE, EROS, ERZULIE, FREYJA, FREYR, HYMENAEUS, KAMA, KRISHNA, SAINT MARINA, OSHUN, PAN, RADHA, XOCHIPILLI, and XOCHIQUETZAL. In a tenth-century northern Italian lyric, a young man loved by the poet is described as a "wondrous idol of Venus," and in "Venus Transiens," the poet Amy Lowell (1874-1925) writes of a woman she loves, "Tell me, / Was Venus more beautiful . . . / When she topped / The crinkled waves . . . ?"

Vesta Roman goddess of the hearth, akin to the Greek goddess Hestia. While it is not clear whether or not ritual lesbianism occurred in her cult, it is conceivable, considering that she was primarily served by unmarried women known as the "vestal virgins," often in female-only rites. This possibility is strengthened by the fact that in the eighteenth and nineteenth centuries, especially in France among the ANANDRYNES, Vesta came to be considered, or was reclaimed as, a patron of lesbian love. By the late nineteenth century, especially in bohemian circles in Paris, *vestale* (vestal) had become a slang term for "lesbian."

Village Old Woman Triune female divinity or spirit revered by the MIATI, or TWO-SPIRIT shamans, of the Hidatsa tribe of North America. Her aspects are Village Old Woman, Holy Woman of the Four Directions, and Holy Woman Above. She often manifests herself as a magpie. In the past, among the Hidatsa, young men destined to become *miati* dreamed that the triune Village Old Woman instructed them to leave behind traditionally masculine attire, speech, behavior and pursuits and to adopt those of individuals of alternate gender. Following such dreams, the young men came to be viewed as "mystic possessors of unique ritual instructions secured directly from the mysterious Holy Woman [Above]" and were "treated as a special class of religious leaders." Miati often became possessed by Village Old Woman during the course of dance rituals; when this occurred, they would chant, "You can't kill me, for I am holy. I am holy, I can do anything."

Vinayaki Feminine manifestation of the elephant-headed Hindu god GANESHA.

Violet In the religion of the Roman goddess CYBELE, violets were a sacred attribute of ATTIS, the Goddess's male consort and the beloved of AGDISTIS. The flowers were said to have emerged from the blood of Attis upon his death. Violets were also incorporated into garlands worn by the poet SAPPHO (b. c. 630/610 BCE) and the women of her THIASOS, or religious household, on the island of Lesbos. Thus, violets have been associated with gender and sexual variance and the sacred since classical antiquity. In the European Middle Ages, violets also signified loyalty and were exchanged by friends and lovers in the springtime. Sixteenth-century Englishmen and women who desired lovers but not marriage carried violets. Jane Barker's 1688 poem of romantic friendship, "On the Death of my Dear Friend . . . Mrs. E. D.," described how the women, "When weary . . . supinely laid / On Beds of Vi'lets under some cool shade." As the nineteenth century drew to a close, the French lesbian poet and fiction writer Renée VIVIEN, known as the "Muse of the Violets," wrote in "Epitaph," "Earth holds you; on your forehead violets weep," and in "The Rocket," "In a fleeting hymeneal kiss, I was the lover / Of the night, her hair tangled with violets." The Sapphic symbolism of violets survived into the 1930s, popularized by the play *The Captive* (1926) by Edouard Bourdet. In the twentieth century, violets came to be associated with effeminacy and male homosexuality in western Europe, the United States, Guatemala, and elsewhere.

Virgo In Euro-western ASTROLOGY, zodiac sign ruling from (approximately) August 23 until September 22, associated with a critical, discriminating nature and with eloquence, typically depicted as a maiden, sometimes carrying a sheaf of wheat. Figures associated with Virgo and with gender and/or sexual variance include: ATALANTA, ATTIS, BRITOMARTIS, CAMILLA, HERMES, NARCISSUS, and the PLEIADES.

Vishnu In Hinduism, the deity who maintains and restores cosmic order. While Vishnu shares many relationships with female beings, he also shares an intimate relationship with the god SHIVA, who becomes enamoured of him when he assumes the form or persona of a beautiful, seductive woman named MOHINI. From the union of Vishnu and Shiva, the god HARIHARA is born.

Vivien, Renée (1877-1909) American-born lesbian writer who settled in Paris, her primary lover being the writer Natalie Clifford BARNEY (1876-1972). Profoundly influenced by SAPPHO and by the Symbolist and Decadent writers and artists of *fin de siècle* Paris, Vivien was an ardent pagan for the greater part of her life, converting to Christianity only on the brink of death – a conversion common to many artists of the late nineteenth and early twentieth centuries. A devotee of both Goddess Reverence and Buddhism and a believer in REINCARNATION, Vivien's writings offer a veritable treasure of lesbian-spiritual imagery. She and Barney shared a vision of lesbian women reconstructing the THIASOS of SAPPHO at MYTILENE on the island of LESBOS; unfortunately, this dream failed to materialize, due in large part to difficulties the two women were experiencing in their relationship.

Becoming known as the "Muse of the VIOLETS," Vivien's works are rich in the imagery of flowers and perfumes (the writer Colette complained of the "funereal perfumes" permeating her friend Vivien's home), and in which the controlling atmosphere is one of melancholy. Perhaps due in part to this sensibility, many lesbian-feminists of the 1970s failed to appreciate her important contributions to lesbian literature and to Women's Spirituality, indeed, some even condemned her as a "sell-out" because she treated subjects such as the VAMPIRE and SADOMASOCHISM, insisting that feminist women would not of their own accord venture into these areas – a peculiar essentialist notion found among social constructionist theorists. In the 1990s, however, a younger generation of lesbians and other queer-identified persons are reclaiming Vivien as an erotico-spiritual radical ancestor. One of the finest works on Vivien is Karla Jay's *The Amazon and the Page: Natalie Clifford Barney and Renée Vivien* (1988). Exemplary of Vivien's writing is a passage from *A Woman Appeared to Me* (*Une Femme m'apparut,* 1904) which reads, "At other times she would dress as a Greek shepherd, and the music of the invisible pipes of PAN would seem to follow her footsteps and her eyes would glitter as if at the lascivious nakedness of maenads . . . She was another Androgyne, vigorous as an ephebe, graceful as a woman. I fervently adored her . . . as a priestess serving a cult of abandoned altars."

Vogel, Karen (1950-   )   Sculptor painter, stone carver, stained glass artist, jeweler, and furniture maker, Vogel, born in New York City and living in northern California, is best known for the *Motherpeace* TAROT deck, which she co-created with Vivki NOBLE. "Inspiration for my work," Vogel explains, "comes from being in wild places, especially in California and in the desert of the American Southwest. I also draw inspiration from my love for women and for the Goddess in all Her forms . . . My other primary source of inspiration is a deep and mysterious feeling which I attribute to the ancestors, who lean on me, waiting to be embodied in artistic forms." Vogel's works include: *The Corn Mother*, a doll over seven feet tall, made of wood, beads, kernels of corn, and other media, to be used in rituals; *Temple of My Familiar*, a wood carving simultaneously depicting an ancestor in female human and other manifestations, including a coyote, mountain lion, rattlesnake, and whiptail lizard, an artwork inspired by Alice Walker's novel of the same title; *Guardians of the Sacred*, a wood sculpture depicting the spiralling dance of two rattlesnakes; *The Gatekeepers*, a relief made of black walnut depicting two women in a loving embrace; and *Javelina Asked Me to Dance*, a painting portraying a wild pig and an equally wild woman dancing in the Arizona desert. Vogel is also the author-creator of a handmade book entitled *17,000 Years of Lesbian Tantric Art*.

W

Wahineomao "Thrush Woman," a goddess of Hawaiian mythology who is the intimate companion (AIKANE) of the goddess HI' IAKA or the goddess HOPOE.

Wairaka Lengendary Maori AMAZON (*wahine toa*) who saves a male hero from drowning as she chants. She marries but ultimately leaves her husband. She is accompanied by a troupe of women and settles with them at Owairaka. Due to her transgenderism and her apparent preference for female companionship, some contemporary Maori women-living women have begun to claim Wairaka as an archetypal Maori lesbian, *takatapui wahine*, as N. Te Awekotuku (1991) suggests.

Wakdjunkaga Nicknamed the "First Born," this figure, whose name means "tricky one," is linked to the Native American Winnebago tribe TWO-SPIRIT shaman called *siange* (or *shiange*). Wakdjunkaga is an archetypal Fool and TRICKSTER, who through his exploits learns one lesson after another. Wakdjunkaga is associated with hunting, fishing, and agriculture and sometimes becomes identified with "the Devil" in the beliefs of the Peyote ritualist. During his many adventures Wakdjunkaga transforms himself into a woman. In one tale Wakdjunkaga marries the son of a chief with whom he bears three sons. He sometimes is said to have a "false vulva" which one time he lost jumping over a ditch, and sometime carries around his enormous penis, which he calls "Little Brother," in a box. In another tale, Wakdjunkaga is traveling with Fox and other companions during the winter who have failed to store enough food. They hear that the son of the chief of a nearby village is single and a good hunter, so Wakdjunkaga decides to seduce and marry the son in order to obtain food for his traveling companions. This time Wakdjunkaga makes a vulva from an elk's liver, and breasts from elk's kidneys. Then he has intercourse with Fox and Jaybird to make him pregnant. Soon after he sets out towards the village to seduce the chief's son. Wakdjunkaga meets an old woman who is charmed by him (as a beautiful woman) and introduces him to the village women. Having seduced the chief's son, a wedding feast of corn and bear-ribs is prepared and the marriage takes place. Wakdjunkaga gives birth to three sons and all goes fine for a year till Wakdjunkaga's false vulva again falls off and his true identitiy is discovered. Wakdjunkaga, Fox and companions leave the village, but Wakdjunkaga is not totally condemned. Indeed, some elders say that despite his trickery, he "loved all things, and was genial and good-natured."

Wakea Sky father of the indigenous religion of Hawaii with the Mother Goddess PAPA, Wakea created all life. According to some, they both share an intimate relationship with their servant HAAKAUILANANI.

Walker, Ethel (1861-1951) English lesbian painter influenced by Eastern spiritual traditions as well as the mystical teachings of Emanuel Swedenborg (1688-1772), subtly expressed in works such as *Zone of Hate* (1914-1915) and *Zone of Love* (1930-1932), the latter depicting the soul as a young woman awakening.

Walker, Mitch (1951-) One of the originators of the contemporary Gay Spirituality movement and also of the Radical Faeries, a writer, and a psychologist in the Jungian, or archetypal, tradition. Walker's essay "The Double: An Archetypal Configuration" (1976) and *Visionary Love: A Spirit Book of Gay Mythology* (1980) are considered seminal texts on Gay Spirituality. Since the early 1980s, Walker has facilitated workshops on gay male spirituality and dreamwork, first in his "Visions and Voices" workshops in Berkeley, California and later, together with Chris Kilbourne, Don Kilhefner, and others, in "Treeroots," a non-profit gay-centered organization. One of Walker's primary concerns in the 1990s is that many gay men are drawn to spirituality not in order to explore inner processes but rather, ironically, to avoid focusing on them. He sees this as especially evident in spiritual movements which avoid discussion of the more disturbing aspects of human experience. Receiving a doctorate in psychology in 1987, Walker is currently completing *The Uranian Soul: Studies in Gay-Centered Jungian Psychology*.

Ward, Drew (1950-) Master of the art of making incense and Founder of Light and Shadow, a San Francisco-based supplier of metaphysical merchandise. Ward is among an emerging group of merchants who are "out of the closet" in terms of both their sexuality and their practice of Neopaganism and/or related spiritual traditions. "My personal spiritual practices," says Ward, "include elements of Celtic, Egyptian, Hindu, Norse, and Slavic paganism." Ward is especially drawn to the Egyptian god MIN, whose erect phallus and flail associate him with "leather" or "S/M" (i.e. SADOMASOCHISM). Ward is also drawn – as are many contemporary queer-identified Neopagans – to manifestations of the so-called "shadow" aspect of the Great Goddess, including HECATE and KALI.

Ward, Jim (1941-) Founder and president of Gauntlet, Inc. Like his lover Drew WARD, Jim is an openly gay and openly pagan businessperson. Inspired by various spiritual paths including Buddhism, Witchcraft, and Native American religions, as well as by the ideas of the renowned mythologist Joseph Campbell, Ward looks upon body modification through piercing and TATTOOING, especially when performed in a ritual context, as an aesthetic response to a need among queer-identified persons to experience initiation into a kind of tribal community.

Warner, Sylvia Townsend (1893-1978) English lesbian writer who often used imagery of Witchcraft and the supernatural in her works, as in *Lolly Willowes* (1926) and *The Kingdoms of Elfin* (1976). She was the intimate companion of Valentine Ackland (1906-1969) for many years.

We' wha (1849-1896) Zuni TWO-SPIRIT *lhamana* who served as a spiritual guide, dressing in traditional female dress and excelling at sacred arts and crafts. One of the most renowned two-spirit leaders, lauded by President Grover Cleveland and others, We' wha is the subject of Matilda Coxe Stevenson's "The Zuni Indians" (1901-1902) and of Will Roscoe's acclaimed anthropological treatise *The Zuni Man-Woman* (1991).

Weasel Sacred attribute of the Greek goddess DEMETER and the favored animal form assumed by the Thessalian witches. Ancient Greeks believed that the weasel produced young through its mouth; in this way it became associated with oral intercourse. Perhaps due to these associations as well as to the European Renaissance folkloric belief that female weasels often engaged in same-sex coupling, the weasel became a signifier of lesbianism in sixteenth-century France.

Wendi Xiao (reigned 179-157 BCE) Chinese emperor and religious eclectic who sought to syncretize shamanistic practices with Taoism (especially Taoist alchemy) and Confucianism. He is most remembered, however, for a homoerotic dream. In this dream, a handsome young boatman ferried him across a celestial river to the abode of the Immortals. Several days after the dream occurred, the emperor encountered a boatman whom he recognized as the young man of his dream. Without hesitating, he asked the young man, nicknamed Deng Tong, to be his lover. The two lived together in the palace until the emperor's death.

Wheat Sacred attribute of the Greek goddesses DEMETER and PERSEPHONE, employed in the ELEUSINIAN MYSTERIES. The homoerotically inclined Spanish writer Federico García LORCA (1898-1936), knowledgeable of the ancient mysteries, uses this symbol in his "Ode to Walt Whitman" in the expression "the truths of the wheat" (*las verdades del trigo*), an expression which refers to the association of Nature and the sacred with "manly love" in the life and work of the poet Walt WHITMAN (1819-1892) as opposed to the absence of these in the lives of gay men living in the urban jungle of New York City in the early twentieth century. Lorca writes, "New York of wires and death: / What angel do you carry hidden in your cheek? / What perfect voice will tell the truths of the wheat?"

When Night Is Falling (1995) Film written and directed by Calvinist-reared Patricia Rozema which depicts an interrelationship of lesbian desire and the spiritual or mythic. The narrative focuses on Camille, a professor of mythology, a Christian, and the wife of Martin, who dreams of women making love under water and then encounters Petra, a circus performer who introduces her to a magical universe. Critic Paula Nechak describes the film as a "phantasmagorical chaotic clash of cultures, sex, art and religion."

White, T(erence) H(anbury) (1906-1964) Homoerotically inclined English writer best known for his tetralogy *The Once and Future King* (1939-1958), a contemporary retelling of the legend of King Arthur, MERLIN, and other inhabitants of Camelot, inspiring the musical *Camelot* (1960) and the animated Disney film *The Sword in the Stone* (1963). The deep friendship of the mentor-wizard Merlin and the young Arthur as well as the wizard's shapeshifting capabilities may subtly reflect White's concern with the interrelationship of homoeroticism, transgenderism, and the mythic.

White Whale Woman Inuit (or Eskimo) deity or spirit most often associated with female gender variant or TWO-SPIRIT shamans. White Whale Woman is said to have married a woman of the Fly Agaric clan. Her marriage to this woman suggests that White Whale Woman may have been associated with the ritual use of fly agaric, the *amanita muscaria* mushroom.

Whitman, Walt (1819-1892) Homoerotically inclined or bisexual American Transcendentalist writer, acclaimed for his epic poem *Leaves of Grass* (1855), including *Song of Myself*, the bisexual "Children of Adam" and the homoerotic "Calamus" poems. While Whitman loved many men and perhaps also a number of women, his primary lover was a streetcar driver named Peter Doyle. Whitman celebrated the body and found it indivisible from spirit, writing in *Song of Myself*: "Divine am I inside and out, and I make holy whatever I touch or am touch'd from, / The scent of these arm-pits is aroma finer than prayer, / This head more than churches, bibles, and all the creeds. / . . . / If I worship one thing more than another it shall be the spread of my own body." Whitman's spiritual vision was rooted not only in the body and nature but more specifically in the power to transform oneself into or to radically identify with another person, plant, animal, or other entity, a process recalling shamanic transformation – including gender metamorphosis as well as theriomorphic (animal) and vegetal transformation – and priestly embodiment of the divine. "I am the man," he tells us, ". . . I suffer'd, I was there. / . . . / We are Nature . . . / We become plants, trunks, foliage, roots, bark, / We are bedded in the ground, we are rocks, / We are oaks . . . / . . . we are two among the wild herds . . . / We are two fishes swimming in the sea together, / . . . / We are snow, rain, cold, darkness . . ." In the late nineteenth and early twentieth centuries, Whitman's vision came to be called "cosmic consciousness," a term coined or at least popularized by the Canadian psychiatrist Richard Bucke. In *Cosmic Consciousness*, published in 1901, Bucke wrote: "The prime characteristic of cosmic consciousness is . . . a consciousness of the cosmos . . . Along with [this] . . . there occurs an intellectual enlightenment or illumination which would place the individual on a new plane of existence – would make him a member of a new species." For Bucke, Whitman was "the best, most perfect, example the world has so far had of the Cosmic Sense." Bucke believed that Whitman had attained this state of consciousness in June 1853 and that this experience had led to the writing of *Leaves of Grass*. For Whitman, nature was a sanctuary in which to celebrate the love of men for each other. Byrne S. Fone describes this sanctuary in terms of a homoerotic ARCADIA. Of the rituals undertaken in this homoerotic paradise, he writes: "These rites are transformational and involve the union of lovers, the loving and sexual fraternity of men, and the washing away of societal guilt." "In paths untrodden, / In the growth by margins of pond-waters," Whitman "celebrate[s] the need of comrades" by singing songs "of manly attachment" and by distributing, in a ritualistic manner, tokens of homoerotic intimacy: lilacs, branches of pine, moss, laurel leaves, sage. Foremost of these is the phallic calamus: "And this, O this shall henceforth be the token of comrades, this CALAMUS-root shall, / Interchange it youths, with each other! let none render it back!" Of this ritual, Fone writes: "Memory and desire flood in as he offers the calamus to his troop of young men in a sacred ceremony . . . [by which all are joined] in wedlock . . . The vow is eternal fidelity not only to one another but to the homosexual life itself, for the calamus is the symbol of that life." While nature offered the poet a sanctuary in which to express his love of comrades, Whitman, who refused to be "outed" during his lifetime, dreamed of an American city of the future in which nothing would be "greater . . . than the quality of robust love." This was to be the "new city of Friends," a UTOPIA "invincible to the attacks of the whole rest of the earth," ruled by "the love of comrades / By the manly love of

comrades." One wonders if Whitman imagined what an enormous role his work would play in the creation of the early homosexual rights movement, the later homophile and gay liberation movements, and the Gay Spirituality and Queer Spirit movements, as forecast in a letter written by John Addington SYMONDS to Havelock Ellis on May 6, 1890: "In one word, does Whitman imagine that there is lurking in manly love the stuff of a new spiritual energy, the benefit of which would prove of benefit to society?" Within two years of this letter, Whitman's vision of comradeship had been nicknamed "the new religion." According to William James, by 1902 many persons had come to "regard Walt Whitman as the restorer of the eternal natural religion. He has infected them with his own love of comrades, with his own gladness that he and they exist. Societies are actually formed for his cult; a periodical organ [*The Conservator*] exists for its propagation . . . hymns are written by others in his peculiar prosody; and he is even explicitly compared with the founder of the Christian religion."

Wikiga-Winagu   In Okinawa, where Shamanism has been practiced primarily by females, there was in the past a ceremony known as *winagu nati*, "becoming a woman," in which males were dressed in feminine attire and by which they were allowed to enter sacred groves and to become shamans. According to William P. Lebra, "male shamans [in Okinawa] tend to be regarded as more deviant than their female counterparts," and their "assumption of a role identified with females . . . may suffice to categorize them as effeminate." He also notes that one informant told him: "There are not many male *yuta* [shamans], and some of them seem like *wikiga-winagu*," that is to say, gender variant males engaging in same-sex eroticism.

Wildan (or **Ghilman**)   In Islam, handsome youths resembling the Greek GANYMEDE who serve as CUPBEARERS to the souls of deceased faithful Muslim males in Paradise. In the Holy Qur'an, they are mentioned on three occasions; in one of these passages, they are described as appearing "to the beholder's eyes . . . like sprinkled pearls." The anonymous authors of the entry on "Liwat" ("Sodomy") in *The Encyclopaedia of Islam* stress that while in general, homoeroticism is condemned in the Qur'an, it "indeed allows a certain ambiguity in passages where the believers are promised that in paradise they will be attended by menservants."

Wild Women   In Germanic mythology, elf- or fairy-like female beings who dwell together inside a hollow hill called Wunderberg (or Underberg). They are depicted as being very beautiful, with long, flowing, shining hair. They live in a magnificent palace surrounded by a stately garden within the hill. Those who honor them with offerings are rewarded with help in farm labor. While they occasionally "adopt" children who are abused by their parents, and occasionally have love affairs with men, they prefer the companionship of each other.

Wilde, Oscar (1854-1900)   Homoerotically inclined, possibly transgendered, British Aesthete and Decadent writer who was betrayed by his lover, Lord Alfred Douglas (1870-1945), and was imprisoned for homosexuality. While his novel *The Picture of Dorian Gray* (1891), his play *Salomé* (1893), and other works give expression to the interrelationship of same-sex eroticism, transgenderism, and the sacred or mythic, few people are aware of the depth of Wilde's spirituality. In *De Profundis* (1897), for example, he writes: "I am conscious . . . that behind all this [artistic] beauty . . . there is some spirit hidden of which the painted forms and shapes are but modes of manifestation, and it is with this spirit that I desire to become in harmony . . . The Mystical in Art, the Mystical in Life, the Mystical in Nature – this is what I am looking for." Focusing on the reverence for Nature, he continues: "I have a strange longing for the great simple primeval things, such as the sea, to me no less of a mother than the Earth . . . the Earth [that] is mother to us all . . . I feel sure that in elemental forces there is purification, and I want to go back to them and live in their presence . . . Nature . . . will hang the night with stars so that I may walk abroad in the darkness without stumbling . . . she will cleanse me in great waters, and with bitter herbs make me whole." Like other poets of the *fin de siècle*, Wilde associated reverence for Nature with Greco-Roman paganism. He mourned the passing of paganism, struggled with Christianity, and awaited the rebirth of the old religion. In "Santa Decca," he laments: "The Gods are dead: no longer do we bring / To grey-eyed Pallas crowns of olive-leaves! / Demeter's child no more hath tithe of sheaves, / And in the noon, the careless shepherds sing, / For Pan is dead, and all the wantoning / By sweet secret glade and devious haunt is o'er: / Young Hylas seeks the water-springs no more; / Great Pan is dead, and Mary's son is King." In *De Profundis*, Wilde honored MARSYAS, apostle of CYBELE, satyr, musician, lover of males, defeated by APOLLO, flayed. For Wilde, Marsyas became a polyvalent symbol of all these components, as well as an archetypal condensation of the Aesthetic-Symbolist-Decadent aesthetic: "When Marsyas was 'torn from the scabbard of his limbs . . . he had no more song,' the Greek said. Apollo had been victor. The lyre had vanquished the reed. But perhaps the Greeks were mistaken. I hear in much modern art the cry of Marsyas. It is bitter in Baudelaire, sweet and plaintive in Lamartine, mystic in Verlaine."

Wilgefortis, Saint (aka **Wylgeforte, Uncumber, Ontkommena, Kümmernis, Librada, Livrade,** dates uncertain)   Saint Wilgefortis, said to be a daughter of a king of Portugal, appears to have lived during the early Middle Ages. When an adolescent, she decided to devote herself to religious life. Her father, however, would have none of this, insisting that she be married to the king of Sicily. Wilgefortis, whose name means "strong virgin," prayed to JESUS Christ to save her from the marriage. He answered her prayer by giving her the long beard of an old man. Her father, accusing her of sorcery, forced her to wear a veil and continued with the wedding plans. When, at the wedding ceremony, her face was revealed, the king of Sicily cried out in horror, refusing to marry her. Her father then had Wilgefortis crucified. St Wilgefortis has been revered since the ninth century. As a healer, Wilgefortis takes away pain and illness, aids women in childbirth, and watches over the dying. She is also a patron of the physically disabled. As a liberator she frees political prisoners and liberates women from abusive marriages. Offerings to her include oats, which, according to some scholars, link her to DEMETER and other grain goddesses of antiquity; and DOVES, which link her to APHRODITE, especially the Bearded Aphrodite, APHRODITOS. She is fêted on July 20.

William Rufus (1056-1100)   Homoerotically inclined king of England from 1087 until 1100. William Rufus was in many ways a wise ruler, and it is not surprising that more conservative scholars would wish to whitewash his image in order to restore to him the respect he deserves. Unfortunately, these scholars are too often guided by homophobic, pro-Christian, and chauvinistic agendas, which encourage them to ignore or deny certain aspects of Rufus's character. Rufus has been described as a "powerfully built, thick-set" man, "red-haired and ruddy in complexion," who dressed in the "latest foppish fashions, his long locks framing a clean-shaven face." According to Jack Lindsay in *The Normans and Their World*, "Rufus seems certainly to have been homosexual." Lindsay reminds us that "sodomy was . . . a common practice" among Norman nobles. Rufus appears to have been attracted to other men like himself who displayed a mixture of traditionally feminine and masculine traits. While, like himself, they wore their hair long and wore colorful, form-fitting clothes, they were also expert soldiers. One of Rufus's lovers may have been his nephew, Prince William, who died in 1120 in the famous wreck of the White Ship, a catastrophe believed by Christian zealots to have been a divine punishment for homoerotic orgies occurring on board. Rufus was despised by Christian authorities not only for his homoerotic and gender variant behavior but also for his respectful treatment of Jews and his alleged worship of pre-Christian deities, including LOKI, by whose face he was said to swear. While Margaret Murray's theory that Rufus was one of a long line of kings who were ritually sacrificed strikes us as farfetched, certain instances surrounding his death do strike us as peculiar. Not only did his final words suggest that he may have known he was to die, but, if we may trust the Abbot of Clugny, the latter had a prophetic dream of the King's death the night before he died. Furthermore, Rufus died on Lammas morning, the date of an important Celtic festival concerning sacrifice and the harvest. Still further, the Earl of Cornwall claimed to have seen, shortly after Rufus's death, a goat carrying the corpse of the King on its back. One of those Christian authorities who viciously attacked the court of Rufus was Anselm, who participated in a reactionary movement against the homoerotic, gender variant, and possibly pagan expressions of Rufus's court. This movement culminated in the mid-twelfth century, with the Council of Nablus declaring burning alive as the penalty for sodomy. An old homophobic belief of Roman converts to Christianity, that sodomy causes earthquakes, was also resuscitated at this time.

Winant, Fran (1943-)   New York lesbian artist and poet who incorporates in her work images of ancient goddesses such as TIAMAT, the theme of metamorphosis, and a system of "secret hieroglyphics."

Winckelmann, Johann Joachim (1717-1768) Homoerotically inclined German art historian, his magnum opus being the *History of the Art of Antiquity* (1764). Drawn primarily to castrati who sang in the OPERA and inspired by Greek religion, mythology, philosophy, and art, as well as by European Renaissance Neoplatonism, he celebrated the male nude as an embodiment of the Divine and homoerotic love as a form of intimacy leading (ideally) to spiritual enlightenment. Simon Richter notes that in terms of the *History*, Winckelmann was proudest of the aesthetic section, wherein he argues that ideal "beauty is realized within a homosexual and desiring gaze trained on the bodies of eunuchs and castrati." In Richter's view, this is a "philosophical treatment of beauty that is distinctly gay." G. S. Rousseau (1987) suggests that while Winckelmann served as librarian to Cardinal Allesandro Albani (1692-1779) at Rome, he and the Cardinal as well as the bisexual painter Anton Rafael Mengs (1728-1779) participated in a cult honoring the Greek gods PAN and PRIAPUS and the divinized lover of the Roman emperor HADRIAN, ANTINOUS (110-130).

Wind, South (or **Southern Wind**)   The Chinese term "*nan feng* ," akin to expressions (*nan seh, yi nan wei ming*) meaning male custom or fashion (i.e. sodomy), was used as a metaphor during the Ming dynasty (1368-1644) to refer to a sudden and explosive cultural phenomenon centering on male gender variant and homoerotic behavior. This was written about by Shen Te-fu and Hsieh Chao-che, contrasting what was seen as situational homosexuality with this new, permanent "*nan feng*" of the fashionable upper class "gentlemen of ambition." This phenomenon was said to have spread like a strong wind from its origins in southern China to the entertainment district of Nanking and thence to other economic classes. It was also seen as a revival of older Taoist and Buddhist practices disapproved of by Neo-Confucianism. Hsieh Chao-che's conclusion concerning this phenomenon was "the whole world has gone crazy." When African-American Texan feminist Dottie Curry visited China in 1995 to participate in the International Women's Conference there, she observed that *nan feng* is still being used in late twentieth-century China as a label for gay persons.

Wine   Beverage symbolic of blood, the life force or *élan vital*, eroticism, sacrifice, eternal life and the "divine intoxication of the soul." In Greek religion and myth, wine is especially associated with DIONYSUS, the god of ecstasy, and with SATYRS, who are in turn linked to homoeroticism and transgenderism. In classical symbology, the goatskin in which wine is kept is itself symbolic of androgyny, with the neck being phallic and the body of the container being likened to the womb. In Islamic and especially in Sufi poetry, wine often signifies homoerotic love, with a young man's lips being compared to wine, and the cupbearer as a handsome youth reminiscent of the WILDAN, who serve the faithful in Paradise. The poet Al-Gobari writes: "The boy who pours the wine / gives off an enchanting perfume. / Ah, just to place your lips / on his lips the color of wine." Lesbian poetry is not without its references to wine. In "Come, Goddess of Kypros," Renée VIVIEN writes, "Pour the wine of Cyprus and the wine of LESBOS, whose hot languor smiles and insinuates itself," and Amy Lowell, in "A Decade," writes, "When you came you were like red wine and honey, / And the Taste of you burnt my mouth with its sweetness."

Winkte   Name given to TWO-SPIRIT shamans by the Lakota people of North America. *Winktes* were believed to be especially powerful healers and magicians, often effecting transformation through chants. When *winktes* died, according to the Lakota shaman Lame Deer, they "had a special hill where they were buried." Lame Deer remembered asking a *winkte* "what he would be in the spirit land, a man or a woman." "Both," the *winkte* replied.

Wittig, Monique (1935-)   French lesbian philosopher and writer whose experimental and speculative fictions foreground a unique lesbian vision. While *Les Guérillères* (1969) centers on the struggle of Amazons against patriarchy, *The Lesbian Body* (1973) celebrates the interrelationship of lesbian passion and the spiritual dimension of life. Drawing upon narratives from classical antiquity and other sources and reinterpreting them in the light of woman-centered desire, Wittig introduces us to such characters as Ulyssea and Christa. We also encounter SAPPHO, who has been deified in Wittig's universe. Of the goddess INANNA/ISHTAR, embodied by a lover, Wittig writes, "You are the tallest, Ishtar goddess of goddesses you are the powerful one, blessed be your name over centuries of centuries. You are the possessor of all power, you are strong impassive while you abide in the green in the violet of the heavens . . . desire for you overwhelms m/e once for all together with terror as befits all your adorers" In *Lesbian Peoples: Material for a Dictionary* (1976), Wittig, in weaving together traditional and speculative mythic figures, symbols and narratives, constructs a lesbian-centered ARCADIA or UTOPIA.

Wiya Numpa "Double Woman," a Native American Indian, Lakota female spiritual being linked to ANOG ITE and associated with women-loving women. Wiya Numpa "links two women together, making them one in Her power." These women, her devotees, are called *koskalaka* and are described as "Double Woman's daughters."

Wizard of Oz, The Film of 1939 delighting children, those young at heart, and queer-identified persons, especially gay men, for generations. The film stars Judy Garland, a gay icon, and is based upon the 1900 novel by L. Frank Baum. A number of gay analyses of the film, most notably that by Jungian writer Robert Hopcke, suggest that while this sentimental film is appreciated by many individuals, it holds a special resonance for queer-identified persons in juxtaposing everyday reality, i. e., homophobic, lesbophobic, biphobic, and transgender-phobic reality, represented by Kansas, to a magical land of acceptance somewhere "Over the Rainbow," represented by Oz. Queer-identified persons discover kinship in a majority of the characters. While dazzled by the Emerald City, they (we), like Dorothy, long for "home." Gay men discover aspects of themselves in both the compassionate Glenda, the Good Witch of the North, and the vengeful Wicked Witch of the West, as well as in the kind-hearted and helpful Scarecrow and Tin Man and the sissyish Cowardly Lion. Women-identified women note that the Land of Oz is not run by the Wizard, a well-meaning humbug, but by female Witches. The authors of this encyclopaedia have also been told that some "butch dykes" feel kinship with the Munchkin lads. When the film is shown in a theatre like the Castro Theatre in San Francisco, it is transformed into a rite celebrating the discovery of acceptance and community. This reading of the film and especially of the song "Over the Rainbow" appears to have been acknowledged by the elder Garland as well as by the diva Patti Labelle, who sang it in tribute to the African-American gay singer Sylvester upon his death. Radical Faeries and lesbian devotees of the Goddess are among those whose ALTARS often display images and objects, especially the Ruby Slippers, drawn from the film. Contemporary lesbian poet Gerry Gomez Pearlberg employs the mythos of Oz as a metaphor for lesbian sexual passion, writing, "There was a ruby slipper between my thighs, / a poppy field in the back of my brain. / Though Kansas might as well have been a globe away."

Women's Country In this country of Chinese legend, sometimes described as an island, women bathing in the waters often become pregnant. In the event that one gives birth to a male child, the child dies before it has reached the age of three. Thus the only relationships existing in Women's Country are those between and among women.

Women's Kingdom Chinese mythical land, different from Women's Country. It was described in the eighteenth-century novel *Ching hua yüan* (*Romance of the Flowers in the Mirror*) by Li Ju-chen. In this kingdom there are both men and women but they perform reversed gender roles. Men call themselves "women," wear skirts and run households. Women call themselves "men," wear boots and tall hats, and preside over public affairs.

Wrestling Sport patronized by the Amazonian Greco-Roman goddess PALAESTRA. Wrestling schools were believed by ancient Greeks and Romans to foster homoerotic and perhaps also lesbian relationships and democratic attitudes. Consequently, tyrants fearing that same-sex lovers would attempt to depose them frequently set fire to wrestling schools. In the pantheon of the African-diasporic spiritual tradition of Vodou, BARON LIMBA and BARON LUNDY open a wrestling school embracing cultic homoeroticism as a form of magical practice.

Wu Tsao (fl. c. 1830) Chinese poet-lyricist and Taoist priestess. According to A. and W. Barnstone (1981), "She may be considered China's major lesbian poet"; Kenneth Rexroth and Ling Chung (1972) describe Wu Tsao as "one of the great lesbian poets of all time." Wu Tsao was the daughter of a merchant and later the wife of a merchant; neither seemed to understand her or her work. Around 1837 she retired to a secluded monastery, where she attained renown as a poet and a priestess. Her lyrics are addressed to intimate female companions. Wu Tsao, in "For the Courtesan Ch'ing Lin: To the Tune 'The Love of the Immortals'", drawing upon symbols from Taoist ALCHEMY (which in major respects resembles Hindu TANTRA), compares her lover to a "celestial companion / Come from the Green Jade City of Heaven." She depicts her as a young woman, also a poet or lyricist, dressed in green and wearing jade and coral ornaments around her waist. They meet on a misty spring evening to "play wine games," to recite poems, and to sing to each other, with the lover singing the melancholy "Remembering South of the River." Then they "paint each others' beautiful eyebrows." "I want to possess you completely," Wu Tsao whispers to her beloved Ch'ing Lin, "let me buy you a red painted boat / And carry you away." Wu Tsao is remembered by the late twentieth-century Chinese-American lesbian writer Kitty Tsui in "Give Joan Chen My Phone Number Anytime" (1995).

Wudi Xiao (reigned 140-87 BCE)   Homoerotically inclined Chinese Emperor known for his spiritual eclecticism. He is credited with the founding of China's first universities and with the institution of certain rites honoring the spirits of the earth known as the *feng shan* rites. Wudi spent a great amount of time studying Taoist alchemy. Through this study, he hoped to discover an elixir of immortality. Among Wudi's male lovers was the eunuch Li Yannian. Eunuchs, however traditionally masculine they might behave, were, due to the loss of genitalia, considered transgendered persons. Bestowed with the official title of "Harmonizer of Tunes," Li Yannian was a musician who composed and performed hymns for use in the *feng shan* rites.

X

Xian (or **Hsien**) "FAIRY" men of Chinese myth, who were often attracted to mortal men. Occasionally they were given leave by the Lord of the Fairies (sometimes identified with Buddha) to seek handsome young lovers and to remain with them for a brief time. Since, however, time passes much more slowly in the heavens than on the earth, these relationships between fairies and humans sometimes lasted for years, without the Lord of the Fairies noticing. Frequently, however, they were fleeting relationships, bringing great melancholy to the mortal lover upon the fairy's return to the heavens.

Xochipilli (also **Naxcit-Xuchitl**) AZTEC Prince of FLOWERS, consort of the goddess XOCHIQUETZAL. Xochipilli is known by various names, including Makuil-Xochitl, Xochiwitl, Chikome-Xochitl, Xocbitun, Piltzintekutli, H Kinxoc, and Balon-Mayel; several of these appellations indicate that his worship spread beyond the Aztecs. Xochipilli is a god of flowers and sensual pleasures. He is the patron of entertainers – dancers, singers, actors, jugglers, gymnasts, and game-players (especially of the *nexoxochitlaxiliztli*, the "game of throwing flowers"). He is also the patron of perfumers. He delights in perfumes containing many exotic essences, called *xochitlanamactli*. Like other deities, Xochipilli brings not only joy but also suffering, especially to those who fail to make sacrifices to him. They are likely to be stricken with venereal disease or hemorrhoids. In Nahuatl, hemorrhoids are referred to as *xochiciutzlil*, "the flowers of the anus." Offerings to Xochipilli include toasted CORN and BUTTERFLY-shaped breads. Xochipilli was honored with Xochiquetzal at the Xochilhuitl festival as well as at the Tecuilhuitontli. Held in the seventh month of the Aztec year, the Tecuilhuitontli was an unusual festival in that human sacrifice played no part in it. It was, in the words of Father Durán, "an occasion for enjoying the flowers which abounded in that season," and in ancient texts was represented by "a man arranging [or men exchanging] flowers." It was a time when great banquets were held which emphasized dainty and exotic dishes and when flowers, "mantles, breechcloths, and jewels" were exchanged. HIERODULES wearing flower garlands and "elaborately embroidered *huipils*" danced in the streets, while noblemen reclined on couches, "surrounded by flowers, picking one up and laying it down, [then] taking another and abandoning it." As the god of dance, Xochipilli was honored with the *cuecuechcuicatl*, the "dance of the itch." This dance was compared by Durán to the Spanish saraband, "with all its wriggling and

grimacing and immodest mimicry." It was performed by hierodules and by transgendered *cihuayollo* males "dressed as women." As David F. Greenberg states, Xochipilli is "the patron of male homosexuality and male prostitution." His patronage of individuals engaging in these behaviors suggests a complex set of associations including the role of entertainer, the love of exotic foods and perfumes, male gender variance, and same-sex eroticism. Xochipilli has been identified with the Mesoamerican deity Naxcit-Xuchitl. This god's name means "Four Foot Flower," suggesting the flowering tree of Tamoanchan and perhaps thereby linking the deity with both Xochipilli and Xochiquetzal. Naxcit-Xuchitl appears to be a synthesis of several Mesoamerican deities including Xochipilli, Quetzalcoatl, and Kukulcan, a Yucatec culture hero. Naxcit is regarded as a legendary founder of Chichen Itzá. He is variously claimed to have been of Itzá, Toltec, or Mayan heritage. Naxcit is among those divine beings considered to have introduced homoerotic practices to the MAYAS. According to José Imbelloni, same-sex eroticism, at various times tolerated and punished by the Mayas, became known as the "sin" of Naxcit-Xuchitl.

Xochiquetzal Precious Flower, the AZTEC goddess of spring, the underworld, and non-procreative sexuality. She is commonly depicted as wearing a blue tunic woven with flowers, a garland of green feathers and red and yellow flowers, and golden earplugs and pendants. Flowers emerge from her mouth, symbolizing eloquence. A knife also emerges from her mouth, suggesting her ability to cut through chatter and lies. A red serpent, signifying unbridled passion, emerges from her vagina. Beneath her ocelot throne are marigolds and a skull, symbolic of the underworld. Marigolds, or *cempoalxochitl* ("twenty flowers"), continue to be offered to Xochiquetzal (albeit in the guise of the Virgin Mary) and to the deceased, whom she protects, on the Día de los Muertos (the Day of the Dead) in Mexico, the United States, and elsewhere. Other symbols sacred to Xochiquetzal are spiders, signifying the art of weaving and the interrelatedness of all life, and thorns, used to pierce the ears and other parts of the body during penance. Father Durán explains that Xochiquetzal is the patron of weavers, embroiderers, silversmiths, sculptors, and painters. She is also the patron of poets, "word weavers" who utter "flower words." As a patron of poets, Xochiquetzal is also the ruler of those who employ lyrical speech or song – in other words, charms – to work magic. Called *xochihua*, or "flower persons", the males among these artists are depicted as homosexually or bisexually inclined males who excel in amatory magic. According to Jésus Arango Cano, Xochiquetzal is a patron of HIERODULES and "hermaphrodites." He refers here not to a biological hermaphrodite but to a transgendered individual who may engage in same-sex eroticism. Depictions of male couples associated with Xochiquetzal, appearing in the *Codex Vaticanus* (Rios 3738) and *Codex Borbonicus*, with their legs touching or intertwined and their bodies covered by a single blanket, also indicate her linkage with homosexuality, especially when these images are compared with similar depictions of heterosexual couples. Astrological texts also indirectly suggest that *cihuayollo* males may have been born on "flower days" sacred to Xochiquetzal. In the *Florentine Codex* is an illustration depicting two men conversing with each other. The man on the left wears masculine clothing, has short hair, and sits on a stool. The man on the right – we know he is male because of his description in the text as a "pervert," "sodomite," and "effeminate . . . womanish" male – wears feminine clothing, has the knotted braids of Xochiquetzal, and sits gracefully on the ground. A large red flower, sacred to Xochiquetzal, looms between them suggestive of both poetic speech and amatory magic. This illustration, unfortunately, has a companion. In the picture to the right, the *cihuayollo* male no longer sits on the ground, but lies on a pile of burning logs. The illustrations were clearly meant to function as a warning to those who would follow the path of the *cihuayollo* male. In terms of her association with transgendered and woman-loving women, Xochiquetzal resides in the celestial paradise of Tamoanchan, also known as Ciutlampa, "the Place of Women," which appears to be inhabited primarily by women and transgendered males bearing BUTTERFLY wings. Of the Aztec transgendered, woman-loving woman, the *patlache*, it was said, "She follows the broad road, the path of the rabbit, of the deer." To Aztecs, this meant that the goddesses Xochiquetzal, represented by the deer, and Tlazolteotl, represented by the rabbit, were the protectors of *patlaches*. The Aztecs believed that Xochiquetzal, with XOCHIPILLI at her side, had governed the earth during that cosmic period known as the Fourth, Black, or Flower Sun. This Age of Xochiquetzal is depicted in the *Codex Vaticanus* (*Rios* 3738). Beneath Xochiquetzal, two figures dressed in masculine clothing and a third dressed in feminine clothing each hold a banner in one hand and a bouquet of flowers in the other. In the heavens, just above Xochiquetzal, float two flint knives, *tecpatl*, used to ritually wound the phallus. To the right of the Goddess and above one of the figures are thirteen stones, *tetl*, signifying male impotence or sterility. In Aztec culture, both flint knives and stones signify male gender variance. The Mayas also spoke of the Age of Flowers, which they called the Nikte Katun, the "Cosmic Cycle of the Four-Petalled Flower." This epoch was ruled by Naxcit-Xuchitl (the Mayan equivalent of Xochipilli). Unfortunately, our only descriptions of this age occur in texts hostile to the legendary epoch. An extremely hostile passage from the *Book of Chilam Balam* depicts the age as one ruled by "the [ass]hole suckers [*Ah calam chuuch*], / . . . the asshole sinners [*Ah cal pach*]." In spite of the Mayan perception of the Flower *katun*, José Imbelloni, Antonio Requeña, Clark Taylor and others have analyzed the data concerning this epoch from a less hostile position. They have concluded that this was an age in which the goddess Xochiquetzal (or her Mayan counterpart) was revered, in which women held political power or fought as warriors, and in which men became *cihuayollo* or "effeminate," spending their days weaving, painting, singing, dancing the "Dance of the Flowers," and engaging in same-sex eroticism. The Epoch of Flowers was said to have ended when a river of blood flooded the earth; it has been suggested that this refers to a disease of the blood which proved fatal to many persons.

Xolotl AZTEC god of Venus as the evening star, an intermediary between the earth and the underworld, and assistant to XOCHIQUETZAL and Citlalinicue, goddess of the Milky Way, in the creation of recycled human beings. Xolotl is also sometimes identified with Nanahuatl, who is "covered with running sores" and who both bestows and heals "diseases of the skin." In another aspect, he is the "dark twin" of the plumed serpent Quetzalcoatl; as such, he is the god of suicide. In another aspect, he is a handsome, unmarried young man who rules the paradise of Xolotlan, the "Land of Young Men." He is a patron of all those who engage in variant forms or eroticism. The literature suggests that he may have been especially associated with practitioners of SADOMASOCHISM.

Y

Yakkidhaalyk Among the Mohave of the American Southwest, a "welcome feast for warriors returning from a raid" which, in the past, was presided over by women and TWO-SPIRIT males, or ALYHAS.

Yakshas Mysterious fairy-like beings of Hindu mythology and religion who commonly dwell in trees or among plants of various kinds. They hold the powers of blessing and cursing, and also of shapeshifting, able to manifest themselves in male, female, or transgendered shapes at will.

Yao Jen "Monster." A term still used in eighteenth-century China to refer to transgendered persons. *Yao jen* were often alleged to practice magic or sorcery.

Yao Sabaoth Manifestation of the Biblical Lord invoked in a sixth-century CE Coptic spell for a man to obtain a male lover. The name Yao Sabaoth suggests the ineffable name of the Hebrew God, YHWH, in Greek letters. The "Lord of Hosts" is a frequently occurring name of God in the Hebrew Scriptures.

Yeats, William Butler (1865-1939) Irish writer known especially for his poems and tales inspired by Celtic mythology and folklore. During his lifetime, Yeats belonged to a number of occult organizations, including the Hermetic Order of the Golden Dawn. As head of the Order, Yeats's homophobia found a target in the person of Aleister CROWLEY, a ritual magician who dared to challenge him. With other members of the Order, Yeats forbade Crowley from initiation into the grade of Adeptus Minor, an initiation, Francis King explains in *The Magical World of Aleister Crowley* (1978) to which Crowley "was formally entitled." King continues, "The reason for this refusal was simple enough; the London adepts had heard that Crowley was a practicing homosexual and decided that, in the words of Yeats, a mystical society was not a moral reformatory."

Yellamma A form of the Hindu goddess Renuka, who is the mother of Parashurama (a manifestation of VISHNU). Her worship is centered in South India, where she is worshipped by JOGAPPA, transgendered males, and JOGAMMA, transgendered women. Like SHIVA, Yellamma has both erotic and ascetic aspects. She is sometimes associated with the goddess PARVATI. Those who neglect Yellama are often visited with *kadata* (troubles), as are those whom she chooses to possess or embody. While both groups may experience loss of appetite, sleeplessness, muscular problems in the fingers and legs, dizziness, vertigo, skin sores or ulcers, the latter, if male, may find himself impotent and/or confused as to his gender and/or sexual identity. He may also find that his hair has become matted (*kannada*). If these things happen to him, it is presumed that his troubles will cease when he is inititated into the cult of the goddess as a *jogappa*, a transgendered priest.

Yellow Color frequently associated with vitality and the healing power of the sun. In Euro-western symbolism, it has also been linked, especially since the nineteenth century, to madness. In ancient Greece, yellow was especially linked to the CROCUS, a typically yellow flower, the autumnal variety of which yields SAFFRON, believed to have obtained its name from a handsome youth loved by the god HERMES. Yellow was also associated with HYMENAEUS, a god of song and the lover of HESPERUS, and as such was employed in ceremonies of UNION. It was also the color of the KROKETOS, a sacred garment worn by priestesses and transgendered male priests. In Hinduism, and especially in TANTRA, yellow is also linked to saffron, which is employed in cultic homoeroticism and lesbianism as well as in heterosexual lovemaking. In the Yoruba-diasporic pantheon, yellow is linked to honey, as an aphrodisiac and medicine, and wealth and is assigned to the *orishá* OSHUN, a patron of same-sex as well as heterosexual lovers. Among the Navaho, yellow is among the attributes of the TWO-SPIRIT deity CALLING GOD, who wears yellow OWL feathers in his headdress and who was created from CORN.

Yemaya (or **Yemonjá, Iemanjá**) In the Yoruba-diasporic pantheon, the *orishá* Yemayá, identified with Our Lady of Regla, rules the sea and maternal compassion. In one of her aspects, however, she is a sorceress, capable of transforming herself into a man or a mouse. In this aspect, as Yemayá Okutí, she is referred to as an *obiní ologun*, a woman warrior; here, she is linked to transgendered and lesbian women. As Yemayá Olokun, she merges with Olokun, the *orishá* who rules the depths of the sea. Yemayá's association with homosexuality has not always been – and is not universally – positive. For instance, she is said to have divorced her husband ORÚNMILA, the god of divination, upon discovering him to be an *adodi*. In our own day, however, her association with homosexuality and male gender variance is generally positive. In *El Monte*, Lydia Cabrera relates a story told to her by a Lucumí priest. According to this priest, Yemayá once ventured into the country – or perhaps onto the island – of Laddo, inhabited solely by *adodis*. Yemayá, in spite of this, fell in love with one of the men; the *adodi*, in spite of himself, also fell in love with her. Since that time, she has been viewed as a patron of gay, bisexual, and gender variant men. In this aspect, she is commonly referred to as Yemayá Oddo, "of the river," indicating her association with Oshún. In a conversation the authors shared with a priestess of Lucumí, she spoke of Yemayá's special concern for persons with HIV/AIDS. "Endless appeals," she said, "should be made to Yemayá. Go to her and speak as a child to its mother. Tell her you did nothing to deserve this [i.e. HIV/ AIDS] and ask her to wash it away."

Yewá (or **Yegguá**) *Orishá*, in the Yoruba-diasporic pantheon, of death, identified with Our Lady of Montserrat. According to Migene González-Wippler, she "feeds on the dead," this feeding referred to as the "dark meal," suggesting a VAMPIRIC character. Yewá insists that her priestesses abstain from sexual intercourse with men. This has led to the belief that Yewá is a patron of lesbian women. Certain accounts indicate that lesbian women have numbered among her spiritual daughters.

Yin and Yang In Taoism, the Tao, or source of all life, is perceived as existing beyond gender. Nevertheless, it is often described as being comprised of yin and yang energies, with yin basically signifying the feminine and/or receptive and yang signifying masculine and/or active (assertive, aggressive). By way of the theory of correspondences, yin is linked to such things as the earth, water, the night, the moon, and winter, while yang is linked to the heavens, fire, daytime, the sun, and summer. Taoists hold that just as the Tao embraces both yin and yang, so every female being contains an element of the male or masculine, while every male being contains an element of the female or feminine. Nevertheless, in women, Taoists say, yin predominates, while in men, yang predominates. One may, however, alter the balances of yin and yang within the Self if one is learned in Taoist ALCHEMY or MAGIC. R. H. van Gulik (1961) observes that in terms of Taoist alchemy, homoerotic lovemaking was deemed acceptable in the sense that "intimate contact between two yang elements" does not result in a loss of vital force for either of the men, but rather in an "exchange of yang" energy. In terms of lesbian lovemaking, Fang Fu Ruan relates in *Sex in China: Studies in Sexology in Chinese Culture* (1991) that lesbianism was likewise accepted by

Taoist alchemists, due to the notion that "women's supply of yin . . . was believed to be unlimited in quantity." In her 1975 manifesto *Ask No Man Pardon*, lesbian writer Elsa GIDLOW, a student of Taoism and other Asian spiritual traditions, here linking lesbian desire and transgenderism, writes: "Women who are lovers of one another increase their yang energies while fully living their yin, thus inwardly harmonizing these aspects of themselves and of the universe." Taoist sources suggest that reincarnation may play a role in both transgenderism and erotic inclination. If an individual who spent his previous incarnation as a male is born into this life as an anatomical female, he may express transgendered behavior (and vice versa). If a person has found and loved a "soulmate" in a previous lifetime, that person will seek and may fall in love with that soulmate in this lifetime as well, regardless of that person's sex or gender in the current incarnation.

Yirka' la 'ul Name for TWO-SPIRIT or transgendered shamans among the Aleuts of northeastern Siberia. The term means "a male transformed into the softer sex." Yirka' la 'ul typically shared intimate relationships with traditionally masculine men.

Ymir In Teutonic myth and religion, Ymir is a transgendered giant composed of fire and ice who arose from chaos (*ginnungagap*) at the beginning of time. Ymir gave birth to those beings responsible for the remainder of creation. These beings slew Ymir, forming earth from her-his body, ocean from her-his blood and the heavens from her-his skull.

Yourcenar, Marguerite (1903-1987) Belgian-born writer of French literature, lover of American professor and translator Grace Frick. Two of Yourcenar's works which depict the interrelationship of the homoerotic and the spiritual are: the *Memoirs of Hadrian* (1951), which tells the tale of HADRIAN and ANTINOUS; and *The Abyss* (1969), wherein homoeroticism and ALCHEMY converge in the figure of Zeno.

Yu In Chinese Shamanism (also referred to as Chinese traditional religion), a deity described as a shaman and a wanderer. He is also a musician who introduces humanity to the art of music; as such, he is credited with the authorship of several *nan-yin*, or "shaman-songs." He is said to have founded the Hsia Dynasty. Yu is alternately depicted as the son or intimate male companion of the god GUN.

Z

Zabeta In a masque of the English Renaissance, the name of a nymph loved by the classical goddess ARTEMIS/DIANA. Both goddess and nymph appear to have alluded to Queen ELIZABETH I (1533-1603), with "Zabeta" resonating with "Elizabeth."

Zacynthus Beloved of the Greek god APOLLO and also of the divinized hero HERACLES. While taking care of Heracles's flocks, Zacynthus was bitten by a serpent and died. The grieving Heracles named an island in memory of his love for the young man.

Zaggala Unmarried Islamic men encountered by English writer Robin Maugham at Siwa in North Africa in the mid-twentieth century. According to Maugham in *Journey to Siwa* (1950), "there was a rule [at Siwa] that no unmarried man might remain inside the walls of the town after sunset . . . The *zaggalas* slept at night in . . . thatched shelters outside the walls." The *zaggalas*, described by Maugham as "fierce," were "responsible for the defense of Siwa." In the evening, near 10 p.m., Maugham relates, the *zaggalas* would gather together to take part in a ritual dance. As the rite commenced, they would drink palm wine, listening to one of their fellows playing a flute and another playing drums. Gradually they began to chant or sing and dance. Some of their chants or songs were love lyrics: "My love is like a flaming torch, and sometimes I take him to my breast." Others were more religious in character, as, "Oh, power of God, oh, power of God!" Maugham writes that they would enter into an ecstatic state as they danced while tearing off their clothes. The dance was extremely sensuous, described by Maugham in terms of "jerking circles of men's bodies." "Quivering with the intensity of their excitement," Maugham reports, "the *zaggalas* poured their virility into the dance as a libation to freedom."

Zarex Young man of Greek legend who was believed to have been instructed in music and loved by APOLLO. Upon his death, a shrine was dedicated to Zarex near Eleusis.

Zat al-Dawáhí Arabic folk character known as the "Lady of Calamities." Zat al-Dawáhí was said to have practiced witchcraft and lesbian eroticism. It was she who taught women the art of anointing themselves with SAFFRON and then rubbing clitoris against clitoris until they fainted in ecstasy.

Zeesar In the NAASSENE tradition/path of Gnosticism, a mysterious transgendered being also known as the "celestial horn of the moon." Zeesar is associated with the divining cup of the Biblical JOSEPH as well as with the unicorn.

Zeffirelli, Franco (1923-) Italian filmmaker and designer-producer of operas, perhaps best known for his cinematic adaptations of Shakespeare. When interviewed by Edward Guthmann in 1983, Zeffirelli made a remark pertaining to the interrelationship of homoeroticism, the spiritual, and the arts. He suggested that gay people "are forced to refine certain receptive instruments in the mind and soul. They become much more sensitive, more ready [than others] to talk [about] and to deal with the things of the spirit."

Zenil, Nahum (1947-) Mexican gay male artist, many of whose works explore the interrelationship of homoeroticism and, to a somewhat lesser extent, transgenderism and the sacred. A native of Veracruz, Zenil has been profoundly inspired by the paintings of Frida KAHLO, as exemplified by his painting *Frida Kahlo with Devil* (1985). He has also been deeply inspired by the Mexican celebration of the Dia de los Muertos (the Day of the Dead), as is apparent in *Clock* (1990), an antique clock painted with skull faces inside hearts, its insides filled with artificial flowers. Of religion in general and of Catholic saints and the Virgen of Guadalupe in particular, Zenil has said, "Religion has always been very important to me . . . I looked to religion as a form of strength. I look to the saints for protection. I have always thought of the Virgen de Guadalupe as my protectress. I have special devotion to her image. She has helped me to survive." His devotion to the Virgen is especially noticeable in his painting *Gracias Virgencita de Guadalupe* (1984). In this painting, two twin-like male lovers (which appear to be a double self portrait) lie in bed gazing at the Virgen who floats above them. Among Zenil's paintings which represent the juxtaposition or interpenetration of Catholicism, Mesoamerican spirituality, and homoeroticism are: *Saint Sebastian* (1982), depicting the martyred saint's voluptuous torso pierced by arrows, his groin and nipples picked at by crows; *Jacob Wrestling with the Angel* (1985), in which these two are portrayed as lovers engaging in "69" lovemaking; *The Two Adams* (1986), another Biblical re-visioning portraying a primordial male couple rather than Adam and Eve, surrounded by Biblical passages; *Self-Portrait as an Angel* (1991), depicting Zenil as an angel lifting his robes and clutching his erect penis; *Angel-Devil* (1991), portraying the artist as both angel and devil, suggesting a pair of male lovers; and *Flying Over New York* (1991), yet another double self-portrait, this time Zenil as two angels, loins bared, soaring over New York City.

Zeno of Citium (or **Zeno of Kition**, 335-263 BCE) Founder of the philosophical tradition of STOICISM who was said to have "never resorted to a woman" but to have loved a number of other men and to have given wild parties for other man-loving friends, including Antigonus Gonatus, King of Macedonia (d. 239 BCE).

Zeno of Elea (c. 490-c. 430 BCE) Disciple and beloved of PARMENIDES, who founded the Eleatic school of Greek philosophy. Zeno demonstrated, by way of a series of paradoxes, Parmenides' notion that "unchanging being is the material substance of which the universe is composed" and that growth and destruction are "illusions of the senses." Zeno and Parmenides captured public attention at a festival of the goddess MINERVA, when the former was past thirty and the latter nearly fifty-five years of age. Their presence was remarked not only because their relationship had lasted so many years but also because of their striking physical appearance; Zeno was described as "tall and handsome," Parmenides as "gray-haired, and of a beautiful and comely aspect."

Zephyrus The west wind, who, like the Greek god APOLLO, was in love with HYACINTHUS. When it became obvious to Zephyrus that the young man preferred the company of Apollo, he caused the wind to shift so that Apollo's discus would strike his beloved's head, causing the death of Hyacinthus.

Zetes The "Searcher" was, in Greek mythology, the twin brother of CALAIS. Like the latter, Zetes was an ARGONAUT and an admirer of HYLAS, a young prince who was loved by HERACLES.

Zeus Greek ruler of the gods, a lover of both women, as Hera (and countless others), and men, as GANYMEDE. As Zeus Arrhenothelus, the deity is perceived as transgendered, bearing, like the Ephesian ARTEMIS, multiple female breasts. An Orphic text depicting Zeus in this manifestation reads: "Zeus is male, Zeus is the immortal wife . . . Thou art father, and lovely mother."

Bibliography

Adler, Laure. *La vie quotidienne dans les maisons closes, 1830-1930*. Paris: Hachette, 1990.

Adler, Margot. *Drawing Down the Moon: Witches, Druids, Goddess-Worshippers, and Other Pagans in America Today*. Boston: Beacon Press, 1986.

Agrippa, Henry Cornelius, von Nettesheim. *The Philosophy of Natural Magic*. Seacacus, NJ: University Books, 1974.

AIDS Bhedbav Virodhi Andolan (ABVA). "Homosexuality in India: Culture and Heritage." In *A Lotus of Another Color: An Unfolding of the South Asian Gay and Lesbian Experience*, ed. Rakesh Ratti. Boston: Alyson Publications, Inc. 1993.

Aizawa, Keizo. "Interview with Mutsuo Takahashi." *Gay Sunshine Interviews: Vol. II*, ed. Winston Leyland. San Francisco: Gay Sunshine Press, 1982.

Albertson, Chris. *AC-DC Blues: Gay Jazz Reissues*. Brooklyn, New York: Stash Records, Inc., 1977, St-106.

Albright, W. F. "Historical and Mythical Elements in the Story of Joseph." *Journal of Biblical Literature* 37, pts. 3, 4 (September-December 1918), 115-116.

Alekseychuk, Leonid. "A Warrior in the Field." *Sight and Sound* 60, no. 1, 1991.

Alexander, H. B. *North American Mythology*. Boston: Marshall Jones Company, 1916.

Allen, Jeffner. *Lesbian Philosophy: Explorations*. Palo Alto, California: Institute of Lesbian Studies, 1986.

Allen, Paula Gunn. "Lesbians in American Indian Cultures." *Conditions: Seven* 7 (1981), 67-87.

Allen, Paula Gunn. *Shadow Country*. Los Angeles: University of California Press, 1982.

Andersen, Johannes C. *Myths and Legends of the Polynesians*. New York: Farrar and Rinehart, 1928.

Ann, Martha and Dorothy Myers Imel. *Goddesses in World Mythology*. Santa Barbara, California: ABC-CLIO, 1993.

Anzaldúa, Gloria. *La Frontera / Borderlands: The New Mestiza*. San Francisco: Spinsters/Aunt Lute, 1987.

Arboleda, Manuel. "Representatciones Arísticas de Actividades Homoeróticas en la Cerámica Moche." *Bulletin de Lima*, Edicions Especial, nos. 16, 18 (December 1981), 98-107.

Arnobius. *Adversus Gentes* (*Against the Pagans*), ed. Rev A. Roberts. Edinburgh: T. and T. Clark, 1861.

Arthur, Gavin (Chester Allen III). *The Circle of Sex*. New York: University Books, 1966.

Arthur, Gavin (Chester Allen III). "Document received from the hands of Gavin Arthur and its authenticity voched for by Allen Ginsberg, San Francisco 1967 [previously unpublished]." *Gay Sunshine: A Journal of Gay Liberation*, no. 35 (Winter 1978), [29].

Arwas, Victor. *Alaistair: Illustrator of Decadence*. London: Thames and Hudson, 1979.

Astour, Michael C. "Tamar the Hierodule: An Essay in the Method of Vestigial Motifs." *Journal of Biblical Literature* 85 (1966), 188-191.

Aurora. *Lesbian Love Signs*. Freedom, California: Crossing Press, 1991.

Austin, Alfredo López. *The Human Body and Ideology: Concepts of the Ancient Nahuas*. Trans. Thelma and Bernard Ortiz de Montellano. Salt Lake City: University of Utah, 1988.

Baker, Rob. *The Art of AIDS: From Stigma to Conscience*. New York: Continuum, 1994.

Balka, Christie and Andy Rose, eds. *Twice Blessed: On Being Lesbian, Gay, and Jewish*. Boston: Beacon Press, 1989.

Barkan, Leonard. *The Gods made Flesh: Metamorphosis and the Pursuit of Paganism*. New Haven: Yale University Press, 1986.

Barnstone, Aliki and Willis, eds. *A Book of Women Poets from Antiquity to Now*. New York: Schocken Books, 1981.

Baroja, Julio Caro. *The World of the Witches*. Trans. O. N. V. Glendinning. Chicago: University of Chicago Press, 1975.

Bascom, William R. *Sixteen Cowries: Yoruba Divination from Africa to the New World*. Bloomington: Indiana University Press, 1980.

Baskin, Wade. *Dictionary of Satanism*. New York: Philosophical Library, 1972.

Bastide, Roger. *The African Religions of Brazil*. Baltimore: Johns Hopkins University Press, 1978.

Bataille, Gretchen M. *Native American Women: A Biographical Dictionary*. New York: Garland Publishing, 1993.

Beck, Evelyn Torton, ed. *Nice Jewish Girls: A Lesbian Anthology*. Watertown, Mass: Persephone Press, 1982.

Beckwith, Martha W. *Hawaiian Mythology*. Honolulu: Univeristy of Hawaii Press, 1970.

Begg, Ean. *The Cult of the Black Virgin*. Boston: Arkana, 1985.

Bell, Robert E. *Dictionary of Classical Mythology: Symbols, Attributes, and Associations*. Santa Barbara, California: ABC-CLIO, 1982.

Bell, Robert E. *Women of Classical Mythology: A Biographical Dictionary*. Santa Barbara, California: ABC-CLIO, Inc., 1991.

Beltz, Walter. *God and the Gods: Myths of the Bible*. Trans. Peter Heinegg. New York: Penguin Books, 1983.

Bennett, Paula. *Emily Dickinson: Woman Poet*. Iowa City: University of Iowa Press, 1990.

Bently, Peter, ed. *The Dictionary of World Myth*. New York: Facts of File, 1995.

Berger, Pamela. *The Goddess Obscured*. Boston: Beacon Press, 1985.

Bertiaux, Michael. *The Voudon Gnostic Workbook*. New York: Magickal Childe, 1988.

Besmer, Fremont E. *Horses, Musicians, and Gods: The Hausa Cult of Possession-Trance*. Zaria, Nigeria: Ahmadu Bello University Press, 1983.

Betz, Hans Dieter, ed. *The Greek Magical Papyri in Translation*. Chicago: University of Chicago Press, 1992.

Beurdeley, Cecile. *L'Amour Bleu*. Trans. Michael Taylor. New York: Rizzoli, 1978.

Biedermann, Hans. *Dictionary of Symbolism: Cultural Icons and the Meanings Behind Them*. Trans. James Hulbert. New York: Facts on File, 1992.

Binding, Paul. *Lorca: The Gay Imagination*. London: GMP Publishers, 1985.

Birrell, Anne. *Chinese Mythology: An Introduction*. Baltimore: Johns Hopkins University Press, 1993.

Blacker, Carmen. *The Catalpa Bow: A Study of Shamanistic Practices in Japan*. London: George Allen and Unwin, 1986.

Blackmer, Corinne E. and Patricia Juliana Smith, eds. *En Travesti: Women, Gender Subversion, Opera*. New York: Columbia University Press, 1995.

Blackwood, Wvelyn. "Sexuality and Gender in Certain Native American Tribes: The Case of Cross-Gender Females," *Signs* 10, no. 1 (Autumn 1984), 27-42.

Blundell, Sue. *Women in Ancient Greece*. London: British Museum Press, 1995.

Bogoras, Vladimir (Waldemar). *The Chukchee. Reports of the Jessup North Pacific Expedition*. New York: Memoirs of the American Museum of Natural History, 1907.

Bogus, SDiane. "The Myth and Tradition of the Black Bulldagger." In *Dagger: On Butch Women*, ed. Lily Durana, Roxxie, and Linnea Due. San Francisco: Cleis Press, 1994.

Bogus, SDiane. "The 'Queen B' Figure in Literature." In *Lesbian Texts and Contexts: Radical Revisions*, ed. Karla Jay and Joanne Glasgow. New York: New York University Press, 1990.

Boime, Albert. "The Case of Rosa Bonheur: Why Should A Woman Want to Be More Like a Man?" *Art History* 4, no. 4 (December 1981), 384-409.

Bolivar-Aróstegui, Natalia. *Los Orishas en Cuba*. Ciudade La Habana: Ediciones Union, 1990.

Bonnet, Marie-Jo. *Un choix sans equivoque: recherches historiques sur les relations amoureuses entre les femmes, XVIe-XX siecle*. Paris: Dènoël, 1981.

Borgeaud, Philippe. *The Cult of Pan in Ancient Greece*. Trans. Kathleen Atlass and James Redfield. Chicago: University of Chicago Press, 1988.

Bornstein, Kate. *Gender Outlaw: On Men, Women and the Rest of Us*. New York: Routledge, 1994.

Boswell, John. *Christianity, Social Tolerance, and Homosexuality*. Chicago: University of Chicago Press, 1980.

Boswell, John. *Same-Sex Unions in Premodern Europe*. New York: Villard Books, 1994.

Bosworth, C. E., *et al. The Encyclopedia of Islam*. Leiden: E. J. Brill, 1983.

Bothmer, Dietrich von. *Amazons in Greek Art*. Oxford: Clarendon Press, 1957.

Bouhdiba, Abdelwahab. *Sexuality in Islam*. London: R. K. P. Inc., 1985.

Bouldrey, Brian, ed. *Wrestling with the Angel: Faith and Religion in the Lives of Gay Men*. New York: Riverhead Books, 1995.

Boyd, Malcolm. "Was Jesus Gay?" *The Advocate* no. 565 (December 4, 1990), 90.

Bradford, Nicholas J. "Transgenderism and the Cult of Yellamma: Heat, Sex, and Sickness in South Indian Ritual." *Journal of Anthropological Research* 39, no. 3 (Fall 1983), 307-322.

Bramly, Serge. *Macumba: The Teachings of Maria-Jose, Mother of the Gods*. New York: St Martin's Press, c. 1977.

Brant, Beth, ed. *A Gathering of Spirit: a Collection by North American Indian Women*. Ithaca, NY: Firebrand Books, 1988.

Brant, Beth, ed. *Writing As Witness: Essay and Talk*. Toronto: Women's Press, 1994.

Bremmer, Jan. "Poseidon." In *The Encyclopedia of Religion*, ed. Mircea Eliade. New York: Macmillan, 1987, Vol. 11, 457-458.

Brett, Philip. "Britten's Dream." In *Musicology and Difference: Gender and Sexuality in Music Scholarship*, ed. Ruth Solie. London: University of California Press, 1993.

Briggs, Katherine. *An Encyclopedia of Fairies: Hobgoblins, Brownies, Bogies, and Other Supernatural Creatures*. New York: Pantheon Books, 1976.

Brinker, Ludger. "Jewish-American Literature." In *The Gay and Lesbian Literary Heritage*, ed. Claude J. Summers. New York: Henry Holt and Company, 1995.

Brisson, Luc. *Le Mythe de Tiresias*. Leiden: E. J. Brill, 1976.

Brooks, Beatrice. "Fertility Cult Functionaries in the Old Testament." *Journal of Biblical Literature* 60, pt. 3

(September 1941). Philadelphia: Society of Biblical Literature and Exegesis.

Brown, Judith C. *Immodest Acts: The Life of a Lesbian Nun in Renaissance Italy*. New York: Oxford University Press, 1986.

Brundage, Burr Cathwright. *Lords of Cuzco: A History and Description of the Inca People in Their Final Days*. Norman: University of Oklahoma Press, 1967.

Brunel, Pierre. *Companion to Literary Myths, Heroes and Archetypes*. Trans. Wendy Allatson, *et al*. New York: Routledge, 1992.

Bucke, Richard, M. D. *Cosmic Consciousness*. New York: E. P. Dutton, 1969 (1901).

Buckle, Richard. *Nijinsky*. New York: Simon and Schuster, 1971.

Budapest, Zsuzsanna. *The Holy Book of Women's Mysteries*. Berkeley: Wingbow Press, 1989.

Budge, Ernest Alfred Wallis. *The Gods of the Egyptians: Volumes I and II*. New York: Dover, 1969 (1904).

Buffière, Félix. *Eros adolescent: la pédérastic dans la Grèce antique*. Paris: Societé d'Edition 'Les Belles Lettres,' 1980.

Bullough, Vern. *Sexual Variance in Society and History*. Chicago: University of Chicago, 1976.

Bullough, Vern L. and Bonnie Bullough. *Cross Dressing, Sex, and Gender*. Philadelphia: University of Pennsylvania Press, 1993.

Burkert, Walter. *Structure and History in Greek Mythology and Ritual*. Berkeley: University of California Press, 1982.

Burton, Sir Richard F. *The Book of the Thousand Nights and a Night*. New York: The Hertiage Press, 1962.

Burton, Sir Richard F. *Terminal Essay to "The Thousand and One Nights."* London: privately printed publication, 1901.

Butler, Becky, ed. *Ceremonies of the Heart: Celebrating Lesbian Unions*. Seattle: Seal Press, 1990.

Cabezón, José Ignacio. *Buddhism, Sexuality, and Gender*. Albany: State University of New York Press, 1985.

Cabezón, José Ignacio. "Homosexuality and Buddhism." In *Homosexuality and World Religions*, ed. Arlene Swidler. Valley Forge, Pennsylvania: Trinity Press International, 1993.

Cabrera, Lydia. *Anago: Vocabulario lucumí*. Miami: Cabrera y Rojas, 1970.

Cabrera, Lydia. *El Monte*. Miami: Colección del Chicherekú, 1968.

Cabrera, Lydia. *Otán Iyebiyé: Las Piedras Preciosas*. Miami: Ediciones Universal, 1986.

Cabrera, Lydia. *Yemayá y Ochún: Kariocha, Iyalorichas, y Olorichas*. New York: Eliseo Torres, 1980.

Calame, Claude, *Les choeus de jeunes filles en Grèce archaïque*. Rome: Edizioni dell'Ateneo and Bizzarri, Istituto di Filologia Classica, 1977.

Campbell, Joseph. *The Way of the Animal Powers*. San Francisco: Harper and Row, 1983.

Canan, Janine, ed. *She Rises Like the Sun: Invocations of the Goddess by Contemporary American Women Poets*. Freedom, California: The Crossing Press, 1989.

Cano, Jésus Arango. *Mitologia en America Precolombina*. Bogotá: Plaza & Janes, 1989.

Caputi, Jane. *Gossips, Gorgons and Crones: The Fates of the Earth*. Santa Fe, New Mexico: Bear and Company Publishing, 1993.

Caputi, Jane. "Interview with Paula Gunn Allen." *Trivia: A Journal of Ideas* 16/17 (1990), 50-67.

Caputi, Jane. "On Psychic Activism: Feminist Mythmaking." In *The Feminist Companion to Mythology*, ed. Carolyne Larrington. London: Pandora, Harper Collins, 1992.

Carpenter, Edward. *Intermediate Types among Primitive Folk*. New York: Arno Press, 1975 (1919).

Carpenter, Edward. "On the Connection Between Homosexuality and Divination and the Importance of the Intermediate Sexes Generally in Early Civilizations." *The American Journal of Religious Psychology and Education* 4 (March 1910-July 1911), 229-243.

Carstairs, George M. "Hinjra and Jiryan: Two Derivatives of Hindu Attitudes to Sexuality." *The British Journal of Medical Psychology* 29, pt. 2 (1956), 75-175.

Case, Sue-Ellen. "Tracking the Vampire." *Differences: A Journal of Feminist Cultural Studies* 3 (Summer 1991), 1-20.

Castelo, Hernán Rodriquez. *Lexico Sexual Ecuatoriano y Latinoamericano*. Quito Ediciones Libri Mundi, Instituto Otavaleño de Antropología, 1979.

Castle, Terry. "The Culture of Travesty: Sexuality and Masquerade in Eighteenth Century England." In Rousseau, G. S. and Roy Porter, eds., *Sexual Underworlds of the Enlightenment*, Manchester University Press, 1987.

Chan, Ping-leung. "'Ch'u Tzu' and Shamanism in Ancient China." Diss. Ohio State University, 1972.

Chevalier, Jean and Alain Gheerbrant. *A Dictionary of Symbols*. Trans. John Buchanan-Brown. Cambridge, Mass.: Basil Blackwell, 1994.

Christ, Carol P. *Diving Deep and Surfacing: Women Writers on Spiritual Quest*. Boston: Beacon Press, 1980.

Christie-Murray, David. *Reincarnation: Ancient Beliefs and Modern Evidence*. London: David and Charles, 1981.

Cirlot, J. E. *A Dictionary of Symbols*. New York: Philosophical Library, 1962.

Cohen, Paul T. and Gehan Wijeyewardene. "Introduction on Spirit Cults and the Position of Women in Northern Thailand." *Mankind* 14, no. 4 (August 1984), Special issue #3, 249-262.

Collcutt, Martin. *Five Mountains: The Rinzai Zen Monastic Institutions in Medieval Japan*. Cambridge: Harvard University Press, 1981.

Conner, Randolph P. *Blossom of Bone: Reclaiming the Connections Between Homoeroticism and the Sacred*. San Francisco: Harper/Collins, 1993.

Conner, Randolph P. *Coals of an Ancient Fire: The Pagan Tradition in Western Literature*. mss, forthcoming.

Conner, Randolph P. "Homoeroticism in the Works of D. H. Lawrence." Unpublished paper, 1975.

Conner, Randolph P. "Les Molles et les Chausses." In *Queerly Phrased*, ed. Anna Livia and Kira Hall. New York: Oxford University Press, 1996 (forthcoming).

Conner, Randy P. and Stephen Donaldson, "Buddhism." In *Encyclopedia of Homosexuality*, Vol. 1, 168-171, ed. Wayne Dynes and Stephen Donaldson. New York: Garland Press, 1990

Cooper, Emmanuel. *The Sexual Perspective: Homosexuality and Art in the Last 100 Years in the West*. New York: Routledge, 1994.

Coote, Stephen, ed. *The Penguin Book of Homosexual Verse*. Harmondsworth: Allen Lane, Penguin, 1983.

Cosman, Carol, Joan Keefe, and Kathleen Weaver, eds. *The Penguin Book of Women Poets*. New York: Viking Penguin, 1988.

Couliano, Ioan. "Sexual Rites in Europe." In *The Encyclopedia of Religion*, ed. Mircea Eliade. New York: Macmillan, 1987, Vol. 13, pp. 186-189.

Courtright, Paul B. *Ganesa: Lord of Obstacles, Lord of Beginnings*. New York: Oxford University Press, 1985.

Craig, D. *Dictionary of Polynesian Mythology*. New York: Greenwood, 1989.

Crompton, Louis. "An 'Army of Lovers': The Sacred Band of Thebes." *History Today* (November 1994), 23-29.

Crowell's Handbook of Classical Mythology, ed. Edward Tripp. New York: Crowell, 1970.

Cumont, Franz. *Oriental Religions in Roman Paganism*. New York: Dover, 1956.

Curb, Rosemary and Nancy Manahan, eds. *Lesbian Nuns: Breaking Silence*. Tallahassee, Florida: Naiad Press, 1985.

D'Alviella, Goblet. *The Mysteries of Eleusis*. Wellingborough, Northamptonshire: Aquarian Press, 1981.

Daly, Mary. *Pure Lust: Elemental Feminist Philosophy*. Boston: Beacon Press, 1984.

Daly, Mary and Jane Caputi. *Websters' First New Intergalactic Wickedary of the English Language*. Boston: Beacon Press, 1987.

Dange, Sadashiv Ambadas. *Sexual Symbolism from the Vedic Ritual*. Delhi: Ajanta Publications, 1979.

Daniel, Marc. 1977. "Arab Civilization and Male Love." Trans. Winston Leyland. *Gay Sunshine: A Journal of Gay Liberation* 32 (Spring 1977), [1-11].

Daniel, Robert W., and Franco Maltomini, eds. *Supplementum Magicum*, 1. Cologne: Westdeutscher Verlag, 1990.

Daniélou, Alain. *Fools of God*. Trans David Rattray. New York: Hanuman Books, 1988.

Daniélou, Alain. *Hindu Polytheism*. New York: Bollingen Foundation, Pantheon, Random House, 1964.

Daniélou, Alain. *The Phallus: Sacred Symbol of Male Creative Power*. Rochester, Vt.: Inner Traditions, 1995.

Daniélou, Alain. *Shiva and Dionysus: The Religion of Nature and Eros*. New York: Inner Traditions International, 1984.

Daniélou, Alain. *The Way to the Labyrinth: Memories of East and West*. Trans. Marie-Claire Cournand. New York: New Directions, 1987.

Daniélou, Alain. *While the Gods Play*. Rochester, Vt.: Inner Traditions International, 1987.

Davidson, H. R. Ellis. *Gods and Myths of the Viking Age*. New York: Bell Publishing Co., 1981.

Delaney, John J. *Dictionary of Saints*. Garden City, New York: Doubleday, 1980.

Delcourt, Marie. *Hermaphrodite: Myths and Rites of the Bisexual Figure in Classical Antiquity*. Trans. Jennifer Nicholson. London: Studio Books, 1961.

Delesalle, Georges. *Dictionnaire argot-francais et francais-argot*. Paris: s.n., 1895.

Delvau, Alfred. *Dictionnaire Erotique Moderne*. Bale: Karl Schmidt, 1891.

Demetrakopoulos, Stephanie A. "Colette, Clairvoyance, and the Medium as Sibyl: Another Step Towards a Female Metaphysics." *Trivia: A Journal of Ideas* 4 (Spring 1984), 62-79.

Deren, Maya. *Divine Horsemen: The Living Gods of Haiti*. New Paltz, New York: Documentext, McPherson and Company, 1983.

Desmangles, Leslie G. *The Faces of the Gods: Vodou and Roman Catholicism in Haiti*. Chapel Hill: University of North Carolina Press, 1992.

Detienne, Marcel. *Dionysos à ciel ouvert*. Paris: Hachette, 1986.

Detienne, Marcel. *Dionysus Slain*. Trans. Mireille Muellner and Leonard Muellner. Baltimore: Johns Hopkins University Press, 1979.

Devereux, George. "Institutionalized Homosexuality of the Mohave Indians." *The Problem of Homosexuality in Modern Society*, ed. Hendrik M. Ruitenbeck. New York: E. P. Dutton, 1963.

Dimmit, Cornelia and J. A. van Buitenen. *Classical Hindu Mythology*. Philadelphia: Temple University Press, 1978.

Dixon, Roland B. *Oceanic Mythology*. (*The Mythology of All Races*). Boston: Marshall Jones Company, 1916.

Donoghue, Emma. *Passions Between Women: Britsh Lesbian Culture* 1668-1801. New York: Harper

Collins, 1993.

Dover, Kenneth James. *Greek Homosexuality*. Cambridge: Harvard University Press, 1978.

Downing, Christine. "Lesbian Mythology." *Historical Reflections / Reflexions Historiques* 20, no. 2 (1994), 169-199.

Drewal, Margaret Thompson. "Trance Among Yoruba Shango Devotees." *African Arts* 20 (1986), 61–62.

Drury, Nevill. *Dictionary of Mysticism and the Esoteric Traditions*. England: Prism Press, 1992.

Duffy, Maureen. *The Erotic World of Faery*. New York: Avon Books, 1980.

Dunham, Katherine. *Dances of Haiti*. Los Angeles: Center for Afro-American Studies, Universities of California, Los Angeles, 1983.

Duran, Khalid. "Homosexuality and Islam." In *Homosexuality and World Religions*, ed. Arlene Swidler. Valley Forge, PA.: Trinity Press Int., 1993.

Durdin-Robertson, Lawrence. *The Goddesses of Chaldea, Syria and Egypt*. Eire: Cesara Publications, 1975.

Dynes, Wayne R., ed. *Encyclopedia of Homosexuality*. New York: Garland Publishing, 1990.

Dynes, Wayne R. and Stephen Donaldson, eds. *Asian Homosexuality. Studies in Homosexuality, Volume III*. New York, London: Garland Publishing, 1992.

Dynes, Wayne R. and Stephen Donaldson, eds. *Ethnographic Studies of Homosexuality*. New York: Garland Publishing, 1992.

Eberhard, Wolfram. *A Dictionary of Chinese Symbols: Hidden Symbols in Chinese Life and Thought*. New York: Routledge, 1986.

Ecun, Oba. *Orichá: Metodología de la Religion Yoruba*. Miami: Editorial SIBI, 1986.

Edwardes, Allen. *The Jewel in the Lotus: A Historical Survey of the Sexual Culture of the East*. New York: The Julian Press, Inc., 1959.

Edwards, Gary and John Mason. *Black Gods: Orisa Studies in the New World*. Brooklyn: Yoruba Theological Archministry, 1985.

Elderkin, George W. Kantharos: *Studies in Dionysiac and Kindred Cult*. Princeton: Princeton University Press, 1924.

Eliade, Mircea, gen. ed. *Encyclopedia of Religion*. New York: Macmillian, 1987.

Eliade, Mircea. *Shamanism: Archaic Techniques of Ecstasy*. Princeton: Princeton University Press, 1974.

Eliade, Mircea. *The Two and the One*. Trans. J. M. Cohen. Chicago: University of Chicago Press, 1979.

Ellis, Havelock. *Studies in the Psychology of Sex: Sexual Inversion*. Philadelphia: F. A. David Company, 1901.

Ellis, Peter Berresford. *Dictionary of Celtic Mythology*. Santa Barbara: ABC-CLIO, 1992.

Ellis, Peter Berresford. *A Dictionary of Irish Mythology*. London: Constable, 1987.

Ellwood, Robert S. "A Japanese Mythic Trickster Figure: Susa-no-o." In *Mythical Trickster Figures: Contours, Contexts, and Criticisms*, ed. William Hynes and William G. Doty. Tuscaloosa: University of Alabama Press, 1993.

Emerson, Nathaniel B. *Unwritten Literature of Hawaii: The Sacred Songs of the Hula*. Rutland, Vt: Charles E. Tuttle Company, 1986.

Ericson, Eric. *The World, the Flesh, the Devil: A Biographical Dictionary of Witches*. New York: Mayflower Books, 1981.

Evans, Arthur. *The God of Ecstasy: Sex Roles and the Madness of Dionysus*. New York: St Martin's Press, 1988.

Evans, Arthur. *Witchcraft and the Gay Counterculture*. Boston: Fag Rag Books, 1978.

Evans-Pritchard, Edward E. *The Azande: History and Political Institution*. Oxford: Oxford University Press, 1971.

Evans-Pritchard, Edward E. "Sexual Inversion among the Azande." *American Anthropologist* 72 (1970), 1428-1434.

Evans-Wentz, W. Y. *The Tibetan Book of the Dead*. New York: Oxford University Press, 1960.

Evola, Giulio. *Eros and the Mysteries of Love: The Metaphysics of Sex*. Rochester, Vt: Inner Traditions, 1991.

Faderman, Lillian, ed. *Chloe Plus Olivia: An Anthology of Lesbian Literature from the Seventeenth Century to the Present*. New York: Viking, Penguin, 1994.

Fang Fu Ruan. *Sex in China: Studies in Sexology in Chinese Culture*. New York: Plenum Press, 1991.

Fang Fu Ruan, M. D. and Vern L. Bullough. "Lesbianism in China." *Archives of Sexual Behavior* 21, no. 3 (June 1992), 217-226.

Farmer, Henry George. *A History of Arabian Music to the Thirteenth Century*. London: Luzac, 1967.

Fernandez, Dominique. *Le rapt de Ganymède*. Paris: Bernard Grasset, 1989.

Fernbach, David. *The Spiral Path: A Gay Contribution to Human Survival*. Boston: Alyson Publications, 1981.

Fichte, Hubert. "La Lame de Rasoir et l'Hermaphrodite." *Psychopathologie Africaine*. 11, no. 3 (1975), 395-406.

Fichte, Hubert and Leonore Mau. *Xango*. Frankfurt am Main: S. Fishcher Verlag, 1976.

Fiedler, Leslie. "Come Back to the Raft Ag'in, Huck Honey!" In *The Collected Essays of Leslie Fiedler*. New York: Stein and Day, 1971.

Fleras, Jomar. "Reclaiming Our Historic Rights: Gays and Lesbians in the Philippines." In *The Third Pink Book: A Global View of Lesbian and Gay Liberation and Oppression*, ed. Aart Hendriks, Rob Tielman, and Evert van der Veen. Buffalo, NY: Prometheus Books, 1993.

Fone, Byrne R. S. "This Other Eden: Arcadia and the Homosexual Imagination." In *Literary Visions of Homosexuality*, ed. Stuart Kellogg. New York: Haworth Press, 1983.

Forberg, Fred. Charles. *Manual of Classical Erotology*. New York: Grove Press, 1966.

Foster, David William. *Gay and Lesbian Themes in Latin American Writing*. Austin: University of Texas Press, 1991.

Foster, Jeannette H. *Sex Variant Women in Literature*. Tallahassee, FL: Naiad Press, 1985.

Fraser, Antonia. *The Warrior Queens*. London: Weidenfeld and Nicolson, 1988.

Frazer, Sir James George. *The Golden Bough*. New York: Macmillan, (1935) 1980.

Frédéric, Louis. *Encyclopaedia of Asian Civilizations*. Villecresnes: Louis Frédéric, 1977.

Freedman, Estelle B., Barbara C. Gelpi, Susan L. Johnson and Kathleen M. Weston, eds. *The Lesbian Issue: Essays from SIGNS*. Chicago: University of Chicago Press, 1985.

Fry, Peter. "Male Homosexuality and Spirit Possession in Brazil." *The Journal of Homosexuality* 11, nos. 3-4 (1985), 137-153.

Fuchs, Hanns. *Richard Wagner und die Homosexualität*. Berlin: H. Barsdof, 1903.

Furth, Charlotte. "Androgynous Males and Deficient Females: Biology and Gender Boundaries in Sixteenth and Seventeenth Century China." *Late Imperial China* 9 (2) 1988.

Garber, Eric and Lyn Paleo, eds. *Uranian Worlds: A Guide to Alternative Sexuality in Science Fiction, Fantasy, and Horror*. Boston: G. K. Hall, 1990.

Garde, Noel I. *Jonathan to Gide: The Homosexual in History*. New York: Nosbooks, 1969.

Gardner, Kay. *A Rainbow Path*. Durham, NC: Ladyslipper Records, LR-103. 1984.

Gardner, Kay. *Sounding the Inner Landscape: Music as Medicine*. Stonington, ME, 1990.

Gargaetas, Patricia. "Altared States: Lesbian Altarmaking and the Transformation of Self." *Women and Therapy: A Feminist Quarterly*, Special Issue 16 (2-3) (1995) 95-105.

Garrity, Jane. "Encoding Bi-Location: Sylvia Townsend Warner and the Erotics of Dissimulation." In *Lesbian Erotics*, ed. Karla Jay. New York: New York University Press, 1995.

Gayatri, B. J. D. "Female closeness and lesbian identity in Indonesia." *Connexions* 46 (Summer 1994).

Gerstein, Mary R. "Germanic Warg: The Outlaw as Werwolf." In *Myth in Indo-European Antiquity*, ed. Gerald James Larson. Berkeley: University of California Press, 1974.

Gettings, Fred. *Dictionary of Astrology*. Boston: Routledge and Kegan Paul, 1985.

Gidlow, Elsa. *Ask No Man Pardon: The Philosophical Significance of Being Lesbian*. Mill Valley, CA: Druid Heights Books, 1975.

Giles, Herbert. *A Chinese Biographical Dictionary*. Tapei: Literature House, 1964.

Gill, John. *Queer Noises: Male and Female Homosexuality in 20th Century Music*. London: Cassell, 1995.

Gill, Sam D. and Irene F. Sullivan. *Dictionary of Native American Mythology*. New York: Oxford University Press, 1992.

Ginn, Victoria. *The Spirited Earth: Dance, Myth, and Ritual from South Asia to the South Pacific*. New York: Rizzoli, 1990.

Ginsberg, Allen. *Gay Sunshine Interview with Allen Young*. Bolinas, CA: Grey Fox Press, 1974.

Ginzburg, Carlo. *Ecstasies: Deciphering the Witches' Sabbath*. New York: Pantheon Books, 1991.

Givry, Grillot de. *Witchcraft, Magic, and Alchemy*. New York: Dover Publications, 1971.

Glob, P. V. *Denmark: An Archaeological History from the Stone Age to the Vikings*. Ithaca: Cornell University Press, 1971.

Goodich, Michael. *The Unmentionable Vice: Homosexuality in the late Medieval Period*. Santa Barbara, CA: Ross-Erikson, 1979.

Goodrich, Norma Lorre. *Priestesses*. New York: Harper Collins, 1990.

Goodwin, Joseph P. *More Man Than You'll Ever Be: Gay Folklore and Acculturation in Middle America*. Bloomington: Indiana University Press, 1989.

Gordon, Richard. "Religion in the Roman Empire: The Civic Compromise and Its Limits." In *Pagan Priests: Religion and Power in the Ancient World*, ed. Mary Beard and John North. London: Duckworth, 1990.

Gordon, Stuart. *The Encyclopedia of Myths and Legends*. London: Headline Books, Harper Collins, 1993.

Goss, Robert. *Jesus Acted Up: A Gay and Lesbian Manifesto*. San Francisco: Harper Collins, 1993.

Govinda, Lama Anagarika. *The Way of the White Clouds: A Buddhist Pilgrim in Tibet*. Boulder: Shambhala, 1970.

Graff, Fritz. "Prayer in Magic and Religious Ritual." In *Magika Hiera: Ancient Greek Magic and Religion*, ed. Christopher A. Faraone and Dirk Obbink. New York: Oxford University Press, 1991.

Grahn, Judy. *Another Mother Tongue: Gay Words, Gay Worlds*. Boston: Beacon Press, 1984.

Grahn, Judy. *Blood, Bread, and Roses: How Menstruation Created the World*. Boston: Beacon Press, 1993.

Grahn, Judy. *The Highest Apple: Sappho and the Lesbian Poetic Tradition*. San Francisco: Spinsters Ink, 1985.

Grahn, Judy. *The Queen of Swords*. Boston: Beacon Press, 1987.

Grahn, Judy. *The Queen of Wands*. Trumansburg, NY: Crossing Press, 1982.

Graillot, H. *Le culte de Cybele, mére des dieux*. Paris: Bibl. Ec. F, 1912.

Grant, Michael, and John Hazel. *Gods and Mortals in Classical Mythology*. New York: Dorset Press, 1979.

Graves, Robert. *The Greek Myths*. New York: George Braziller, 1957.

Graves, Robert. *The White Goddess: A Historical Grammar of Poetic Myth*. New York: Farrar, Straus and Giroux, 1981.

Green, Miranda J. *Dictionary of Celtic Myth and Legend*. London: Thames and Hudson, 1992.

Greenberg, David F. *The Construction of Homosexuality*. Chicago: University of Chicago, 1988.

Grey, Morgan and Julia Penelope. *Found Goddesses: Asphalta to Viscera*. Norwich, VT: New Victoria Publishers, 1988.

Griffin, Gabriele. *Heavenly Love? Lesbian Images in Twentieth-Century Women's Writing*. New York: Manchester University Press, 1993.

Grimal, Pierre. *Larousse World Mythology*. New Jersey: Chartwell Books, 1965.

Grimal, Pierre. *The Penguin Dictionary of Classical Mythology*, ed. Stephen Kershaw, trans. A. R. Maxwell-Hyslop. New York: Penguin Books, 1991.

Grottanelli, Cristiano. "Archaic Forms of Rebellion and Their Religious Background." In *Religion, Rebellion, Revolution*, ed. Bruce Lincoln. Houndmills, England: Macmillan, 1985.

Gubar, Susan. "Sapphistries." *The Lesbian Issue: Essays from SIGNS*, ed. Estelle B. Freedman, *et al.* Chicago: University of Chicago Press, 1985.

Guerra, Francisco. *The Pre-Columbian Mind*. London: Seminar Press, 1971.

Guiley, Rosemary Ellen. *The Encyclopedia of Witches and Witchcraft*. New York: Facts on File, 1989.

Gulik, Robert Hans van. *Sexual Life in Ancient China: A Preliminary Survey of Chinese Sex and Society from ca. 1500 B. C. till 1644 A. D.* Leiden: E. J. Brill, 1961.

Gundarsson, Kveldulf. *Teutonic Magic: The Magical and Spiritual Practices of the Germanic Peoples*. St Paul, Minn.: Llewellyn, 1990.

Halifax, Joan. *Shamanic Voices: A Survey of Visionary Narratives*. New York: E. P. Dutton, 1979.

Haller, Robert A. *Kenneth Anger: A Monograph*. New York: Mystic Fire Video, Film in the Cities, 1980.

Halliday, William R. *Greek Divination: a Study of its Methods and Principles*. London: Macmillan, 1913.

Halsall, Paul. *Calendar of Lesbian, Gay, Bisexual, and Transgender Saints*. (Version 2). Electronically published on the *Queer Studies List*, August 9, 1994.

Halsberghe, Gaston H. *The Cult of Sol Invictus*. Leiden: E. J. Grill, 1972.

Hanon, Geraldine Hatch. *Sacred Space: A Feminist Vision of Astrology*. Ithaca, NY: Firebrand Books, 1990.

Hart, Donn V. "Homosexuality and Transvestism in the Philippines: The Cebuan Filipino Bayot and Lakin-on." In *Behavioral Science Notes* 3 (1968), 211-248.

Hawkins, Peter S. "Naming Names: The Art of Memory and the Names Project AIDS Memorial Quilt." *Critical Inquiry* 19, no. 4 (Summer 1993), 752-774.

Hay, Harry. "A Separate People Whose Time Has Come." Los Angeles, CA: Christopher Street West Gay Pride Festival Souvenir Program, 1983.

Heard, Gerald (as D. B. Vest). "The Isophyl as a Biological Variant." *ONE: Institute Quarterly of Homophile Studies* 1, no. 2, 1958.

Heflin, Llee. *The Island Dialogues*. San Francisco: Level Press, 1973.

Helminiak, Daniel A. *What the Bible Really Says About Homosexuality*. San Francisco: Alamo Square Press, 1994.

Henderson, Hamish. "The Women of the Glen: Some Thoughts on Highland History." In *The Celtic Consciousness*, ed. Robert O'Driscoll. New York: G. Braziller, 1982.

Henderson, Joseph L. and Maud Oakes. *The Wisdom of the Serpent: The Myths of Death, Rebirth, and Resurrection*. New York: George Braziller, 1963.

Herbert, Jean. *Shinto: At the Fountainhead of Japan*. New York: Stein and Day, 1967.

Herdt, Gilbert H. *Guardians of the Flutes: Idioms of Masculinity*. New York: McGraw-Hill Book Company, 1981.

Herdt, Gilbert H., ed. *Ritualized Homosexuality in Melanesia*. University of California Press: Berkeley, 1984,

Herdt, Gilbert H., ed. *Third Sex, Third Gender: Beyond Sexual Dimorphism in Culture and History*. New York: Zone Books, 1994.

Herdt, Gilbert and R. J. Stroller, eds. *Intimate Communications: Erotics and the Study of Culture*. New York: Columbia University Press, 1990.

Hinsch, Bret. *Passions of the Cut Sleeve: The Male Homosexual Tradition in China*. Berkeley: University of California Press, 1990.

Hirschfeld, Magnus *Transvestites: The Erotic Drive to Cross-Dress*. Trans. Michael A. Lombardi-Nash. Buffalo, New York: Prometheus Books, 1991.

Hirschfelden, Arlene and Paulette Molin. *The Encyclopedia of Native American Religions*. New York: Facts on File, 1992.

Humphreys, Christmas. *Buddhism*. Baltimore: Penguin, 1969.

Huneker, James. *Overtones: A Book of Temperaments*. ("Parsifal: A Mystic Melodrama.") New York: Charles Scribner's Sons, 1904.

Hurbon, Laënnec. *Voodoo: Search for the Spirit*. Trans. Lory Frankel. New York: Harry N. Abrams, 1995.

Huxley, Francis. *The Invisibles: Voodoo Gods in Haiti*. New York: McGraw-Hill, 1966 (1969).

Imbelloni, J. "La 'Essaltatione delle Rose' del Codice Vaticano Mexicano 3738." In *Anales del Instituto de Ethnografia Americana* 4 (1943), 161-201. Universidad Nacional de Cuyo.

Ives, George Cecil. "The Urning," and "Eocene." Original manuscripts. Harry Ransom Humanities Research Center, University of Texas at Austin, British Sexological Society / George Cecil Ives Collection.

Jamal, Michele. *Deerdancer: The Shapeshifter Archetype in Story and in Trance*. New York: Arkana, Penguin, 1995.

Jeanmaire, Henri. *Couroi et Courètes*. New York: Arno Press, 1975.

Jensen, Eric. *The Iban and Their Religion*. Oxford: Clarendon Press, 1974.

Jochelson, Vladimir I. *The Koryak. Report of the Jessup North Pacific Expedition*. New York: Memoirs of the American Museum of Natural History, 1905.

Jones, George Fenwick. "The Kiss in Middle High German Literature." *Studia Neophillologica* 38, no. 2 (1966), ed. Bengt Hasselrot (Uppsala: Ab Lundeguistka Bokhandeln).

Jüdell, Brandon. *"Hell's Angel."* (An Interview with Clive Barker). *10 Percent* (March-April 1995), 53-55, 73.

Jullian, Philippe. *Dreamers of Decadence: Symbolist Painters of the 1890s*. New York: Praeger, 1975.

Jung, Carl G. "On the Psychology of the Trickster Figure." In *The Trickster: A Study in American Indian Mythology*, ed. Paul Radin. London: Routledge and Kegan Paul, 1956.

Jung, Carl G. *Psychology and Alchemy*. Trans. R. F. C. Hull. Princeton: Princeton University Press (Bollingen Series), 1968.

Juno, Andrea and V. Vale, eds. *Angry Women: Re/Search #13*. San Francisco: Re/Search Publications, 1991.

Kafi, Hélène. "Tehran: Dangerous Love." In *Sex and Eroticism Among Males in Moslem Societies*, ed. Arno Schmitt and Jehoeda Sofer. New York: Haworth Press, 1992.

Karlen, Arno. *Sexuality and Homosexuality: A New View*. New York: W. W. Norton, 1971.

Karlinsky, Simon. "Russian Literature." In *The Gay and Lesbian Literary Heritage*, ed. Claude J. Summers. New York: Henry Holt, 1995.

Katz, Jonathan. *Gay American History: Lesbians and Gay Men in the U.S.A*. New York: Thomas Y. Crowell Company, 1976.

Kaye, Richard. "Saint Sebastian." In *The Gay and Lesbian Literary Heritage*, ed. Claude J. Summers. New York: Henry Holt, 1995.

Keating, AnnLouise. "Myth Smashers, Myth Makers: (Re)Visionary Techniques in the Works of Paula Gunn Allen, Gloria Anzaldúa, and Audre Lorde." *Journal of Homosexuality* 26, nos. 2/3 (1993), 73-95.

Keesey, Pam. *Dark Angels: Lesbian Vampire Stories*. San Francisco: Cleis Press, 1995.

Keightley, Thomas. *The Fairy Mythology*. London: H. G. Bohn, 1860.

Kennedy, Hubert. *Ulrichs: The Life and Works of Karl Heinrich Ulrichs, Pioneer of the Modern Gay Movement*. Boston: Alyson Publications, 1988.

Kepner, Jim. *Becoming a People: A 4,000 Year Gay and Lesbian Chronology*. Los Angeles: National Gay Archives, 1983.

Kepner, Jim. "A Memory of Gerald Heard." *Lewd Conduct: Gay Community Alliance News Magazine* (Los Angeles) 1, no. 1 (October 1971), 14-15.

Kepner, Jim. *Seeking the Spark: Exploring Various Paths to Gay Spirit*. Unpublished manuscript, 1996.

Kerényi, Carl (or Karoly). *Dionysos: Archetypal Image of Indestructible Life*. Princeton: Princeton University Press, 1976.

Kerényi, Carl. *Eleusis: Archetypal Image of Mother and Daughter*. Trans. Ralph Manheim. New York: Bollingen, Pantheon, 1967.

Kerényi, Carl. *Hermes, Guide of Souls: The Mythologem of the Masculine Source of Life*. Trans. Murray Stein. Zurich: Spring Publications, 1976.

Kerényi, Carl. "The Trickster in Relation to Greek Mythology." In *The Trickster: A Study in American Indian Mythology*, ed. Paul Radin. London: Routledge and Kegan Paul, 1956.

Keuls, Eva C. *The Reign of the Phallus: Sexual Politics in Ancient Athens*. New York: Harper and Row, 1985.

Kiefer, Thomas M. "A Note on Cross-Sex Identification Among Musicians." *Ethnomusicology* 12, no. 1 (1968), 107-109.

Kim, Young Ja. "The Korean Namsadang." In *The Drama Review* 25 (1981), 9-16.

Kinsley, David. *Hindu Goddesses: Visions of the Divine Feminine in the Hindu Religious Tradition*. Berkeley: University of California Press, 1986.

Kinsley, David. *The Sword and the Flute: Kali and Krishna, Dark Visions of the Terrible and the Sublime in Hindu Mythology*. Berkeley: University of California Press, 1975.

Kneeland, J. E. *Gay Signs: An Astrological Approach to Homosexuality*. Santa Monica, CA: Hay House, Inc., 1988.

Kodansha Encyclopedia of Japan. (Vols. 3, 4). New York: Kodansha 1983.

Koestenbaum, Wayne. *The Queen's Throat: Opera, Homosexuality, and the Mystery of Desire*. New York: Poseidon Press, 1993.

Koskoff, Ellen. *Women and Music in Cross-Cultural Perspective*. Urbana: University of Illinois Press, 1989.

Kramrisch, Stella. *Manifestations of Shiva*. Philadelphia: Philadelphia Museum of Art, 1981.

Kristeller, Paul Oskar. *The Philosophy of Marcilio Ficino*. Trans. Virginia Conant. Gloucester, Mass.: Peter Smith, 1964.

Kroef, Justus M. van der. "Transvestitism and the Religious Hermaphrodite in Indonesia," *University of Manila Journal of East Asiatic Studies* 3, no. 3 (April 1954), 257-265.

Kunz, George Frederick. *The Mystical Lore of Precious Stones*. North Hollywood, California: Newcastle Publishing Company, 1986.

Lacarrière, Jacques. *The Gnostics*. Trans. Nina Rootes. New York: E. P. Dutton, 1977.

Lambert, Royston. *Beloved and God: The Story of Hadrian and Antinous*. New York: Viking, 1984.

Lambourne, Lionel, *et. al. Solomon: A Family of Painters*. London: Publication of the Geffrye Museum, London, and the Birmingham Museum and Art Gallery, 1986.

Larivière, Michel. *Les Amours Masculines: Anthologie de l'homosexualité dans la littérature*. Paris: Lieu Commun, 1984.

Larivière, Michel. *A poil et à plume, Homosexuels et bisexuels célèbres*. Paris: R. Deforges, 1987.

Larrington, Carolyne, ed. *The Feminist Companion to Mythology*. London: Pandora Press, Harper Collins, 1992.

Lattin, Don. "AIDS and the Healing Spirit." *San Francisco Chronicle,* Vol. 125, no. 36 (Feburary 27, 1989), A-1, 8-9.

Lawler, Lillian B. *The Dance of the Ancient Greek Theatre*. Iowa City: University of Iowa Press, 1964.

Lawton, George. "The Psychology of Spiritualist Mediums." *Psychoanalytic Review* 19 (1932), 418-445.

Layard, John. *Stone Men of Malekula:Vao*. London: Chatto and Windus, 1942.

Lea, Henry Charles. *A History of the Inquisition of Spain*. New York: Macmillan, 1922.

Leach, Maria, ed. *Funk and Wagnalls Standard Dictionary of Folklore, Mythology and Legend*. New York: Funk and Wagnalls, 1972.

Leach, Marjorie, *et al.*, eds. *Guide to the Gods*. Santa Barbara, California: ABC-CLIO, 1992.

Leacock, Seth and Ruth Leacock. *Spirits of the Deep: A Study of an Afro-Brazilian Cult*. New York: Doubleday, 1972.

Leão Teixera, Maria Lina. "Lorogun: Identidades sexuais e peder no Candomblé." In *Candomblé Desvendando Identidades: Novos escritos subre a religião dos orixas*, ed. Carlos Eugenio Marcondes de Moura. São Paulo: EMW Editiones, 1987.

Leick, Gwendolyn. *Sex and Eroticism in Mesopotamian Literature*. New York: Routledge, 1994.

Lever, Maurice. *Le Sceptre et la Marotte: Histoire des Fous de Cour*. Paris: Fayard, 1983.

Lever, Maurice. *Les bûchers de Sodome: Histoire des "infâmes."* Paris: Fayard, 1985.

Lewis, James. R. *The Astrology Encyclopedia*. Detroit: Gale Research, 1994.

Licht, Hans. *Sexual Life in Ancient Greece*. London: The Abbey Library, 1971.

López-Austin, Alfredo. *The Human Body and Ideology: Concepts of the Ancient Nahuas*. Trans. Thelma and Bernard Ortiz de Montellano. Salt Lake City: University of Utah Press, 1988.

Lorde, Audre. *Uses of the Erotic: The Erotic as Power*. Trumansburg, NY: Out and Out Books, 1978.

Loulan, JoAnn. *The Lesbian Erotic Dance: Butch, Femme, Androgyny, and Other Rhythms*. Minneapolis: Spinsters Ink, 1990.

Lucas, Ian. *Impertinent Decorum: Gay Theatrical Manoeuvres*. London: Cassell, 1994.

Lucie-Smith, Edward. *Eroticism in Western Art*. New York: Praeger Publishers, 1972.

McClary, Susan. *Feminine Endings: Music, Gender and Sexuality*. University of Minnesota Press, 1991.

Malaurie, Jean. "Note sur l'homosexualité et le chamanisme chez les Tchouktches et les Esquimaux d'Asie." *Nouvelle Revue d'Ethnopsychiatrie*, no. 19 (1992), 173-214.

Marcelin, Milo. *Mythologie Vodou: Rite Arada*. Port-au-Prince: Les Editions Haitiennes, 1950.

Marcus, Jane. "Sapphistory: The Woolf and the Well." In *Lesbian Texts and Contexts: Radical Revisions*, ed. Karla Jay and Joanne Glasgow. New York: New York University Press, 1990.

Marcuse, Herbert. *Eros and Civilization: A Philosophical Inquiry into Freud*. New York: Vintage; Random House, (1955) 1962.

Mariechild, Diane and Marcelina Martin. *Lesbian Sacred Sexuality*. Oakland: Wingbow Press, 1995.

Markale, Jean. *Le druidisme: Traditions et dieux des Celtes*. Paris: Payot, 1985.

Markale, Jean. *Mélusine, ou l'androgyne*. Paris: Editions Retz, 1983.

Marriott, McKim. "The Feast of Love." *Krishna: Myths, Rites, and Attitudes*, ed. Milton Singer. Chicago: University of Chicago, 1968.

Martin, Robert K. *The Homosexual Tradition in American Poetry*. Austin: University of Texas Press, 1979.

Mass, Laurence. "Homosexuality and Music: A Conversation with Philip Brett." *Christopher Street* 115 (1987), 12-26.

Masson, Olivier and Maurice Sznycer. *Recherches sur les Phéniciens à Chypre*. Hautes Etudes Orientales II, 3. Paris: Librairie Droz, 1972.

Masters, R. E. L. *Eros and Evil: The Sexual Psychology of Witchcraft*. Baltimore: Penguin Books, 1974.

Mayne, Xavier [pseudonym of Edward Irenaeus Prime-Stevenson]. *The Intersexes: A History of Similisexualism as a Problem in Social Life*. Florence: privately printed, 1908.

Mercatante, Anthony S. *The Facts on File Encyclopedia of World Mythology and Legend*. New York: Facts on File, 1988.

Meyer, Marvin, Richard Smith, and Neal Kelsey, eds. *Ancient Christian Magic: Coptic Texts of Ritual Power*. San Francisco: Harper Collins, 1994.

Michaelides, Solon. *The Music of Ancient Greece: An Encyclopedia*. London: Faber and Farber, 1978.

Mitchell, Larry. *The Faggots and Their Friends Between Revolutions*. Ithaca, NY: Calamus Books, 1977.

Mohr, Richard D. *Gay Ideas: Outing and Other Controversies*. Boston: Beacon Press, 1992.

Monaghan, Patricia. *The Book of Goddesses and Heroines*. Minnesota: Llewellyn Publications, 1990.

Monter, E. William. *Witchcraft in France and Switzerland: The Borderlands during the Reformation*. Ithaca: Cornell University Press, 1976.

Mookerjee, Aiit. *Kali the Feminine Force*. Boulder: Inner Traditions, 1989.

Moore, Robert and Douglas Gillette. *The Magician Within: Accessing the Shaman in the Male Psyche*. New York: William Morrow, 1993.

Morgan, Ffiona. *Goddess Spirituality Book: Rituals, Holydays, and Moon Magic*. Graton, CA: Daughters of the Moon, 1995.

Morgan, Ffiona. *Mysteries of the Godess: Astrology, Tarot, and the Magical Arts*. Graton, CA: Daughters of the Moon, 1995.

Morgan, Raleigh, Jr. "Old French *jogleor* and Kindred Terms: Studies in Medieval Romance Lexicology." *Romance Philology* 7, no. 4 (May 1954).

Morgan, Robin. *Lady of the Beasts*. New York: Random House, 1976.

Morris, Robert J. "Same Sex Friendships in Hawaiian Lore: Constructing the Canon." In *Oceanic Homosexualities*, ed. Stephen O. Murray. New York: Garland Publishing, 1992.

Morris, Rosalind, C. "Three Sexes and Four Sexualities: Redressing the Discourse on Gender and Sexuality in Contemporary Thailand." *Positions: East Asian Cultures Critique* 2, no. 1 (Spring 1994), 15-43.

Mott, Luiz. "Brazil." In *The Encyclopedia of Homosexuality* (Vol. I), ed. Wayne Dynes and Stephen Donaldson. New York: Garland, 1990.

Mullaney, Steven. "Strange Things, Gross Terms, Curious Customs: The Rehearsal of Cultures in the Late Renaissance." *Representing the English Renaissance*, ed. Stephen Greenblatt. Berkeley: University of California Press, 1988.

Murray, Raymond. *Images in the Dark: An Encyclopedia of Gay and Lesbian Film and Video*. Philadelphia: TLD Publishers, 1994.

Murray, Stephen O., ed. *Oceanic Homosexualities*. New York: Garland Publishing, 1992.

Nadel, S. F. *The Nuba: An Anthropological Study of the Hill Tribes in Kordofan*. London: Oxford University Press, 1947.

Nanda, Serena. "The Hijras of India: A Preliminary Report." *Medicine and Law* 3 (1984): 59-75.

Nanda, Serena. *Neither Man nor Woman: The Hijras of India*. Belmont, CA: Wadsworth Publishing Co., 1990.

Nelson, Ida. *La Sottie San Souci*. Paris: Editions Honore Champion, 1976.

Newall, Venetia. "Folklore and Male Homosexuality." *Folklore* 97, no. 2 (1986), 123-147.

Ngubane, Harriet. *Body and Mind in Zulu Medicine*. New York: Academic Press, 1977.

Nightlinger, Elizabeth. "The Female Imitatio Christi and Medieval Popular Religion: The Case of St. Wilgefortis." In *Feminea Medievalia 1: Representations of the Feminine in the Middle Ages*, ed. Bonnie Wheeler. Dallas: Academia Press, Derek Baker, 1993.

Nightlinger, Elizabeth. "Images of Divine Unity: Cross-Cultural Aspects of Androgyny and Sacred Female Hirsutism." Unpublished manuscript, 1993.

Nightlinger, Elizabeth. "The Powers of an English Female Imitatio Christi: Miracles or Magic?" Unpublished manuscript, 1995.

Nightlinger, Elizabeth. "Symbols of Repressed Feminine Power: The Destructive Regenerative Solar Gorgoneion Complex as Athena's Shield Devices." Unpublished manuscript, 1995.

Noble, Vicki. *Shakti Woman: Feeling Our Fire, Healing Our World: The New Female Shaman*. San Francisco: Harper Collins, 1991.

Noble, Vicki, ed. *Uncoiling the Snake: Ancient Patterns in Contemporary Women's Lives*. San Francisco: Harper Collins, 1993.

Norton, Rictor. *The Homosexual Literary Tradition: An Interpretation*. New York: Revisionist Press, 1974.

Norton, Rictor. *Mother Clap's Molly House: The Gay Subculture in England 1700-1830*. London: Gay Men's Press, 1992

Nykl, Alois Richard. *Hispano-Arabic Poetry and Its Relations with the Old Provençal Troubadours*. Baltimore: J. H. Furst Co., 1946

O'Brien, Maire Cruise. "The Role of the Poet in Gaelic Society." In *The Celtic Consciousness*, ed. Robert O'Driscoll. New York: George Braziller, 1982.

Ochshorn, Judith. "Ishtar and Her Cult." *The Book of the*

Goddess: Past and Present, ed. Carl Olson. New York: Crossroad, 1983.

O'Flaherty, Wendy Doniger. *Asceticism and Eroticism in the Mythology of Shiva.* New York: Oxford University Press, 1973.

O'Flaherty, Wendy Doniger. *Hindu Myths.* Baltimore: Penguin Books, 1975.

O'Flaherty, Wendy Doniger. *Women, Androgynes and Other Mythical Beasts.* Chicago: University of Chicago Press, 1980.

Opie, Iona and Peter Opie, ed. *The Oxford Dictionary of Nursery Rhymes.* Oxford: Oxford University Press, 1983.

The Oxford Annotated Bible. Revised Standard Version. Oxford: Oxford Unversity Press, 1965.

Paglia, Camille. *Sex, Art, and American Culture: Essays.* New York: Vintage, Random House, 1992.

Paglia, Camille. *Sexual Personae: Art and Decadence from Nefertiti to Emily Dickinson.* New York: Vintage Books, Random House, 1991.

Palmer, Susan Jean. *Moon Sister, Krishna Mothers, Rajneesh Lovers: Women's Roles in New Religions.* Syracuse, New York: Syracuse University Press, 1994.

Parrinder, Geoffrey, ed. *Sex in the World's Religions.* New York: Oxford University Press, 1980.

Patai, Raphael. *The Hebrew Goddess.* New York: Ktav Publications, 1968.

Patterson, Rebecca. *The Riddle of Emily Dickinson.* New York: Cooper Square, 1973.

Paul, Rick. "Carnival Gay Balls: Gay Urban Folk Art." *RFD* no. 39 (Summer 1984), 46.

Pellat, Charles. "Liwat." In *Sex and Eroticism Among Males in Moslem Societies,* ed. Arno Schmitt and Jehoeda Sofer. New York: Haworth Press, 1992.

PenDragon, Valkyrie Cougar. "TS and Wiccan Spirituality." *Transgender* no. 74 (Winter 1995).

Penelope, Julia and Morgan Grey. *Found Goddesses.* Norwich, Vermont: New Victoria Publishers, 1988.

Perella, Nicolas. *The Kiss, Sacred and Profane: An Interpretative History of Kiss Symbolism and Related Religio-Erotic Themes.* Berkeley: University of California Press, 1969.

Perry, Troy D. "A Meditation on Religion and Leatherspace." In *Leatherfolk: Radical Sex, People, Politics, and Practice.* Boston: Alyson Publications, 1991.

Persson, Axel W. *The Religion of Greece in Prehistoric Times.* Berkeley: University of California Press, 1942.

Plante, David. "Images of the Body from My Religion." In *Wrestling with the Angel: Faith and Religion in the Lives of Gay Men,* ed. Brian Bouldrey. New York: Riverhead Books, G. P. Putnam's Sons, 1995.

Plaskow, Judith and Carol P. Christ, eds. *Weaving the Visions: New Patterns in Feminist Spirituality.* San Francisco: Harper and Row, 1989.

Pollack, Sandra and Denise D. Knight, eds. *Contemporary Lesbian Writers of the United States: A Bio-Bibliographical Critical Sourcebook.* Westport, CT: Greenwood Press, 1993.

Popescu-Judetz, Eugenia. "Kocek and Cengi in Turkish Culture" *Dance Studies* 6. Jersey, CI: Centre for Dance Studies Publications, 1982.

Povert, Lionel. *Dictionnaire Gay.* Paris: Jacques Grancher, 1994.

Pratt, Annis. *Dancing with Goddesses: Archetypes, Poetry, and Empowerment.* Bloomington: Indiana University Press, 1994.

Praz, Mario. *The Romantic Agony.* Trans. Angus Davidson. New York: Meridian Books, World Publishing Company, 1963.

Pressel, Esther. "The Clique: Two Children of Mamae Oxum." Goodman, Felicitas D. *et al. Trance, Healing, and Hallucination: Three Field Studies in Religious Experience.* New York: John Wiley and Sons, 1974.

Provost, Bert (aka Corona). "Discovering Queer Archetypes." *Lavender Pagan Newsletter* 1.2 (1991), p. 1.

Purkiss, Diane. "Women's Rewriting of Myth." In *The Feminist Companion to Mythology,* ed. Carolyne Larrington. London: Pandora, Harper Collins, 1992.

Purusha (Christopher Larkin). *The Divine Androgyne.* San Diego: Sancturary Publications, 1981.

Qualls-Corbett, Nancy. *The Sacred Prostitute: Eternal Aspect of the Feminine.* Toronto: Inner City Books, 1988.

Quasten, Johannes. *Music and Worship in Pagan and Christian Antiquity.* Trans. Boniface Ramsey. Washington, DC: National Association of Pastoral Musicians, 1983.

R. C. *La Nouvelle Sapho, ou Histoire de la Secte Anandryne.* Paris, 1791.

Radin, Paul. *The Trickster: A Study in American Indian Mythology.* London: Routledge and Kegan Paul, 1956.

Ratti, Rakesh, ed. *A Lotus of Another Color: An Unfolding of the South Asian Gay and Lesbian Experience.* Boston: Alyson Publications, 1993.

Raymond, Janice G. *A Passion for Friends: Toward A Philosophy of Female Affection.* Boston: Beacon Press, 1986.

Reade, Brian. *Sexual Heretics: Male Homosexuality in English Literature from 1850 to 1900.* New York: Coward-McCann, 1971.

Rehmus, E. E. *The Magician's Dictionary.* Los Angeles: Feral House, 1990.

Reichard, Gladys A. *Navaho Religion: A Study of Symbolism.* Tucson: University of Arizona Press, 1983.

Requena, Antonio. "Sodomy among Native American Peoples." *Gay Sunshine* 38/39 (Winter 1979), 37-39.

Rhoads, Heather. "Cruel Crusade: The Holy War Against Lesbians and Gays." *The Progressive* 57, no. 3 (1993): 18-23.

Richards, Dell. *Lesbian Lists*. Boston: Alyson Publications, 1990.

Richlin, Amy. *The Garden of Priapus: Sexuality and Aggression in Roman Humor*. New Haven: Yale University Press, 1983.

Roberts, J. R. *Black Lesbians: An Annotated Bibliography*. Tallahassee, Florida: Naiad Press, 1981.

Robertson, Carol E. "The Ethnomusicologist as Midwife" In *Musicology and Difference: Gender and Sexuality in Music Scholarship*, ed. Ruth Solie. London: University of California Press, 1993.

Roscoe, Will. "Bibliography of Berdache and Alternative Gender Roles Among North American Indians." *Journal of Homosexuality* 14 (3-4), 1987.

Roscoe, Will. *Making History*. San Francisco: Vortex Media, 1985.

Roscoe, Will. *The Zuni Man-Woman*. Albuquerque: University of New Mexico Press, 1991.

Roscoe, Will, ed. (with Gay American Indians). *Living the Spirit: A Gay American Indian Anthology*. New York: St Martin's Press, 1988.

Rosen, Susan Grant. "The NAMES Project Quilt: Sacred Symbol for the Age of AIDS?" Unpublished paper delivered at the American Academy of Religion (November 21, 1993).

Ross, Margaret Clunies. "Hildr's Ring: A Problem in the Ragnarsdrápa, strophes 8-12." *Mediaeval Scandinavia* 6 (1973). Odense, Denmark: Odense University Press.

Roth, Norman. "Deal Gently with the Young Man: Love of Boys in Medieval Hebrew Poetry of Spain." *Speculum* 57 (1982), 20-51.

Rousseau, G. S. "The Pursuit of Homosexuality in the Eighteenth Century," and "The Pursuit of Homosexuality in the Eighteenth Century: 'Utterly Confused Category' and/or Rich Repository?" In *'Tis Nature's Fault': Unauthorized Sexuality during the Enlightenment*, ed. Robert Maccubbin. Cambridge: Cambridge University Press, 1987.

Rowse, A. L. *Homosexuals in History: A Study of Ambivalence in Society, Literature and the Arts*. Dorset Press, 1983 (orig. 1977).

Rucker, Paul B. "People of the Rainbow: Transgender in Magick and Ritual." *Tapestry Journal* 73 (Fall 1995), 56-59.

Ruggiero, Guido. *The Boundaries of Eros: Sex Crime and Sexuality in Renaissance Venice*. Oxford: Oxford University Press, 1985.

Russell, Kenneth C. "Aelred, the Gay Abbot of Rievaulx." *Studia Mystica* 5, no. 4 (Winter 1982), 51-64.

Russo, Vito. *The Celluloid Closet: Homosexuality in the Movies*. New York: Harper and Row, 1985.

Russo, William. "Nijinsky." *Mandate* (April 1978), 38-45.

Rutledge, Leigh W. *The Gay Book of Lists*. Boston: Alyson Publications, 1987.

Rutt, Richard. "The Flower Boys of Silla (*Hwarang*): Notes on the Sources." *Royal Asiatic Society, Transactions of the Korean Branch* 38 (1961), 1-66.

Sager, John G. *Curse Tablets and Binding Spells from the Ancient World*. New York: Oxford University Press, 1992.

Sahuquillo, Angel. *Federico García Lorca y la Cultura de la Homosexualidad masculina: Lorca, Dali, Gil-Albert, Prados y la voz silenciada del amor homosexual*. Alicante: Instituto de Cultura "Juan Gil-Albert," Diputacion de Alicante, 1991.

Sakoian, Frances and Louis S. Acker. *The Astrologer's Handbook*. New York: Harper and Row, 1973.

Saladin d'Anglure, Bernard. "Du foetus au chamane: la construction d'un 'troisième sexe' inuit." *Etudes / Inuit / Studies*. 10, nos. 1-2 (1986), 25-113.

Saladin d'Anglure, Bernard. "Du Projet 'Par ad i' : au sexe des anges: notes et débats autour d'un 'troisième sexe'." *Anthropologie et Sociétés* 9, no. 3 (1985), 139-176.

Saladin d'Anglure, Bernard. "Penser le 'féminin' chamanique, ou le 'tier-sexe' des chamanes inuit." *Recherches Amérindiennes au Québec* 18 (1988), 19-50.

Salmonson, Jessica Amanda. *The Encyclopedia of Amazons: Women Warriors from Antiquity to the Modern Era*. New York: Paragon House, 1991.

Salmonson, Jessica Amanda and Jules Remedios Faye. *Wisewomen and Boggy-boos: A Dictionary of Lesbian Fairy Lore*. Austin, Texas: Banned Books, 1992.

Samshasha (Xiaomingxiong). *History of Homosexuality in China*. Chinese edition. Hong Kong: Pink Triangle Press, 1984.

Sangirardi Junior. *Deuses da Africa e do Brasil: Candomble and Umbanda*. Rio de Janeiro: Civilizacao Brasileira, 1988.

Saslow, James M. *Ganymede in the Renaissance: Homosexuality in Art and Society*. New Haven: Yale University Press, 1986.

Schärer, Hans. *Ngaju Religion: The Conception of God among a South Borneo People*. The Hague: Martinus Nijhoff, 1963.

Schechter, Harold. "Symbols of Initiation in Adventures of Huckleberry Finn." In *Betwixt and Between: Patterns of masculine and Feminine Initiation*, ed. Louise Carus Mahdi *et al*. La Salle, Illinois: Open Court, 1987.

Schieffelin, E. L. "The *Bau A* Ceremonial Hunting Lodge: An Alternative to Initiation." In *Rituals of Manhood: Male Initiation in Papua New Guinea*, ed. Gilbert H. Herdt. Berkeley: University of California Press, 1982.

Schieffelin, E. L. *The Sorrow of the Lonely and the Burning of the Dancers*. New York: St Martin's Press, 1976.

Schmitt, Arno and Jehoeda Sofer, eds. *Sexuality and Eroticism Among Males in Moslem Societies*. New York: Haworth Press, 1992.

Schneider, David. *Street Zen: the Life and Works of Issan Dorsey*. Boston: Shambhala, 1993.

Schultes, Richard Evans and Albert Hofmann. *Plants of the Gods*. New York: McGraw-Hill, 1979.

Sébillot, Paul. *Le Folk-Lore de France*. Paris: Editions G.-P. Maisonneuve et Larose, 1968.

Sendrey, Alfred. *Music in the Social and Religious Life of Antiquity*. Rutherford: Fairleigh Dickinson University Press, 1974.

Sergent, Bernard. *L'homosexualité initiatique dans l'Europe ancienne*. Paris: Payot, 1986.

Sergent, Bernard. *Homosexuality in Greek Myth*. Trans. Arthur Goldhammer. Boston: Beacon Press, 1986.

Serinus, Jason, ed. *Psychoimmunity and the Healing Process: A Holistic Approach to Immunity and AIDS*. Berkeley: Celestial Arts, 1986.

Sharma, Arvind. "Homosexuality and Hinduism." In *Homosexuality and World Religions*, ed. Arlene Swidler. Valley Forge, PA: Trinity Press International, 1993.

Shepard, Leslie A., ed. *Encyclopedia of Occultism and Parapsychology* (3rd edition). Detroit: Gale Research, 1991.

Sherman, Suzanne, ed. *Lesbian and Gay Marriage: Private Commitments, Public Ceremonies*. Philadelphia: Temple University Press, 1992.

Shetty, Kavitha. "Eunuchs: A Bawdy Festival." *India Today* 15, nos. 1-2 (June 15, 1990), 50-55.

Shulman, David D. *Tamil Temple Myths*. Princeton: Princeton University Press, 1980.

Simek, Rudolf. *Dictionary of Northern Mythology*. Trans. Angela Hall. Cambridge: D. S. Brewer, 1993.

Simons, Patricia. "Lesbian (In)Visibility in Italian Renaissance Culture: Diana and Other Cases of *donna con donna*." In *Gay and Lesbian Studies in Art History*, ed. Whitney Davis. New York: Harrington Park Press, The Haworth Press, 1994.

Simpson, Jacqueline. *European Mythology*. New York: Peter Bedrick, 1987.

Singer, Milton. "The Radha-Krishna Bhajanas of Madras City." In *Krishna: Myths, Rites, and Attitudes*, ed. Milton Singer. Chicago: University of Chicago, 1968.

Sjoo, Monica and Barbara Mor. *The Great Comic Mother*. San Francisco: Harper Collins, 1987.

Slater, Herman, ed. *The Magickal Formulary*. New York: Magickal Childe, 1981.

Smith, Morton. *Jesus the Magician*. New York: Harper and Row, 1978.

Smith, Morton. *The Secret Gospel: The Discovery and Interpretation of the Secret Gospel According to Mark*. New York: Harper and Row, 1973.

Smith, Pauline M. *The Anti-Courtier Trend in Sixteenth Century French Literature*. Geneva: Librairie Droz, 1966.

Smith, Timothy d'Arch. *The Books of the Beast: Essays on Aleister Crowley, Montague Summers and others*. Oxford: Mandrake, 1991.

Smith, Timothy d'Arch. *Love in Earnest: Some Notes on the Lives and Writings of English 'Uranian' Poets from 1889 to 1930*. London: Routledge and Kegan Paul, 1970.

Sobol, Donald J. *The Amazons of Greek Mythology*. South Brunswick and New York: A. S. Barnes and Company, 1972.

Solomon, Maynard. 1981. "Franz Schubert's 'My Dream'." In *Homosexuality and Homosexuals in the Arts*, ed. Wayne Dynes and Stephen Donaldson. New York: Garland Publishing, 1992.

Spicer, Jack. "Some Notes on Whitman." *Angels of the Lyre: A Gay Poetry Anthology*, ed. Winston Leyland. San Francisco: Panjandrum Press, 1975.

Stapleton, Douglas and Beth Tanner. *Our Whirling Endures*. Photocopy manuscript from authors, 1996.

Starhawk. *Dreaming the Dark: Magic, Sex and Politics*. Boston: Beacon Press, 1982.

Starhawk. *The Spiral Dance: A Rebirth of the Ancient Religion of the Great Goddess*. San Francisco: Harper and Row, 1979.

Starr, Kevin. "Indulging the Sisters." *The Nun Issue* 1, no. 2 (1993) 3. (Originally appeared in *San Francisco Examiner*, October 12, 1981.)

Stehling, Thomas. *Medieval Latin Poems of Male Love and Friendship*. New York: Garland Publishing, 1984.

Stein, Diane. *Casting the Circle: A Women's Book of Ritual*. Freedom, California: Crossing Press, 1990.

Stein, Diane. *The Goddess Book of Days: A Perpetual 366 Day Engagement Calendar*. St Paul, Minn.: Llewellyn Publications, 1989.

Stein, Diane. *The Kwan Yin Book of Changes*. St Paul, Minn.: Llewellyn Publications, 1989.

Stein, Diane. *The Women's Spirituality Book*. St Paul, Minn.: Llewellyn Publications, 1988.

Stemmeler, Michael L. and José Ignacio Cabezón. *Religion, Homosexuality and Literature*. Las Colinas: Monument Press, 1992.

Stewart, Jean. *Warrior of Isis*. Huntington Station, NY: Rising Tide Press, 1995.

Stewart, William, ed. *Cassell's Queer Companion*. London: Cassell, 1995.

Stone, Laura M. *Costume in Aristophanic Poetry*. New York: Arno Press, 1981.

Stone, Merlin. *Ancient Mirrors of Womanhood: A Treasury of Goddess and Heroine Lore from Around the World*. Boston: Beacon, 1984.

Stone, Merlin. *When God was a Woman*. New York, Harcourt Brace Jovanovich, 1976.

Ström, Folke. *Nidh, Ergi and Old Norse Moral Attitudes*. Dorothea Coke Memorial Lecture Delivered 10 May 1973. London: University College by Viking Society for Northern Research, 1974.

Stroumsa, Gedaliahu A. *Another Seed: Studies in Gnostic Mythology*. Leiden: E. J. Brill, 1984.

Stutley, Margaret and James Stutley. *Harper's Dictionary of Hinduism: Its Mythology, Folklore, Philosophy, Literature, and History*. New York: Harper and Row, 1977.

Summers, Claude J., ed. *The Gay and Lesbian Literary Heritage: A Reader's Companion to the Writers and Their Works, from Antiquity to the Present*. New York: Henry Holt and Company, 1995.

Surieu, Robert. *Sarv-e naz: An Essay on Love and the Representation of Erotic Themes in Ancient Iran*. Geneva: Nagel, 1967.

Swift, Michael. "For the Homoerotic Order," *Gay Community News*. (Feb 21, 1987), 5

Swidler, Arlene, ed. *Homosexuality and World Religions*. Valley Forge, PA: Trinity Press International, 1993.

Symonds, John Addington. *The Letters of John Addington Symonds*, ed. Herbert M. Schueller and Robert L. Peters. Detroit: Wayne State University, 1967-1969.

Symonds, John Addington. *Male Love: A Problem in Greek Ethics and Other Writings*, ed. John Lauritsen. New York: Pagan Press, 1985.

Symonds, John Addington. *Studies of the Greek Poets*. New York: Harper and Brothers, 1920.

Te Awekotuku, Ngahuia. "Dykes and Queers: Facts, Fairytales and Fictions." In *Mana Wahine Maori: Selected Writings on Maori Women's Art, Culture and Politics*. Auckland, New Zealand: New Women's Press, 1991.

Teish, Luisah. *Carnival of the Spirits: Seasonal Celebrations and Rites of Passage*. San Francisco: Harper Collins, 1994.

Teish, Luisah. *Jambalaya: The Natural Woman's Book*. San Francisco: Harper and Row, 1985.

Thomas, E. Winton. "Kelebh 'Dog': Its Origin and Some Usages of It in the Old Testament." *Vetus Testamentum* 10, no. 4 (October 1960).

Thompson, Mark. *Gay Soul: Finding the Heart of Gay Spirit and Nature*. San Francisco: Harper Collins, 1994.

Thompson, Mark. *Gay Spirit: Myth and Meaning*. New York: St Martin's Press, 1987.

Thompson, Mark. *Leatherfolk: Radical Sex, People, Politics, and Practice*. Boston: Alyson Publications, 1991.

Thompson, Robert Farris. *Flash of the Spirit: African and Afro-American Art and Philosophy*. New York: Vintage Books, 1983.

Thorsten, Geraldine. *The Goddess in Your Stars: The Original Feminine Meanings of the Sun Signs*. New York: Fireside, Simon and Schuster, 1989.

Timmons, Stuart. *The Trouble with Harry Hay: Founder of the Modern Gay Movement*. Boston: Alyson Publications, 1990.

Touliatos, Diane. "The Traditional Role of Greek Women in Music from Antiquity to the End of the Byzantine Empire." In *Rediscovering the Muses: Women's Musical Traditions*, ed. Kimberly Marshall, 1992.

Traub, Valerie. "The (In)Significance of 'Lesbian' Desire in Early Modern England." In *Queering the Renaissance*, ed. Jonathan Goldberg. Durham: Duke University Press, 1994.

Trevisan, João. *Perverts in Paradise*. Trans. Martin Foreman. London: GMP Publications, Inc., 1986.

Tsui, Kitty. "Give Joan Chen My Phone Number Anytime." In *Lesbian Erotics*, ed. Karla Jay. New York: New York University Press, 1995.

Tsuneo Watanabe and Jun'ichi Wata. *The Love of the Samurai: A Thousand Years of Japanese Homosexuality*. Trans. D. R. Roberts. London: GMP Publishers, 1989.

Turner, Kay. *I Dream of Madonna: Women's Dreams of the Goddess of Pop*. San Francisco: Collins Publishers, 1993.

Tyrrell, William Blake. *Amazons: A Study in Athenian Mythmaking*. Baltimore: Johns Hopkins University Press, 1984.

Ulrichs, Karl Heinrich. *The Riddle of "Man-Manly" Love* (Vols 1-2). Trans. Michael A. Lombardi-Nash. Buffalo, New York: Prometheus Books, 1994.

Velde, H. Te. *Seth, God of Confusion*. Leiden: E. J. Brill, 1977.

Venker, Joseph. "The Goddess of Every Man." *White Crane Newsletter* no. 2 (1989) 1–3.

Verger, Pierre. *Notes sur le culte des Orisa et Vodun: a Bahia, la Baie de tous le Saints, au Bresil et l'ancienne Cote de esclaves en Afrique*. Dakar: Ifan, 1957.

Vermaseren, Maarten J. *Cybele and Attis: The Myth and the Cult*. London: Thames and Hudson, 1977.

Vitiello, Giovanni. "Taoist Themes in Chinese Homoerotic Tales." *In Religion, Homosexuality and Literature*, ed. Michael L. Stemmeler and José Ignacio Cabezón. Las Colinas: Monument Press, 1992.

Volpp, Sophie. "The Discourse on Male Marriage: Li Yu's 'A Male Mencius's Mother'." *Positions: East Asia Cultures Critique* 2, no. 1 (Spring 1994), 113-132.

Waddell, Helen. *Medieval Latin Lyrics*, New York: 1948.

Waddell, Helen. *The Wandering Scholars*. New York: Constable; Lord, Barnes and Noble, 1966.

Wafer, Jim. *The Taste of Blood: Spirit Possession in*

Brazilian Candomblé. Philadelphia: University of Pennsylvania Press, 1991.

Waley, Arthur. *The Nine Songs: A Study of Shamanism in Ancient China*. London: George Allen and Unwin, 1955.

Walker, Barbara. *The Woman's Dictionary of Symbols and Sacred Objects*. San Francisco: Harper Collins, 1988.

Walker, Barbara. *The Woman's Encyclopedia of Myths and Secrets*. New York: Harper Collins, 1983.

Walker, Benjamin. *Hindu World: An Encyclopedic Survey of Hinduism*. London: George Allen and Unwin, 1968.

Walker, Benjamin. *Man and the Beasts within: The Encyclopedia of the Occult, the Esoteric, and the Supernatural*. New York: Stein and Day, 1977.

Walker, Mitchell. "The Double: An Archetypal Configuration." *Spring* (1976), 165-175.

Walker, Mitchell. *Men Loving Men*. San Francsico: Gay Sunshine Press, 1977.

Walker, Mitchell. *Visionary Love: A Spirit Book of Gay Mythology*. San Francisco: Treeroots Press, 1980.

Weinreb, Ben and Christopher Hibbert, eds. *The London Encyclopedia*. London: Papermac, Pan Macmillan 1993.

Weiss, Andrea. *Vampires and Violets: Lesbians in Films*. New York: Penguin Books, 1993.

Werner, Edward T. C. *A Dictionary of Chinese Mythology*. New York: Julian Press, 1961.

West, Celeste. *A Lesbian Love Advisor: The Sweet and Savory Arts of Lesbian Courtship*. San Francisco: Cleis Press, 1989.

Whitam, Frederick L. and Robin M. Mathy. *Male Homosexuality in Four Societies: Brazil, Guatemala, the Philippines, and the United States*. New York: Praeger Publishers, 1986.

Wigoder, Geoffrey, ed. *The New Standard Jewish Encyclopedia*. New York: Facts on File, 1992.

Wijeyewardene, Gehan. *Place and Emotion in Northern Thai Ritual Behavior*. Bangkok: Pandor, 1986.

Williams, Robert. *Just as I Am: A Practical Guide to Being Out, Proud, and Christian*. New York: Crown Publishers, 1992.

Williams, Walter. *The Spirit and the Flesh*. Boston: Beacon, 1986.

Willoughby, Harold R. *Pagan Regeneration*. Chicago: University of Chicago, 1929.

Wilson, Nancy. *Our Tribe: Queer Folks, God, Jesus, and the Bible*. San Francisco: Harper Collins, 1995.

Wilson, Peter Lanborn. *Scandal: Essays in Islamic Heresy*. New York: Autonomedia, 1989.

Wittig, Monique. *The Lesbian Body*. Trans. David Le Vay. New York: Avon Books, 1975.

Wittig, Monique and Sande Zeig. *Lesbian Peoples: Material for a Dictionary*. New York: Avon, 1979.

Wittman, Carl. "In Search of a Gay Tarot." *RFD* 1, no. 2 (Winter 1974-1975), 33-37.

Wolkstein, Diane and Samuel Noah Kramer. *Inanna: Queen of Heaven and Earth*. New York: Harper and Row, 1983.

Wood, Leona, and Anthony Shay. "Danse du Ventre: A Fresh Appraisal." *Dance Research Journal* 8, no. 2 (1976), 18-30.

Woods, Gregory. *Articulate Flesh: Male Homo-eroticism and Modern Poetry*. New Haven: Yale University Press, 1987.

Woods, Richard. *Another Kind of Love: Homosexuality and Spirituality* (Revised edition). Garden City, New York: Doubleday and Company, 1978.

Yohalem, John. "Coming Out of the Broom Closet." *The Advocate*, issue no. 589 (November 5, 1991), 70-72.

Zolla, Elémire. *The Androgyne: Reconciliation of Male and Female*. New York: Crossroad, 1981.

Zoller, Robert. *The Arabic Parts in Astrology*. Rochester, Vt: Inner Traditions, 1989.

Zuntz, Günther. *Persephone: Three Essays on Religion and Thought in Magna Graecia*. Oxford: Clarendon Press, 1971.

Thematic Index

AFRICAN AND
AFRICAN-DIASPORIC TRADITIONS

Abattá; Abrao; Agule; Aido Hwedo; Aku; Altar; Amazon; Amen; Avery, Shug; Awo; Ayizan; Babaluayé; Baldwin; Baleine, La; Banana and Plantain; Banda; Barbara, Saint; Baron Limba; Baron Lundy; Baron Oua Oua; Baron Samedi; Bee and Honey; Black; Blackberri; Blues; Bori; Bulldagger; Carnival, Carnivalesque; Civet-Cat; Cross; Cullen; Damballah; Deer; Duck; Eroticism; Erzulie; Faro; Fichte; Fire; Fish and Fishing; Flute; Gallina; Ghede; Ghede Masaka; Ghede Nibo; Ghede Oussou; González; Gouillé; Hair; Haring; Hunting; Inlé; Inyangba; Isangoma; Jones; Jupiter; Kimbanda; Kosio; Labrys; Lee; Legba; Lewis, M. E.; Logunedé; Lorde; Machlyes; Madivinèz; Massissi; Mawu-Lisa; Moon; Moret; Mukasa; Music, Contemporary Popular; Mwari; Nanan-bouclou; Neith; Neptune; Nyame; Nzambi; Obatalá; Ogún; Olokun; Orúnmila; Osanyin; Oshumaré; Oshún; Owu; Oyá; Peach; Photography; Pisces; Pluto; Pomba Gira; Pukkumina; Queen B(ee); Rainbow; Ram; Raphael the Archangel, Saint; Riggs; Rooster; Sapphire; Scorpio; Seabrook; Serpent; Shangó; Silibo-Gweto; Sirène, La; Soul Windows; Stapleton; Sun; Tano; Tortoise and Turtle; Trickster; Tutu; Ulanah; Ungud; Union; Uranus; Venus; Wrestling; Yellow; Yemayá; Yewá.

ALCHEMY, DIVINATION, MAGIC

A'anon'nin; Aakulujjuusi and Uumarnituq; Abaris; Abban, Saint; Abbot of Drimnagh; Abraxas; Adonai; Adonis; Adrasteia; Aelia Laelia Crispis; Agate; AIDS/HIV and Spirituality; Alchemy; Alexander, Follower of Apollonius of Tyana; Altar; Amathaon; Ame No Uzume; Amphion; Anger; Asushunamir; Ayizan; Baphomet; Beccarelli; Bran; Budapest; Burroughs; Caduceus; Canidia; Capon; Cerberus; Channeling; Choronzon; Cottabus; Crowley; Cybele; Daniel; Diaghilev, T.; Ephesian Letters; Ereshkigal; Erinyes; Eroticism; Feathers; Fey Shamanism; Fortune; Freyja; Freyr; Furfur; Gallos/Galli; Glow-Worm; Goat; Grant; Haecke; Hecate; Hermes; Hermes Trismegistus; I Ching; Ilpindja; Inlé; Irinaliutiit; Isis; Jade; Johnson, Tom; Joseph; Jupiter; Kahl; Kapo; Knight, Gareth; Kumukahi; Laka; Leadbeater; Lily; Lu Yi Jing; Maenad; Magic, Ancient Love and Sex; Magic and Ritual, Contemporary; Magodus; Mars; Martello; Mathurine; Meliouchos; Melusine; Mercurius; Mercury; Merlin; Midwife's Tale;

Morgan, Ffiona; Nadle; Neboutosoualeth; Netzach; Neuburg; Niantiel; Odin; Orpheus; Orúnmila; Osiris; Padmasambhava; Paimon; Pakaa; Pala-Moa; Peacock; Péladan; Phoenix; Pomba Gira; Prospero; Puck; Qabbalah; Quicksilver; Radegunde; Rebis; Red; Regardie; Rose; Sahaykwisa; Sapphire; Saturn; Seabrook; Seidr; Shrieking Scorpion; Silibo-Gweto; Starhawk; Stein, Diane; Summers; Tages; Taliesin; Tarot; Tezcatlipoca; Thoth; Tiresias; Trophonius; Vampire; Venus; Wendi Xiao; Wizard of Oz; Wudi Xiao; Wu Tsao; Yao Jen; Yao Sabaoth; Yin and Yang; Yeats; Zat al-Dawáhí.

AMAZONS, HEROES, WARRIORS

Abderus; Acca; Achilles; Aegea; Aegis; Albina; Alfhild; Al-Lat; Amaterasu Omi Kami; Amazon; Amazonium; Amis and Amile; Amphiaraus; Anahita; Anahita; Anat; Anandryne; Andro; Antheus; Antony; Anticleia; Antilochus; Antiope; Areis; Ares and Memlippa; Argonauts; Aristogeiton; Astrology; Atalanta; Athena; B(ee), Queen; Baleine, La; Barbara, Saint; Baton; Bear; Bec; Bellona; Beowulf; Berenice; Boudicca; Bradamante; Bull; Bulldagger; Calais; Califia; Cancer; Carneius; Chalcon of Cyparissus; Chariton and Melanippus; Chrysippus; City West of Urs; Couros and Couretes; Cratinus; Cú Chulainn and Fer Diadh; Cymbals; Cyrene; Damon and Pythias; Danaids; Daniel; David and Jonathan; Deer; Diomus; Doris; Durga; Elizabeth I; Epaminondas; Erauso; Euryalus and Nisus; Féithlinn; Furies; Gilfaethwy and Gwydion; Gilgamesh and Enkidu; Gorgoneion; Groa; Gullveig; Gwarach y Rhibyn; Gwidinot; Hatshepsut; Hé-é-é; Heracles; Hinemoa; Hippo; Hippolyta; Hwame; Ianthe; Idomeneas; Iolaus; Jeanne d'Arc; Joseph; Kartikkeyeh; Kauxuma Nupika; Keawe-nui-a-'umi; Knight; Kolhamana; Kumarbi; Kwe'rhame, Kwiraxame; Labarindja; Labrys; Lakshmi; Leucippe/Leucippus; Lithben; Lono; Macha; Maeve; Mars; Medusa; Melanippe; Menestratus; Meriones; Metis; Miletus; Mishima Yukio; Mitra-Varuna; Music, Ancient Near Eastern and Mediterranean; Mytilene; Nemien; Nestor; Noah; Odin; Omphale; Order of Chaeronea; Orestes and Pylades; Otrera; Oyá; Palaestra; Pamano; Parsifal; Patroclus; Peirithous; Peleus; Penthesilea; Philoctetes; Philolaus; Pollux; Procris; Rhodogune; Rusla; Sacred Band of Thebes; Sahaykwisa; Sarpedon; Scáthach; Semiramis; Sergius and Bacchus, Saints; Shugia; Skadi; Srikandi; Stikla; Strirajya; Talos; Theseus; Tiamat; Tiki; Tripurasundari; Tutanekai; Valkyries; Wairaka; Zetes.

ANCIENT MEDITERRANEAN TRADITIONS
(including Greek, Roman, and Hellenistic)

Abaris; Abderus; Abraxas; Acca; Achilles; Acoetes; Actaeon; Admetus; Adonai; Adonis; Adrasteia; Aegea; Aegis; Agamemnon; Agate; Agathon; Agdistis; Agido; Agnodice; Albina; Alcibiades; Alexander the Great; Alexander, Follower of Apollonius; Alexandria; Alimontian Mysteries; Almond; Altar; Amaesia Sentia; Amazon; Amazonium; Amber; Ambrosia; Ameinas; Amethyst; Ampelus; Amphiaraus; Amphion; Amyclas; Anactoria; Anahita; Anaxagoras; Andro; Androphonos; Anemone; Anethus; Angel; Anise; Ant; Antheus; Anticleia; Antilochus; Antinous; Antiope; Antony; Anubis; Aotis; Aphrodite; Aphroditus; Apollo; Apollonius of Tyana; Apple; Aquarius; Aquila; Arcadia; Ares and Menelippa; Arescontes; Arete; Argonauts; Argynnus; Ariadne; Aries; Aristodemus; Aristogeiton; Arsenothelys; Artemis; Asclepius; Astrology; Atalanta; Ate; Athena; Atlantius; Atthis; Attis; Atymnius; Augustus; Aulos; Aurora; Baptai; Bassareus; Baton; Baubo; Bear; Beard; Beaver; Bee and Honey; Bellona; Bird; Bitter, Bittersweet; Bona Dea; Branchus; Britomart; Britomartis; Bryallicha; Bull; Bushido; Butterfly; Cabeiri; Caduceus; Caenis; Calais; Calamus and Carpus; Callisto; Camilla; Campus Martius; Cancer; Canidia; Capon; Capricorn; Carneius; Cavafy; Cerberus; Cervula; Cestos; Chalcis; Chalcon of Cyparissus; Chariclo; Charites; Chariton and Melanippus; Chios; Chiron; Chloris; Chryses; Cithara; Clazomenae; Commodus; Comus; Constantine the Great; Constitius; Corydon; Corythus; Cossitius; Cottabus; Couros and Couretes; Cratinus; Crocale; Crocus; Crone; Cross; Cupbearer; Cybele; Cycnus; Cymbals; Cyparissus; Cypress; Cyrene; Damon and Pythias; Danaids; Daphne; Daphnis; Dates; Deer; Demeter; Dictynna; Diocles; Diomus; Dionysia; Dionysus; Diotima; Dog; Dolphin; Doris; Dove; Drill; Drum; Dryops; Eagle; Earthquake; Elagabalus; Eleusinian Mysteries; Empedocles; Endymion; Epaminondas; Ephesian Letters; Ephesus; Epimenides; Erikepaios; Erinyes; Eros; Erotes; Eroticism; Euphorion; Eurotas River; Euryalus and Nisus; Fanatici; Fates; Fig; Fire; Fish and Fishing; Flora; Flower; Flute; Furies; Gallos/Galli; Ganymede; Gemini; Giton; Glaucon; Glyphius; Goat; Goose; Gorgoneion; Gorgons; Graces; Green; Grey; Gymnopedia; Gypones; Hades; Hadrian; Hagésichora; Hair; Hamilton; Hare and Rabbit; Harpagmos; Harrison, Jane Ellen; Hecate; Helen; Helenus; Hephaestus; Hera; Heracles; Herm; Hermaphroditus; Hermes; Hermes Trismegistus; Hesperus; Hetaira and Female Hierodule; Hierodule, Male; Himerus; Hippo; Hippolyta; Hippolytus; Hispo; Horse; Hortensius; Hunting; Hyacinth (flower, gem); Hyacinthus; Hyena; Hylas; Hymenaeus; Hypnos; Ianthe; Idomeneas; Iolaus; Iphigenia; Iphis; Isis; Ithyphalloi; Ivy;

Jupiter; Justinian the Great; Kalathiskos; Kallabis; Kalogheri; Kalos Vase; Komos; Kordax; Kothornos; Kotys; Kroketos; Labrys; Laius; Lambda; Leo; Lesbos; Leto; Leucippe/Leucippus; Leuké; Libra; Lily; Lion; Lizard; Lotus; Lygismos; Lyra; Lyre; Mâ; Macareus; Machlyes; Maenad; Magic, Ancient Love and Sex; Magodus; Maron; Marsyas; Massalia; Mastic; Medusa; Megabyzos; Melanippe; Meliouchos; Menestratus; Mercurius; Mercury; Meriones; Mestra; Metamorphoses; Metis; Midas; Miletus; Minerva; Minos; Mirror; Misa; Moon; Moonstone; Moth; Mothon; Musaeus; Music, Ancient Near Eastern and Mediterranean; Myrmex; Myrtle; Mytilene; Narcissus; Neboutosoualeth; Nemesis; Neptune; Nereids; Nestor; Niobe; Nymph; Olive; Olympus; Omphale; Order of Chaeronea; Orestes and Pylades; Orpheus; Oschophoria; Otrera; Owl; Palaestra; Pales; Pallas; Pan; Panther; Papaver; Parasol; Parenting and Mentoring; Paris; Parmenides; Patroclus; Peirithous; Peleus; Pelops; Penthesilea; Persephone; Phaenon; Phaeton; Phanes; Philoctetes; Philolaus; Phoenix; Pine; Pisces; Plague; Plato; Pleiades; Pollux; Polyphemus; Pomona; Poppy; Poseidon; Pothos; Priapus; Procris; Prosymnus; Purple; Pyrrha; Rain; Rainbow; Ram; Raven; Red; Regkeis; Reincarnation; Rhadamanthys; Rhodogune; Rhodopis; Rome; Rooster; Rose; Sacred Band of Thebes; Sadomasochism; Saffron; Sagana; Sagittarius; Salmacis; Sandyx; Sapphire; Sappho; Sarapis; Sarpedon; Saturn; Satyrs and Silenoi; Semnotatoi; Serpent; Shepherd; Silvanus; Siproites; Sirius; Sithon; Smyrna, Female-Male of; Sol Invictus-Elagabal; Sphinx; Stoicism; Strophios; Swan; Syrinx; Tages; Talos; Tattoo; Taygete; Telines; Temple of Peace; Thamyris; Theseus; Thiasos; Tiresias; Tree; Troilus; Trophonius; Union; Ursa Major; Venus; Vesta; Violet; Virgo; Weasel; Wheat; Wine; Wrestling; Yellow; Zacynthus; Zarex; Zeno of Citium; Zeno of Elea; Zephyrus; Zetes; Zeus.

ANCIENT NEAR EASTERN TRADITIONS
(including Canaanite,
Egyptian, Mesopotamian, and Phoenician)

Adonis; Ahriman; Akhenaton; Aldinach; Alexandria; Amun; Anat; Anubis; Aquarius; Assinnu; Astrology; Asushunamir; Atargatis; Athirat; Attr; Atum; Baal; Beard; Berenice; Bull; Crone; Cupbearer; Cymbals; Dog; Dove; Dumuzi; Ereshkigal; Eroticism; Galaturra; Gilgamesh and Enkidu; Hadad; Hapy; Hatshepsut; Hyena; Ibis; Imsety; Inanna/Ishtar; Isis; Kalaturru; Kalbu; Kalebh; Kalum; Kelab; Khepera; Khonsu; Kombabos; Kulu'u; Kumarbi; Kurgarru; Lettuce; Lotus; Magic, Ancient Love and Sex; Manat; Me; Min; Music, Ancient Near Eastern and Mediterranean; Mut; Neboutosoulaeth; Neith; Osiris; Papyrus; Partridge; Pilpili; Ptah; Qadesh; Queen; Rain; Sag-ur-sag; Sarapis; Sardanapalus;

Sekhmet; Semiramis; Set; Shepherd; Shugia; Sinnishanu; Sirius; Sphinx; Thoth; Tiamat; Vampire.

ARTISTS AND THE ARTS
(including Crafts, Dance, Dramatic Arts, Film, Fine Arts, Literature, and Music)

Abbott, Franklin; Abu Nuwas; Agathon; Al-Jink; Al-Marini; Alastair; Albani; Alcibiades; Alcuin of Tours, Saint; Aldinach; Alger; Allen; Altar; Alyha; Ame No Uzume; Amphion; Anandryne; Anderson; Anger; Anog Ite; Apollo; Anzaldúa; Apollonius of Tyana; Arthur; Assinnu; Augustine; Aulos; Ausonius; Austen; Baldwin; Ballanche, Pierre; Banda; Bankhead; Barker; Barney; Basava; Basket; Bazzi; Beardsley; Beat Movement; Bell; Bernhard; Berthelot; Biaggi; Blackberri; Blavatsky; Blues; Bly; Bonfire of the Vanities; Bonheur; Boy George; Boyd; Brant; Breeden; Britten; Broughton; Broumas; Bryallicha; Budapest; Burroughs; Caravaggio; Carlos; Carmina Burana; Casper von Lohenstein; Cavafy; Cellini; Cernuda; Chiabiabos; Chrystos; Chubb; Cithara; Clark; Cocteau; Colette; Corelli; Crowley; Cuadros; Cullen; Cymbals; Daly; Daniélou; Dante Alighieri; Daphnis; Day; Diaghilev, Sergei; Dickinson; Dillard; Dionysia; Dolben; Drum; Duncan; Duquesnoy; Dykewomon; Dzonokwa; Engstrom; Epimenides; Erasmus; Erzulie; Evans; Evola; Fellini; Ferro; Fichte; Ficino; Fidus; Fife; Filidh; Filiger; Fini; Flute; Forster; Fortune; Frances; French; Galás; Gallina; Ganneau/Le Mahpah; Gardner; Gearhart; Genet; George; Ghazali; Gide; Gidlow; Ginsberg; Girodet de Roucy; Gleim; González; Gouillé; Grahn; Grant; Graves; Gypones; H.D. Hall; Hamilton; Haring; Harjo; Harp; Harrison, Jane Ellen; Harrison, Lou; Hartley; Harvey; Hay; Heard; Hennessy; Herrman; Hesperus; Hosmer; Hula; Humboldt; Hwarang; Hymenaeus; Ibn Dawud al-Zahiri; Isherwood; Ishquicuink; Isis; Ithyphalloi; Jarman; Johnson, Toby; Johnson, Tom; Jones; Kahl; Kahlo; Kalathiskos; Kallabis; Kalmakoff; Kalogheri; Kalos Vase; Kapo; Kenny; Kepner; Klah; Klyuev; Knight, Gareth; Kocek; Komos; Kordax; Kotys; Kramer; Krishna; Kuzmin; Laka; Lan Caihe; Lawrence; Leadbeater; Leblanc; Leonardo da Vinci; Lewis, Mary Edmonia; Lewis, Matthew G.; Lorca; Lorde; Lorrain; Ludlam; Lygismos; Lyre; Madonna; Magodus; Marées; Margherita de Parma; Mariechild; Marlowe; Marsyas; Martello; Mastamho; Mawu-Lisa; Merrill; Michelangelo Buonarroti; Mihri Hatun; Minstrel; Mishima Yukio; Moraga; Moreau; Moret, Alfonso; Morgan; Morris; Mothon; Mujun; Mukhannath; Murphy; Musaeus; Music, Ancient Near Eastern and Mediterranean; Music, Contemporary Popular; Nadle; Namsadang; Narada; Neo-Gothic Movement; Neuburg; Nijinsky; Noble; Nureyev; Oliveros; Olympus; Opera; Orpheus; Oshún;

Pamano; Pan; Paradjanov; Paulinus of Nola; Péladan; Photography; Poliziano; Ptah; Purusha Queen B(ee); Quilt, Names Project AIDS Memorial; Rakusin, Sudie; Ram Dass; Ramer; Ravarour; Regardie; Renvoisy; Rich; Riggs; Rimbaud; Rolfe; Roscoe; Rôti le balal; Rubinstein; Rumi; Sappho; Schlegel; Schubert; Seabrook; Sebastian, Saint; Seises; Shiva; Sjoo; Slater; Smyth; Solomon; Sots and Sotties; Sprinkle; Stapleton; Starhawk; Stein; Subrahmanya; Summers; Symonds; Syrinx; Szymanowski; Takahashi Mutsuo; Taledhek; Taliesin; Tarot; Tattoo; Tchaikovsky; Tchelitchew; Thamyris; Thompson; Thoreau; Thorn; Tiki; Tristan; Tupilak; Turner; Tutanekei; Tuwais; Ulanah; Uranian Poets; Venus; Vivien; Vogel; Walker, Ethel; Walker, Mitch; Ward, Drew; Ward, Jim; Warner; White, T. H.; Whitman; Wilde; Winant; Winckelmann; Wittig; Wu Tsao; Xochipilli; Xochiquetzal; Yeats; Yourcenar; Yu; Zarex; Zeffirelli; Zenil.

ATHLETICS, GAMES

Abderus; Amphiaraus; Antinous; Apollo; Atalanta; Cottabus; Couros and Couretes; Cyrene; Eros; Gambling; Himerus; Iolaus; Lieblingminne; Macha; Mishima Yukio; Palaestra; Philolaus; Plato; Sebastian, Saint; Utah Game; Wrestling; Xochipilli.

BODY AND ADORNMENT

Addaura; Adhesiveness; Anog Ite; Antenna; Armpit; Bahucharamata; Baron Samedi; Bassareus; Baubo; Beard; Bee and Honey; Bindhu; Breechcloth; Bryallicha; Caribou Carmina Burana; Cestos; Eroticism; Erzulie; Frog Earrings; Gallina; Gymnopedia; Hair; Hijra; Himerus; Intestines; Kothornos; Kroketos; Menstruation; Mirror; Murphy; Neo-Gothic Movement; Oshún; Parasol; Purple; Regkeis; Ring; Rose; Rôti le balal; Sadomasochism; Sandyx; Sardanapalus; Sirène, La; Sleeve, Cut; Sprinkle; Strophios; Tattoo; Thoth; Vampire; Vasanta; Ward, Drew; Ward, Jim; Zaggalas.

BUDDHISM AND RELATED TRADITIONS
(*see also*: **Chinese and Korean Shamanism, Taoism, Confucianism, and Chinese Syncretism; Shinto**)

Amitabha; Avalokiteshvara; Bodhisattva; Bushido; Chai T'ang; Chigo; Dorsey; Ginsberg; Golden Orchid Association; Hagakure; Han Temple; Hwarang; Kannon; Kathoey; Kuan Yin; Kukai; Lord Abbot of Ninnaji; Maitreya; Miao Shan; Mishima Yukio; Namsadang; Nun; Orchid; Padmasambhava; Saicho; Senju; Shirabyoshi; Tara; Tompa, Uncle.

CELESTIAL BODIES AND ASTROLOGY

Abrao; Abraxas; Aku; Amen; Antinous; Aquarius; Aquila; Aries; Artemis/Diana; Asclepius; Astrology; Callisto; Cancer; Candi; Capricorn; Cycnus; Dictynna; Gemini; Hera; Hesperus; Jupiter; Kotys; Kumukahi; La; Leo; Libra; Lyra; Mars; Mawu-Lisa; Mercury; Moon; Neptune; Phaenon; Phaeton; Pisces; Pleiades; Pluto; Sagittarius; Saturn; Scorpio; Sirius; Sol Invictus-Elagabal; Soma; Srikandi; Sun; Taurus; Uranus; Ursa Major; Venus; Virgo; Zeesar; Zeus.

CHINESE AND KOREAN SHAMANISM, TAOISM, CONFUCIANISM, AND CHINESE SYNCRETISM
(see also: **Buddhism**)

Altar; Apricot; Black Teeth Country; Chai T'ang; Chao Tian Gong; Ch'i-Lin; Chou Wang; Chrysanthemum; Dragon; Duck; Eel; Eroticism; Eunuchs, Chinese; Fish and Fishing; Flute; Golden Orchid Association; Gun; Hare and Rabbit; He-xiang-gu; Hu Hsien; Hwarang; I Ching; Iris; Jade; Kuan Yin; Lan Caihe; Li-Liang-Yü; Lu Yi Jing; Magnolia; Men's Country; Miao Shan; Mirror; Mojing Dang; Moon; Mother of the First Cause; Mushroom; Namsadang; Na Thu Pen Do; Onion; Orchid; Paksu Mudang; Peach; Phoenix; Plum; Qu Yuan; Reincarnation; Scholar and the Flower Spirit; Serpent; Seven Sages of the Bamboo Grove; Shan Gui; Shih-Niang; Sleeve, Cut; Stone Maiden; Stone Man; Ta-chueh and Chih-yan; Tan, the Lord of An-Ling; Tiger; Toad; Tofu; Tsze-Too; Two Flower Temple; Unions; Wendi Xiao; Wind, South; Women's Country; Women' Kingdom; Wudi Xiao; Wu Tsao; Xian; Yao Jen; Yellow; Yin and Yang; Yu.

CHRISTIANITY
(see also: **Judaism**)

Abban, Saint; Abbot of Drimnagh; Aelred of Rievaulx; Albani; Alcuin of Tours; Alexander VI; Alger; Amis and Amile; Anastasia the Patrician; Angel; Anselm of Canterbury; Apollinaris; Apostle; Augustine; Ausonius; Baader; Baldwin; Barbara; Baudri of Bourgueil; Bavent; Beccarelli; Bernard of Clairvaux; Bogomil; Bohme; Bonfire of the Vanities; Boniface; Boris; Boyd; Buonamici; Bryant; Carlini; Cathars; Catherine of Genoa; Catherine of Siena; Church, the Reverend John; Clement of Alexandria; Constantine the Great; Convent; Cross; Daly; Dolben; Dominicus; Dorotheus; Duquesnoy; Erasmus; Erauso; Erigena; Eugenia of Alexandria; Euphrosyne; Flora; Foutin; Gabriel the Archangel; Galatians, Letter to the; Galla, Saint; Gospel of Philip; Gospel of Thomas; Haecke; Hair; Iscariot; Jeanne d'Arc; Jesuit; Jesus; Joan, Pope; John the Evangelist; John XII; Juan de la Cruz; Juana Inéz de la Cruz; Julius II; Julius III; Justinian the Great; Khlysts; Lazarus; Leadbeater; de Ledefron; Lee; Lily; Luke; Margarita; Marina; Martha-Mary; Maximus the Confessor; Meredites; Michael the Archangel; Nun; Partridge; Paul II; Paula of Avila; Paulinus of Nola; Pelagia, and Saint Pelagia; Perpetua, Saint and Saint Felicitas; Perry; Plague; Polyeuctus, Saint and Nearchus; Popovici; Prieuré Notre-Dame de Sion; Pukkumina; Rahere; Raphael the Archangel; Renvoisy; Rolfe; Rose of Lima; Santa Maria del Carmine; Satan; Sebastian; Secret Gospel of Mark; Segarelli; Sergius and Bacchus; Seuse; Shepherd; Sixtus IV; Sophia; Spighi; Summers; Terésa de Avila; Toledoth Yeshu; Turlupins; Tutu; Ultramontanist; Unification Church; Wilgefortis.

COLORS, LETTERS, SHAPES

Black; Blue; Cross; Diamond; Green; Grey; Hexagram; Lambda; Purple; Red; Saffron; Triangle; Yellow.

CREATION, BIRTH, PARENTING AND MENTORING

Aakulujjuusi and Uumarnituq; Abban, Saint; Adam; Agni; Ame No Uzume; Amun; Anat; Aphrodite; Ariadne; Artemis; Athena; Athirat; Baal; Baubo; Begochidi; Bryallicha; Bull; Cernunnos; Chiron; Couros and Couretes; Cybele; Damballah; Demeter; Dionysus; E'chûk; First Man and Woman; Flora; Freyja; Freyr; Ganesha; Hapy; Hera; Inanna/Ishtar; Isis; Khepera; Kuan Yin; Kucumatz; Kumarbi; Macha; Malini; Mastamho; Mawu-Lisa; Midwife's Tale; Min; Mother of the First Cause; Mut; Mwari; Naarjuk; Nadle; Neith; Nous; Numboolyu; Nyame; Nzambi; Obatalá; Oyamakui; Pales; Pan; Papa; Parenting and Mentoring; Parjanya; Parvati; Persephone; Phaenon; Phanes; Plato; Poseidon; Priapus; Sarapis; Satyrs and Silenoi; Shiva; Silibo-Gweto; Tano; Taqqiq; Te Rongo; Tiamat; Tlazolteotl; Wakdjunkaga; Weasel; Women's Country; Yemayá.

DEATH AND AFTERLIFE

Abderus; Adonis; Adrasteia; Alké'na'a'ci'; Altar; Angel; Antheus; Antilochus; Anubis; Argynnus; Aristodemus; Asclepius; Asushunamir; Bavent; Bonheur; Boris, Saint; Bran; Calamus; Cerberus; Cernunnos; Chalcon; Coatlicue; Cybele; Daath; Durga; Dwarf, Hermaphrodite; Ereshkigal; Ghede; Ghede Masaka; Ghede Nibo; Ghede Oussou; Hades; Hapy; Hecate; Imsety; Iolaus; Isis; Kali;

DESTINY, FATE, FORTUNE, LUCK, PROSPERITY

DIVINE AND SUPERNATURAL BEINGS
(including saints with popular cults)

FAUNA

Abraxas; Acoetes; Actaeon; Addaura; Admetus; Alexis; Ant; Ape; Aquila; Artemis/Diana; Baleine, La; Bear; Beaver; Bee and Honey; Bird; Bonheur; Britomartis; Bull; Butterfly; Callisto; Capon; Caribou; Cerberus; Cernunnos; Ch'i-Lin; Chiron; Civet-Cat; Corydon; Coyote; Crab; Cyparissus; Cyrene; Damballah; Daphne; Daphnis; Deer; Dictynna; Dog; Dolphin; Dove; Dragon; Duck; Eagle; Eel; Elephant; Fish and Fishing; Freyja; Frog Earrings; Glow-Worm; Golden Bird; Goose; Hare and Rabbit; Horse; Hu Hsien; Hunting; Hyena; Ibis; Inlé; Jaguar; Kalbu; Kanyotyotse; Kiha (-nuilulumoko); Kitsune; Lion; Lizard; Logunedé; Magpie; Mahatala-Jata; Mastamho; Min; Moth; Mule; Myrmex; Nereids; Nihooleki; Onkoy; Owl; Oshún; Owu; Pala-Moa; Pales; Pan; Panther; Partridge; Peacock; Pelops; Phoenix; Pikoe Sendo; Pikoi; Poseidon; Ram; Raven; Rhinoceros, Lavender; Robin; Rooster; Satyrs and Silenoi; Sebastian, Saint; Sedna; Serpent; Silvanus; Sparrow; Sphinx; Swan; Taqqîq; Taygete; Tiger; Toad; Tortoise and Turtle; Tvastr; Uroborus; Ursa Major; Weasel; Yemayá.

FLORA, AGRICULTURE, FOODS, AND BEVERAGES

Acoetes; Adonis; Almond; Amathaon; Ambrosia; Anemone; Anise; Antinous; Apple; Arepa; Arroweed; Banana and Plantain; Bee and Honey; Berry; Butter; Calamus and Carpus; Carnation; Cassia; Cauliflower; Cherry; Chrysanthemum; Coffee; Columbine; Corn; Crocus; Cupbearer; Cyparissus; Cypress; Dates; Demeter; Dionysus; Dryops; Fig; Flower; Hyacinth; Iris; Ivy; Lad's Love; Lettuce; Lily; Linden; Lono; Lotus; Madrone; Magnolia; Maron; Mastic; Mushroom; Myrtle; Nadle; Narcissus; Olive; Onion; Orchid; Pansy; Papaver; Papaya; Papyrus; Pauopalae; Pea; Peach; Peony; Pine; Plum; Pomona; Poppy; Rice with Pork; Rose; Saffron; Scholar and the Flower Spirit, The; Selu; Silvanus; Sweetgrass; Syrinx; Talan; Tofu; Tortilla; Tree; Violet; Wheat; Wine.

GAY AND QUEER LIBERATION AND SPIRITUALITY
(including forerunners)

Abbot, Franklin; Adhesiveness; AIDS and Spirituality; Altar; Angel; Armpit; Arthur; Assimilation; Beat Generation; Beauty and the Beast; Bifrost; Bilitis; Blackberri; Boy George; Boyd; Broughton; Camp; Carnival, Carnivalesque; Carpenter; Chubb; Clark; Diaghilev, Tamara; Double, the; Engstrom; Eroticism;

Evans; Faggot; Fairy; Fey Shamanism; Gemeinschaft der Eigenen; Ginsberg; Grahn; Green; Han Temple; Harvey; Hay; Heard; Hennessy; Herrman; Island Dialogues; Johnson, Toby; Johnson, Tom; Karezza; Kenny; Kepner; Klaristiche Movement; Kramer; Lambda; Lieblingminne; Madrone; Magic and Ritual, Contemporary; Mardi Gras; Music, Contemporary Popular; Neo-Gothic Movement; Order of Chaeronea; Purple; Purusha; Quilt, Names Project AIDS Memorial; Rainbow; Ram Dass; Ramer; Rhinoceros, Lavender; Ring; Roscoe; Sadomasochism; Sisters of Perpetual Indulgence; Sprinkle; Stapleton; Symonds; Tantra; Tattoo; Tayu; Thompson; Thorn; Triangle; Union; Uranian; Urning; Uranian Poets; Utopias and Dystopias; Vampire; Walker, Mitch; Ward, Drew; Ward, Jim; Whitman; Wizard of Oz.

GEMSTONES

Agate; Amber; Amethyst; Carnelian; Diamond; Hyacinth (Jacinth); Jade; Moonstone; Sapphire.

GNOSTICISM

Adam; Adonai; Arsenothelys; Autopator; Bythos; Cainites; Eon; Eroticism; Geryon; Kadesh Barnea; Naas, Naassenes, Ophites; Nous; Phanes; Phibionites; Serpent; Sophia, Saint; Uroborus; Yao Sabaoth; Zeesar.

GUARDIANS AND PROTECTORS

Aegea; Agdistis; Agni; Alexis; Anubis; Arcadia; Artemis; Athena; Attr; Branchus; Britomartis; Cyparissus; Cyrene; Daphne; Daphnis; Dictynna; Dzonokwa; Fish and Fishing; Freyr; Glaucon; Guardian; Harbor; Hecate; Hera; Hunting; Hyacinthus; Isis; Kuan Yin; Macha; Min; Minerva; Neith; Odin; Pala-Moa; Pales; Panther; Pashupata; Pavatairayan; Pelops; Pikoe Sendo; Pollux; Poseidon; Sailor; Shepherd; Silibo-Gweto; Silvanus; Talking God; Taqqiq; Theseus; Wakdjunkaga.

HEALING AND ILLNESS

Abban, Saint; Aegea; Aegis; Agnodice; AIDS and Spirituality; Alexander, Follower of Apollonius of Tyana; Apothecary; Asclepius; Ayizan; Babaluayé; Battersea'd; Bran; Branchus; Caduceus; Chiron; Cybele; Fey Shamanism; Inlé; Iolaus; Kapo; Kumukahi; Laka; Menjaya Raja Manang; Mitra-Varuna; Musaeus; Nanan-bouclou; Na Thu Pen Do; Osanyin; Oshún; Pauopalae; Plague; Quilt, Names Project AIDS Memorial; Radegunde; Raphael the Archangel, Saint; Rooster;

Sahaykwisa; Stein; Tezcatlipoca; Vishnu; Wilgefortis, Saint; Willow; Yemayá.

HINDUISM AND OTHER SOUTH ASIAN TRADITIONS
(see also: **Islam***)*

Agni; Agnicayana; Agnidhra; A-Jami, Jami; Arani; Aravan; Ardhanarishvara; Arjuna; Asanga; Bahucharamata; Basava; Bhakti; Bhutamatr; Bindhu; Bissu; Blue; Boy George; Brahma; Butter; Caitanya; Candi; Crone; Daksha; Daniélou; Devi; Diamond; Drum; Durga; Elephant; Eroticism; Fire; Gandarva; Ganesha; Ganga; Gardner; Goat; Gopi; Hair; Han Temple; Harihara; Hierodule, Male; Hijra; Holi; Huligamma; Ila/Sudyumna; Indra; Jeto; Jogamma; Jogappa; Kali; Kama; Karezza; Kartikkeyeh; Khandoba; Khoja; Krishna; Lakshmi; Lalita; Leadbeater; Leo; Lion; Lotus; Malini; Mithuna; Mitra-Varuna; Mohini; Napunsaka; Narada; Nestr; Parenting and Mentoring; Parjanya; Parvati; Pashupata; Pavatairayan; Peacock; Prajapati; Prakriti-Purusha; Prthivi; Purusha; Radha; Rain; Raja's Daughter; Raja-suya; Rajneesh Movement; Rama; Ram Dass; Red; Rooster; Sadhana Brothers; Sakhibhava; Serpent; Shakta; Shakti; Shamba; Shikhandin; Shiva; Singh, Ranjit; Soma; Srikandi; Strirajya; Subrahmanya; Talan; Tantra; Tara; Thug; Tree; Tripurasundari; Trititya Prakriti; Tvastr; Upanaya; Vallabha; Vasanta; Vinayaki; Vishnu; Yakshas; Yellamma.

ISLAM AND PRE-ISLAMIC ARABIC TRADITIONS
(including Sufism)

Abraham; Abu Nuwas; Adam; Al-Basri, Abu Abdallah; Al-Jink; Al-Lat; Al-Marini; Al-Uzza; Al-Zahara; Assassins; Budur, Lady; Cupbearer; Cymbals; Eroticism; Fig; Ghazali, Mehemmed; Hair; Ibn Dawud al-Zahiri; Jinn; Khunsa; Khurafa; Kocek; Liwat; Manat; Mihri Hatun; Mujun; Mukhannath; Neptune; Peacock; Relaxation of the Poor; Rose; Rumi, Jalal al-Din; Sa'd and Isa; Saffron; Shahed; Shams al-Din Tabrizi; Sodom; Sorcerer and the Young Cook of Baghdad, The; Tuwais; Wildan; Wine; Zaggala; Zat al-Dawahi.

JUDAISM
(including Qabbalah)

Abraham; Adam; Aristobulus; City West of Urs; Daath; Daniel; David and Jonathan; Dykewomon; Faggot; Ginsberg; Gomorrah; Herrman; Joseph; Kadesh Barnea; Netzach; Niantiel; Noah; Potiphar; Qabbalah; Ramer;

Regardie; Rich; Rochel; Rubinstein; Ruth and Naomi; Shepherd; Sodom; Solomon; Starhawk; Toledoth Yeshu.

JUDGEMENT, JUSTICE, VENGEANCE

Agni; Anat; Anubis; Apollo; Artemis; Asushunamir; Athena; Callisto; Durga; Ereshkigal; Erinyes; Furies; Gorgons; Hecate; Hera; Horus; Kali; Kartikkeyeh; Loki; Nemesis; Odin; Ogún; Pomba Gira; Priapus; Rhadamanthys; Sekhmet; Set; Shangó; Tezcatlipoca; Thamyris; Thoth; Zeus.

KNOWLEDGE AND WISDOM

Amaterasu Omi Kami; Anubis; Apollo; Athena; Chiron; Daath; Ganesha; Hecate; Kadesh Barnea; Merlin; Minerva; Naas, Naasenes, Ophites; Neith; Nous; Odin; Persephone; Qabbalah; Radegunde; Serpent; Soma; Sophia, Saint; Thoth; Uroborus.

MESOAMERICAN AND SOUTH AMERICAN TRADITIONS

Altar; Amazon; Angel; Anzaldúa; Arepa; Astrology; Bird; Butterfly; Cauliflower; Cernuda; Chimu; Chin; Crab; Cuadros; Culiacan; Deer; Giant; Goat; Heisèi; Hierodule, Male; Horse; In P'en; Ishquicuink; Jaguar; Kahlo; Kucumatz; Lache; Lion; Lupacas; Machi; Malinche, La; Manta; Mayas; Mbaya; Moche; Moraga; Ngenechen; Onkoy; Owl; Panuco; Papaya; Piache; Pikoe Sendo; Puná; Rice with Pork; Sabina; Taweakame; Tezcatlipoca; Tlazolteotl; Tortilla; Trujillo; Tupi; Uruhú; Xochipilli; Xochiquetzal; Xolotl; Zenil.

METALLURGY, TOOLS, WEAPONS

Aegis; Caduceus; Drill; Gorgoneion; Hephaestus; Labrys; Ogún; Pan.

METAMORPHOSIS AND SHAPESHIFTING

Aakulujjuusi and Uumarnituq; Abban, Saint; Abbot of Drimnagh; Abraham; Aemilia; Agdistis; Agnodice; Al-Jink; Al-Zahra; Amaesia Sentia; Anethus; Anise; Arescontes; Asanga; Athena; Beccarelli, Abbot; Begochidi; Blavatsky; Caenis; Caieteva; Calamus; Callisto; Civet-Cat; Constitius; Cossitius; Coyote; Crocus; Cycnus; Erigena; Furfur; Glow-Worm; Glyphius; Hinemoa; Hu Hsien; Ianthe; Ila/Sudyumna; Iphis; Khurafa; Kiha (-nuiluliumoko); Kitsune; Krishna; Kumukahi;

Kwe'rhame; Kwiraxame; Leucippe/Leucippus; Li-
Liang-yü; Margarita, Saint; Marina, Saint; Melusine;
Mercurius; Meredites; Merlin; Mestra; Mohini; Myrmex;
Nemesis; Orlando; Padmasambhava; Pala-Moa; Pales;
Papaver; Paula of Avila, Saint; Poppy; Puck; Radha;
Rainbow; Raja's Daughter; Raja-suya; Reincarnation;
Rhodopis; Rochel; Sabina; Sakhibhavas; Salmacis; Scrat;
Shih-Niang; Shikhandin; Silvanus; Sipiniit; Siproites;
Sithon; Smyrna, Female-Male of; Sorcerer and the Young
Cook of Baghdad, The; Svin-fells-âs; Syrinx; Taliesin;
Taweakame; Taygete; Tezcatlipoca; Tiresias; Tvastr;
Vampire; Water; Wilgefortis, Saint.

NATIVE AMERICAN INDIAN AND
NORTH ASIAN SHAMANIC TRADITIONS

Aakulujjuusi and Uumarnitug; Ahsonnutli; 'Alké 'na 'a ci';
Allen; Altar; Alyha; Amazon; Angakkuq; Anog Ite;
Assiniboin Woman; Awonawilona; Begochidi; Black;
Brant; Breechcloth; Calling God; Caribou; Chibiabos;
Chrystos; Corn; Coyote; Double Woman; Dwarf,
Hermaphrodite; Dzonokwa; East; E' chûk; Elxa;
Eroticism; Fife; First Man and Woman, Myth of; Frog
Earrings; Gambling; Hair; Harjo, Joy; Hé-é-é; Hwame;
Intestines; Irinaliutiit; Itijjuaq; Kannaaluk;
Kanyotsanyotse; Katsotsi'; Kauxuma Nupika; Ke'let;
Kenny; Ke'yev; Klah, Hosteen; Koe'kcuc; Kokk'okshi;
Kokopelli Mana; Kolhamana; Koskalaka; Kossa and
Kwirana; Koyemshi; Kwe'rhame; Kwiraxame; Lhamana;
Magpie; Mastamho; Menstruation; Miati; Mihdacke;
Minquga; Miti; Mountain Person; Naarjuk; Nadle; Ne-
uchica; Owl; Parenting and Mentoring; Pikoe Sendo;
Prayer Stick; Qa'cikicheca; Qailertetang; Rain; Raven;
Red; Rope Baby; Roscoe; Sahaykwisa; Sedna; Selu;
Shooting God; Sipiniit; Soft Man; Sweetgrass; Sx'nts;
Talking God; Taqqiq; Tattoo; Tewa; Tornaq; Tortoise
and Turtle; Trickster; Tsilth-'tsa-assùn; Tupilak; Two-
Spirit; Union; Utah Game; Village Old Woman;
Wakdjunkaga; We' wha; White Whale Woman; Winkte;
Wiya Numpa; Yakkidhaalyk; Yellow; Yirka' la' ul.

NATURAL PHENOMENA, ELEMENTS,
GEOGRAPHICAL DIRECTIONS,
SEASONS, TIMES

Aldinach; Aurora; Calling God; Damballah; Earthquake;
East; Erzulie; Fire; Ganga; Hapy; Hesperus; Kahukura;
Koolau; Limaloa; Lono; Makanikeoe; Mawu-Lisa;
Naarjuk; Olokun; Oshumaré; Oshún; Pele; Rain;
Rainbow; Shangó; Silibo-Gweto; Sirène, La;
Subrahmanya; Tiresias; Tsilth-tsa-assùn; Water; Wind,
South; Zephyrus.

NEW AGE
(including forerunners)

AIDS and Spirituality; Angel; Astrology; Blavatsky; Bly;
Channeling; Diaghilev, Tamara; Fortune; Johnson, Toby;
Leadbeater; Mariechild; Music, Contemporary Popular;
Ram Dass; Ramer; Regardie; Reincarnation; Tantra;
Tarot; Union.

NORTHERN AND
EASTERN EUROPEAN TRADITIONS
(including Germanic, Norse, Scandinavian, Scythian, and
Teutonic)

Alfhild; Amazon; Artimpasa; Bifrost; Bogomils; Calusari;
Dragon; Enaree; Fairy; Fates; Fey Shamanism; Fire;
Freyja; Freyr; Groa; Gullveig; Khlysts; Linden; Loki;
Meredites; Odin; Rusla; Seidr; Skadi; Stikla; Svin-fells-âs;
Thokk; Tuisto; Valkyries; Vampire; Wild Women; Ymir.

PACIFIC TRADITIONS
(including Australian, Micronesian, Oceanic, Polynesian,
and Southeast Asian)

Aikane; Angamunggi; Assimilation; Bajasa; Bantut;
Bathala; Bayoguin; Big Nambas; Eroticism; Fire; Flute;
Haakaulianani; Hi'iaka; Hiiakalalo and Hiiakaluna;
Hinemoa; Hintubuhet; Hopoe; Hula; Ilpindja; Ingiet; Ini;
Kahukura; Kaluli; Kamapua'a; Kanekoa; Kapa'ihi; Kapo;
Kathoey; Kaw phii; Keawe-nui-a-'umi; Keputren;
Keraki; Kiha (-nuilulumoko); Kiwai; Koolau;
Kumahumahuka'aka, Kumahumahukole, and
Kumahumaliukole; Kumukahi; La; Labarindja; Laka;
Liloa; Limaloa; Lohiau; Lono; Lonoikiaweawealoha;
Mahatala-Jata; Mahu; Makanikeoe; Makanoni; Malyari;
Manang Bali; Menjaya Raja Manang; Neptune; Nihooleki;
Numboolyu; Omeo; Pakaa; Pala-Moa; Pamano; Paoa;
Papa; Pauopalae; Pele; Pikoi; Puuhele; Remember the
Tarantella; Sanghyang Tjintiya; Srikandi; Taledhek; Te
Rongo; Tiki; Tree; Tutanekai; Ungud; Wahineomao;
Wairaka; Wakea.

PEACEMAKERS AND MEDIATORS

Aido Hwedo; Amaterasu Omi Kami; Artemis; Athena;
Damballah; Freyr; Ganesha; Kauxuma Nupika; Minerva;
Neith; Obatalá; Palaestra; Temple of Peace; Two Flower
Temple; Vishnu.

Vallabha; We' wha; Wendi Xiao; Wikiga-Winagu; Wilgefortis; Winkte; Wudi Xiao; Wu Tsao; Yao Jen; Yirka'la'ul; Zaggala; Zeno of Citium; Zeno of Elea.

TEXTS AND LITERARY PERSONAE
(including Film Texts;
see also: **Artists and the Arts**)

Avery; Beauty and the Beast; Berenice; Bilitis; Bradamante; Britomart; Bulldagger; Califia; Chibiabos; Dante Aligheri; Falling Woman; Found Goddesses; Galatians, Letter to the; Goblin Market; Golden Bird; Gospel of Philip; Gospel of Thomas; Hagakure; Hansel and Gretel; Huckleberry Finn; Island Dialogues; Lee; Metamorphoses; Midwife's Tale; Neo-Gothic Movement; Nursery Rhymes; Orlando; Prospero; Puck; Qabbalah; Queen B(ee); Radegunde; Rapunzel; Remember the Tarantella; Renart; Rocky Horror Picture Show; Scholar and the Flower Spirit, The; Secret Gospel of Mark; Séraphita; Sexual Secrets: The Alchemy of Ecstasy; Shrieking Scorpion; Snow Queen; Snow White; Sorcerer and the Young Cook of Baghdad, The; Tadzio; Toledoth Yeshu; Vampire; Vathek; When Night Is Falling; Wizard of Oz; Zabeta.

TRICKSTERS, CAMP, AND THE CARNIVALESQUE

Altar; Ame No Uzume; Baubo; Begochidi; Bernhard, Sandra; Camp; Carnival, Carnivalesque; Cervula; Comus; Coyote; Crokesos; Crone; Ghede Nibo; Hairy Meg; Hermes; Hijra; Hu Hsien; Kitsune; Kokk'okshi; Kokopelli Mana; Kossa and Kwirana; Koyemshi; Legba; Loki; Madonna; Mardi Gras; Mathurine; Mercurius; Mère Sotte; Molly; Nun; Pan; Puck; Punchinello; Rahere; Renart; Schemen; Scorpio; Scrat; Seigneur de Joye; Sisters of Perpetual Indulgence; Sots and Sotties; Tompa, Uncle; Trickster; Tsze-Too; Wakdjunkaga.

WESTERN EUROPEAN TRADITIONS
(including Celtic, Medieval, Renaissance, and Pre-Modern)

Abraxas; Addaura; Aelia Laelia Crispis; Aemilia; Alchemy; Amathaon; Amis and Amile; Aquarius; Arcadia; Aries; Astrology; Baphomet; Barnariccia; Beauty and the Beast; Bec; Bee and Honey; Bell; Beowulf; Berry; Berthelot; Bird; Bohme; Bonfire of the Vanities; Boudicca; Bradamante; Bran; Britomart; Butterfly; Caieteva; Califia; Cancer; Capricorn; Caravaggio; Carmina Burana; Carnival, Carnivalesque; Cathars; Cellini; Cernunnos; Cervula; Chartres; Cherry; Christsonday; Civet-Cat; Cú

Chulainn and Fer Diadh; Cupbearer; Dante Alighieri; Dove; Elizabeth I; Faggot; Fairy; Fates; Féithlinn; Ficino; Fig; Filidh; Flora; Flower; Furfur; Gemini; Gilfaethwy and Gwydion; Glow-Worm; Goat; Golden Bird; Green; Gwidinot; Gwrach y Rhibyn; Hag; Hairy Meg; Hansel and Gretel; Hare and Rabbit; Henri III; Hexagram; Horse; Hunting; Hyena; James I; Jeanne d'Arc; Jupiter; Knight; Leo; Leonardo da Vinci; Libra; Lily; Lithben; Macha; Maeve; Margherita de Parma; Marlowe; Mars; Massalia; Mathurine; Melusine; Mercurius; Mercury; Mère Sotte; Merlin; Mermaid; Michelangelo Buonarroti; Minstrel; Moon; Morgaine of the Fairies; Mule; Muret; Nemien; Neptune; Nursery Rhymes; Opera; Orleans; Paimon; Pan; Pansy; Paris (City); Parsifal; Peacock; Pisces; Plague; Pluto; Poliziano; Prieuré Notre-Dame de Sion; Prospero; Puck; Punchinello; Queen; Quicksilver; Radegunde; Rahere; Rainbow; Rapunzel; Rebis; Red; Renaissance; Renart; Renvoisy; Rose; Rôti le balal; Sagittarius; Sailor; Saint-Simonism; Sapphire; Satan; Scáthach; Schemen; Scorpio; Scrat; Seigneur de Joye; Seises; Sens; Shepherd; Snow Queen; Snow White; Sots and Sotties; Sun; Swan; Taliesin; Tarot; Taurus; Templar, Order of the Knights; Terragon; Tortoise and Turtle; Triangle; Trickster; Ultramontanist; Utopias and Dystopias; Vampire; Vathek; Venus; Virgo; William Rufus; Zabeta.

WITCHCRAFT AND WICCA

Altar; Artemis/Diana; Budapest; Canidia; Cernunnos; Christsonday; Crone; Diaghilev, Tamara; Engstrom; Evans; Faggot; Fairy; Fortune; Hag; Hecate; Henri III; Johnson, Tom; Magic, Ancient Love and Sex; Magic and Ritual, Contemporary; Martello; Midwife's Tale; Morgan; Music, Contemporary Popular; Owl; Rôti le balal; Sagana; Slater; Starhawk; Stein; Summers; Tantra; Tarot; Thorn; Union; Ward, Drew; Ward, Jim; Warner.

WOMEN'S LIBERATION AND SPIRITUALITY
(including forerunners)

Allen; Altar; Amazon; Anandryne; Antenna; Anzaldúa; Armpit; Artemis/Diana; Assimilation; Astrology; Austen; Avery; Barney; Biaggi; Bilitis; Brant; Broumas; Bulldagger; Chrystos; Convent; Crone; Daly; Diaghilev, Tamara; Dykewomon; Eroticism; Falling Woman; Fates; Fortune; Found Goddesses; Frances; Furies; Gallina; Gardner; Gearhart; Gidlow; Gorgons; Grahn; Graves; Hag; Labrys; Lorde; Madrone; Magic and Ritual, Contemporary; Mariechild; Menstruation; Mermaid; Metamorphosphere; Midwife's Tale; Moraga; Morgan; Music, Contemporary Popular; Noble; Nun; Oliveros; Queen B(ee); Rakusin; Remember the Tarantella; Rich; St